THE NEW OXFORD HISTORY OF ENGLAND

General Editor · J. M. ROBERTS

A Mad, Bad, and Dangerous People?

ENGLAND

1783–1846

BOYD HILTON

CLARENDON PRESS · OXFORD

OXFORD

UNIVERSITY PRESS

Great Clarendon Street, Oxford OX2 6DP

Oxford University Press is a department of the University of Oxford.
It furthers the University's objective of excellence in research, scholarship,
and education by publishing worldwide in

Oxford New York

Auckland Cape Town Dar es Salaam Hong Kong Karachi
Kuala Lumpur Madrid Melbourne Mexico City Nairobi
New Delhi Shanghai Taipei Toronto

With offices in

Argentina Austria Brazil Chile Czech Republic France Greece
Guatemala Hungary Italy Japan Poland Portugal Singapore
South Korea Switzerland Thailand Turkey Ukraine Vietnam

Oxford is a registered trade mark of Oxford University Press
in the UK and in certain other countries

Published in the United States
by Oxford University Press Inc., New York

British Library Cataloguing in Publication Data

Data available

Library of Congress Cataloging in Publication Data

Data available

Typeset by Newgen Imaging Systems (P) Ltd., Chennai, India
Printed in Great Britain
on acid-free paper by
Biddles Ltd., King's Lynn, Norfolk

ISBN 0-19-822830-9 978-0-19-822830-1

1 3 5 7 9 10 8 6 4 2

FOR

MARY

TOM ELIZA ZOË

General Editor's Preface

The first volume of Sir George Clark's *Oxford History of England* was published in 1934. Undertaking the General Editorship of a *New Oxford History of England* forty-five years later it was hard not to feel overshadowed by its powerful influence and well-deserved status. Some of Clark's volumes (his own among them) were brilliant individual achievements, hard to rival and impossible to match. Of course, he and his readers shared a broad sense of the purpose and direction of such books. His successor can no longer be sure of doing that. The building-blocks of the story, its reasonable and meaningful demarcations and divisions, the continuities and discontinuities, the priorities of different varieties of history, the place of narrative—all these things are now much harder to agree upon. We now know much more about many things, and think about what we know in different ways. It is not surprising that historians now sometimes seem unsure about the audience to which their scholarship and writing are addressed.

In the end, authors should be left to write their own books. Nonetheless, the *New Oxford History of England* is intended to be more than a collection of discrete or idiosyncratic histories in chronological order. Its aim is to give an account of the development of our country in time. It is hard to treat that development as just the history which unfolds within the precise boundaries of England, and a mistake to suggest that this implies a neglect of the histories of the Scots, Irish, and Welsh. Yet the institutional core of the story which runs from Anglo-Saxon times to our own is the story of a state structure built round the English monarchy and its effective successor, the Crown in Parliament, and that provides the only continuous articulation of the history of the peoples we today call British. It follows that there must be uneven, and sometimes discontinuous, treatment of much of the history of those peoples. The state story nevertheless, is an intelligible thread and to me appears still to justify both the title of this series and that of its predecessor.

If the attention given to the other kingdoms and the principality of Wales must reflect in this series their changing relationship to that central theme, this is not only way in which the emphasis of individual volumes will be different. Each author has been asked to bring forward what he or she sees as the most important topics explaining the history under study, taking account of the present state of historical knowledge, drawing attention to areas of dispute and to matters on which final judgement is at present difficult (or, perhaps, impossible) and not merely recapitulating what has recently been the fashionable centre of professional debate. But each volume, allowing for its special approach and proportions, must also provide a comprehensive account, in which politics is always likely to be prominent. Volumes have to be demarcated chronologically but continuities must not be obscured; vestigially or not, copyhold survived into the 1920s and the Anglo-Saxon shires until the 1970s (some of which were to be resurrected in the 1990s, too). Any single volume should be an entry-point to the understanding of processes only slowly unfolding, sometimes across centuries. My hope is that in the end we shall have, as the outcome, a set of standard and authoritative histories, embodying the scholarship of generation, and not mere compendia in which the determinants are lost to sight among the detail.

J. M. ROBERTS

Preface

The pen might be mightier than the sword, but it is not always as quick. This book has taken a third as long to write as the events that it describes took to happen, or, to put it another way, about as long as the 'Great War' that led to the creation and then destruction of a French imperium throughout most of continental Europe. During this book's laboured gestation I have incurred so many debts to colleagues, students, and others that it is impossible to mention all of them by name. My first draft of a thank-you list was so long as almost to devalue the quality of the thanks on offer, besides which the longer the list the greater the solecism of inadvertently dropping someone off it. So I hope that my legion of intellectual creditors will understand if I pare this section down to bare essentials.

I must start with five people who are no longer alive to receive my thanks. Angus Macintyre was my first mentor. Anyone lucky enough to have been tutored or supervised by Angus will know how wonderfully inspiring and uplifting he could be. Bob Robson did not do uplift exactly, but he had an encyclopedic knowledge of eighteenth- and nineteenth-century Britain, and was endlessly solicitous as I started on my long task. Colin Matthew was not so much solicitous as chivvying, but for thirty years I regarded him as my alter ego, the person with whom I shared all my thoughts about the nineteenth century, a period we gossiped about as though its inhabitants were alive and kicking among us. Arguably John Roberts, the general editor of this series, should have chivvied harder in the earlier stages. Like some other contributors, I feel guilty about the time I took to bring things to the boil. But no one could have asked for a wiser, shrewder, or kinder editor when at last the prose began to flow. This manuscript must have been almost the last thing John read. Perhaps the most moving letter I have ever received is the stoical, encouraging, and wholly unself-regarding one in which he informed me, two weeks before his death in 2003, that he physically could not read any further. A very recent loss is that of Maurice Cowling, a mesmerising colleague, sometimes brutal and alarming but always funny and endearing.

My colleagues Peter Mandler and Martin Daunton read and commented on the typescript in full. They and I know just how much they have contributed to the outcome, and I am particularly grateful to Martin for his tuition in economic history, some of it pretty basic. Tim Blanning read the early bits and saved me from many inaccuracies and infelicities. I deliberately did not ask Jon Parry to read the typescript because I knew that he would do so with such expert devotion to duty that not only would his own research suffer unduly, but this book's publication would be delayed a great deal longer. Nevertheless, I am conscious of how much I have learned from him, especially in our graduate and undergraduate seminars. He has taken over the role that Colin Matthew played in persuading me that the nineteenth-century world lives and breathes. William Thomas and John Walsh have the same gift of being able to bring the past alive, and I have benefited enormously over the years. John Ehrman and Leslie Mitchell responded to specific queries with great generosity. The 'Sussex three' (as they continue to be considered)—John Burrow, Donald Winch, and Stefan Collini—helped to turn my thought to new directions. My nervous attempts to penetrate the world of the history of science were aided enormously by Pietro Corsi, Adrian Desmond, David Knight, Jim Moore, John Pickstone, Simon Schaffer, Jim Secord, and Alison Winter. The classes that I gave with the last two have been among the most rewarding in a long teaching career. I have enjoyed discussions about the period with (among many others) Will Ashworth, Derek Beales, Eugenio Biagini, Joe Bord, Jonathan Clark, Peter Clarke, Jonathan Conlin, David Eastwood, Anna Gambles, Vic Gatrell, Lawrence Goldman, Peter Gray, Neil Hitchin, Larry Klein, David McKitterick, Danny Mansergh, Rachel Martin, Rose Melikan, Pablo Mukherjee, Michael Murphy, the late Roy Porter, Jennifer Ridden, Reba Soffer, Peter Spence, Gareth Stedman Jones, William St Clair, and Luke Wright. Though they mainly specialize in different periods, Margaret Pelling and Ross McKibbin were for many decades fellow members of the circle that gathered round Colin Matthew in Oxford, and they and Sue Matthew continue to offer both friendship and scholarly stimulus. Although this is not the place for expressions of purely personal devotion, I must also pay tribute to the first of this book's dedicatees, Mary Hilton, for her intellectual input, especially in those aspects of the period with which I am least at ease.

My colleagues at Trinity (too numerous to mention by name) have never let me forget that history should first and foremost be fun. More formally I should record my debt to the Master and Fellows of that College for material support in all sorts of ways. I acknowledge the two additional terms of sabbatical leave that were paid for by the British Academy and by the Arts and Humanities Research Council. I have been helped by a succession of editors at Oxford University Press, but must thank in particular Matthew Cotton and Kay Rogers for steering the book to completion, and also my eagle-eyed and endlessly indulgent copy-editor, Laurien Berkeley. As ever I owe a great deal to the patience of librarians, especially those at the Cambridge University Library, the Seeley, and Trinity College. Laura Cordy has been an expert adviser in matters of word-processing, and Traci Cullen has put up with my inadequacies at the computer. I thank Tom Hilton warmly for devising the graphs and bar chart, and also Reginald Piggott, who drew the three maps in Chapter 4 at very short notice.

Anyone who works on a book of this scale, and for such a long time, and who is forced to touch on so many topics outside his or her own expertise, must be in danger of committing unconscious acts of plagiarism. 'Can this choice phrase, scribbled on this torn and yellowing scrap of paper, really be my own, or did I copy it from someone else?' I can only hope that, if I have erred in such respects, offended authors will understand and forgive.

B. H.

Acknowledgements

For permission to quote from manuscript materials in their possession I wish to thank the responsible officers of the following institutions: The National Archives of England, Wales, and the United Kingdom; the National Library of Wales; the National Museum of Wales; the Public Record Office of Northern Ireland; the County Record Offices of Cornwall, Devon, Kent, Staffordshire, and Surrey; the West Yorkshire Archives Service, Leeds; Canterbury Cathedral Archive; the British Library; the Cambridge University Library; Trinity College, Cambridge; the University of Durham Archives; Edinburgh University Library; the John Rylands University Library of Manchester; the Nottingham University Library; the Bodleian Library, Oxford; Oriel College, Oxford; the University of Southampton Library; and University College London. Also Sir James Graham, Bt., the Earl of Harewood, the Earl of Harrowby, Mr P. L. V. Mallet, and the Duke of Wellington. I am grateful to the following publishers and distribution firms for permission to adopt or adapt certain figures and tables: Elsevier, Harcourt and Butterworth-Heinemann (Map 1.1, Turnpike road network, 1770); Manchester University Press (Table 3.5, Membership of the Leeds Philosophical and Literary Society by occupation, 1834); Palgrave Macmillan and Stanford University Press (Table 8.5, Voting records of Whig, Liberal, and Radical MPs, 1831–1841); Yale University Press (Table 8.11, Number of Sunday Schools built or founded, 1780–1851); Cambridge University Press (Figure 9.1, Mean height of working-class 13-, 14-, 15-, and 16-year olds, 1758–1940); and Oxford University Press (Map 1.2, Inland navigation, c.1830; Table 8.10, Number of Protestant Nonconformist worshippers in England, 1851; Table 8.15, Percentage of British manufactured exports by destination, 1699–1856).

Contents

Plates

Figures

Maps

Tables

Abbreviations

Add. MSS	British Library Additional Manuscripts
Arbuthnot, *Journal*	*The Journal of Mrs Arbuthnot 1820–1832*, ed. F. Bamford and the Duke of Wellington, 2 vols. (1950)
BIHR	*Bulletin of the Institute of Historical Research*
BL	British Library
Burke, *Correspondence*	*The Correspondence of Edmund Burke*, ed. Thomas W. Copeland *et al.*, 9 vols. (Cambridge, 1958–70)
Burke, *Noble Lord*	*A Letter to a Noble Lord on the Attacks made upon Him and his Pension* (1796), in *The Writings and Speeches of Edmund Burke*, ix: *The Revolutionary War, 1794–1797*, ed. R. B. McDowell (Oxford, 1991)
Burke, *Philosophical Enquiry*	*A Philosophical Enquiry into the Origin of our Ideas of the Sublime and Beautiful* (1757), in *The Writings and Speeches of Edmund Burke*, i: *The Early Writings*, ed. T. O. McLoughlin and James T. Boulton (Oxford, 1997)
Burke, *Reflections*	*Reflections on the Revolution in France and on the Proceedings in certain Societies in London relative to that Event* (1790), in *The Writings and Speeches of Edmund Burke*, viii: *The French Revolution 1790–1794*, ed. L. G. Mitchell (Oxford, 1989)
Burke, *Regicide*	*Three Letters on the Proposals for Peace with the Regicide Directory of France* (1796–7), in *The Writings and Speeches of Edmund Burke*, ix: *The Revolutionary War, 1794–1797*, ed. R. B. McDowell (Oxford, 1991)
Burke, *Thoughts*	*Thoughts on the Cause of the Present Discontents* (1770), in *The Writings and Speeches of Edmund Burke*, ii: *Party, Parliament, and the American Crisis 1766–1774*, ed. Paul Langford (Oxford, 1981)
Canning MSS	The West Yorkshire Archives Service, Leeds (Harewood Papers)
CPD	*Cobbett's Parliamentary Debates 1803–12*
CPH	*Cobbett's Parliamentary History of England to 1803*
Croker Papers	*The Croker Papers: The Correspondence and Diaries of John Wilson Croker*, ed. L. J. Jennings, 3 vols. (1885)
CUL	Cambridge University Library
DNB	*Dictionary of National Biography*, ed. Leslie Stephen and Sidney Lee, 63 vols. (1885–1900)
EconHR	*Economic History Review*, 2nd ser.
EHR	*English Historical Review*

Ehrman i — John Ehrman, *The Younger Pitt*, i. *The Years of Acclaim* (1969)

Ehrman ii — John Ehrman, *The Younger Pitt*, ii. *The Reluctant Transition* (1983)

Ehrman iii — John Ehrman, *The Younger Pitt*, iii. *The Consuming Struggle* (1996)

ER — *Edinburgh Review*

George III, *Correspondence* — *The Later Correspondence of George III*, ed. A. Aspinall, 5 vols. (Cambridge, 1962–70)

Graham MSS — Netherby Hall, Papers of Sir James Graham (series and bundle number followed by the microfilm MS number in CUL)

Greville, *Memoirs* — *The Greville Memoirs: A Journal of the Reigns of George IV and William IV*, ed. Henry Reeve, 3 vols. (1875)

Herries MSS — British Library, Add. MSS (provisional foliation)

HJ — *Historical Journal*

HO — Home Office Papers

Holland MSS — British Library, Add. MSS (Holland House Papers) (provisional foliation)

HPD1 — *Hansard's Parliamentary Debates 1812–20*, produced under the direction of Luke Hansard from 1813

HPD2 — *Hansard Parliamentary Debates*, 2nd ser. (1820–30)

HPD3 — *Hansard Parliamentary Debates*, 3rd ser. (1830–91)

Huskisson MSS — British Library, Add. MSS

JBS — *Journal of British Studies*

Liverpool MSS — British Library, Additional Manuscripts

Namier & Brooke — *The History of Parliament: The House of Commons 1754–1790*, ed. Lewis Namier and John Brooke, 3 vols. (1964)

ODNB — *Oxford Dictionary of National Biography*, ed. H. C. G. Matthew and Brian Harrison, 60 vols. (Oxford, 2004)

P&P — *Past & Present*

Parker, *Peel* — *Sir Robert Peel from his Private Papers*, ed. Charles Stuart Parker, 3 vols. (1891–9)

Peel, *Memoirs* — *Memoirs by Sir Robert Peel*, ed. Earl Stanhope and E. Cardwell (1857)

Peel MSS — British Library, Additional Manuscripts

PP — *Parliamentary Papers*

PRO NI — Public Record Office of Northern Ireland

QR — *Quarterly Review*

RO — Record Office

Stanhope, *Pitt* — Philip Henry, Earl Stanhope, *Life of the Right Honourable William Pitt*, 4 vols. (1861–2)

Thorne   *The History of Parliament: The House of Commons 1790–1820*, ed. R. T.
            Thorne, 5 vols. (1986)
TNA   The National Archives, Kew, London
WND   *Despatches, Correspondence, and Memoranda of Arthur Duke of Wellington,*
            1819–1832, ed. second Duke of Wellington (1867–80)

CHAPTER I

England 1783–1846: a preview

Published in 1781, the third volume of Edward Gibbon's *Decline and Fall* closed on a portentous note. The loss of ancient Rome's western empire had been due, not to the anger of gods or the flight of vultures, but to the corruption of republican virtue by commerce and its concomitant, effeminate luxury.

> The taxes were multiplied with the public distress; œconomy was neglected in proportion as it became necessary; and the injustice of the rich shifted the unequal burden from themselves to the people . . . Imperial ministers pursued with proscriptive laws, and ineffectual arms, the rebels whom they had made . . . and if Rome still survived, she survived the loss of freedom, of virtue, and of honour.[1]

None of Gibbon's readers could have failed to draw the message. Since 1763 Britain had been the world's most powerful nation, with a dominion stretching from the eastern seaboard of India to the Great Lakes of North America. But now a large part of its western empire was in revolt, leaving the imperial State traumatized. In 1783 the Treaty of Paris formally ceded independence to the thirteen rebel colonies of the new United States of America. Some attributed the disaster to divine chastisement, others like Gibbon blamed internal decay. Yet the forebodings proved false. Over the following decades Britons established a second, more dispersed, mainly maritime, and (in their own eyes) moral empire, blessed by providence and devoted to peace, freedom, and Christian mission. In 1850, by which date about one-quarter of the world's population was governed from London, a Foreign Secretary could boast that Britons were like ancient Romans before the fall, world citizens able to call on the protection of Her Britannic Majesty's Government wherever they might be.

> As the Roman, in days of old, held himself free from indignity, when he could say *Civis Romanus sum*; so also a British subject, in whatever land he may be, shall feel confident that the watchful eye and the strong arm of England, will protect him against injustice and wrong.[2]

---

[1] Edward Gibbon, *The History of the Decline and Fall of the Roman Empire*, ed. David Womersley (1994), ii. 355–6.   [2] Lord Palmerston, in *HPD*3 cxii. 444 (25 June 1850).

His self-confidence rested partly on brute power. By exploiting its economic strength, Britain was able to bankroll the military coalition that battled for two decades to prevent Napoleon from conquering the whole of Europe. In 1815 an Anglo-Irish officer commanded the armies that finally humbled the French emperor at Waterloo. And in 1848 the country escaped the wave of revolutions that brought down monarchical regimes across much of the Continent. But it was not only a matter of guineas, gunboats, and good governance. For once British learning, literature, and painting were admired throughout Europe. Shakespeare came to be regarded as, not just the supreme master of English letters, but the towering genius of world literature. Walter Scott became the first international best-selling novelist, whose books sold in huge numbers and in many languages, while everyone everywhere remembered what they had been doing when they heard the news that Lord Byron had expired at Missolonghi on 19 April 1824. A would-be freedom fighter in the Greek war of independence, Byron was revered by almost all the Continent's leading writers, artists, composers, and intellectuals—Goethe, Heine, Hugo, de Vigny, Lamartine, Rossini, Schumann, Delacroix, Géricault, Berlioz, Pushkin, Lermontov, and Mazzini among others. If Paris easily outstripped London as a centre of culture, fashion, and pleasure, even the French were forced to acknowledge that power, dynamism, and intellect now resided on the northern side of the Channel. Above all, Britain seemed 'modern', a concept that was itself modern, having its origins in the revolutionary decade of the 1790s.

THE ECONOMY: CRISIS AND SURVIVAL

Outwardly at least, England was transformed between 1783 and 1846. The development of new coalfields in South Wales, the Midlands, and Lancashire to supplement the historic collieries of the North-East, enabled total output to increase three-and-a-half times between 1775 and 1830, and helped to keep the price stable despite rising demand. As a replacement for timber, coal succeeded in galvanizing the iron industry, and it played an essential role in the development of steam-driven textile mills, but just as importantly it provided the domestic fuel without which a megalopolis such as London could not have operated.[3] Since no other industries enjoyed the same pace of development as iron and textiles, precisely how fast the economy grew in *aggregate* terms remains disputed,[4] but the value of domestic exports demonstrably increased by

---

[3] E. A. Wrigley, *Continuity, Chance and Change: The Character of the Industrial Revolution in England* (Cambridge, 1988), 51-9.

[4] A conservative estimate puts growth as low as 1.3% per annum at the start of the period and about 2.5% at the end, but even this was twice what any previous country had been able to sustain over such a long period (N. F. R. Crafts and C. K. Harley, 'Output Growth and the British Industrial Revolution', *EconHR* 45 (1992), 702-30). The statistics in this chapter refer to all of Britain but not Ireland, unless otherwise stated.

a factor of six-and-a-half, and that of cottons by thirty-two. Pig-iron output rose by thirty-five times, while sales abroad of iron products more or less doubled. In 1850 exports of pig- and bar iron exceeded the production of the whole of the rest of Europe, while by 1873 British output was equal to that of Europe and the United States combined. Such statistics justified this country's mid-nineteenth-century designation as 'the workshop of the world', and while contemporaries were only partially aware of them, they could hardly fail to notice the proliferation of steam engines, iron bridges, canals, and railways, or the haemorrhaging of population from the countryside and the corresponding growth of great towns. The most awe-inspiring of many industrial icons were the fiery furnaces of Merthyr Tydfil in the neighbouring Welsh valleys. A tiny village in 1750, Merthyr was home to 46,000 by 1851. It boasted the largest site of iron production in the world, as well as its largest factory, the 5,000-strong Dowlais Iron Works.

This period has been described as a 'Great Transformation', and more recently a 'Great Divergence'.[5] The terms are apt, whereas the once common designation of 'the first Industrial Revolution' now appears problematic, if only because it suggests that there was an inevitable and integrated process of transition from an organic or agriculturally based economy reliant on handicraft, to one based on manufactures and machine production. Analyses based on this latter assumption have often turned on the relative importance of supply- and demand-side factors in explaining the revolution. The former category would include the abundance of cheap labour, capital investment, technological inventions, economies of scale, improvements to internal and coastal transport, and ready access to raw materials, especially coal. Further in the background, but possibly just as important, was the vibrant entrepreneurial culture, due in part to the fact that many industrialists strove not for financial gratification but to establish their families socially, which often induced them to live frugally and to reinvest profits. This may have applied especially to Nonconformists, who were legally barred by the Test and Corporation Acts from accepting public office, but it also obtained more generally in England's relatively fluid society, where status could be won through the patient accumulation of wealth.

Demand-side factors included the growth of domestic consumption due to a habit of social emulation, and a surge in overseas markets thanks to colonial acquisitions and a vibrant Atlantic trade. As to their relative importance, internal demand was much the greater in absolute terms, but it could be argued that foreign commerce offered more opportunities for dynamic spurts of growth of the sort which excited entrepreneurs into more imaginative ways of doing

[5] Karl Polanyi, *Origins of our Time: The Great Transformation* (1945); Kenneth Pomeranz, *The Great Divergence: China, Europe, and the Making of the Modern World Economy* (Princeton, 2000).

things. Again, foreign trade provided an opportunity for a technologically superior country suddenly to seize another's export markets, or to supplant a Third World country's indigenous manufactures. (There is a certain circularity here, of course, in that these two arguments for the superior importance of external demand are really arguments in favour of supply-side factors like entrepreneurship and technology.) Anyway, by playing with variables of this sort, economic historians have constructed models to test any number of explanations for economic growth, including leading-sector analysis, forward and backward linkages, exogenous and endogenous stimuli, factor scarcities, and human capital formation. Unfortunately, many of their analyses have been too sophisticated for the flimsy statistics on which they are based, besides which such approaches hardly do justice to the haphazard and contingent nature of what actually happened.

A second problem with the 'first Industrial Revolution' approach is that, in so far as the economy underwent a *structural* transformation, that had already taken place during the last quarter of the seventeenth century and the first half of the eighteenth, and was based on developments in commerce, finance, and agriculture rather than manufacturing. Here the crucial variables were those of population and production. During the medieval and early modern eras, the size of the population and the level of economic activity had broadly risen and fallen together over the course of a generation or two. There had been periods (such as the early fourteenth and early seventeenth centuries) during which the population had expanded and so had the national product, but since the increased product had had to be shared among more people, welfare had collapsed, death rates had risen, and population had fallen back again. The pattern was therefore one of ups and downs rather than a rising spiral. Yet between about 1675 and 1750 demand for—and production of—goods and services increased *without* any significant rise in population. This was mainly because Britain was able to dominate the rapidly growing Atlantic and Caribbean trades, in particular the market for slaves and colonial groceries (coffee, tea, sugar).[6] That it was able to do so was partly owing to its abstention from the Thirty Years War (1618–48), which gave it advantages in the carrying trade, and also to the Navigation Code (1651–63), which restricted a large proportion of imports and exports to British merchant ships. But whatever the antecedent causes, the accumulation of profits ahead of population led in the mid-eighteenth century to surplus wages, increased consumption, upward social mobility, and emulation.[7]

[6] E. J. Hobsbawm, *Industry and Empire: An Economic History of Britain since 1750* (1968), 10–39; Joseph E. Inikori, *Africans and the Industrial Revolution in England: A Study in International Trade and Economic Development* (Cambridge, 2002), 405–86.

[7] D. E. C. Eversley, 'The Home Market and Economic Growth in England, 1750–1780', in E. L. Jones and G. E. Mingay (eds.), *Land, Labour and Population in the Industrial Revolution* (1967).

Agricultural production also increased during the first half of the century, despite the minimal population growth, depressed demand, low rents, and falling prices. The result was that Britain in 1750 had briefly become a significant net exporter of wheat. This happy situation came about in part fortuitously through the extension of arable farming from the heavy clays of the Midland Plain to the lighter and more suitable soils of the South and East, but it was also due to investment in new techniques of 'convertible husbandry', including sophisticated rotations, improved fertilization, and drainage.[8] There has been much debate as to whether this was a 'yeoman farmer's revolution', or whether the main cost was borne by landlords, who might be relatively independent of the market, especially if they were in receipt of favours from government. Like some entrepreneurs, many improving estate owners seem to have been motivated by the desire for social esteem rather than for financial profit.[9] But whatever the motive, the creation of a surplus in wheaten bread was enormously significant for the future. The high real wages that resulted stimulated domestic demand for non-agricultural goods, while self-sufficiency created the conditions for the population to expand beyond its conventional Malthusian limits.

The decades before 1783 thus left a benign legacy, the fruits of which would be enjoyed during the mid-Victorian boom in the third quarter of the nineteenth century. The significance of the intervening years from 1783 to 1846, however, is not that England forged ahead into self-sustained growth, but that it just about managed to avoid a demographic catastrophe. In 1783 the population of the British Isles was a little over 13 million. By 1841 it had more than doubled to about 26.7 million, an increase of 1.8 per cent per annum as compared with about 0.7 for France (see Table 1.1). Since this population growth was due to increased fertility rather than falling mortality—births exceeded deaths by more than 10 million between 1781 and 1851—Britain became a very much younger country. As with all such phenomena, the reasons are much disputed. Optimistic historians claim that the rise in real wages that had occurred earlier in the eighteenth century enabled people to marry younger, and that they had more children because they could afford them. Pessimists retort that the rising generation of males married earlier because they had been 'proletarianized'—that is to say, they had no reason to postpone marriage, because they saw no prospect of inheriting a smallholding or of succeeding their fathers as independent artisans—and also that they *needed* children to bring in wages, for example by working on textile looms. Whatever the reasons, more than 60 per cent of people were less than 24 years old during the first half of the nineteenth century.[10]

[8] Eric Kerridge, *The Agricultural Revolution* (1967), 181–267.
[9] E. L. Jones, *Agriculture and the Industrial Revolution* (Oxford, 1974), 67–84.
[10] As compared with 44.4% in France in 1851.

TABLE 1.1. *Population of the United Kingdom, 1781–1851*

Date	England	England, Wales, and Scotland	Ireland
1781	7,050,000		4,048,000
1791	7,750,000		4,753,000
1801	8,650,000	10,501,000	
1811	9,900,000	11,970,000	
1821	11,500,000	14,092,000	6,802,000
1831	13,300,000	16,261,000	7,767,000
1841	15,000,000	18,534,000	8,175,000
1851	16,750,000	20,817,000	6,552,000

TABLE 1.2. *Population of nine fast-growing towns, 1801 and 1851*

Town	Population (1801)	Population (1851)	Average annual % increase
Bradford	13,000	104,000	14.00
Liverpool	82,000	376,000	7.17
Huddersfield	7,000	31,000	6.86
Manchester	75,000	303,000	6.08
Blackburn	12,000	47,000	5.83
Wolverhampton	13,000	50,000	5.69
Birmingham	71,000	233,000	4.56
Leeds	53,000	172,000	4.49
Sheffield	46,000	135,000	3.87

Population explosion can of course occur in rural societies, such as twentieth-century India, but in England's case, just as significant as the explosion itself was the spectacular growth of towns in formerly backward regions like the West Riding, the North-West, and the Midlands. With the possible exception of Liverpool, the towns listed in Table 1.2 were all relatively new, possibly because industrialists found it easier to expand in places that were unencumbered by restrictive guild regulations and corporation red tape. (It might explain why, unusually in Europe, Britain's major cities contain so little medieval or early modern architecture,[11] and conversely why Britain's medieval and early modern towns have remained relatively small.) London meanwhile merely doubled

---

[11] Pre-1940 Coventry being a notable exception.

in size, but did so from a very much higher base, reaching almost 2.5 million in 1846, or two-and-a-half times the size of its nearest European rival, Paris. All in all, by 1851 slightly more than half the English lived in towns, as compared with less than one-third in 1801 and about 10 per cent in the world as a whole.

Population growth and urbanization inevitably caused severe social problems.[12] Already by 1783 Britain had reverted to being a net importer of wheat, while during the 1830s imports of that vital commodity outstripped exports by more than fourteen times. Further strain was evident in the dramatic rise in food and other prices during wartime (1793–1815). These trends threatened to confirm the dire message of the *Essay on the Principle of Population* (1798), in which Robert Malthus predicted demographic disaster, as the number of mouths to be fed increased at a much faster pace than farmers could grow food. Disaster did indeed strike in Ireland, with the Great Famine of the 1840s, but not in Britain. Although there was no growth in income per capita until almost the end of the period, there was throughout just enough increase in output to avoid a social catastrophe. It was an economic triumph of sorts, but it was also—to quote the Duke of Wellington's famous words on the battle of Waterloo—'a damned close run thing'.

So the question to be asked is not why this country pioneered an economic revolution and a new form of social organization, but how it managed to pull through during a period of grave economic strain. To what extent did increased productivity in manufacturing enable food and other necessaries to be purchased from abroad? How big a part did infrastructural factors play, or the service industries, or the State in both its central and local manifestations? And given the dramatic exodus from the land—agriculture employed only about 22 per cent of

TABLE 1.3. *Price of wheat and commodity price index by decade, 1781–1850*

Decade	Average price of wheat (s. per quarter)	Commodity price index
1781–1790	47.9	
1791–1800	63.5	109.4
1801–1810	84.0	138.1
1811–1820	87.5	139.4
1821–1830	59.4	98.6
1831–1840	56.9	94.1
1841–1850	53.3	84.3

[12] See below, pp. 573–8.

the workforce in 1851 compared with 35 per cent fifty years earlier—how on earth did agricultural output manage to rise to meet the needs of townsfolk?

Of these four factors, the last is the most problematic since, with hand and horse power continuing to dominate arable farming, there were no major technological breakthroughs, no significant productivity gains, and no net inward investment. It is going too far to say that agriculture 'seemed unchanging, and indeed unchangeable, in the hundred years before 1850',[13] since the steady increase in farm size over the period must have facilitated economies of scale in the use of labour, while the hand tools used became substantially more efficient, but it *is* the case that this was a period of agricultural expansion rather than revolution. The number of acres under cultivation increased from about 10 to 15 million between 1770 and 1850, while the area under wheat rose from about 2.8 to 3.8 million. This was partly owing to the release of former woodland for crops—a consequence of coal substituting for timber as the main source of fuel—but most of the increase took place between 1790 and 1812, when scarcity prices due to population pressure and the difficulty of importing food in wartime led the margin of cultivation to be pushed up the hillsides. Social commentators complained about 'overgrown' and grasping farmers, who sought to turn themselves into minor gentry, and whose wives fancied themselves in lace and silk, but the landlords were still more avaricious, and rents rose even faster than prices. Unfortunately, much of the newly ploughed land was on stony ground that had hitherto lain waste. Once the natural protection afforded by war had been removed, much of this poorer soil fell out of use, causing grave distress, while many traditional Midlands producers were simply unable to compete. Again the landlords did better than their tenants, since rents fell far less quickly than prices. There was a further spurt in wheat production between 1836 and 1846, but this was mainly at the expense of meadows, with the result that the area of pasture came down from over 16 million acres in 1836 to nearer 13 million in 1851, while the number of cattle and sheep fell commensurately. Even in the modernized South-East there remained a considerable number of small and relatively inefficient family farms.[14]

The most visible changes to the countryside resulted from the enclosure of common land. This process went back to Tudor times but intensified in the Hanoverian period, with a further 7 million acres or so affected. More than 4,000

[13] G. E. Mingay, 'The Progress of Agriculture, 1750–1850', 30–6; Hugh C. Prince, 'The Changing Rural Landscape, 1750–1850', 128–9; B. A. Holderness, 'Prices, Productivity, and Output', 971; all in Mingay (ed.), *The Agrarian History of England and Wales*, vi: *1750–1850* (Cambridge, 1989); Gregory Clark, 'Agriculture and the Industrial Revolution: 1700–1850', in Joel Mokyr (ed.), *The British Industrial Revolution: An Economic Perspective* (Boulder, Colo., 1993), 249.

[14] Mick Reed, 'The Peasantry of Nineteenth-Century England: A Neglected Class?', *History Workshop*, 18 (1984), 53–76.

Enclosure Acts were passed between 1750 and 1850, encouraged in part by a streamlining of parliamentary procedures, and of these about half occurred during the French revolutionary and Napoleonic wars. Historians dispute whether enclosed land enjoyed significantly higher yields than the remaining open fields,[15] but most agree about the malign social consequences. Enclosures led to the break-up of many existing leases, which led in turn to shorter leases and higher rents. They deprived labourers of common or shared-use rights, not just to grazing but to crops, brushwood, and fuel. Many cottagers and smaller yeomen were turned into landless labourers, though victims able to claim a legal as distinct from customary right to commons were usually granted a very small allotment by way of compensation. It is hardly surprising that contemporary debate over the merits or otherwise of capitalism should have focused so frequently on agriculture, since this was a sphere in which most of the benefits accrued to the landowners, few to the tenant farmers, and none whatever to the labourers and consumers. Enclosures also had political and cultural overtones, in so far as the planting of some 200,000 miles of quickset hedge between 1750 and 1850[16] created what now passes for traditional English countryside. Many Tory and Conservative diehards railed against what they saw as a desecration of the landscape, while most Whigs, as advocates of 'improvement', rejoiced. T. B. Macaulay, for example, was scornful about the absence of hedgerows in the Île de France: 'None of the drapery which makes even tame English scenery so charming.'[17]

If there were few technological breakthroughs to record in agriculture, accounts of manufacturing, and especially cotton textiles, have often been dominated by the rise of mass production and steam-driven machinery.[18] It is an oft-told and heroic story of enterprising giants. Traditional manufacturing was based on the so-called 'domestic', 'cottage', or 'putting-out' system, where capitalist masters deposited raw material at labourers' homes and collected finished goods in return. Yet in the eighteenth century a number of these masters scaled down their 'putting-out' operations in order to centralize some cotton and iron production in factories. There are as usual divergent explanations, one of which is the conjunction between 1680 and 1750 of increased demand and a static level of population, leading to labour shortages and a shift in the balance of power from masters to workers. Some of these workers (it is often argued) took advantage, either by embezzling raw materials in order to

[15] Robert C. Allen, 'The Two English Agricultural Revolutions, 1450–1850', in Bruce M. S. Campbell and Mark Overton (eds.), *Land, Labour and Livestock: Historical Studies in European Agricultural Productivity* (Manchester, 1991).

[16] Oliver Rackham, *The History of the Countryside* (1997), 190.

[17] T. B. Macaulay, diary, 21 Oct. 1838, Trinity College, Cambridge, MSS, i. 3.

[18] Such as Crompton's spinning mule (1779), Watt's rotary steam engine (1782), Cartwright's power-loom (1785).

produce goods on the side, or else by taking unscheduled days off. The latter malpractice would have been especially frustrating for the capitalists, who were seeking not only to boost supply but to make it more regular, as widening markets made them more dependent on precise transport schedules. The main attraction of factories, according to this version of events, was not the prospect of technological improvement, or economies of scale, or the opportunity to replace piece-rates by a flat wage, but rather that masters would find discipline easier to enforce, and would thereby regain control over the production process.[19] Admittedly, very few cotton textile or iron entrepreneurs centralized production in this way before 1783, but that is perhaps beside the point, since the fact that some did so meant that their rivals would be likely to follow suit before long.

If this narrative is correct, then the impulse to mechanize was a consequence rather than a cause of the movement into factories. Initially the working methods adopted in centralized production units would have been much the same as in the outworkers' cottages: Arkwright's cotton mills at Cromford from 1771 onwards were organized on factory-type lines, yet were wholly dependent on water power, while even as late as 1830 the Leeds wool merchant Benjamin Gott employed 1,300 hand-loom workers in his mills.[20] However, once the business had been concentrated on a single site it naturally became more feasible to experiment with new processes, the most visible of which, so far as the cotton industry was concerned, was the application of the Boulton–Watt rotary steam engine to a spinning mule by Manchester's McConnel and Kennedy in 1798. And as with centralization itself, once certain firms had introduced these labour-saving machines, rivals would have felt pressured to do the same. Historians have often wondered why British entrepreneurs should have proved so much more imaginative in adopting new industrial technology than the more scientifically oriented French, and some have put the answer down to 'uneducated empiricism' or 'inspired tinkering'.[21] But a more convincing answer might be that, whereas the French were required to make two leaps of imagination, some Britons found technological innovation easier because they had already centralized production.

However, while the spread of factories and machines (like that of enclosures) was important politically and culturally, its contribution to economic growth is more uncertain. Even in textiles, metalworking, and engineering, mechanization

[19] David S. Landes, *The Unbound Prometheus: Technological Change and Industrial Development in Western Europe from 1750 to the Present* (Cambridge, 1969), 41–123; Sidney Pollard, *The Genesis of Modern Management: A Study of the Industrial Revolution in Great Britain* (1965).

[20] Herbert Heaton, *The Yorkshire Woollen and Worsted Industries*, 2nd edn. (Oxford, 1965), 437.

[21] For a comprehensive and subtle analysis, see A. E. Musson and Eric Robinson, *Science and Technology in the Industrial Revolution* (Manchester, 1969), 87–189.

was fairly limited, and much of the increased production came from traditional domestic handicraft in small towns and villages. Only twenty-five out of Lancashire's 975 spinning and weaving firms employed more than a thousand workers in 1841, the average number being 193,[22] while woollen factories in the West Riding employed fewer than fifty. As for steam-powered machines, although the mule was adapted for cotton-spinning from 1785, there is no evidence that it was any more cost-effective than water power before the 1840s.[23] Cotton-weaving was not seriously affected by power-looms until the 1810s,[24] worsteds not until the 1830s,[25] and woollens with their fragile fibres not until the 1850s. Aside from textiles, more than three-quarters of British industry remained small-scale, hand- and cottage-based throughout the period,[26] and there were spectacular examples of deindustrialization to balance those in the opposite direction, notably in old woollen counties such as Wiltshire, Norfolk, and Suffolk. Finally, London rather than Lancashire remained the greatest manufacturing centre, producing clothes, boots, shoes, light metals, earthen-ware, leather, soap, chemicals, processed food, beer, paper, furniture, and timberware, all on a small scale and by traditional hand tool methods.

As for the argument about worker discipline, some historians have objected that factories merely brought new problems of control, and also that by the late eighteenth century it was unnecessary to enforce discipline on domestic workers because they were working harder anyway. Certainly, it seems that even outworkers put in considerably longer hours and took fewer casual holidays, while wives and children switched from predominantly household chores to producing goods for market. As usual, the cause of this so-called 'industrious revolution' is disputed. Perhaps workers took advantage of developing markets in order to maximize earning power, and to purchase consumer goods such as tea, tobacco, sugar, and the new 'wave of gadgets' that were available.[27] That

[22] V. A. C. Gatrell, 'Labour, Power and the Size of Firms in Lancashire Cotton in the Second Quarter of the Nineteenth Century', *EconHR* 30 (1977), 95–139.

[23] G. N. von Tunzelman, *Steam Power and British Industrialization to 1860* (Oxford, 1978), 47–97, 175–251.

[24] Almost 110,000 power-looms were operational in the Lancashire cotton industry in 1836, almost 250,000 in 1850.

[25] Though when such machines did come, they came exceeding fast. In 1836 there were 2,768 power-looms in the West Riding; nine years later there were 19,121, and hardly any hand-looms left (Herbert Heaton, *The Yorkshire Woollen and Worsted Industries from the Earliest Times up to the Industrial Revolution* (Oxford, 1920), 356–8).

[26] Raphael Samuel, 'The Workshop of the World: Steam Power and Hand Technology in Mid-Victorian Britain', *History Workshop*, 3 (1977), 6–72; Maxine Berg, *The Age of Manufactures: Industry, Innovation and Work in Britain 1700–1820* (Oxford, 1985).

[27] Jan de Vries, 'Between Purchasing Power and the World of Goods: Understanding the Household Economy in Early Modern Europe', in John Brewer and Roy Porter (eds.), *Consumption and the World of Goods* (1993).

would be the optimistic explanation. However, it is more likely that they were driven to work harder by the pressure of rising prices from the 1790s, and the consequent squeeze on real wages.[28]

There are further disagreements over the relative impact on the economy of high- and low-tech industry. The West Midlands region centred on Birmingham underwent structural changes *before* 1760 and *after* 1850 but not in between,[29] prompting the historian Eric Hobsbawm to write, 'it was not Birmingham, a city which produced a great deal more in 1850 than in 1750, but essentially in the old way, which made contemporaries speak of an industrial revolution, but Manchester, a city which produced more in a more obviously revolutionary manner'.[30] Even so, Birmingham's economic contribution should not be discounted. Its so-called toy trade encompassed a multitude of small articles made from iron, brass, and steel: buttons, pins, keys, buckles, jewellery, guns. What mattered was not mass manufacture but short production runs and above all flexibility, allowing firms to introduce novelties and to take advantage of sudden changes in fashion (instance the 1780s, when a vogue for shoelaces destroyed the buckle trade). Many of these products were of high value, but there was also money to be made out of populuxe goods, meaning cheap copies of luxury items: jewellery, watches, snuffboxes, books. As the Birmingham experience shows, labour being plentiful and cheap, it was often unnecessary for entrepreneurs to undertake expensive investment in machinery. It also explains how there could be a notable rise in national output, despite the fact that capitalization was remarkably low by subsequent standards.[31] Perhaps, as another historian has suggested, 'the triumph of the industrial revolution lay in getting a lot of workers into industry rather than obtaining high productivity from them once there'.[32]

Even this cautious verdict may overstate the significance of manufacturing. Despite the country's status as the workshop of the world, worsening terms of trade meant a consistently adverse balance between imports and domestic exports. The last recorded surplus ever (a mere £200,000) was notched in 1822, and by the 1840s the deficit on visible trade was running at about £23 million per annum. That the current account was nevertheless in credit by nearly £5 million per annum was thanks to invisibles, which on average brought in nearly

[28] For discussion of possible causes, see Hans-Joachim Voth, *Time and Work in England, 1750–1830* (Oxford, 2000), 161–241.

[29] Marie B. Rowlands, 'Continuity and Change in an Industrialising Society: The Case of the West Midlands Industries', in Pat Hudson (ed.), *Regions and Industries: A Perspective on the Industrial Revolution in Britain* (Cambridge, 1989).

[30] Hobsbawm, *Industry and Empire*, 20.

[31] H. J. Habakkuk, *American and British Technology in the Nineteenth Century: The Search for Labour-Saving Inventions* (Cambridge, 1962), 132–88.

[32] N. F. R. Crafts, *British Economic Growth during the Industrial Revolution* (Oxford, 1985), 156.

£28 million during the 1840s, more than a quarter of which came from earnings on overseas investments. The City of London shared with Paris the role of clearing house for financial transactions, and was the leading market for insurance services and securities.[33] Yet even these activities were less important than the entrepôt trade, for London was unquestionably the *warehouse* of the world, handling £3.7 million of foreign and colonial tonnage in 1841, as well as £4.1 million of coastal trade. (It was estimated in 1818 that at any one time the river Thames, with its almost 4 miles of dockyards stretching as far as Limehouse and Deptford, played host to 1,100 ships, 3,000 barges, 2,288 small coastal craft, 3,000 passenger vessels, 3,000 watermen or navigators, 4,000 labourers to load and unload, and 12,000 revenue officers.[34]) By 1846 re-exports of raw cotton were valued at over £4 million, dyewood and dyestuff at nearly £2 million, coffee, sugar, and tea each at well over half a million. By such criteria, foreign commerce easily trumped manufacturing in importance.

Internal trading was also highly developed, but once again there is uncertainty over causes and chronology. It used to be supposed that the main development of retailing at fixed points of sale occurred in the early nineteenth century, i.e. just *after* Napoleon called the English 'a nation of shopkeepers',[35] yet recent research has demonstrated that many of the most important innovations had occurred a hundred years earlier, alongside the commercial and consumer revolutions. By 1750 there was already a shop for every thirty to forty people in the South of England, a far higher density than exists today, and that statistic excludes markets and alehouses. Establishments ranged from posh town centre drapers and milliners to corner shops and back-street stores. Already many retailers were specializing in particular types of goods and making use of sophisticated transport and credit systems, advertisements, promotional gimmicks, postal sales, free deliveries, pre-packaging, and branding.[36] It seems that Napoleon knew what he was talking about. What mainly took place between 1783 and 1846 was that all these practices spread rapidly from London, Bristol, Norwich, and the South generally to the developing areas of the Midlands and North. However, it would be untrue to say that *no* structural changes took place during this period. Transaction costs certainly fell as retailing became almost entirely differentiated from wholesale, and the process of producing goods was separated from that of distributing them.

---

[33] For the superior efficiency of the finance and service sectors over those of the United States and Germany, see S. N. Broadberry, *The Productivity Race: British Manufacturing in International Perspective, 1850–1990* (Cambridge, 1997), 64–5.

[34] [Samuel Leigh], *Leigh's New Picture of London* (1818), 229–31.

[35] Peter Mathias, *The Brewing Industry in England 1700–1830* (Cambridge, 1959), 100.

[36] Hoh-cheung and Lorna H. Mui, *Shops and Shopkeeping in Eighteenth-Century England* (Kingston, 1989).

The growth of the retail sector may have had a homogenizing effect, but in other respects there was increasing regional specialization.[37] Lancashire textile masters focused almost exclusively on cottons, leaving woollens and worsteds to the West Riding, silk to Coventry, and lace to the East Midlands. The great western ports of Liverpool and Bristol retained their interest in sugar, slaves, and increasingly palm oil. Birmingham concentrated on the metal trades, Sheffield on cutlery, north Staffordshire on pottery, Newcastle on coal and ships, and the Black Country on coal and pig-iron. There were various reasons for this differential pattern of development, one of which relates to what economists call externalities. The towns referred to were notoriously blighted by crime, pollution, and disease, but they were also centres of sociability, with clubs and societies where members could do business almost without realizing it over port and pork pie. Such personal contacts were necessary because the traditional capital markets were highly localized, and there was need for inter-firm cooperation in matters like price-fixing and wage cuts.[38] Another reason is that historically England's waterways had been more successful in facilitating contact within regions than between them. A crucial factor in the creation of an integrated market was the development, from the 1770s onwards, of an impressive network of canals for carrying freight (see Map 1.2). This undoubtedly lowered distribution costs, but if traders were to buy and sell goods nationally, a sophisticated credit network was also vital. After 1783 the banking system became increasingly integrated via London,[39] while the rise of railway finance after 1830 meant that local banking networks diminished in importance, and successful businessmen opened branches in far-flung parts of the country. This was recognized symbolically in the 1840s when it was decided that all of Britain should adopt standard Greenwich time in order to allow the new railway network to function efficiently. Even so, the country remained a disparate collection of local economic communities.

One consequence of regional specialization was that aristocrats and manufacturers often pulled together to promote a common interest.[40] Pressure groups, lobbies, trade associations, and chambers of commerce played an increasingly important part in local affairs, and formed a link with central government by petitioning Parliament and lobbying the Board of Trade. Because of this it has been suggested that regions developed different cultural as well as economic identities,[41] but this seems unlikely, if only because the rapidly expanding

[37] Pat Hudson, 'The Regional Perspective', in Hudson (ed.), *Regions and Industries*.

[38] Robin Pearson and David Richardson, 'Business Networking in the Industrial Revolution', *EconHR* 54 (2001), 677.   [39] See below, pp. 152–3.

[40] Richard H. Trainor, *Black Country Elites: The Exercise of Authority in an Industrialized Area 1830–1900* (Oxford, 1993), 86–90.

[41] John Langton, 'The Industrial Revolution and the Regional Geography of England', *Transactions of the Institute of British Geographers*, 9 (1984), 145–67.

transport network made the English much more mobile. Already by 1783 there was a dense spider's web of turnpike roads (see Map 1.1). Isolated communities measured their distance to the nearest staging posts, which were linked to each other by coaches, usually provided by neighbouring innkeepers and pulled by two or four horses. From 1784 expensive six-horse mail coaches began to be introduced on key business routes in a public–private partnership involving armed guards and a Post Office subsidy, while smaller branch carriers ferried passengers between these routes and more remote localities. Where possible, timetables were coordinated to ensure speed of transfer from one major route to another. Gradually roads were straightened and drained, their foundations strengthened, and their surfaces made smoother. New bridges—sometimes of iron—carried them over rivers and gullies. As a result of these developments the journey time from London to Bristol came down from forty hours in 1750 to less than twenty-four in 1783 and under twelve in 1811, while by 1830 as many as thirteen coaches a day crossed the Pennines between Leeds and Manchester. In addition to stage coaches, about 1,000 goods wagons entered or left London each week, many carrying loads of up to 6 tons.[42] Even more significant advances in passenger transport occurred after 1830 with the beginning of the steam railway. Over 3,000 miles of permanent track had been built by 1846 (Map 1.3), when it was possible to travel from London to Bristol in less than four hours, and to Manchester in just over eight (Figure 1.1). In that year more than 20 million passengers were recorded, of whom at least a third were cramped into cheap third-class coaches, prompting the Duke of Wellington to complain that railways 'encourage the lower classes to travel about'.

News too travelled faster than ever before, thanks to the introduction of mail coaches, and people in different parts of the country got to know far more about each other. Although the penny post[43] was not introduced until 1840, long before then private letter-writing became something of a craze, especially among women, and led to an obsession with the weather as correspondents in different regions speculated on prospects for the next harvest. There was also an explosion of print culture: by the 1790s more than half a million copies of morning newspapers were sold in London alone. Book production had grown considerably throughout the eighteenth century, but it leaped dramatically during the last quarter, when it has been estimated that sales rose by a factor of four, and 'acts of reading' by a factor of fifty. An important catalyst was an Act of 1774, which abolished perpetual copyright, and limited to just fourteen years

[42] E. Pawson, *Transport and Economy: The Turnpike Roads of Eighteenth Century Britain* (1977), 286–91; Dorian Gerhold, *Road Transport before the Railways: Russell's London Flying Wagons* (Cambridge, 1993), 1.
[43] Which led before long to a uniform cost for internal deliveries irrespective of distance (M. J. Daunton, *Royal Mail: The Post Office since 1840* (1985), 36–49).

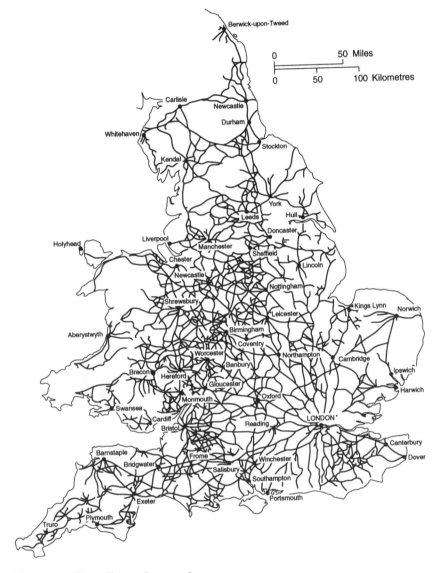

MAP 1.1. Turnpike road network, 1770

Source: Eric Pawson, *Transport and Economy: The Turnpike Roads of Eighteenth Century Britain* (1977), 151.

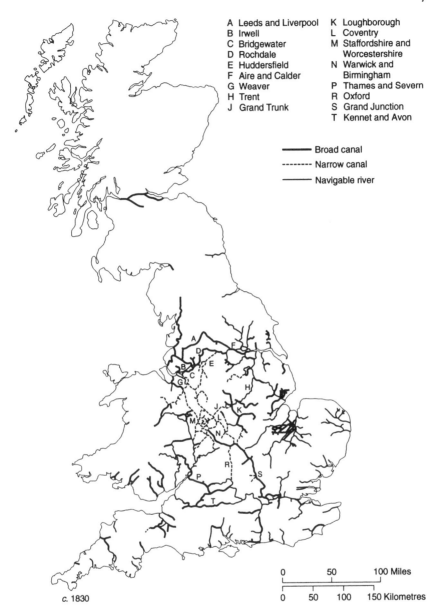

A Leeds and Liverpool
B Irwell
C Bridgewater
D Rochdale
E Huddersfield
F Aire and Calder
G Weaver
H Trent
J Grand Trunk

K Loughborough
L Coventry
M Staffordshire and
   Worcestershire
N Warwick and
   Birmingham
P Thames and Severn
R Oxford
S Grand Junction
T Kennet and Avon

———— Broad canal

- - - - - - Narrow canal

———— Navigable river

c. 1830

MAP 1.2. Inland navigation, *c.*1830

Source: M. J. Daunton, *Progress and Poverty: An Economic and Social History of Britain 1700–1850* (Oxford, 1995), 293.

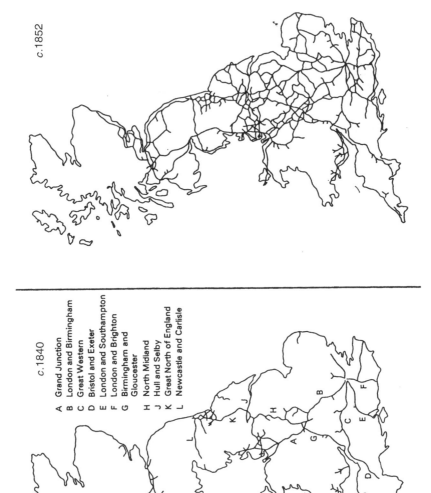

c.1852

c.1840

   A Grand Junction
   B London and Birmingham
   C Great Western
   D Bristol and Exeter
   E London and Southampton
   F London and Brighton
   G Birmingham and
      Gloucester
   H North Midland
   J Hull and Selby
   K Great North of England
   L Newcastle and Carlisle

MAP 1.3. Railway network, *c*.1840 and *c*.1852

Source: Harold Pollins, *Britain's Railways: An Industrial History* (Newton Abott, 1971), 32, 42.

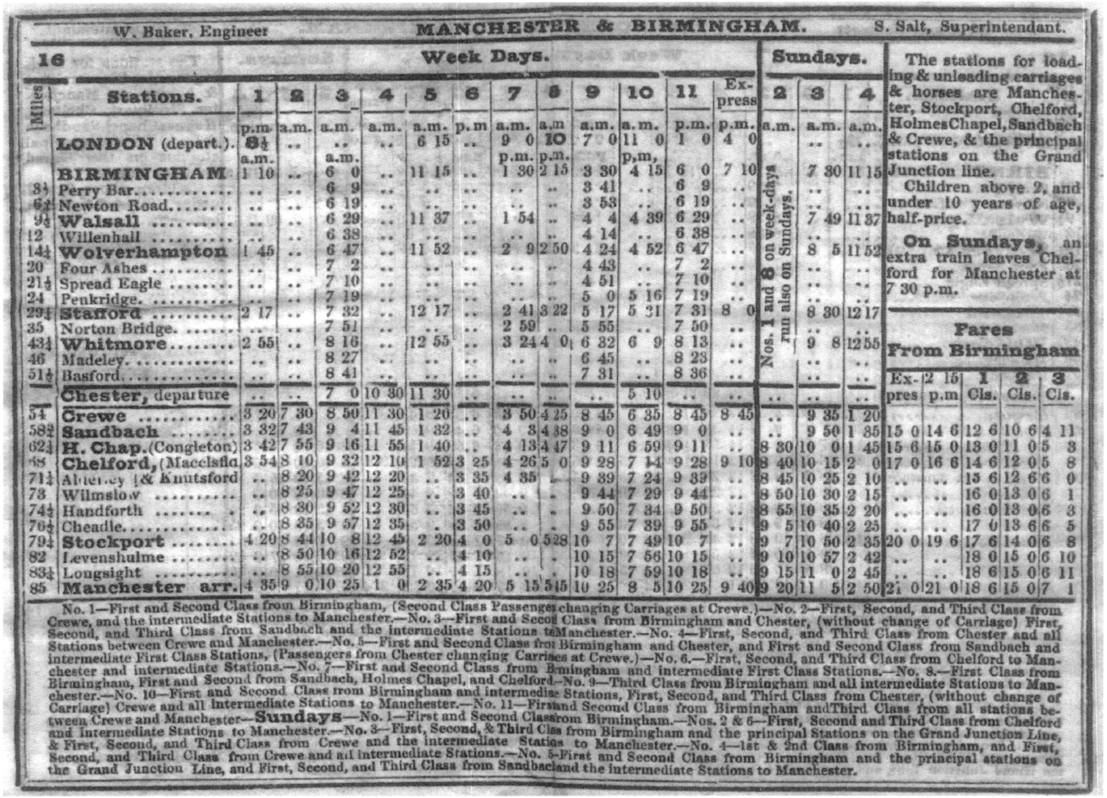

W. Baker, Engineer — **MANCHESTER & BIRMINGHAM.** — S. Salt, Superintendant.

16 — **Week Days.** / **Sundays.**

Miles	Stations.	1	2	3	4	5	6	7	8	9	10	11	Express	Sun. 2	Sun. 3	Sun. 4
		p.m.	a.m.	a.m.	a.m.	a.m.	p.m	a.m.	a.m	a.m.	a.m.	p.m.	p.m.	a.m.	a.m.	a.m.
	LONDON (depart.).	8½	..	..	..	6 15	..	9 0	10	7 0	11 0	1 0	4 0		..	..
		a.m.		a.m.				p.m.	p.m.		p.m.					
	BIRMINGHAM	1 10	..	6 0	..	11 15	..	1 30	2 15	3 30	4 15	6 0	7 10		7 30	11 15
3¼	Perry Bar	..	..	6 9	..	..	..	..	..	3 41	..	6 9	..		..	..
6¾	Newton Road	..	..	6 19	..	..	..	..	..	3 53	..	6 19	..		..	..
9½	**Walsall**	..	..	6 29	..	11 37	..	1 54	..	4 4	4 39	6 29	..		7 49	11 37
12	Willenhall	..	..	6 38	..	..	..	..	..	4 14	..	6 38	..		..	..
14¼	**Wolverhampton**	1 45	..	6 47	..	11 52	..	2 9	2 50	4 24	4 52	6 47	..		8 5	11 52
20	Four Ashes	..	..	7 2	..	..	..	..	..	4 43	..	7 2	..		..	..
21½	Spread Eagle	..	..	7 10	..	..	..	..	..	4 51	..	7 10	..		..	..
24	Penkridge	..	..	7 19	..	..	..	..	..	5 0	5 16	7 19	..		..	..
29¼	**Stafford**	2 17	..	7 32	..	12 17	..	2 41	3 22	5 17	5 31	7 31	8 0		8 30	12 17
35	Norton Bridge	..	..	7 51	..	..	..	2 59	..	5 55	..	7 50	..		..	..
43¼	**Whitmore**	2 55	..	8 16	..	12 55	..	3 24	4 0	6 32	6 9	8 13	..		9 8	12 55
46	Madeley	..	..	8 27	..	..	..	..	..	6 45	..	8 23	..		..	..
51½	Basford	..	..	8 41	..	..	..	..	..	7 31	..	8 36	..		..	..
	Chester, departure	..	..	7 0	10 30	11 30	..	..	..	..	5 10	..	..	..	..	..
54	**Crewe**	3 20	7 30	8 50	11 30	1 20	..	3 50	4 25	8 45	6 35	8 45	8 45	..	9 35	1 20
58¾	**Sandbach**	3 32	7 43	9 4	11 45	1 32	..	4 3	4 38	9 0	6 49	9 0	..	..	9 50	1 35
62¼	**H. Chap.** (Congleton)	3 42	7 55	9 16	11 55	1 40	..	4 13	4 47	9 11	6 59	9 11	..	8 30	10 0	1 45
68	**Chelford,** (Macclsfld	3 54	8 10	9 32	12 10	1 52	3 25	4 26	5 0	9 28	7 14	9 28	9 10	8 40	10 15	2 0
71¼	Alderley [& Knutsford	..	8 20	9 42	12 20	..	3 35	4 35	..	9 39	7 24	9 39	..	8 45	10 25	2 10
73	Wilmslow	..	8 25	9 47	12 25	..	3 40	..	..	9 44	7 29	9 44	..	8 50	10 30	2 15
74½	Handforth	..	8 30	9 52	12 30	..	3 45	..	..	9 50	7 34	9 50	..	8 55	10 35	2 20
76½	Cheadle	..	8 35	9 57	12 35	..	3 50	..	..	9 55	7 39	9 55	..	9 5	10 40	2 25
79¼	**Stockport**	4 20	8 44	10 8	12 45	2 20	4 0	5 0	5 28	10 7	7 49	10 7	..	9 7	10 50	2 35
82	Levenshulme	..	8 50	10 16	12 52	..	4 10	..	..	10 15	7 56	10 15	..	9 10	10 57	2 42
83¾	Longsight	..	8 55	10 20	12 55	..	4 15	..	..	10 18	7 59	10 18	..	9 15	11 0	2 45
85	**Manchester arr.**	4 35	9 0	10 25	1 0	2 35	4 20	5 15	5 45	10 25	8 5	10 25	9 40	9 20	11 5	2 50

Nos. 1 and 8 on week-days run also on Sundays.

The stations for loading & unloading carriages & horses are Manchester, Stockport, Chelford, Holmes Chapel, Sandbach & Crewe, & the principal stations on the Grand Junction line.

Children above 2, and under 10 years of age, half-price.

On Sundays, an extra train leaves Chelford for Manchester at 7 30 p.m.

Fares From Birmingham

Stations	Express	2 15 p.m	1 Cls.	2 Cls.	3 Cls.
Sandbach	15 0	14 6	12 6	10 6	4 11
H. Chap.	15 6	15 0	13 0	11 0	5 3
Chelford	17 0	16 6	14 6	12 0	5 8
Alderley	..	..	15 6	12 6	6 0
Wilmslow	..	..	16 0	13 0	6 1
Handforth	..	..	16 0	13 0	6 3
Cheadle	..	..	17 0	13 6	6 5
Stockport	20 0	19 6	17 6	14 0	6 8
Levenshulme	..	..	18 0	15 0	6 10
Longsight	..	..	18 6	15 0	6 11
Manchester	21 0	21 0	18 6	15 0	7 1

No. 1—First and Second Class from Birmingham, (Second Class Passenger changing Carriages at Crewe.)—No. 2—First, Second, and Third Class from Crewe, and the intermediate Stations to Manchester.—No. 3—First and Secoi Class from Birmingham and Chester, (without change of Carriage) First, Second, and Third Class from Sandbach and the intermediate Stations toManchester.—No. 4—First, Second, and Third Class from Chester and all Stations between Crewe and Manchester.—No. 5—First and Second Class fro Birmingham and Chester, and First and Second Class from Sandbach and intermediate First Class Stations, (Passengers from Chester changing Carriaes at Crewe.)—No. 6.—First, Second, and Third Class from Chelford to Manchester and intermediate Stations.—No. 7—First and Second Class from Bmingham and intermediate First Class Stations.—No. 8.—First Class from Birmingham, First and Second from Sandbach, Holmes Chapel, and Chelford.—No. 9—Third Class from Birmingham and all intermediate Stations to Manchester.—No. 10—First and Second Class from Birmingham and intermediae Stations, First, Second, and Third Class from Chester, (without change of Carriage) Crewe and all intermediate Stations to Manchester.—No. 11—Firsand Second Class from Birmingham andThird Class from all stations between Crewe and Manchester—**Sundays**—No. 1—First and Second Classrom Birmingham.—Nos. 2 & 6—First, Second and Third Class from Chelford and Intermediate Stations to Manchester.—No. 3—First, Second, & Third Clas from Birmingham and the principal Stations on the Grand Junction Line, & First, Second, and Third Class from Crewe and the intermediate Statios to Manchester.—No. 4—1st & 2nd Class from Birmingham, and First, Second, and Third Class from Crewe and all intermediate Stations.—No. 5-First and Second Class from Birmingham and the principal stations on the Grand Junction Line, and First, Second, and Third Class from Sandbacland the intermediate Stations to Manchester.

FIG. 1.1. Railway timetable, 1844

Source: *Bradshaw's Railway Companion 1845*.

the length of time for which printers and publishers could prevent unauthorized copies of their books. In 1808 that period was extended to twenty-eight years, in 1814 it was extended further in certain cases to include the life of the author, and in 1842 long copyrights were introduced, but meanwhile there had been sixty-five years of intense cultural fermentation thanks to the open market in cheap popular editions of traditional texts.[44] In this context the word 'pirate' came to have publishing rather than maritime connotations. Thomas Tegg, who launched his business in 1826, more or less created a market in remainders, and was rivalled later by Henry Bohn. Meanwhile, the circulation of non-fiction (or 'rational information') was also increasing at an incredible rate. The Society for the Diffusion of Useful Knowledge, founded in the same year, charged just sixpence for a series of publications by an enterprising Whig sympathizer, Charles Knight. His Tory counterpart John Murray responded to these initiatives with fifty-three pocket-sized volumes of the *Family Library* (1829–34). Soon afterwards Longmans brought out the *Cabinet Cyclopædia*, 133 volumes edited by the Irishman Dionysius Lardner, and this was followed by Knight's illustrated *Penny Magazine* (1832–45), which began with a circulation of about 200,000 and a readership of over a million, though these levels were not sustained. Before long books became cheaper still, thanks to the rapid spread of steam printing in the 1830s and to distribution by railway. Among the first to take advantage were William and Robert Chambers, whose *Edinburgh Journal* (1832) and People's Editions of famous books established them as forerunners in the field.[45] All these improving volumes were aimed at the working classes, and were motivated by political and didactic considerations as well as commercial ones, but they were mainly bought by the middle classes, who were as ever alive to a bargain. Nevertheless, there is no doubt that the ideas and information contained in them reached a wide audience, being disseminated by local journalists, itinerant lecturers, and those who addressed the mechanics institutes that were established in almost every industrial centre. A thirst for knowledge contributed to what was sometimes admiringly and sometimes disparagingly called 'the march of mind'. England was a country obsessively communicating with itself, one consequence of which was a nationwide marketplace in ideas, or what the social philosopher Jürgen Habermas has called a public sphere.

[44] William St Clair, *The Reading Nation and the Romantic Period* (Cambridge, 2004), 103–21; James Raven, *Judging New Wealth: Popular Publishing and Responses to Commerce in England, 1750–1800* (Oxford, 1992), 32–5.

[45] James A. Secord, *Victorian Sensation: The Extraordinary Publication, Reception, and Secret Authorship of 'Vestiges of the Natural History of Creation'* (Chicago, 2000), 41–76; John Sutherland, 'The British Book Trade and the Crash of 1826', *The Library*, 9 (1987), 148–61; Simon Eliot, *Some Patterns and Trends in British Publishing 1800–1919* (1994), 7–20, 44–6.

One idea which prospered in that market was that of the market itself. By the end of the period, the proposition advanced by Adam Smith at the beginning— that economic growth was best advanced by a minimal State and the free play of competition—was in the process of becoming accepted as an orthodoxy. By then most economists had come to deride as corrupt and inefficient the mercantilist states of the eighteenth century. In the same vein, some historians have attributed Britain's economic growth to its government's hands-off approach in comparison with other countries. However, this may be to muddle cause and effect. If, instead of seeking reasons for the 'first Industrial Revolution', one asks 'How did Britain weather the demographic storm?', part of the answer lies in the beneficial effects of mercantilism—or, as it is now called, the 'fiscal–military state'.[46]

It will be evident from the figures in Table 1.4 just how fiscal the Hanoverian state was. The regime had always relied heavily on indirect taxes, which encouraged exports and import substitution, but by 1783 the intention was clearly as much protective as fiscal, with heavy duties on corn and other produce and a ban on the import of silk and Indian calicoes. It was also forbidden to export machinery, while artisans primed with industrial secrets were not allowed to emigrate. Then during the French wars the schedule became more protective still, not always by design but as a spin-off from the need to raise additional revenue. (It is sometimes claimed that government borrowing in wartime crowded out productive private investment,[47] but the increased tariffs which were necessary to pay the interest on public loans may paradoxically have had a contrary effect.) The Navigation Laws had long guaranteed British ships a huge slice of the coastal, Continental, and imperial trades. Aimed initially against the Dutch, they were the means of building up a huge merchant marine, which was in turn regarded as a nursery for naval seamen in time of war. Most of Britain's eighteenth-century wars led to the conquest of new territory and new markets along the world's shipping routes. Colonial acquisitions, it has been argued, provided a much-needed injection of resources into the domestic economy, not least the calorific content of Caribbean sugar. Without this 'ecological windfall', according to one historian, the country might not have overcome the constraints implied by limits on the amount of available land.[48] The French wars in particular, while their impact on manufacturing industry was broadly neutral, gave a further enormous fillip to commerce, shipping, banking, and insurance.

---

[46] John Brewer, *The Sinews of Power: War, Money and the English State, 1688–1783* (1989).

[47] For the 'crowding-out' argument, see Jeffrey G. Williamson, 'Why was British Growth so Slow during the Industrial Revolution?', *Journal of Economic History*, 44 (1984), 687–712. For the opposite view, see Carol E. Heim and Philip Mirowski, 'Interest Rates and Crowding-Out during Britain's Industrial Revolution', *Journal of Economic History*, 47 (1987), 117–39; Larry Neal, *The Rise of Financial Capitalism: International Capital Markets in the Age of Reason* (Cambridge, 1990), 216–22.

[48] Pomeranz, *Great Divergence*, 274–97, 313–15.

TABLE 1.4. *Estimated national income, total revenue, and indirect tax revenues,
1712–1810*

Year	Estimated national income at current prices (£m.)	Total revenue at current prices (£m.)	Total revenue as % of national income	Indirect taxes[a] as % of total taxes
1712	60.77	5.83	9.59	57.2
1741	72.74	6.24	8.58	64.4
1759	82.43	8.05	9.77	66.8
1779	112.21	11.29	10.06	68.7
1782	118.29	12.90	10.91	67.7
1791	153.92	17.89	11.62	67.3
1799	232.48	32.47	13.96	59.5
1806	271.41	51.77	19.07	60.5
1810	358.98	63.49	17.68	56.9

[a] Customs, excise.

Source: Patrick K. O'Brien and Philip A. Hunt, 'The Rise of a Fiscal State in England, 1485–1815', *Histrorical Research*, 66 (1993), 175.

The fiscal–military state also adopted a paternal role in mitigating some of the worst consequences of economic change. The most important instrument for the relief of suffering was the Poor Law, a traditional system of legal charity or social security paid for from local taxes.[49] Malthus blamed its existence for the falling age of marriage, and certainly it might explain why so many people were willing to risk moving off the land. However, as rising prices began to pinch in wartime, in southern counties especially poor relief was increasingly used to supplement wages as well as to support the old and indigent, its main customary function. As will be seen, the strains this placed on the local tax base was one of the main reasons why the old assumptions of 'moral economy' came to be discarded. A more repressive type of interventionism was the policy of transporting criminals to Australia, which began in 1787. The consequences for that industrializing society must surely have been grim, had it not been able to flush out its most antisocial members.

Given the constraints on agriculture, and the unwillingness of governments to do more than mop up at the margins of society, economic survival depended on its men of business in the widest sense, but for them the period was marked

---

[49] For the contrast with Scotland, Ireland, and most of the rest of Europe, where relief was wholly or almost wholly voluntary, see Joanna Innes, 'The Distinctiveness of the English Poor Laws, 1750–1850', in Donald Winch and Patrick K. O'Brien (eds.), *The Political Economy of British Historical Experience, 1688–1914* (Oxford, 2002).

by failure as much as by prosperity. Even in successful sectors the line between winners and losers could be very narrow. For example, the cotton industry grew dramatically between 1780 and 1815, yet that did not prevent four out of every five of Manchester's manufacturers from failing.[50] Such reverses were inevitable because of the violent way in which the economy fluctuated, and the banks did not help, since many were only too willing to lend money in booms and cut back viciously in downturns, thereby reinforcing rather than dampening cycles. There were huge commercial and financial crises in 1811, 1825, 1837, and 1847, with lesser shocks in between, all of which created a sense of disorientation and insecurity. In 1846, when this volume closes, the economy was on a roll, but four years earlier it had still been mired in the worst manufacturing recession of the century. These conditions help to explain why, during the period as a whole, there was a surge in suicides, which more than balanced the decline in deaths from duelling.

What most alarmed businessmen was their enhanced exposure to risk. Increasingly manufacturers had to give very long credit in order to secure markets. Merchants were forced to sell goods to customers outside their own regions, or to trade bills of exchange with parties whom they did not know, even by repute. Others might invest in what turned out to be worthless enterprises, in which case the risk of bankruptcy and incarceration was very real. Debtor's prisons like King's Bench, the Fleet, the Marshalsea, and Newgate received 13,586 new inmates in 1843 alone. For some they were living hells, for others safe havens from creditors, while for society at large they symbolized the pitfalls attaching to insubstantial wealth.[51] Various strategies were attempted for cutting risk, such as life insurance policies, land purchase, marriage settlements in benefit of wives, and recourse to specialized bill-brokers, but the only effective prophylactic was the joint-stock company, since such bodies were able to achieve limited liability status by private (and costly) Act of Parliament. Without their proliferation in the 1830s, it is unlikely that private capital would have been attracted into large and uncertain undertakings such as railways or utilities (gas and water).

Such was the prevalence of risk and insecurity that the business cycle came to displace the harvest as the most portentous variable in the eyes of nineteenth-century policy-makers. Increasingly their aim was to promote effective market behaviour, to persuade capitalists to invest in utilities, and to prevent those utilities from exploiting monopoly powers to the detriment of consumers. They might have presented policy in more emotive terms—as a means to achieve

[50] Stanley Chapman, *The Rise of Merchant Banking* (1984), 10–11.

[51] Margot C. Finn, *The Character of Credit: Personal Debt in English Culture, 1740–1914* (Cambridge, 2003), 109–51; Timothy L. Alborn, *Conceiving Companies: Joint-Stock Politics in Victorian England* (1998), 79–115.

freedom, morality, and responsibility—but their underlying concern was the difficulty of managing the country at this time of overwhelming demographic challenge.

AN OLD OR NEW REGIME?

Outwardly England was transformed between 1783 and 1846, but what about inwardly? The previous volume in this series closed with the comment that a period of apparent stability had in fact experienced striking changes. 'The polite and commercial people of the 1730s was still polite and commercial in the 1780s [but] did not, in any fundamental sense, inhabit the same society.'[52] There was to be an equally marked shift in perspective during the years 1846–86, which are covered in the following volume.[53] Yet it is probably *not* the case that someone who went to sleep in 1783 and woke up in 1846 would have felt significantly out of place, despite the railways and chimney stacks and associated soot and smoke. In term of basic attitudes and culture, England changed greatly during the last two decades of the eighteenth century, and again at the middle of the nineteenth, but the years in between—the years covered here—formed what in many ways was a distinctive period.

Some weighty historians have rejected this perspective in favour of what they call the 'long eighteenth century'. To them the first fifty or so years of the period should really be interpreted as the tail-end of an *ancien régime*, a term which also serves to emphasize its affinity with much of Continental Europe. From 1660 until about 1830, it is argued, England was governed—mentally as well as in fact—by three great institutions: the monarchy, which was accorded the status of divine right; the Church of England as by law established, otherwise known as the Anglican Communion, whose priests were assumed to possess sacramental and sacerdotal powers; and a hereditary and territorial aristocracy at whose apex was the peerage. (A fourth institution, not often cited in this context, was patriarchy.) By comparison, it is claimed, innovations like the Industrial Revolution, political radicalism, secularism, and middle-class consciousness made little impact, notwithstanding the growth of towns and the spread of religious (and civil) Dissent. Again according to the theory, the end of the *ancien régime*, when it finally came, was sudden. 'In 1827, no one could have foreseen the destruction of the old society between 1828 and 1832.' But suddenly in 1828, quite out of the blue, Anglican privileges were legislated away. Protestant privileges went the following year, and three years after that the Great Reform Act destroyed the influence of the monarch and the House of Lords.

---

[52] Paul Langford, *A Polite and Commercial People: England 1727–1783* (Oxford, 1989), 725.
[53] K. Theodore Hoppen, *The Mid-Victorian Generation, 1846–1886* (Oxford, 1998).

These events amounted to 'the shattering of a whole social order, and its appropriate values and modes of behaviour. What was lost at that point . . . was not merely a constitutional arrangement, but the intellectual ascendancy of a world view, the cultural hegemony of the old elite.'[54] From that point on, it is claimed, the old patriarchal regime was effectively challenged by the forces of religious pluralism, liberalism, and political reform, the most signal defeat of all coming at the very end of the period, in 1846, when the Corn Laws were repealed and the landlords' guarantee of rich remuneration ended.

All historical interpretations are partly matters of perspective. The above version is worth taking seriously, not least because it has been immensely influential, provoking assent and rejection in roughly equal measure. Probably the most serious criticisms are that it mistakes revival for survival, and mistakes for consensus that which was actually just one side of a fierce ideological divide. Those who propagated *ancien régime* values were indeed on heat during this period, but mainly as a reaction against what they perceived to be a new and destructive and all-consuming ideology of progress and Enlightenment.

One reason why traditional values revived, according to a powerful recent account, was technical rather than ideological: the ending of perpetual copyright in 1774. At a time when new books were becoming dearer, and also subject (from the 1790s onwards) to formal and informal censorship, there was money to be made by publishing cheap editions of old texts. This led to the establishment of an 'old canon' comprising writers such as Addison, Baxter, Bunyan, Chesterfield, Defoe, Goldsmith, Gray, Johnson, Milton, Pope, Shakespeare, Spenser, and Steele. These authors were also endlessly anthologized, not least in the new wave of school textbooks, as a result of which 'English literature entered the educational and imaginative space which had traditionally been occupied by the Bible'.

Although taken together, the poetry, the novels, the essays, the conduct literature, and the other works were by no means a fully coherent body of texts, they shared many common features. The old-canon writers had written mainly about their own times and about England, especially about life in the country villages in the southern counties. The poets had written on topics regarded as particularly suitable for poetry: love of God, moral lessons, family love and affection, elegies for the dead. They celebrated, or occasionally satirised or lamented, the values of the (still largely pre-industrial) society as it had existed at the time the poems were written. The benevolence of God, the poetry of the three favourites, Young, Thomson, and Cowper, implied and proclaimed, is proved by the design of the natural world, especially by the extraordinary variety and beauty of

---

[54] J. C. D. Clark, *English Society 1688–1832: Ideology, Social Structure and Political Practice during the Ancien Regime* (Cambridge, 1985), 90, 409. See Bibliography. More recently the notion of continuity has been taken even further to embrace the whole period from the 1680s to the 1880s (Richard Price, *British Society, 1680–1880: Dynamism, Containment and Change* (Cambridge, 1999)).

living things. God is good and so is Nature, and by extension agriculture and rural life has its own beautiful rhythms which follow the rhythm of the seasons. God made the country, man made the town...The publishers of the old-canon lists...not only ignored the discoveries of the Enlightenment, but offered a Counter-Enlightenment to readers who knew nothing of the Enlightenment.[55]

It is impossible to say how far the revival of *ancien régime* values was due to technical factors like this, and how far they were a defensive reaction against more 'modern' ideas. Either way it is clear that, while Throne and Altar beliefs were current in the early nineteenth century, they could hardly be said to have been inherited from the seventeenth, since outside Oxford these strains had almost completely dried up between 1720 and 1780. High Church bishops and clergy in particular, however individually devout and locally esteemed, had contributed little to the *public* doctrine of those years. They only came into their own towards the end of the century when they bombarded their flocks with charges and sermons, exhorting them to loyal obedience and moral reformation in time of war. Likewise two decades of warfare from 1793 onwards gave titled soldiers and sailors an opportunity to serve the nation as a new species of *noblesse de l'épée*. Seventy-seven baronetcies were created in the 1790s as compared with only sixty-one in the four decades from 1720 to 1760. Even so, neither the clergy nor the nobility seriously tried to reassert themselves politically until immediately *after* the reforms of 1828–32, which, so far from destroying the old beliefs, gave them a new and final lease of life. The peerage, its blue blood diluted by the new creations, had more or less abdicated politically, and only sprang to action in a desperate attempt to block the 1832 Reform Bill, while in the subsequent decade Tories such as Lyndhurst fought hard to restore the Upper House as an equal partner in the legislature. Again, it was not until the 1830s that a young High Churchman and high Tory, William Gladstone, tried to revive the theocratic ideals of Robert Filmer (1588?–1653) and Charles Leslie (1650–1722), last current in the reign of Queen Anne. At the same time, the Oxford Movement revived the old nonjuring tradition and sought to rediscover pre-Reformation theology, while a group of Conservative politicians styling itself Young England sought to reawaken aristocratic paternalism. Admittedly, these longings for a chivalric 'olden time' were reactive rather than consensual, being balanced by an equally powerful vogue for progress, evolution, and reform, but they were undoubtedly revivalist—not survivalist—in mode, and would not have emerged but for the traumas of the late eighteenth-century revolutions. An architectural analogy might be helpful in establishing the argument. It is *possible* to trace a continuous tradition of vernacular Gothic from the later Middle Ages, through the seventeenth and eighteenth centuries, and finally picking up speed

---

[55] St Clair, *Reading Nation*, 133–4.

in the Victorian period. Yet the iconic mansions of the early 1800s, such as turreted Belvoir and battlemented Panshanger, are more appropriately thought of as a new phase of Gothicism, tentative at first but becoming more confident in the 1830s and 1840s under the influence of Pugin, whose idealized buildings were more philosophically charged and altogether more full-blooded in their muscular pointedness than the anaemic survivals of the eighteenth century. According to one historian, the competition for a new Palace of Westminster in 1836 'established Gothic as the national style, took it away from the eccentrics and made it official'.[56] Such a victory must be seen as a revival of old-regime ideals, not their survival.

Whereas it is possible to generalize about the status of aristocracy and clergy, the reputation of the monarchy was bound to be affected by the vagaries of individual incumbents. George III was in the twenty-third year of his reign when this volume begins. Routinely denounced as a tyrant, he was heavily implicated in the policy that had led to defeat at the hands of America, while his priggish assault on lax aristocratic values, and his prating about the need for morality in public affairs, had made him odious to many of his subjects. Although he remained a fitfully significant political player, his role in executive decision-making was much reduced from 1783 onwards. This was partly because the dramatic growth of business (especially in wartime) made it impossible for anyone to maintain an overview of all that was going on, but a more immediate reason was the King's illness, which was probably a metabolic form of porphyria but may have been psychotic in origin. The symptoms included bouts of depression which gave way to florid behaviour in the manic phases. Then he would foam at the mouth, his eyes would bulge like blackcurrant jellies, he would gabble dementedly, shriek obscenities (which were all the more shocking for the fact that his normal discourse was so prim), chase girls, insist that he was really married to Lady Pembroke, and often end up in a straitjacket or else strapped to a chair. The illness struck first in 1765 but did not cause serious problems until 1788, when it seemed as though his authority might have to be vested elsewhere. He recovered quite suddenly, but relapsed briefly in 1801 and 1804 before succumbing permanently in 1810, and in the following year his son the Prince of Wales was installed as Regent.

Yet the more the King's health and influence declined, the more his popularity soared. Partly this was because he became a focus of national endeavour in time of war, a symbolic John Bull defying invasion. He benefited from the slipstream of royalist feeling which followed the French king Louis XVI's execution in 1793.

---

[56] R. Furneaux Jordan, *A Concise History of Western Architecture* (1969), 291. However, this national style—like nationalism itself—would not become fashionable until after mid-century. See below, pp. 475–7, 479–81.

He was also boosted by the evangelical revival, which brought with it a new emphasis on family values, another sphere in which George ('the father of the nation' as well as of fifteen legitimate children) was thought to excel. Two of his womenfolk helpfully reinforced the impression of domestic bliss. Queen Charlotte Sophia from Germany was a cipher, but she enjoyed a favourable public image owing to her genuine concern for the poor. (She went one better than Marie-Antoinette by inventing a cake for them to eat, a cheap and cheerful dish called apple charlotte.) A more alluring advertisement was George's favourite grandchild, the beautiful Charlotte Augusta, daughter of the Prince Regent and the only credible heir to the throne. Her death in childbirth in 1817 provoked nationwide grief. Buildings were draped in black, shops closed for a fortnight, the press pumped out lamentations, and poets versified ad lib, Byron dubbing her the 'fair-hair'd Daughter of the Isles' and the 'love of millions'. A prominent politician thought that it was 'as if every household throughout Great Britain had lost a favourite child', while a lady-in-waiting bewailed, 'There is now no object of great interest to the English people, no one great rallying point, round which all parties are ready to join.'[57] Such extremes of approbation almost always signify some deeper feeling than that of mere loss. It seems likely that Charlotte was mourned as someone who might have redeemed her line and her country. None of the other younger royals was likely to do this, since all but one of the King's seven sons who reached adulthood became conspicuous adulterers.[58] His dissolute heir and successor George IV, who reigned from 1820 to 1830, was amiable but egotistical and capricious, and he became even more unpopular when sordid details emerged during the trial of his wife, Queen Caroline, before the House of Lords. The Duke of Wellington called him 'the worst man he fell in with in his whole life, the most selfish, most false...most entirely without redeeming qualities', while the well-connected courtier and diarist Charles Greville wrote that 'a more contemptible, cowardly, selfish, unfeeling dog does not exist'.[59] As in the case of Charlotte, such hyperbole arouses suspicion, and 'unfeeling' misses the mark since George was soft-hearted and affectionate, but there is no denying that he was widely despised.

Putting all such personal factors aside, it is clearly *not* the case that divine right ideas survived from the seventeenth to the nineteenth centuries.

---

[57] *The Life and Times of Henry Lord Brougham, Written by Himself* (Edinburgh, 1871), ii. 332; Lady Charlotte Bury, *The Diary of a Lady-in-Waiting* (1908), ii. 144. The posthumous 'commodification' of Charlotte, and the manipulation of mourning by politicians and publicists, is extensively analysed in Stephen C. Behrendt, *Royal Mourning and Regency Culture: Elegies and Memorials of Princess Charlotte* (Houndmills, 1997).

[58] The Prince of Wales and the dukes of York, Clarence, Kent, Cumberland, and Sussex. The Duke of Cambridge was the solitary white sheep.

[59] Greville, *Memoirs*, i. 155 (12 Jan. 1829). Wellington cannot have been mollified by George IV's insistence, even to his own face, that *he* and not the Duke had won the battle of Salamanca.

AN OLD OR NEW REGIME?

Attendance at the annual 30 January sermons to mark the execution of King Charles the Martyr was minimal during the reigns of George I and II, the atmosphere perfunctory.[60] Moreover, when towards the end of the century there was a revival of royalist sentiment, it had much less to do with reverence for a legitimate Stuart line than with a Burkeian belief in monarchy as a useful bulwark against liberalism and revolution. Events in France, it has been suggested, led many in Britain to fantasize about 'encompassing the King's death'. Radicals did so with tumescent anticipation and conservatives with horror, but both conspired to created a sense that royalty was symbolic and mysterious.[61] George's madness might even have helped in this respect, since an evangelically inclined public saw his affliction as a sign of divine affection, giving him the status of a holy fool. Sensations of atonement were also aroused by the death of Princess Charlotte. 'The Almighty sometimes, for the most benevolent purposes, deals severe chastisement on mankind,' intoned the editor of *The Times* and a thousand other pundits.

This new pseudo-medieval reverence for majesty required the British to distinguish the person from the office. As it happened, there was a legal basis for doing so, since the Crown Estates Act of 1800 effectively separated the official and private personalities of the King, allowing him to own land in his own name for the first time. Both sides of the political and ideological divide now sought to appropriate royalty for its own purposes.

By the 1790s, the King was sufficiently idealized to allow clergymen to place him next to God and sufficiently earthy for caricaturists to place him on the privy. The Monarchy developed a multifaceted character that gave it the potential to appeal to a wide range of groups, interests, and individuals. A neo-Filmerite of the 1790s could look at George III and see a semidivine bastion of church and state, while a member of the London Corresponding Society could see him as a potential ally in the fight for republican reform of the Commons against the corrupt practices of politicians.[62]

In the event the monarchy successfully steered a middle course between these two extremes. William IV's Civil List in 1830 set another precedent by being limited to legitimate court expenses.[63] Now that he was no longer responsible for paying the salaries of various political appointees, his direct financial influence

[60] James J. Sack, *From Jacobite to Conservative: Reaction and Orthodoxy in Britain, c.1760–1832* (Cambridge, 1993), 129–31.

[61] John Barrell, *Imagining the King's Death: Figurative Treason, Fantasies of Regicide 1793–1796* (Oxford, 2000).

[62] Marilyn Morris, *The British Monarchy and the French Revolution* (New Haven, 1998), 193; Peter Spence, *The Birth of Romantic Radicalism: War, Popular Politics, and English Radical Reformism, 1800–1815* (Aldershot, 1996).

[63] William IV was George III's third son and succeeded his brother George IV in 1830. He was succeeded in turn by his niece Victoria in 1837.

over Parliament was ended. The idea of an executive working monarchy was to be taken further by Prince Albert, the earnest and statesmanlike German whom Queen Victoria married in 1840, but some credit should go to George IV and his ducal brothers, who played a part in developing the royal family's reputation for philanthropy and good works.[64] Monarchy was undoubtedly in good shape at mid-century, but by then its appeal was far more social and domestic than medieval or 'sacral'.

To recap, this book starts from the premiss that neo-conservative ('Throne and Altar') ideology, so far from representing an *ancien régime*, was a *new* development following the American and French revolutions; that it was a reaction against the 'progressive' ideologies associated with those events; and that 'a real change in sensibility'[65] occurred at that time. In London the new mood was signalled by the Gordon riots of 1780, a week of anti-Catholic hysteria and looting that was wholly out of character with the broadly tolerant decades preceding, and clearly suggestive of a nation in the throes of military defeat. They marked the breakdown of a consensus which had previously united at least the elite sections of society. Admittedly, the 'peace of the Augustans'—a term once routinely used to describe the political and intellectual scene between 1720 and 1770—must not be exaggerated, since it was partly stylistic, resulting from a disinclination to use extreme language or to appear enthusiastic. Even so it is evident that political, religious, and intellectual disputes cut much more deeply after 1783, as the English became locked in 'a war of ideas' (or rather a number of 'wars of ideas', since there were no simple battle lines and several competing paradigms). Politically, it will be argued, the most disruptive elements were two competing versions of liberalism. The first concentrated on civil rights, and sparked off a violent conservative backlash, as already noted. The second was a socio-economic version based on market values, and it too provoked a backlash in the form of a revived paternalism. Eventually these two branches of liberalism would merge to establish a degree of consensus once again, but this did not happen until the 1850s, when another profound shift in sensibility occurred.

In other words, the years covered here are presented as a distinctive period in the nation's political and cultural history. In many ways, indeed, what happened during the last quarter of the eighteenth century set the agenda for the first half of the nineteenth. In 1776 Adam Smith's *Wealth of Nations* more or less 'founded economic discourse' in a way that affected people's imaginations powerfully, as did James Watt's successive developments of the steam engine. The 1780s inaugurated a working alliance between the bulk of the landed gentry

[64] Frank Prochaska, *Royal Bounty: The Making of a Welfare Monarchy* (New Haven, 1995), 38–66.

[65] The phrase comes from Thomas H. Haskell, 'Capitalism and the Origins of the Humanitarian Sensibility', *American Historical Review*, 90 (1985), 339–61, 547–66.

and the haute bourgeoisie that was to dominate political life until 1846, while Pitt's rhetoric initiated a drive for administrative reform and retrenchment that was gradually to capture the official mind and help create a minimal State. In 1790–1 Burke and Paine launched the most passionate and widespread political debate since the mid-seventeenth century, and in 1792 Thomas Hardy founded the London Corresponding Society, an event which was followed by 'the most prolonged period of recurrent social disorder in modern British history'.[66] In 1793 the nation entered into possibly the most dangerous war in its history, and as a result, four years later, the Bank of England was forced to suspend cash payments, a move which caused severe dislocation and had major repercussions. Just as portentous were the food shortages and high prices, which prompted magistrates across southern England to boost the amount of poor relief in the hope of preventing a French-style revolution. In 1797 William Wilberforce's *Practical View of Christianity* added momentum to the evangelical revival, a sort of 'Victorianism' *avant la lettre* which was already in the process of transforming English manners, and forcing its devotees to apologize for the behaviour of their more worldly parents. In 1798 the *Lyrical Ballads* of Coleridge and Wordsworth presaged a shift in literary sensibility that would eventually open up an equally wide chasm of comprehension between generations. In the same year Malthus' *Essay on Population*, by seeming to postulate the inevitability of wars, famines, and pestilence in a world of finite resources, critically undermined those optimistic visions of economic growth, social development, and general improvement which Smith's managerial and Watt's technological discoveries had but so recently excited. Finally, in 1800–1 the British Government responded to a decade of turbulence in Ireland by securing the dissolution of the Dublin Parliament, and handing legislative sovereignty over to Westminster. For the next fifty years political life was to be dominated by monetary, fiscal, and welfare issues, by a battle for preponderance between industry and agriculture, and by efforts to make the Union with Ireland work. And all this took place against a constant sensation of fear—fear of revolution, of the masses, of crime, famine, and poverty, of disorder and instability, and for many people fear even of pleasure.

THE POLITICS OF THEATRE AND THE THEATRE OF POLITICS

The late eighteenth-century revolutions are often said to have led to the 'birth of political ideology', one consequence of which was the politicization of society as a whole.[67] Before then Lewis Namier's classic model of mid-Hanoverian

---

[66] Norman Gash, *Aristocracy and People: Britain 1815–1865* (1979), 5.

[67] Which explains why this book contains more conventional political narrative than the previous volume in the series.

Westminster retains, for all its shortcomings, a good deal of saliency. Well-developed structures of popular politics existed, but they rarely exerted pressure on the elite, for whom what mainly mattered was procuring jobs for family, friends, and self, and whose behaviour was governed by considerations of pragmatism, habit, custom, and routine rather than by concern for society or commitments to principle. Even the crisis with which this volume opens was, for all the sense of national catastrophe engendered, a high political and constitutional affair. Set off by external events in America, and largely confined to the political nation, it was resolved by a royal coup which was later endorsed at the polls. Calls for reform and an end to corruption were everywhere in the air, but were largely meaningless rhetoric, while so far as the mass of ordinary people was concerned, their lives would not have been much altered had Fox won the Election of 1784 rather than Pitt. Hugely different was the crisis of 1830, which was no mere squabble over the benches at Westminster but was generated by structural conflicts in society. One might even crudely say that it was a struggle for control over policy—and for the spoils of a burgeoning economy—between different interest groups, and it was not finally resolved until 'the field of coal defeated the field of barley' (a reference to the repeal of the Corn Laws) in 1846.[68] Once again there were calls for reform and an end to corruption, but this time they penetrated all areas of institutional life—cathedral chapters, parishes, courts of law, universities, schools, hospitals, literary and scientific associations, charities, livery companies, municipal bodies.[69] Everything seemed to have become political.

This was nowhere more apparent than in the republic of letters. It is now recognized that what distinguished the so-called Romantics from their predecessors was not so much a preoccupation with sensibility or subjectivity as an engagement with public affairs (including issues such as slavery and gender) and with the 'production of social order'.[70] Whereas Jane Austen's domestic romances were once thought to have ignored the outside world, she is now considered one of the most acute social commentators of her time. Even John Keats, formerly regarded as the most purely aesthetic of poets, is nowadays routinely contextualized in terms of contemporary medical theory and 'the culture of Dissent'. Shakespeare had long been thought to embody the peculiar genius of the English nation, but in the early nineteenth century a fierce struggle broke out over just whose nation he represented, as cartoonists and critics sought

---

[68] See below, pp. 552–8.

[69] G. F. A. Best, 'The Road to Hiram's Hospital: A Byway of Early Victorian History', *Victorian Studies*, 5 (1961–2), 135–50.

[70] Kelvin Everest, *English Romantic Poetry: An Introduction to the Historical Context and the Literary Scene* (Milton Keynes, 1990).

to appropriate the Bard for their own political purposes. Where Coleridge saw an authoritarian hero-worshipper, reformers like George Cruickshank celebrated his subversive humanity, his hatred of arbitrary power and cruelty. Hence the charged political connotations of different styles of acting—the statuesque authoritarianism of John Philip Kemble, for example, as against the naturalistic but melodramatic histrionics of his younger rival Edmund Kean.[71] Such differences of interpretation frequently took on a party-political aspect, since productions at Covent Garden invariably supported the Pitt, Portland, and Liverpool governments, while those at Drury Lane took the part of the Opposition Whigs.[72] (Incidentally the Covent Garden 'old price' riots of 1809 constituted one of the last successful episodes of mob power in London. After the theatre had been rebuilt following a fire, its actor–manager Kemble sought to recoup his losses by raising the price of seats, but was forced to back down after several months of audience rioting.) Such was the centrality of theatre to public consciousness that one historian has referred to 'the transforming power of the stage'.[73]

But if theatre was political, it is equally the case that politics was theatrical. The most obvious manifestation of this was the growing taste for pageantry. A royal Jubilee in 1809 was followed by a series of military successes on the Continent, each giving rise to victory parades. Meanwhile, a succession of royal weddings led to the honing of official ceremonial. Life at court was characterized by fêtes, mock battles, levees, and parties, and the national anthem began routinely to be sung at theatrical performances. The Prince Regent, obsessed by orders, insignia, and real or made-up uniforms, sought to emulate Continental despots by building up collections of paintings, sculpture, weapons, and furniture. He also threw himself into grand architecture, notably at Windsor and Brighton, and patronized indigenous artists such as Lawrence, Reynolds, Hoppner, and Wilkie. His Coronation in July 1821, a five-hour service in the Abbey followed by a grand banquet in Westminster Hall, set new standards of pseudo-medieval pomp. It cost £238,238 0s. 2d., or getting on for £10 million in today's money,

---

[71] Jonathan Bate, *Shakespearean Constitutions: Politics, Theatre, Criticism 1730–1830* (Oxford, 1989), 34–44, 102–4, 134–84.

[72] In London only Covent Garden, Drury Lane, and the Haymarket were licensed for performances of 'serious' theatre (tragedy and comedy), the remaining venues being restricted to melodrama, burlesque, pantomime, and visual spectacle. From the 1790s onwards a growing number of 'illegitimate' theatres challenged the monopoly of the three 'patent' theatres, and were eventually rewarded with the Theatre Regulation Act of 1843, which finally brought free trade (actually *de*regulation) to the stage. Jane Moody, *Illegitimate Theatre in London, 1770–1840* (Cambridge, 2000), 10–47.

[73] Marc Baer, *Theatre and Disorder in Late Georgian London* (Oxford, 1992); Gillian Russell, *The Theatres of War: Performance, Politics, and Society, 1793–1815* (Oxford, 1995); Julia Swindells, *Glorious Causes: The Grand Theatre of Political Change, 1789 to 1833* (Oxford, 2001).

and his own costume alone was worth £24,704 8s. 10d. (it needed to be if it was to stand out against all the other crimson, scarlet, and gold on display).[74] All in all the jewels, coronets, balloons, and fireworks made it a most splendiferous affair, and many that came to mock stayed on to marvel. In the following year he made a famous and symbolic 'jaunt' to Edinburgh during which he wore a tartan kilt.[75] That occasion inaugurated both a royal love affair with Scotland and a Scottish love affair with its Jacobite past. Of course, many argued that these robes and furred gowns hid all sorts of rottenness in the State, just as their elegant pilasters, porticoes, and pediments hid the fact that many of the West End's new and fashionable John Nash-style terraces were pretty gimcrack under the stucco. Nevertheless, royalty and ceremonial were now inextricably intertwined. William IV and Victoria both followed George IV in their taste for ceremonial, as exemplified by the annual state opening of Parliament.[76]

All this led the journalist Walter Bagehot in 1867 to distinguish 'efficient' aspects of the Constitution like the House of Commons from its 'dignified' or 'theatrical' aspects ('that which is mystic in its claims; that which is occult in its mode of action; that which is brilliant to the eye') such as the monarchy and House of Lords.[77] Yet almost all aspects of public life during the first half of the century were dignified in that theatrical sense. Certainly, many of the individuals, movements, and incidents featured in the pages below were acutely histrionic: for example, the inaptly named 'delicate investigation' into the conduct of Caroline Princess of Wales in 1806–7, the appearance of the Duke of York's ex-mistress Mrs Clarke at the bar of the House of Commons in 1809, and the trial of Queen Caroline in 1820 ('staged as for Grand Opera').[78] Equally theatrical were O'Connell's monster meetings, the romantic outpourings of Young Ireland, the nostalgic vapourings of Young England, the florid advertising campaigns of the Anti-Corn Law League, the Chartists' torchlight processions, O'Connor's emergence from gaol wearing fustian, Admiral Sir Sidney Smith's sporting himself in Ottoman costume and flamboyant Turkish moustache, the dramatic walkout of evangelicals from St Andrew's Church in Edinburgh that precipitated the Scottish Disruption, the saga of J. H. Newman's juddering movements towards the Roman Catholic Church, and Disraeli's parliamentary destruction of Peel in 1846. While actors became public celebrities—one of

[74] Steven Parissien, George IV: The Grand Entertainment (2001), 152–62, 245–63, 303–15; E. A. Smith, George IV (New Haven, 1999); Christopher Hibbert, George IV: Regent and King 1811–1830 (1973), 189–201.
[75] John Prebble, The King's Jaunt: George IV in Scotland, August 1822: 'One and Twenty Daft Days' (1988); J. H. Plumb, The First Four Georges (1956), 178.
[76] Walter L. Arnstein, 'Queen Victoria Opens Parliament: The Disinvention of Tradition', Historical Research, 63 (1990), 178–94.
[77] Walter Bagehot, The English Constitution (1867), in The Collected Works of Walter Bagehot, ed. Norman St John-Stevas (1965–86), v. 206–9.   [78] Plumb, First Four Georges, 177.

them, the comic player Dora Jordan, lived blissfully with the future William IV
long enough to bear him ten children—politicians became more like thespians.
It is true that superficially Parliament became greyer over the period as
wigs, coloured silks, and spurs gradually gave way to black trouser suits and top
hats, but this was deceptive. Many of the leading parliamentarians such as
Canning, Grey, Brougham, Stanley, Lyndhurst, and Disraeli were all actors at
heart. It is more surprising to find the same quality in some official parliamentary
papers known as blue books, a genre normally redolent of utilitarian dryness.
Yet, as will be seen, Michael Thomas Sadler's *Select Committee Report on the
Labour of Children in Factories* (1832) deliberately sought to convey poetic rather
than literal truths, while a recent historian has referred to the 'soap opera
quality' of Edwin Chadwick's *Report on the Sanitary Condition of the Labouring
Population* (1842), with its 'alternation between chaos and control, horror and
security'. 'The narrative ... has a plot, heros and villains, and a happy ending.'[79]

Even the Army showed signs of becoming dignified and inefficient once the
long French wars had ceased. As police forces gradually took over responsibility
for dealing with strikers and rioters, its domestic function grew increasingly
symbolic—to glamorize rather than safeguard the State. Its obsession with
ceremonies, parades, reviews, bands, uniforms, buttons, headgear, shoes, bright
colours, and height—one noble officer, surveying his troops, wanted all the 'ugly
little fellows' killed off quickly—undoubtedly caught the public's imagination,
so that whereas in 1800 Britons had 'hated and feared the sight of soldiers',
by 1850 their conception of England was based very largely on a 'military
paradigm'.[80] Even potentially subversive sections of the population could fall
under the spell. On several occasions when the Army was called on to deal with
Chartist demonstrators, it deployed military spectacle in an effort to 'awe and
intimidate' the rioters, only for the latter to respond, in an ironic act of mimesis,
with parades and marches of their own.[81] Likewise, it has been argued that 'the
crowd, and particularly the carnivalesque crowd, was the central actor in English
executions', which were carried out in public, though with declining frequency,
until 1868. Public hangings made ordinary people feel that they were involved in
the dispensation of the most solemn justice, which was therefore not simply the
act of an impersonal executive. Publicity was also due to the felons who, it was
often argued, had a right to occupy the limelight when being dispatched.[82] Even

---

[79] Christopher Hamlin, *Public Health and Social Justice in the Age of Chadwick: Britain, 1800–1854*
(Cambridge, 1998), 186–7.

[80] Scott Hughes Myerly, *British Military Spectacle: From the Napoleonic Wars through the Crimea*
(Cambridge, Mass., 1996), 14–29, 139–65.

[81] Ibid. 120–38; Kenneth O. Fox, *Making Life Possible: A Study of Military Aid to the Civil Power in
Regency England* (Kineton, 1982).

[82] Thomas W. Laqueur, 'Crowds, Carnival and the State in English Executions, 1604–1868', in A. L. Beier,
David Cannadine, and James M. Rosenheim (eds.), *The First Modern Society* (Cambridge, 1989).

the unreformed system of parliamentary representation seems less absurd once its theatrical purpose is appreciated. The treating, violence, and near-hysteria which were associated with the hustings in Georgian England made later Victorians shudder, but it could be argued that elaborate campaign rituals and ceremonies created a sense of popular participation, and so helped to legitimize a system in which very few of the population exercised formal power through the franchise.[83] Much later in the century, when voting was extended and made private, and when civil servants armed with blue books and social science manuals came to dominate decision-making, Britons seeking dramatic fantasies would turn to empire as an alternative theatre of dreams,[84] but for the time being there was sufficient drama to be had at home.

If public life was a stage, so too was the society it mirrored. London especially offered an endless round of extravaganzas, burlesques, melodramas, spectacles, pantomimes, street theatre, shows, panoramas, carnivals, and circuses, of which Astley's was the oldest and most famous. One could pay to witness scientific experiments (including controlled explosions), mesmeric demonstrations, apocalyptic preaching (with or without 'speaking in tongues'), and legal histrionics, confined at first to political causes, but spreading to criminal cases once defence counsel were permitted to speak on behalf of accused felons (1836). The taste for sensationalism and excess probably reflected widespread feelings of insecurity at a time when established codes were contested and no one really knew his or her place. A combination of war, roller-coaster economies, and physical and social mobility created a fluid and anonymous society in which acres and armorial bearings carried less cachet than money, fashion, and panache. Jane Austen's novel *Persuasion* (1818) opens by remarking that 'Sir Walter Elliot, of Kellynch Hall, in Somersetshire, was a man who, for his own amusement, never took up any book but the Baronetage.' In other words, he was prepared to 'know' only those whom he could place in social terms, and regarded those whom he could not place as belonging to an inferior species.[85] At least, that was the case until reduced circumstances forced him to let out his estate and retire to Bath with his eldest daughter, Elizabeth. Happily,

Bath more than answered their expectations in every respect. Their house was undoubtedly the best in Camden Place; their drawing-rooms had many decided advantages over all the others which they had either seen or heard of; and the superiority was not less in the style of the fitting-up, or the taste of the furniture. Their acquaintance was exceedingly sought

[83] Frank O'Gorman, 'Campaign Rituals and Ceremonies: The Social Meaning of Elections in England 1780–1860', *P&P* 135 (1992), 79–115.

[84] David Cannadine, *Ornamentalism: How the British Saw their Empire* (2001).

[85] The prevalence of armed camps along the south coast threw up any number of fetching young officers whose charms excited the local maidenry but whose backgrounds were unknown.

after. Every body was wanting to visit them. They had drawn back from many introductions, and still were perpetually having cards left by people of whom they knew nothing.

They discovered, in other words, that the competitive anonymity of urban life suited their superficial personalities. And, if Bath was like this, how much more so the capital. Anonymity and transience were recurring motifs in the writings of Dickens and Thackeray, as well as of numerous commentators whose words were as ephemeral as the people they wrote about. *Punch*, for example, carried a column devoted to a fictional socialite couple, the Spangle Lacquers.

You will always be certain to meet at the Lacquers' a great many persons with whom you are perfectly well acquainted by sight, but to whom you can assign no fixed position in society, having generally met them in places where distinction was acquired by paying for it. You will see them sailing up the avenues of a morning concert; they cross your pathway in going to their carriages from Howell and James's; they brush against you at the conclusion of the performance at the Opera; and they put their faith in Gunter, firmly believing that his ice is much colder than even that of Wenham Lake—at all events it is expensive, which, placing it more out of the power of the common-place million, must of course endow it with superior attributes.[86]

In a society where men especially strove to fashion, promote, and advertise themselves, public life became a site on which individuals and groups negotiated roles. Not everyone could amass great wealth, but there was endless scope for celebrity in civic or national affairs, especially as participation in public life no longer depended so acutely on the possession of property or the receipt of patronage, nor yet on subservience to a party line.

The previous volume in this series characterized eighteenth-century Englishmen and -women as 'polite and commercial'. 'Politeness' was a term associated with early eighteenth-century writers like Addison and Shaftesbury, who insisted that the good life was to be attained privately, in civil and sociable activities such as coffee-house conversation, companionship and courtship, affectionate family relationships, leisure activities, and business dealings. Military and political activity, meanwhile, was to be left to professionals. Well-to-do people in the nineteenth century, being no less obsessed with private consumption, continued to buy pottery, earthenware, books, magazines, maps, paintings, engravings, toys, and other fashion accessories. However, their satisfaction was tempered by an awareness of environmental squalor, by the overcrowding, putrefaction, smoke, smells, noise, chaos, and intemperance that disfigured the public sphere. Even worse was an apprehension that the polite sections of society were about to be attacked by the bestial mob. Many were

---

[86] Later republished as Albert Smith, *The Natural History of Stuck-Up People* (1847), 53.

terrified of an ultra-radical, revolutionary, and mainly artisanal tradition which from 1792 onwards pursued the violent overthrow of government and the corporate ownership of land: the Spenceans (or followers of Thomas Spence), Colonel Despard and his desperadoes, who plotted an intended coup in 1802, the Luddites of the early 1810s, the Spa Fields rioters of 1816, the prospective insurrectionists of St Bartholomew's Fair in 1817, the Cato Street conspirators of 1820, the Swing rioters a decade later, and finally and most explosively the Chartists. In the eyes of the polite and commercial sections of society, the town labourers especially were carriers of a revolutionary germ so contagious that it made them 'dangerous to know'.[87] But were they right to think so? For some historians their reaction was simply establishment paranoia, since in reality the people were undergoing

what may be called the Moral Revolution, that profound change in the national character which accompanied the Industrial Revolution. Between 1780 and 1850 the English ceased to be one of the most aggressive, brutal, rowdy, outspoken, riotous, cruel and bloodthirsty nations in the world and became one of the most inhibited, polite, orderly, tender-minded, prudish and hypocritical.[88]

This claim is not wrong exactly, but it relies too much on hindsight. It would have astounded not just the frightened members of the elite, but the lower orders themselves. There *was* a moral revolution at work, but subliminally. Consequently, it was not until about 1850 that the mad, bad, and dangerous people woke up, as it were one morning, to find themselves respectable.

[87] David Worrall, *Radical Culture: Discourse, Resistance and Surveillance, 1790–1820* (New York, 1992).
[88] Harold Perkin, *The Origins of Modern English Society 1780–1880* (1969), 280. See also Robert B. Shoemaker, *The London Mob: Violence and Disorder in Eighteenth-Century England* (2004), 151–2, 175–6, 290–9.

CHAPTER 2

Politics in the time of Pitt and Fox, 1783–1807

'England does not love coalitions', as Disraeli famously said in 1852. He may well have had in mind the Duke of Portland's first ministry, always referred to as the Fox–North Coalition after its leaders in the Commons, and formed in response to a long-running political crisis. In March 1782 the 12-year-old Government of Lord North ended ignominiously following the disasters in America. Lord Rockingham and Charles James Fox, who had denounced the war emphatically from the Opposition benches, then took the opportunity to 'storm the closet', meaning that they forced themselves into office against the wishes of the King. Four months later Rockingham died and was replaced by the Earl of Shelburne. But so bitter were the recriminations caused by military failure that in April 1783 Shelburne too fell from power, at which point North and Fox agreed to bury past hatreds and to enter into coalition under Portland. Their initiative met with approbation by some but with fanatical condemnation from others.[1]

These different reactions reflected the fact that contemporaries were divided in their understanding of how the eighteenth-century political system should work. In the same way, historians are divided over how it actually *did* work. For many decades the dominant view, as established by Lewis Namier, was that politicians operated within the closed world of the court. England was ruled not only by the King but by a federation of great estates, whose representatives congregated at Westminster for significant parts of the year. Their actions might have the effect of winning and losing empires, but they had much less effect on the lives of ordinary people at home than parish overseers, corporation officers, and justices of the peace. Their overriding objective was not governance as such, but simply to maintain parliamentary support, the key being successful management of the House of Commons through patronage, clientage, and personal relationships.[2] Based on an instrumental view of politics, this 'court versus country' interpretation is consistent with the more recent description of

---

[1] See below, p. 48–9.
[2] Lewis Namier, *The Structure of Politics at the Accession of George III* (1929).

Hanoverian England as a 'fiscal–military state'. Viewed from these Namierite and bureaucratic perspectives, it was perfect natural for North and Fox to come together to provide the King and country with stable government at a time of crisis. However, there is an alternative interpretation which emphasizes the importance of principle and ideology, and the emergence—in embryo at least—of party. The belief that George III had subordinated Parliament to his will, by bribing MPs with offices and favours, had led to calls for reform. Accordingly the American Revolution was not so much a colonial as a civil war, and in fighting under the banner of 'No taxation without representation', the colonists were seen to be standing up for the rights of free-born Englishmen as well as for themselves. Then, as the war went disastrously wrong, opinion polarized sharply between those who supported the royal prerogative and those who upheld the rights of citizens. From this second perspective, the accommodation between North and Fox, between the King's Minister and the champion of the people, looked highly unprincipled.

What is not in dispute is that George III loathed the Coalition and took the first opportunity to destroy it. It came on 8 December 1783, when a Government Bill for the 'management of the territorial possessions, revenues, and commerce' of the East India Company passed the Commons by 208 votes to 102. Its purpose was to transfer control of British India to seven named commissioners, all friends of ministers. William Pitt, in opposition, described it as the 'most unconstitutional measure ever attempted, transferring at one stroke . . . the immense patronage and influence of the East to *Charles Fox, in or out of office*'.[3] Seizing the moment, the King let it be known, through what today might be called the usual channels, that any peer who supported the Bill 'would be considered by him as an enemy'. On 17 December the Lords threw it out by 95 to 76, whereupon the King gleefully dismissed the Coalition and installed Pitt. The news that a 24-year-old had become Prime Minister was greeted with hilarity, and few thought that the 'mince pie' administration could last much longer than the festive season. Pitt himself was sufficiently despondent to make immediate overtures to his rival. If Fox would only modify the Bill and give up North it might be possible to include him within the new administration. But Fox was too confident and too loyal to ditch North. 'Why don't they advise us to pick pockets,' he snorted.[4] It was an impetuous refusal which Fox was able to regret at leisure, for against all odds 'Master Billy' survived as Prime Minister for more than seventeen years, before he too fell foul of a royal warning that any-one who voted for a particular measure would be reckoned a 'personal enemy'.

---

[3] Pitt to Rutland, 22 Nov. 1783, in *Correspondence between William Pitt and Charles Duke of Rutland, 1781–1787*, ed. seventh Duke of Rutland (Edinburgh, 1890), 4–5.

[4] *Diaries and Correspondence of James Harris, 1st Earl of Malmesbury*, ed. third Earl of Malmesbury (1844), ii. 59.

THE LAUNCHING OF PITT AND THE DESTRUCTION OF FOX

The King was undoubtedly playing for high stakes. He had taken much of the blame for defeat in America, and in 1780 Dunning's famous motion—'that the influence of the Crown has increased, is increasing, and ought to be diminished'—had been carried by 233 votes to 215, a significant act of defiance given the axiom that kings could do no wrong, only their advisers. The Association movement, a gentry-based protest led by a Yorkshire landowner, the Revd Christopher Wyvill, had also targeted the monarch personally in pressing for economic reform to curb executive power. In 1782 the King's stipend had been frozen at its then level, a move inspired by Fox's colleague Edmund Burke. It was designed both to limit the monarch's powers of patronage, and to force economy on his advisers by stipulating that their own salaries should have last call on payments from the Civil List.[5] Given the widespread animus against him, George III could hardly be sure that the political nation would support his attack on the Coalition, which is why he went so far as to draft a message of abdication, just in case. True, North was also implicated in the military disaster, but Fox and Portland had strenuously opposed the American war, and might reasonably have expected to be given some credit for their caution.

Except that nations in defeat do not usually thank their Jeremiahs and Cassandras. Increasingly blame shifted from the Crown to the aristocracy, perhaps because the latter was thought to be responsible for military success or failure. This damaged the Foxites, who were widely perceived to be the most aristocratic faction, while Fox himself was condemned as a second Catiline whose seditious opposition to the war had stabbed the country in the back.[6] 'Has there been one officer, either naval or military; one coward, who from fear; or one traitor, who from treachery, has neglected his duty to his country, whom *you have not embraced, justified, and defended*?' Nor would caricaturists allow him to forget that he had once attended the Commons wearing the American uniform of buff and blue. Meanwhile, the King managed to metamorphose from villain of the piece into potential saviour. At this stage Pitt was little more than a tool in the struggle between monarch and aristocracy. The veteran Dr Samuel Johnson was probably typical in declaring, 'I am for the King against Fox, but I am for Fox against Pitt.'[7]

Just how George III and his young minister turned the tables on Charles James Fox and his huge Commons majority remains something of a mystery. Viewed in retrospect the events of 1783–4 can easily take on an air of inevitability, but this is illusory for the launching of HMS Pitt was a precarious business, shot through with contingency and luck.

[5] J. Steven Watson, *The Reign of George III, 1760–1815* (Oxford, 1960), 247–8.
[6] [Joseph Galloway], *Letters from Cicero to Catiline the Second* (1781), 49.
[7] *Boswell's Life of Johnson*, ed. R. W. Chapman (1953), 1292 (11 June 1784).

To start with, George III won the constitutional argument. His blatant attempt to influence the Lords' debate on the India Bill was improper, but it was justified in his own eyes by what had happened in 1782. Then, Lord North had resigned as Prime Minister rather than waiting to be beaten on a vote of no confidence. 'Remember, my Lord, that it is you who desert me, not I you,' the King is reported to have told him on that occasion.[8] Soon afterwards North's fiercest opponents, Rockingham and Fox, had 'stormed the closet', dictating to the King who his own ministers should be. '[T]he political struggle is not as formerly between two factions for power, but it is no less than whether a desperate faction shall not reduce the Sovereign to a mere tool in its hands' was George's comment on that piece of temerity.[9] In 1784 many MPs seem to have swung round to the King's view, for division lists showed a gradual attrition of Fox's support. In mid-February his majority was down to only twelve when he moved to delay the vote of supply, whereas in the previous session it had been in three figures. By early March it was down to nine on a motion to postpone the Mutiny Bill, and then to just a single vote on a resolution declaring that the King's 'new system of executive administration' was inimical to 'the liberties of the people'. 'The enemy seem indeed to be on their backs,' chortled Pitt.[10] On the following day Fox's nerve broke, and he allowed the Mutiny Bill to pass. It was a defining moment.[11]

Pitt's success in whittling away Fox's majority was partly due to manipulation. George had granted the Coalition no British peerages and very little other patronage, but he was willing to turn the hose of royal favour full in Pitt's direction, and the big borough patrons in particular were showered with benefits. The Duke of Northumberland, who controlled six or seven seats in the Commons, was given a barony with remainder to his second son; Edward Eliot, disposer of six Cornish borough seats, was created a baron; and Sir James Lowther, who returned nine mainly northern MPs, became Baron Lowther of Lowther, Baron of the barony of Kendal, Baron of the barony of Burgh, Viscount Lonsdale, Viscount Lowther, and the first Earl of Lonsdale. Unsurprisingly this 'Jimmy Grasp-all' at once abandoned the Rockinghams and became a loyal tool of Pitt.[12] In all, eleven new peers were created and eleven existing peers promoted within a year of Pitt taking office. Fox had every reason to resent the King's partiality, but could only blame his own friends for the Government's other main opportunity to dispense patronage. Seventeen peers

---

[8] Horace Walpole, *Journal of the Reign of King George III, from the Year 1771 to 1783*, ed. Dr Doran (1859), ii. 521.

[9] George III to the Duke of Marlborough, 29 Dec. 1783, in George III, *Correspondence*, i. 15.

[10] Pitt to Rutland, 10 Mar. 1784, in *Correspondence between Pitt and Rutland*, 7–8.

[11] L. G. Mitchell, *Charles James Fox and the Disintegration of the Whig Party, 1782–1794* (1971), 82–3.

[12] But he considered withdrawing support from Pitt in 1792 because he had not been made a duke.

and twenty-nine office-holding MPs (of whom seventeen were Foxites and twelve were Northites) expressed their solidarity with their chiefs and their contempt for the King by quitting their posts.[13] This collective resignation gave Pitt an immediate chance to win adherents by appointing them to the situations vacated.

By March the lure of office had induced more than fifty Northite MPs to desert the Coalition. Just as significant was the swing among the country gentlemen on the back benches. At first they had seemed divided over whether liberty was more at risk from 'the influence of the Crown' or from 'the spirit of party', and it was by no means obvious that a majority would rally to the King. However, in seeking to abort Pitt's administration, Fox—a compulsive gambler—overplayed his hand. In particular, his attempts to withhold supply and to prevent the annual renewal of the Mutiny Act made him seem irresponsible, especially as the latter move, if successful, would have deprived the King of legal authority to enforce discipline in the armed services. He also tried to prevent a dissolution of Parliament, being afraid that royal influence would be used to secure the election of MPs favourable to Pitt, but unfortunately this contradicted Fox's own heady rhetoric about the rights of the 'people'.

In playing these three cards Fox was attempting to tap folk memories of the Bill of Rights and Revolution Settlement of 1689, when the monarch had been warned against violating the freedom of elections. 'Had not a majority of the House of Commons, almost from time immemorial, governed this country,' asked Fox rhetorically. 'Was it not in clashing with this radical and primary principle that so many calamities had happened in some of the reigns prior to the Revolution?'[14] Yet Fox's attempt to drink from the well of seventeenth-century Whiggism proved disastrous for, by polarizing the issue in terms of 'Parliament versus the prerogative', he reminded many of his hearers that republican regicides had been at least as much to blame for those calamities as had kings. The engraver James Sayers made this point when he showed Fox seated in front of a looking glass with an armour-plated Lord Protector reflected back at him,[15] while in Yorkshire apparently 'the received notion among the inferiors in many parts is that Mr. Fox was attempting to dethrone the King and make himself an Oliver Cromwell'.[16] Well over 200 petitions and as many addresses were sent from London, from other large towns, from counties, and from Scotland congratulating the King and Pitt for having got the better of a corrupt aristocracy, while hardly any took the other side. There is no evidence to suggest that this cascade of support for Pitt was stage-managed, but if any of his

---

[13] They included St Andrew St John (Fox's 'beloved apostle' and gambling partner), Edmund Burke, and William Eden (Paul Kelly, 'British Politics 1783–4: The Emergence and Triumph of the Younger Pitt's Administration', *Historical Research*, 54 (1981), 68–9).   [14] *CPH* xxiv. 597 (18 Feb. 1784).
[15] James Sayers, *The Mirror of Patriotism* (1784).   [16] Namier & Brooke, ii. 460.

contemporaries thought that it was, then their suspicions must have been dispelled by the results of the general election held in April.

According to the *Annual Register*, 'so complete a rout [was] scarcely to be credited'. Even Burke conceded that 'the demolition is very complete'. Nearly 100 Foxites and about sixty-five other MPs who had supported the Coalition were unseated, either beaten at the polls or forced by their patrons to withdraw. Many of these, admittedly, were North's friends who had been elected with the help of official influence in 1780, so their rejection now was hardly surprising. Even so the 1784 election marked an unusually swift turnaround and was clear evidence that voter opinion was running powerfully for George and Pitt. Some historians have resisted this conclusion by stressing the fact that no government had lost an election since 1708, and by pointing to the assiduous way in which the Treasury Secretary George Rose and his predecessor, John Robinson, worked behind the scenes to secure victory. Yet in fact the Treasury's attempts to buy political support were less strenuous and less successful than usual. Just over £30,000 of secret service money was spent in trying to secure nineteen seats,[17] compared with £62,000 spent on thirty-three seats in 1780. The number of gains in close boroughs was disappointing, and even the Scottish boroughs, which were notoriously susceptible to Government influence, divided only 24–21 in Pitt's favour. Probably the suddenness of the dissolution meant that the Treasury had less time than usual to make the necessary preparations.

More importantly, this was the only general election between 1710 and 1831 which can be regarded as an appeal to the nation. In many places, admittedly, personal, family, and local rivalries decided the outcome, but national politics predominated in at least nine out of forty counties and in thirty-two out of the 203 English boroughs. Significantly, these were mainly the larger and more open constituencies, representing nearly half of the total borough electorate,[18] and it was in just such places that Foxites did so badly, to an extent that surprised even John Robinson. Lord John Cavendish, for example, had been the member for York since 1768 and Chancellor of the Exchequer in the Coalition, but in 1784 he came third after Viscount Galway and R. S. Milnes. His failure was a defeat for most of the Corporation of York, and even more for the Earl of Fitzwilliam, who had succeeded to Rockingham's estates but not his influence. Things went just as badly for the Coalitionists in London, for although Fox just held on in Westminster, his ally Byng was ejected in Middlesex.

Overall, Pitt won 48 county seats to Fox's 29, including 12 gains, all but two of which lay in the eastern half of England. He won 125 seats in open boroughs

---

[17] More than a third of the amount was spent in trying and narrowly failing to unseat Fox at Westminster.

[18] Frank O'Gorman, *Voters, Patrons, and Parties: The Unreformed Electorate of Hanoverian England 1734–1832* (Oxford, 1989), 295–7.

as against only 96 for Fox. As usual, fewer than one-third of constituencies proceeded to a contest, but this does not indicate any lack of intensity since, when an outcome was predictable, it was in everyone's interest financially for the losing candidate to withdraw. In 1784 the single most significant contest was aborted in just such a way. That was in Yorkshire, where a county meeting voted overwhelmingly to thank the King for having quashed the India Bill. Such was the strength of feeling that Fitzwilliam declined the contest, Henry Duncombe and William Wilberforce were elected unopposed, and the Rockinghamite domination of Yorkshire came to a sudden end.[19]

Galway, Milnes, Duncombe, and Wilberforce all stood for reform, a word invested with talismanic qualities even though its meaning was unclear. Retrenchment, shorter parliaments, more county seats, abolition of rotten boroughs, and some widening of the franchise were all implied. Fox had championed reform since 1779, Pitt had made notable speeches on the subject in 1781–2, and now they competed to catch the public mood, but almost invariably it worked to Pitt's advantage. This was partly because of Fox's greater maturity. He was only ten years older, but at a time when everyone was anxious to shut the door on the past, Pitt's schoolboy image was an asset. It was partly because of Fox's association with North, who was widely if unfairly caricatured as 'the father of corruption'. It was partly that the word 'reform' implied moral reformation, seen as an essential prerequisite of national redemption, and that Fox's personality was unsuited to a crusade for virtue. His India Bill was particularly maladroit in this context since it seemed like a classic case of politicians grubbing for patronage. Probably the most powerful cartoon of the year was one by Sayers showing Charles James Fox decked out as Carlo Khan, master of all the wealth of the East, riding into Leadenhall Street on an elephant.

In Yorkshire a struggle between lesser gentry and great magnates '*merged into* that between the supporters of Pitt and those of Fox',[20] while in Great Yarmouth two Pittites managed to oust two Coalitionist MPs by taking the side of the merchants and Dissenters against the Anglican Corporation.[21] Although no one thought in such terms at the time, these attacks on aristocracy indicate a stirring middle-class awareness. It had long been accepted that county freeholders and clergy could deliver 'instructions' to their MPs. To this extent the Association movement of the early 1780s was not unprecedented. However, since about 1760 there had been an increasing tendency for common townsfolk, such as unenfranchised craftsmen and journeymen, to assert their own ideas about government. It was a logical development given that excise and other taxes now

[19] K. J. Allison and P. M Tillott, 'York in the 18th Century', in *The Victoria History of the Counties of England. Yorkshire: City of York*, ed. P. M. Tillott (1961), 244; Namier & Brooke, i. 431.

[20] Namier & Brooke, i. 431 (italics added).

[21] This was paradoxical in view of Fox's later alignment with the Dissenters and Pitt's with the Church.

affected large swathes of the population, but it meant that the gentry leaders of the Association movement had to tread a fine line between attacking the Government and defending the political system against outsiders. Wyvill was more or less able to contain the clothiers and other industrialists in Yorkshire, but the social hierarchy was seriously challenged by the Middlesex Committee, whose active members were mainly lawyers and businessmen. In 'radical Westminster' religious Dissent and even scepticism was breeding a bitterer and more extreme form of protest politics, and Fox was identified with it as the constituency MP. He was therefore caught in a double bind, for while the country gentry thought him not enough of a moderate reformer to carry out the necessary regeneration of public life, they also regarded him as tainted by association with reform in its more populist and disreputable guise.

The political nation had been in turbulence since 1780, and no brief account can do justice to the scores of motives, principled and selfish, which moved the various participants, but what is clear is that Fox lost the goodwill of a great part of the political establishment. To take the case of one notable defector, who may not have been wholly idiosyncratic: Cecil Wray was a Lincolnshire baronet and fiercely independent MP, a former supporter of Wilkes and the Bill of Rights Society, and a member of the Yorkshire Association in 1780. He felt 'the most enthusiastic reverence' for Fox and consistently voted against North, whose 'high prerogative principles' had involved the country in 'the cursed American war, the cause of all our ruin'. Wray's populist sympathies were rewarded in 1782 when the committee of the Westminster Association—Fox's local political machine—urged him to stand in a by-election, and even paid his expenses. Once re-elected, however, Wray drifted quickly away from the Rockingham party. First he objected to the peace treaty with America, not because it was humiliating (the usual complaint) but because it was not humiliating enough! Wray felt that the degraded state of Britain called for peace 'almost at any rate', and he therefore condemned the retention of Gibraltar and Quebec. Fox's junction with North left him 'thunderstruck', and he disliked the Coalition's proposal to raise revenue from a receipts tax, which he thought would fall unfairly on 'the middling ranks'. The ruling classes had started this wicked war and they should now pay for it through an increase in the land tax, which 'far from being too great was in his opinion too low'. Wray's gradual defection from Fox was sealed by the India Bill, 'the most violent, arbitrary, and unprincipled Bill he ever saw brought into the House'. Its sponsors 'ought to have been brought to the scaffold'. Pitt and his ministers, on the other hand, seemed 'a wise, an honest and virtuous set of people'. He stood as a Pittite in the Westminster election of 1784, and was narrowly beaten by Fox into third place.[22] The route by which he had picked his way through the shifting sands of the early 1780s was his own, but in one respect it was representative. Having been highly suspicious of the prerogative in 1780, Wray had come to regard George III as the nation's best safeguard against an even more dangerous clique of aristocrats.

PARTY GOVERNMENT OR BROAD BOTTOM?

English politics entered a new phase when Pitt supplanted Fox. Whereas previously there had been a number of informal groupings under individuals such as North, Rockingham, Shelburne, Grenville, Rutland, and Portland, now two distinct and fairly coherent parties faced each other in Parliament. Government had changed hands four times in rapid succession, and on three of those occasions a whole team of Cabinet ministers left office together and was replaced by another: March 1782 when North fell and was replaced by Rockingham; April 1783 when Shelburne fell and was replaced by the Coalition; and December 1783 when the King installed Pitt.[23] Such wholesale turnabouts had never happened before, even during the so-called 'rage of party' under Queen Anne. In addition, there were substantial changes of personnel among the minor office-holders, thereby challenging the convention that placemen were permanent officials who served the King rather than a particular Prime Minister. Thus of the thirty-two MPs holding junior posts who left office with Fox and North in December 1783, only eleven had held office under Shelburne, the other twenty-one having been appointed in April. These events marked an important turning point. 'After this', it has been said, 'administrations fall and are succeeded by others instead of melting into new shapes.'[24] They also marked the beginning of a process which has been called 'the waning of the influence of the crown',[25] for if ministers came and went in packs, instead of individually as heretofore, there was a limit to the King's freedom to choose who his individual servants should be. There was a rich paradox in all this. George hated Fox for having challenged his right to choose his own ministers, yet in sacking the Coalition so peremptorily he helped to perpetuate a system of separate administrations, and thereby undermined his own freedom of action. This long-term threat to royal power was not apparent at the time, however, being masked by George's triumph in ousting Fox.

North's ministry (1770–82) had been a traditional broad bottom. He was supported by the Bedford, Gower, and Sandwich factions, by a small number of friends who had attached themselves to his colours in office, and by the

---

[23] Except that Lord Thurlow, Lord Chancellor since 1778, survived the change of government in March 1782. The Great Seal was put in commission under the Coalition, but Thurlow resumed his post under Pitt.   [24] Watson, *Reign of George III*, 574.
[25] A. S. Foord, 'The Waning of "the Influence of the Crown" ', *EHR* 62 (1947), 484–507.

placemen—about 140 MPs who occupied situations of profit under the Crown. In addition he enjoyed the regular support of over sixty so-called independents. To describe those who usually voted with him as forming a party would be anachronistic. Nevertheless, North made an important innovation when he inaugurated the doctrine of collective Cabinet responsibility. In 1778–9 the Commons attempted to censure a Secretary of State and then the First Lord of the Admiralty for their alleged contributions to various operational setbacks in America. North was adamant that the whole Government was to blame and not just the ministers officially responsible. 'He himself was equally criminal . . . So was every other efficient member of the cabinet . . . It was a crime in common, or no crime.'[26] The doctrine quickly took effect, being used to justify Pitt's ejection of Thurlow from his Cabinet in 1792, and Wellington's virtual dismissal of Huskisson in 1828. After North it was no longer possible for Parliament to censure an individual minister because it disliked his policies, and this marked another important step in the transition from departmental administration to Cabinet government. Indeed, it was because of the authority which they could wield in united cabinets that future prime ministers like Liverpool (1812–27) and Salisbury (1885–92, 1895–1902) were able to run effective governments from the Lords, whereas it had proved impossible to do this in the eighteenth century when ministries had been so much less cohesive. Then, in order to be effective, a Prime Minister had had to sit in the Commons, since that was where any lethal attacks on his government were likely to be mounted.

The 'invention' of party has usually been attributed to the Rockingham Whigs, who had formed the main opposition to North, and especially to Burke, who argued that party was the only way to combat royal despotism and secret influence. 'When bad men combine, the good must associate,' he had written. 'Party is a body of men united, for promoting by their joint endeavours the national interest, upon some particular principle in which they are all agreed.'[27] Measures not men, in other words. This high-flown rhetoric has often been disparaged as a mere device to justify the Rockinghams' anti-Government tirades at a time when 'formed opposition' was frowned on. A more important explanation for the emergence of party may have been Rockingham's refusal three times—in 1766, 1767, and 1780—to enter into coalition ministries. His devoted 'knot of stainless friends' blamed their frustrations on the King, who they were sure was out to exclude them, but they might more justly have blamed their leader's determination to maintain party exclusivity.

Rockingham died in July 1782. When nine months later Fox formed a junction with North, he found himself hoist with his old leader's petard. But for the latter's pious rhetoric about party purity, Fox might have got away

---

[26] *CPH* xx. 198 (3 Mar. 1779).   [27] Burke, *Thoughts*, 315–17.

with the Coalition. When the news came through that he had shaken hands with the man whom he had once described as 'a blundering pilot', 'void of every principle of honour and honesty', it provoked cynicism and even outrage in some quarters,[28] but many observers thought it entirely appropriate that enemies should unite to provide stability in time of crisis. This, it could be argued, was how eighteenth-century government was supposed to work. As late as January 1784 a meeting of over fifty independents at Westminster's St Alban's Tavern sought to bring about just such a junction between Pitt and Fox. It was only in the fevered and bipolar atmosphere of pre-election propaganda that the Fox–North Coalition came to be stigmatized in the Pittite press as the father and mother of all unnatural acts.[29] But if it was, the turpitude clearly extended from the two leaders down to their adherents. It is a striking fact that several of North's closest supporters emerged from the Coalition as dedicated followers of Fox: his son George North, for example, and William Adam, who had earlier fought a duel with Fox and nearly killed him, but was shortly to become his main party organizer. This suggests an awareness, even at the time, that the old political slate had been wiped clean and a new dispensation begun.

Nominally both Pitt and Fox were Whigs, like North and all other frontbench politicians. Pitt sometimes called himself an independent Whig. The label 'Tory' had fallen out of use in national politics during the 1760s, and became little more than a term of abuse used by some to describe the supporters of North and the American war. But if Pitt and Fox were on opposite sides of a two-party system, then which was the *true* Whig and which was *really* a Tory? Approached from a nineteenth-century perspective, the answer to this question is clear: Pitt refounded the Tory Party while Fox inspired generations of Whigs. The same perspective pushed further back suggests that North was also a Tory, and many historians have called him one without a second thought. A much more pertinent consideration is how the antagonism between Pitt and Fox related to the struggle between Whigs and Tories during the first half of the eighteenth century, but unfortunately there is no consensus on that point. Some historians maintain that the Rockingham and Foxite Whigs were heirs of the Court Whigs under Pelham and Newcastle, and that the supporters of North and Pitt were descended from those Tories and Country Whigs who had opposed the ministries of George II. Other historians are equally adamant that Rockingham and Fox followed in the tradition of early Hanoverian Tories and Country Whigs, and that North and Pitt possessed the same Court mentality as Pelham and Newcastle. The dispute cannot be settled by trying to

---

[28] *The Diary of a Country Parson: The Reverend James Woodforde (1758–1802)*, ed. John Beresford (Oxford, 1924–31), ii. 63; Ian R. Christie, *Wilkes, Wyvill and Reform: The Parliamentary Reform Movement in British Politics 1760–1785* (1962), 190–7.   [29] Mitchell, *Fox and the Disintegration*, 52.

trace continuities among the personnel, if only because a high proportion of MPs died or retired from Parliament between the ministries of Pelham and North. Moreover, no conclusive trend can be discerned from among the few prominent politicians whose careers did straddle the interval. William Dowdeswell and Thomas Pelham were Rockinghamites who had previously been Tory or Country members, whereas Viscount Duncannon, second Earl of Bessborough, was a Rockinghamite who had previously been with the Court.[30]

In the circumstances, an ambiguous conclusion is called for. If the struggle between Pitt and Fox is considered ideologically, as an episode in the battle that was waged between 'freedom' and 'authority' from the seventeenth to the nineteenth centuries, then Fox will appear to be the Whig and Pitt the Tory.[31] If, on the other hand, Pitt's administration is regarded as merely the latest instalment of broad-bottomed government under a Hanoverian monarch, then Pitt looks like a Whig and Fox looks more like a Tory. This second perspective explains how Pitt's successors in the 1820s, despite coming to think of themselves as Tories or Conservatives, could defend the Whig settlement of 1689 against reformers. It also explains how, when he was execrated almost everywhere else, Fox retained a loyal base in radical Westminster, that old Tory hideout and scourge of the Walpole and Pelham Courts. For all his aristocratic disdain and contempt for democracy, Fox's instinctive populism and hostility to an oligarchic Court were worthy of his Jacobite forenames. As the Earl of Carlisle observed, 'He was ever in his heart more inclined to Tory, than what in these times are called Whig principles.'

Party labels aside, Pitt undoubtedly thrived in the hot two-party atmosphere. Even after 1784 there were still about 130–40 loyal followers of Fox and Portland, as well as a depleted band of about seventeen Northites.[32] And though only about thirty MPs were attached to Pitt personally, he had the sympathy of at least 350 who loathed the Opposition leader. The practice of canvassing sympathizers and posting circular letters increased on both sides, and there were attempts to whip backbenchers into division lobbies or else force them into pairs. A number of local party associations were established, the most famous of which was the Whig Club, founded at Westminster in 1784 to facilitate Fox's election. In so far as it provided an opportunity for MPs to mix with sympathetic businessmen and professionals, it may be regarded as the first glimmering of an extra-parliamentary party identity. It

[30] Dowdeswell was a Tory under George II and leader of the Rockinghams in the Commons during 1767–75, Pelham was an important Newcastle Whig who later supported North, and Duncannon held office under Pelham and was later devoted to Rockingham. No old Tory became an active Northite, however, though Thomas Grosvenor was one who lent North independent support.

[31] B. W. Hill, *British Parliamentary Parties 1742–1832: From the Fall of Walpole to the First Reform Act* (1985), 35–52.

[32] All such estimates must be tentative given the fluidity of party allegiance, the inadequacy of division list evidence, and the wide variation of contemporary estimates.

was also an early indication that the term 'Whig' would come to be appropriated by the Foxites.

The 1780s experienced an explosion of political satire, invective, and caricature. This happens periodically, and when it does it is hard to know whether it is a cause of political excitement, or merely a response to it. With at least nine London dailies and perhaps as many as a quarter of a million readers, pressmen and publishers became thoroughly embroiled in party warfare.[33] The Government provided handouts from the secret service account, which forced the Opposition to set up its own fund. On 17 July 1788, for example, the *London Evening Post* and the *St. James' Chronicle* each received £100 from the taxpayer, and this was matched by £200 of Foxite money for the *General Advertiser*. A snapshot taken in 1790 shows the Treasury controlling nine dailies including the *Morning Herald* and *The Times*, while the Opposition ran the *Morning Chronicle* and four others.[34] There was scope here for venality, as when in 1784 the Treasury offered the *Morning Post* a financial inducement to support Pitt, and then five years later when the Prince of Wales's entourage inveigled it back into Opposition,[35] but most editors seem to have been consistent in their partisanship. Meanwhile, the reporting of parliamentary proceedings improved considerably after 1783, when journalists were permitted to take notes for the first time. The printer John Stockdale received a Treasury subsidy, and his version of what was said, as recorded in *Parliamentary Debates*, sometimes differed from that in John Debrett's *Parliamentary Register*, which was patronized by the Opposition. Such intensive coverage may have helped to make debates more polemical, with speeches increasingly being directed at the public.

Party feeling was especially intense at the time of the 1790 election. Eighteenth-century governments had always orchestrated their electoral resources; what made this occasion different was that Opposition politicians did so too. Portland, Fitzwilliam, and William Adam went to unprecedented lengths in setting up election funds and commissioning local canvasses, surveys, and flysheets (even in Scotland, which was usually considered a lost cause).[36] The consequence was a high degree of partisan behaviour, at least in the boroughs: for example, fewer electors than usual split their two votes between candidates of different parties, while many others plumped [37] if only one candidate of their own preferred party was standing in a particular constituency.[38]

---

[33] Hannah Barker, *Newspapers, Politics, and Public Opinion in Late Eighteenth-Century England* (Oxford, 1998), 23.

[34] Lucyle Werkmeister, *The London Daily Press 1772–1792* (Lincoln, Nebr., 1963), 139, 268, 317–18, 331.

[35] Ibid. 78–108; A. Aspinall, *Politics and the Press, c.1780–1850* (1949), 126–7.

[36] Donald E. Ginter, *Whig Organization in the General Election of 1790* (Berkeley, Calif., 1967); id., 'The Financing of the Whig Party Organization, 1783–1793', *American Historical Review*, 71 (1965–6), 421–40.   [37] See App. 6.2.

[38] That is, they forfeited one of their two votes. See below, p. 437–8; J. Phillips, *Electoral Behaviour in Unreformed England: Plumpers, Splitters, and Straights* (Princeton, 1982), 212–52, 306–8.

It is possible to see all this as marking the origin of the modern party system, but there are grounds for caution. In the first place, Fox's leadership in the Commons during 1784–90 was fitful at best, while his support in division lobbies was wobbly.[39] Even the organizational improvements can be seen as signs of weakness rather than strength; at any rate, it is usually Opposition parties that advance fastest in this respect, the Conservatives in the 1830s and 1860s, for example, and the Liberals in the later 1870s. Fitzwilliam certainly worked furiously, as did another of 'Fox's martyrs', Tom Coke in Norfolk, but in both cases they were seeking to claw back ground which the aristocracy felt it had lost to the gentry, farmers, graziers, and country townsmen in 1784. And in spite of all their efforts the Foxites did little more than hold their own in 1790, while Pitt strengthened his position at the expense of the independent section of the House. Whether a united Opposition could have bounced back after this disappointment cannot be known, for Portland and some other grandees broke with Fox soon afterwards, taking their money with them. Adam was therefore much less active in the 1796 election, when virtually everything was left to local patrons and activists, and the heroic push into Scotland was not repeated.

If the conduct of elections hardly justifies claims for a two-party system, it is equally difficult to draw any clear distinction of principle between Pitt and Fox. Both were committed to aristocratic governance and neither had any real enthusiasm for reform, despite what they pretended. The most controversial issues—electoral reform, slave trade abolition, Test and Corporation Act repeal, Warren Hastings' impeachment—divided each of the parties rather than distinguishing between them. Pitt was popular with a majority of country gentlemen, but there was no question of their regarding him as their leader whose opinions on policy they should defer to. This became clear in 1785–6, when Pitt was defeated on four important issues. The first was an attempt to 'scrutinize' the legality of Fox's victory over Wray at Westminster; for once it was Pitt who appeared the more vindictive. The second was a proposal to introduce an Anglo-Irish preferential trading area; it aroused the opposition of the General Chamber of Manufactures and was dropped, leaving Pitt to lament the 'evils of a nation dominated by shopkeepers'. The third was a plan by the Duke of Richmond, Master-General of the Ordnance, to fortify the naval dockyards in Plymouth and Portsmouth; it was defeated, partly because of the expense, partly because MPs did not wish to shift responsibility for defence from the Royal Navy (which they adored) to a 'standing Army' (which they dreaded), and partly because—like Fox's India Bill—it was seen as a bid to increase the scope for ministerial patronage. The most important defeat was on an attempt to take parliamentary representation away from thirty-six small

---

[39] Paul Kelly, 'British Parliamentary Politics, 1784–1786', *HJ* 17 (1974), 749–50.

boroughs, and compensate their patrons financially. With the King known to be hostile, Pitt made no attempt to claim that the Bill was the collective responsibility of ministers, and it failed by seventy-four votes. Possibly he only introduced it in the first place in order to gratify reforming friends like Wyvill. At any rate, he never raised the question again. These four defeats taught him how to trim in policy matters (as Walpole had done before him), and demonstrated how far his situation was from that of a modern party leader.

Stable government required the support of the King and a reasonably broad bottom. During 1784–90 the core of the ministry was composed of Pitt's personal supporters and those of Shelburne, Dundas, and Gower. Beyond them were about 185 MPs on the court or government payrolls, and beyond them about 100 who prided themselves on their independence but were fundamentally loyal. When Fox complained that 'the country gentlemen oppose [Pitt] upon one occasion, only to give him more strength upon another', he was stating what should have been obvious to anyone who understood eighteenth-century politics. Pitt's setbacks flattered the country gentlemen by making them feel important, and since he responded to rebuffs graciously they even strengthened his position. He also benefited from the services of a 'Mr Fix-it' figure, the former Northite Henry Dundas. Through personality and perseverance Dundas got to play broker in most of the parliamentary seats of Scotland, where he was known as Harry the Ninth; as a commissioner of the Board of Control (1784–93) he became the greatest dispenser of jobs in India (Canning referred to his system of 'pillage and patronage'); and as an intimate of the Duke of York he influenced some Army appointments. Later Dundas would develop strong views on policy, but at this point he was willing, like the old Duke of Newcastle, to concentrate on men and let the Prime Minister take care of measures.

In many ways Pitt and Fox seemed complete opposites. One was the son of the patriot Chatham, who had won America, the other the son of Henry Fox, epitome of that political sleaze which had lost it again. Pitt was tall, wafer-thin, fastidious in manner, and slightly androgynous in appearance; his rival was swarthy, fat, and (like many fat men in the eighteenth century) irresistible to women. Despite a fondness for boyish horseplay in private, Pitt's public demeanour was cool and aloof, Fox's mercurial and sloppy. Sir Robert Walpole was mocked 'for having such a passion to the House of Commons, because he shined so well in the debates, that he dressed himself out every morning to appear there, as if it were to see his mistress',[40] whereas Fox by contrast, dishevelled and unshaven, always looked as though he had just come from his mistress. Pitt had no mistress,[41] and it has sometimes been suggested that he

---

[40] *Diary of Viscount Percival, Afterwards First Earl of Egmont*, ed. R. A. Roberts (1920–3), i. 31–2.
[41] A contemporary joke had it that 'Pitt was stiff with everyone but women.'

threw himself into work as a way of sublimating repressed homosexual instincts, but it seems more likely that he had little sexual appetite. He knew how to flatter MPs by preparing furiously for the following day's debate, whereas Fox would blunder in from a night's dissipation, utterly unprepared, and was arrogant and ingratiating by turns. 'Mr. Pitt conceives his sentences before he utters them,' commented Richard Porson. 'Mr. Fox throws himself into the middle of his, and leaves it to God almighty to get him out again.' True, Fox was a magnificent orator—even Pitt acknowledged 'the wand of the magician'—and in private he could be as charming as only a dedicated egotist can be when he decides to flatter an inferior with his attention or concern, but the brilliance of his conversation could intimidate those with whom he was not intimate. He was damaged by his friendship with the Prince of Wales, especially in 1787 when the Hanoverian rat pack and paparazzi revealed that the Prince was secretly married to a Catholic woman. Nor did the ostentatious support of Georgiana, Duchess of Devonshire, help Fox's cause in the 1784 election. Apart from the rumour that she had traded kisses for votes, it was widely condemned as unnatural that a woman should neglect her domestic duties in order to interfere in politics.[42]

Most importantly, Fox was widely thought to be corrupt while Pitt enjoyed a reputation for integrity. Neither was well off, and yet just before the 1784 election Pitt ostentatiously refused to accept the Clerkship of the Pells, a sinecure worth £3,000 a year (Fox called the gesture 'a priggish piece of political legerdemain'). The impression of purity was further strengthened by his willingness to suppress some of the patronage available to him as First Lord of the Treasury. Moreover, he understood that if one has to deceive, one might as well be blatant about it. For example, he was accused of having had foreknowledge of the King's intention to try to influence the Lords' debate on Fox's India Bill. The charge was true, yet Pitt worked up so much righteous indignation in rebutting it that he managed to augment his reputation for rectitude.

I came up no backstairs . . . Little did I think to be ever charged in this House with being the tool and abettor of secret influence. The novelty of the imputation only renders it so much the more contemptible. This is the only answer I shall ever deign to make on the subject, and I wish the House to bear it in their mind, and judge of my future conduct by my present declaration: the integrity of my own heart, and the probity of all my public, as well as my private principles, shall always be my sources of action.[43]

As the historian of this incident has written, 'It was the lie of a master, perfect of its kind, superb in its insolence, and totally successful; its very unctuousness

---

[42] Linda Colley, *Britons: Forging the Nation 1707–1837* (New Haven, 1992), 242–8.

[43] A pretty straight kind of guy in other words (*CPH*, xxiv. 294 (12 Jan. 1784)).

carried the war into the enemy's camp, smearing them as the purveyors of shabby slanders and cheap rumours.'[44]

And yet it was Fox who was supposed to be unprincipled. Worse still, his exaggerated attempts to defend himself against the charge often led him into deeper and deeper holes, a tendency exemplified by the saga of the Warren Hastings impeachment. A ruthless and high-handed Governor-General of Bengal (1773–85), Hastings' record was held up to intense scrutiny during 145 days of impeachment proceedings, which dragged out over seven years before he was acquitted in 1795. He was a victim of personal vendettas, not to say 'hypocrisy and hysteria'—a feeling that the nation had erred and that scapegoats must be pilloried—but his case gave rise to a useful debate on imperial responsibilities. Hastings' resourcefulness might have saved the Indian empire but 'His principles were somewhat lax. His heart was somewhat hard.'[45] This judgement was delivered by someone who belonged to a younger generation fed on concepts of probity, responsibility, and the need to show humanity to lesser breeds. Hastings became the first casualty of this new sensibility when, in 1787, the Commons decided on impeachment by a majority of three to one. Pitt supported the initiative at this stage, but refused to manage the prosecution and before long was throwing obstacles in its way. Fox, Burke, and Sheridan, on the other hand, persisted long after the point at which the trial began to discredit them by making them appear obsessive and vindictive. Burke was genuinely outraged that Hastings (the 'Captain-General of Iniquity') should have let down aristocracy by his autocratic methods. His trampling on Indian laws and customs prefigured what the Jacobins would do to France. Also, as an Irishman Burke was especially sensitive on the subject of colonial misrule. The main reason for Fox's persistence, however, was a determination to vindicate his India Bill. Having justified it on the grounds that East India Company rule was a 'system of despotism, unmatched in all the histories of the world', he now felt obliged to prove the point by pressing the impeachment. (Later, when it began to look as though Hastings might be exonerated, he tried to abort the prosecution.) It is hard to imagine Pitt embroiling himself in a cause so detrimental to himself *merely* in order to justify earlier conduct, but then Pitt was too cocksure of his own integrity to worry about what others might think about matters long since past.

It helped, of course, that he was in office. As a contemporary remarked, in the 1780s Pitt 'composed himself the Administration'.[46] Until 1789, when he was joined by his cousin William Grenville, he was the only Cabinet minister in the

---

[44] John Cannon, *The Fox–North Coalition: Crisis of the Constitution, 1782–4* (Cambridge, 1969), 165.

[45] [T. B. Macaulay], 'Warren Hastings', *ER* 74 (1841), 255.

[46] *The Historical and Posthumous Memoirs of Sir Nathaniel William Wraxall 1772–1784*, ed. Henry B. Wheatley (1884), v. 164.

Commons, like Walpole before 1730, and therefore spoke on all Government policies, domestic, imperial, and foreign, in the only arena that really mattered, while noble colleagues such as Gower, Sydney, Carmarthen, and Richmond were relative ciphers. It meant that the King became dependent on him, since only he stood between the Crown and a vengeful Fox. George's hatred of the man who had denounced the American war, stormed his closet, and debauched his eldest son was unremitting, perhaps pathological. But if the King needed Pitt, Pitt needed the King. Just how much Pitt needed the King became clear during the Regency crisis of 1788–9.

It followed a difficult parliamentary session during which Pitt had been forced to trample on one of his own most important measures. The India Act of 1784, establishing a Board of Control to oversee affairs, had avoided the criticism directed at Fox's Bill by allowing the King rather than Parliament to appoint its members, and by leaving most patronage and all routine administration to the East India Company. It was to be the basis of Indian government for the next half-century, but in 1788, following a military threat to the Subcontinent, Pitt was induced to force through a Declaratory Act giving the Government authority to dispatch regiments at Company expense and without reference to the directors. Worse than the measure itself was the fact that, tired and hung over, he failed for once to prepare his case and delivered 'one of the worst speeches of his career'.[47] Shortly afterwards there was a row over naval appointments, leading six peers and twenty-four independent MPs to clamour for the formation of a third party. It was a minor irritant but more troubling than anything Pitt had suffered so far, and to make matters worse early in November the royal doctors announced something which had already become clear to those in high society—that George III was seriously unwell. He was to recover quite suddenly in February 1789, but throughout the winter it looked as though there would have to be a Regency, in which case the Prince would probably knife Pitt just as the King had knifed Fox and North. Politics suddenly seemed to be in flux once more.

The constitutional question, of course, was how to proceed when the monarch was incapacitated. Did the heir to the throne automatically inherit the powers of the Crown by right, or did authority pass from the King *in* Parliament to Parliament *without* the King, leaving the two Houses to make whatever arrangements they thought fit? Unsurprisingly, Fox argued that a regent should enjoy the powers of a monarch, and just as unsurprisingly Pitt demurred. Lord Chancellor Thurlow, the ministry's chief spokesman in the Lords, began to flirt openly with Opposition, and some who had ratted from Fox to Pitt in 1784 now ratted back, notably the Earl of Lonsdale, who ordered his 'ninepins' in the

---

[47] Ehrman i. 454–5.

Commons to vote against the Government. While Fox fantasized about the shape of his Cabinet, Pitt's only trick was to play for time, so he called for a lengthy investigation into constitutional precedents, and insisted on proceeding by legislation rather than by an address. This tactic succeeded. The King recovered just in time, and Pitt not only survived but probably gained from the episode. For Fox had been too eager, too expectant, too reckless in his demands on behalf of the Prince, too careless of historical precedent and formal procedure, whereas Pitt—though no less self-interested—had managed to appear reasonable and altruistic.[48]

The Regency crisis illustrates the interplay of 'myth and reality' in eighteenth-century politics. Pitt claimed to have 'un-Whigged' his rival by exposing the inconsistency between Fox's demands on behalf of the Prince and his normal rhetoric calling for limits to royal power. Yet Pitt 'un-Whigged' himself as well, for in arguing that the Prince should not enjoy his father's rights and privileges, he was forced to claim that the person and office of the Crown were inseparable. This doctrine, denounced by Fox as 'legal metaphysics', seemed tantamount to a Tory belief in the divine right of kings, and was hardly an appropriate way for a Whig to celebrate the centenary of the Glorious Revolution. Such blatant shadow boxing was only possible because of the relaxed nature of constitutional debate, but this was shortly to change. On 14 July 1789, just five months after the King's recovery, a Paris mob stormed the Bastille, and thereby precipitated the dramatic series of events known as the French Revolution.

THE FRENCH REVOLUTION AND POLITICAL REALIGNMENT

Like all Hanoverian prime ministers, Pitt received begging letters almost daily. One from Nathaniel Wraxall in 1792 was typical, and conveys the extent to which politics was still a matter of seeking jobs in return for services rendered.

Next November, I [shall] have supported your Government nine years complete through three Parliaments. In two of those, I did not procure my seat, without the greatest personal exertion. In 1784, at the *express request* of the Treasury, I seated Heneage and Nicholas for Cricklade, and turned out Adamson and Coxe, on the petition, by invalidating no less than 97 votes. I was enabled to do Government so essential a service, by having in my own hands, at that time, the exclusive management of Cricklade. During the winter of the Regency, I adhered to you, Sir, steadily, in defiance of every solicitation, and of the most flattering offers . . . I now ask for a situation, which I am competent to fill.[49]

48 John W. Derry, *The Regency Crisis and the Whigs 1788–9* (Cambridge, 1963).
49 N. W. Wraxall to Pitt, 7 Aug. 1792, TNA, Pitt MS 30/8/192, fos. 119–20.

Bribes and blandishments would remain a feature of political life for a long time to come, and yet it is hard to imagine that a letter quite so innocent of principle or ideology could have been written much later than 1792. For that was when the French Revolution, after simmering for three years, suddenly bubbled over with sickening violence. The invasion of the Tuileries took place in June, the massacre of the Swiss Guard in August, the prison massacres in September, the execution of Louis XVI in the following January, and then the Reign of Terror during 1793–4. French politics was now literally a matter of life and death! The events were reported in England in grisly detail, with rumours of cannibalism, as well as fully accredited accounts of aristocratic men, women, and children being wheeled through the streets to have their heads sliced off, and—what was almost worse—being mocked and spat at by a 'carnivorous rabble howling around', faces distorted with hatred. Nor were these seen as merely local events. In April 1792 the French Legislative Assembly declared war on Austria, in May the rulers of Austria and Prussia declared war on France, and in November the Jacobin-dominated National Convention declared its mission to export the Revolution by promising 'fraternity and assistance to all people who wish to recover their liberty'.[50] It would be an exaggeration to say that these events made ideologues of everyone, but they certainly heightened consciousness about the Revolution and its implications. Never again would politics turn on jobbery or 'the exclusive management of Cricklade'.

For many in England the Revolution had been regarded as demonic even before these terrible developments, owing to the passion with which writers such as Edmund Burke had denounced it. For most of 1790 foreign affairs had been dominated by events elsewhere, notably the Nootka Sound where Spain had briefly threatened to grab possession of a rich whaling area off Vancouver Island. There was then the 'Ochakov incident', when Pitt mobilized the fleet to go to war against Russia in an abortive attempt to force her to surrender a Black Sea port which she had seized from Turkey. Attention turned to France only because of Burke's *Reflections on the Revolution in France*, which went through eleven editions and sold a record number of 32,000 copies within a year of its publication in November. Like most of Burke's writings, it combined crudely sensationalist polemic with sophisticated analysis. His aim was to show that the Revolution was both destructive in its effects and dangerously contagious. Just as financial speculation had led to an accursed credit system, which debased true value and destabilized the State, so the political speculations of the *philosophes*, based on enlightened individualism, had corroded old habits of communal association, respect, and deference. The hallmark of the Revolution was its unstoppable energy, which would destroy not just property—the lands

---

[50] Decree of Fraternity and Assistance to all People, 19 Nov. 1792.

belonging to the French Church had been nationalized as early as 1789—but even commerce, since markets depended on religion and civility for their successful operation.

Burke undoubtedly idealized France's Ancien Régime, its royal splendour, glorious aristocracy, religious devotion, and spirit of chivalry. His elegiacs prompted Thomas Paine's famous remark that Burke 'pities the plumage but forgets the dying bird', meaning that he neglected the mass of poverty and wretchedness existing beneath the glitter of Versailles. This was to miss the point, however, for Burke was less bothered by the material or even the constitutional consequences of what was happening in France than by the attempted cultural 'revolution in sentiments, manners, and moral opinions',[51] the Jacobin plan to brainwash the public through revolutionary festivals and symbols. Such 'little things', he wrote later, 'made a schism of the whole universe'. 'Nothing in the Revolution, no, not to a phrase or a gesture, not to the fashion of a hat or a shoe, was left to accident.' Coercion in such matters was dangerous, because 'manners are what vex or soothe, corrupt or purify, exalt or debase, barbarize or refine us, by a constant, steady, uniform, insensible operation, like that of the air we breathe in. They give their whole form and colour to our lives.'[52]

Yet for all the book's elevation of habit, passion, and feeling above abstract reason, its central message was the utilitarian, even Hobbesian, one that no rebellion is legitimate unless it succeeds, in which case the sanction of providence combines with prudence to render it sacred. What Burke wrote about the court of Versailles may have been 'pure foppery',[53] but it reflected his sensationalist understanding that because people's appetites and aspirations are conditioned by the environment in which they are nurtured, and because they have a prejudice in favour of prescriptive rights, rapid non-evolutionary change must by definition make them unhappy. And because there is an implicit contract between past, present, and future, the only *rights* that we in the present generation are entitled to claim are those that have come down as 'an *entailed inheritance* derived to us from our forefathers . . . without any reference whatever to any other more general or prior right'.[54] In other words, there are no natural rights or 'rights of man'.

Burke's *Reflections* included a warning that excess of liberty always leads to licence, licence to anarchy, and anarchy to military despotism. He wrote it during the spring and summer of 1790, when the Revolution was going through what one historian calls a 'period of constitution-making, of benevolent rhetoric and of peaceful jubilation'.[55] To have prophesied so early that it would lead to the

---

[51] Burke, *Reflections*, 131.   [52] Burke, *Regicide*, 242.
[53] Philip Francis to Burke, 19 Feb. 1790, in Burke, *Correspondence*, vi. 85–7.
[54] Burke, *Reflections*, 83.   [55] Conor Cruise O'Brien, *The Great Melody* (1992), 402.

'assassination' of Louis XVI and Marie-Antoinette,[56] and from there to a Reign of Terror followed by a whiff of grapeshot and the dictatorship of 'some popular general', was a singular scoop that won Burke a reputation for great foresight,[57] but as always his arguments operated at different levels. In crude terms his prophecy was no more than guesswork, an extrapolation from seventeenth-century English history when civil war had led to Cromwell's military dictatorship. As such, it turned out to be accurate but might just as easily have proved false. However, Burke was making a more subtle point when he observed that 'men cannot enjoy the rights of an uncivil and of a civil state together'.[58] If states allow their citizens rights outside society, or recognize a private sphere in which they may not legally interfere, then dictatorship must be the outcome. This is because all states are forced willy-nilly to adjudicate between the incompatible rights of individuals, yet if such intervention has been declared unconstitutional, those states must then *by definition* be acting dictatorially. In this sense the *Reflections* can be understood as either a Tory or a Foxite text—but not as a 'True Whig' or Pittite one—because it recognized no distinction between public and private morality, and saw that such a distinction if made would ultimately be subversive of all practical authority.

There is a danger of exaggerating Burke's influence, since several writers anticipated him or expressed their views independently. Pamphlets and newspaper articles by High Church bishops such as George Horne and Samuel Horsley had already begun to propagate a counter-enlightenment among younger members of the elite in the 1780s. Their appeals to Revelation and to the authority of the Fathers, and their attacks on the rational philosophies of Hume and Priestley, are said to have 'helped the Church to retain its prominence in the life of the nation by preparing the ground for the popular conservatism of the war years well before 1793'.[59] The laymen John Reeves and John Bowles wrote at least thirty-three loyalist and bellicose pamphlets between them. They echoed Burke's appeal to 'the accumulated wisdom of our ancestors', but mingled it with a strident anti-Catholicism that was deeply un-Burkean. Like Hannah More, another prolific pamphleteer, they have been charged with disseminating a 'vulgar conservatism' which backfired on itself. It was one thing to tell the populace what to think, but by addressing them so frequently, so urgently, and so directly, these writers unwittingly acknowledged the masses as agents. They 'breached the traditional boundaries of the political nation and thereby advanced a process of mass participation which they had come into existence

---

[56] As Burke did in his *Letter to a Member of the National Assembly* (Jan. 1791).

[57] The 'popular general' was Napoleon Bonaparte, who subsequently used the phrase 'whiff of grapeshot' to describe his dispersal of the Paris mob in October 1795.   [58] Burke, *Reflections*, 110.

[59] Nigel Aston, 'Horne and Heterodoxy: The Defence of Anglican Beliefs in the Late Enlightenment', *EHR* 108 (1993), 918.

to prevent'.[60] This was also a problem with Archdeacon William Paley's *Reasons for Contentment Addressed to the Labouring Part of the British Public* (1792), which was both warmly celebrated and bitterly reviled. From a conservative's point of view, he should simply have told the poor to be content, and not tried to reason with them as to why. But if this is so, then maybe the vulgarity began with Burke himself, and especially with his language. For in the *Reflections* Burke abandoned the abstract rationalist mode in which political argument had traditionally been conducted, and which had effectively restricted it to an elite, in favour of highly charged metaphor and figurative diction. Perhaps this reflected his own furious emotions, perhaps it was a cynical attempt to manipulate those of his readers. Whichever, its radical format may have undermined the *Reflections'* conservative content by breaking down the barriers of polite discourse. Moreover, Burke's discarding of traditional modes allowed Paine to follow suit in *Rights of Man*. His combination of plain man's demotic and colloquial bluntness was even more subversive than his republican ideology.[61]

Burke began *Reflections* in response to a speech by the Dissenter Richard Price to the Revolution Society,[62] congratulating the French and calling for civil and religious liberty at home. It coincided with a campaign for the repeal of the Test and Corporation Acts. Fox had supported repeal enthusiastically, but Pitt argued that Dissenters had a right to freedom of worship only, not to 'a complete equality of participation'. This was ingratitude, given that Pitt had enjoyed Nonconformist support in the 1784 election, but it led Burke to wonder whether Pitt might not be a fitter statesman than Fox. For in Burke's view it would be dangerous to allow full civil and political rights to people who refused to subscribe to the state religion. It would be tantamount to recognizing a private religious sphere that was separate from the public realm.

It is hardly surprising that the French Revolution should have led to the break-up of the Opposition Whig Party. A lover of all things Parisian, an enemy of all monarchs but especially Bourbons, and an old friend of the French Whig Lafayette, Charles Fox was genuinely exhilarated by the storming and fall of the Bastille: 'How much the greatest event it is that ever happened in the world, and how much the best!'[63] More to the point, his stubbornness and loyalty to causes once taken up prevented him from beating the conventional retreat when events turned nasty. He can hardly have liked the principles of the Parisian *sans-culottes*, but he showed his sympathy by cultivating a grizzled chin, greasy

[60] Mark Philp, 'Vulgar Conservatism, 1792–3', *EHR* 110 (1995), 45; Kevin Gilmartin, 'In the Theater of Counterrevolution: Loyalist Association and Conservative Opinion in the 1790s', *JBS* 41 (2002), 291–328.   [61] Olivia Smith, *The Politics of Language 1791–1819* (Oxford, 1984), 36–51.

[62] Revolution societies were founded in London, Manchester, Norwich, and elsewhere to celebrate the centenary of the Glorious Revolution.

[63] Fox to Richard Fitzpatrick, 30 July 1789, in *Memorials and Correspondence of Charles James Fox*, ed. Lord John Russell (1853–7), ii. 361.

locks, and sub-demotic pseudo-libertarian rhetoric. He seemed to be imitating Danton. Burke was appalled.

By late 1792 there were over 10,000 French émigrés clustered in London,[64] and the Home Office was receiving reports from Bourbon partisans that an army of Jacobins disguised as *abbés* and waiters was plotting with home-grown radicals to attack the Bank of England and the Tower of London.[65] Government officials almost certainly fed these rumours to the loyalist press in order to prepare the ground for a Royal Proclamation (1 December) calling out the militia of ten counties to quell the anticipated insurrection.[66] Richard Brinsley Sheridan, the brilliant playwright politician, claimed that the danger existed only in Pitt's 'foul imagination', and Fox dismissed it as a fraud, a snare, and a delusion, a latter-day Popish Plot but aimed at republicans and Dissenters.[67] His aspersion was almost certainly justified, but it led to the first wave of defections from his party. His motion to reject the King's Speech at the opening of the parliamentary session was opposed by most of his more conservative and aristocratic followers, who did not wish to divide against the Government at a time of national danger, and a few days later Burke announced a formal separation from the man he had once described as 'born to be loved'. Replying to Fox, he took a dagger from a brown paper bag and hurled it melodramatically onto the floor of the Commons. There were hoots of laughter, but Burke was deadly sincere:

It is my object to keep the French infection from this country; their principles from our minds, and their daggers from our hearts. . . . When they smile, I see blood trickling down their faces; I see their insidious purposes; I see that the object of all their cajoling is—blood! I now warn my countrymen to beware of these execrable philosophers, whose only object is to destroy every thing that is good here, and to establish immorality and murder by precept and example—*Hic niger est hunc tu Romane caveto.*[68]

Fox was probably correct to claim that the Government's fear of an imminent insurrection was simulated and that the Royal Proclamation was a charade, but his own exaggerated rhetoric and Burke's histrionics were designed to mask the uncomfortable truth that their relationship had been under strain for a long time. Burke had felt increasingly isolated since Rockingham's death. In 1787 he had joined with Loughborough and Windham in forming a cabal of 'New

[64] Between 1789 and 1815 Britain admitted a substantial proportion of the roughly 150,000 émigrés, including about 7,000 exiled Roman Catholic priests (D. A. Bellenger, *The French Exiled Clergy in the British Isles after 1789* (Bath, 1986), 1).

[65] Clive Emsley, 'The London "Insurrection" of December 1792: Fact, Fiction, or Fantasy', *JBS* 17 (1978), 66–86; Jennifer Mori, 'Responses to Revolution: The November Crisis of 1792', *Historical Research*, 69 (1996), 284–305; ead., *William Pitt and the French Revolution 1785–1795* (Edinburgh, 1997), 121–30.

[66] But not the Middlesex and Westminster militias, which were considered too untrustworthy.

[67] 'An Invasion? Where Is It?' *CPH* xxx. 12–34 (13 Dec. 1792).

[68] *CPH*, xxx. 189 (28 Dec. 1792).

Whigs' against Fox's leadership, following a long wrangle over the Prince of Wales.[69] He was further dismayed when in April 1792 Fox complaisantly allowed his henchmen Charles Grey and Sheridan to link his name to a new Association of the Friends of the People, and when Grey proposed reform in the Commons Burke and Windham spoke violently against. In the following winter some of the more liberal Foxites moved resolutions which would have given them control of the Whig Club. Their language of intimidatory virtue and refusal to countenance dissent was reminiscent of the Jacobin Club in Paris, and prompted some forty of the more conservative members to resign en bloc in February and March 1793.[70]

Encouraged by the emergence of Windham's third party, now about thirty strong, Pitt had already begun to look about for recruits. His first step was to prise Thurlow out of the Cabinet for failing to support official policy. Since the Lord Chancellor was widely known to be a royal spy, this démarche was almost certainly timed to appeal to the more 'respectable' members of the Opposition. Pitt then invited Portland to a Privy Council and sought his advice on the wording of the 21 May Proclamation against 'tumultuous meetings and seditious writings'.[71] Egged on by Burke and Windham, Pitt encouraged rumours of an impending junction with Fox, and held out tantalizing prospects of jobs for penitent members of the Opposition. Desperate to keep his followers loyal, Fox scotched these rumours by demanding impossible conditions, such as Pitt's removal from the Treasury.[72] In November 1792 Loughborough coyly declined an offer of the Great Seal[73] on the grounds that impartial observers 'might find reason to question the sincerity with which I have always maintained this doctrine, that in times of difficulty every man owed a *disinterested* support to the Government, if they found me inclined to make a distinction in favor of what would be called my own ambition'.[74] George III took this gobbledygook to mean that Loughborough would have liked to accept, but that Portland and Fox would not let him.[75] In December Loughborough assured Pitt that Portland was less intransigent than the Foxite press made out,[76] and towards the end of January 1793 he at last agreed to become Lord Chancellor.

[69] In attempting to persuade the Commons to settle the Prince's debts, Fox had recklessly denied a fact known to everyone in social circles, that the Prince had entered a secret and illegal marriage with Maria Fitzherbert, illegal because as a Roman Catholic she was ineligible to marry the heir to the throne.

[70] F. O'Gorman, *The Whig Party and the French Revolution* (1967), 120–1.

[71] *The Journal and Correspondence of William, Lord Auckland*, ed. third Baron Auckland (1861–2), ii. 401–2; J. Holland Rose, *Pitt and Napoleon* (1912), 249; Portland to Pitt, 13 and 24 May 1792, CUL Pitt MSS 6958/1087, 1090.

[72] L. G. Mitchell, *Charles James Fox* (Oxford, 1992), 122–9; Portland to Fitzwilliam, 22 July 1792, in George III, *Correspondence*, i. 608 n.   [73] The Great Seal is the office of Lord Chancellor.

[74] Loughborough to Pitt, 24 Nov. 1792, CUL, Pitt MS 6958/1154.

[75] George III to Pitt, 26 Nov. 1792, CUL, Pitt MS 6958/1155; Stanhope, *Pitt*, vol. ii., app., p. xvi.

[76] Loughborough to Pitt, 9 Dec. 1792, CUL, Pitt MS 6958/1166.

In February Britain entered the war against France, and from that point on it was only a matter of time before a general reconstitution of the ministry took place. Rather surprisingly it did not happen until July 1794, by which time the European war was at a crisis point and most Opposition backbenchers had already switched allegiance. The appointment of Portland (Home Secretary),[77] Fitzwilliam (Lord President), Windham (Secretary at War), Spencer (First Lord of the Admiralty), Mansfield (without portfolio), and Loughborough meant that the whole of Pitt's first Cabinet had been dismissed within a space of six years, and that of its thirteen members six had until recently been Foxites. The new ministry was unmistakably a coalition, but because Pitt remained Prime Minister while Fox was firmly outside, and because historians, like contemporaries, are obsessed with the Pitt–Fox duel, it is not usually thought of as such, but rather as a humiliating capitulation by a large section of the Opposition to the Government of the day.

The effect of these developments was that the Foxites were reduced from about 180 MPs to about fifty-five. Most of the latter were socialites and gamblers, most were either Old Etonians or Westminsters, and all were close personal friends of Fox. At least twenty-five were closely connected to the peerage either by birth or by marriage, while many belonged to established Whig families and had married into others. More than half represented constituencies with fewer than 200 voters, and one-third owed their seats to aristocratic patrons. For example, most of the forty-four MPs who voted for Fox's motions against the war in February 1793 and May 1796 sat for rotten or nomination boroughs with few constituents to worry about.[78] It may seem incongruous that aristocratic politicians should have excluded themselves from power by supporting a popular revolution, but the explanation lies in what they were *against* rather than in what they *hoped for*. As Fox put it to Fitzwilliam as early as March 1792, 'Our apprehensions are raised by different objects: *you* seem to dread the prevalence of Paine's opinions (which in fact I detest as much as you do) while I am much more afraid of the total annihilation of all principles of liberty and resistance, an event which I am sure you would be as sorry to see as I.'[79] True Foxites *loathed* the Crown, and they opposed the war because they saw it as a pretext to undermine still further the liberties of the English people. It proved to be a justified concern, since the next six years were to be characterized by an unprecedented amount of repressive legislation.

---

[77] In place of Dundas, who became Secretary of State for War and the Colonies.

[78] Mitchell, *Fox and the Disintegration*, 247–54; George III, *Correspondence*, ii. p. xiii.

[79] H. Butterfield, 'Charles James Fox and the Whig Opposition in 1792', *Cambridge Historical Journal*, 9 (1947–9), 296.

'PITT'S TERROR'

Whether there was a serious threat of subversion in the early to mid-1790s is uncertain. What is certain is that the Government responded as though there was. According to one provincial magazine, Pitt instituted 'a system of TERROR almost as hideous in its features, almost as gigantic in its stature, and infinitely more pernicious in its tendency than France ever knew'.[80] While this was baloney, it *is* the case that there was a significant increase in the coercive powers of the State, or what Windham unapologetically called 'vigour beyond the law'.[81]

The trigger for this development was the reports of an imminent insurrection in London in December 1792. It might be going too far to suggest that Pitt cold-bloodedly exploited for political purposes intelligence which he knew to be false, but it is surely fair to say that he did not investigate as critically as he might have done a rumour which he knew would be convenient. He was perfectly aware that Portland, Loughborough, Windham, and suchlike were far more aristocratically minded and anti-democratic than he was himself, so this was just the sort of rumour to prise open the crack which was developing within the Opposition. There is also evidence to suggest that the rising sense of panic, especially but not only among the propertied classes, was magnified by Government manipulation. Surviving secret service accounts reveal that in the early 1790s the Government spent about £5,000 a year on press subsidies, and that the two most alarmist newspapers, the *Sun* and *True Briton*, were both started with ministerial help in 1792–3.[82] Three junior ministers—George Rose (Treasury), Bland Burges (Foreign Office), and Francis Freeling (Post Office)—masterminded these links with the press. The Archbishop of Canterbury acknowledged privately that the Royal Proclamation of May 1792 was intended to spread alarm, and that it presumed 'more disposition in the country to tumult than exists in fact'.[83] Even so, there was some legitimate cause for alarm, and ministers could hardly be expected to discuss how close the country had come to revolution with the detachment of historians. The nature of the radical movement changed dramatically in 1792. Until then membership of the various reform groups like the Society for Promoting Constitutional Information (SCI) had been confined to men of at least some substance, but the Sheffield Constitutional Society, founded in November 1791, broke with tradition by waiving subscriptions and entry fees. It claimed about 2,500 members within six months, which if true meant that more than one in ten of the town's population

[80] *The Cabinet*, produced in Norwich by a society of young gentlemen infatuated with the Revolution (C. B. Jewson, *Jacobin City: A Portrait of Norwich 1788–1802* (Glasgow, 1975), 58).

[81] *CPH* xxxii. 386 (23 Nov. 1795).

[82] Aspinall, *Politics and the Press*, 68–9, 78–9, 203–6; Lucyle Werkmeister, *A Newspaper History of England 1792–3* (Lincoln, Nebr. 1967), 118–19, 170–2.

[83] Archbishop John Moore to Auckland, 22 May 1792, in Auckland, *Journal*, ii. 407–8.

must have joined. Then in January 1792 Thomas Hardy founded the London Corresponding Society (LCS), which was also phenomenally successful, and spawned hundreds of affiliates all seeking 'members unlimited'.[84] Particularly alarming was the fact that its numbers more than doubled in the month following the battle of Valmy, a strategic victory for French arms which was celebrated enthusiastically by English radicals. For the first time ordinary working men took part in organized political activity entirely on their own initiative. For the first time in a century radical societies in different regions coordinated their campaigns, largely thanks to the initiative of John Horne Tooke of the SCI. And for the first time there was a neighbouring Great Power willing to egg these radicals on. In November 1792 the French envoy Chauvelin ostentatiously received deputations from the Norwich Revolutionary Society, the Manchester Constitutional Society, the London Independent Whigs, and the LCS,[85] while English radicals sent money and armaments to help the revolutionary armies in Belgium. By Christmas it looked as though the notorious Edict of Fraternity and Assistance might claim its first international success in England.

It was in this feverish atmosphere that the country was inexorably sucked into war. There was no awareness to begin with that the conflict would last a generation, encompass most of Europe, involve parts of the New World and Asia Minor, or bring threats of invasion and conquest. Indeed Pitt, who was inclined to be sanguine in military matters, expected a quick victory. In theory the rulers of Austria and Prussia had declared war on France for dynastic and ideological reasons—to save Louis XVI and to destroy the Revolution. In reality they were motivated by the usual pragmatic considerations. The spur was not that France was strong, as they alleged, but that she *appeared* to be weak. Probably they calculated that, if only they could crush her completely, they would be freer to dismember Poland.[86] English ministers did not even pretend to be mounting an ideological crusade, except, that is, for Windham, who was keen to encourage counter-revolution. Though they occasionally made statements which seemed to chime with Burke's anti-Jacobinical rhapsodies—for example, Pitt warned of the dangers of universal anarchy after Louis XVI's execution—these were deliberately kept vague and were obviously intended to reconcile the country to a war being fought for more practical reasons.

The traditional objectives of British foreign policy were strategic and mercantilist: to prevent any single Continental power from dominating Europe,

---

[84] Jenny Graham, *The Nation, the Law and the King: Reform Politics in England, 1789–1799* (Lanham, Md., 2000), i. 273–83. Membership peaked at about 3,000 in 1795 (*Selections from the Papers of the London Corresponding Society 1792–1799*, ed. Mary Thale (Cambridge, 1983), p. xxiv; Albert Goodwin, *The Friends of Liberty: The English Democratic Movement in the Age of the French Revolution* (1979), 136–70).

[85] T. C. W. Blanning, *The Origins of the French Revolutionary Wars* (Harlow, 1986), 142–52; J. T. Murley, 'The Origin and Outbreak of the Anglo-French War of 1793', D.Phil. thesis (Oxford University, 1959), 145.   [86] Blanning, *Origins*, 206–7.

and to safeguard the country's overseas possessions and trade. It was thought especially important to protect the Low Countries[87] against French aggression, not least because the Dutch controlled the Cape of Good Hope, a key station on England's vital sea route to India. Burke said that the Netherlands were 'as necessary a part of this country as Kent'. In 1787 the British representative at The Hague, James Harris, had assisted the Anglophone Stadtholder to defeat the Patriots, a French-backed republican party, and to re-establish the Orange regime, while in 1789 Pitt was almost certainly less worried about events in Paris than he was about the revolution of Brabant, when Belgian nationalists rebelled against Austrian rule. His diplomatic support had helped the Austrians to reassert their authority by the end of 1790, but he remained anxious about the precarious situation in both parts of the Low Countries.

When Continental war broke out in the summer of 1792, it seemed obvious at first that Britain should keep aloof and let the two sides slog it out, especially as it was confidently believed that the Duke of Brunswick would easily defeat the armies of the chaotic and bankrupt Republic. But this non-strategy was discredited when French troops rapidly overran the Low Countries as well as Savoy and Nice. The Duke of Brunswick was defeated by Dumouriez at Valmy[88] in September and at Jemappes in November, whereupon the French occupied Brussels and opened the river Scheldt to navigation. This last was in defiance of the Treaty of Westphalia (1648), which had given commercial rights exclusively to the Dutch, a monopoly which Pitt had guaranteed as recently as 1788. It was not intrinsically so important as to constitute a *casus belli*, but it was symbolic of France's contempt for international treaties and determination to dominate the Low Countries.[89] From this point on, and with prominent revolutionaries proclaiming that the Rhine was France's true border, it seemed ever more likely that Britain would be provoked into joining the Coalition powers, though after several weeks of stand-off it was actually the French who declared war first in February 1793.

It is sometimes said that Pitt allowed Britain to drift into war for the same reason that he overreacted to the rumour of a London insurrection—i.e. to widen divisions within the Opposition. It seems more likely that he had to go to war in order not to alienate those disaffected Foxites whom he was seeking to attract.[90] For there can be little doubt that Portland, Loughborough, and Windham were keener to fight against revolutionary France than he and

---

[87] The Low Countries, or Netherlands, consisted of Belgium in the south and the United Provinces in the north. By the 18th century the term 'the Netherlands' was often applied to the northern part exclusively, which was also sometimes called Holland after its most important province.

[88] The significance of Valmy (20 Sept. 1792) was noted in Sir David Creasy's *Fifteen Decisive Battles of the World* (1851). Although nearly four times as many Frenchmen were killed as Prussians, it lifted the immediate danger to Paris from the allied armies.   [89] Blanning, *Origins*, 140–1.

[90] Ibid. 151–2.

Grenville were. Pitt may even have feared that, unless he went with the tide, he would be outflanked on the Right[91] in an increasingly combative and xenophobic Parliament. He was also under pressure from the King, and may have felt some from the country as well, since (at least according to a Foreign Office minister) there was only 'one sentiment throughout the country' by December 1792, 'that of loyalty to the King—affection to the existing constitution—ardor to support it and an earnest desire to go to war with the French'.[92]

The outbreak of war combined with fears of insurrection led to a strengthening of the executive. The idea of paid magistrates had until now been vigorously opposed, partly on grounds of economy, but in June 1792 the Middlesex Justices Act finally established London stipendiaries.[93] Though initiated locally, it was enthusiastically supported by ministers and opposed by Fox. Hitherto, troops intended for use against the civilian population had been billeted in alehouses, but this was now thought to be dangerous, so Army barracks began to be erected. In November Treasury solicitors laid plans to prosecute seditious libellers, and local agents were appointed to collect the necessary evidence.[94] Soon afterwards the Government established an Alien Office under the wing of the Home Secretary.[95] Inevitably denounced by Fox, its ostensible function was counter-espionage, but it quickly spread its surveillance from foreign spies to suspected rebels at home. According to one of its agents, William Wickham, it constituted a 'system of *preventitive* police'. 'Without bustle, noise or anything that can attract public attention, Government possess here the most powerful means of observation and information . . . that was ever placed in the hands of a free government.'[96]

Not all aspects of the new bureaucracy were repressive. The collapse of a long economic boom in 1792 precipitated bankruptcies and strikes, while a series of poor harvests caused wheat prices to rise dramatically during 1794–6, finally reaching crisis levels of 80s. per quarter. Faced with famine and food riots, and with merchants hesitating to import grain because of wartime uncertainty, the

---

[91] Although the terms 'Left' and 'Right' are anachronistic, the concepts behind them were well understood as a result of the French Revolution.

[92] Burges to Auckland, 18 Dec. 1792, Auckland Papers, Add. MS 34446, fo. 161.

[93] Leon Radzinowicz and Roger Hood, *A History of English Criminal Law and its Administration from 1750* (1948–86), iii. 123–37.

[94] Robert R. Dozier, *For King, Constitution, and Country: The English Loyalists and the French Revolution* (Lexington, Ky., 1983), 51–4; Ehrman ii. 213–27.

[95] It was an extension of the Foreign Letter Office, which had operated unofficially under the aegis of the Post Office, and its first superintendent was William Huskisson. The Act which authorized the Alien Office had to be renewed each year and re-enacted every five. In the event it was re-enacted only once (in 1798), although the Office seems to have been operative at least as late as 1806. Elizabeth Sparrow, 'The Alien Office, 1792–1806', *HJ* 33 (1990), 361–84.

[96] Bernard Porter, *Plots and Paranoia: A History of Political Espionage in Britain 1790–1988* (1989), 29–32; Roger Wells, *Insurrection: The British Experience 1795–1803* (Gloucester, 1983), 28–43.

Government bought up overseas wheat through the Committee (later Board) of Trade.[97] Then, having been criticized for this initiative by free-marketeers, it resorted instead to temporary import bounties in the hope of encouraging private speculation. In France a similar situation had led to the Law of the Maximum. In England few people demanded price-fixing, but there were demands for a minimum wage, with the Foxite Samuel Whitbread bringing forward a Bill in 1795–6. Pitt scotched that idea, but instead introduced a comprehensive measure which aimed to increase the total amount spent on poor relief and provide extra allowances for large families. It was badly drafted and had to be withdrawn, but at least he secured a provision requiring JPs to grant relief to anyone in sickness or temporary distress, without their having to enter a workhouse.[98]

Bureaucratic developments could help, but it was plain that some coercive persuasion would also be needed. Lord Auckland[99] called for 'every possible form of proclamation to the people, orders for fast days, speeches from the Throne, discourses from the pulpit, discussions in Parliament'. In May 1792 a Royal Proclamation prohibited seditious meetings and publications. It might have looked like a sledgehammer, but the book it mainly aimed to crack was no nut. The two parts of Thomas Paine's *Rights of Man* (1791–2), a radical riposte to Burke, was selling in huge quantities and cheap editions. Part I appealed to natural rights, and Part II anticipated a fundamental revolution in social relationships, including the end of monarchy and aristocracy.[100] An official press campaign was mobilized to discredit Paine, and secret service money disbursed to loyal propagandists such as the placemen John Bowles and John Reeves. Even more than Burke, Reeves can be regarded as the godfather of popular loyalism. Whether or not Fox was correct to rubbish him as a 'ministerial hireling', he almost certainly acted with ministerial connivance when he founded an Association for Preserving Liberty and Property against Republicans and Levellers in November 1792 (henceforward the Association). Working from the Crown and Anchor in the Strand, it proved staggeringly successful, outstripping even the Constitutional societies. Before long there were more than 2,000 local branches or Reeves societies, whose function was to disrupt radical

[97] Ehrman ii. 464–6.

[98] The Poor Law of 1722 had authorized parishes to build workhouses and to deny relief to anyone who refused to enter one. Thomas Gilbert's Act in 1782 had sanctioned outdoor relief but did not apply to towns or other places with incorporated Poor Law guardians. J. R. Poynter, *Society and Pauperism: English Ideas on Poor Relief, 1795–1834* (1969), 55–76; Raymond G. Cowherd, *Political Economists and the English Poor Laws* (Athens, Ohio, 1977), 4–6, 10.

[99] The Ambassador to the United Provinces, and personally very close to Pitt.

[100] It has been suggested that 'many working men must have come to political consciousness by reading Paine' (Marilyn Butler (ed.), *Burke, Paine, Godwin, and the Revolution Controversy* (Cambridge, 1984), 108).

meetings, beat up Paineite printers, initiate prosecutions for sedition, and distribute loyalist tracts.[101]

Radicalism and loyalism enjoyed something of a symbiotic relationship throughout the Hanoverian period, in that when one was strong the other was too. It was therefore not a question of large numbers of people changing their views, but one of a cycle of tumescence and quiescence affecting both sides together. On any simple head count it would seem that there were many more loyalists than radicals, but the matter is complex. Some radical activity was presumably a cover for criminal behaviour and private vendettas, but then much loyalist activity was obviously manipulated from above. Even where the latter was spontaneous, it often took ritualistic and carnivalesque forms whose meaning is difficult to assess. For example, when effigies of Paine were burned, hanged, beheaded, or horse-whipped through the streets,[102] it is not clear that such symbolic violence indicated vicious intentions, any more than with Guy Fawkes. Finally, and paradoxically, popular loyalism may have had radical implications in the longer term by inducting the poor in political action.

But whatever were the consequences, the propertied classes undoubtedly went to enormous lengths to create the necessary climate of opinion. This enabled the Anglican clergy to come in from the relative cold. National as distinct from local life in the eighteenth century had been essentially secular, but in its anxieties about radicalism the regime was willing to employ spiritual weapons. Paley's *Reasons for Contentment*, already referred to, appeared as an Association pamphlet in 1792 and was very widely distributed. The ancient universities too began to escape from decades of internal torpor and external indifference,[103] and were welcomed on board by an establishment anxious to rope them into the ideological work of conservatism. At the same time a subtle shift took place in the thrust of clerical polemic generally. As well as age-old admonitions on 'the duty of submission to higher powers', there came a new emphasis on what has been called 'eschatological policing': warnings to the poor that if they did not behave themselves they would go to Hell.[104] It was an effective message, and helped to raise the public profile of the lesser clergy.

Coercive methods were also thought to be necessary. In 1794 permission was given for raising Volunteer corps, to be used 'for the suppression of riots

---

[101] Austin Mitchell, 'The Association Movement of 1792–3', *HJ* 4 (1961), 56–77.

[102] John Keane, *Tom Paine: A Political Life* (1995), 336–40; Dozier, *For King, Constitution*, 90–2.

[103] In Oxford, which was the more torpid, a number of colleges established stricter methods of selection and assessment between 1790 and 1810, while statutes of 1800 and 1807 established an efficient system of University examinations for both honours and pass degrees.

[104] Robert Hole, *Pulpits, Politics and Public Order in England 1760–1832* (Cambridge, 1989), 97–144. For a related discursive shift from questions of rights and precedent to questions of civilization and utility, see Gregory Claeys, 'The French Revolution Debate and British Political Thought', *History of Political Thought*, 11 (1990), 59–80.

and tumults' as well as against invaders. In May the Habeas Corpus Act was suspended, enabling ministers to detain a number of prominent radicals, twelve of whom were promptly indicted for high treason ('compassing and imagining the King's death'). The prosecution did not claim that the accused had literally plotted to kill George III; rather that, by calling for a Convention and for universal suffrage, they had issued a challenge to royal authority which the King would be obliged to resist, thereby setting in train a process of events which might jeopardize his life.[105] There were precedents for this doctrine of constructive treason, though the best legal authorities such as Coke and Hale had all frowned on it. Perhaps the law officers assumed that juries would be influenced by events in France, where the calling of the Estates General had indeed led on to regicide. If so, they were to be disappointed. First Thomas Hardy and then John Horne Tooke and John Thelwall were acquitted, the jury taking less than ten minutes in Tooke's case, whereupon charges against the other nine defendants were abandoned. On the face of it, this outcome was a savage blow for the Government, especially as defending and prosecuting counsel were respectively cheered and booed. Ministers would almost certainly have succeeded with lesser charges of sedition, and it may simply be that they miscalculated. If so, Pitt's political luck held. The events further consolidated his support among the propertied classes, who readily identified the defendants with Fox, especially as he was voluble on their behalf and the defence counsel Thomas Erskine was a Foxite; while so far as the public at large was concerned, the failure of these show trials may have helped to legitimize the Constitution by demonstrating the impartiality of the judicial process. Suddenly Magna Carta seemed to be more than just a historical curiosity.

In 1796 the Government brought a charge of libel against John Reeves of all people. His loyalty was never remotely in doubt, but he had fallen foul of a technicality, and Opposition MPs were demanding his blood. In arguing that the nation was vested in the King and in the law, that constitutions were chimeras seen only in dreams and visions, and that Parliament was merely a branch of the sovereign power and could be 'lopped off', he appeared to defy the 1689 Revolution Settlement, which had firmly placed the King *in* Parliament.[106] Such strongly monarchist notions had hardly been heard since the reign of Queen Anne, and anticipated those of the Ultra Tories, who argued in the 1820s that the King should thwart Parliament in the name of the people. So whereas Hardy and Tooke were targeted for subordinating Parliament to the people, Reeves's offence was that he subordinated it to the King. His prosecution was probably a

[105] Alan Wharam, *The Treason Trials, 1794* (Leicester, 1992); John Barrell, *Imagining the King's Death: Figurative Treason, Fantasies of Regicide 1793–1796* (Oxford, 2000).
[106] [John Reeves], *Thoughts on the English Government, Addressed to the Quiet Good Sense of the People of England* (1795), 9–13.

case of shadow boxing, indicating a disposition by ministers to appear even-handed, but never really intended to secure a conviction. At all events the Attorney-General,[107] prosecuting, pulled his legal punches wherever possible, while the presiding judge declined to read the offending pamphlet and lectured the special jury on the importance of free speech. Reeves was duly acquitted and resumed his career as a placeman, becoming King's Printer in 1800 and Superintendent of Aliens (1803–14).[108]

Meanwhile the not guilty verdicts on Hardy, Tooke, and Thelwall, together with a trifling incident when someone threw a stone at the King's coach, gave Pitt and Grenville an excuse to introduce some fairly draconian legislation. In December 1795 they rushed the Treasonable and Seditious Practices and the Seditious Meetings and Assemblies Bills through Parliament. Fox compared this systematic attack on liberty to Stuart despotism, and for once managed to put ministers on the defensive. (One reason why they turned against Reeves might have been to dissociate themselves from his call for arbitrary royal government.) Nevertheless, the Bills passed speedily and easily, and incorporated the doctrine of constructive treason, which had been challenged in the courts, into statute law. Then, in the wake of naval mutinies, the Seduction from Duty and Allegiance Act (1797) made it a capital offence to suborn servicemen. It was followed by two Newspaper Publications Acts (1798–9), which required the registration of printing presses, an Act against Administering Unlawful Oaths (1797), and an Act for the more Effective Suppression of Societies established for Seditious and Treasonable Purposes (1799). Finally, two Combination Laws (1799–1800) reinforced existing controls to prevent workers from uniting to act in restraint of trade.

The phrase 'Pitt's Terror' was coined retrospectively by radicals to explain why their movement never fulfilled the promise of the early 1790s, yet compared with what happened in France the forces of repression were obviously puny.[109] Political prisoners were pilloried, shipped out to Botany Bay, or sentenced to two years in prison, but very few were hanged, there were no tumbrils and no place de la Guillotine. In France the Law of Suspects and the Law of the Maximum laid down prohibitions which it was difficult not to break, if only inadvertently, and so everyone was at risk of being denounced. Pitt's Terror, by contrast, was avoidable. No one was forced to write or publish, and political clubs could continue to meet by restricting their attendance to forty-nine members at any one time. Although at nearly 200 the number of prosecutions for treason and

---

[107] Sir John Scott, the future Lord Eldon.

[108] A. V. Beedell, 'John Reeves's Prosecution for a Seditious Libel, 1795–6: A Study in Political Cynicism', *HJ* 36 (1993), 799–824.

[109] Repression was most severe in Scotland, where Dundas used his grip to clamp down hard on free speech, and where 'Judge Jeffreys' Braxfield conducted sedition trials with bullying brutality.

sedition was very much higher than in previous decades, that was nothing like as many as during the 1715 and 1745 Jacobite rebellions.[110] Anyway, most were brought under traditional laws and were unaffected by Pitt's legislation. In one respect the balance of power had even tipped in favour of the radicals. Before Fox's Libel Act of 1792, juries had merely pronounced on factual matters, such as whether the accused had published an offending passage. As a result of Fox's Act, which Pitt supported, juries were given the power to decide whether a passage was actually libellous. This change, widely hailed as a charter of free speech, undoubtedly helped defendants by exalting juries into something more than tools of the judiciary. Of course, Pitt's Terror *might have been* carried much further if the juries had found Hardy and his colleagues guilty of high treason in 1794. Hardy himself claimed that 800 warrants were in the pipeline, [111] but there is no evidence for this. Policy was notably unsystematic anyway, with a great deal of muddled and last-minute decision-taking. The law officers, uncertain as to how far they could enforce their own statutes, were cautious about following up cases initiated by over-zealous magistrates, and anxious not to give away their own sources of secret intelligence in the course of futile prosecutions.

On the other hand it could be argued that, although Pitt's Terror was mild compared with that in France, so too was the threat with which it had to deal. Nor did it *have* to be as bloody since the ordinary penal code was already (in theory at least) the bloodiest in Europe. The number of capital statutes had grown under the Hanoverians from under fifty to over 200, most of them relating to property and many covering very trivial amounts. It was not the case that every convicted felon hanged, since judges had discretion to recommend mercy and the King in Council to grant it, so the result was continuous low-level terror, with even the pettiest criminal liable to execution, while the highly ritualistic aspects of the judicial process reinforced its awful message. [112] There was therefore less need of additional sanctions at times of social unrest, less justification for packing juries, or for using ex officio information in order to impose legal costs on suspects and detain them without trial. Then again, the scope of Pitt's Terror should perhaps be measured, not in terms of actual prosecutions but by the licence which his Acts gave to bully-boys. Exhortations to loyalists could easily turn into the intimidation of minorities and misfits. Thanks to the climate created by legislation, a radical, a Dissenter, or a publisher beaten up in the night had even less hope of redress than he might have expected in ordinary times. A Quaker member of the Sheffield SCI was threatened with eviction by the Earl of Fitzwilliam, the radical Thomas Beddoes was denied a Chair of Chemistry at Oxford, the

[110] Clive Emsley, 'An Aspect of Pitt's "Terror": Prosecutions for Sedition during the 1790s', *Social History*, 6 (1981), 155–84.   [111] *Memoir of Thomas Hardy Written by Himself* (1832), 42–3, 121.
[112] Douglas Hay, 'Property, Authority and the Criminal Law', in Hay et al., *Albion's Fatal Tree: Crime and Society in Eighteenth-Century England* (1975).

Unitarian William Frend was forced to live out of residence at Jesus College, Cambridge, and many minor public office-holders were forced to quit, all of which added to an atmosphere of stifling conformity.[113]

Faced with an insurrectionary threat, and forced to rely on unpaid local magistrates, Pitt had responded in two distinct ways. On the one hand there was his very public recourse to statute law, defining the limits of public behaviour as though there was a state of emergency; and on the other hand a recourse to executive management, using a panoply of Home Office spies, informers, and agents provocateurs. The trouble with the first policy was its publicity: prohibiting certain political rights merely fed people's desire to exercise them. For example, the Combination Acts probably stimulated working-class consciousness by treating workers as a distinct section of the community. The trouble with the second policy was its secrecy, which offended against a long-held belief that English liberties were safe because there were no *lettres de cachet* or knocks on the door at night. The two approaches were to prove incompatible when taken further, which is why, thirty years later, politicians of opposing views would squabble over which of them kept the true Pittite flame, but in the 1790s it was just possible to combine a paternalist and authoritarian approach with a parliamentary and liberal one. The distinction, it should be emphasized, had nothing to do with tough versus tender responses to social unrest. Indeed the paternalist and authoritarian side of Pitt, though generally tough, included some tender elements, such as his generous ideas on poor relief. The difference was rather between dealing with crises in an executive or managerial or (as Fox would have said) arbitrary way, and governing by means of statute law, where Parliament laid down the rules of what was permissible, and juries decided whether those rules had been transgressed. From the latter point of view, the acquittals of Hardy, Tooke, and Thelwall showed that the rule of law still operated. Likewise, Pitt's counter-terrorist legislation was a welcome attempt to restore the scope of public law as against the arbitrary actions of local and central officials. While it might seem paradoxical to describe such legislation as a germ of nineteenth-century liberalism, this is only because it is not sufficiently appreciated that liberalism could be and often was highly repressive, its main characteristic being a dislike of arbitrary governance, whether tough or tender.[114]

IRISH PROBLEMS

If the state of the mainland gave the Government cause for alarm, that of the other country for which it had responsibility was very much worse. Ireland's fundamental problem was the gap between a small landholding, mainly settler,

---

[113] Clive Emsley, 'Repression, "Terror" and the Rule of Law in England during the Decade of the French Revolution', *EHR* 100 (1985), 801–25.   [114] See below, Ch. 5.

and mainly Anglican ruling class (the Ascendancy) and the vast mass of the population. This was composed for the most part of Catholic peasants, though by the third quarter of the eighteenth century there were significant pockets of articulate middle-class Presbyterians among the legal and commercial circles of Dublin and Belfast, as well as working-class Presbyterians in the industrialized parts of Ulster. The Irish Parliament was notoriously corrupt, and was wholly subordinate to Westminster, its members being in effect nothing more than a colonial elite and Ireland a client state. Then came the American Revolution. When the French navy intervened on behalf of the Americans in 1778, an invasion of Ireland looked on the cards, and in order to prevent this a pan-Protestant Volunteer movement was formed, mostly made up of farmers, trades-men, and merchants responsive to their local gentry. It was these mainly Presbyterian Patriots who, once the crisis was over, took the lead in campaigning for an independent Irish legislature. The first step was taken in 1782 when Rockingham's ministry repealed the Declaratory Act.[115] It led to the election of 'Grattan's Parliament' (1782–1800) and to a period of relative independence for Ireland under the dominance of the Protestant Ascendancy.

Despite the existence of some futile Penal Laws, the purpose of which was to de-Catholicize the majority population, eighteenth-century Ireland was relat-ively tolerant, the bloody sectarian battles of the Stuart period apparently forgiven. Annual celebrations of the battle of the Boyne kept plebeian folk memories alive, but there was little Protestant triumphalism or Catholic subversion, and in 1789 the centenary of the siege of Derry was apparently celebrated by both in unison. The main problems were social rather than religious, for though the 1780s were relatively prosperous, the countryside was clearly overpopulated, while the wool, linen, and cotton textile industries—the only alternative sources of employment—were entering a long period of decline. The Ascendancy was therefore more hostile to Presbyterian artisans and labourers, especially in Belfast, than to the Popish peasants, who thus found themselves courted by London and Dublin in turn. The British Government would play a 'Catholic card' (such as the 1778 Relief Act) in order to keep the Protestants in line, and the Irish Parliament would respond with another Relief Act (as in 1782) in order to ingratiate itself with the peasantry.[116] The most significant act in this pas de deux came in 1793 when Dundas and Pitt more or less forced Grattan's Parliament to allow Catholics with a forty shilling freehold to exercise a county vote.[117] This was the umpteenth relaxation of the Penal Laws, and politically the most significant.

[115] The Declaratory Act (1720) had established the right of Westminster to legislate for Ireland.
[116] Thomas Bartlett, *The Fall and Rise of the Irish Nation: The Catholic Question 1690–1830* (Dublin, 1992), 91–103.
[117] Dundas's powerful urge to gratify the Catholics was related to his hopes for a British empire of politically independent but economically dependent colonies.

At first this official ecumenism was matched by that of the reformers. In 1791 a dozen or so of the younger members of the Catholic Committee, a Dublin pressure group,[118] joined forces with the northern Presbyterians, who were themselves barely represented in the Irish Parliament, increasingly alienated from Britain, and highly susceptible to French influence. This led to the formation of the United Irishmen, first in Belfast, then in Dublin and elsewhere, a network of societies mainly dominated at this stage by middle-class Presbyterians, with Catholics probably making up the more conservative elements. Many of its leaders were Belfast Club Whigs and some were Jacobins, though the most important one was a Dublin lawyer, Wolfe Tone. Although a Protestant, Tone became secretary of the Catholic Committee in 1792, further emphasizing the non-sectarian nature of Irish affairs at this stage. From the start the United Irishmen demanded full Catholic emancipation and various other parliamentary reforms, but their approach remained constitutional and their methods moderate. They derived inspiration from the Commonwealthmen and from John Locke, yet they can also be seen as prototype Victorian Liberals.[119] Living in such a tightly closed and privileged society, and feeling a breeze of economic opportunity, they had naturally pressed for more a meritocratic administration and greater freedom of trade.[120] The years 1791–3, however, brought a rapid polarization along both class and sectarian lines. This was partly due to the economic downturn and partly to heady messages of support from the French National Convention. It was also partly due to a tactless (and rapidly withdrawn) attempt by the Government to compel lower-class Irishmen into militia ballots.[121] But the fundamental cause was that the United Irish leaders lost the initiative as their rank and file became increasingly intermingled with the Defender Movement.

Defenderism originated in a sectarian land war but was also a reaction against growing Protestant aggression. It began in Armagh, a prosperous county but with a large body of land-hungry weavers and small farmers, and with roughly equal numbers of Catholics and Protestants. The Relief Acts of 1778 and 1782 had permitted Catholics to buy and lease land on equal terms with others, and, since they were accustomed to a lower standard of living, many were ready to outbid Protestants by offering to pay higher rents. Catholics also moved into the local linen industry where they were again able to undercut the older independent weavers by taking meagre wages.[122] Protestants were also provoked by

---

[118] Pitt was in touch with the Catholic Committee through Edmund Burke's son Richard, who was its London agent.

[119] N. J. Curtin, *The United Irishmen: Popular Politics in Ulster and Dublin 1791–1798* (Oxford, 1994), 13–37, 47–53, 282–7.   [120] Such as would have resulted from Pitt's abortive trade proposals of 1785.

[121] Thomas Bartlett, 'An End to Moral Economy: The Irish Militia Disturbances of 1793,' in C. H. E. Philpin (ed.), *Nationalism and Popular Protest in Ireland* (Cambridge, 1987).

[122] Hereward Senior, *Orangeism in Ireland and Britain, 1795–1836* (1966), 1–21; Peter Gibbon, *The Origins of Ulster Unionism: The Formation of Popular Protestant Politics and Ideology in Nineteenth-Century Ireland* (Manchester, 1975), 22–43.

the increasingly common sight of Catholics in uniform as the revived Volunteer companies sought to broaden their recruitment, and by the formation of Catholic militias alongside the mainly Protestant yeoman cavalry. These aggravations spurred some (mainly Anglican) Protestants to form a secret armed society known as the Peep O'Day Boys because of their propensity for dawn raids. Defenderism was a Catholic counter-response,[123] but as it spread beyond Armagh it took many different forms. In some places it emerged as peasant violence, or jacquerie, drawing on the traditions of *banditti* such as the Whiteboys and Rightboys, but also pointing forward to the more nationalist and sectarian Ribbonmen. Elsewhere it might take the form of protests against tithe, or against labour-saving machinery in the agrarian and artisan economies, or it might take the guise of a messianic belief in Ireland's providential deliverance. But in all its varieties the movement involved oath-taking, the ritual humiliation of scapegoats, armed raids on isolated country houses, hatred of Protestantism, and hatred of the State.[124] So powerful was it that over the next few years the middle-class leaders of the United Irishmen were unable to prevent their predominantly Protestant, liberal, and civic humanist movement from being swamped by this much more violent creed of Catholic republican nationalism.[125]

These problems would have tested any government. Unfortunately Ireland was experiencing a crisis of authority anyway. Successive lords lieutenant (viceroys) and chief secretaries found themselves caught in no man's land between an increasingly intransigent executive at Dublin Castle, mistrustful Protestant 'friends', an increasingly truculent Catholic minority, and a distracted Prime Minister. It is possible to convey some sense of the strain by quoting, more or less at random, from the frequent, copious, and panicky letters which one of them (Westmorland) wrote to Pitt during 1792, as events on the ground spun rapidly out of control. Several times he accused Pitt of playing a 'Catholic game', and of wishing 'to punish the Protestant Aristocracy' for the fact that the Irish Parliament had taken Fox's side in the Regency crisis. Could Pitt not see that Catholic shopkeepers and other 'middling ranks', having 'caught in a degree the French mania', were seeking a 'discharge from rents, tythe, and taxes'? Worse still, they were circulating maps of Ireland as it had been before the Cromwellian land forfeitures, with obvious intent. However, the *immediate* danger came not from Catholics but from a pre-emptive backlash by Protestants, who were even now smuggling arms into Belfast because they feared that the British Government did not care for them. 'You cannot manage

---

[123] Curtin, *United Irishmen*, 149–53.

[124] Thomas Bartlett, 'Defenders and Defenderism in 1795', *Irish Historical Studies*, 24 (1984–5), 373–94.

[125] M. Elliott, 'The Origins and Transformation of Early Irish Republicanism', *International Review of Social History*, 23 (1978), 405–28.

Ireland without the confidence of the Protestants!' 'Man, woman, and child dream of 1641' (a reference to the bloody slaughter of Ulster Protestant settlers by Catholics). In November, with the situation palpably deteriorating by the hour, Westmorland asked to be sent 11,000 men at once, if only to show the Protestants that the Government was on their side.[126] Pitt did not bother to respond to Westmorland's alarms very often, and when he did he was hardly reassuring.

> The idea of our wishing to play what you call a Catholic Game is really extravagant. We have thought only of what was the most likely plan to preserve the security and tranquillity of a British and Protestant Interest. . . . As to what may be wise for the future, I still believe that the not excluding a possibility even of further concessions if circumstances should admit of it would be the best security for the Protestant Interest. But I have no difficulty in saying to you that my opinion will never be for bringing forward any concession beyond what the public mind and the opinion of those who are the supporters of British Government, or its present Establishment are reconciled to. I may have my own opinion as to expediency, but I am inclined myself to follow theirs, not to attempt to force it.[127]

Not for the last time England's Irish policy was one that dared not speak its name: to promote the Catholic cause, but without admitting as much to the Protestants.[128]

By 1794 the situation seemed to have calmed, but the authorities remained jittery. First they arrested an Anglican clergyman and French Government agent who had been sent to Ireland to assess how much revolutionary potential there was, and shortly afterwards they suppressed the Dublin Society of United Irishmen. This action no doubt cowed the moderates into silence while it aggravated but did not deter the militants, who simply went underground where they were more dangerous. There then occurred a spectacular exercise in political ham-fistedness which might or might not have constituted a missed opportunity. In December 1794, five months after the Pitt–Portland Coalition was formed, Fitzwilliam was appointed to replace Westmorland as Lord Lieutenant. Having personally succeeded to Rockingham's estates in Wicklow as well as Yorkshire, Fitzwilliam may have felt that he was authorized to take matters into his own hands. The Foxites had always claimed to have a special rapport with the Patriots, and Fitzwilliam had been well tutored in Irish affairs

---

[126] Westmorland to Pitt, 1 and 30 Jan., 18 Feb., 3, 13, and 19 Nov., 4 Dec. 1792, CUL, Pitt MSS 6958/1038, 1056, 1064, 1142, 1145, 1151, 1161.

[127] Pitt to Westmorland, 29 Jan. 1792, CUL, Pitt MS 1055.

[128] Two years later the Chief Secretary, Glenbervie, complained that Pitt wanted to extend full civil rights to Catholics, 'but he seems to wish this plan not to be known to be his by the Irish government', and insists that this 'must be done as it were insensibly to the Protestants' (*The Diaries of Sylvester Douglas (Lord Glenbervie)*, ed. Francis Bickley (1928), i. 35–6).

by Edmund and Richard Burke. During the previous summer he and two prominent Irish Whigs (Henry Grattan and George Ponsonby) had concocted a strategy: a clampdown on Defenderism and other manifestations of disorder, Catholic relief, and the replacement of the Volunteers by an expanded yeomanry open to the propertied of all religions.[129] It was a well-thought-out and comprehensive programme, but unfortunately it had not been coordinated with Pitt. On 15 January, just eleven days into his mission, and after sacking several senior and long-serving members of the executive, Fitzwilliam sent a dispatch to London announcing that the majority population *had* to be reconciled, and that unless he received 'very peremptory directions to the contrary' he would instigate a full emancipation without further hesitation. Hearing nothing back, he then encouraged Grattan to bring in a bill for Catholics to be allowed to sit in Parliament and hold high office. Unfortunately, bad weather had delayed communications, and it was not until two days before the bill was introduced that Fitzwilliam learned of London's horrified opposition to his plan.[130] Forced to resign, he left Ireland in March nursing a grievance, and leaving behind a bundle of thwarted hopes. 'The day of his departure was one of general gloom; the shops were shut; no business of any kind was transacted; and the greater part of the citizens put on mourning, while some of the most respectable among them drew his coach down to the water-side.'[131] As for the Catholic Relief Bill, it would probably have passed the Irish House of Commons if Fitzwilliam had remained. In the event it failed by 155 votes to 84.

The possibility of union between Britain and Ireland as a way out of the maelstrom had occasionally been mooted in private. For example, Westmorland had written to Pitt in 1792:

The Protestants frequently declare they will have an Union, rather than yield the franchise to the Catholics. The Catholics will cry out for Union rather than submit to their present state of subjection, it is worth turning in your mind, how the violence of both parties might be turned on this occasion to the advantage of England.[132]

Shortly after this letter was written, Catholics had been allowed to vote, which left them in the anomalous situation of being able to *choose* but not to *be* MPs. Pitt must have realized that this was an untenable position, but he probably

---

[129] Fitzwilliam to Portland, 10 and 15 Jan. 1795, TNA, HO/100/56, fos. 58, 82–5; Danny Mansergh, 'Grattan's Failure: Parliamentary Opposition and the People in Ireland, 1779–1800', Ph.D. thesis (Cambridge University, 2002), 137–53; David Wilkinson, 'The Fitzwilliam Episode, 1795: A Reinterpretation of the Role of the Duke of Portland', *Irish Historical Studies*, 29 (1994–5), 315–39.

[130] R. B. McDowell, 'The Age of the United Irishmen: Revolution and the Union, 1794–1800', in T. W. Moody and W. E. Vaughan (eds.), *A New History of Ireland, iv: Eighteenth-Century Ireland, 1691–1800* (Oxford, 1986), 343–6.

[131] Stanhope, *Pitt*, ii. 307; Edith M. Johnston, *Great Britain and Ireland 1760–1800: A Study in Political Administration* (Edinburgh, 1963), 104–16. For comparable reactions to the recall of Viceroy Anglesey, see below, pp. 388–9.   [132] Westmorland to Pitt, 13 Nov. 1792, CUL, Pitt MS 6958/1145.

wished to move delicately by easing forward on the two fronts (emancipation and Union) together. If so, he failed to explain this somewhat ambiguous policy to Fitzwilliam, whose impetuous determination to make up for lost time was typically Foxite, but whose raising and dashing of hopes greatly exacerbated the sectarian divide. His subsequent replacement by Lord Camden was exactly the sort of thumbs-up gesture to the Protestants for which Westmorland had pleaded, but which Pitt had until then adroitly avoided making. From this point the situation swung quickly out of control. In 1795 the Orange Order was secretly founded in Armagh, and many old masonic Boyne lodges were revived, sometimes by country gentlemen. Their violent menacing rituals soon forced several thousand Catholic tenants to flee Armagh.[133] Then in September 1796 a part-time Irish Yeomanry was formed to act as a volunteer Protestant defence force.[134] To Catholics it suddenly seemed as though the forces of law and order were dominated by sectarian bigots.

The United Irishmen (UI) responded to this 'Orange fear' by turning itself into a military organization for the first time. A national executive directory was set up, largely the instigation of Fox's friend Lord Edward Fitzgerald, and a decision taken to seek help from France. Wolfe Tone, Napper Tandy, and other UI leaders exiled in Paris succeeded in persuading the regime there that the Irish back door was worth exploiting. Accordingly, in December 1796 General Hoche tried to land 14,500 men at Bantry Bay in County Cork, but the winds were unkind, the Irish were unready to receive them, and the attempt failed. Then in October of the following year a Dutch fleet carrying 15,000 French troops was destroyed at the battle of Camperdown by Admiral Duncan. It is not entirely clear that the expedition had been bound for Ireland in the first place, but even so the engagement was decisive in that it effectively isolated the Irish rebels. Many of the more respectable United Irishmen were unwilling to rise until they could be sure that the French would invade, while the French were reluctant to invade unless they could be sure that enough Irishmen would rise— the same dilemma that had faced the Jacobites in 1744–6.

This fortunate stalemate might well have persisted if it had not been for some over-anxious blundering. In 1796 the Dublin Government embarrassed London by passing an Insurrection Act, which gave the Lord Lieutenant power to 'proclaim' a district, leading to curfews and armed searches. For more than a year much of Ulster was proclaimed, allowing General Lake to undertake a massive programme of disarmament accompanied by mass arrests, house burnings, and floggings. Meanwhile, William Wickham at the Alien Office planted agents throughout the country to infiltrate the UI, and as a result of

---

[133] Bartlett, *Fall and Rise*, 216. At the apex of the Orange Order was the Grand Lodge of Ireland, formed in Dublin in 1798.

[134] Allan Blackstock, *An Ascendancy Army: The Irish Yeomanry, 1796–1834* (Dublin, 1998), 55–74.

intelligence received the Dublin Government was able to arrest sixteen out of eighteen members of the UI's provincial committee in Leinster on 12 March 1798.[135] Soon afterwards Fitzgerald and other Dublin leaders were also arrested, and martial law imposed. Such heavy-handed tactics by the authorities more or less forced the UI to fight back, since otherwise it could have been wiped out without a whimper. Two months later (23–4 May) the hardline rebels swept their more cautious colleagues aside and, without waiting for the French, embarked on a savage rising in the counties around Dublin.

The disarming of known rebels had obviously been intended to pre-empt a rebellion. In practice it meant that the rebellion, which happened anyway, took place without the restraining (and relatively ecumenical) hand of the UI leadership. The result was a civil war of terrible ferocity. Only in Ulster was much attention paid to political demands. Elsewhere the violence was visceral— and often directed against unpopular landlords and clergy—but what was quite unprecedented (at least in anything like its present intensity) was the element of holy war, fuelled by waves of apocalyptic pre-millenarianism which swept through both the Catholic and Protestant populations. In one example of what would now be called ethnic cleansing, between 100 and 200 Protestants were either shot or burned alive in a barn at Scullabogue, co. Wexford. In all, perhaps as many as 30,000 were massacred on sectarian lines. 'The People could not be described,' commented the Catholic bishop of Ferns: 'The Devil was roaring among them . . . They would make it a religious war which would ruin them.'[136] By the beginning of June the insurgents had captured control of the county of Wexford, but were savagely crushed at Vinegar Hill on the 21st, and by mid-July the rebellion had been almost entirely suppressed.[137] Just weeks later a small French force landed and was easily defeated at Killala.

The nationalist movement stuttered on for a while—Emmet's rebellion in 1803 has been called 'the dying spasm of United Irishism'[138]—but with most of its leaders executed, gaoled, or exiled, its first phase was effectively over. It had, however, achieved a mass basis, garnered its first myths and martyrs (notably Tone and Fitzgerald), and established its ethos as Roman Catholic, its methods as underground—very different, in other words, from that mainly Protestant,

[135] Sparrow, 'Alien Office', 374; Marianne Elliott, *Partners in Revolution: The United Irishmen and France* (New Haven, 1982), 194.

[136] Thomas Pakenham, *The Year of Liberty: The Story of the Great Irish Rebellion of 1798* (1969), 190; J. C. D. Clark, *The Language of Liberty 1660–1832: Political Discourse and Social Dynamics in the Anglo-American World* (Cambridge, 1994), 288; Jim Smyth, *The Men of No Property: Irish Radicals and Popular Politics in the Late Eighteenth Century* (Basingstoke, 1992), 178–81.

[137] McDowell, 'The Age of the United Irishmen', 351–60.

[138] Oliver MacDonagh, 'Ireland and the Union, 1801–70,' in W. E. Vaughan (ed.), *A New History of Ireland*, v: *Ireland under the Union, pt. 1: 1801–70* (Oxford, 1989), p. xlix. Robert Emmet, an Irish Protestant republican who had played a minor role in the '98, led a rebellion in Dublin in July 1803. It was put down quickly and Emmet was hanged.

liberal, and classical republican movement which had been inaugurated just a decade earlier.

FRENCH WARS

English Radicals and Irish rebels seemed all the more dangerous in the context of the Continental war, which proceeded in phases as defined by the successive alliances formed against France. The War of the First Coalition, lasting until the autumn of 1797, was a fairly unmitigated disaster. George III's second son was made commander-in-chief of an expedition to Flanders, where he enjoyed some initial successes, but his lack of purposeful progress was summed up in a well-known ditty ('The Grand Old Duke of York'), and he was eventually beaten into retreat. Indiscipline (a euphemism for dissipation) having set in among the ranks, he was quickly replaced amid some bitterness. In August 1793 the port of Toulon was taken by British, Spanish, and French émigré troops under Admiral Lord Hood, but this triumph was reversed four months later and the garrison forced to evacuate. It was another shot in the arm for the struggling French Republic, and a first conspicuous success for a 24-year-old officer, Napoleon Bonaparte. The record in 1794 was even worse, being in Auckland's words a catalogue of 'numberless and strange defeats, treacheries, retreats, capitulations, incapacities and disgraces'.[139] Worse still, the Austrian army was forced to retreat after having looked set at one time to capture the fortresses guarding the northern routes to Paris. In June they were defeated again at Fleurus and made to withdraw from the Netherlands altogether. Even Pitt became despondent at this point.

A possible alternative to tackling the French Republic head on offered itself in the counter-revolutionary movements that were raging in various parts of France, such as Brittany and La Vendée. The most ardent British proponents of ideological warfare were two former Foxites, the War Secretary, Windham, and his mentor, Burke. William Windham was the first in a line of brilliant but maverick right-wing politicians—Lyndhurst, Randolph Churchill, F. E. Smith— who operated too far outside the consensus to be effective. He had a scintillating personality, and political convictions so strong that they belied his otherwise scholarly and discriminating characteristics, but he lacked judgement and had a streak of melancholic instability. Now in his forties and sexually frustrated, he led a life of 'dodging with the world and playing at whoop with all his friends', as one of them wearily put it,[140] and he may also have been willing to play at whoop with his country's destiny. At any rate, for Windham the root of all evil

[139] Auckland, *Journal*, iii. 247.
[140] Sir Gilbert to Lady Elliot, 12 July 1798, in *The Windham Papers*, ed. Earl of Rosebery (1913), ii. 77. He calmed down somewhat following his marriage in 1798.

was Jacobinism: 'Nothing is a cure for the evil . . . but a counter Revolution', which could 'never be effected by mere external force', but only in France itself.[141] However, Dundas had no interest in royalism. Grenville had some but was irresolute. Pitt was prepared to go along with the plan to some extent, though possibly his objective was not so much to restore monarchy in France as to keep the French divided by civil war.

Few in Britain had much appetite for ultra Bourbons such as Condé and d'Artois, but there was considerable support for moderates. Two such—an émigré, J. J. Mounier, and a Genevan, Jacques Mallet du Pan—had put forward a plan for the Bourbons to become constitutional monarchs on English lines, and for aristocrats to regain their lands but not their feudal privileges. Having decided to give these moderate royalists physical support, in December 1793 Pitt sent a force to Brittany under Lord Moira. Although the invasion petered out ineffectually, the idea of a landing in north-western France remained his 'dream' strategy,[142] and he was therefore sympathetic when nine months later another royalist came to lobby ministers. Joseph, comte de Puisaye, was a leader of the movement known as *chouannerie*, a network of peasant insurrectionary cells dispersed throughout the Breton countryside. Grenville and Windham seem to have thought him an important counter-revolutionary contact, yet it was probably only his influence with them, and his consequent access to English money and muskets, which gave him any clout in Brittany. Whatever the truth of the matter, in June 1795 Puisaye and Windham hatched a plan for a French émigré corps and a small British naval squadron to land at Quiberon Bay. It was a promising move, and might have sparked off a *chouan* rebellion, but it came to nothing when the invasion force was smashed by republican forces under the far more enterprising Hoche (July 1795), following which 690 émigré prisoners were sentenced to death by a republican court martial.[143]

This debacle was just one manifestation of a strategic error which dogged British policy throughout the 1790s—that of frittering resources on disparate and half-hearted projects, what George III called 'orders and counter-orders'. There were forays in Flanders, expeditions to the West Indies, and attempts to land in this or that port culminating in fiascos at Ferrol (1799) and Cadiz (1800). It would have been more sensible to concentrate on La Vendée, in revolt since 1793 and offering better prospects for counter-revolution than Brittany. There was a Vendéan lobby, particularly among the Portland Whigs, and Francis Drake, the energetic British minister at Genoa, was urgent in appeals for money to assist the Catholic and royalist armies there. Ministers dithered, however, and

[141] Windham to Grenville, 2 May 1799, Windham Papers, BL, Add. MS 37846, fo. 75.
[142] Dundas to Pitt, 13 Oct. 1794, CUL, Pitt MS 6958/1511.
[143] Maurice Hutt, *Chouannerie and Counter-Revolution: Puisaye, the Princes and the British Government in the 1790s* (Cambridge, 1983), ii. 269–323.

by the time that Major-General Doyle took an expedition to the Île d'Yeu, it was too late. The Vendée rebellion was betrayed and had effectively been scuppered by the end of October 1795, in which month Bonaparte dispersed a royalist-inspired rising of the Paris sections with the 'whiff of grapeshot', and any hopes for a Bourbon restoration in the short term were dashed.

These failures in arms led some British statesmen to pin their hopes on underground warfare. It involved a dramatic increase in foreign espionage to match what was happening at home, and in both cases operations were directed by William Wickham from the Alien Office. Wickham had been friendly with Grenville since Christ Church days, and shared Windham's hatred of revolution and popular movements generally. In December 1794 he was seconded from his post in order to become chargé d'affaires in Berne, from where he sought to organize subversion throughout the Continent and to forge links with French royalists, including one in particular, A. B. J. d'André. Using as many as thirty-one aliases, Wickham soon spun a huge web of (mostly French) agents and informants centred on the 'police office' at Hamburg, a town which also attracted a large number of Irish rebels.[144] Secret service funds could be authorized by Portland, Grenville, and Dundas among others, and then remitted to agents and informers via Continental banks.[145] Wickham might have lacked the suave glamour of the fictional Sir Percy Blakeney, but no other Englishman came as close to playing the counter-revolutionary part credited by Baroness Orczy to the Scarlet Pimpernel.

Certainly he was an indefatigable schemer and quite irrepressible, 'a cork on the murky, troubled waters of Counter-Revolution'.[146] Whenever one of his grand designs collapsed, he simply erected another: an attempt to suborn a republican general (Pichegru), a scheme to provoke a royalist rising in Lyon, a cunning plan to disrupt France by manipulating elections to the Council of the Five Hundred (this at a cost to the British taxpayer of £34,000), a bid to mobilize the cantons of Switzerland, a wheeze to infiltrate the Paris gendarmerie with British agents, and another to disseminate propaganda via the French internal postal systems. All these schemes were thwarted, some by Le Clerc de Noisy, a mole who served in the London Alien Office for several years but was really working for France. Finally, when incitements to rebellion and efforts to influence elections had failed, attention turned to assassination. A royalist organization in Paris, known as the English Committee because it received money and instructions from London, successfully bribed and

---

[144] Paul Weber, *On the Road to Rebellion: The United Irishmen and Hamburg 1796–1803* (Dublin, 1997).

[145] Elizabeth Sparrow, 'The Swiss and Swabian Agencies, 1795–1801', *HJ* 35 (1992), 861–84; ead., 'Alien Office', 381–2.

[146] Richard Cobb, 'Our Man in Berne', in Cobb, *A Second Identity: Essays on France and French History* (1969), 189.

infiltrated both the *haute police* and the local gendarmerie. This *contre-police*, as it was known, master-minded several attempts on Bonaparte's life, the most promising of which was the bomb which just missed him and Josephine in the rue Niçaise on Christmas Eve 1800.[147] British officialdom, acting through the Alien Office's Swiss Agency, may also have been behind the murder of two French delegates by a detachment of Austrian hussars at the Rastadt Conference in April 1799. If so, the intention must have been to incriminate Austria in the hope—successful as it turned out—that that country would pull out of a temporary understanding with France and join Britain once more.[148]

As with any secret war, it is difficult to assess just what was going on. There are extensive archives, replete with code names and records of down payments, but it is difficult to sift fact from fantasy, intelligence from disinformation, agents from double agents. Some historians have taken Wickham's plans almost as seriously as he did himself.[149] Others contend that the whole thing was an exercise in futility. What is certain is the enormous financial cost of all these plots, intrigues, rendezvous, assignations, and secret missions. According to one calculation, the Foreign Office spent £665,222 on His Majesty's Secret Service operations during the 1795–9 quinquennium, as compared with £76,759 in the previous one. Wickham and James Talbot, his successor at Berne, were responsible for 80 per cent of all secret service moneys spent by British envoys in Europe during the period 1790–1801,[150] and in addition there were a number of hidden or camouflaged accounts, many of which have never been brought to light. The term applied to all this expenditure was Pitt's Gold, but it was really the taxpayer's.

The underground war may have helped to keep royalism alive, and may even have contributed to the success of the Constitutional Monarchists in the 1797 elections, but otherwise it achieved very little. Nevertheless, the sheer size of the operation was significant in itself. As with the Second World War, there is a tendency to suppose that the conflicts of the 1790s pitted a plucky but amateurish Albion against a state geared to all-out war and the *levée en masse*. Yet in both cases the British could claim to have been more professional than the enemy. The cooperation achieved between such fiercely independent bodies as the Foreign, War, and Home offices, and the undertaking of operations, keeping

[147] Elizabeth Sparrow, *Secret Service: British Agents in France 1792–1815* (Woodbridge, 1999), 217–22.

[148] Ibid. 169–71; Sparrow, 'Swiss and Swabian Agencies', 876–84.

[149] Harvey Mitchell, *The Underground War against Revolutionary France: The Missions of William Wickham 1794–1800* (Oxford, 1965), 237–43.

[150] Ibid. 256–60. According to one official account (TNA, A.O. 1/2121, roll 5), Foreign Office demands on the Civil List for the secret service averaged about £24,000 annually during 1784–92, though that figure was biased upwards by large outlays to Holland in 1787–8, when Harris sought to boost the standing of the house of Orange. Spending remained at about that average level in 1793–4, but then soared to £90,232 in 1795, £129,951 in 1796, and £182,227 in 1797.

them secret, and if necessary shredding files,[151] all required sophisticated planning. These departments could all draw on secret service funds to whatever extent they thought was necessary for national security, and without any scrutiny by the Treasury.[152] England in the 1790s not only possessed a fiscal–military state but a highly clandestine one.

However, it was no substitute for success on the battlefield, and this was elusive. In the summer of 1795, after something of a lull, Prussia and Spain made separate peace terms with France, and shortly afterwards, much to George III's disgust, the British withdrew their cavalry from Germany, leaving Austrian forces alone to face Bonaparte, who then embarked on a spectacular romp through northern Italy. The Austrian Emperor's resolve was further sapped by Britain's failure to keep up with promised subsidy payments, so it is hardly surprising that in October 1797 the War of the First Coalition came to an end. In signing the Treaty of Campo Formio, the Austrians agreed to the setting up of the Ligurian and Cisalpine Republics as French client states covering most of northern Italy,[153] and also acknowledged France's right to Belgium, Lombardy, and a stretch of the left bank of the Rhine. The Republic was triumphant, while Britain's only trophies were a few West Indian islands annexed from the French.

Meanwhile, events inside France, starting with the fall of Robespierre (July 1794) and culminating in the installation of the Directory (October 1795), had greatly lowered the ideological temperature. Pitt openly admitted his desire to make an 'honourable' peace, while junior ministers and Government supporters issued pamphlets designed to prepare the public for a peace that might be less than honourable.[154] In the summer of 1796 Grenville proposed a 'scheme of pacification', and in October Malmesbury was sent to Paris to be rebuffed and humiliated by a French Government which sensed that events were moving in its direction. Even as negotiations were broken off in December, Pitt repeated his willingness to start them up again on the basis that Britain should surrender all its overseas gains in return for a restoration of the *status quo ante bellum* in Europe. In April 1797, with public bankruptcy staring it in the face, the Cabinet decided to make yet another peace overture to the Directory, though this time Grenville was strongly opposed. Naturally Burke was distraught by all this 'mendicant diplomacy', these 'oglings and glances of tenderness' in France's direction.[155] Much of what he wrote at this time bordered on hysteria. The Revolution was a product of metaphysical philosophy, described as 'incorporeal,

---

[151] Why were so many of the Alien Office's records destroyed? Was it to protect Whig patriots from suspicion of treason, or to conceal the extent to which the Government was willing to trample on cherished British freedoms?

[152] R. R. Nelson, *The Home Office, 1782–1801* (Durham, NC, 1969), 72–5.

[153] In fact, the whole of northern Italy west of the Adige and stretching as far as Rimini in the south.

[154] [Lord Auckland], *Some Remarks on the Apparent Circumstances of the War* (1795); Charles Long, *The New Era of the French Revolution* (1795).   [155] Burke, *Regicide*, 204, 344.

pure, unmixed, dephlegmated, defecated evil'.[156] Members of the Directory were 'the very same Ruffians, Thieves, Assassins, and Regicides, that they were from the beginning'. Britain was 'at war with a system', 'an *armed doctrine*' that could be summed up as '*regicide by establishment*', '*atheism by establishment*', and 'systematick unsociability'.[157] The world had changed for ever in 1789, and Britain had to confront 'not only new men, but what might appear a new species of men'.[158] However, apart from Windham and Fitzwilliam (and also the King, whose views hardly counted any more), no one in Government had any relish left for an ideological war *à outrance*.

On the other hand, it does seem to have occurred to the British at last that they were engaged—if not in an ideological war—at least in a war to the death. For peace ceased to be an option in October 1797 when Bonaparte, fresh from his stunning victories in Italy, was put in charge of the Army of England. By December there was a force of 120,000 men spread along the coast from Boulogne, waiting for favourable conditions in which to invade. The immediate threat receded in the following March, when the Directory decided to send Napoleon off to Egypt instead, but the potential danger was obvious. For the first time in a hundred years England faced a serious prospect of invasion and conquest by a Continental power. But if passivity was not an option, it was far from obvious what steps should be taken, especially as the two strongest members of Pitt's Cabinet disagreed fundamentally. Grenville called for a European land war in the Whig tradition, Dundas for a Tory, or 'blue-water', policy, seeking to turn the enemy's flank by maritime expeditions that would pay for themselves. Grenville advocated a 'strategy of overthrow' on the grounds that Britain would never be secure until France was humbled, whereas Dundas believed that the two powers were not incompatible. Grenville argued that, since the enemy was 'completely exhausted', another coalition would surely do the trick, but Dundas objected that the French were resilient and the allies unreliable. These disagreements reflected different political economies. Grenville was a wholly committed free-trader who was even willing to allow Americans to trade with the West Indian colonies in defiance of the Navigation Laws.[159] Dundas, by contrast, called for amphibious assaults on French colonies in order to open up commercial opportunities, and so enhance Britain's economic empire, plans for which he had begun to formulate before the war in respect of India, China, and the Cape.[160] His imperial vision was sincerely held but it was also self-serving, for the quarrel over strategy can also be seen as a demarcation dispute between two politicians with an urge to dominate. As Foreign Secretary,

[156] Burke, *Noble Lord*, 176.   [157] Burke, *Regicide*, 72, 199, 241, 257.   [158] Ibid. 358.
[159] Peter Jupp, *Lord Grenville 1759–1834* (Oxford, 1985), 368.
[160] Michael Fry, *The Dundas Despotism* (1992), 197–9; Edward Ingram, *Commitment to Empire: Prophecies of the Great Game in Asia 1797–1800* (Oxford, 1981), 41–57, 345–9.

Grenville was in charge of relations with the Great Powers, while Dundas, as Secretary of State for War, was unofficially in charge of the colonies.

Dundas's idea of pilfering sugar islands, to be used as bargaining counters when the time came for a diplomatic reckoning with France, was hardly a new one. This was the sixth Anglo-French war within a hundred years and all had featured a struggle for possession in the West Indies. This time Britain had the advantage, thanks to the fact that Pitt and Sir Charles Middleton had rebuilt the Navy since 1783, with forty-three new ships of the line and eighty-five others repaired.[161] Their reward came in 1794 with Admiral Howe's victory at the battle of the Glorious First of June, the first serious naval engagement of the war. It was therefore expected that the several expeditions to the West Indies (1793–4, 1795–6, and 1796–7) would carry all before them. However, delays in setting out, due among other things to squabbles between Army and Navy over which should be responsible for disciplining troops on board, meant that the ships reached the Caribbean during the rainy season, with the consequence that yellow fever ravaged the troops terribly. The invaders also encountered unaccustomed resistance from the slaves, who, having been liberated by the French, did not wish to lose their freedom under British rule. Nevertheless, by 1800 a number of islands had been gained from France including Martinique, St Lucia, Trinidad, and Tobago, as well as the mainland colony of Guiana from the Dutch. Britain also dominated the international sugar trade, having destroyed France's commercial position in the Atlantic. On the other hand she had failed to capture Guadeloupe, while her main objective, Saint-Domingue, was on its way to independence. She had lost about 45,000 men (mainly to disease) and had spent a great deal of money, about one-half of total military expenditure to date. As for whether the strategy pursued by Dundas can be accounted a success overall,[162] it depends on how useful all that money and manpower would have been if it had been applied elsewhere, to the Flanders campaigns for example, and on whether the same economic gains could have been made by a simple naval blockade without attempt at occupation.

Meanwhile, the French had also embarked on diversionary tactics. In May 1798, with that audacious rapidity which was his most striking characteristic, Bonaparte set sail with an Army of the Orient (40,000 men in 300 ships) and quickly occupied Malta and Egypt. Obviously, this was a less immediate danger to Britain than invasion, but it was worrying geopolitically since it jeopardized trade with the Levant, as well as posing a threat to the Ottoman Empire and

---

[161] P. L. C. Webb, 'The Rebuilding and Repair of the Fleet, 1783–1793', *BIHR* 50 (1977), 202. Middleton was Comptroller of the Navy Board (1778–90).

[162] As argued by M. Duffy, *Soldiers, Sugar and Seapower* (1987). The opposite view is taken by J. W. Fortescue, *A History of the British Army* (1910–21), iv. 350–85, 424–96, 537–66, and by J. Holland Rose, *William Pitt and the Great War* (1912), 219–49.

British India. Rear-Admiral Sir Horatio Nelson was sent on the chase, which ended on 1 August at the battle of the Nile and the destruction of the French fleet, anchored in an apparently impregnable position in Aboukir Bay. The victory put an end to Bonaparte's designs on India, and had an exhilarating psychological effect at home, just when prospects seemed bleakest. It did not stop Bonaparte from securing his hold over Egypt or launching a campaign in Syria and Palestine, but being cut off from base he could make little permanent headway. In May 1799 he was checked at the old crusader fortress of Acre on the Mediterranean coast by a Turkish force and a small British squadron, brilliantly orchestrated by Sir Sidney Smith. Bonaparte said later that the reverse had 'made me miss my destiny', though the cause of his return to Europe shortly afterwards, leaving his troops behind, was news of a threat to the French Republic, whose armies were in some danger of being expelled from Italy and Germany. His departure gave the British scope for further amphibious operations and at last allowed the infantry to score some victories. The most famous of these were the veteran general Sir Ralph Abercromby's at Aboukir and Alexandria in March 1801. According to one historian, it 'marked the turning point in the British Army's regeneration'.[163] Abercromby himself, a Scotsman, was killed in action. He had been largely responsible for the restoration of military morale following the disasters in America, and in death he became an inspiration to many younger British generals such as John Moore and John Hope. The practical result of the campaign was that French troops were forced to hand over Malta in September 1800, and then to evacuate Egypt in September 1801. However, as often happens, victory brought further responsibility since, having secured a strategic dominance in the central Mediterranean, it then became a major British interest to retain it.

Meanwhile, Continental fighting had broken out again. The War of the Second Coalition (January 1799–October 1801) was primarily a struggle between Austria and France. The former was desperate to recover her losses, while for the Directory war had become 'a matter of necessity', the only way to feed its armies, justify its abuses of the Constitution, gain badly needed prestige, and keep disruptive generals out of France.[164] For Britain, by contrast, war was a peril and a burden. There was no need for her to become involved at this point, and that she did so was mainly due to the determination of the Foreign Secretary. From the British perspective the next stage of the conflict was Grenville's war. He has been called 'a statesman of European vision', indifferent to empire but determined to liberate the Low Countries[165] and drive

---

[163] Piers Mackesy, *British Victory in Egypt, 1801: The End of Napoleon's Conquest* (1995), 240.

[164] Blanning, *Origins*, 196.

[165] France now occupied Belgium, and in 1795 had set up a client state in the Netherlands (the Batavian Republic).

France back to its old frontiers. Realizing that the First Coalition had failed for lack of strategy, he set out clinically to devise one. Austria, Prussia, and Britain—together with Russia, which felt threatened by Bonaparte's Near Eastern adventures—should enter on a Quadruple Alliance, establish a joint headquarters, and continue to meet once France had been defeated to administer the peace.[166] This attempt to revive the Grand Alliance against Louis XIV would eventually materialize in 1814, but Grenville's ideals were premature, especially as Austrian and Prussian diplomats were more suspicious of each other than they were of Bonaparte.[167] Even so, it might have been possible to cajole the allies into his point of view, but this was not the Foreign Secretary's style. Stiff, marmoreal, and colder even than Pitt, 'Bogey' (as he was sometimes known) did not know the meaning of the word diplomacy and treated foreign counterparts like servants. There were also recriminations over money, Austria complaining that Britain had not delivered on a promised loan, Britain that Austria had failed to acknowledge a previous debt.

Britain's part in the War of the Second Coalition—Grenville's 'western offensive'—was brief and derisory. The Duke of York landed in Holland in late August 1799, conducted a fruitless campaign, and left it again in mid-November. The fault lay with Grenville as much as the Duke, who found himself with overstretched supply lines and insufficient reinforcements among a population which did not want him. Elsewhere, with Bonaparte tied up in the Near East, the allies were initially triumphant. The Russians, led by General Suvorov, won important victories in Italy, and by the end of August all of Bonaparte's earlier gains had been lost. However, at this propitious moment the allies failed to coordinate strategy, partly because the Austrians were envious of the Russians' success, and this allowed the French to bounce back with a vengeance. The Tsar quit the Coalition in October following defeat in Switzerland. As for the Austrians, a series of humiliating reverses culminated in the battle of Marengo (June 1800) and restored most of northern Italy to France, and this was followed by further demoralizing defeats in Germany. If the Austrians' departure from the First Coalition had been calculating, this time it was abject, yet the terms of the Peace of Lunéville (February 1801) were again remarkably generous, essentially a reaffirmation of Campo Formio. It left Britain alone to fight Bonaparte, now First Consul of the Republic. Although she had not been trounced like her allies, there was a desperate yearning for the war to stop. Pitt had fallen from office by this time, but lent his support to the Preliminaries of Peace, which were signed in the autumn of 1801 and ratified at Amiens in March 1802. The terms, which were much less generous than those

---

[166] Piers Mackesy, *Statesmen at War: The Strategy of Overthrow 1798–1799* (1974), 4–10; J. M. Sherwig, 'Lord Grenville's Plan for a Concert of Europe, 1797–99', *Journal of Modern History*, 34 (1962), 284–93.   [167] In the event Prussia stayed neutral during the War of the Second Coalition.

offered to Austria, show just how badly the English wanted that respite. France was to keep Savoy and Nice, Piedmont, her acquisitions on the left bank of the Rhine, and Holland—nearly all her Continental conquests in fact. Britain was to retain only Trinidad and Ceylon of the many overseas gains she had made during the 1790s, and was to give up the Cape, Egypt, Malta, Tobago, Martinique, Demerara, Berbice, and Curaçao. Yet such was the state of public opinion that the Peace of Amiens led to great relief and rejoicing. The beau monde, with Foxites to the fore, took the chance to revisit Paris, where Bonaparte was now made Consul for Life. Fox managed to have an interview with the man whom he had consistently cast in the role of a misunderstood adolescent, but the two did not hit it off as well as he had hoped.[168] More fruitfully, peace gave a 27-year-old artist, J. M. W. Turner, an opportunity to leave the country for the first time. Visiting the Alps, and especially Mont Blanc, he came home with a sense of vaster immensities and more ethereal light than had been available to him in the Lake District.

THE FALL OF PITT

To understand why the English should have rejoiced at such unfavourable peace terms, it is necessary to appreciate the previous sense of foreboding. Waves of despair had alternated with sudden bursts of patriotic elation, such as after Nelson's victory at the Nile when the entire Commons was roused to a rendering of 'Britons, Strike Home!' The most immediate fear, giving rise to apocalyptic fantasies, was of invasion. Dundas ordered a hunt for documents as far back as the Spanish Armada in an attempt to find out how such threats had been handled before. Worryingly, England's safety depended on naval defences, the thin blue line, but in May and June 1797 there were serious mutinies in the Channel fleet at Spithead and the Nore. Real terror gripped the southern coastal areas, and all through that winter naughty children were sent to bed to have nightmares about what 'Bony' would do to them. There was a respite in the following March when the French demon was diverted to Egypt, but the primal fear remained at least until Nelson's victory at Trafalgar in October 1805. The greatest panic was in 1803–4, but there was also a heightened scare in July 1801, another reason for the craven sense of relief when peace was signed.

Economic and social conditions contributed to the alarm. By 1797 the price of Government stock had fallen to 50 below par, and its main loan contractor, Walter Boyd, nearly went bankrupt. In Black February a rapid drain of money from the country forced Parliament to suspend the convertibility of banknotes into gold and silver coin, effectively declaring a national bankruptcy and

---

[168] Burdett also went to Paris but refused to be presented to Bonaparte, his brand of patrician radicalism being miles away from Fox's anti-patriotic Whiggism. See below, pp. 207–8.

puncturing Pitt's reputation as a financier (another reason why he was keen for a negotiated peace).[169] As it happened, the financial storm was weathered more easily than anticipated. Not for the last time the British currency was ejected from a fixed parity system by market forces, and the economy was invigorated as a consequence. Even so, the Bank restriction made it harder to raise fresh loans, so in 1797–9 Pitt was forced to introduce assessed taxes and then an income tax, the first time such an impost had been resorted to in peacetime. It was naturally far from popular, but the sense of national danger and consequent resolve were sufficient to ensure its acceptance by Parliament. A still worse threat was the return of famine, as poor harvests in 1799–1800 led to a series of 'hypercrises' (see Table 2.1) as wheat prices rose.[170]

Against this background the London Corresponding Society, the United Britons, and United Englishmen became more active than ever, and were all the more dangerous for having to operate underground. Some historians claim that 'a state of virtual war existed between the upper and lower levels of English society'.[171] Whatever the truth of this, it is certainly the case that the authorities were more than ever alarmed about radicalism, partly because it was no longer visible. There were industrial riots and looting, leading to a further wave of prosecutions for sedition and the outlawing of combinations. In some ways this period marked the climax of Pitt's Terror, with scores of arrests and five treason trials.[172] The Royal Proclamation of September 1800 exceeded all previous ones in its calls for JPs to use military force against rioters, although (except in the case of certain regiments which had tasted Irish blood in 1798) the reality of repression fell short of ministerial rhetoric.

TABLE 2.1. *Movement of grain prices (per imperial quarter), 1796–1803*

Year	s.	d.
1796	78	7
1797	53	9
1798	51	10
1799	69	0
1800	113	10
1801	119	6
1802	69	10
1803	58	10

[169] George III, *Correspondence*, ii. 560.
[170] Roger Wells, *Wretched Faces: Famine in Wartime England 1763–1801* (Gloucester, 1988), 46–50, 120–32.   [171] Elliott, *Partners in Revolution*, 282; Wells, *Insurrection*, 131–61, 188–219.
[172] Emsley, 'Repression, "Terror" and the Rule of Law', 816.

To add to Pitt's worries there was also a rupture with the Baltic powers. Not surprisingly Russia (an ally) and Denmark, Sweden, and Prussia (neutrals) resented the way in which the Royal Navy, in its attempt to enforce a blockade of French commerce, stopped and searched their ships for contraband, and in December 1800 they retaliated by forming an Armed Neutrality, the effect of which was to impose a similar blockade on Britain. It was seen here as a dreadful stab in the back, coming as it did when Britain stood alone and had only the economic weapon at her disposal. Worse still it deprived her of grain imports in time of famine, and also of vital naval supplies such as timber, hemp, and pitch. Early in 1801 Grenville sent a large fleet into Danish waters with an ultimatum. Its rejection led to the first battle of Copenhagen (2 April), when Nelson is popularly but mistakenly thought to have turned his famous blind eye to orders before destroying the Danish fleet. This act of retribution, together with the assassination of the Tsar in March,[173] led to the collapse of the Armed Neutrality and successfully inaugurated nineteenth-century gunboat diplomacy. Nonetheless, the crisis had demonstrated this island nation's vulnerability to wartime blackmail. The need to secure a guaranteed supply of food would dominate government policy for the next fifty years. Meanwhile, the northern crisis had so disrupted trade that mercantile opinion was stirred to move for peace at any price, even the price exacted at Amiens.

It is hardly surprising that Ireland, the war, the economy, and social unrest should have taken their toll of Pitt politically. Everything came to a head in 1797. In February there was the suspension of cash payments, which led to delays in paying naval seamen's wages, followed by the mutinies already referred to. The United Irishmen were openly fomenting rebellion, Bonaparte's Army of England was straining at the leash, and there was an actual though ineffectual enemy landing at Fishguard in South Wales. A self-styled 'Armed Neutrality'— that is, a large band of disgruntled country gentlemen led by a maverick backbencher, John Sinclair—presented numerous petitions and addresses calling for Pitt to be dismissed in favour of a government of national unity. Even so the Prime Minister was impregnable in the Commons, where there were now only fifty-five or so real Foxites. Support from some independents (including occasionally Wilberforce) on the issues of war and repression boosted the Opposition's strength by about twenty during 1795–6, but to little avail since, whenever its vote increased, so did that of the Government. Moreover, whenever Fox, Grey, or Sheridan roared for peace, they merely invited pamphleteers to describe them as 'enemies within', and cartoonists to depict them as sans-culottes, signalling with lanterns to the French fleet as it approached

---

[173] There is some evidence to suggest that the British secret service might have been behind the assassination (Sparrow, 'Alien Office', 384).

British shores. The 1796 election merely confirmed Pitt's supremacy, with 424 ministerial supporters returned as against 95. It is therefore hardly surprising that at the end of May 1797, frustrated and disgusted, Fox and about thirty of his hard-core supporters seceded from the Commons.[174]

Yet despite his parliamentary strength, Pitt's position had been getting weaker for a long time, mainly due to changes at the heart of government. During the 1780s he had benefited from being the only commoner in Cabinet. Then in 1789 Grenville had become Home Secretary, and for the next four years these two took all the important decisions. Grenville went to the Lords in 1790 and to the Foreign Office in 1791, when two other commoners, Henry Dundas and Lord Hawkesbury, entered the Cabinet[175] Pitt's authority had therefore been diluted even before the realignment of parties, but the admission of Portland, Loughborough, Fitzwilliam, Spencer, Mansfield, and the effervescent Windham rendered his ministry more diffuse than ever. In an often quoted memorandum Bland Burges opined that before 1789 Pitt 'had no person in the Cabinet to influence or oppose him, and things went on prosperously'. Along came Grenville, who 'gradually gained an ascendancy', and then all the rag, tag, and bobtails 'after which every thing went on worse, and he gradually was ruined'.[176] Now it needs to be borne in mind that Burges disliked Grenville, but even so he had a point. Pitt had maintained a tight power base in the 1780s, when he had seemed incapable of delegating, but in the following decade many important decisions were devolved on others. In foreign affairs, especially, the Prime Minister was increasingly marginalized by Grenville and Dundas. (Apparently he had to rely on a devoted Foreign Office mole, Under-Secretary George Canning, to penetrate Grenville's elaborate network of overseas information.) The combination of Grenville's intellectual rigidity, Dundas's opinionated truculence, and Pitt's shyness in small gatherings inevitably made for distracted counsels, and Pitt himself was more and more inclined to agree with whichever of the others he had last spoken to.[177] ('I do not see any particular use that he can be,' wrote Grenville in 1801, with reference to some military conferences.) Meanwhile, it was obvious in debates on the Combination Acts that he was not on top of the subject, and he was also increasingly fretful. His health had been damaged by overwork, worry, and too much alcohol, and his reputation was at its lowest point.

---

[174] In theory the secession lasted until Pitt's fall in 1801, but it was not rigidly adhered to and was frequently flouted by 'ambitious lieutenants' such as Tierney and Sheridan (Thorne, i. 153–4).

[175] As Home Secretary and President of the Committee of Trade respectively.

[176] Bodleian Library, Burges MSS, Concise Diary of Events; Michael Duffy, 'Pitt, Grenville and the Control of British Foreign Policy in the 1790s', in Jeremy Black (ed.), *Knights Errant and True Englishmen: British Foreign Policy, 1660–1800* (Edinburgh, 1989).

[177] Piers Mackesy, *War without Victory: The Downfall of Pitt 1799–1802* (Oxford, 1984), 39, 179; for a condemnation of Pitt's ignorance on such subjects, see *Diaries of Sylvester Douglas (Lord Glenbervie)*, i. 159–60.

The biggest single clue to Pitt's loss of authority was his relationship with the King. The huge increase in public business brought on by war and his own precarious health meant that George became excluded from day-to-day decision-making, especially as Pitt used committees to streamline procedures and bypass Windsor Castle. As for foreign policy, it is only necessary to compare the King's role in the American war with his role in this one to demonstrate how far his executive power had declined. But being squeezed out of government left the King with more time for politics, and here he indulged himself abundantly, holding levees and granting audiences, dropping hints, raising and dashing hopes. In terms of high political intrigue he could claim to be a dominant player, and the harsh fact was that he no longer cared very much whether Pitt survived or not. He had never been very fond of him personally but had needed him desperately as a safeguard against Fox. Now that Fox was impotent, Pitt was dispensable. The King did not deliberately set out to undermine him, but the fact that he no longer needed him meant that there was daylight between himself and Pitt, so that other ministers now had to ask themselves which of the two it was in their own interest to please. This was like the 1760s, when the combination of a capricious monarch and jockeying ministers had caused a similar fragmentation of power.

So it was that, during the multiple crises of 1797, the danger to Pitt came not from Parliament but from the closet and the back stairs. (At one point even Fox was granted a royal audience, though the King 'said not one word'.[178]) There was much talk of a coalition ministry or government of national unity, to be led by Lansdowne and to include Dundas, Windham, two of the Prince's friends (Moira, Northumberland), two of the King's (Thurlow, Pulteney), and some of Fox's (Grey, possibly Sheridan).[179] It is impossible to say whether the plan was realistic or pure fantasy. The plotters needed George's complicity, but one of their arguments—that the Directory was more likely to make a reasonable peace if Pitt were deposed—was unlikely to appeal to the King, who wanted war to the death. Whatever, in June George seems to have dissuaded Grenville from the resignation that would have set the game of ministerial chairs in motion. From then on, however, all semblance of Cabinet solidarity was gone. The King blatantly intrigued with Cabinet ministers behind Pitt's back, and especially with the Speaker, Henry Addington. After 1797, according to Lord Holland, 'the Court more frequently thwarted the ostensible Ministers in small matters, and resorted with greater success to those little arts which had distinguished and

---

[178] Thorne, iii. 816.
[179] George III, *Correspondence*, vol. i, pp. xxiv–xxix. It was rumoured that George III, in order to secure a declaration of war against France, had been prepared to supplant Pitt by someone like Moira in 1793 (Howard V. Evans, 'William Pitt, William Miles and the French Revolution', *BIHR* 43 (1970), 210–11).

disgraced the early part of George the Third's reign'.[180] Pitt in return was recklessly neglectful of the King and heedless of his opinion.[181]

In which case it is surprising that Pitt remained in office as long as he did. Exactly what brought about his fall has always been controversial, though the outlines are clear enough. Following the rebellion, Ireland needed a fresh start. The Dublin Parliament was increasingly dysfunctional,[182] and in December 1798 Pitt's Cabinet agreed on a plan for a Union between the kingdoms of Great Britain and Ireland. Since it would need Irish Catholic support, eleven months later, and after a great deal of shilly-shallying, the Cabinet also agreed in principle (though without telling the King) that this measure should be accompanied by the second stage of Catholic emancipation—i.e. having achieved the vote in 1793, Catholics should now be allowed to sit in Parliament.

It remains unclear quite how the Act of Union was carried against the wishes of the Patriot Party,[183] though corruption and management certainly played a part. At all events, the Parliament on College Green finally dissolved itself in 1800, 100 Irish MPs were invited to attend the House of Commons (thereby adding unbearably to what was already an overcrowded assembly), and it was enacted that four Irish bishops and twenty-eight members of the Irish aristocracy should sit as representative peers in the House of Lords. Shortly afterwards Pitt brought forward a plan for Catholic relief, to which he clearly felt himself pledged, and at this point the King metaphorically stamped his foot, pleading the terms of his Coronation Oath as a reason why he could never consent, and hinting that he might have another mental relapse if his wishes were thwarted. 'None of your d——d Scotch metaphysics', he expostulated, when the fervently pro-Catholic Dundas tried to reassure him that the Coronation Oath applied only to his executive and not to his legislative capacity. Then, in a chilling phrase which recalled the crisis over the India Bill in 1783, he announced in a loud voice at one of his levees that those who opposed him on the matter were his 'personal enemies'. This was enough. The bishops rallied round him like rugby players in a ruck, and it quickly became clear that Pitt must either back down or back out. He finally signalled his resignation in February 1801, after which the King made

[180] *Memoirs of the Whig Party During My Time, by Henry Richard Lord Holland*, ed. fourth Baron Holland (1852–4), i. 92–3.

[181] 'He has regularly been 6 weeks, in London, without going to the Levée. A long train of this conduct certainly in a degree estranged the King from him and induced him to think of him personally with less interest' (second Earl Camden, 'Memorandum on Pitt's Retirement', Kent RO, Pratt MS U840/0127). Camden was a supporter of Pitt.

[182] The Irish Whig Party had seceded from the Dublin Parliament in the same month (May 1797) as the Foxites had seceded from Westminster.

[183] Patrick M. Geoghegan, *The Irish Act of Union: A Study in High Politics 1798–1801* (Dublin, 1999); G. C. Bolton, *The Passing of the Irish Act of Union: A Study in Parliamentary Politics* (1966). Opposition at Westminster was muted, though the Foxites protested that the Act would be prejudicial to Ireland.

Speaker Addington Prime Minister, even though he had never held government office.[184] Pitt asked his friends to remain in office but Grenville, Dundas, Spencer, Windham, Camden, Castlereagh, Canning, and Charles Cornwallis[185] would have none of it, and promptly resigned in sympathy.

The Irish question and the Catholic question were obviously intertwined, but in fairly complex ways. The King wanted a Union in order to *prevent* emancipation. Apparently he thought that the association of the Established churches of England and Ireland would help to marginalize the Irish Catholics and prevent any further concessions to them. Pitt wanted both. Union was deemed necessary for the good government of Ireland and the defence of Great Britain,[186] and emancipation was the only way to reconcile Catholics to the Union. He may also have been motivated by the need for military recruits. The incorporation of Ireland would increase the size of the United Kingdom's population by half as much again, and Irish soldiers were later to play a disproportionately large role in Wellington's armies. But then again, and especially in the light of Defenderism, Pitt may have thought that emancipation was necessary, with or without Union, simply in order to pacify Ireland. However, since emancipation *without* a Union would have resulted in a Catholic-dominated Parliament in Dublin, it would be expedient to pass the Union first. That way, instead of Catholics swamping Protestants on College Green, Protestants could swamp Catholics at Westminster. Whichever way one looks at it, the two policies were complementary, but the first interpretation subordinates emancipation to the Union and the second subordinates the Union to emancipation.

On the face of it, Pitt was the first of seven nineteenth-century prime ministers to fall as a result of the Irish question.[187] Yet the first Lord Liverpool is reported to have laughed when he heard someone say that Pitt had resigned over emancipation,[188] and it is a fact that he resumed his post three years later with a promise not to raise the issue. Contemporaries felt that there must be more to his resignation, perhaps that he knew of some impending crisis, and wished to get out before the going got worse. Some said that he wanted to detach himself from Grenville, others that he wanted to avoid responsibility for a humiliating peace treaty. None of this is convincing. Rather than running away from difficulties, it is more likely that Pitt was courting them. Having lost the confidence of the King and of several of his colleagues, he may deliberately have engaged in

---

[184] Addington had been the Recorder of Devizes and also its MP since 1784.

[185] Viceroy of Ireland (1798–1801).

[186] Especially as there were rumours of an impending concordat between Bonaparte and the Irish Catholic hierarchy.

[187] The others were Grenville (1807), Wellington (1830), Grey and Melbourne (1834), Disraeli (1868), Gladstone (1886).

[188] Addington also believed that the Catholic question was 'but the pretext' (*Diaries of Sylvester Douglas (Lord Glenbervie)*, i. 279, 294–5).

a battle of wills over emancipation in the hope of restoring his authority. That, at any rate, was what Canning apparently told Lord Malmesbury, who recorded in his diary:

For . . . three years back so many concessions . . . had been made, and so many import-ant measures overruled, from the King's Opposition to them, that Government had been weakened exceedingly; and if on this particular occasion a stand was not made, Pitt would retain only a nominal power, while the real one would pass into the hands of those who influenced the King's minds and opinion out of sight.[189]

There was a touch of Canning's habitual hypersensitivity to intrigues in the last phrase, since George's mind was incapable of being influenced systematically by anyone, but the main point was correct. Pitt stood up to the King and lost. The monarch's influence had not yet waned to the point where a prime minister could force through a constitutional change which he abhorred.

PEACE AND WAR

There was something self-consciously old-fashioned about Addington (he even called himself 'the last of the port-wine faction'[190]). Cartoonists drew him as a pigmy in clothes too big for him, while lampoonists referred to him as 'the Doctor' because his father was one. There was an element of snobbery in this sobriquet, but the main implication was that Addington was a quack, not quite the real thing. His first task was to make peace with Bonaparte, in which he was supported by Fox and Pitt. The Peace was wildly popular and only twenty MPs voted against it, but the quality of the opposition was more impressive than its size. Grenville and Spencer denounced the terms as humiliating, Dundas spoke against them in private, while Windham was said to be 'absolutely raving' about what he called a 'death blow' to the country.[191] These disgruntled ex-Pittites soon came to be known as the New Opposition to distinguish them from Foxites, whose own secession from Parliament now came to an end. In many ways it had been little more than a petulant gesture, but for Fox himself also a merciful release. Politics was only ever his hinterland, and less important to him than life and literature. And since he had a homely as well as a raffish side, his final decade of semi-retirement in the bosom of Mrs Armitstead, whom he married in 1795, was probably his most contented. What is more, his party held together without

---

[189] Those who were thought to influence the King's mind included Loughborough, Auckland, and the Bishop of Lincoln (George Pretyman, later Pretyman-Tomline) (Malmesbury, *Diaries and Correspondence*, iv. 4; Richard Willis, 'William Pitt's Resignation in 1801', *BIHR* 44 (1971), 239–57).

[190] Port was an 18th-century tipple, now being challenged by the craze for claret.

[191] Thorne, v. 620–1. Grenville, Dundas, and Spencer had provisionally agreed to similar terms as members of Pitt's Government, but since then France had been ousted from Egypt, Britain had captured Malta, and the Armed Neutrality had been broken, so better terms might have been hoped for.

him, and even embarked on a rehabilitation which would see it win about 125 seats in the general election of 1802 and nearly 200 in 1812.

The 1802 election was fought mainly over the Peace, and significantly the Foxites (the main peace party) did quite well in the larger boroughs. Radicalism also reasserted itself in obvious places like Westminster, Southwark, and Middlesex, where Francis Burdett was elected. The latter was genuinely popular out of doors, and had taken the opportunity afforded by the Foxite secession to make his mark in the previous Parliament. The New Opposition comprised about thirty MPs, many of whom represented small boroughs and about ten of whom were connected to Grenville. A fourth opposition group of about forty, led by Sheridan, Moira, and George Tierney, expressed allegiance to the Prince of Wales. Contemporaries considered the 'confusion of the state of parties greater than ever'. 'The whole House of Commons seems to be individualised.'[192] 'The Government, the Parliament, the people are all loose, incoherent atoms.'[193]

In retrospect it is clear that Addington left Britain much stronger than he found it. Given this and his enormous majority, he ought to have been secure, but the country was in a twitchy mood. As soon as the Peace was signed, there was a palpable sense that it was about to be broken. As Bonaparte annexed Elba, Piedmont, and then Parma, mediated a new constitution for Switzerland, seized Hanover, and sought to reconquer Saint-Domingue from the native population, Addington was accused first of dilatoriness in declaring war and then of vacillation in prosecuting it. This was to ignore his deliberate coup in declaring war before Bonaparte expected him to (May 1803), commencing with a blockade of French ports. Moreover, in concert with Hawkesbury, who proved to be a capable and level-headed Foreign Secretary, and also Portland (Lord President), Addington brought a new clarity and purpose to military and foreign policy. Since Britain stood alone against France and her satellites, the only option was to fight a commercial and naval war of attrition, with the object of bringing about France's internal collapse. If Bonaparte could be thwarted at sea, he might seek to gobble up even more of central Europe, so forcing Austria and Prussia to react in self-defence. That in itself would not be enough, however. Addington was one of the first to appreciate the importance of Russia as a potential ally, and as one of the world's three greatest powers, occupying like Britain a strategically impregnable place on the fringe of Europe.[194] And being much more adept than Grenville at personal diplomacy, he also had the wit to see that the impressionable young Tsar Alexander, though likely to prove malleable, would need to be worked over tactfully.

---

[192] Thorne, i. 348 (Dec. 1802).

[193] *Life and Letters of Gilbert Elliot, 1st Earl of Minto, from 1751 to 1806*, ed. Countess of Minto (1874), iii. 271 (9 Feb. 1803).

[194] Paul W. Schroeder, *The Transformation of European Politics 1763–1848* (Oxford, 1994), 244–5.

Before a sea war could be sustained, it was necessary to tackle the notorious abuses taking place in naval dockyards, a scandal Pitt had ignored. For example, one piece of cooperage costing £37 2s. 3d. at Deptford was charged at £1,020 10s. 5d. in the Navy Board's accounts, a mark-up which meant that it cost more (officially) to repair a ship than to build a new one. Nothing could be done until after the 1802 election for fear of prejudicing 'the interest of Government in all the Western Boroughs',[195] but immediately afterwards the new First Lord of the Admiralty, Earl St Vincent, who had long chafed under the Navy Board's corruption and incompetence, set up a thoroughgoing if heavy-handed investigation.[196] Unlike his predecessor, Lord Spencer, St Vincent was a professional naval officer, who as Sir John Jervis had won a famous victory over the Spanish at the cape from which he took his title in 1797. It was largely thanks to his energy that there were soon enough ships available, both to defend home waters and to send a contingent off to the West Indies, where they quickly recaptured St Lucia, Tobago, Demerara, and Berbice from the French.[197]

There was less success on the diplomatic front, since despite a promise of subsidies Austria and Prussia refused to engage in another bout against Bonaparte, but at least Addington's financial measures laid the basis for future subsidies. He revised the income tax by deducting at source, which simplified the impost and reduced evasion. His tax of 1s. in the pound netted £4.76 million in its first year, whereas Pitt's had only averaged £5.6 million per annum over three years, despite being levied at twice the rate.[198] Ministers could also be credited for their prompt and vigorous action in checking internal revolutionaries. After the execution of Despard in 1803, it has been observed, 'the rumours of conspiracy and oath-taking, the night meetings, the reports of secret conferences in the back rooms of London taverns, all died away'.[199] Addington's most prodigious achievement, however, was in strengthening the home guard. By January 1804 he had raised 85,000 men for the militia and over 400,000 Volunteers. Service in the first was for five years and was subject to ballot, though a balloted person could escape by paying a fine or finding a substitute. It was of course unpopular, but less so than in 1757 and 1796, such was the zeal to

[195] St Vincent to George Grey, 6 Aug. 1802, *Letters of Admiral of the Fleet the Earl of St Vincent whilst First Lord of the Admiralty 1801–1804*, ed. David Bonner Smith (1922–7), ii. 191.

[196] A. D. Harvey, *Britain in the Early Nineteenth Century* (1978), 128–30.

[197] But for a negative view of St Vincent's contribution, see N. A. M. Rodger, *The Command of the Ocean: A Naval History of Britain, 1649–1815* (2004), 476–88.

[198] Christopher D. Hall, *British Strategy in the Napoleonic War 1803–15* (Manchester, 1992), 1–26, 102–12, 127–8; Philip Ziegler, *Addington: A Life of Henry Addington, First Viscount Sidmouth* (1965), 148. For Pitt's income tax, see below, p. 118.

[199] Harvey, *Britain in the Early Nineteenth Century*, 92. Colonel Edward Despard, an Irishman and former Army officer with a legitimate private grievance against government, had devised an improbable plot to kill the King and his ministers. His fantastical sort of rebellion was a boon to any government wishing to crack down on subversives.

defend the country. The Volunteering movement was more popular than expected, probably because the terms of service were fairly light and it carried exemption from the militia ballot. In the vulnerable southern counties about 50 per cent of all men aged between 17 and 55 put themselves forward,[200] with the result that it was difficult to arm or train recruits properly, but as a fighting force it gave some reassurance, both to repel invaders and to keep the peace at home, and it was backed up by a reserve army of organizers, subscribers, women's committees, and well-wishers generally. This spate of volunteering has been described as 'the greatest popular movement in Georgian Britain',[201] one of the sources of that sense of civic consciousness and public responsibility which was to develop as the century progressed. The Army of Reserve also contributed to defence because, although only 30,000 men were raised out of a projected 50,000, two-thirds of these went on to join the regular Army at a time when full-time recruitment was extremely difficult.

Yet however capable the ministers proved to be, they received little credit.[202] During more than a year of phoney war Addington, like Chamberlain in 1940, was blamed for a situation which was more tense than actual conflict. Meanwhile, like Churchill, Pitt was suddenly relieved of past suspicions and came to be invested with the aura of a national saviour. That he refrained from harrying his successor was held to his credit (though he did nothing to hold back his cronies in the Lords). A Pitt Club was founded (1802) and birthday dinners began to be held, with toasts and tributes. Canning, who was desperate to wean him away from Addington's 'wretched, pusillanimous, toadeating, beshitten administration', composed a song to 'the Pilot that weathered the Storm'.[203] The sentiment was risible given Pitt's record as war leader, but it struck a chord and damaged his successor. Emmet's rebellion (July 1803), although short-lived, was a reminder of the country's vulnerability to events in Ireland, and, however unfairly, an impression gained ground that the Government was drifting. Most damaging of all were Pitt's alienation from Addington and a junction between the Old and New Oppositions.

It is not clear just when Pitt began to resent his successor—whose temerity in daring to improve the income tax[204] may have been a factor—but envy was soon eating him up. Maybe he had expected Addington to be more deferential or to use him as a minister behind the curtain. He may even have swallowed the claim of his protective protégé, Canning, that Addington had 'squeezed [him] like

---

[200] Colley, *Britons*, 292.

[201] J. E. Cookson, 'The English Volunteer Movement of the French Wars, 1793–1815: Some Contexts', *HJ* 32 (1989), 867–91.

[202] This was especially true in the case of St Vincent, whose strict enforcement of naval discipline and eradication of abuses were as unpopular as they were effective.   [203] Thorne, iii. 383.

[204] Improvements which Pitt nevertheless perpetuated in his 1805 Budget.

an orange'.[205] The shrewd, fair-minded, and well-informed Burges considered that the more Pitt 'felt frustrated on the back benches and increasingly contemptuous of his successor', the more 'his disgruntlement swelled'. In April 1804 he went into overt opposition, rebuffed all Addington's attempts to placate him, and was clearly bent on regaining his former position. It was understandable. He had been Prime Minister since the age of 24 and could hardly breathe out of office.

In a cruel way Addington was also the victim of his own success. For what happened during 1803–4 was nothing less than a successful appeal to the nation in arms, with the result that during 1803 over 800,000 men, more than one in five of the male population of military age, was in armed service.[206] Some of the impetus came from that year's Levy en Masse Act, which led to the preparation of lists to identify all those who could be called up for military training should volunteer forces fall short. Doctors, clergymen, and Quakers were exempted, but every other fit male aged between 17 and 55 was rendered liable, while unmarried and childless men under 30 were placed in Category A. Such an unprecedented degree of mobilization was not without its dangers, of course. The Volunteer forces, which had hitherto been overwhelmingly middle-class, now took on a more plebeian aspect, and pikes were handed out to all and sundry. The explanation of course was fear. With the Grande Armée of 130,000 men and 2,240 barges rapidly assembling at Boulogne, the invasion scare was even greater than in 1797–8, and the whole of southern and eastern England began to resemble an armed camp.[207] It was believed that Bonaparte's engineers were constructing a bridge from Calais to Dover, and Eastbourne was said to be completely deserted one August day in 1803 when it was rumoured that the French had landed, perhaps in their flat-bottomed boats, possibly by balloon. Yet while fear was important, there was something else, something imponderable, something which had not been manifested six years earlier. Small events can affect the public mood disproportionately, and Bonaparte's decision to intern British tourists[208] stranded in France when war was declared convinced many that they were dealing with a fiend rather than just an enemy. There was also the murder of the duc d'Enghien in March 1804, a rare example of a Napoleonic

[205] Canning to Leveson Gower, 6 Apr. 1802, in *Lord Granville Leveson Gower: Private Correspondence 1781–1821*, ed. Castilia, Countess Granville (1917), i. 338.

[206] J. E. Cookson, *The British Armed Nation 1793–1815* (Oxford, 1997), 95. The figures include Volunteers and sea fencibles.

[207] H. F. B. Wheeler and A. M. Broadley, *Napoleon and the Invasion of England: The Story of the Great Terror* (1908), ii. 37–76.

[208] The tourists included Lord Elgin, on his way home from Athens to be reunited with his Parthenon marbles (William St Clair, *Lord Elgin and the Marbles: The Controversial History of the Parthenon Sculptures*, 3rd edn. (Oxford, 1998), 121). It was a convention of 18th-century warfare that civilians should be left undisturbed.

atrocity. Whatever the reasons, for the first time the war seemed popular, and pacifist protest faded away. Nottingham was a revolutionary town which had previously been divided on the issue, but now there was a 'remarkable consensus' in favour of hostilities. Although it was nowhere near the south coast, the Corporation raised 400 guineas for the war effort in July alone.[209] Equally telling was the turnaround in Sheridan's opinions. Having been an anti-war Foxite and a heartfelt admirer of Bonaparte, he now turned out a patriot at last, becoming a lieutenant-colonel in the St James's Volunteers corps. Political motives might have operated here. He was a pal of the Prince, and with the King once more showing promising symptoms of madness he may have sensed that his time was about to come.[210] He may also have dreamed of becoming leader of an Irish parliamentary party, such as was expected to form in the wake of the Union (though never did). But equally he was galvanized by the prospect of invasion, and disgusted by Bonaparte's despotic behaviour in and outside France. At any rate, he became the leading patriotic cheerleader, with broadsides such as *Our King! Our Country! And Our God* (1803):

[The French], by a strange Frenzy driven, fight for Power, for Plunder, and extended Rule—WE, for our Country, our Altars, and our Homes.—They follow an ADVENTURER, whom they fear—and obey a Power which they *hate*—WE serve a *Monarch* whom we love, a GOD whom we adore.

This was certainly a volte-face on Sheridan's part, but it was not turncoat behaviour of the type perpetrated by more dilettante literary revolutionists such as Wordsworth, Coleridge, and Southey. Rather, it showed that it was still possible to be a radical patriot, and that loyalism was not inherently conservative.

'Britons Strike Home! Or your Fame is for ever blasted,—your Liberties for ever lost!!!'[211] Judging by all the sermons, tracts, handbills, songs, and newspaper articles, the period of maximum panic, which was also that of the greatest martial fervour, occurred during the second half of 1803. Cartoonists habitually showed John Bull or Jack Tar fighting against a pygmy with an enormous nose, while French slaves were contrasted with free-born Englishmen (or Britons, the two terms being interchangeable). *Rule Britannia* was sung at the slightest provocation, the *Gazette* reported battles in graphic detail, and the crowd fêted George III whenever he reviewed the Volunteers. The London stage was monopolized by invasion drama and anti-French exhortation. Between August and December theatregoers could see *The Maid of Bristol*, *Henry V*, *Edward the Black Prince*,

---

[209] John Beckett, 'Responses to War: Nottingham in the French Revolutionary and Napoleonic Wars, 1793–1815', *Midland History*, 22 (1997), 77.

[210] Finlan O'Toole, *A Traitor's Kiss: The Life of Richard Brinsley Sheridan* (1997), 354–72.

[211] Frank J. Klingberg and Sigurd B. Hustvedt (eds.), *The Warning Drum: The British Home Front Faces Napoleon* (Berkeley and Los Angeles, 1944), 24–5, 169.

Sheridan's *Pizarro* (starring Kemble and Siddons), *The English Fleet in 1342*, *Britons Strike Home*, *The Surrender of Calais*, *The Camp*, and a score of similarly tonic dramas.[212] Much has been written about the gradual rise of English nationalism over the preceding half-century, but this was more like a *revanche*, equivalent to what occurred in France in 1792–3, Prussia in 1806–7, and Russia in 1812, a heightened mood combining elements of apocalyptic despair, epiphany, and catharsis. Fortunately for Pitt it was not a mood that Addington could live up to. It was time for the pilot to return, and this he did 'with some at least of the quality of legend that would gather round him in his final phase'.[213]

Addington's other bugbear was the so-called 'cooperation' between Fox and Grenville. Considering their past enmity and disagreement over almost everything except Catholic emancipation, it was as remarkable in its way as that between Fox and North twenty years previously.[214] Having operated under the shadow of his cousin for so long, Grenville was beginning to emerge as the head of his own party. It was the last of the eighteenth-century connections to survive, a compact family grouping with territorial influence in Buckinghamshire and an appetite for public emoluments.[215] Like all such faction leaders, Grenville now craved a broad-based coalition of 'talents', preferably with Pitt in it. However, by the time that Pitt agreed to desert Addington, Grenville had reluctantly given up on him and committed himself to Fox. Fox himself had lost any residual sense of obligation to Addington once war had broken out again, and a juncture with Grenville was the only way he could think of to rally his restive troops.[216] At all events, once the parties of Fox, Grenville, and the Prince had joined forces to attack the ministry's supposed inadequacies in homeland defence, it was inevitable that the country gentlemen would desert. In May 1804, having seen his majorities slashed on a succession of defence issues, Addington made way for Pitt, who vindictively insisted, against the King's wishes, that the outgoing Prime Minister should also quit the Cabinet. However, after failing to include Grenville and Fox in a government of national unity—the King would not have Fox, and Grenville would not come in without him—Pitt was more or less forced to take Addington back in January 1805, though he also bullied him into taking a peerage as Viscount Sidmouth.

Pitt's second administration was weak in the Commons from the start. His Additional Force Act, which passed by very narrow majorities in June 1804, returned to the failed principle of local (i.e. parish) recruitment and was

---

[212] Wheeler and Broadley, *Napoleon and the Invasion*, ii. 259–68.   [213] Ehrman iii. 643.

[214] They differed especially on foreign policy, since Fox was reluctant to fight France at all, while preferring 'old Tory', or 'blue-water', strategy should fighting become necessary. However, 'the situation they inherited narrowed the ground between them' (Jupp, *Grenville*, 370).

[215] James J. Sack, *The Grenvillites 1801–29: Party Politics and Factionalism in the Age of Pitt and Liverpool* (Urbana, Ohio, 1979), 3–101.

[216] Richard E. Willis, 'Fox, Grenville, and the Recovery of Opposition, 1801–1804', *JBS* 11 (1972), 24–43.

intended to show how inept his predecessor's recruitment drive had been. In fact it showed the opposite, for instead of the expected 20,000 men in two months, it raised just 13,000 men in two years! A report of September 1804 recommended the building of Martello towers, an initiative that was to dot the southern coast with short, stout forts and do wonders for the brick industry. By this time, however, attention was shifting from defence to attack. A Third Coalition was formed in April 1805 with the signing of that Anglo-Russian alliance which Addington had envisaged. It became effective in August when Austria joined up to it. In planning and execution it performed just as badly as its two predecessors, but it brought an immediate respite for England by forcing Napoleon[217] to switch his army from Boulogne to the Rhine. Meanwhile, Nelson chased Admiral Villeneuve all the way to the West Indies and back before their respective fleets finally came within sight of each other off Trafalgar. Battle was fought on 21 October, and the result was crushing. The details are disputed, but the British seem to have lost 1,500 men including Nelson himself, the French and Spanish allies about 14,000, while of their thirty-three ships of the line, one was sunk and another seventeen were captured. It was final proof of the superiority of mêlée tactics over the enemy's more traditional 'line ahead' methods. The latter meant that opposing fleets sailed in parallel lines and bombarded each other laterally, whereas in a mêlée a detachment of vessels from one of the fleets attacked head on, breaking the enemy line and engaging in ship-to-ship combat, a tactic pioneered by Howe and Jervis, and only available to the fleet with the superior gunpower and the more skilled and experienced captains and crews. It was a mode of battle which made top brass vulnerable to sniper fire, as was demonstrated when Nelson was felled by a French musket, but it also contributed to the national myth. The initiative that it gave to individual captains was held to epitomize the individualism of an enterprising island race by comparison with the enslaved populations of the Continent, and equality of danger was also felt to be appropriate to a land of free peoples.

Like one or two previous admirals, Nelson had become something of a public figure, cheered when he entered a theatre and fêted on his occasional tours of the country. Unlike some previous ones, however, his glory was there to be exploited by the government of the day, rather than used in opposition to it, and on this occasion ministers were determined to make the most of his obsequies, declaring that his burial should be a state occasion, despite his own request to the contrary. Held in early January, and costing £14,000, it has been described as 'the most magnificent funeral ever staged'.[218] As well as cheering everyone up, it

---

[217] Bonaparte had become Napoleon, Emperor of the French, on 18 May 1804, though some historians call him Napoleon from the time that he became Consul for Life in August 1802.

[218] Andrew Lambert, *Nelson: Britannia's God of War* (2004), 311–17; Gillian Russell, *The Theatres of War: Performance, Politics, and Society, 1793–1815* (Oxford, 1995), 80–7.

set the tone for much subsequent pageantry, including a great deal of squabbling over rank and precedence.[219] After four days of lying-in-state, the body was borne from Greenwich to Whitehall Steps in Charles II's royal barge. Followed by a flotilla of sixty or more boats, it wove its way through countless vessels moored along the route, their ensigns flying and each one firing a salute as the corpse came by. The following day the cortège—designed to look like a replica of Nelson's flagship, the *Victory*—processed through silent multitudes from the Admiralty to St Paul's, where temporary seating had been arranged for 7,000. The King was not present by convention, but there were seven royal dukes and what seemed like half the aristocracy, as well as forty-eight able seamen to register Nelson's common touch. The service was turgid, but it ended movingly with the body being lowered by mechanical winch into the cathedral crypt under the huge dome. Prints of the occasion and other assorted memorabilia continued to be sold for years to come, and there were any number of re-enactments staged in exhibition halls throughout the country.

Nelson had not been a nice man. His dalliance with Emma Hamilton in Naples and 'frolicking' with 'dollies' generally, and his heartless neglect of a dutiful and long-suffering wife, are hard to reconcile with his ostentatious piety. He was also ruthless, crude, and egotistical, a hanger and flogger of his own men, and merciless towards the enemy. (It says something that, although thirty-six admirals attended his funeral, St Vincent and seventeen others who were in the country refused to do so, in many cases pleading coughs and colds and prior engagements.) Yet he had undoubtedly been the man for the hour. He was fearless and single-minded, passionately loyal to his King (whom he believed to rule by divine right), convinced that he himself was an instrument of providence, and very possibly a deliberate martyr—it has often been suggested that he willed his own death at Trafalgar by wearing gaudy apparel. All in all he was a worthy antagonist of the French Emperor.[220]

In the short term Trafalgar made little difference, since Napoleon had already called off the invasion, but like the battle of the Nile it was a great psychological fillip and effectively guaranteed British naval supremacy for the remainder of the war. Meanwhile the Grande Armée had crossed the Rhine and Danube and had penetrated Bavaria. On the day before Trafalgar, Napoleon won one of his most stunning coups when he enveloped an Austrian army and forced its commanders to hand over 50,000 men out of a total of 72,000 (the Capitulation of Ulm). In mid-November he took Vienna and then routed the Russians and Austrians at Austerlitz (2 December). It was said that news of this defeat precipitated Pitt's final illness. The Third Coalition was effectively broken, and in the

---

[219] State funerals had been common during the Interregnum (1649–60) and would become so again in the later 19th century.

[220] Terry Coleman, *Nelson: The Man and the Legend*, 2nd edn. (2002), 331–4.

ensuing Peace of Pressburg, Austria was denied the relatively easy terms which she had been granted twice before. She was virtually excluded from Germany and Italy, while her titular headship of the Holy Roman Empire ended the following August when it was dissolved. Once again Britain was left to fight alone.

Even more demoralizing for Pitt was a charge of sleaze against the man who had once been his most (even perhaps his only) intimate colleague. Dundas (now Viscount Melville) returned to office with Pitt as First Lord of the Admiralty, but in 1805 he was criticized in the tenth report of the Public Accounts Commissioners for alleged malversation of public funds, and was subsequently censured in the Commons. 'We can get over Austerlitz', wailed Pitt, 'but we can never get over the tenth report.'[221] Deserted by the Addingtonians (or Sidmouthites), Pitt was defeated on a number of minor issues that autumn. His energy and grip on business, which had been weakening before 1801, had now almost completely gone, and it was thought that he would be decisively defeated in the following session. In fact he died on 23 January 1806, aged 46, from a gastro-intestinal lesion, possibly cancer of the bowel.[222] Fox felt cheated of the political victory he had felt sure was about to be his at last, but he also felt that there was 'something missing in the world'. The funeral was grand naturally, but fell short of Nelsonian proportions. For example, only three royal dukes were present in the Abbey.

George III now turned to Grenville, who turned to Fox, Sidmouth, and the Prince's friends. The new Government was dubbed 'All the Talents',[223] but did not include Hawkesbury or Canning since Pittites were vetoed by Windham and Grey. Fox was proposed for Foreign Secretary and Leader of the Commons, and this time the King had to 'swallow the pill'.[224] Whereas the appointment of Addington in 1801 and the return of Pitt in 1804 had involved only a small number of changes in the ranks of minor office-holders, the return of the Foxites naturally involved many more, though except in Scotland[225] there were nothing like as many as had taken place on three separate occasions during 1783–4. Maybe it was thought that wholesale changes would be disruptive of the war effort. At all events, the continuation of so many officers in their posts marked a return to pre-1783 traditions of permanent placemanship, and disappointed many aspirants. Another traditional touch was the way in which the new administration immediately strengthened its position at the polls. The election

---

[221] Thorne, iii. 642. It was reported that Pitt forgot his reserve so far as to cry in the Commons, and that he covered his face in his hat to hide the tears.

[222] For the gory details, see Ehrman iii. 549–51, 825–6.

[223] A double-edged sobriquet in a country where it was felt that talent and virtue did not mix easily.

[224] He had refused to consider himself for the premiership, but was widely regarded as the real Prime Minister (Thorne, iii. 822–3).

[225] Where there was something of a vendetta against the Dundas regime.

TABLE 2.2. *Composition of the House of Commons before and after the 1806 general election*

	Before	After
Supporters of the Talents Ministry	260	308
Independent but friendly to the ministry	176	151
Opposition (Pittites)	108	90
Independent but friendly to the Opposition	110	102

held in October 1806 was a quiet affair, but it increased support for ministers substantially and left the Pittites in disarray (see Table 2.2).

However, in terms of policy Grenville's administration was more or less a disaster. The one great achievement, abolition of the slave trade, would have happened anyway. Henry Petty's budget, raising the rate of property tax from 6½ to 10 per cent, was naturally unpopular, but less so than Windham's proposed Army reforms, which would have undermined the role of the county in Volunteer training.[226] Worse still, Fox's attempt to end the war, if necessary on abject terms, also foundered. Although he was willing to accept a France far more powerful than even Louis XIV could have dreamed of, it soon became obvious that Lord Lauderdale's peace mission to Paris was futile. To ram that point home, Napoleon annihilated the Prussians at Jena and extended the blockade of German ports against Britain. The possibility of peace meanwhile had compromised British policy in South America, where Sir David Baird and Sir Home Popham, having captured Buenos Aires, were keen to encourage the Argentine colonists to rise against Spain. Not wanting to offend Napoleon, the Cabinet in London instructed them to stay their hand, with the result that before long the British had been ignominiously expelled, not only from Buenos Aires but from Montevideo. This humiliation caused a good deal of soul-searching back home—literally so in some devout circles—and also disappointed British merchants, who were anxious to find a recompense in South American markets for loss of trade with the Continent.

Grenville was also hamstrung by a scrupulous desire to avoid attacking his dead cousin. It showed delicacy but meant that when things went wrong he could not blame the previous administration. The Pittites themselves (Portland, Canning, Hawkesbury, Perceval, Castlereagh, Eldon, and Wellesley) could hardly believe that he was really in control, and expected the Foxites to seize command at any moment. Then it became clear that Fox was dying. Grenville made an offer to Canning as the only man big enough to lead the Commons, but as none of the other Pittites were to be offered anything he, after some

---

[226] See below, p. 225.

prevarication, refused. 'With the exception of Ld G and Ld Spencer', he told his wife, 'I objected to *all* the present people, as the persecutors of Ld Melville, and consequently the slayers of Mr Pitt.' The proposal also foundered on the animosity, which had now reached boiling point, between himself and Windham. Then, when Fox died in September from cirrhosis of the liver and gallstones, the Government lost its only commanding presence in the Commons. All in all it was a shambles, and the end was particularly bathetic. Fox and Grenville had of course been committed to Catholic emancipation, but in view of the King's outright hostility the matter was quietly dropped. Something had to be done to appease the Government's supporters, however, and so a measure was introduced allowing Roman Catholics to take up commissions in the armed forces. Even this sop was vetoed by the King, who demanded a pledge from ministers that they would never raise the Catholic issue again in any form, and as a result the Cabinet felt obliged to resign in March. The Foxites' taste of office had lasted just over a year, a few months longer than in 1783. On both occasions they foundered over opposition from the King, though on this occasion they threw away their own seals of office instead of waiting for them to be snatched back. On both occasions the price was to be more than twenty years in opposition.

'What is become of all the shyness in the world?', Jane Austen asked her sister in February 1807. 'Moral as well as natural diseases disappear in the progress of time, and new ones take their place. Shyness and the sweating sickness have given way to confidence and paralytic complaints.'[227] There was a spurious confidence in the air that winter, a slight hysteria, the flip side perhaps of that patriotic *revanche* that had characterized the three previous seasons. As the immediate danger of invasion receded, sheer relief caused the blanket of deference to lift, and people began to turn inwards and question what their politicians were up to. Political disarray was matched by perceptions of moral decay and dissolution, and Melville's impeachment took on symbolic significance if only because, as Mr Secretary Dundas, he had seemed the embodiment of rectitude. There was nothing new about political gossip, scandal-mongering, lampoons, and satire, but contemporaries noted a new viciousness, and this was matched in popular literature by a craze for sensation as well as for Gothic horror from the Minerva Press, sentimental potboilers, and *romans-à-clef*, especially ones that highlighted scandals among the royal family and in high life generally.[228] A generation inured to Pittite solemnity and weaned on endurance seemed to have lapsed into a temporary fit of noisy levity now that Pitt was dead.

[227] *Jane Austen's Letters*, ed. Deirdre Le Faye, 3rd edn. (Oxford, 1995), 119.
[228] Peter Garside, 'J. F. Hughes and the Publication of Popular Fiction, 1803–1810', *The Library*, 6th ser., 9 (1987), 240–58.

CHAPTER 3

Pittism and plutocracy: the social and psychological foundations

It will be clear by now that, viewed in strictly high-political terms, Pitt was much weaker during the last ten years of his life than he had been previously. Even so, mere possession of office sometimes enables politicians to create self-serving mythologies and otherwise bend opinion in their own favour. In retrospect it is evident that Pitt secured a working partnership between a cadre of executive-minded ministers like himself and a majority of country gentlemen in Parliament. Despite rocky moments, this alliance guaranteed the Conservative Party (as it eventually came to be called) a near-monopoly of office from 1783 to 1830, and a last but notable election victory in 1841. But what was the basis of this achievement? It seems unlikely that Pitt could have inaugurated such a durable regime if he had stood for nothing more than merely 'carrying on the King's government', like so many of his predecessors. Nor does the obvious high-political explanation, based around Fox's mistakes and misfortunes, account for the fact that Pittite governance ultimately proved to be popular as well as possible. The purpose of this chapter is to probe the reasons, part social and part psychological, for this success. It moves beyond Pitt, in other words, to the more complex phenomenon of Pittism.

COURT WHIGS, COUNTRY WHIGS, AND THE CONSERVATIVE REACTION

Some contemporaries refused to accept that there was any such phenomenon. William Hazlitt, for example, accused Pitt of 'weakness', 'imbecility', and 'a defect of understanding bordering on idiotism'. He had 'no strong feelings, no distinct perceptions', 'no general principles', 'no comprehensive views of things, no moral habits of thinking, no system of action', 'no insight into human nature, no sympathy with the passions of men, or apprehension of their real designs'. Every new subject which came up for consideration 'presented to him nothing more than a *tabula rasa*, on which he was at liberty to lay whatever colouring of language he pleased'. Rhetoric was his only weapon, 'an artful use of words, and a certain dexterity of logical arrangement. In these alone his power consisted.'[1] Of course Hazlitt, as a radical writer, was hardly impartial, but his caricature carries some force. Part of the problem was that Pitt never had to declare where he stood, having been catapulted to the top so soon, and he therefore carried little of what is now called ideological baggage. He once said that 'there was no wisdom in establishing general rules or principles in government or policy'.[2] His demeanour, incongruous in such a young man, was that of the world-weary pragmatist exasperated by Fox's utopian idealism and habit of playing to posterity. To Hazlitt, on the other hand, Fox represented an ideal of 'pure good nature' and 'refined humanity', thanks to his love of 'whatever was generous or liberal'.[3]

If Fox strove to demonstrate his own consistency it was partly because his detractors made so much of his chops and changes,[4] whereas Pitt's inconsistencies were generally condoned as evidence of common sense. No doubt this was partly because one was 'in' and the other was 'out', but it was also the case that Fox and his friends had less scope for prevarication, since unlike Pitt they had constantly proposed that politics should have what would now be called an agenda, that government should be about more than balance sheets and the balance of power. This does not mean that Fox was doctrinaire. His speeches were often incoherent and contradictory, delivered extempore and without reflection. Yet Hazlitt was right to point to his sublimer longings, his 'innate love of truth, of justice, of probity'. He was proud of the name 'Whig', but paradoxically he had something in common with early eighteenth-century Tories, who had argued that, since public life was subject to providence, only the party of the Church was equipped to understand God's wishes. The contrary view had been pressed by Whigs such as Walpole, who had insisted that government was a secular and pragmatic business which should be left to those with knowledge of worldly affairs. By winning this rhetorical battle, the Whig Party had marginalized the Churchmen and had established a hold over political life. By the 1780s it was the Pittite branch of the Whig Party that claimed Walpole's Court Whig inheritance and took refuge in managerial expediency, while Foxite Whigs, heirs to the old country tradition, called for political sincerity. They did not, of course, seek to return to the Church Toryism of Queen Anne's reign— sacerdotal politics would not come back into currency until the 1830s—but they craved a similar commitment to ultimate values, to Hazlitt's 'general principles' and 'comprehensive views of things'. Accordingly they condemned Pitt's

[1] *The Complete Works of William Hazlitt*, ed. P. P. Howe (1930–4), vii. 322–3.
[2] *The Diaries of Sylvester Douglas (Lord Glenbervie)*, ed. Francis Bickley (1928), i. 152 (2 Feb. 1801).
[3] *Works of Hazlitt*, vii. 316, 321–2.
[4] e.g. *Fox against Fox!!! Or, Political Blossoms of the Rt. Hon. Charles James Fox* (1788).

'system' as amoral and cynical in the same way that Bolingbroke had disparaged Walpole. Fox's problem was that, lacking all religious sense, he could not devise any other basis for his moralism. It was possible to thrive as a secular politician, it was equally possible to be lax in one's behaviour, but it was hard to combine moral politics with a secular and amoral private ethic. Fox was therefore unable to move from negative rage to positive vision. It was something which his devotees found easier to do after he had died.

Some historians would argue that although Pitt started out as a Court Whig in the Walpole–Pelham tradition, maintaining power by cultivating the King and with the conditional support of a broad-bottomed coalition in Parliament, the wave of reactionary loyalism which swept across the country after 1792 provided him with a social and ideological constituency, and that he became in effect the progenitor of a new Burkean conservatism with a mission to defend throne, Church, and aristocracy against the rights of man.

There are two problems with this argument. The first is that Pitt enjoyed less wholehearted support within the political nation in the 1790s than he had in the previous decade. *Elijah's Mantle* (1806), James Sayers' obituary poem comparing Pitt with the Hebrew prophet and forerunner of the Messiah, was pure myth-making. Many who supported him did so *faute de mieux*, while resenting the income tax and his abortive plan to sell off the Church tithe.[5] Many were also dismayed by his wretched performance as a war leader, and would have agreed with Macaulay's later comment that his military administration 'was that of a driveller', his Army the laughing-stock of Europe. ('It had never shown itself on the Continent but to be beaten, chased, forced to re-embark, or forced to capitulate'.[6]) When his political difficulties reached a peak in 1797–8, innuendoes began to circulate about Pitt's love of alcohol and his bachelor status. He was burned in effigy at demonstrations up and down the country, just as the King came increasingly into focus as the symbol of national pride and devotion. Finally, in proposing Catholic emancipation Pitt challenged the landed elite's cherished Protestantism. Whatever might have seemed to be the case in retrospect, there was little identification between Pitt and the landed establishment at the time.

As for the notion that Pitt pursued a Burkean strategy of counter-revolution, undoubtedly a *ralliement* of conservative forces took place. Louis XVI's execution, the Civil Constitution of the Clergy, and the Reign of Terror all increased the esteem in which monarchy, Church, and aristocracy were held in England. Burke's *Reflections* and Paine's *Rights* so polarized debate that for the first time English politics could be described in terms of Left and Right, and Pitt was posthumously identified with the Right just as he was remembered as a great

[5] By allowing tithe-payers to redeem their obligations through the payment of stock into the sinking fund.

[6] Lord Macaulay, 'Pitt', in *Encyclopedia Britannica*, 8th edn. (1859); 9th edn. (1885), xix. 144–5.

war leader. Yet the war for him was all about the balance of power, not ideology, and he could not bear to listen to Burke's post-prandial effusions on the glories of the French aristocracy. Like Hazlitt, Macaulay was scornful of Pitt's failure even to recognize that a war of ideals was being waged.

He should have proclaimed a holy war for religion, morality, property, order, public law, and should have thus opposed to the Jacobins an energy equal to their own . . . He was obstinately blind to the plain fact that he was contending against a State which was also a sect . . . It was pitiable to hear him, year after year, proving to an admiring audience that the wicked republic was exhausted, that she could not hold out, that her credit was gone . . . as if credit was necessary to a government of which the principle was rapine, as if Alboin could not turn Italy into a desert till he had negotiated a loan at five per cent., as if the exchequer bills of Attila had been at par.[7]

However, to say that Pitt did not identify with a Burkean conservatism is not to say that his power rested only on expediency. He did after all inaugurate a regime which survived him by forty years, and he could hardly have done this if his power had rested solely on pragmatism and patronage.

VIRTUOUS ECONOMICS

'The salvation of the country required virtue as well as talents.'[8] Asked why they supported Pitt in preference to Fox, contemporaries cited these two qualities again and again. This prompts two further questions. Virtue is useful in a bishop, but why was it thought so in a statesman? Walpole, after all, had made political capital out of boasting that he was 'no saint, no spartan, no reformer'. Secondly, *how* did Pitt garner his reputation for talent, given that he had little aptitude for administration and was wayward in his office habits, often leaving letters unanswered or undealt with for weeks.

Both questions can be approached obliquely through a consideration of economic policy. People certainly persuaded themselves that Pitt was a sound financier. They hoped beyond hope that he could solve the problem of the public debt, which had grown inexorably and was at alarming levels. Unredeemed capital on the national debt had risen from about £127 million just before the American war to £243 million in 1784, when the Government spent £8 million simply paying interest charges. This was out of a total net income of £13 million and a total net expenditure of £24 million. The debt held steady over the following decade, being at almost exactly the same level when the French wars started in 1793, but by 1801 it had climbed to £456 million and then soared to a peak in 1819 at over £844 million (more than double the nation's gross

---

[7] Ibid.
[8] Lord Mulgrave, 3 Feb. 1784, quoted in John Debrett, *The Parliamentary Register, 1780–1799*, xiii. 46.

national product).[9] A distinguishing feature of the period 1783–1850 was that the public debt was almost universally thought to portend calamity or 'shipwreck'. As well as being an impediment to productive enterprise and a motor of corruption, it was seen as a harbinger of national bankruptcy, social collapse, and even religious apocalypse.[10]

The national debt was the accumulated amount of money borrowed by successive governments since 1691 and not yet repaid. Before 1740 most of it had been incurred through loans from three great corporations—the Bank of England and the South Sea and East India companies—but since then it had expanded mainly by means of public loans raised in the London money market in return for various types of government stock, mostly perpetual annuities, and carrying various rates of interest. Share certificates representing government stock were bought and sold like bills of exchange, usually at a premium or discount, that is above or below the par value (the price at which the Government undertook to buy them back). When it was desperate for money, as in 1781–2, the Government was forced to issue stock at a high rate of interest and to a much greater amount than the nominal value of the loans raised, and in this way its liabilities increased very rapidly. For less than £92 million borrowed during 1776–85, it had to pay back over £115 million. This meant that the purchaser of the stock—the so-called fundholder—might receive a high real rate of return on the sum invested, even though the nominal rate was low. In 1797, for example, investors paid £100 for each £219 of stock issued, which stretched their nominal dividend of 3 per cent to more than 6 per cent.

By far the greater part of the national debt was funded, meaning that, for each tranche of money raised, taxes were imposed to defray the additional interest charge. The growth of the debt therefore automatically entailed an increase in taxation, over 75 per cent of which sometimes went on paying off interest. A minuscule part of the debt (about £14 million in 1784) was *un*funded, and took the form of Exchequer, Navy, and Ordnance bills which were used by the respective spending departments to raise supply on a short-term basis in anticipation of the following year's revenue. These bills were exchanged by the Bank of England in return for ready money, and though the amount was relatively small (just over £60 million at its peak in the mid- to late 1810s) it was this floating or unfunded debt that chancellors of the Exchequer regarded as a sword of Damocles, threatening national bankruptcy.

The centrepiece of Pitt's financial policy was the sinking fund. In 1786 he told Wilberforce that he was 'half mad with a project which will give our supplies the

---

[9] In 1819 well over half of the Government's annual expenditure went to defray interest on the national debt (i.e. £31.3m out of £57.6m).

[10] Some of those who disliked economic growth regarded the impediment to productive enterprise as an argument in its favour.

effect almost of magic in the reduction of debt'.[11] It was usual to apply any surpluses that might accrue to the redemption of funded debt. However, under the new plan £1 million of tax revenue was to be vested every year in commissioners, who would use it not to redeem but to buy stock (preferably when it was below par), and to invest it at compound interest until the fund was worth £4 million per annum, it was hoped in about twenty-eight years' time. Since the current market price of stock was some way below par—in 1786 most of the three per cents were circulating at about 70–75 per cent of their nominal value: the commissioners could purchase £100 of stock for only £70–75 of revenue, which was a good bargain for the public. By this means the principal of the funded debt was reduced by £10 million between July 1786 and December 1793, at a cost to the taxpayer of only £7.5 million (though, since the actual surplus of revenue was only £4.4 million, the unfunded debt was forced upwards by nearly £7 million in the same period, making the overall achievement less than heroic). In 1792 Pitt set up a new sinking fund alongside the first. It was to be financed by the imposition of a 1 per cent annuity on all new loans, except in cases where Parliament made initial provision for redeeming those loans within forty-five years. Had there been no more wars, it might eventually have been possible to eliminate the whole debt in something like the same time scale.

It was always recognized that a sinking fund only made sense if it could be financed out of a genuine surplus of revenue over expenditure. Yet it was to be persisted with throughout the war and was only finally abandoned, discredited and derided, in 1829. Between 1793 and 1815, £578 million of new funded debt was created, of which £81 million went into the sinking fund, that is to pay off the capital of older debt which mostly bore a lower rate of interest than the new debt which was created. Moreover, because stock was selling at 50 below par in 1797, each extra £1 million borrowed increased the capital of the debt by £2 million. There were some practical justifications for this apparent madness. The war might have ended at various points before it did, and there was reluctance to throw away the sacrifices already made on behalf of the sinking fund. And since governments at war must raise money quickly, potential lenders had to be reassured that debt would not be repudiated as in France. More than anything else the sinking fund was indicative of national resolve: 'the great prop, the hope, and consolation of the country', as Addington described it.

To pay for it Pitt made strenuous attempts to increase revenues. In his pre-war budgets he either introduced or raised excise taxes on servants, bachelors (according to the number of their servants), gamekeepers, gentlemen's hats, ladies' ribbons, silk gloves, hackney carriages, post horses, pleasure horses,

---

[11] *The Letters of Lady Harriot Eliot, 1766–1786*, ed. Cuthbert Headlam (Edinburgh, 1914), 140.

racehorses, shooting licences, cards, dice, spirits, armorial bearings, sporting dogs, wig powder, newspapers, letter franks, legacies, wills, probates, and houses (the amount of tax to depend on the number of windows). All this can be seen as an attack on old money, but also on luxury and the macaroni manners of the beau monde, and it strengthened the image of austerity, from which Pitt benefited politically. To balance these additional excise taxes he reduced some customs duties. The subsequent increase in consumption and revenue was often impressive (for example, a reduction in the duty on tea from an average of 119 per cent to 25 per cent was followed by a rise in the official value of imports from an average of £462,000 in 1775–84 to £1,830,000 in 1785–94), but this was partly due to a cyclical economic upturn. In 1786 William Eden (later Lord Auckland) negotiated a treaty by which England and France agreed to accept each other's products except silk on easy terms. Since silk was a French speciality, this was accounted a diplomatic triumph.

Complementing the shift from indirect to direct taxes was retrenchment, a policy which dominated the political agenda from 1782 (when Rockingham stormed the closet crying, 'peace, retrenchment, and reform'), until Gladstone's budgets of the mid-nineteenth century. Pitt's contribution included the opening of public contracts to competitive tender and the exclusion of government contractors from sitting as lobby fodder in the Commons. In 1785 he ensured that nearly 200 patent offices in the Customs Department should not be filled when they became vacant, and it appears that between 1783 and 1799 the number of excise officers fell by 747, despite a doubling of the revenue which they had to manage.[12] Those who retained office had their salaries increased in order to discourage them from accepting fees and bribes, they were required for the same reason to change location at regular intervals, methods of assessment and collection were simplified, and the old Salt Board was abolished. Admittedly, Pitt was cautious in retrenchment and his practice often fell short of his rhetoric. He constantly sought the advice of financiers and was willing to withdraw schemes that were not working. Although he sometimes referred to theorists such as Adam Smith and Josiah Tucker, this was more by way of justification than inspiration, and for the most part he followed precedent. Walpole had devised a sinking fund, North and Cavendish had introduced sealed competitive tendering when allotting subscriptions to public loans, while Rockingham and Burke had commenced retrenchment, though whereas they had been motivated by a desire to reduce Crown patronage, he acted out of economic necessity. Even customs reform reflected a common-sense desire to simplify the tariff after two decades in which numerous ad hoc duties had been imposed purely to guarantee the interest on wartime loans. Similar problems

---

[12] Ehrman iii. 472.

were tackled in similar ways elsewhere, by Cameralists in Austria, for example, and by Necker, Turgot, and Calonne in France. All of which suggests that Pitt's fiscal policies were arrived at pragmatically,[13] except that he was close to his former mentor Lord Shelburne, now Marquess of Lansdowne. One of the few politicians who could confidently be called doctrinaire, and arguably the first 'liberal' statesman in the sense of being a free-marketeer, Shelburne was an enigmatic figure. Wildly unpopular and personally ineffectual, he nevertheless exercised considerable influence over the following generation. If there *was* a theoretical tinge to Pitt's economic policies, it was probably due to Shelburne's influence.

Pitt's policies were successful in that by 1792, the last year of peace, he could boast a healthy surplus. However, the outbreak of war had an immediate and devastating effect on the public finances. As reported in Chapter 2, the war forced Pitt to borrow so much and so fast that the price of government stock plummeted and the Bank was forced to suspend cash payments in February 1797. This turn of events would now be called a U-turn, but Pitt neatly called it 'a new turn to our operations'. 'The crisis, though difficult, may, I think, furnish the remedy.' He was not only unabashed but seemed pleased to be blown off course, and he and Auckland were soon concocting another 'great scheme of

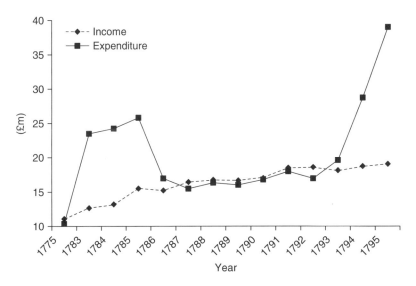

FIG. 3.1. Public income and expenditure, 1783–1795

[13] John Ehrman, *The British Government and Commercial Negotiations with Europe 1783–1793* (Cambridge, 1962), 177–81.

finance'.[14] As interest rates soared above 6 per cent, he vowed to bring them down by borrowing less and taxing more. In 1798 he introduced the triple assessment, under which about 60 per cent of better-off households would pay a multiple of the assessed taxes they had previously paid. Following widespread evasion, however, Pitt replaced this complicated expedient with the first income tax in 1799. It was a graduated levy on all incomes over £60, and targeted many people who had not paid assessed taxes.[15] The intention was that it should continue after the war until all post-1798 debt had been redeemed, the sinking fund being relied on to clear all earlier liabilities. Although this hope proved utopian, the policy meant that, notwithstanding the continued huge increase in borrowing, 60 per cent of the cost of the French wars would be met from taxation, as compared with only 20 per cent of the cost of the American war.

As a result the State expanded fiscally to a degree that made it qualitatively different from anything it had been before. This massive tax increase was not regressive, since efforts were made to spare the poor and to tax luxuries rather than necessaries, but the net was spread widely, which may explain why society became more politicized. It does *not* explain why Pitt and his successors should have been political beneficiaries, especially as the money no longer went to

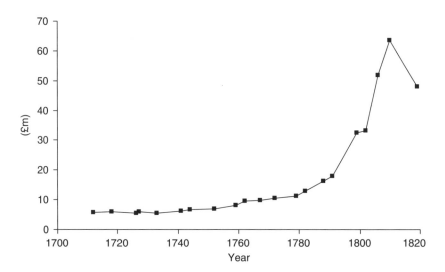

FIG. 3.2. Estimates of total revenue from taxation at current prices, 1712–1819

[14] *The Journal and Correspondence of William, Lord Auckland*, ed. third Baron Auckland (1861–2), iii. 379–84.

[15] Child allowances were included in recognition of the fact that those who 'enriched their country with a number of children' had a 'claim upon its assistance for their support'.

reward political supporters. The fact that Pitt cut patronage enhanced his reputation for public virtue, but in view of the role which preferment played in public life it makes it all the more remarkable that he should have been able to build up a successful political regime. Indeed, one of his successors, Lord Liverpool, would frequently complain that there was not enough patronage at his disposal to secure a compliant House of Commons.

A partial explanation is that, like Napoleon, Pitt gratified his supporters' need for status. Ninety-one new peers were created during 1783–1801 compared with only forty-three during 1760–83. Expansion was to continue under Lord Liverpool, so that the size of the Upper House increased from 195 in 1784 to 372 in 1830.[16] Pitt also had an eye to timing. There were no adjustments to the British peerage in 1794 and only one promotion in 1795, as compared with twenty creations or promotions in the run-up to the 1796 election. Such promiscuity was one way to build up a regime, though if the economy had been in the doldrums it would probably have been necessary to offer pensions, sinecures, and other material blandishments, as Walpole had done in building a Whig oligarchy in the early Hanoverian period. The scramble for honours may partly account for the rise in George III's influence, since he had final say over the composition of the peerage, but it hardly explains Pitt's political allure. Intriguingly, contemporaries seem actually to have relished the belt-tightening that he offered them. To understand why so many of them believed in the possibility of salvation though austerity, it is necessary to dig below the technicalities of financial policy to the social, cultural, and psychological underpinnings of the regime.

A NEW VISION OF GOVERNMENT

A remarkable blueprint for economic and administrative policy was elaborated in a series of fifteen reports by the Commissioners for Examining the Public Accounts (1780–6).[17] Established by North in an attempt to stave off criticism over America, it was (most unusually) granted full access to documents and allowed to interrogate ministers and officials on oath. Although for North the Commission was merely a face-saver, Shelburne took its reports seriously, and many of Pitt's policies were adumbrated in them. In particular the eleventh report (1783) enunciated ideas for a sinking fund and income tax. 'It is expedient that the true state of the national debt should be disclosed to the public; every subject ought to know it, for every subject is interested in it . . . The evil

---

[16] Of whom, however, thirty-two were Irish peers added in 1801.

[17] For a memorable analysis, see John Torrance, 'Social Class and Bureaucratic Innovation: The Commissioners for Examining the Public Accounts 1780–1787', *P&P* 78 (1978), 56–81. For details, see J. E. D. Binney, *British Public Finance and Administration 1774–92* (Oxford, 1958), 7–15.

does not admit of procrastination, palliatives, or expedients.' The Commissioners repeatedly urged good husbandry in all branches of public service, arguing that 'the character of national justice, the support of national credit, and the preservation of the public welfare' depended on the 'principle of public œconomy'. Other reports recommended that the Customs, Audit, and Inland Revenue should be raised to the level of the Excise, reputedly the most efficient and economically run department in Europe. This in itself indicated a significant shift, since before the American war the Excise had been hated precisely because it *was* efficient, inquisitorial, and centralizing. The free-born but taxpaying Englishman had always preferred the land tax, which by virtue of its county-based mode of assessment and collection helped to cement local communities, whereas excise duties threatened to disrupt them. Yet now, at a time of national crisis, the Excise was held up for imitation, especially the simple and regular procedures which rendered its officers accountable.

As this suggests, the Commissioners envisaged a more bureaucratic breed of public servant. Instead of continuing to receive fees for services rendered, officials should draw fixed salaries, so facilitating estimates of future spending. Instead of having to depend on parliamentary goodwill for retirement pensions, they should be entitled to superannuation. Rather than performing their duties when and how they pleased, they should observe regular office hours and annual holidays, and if performance was unsatisfactory they should be dismissed. Utility, rationality, uniformity, and accountability—these were all principles which the Commissioners thought would make public administration better and cheaper. There was clearly a centralizing ethos behind these recommendations. According to the demonology of the Commissioners, State servants had customarily treated their offices as personal property or fiefdoms, in some cases even enjoying a right of reversion by which they could choose their successors. In exercising greater authority over these private barons, the State would regain control over many important administrative functions. However, strong government in that sense cohabited with a desire for weak government in another and more conventional one, for the corollary was that the new bureaucrats would exercise *less* control and above all less arbitrary control over ordinary citizens. The Commissioners' bureaucratic vision was thus the antithesis of welfare state ideology, since their administrative dirigisme complemented the emerging science of political economy with its emphasis on individual market choice.[18]

The significance of the Public Accounts Commission is hard to estimate. Demands for public probity and efficiency were hardly new, though except with regard to India there had been little fuss about such matters previously. The immediate trigger for the Commissioners' brand of moralism was undoubtedly

---

[18] This point is developed below, pp. 590–1.

the sudden escalation of the national debt, and on this point anxieties waned temporarily as trade recovered in the later 1780s, before being swamped by greater and different anxieties after 1792. It came back into fashion from about 1808, but was not fully reinstated until the 1830s. Yet although Pitt's tone of voice often mimicked theirs, and his ostentatious refusal of patronage for himself appealed to their ethos, in actuality he took retrenchment only so far, even *before* the outbreak of war stymied it completely.[19] As one historian has written, Pitt shared the perspective of the Commissioners, 'but he responded to their reports in a piecemeal and undramatic fashion that was at variance with the boldness and urgency of their pronouncements'.[20] Sometimes he abolished posts but fobbed their holders off with generous pensions, and though he got rid of many sinecures in the Customs, he waited for the offices to fall in before doing so.[21] He was also disinclined to act on the recommendations of a Commission which met during 1785–9 to investigate the fee and salary structure in twenty-four offices of State. Having suppressed its report on corruption in the Post Office, and shelved its recommendations on the Navy Board for a decade before implementing them in watered-down form,[22] he finally dismissed the Commission with fourteen offices still to be looked at. Admittedly, the Navy was vital to national defence, while the Post Office acted as 'the government's mouthpiece, eyes, and ears', at least until the establishment of the Alien Office.[23] It was where the letters of known radicals were opened, and intelligence passed upwards via resident surveyors to the Home Secretary. Even so, it says something that under Pitt only six Government departments were subjected to reform.[24]

All in all it is hard to avoid the suspicion that Pitt wanted the credit for setting up such inquiries but was not keen to act on them. He liked to order hair shirts but did not wish to wear them. No matter. At a time when popular interest in politics was growing rapidly thanks to the circulation of cheap broadsheets, image and rhetoric often counted for more than reality. Two centuries later Margaret Thatcher would successfully propagate a similar image of ruthless frugality, thrift, and what was called corner-shop economics, even while she presided over a credit boom and consumer spending spree of unprecedented proportions. Although the Public Accounts Commissioners did not alter the way in which governments operated overnight, they did signal a new

[19] On the other hand it may be more significant that the war was not allowed to lead to a huge expansion of bureaucracy as in France (Ehrman iii. 473).

[20] Philip Harling, *The Waning of 'Old Corruption': The Politics of Economical Reform in Britain, 1779–1846* (Oxford, 1996), 31–88: 61.   [21] Ehrman i. 282–92.

[22] Ehrman i. 316–17, ii. 494–500, iii. 460–4.

[23] Kenneth Ellis, *The Post Office in the Eighteenth Century: A Study in Administrative History* (1958), p. viii.

[24] John R. Breihan, 'William Pitt and the Commission on Fees, 1785–1801', *HJ* 27 (1984), 59–81.

rhetoric—a new way of thinking and talking about public affairs—which was to have a momentous effect in the long term.

Most of the Commissioners' reports were written by Thomas Anguish, Accountant-General of the Court of Chancery. When Charles Dickens wrote *Bleak House* in the mid-nineteenth century, Chancery was thought to epitomize all that was sclerotic, corrupt, and inefficient, but in the 1780s its reputation was very much higher because its procedures were based on equity law, which was then widely regarded as a model of modernity and good sense compared with the pedantic and precedent-bound common law. Anguish's reports employed the language and concepts of the equity law of trusts which, 'with some over-simplification', can be regarded as a vehicle of middle-class aspirations.[25] Whereas statute and common law mainly protected the rights of real or landed property-owners, with emphasis on issues such as trespass, poaching, and the preservation of game, equity had developed largely to protect business rights. While property remained the basis of participation in public life, in the course of the century it had come to embrace not only real but movable property, not only land but money, shares, market shares, professional skills, and intellectual property.[26] Equity was a means of settling disputes over wills and testaments, family settlements, trading and monopoly rights, breaches of patent, and corporate privileges. It was resorted to by Dissenting sects, bankers and stockbroking firms, by chartered companies and the London Stock Exchange, by local government corporations, by trade unions and combinations, by political clubs and associations, and by the hundreds of charitable trusts established to provide for the welfare of foundlings, orphans, single parents, and the elderly. In this way, equity law became *the* law for protecting the personal, associational, and institutional rights of the middling classes. And whereas it was a commonplace that landed property was part of the providential order, and that the rights and duties attaching to it were sacred, the Commissioners' more novel message was that rights and duties attaching to contracts were equally sacred, and especially those contracted by the State. In this way, policies which in one sense might be regarded as commonsensical—such as retrenchment and the reduction of national debt—came to be invested with intense moralism, while office-holding was increasingly understood as a 'sacred trust'.

Country members had always favoured public frugality, partly to get at the court and partly to get lower taxes, but now money saved on court appointments would go not to relieve taxpayers, at least not in the short term, but rather to swell the sinking fund. Hitherto governments had paid interest on the debt but

---

[25] 'With some simplification one may say that, when English capitalism needed to assert its form of life against feudal common law, it found a vehicle in equity; when its bearers wished to associate, they created the public trust; and when the bourgeoisie proclaimed its class interest as the universal interest, it invented the ideology of public trust' (Torrance, 'Social Class and Bureaucratic Innovation', 71).

[26] Paul Langford, *Public Life and the Propertied Englishman 1689–1798* (Oxford, 1991), 1–70.

had not worried unduly about reducing the principal. Now it became an axiom of policy that the present generation should pay for itself—indirectly in the form of spending cuts and directly in the form of higher taxes—rather than shove the burden onto posterity. 'Justice to the public creditor' came to be equated with economic righteousness, and debt redemption a touchstone of national sacrifice and morality.

As with the Excise, this signalled a remarkable shift in attitudes. For eighty years fundholding, like paper money, had been strongly resented. In old country party demonology, fundholders were drones with wealth amassed on the enterprise of others, leeches sucking the blood of honest toilers, usurers whose power over the State undermined civic virtue. Like other aspects of early eighteenth-century ideology, this critique would resurface in the 1820s, especially among Ultra Tories and Radicals, but in polite circles from the 1780s onwards *investing* in the funds—possessing financial assets—being in credit—all came to be esteemed as virtuous. Correspondingly, being in debt came to be regarded unfavourably, even when it occurred because individuals had borrowed money in order to build up businesses and create employment. Whereas public creditors paid for the Army, Navy, court, and Church, all establishments necessary for security and the promotion of civilization, entrepreneurs were routinely condemned as speculators, the begetters of exploitation, economic and social instability, and ugliness. Of course, far from being universal, such attitudes were hotly contested, like all others in that polarized society, and there were also signs of the beginning of a shift in attitudes towards the end of the period, for example among the judiciary. Whereas more than two-thirds of would-be patentees lost their cases at common law in the first three decades of the nineteenth century, more than three-quarters were successful during the 1830s and 1840s,[27] a turnaround which might possibly have reflected the new prestige of the manufacturing classes. Until then, however, it would seem that rentier interests were promoted by those responsible for disseminating public doctrine, precisely because they subserved a culture of stability and restraint at a time when Britain seemed to be developing so much faster than everywhere else, and dangerously so. It was only after 1850, when the country's economic performance was perceived to falter relative to its rivals, that an unequivocally positive attitude to growth set in, and that fundholders came to be derided once more as drones, seeking safe outlets for their capital in three per cent consols when what the nation needed was enterprise and speculation if it was to regain its competitive edge.[28]

---

[27] H. I. Dutton, *The Patent System and Inventive Activity during the Industrial Revolution 1750–1852* (Manchester, 1984), 78–9; Christine MacLeod, *Inventing the Industrial Revolution: The English Patent System, 1660–1800* (Cambridge, 1988), 201–22.

[28] Not until after the First World War, and then only very briefly, and again in the Thatcherite 1980s, would reduction of the capital of the national debt become once more a major object of policy.

It seems, then, that the prestige attached to fundholding reflected a particular stage in the country's development, when economic growth was regarded as neither normative nor particularly desirable. If so, it may provide a clue to the nature of the regime which monopolized power during those same years.

CLASS DISTINCTIONS AND RENTIER CAPITALISM

As de Tocqueville observed, England differed from France in possessing a class rather than a caste system.[29] There were no impenetrable legal barriers separating the various layers of society, and the differences between them were blurred so that people's status largely depended on how they behaved, whom they associated with, and how they esteemed themselves. The concept of class formation is currently unfashionable, but since it was in this period that the language of class began to supersede that of orders,[30] the topic must be addressed, however tentatively.

Historians have long been divided over the nature of eighteenth-century society. There is a two-class model which pits patricians against plebs, landowners against the propertyless. From this perspective there could not be a middle *class*. The so-called 'middling people' were merely elevated plebs, lacking an autonomous culture and in many cases seeking through wealth to be accepted in patrician society. The relationship between patricians and plebs is sometimes seen as having been brutal and exploitative, revolving around the Black Acts, press-gangs, and the Bloody Code.[31] Alternatively, it has been depicted in terms of a comfortable reciprocity between deference and paternalism, 'a massive consensus, based upon the widespread acceptance of aristocratic values and aristocratic leadership' by the tenants, estate workers, shopkeepers, innkeepers, country attorneys, and others who made up the large segment of the population that lived in villages and small rural towns.[32] Different again is the three-class model, which places more emphasis on towns and allots a role to the middle class,[33] those 'polite and commercial people' who were fast developing tastes and

[29] Alexis de Tocqueville, *L'Ancien régime*, ed. G. W. Headlam (1968), 89–91.

[30] A. Briggs, 'The Language of "Class" in Early Nineteenth-Century England', in M. W. Flinn and T. C. Smout (eds.), *Essays in Social History* (Oxford, 1974).

[31] E. P. Thompson, *Whigs and Hunters: The Origin of the Black Act* (1975); id.,*Customs in Common* (1991); Douglas Hay *et al.*, *Albion's Fatal Tree: Crime and Society in Eighteenth-Century England* (1975); Roy Porter, *English Society in the Eighteenth Century* (Harmondsworth, 1982).

[32] John Cannon, *Aristocratic Century: The Peerage of Eighteenth-Century England* (Cambridge, 1984), p. viii; W. A. Speck, *Stability and Strife: England 1714–1760* (1977); Ian R. Christie, *Stress and Stability in Late Eighteenth-Century Britain: Reflections on the British Avoidance of Revolution* (Oxford, 1984), 54–93; J. C. D. Clark, *English Society 1688–1832: Ideology, Social Structure and Political Practice during the Ancien Regime* (Cambridge, 1985), 93–118.

[33] Paul Langford, *A Polite and Commercial People: England 1727–1783* (Oxford, 1989), 61–121; John Money, *Experience and Identity: Birmingham and the West Midlands 1760–1800* (Manchester, 1977),

values independent of aristocracy. The popularity of the reformed grammar schools, the 'rise of public science', the emphasis on hygiene, the growth of assembly room culture, the social space accorded to women, the consumer revolution, the conceptualization of leisure, and the market for books (especially novels and histories) all helped to propagate the notion of gentility, a bourgeois quality in so far as it could be acquired by any ambitious bookseller, clerk, or dancing master. Metropolitan London, with its French food and Italian opera, had for a long time offered such glittering attractions to the professional and business elite that many of its members had long since ceased to aspire to county status,[34] but by the end of the century many provincial centres were beginning to do the same, not just the flourishing ports of Whitehaven, Bristol, and Liverpool, and the fashionable spa towns and seaside resorts of Harrogate, Bath, Scarborough, Weymouth, and Brighton, but even the new industrial centres of the north and midlands—Manchester, Leeds, Bradford, Huddersfield, Birmingham, and Wolverhampton. All these towns built market halls, dispensaries, schools and Sunday schools, chapels, asylums, workhouses, hospitals, and cemeteries. All had their service, business, and administrative sectors, whose members had incomes similar to those of the small and middling gentry with whom they danced and sometimes hunted. Their leading inhabitants cultivated the accoutrements of a polite lifestyle such as charitable giving, assembly rooms, debating societies, musical ensembles, couturiers, coiffeurs, and bookshops, the latter often serving as centres of intellectual discussion. They hired fashionable architects, sculptors, and portraitists, read London papers and the latest novels, and built up collections of china and porcelain. How far this urban lifestyle bestowed cultural autonomy might depend on the pulling power of county society in different localities. So, for example, the fact that there were few resident peers and smart gentry in south Lancashire may help to explain why bourgeois culture was more developed in Manchester and Liverpool than in Nottingham or Northampton. Again, in small single-industry towns the service sector might amount to no more than the occasional banker and lawyer, in which case a vibrant commercial culture would not develop until well into the nineteenth century. But everywhere the trend was similar.

The two- and three-class models may both be valid, but the second has the merit of pointing up the contrast with other countries and with what England itself had been like a hundred years earlier. However, it is essential to recognize that the middle class was itself divided, at the very least into upper and lesser

8–50; Peter Earle, *The Making of the English Middle Class: Business, Society and Family Life in London, 1660–1730* (1989), 227–37; Peter Borsay, *The English Urban Renaissance: Culture and Society in the Provincial Town, 1660–1770* (Oxford, 1989), 199–308.

[34] Nicholas Rogers, 'Money, Land and Lineage: The Big Bourgeoisie of Hanoverian London', *Social History*, 4 (1979), 437–54.

strata, and also that the boundary between the upper-middle class and landed society was blurred, as was that between landed society and the aristocracy. In what follows a great deal of weight will be placed on this concept of an upper-middle class, for which reason the following caveat is necessary. The word 'class' traditionally implies self-consciousness on the part of its members, while the words 'upper-middle' seem to indicate a particular horizontal segment of society as defined economically. Yet, as will become clear, the term 'upper-middle' is intended here to include unself-conscious mental criteria as well as material self-interest, and as such it distinguishes between people vertically as well as horizontally.

Any discussion of social structure must start with the calculations for England and Wales in 1801–3 made by Patrick Colquhoun. They imitated Gregory King's statistics of 1688, and may be biased upwards by Colquhoun's desire to show how greatly the two countries had prospered in the interim. Still, they were based on information provided by the recent census, the income tax returns, and the 1802–3 survey of paupers, and modern historians have seen little reason to challenge them.[35] Impressionistically, it seems that a line might be drawn between less well-off middling persons earning £120 a year (farmers, lower clergymen, and Dissenting ministers) and well-paid working people such as clerks on an average of £75 and artisans or craftsmen on £55. Forty years earlier it had been possible to estimate that those at the lower end of the middle-class spectrum earned about twice what they needed for subsistence.[36] It is more difficult to compute such a figure for 1801–3 because of the sharp fluctuations in prices caused by bad harvests. (These fluctuations may account for the large gap between £75 and £120, the licensed innkeepers and lesser freeholders or yeomen[37] who occupied it being to some extent insulated from price rises by the nature of their employment.) Moving up Colquhoun's table to farmers, vicars, and military officers, these are people who even in times of scarcity would have had enough disposable income to participate in consumer society. They could rent a decent house and purchase furniture, clothes, education, medical treatment, and holidays. Roughly speaking, nearly one in four of the population belonged to families with an income of at least £120 per annum. However, in order to have pretensions to *upper*-middle-class gentility it was necessary to have

[35] Patrick Colquhoun, *A Treatise on Indigence* (1806), 23; P. H. Lindert and J. G. Williamson, 'Revising England's Social Tables 1688–1812', *Explorations in Economic History*, 19 (1982), 399–408, revise the number of heads of families as follows: persons employed in theatrical pursuits etc. 1,000; naval officers etc. 7,000; military officers etc. 13,064; clerks and shopmen to merchants etc. 60,000; seamen in merchant service etc. 49,393; marines and seamen in Navy etc. 52,906; common soldiers 121,985; vagrants 175,218.

[36] In 1759 it was estimated that one family in five earned £50 and that two families in five earned £40, which was about twice what was required for mere subsistence (Langford, *Polite and Commercial People*, 62–3).   [37] A smallholding of 300 acres brought in about £100 p.a.

TABLE 3.1. *Patrick Colquhoun's calculation of the social structure of England and Wales, 1801–1803*

Occupational category	No. of heads of families	Aggregate no. of persons in the family of each rank	Average annual income (£)
The King	1	50	200,000
Temporal peers and peeresses	287	7,175	8,000
Spiritual lords or bishops	26	390	4,000
Baronets	540	8,100	3,000
Eminent merchants, bankers, etc.	2,000	20,000	2,600
Knights	350	3,500	1,500
Esquires	6,000	60,000	1,500
Persons in higher civil offices	2,000	14,000	800
Lesser merchants, trading by sea	13,000	91,000	800
Principal warehouseman, selling by wholesale	500	3,000	800
Manufacturers employing capital in all branches (wool, cotton, iron, etc.)	25,000	150,000	800
Gentlemen and ladies living on income	20,000	160,000	700
Persons employing capital in building and repairing ships, etc.	300	1,800	700
Persons educating youth in universities and chief schools	500	2,000	600
Eminent clergymen	1,000	6,000	500
Shipowners letting ships for freight only	5,000	25,000	500
Persons keeping houses for lunatics	40	400	500
Persons of the law, judges down to clerks	11,000	55,000	350
Liberal arts and sciences	16,300	81,500	260
Persons in lesser civil offices	10,500	52,500	200
Persons employed in theatrical pursuits, musicians, etc.	500	2,000	200
Persons employing professional skill and capital as engineers, surveyors, master builders, etc.	5,000	25,000	200
Freeholders of the better sort[a]	40,000	220,000	200
Persons in the education of youth of both sexes	20,000	120,000	150
Shopkeepers and tradesmen dealing in goods	74,500	372,500	150
Persons employing capital as tailors, mantua makers, milliners, etc.	25,000	125,000	150
Naval officers, marine officers, surgeons, etc.	3,000	15,000	149
Military officers, including surgeons, etc.	5,000	25,000	139
Lesser clergymen	10,000	50,000	120
Dissenting clergymen and itinerant preachers	2,500	12,500	120

TABLE 3.1. (*Continued*)

Occupational category	No. of heads of families	Aggregate no. of persons in the family of each rank	Average annual income (£)
Farmers	160,000	960,000	120
Innkeepers and publicans, licensed	50,000	250,000	100
Lesser freeholders	120,000	160,000	90
Clerks and shopmen, to merchants, manufacturers, shopkeepers, etc.	30,000	150,000	75
Artisans, handicrafts, mechanics, and labourers, employed in manufactures, buildings, and works of every kind	445,726	2,005,767	55
Military and naval half-pay officers, pensioned	4,015	10,000	45
Labouring people in mines, canals, etc.	40,000	130,000	40
Hawkers, pedlars, duffers, etc.	800	4,000	40
Seamen in the merchant service, fisheries, rivers, canals, etc.	67,099	299,663	40
Marines and seamen, in the Navy and revenue	38,175	150,000	38
Labouring people in husbandry, including earnings of the females	340,000	1,530,000	31
Confined lunatics	2,500	2,500	30
Common soldiers, including non-commissioned officers and militia	50,000	200,000	29
Persons imprisoned for debts	2,000	10,000	25
Paupers producing from their own labours in miscellaneous employments	260,179	1,040,716	10
Vagrants, Gypsies, rogues, and vagabonds, thieves, swindlers, coiners of base money, in and out of prisons, and common prostitutes (including wives and children)	?	222,000	10
Chelsea, Greenwich, Chatham pensioners	30,500	70,500	10
Labour earnings of the above pensioners	?	?	10

[a] i.e. those who were freeholders only, though some of them may also have been farmers on the side. Many of the better-off persons in other categories would also have owned freehold property.

an income of at least £200 per annum and preferably £300, a qualification which excluded retail tradesmen and schoolteachers. The pension awarded to a former senior commander in the Royal Navy in 1816 was roughly £250.

According to this analysis the upper-middle class comprised a much wider band than the others in terms of income, though smaller in terms of numbers. For although £250 was a great deal less than the £10,000 and more earned by wealthy lawyers and merchant bankers, moving in the penumbra of aristocratic society, it was sufficient to enable its possessor to join the ranks of those who invested capital. This is important because, while conventional definitions of wealth have centred on property ownership, the single most important characteristic of the late eighteenth-century upper-middle class was not to own real property but to possess or have access to capital assets for investment. The most extensive and important research on probate records has revealed the extent to which the owners of such liquid wealth were landowners, merchants, and professional people from London and the South of England rather than provincial industrialists. Between 1809 and 1839 just over 900 Britons died leaving more than £100,000 in personal unsettled property, and of these almost 800 can be identified by occupation.[38] The inescapable conclusion to be drawn from Table 3.2 is that bankers, financiers, and wealthy merchants dominated the financial elite, followed by landowners, professional men, and public administrators, with manufacturers lagging far behind. Again, out of 565 non-landed wealth-owners in England whose business venues are known, London and the Home Counties claimed 425, the rural South 26, and East Anglia 20. Lancashire mustered 25, the West and East Midlands 24, but Yorkshire and the remainder of the North only 15.[39] Admittedly, £100,000 was a lot of money, and a lower threshold might well net more northern industrialists. Yet in 1859 there was still a markedly higher proportion of residents earning more than £100 in London

TABLE 3.2. *Persons leaving more than £100,000 in personal unsettled property, 1809–1839*

	No.	%
Landowners (including West India planters)	178	22.3
Merchants and financiers	344	43.2
Professionals and public administrators	158	19.2
Manufacturers and industrialists	78	9.8
Food, drink, and tobacco suppliers, brewers	33	4.1
Miscellaneous	6	0.8
TOTAL	797	

[38] W. D. Rubinstein, 'The Structure of Wealth-Holding in Britain, 1809–39: A Preliminary Anatomy', *Historical Research*, 65 (1992), 74–89 (where these aggregates are broken down into the three decades, without significant variation). See also id., *Men of Property: The Very Wealthy in Britain since the Industrial Revolution* (1981), 56–116; id., *Elites and the Wealthy in Modern British History* (Brighton, 1987), 17–118.

[39] There were four in the port of Hull, but none in the manufacturing towns of Leeds, Bradford, and Sheffield.

and the other southern towns than in the northern manufacturing districts.[40] It is equally striking that of all those dying in Bradford between 1838 and 1857 with personal property worth £100 or more, the vast majority received their income as dividends, interest, shares, fees, and rents rather than as profits, even though this was a town whose economic wealth was almost entirely derived from industrial production.[41]

Of course, the exclusion of real property from probate records renders all such calculations seriously misleading to the economic historian as an index of wealth per se. Between 1809 and 1839 about 1,200 landowners left estates with a capital value of at least £100,000, whereas only 178 left personalty to that amount. Probate also underestimates the real wealth of entrepreneurs by excluding valuations of plant and other fixed assets. However, the focus here is on disposable incomes. Land that was mortgaged or otherwise encumbered was often a financial liability, while the need to keep a factory open through periods of recession frequently forced its owner into debt. In seeking to draw up a profile of capital-owning society, it is precisely an individual's personal assets or liquid wealth that counts.

And there was an enormous amount of surplus capital splashing about. Some of it was absorbed by savings banks, by life, fire, and marine insurers, and by trust companies. However, by far the most important outlet for investment was the national debt. A portion was traditionally taken out by foreigners, particularly the Dutch, but as much as nine-tenths may have been held by British fundholders (or rentiers).[42] It is impossible to be sure how many there were, for they often conducted business through London dealers and brokers. One estimate suggests about 60,000 in 1760, of whom one-quarter held about three-quarters of the whole. The number may have risen to about 100,000 by the 1780s, and then to about a quarter of a million by 1815. If so, it would mean that roughly one citizen in forty-five was a fundholder, and that England had at last caught up with France, where the urban bourgeoisie had enjoyed rentier status since the seventeenth century. A banker informed his fellow MPs in 1830 that at least 1,374,000 people had a stake in the public securities, a figure which presumably included wives, children, and sundry dependent relatives. Traditionally most fundholders lived in or near London, while provincials were more likely to invest in local toll roads, bridges, and canals, but the expansion of the debt after 1783 almost certainly coincided with a wider geographical distribution as

---

[40] W. D. Rubinstein, 'The Size and Distribution of the English Middle Classes in 1860', *Historical Research*, 61 (1988), 65–89. By 1859 an income of £100—the point at which liability to income tax began—just about conferred middle-class status. This is less than in 1801–3, mainly because of falling prices in the interim.

[41] Theodore Koditschek, *Class Formation and Urban-Industrial Society: Bradford, 1750–1850* (Cambridge, 1990), 137–43.   [42] Not to be confused with rent-*receivers* or landlords.

regional elites increasingly interacted with the metropolis. High interest rates tempted small investors into the market, especially in the three per cents, whose low nominal yield made them cheap to buy. Just as important was the growing number of pension funds designed to cushion beneficiaries against downward social mobility and to protect persons (women especially) who were dependent on the life of a breadwinning relative. The National Benevolent Institution, for example, was founded in 1812 to dispense nearly £200,000 to 'distressed persons in the middle ranks of society', such as ex-service officers, clergy widows, indigent gentry, and 'persons of education and talent in the professions, and the more reputable departments of trade'. There were individual funds for particular groups such as Old Etonians and 'decayed governesses'.[43] A market in securities had been in fairly sophisticated operation since at least 1750, though the Stock Exchange was not formally established as a trust until 1808. It too was metropolitan-based until after 1830, when the spectacular growth of railway finance led to the establishment of formal exchanges in Liverpool, Manchester, and elsewhere.

After the national debt, nothing did more to create the habit of investment than canals, which absorbed large amounts of private capital. Most of the first generation had been financed locally by businessmen who hoped to benefit economically; for example, the third Duke of Bridgewater built his waterway from Worsley to Manchester (1759–61) in order to reduce the cost of transporting coal, and Josiah Wedgwood promoted the Trent and Mersey to speed up the distribution of earthenware. However, these ventures often attracted some London investors, whose interest in canals was purely financial. For while the Usury Laws effectively limited the rate of interest on simple loans to 5 per cent, many canal companies paid dividends of over 20. Out of more than fifty companies formed during the so-called canal mania of 1792, a mainly Midlands phenomenon, only eight imposed a limit on dividends; significantly, these were ones which had a greater than average number of economically motivated shareholders. And when Pitt proposed a tax on inland navigation in 1796, opposition was based much more on the threat to share prices than on the prospect of canalusers having to pay higher rates. All this suggests that by 1800 financial motives were predominant, and this was certainly the case with the speculative and almost entirely metropolitan joint-stock boom of 1807–11, which led to many new canals, mainly in the South.[44]

The projection of new canals virtually ceased after 1814, which prompted many non-metropolitan wealth-owners to invest for the first time in public securities, public utilities, and fire and life insurance companies. For example,

[43] E. Evelyn Barron, *The National Benevolent Institution 1812–1936* (1936), 74–9; Frank Prochaska, *The Voluntary Impulse: Philanthropy in Modern Britain* (1988), 39–40.
[44] J. R. Ward, *The Finance of Canal Building in Eighteenth-Century England* (1974), 18–78, 136–7.

about 200 provincial gas companies were founded between 1816 and 1830.[45] Taking companies of all types, as many as 624 with a total capitalization of £372 million were floated during the boom of 1824–5 alone. At the same time, large numbers of Manchester cotton merchants and Leeds woollen merchants diversified by switching capital from textiles to insurance. Why? There were few financial gains to be made in the short or even medium term. Since consols fell steadily from 5 per cent in 1816 to 3.3 in 1824, while the hugely successful Manchester Fire and Life Assurance Company was only able to pay its shareholders dividends of 4.5 per cent (1828–39), these merchants would almost certainly have done better by continuing to concentrate on cotton. One answer may be that they preferred to spread their risks at a time when textiles were perceived to be volatile. If so, it would indicate that local businessmen were beginning to behave in a way that was typical of an established financial class, to whom stability and long-term growth matters more than the opportunity for short-term speculative gain. Or perhaps they were genuinely keen to improve their region's economic infrastructure, and establish their own claim to leadership in the process.[46] Whatever the reason, a substantial number of northern businessmen were becoming rentiers for the first time. The railway mania of the 1830s and 1840s was to consolidate this tendency, and Liverpool and Manchester capital was very prominent in the joint-stock banking boom of the mid-1830s.[47]

This was important politically given that capital investment, especially in the funds, was the hallmark of the regime that was consolidated under Pitt and his successors. One historian has inferred from this that the 1780s witnessed 'the making of the *haute bourgeoisie*' or 'upper-middle class' as 'a horizontal interest'.[48] Others have employed the term 'gentlemanly capitalism' to make the point that metropolitan and financial interests dominated much important decision-making.[49] Although 'upper-middle class' and 'gentlemanly capitalism' are slightly clumsy terms, the implication is evident—that while the age-old accommodation between land and money continued to operate, the terms of trade between them had shifted perceptibly. It is true that some bankers continued to see their destiny in terms of landownership and a barony, the Opposition Whig Francis Baring being a case in point, but more typical now was the Pittite Walter Boyd, who craved neither estates nor family dynasty. What *he* wanted was

[45] Philip Chantler, *The British Gas Industry: An Economic Study* (Manchester, 1938), 4.

[46] Robin Pearson, 'Collective Diversification: Manchester Cotton Merchants and the Insurance Business in the Early Nineteenth Century', *Business History Review*, 65 (1991), 379–414.

[47] B. L. Anderson and P. L. Cottrell, 'Another Victorian Capital Market: A Study of Banking and Bank Investors on Merseyside', *Economic History Review*, 28 (1975), 598–615; Seymour A. Broadbridge, *Studies in Railway Expansion and the Capital Market in England 1825–1873* (1970), 79–150.

[48] Torrance, 'Social Class and Bureaucratic Innovation', *P&P* 78 (1978), 56–81.

[49] P. J. Cain and A. G. Hopkins, *British Imperialism: Innovation and Expansion, 1688–1914* (1993).

yet more capital.[50] Nor is this surprising given that high society was centred on London and its satellites, Bath and Brighton. That was where the beau monde, the avant-garde, the bloods, the dandies, the rattles, the bucks and blades, and clubmen, as well as the court and almost the whole of the political and judicial worlds were congregated. Of course, many of these were sons and daughters of aristocrats, but they moved in circles whose ethos was increasingly urban and plutocratic. A small but telling point was the growing fashion for landed offspring to take legal qualifications without ever intending to practise law. It exemplifies the way in which some members of the old elite sought to appropriate the status symbols of their erstwhile challengers, rather than the other way around.

THE LATE HANOVERIAN ARISTOCRACY: DOMINATION OR ACCOMMODATION?

It is possible to see things differently. One historian has argued forcefully that the aristocracy 'renewed, re-created, re-invented, and re-legitimated' itself between 1780 and 1830 by investing heavily in government stock, turnpikes, and canals, and otherwise diversifying. Here the fusion of land and money in a united ruling class is presented as a case of noble families absorbing and there-fore still dominating the moneyed interest.[51] Other historians have applied this interpretation to the political sphere by suggesting that the creation of a second British empire between 1790 and 1850 was the work of an 'aristocratic reaction', and further that the imperial regime was statist, militaristic, authoritarian, and agrarian, with trade playing second fiddle.[52]

Before considering these claims it will be as well to define terms, many of which are notoriously ambiguous. 'Aristocracy' is usually taken as a synonym for 'peerage', the size of which increased rapidly as a result of the creations already referred to (see Table 3.3).[53] Traditionally Britain's was a territorial rather than a service aristocracy. Pitt reinforced this bias with a cascade of creations, but after his time only about one-fifth of new peerages went to established gentry families, while as many as one-half went to reward prominent politicians, judges, diplomats, generals, and admirals.[54] All this naturally created an obsession with titles and honours: Debrett's *Peerage* (which went through fifteen editions

[50] S. R. Cope, *Walter Boyd: A Merchant Banker in the Age of Napoleon* (Gloucester, 1983), 174–8.
[51] David Cannadine, 'The Making of the British Upper Classes', in Cannadine, *Aspects of Aristocracy: Grandeur and Decline in Modern Britain* (New Haven, 1994). See also Linda Colley, *Britons: Forging the Nation 1707–1837* (New Haven, 1992), 155–64.
[52] C. A. Bayly, *Imperial Meridian: The British Empire and the World 1780–1830* (1989), 80–1. See below, pp. 241, 244.   [53] J. V. Beckett, *The Aristocracy in England 1660–1914* (Oxford, 1986), 487.
[54] Michael W. McCahill, 'Peerage Creations and the Changing Character of the British Nobility, 1750–1850', in Clyve Jones and David Lewis Jones (eds.), *Peers, Politics and Power: The House of Lords, 1603–1911* (1986), 409, 419.

TABLE 3.3. *Increase in the size of the aristocracy, 1780–1840*

Aristocrats	1780	1840
Dukes	21	21
Marquesses	1	20
Earls	78	113
Viscounts	14	20
Barons	65	209
TOTAL	179	383

between 1802 and 1823) and *Baronetage* were pored over by many who would never appear in them. However, becoming a peer had little practical significance, and probably entailed a reduction in political clout (Foxites frequently complained that creations strengthened the power of the court by preventing influential and independent-minded country gentlemen from sitting in the Commons, where they could act as a check on the executive). The term 'landed interest' includes a wider penumbra of families that moved, sometimes uncomfortably, in aristocratic circles. According to Colquhoun, 1.4 per cent of English and Welsh families could be classified as belonging to the aristocracy *and* gentry at the turn of the century, but most other reliable estimates lie outside the period. It was calculated in the 1870s, for example, that 0.2 per cent of all landowners owned about 43 per cent of the land. That is to say, there were about 1,700 with more than 3,000 acres, including thirty-five magnates with upwards of 100,000. Below them came the squirearchy, or gentry, comprising about 12,000 families with acreages of between 300 and 3,000. Anything less than 300 acres would have made it hard for someone to call himself a landed gentleman. Further down still came freeholders with fewer than 300 acres, comprising about 180,000 families in 1803, though some of these were gradually being squeezed out by enclosure. Most will have worked their own estates, being not much superior to tenant farmers and well below merchants and professional people in social rank.[55] Even excluding this last category, it is clear that the landed interest comprised a very broad band.

Unlike that of many Continental countries British law included the principle of primogeniture, whereby the eldest male heir inherited the whole of the estate. This had traditionally forced younger sons to seek employment in the Church or

---

[55] J. V. Beckett, 'Landownership and Estate Management', in G. E. Mingay (ed.), *The Agrarian History of England and Wales*, vi: *1750–1850* (Cambridge, 1989), 547–8; G. E. Mingay, *English Landed Society in the Eighteenth Century* (1963), 19–107; F. M. L. Thompson, *English Landed Society in the Nineteenth Century* (1963), 109–50.

State or armed services, or failing that in commerce, finance, or the service sector, thereby lending a *ton* to those avocations which was not always found elsewhere. Together with the widespread use of strict settlements, primogeniture also helped to prevent the subdivision of landed properties and their consequent impoverishment, one reason why noble families proved more robust than in many other European countries, even though they faced the greatest challenge from new forms of wealth. Another factor was the 'marked trend towards territorial amalgamation' as a result of intermarriage.[56] For example, the third Earl Gower, a large landowner in Staffordshire and Shropshire, gained over 800,000 Scottish acres when he married the Countess of Sutherland in 1785. His father's earlier marriage to Lady Louisa Egerton in 1748 was to bring the family considerable funds from the Bridgewater estate fifty-five years later,[57] while in 1819 his second daughter also did her bit when she married Richard Grosvenor, the future Marquess of Westminster.

The landed interest naturally benefited from the soaring price of wheat in wartime (an average of 53*s*. per quarter in 1789, 114*s*. in 1800, 102*s*. during 1810–14). There were powerful longings for agricultural 'improvement', and the Whig agronomic expert Thomas Coke of Norfolk became something of an icon. Under Sir John Sinclair and Arthur Young the Board of Agriculture (1793–1822) sought to promote scientific farming, starting with a series of detailed county-by-county reports. Landlords and farmers kept up to speed by perusing the *Farmers' Journal* and *Farmer's Magazine*, and vied with each other to introduce new breeds and methods of husbandry, to create water meadows and improve drainage. In particular there was a revival of interest in pastoral farming, and fierce arguments over the merits of merino sheep (whose Spanish provenance was in their favour) and shorthorn cattle. The post-war agricultural depression put a temporary dampener on these efforts, but there was a sudden revival from the late 1830s. Several county societies were formed towards the end of the period (e.g. North Lincolnshire 1836, Yorkshire and Nottinghamshire 1837), stimulated in part by the building of railways, which opened up fresh opportunities for marketing produce and showing off livestock, as well as providing hefty financial compensation for the many owners whose land was taken over for track.[58] These developments were matched at national level by the Farmers' Club (1844) and especially the Royal Agricultural Society of England (1838), whose aims were to investigate and disseminate technical information such as the application of Liebigian chemistry to agriculture, plant nutrition, and the use of bones and bird droppings for fertilizer.[59]

[56] Cannadine, 'Making of the British Upper Classes', 10.

[57] Eric Richards, *The Leviathan of Wealth: The Sutherland Fortune in the Industrial Revolution* (1973), 7–9.   [58] Vance Hall, *A History of the Yorkshire Agricultural Society 1837–1987* (1987), 23.

[59] Nicholas Goddard, *Harvests of Change: The Royal Agricultural Society of England 1838–1988* (1988), 1–94.

These developments would all bear fruit after 1850. Until then, agricultural improvement was more of a cultural statement than a practical contribution to economic growth. Moreover, its practitioners were mostly ecumenical in their interests rather than dyed-in-the-wool agrarians. As the economy moved from its wood and water phase to a dependence on coal and iron, landlords cashed in on mineral rights, either in partnership with companies or else by leasing land out to exploiters. In Lancashire the Derbys, Seftons, and Crawfords; in the Midlands the Dudleys, Hathertons, Sutherlands, Portlands, Scarboroughs, Dartmouths, and Clevelands; in Yorkshire the Norfolks and Fitzwilliams; in the North-East the Londonderrys, Wharncliffes, and Durhams; such families milked coal mines for all they were worth.[60] Many peers besides Bridgewater took an interest in canals for carrying coal, and aristocrats joined with entrepreneurs to defeat Pitt's proposed tax on that commodity in 1784. While disdain for *trade* remained characteristic (if only because too many landed families had risen by that embarrassing route), manufacturing struck a more powerful chord. Rockingham saw himself as the protector of the Yorkshire woollen industry, while Dartmouth identified with Matthew Boulton, Samuel Garbett, and other industrialists in the Birmingham area.[61]

Historians wishing to argue the case for an aristocratic revival can also point to cultural factors, beginning with architecture. There was a return to building great country houses, often surrounded by spacious parkland to the designs of landscape gardeners such as Humphry Repton and John Loudon. Many were open to tourists, their numbers boosted by the difficulty of foreign travel in wartime, and by a vogue for discovering England, its history and antiquities.[62] Lavish new palaces went up in London; Lancaster House (c.1825–1840) by Wyatt and Smirke cost its first owner, the Duke of York, £65,155. Soane's Bank of England (1788–1827) was matched by Nash's stuccoed Palladianism, stretching all the way from Carlton House Terrace via Regent's Street to Regent's Park (1812–33). Cubitt's Belgravia was developed between 1821 and 1840, and superior town houses went up around Hyde Park. It was also a time when at last English aristocrats caught up on their collections of European furniture, porcelain, books, paintings, and statuary, taking advantage not only of their own wealth but of the buyer's market resulting from the pillage of French chateaux by revolutionaries. The Orléans collection, for example, was sold for $43,000 in

[60] Phyllis Deane, *The First Industrial Revolution* (Cambridge, 1965), 129–30; J. T. Ward, 'Landowners and Mining', in J. T. Ward and R. G. Wilson (eds.), *Land and Industry: The Landed Estate and the Industrial Revolution* (Newton Abbot, 1971).

[61] Michael W. McCahill, 'Peers, Patronage, and the Industrial Revolution, 1760–1800', *JBS* 16 (1976–7), 84–107; Richard H. Trainor, *Black Country Elites: The Exercise of Authority in an Industrialized Area 1830–1900* (Oxford, 1993), 86–90.

[62] A vogue pandered to in John Preston Neale, *Views of the Seats of Noblemen and Gentlemen in England, Wales, Scotland, and Ireland*, 11 vols. (1818–29).

1798 to a syndicate comprising the Bridgewater, Carlisle, and Gower families. As with their mansions, some collectors began to let the public in, one such being the second Marquess of Stafford at Bridgewater House. At the same time, many aristocrats developed a new sense of service to the community, by engaging in local government for example, while the proportion of Army officers with landed connections rose from 40 to 53 per cent between 1780 and 1823.[63]

All this adds up to a strong case for aristocratic revival and reinvention, but there is an opposite way of looking at the picture. Although primogeniture and strict settlement helped families to preserve the patrimony, it often meant that the first-born had to maintain his brothers as well as female dependants. Since more of these were surviving infancy and living longer, many estates became indebted, in some cases forcing the owner to sell out to new wealth.[64] One way out of the dilemma was for younger sons to find gainful employment off the land. This was not problematic in wartime but became so afterwards owing to government retrenchment. In this context, the aristocracy's love affair with the colonies may have been a defensive retreat rather than a confident assertion (the Radical John Bright famously dismissed empire 'as a system of outdoor relief for the upper classes'). The difficulties were of course exacerbated by the collapse of prices and rents after 1815, leaving many landlords crippled by mortgage repayments and other debts. That the Board of Agriculture could be wound up in 1822 with very little protest suggests that there was little interest in scientific agriculture just then. Even the flurry of interest in high farming from the late 1830s onwards might be regarded as a mainly defensive response to several years of acute rural crisis. Public opinion was beginning to turn decisively against agricultural protection, and the effects of the Tithe Commutation Act of 1836 were widely feared.[65] Many of the county societies formed at that time were in especially hard-hit areas such as the North and Midlands, and many were short-lived and ineffectual, while most of their support came from small gentry[66] and middle-class farmers rather than from great magnates. It was significant, for example, that Nottinghamshire's most important and most improving landlord, the Duke of Portland, would have nothing to do with its agricultural society.[67]

The cultural evidence in favour of an aristocratic revival is equally ambiguous. To start with, the wartime boom in architecture, like that in agriculture, was notable more for quantity than quality. No one could seriously compare the results with the great age of baroque and Palladian houses between 1614 and

---

[63] Cannadine, 'Making of the British Upper Classes', 22.

[64] John Habakkuk, *Marriage, Debt, and the Estates System: English Landownership 1650–1950* (Oxford, 1994), 77–142, 243–358.   [65] See below, p. 525.

[66] Notably William Shaw, co-founder of the Royal Agricultural Society.

[67] J. R. Fisher, 'The First Nottinghamshire Agricultural Association, 1837–1850', *Transactions of the Thoroton Society of Nottinghamshire*, 94 (1990), 64.

1750. It may, however, be significant that many noble patrons abandoned the neo-classical mode, previously de rigueur among the cosmopolitan aristocracy, in favour of a picturesque Gothic or Tudorbethan that would once have been associated with mere gentry. Panshanger (1806–21), Belvoir (1801–30), and Lowther Castle (1806–11) are cases in point. Similarly, while Repton and Loudon were prolific, their work hardly compares with that of Capability Brown, who died in 1783. The first person to style himself a landscape gardener, Repton graced the estates of the dukes of Bedford and Portland, but unlike Brown's most of his work was clustered around London and certain provincial towns. Many of his later designs were for nouveaux riches financiers who lived in the capital but week-ended in the Thames Valley, and here his parks were frequently dotted with flowers, cottages, follies, and pergolas.[68] Again, the new town mansions and houses were impressive, but less so than those by the Adam brothers and Chambers, the dominant architects of the third quarter of the eighteenth century, or the still more splendid earlier work of the elder Wood at Bath. Nash's Regency crescents and terraces were elegant, while Soane's Bank of England was ingenious, but neither were grandiloquent in the Continental manner. Anyway, urban development might more plausibly be seen as an accommodation with bourgeois priorities than an assertion of aristocratic ones (most 'Grand Whigs' were attracted to the glitter of metropolitan life while paying lip-service to the charms of the countryside). Finally, while involvement in government and support for local manufacturers could be seen in terms of aristocrats extending their hegemony over other areas of national life, and as illustrating 'a heightened sense of privilege and extended sense of identity',[69] it could also be seen as a capitulation, a recognition that they now had to earn their moral as well as physical keep, even if that meant behaving in non-aristocratic ways.

Of course, it is impossible to generalize about people whose main characteristic was their eccentricity. The two most compulsive connoisseurs and collectors were Lord Yarmouth, third Marquess of Hertford (1777–1842) and George Wyndham, third Earl of Egremont (1751–1837), but there all likeness ends. The former was an archetypal Regency bohemian and scapegrace, the model for Lord Monmouth in Disraeli's *Coningsby*, for the Marquess of Steyne in Thackeray's *Vanity Fair*, and for Lord Dudley in Balzac's *La Fille aux yeux d'or*. A quaffing partner of the Prince Regent, he was considered by the diarist Charles Greville to be 'without a serious thought or a kindly feeling, lavishing sums incalculable on the worthless objects of his pleasures or caprices, never doing a generous or a charitable action, caring and cared for by no human

---

[68] Repton has been described as pointing in 'the deadly direction of the interior decorator let loose outdoors' (Robert Lane Fox, *Financial Times*, 19 Sept. 1999, p. v. Stephen Daniels, *Humphry Repton: Landscape Gardening and the Geography of Georgian England* (New Haven, 1999), 207–54).

[69] Cannadine, 'Making of the British Upper Classes', 33.

being'.[70] Having settled early into a life of extravagance and debauchery, Hertford eloped at the age of 21 with an illegitimate and half-Italian ballet dancer. At the Peace of Amiens they dashed over to Paris, where his wife consorted with senior members of the imperial regime, while Hertford was interned by Bonaparte at Verdun for three years. After succeeding to the marquessate in 1822 he became known as 'the Caliph of Regent's Park', where his villa—a bizarre design by Decimus Burton with spectacular Corinthian columns, tent-shaped roof, gilded pillars, and Roman antiquities—became a centre of high Tory intrigue and was famous for all-night fêtes.[71] By contrast George Wyndham, third Earl of Egremont, though gruffly affable, was fundamentally shy, and certainly he shied away from fellow grandees. Disdainful of the aristocratic scramble for honours, he several times turned down the Garter, blaming 'something wrong in my natural construction' for this eccentricity. He did not drink or gamble, and although not personally religious[72] he engaged to the hilt in charitable do-gooding and all sorts of evangelical societies. A highly developed sense of duty towards the people of his estate and neighbourhood meant that he was adored locally. If the rakish and raffish Hertford exemplifies the Hanoverian peerage, which one historian has called 'the most licentious Aristocracy that England has known since the Middle Ages',[73] Egremont seems to point towards a more sober and responsible breed of Victorian aristocrat, and yet he was senior to Hertford by a quarter of a century. Their ages were also reversed in matters of taste. The younger man followed the aristocracy's traditional love affair with Continental art, with a preference for French seventeenth and eighteenth century,[74] whereas Egremont was a sturdy patron of British painters such as John Constable, Benjamin Robert Haydon, and especially J. M. W. Turner, who spent much time at Petworth as artist-in-residence.

Clearly, the landed interest could still outface the financial elite in terms of social esteem, but the question at issue here is political, to discover whether there was a social basis to the ruling regime. A large number of aristocrats supported the Pitt, Portland, Perceval, and Liverpool governments, of course, but it seems inappropriate to describe the regime as aristocratic, since so many of the grandest families took the other side—the Howard, Cavendish–Devonshire, and Grosvenor–Westminster clans for instance, and after 1830 the

---

[70] *The Greville Memoirs: A Journal of the Reign of Queen Victoria from 1837 to 1852, by Charles C. F. Greville*, ed. Henry Reeve (1885), ii. 92 (19 Mar. 1842).

[71] Donald Mallett, *The Greatest Collector: Lord Hertford and the Founding of the Wallace Collection* (1979), 3–25.

[72] At least, not according to his close friend Arthur Young, but then Young was a fervent evangelical (Lord Egremont, *Wyndham and Children First* (1968), 27–42; Ford K. Brown, *Fathers of the Victorians: The Age of Wilberforce* (Cambridge, 1961), 353 n.).

[73] J. H. Plumb, *The First Four Georges* (1956), 180.

[74] His acquisitions form part of today's Wallace Collection.

Stafford–Sutherlands as well. On the other hand, the term 'gentlemanly capitalist' seems justified, for while not all rentiers supported successive governments, a majority almost certainly did so. Conversely, lack of access to capital explains why certain sections of their landed supporters turned against them in the early and late 1820s.[75]

To clarify, it is not being suggested that political allegiance was mainly a case of material self-interest. Pitt won the support of capitalists as much because his rhetoric flattered their self-esteem as anything. Similarly, high farming sometimes appealed or repelled for cultural rather than economic reasons. Improving landlords were demonstrating expertise, responsibility, and professionalism rather than simply seeking to maximize profits. Some who could not afford to do so borrowed like mad in order to get in on the act, determined to improve their estates even if it ruined them, which was more than likely during the post-war depression, when agricultural land rarely provided a return of 3 per cent on the purchase price.[76] Their ranks included Sir James Graham, a Cumbrian squire and later Peel's Home Secretary (1841–6). A heroic not to say foolhardy high farmer, he spent £93,000 on plantations, buildings, enclosures, and drainage between 1817 and 1844, which required him to borrow £100,000 at 3½ per cent. By 1845 he had managed to increase the rental value of his estates from £18,000 to £21,000, but was paying £7,650 in debt charges, and had made virtually no productivity gains. Yet improvement remained an imperative for him and an end in itself. At the opposite extreme there were wealthy backwoodsmen[77] who desisted from 'fancy' or 'new-fangled farming' simply because it was destroying the old ways, eliminating yeomen, and throwing farmhands on the parish. The most theatrical gesture of cultural disgust was made by the second Duke of Buckingham and Chandos, acknowledged leader of the landed interest in Parliament at a time when it already suspected that it was about to be dished by the Establishment. In 1839 he succeeded to rent rolls of £100,000 a year on estates that were heavily encumbered. He at once bought enormous amounts of additional land with borrowed money, on which interest payments exceeded the acquired rental. He made no attempt to retrieve the situation through profit maximization, but instead invited Queen Victoria and Prince Albert to a lavish entertainment at Stowe, a defiant gesture of conspicuous expenditure which led directly to financial collapse. The house was shut and its contents sold, but at least 'the family pride had been satisfied in one last great orgy of indulgence'.[78]

---

[75] See below, pp. 270–4, 407–11.

[76] E. L. Jones, *Agriculture and the Industrial Revolution* (Oxford, 1974), 160–81; Thompson, *English Landed Society*, 231–52.

[77] Or 'Blackwoodsmen'. *Blackwood's Edinburgh Magazine* provided a forum for their jeremiads against 'fancy farming'.

[78] John Beckett, *The Rise and Fall of the Grenvilles: Dukes of Buckingham and Chandos, 1710 to 1921* (Manchester, 1994), 192–225.

With debts of over £1,500,000, Buckingham solaced his poverty by burying himself in historical scholarship.

COMMERCE AND THE QUASI-PROFESSIONS

George Canning, the most brilliant of later Pittites, had no wish to be a landed proprietor, was bored by the country, refused to hunt, and was no admirer of hills, vales, woods, or water for their own sakes. 'They must be well tenanted to make me look at them with delight.'[79] The source of delight was probably a sense that England was doing well, that food supplies were safe, that society was prospering harmoniously, and that the earth was being utilized efficiently. For people like him, professional imperatives were at least as strong as commercial ones, though as will become clear the dividing line was often blurred.

Because farming was increasingly regarded as an industry rather than a way of life, large landlords now relied on stewards, the most famous of whom was James Loch, overseer to the vast Sutherland holdings as well as helping to manage the Egerton, Carlisle, Bridgewater, Dudley, and Keith estates. Stewards were backed up by a panoply of estate agents, auctioneers, auditors, land and tithe surveyors, enclosure commissioners, and attorneys. These agricultural professionals lived mainly in country and market towns like the fictional cathedral city of Barchester, but from about 1790 it was increasingly common for them to join the throng of ex-businessmen building villas with substantial gardens, or even ten-acre farms, a few miles outside town. Some of them became cultivators in their own right, and some eventually found their way into the ranks of the gentry. Almost all of Jane Austen's real-life neighbours in Hampshire were nouveaux riches rather than old gentry.[80]

According to Colquhoun, there were about 1,000 'eminent clergymen' of the Established Church, most of them based in rural areas and earning on average £500 per annum. Traditionally the vast majority had been men of humble birth, incorporated into polite society by way of Oxford and Cambridge, like mid-twentieth-century grammar school boys. They were lackeys of the landed class, complicit but subordinate members of a squire–parson alliance, and their implicit role was to preach deference in the countryside. By the 1790s, however, a growing number of wealthier clergymen were becoming landowners in their own right. With the tendency for squires to move to new manor houses some way outside the village, many vicars followed suit, abandoning their old dwellings by the church and building new stone houses alongside their patrons, while those that stayed put 'improved' their rectories and parsonages with

---

[79] Wendy Hinde, *George Canning* (1973), 89.
[80] Claire Tomalin, *Jane Austen: A Life* (1997), 85–100.

extensions and sash windows.[81] There was also a striking increase in the number of clergy who doubled as JPs, from about 11 per cent of all magistrates in 1761 to over 25 per cent in 1831. By then, conversely, as many as one in six of all beneficed clergymen was also an active magistrate, leading critics to complain that such 'squarsons' were engaged in the contradiction of punishing parishioners with one hand and absolving them with the other. The rise in clerical status meant that landlords were increasingly inclined to present their own sons to livings in their gift, with the result that by the end of the period probably one in five of clergymen was related by birth or marriage to the aristocracy or gentry.[82] There was still a squire–parson alliance, but on subtly more equal terms than before. The 'new clergyman' invested in the funds, leading to the witticism that he had 'forsaken Scripture for scrip', but many of them, and especially those of an evangelical bent, took a far more professional approach to the vocation of saving souls than their huntin', shootin', and fishin' predecessors.

Superficially at least, professionalism was a marked feature of the period. For example, in the eighteenth century there were farriers. But then in 1791 a college was opened in London offering a three-year course of study in animal medicine, and five years later the Army Board formally recognized the category of veterinary surgeons. In 1828 two periodicals were founded, the *Farrier and Naturalist* (which soon changed its name to the more clinical sounding *Hippiatrist*) and *The Veterinian*. In 1844 the Privy Council granted the London College a charter, so that it became the Royal College of Veterinary Surgeons with its own coat of arms, and in 1852 the first register of veterinary practitioners was published. It contained 1,733 names.[83]

This chronology was fairly typical, and many other so-called professions followed a similar trajectory. Although it is impossible to be sure how many practitioners there were, the mid-nineteenth-century estimate shown in Table 3.4 is probably fairly accurate.[84] Army and Navy officers are slightly anomalous inclusions in this context, although a degree of professionalization was forced on them by the protracted state of warfare. Their main shortcomings related to education and training, where a certain amateurishness was encouraged as a riposte to Napoleon's military dictatorship. Like most young officers, Wellington learned his craft on the job, and neither the Royal Military College at Sandhurst[85] nor the Royal Military Academy at Woolwich brought much improvement before the 1840s, when it began to dawn on officers that the other

---

[81] Irene Collins, *Jane Austen and the Clergy* (1993), 68–9. For a fictional case, see below, pp. 255–7.

[82] Peter Virgin, *The Church in an Age of Negligence: Ecclesiastical Structure and Problems of Church Reform 1700–1840* (Cambridge, 1989), 81, 115–25, 261.

[83] Iain Pattison, *The British Veterinary Profession 1791–1948* (1983), 1–47.

[84] H. Byerley Thomson, *The Choice of a Profession* (1857), 6–8.

[85] Founded in 1801–2, transferred to Sandhurst in 1812.

TABLE 3.4. *Estimated number of 'professional workers', 1857*

Barristers	3,111
Attorneys, solicitors	13,256
Physicians	2,238
Apothecaries, surgeons	15,163
Army, Navy officers	11,087
Local government officers	29,785
Indian civil servants in UK	3,708
Home civil servants	37,698
Anglican clergymen	18,587

ranks were frequently better informed than themselves. This failure to professionalize is often blamed on post-Waterloo complacency and the dead hands of the commanders-in-chief, Hill and Wellington, but the real problem was that opportunities for promotion and achievement had come to a sudden halt. In 1815 the total number of non-commissioned officers and men was very nearly 234,000, or 2.5 per cent of the population, but this had fallen by 1820 to under 115,000, or 1.1 per cent, and by 1825 to under 100,000, or 0.9 per cent. In the same period hundreds of officers had to be put on the retired list: in 1831 there were fewer than 6,000 serving officers, while more than 8,500 languished on half-pay. It was only later with the establishment of permanent colonial garrisons abroad that the Army could begin to be regarded as a regular career.[86]

On the other hand, the social composition of the officers' mess was broadening gradually. Most commissions and promotions in the Army had to be purchased, and it might cost anything up to £10,000 to become a cavalry officer.[87] Since at the same time pay was low and mess life expensive, all but the wealthy were excluded. Traditionally it had been argued that the Army needed to be led by aristocratic officers, if only because it was the thin red line that would protect the propertied classes from social upheaval like that of the 1640s, but by the nineteenth century this argument was seldom heard and in fact the military absorbed a good deal of new wealth. Only 21 per cent of British officers were aristocrats in 1830, 32 per cent were landed gentry, while the remaining 47 per cent were from professional or business backgrounds. By 1854 the corresponding figures were 13, 25, and 62 per cent.[88] The Army provided a means by which new

[86] Hew Strachan, *Wellington's Legacy: The Reform of the British Army 1830–54* (Manchester, 1984), 109–45; Edward M. Spiers, *The Army and Society 1815–1914* (1980), 1–96.

[87] C. B. Otley, 'The Social Origins of British Army Officers', *Sociological Review*, 18 (1970), 213–39.

[88] P. E. Razzell, 'Social Origins of Officers in the Indian and British Home Army, 1758–1862', *Journal of the Society for Army Historical Research*, 37 (1959), 186.

wealth could attain immediate status, while less well-off aristocrats chafed to find that they could not keep up with the buoyant market price of commissions. Paradoxically the abolition of purchase in 1871 may have led to a narrowing of social intake, as public school and university-based recruitment served to filter out socially unacceptable aspirants more efficiently than money had been able to do.

The Navy was more socially exclusive than the Army (which might explain why a greater proportion of its leading officers were Foxite Whigs). Statistics are available for only just over half of those who became officers, but on that basis 39.4 per cent came from aristocratic or gentry families during the war years, and 45.4 per cent in the thirty-five years following. About one-third of entrants had fathers who were themselves naval officers, while 20 per cent or so came from other professions. As for the sons of businessmen and merchants, the need for talent wherever it could be found boosted this figure to about 4 per cent in wartime, but between 1814 and 1849 it was less than 0.5 per cent. Finally 120 officers are known to have had working-class backgrounds in wartime, a staggering 6.7 per cent, but none at all were appointed during the following thirty-five years.[89] In 1814 the Secretary to the Admiralty, J. W. Croker, reassured one of the Government's titled supporters that, 'except in extraordinary instances where officers may have acquired publick notice by some distinguished service, promotion is obtained by Interest'.[90]

Perhaps because they were centred on the metropolis, barristers led the move towards professionalization, being the first to issue an annual register of practitioners. Traditionally the best preparation for a legal career was a classical education, the best hope of advancement was an influential patron, and the usual object was to achieve social status, leisure, respect, and possibly public office.[91] From the 1780s, however, an alternative ideal began to develop based on 'service to society'. Skill and success became the main criteria for promotion, while training and testing came to be regarded as indispensable. True, some of these developments took place very slowly—in particular, examinations were fiercely resisted—but they established norms which other occupations would seek to emulate. The driving force behind all this was probably increased competition. According to the *Law Lists* the number of barristers rose from 257 in 1780 to 880 in 1810 and 3,268 in 1850 (all but sixty of whom operated in London). Admittedly, these figures are deceptive in so far as the number of *practising* barristers in 1850 was probably lower than 1,000. The rest were sons of aristocrats and gentry, who studied at the Inns of Court in order to gain expertise that

[89] Michael Lewis, *The Navy in Transition 1814–1864: A Social History* (1965), 21–6.

[90] *The Diary of Joseph Farington*, ed. Kenneth Garlick, Angus Macintyre, Kathryn Cave, and Evelyn Newby (New Haven, 1978–98), xiii. 4547.

[91] An exemplar was John Scott, Earl of Eldon (1751–1838), a coal-fitter's son who rose via the Bar to be Solicitor-General and then Attorney-General and finally Lord Chancellor.

might prove useful to them in estate management, or else to gain paper qualifications that might enhance their claims to become a JP or MP. Even so, there was a significant real increase in the number of practitioners, meaning that they were forced to hone their skills and vie for business. Besides riches, it would seem that most barristers' ambition was no longer to be accepted by landed society, but to rise to the head of the profession. In the central superior courts, the proportion of judges whose fathers had been landed gentry declined from nearly half of those appointed during 1727–60, to 30 per cent during 1760–90, and less than 20 per cent during 1790–1820. In the latter period there was also, conversely, a dramatic change in the career choices of judges' sons, who, instead of becoming country gentlemen and cashing in on high wartime prices, mainly followed their fathers into the law. This may explain why, during the second quarter of the century, judges reduced their investments in land and ceased to practise primogeniture, another trend which other professionals would later follow.[92]

Something which did not change was the refusal of barristers to take fees directly from clients, which would have looked too much like common trading. Instead they insisted on dealing through attorneys, almost two-thirds of whom in the eighteenth century were younger sons with gentry and mainly lesser gentry backgrounds.[93] Even so, attorneydom had never enjoyed the prestige of the Bar, being almost a byword for sharp practice or 'pettifogging'. There was now pressure to increase its status by introducing formal education and examinations in place of apprenticeship, which Parliament had stipulated as a necessary preliminary to qualification. As far back as 1739—and possibly earlier— a Society of Gentlemen Practisers in the Courts of Law and Equity had been set up to enforce standards and exclude mountebanks, but little changed until the establishment of local law societies after 1786.[94] By this time attorneys were so far along the road to respectability and wealth that there was no danger of them playing a revolutionary role like their counterparts in France, while fewer joined Corresponding societies than served as officers of the militia, or as secretaries to Church and King clubs and Reeves associations for the Protection of Property.[95] Increasing respectability was monitored by a shift in terminology ('There are no such things as *attorneys* now in England, they are all turned into solicitors and agents, just as every *shop* is become a *warehouse*, and every *service* a *situation*'[96]) and by the formation of national organizations such as the Law Society, founded in 1823 and chartered in 1831. Lest this suggestion of an inherent

---

[92] Daniel Duman, *The Judicial Bench in England 1727–1875* (1982), 8, 25–6, 175–82; id., *The English and Colonial Bars in the Nineteenth Century* (1983), 203.

[93] Michael Miles, ' "A Haven for the Privileged": Recruitment into the Profession of Attorney in England, 1709–1792', *Society History*, 11 (1986), 197–210; Robert Robson, *The Attorney in Eighteenth-Century England* (Cambridge, 1959), 35–51.

[94] At least seventeen, including societies in Yorkshire (1786), Leeds (1805), and Manchester (1809).

[95] Robson, *The Attorney*, 153–4.   [96] Maria Edgeworth, *Patronage* (1814), ii. 269.

tendency towards professionalization should seem too whiggish, it is worth adding that some of the salient developments happened accidentally. For example, Pitt had no other object in mind but to raise revenue when he imposed a stamp duty on the annual practice licences of attorneys, solicitors, and articled clerks, but when he followed this up with a duty on conveyances, he was forced for practical reasons to exempt those that had been drawn up by unqualified persons. This was naturally resented by the attorneys, who lobbied furiously for several years, and when the time came for him to increase the duty in 1804, he agreed in return to grant qualified lawyers a monopoly of conveyancing for profit. This species of work required large amounts of deeds and other papers to be filed, which in turn forced attorneys to spend more time at their office desks instead of hanging around Nandos (just one of the many taverns and coffee-houses where they had once been used to tout for clients). And so gradually it came about that the public was forced to go to law instead of the other way around.

Eighteenth-century medicine, like the law, was highly stratified. The university-trained physicians enjoyed much more status than surgeons and apothecaries. The former were widely regarded as manual workers, while the latter were classed as salesmen, dispensing physic to the nation with as much discrimination as Coleridge dispensed metaphysics. But even Fellows of the Royal College of Physicians, despite their wealth and social acceptability, enjoyed less professional deference than barristers. There were many reasons for this, not least their own helplessness in the face of most diseases, especially cholera and the other fevers which regularly ravaged urban areas. And, whereas lawyers increasingly presented themselves as mediators between their clients and some impartial notion of justice, doctors were themselves more like clients, competing by means of advertisements for the custom of aristocratic patrons, who dictated the terms of the relationship. In such a climate fashionable doctors came and went as rapidly as fashionable cures. Above all a successful doctor needed ingratiating manners, fluency in Latin, and a taste for medico-philosophical speculation. Partly because social codes made a taboo of physical examination, and partly because of religious prejudice against experiments on corpses, English medicine was slow to absorb the developments in anatomical pathology that were exciting the clinical schools of Paris. This is not to say that doctors were uninterested in the scientific side of medicine—many of them experimented in the privacy of the laboratory—but their first duty was simply to cure or relieve symptoms, however temporarily, and they tended to keep such therapeutic discoveries to themselves, rather than adding to the stock of clinical knowledge.[97] Finally, whereas the legal profession was largely able to control the

---

[97] N. D. Jewson, 'Medical Knowledge and the Patronage System in 18th Century England', *Sociology*, 8 (1974), 369–85.

teaching of common law and equity in the Inns of Court, allowing the universities a foothold only in civil law, outside Scotland most formal medical education was restricted to Oxford and Cambridge, neither of which was well geared to the promotion of applied science.

Important steps towards a more professional approach were taken in the early nineteenth century, partly as a consequence of the conflict with France, which, like most wars, led to important medical advances. Surgery benefited from more than two decades of battlefield carnage, while physicians learned from the West Indies campaigns, in which the overwhelming majority of casualties were caused by malaria, yellow fever, typhus, and dysentery. Of 18,000 soldiers sent to Saint-Domingue in 1795–6, more than 12,000 died; one regiment of 494 light dragoons lost 305 men to disease and only one to the enemy. The Army Medical Board (established in 1793) responded by ordering that soldiers be inoculated against smallpox, and then made a deliberate attempt to improve the status of Army doctors—physicians only ranked as captains and surgeons as lieutenants— by restricting military appointments to graduates of Oxford and Cambridge or members and licentiates of the London College of Physicians.[98]

Like attorneys, surgeons and apothecaries sought to enhance their status through new institutional practices, which the physicians by and large resisted. The Royal Society of Surgeons was chartered in 1800, and an Act of 1815 empowered the Society of Apothecaries to determine qualifying standards, examine candidates, and fine unauthorized practitioners. It has rightly been described as providing 'a model for nineteenth-century professional organisa- tion' and as marking 'the emergence' of the general practitioner,[99] though the speed with which it took effect should not be exaggerated, and it was not until after the Medical Act of 1858 that any effective rooting-out of charlatans took place. Meanwhile, medical societies proliferated—the Provincial Medical and Surgical Association (now the British Medical Association) held its first meeting at the Worcester Infirmary in 1832—and medical journals began to report clin- ical findings impartially and for the common benefit. More than any other it was *The Lancet*, founded in 1823 by radicals Thomas Wakley and William Cobbett, that made clinical research seem central to orthodox medical practice, though it was bitterly attacked for doing so by some elite doctors, who protested that only they should be allowed to dispense medical wisdom to fledgling doctors.

Like medics, engineers benefited from being useful in wartime, but their more lasting contribution was domestic, for Britain's industrial lead owed a great deal to applied technology. The new roads, canals, railways, tunnels, bridges,

---

[98] Michael Duffy, *Soldiers, Sugar, and Seapower: The British Expeditions to the West Indies and the War against Revolutionary France* (Oxford, 1987), 326–67.

[99] W. J. Reader, *Professional Men: The Rise of the Professional Classes in Nineteenth-Century England* (1966), 41, 51–3, 164.

cuttings, viaducts, mines, harbours, factories, furnaces, engines, and steamships ensured that earlier nineteenth-century engineers were invested with a prestige that would surprise and gratify their twenty-first-century successors. Among the most iconic figures of the age were the elder John Rennie (1761–1821), who has been described as 'a new type of engineer, in whom theory and practice were blended';[100] Thomas Telford, designer of breathtaking roads and bridges; and Isambard Kingdom Brunel, who masterminded the Great Western Railway from 1833 to 1846 and launched the first giant steamship (236 × 35 feet) in 1838. More prosaically, the spread of advanced industrial technology created a breed of travelling mechanics whose role it was to service new machinery. Some classic symptoms of the professionalization process were also evident, including a gradual differentiation as sub-specialities were recognized in turn (e.g. the Institution of Civil Engineers in 1818, the Institute of Mechanical Engineers in 1847).

Architects profited immensely from the growth of towns and of population generally, which naturally led to a great deal of speculative development for housing. Before the 1780s it had not always been easy to distinguish them from builders, masons, and other craftsmen, but gradually the concept of design led to a functional differentiation as John Eveleigh, John Nash, and others were commissioned to provide elegant façades to bog-standard and often sub-standard structures. Hull was just one of many corporations that began to employ their own architects, and so too did some improvement commissions. So, whereas in order to flourish it had once been necessary to have aristocratic patrons or contacts in the building trade, it was now possible to rely on reputation, the important thing being to win favourable reviews in the growing number of magazines devoted to building aesthetics. Successful architects could now live handsomely from fees—Robert Smirke's estate was valued for probate at £90,000—and it therefore became necessary to police the profession.[101] For a long time there were only a few informal clubs and societies to bolster a sense of exclusiveness, but the Institute of British Architects was founded in 1835 and chartered two years later. As a result it gradually became possible to establish controls over recruitment and pupillage, to prevent poaching, and to protect members from dissatisfied customers—except that it was no longer fashionable to think of them as customers, 'client' being increasingly the term of preference.

Society doctors, lawyers, architects, and engineers clearly belonged to the fundholding upper-middle class, and it is customary to refer to them as members of the new 'professions', a useful but possibly misleading term. The trends

[100] W. H. G. Armytage, *A Social History of Engineering*, 4th edn. (1976), 90–1.

[101] Howard Colvin, *A Biographical Dictionary of British Architects 1600–1840*, 3rd edn. (New Haven, 1995), 29–46.

outlined here quickened after 1846, so that by the later nineteenth century almost every branch of white-collar employment from academia to accountancy had divided into sub-specialities, founded societies, launched journals, begun to discipline members, and closed ranks by imposing qualifications, standards, and other restraints on trade.[102] These trends, a middle-class variant of trade union-ism, were so powerful that it is all too easy to assume that developments in the first half of the nineteenth must have foreshadowed them. However, it is questionable whether the modern concept of professionalism throws any helpful light on atti-tudes in the late Hanoverian period. Certainly the *idea* was widely subscribed to, which is why the rhetoric of the Public Accounts Commissioners was so effective politically. It may be, however, that the ideal was so strong simply because the real-ity was weak, that professionalism was a theory before ever it was a fact, and that it was a mainly defensive response to rampant consumerism and commercial exploitation. The fourfold increase in practising barristers, especially in Chancery, might in theory have led to a reduction in fees, but in fact it led to a cut-throat com-petition in which rewards for the successful rose enormously while others failed altogether. The rise in the number of attorneys was less rapid, from about 5,300 in 1800 to 8,700 in 1832, but much greater than that of those sections of the popula-tion which provided them with business.[103] Since the nature of their business was less obviously cut-throat, the only way to maintain fees was by controlling recruit-ment, and the development of such controls almost certainly had more to do with commercial calculation than with a desire for professional efficiency.

It has also been argued that in some ways legal practice had become *less* professional since 1700, and that despite improvements from the 1820s it was not until after 1850 that the law reached seventeenth-century levels of efficiency and fairness. One measure of this was the declension in legal education under the apprenticeship system; another was the very low level of litigation as com-pared with the Elizabethan and early Stuart periods. There are various possible reasons. Perhaps attorneys encouraged clients to seek other means of settling disputes, as they themselves took on more conveyancing and work connected with wills, trusts, and marriage settlements.[104] The funding system probably reduced the need for private debt litigation, while economic expansion may have enabled disputes to be reconciled more easily without recourse to law. But it might also have been that potential litigants lost confidence in civil justice because of its procrastinations, perceived arbitrariness, and the general 'ossification' of its 'bureaucratic practices'.[105] Whatever the cause, if the

[102] Harold Perkin, *The Rise of Professional Society: England since 1880* (1989).

[103] About one-third of attorneys were in London.

[104] M. Miles, 'Country Attorneys c.1750–1800', in G. R. Rubin and David Sugarman (eds.), *Law, Economy and Society, 1750–1914: Essays in the History of English Law* (1984).

[105] Christopher W. Brooks, *Lawyers, Litigation and English Society since 1450* (1998), 27–147, esp. 61.

revisionist view is correct, historians will have to revise the common assumption that a stable judicial system was one of the factors conducive to economic enterprise.

Again, the Apothecaries Act of 1815 was described above as providing a model for professional organization, but it may also have been a response to the fact that a huge number of medics—perhaps as many as 300—faced discharge from the Army and into civilian practice. Overcrowding led to a reduction in fees,[106] one reason why doctors were more likely to adopt a radical political line than lawyers (their employment as Poor Law officers was another). As with the law, medical practice was in many respects less well regulated than it had been before 1700 when, albeit on a strictly local basis, craft and mercantile guilds had exercised some of the controls now regarded as professional, imposing standards, arbitrating internal disputes, establishing criteria for qualification, and eliminating incompetent or unlicensed practitioners.[107] These regulations declined rapidly during the eighteenth century, even in old market towns, while in the new rapidly growing centres of population there were no such restrictions at all. Consequently, even successful doctors had to compete with the pedlars of fringe and fairground cures for the favours of a susceptible public. This was the golden age of patent medicines—Morisons Pills, Dr Norris's Fever Drops, Squire's Original Grand Elixir, and Graham's Celestial or Magnetico-electrico bed (1780), inspired by the seraglio. ('Any gentleman and his lady desirous of progeny, and wishing to spend an evening in the Celestial apartment, which coition may, on compliment of a £50 bank note, be permitted to partake of the heavenly joys it affords by causing immediate conception, accompanied by the soft music.'[108]) In an age of rampant consumerism and unrestrained market forces, commercial priorities characterized all medical practice, and not just that of the quacks.[109] Likewise engineers, architects, brokers, and accountants were first and foremost businessmen, some of whom grew rich from speculative developments, while others suffered in terms of income and prestige as more and more middle-class sons competed for business.[110] In all three cases recruitment was mainly by apprenticeship, conventionally a hallmark of trade and industry, while its role in medical education actually increased during much of the nineteenth century. Indeed, if being trained in dedicated institutions is considered a prerequisite of professional status, only lawyers and clergy qualified. But while the religious

---

[106] Irvine Loudon, *Medical Care and the General Practitioner 1750–1850* (Oxford, 1986), 208–27.

[107] Margaret Pelling, 'Medical Practice in Early Modern England: Trade or Profession?', in Wilfrid Prest (ed.), *The Professions in Early Modern England* (Beckenham, 1987).

[108] Roy Porter, *Health for Sale: Quackery in England 1660–1850* (Manchester, 1989), 161–2.

[109] Ibid. 1–59, 222–39.

[110] F. Musgrove, 'Middle-Class Education and Employment in the Nineteenth Century', *EconHR* 12 (1959–60), 99–111.

revival undoubtedly bred a number of highly dedicated ministers, this was matched by a competition for rich benefices and a vogue for fashionable preaching, especially in London. For all these reasons it may be proper to conclude that a commercial ethos was more significant than the cult of professionalism, which in turn may have been a defensive response to the fact that commercial monopolies were coming under attack.

If it is granted that the groups discussed in this section belonged to an haute bourgeoisie or upper-middle class, can it be said that that class was 'made' from the 1780s onwards? After all, 'property' had long since signified not just real estate but paper securities, trading rights, deposits with insurance companies, and scientific discoveries, while engineers, architects, attorneys, sea captains, and music teachers had existed for centuries. On the other hand, it was only in the 1780s that such people began to identify themselves as like-minded, or presumed to formulate public opinion independently (and sometimes in defiance) of aristocratic norms; only then that they established professional and commercial associations with the aim of asserting a national as well as merely local importance; only then that their voice—sonorous, knowing, oracular, collusive—began to prevail in the public consciousness, largely via new periodicals such as *The Quarterly, Edinburgh, London, Westminster*, and *British and Foreign*. The reasons—largely top-down and political—why this happened at that time are complex, but in a nutshell the American debacle discredited the aristocracy and created a moral vacuum, which the moralistic upper-middle classes were able to fill, thanks in part to the fact that the staggering growth of the national debt had placed them as fundholders in a creditor, that is morally superior, relationship to the State.

It may be helpful to clarify the argument at this point by emphasizing three things. First, and as already stated, the categories 'upper-middle class' and 'gentlemanly capitalist' do not exclude the landed interest as such, but only those members of it who felt left behind by the development of fundholding and financial investment. Secondly, while the upper-middle classes and gentlemanly capitalists identified with metropolitan values, a number of them actually lived in the English regions. For them the culture of the West End was a form of false consciousness, while they themselves might be described as subaltern members of the upper-middle class. Lastly, it is common for gentlemanly capitalism to be identified with the 'City interest', meaning the worlds of high finance and international commerce, but this too is problematic for any period before the late nineteenth century, since the 'City' remained diversified throughout the period, with many firms dependent on mercantilist regulations and strongly resistant to the policies pursued by Pitt and his successors. The values of capitalism and professionalism divided the business world just as they did landed society.

BUSINESS CLASSES

Businessmen, meaning those who engaged in finance and commerce, made up the third and final category of upper-middle-class membership. By 1783 London had taken over from Amsterdam as the world's leading financial centre. In addition to the Bank of England (from now on the Bank for short) there were some seventy private banks with a combined daily turnover of about £5 million. Some were located in the West End, their main function being to furnish lawyers and landlords with loans and mortgages. The rest were City-based, and handled commercial bills or served the stock market. Some had restricted functions, such as Cocks & Co., the nabobs' bank,[111] and later on Glyn Mills & Co., known as the railway bank. The money market ('Change Alley') institutionalized rapidly after the reorganization of the Stock Exchange in 1802,[112] when firms began to specialize as stockbrokers, bill-brokers, discount houses, or whatever. In the rest of England and in Wales (but not Scotland) banking facilities had traditionally lagged well behind, but the situation was changing as the number of country banks rose from about 120 in 1784, to 280 in 1793, and then to nearly 700 by 1815.[113] A number of local banking networks grew up, such as the Gurneys in Norwich and Backhouse and Co. in Darlington (both Quaker), Beckett's Bank in the West Riding, Jones Loyd & Co. in Manchester. Many were started by tradesmen, attorneys, and tax-receivers who wished to do a little banking on the side.

Nearly all commercial transactions of any size were conducted with banknotes, bills of exchange, or accommodation paper rather than in cash (or coin). Circulation tended to be restricted to particular regions, Bank of England notes (Bank notes for short) circulating in and around London,[114] and country banks providing paper currency for their own districts. By depositing sums with London banks, which they were then allowed to make drafts on, the latter were able to conduct business with distant parts where their own notes were unacceptable. Conversely, by giving or receiving coin and Bank notes to settle the accounts of their country correspondents, the London banks acted as clearing houses for business deals throughout the country. This all amounted to a complex series of transactions, but the main effect was that banks in the agricultural South and East, where there were surplus funds, deposited money in London by investing in bills of exchange, while in the industrial areas banks which had lent too much maintained liquidity by sending bills to London for rediscount.

---

[111] 'Nabob' was the name given to men who had made their pile in India and had come back home to flaunt it.

[112] E. Victor Morgan and W. A. Thomas, *The Stock Exchange: Its History and Functions* (1962), 68–77.

[113] L. S. Pressnell, *Country Banking in the Industrial Revolution* (Oxford, 1956), 11.

[114] The other London banks did not issue notes.

So, despite its width, the system was remarkably centralized, with the country banks dependent on the London banks and the London banks dependent on the Bank of England. The suspension of cash payments in 1797 increased this tendency since it made country banknotes convertible into Bank notes, which were themselves made legal tender. After the 1825–6 financial crisis, partly blamed on excessive country issues, the Bank of England sought to tighten its grip on the system even further by opening branches in Manchester, Liverpool, Bristol, Birmingham, Leicester, and Leeds, while in the 1830s it took tentative steps towards its later role as a central bank by maintaining its rate of discount slightly above the market rate, becoming in effect the lender of last resort. Contrariwise, the system opened out to some extent with the rapid spread of joint-stock banking after 1826, notably around Liverpool and Manchester.

By 1844 about 170 out of 950 joint-stock companies were life and or fire insurance offices with limited liability. Insurance selling had been established long before 1783, but there was now an explosion of business amounting to what has been called 'a minor social revolution'.[115] The boom in marine insurance, dominated by Lloyds of London, was naturally war-related, with a tremendous crescendo during 1810–14 and an even more dramatic diminuendo thereafter. The value of property insured against fire rose by about 50 per cent in real terms during 1788–1808, and then more than doubled in the following twenty years. This was due partly to the greater number and size of warehouses and industrial premises, but also to an increased demand for security: according to contemporary estimates the proportion of all property insured rose from about one-third to two-thirds between 1800 and the 1860s. The really dramatic surge, however, came in life insurance, although precise values are unavailable. At the start of the Napoleonic wars there were only five firms offering this facility, but about fifteen new offices were founded during the wars, another twenty-nine during 1815–30, and fifty-six more during 1830–44. The value of life insurance per head of the population increased by at least five times during the first half of the nineteenth century, standing at more than £5 in 1852, comfortably in advance of Germany (£0.1), France (£0.05), and all other countries. This could not have happened without the development of sophisticated mathematics to facilitate the compilation of actuarial tables,[116] nor would it have happened without a growing desire for security (the consequence perhaps of increased *in*security due to economic

---

[115] Barry Supple, *The Royal Exchange Assurance: A History of British Insurance 1720–1970* (Cambridge, 1970), 103–20.

[116] Notably by Benjamin Gompertz in 1825. The first published table of life assurance mortality based on data pooled from a range of companies was in 1843. Before that insurers did business on the basis of private estimates which they kept to themselves in the same way that 18th-century doctors guarded their treatments. An Institute of Actuaries was formed in 1848. Steven Haberman and Trevor A. Sibbett (eds.), *History of Actuarial Science* (1995), vol. i, pp. xx, xxvi–xxvii.

and political changes), but supply-side factors must also have been at work. Selling life, marine, or fire insurance was a means of mobilizing spare capital, and by the second quarter of the century it was common for lenders to make loans conditional on taking out a life insurance policy as security. At the same time the Sun Life and Fire Offices supplemented their traditional mortgage business with large landlords by lending to leaseholders, dock companies, and a number of public commissioners (e.g. Woods and Forests, the Metropolitan Commissioners of Sewers).[117] The development of with-profits endowment policies attracted many investors and further accentuated the extent to which, as a witness to the Select Committee on Joint-Stock Companies commented in 1841, 'insurance has become an adjunct to money-lending'.[118]

There was no clear demarcation between banking, insurance, and commerce, with businessmen moving easily among all three. In Leeds, for example, leading merchants anticipated the role of banks, circulating cash and bills throughout West Yorkshire, accepting deposits or lending money to each other on bond and to the gentry on mortgage. Many also became partners in the rash of local banks that were founded after 1790. These dealt increasingly in government securities, which with land was the main area of mercantile investment until the 1820s.[119] As for commerce proper, there were enormous fortunes to be made in international trade as it expanded rapidly after 1783, with firms specializing either functionally—e.g. in shipping, sugar, tobacco, and textiles—or else regionally in Europe, the Levant, Hudson's Bay, the East Indies, the West Indies, South America, or the United States. Below the merchant princes came various sorts of middlemen: wholesalers, corn factors, brokers, acceptance men, commission agents, the latter mainly persons on the make who lived abroad. Networks were established in all the leading ports with the result that, whereas before 1750 and after 1870 mercantile wealth was concentrated in the hands of a relatively small number of mainly London-based firms, in the period under review it was distributed much more widely. As a result London lost some of its market share of international trade to ports such as Liverpool, and to inland warehouse centres such as Manchester. To counteract this trend, however, after 1815 the provinces became increasingly dependent on a new breed of specialists based in London, the merchant bankers. Their most important function was to accept (guarantee) short-term bills—mainly provincial merchants' bills on London—thereby effectively financing Britain's international trade. A secondary function was to issue long-term securities to governments and increasingly the utilities, such as gas and water companies.

---

[117] P. G. M. Dickson, *The Sun Insurance Office 1710–1960: The History of Two and a Half Centuries of British Insurance* (1960), 249–51.   [118] *PP* 1844 vii. 21; Supple, *Royal Exchange Assurance*, 116.
[119] R. G. Wilson, *Gentlemen Merchants: The Merchant Community in Leeds 1700–1830* (Manchester, 1971), 153–9.

By far the most important merchant bankers were Nathan Mayer Rothschild and Alexander Baring. Born in Frankfurt the third of five brothers, Rothschild moved in 1798 to Manchester where he set up as a warehouseman, importing goods from all over in return for cottons. He expanded very rapidly, mainly thanks to his amazing liquidity, which in turn was due to his fraternal contacts and especially Amschel, the investment broker to the Elector of Hesse-Cassel, the biggest moneylender in Europe. Drawing on extensive credit facilities in Hamburg and Frankfurt, Rothschild would pay in cash while prices were low and accept tiny profit margins, relying on volume and rapid turnover to outdistance his rivals. In the same way, after setting up a discount business, he deliberately charged low rates of commission. He gradually moved to London between 1808 and 1811, made killings in the bullion and securities markets, and turned himself into first the British Government's and then the allies' unofficial banker. He amassed gold by buying small amounts at a time, so as not to disturb the money markets unduly, and by the time the war ended he was owed well over £1 million by the British Government alone. Alexander Baring was the son of Sir Francis Baring, who in 1763 had helped to found a firm of import and export agents that later metamorphosed into a merchant bank. By the time of Francis's death in 1810 Barings had unrivalled worldwide investments, was helping to finance Anglo-American trade, and was acting as banker to the US Government. The rise of Rothschild and Barings was a serious challenge to the old monopolistic corporations that had previously dominated the City, such as the East India Company, the shipping interest, and the Bank of England. More internationally focused than those older interests with their strong colonial links, the new breed of merchant bankers nevertheless shared with them a close—enemies said cosy—relationship with the Government.

Thanks to its merchant bankers, the City of London turned into a market for discounting bills and for settling international payments in sterling. This undoubtedly set the stage for England's dominance of international trade, though a price to be paid was that their business, being international, was not geared to the needs of the domestic economy. The function of merchant bankers was usually to guarantee the final payment of bills for a commission, while others—landlords, insurers, or joint-stock bankers—provided the actual working capital and held the bills until maturity. Merchant bankers needed a reputation for honest dealing and contacts with the rich, but since most were not wealthy themselves, they constituted a source of instability. Eighty per cent of London merchants went bankrupt during 1781–3. Many who switched out of European markets during the wars were ruined in Buenos Aires (1806) and Rio (1808–9). Ninety per cent of London's Continental houses, and 80 per cent of Manchester's manufacturers (many of whom had dabbled in merchanting) were eliminated within twenty years of the battle of Waterloo, while of the nineteen largest Leeds merchant firms in 1781, only five still existed in 1830.[120] There were more or less severe commercial crises in 1793, 1803, 1807–8, 1810–11, 1816, 1819, 1826, 1837, and 1841–2. Share prices collapsed spectacularly in 1793, 1797, and again in 1825–6 when 145 banks (including eighty country banks) failed. Even the Bank of England was in periodic jeopardy, forced to suspend payments in 1797, baled out in 1826 by Rothschild, and again by Baring in 1839. Throughout the period, most capital investment was subject to unlimited liability, the main exceptions being joint-stock utilities, a situation which naturally attracted investments by adventurers who did not possess too much capital of their own, and so did not have much to lose.

This is important, because insecurity was endemic among the upper-middle classes as business crashes and rumours of crashes spread anxiety throughout the community. (Even holdings in the funds did not bring reassurance, given the underlying fear of revolution and radical demands for debt repudiation.) So-called gentlemanly capitalism turns out to have been a roller coaster, on which it was possible for individuals to rise to huge prosperity, only for the next wave of bankruptcies to plunge them into economic doom and social obloquy.

PRODUCERS AND DEALERS: THE MAKINGS OF A LESSER–MIDDLE CLASS?

Generally speaking bankers, merchants, and professionals distanced themselves, not only from less prosperous tradesmen and retailers (Cobden's 'shopocracy'), but also from the master manufacturers or industrial bourgeoisie, described here as a *lesser*-middle class.[121] Previously the line between manufacturing and trading had been blurred, and the word 'entrepreneur' had implied a whole range of economic activities: inventing machines, managing labour, buying raw materials, transporting and selling finished goods, accounting, and advertising. This remained the case in many of the smaller provincial industrial centres like Halifax, Bradford, and Huddersfield, where the larger clothiers continued to function as merchant–manufacturers. In the larger provincial centres, however, a marked specialization of functions occurred.

Whereas merchants and financiers were locked into national and international systems, entrepreneurs were bound to their own industries and regions, and attempts to generalize about them have invariably foundered on problems of definition and comparison.[122] It made a difference whether they were

---

[120] Wilson, *Gentlemen Merchants*, 115.

[121] To distinguish it from the 'lower-middle class', a term used to depict white-collar working men such as clerks from the 1840s onwards. The term 'shopocracy' was apparently coined by the *Poor Man's Guardian* in 1832.

[122] One of the most honest attempts in this direction is François Crouzet, *The First Industrialists: The Problem of Origins* (Cambridge, 1985).

first-, second-, or third-generation, and whether they were still striving to succeed or had made their fortunes and now wished to relax and enjoy. Unlike the merchants and bankers dealing with goods, money, balance sheets, and bills, factory owners were primarily concerned with managing people, which naturally gave scope to personality differences. For every tyrannical and philistine Josiah Bounderby there was probably a John Thornton, honest, responsible, and caring of his workforce.[123] A further problem is that only a fraction of business records survive, and those that do tend to belong to the more resilient firms. Even the most distinguished sectoral study to date (Anthony Howe's on the Lancashire cotton magnates between 1830 and 1860) is based on only 351 out of what must have been up to 4,000 owners or partners, many of whom will have been less successful. These textile masters—mostly cotton-spinners and -weavers but also some calico-printers and -bleachers—are said to have composed 'the first distinctive industrial elite in British society'. They were mainly second- and third-generation entrepreneurs whose political time had come. The 1832 Reform Act ensured them a parliamentary vote, the Municipal Corporations Act of 1835 handed them control over local government, and the movement for the repeal of the Corn Laws provided cohesion and a sense of irresistible righteousness. Politically they were divided (with a modest preponderance towards the Liberal Party), and they differed on most issues other than free trade. Denominationally too they were a mixed bag—about half subscribed to the Church of England, 19 per cent were Unitarians, and 5 per cent Quakers (though thirty years earlier, before respectability set in, many more of their forebears would have been Dissenters). Even so, they were broadly at one in their basic values. They had no desire to overthrow the existing political system, being conscious of their growing muscle within it, as well as being conservative with a small 'c'. Having won esteem through local office-holding and charitable activity, they bristled with civic pride and municipal responsibility. They were rarely moved to sink their profits into land, as the Arkwrights and Peels had done in an earlier period, nor did they seek to assimilate into aristocratic society or adopt its values.[124] More pertinent for the present analysis is the fact that the cotton masters equally resisted metropolitanization. South Lancashire and north Cheshire formed their world, a cohesive world within which they mainly intermarried and were culturally self-sufficient—though it would also appear that by the 1850s some of them were investing heavily in railways and insurance, while others were increasingly reliant on rentier wealth.

---

[123] Bounderby was the odious industrialist in Charles Dickens's *Hard Times* (1854); Thornton was the firm but fair mill-owner in Elizabeth Gaskell's *North and South* (1854–5).

[124] Howe is emphatic on this point, though it would be interesting to know whether they did so after 1860, when more and more manufacturers' sons were sent away to public school (Anthony Howe, *The Cotton Masters 1830–1860* (Oxford, 1984), 62, 310–15).

Even before Samuel Smiles published *Self Help* in 1859, Victorians had convinced themselves that industry and engineering provided avenues for heroic individuals to climb from rags to riches. How far this actually happened is hard to say because of the different stories people told about themselves. Some, like the fictional Bounderby, will have exaggerated the poverty of their origins in order to emphasize their own merits, while others will have tried to pretend that their ancestors were gentler folk than was really the case. Probably just enough individuals made the great ascent to justify the myth, but very few, while equally few stooped downward from the landed classes to become entrepreneurs. The vast majority of the latter, unsurprisingly, came from that third of the total population which might be called middling. Of these, probably rather more than half were the sons of bankers, merchants, and other manufacturers, and rather less than half were born to farmers, clerks, managers, and craftsmen. Also, the proportion coming from better-off parents probably increased over time, as more and more industrialists inherited rather than fashioned their positions. By 1815 the amount of capital required to set up in cotton-spinning and lace-making was already sufficient to deter the small beginner.[125]

It was suggested above that factory owners, entrepreneurs, and industrialists (the terms are used here interchangeably) made up a lesser-middle class in order to differentiate them from the commercial and professional people, but this requires some explanation. It was certainly not a simple matter of wealth and lifestyle. Until quite recently it was assumed that entrepreneurs lived frugal lives so that they could plough profits back into the firm. The belief went with Weberian ideas of capitalist enterprise as a function of the Protestant ethic. It also seemed to make sense that Dissenters, being denied the status that went with office-holding, should have become manufacturers with the intention of building up the family business rather than to make quick money. And, of course, this *was* often the case, especially in a firm's early stages. To cite just one example, George Philips belonged to a younger branch of a landowning Methodist family. Having been left a lump sum but no estate, he proved willing to risk his capital in technological innovation. However, instead of seeking immediate gratification, he built his cotton firm up in the most frugal and gradual manner, eventually becoming the richest man in his native Manchester and a landed baronet in his own right.[126] On the other hand, there were other entrepreneurs who, so far from 'ploughing back', paid themselves handsome salaries and lived sumptuously.

---

[125] Katrina Honeyman, *Origins of Enterprise: Business Leadership in the Industrial Revolution* (Manchester, 1982), 57–171.

[126] D. Brown, 'From "Cotton Lord" to Landed Aristocrat: The Rise of Sir George Philips Bart., 1766–1847', *Historical Research*, 69 (1996), 62–82.

   The crucial distinction was that merchants, bankers, and professionals lent their profits by investing them—occasionally in industrial concerns—whereas manufacturers themselves were typically in the business of borrowing. However wealthy they might be, they were constantly required to *raise* both fixed and working capital in order to expand, re-equip, purchase raw materials, pay the weekly wage bill, or tide their firms over depressions. In so far as investing was a hallmark of the upper-middle class, entrepreneurs—being borrowers rather than lenders, and lacking liquid capital—did not qualify. So it was that in London, for example, overseas merchants (but not manufacturers) switched readily into high finance, while in Yorkshire too they moved their money increasingly into landed property, the funds, and canal shares. According to literary evidence it also seems that more members of the upper- than the lesser-middle class sought security for their families by purchasing life insurance policies. If so, one reason might be that manufacturers could expect their firms to provide for their dependants, whereas men who relied on their skills and know-how to bring in salaries, fees, or profits naturally fretted about what would happen after they died. In this respect, taking out insurance was an attempt to mitigate economic insecurity, hence the founding of such life insurance offices as the Clergy Mutual (1829), the Provident Clerks (1840), the Architects and Builders (1847), and the Schoolmasters and General (1851).

   The West Riding woollen and worsted industries provide two examples of how complex credit networks could be. The fast-growing worsted industry, which was based on 'putting out', dominated the infertile uplands north and west of Halifax, where a system of partible inheritance existed. Substantial cloth merchants supplied raw materials to hordes of domestic workers, who worked for wages while also practising small-scale subsistence agriculture. The woollen industry went back much further but advanced more slowly. Whereas merchant capital financed innovation in worsteds, woollens were mainly produced by small independent craftsmen. They owned their own tools and materials, but had little spare capital and operated on short-term credit supplied to them by import merchants and wool staplers. These artisans were mainly concentrated to the east of the worsted belt, in the more fertile valleys of the Aire and Calder, and they too operated as family units, combining textile production with commercial farming, either as freeholders or as tenants. In both industries these working arrangements came under great pressure from the 1790s onwards, owing to a massive expansion of overseas trade. Increasingly wool was imported on consignment from Europe and Australia, instead of being purchased in local markets and cloth halls, while more and more of the finished product was shipped to Europe, then after 1815 to America, and later still to the Far East. Eventually these developments would lead to concentration in large mills, but this process did not even begin to get under way until the 1820s, much later than in cotton, and in the meantime there was an urgent need for credit in order to increase production in line with the demand for exports.

In the case of worsteds the necessary facilities were provided by the importers and exporters who, although they contributed very little in the way of fixed capital, extended crucially important short-term credit. This meant that by 1846 the export trade was largely in the control of Bradford's merchants, many of them immigrants such as the Scotsman Robert Milligan and the German Jacob Behrens. The situation in the woollen industry was more complicated. The new market opportunities enabled many of the more ambitious independent clothiers to turn themselves into entrepreneurs, employing dozens or even scores of workers.[127] How did they find the wherewithal to do this? It appears that a relatively small proportion of the requisite fixed capital was supplied by producers ploughing back profits, and that no more than 10 per cent came from the agricultural sector. The workforce contributed unwittingly to expansion, as many fledgling employers raised credit by delaying the payment of wages, or else by paying their workers with tokens or in kind. But perhaps the most important factor was the clothiers' ability to raise money by mortgaging their freeholds,[128] or by raising loans on the security of copyholdings. Many of these transactions were underwritten by lawyers, while the vital credit came ultimately from banks and discount houses operating in a highly localized capital market, based mainly on Leeds. So whereas the worsted trade became directly dependent on mercantile houses, in woollens the 'web of indebtedness' was more complicated but no less decisive. Effectively what happened was that financial institutions directed the proceeds of trusts and rentier wealth towards the manufacturers, in order to provide them with essential circulating capital.[129]

A comprehensive survey of English industry would need to take in other textiles such as linen, flax, and lace; the primary and secondary metal trades; house-building, engineering, transport, shipbuilding, and railway development; coal-, lead-, and copper-mining; food-processing, brewing, chemicals, glassmaking, pottery, and leather. Concentration on cotton and woollens is justified only in so far as they were the most dynamic elements in the economy, their growth was all too visible to contemporaries, and they threw up human problems which politicians were forced to deal with in the 1830s.

Urbanization spawned a hugely expanded salariat: schoolteachers, dancing masters, journalists, local government officers, accountants, clerks, guards,

---

[127] Though, as in cottons, by 1815 the amount of capital required for entry was sufficient to deter humble newcomers.

[128] Enclosures might actually have helped by giving smallholders a clear title to land which could then be used to raise credit for industry (Pat Hudson, *The Genesis of Industrial Capital: A Study of the West Riding Wool Textile Industry c.1750–1850* (Cambridge, 1986), 97).

[129] Ibid., 25–84, 260–70.

cleaners, bouncers, and increasingly industrial managers. After 1800 it began to be recognized that managers could play a different role from that of owner–entrepreneurs. They came to form a distinctive group in several sectors, in many cases earning as much as £250 (£2,000 if they were taken on as managing partners). However, large textile firms lagged behind, and a recognized managerial profession, capable of transferring skills across industrial boundaries, did not emerge until after 1850.[130] A much more significant addition to what is defined here as a lesser-middle class came with the emergence of a shopocracy. Although there was no structural transformation in retailing, the most significant changes having taken place before 1750,[131] in urban history terms—socially, spatially, and politically—important developments did occur from 1820 onwards, especially in the new industrial towns. Markets disappeared as roads were paved and widened, street traders were forced out to the suburbs, while shops and warehouses replaced fashionable town centre residencies, as in Manchester's Mosley Street. A few large stores were built, especially in draperies, and some retailers established multiple outlets.[132] All this made for a large though dispersed and often exploited workforce. For example, Birmingham's wholesale and retail trades employed 20,000 men and women in 1861, about 13 per cent of the total.[133] It is hard to generalize about the social and political attitudes of such a multitude, especially as there was a vast gulf in earnings between the fashionable milliner and the humble grocer or shop assistant. Those who served a privileged clientele might have been forced, in those days of open ballots, to vote for Conservative candidates at election time, while almost all the less well-off shopkeepers were Radicals, and many became Chartists in the late 1830s and 1840s,[134] but the term 'shopocracy' refers to those in the middle who wielded formal political power rather than pikestaffs, and who were predominantly Liberals. Being well known in the community, shopkeepers had their fingers on the pulse, and were often prominent in the fight for ratepayers' interests, e.g. as Poor Law Guardians.[135] They were at the forefront of grass-roots radicalism in the North-East, they accounted for one-third of Leeds voters following the Reform Act of 1832, and they captured eighteen out of sixty-four places on Manchester's first council in 1838.[136] Obviously the shopocracy lacked the prestige of most factory owners, but politically it counted.

[130] Sidney Pollard, *The Genesis of Modern Management: A Study of the Industrial Revolution in Great Britain* (1965), 104–59.   [131] See above, p. 13.

[132] David Alexander, *Retailing in England during the Industrial Revolution* (1970), 89–109.

[133] Eric Hopkins, *Birmingham: The First Manufacturing Town in the World 1760–1840* (1989), 79.

[134] Dorothy Thompson, *The Chartists* (1984), 152–72.

[135] Trainor, *Black Country Elites*, 82–6, 287–92.

[136] Derek Fraser, *Urban Politics in Victorian England: The Structure of Politics in Victorian Cities* (Leicester, 1976), 121.

CIVIC CULTURES: A LITERARY AND PHILOSOPHICAL PEOPLE

The distinction between a mercantile and moneyed elite on the one hand and manufacturers and retailers on the other was particularly stark in Leeds, where it was also mirrored by religious and political differences. In 1831 the former category numbered several hundred out of a total population of about 124,000. William Milner, Henry Ibbetson, and most of the other leading merchants were descended from landed families. Fewer than a dozen were Dissenters, though some (including the two just mentioned) had only recently joined the Establishment. Many came from old established Anglican stock like the Oateses, Becketts, Ibbetsons, and Denisons, and many were highly evangelical. They lived in fine houses with fine furniture, and patronized the local surgeons and lawyers. They ate good food off silver and drank French wine. They kept butlers, footmen, and carriages and were sensitive about their accents. They read novels, had portraits painted of their families, and regarded themselves as leaders of local taste. They made excursions to Bath and Scarborough, looked to London for the latest fashions, and affected a cosmopolitan outlook. Their sons attended Oxford and especially Cambridge universities, after which they might go into the law or the Church, while their daughters married into other merchant families, all of which they knew intimately, and sometimes into the gentry. In politics they supported Pitt and his successors.

Leeds manufacturers or clothiers, on the other hand, were nearly always Foxite Whigs and later Liberals. They were more likely to have become wealthy since 1780, and also far more likely to be Nonconformists. Running a factory or large workshop for fifteen hours a day six days a week left them so little time for leisure and sport that they could hardly aspire to the same degree of social status as merchants, and many dared not devolve day-to-day responsibility for their factories onto salaried managers because there were too many cases of industrial usurpation. If their children received formal education they would have the advantage of attending a Dissenting academy, where the instruction was much superior to that of the universities. They were then more likely to became apprentices than to enter the professions. Finally, the entrepreneurs' loyalties were to their region rather than metropolitan or national.[137] No doubt all such generalizations should be taken with a pinch of that snuff which merchants but not manufacturers were wont to inhale after dinner, but for Leeds at least this one is far from being a caricature.

Prior to 1810 merchants dominated the Leeds Corporation as well as every other administrative body in the town: the parish vestry, the Poor Law overseers, charitable societies, improvement commissions, the infirmary, the grammar school, the lordship of the manor. By contrast industrialists and tradespeople

[137] R. J. Morris, *Class, Sect and Party: The Making of the British Middle Class, Leeds 1820–1850* (Manchester, 1990), 123–60; Wilson, *Gentlemen Merchants*, 212–15.

enjoyed very little formal influence. Gradually tensions increased between the two groups, thanks in part to Edward Baines's *Leeds Mercury*, which constantly assailed the Anglican merchants' hold over the Corporation. As the population rose (by almost 100,000 during 1801–41) and also the number of firms (by almost 3,500), merchants increasingly decamped to the countryside to escape the excrement and smoke, allowing the manufacturers to supplant them as leaders of the town's woollen interest. In alliance with engineers and shopkeepers, and abetted by a small number of Whig Dissenters among the merchant body, this new class of manufacturers gradually began to assert itself politically.[138] A hardening of sectarian differences in the 1820s and 1830s further sharpened the struggle. Although merchants, bankers, and professional men continued to predominate in most of the voluntary organizations devoted to working-class temperance, thrift, and education,[139] the balance of power shifted tectonically when Whig Dissenters captured control of the vestry and the Poor Law commission. The conflict was resolved in the 1830s with a decisive defeat for the merchant–Pittites, latterly called Tories. The first parliamentary election in 1832 dealt them a crushing blow, and three years later, following the Municipal Corporations Act, the Whig reformers secured a four to one majority on the new council. As a result, 'The way was left wide open for the great Liberal captains of industry who dominated Victorian Leeds. The names of the prominent eighteenth-century merchants were soon forgotten in Leeds by all save a few of their remoter female descendants who could not afford the comforts of Cheltenham or the south coast.'[140]

The situation in Bradford 9 miles away was similar but subtly different. Here, it will be remembered, the merchants had traditionally enjoyed a hands-on relationship with the worsted producers to the west, unlike in Leeds where the merchants and bankers had kept the independent manufacturers at arm's length. This necessarily made Bradford merchants—and particularly those of the second (*c*.1790–*c*.1830) generation like Henry Leah, Joshua Pollard, and John Sturges—more fastidious than their self-assured Leeds counterparts. In their urgent desire for status they ingratiated themselves with the local aristocracy, the Tory Party, and the Anglican Church. They moved into ornate villas set in lavish parkland two miles out of town, only to find suburbia lapping up to and around them. Some moved out to more graceful places like Harrogate. Most remained, but as fast as they could they diversified their assets, so that their industrial–mercantile profits came to mean less than dividends, interest, shares, and rents. Then, as in Leeds, this Pittite clique of gentlemen capitalists found itself rudely dethroned by a 'new bourgeois generation', which came to prominence from the 1830s onwards and made them feel 'like strangers in their own native town'. These challengers

[138] Wilson, *Gentlemen Merchants*, 132–3, 165, 175–6, 207, 215–17.
[139] R. J. Morris, 'Voluntary Societies and British Urban Elites, 1780–1850: An Analysis', *HJ* 26 (1983), 95–118.   [140] Wilson, *Gentlemen Merchants*, 181–2.

were 'generally immigrants' (especially from Scotland and Germany), Nonconformists, and 'frequently children of relatively humble and obscure working- or lower-middle-class parents'. They too were 'upwardly mobile', but for them 'up' meant not land and funds but industry, since, although they were not entrepreneurs, men like Robert Milligan were 'entrepreneurially minded'.[141]

Although the distinction was rarely as clear-cut as in Leeds and Bradford, in early nineteenth-century towns everywhere manufacturing, retailing, and Dissenting groups challenged older elites entrenched in parishes, corporations, courts leet, manors, and street commissions. In London many merchants became aldermen, but apart from brewers very few manufacturers did so.[142] Norwich was known as the 'Jacobin city' for its political and religious radicalism, but its government was dominated by a Pittite Anglican clique comprising gentlemen, professionals, and the mercantile elite. Bristol was run (very badly) by a closed, self-electing Corporation comprising a number of Tory and Anglican or Quaker banking families such as the Mileses and Harfords. In Coventry, despite (or more likely because of) a wide artisanal franchise, the old Corporation was dominated by bankers, lawyers, gentlemen of independent means, and a few aristocrats.[143] Manufacturers were virtually excluded, but as in Leeds they had their revenge after municipal reform, for right from the beginning the boss class—mainly ribbon masters and hosiers—controlled the new City Council. All these places give substance to the gentlemanly capitalist thesis in so far as, broadly speaking, the Anglican upper-middle classes united in power and prestige with local landlords and set themselves somewhat apart from the Dissenting manufacturing and retailing middle classes.[144]

The shock city was Manchester, scene of food riots in 1795 and 1800, a weavers' strike in 1808, machine-wrecking and a breakdown of law and order in 1812, and the notorious Peterloo massacre seven years later.[145] Here the social situation was complicated by two factors. Although it is commonly thought of as the world's first industrial city, with about fifty steam-powered spinning factories in 1816, it was never dominated by cotton mills like its satellites or 'out-towns'—Bolton, Bury, Oldham, Ashton, and Stockport.[146] It was primarily

---

[141] Koditschek, *Class Formation*, 41–81, 135–81.

[142] Rogers, 'Money, Land and Lineage', 439, 442 n.

[143] John Prest, *The Industrial Revolution in Coventry* (1960), 28, 36.

[144] Liverpool was different because its Common Council, dominated by Tory freemen, by and large excluded the wealthier merchants, many of whom were Dissenters (Martin Lynn, 'Trade and Politics in 19th Century Liverpool: The Tobin and Horsfall Families and Liverpool's African Trade', *Transactions of the Historic Society of Lancashire and Cheshire for the Year 1992*, 142 (1993), 108–9). Birmingham differed also because of the relative weakness of its upper-middle-class sector.

[145] John Bohstedt, *Riots and Community Politics in England and Wales 1790–1810* (Cambridge, Mass., 1983), 69–164.

[146] In 1841 about 18% of Manchester's labour force was employed in all branches of the cotton industry, as compared with 50% in Ashton and 40% in Oldham (Alan Kidd, *Manchester* (Keele, 1993), 25).

a centre of commerce and distribution, and later of finance and services. Its warehouses possessed twice as much rateable value as its manufactories, though since (as in Bradford) their function was not storage but wholesale— e.g. to display colourful patterned cloth to dealers from all over the world—their owners should really be designated merchant princes.[147] This was reflected in their increasingly elaborate architecture which, by the 1840s, was beginning to imitate the Florentine and Venetian palazzi of the Cinquecento. Another complication was the high proportion of Unitarians among Manchester's business and professional families. Like some Quakers, these 'gentlemen Dissenters' with names like Potter, Heywood, and Greg were culturally assimilated to the upper-middle classes. The bankers, merchants, physicians, lawyers, engineers, and scientists who worshipped in Cross Street made up a self-consciously intellectual and questioning elite, whose members frequently intermarried. Their opulent chapels and often luxurious lifestyles contradicted Nonconformist stereotypes—not for them the hard work, abstemiousness, and philistinism of the Leeds clothiers, fired by Methodist enthusiasm. Many Unitarians were so assimilated by this time that a steady drip of personnel to the Establishment was inevitable, especially as they were often too proud to proselytize. They served as JPs, town constables, and members of the governing Court Leet jury,[148] and their leadership may explain why there was much less anti-war protest than in other industrial regions—on the contrary, many Unitarians made substantial contributions to the Volunteers and the General Defence Fund.[149]

Culturally, then, the haute bourgeoisie was as powerful in Manchester as in Leeds, and as in Leeds there was an enormous gulf between it and the lesser-middle class of small employers, shopkeepers, and journalists.[150] However, several factors made the situation more complicated than in Leeds. First of all, and as already stated, the line between manufacturing production and commerce was less clear-cut. Secondly, the fact that so many members of the upper-middle class were Dissenting in religion, and therefore Whigs or Radicals in politics, meant that they could not integrate with Anglican Tories as easily as in Leeds, or obtain the same hold over local institutions. Cross Street Unitarians never quite melded with the Church-and-King

[147] Though some retained an interest in putting out production, often in one of the out-towns.
[148] Historically a feudal dependency of the Mosley family, prior to 1838 Manchester was governed by some feeble remnants of medieval manorial jurisdiction, such as a Court Leet and a Boroughreeve. These authorities were supplemented by a Police and Improvement Commission from 1792.
[149] J. E. Cookson, *The Friends of Peace: Anti-War Liberalism in England, 1793–1815* (Cambridge, 1982), 177–9, 186–7, 210–13.
[150] V. A. C. Gatrell, 'The Commercial Middle Class in Manchester, c.1820–1857', Ph.D. thesis (Cambridge University, 1972), 139–206; John K. Walton, *Lancashire: A Social History, 1558–1939* (Manchester, 1987), 126, 133–8; Bohstedt, *Riots*, 100–25.

Anglicans who patronized St Ann's Church and the Parish Church of St Mary, while their daughters were unlikely to marry into local gentry families, further preventing full assimilation between communities whose economic interests and cultural values were similar. This and a common attachment to Dissent also meant that they developed closer links with the lesser-middle class than in Leeds or Bradford.[151]

To round up this survey it is worth considering the situation in two genuine cotton towns. Neither Oldham nor Bolton possessed much of an upper-middle class, but whereas the former's few merchants, bankers, and lawyers looked to their counterparts in Manchester just 5 miles away, those in Bolton, being as far away again, sought assimilation with the Lancashire gentry. Bolton's elite was almost entirely composed of manufacturers and was divided. A first group included nearly all the major employers in the textile-finishing, coal, iron, and engineering industries. Bound up in many cases with local landed families such as the Stanleys and Egertons, they constituted an oligarchy of Church-and-King Tories who had traditionally controlled everything, from poor relief and improvement to policing. Ranged against them was a petite bourgeoisie made up of shopkeepers, traders, and smaller producers, the vast majority of whom were Liberals and Dissenters, with the Bank Street Unitarian Chapel providing a spearhead. Decades of disputation over rates and patronage gave way to a bitter struggle over incorporation in the later 1830s, and then to equally bitter quarrels of competence between the old Court Leet and the new Town Council.[152] This was a more primitive, perhaps pre-gentlemanly capitalist formation.

Even so, and allowing for various permutations, it is clear that the upper-middle classes provided much of the country's urban leadership from the 1780s to the 1830s. Was their contribution in any way distinct? One striking difference between theirs and the preceding and succeeding generations was an apparent indifference to the physical environment, despite mounting demographic pressures. Ensconced in their corporations and courts leet, they regularly fought off the attempts of industrialists and shopkeepers—acting as vestrymen, Poor Law guardians, highway surveyors, improvement commissioners, and charitable trustees—to achieve better lighting, cleansing, and watch facilities. Bristol's Merchant Venturers, for example, operating through a close and self-appointing Corporation, seriously jeopardized health by blocking the development of a central water supply.[153] One reason for their reluctance was that, whereas the

---

[151] Michael J. Turner, *Reform and Respectability: The Making of a Middle-Class Liberalism in Early Nineteenth-Century Manchester* (Manchester, 1995), 7–58.

[152] Peter Taylor, *Popular Politics in Early Industrial Britain: Bolton 1825–1850* (Keele, 1995), 57–103; Paul T. Phillips, *The Sectarian Spirit: Sectarianism, Society, and Politics in Victorian Cotton Towns* (Toronto, 1982), 10–36.

[153] B. W. E. Alford, 'The Economic Development of Bristol in the Nineteenth Century: An Enigma?', in Patrick McGrath and John Cannon (eds.), *Essays in Bristol and Gloucestershire History* (Bristol, 1976), 265–6.

younger generation of entrepreneurs and shopkeepers lived and worked locally, these gentlemen capitalists were not always resident, yet paid the lion's share of rates. A deeper explanation may be that, in looking to either London or landed society for their values, these subaltern members of the upper-middle class detached themselves psychologically from—and so failed to identify physically with—their surroundings. While the capital recladded itself in Palladian elegance, provincial notables took almost no interest in the physical environment. Operatives' houses were thrown together in heaps, creating hopelessly overcrowded and filthy districts like Manchester's 'Little Ireland', and there were hardly any attempts to make town centres look grand.[154] It has been called a 'retreat from planning', and was in marked contrast to the previous century's urban renaissance. At the same time terraces and crescents, which had once facilitated promenading and collective activities, emptied in the early nineteenth century as townspeople adopted a more reclusive lifestyle based on villas. Public subscriptions for racecourse grandstands, bowling greens, promenades, and pleasure gardens all declined after 1780, as did provincial theatre, balls, concerts, and oratorios, and the rounds of fashionable entertainments that had once been held in imitation of the London season.[155] These activities would only reappear, along with ambitious architecture, under *lesser*-middle-class leadership in the 1840s, though by that point provincial culture was much less imitative of the capital.

A similar chronology was evident with respect to the visual arts. The upper-middle classes' relative indifference to aesthetic matters was partly owing to the dominant religion. Evangelicals, it has been said, 'exalted the ear-gate at the expense of the eye-gate of the soul'.[156] There was also an element of inverted snobbery, connoisseurship being for effete aristocrats. Moreover, those businessmen who did collect regarded their acquisitions in a strictly private light. For a long time Britain was the only Great Power not to possess a public collection of old masters, something which heritage Radicals like John Wilkes had long called for. A British Institution for the Promotion of the Fine Arts was established in 1805 under the presidency of the Prince Regent. It encouraged young artists and exhibited privately owned paintings, but proposals for a permanent national collection, though constantly mooted, continued to meet with resistance, partly on commercial grounds (struggling artists were afraid

---

[154] A notable exception was the Newcastle of Grainger and Dobson. Significantly it was a Whiggish and anti-Pittite town, run mainly by landowners and coal barons.

[155] J. Jefferson Looney, 'Cultural Life in the Provinces: Leeds and York, 1720–1820', in A. L. Beier, D. Cannadine, and James M. Rosenheim (eds.), *The First Modern Society: Essays in English History in Honour of Lawrence Stone* (Cambridge, 1989), 506–7. But see C. W. Chalkin, 'Capital Expenditure on Building for Cultural Purposes in Provincial England, 1730–1830', *Business History*, 22 (1980), 51–70.

[156] Horton Davies, *Worship and Theology in England: From Watts and Wesley to Maurice, 1690–1850* (Princeton, 1961), 236; Doreen M. Rosman, *Evangelicals and Culture* (1984), 147–65.

that public access to old masters would damage their sales), but also because it was felt that artistic mercantilism should be left to despots like Catherine the Great and Napoleon.[157] It was not until 1824 that a National Gallery was eventually established, when Parliament voted £60,000 (fortunately the annual budget was in surplus that year) to purchase the private collection of John Julius Angerstein, a Lloyd's underwriter, but thereafter it made only stuttering progress. Though championed by a number of Tories and Radicals, it suffered from Exchequer parsimony and the suspicions of cost-conscious liberals in both main parties. Even for its promoters the purpose was not so much artistic as didactic and social, being to educate and civilize the masses. This was why Peel insisted that admission should be free at all times, why proposals for new acquisitions had to be debated in Parliament to ensure that they were politically and morally suitable, and why most trustees were determined to retain the Gallery at Charing Cross, in reach of the working classes, rather than moving out to Hyde Park or South Kensington, despite evidence that polluted air from Seven Dials was having a deleterious effect on the canvases. The Gallery only really began to take off in the 1850s, thanks to an annual Treasury grant and a much more sympathetic cultural climate. It was much the same locally. In Manchester, for example, there was little interest in painting before 1820, and no one to match Liverpool's William Roscoe (but then the slaving port was a much older town and Roscoe a slightly older man).[158] However, an 'important shift in its cultural economy' set in during the 1820s, when several voluntary associations devoted to music, literature, art, and education were formed, most significantly the Royal Manchester Institution (1823), afterwards the City Art Gallery. At least twenty-six of its leading members in the later 1830s were manufacturers as against fifteen professionals, seven merchants, four gentlemen, and just one banker, and it seems to have heralded a new lesser-middle-class confidence in the idea of art as public culture. It was hoped that common artistic pursuits might heal the town's bitter political divisions, as well as civilizing the working class and showing the world that industry need not equal philistinism.[159]

Although the earlier upper-middle-class leaders failed to patronize art and architecture, they made up for it by founding learned societies. Whereas in the

---

[157] Jonathan Conlin, 'The Origins and History of the National Gallery, 1753–1860', Ph.D. thesis (Cambridge University, 2002), 64–121.

[158] Edward Morris, 'The Formation of the Gallery of Art in the Liverpool Royal Institution, 1816–1819', *Transactions of the Historic Society of Lancashire and Cheshire for the Year 1992*, 142 (1993), 87–98.

[159] John Seed, ' "Commerce and the Liberal Arts": The Political Economy of Art in Manchester, 1775–1860', in Janet Wolff and John Seed (eds.), *The Culture of Capital: Art, Power and the Nineteenth-Century Middle Class* (Manchester, 1988). A Select Committee met during 1835–6 to 'inquire into the best means of extending a knowledge of the Arts and of the Principles of Design among the People (especially the manufacturing population)'. It was followed by the establishment of Art unions, specifically to target the 'masses'.

eighteenth century associational life had revolved around alcohol and sociability, there was now a fashion for geology, palaeontology, natural history, chemistry, and political economy.[160] Since these were subjects which the ancient universities more or less ignored, it is not far-fetched to say that English academia began here. The prototype is often mistakenly thought to be Birmingham's Lunar Society, founded in about 1765 and at its peak in the 1780s.[161] Started by a hard-headed toymaker Matthew Boulton,[162] its distinguished members included Joseph Priestley, James Watt, Erasmus Darwin, Josiah Wedgwood, and Richard Lovell Edgeworth. Its experimental work in chemistry, hydraulics, botany, geology, and mineralogy was often imaginative,[163] and may have assisted the spread of industrial technology, but it was not a template for the hundreds of scientific societies founded between 1790 and 1850. In the first place, although it met in Boulton's house in Soho outside Birmingham, it was not a civic society but a remarkably wide-ranging private and mainly Dissenting network, which spread through mid-western England and took in Liverpool, Manchester, Warrington, Derby, and Lichfield. Membership was by invitation, not subscription as was usually the case with later bodies. Secondly, it was more interested in practical technology than in pure science,[164] and almost not at all in philosophy. Finally, it was 'insensibly dissolved' in the 1790s, disappearing quickly and virtually without trace. During the first half of the nineteenth century Birmingham remained backward in terms of intellectual sodality, lagging behind its rivals in the provision of learned societies and mechanics institutes, but then Birmingham was counter-cultural in many respects, led by Tory–Radicals and resentful of the 'liberal' movement towards free trade, retrenchment, and sound money.

It was from London, not Birmingham, that provincial notables sought inspiration, and especially from bookish Bloomsbury, Paternoster Row, and the Strand, with their bookshops, reading clubs, and debating societies. In contrast to the setbacks faced by the National Gallery as a centre for *art*, the British Museum (1753) as a centre of *intellectual* excellence benefited hugely from major

---

[160] Arnold Thackray, 'Natural Knowledge in Cultural Context: The Manchester Model', *American Historical Review*, 79 (1974), 672–709; Peter Clark, *British Clubs and Societies 1580–1800: The Origins of an Associational World* (Oxford, 2000), has sought to play down the late 18th-century developments by arguing that an 'associational' culture had existed since the 1650s. Nevertheless, one of his own graphs (p. 132) tells its own story by identifying 150 societies (of all types) in England in 1740–9, 450 in 1770–9, and 1,100 in 1790–9.

[161] The best intellectual history is Robert E. Schofield, *The Lunar Society of Birmingham: A Social History of Provincial Science and Industry in Eighteenth-Century England* (Oxford, 1963); the best social and personal history is Jenny Uglow, *The Lunar Men: The Friends Who Made the Future, 1730–1810* (2002).   [162] Toy was the name given to small metalware.

[163] Its most imaginative wheeze was to blow up polar ice caps with gunpowder, and divert them to the tropics in order to lower temperatures there.

[164] One reason, perhaps, why its members clung to Priestley's belief that heat was caused by 'phlogiston', thereby allowing the French scientist Antoine Lavoisier to develop Priestley's observations into a correct account of oxygen.

benefactions and was bathed in general approbation. Its rapidly accumulated collections of minerals, fossils, coins, antiquities,[165] books, charters, and manuscripts made London an intellectual capital second only to Paris even before the foundation of King's and University colleges in 1829–36. There was an obsession with natural philosophy or science, which now came out of the gentleman's private laboratory and into the public sphere, creating a vast metro-politan circuit of teaching and research. The Royal Society was a venerable body presided over by Sir Joseph Banks, but it was now somewhat gentrified, and too closely connected with the blatantly political Board of Agriculture. Faced with demands to become more accessible, it set up a subordinate organization, the Royal Institution (RI, 1799), in order to achieve accessibility at arm's length. Though intended as a sop, the RI had an egalitarian effect thanks to some remarkable individual contributions, especially the chemistry lectures of Humphry (later Sir Humphry) Davy from 1801 to 1812,[166] and it probably helped to stimulate the establishment of many more specialist institutions.[167]

The vogue for chemistry might be said to begin with the Society for Philosophical Experiments and Conversations (1794–7), founded by Dr Bryan Higgins, who had run a 'school of practical chemistry' in Soho for twenty years before that. Its annual subscription was 5 guineas, which was higher than aver-age, and it attracted a number of peers, MPs, lawyers, and businessmen as well as practising apothecaries and chemists.[168] Hitherto the subject had been regarded as the most dangerous and radical of all sciences, thanks in part to the reputations of men like Priestley and Beddoes, but Davy quickly made it respectable.[169] Though radical to start with, and trained by Beddoes, Davy made for London and locked himself into the metropolitan establishment, where he developed into a high Tory. Theoretically his chemistry was not so different from that of Priestley and Beddoes. However, in writing up experiments he eschewed their discursive but accessible narratives in favour of analysis, and

---

[165] In 1816 the marauder Lord Elgin sold it the marbles which he had hacked from the Parthenon in order to save them from Turkish marauders.

[166] Morris Berman, *Social Change and Scientific Organization: The Royal Institution, 1799–1844* (1978), 1–31.

[167] Societies such as the Horticultural (1804), Medical and Chirurgical (1805), Geological (1807), Royal Astronomical (1820), Royal Asiatic (1823), Zoological (1826), Royal Geographical (1830), Entomological (1833), Statistical (1834), London Botanical (1836), Numismatic (1836), Microscopical (1839), Pharmaceutical (1841), Chemical (1841), Philological (1842), and Ethnological (1843). Also the Archaeological Institute (1843) and the Royal College of Chemistry (1845). A. Hume, *The Learned Societies and Printing Clubs of the United Kingdom* (1853), 67–126.

[168] Jan Golinsky, *Science as Public Culture: Chemistry and Enlightenment in Britain, 1760–1820* (Cambridge, 1992), 188–235; Gwen Averley, 'The "Social Chemists": English Chemical Societies in the Eighteenth and Early Nineteenth Century', *Ambix*, 33 (1986), 99–128.

[169] In 1792 Beddoes was effectively forced to relinquish his Readership at Oxford on account of his support for the early stages of the French Revolution.

presented his results for their intrinsic scientific worth rather than for any contribution they might make to social amelioration.[170] His poetical and morally uplifting style of address was appealing, and his galvanic experiments remained immensely popular up until the 1830s, when they were finally overtaken by a fascination with magnetism and electricity, the main exponent being Davy's own protégé Michael Faraday, whose Friday evening lectures at the Royal Institution were even more sensational. For a fee enthusiastic amateurs could now attend an enormous range of scientific lectures, shows, displays, demonstrations, and tutorials, as well as buying textbooks.[171]

Generally speaking, provincial science imitated these metropolitan developments rather than the private science of the Enlightenment. Admittedly, the Manchester Literary and Philosophical Society (1781) and the Derby Philosophical Society (1783–4) began as an extension of the old Lunar tradition, but whereas it succumbed to the political reaction of the 1790s, these bodies managed to survive by changing. An influx of High Church Tories into the Manchester Lit. & Phil. forced a switch of emphasis from political philosophy to antiquarianism, and from human to physical science. Numbering Dr John Dalton, Dr John Ferriar, and Dr Thomas Percival among its members, it made that town pre-eminent in such matters.[172] Elsewhere discussion of religion and politics was prohibited in order to avoid the fate of the Preston Debating Society and the Leeds Reasoning Society, both of which were suppressed under Pitt's anti-terror legislation.[173] As new bodies formed after 1800 they mainly conformed to the new model by specializing in chemistry, geology, and natural history. Many of their luminaries had been trained in chemistry by William Cullen, Joseph Black, or John Robison at Edinburgh or Glasgow. Almost as fashionable was geology, which became a considerable outdoor pursuit in areas like Devon and the Peak District, and which fed off the new Ordnance Survey. The latter was initiated in 1791 by the Duke of Richmond in imitation of earlier developments in Austria, France, India, and North America, but the outbreak of war, and the need to deploy volunteer forces along the south coast, gave it a new urgency.[174] Even more significant in stimulating interest was a great solo effort, the beautiful and coloured geological map of Britain drawn up by William Smith in 1815 after fifteen years of painstaking lone research.[175]

[170] Which makes it paradoxical that he should be remembered chiefly for his miner's lamp.

[171] J. N. Hays, 'The London Lecturing Empire, 1800–50', in Ian Inkster and Jack Morrell (eds.), *Metropolis and Province: Science in British Culture, 1780–1850* (1983).

[172] Robert H. Kargon, *Science in Victorian Manchester: Enterprise and Expertise* (Manchester, 1977), 1–33.

[173] P. D. Brett, 'The Liberal Middle Classes and Politics in Three Provincial Towns—Newcastle, Bristol, and York—*c.*1812–1841', Ph.D. thesis (Durham University, 1991), 157.

[174] W. A. Seymour (ed.), *A History of the Ordnance Survey* (Folkestone, 1980), 24.

[175] Simon Winchester, *The Map that Changed the World: The Tale of William Smith and the Birth of a Science* (2001).

Thanks to the efforts of a local Unitarian, William Turner, Newcastle upon Tyne gained a Lit. & Phil. in 1793 and a Chemical Club in 1796 (which grew to more than 500 members in fifteen years).[176] Elsewhere the campaigns against the Orders in Council[177] galvanized local merchant communities in a way that spilled over into cultural affairs. Many Lit. & Phils. were founded from the later stages of the French wars onwards, including those at Bristol (1809), Liverpool (1812), Leeds (1819), Hull and Sheffield (1822), and Halifax (1830).[178] Naturally there was a great deal of shared membership. The Manchester Lit. & Phil. over-lapped with the Portico Library (1806), the Royal Manchester Institution (1823), and the Manchester Statistical Society (1833); members of the Bristol Lit. & Phil. helped to form the highly exclusive Institution for the Advancement of Science (1823), its satellite the Phil. & Lit., and later the Statistical Society (1836); while the Newcastle Lit. & Phil. spawned a Society of Antiquaries (1813) and a Natural History Society (1829).[179] Several bodies elected honorary mem-bers so as to keep in touch with what was happening elsewhere. Thus in 1829–30 the Leeds Phil. & Lit. had nine London scholars and scientists on its books, as well as five from York, three from Manchester, one from Paris, and one from Cincinnati. This was intellectual networking on a fairly grand scale, and the impetus for it came not from local aristocracy and gentry or from the Liberal-inclined entrepreneurs but mainly from merchants, bankers, doctors, lawyers, and clergy. The Bristol Lit. & Phil. was founded by Anglican middle-class burghers with the support of a few wealthy Unitarians, while in Manchester the Portico's first twenty-two committee members included two bankers, one attorney, seven physicians, six merchants, and only four manufacturers.[180] Most telling is an occupational analysis of the Leeds Phil. & Lit., comparing its membership with a database of all the identifiable well-to-do citizens listed in the *Leeds Directory* for 1834 (see Table 3.5.)[181]

In 1818 the *Leeds Mercury* published a letter calling for a formation of a Lit. & Phil.

How can a young man be more usefully or more honorably employed than in the acquisi-tion of knowledge, which must render him respectable and superior in life, and in the cultivation of those noble powers, which alone exalt man to an infinite height above the brutes, and assimilate him to the image of his Maker? An acquaintance with history, with

---

[176] Joan Knott, 'Circulating Libraries in Newcastle in the 18th and 19th Centuries', *Library History*, 2 (1972), 227–49.   [177] See below, p. 231.

[178] Roscoe had founded an earlier Lit. & Phil. in Liverpool in 1783, but it had folded very quickly.

[179] Michael Neve, 'Science in a Commercial City: Bristol 1820–60', and Derek Orange, 'Rational Dissent and Provincial Science: William Turner and the Newcastle Literary and Philosophical Society', in Inkster and Morrell (eds.), *Metropolis and Province*.

[180] Ann Brooks and Bryan Haworth, *Boomtown Manchester 1800–1850: The Portico Connection* (Manchester, 1993), 121; Thackray, 'Natural Knowledge in Cultural Context', 690.

[181] Morris, *Class, Sect and Party*, 236.

TABLE 3.5. *Membership of the Leeds Philosophical and Literary Society by occupation, 1834*

Members	No.	%	% in 1834 database
Gentlemen	19	12	2
Merchants	49	31	6
Professionals	42	27	3
Manufacturers	21	13	18
Shopkeepers	12	8	21
Craft	3	2	31
Other	11	8	5

Source: R. J. Morris, *Class, Sect and Party: The Making of the British Middle Class, Leeds 1820–1850* (Manchester, 1990), 236.

languages, and with literature places him in a higher rank in intellectual life, and with men of talent, than any intrinsic advantages however great.[182]

Such pronouncements confirm that burghers soaked up scientific lectures and books as a declaration of gentility.[183] It is less likely that learned societies acted as 'cultural outlets for upwardly mobile, largely professional and commercial groups'.[184] These men were already the lords and masters of their own universe, and the first generation of their kind *not* to seek upward assimilation into aristocracy, despite its 'intrinsic advantages'. It was only after the emergence of a more entrepreneurial and less self-confident leadership that a degree of social accommodation occurred. A turning point came in 1831 with the British Association for the Advancement of Science, a proselytizing society of gentlemen scientists which determined to hold its annual circuses in provincial towns.[185] This might be seen as a gesture of condescension towards the industrial middle classes, just then in everyone's consciousness owing to the debate over parliamentary reform, but whatever the motive, it may have turned some provincial heads. Suddenly learned societies sought to hook aristocratic patrons, while several local societies and journals lost their autonomy.

The proliferation of Lit. & Phils. was matched by that of mechanics institutes. The two earliest were inaugurated at Glasgow and London in 1823 by a professor of medicine, George Birkbeck. Manchester, Bristol, and Bolton

---

[182] 'Intrinsic' here referred to mere birth and breeding (E. Kitson Clark, *The History of 100 Years of Life of the Leeds Philosophical and Literary Society* (Leeds, 1924), 5–6).

[183] R. S. Porter, 'Science, Provincial Culture and Public Opinion in Enlightenment England', *British Journal for Eighteenth-Century Studies*, 3 (1980), 20–46.   [184] Golinski, *Science as Public Culture*, 58.

[185] Jack Morrell and Arnold Thackray, *Gentlemen of Science: Early Years of the British Association for the Advancement of Science* (Oxford, 1981), 1–163.

quickly followed suit and by 1850 there were more than 200, not to mention 500 literary institutes, athenaeums, mutual improvement societies, and circulating libraries.[186] While local Tories opposed popular education as being likely to empower the lower orders, liberal-minded commentators argued that scientific knowledge including political economy would tame and moralize them. In practice, however, long working hours, annual subscription rates sometimes as high as 1 guinea, and a tone of middle-class condescension probably put many working men off these adult education initiatives (women were usually excluded anyway). Much the same was true of the Society for the Diffusion of Useful Knowledge, founded by the Whig Henry Brougham and his Utilitarian allies in 1826, though its *Penny Magazine* (1832–45) and *Penny Cyclopedia* (1833–44) filled an important gap at a time when working people had little access to libraries.[187]

The content of all this scientific discussion is considered below.[188] What matters here is the question of culture. Upper-middle-class provincial society was composed of earnest and intellectual citizens, not very interested in art or the physical environment, and inclined to withdraw from organized leisure and public assembly in favour of private life. Well-to-do families still held balls in order to attract business and husbands for their daughters, but the old easygoing intimacy of social visiting seems to have been choked off by ever more elaborate systems of calling cards. Terraces and crescents which had once facilitated promenading and collective activities emptied in the early nineteenth century as townspeople adopted a more reclusive lifestyle based on villas.[189] This tendency on the part of elites to withdraw may have represented a collective shudder at the thought of the mad, bad, and dangerous classes asserting themselves on the public stage, but it also owed something to a wave of religious moralism which swept the country, and which ensured that the newly self-confident upper-middle class would be high-souled as well as high-minded.

THE EVANGELICAL REVIVAL

> The mother looked young and the daughter looked old; the mother's complexion was pink, and the daughter's was yellow; the mother set up for frivolity, and the daughter for theology.
>
> (Charles Dickens, *Great Expectations*)

---

[186] Mabel Tylecote, *The Mechanics Institutes of Lancashire and Yorkshire before 1851* (Manchester, 1957), 258–9.

[187] Mudie's Circulating Library was not established until 1842. The first free (i.e. rate-supported) public libraries were opened at Salford and Manchester in 1850.   [188] See Ch. 7.

[189] Lawrence and Jeanne C. Fawtier Stone, *An Open Elite? England 1540–1880* (Oxford, 1984), 326–8, 344–9; Lawrence Stone, *The Family, Sex and Marriage in England 1500–1800* (1977), 666–80.

The maturation of the upper-middle class from the last two decades of the eighteenth century onwards coincided with the so-called 'evangelical revival'. The epithet is as slippery as it was ubiquitous. When used as a synonym for 'evangelism', meaning the fervent preaching of the Gospel, it had no denominational connotation and could apply as much to Baptists, Congregationalists, and some Quakers as to Anglicans. 'Evangelical revival' sometimes refers to the Methodist movement led by Wesley and Whitefield after 1739. This was an attempt to evangelize the Anglican Church from within, and had affinities with the Great Awakening in North America and with Pietism in Germany, but shortly after Wesley died in 1791 the Methodist Connexion commenced a process of secession from the Establishment. Here 'evangelical revival' refers to a spiritual movement within the Church of England from the 1780s onwards. It originated in the City ministry of John Newton, who was much influenced by the devotional poet William Cowper as well as by Whitefield and Wesley. His very personal sermons, in which he grappled aloud with the dangers of temptation and sin, inspired a number of prominent laymen, notably William Wilberforce and Henry Thornton. Together with the clergymen Henry and John Venn, these two were part of a close-knit group known alternatively as the Clapham Sect[190] or 'Saints'. Two other sources of recruitment were the evangelical redoubts of St Edmund Hall in Oxford and Magdalene College, Cambridge;[191] many an undergraduate at the latter university experienced spiritual rebirth at the hands of the vicar of Holy Trinity Church, Charles Simeon. As numbers grew in successive revivalist waves (e.g. 1807–11), evangelicals ceased to be anything like a party, though detractors supposed them to be so, often misleadingly denouncing them as Methodists. Among ordained Churchmen the movement became a sort of freemasonry, an influential network which struck its enemies as conspiratorial. By 1848, when an evangelical John Bird Sumner became Archbishop of Canterbury, between a quarter and one-third of Anglican clergy were probably of the same persuasion, but the movement was by then so diffuse as to be beyond precise definition. For that reason it does not seem appropriate to describe its members with a capital 'E'.

Because it was centred on the divinity of Christ, evangelicalism was incompatible with what is sometimes called heterodox Dissent (e.g. Socinianism, Unitarianism), since the latter was rooted in a rejection of the Holy Trinity. On the other hand, it was entirely consistent with the doctrines of orthodox or Trinitarian Dissent, as elaborated in the *Evangelical Magazine* (1793), for example. Theologically the only fundamental division *within* evangelicalism lay, not between Church and Dissent, but between followers of the Clapham Sect on

[190] The term was coined by the Revd Sydney Smith and was originally meant to be derogatory.
[191] The river Cam, which 'licks the walls' of Magdalene, was said to be 'rendered unnavigable' because of the tea leaves deposited by the teetotal undergraduates (Ronald Hyam, *Godliness, Hunting and Quite Good Learning* (Cambridge, 1992), 7).

the one hand—enlightened, rationalist, and post-millennial—and a growing minority of apocalyptic and sometimes pentecostal pre-millenarians on the other.[192] This conflict led to serious fragmentation in the 1820s, by which time the two groups had diverged so greatly that historians urgently need to find separate names for them. When the word 'evangelical' is used here without qualification, it refers to the post-millennialism of the Clapham Sect, though with the further proviso that it was a style of religiosity shared by many others who would never have adopted the evangelical label.

That apart, evangelicalism—like most religious movements—was defined, not by the singularity of its doctrines, but by which ones it chose to prioritize. Evangelicals emphasized spiritual conflict, the active agency of the Devil, individual sinfulness in all its intensity and virulence, the possibility of redemption through and only through faith in Jesus Christ, and the certainty of future Judgement. No one has explained the psychological effects of all this better than the historian G. M. Young.

Evangelical theology rests on a profound apprehension of the contrary states: of Nature and of Grace; one meriting eternal wrath, the other intended for eternal happiness. Naked and helpless, the soul acknowledges its worthlessness before God and the justice of God's infinite displeasure, and then, taking hold of salvation in Christ, passes from darkness into a light which makes more fearful the destiny of those unhappy beings who remain without. This is Vital Religion. But the power of Evangelicalism as a directing force lay less in the hopes and terrors it inspired, than in its rigorous logic, 'the eternal microscope' with which it pursued its argument into the recesses of the heart, and the details of daily life, giving to every action its individual value in this life, and its infinite consequence in the next.[193]

As this suggests, evangelicals were intensely pietistic and devotional. The crucial point in a person's life was conversion, the moment of change when light flooded the empty vessel and regeneration occurred. Faith was impossible without conversion, but conversion did not guarantee salvation since there was the ever-present danger of backsliding, of succumbing to the temptations of the world and the Devil. Since Heaven was 'not to be won without labour', Christians were enjoined to concentrate continuously on their own spiritual state, to be *active* believers, and to keep 'the captain-general of salvation'[194] before their mind's eye in every conscious thought. It followed that chatterboxes were in mortal danger since their minds were accustomed to wander from contemplation of Christ's Crucifixion.[195] For 'every idle word that men shall

---

[192] For an explanation of the differences between pre- and post-millennialists, see below, pp. 401–5.

[193] G. M. Young, *Portrait of an Age: Victorian England* (1936), ed. George Kitson Clark (1977), 21–2.

[194] Heb. 2: 10.

[195] 'Talkative people are to be pitied, if old. It is quite an infirmity of old age' (*The Thought of the Evangelical Leaders: Notes of the Discussions of the Eclectic Society of London, 1798–1814*, ed. John H. Pratt, 2nd edn. (Edinburgh, 1978), 304).

speak, they shall give account thereof in the Day of Judgment' (Matt. 12: 36). This quest for continuous faithfulness impelled evangelicals towards good works in a desperate attempt to reassure themselves of their sanctity, but the works themselves were spiritually insignificant. Faith was all.

Judgement was certain and would take two forms. The first concerned the individual, since after death souls were dispatched to Heaven or Hell, both of which were conceived in spatial and exaggerated terms, the one a bejewelled pagoda enlivened by hallelujah choruses, the other a Dantesque phantasmagoria of eternal torment. Judgement also fell on nations in the form of divine rewards and retributions, battles won and lost, plenty and famine, prosperity and pestilence, good and bad rulers. Evangelicals scoured providence for signs of favour and admonition, finding the latter in personal bereavement or the madness of a king. But even such chastisements gave cause for renewed hope for, since 'God smiteth those he loveth', temporal afflictions could be regarded as examples of what is now called tough love on his part, portents carefully designed to awaken the favoured sinner to Christ ere it was too late. Eventually, it was believed, the end would come to nations as well as to individuals. The precise route to the millennium was disputed, but all evangelicals were certain that, as foretold in the book of Revelation, the last trumpet would sound, the Second Coming of Christ would establish a new Jerusalem, Satan would be bound for a thousand years and then cast into the lake of fire and brimstone, and the dead would be resurrected in preparation for the General Judgement that awaited everyone.

Exhilarated by this divine scenario, evangelicals reacted against what they saw as worldliness and indifference. Their disparagement of eighteenth-century religion was often unfair, but they rightly perceived the distance between themselves and older theologians such as Law and Paley. Paley believed that characters were '*formed* by circumstances',[196] a form of environmentalism, whereas evangelicals insisted that people were forever free to choose between good and evil. Paley thought that there were gradations of depravity, whereas for them the tiniest peccadillo was a flagrant rebellion against God, inviting eternal punishment. Indeed, since repentance was always efficacious (so long as it was sincere), murderers might be safer spiritually, their predicament being apparent, than minor sinners who—proud, complacent, and heedless—frequently died unregenerate. Paley was willing to admit that there might be little to choose morally between the best person in Hell and the worst person in Heaven, but this did not bother him because he conceived of the afterlife as stratified, much like human society, meaning that there might also be little to choose between their two conditions.[197] Again this set him apart from evangelicals, for whom

---

[196] William Paley, *Natural Theology; Or, Evidences of the Existence and Attributes of the Deity, collected from the Appearances of Nature* (1802), 564.
[197] William Paley, *The Principles of Moral and Political Philosophy* (1785), bk. I, ch. 7, pp. 41–2.

Heaven and Hell were absolute states and diametrically opposed—an assumption which helps to account for the black-and-white, all-or-nothing mentality of the period.

When, back in the 1760s, George III had pontificated about the need for integrity in public life, and had issued a Proclamation for the Encouragement of Piety and Virtue, he was widely regarded as an odious prig, but now the moral majority appeared to be catching up with him. There was a proliferation of improving organizations, including the century-old and now revivified Society for the Reformation of Manners (1690), the Society of Universal Good Will (1786), the Society for Carrying into Effect His Majesty's Proclamation against Vice and Immorality (1788), the Society for Promoting the Religious Instruction of Youth (1800), the Society for the Suppression of Vice (1802), and the Friendly Female Society, for the Relief of Poor, Infirm, Aged Widows, and Single Women, of Good Character, Who Have Seen Better Days (1802). Much of this philanthropic activity was inspired by Wilberforce, who emerged as the conscience of the age like Lord Shaftesbury in the 1840s. Working from the metropolis, he kept in touch with zealots in the provinces, men like Alderman William Hey, an Anglican evangelical and prominent member of the Leeds Lit. & Phil.[198] All this activity was accompanied by a welter of didactic literature, a collateral purpose of which was to inoculate the poor against Paine-ism and keep them humble. Whereas earlier revivalists like Wesley had had to rely on itinerant preachers, Wilberforce's generation took advantage of the new print culture to launch a massive propaganda drive. The most important publicist was Hannah More, a West Country gentlewoman whose avalanches of morally improving literature included the Cheap Repository Tracts, issued for a penny under the auspices of the Religious Tract Society (1799). Consisting of homely moral parables, they were bought up in enormous quantities, often by Sunday school teachers. But if middle-class evangelicals sought to colonize downwards for God, they also looked upwards. The need for the rich to set a moral example to the poor was hammered home in sermons and expounded in canonical texts by More, Wilberforce, and Thomas Gisborne.[199] Their success was limited, as is obvious from the fact that the Regency peerage was more notable for rakes like Byron and Brummell than for godly nobles such as Hardwicke, Teignmouth, Tavistock, and the Duchess of Beaufort. Even so, there is no

[198] Joanna Innes, 'Politics and Morals: The Reformation of Manners Movement in Later Eighteenth-Century England', in Eckhart Hellmuth (ed.). *The Transformation of Political Culture: England and Germany in the Late Eighteenth Century* (Oxford, 1990), 70, 74.

[199] Hannah More, *Thoughts on the Importance of the Manners of the Great to General Society* (1788); Thomas Gisborne, *An Enquiry into the Duties of Men in the Higher and Middle Classes* (1794); William Wilberforce, *A Practical View of the Prevailing Religious System of Professed Christians, in the Higher and Middle Classes in this Country, Contrasted with Real Christianity* (1797).

denying the gradual permeation of the new Puritanism, even among the aristocracy.[200]

Because they made a fetish of salvation by faith, evangelicals were obliged to elevate the passions, but they were also afraid of them, a tension they sought to resolve by inventing over-elaborate rules of conduct. Their repressive emphasis on self-control led to new ideas about sexuality. Not the least of the many sudden changes in attitude that characterized the late eighteenth century was a swift retreat from the older view that sex (whether conjugal or otherwise) was beneficial, and as 'necessary to a woman's health and happiness' as to that of men.[201] After 1800, by contrast, sexuality was regarded as natural but dangerous in men, while in women it was regarded as merely hysterical or perverted.[202] The message was surely internalized, since evangelicalism as a religion of the heart appealed with particular force to women, who were encouraged to see themselves as possessing more sensibility than intellect, and from them it filtered through to children. While it is important not to exaggerate, another change that seems to have occurred at this time is the greater emotional capital invested in offspring, though the practical effect of their greater fondness was that 'discipline increased markedly in its severity'.[203] Because children were born in sin and might die at any time, punishment was necessary in order to turn them from Satan. This did not necessarily imply physical chastisement. While some evangelicals, like the novelist Samuel Butler's father,[204] beat their children viciously in order to subdue unregenerate flesh, others—including More probably—opposed corporal punishment as degrading and dehumanizing. They would rather lock recalcitrant children in dark closets and coal-holes ('solitary confinement'), or impose tasks of mind-numbing boredom, or set up systematic devices to signify their withdrawal of affection. But whatever the method, punishment was thought to be essential. As More rhetorically inquired, 'Is it not a fundamental error to consider children as innocent beings, whose little weaknesses may perhaps want some correction, rather than as beings who bring into the world a corrupt nature and evil dispositions, which it should be the great end of education to rectify?'[205] There was an eighteenth-century rationalism in More, a confidence that reason and judgement could subdue the errors which the

---

[200] David Spring, 'Aristocracy, Social Structure, and Religion in the Early Victorian Period', *Victorian Studies*, 6 (1962–3), 263–80.

[201] The Earl of Kildare, quoted in Stella Tillyard, *Aristocrats: Caroline, Emily, Louisa and Sarah Lennox 1740–1832* (1994), 58.

[202] Roy Porter and Lesley Hall, *The Facts of Life: The Creation of Sexual Knowledge in Britain, 1650–1950* (New Haven, 1995), 14–105.

[203] James Christen Steward, *The New Child: British Art and the Origins of Modern Childhood, 1730–1830* (Berkeley, 1995), 159; Stone, *Family, Sex and Marriage*, 669–73. G. M. Young was wrong to suppose that the discipline of children became 'milder' under the impact of evangelicalism (Young, *Portrait*, 22).   [204] Fictionalized as Theo Pontifex in Samuel Butler, *The Way of All Flesh* (1903).

[205] Hannah More, *Strictures on the Modern System of Female Education* (1799), i. 57.

passions ('those propensities of our constitution') naturally led to, but with the next generation the evangelical message became more scary. Mary Martha Sherwood had an Enid Blyton-like facility for writing children's stories, and brought out more than 300 books, tracts, and chapbooks, but her genre was much less cosy. Although she regarded herself as 'one of the very happiest old women that ever cumbered the earth', her speciality was psycho-religious terrorism. A particularly obscene but far from untypical episode in her three-volume *magnum opus*, *The History of the Fairchild Family* (1818–47), depicts the paterfamilial Mr Fairchild taking his quarrelsome children to see a corpse strung up on a gibbet. The intention is to impress on them 'that our hearts by nature are full of hatred'. For after all,

> My child... you are not so healthy and gay,
> So young, and so active, and bright,
> That death cannot snatch you away...

According to one authority, 'most children of the English middle-class born in the first quarter of the nineteenth century may be said to have been brought up on the *Fairchild Family*',[206] but there were hundreds of equally intimidating polemics such as the American Mary Belson Elliott's *Grateful Tributes: Or, Recollections from Infancy* (1811), *The Modern Goody Two-Shoes* (1819), and *The Wax Taper: Or, The Effects of Bad Habits* (1819). Then there were the many spine-chilling novels of Charlotte Elizabeth Tonna. 'Be assured, my child, that, although very young, you are a sinner in the sight of God... There is but one hiding-place, and that is Jesus Christ, to whom you must flee, and beseech Him to blot out your sins with his precious blood; and to give you a new heart.'[207] In view of all this propaganda it is easy to see why, as G. M. Young put it, people found themselves 'at every turn controlled, and animated, by the imponderable pressure of the Evangelical discipline'. Bestowing promiscuous affection, on the other hand, was as dangerous as giving too much alms to the poor, an assumption in which some children seem to have been complicit, at least in hindsight. The grown-up Frances Shelley, for example, reflected ruefully on the indiscriminate manner in which her mother had petted her.

> She was not judicious in the management of her 'lambkin' (as she used to call me)... I disliked her impetuous caressing, and early learnt to allow myself, as a favour to *her*, to be kissed; and not, as is usual with most children, to receive a caress as the reward of good conduct and maternal affection.[208]

Evangelicals were frequently in conflict with High (or Orthodox) Churchmen. In the Blagdon Controversy of 1799–1803, for example, More was

---

[206] *DNB, ODNB.*

[207] Charlotte Elizabeth [Tonna], *Tales and Illustrations*, 4th edn. (Dublin, 1844), vol. i, p. xxi.

[208] *The Diary of Frances Lady Shelley 1787–1873*, ed. Richard Edgcumbe (1912–13), i. 1.

accused by local clergymen of hiring a succession of 'methodistical' Sunday school teachers simply because they were given to enthusiasm and extempore prayer. There followed a long Trollopean power struggle in which clerical dignitaries from London were mobilized to sort out a remote Somerset parish. Then there was the Cambridge Controversy (1810–13) over how to preach Jesus Christ to heathens overseas.[209] The exclusively Anglican Church Missionary Society (1799), though successful, resented the still greater success of the inter-denominational British and Foreign Bible Society (BFBS, 1804), which by 1825 had issued 4,252,000 Bibles in 140 languages, starting in Wales but mainly in India and Africa. Tensions spilled over when 200 fired-up undergraduates met in Cambridge to found a BFBS auxiliary branch. Simeon compared the occasion to the day of Pentecost ('Many, many tears were shed ... and God himself was manifestly present'[210]), but High Churchmen strongly disapproved, partly because of the inclusion of Dissenters, more specifically because the Bible Society circulated the Scriptures neat, without the Prayer Book to provide an orthodox leavening of interpretation. The conflict climaxed in an acrimonious dispute between Isaac Milner, a rumbustious and evangelical professor of mathematics, and the controversialist Herbert Marsh, professor of divinity. The latter was not himself a High Churchman—he defied categorization—but like them he put more stress than evangelicals on the Creeds, the Prayer Book, the Catechism, and the sacramental and sacerdotal aspects of religion. A related point of dispute was the importance of the Church as an institution; in the next generation it would be High Churchmen like William Van Mildert, Bishop of Durham (1826–36), and Henry Phillpotts, Bishop of Exeter (1831–69), who mainly drove forward the movement for diocesan revival. The most acute doctrinal dispute arose from the evangelical emphasis on conversion, which seemed to High Churchmen to deny both the necessity of Church attendance and the spiritual validity of baptism as a sacrament. They believed that sinners had to grow in faith gradually through a process of sanctification and purification, a difference of perspective which explains why circulating the Bible proved so controversial. According to a leading High Churchman, Scripture was 'not in the purpose of God, the instrument of conversion—but the repository of divine knowledge for the perfecting of those *already* converted. I mean that it is the children's bread and not to be cast to dogs.'[211]

Historians have sometimes drawn a distinction between High Church worldliness and evangelical enthusiasm, but this is misleading. It is true that followers

---

[209] Brown, *Fathers of the Victorians*, 196–233, 285–316; Anne Stott, *Hannah More: The First Victorian* (Oxford, 2003), 232–57.

[210] *Memoirs of the Life of the Rev. Charles Simeon*, ed. William Carus (London, 1847), 308–13.

[211] H. H. Norris to R. Churton, 4 Mar. 1813, quoted in Peter Benedict Nockles, *The Oxford Movement in Context: Anglican High Churchmanship, 1760–1857* (Cambridge, 1994), 200 (italics added).

of the Clapham Sect despised 'high and dry' religion, by which they meant the routine performance of Christian worship for the purpose of appearing respectable and upholding the social order, but by no means all High Churchmen were dry. Many were affected by the current mood of religious revival and undertook crusades for the reformation of manners; there was more High Church than evangelical involvement in the Vice Society, for example.[212] They too held Justification by Faith to be the central doctrine, and cultivated a practical spirituality based on good works and self-denial.[213] They too published floods of pious tales, poems, and homilies; Sarah Trimmer, who edited the *Family Magazine* (1788–9) and the *Guardian of Education* (1802–6), was some-times referred to as 'the High Church Hannah More'. They too depicted France as an apocalyptic beast or Antichrist, while warning of divine retribution on England.[214] They too formed associations, such as the Society of Nobody's Friends (1800), the National Society for Promoting the Education of the Poor (1811), and the Church Building Society (1818), and it was mainly they who reinvigorated some older outreach organizations such as the Society for the Propagation of the Gospel in Foreign Parts and the Society for the Propagation of Christian Knowledge. And while Clapham had its official magazine in the *Christian Observer* (1802), High Churchmen hit back with the *British Critic*, the organ of a coterie led by Joshua Watson and H. H. Norris and nicknamed the Hackney Phalanx in mockery of Clapham. Finally, evangelicals and High Churchmen were united in their hostility to Latitudinarianism, a lukewarm and lowest-common-denominator religion aimed at pleasing most sects. This bond between them lasted until the 1830s. It was only with the emergence of a more populist and irresponsible evangelicalism, and of a more intense and proselytiz-ing High Churchmanship (Tractarianism),[215] that the two movements came to regard themselves as polar opposites. To emphasize the point, by 1846 Anglican evangelicals had begun to be called Low Churchmen for the first time.

Although Clapham evangelicalism was one of many manifestations of a new religious intensity following the American and French revolutions, it deserves its prominence if only because its tone increasingly informed public morality. Indeed, its sway may be attributable to its political success as much as to its intrinsic appeal. To blame it for the gloomy, philistine, a-sensual, and buttoned-up

---

[212] M. J. D. Roberts, 'The Society for the Suppression of Vice and its Early Critics, 1802–1812', *HJ* 26 (1983), 159–76.

[213] High Churchmen sometimes dismissed evangelicals as Calvinists, which was not true of most of them, but this was little more than 'yah-boo' polemic, besides which outside academia the sting had gone out of the Arminian–Calvinist debate by the 19th century.

[214] e.g. Samuel Horsley, *Critical Disquisitions on the Eighteenth Chapter of Isaiah, in a Letter to Edward King* (1799); John Bowles, *A Dispassionate Inquiry into the Best Means of National Safety* (1806), 54–9. See F. C. Mather, *High Church Prophet: Bishop Samuel Horsley (1733–1806) and the Caroline Tradition in the Later Georgian Church* (Oxford, 1992), 261–8.   [215] See below, pp. 468–75.

atmosphere which the word 'Victorianism' once conveyed would be unfair, since not all evangelicals resembled Theobald Pontifex in Samuel Butler's autobiographical novel *The Way of All Flesh* (1903), and some—like Wilberforce, Henry Venn, Simeon, and Milner—were conspicuously merry. Nor was prudishness its defining characteristic. The often repeated canard that evangelicals ordered piano legs to be covered out of delicacy is wide of the mark: nude mixed bathing remained commonplace until the 1870s. But evangelicalism *did* remind wealthy Anglicans that they were accountable to God for their privileges, and this, together with an emphasis on spiritual indeterminacy—*one could never be sure that one was saved*—increased the sense of anxiety referred to above as characteristic of the capitalist classes in this period. Spiritual insecurity, in other words, complemented commercial insecurity. Sometimes those whose worldly lot is miserable seek comfort in a religion which offers them an assurance of salvation, or recompense in another life. Evangelicalism did the opposite by reminding well-off Anglicans that it was useless to lay up treasure on earth.

Reduced to essentials it was a *contractual* religion. Evangelicals took from Anselm and Calvin the idea that sin constituted a *debt* owed by humans to their divine banker. Individuals stood in a *commercial* relationship with God, whose ultimate *merchandise* was Heaven. Christ, by his sacrifice, had *redeemed* that debt on behalf of all true believers. Those who did not believe would perish in everlasting hellfire. This system was commonly called 'the economy of redemption' or the 'scheme of salvation'. The word 'economy' is appropriate, since the market was the arena in which God's providence operated most obviously in daily life. The word 'scheme' is appropriate because the whole conception was a speculation in faith, a way of making sense of the world by a financial and commercial upper-middle class (including many landlords) with movable property. That is why any number of hymnists and prayer-smiths could write unselfconsciously about the need for sinners to acquire 'a saving interest in the blood of Jesus'. Looking back on the period, Gladstone described the way in which the Atonement had been envisaged as 'a sort of joint-stock transaction'.

Debt was capable of being both *redeemed* and *converted*. If only through the use of such language, evangelical theology made it seem that to be in credit was virtuous and to be in debt immoral. It helps to explain why public creditors were no longer abused as drones and parasites, but instead took on a mantle of righteousness. It also explains why the stigma of indebtedness was even applied to people whose debts were mere technicalities, as was often the case with master manufacturers, borrowing money to install equipment or tide themselves through a depression. Such entrepreneurs might benefit the community, but 'So what?', when what mattered was getting to Heaven, and the worldly community was merely 'an arena of moral trial'. Attitudes were to change in the mid-century when the hegemony of a financial elite gave way to that of manufacturers, who felt that their greatest spiritual duty was to develop their God-given talents, and that missionary work or soul-saving was secondary. It marked a reaction, in Anglican upper-middle-class circles especially, against a cruel evangelical theology based on Hell and the Crucifixion. In its place came a more creationist and incarnational theology, based on an idea of developing God's earth through energy, work, and labour—in short, through manufacturing industry.[216]

Evangelicals would not have recognized the description of themselves as other-worldly. In their own eyes *they* more than anyone cared about improving society here and now. They were motivated to improve it by their belief that Christ would not return until the world was fit to receive him. However, they conceived of improvement in moral rather than material terms, which explains why the great public cause to which they devoted themselves was anti-slavery.

SLAVERY AND NATIONAL MISSION: THE POLITICS OF VIRTUE

In brief, the slave trade was a traffic whereby blacks were torn from their African homelands and indentured to work on sugar plantations in the Americas. Protestations had rumbled on for a long time, channelled mainly through a Quaker-dominated London Committee, but the sudden nationwide explosion of moral indignation was largely due to Thomas Clarkson, an Anglican evangelical and itinerant campaigner, recently down from Cambridge. It was shortly after his visit in 1787 that Manchester mobilized a petition signed by about 11,000 people, nearly one-fifth of the local population, and the first mass petition on any subject.[217] It provoked a wave of imitations from other towns in a spiral of 'competitive philanthropy', converting what had been 'little more than a low-key lobby . . . into the prototype of the modern social reform movement'.[218] Given that the town had a considerable (though not overwhelming) stake in slave-produced raw cotton, the initiative looked like a remarkable declaration of morality over economics.

Manchester was just beginning to feel its strength with a series of political campaigns, successful in the case of Pitt's fustian tax and Irish trade proposals, unrequited with respect to Test and Corporation Act repeal. Along with these, anti-slavery has been seen as an early drumbeat of middle-class radical

---

[216] On these 1850s shifts, see Boyd Hilton, *The Age of Atonement: The Influence of Evangelicalism on Social and Economic Thought 1795–1865* (Oxford, 1988), 255–339.

[217] Only 30% of anti-slave-trade petitions emanated from privileged groups (nobility, corporation, freemen, etc.) in 1788, and 15% in 1792. This compares with 89% of petitions on John Wilkes in 1769–70 and 57% on the dismissal of the Fox–North Coalition. Seymour Drescher, *Capitalism and Antislavery: British Mobilization in Comparative Perspective* (Basingstoke, 1986), 70–4.

[218] Ibid. 67; J. R. Oldfield, *Popular Politics and British Anti-Slavery: The Mobilisation of Public Opinion against the Slave Trade 1787–1807* (Manchester, 1995), 96–124.

politics, and a prelude to the founding of the Chamber of Commerce (1820), the fight for municipal control of the highly profitable gasworks (1823–4), the struggle for parliamentary representation and incorporation (1831–8), and finally the Anti-Corn Law League (1838–46). As usual the reality was more complex. The local business community was fairly evenly divided over the slave trade, while those who supported abolition were motivated less by altruism than by a wish to establish moral high ground over its arch-rival, Liverpool, the world's leading slaving port.[219] Moreover, far from pointing forward, Manchester radicalism dramatically illustrates the caesura caused by Pitt's Terror. It was at a peak in the early 1790s when Thomas Walker, a member of the Society for Promoting Constitutional Information and editor of the reforming *Herald*, held the town's highest office of Boroughreeve, and another monster petition against the slave trade attracted a staggering 20,000 signatures. But then in September 1792 the local authorities suddenly banned all reform meetings, and more than thirty loyal associations were hurriedly got together. A Church and King mob trashed the *Herald*'s offices, forcing it to close down, and laid siege to Walker's house. Although conspiracy proceedings against them eventually collapsed, the radicals were effectively crushed and demoralized. Walker would not hit the local headlines again until 1815, when it was reported that he had grown an 'exceedingly large' melon.[220] The significant point is not that he grew it but that newspapers took any interest. It suggests not so much a switch to the Right as a complete switch-off.

Slavery was one of those issues on which politicians preferred to shelter behind the coat-tails of opinion-formers, which is why Pitt and Grenville urged Wilberforce to raise it in Parliament. In 1791 the Commons threw out a bill to outlaw the trade by a large majority, but in the following year—after more than 500 petitions had registered the nation's disapproval—MPs voted by an even larger majority (230–85) in favour of gradual abolition. Campaigners were euphoric, but momentum was checked, first by stalling tactics in the Lords, then by the war and by brutal rebellions in Saint-Domingue (1791), Grenada, and St Vincent (1794–5). These sparked off an anti-black reaction, which was cleverly exploited by the West India lobby. The latter did not *look* particularly powerful—averaging sixteen planter MPs ('country gentlemen whose estates lay overseas'[221]) and eight merchants, it had less than half the strength of the rival East India interest—but pariah status lent it useful cohesion, and anyway the political system was helpful to vested interests. Planters were able to prevaricate by mooting all sorts of impractical compromises, such as converting the slaves to

[219] Rachel Martin, 'The Manchester Business Community and Antislavery 1787–1833', Ph.D. thesis (Cambridge University, 2002), 52–113. [220] Ibid. 187.
[221] Gerrit P. Judd, *Members of Parliament 1734–1832* (New Haven, 1955), 67–9.

Christianity and taxing the trade until it became unprofitable. Nothing happened therefore until 1806–7, when the issue revived almost as suddenly as it had first erupted, and traffick in slaves was outlawed. This had everything to do with the Foxites' accession to power at last, and nothing to do with developments in Africa and the Caribbean or with popular agitation at home.[222]

The issue resurfaced after 1815 with the coming of peace, one aspect of which was the planned handing back of most of Britain's African and Caribbean spoils to their former European masters, including France. The question arose as to how to prevent the reintroduction of the slave trade in these territories, a move which apart from anything else would give foreign manufacturers an unfair commercial advantage. Abolitionists complained that the British Government was insufficiently enthusiastic about policing the seas to root out the evil, and they were outraged by the violence with which local militias suppressed slave rebellions in Barbados (1816), Demerara (1823), Jamaica (1831–2), and elsewhere. The campaign moved up a notch in 1823 when Wilberforce and Thomas Fowell Buxton founded the Anti-Slavery Society, the object of which was to outlaw not just the trade but slavery itself throughout the British colonies. Wilberforce looked to his friend Canning for leadership, but the latter proved little less temporizing than Pitt had been,[223] and so once again it was not until the Whigs returned to office that anything was done. One of the first acts of the reformed Parliament (1833) was to transmute slaves throughout British territories into apprentices, prior to their achieving complete freedom in 1840, though the pill was sugared for plantation owners by the award of generous compensation.

For a long time it was fashionable to suppose that the religious language used by anti-slavery campaigners was humbug, and that Britain really took the lead in abolition because its colonial sugar islands and the trade which sustained them were no longer profitable to an economy undergoing transformation to industrial capitalism and increasingly dependent on wage labour.[224] From this perspective, abolitionism was merely material self-interest masquerading as morality. However, most historians today believe that Britain derived considerable and still increasing benefit from slave sugar. One has even called abolition 'econocide',[225] though probably not even he would go as far as the contemporary

---

[222] Manchester was the only large town to send a substantial petition (2,356 signatures) in favour of abolition in 1806. Even in Manchester the situation was not like that of 1787, since on this occasion its businessmen were evidently manipulated by the London abolitionists. Martin, 'The Manchester Business Community', 158–98.

[223] Part of the problem was that, as successive MPs for Liverpool, Canning (1812–22) and Huskisson (1823–30) depended on local shipping and African interests.

[224] Eric Williams, *Capitalism and Slavery* (1944).

[225] Seymour Drescher, *Econocide: British Slavery in the Era of Abolition* (Pittsburgh, 1977); David Eltis, *Economic Growth and the Ending of the Transatlantic Slave Trade* (Oxford, 1987).

who hailed it as 'the most altruistic act since Christ's crucifixion'.[226] In fact there can be little doubt that the evangelicals were sincere.[227] This does not mean, however, that they were motivated by humanitarian feelings. It was often pointed out that their concern for negro slaves contrasted markedly with their apparent indifference to so-called wage slaves at home, and it is certainly true that most evangelicals opposed legislation to relieve poverty and working conditions.[228] (Dickens satirized their 'telescopic philanthropy' in *Bleak House*, with its ludicrous portrait of Mrs Jellyby, who is as neglectful of the needs of her own multitudinous children as she is solicitous of the natives of Borrioboola-Gha on the left bank of the Niger.) This is less contradictory than might appear, however, since in both cases it was the souls of the downtrodden and not their material well-being which signified. Wage-earners should be left to fight in the market because it reflected the divine economy, testing human beings and putting them on their moral mettle. The problem with indentured slaves was that, not being free—free to choose between God and Satan—they were incapable of being saved. Abolitionists rarely worried about how black people would manage once they had been emancipated, or whether they would be any better off materially than before. Emancipation was analogous to conversion, that most crucial moment in an evangelical's life when he or she broke free from the bondage of sin.[229]

There was another way in which religion drove the abolitionist campaigns. As the world's leading maritime nation, this country was more steeped in the trade's blood than any other. Its profits had led to luxury and hedonism, causing evangelicals to conclude that national prosperity was not a manifestation of God's favour so much as a mark of degeneration requiring communal humiliation and penitence. Why else had God awarded Bonaparte so many victories?[230] But what better way to atone for national sins than by moving against slavery. The idea had been adumbrated by Granville Sharp[231] and was repeated ad nauseam in Parliament. The slave trade was a 'foul iniquity' which would

[226] David Brion Davis, 'Capitalism, Abolitionism, and Hegemony', in Barbara L. Solow and Stanley L. Engerman (eds.), *British Capitalism and Caribbean Slavery: The Legacy of Eric Williams* (Cambridge, 1987), 215.

[227] Roger Anstey, *The Atlantic Slave Trade and British Abolition 1760–1810* (London 1975), 157–99.

[228] See below, pp. 332–42, 520–3.

[229] Calvinists tended to take a paternalist rather than a salvationist attitude to the lower orders, and were therefore less likely to oppose slavery than Arminians. For example, many members of the Countess of Huntingdon's Connexion supported slavery, as had George Whitefield. Boyd Stanley Schlenther, *Queen of the Methodists: The Countess of Huntingdon and the Eighteenth-Century Crisis of Faith and Society* (Durham, NC, 1997), 90–1.

[230] The thought that God might be on Bonaparte's side niggled, and accounts for the outpouring of relief that greeted Nelson's victory on the biblical river Nile.

[231] Granville Sharp, *The Law of Retribution: Or, A Serious Warning to Great Britain and her Colonies, founded upon Examples of God's Temporal Vengeance against Tyrants, Slave-Holders, and Oppressors* (1776).

'completely justify the avenging angel, in entirely extirpating [this nation] from the face of the earth'.[232] Without abolition Britain would 'look in vain hereafter for the glories of the Nile or of Trafalgar'.[233] 'God has entered unto judgment with us; we must, I repeat, look to Africa, and to the West Indies, for the causes of his wrath.'[234] Or, in Canning's words during a debate on Trinidad, 'Providence had determined to put to the trial our boasts of speculative benevolence and intended humanity... This day is a day of tests. I trust we shall all abide the trial.'[235] These and a hundred other quotations make anti-slavery seem far from altruistic, but not materially selfish in the way that Marxist historians have supposed.

THE POLITICS OF PITTISM: RHETORIC AND REALITY

It is time to return to the question posed earlier: did Pitt have a constituency, and did he identify with particular sections of the political nation?[236] As already noted, the situation in Leeds suggests an affirmative answer. There merchants overwhelmingly favoured Pitt while manufacturers, small tradesmen, and shopkeepers were for Fox.[237] Even as late as the 1834 by-election, when resurgent Whiggism was appealing to middle-class groups everywhere, and especially in newly enfranchised towns like Leeds, 70 per cent of professionals, 61 per cent of men of independent income (including rentiers), and 52 per cent of merchants and bankers voted Tory, while 57 per cent of textile manufacturers voted Whig.[238] Elsewhere the situation was less clear-cut, but there is some general evidence that Pitt's policies, being designed to benefit financial and commercial interests, alienated the lesser-middle class of manufacturers and retail traders. In 1784 he was forced to abandon a proposed coal tax because of demonstrations in Shropshire and Leicester, and he withdrew his new tax on linens and calicoes after only one year following protests in Lancashire and Scotland. Its replacement, a tax on retail shops, was jettisoned in 1789 after riots in London. A graduated rise in window tax in 1784 blatantly penalized mill owners, while the following year's attempt to incorporate Ireland into Britain's home and colonial trade provoked outrage. It prompted Josiah Wedgwood and others to set up a General Chamber of Manufactures to lobby for the protection of domestic industry,

---

[232] Serjeant Adair, *CPH* xxxii. 750–1 (18 Feb. 1796).

[233] Shute Barrington, Bishop of Durham, *CPD* viii. 670–1 (5. Feb. 1807).

[234] James Stephen the elder, quoted in David Brion Davis, *The Problem of Slavery in the Age of Revolution 1770–1823* (Ithaca, NY, 1975), 366–7.   [235] *CPH*, xxxvi. 868 (27 May 1802).

[236] There is little point in attempting to correlate MPs' allegiance with their occupations or material interests since they were all required to be substantial property-holders and were atypical in many other ways. Thus the fact that most manufacturing MPs supported Pitt and his successors rather than the Opposition hardly signifies given how few they were—perhaps four in 1784–90, eight in 1820–6—and that most of them had or would soon have an entry in the *Baronetage* or *Landed Gentry*.

[237] Wilson, *Gentlemen Merchants*, 171–7.   [238] Morris, *Class, Sect and Party*, 132–8.

especially against cheap Irish labour and Irish government subsidies. Correspondingly, Fox attracted lots of lesser-middle-class backing. The only areas to support him during the frenzied early months of 1784 were industrial Lancashire and Middlesex, and the Yorkshire and Nottinghamshire manufacturers also became staunch allies. Part of the reason will have been mere expediency—they opposed Pitt's policies and so did he—but there was more to it than that. Fox consistently professed mercantilist principles, and braved convention by criticizing Adam Smith. As a thoroughgoing mercantilist he argued that commerce, and especially colonial commerce, should be regulated so as to benefit domestic industry. This was the basis of his opposition to the Irish proposals, and before that to the American Intercourse Bill of 1782–3, which Shelburne and Pitt had proposed with Smith's warm approval. Its object was to allow former American colonists to trade with Britain as though they were still His Majesty's subjects, and to carry goods in their own ships between Britain and the West Indies in defiance of the navigation code. Eden, still at that stage a Foxite, had objected that the policy would 'shake' British commerce 'to its very basis, and endanger the whole pile', while Fox's key economic adviser Lord Sheffield had argued that the navigation code was England's Magna Carta, and that Americans must live with the consequences of losing their Britishness.[239] Fox also opposed the Anglo-French trade treaty on the grounds that 'they may gain our skill, but we can never gain their soil and climate'. Admittedly, his objection to the treaty was partly diplomatic. Hating the Bourbon family compact between Catholic France and Spain, and rather admiring the bravura empress Catherine, he asserted that a quadruple alliance with the northern powers of Prussia, Russia, and Denmark comprised 'the whole of my foreign policies'.[240] Fear of French influence in the Low Countries was particularly intense in 1786, and Fox hoped to play on gentry prejudices when he denounced Pitt's compact with the 'natural enemy'. But even the diplomatic motive was partly economic, since one point of a northern alliance was to guarantee Baltic timber for the Navy.

Just how far Pitt's peacetime policies benefited the fundholder interest is problematic. Certainly the yield on consols only fell below 4 per cent in four of the seventeen years of Pitt's first administration, whereas it had been below that level in eleven of the seventeen previous years, while in 1797 it soared to over 6 per cent. Pitt also reversed a long tradition of public finance whereby governments sought to borrow money as cheaply as possible. The hallmark of a

---

[239] *CPH* xxiii. 602 (7 Mar. 1783); Lord Sheffield, *Observations on the Commerce of the American States with Europe and the West Indies* (1783); Lord Sheffield, *Observations on the Manufactures, Trade, and Present State of Ireland* (1785).

[240] Fox to the Duke of Manchester, 12 Sept. 1783, in *Memorials and Correspondence of Charles James Fox*, ed. Lord John Russell (1853–7), ii. 156–7.

successful chancellor of the exchequer had been to convert old debt into new debt bearing lower interest rates. The trick was to persuade holders of old debt to trade it in by offering them a price nearer to its nominal value than it was currently fetching in the market. If, for example, existing 4 per cent stock was trading below par at 60, the Government could offer to buy it back from holders at 80. This would be a good short-term bargain for those stockholders who wanted immediate liquidity, but it would also be a good long-term bargain for the Government (and taxpayer) if the same or other stockholders could be tempted to buy new stock at only 3 per cent. Such operations happened on a small scale throughout the period, and occasionally on a big scale as in 1749, but Pitt did the opposite. He deliberately borrowed money at *high* rates of interest, arguing that 'a four per cent. was preferable to a three per cent. and a five per cent. better than a four'.[241] He was also attracted to the idea of converting upwards by persuading holders of (say) £100 in the three per cents to exchange their stock for £75 in the four per cents, which would yield the same annual interest. The obvious advantage of high interest rates was that the sinking fund would accumulate rapidly and so enable Pitt to cut down on the capital of the debt. The disadvantages were higher taxes and/or public expenditure cuts. (By the late 1780s there were signs of a return to more orthodox funding policies—or what he once called 'the sweet simplicity of the 3 per cents.'—in part perhaps because of the impact that borrowing dear was having on interest rates generally.) The sinking fund too can be depicted as an example of fiscal self-flagellation, since it necessitated higher taxation. Despite his promise that it would have the effect 'almost of magic', he was realistic enough to know that money did not come from nowhere, and he probably sensed that his own masochistic generation would relish the idea of paying for its own extravagances rather than burdening posterity.[242]

In terms of ready cash the net effect of Pitt's policies was a notable transfer of resources from taxpayers to fundholders (see Table 3.6). Judging where the burden fell hardest is, as a modern authority has put it, 'impossible to answer except impressionistically'.[243] Many people will have broken about even, but attorneys with funded wealth and no acres probably benefited, at least in the short term, whereas landlords with mortgages and rates to pay but no share income will have suffered.

[241] *CPH* xxiv. 1022 (30 June 1784).

[242] The rational Dissenter Richard Price apparently sold the sinking fund and upward conversions to Pitt. With his utopian optimism regarding the Creation, he does seem to have thought that compound interest was an alchemic device for creating money, rather than an accounting procedure.

[243] Patrick K. O'Brien, 'The Political Economy of British Taxation, 1660–1815', *EconHR* 41 (1988), 1–32 [8]; Patrick K. O'Brien and Philip A. Hunt, 'The Rise of a Fiscal State in England, 1485–1815', *Historical Research*, 66 (1993), 129–76.

TABLE 3.6. *Percentage of national income taken in taxes, percentage paid in debt charges, yield and price of 3 per cent consols, 1772–1810*

Year	% national income taken in taxes	% paid to fundholders in debt charges	Yield on three per cent consols	Price of three per cent consols
1772	10	4.5	3.3	
1782	11	6.3	5.3	
1788	12	6.9	4.0	
1791	12	6.2	3.6	83.75
1799	14	7.3	5.1	59.17
1802	14	8.1	4.2	70.89
1806	19	8.6	4.9	61.47
1810	18	6.7	4.5	68.41

However, it probably makes more sense to explain Pitt's allure for the upper-middle classes in psychological rather than material terms. Maybe he empowered them simply by talking their language and endorsing their values, as Gladstone was to do for the lower-middle classes in the 1860s. Even this was somewhat incongruous since Pitt was no evangelical, being steeped in religious indifference, and he was not always fastidious in his political dealings, yet he acquired a reputation for 'moral character, high integrity, and indisputable rectitude of intention'.[244] This was partly because, despite fretting over the state of his soul, Wilberforce and Thornton mobilized the evangelical constituency behind him following the former's religious conversion in 1785, and after that they never let up. Perhaps his lack of personality made it easier to project himself in the mirror of public morality. Private austerity was translated as public probity, while emotional restraint came across as rectitude, making him a sort of secular evangelical! For example, evangelicals loathed the games of chance *au courant* in Fox's set because they needed to believe that the world was rationally designed and providence a readable book to those of spiritual discernment. According to Wilberforce, Pitt had played dice, faro, and roulette with 'intense earnestness' until, having 'perceived their increasing fascination...[he] suddenly abandoned them forever'.[245] If this was true, and not just 'Saintly' spin, it suggests that Pitt was anxious about his own appetites, in which case behaviourally and psychologically, though not doctrinally, he might well have been in tune with the spirituality of the age.

[244] *The Historical and Posthumous Memoirs of Sir Nattaniel William Wraxall 1772–1784*, ed. Henry B. Wheatley (1884), iii. 232.
[245] *The Life of William Wilberforce*, ed. Robert Isaac and Samuel Wilberforce (1838), i. 18.

However, Pitt's main tricks were rhetorical, and must have owed much to artifice. In the first place, he was adept at making Fox look highly irresponsible in matters affecting business. Admittedly, Fox opened himself to criticism with his India Bill, which was seen as an implicit threat to all chartered companies including the Bank of England, but Pitt took advantage with a series of low rhetorical feints. He once congratulated Fox on 'having become a proselyte' to the sinking fund. No matter how indignantly Fox spluttered that he had always supported the fund ('How happens it, then, that the right honourable gentleman has discovered that it is a new doctrine in my mouth?'), a damaging impression had been created, and was made worse by Fox's hyperbole in rebuttal: 'No man in existence is, or ever has been, a greater friend to the principle of a sinking fund than I am, and ever have shewn myself from the first moment of my political life.'[246] On another occasion Fox sensibly proposed that there should be binding legislation to prevent chancellors of the Exchequer from raiding the sinking fund. For as things stood, 'What should hinder the House from agreeing to [such a] proposition . . . when so much money could easily be got at, and when they could so readily save themselves from the odious and unpleasant task of imposing new taxes on themselves and their constituents?' What Fox warned against had happened before and would soon happen again, but Pitt turned the polemical tables by insinuating that Fox's fears were children to his wishes. He 'gave the right honourable gentleman credit for having shewn great candour', thereby implying (without actually saying) that Fox had somehow *called for* the sinking fund to be raided in wartime.[247] Fox continued to protest his financial orthodoxy, but the more he did so the more easily rentiers persuaded themselves that this notorious gambler would repudiate the national debt.

Again, once it became obvious that abolitionism was a powerful political force, Pitt and Fox fell over each other in proclaiming devotion to the anti-slavery cause. Fox was magnificent in his denunciations of the abominable 'traffic in human flesh', the 'system of rapine, robbery, and murder', and equally eloquent in his noble-hearted support for 'the principles of justice, humanity, truth, and honour', but it was tactless of him to cite public opinion as a reason for abolition, to praise France as the nation most likely 'to catch a spark from the light of our fire', and to appeal to 'the principles of real liberty', 'the happiness of mankind', and 'the rights of nature' just twenty-five days after France had declared war on England.[248] And however splendid his 'torrent of manly eloquence', crucially Fox would not or could not capture the language of the Saints, whereas the

---

[246] *CPH* xxv. 503, 510, 1315 (29 Apr. 1785, 29 Mar. 1786); *The Speeches of Charles James Fox in the House of Commons* (1815), iii. 162–3, 207.

[247] *The Debate upon the Establishing a Fund for the Discharge of the National Debt, etc.* (1786), 30–42.

[248] *CPH* xxviii. 75 (12 May 1789), xxix. 344–5 (19 Apr. 1781), xxx. 518 (26 Feb. 1793).

mellifluous Pitt did so only too well, as when he reflected that slave-trading Britain had plunged more 'deeply into this guilt' than any other nation.

Thus Sir has the perversion of British commerce carried misery instead of happiness to one whole quarter of the globe . . . How shall we hope to obtain, if it be possible, forgiveness from Heaven for those enormous evils we have committed, if we refuse to make use of those means which the mercy of Providence hath still reserved to us for wiping away the guilt and shame with which we are now covered?

In other words, guilt brought with it the prospect of propitiation. 'It is as an atonement for our long and cruel injustice towards Africa, that the measure . . . most forcibly recommends itself to my mind.'[249] Such sentiments reflected a characteristic ambiguity in the language of retribution. Evangelicals who warned about iniquity always left an escape hatch open marked 'repentance', and an impression was given that, the later repentance was left, the more jubilant would the deliverance be. In this way the ethos of anti-slavery oscillated between an introspective craving for atonement and a crusading humanitarian optimism. Pitt's observation, that 'it depends upon us, whether other countries will persist in this bloody trade or not', struck most Englishmen as self-evidently true, such was their confidence that *despite everything* Britannia occupied the moral high ground. It was especially gratifying to reflect that their ex-colonists in North America still kept slaves, and gratifying too when Napoleon recognized slavery in French law in 1803.[250]

Again, Pitt saw while Fox did not that anti-slavery was a way of renegotiating national identity. Fox often appealed to traditional prejudice against the Continent generally and Bourbon France especially, for example in his opposition to the Eden Treaty of 1786, but his rhetoric failed to resonate. He probably underestimated the extent to which a commercial ethos was superseding his 'country' or republican emphases on agriculture as the source of wealth and esteem. By contrast, Pitt's approach to national identity, like that of evangelicals, was solipsistic in the sense of being fixated on itself rather than on some putative 'other'. As a young man he had almost revelled in the trauma of defeat in America ('The memorable era of England's glory . . . is past.' 'Her power and pre-eminence are passed away.' 'Let us examine what is left, with a manly and determined courage'[251]), yet eight years later Cassandra had transmuted into John of Gaunt.

We have become rich in a variety of acquirements, favoured above measure in the gifts of Providence, unrivalled in commerce, pre-eminent in arts, foremost in the pursuits of

---

[249] *The Speeches of William Pitt*, ed. W. S. Hathaway, 2nd edn. (1808), i. 385–8, 396 (2 Apr. 1792).

[250] As Linda Colley suggests, anti-slavery appealed because it enabled Parliament to fly at least one libertarian flag at a time when it was clamping down on liberties generally (Colley, *Britons*, 354–60).

[251] *CPH* xxiii. 549–50 (21 Feb. 1783).

philosophy and science, and established in all the blessings of civil society; we are in the possession of peace, of happiness, and of liberty; we are under the guidance of a mild and beneficent religion; and we are protected by impartial laws, and the purest administration of justice: we are living under a system of government, which our own happy experience leads us to pronounce the best and wisest which has ever yet been framed; a system which has become the admiration of the world.[252]

Pitt's language of 'manliness' reflected the way in which nationalist sentiment, which had hitherto been claimed by radicals as a means to attack a cosmopolitan elite, was ceasing to be a subversive force and becoming a conservative one instead. It compelled the Foxites to declare themselves as internationalists, and enabled radical patriots to be stigmatized as traitors. Evangelicalism and conservative nationalism were crucial components of upper-middle-class mentality, and closely connected, for if Heaven was often spoken of as though it were a commodity to be purchased, it was also envisaged as a foreign country to be colonized.

War destroyed Pitt's fiscal and economic policies. He needed so much money that, instead of continuing to borrow dear, he was forced to raise loans as cheaply as possible in consols and in three per cents reduced. Worse still, the enforced suspension of cash payments in 1797 led in time to a significant fall in the value of money which, like the income tax, disadvantaged the upper-middle classes especially. After the war was over, Pitt's successors would feel obliged to recompense the moneyed interest for its sacrifices, especially by restoring the value of money. This would severely damage producer interests, including those who made up the Government's other natural supporters, the agriculturists, and although the hurt done to them was only commensurate with the gain they had reaped in wartime, the political consequences were striking. These fluctuations in the value of money were to make the currency a central issue. In this way the politics of the 1820s would throw retrospective light on developments thirty years earlier. Without that light, the social lineaments of the Pittite regime might have remained obscure.

But this is to anticipate. During his lifetime Pitt cornered the market in political virtue by promising to defend property, the currency, the *patria*, the nation, the King, and Whig revolution principles. He also stood for public service, incorruptibility, rational government, and a balance between interests, and he benefited from his deliberately non-committal association with Wilberforce's evangelicals. Much of this may have been cosmetic, but Fox could not compete on this ground being associated with party, vested interests, loose aristocratic morals, Lord North, and the India Bill. Desperation eventually forced him to assert a radical and politically much less rewarding species of virtue based on liberty.

---

[252] Pitt, *Speeches*, i. 394.

CHAPTER 4

Politics in the time of Liverpool and Canning, 1807–1827

Although the threat of invasion had faded, the foreign situation in 1807 was worse than ever, and metropolitan society responded in frivolous mood. Adding to the confusion was the fact that in the last dozen years politicians had fragmented into tiny factions, and now death had removed Pitt and Fox, the only reliable reference points. Few could have predicted that stability would set in very quickly, largely thanks to a solidification of parliamentary allegiances which amounted, or so it could be argued, to a new two-party system.

THE DEVELOPMENT OF TWO-PARTY POLITICS?

To start with nomenclature, the label 'Tory' had never quite died out locally, and even revived slightly in the 1800s,[1] but with the exception of a very few self-conscious Neanderthals like the second Baron Kenyon, all Westminster politicians—if they thought of themselves as anything—thought of themselves as Whigs. As late as 1812 Lord Liverpool assured the Prince Regent that his new and essentially Pittite administration had been formed on 'Whig principles', though this was slightly tongue-in-cheek given that by then the friends of Fox and Grenville had taken out a monopoly on the word 'Whig'. His serious point was to deny that his colleagues were Tories. The terms normally used to describe Government supporters were 'official' and 'ministerialist', while 'Tory' remained a term of abuse hurled at them by the Opposition.

During the late 1810s some independent MPs and commentators began to refer to Tories in a neutral way, but ministers still held the label at arm's length. One of them (Palmerston) dismissed a section of the Government's supporters as 'the stupid old Tory party'.[2] That the word still connoted Stuart absolutism is

---

[1] Bedfordshire, for example, was said to be 'a field of battle for Whig and Tory politics' in 1807 (Thorne, i. 350).

[2] Palmerston to William Temple, 17 July 1826, in Henry Lytton Bulwer, *The Life of Henry John Temple Viscount Palmerston* (1870), i. 171.

clear from the following comment by a prominent public servant:

We are advancing fast to that period when an experiment will be made to stem the tide of innovation with a vigorous hand, and to govern the country upon principles which have never obtained a decided ascendancy since the Revolution of 1688. A True Tory and High Church Government, which a vast proportion of the power and landed property of the country are ready to support.[3]

Significantly, when the term 'Tory' finally did come into day-to-day currency, in 1827, it was used in opposition not to Whiggism but to liberalism, and was applied less to ministers than to an extreme group of Ultra Tory *enragés* that was emerging on the back benches. In that year half the Cabinet resigned following Lord Liverpool's stroke, and the governing party split temporarily into two parts. One of those who left office was the Home Secretary, Robert Peel, who for reasons which will become clear felt obliged to take the more reactionary side, but he only did so with grave misgivings.

I may be a Tory—I may be an illiberal—but the fact is undeniable . . . that there is not a single law connected with my name, which has not had for its object some mitigation of the severity of the criminal law; some prevention of abuse in the exercise of it; or some security for its impartial administration.[4]

As the apologetic 'but' makes clear, the term 'Tory' was still not a positive badge of identity. It is also seriously misleading, for even the Ultras had little in common with the Tories of Queen Anne and the first two Georges, apart from orthodox 'country' attitudes (e.g. dislike of London, high finance, and taxes). They bore no resemblance whatever to the old nonjurors with their belief in divine right or sacral kingship and a confessional State, and so far from sharing any nostalgia for the Stuart cause, they were bigoted Protestants whose constitutional bedrock was the Whig settlement of 1689. When Eldon, Newcastle, the Duke of York, and twenty-one other 'rejoicing Protestants' met at table one evening in 1825, they naturally drank 'the '48, the year 1688, and the glorious and immortal memory of William III'.[5] Eldon and Newcastle are sometimes taken to be archetypal Ultra Tories, but Eldon called himself a Whig and sat with that party during the 1830 session, while Newcastle declared that he would prefer to be called a Whig, since Tories were Jacobites.[6] It was only in the reform crisis of 1831 that Opposition MPs referred to themselves unself-consciously as Tories. J. W. Croker even sought to construct a late eighteenth-century pedigree

---

[3] Balliol College Library, Oxford, Mallet, diary, 5 Dec. 1821, iv. 14. John Lewis Mallet was a clerk in the Audit Office and the son of Mallet du Pan, who had been forced to settle in England in 1798.

[4] *HPD*2 xvii. 411 (1 May 1827).

[5] Eldon to his daughter, 23 May 1825, in Horace Twiss, *The Public and Private Life of Lord Chancellor Eldon* (1844), ii. 554. On the Ultras, see below, pp. 406–11.

[6] Nottingham University, Newcastle Papers, NeC. 5, 143.

for them.[7] Yet in his correspondence of that year Peel preferred 'Conservative',[8] a more accurate word for a party seeking to preserve the Whig constitution settlement. Significantly, the first edition of Dod's *Parliamentary Pocket Companion* (1833) described MPs as being Conservatives, Liberals, or Radicals.

Nevertheless, many historians have described the period 1807–27 in terms of Whig versus Tory, which at least has the merit of conveying the confrontational atmosphere. In retrospect it looks like single-party rule, but at many points the Government seemed likely to fall. In 1826 two Whigs coined the phrase 'His Majesty's Opposition', claiming that they formed, 'to all intents and purposes, a branch of His Majesty's Government'. Their point was that ministers had stolen the Whigs' policies—'the measures are ours, but all the emoluments are theirs'.[9] That was a half-truth at best,[10] but the phrase stuck for different reasons: firstly, it registered the fact that there was now, if not quite a shadow Cabinet, at least a body of MPs waiting to step into ministers' shoes, and secondly, because it signalled that the Opposition was at last an accepted part of the Constitution.[11]

Party feeling was heightened by some highly charged political journalism, beginning with the *Anti-Jacobin* (1797–8), to which Canning and his crony George Ellis contributed brilliant invective, and the *Antijacobin Review and Magazine* (1798–1821), a hysterical rag dominated by loyalist zealots like Reeves and Bowles. In 1802 a group of young Scottish Whigs including Francis Jeffrey, Francis Horner, and Henry Brougham founded the *Edinburgh Review*, which turned itself into a committed party journal in 1807, though the main point was to distinguish Whigs from Radicals like William Cobbett.[12] In 1808 Leigh and John Hunt founded a radical weekly, *The Examiner*, and in 1809 *The Quarterly* was launched by William Gifford as a ministerial riposte to the *Edinburgh*. *Blackwood's Edinburgh Magazine* (1817), first edited by John Lockhart, supplied a mouthpiece to extreme (later Ultra) Toryism, and in 1824 the *Westminster Review* provided the first systematic exposition of Benthamite Radicalism. However, it was mainly the *Edinburgh* and *Quarterly*, with their huge circulations, which set the tone, at once collusive and combative, of early nineteenth-century politics. While taking the form of anonymous book reviews, their contents were implacably partisan, unlike all their eighteenth-century predecessors, the

---

[7] James J. Sack, *From Jacobite to Conservative: Reaction and Orthodoxy in Britain, c.1760–1832* (Cambridge, 1993), 67–74.
[8] Peel to Croker, 28 May 1831, in *Croker Papers*, ii. 116–17; Parker, *Peel*, ii. 186–7; Arbuthnot, *Journal*, ii. 415 (29 Mar. 1831).
[9] George Tierney and J. C. Hobhouse, *HPD*2 xv. 135, 145 (10 Apr. 1826).
[10] Since both parties were divided on most policies.
[11] Stephen M. Lee, ' "A New Language in Politicks": George Canning and the Idea of Opposition, 1801–1807', *History*, 83 (1998), 472–96, pinpoints 1801–7 as a period in which systematic opposition began to be considered acceptable.
[12] John Clive, *Scotch Reviewers: The 'Edinburgh Review', 1802–1815* (1957), 66–7, 104–7.

Monthly Review, the *Critical Review*, the *Analytical Review*, and the *British Critic*. They were subject to strong editorial surveillance—Gifford was described by Hazlitt as 'the Government Critic... the invisible link, that connects literature with the police'.[13] Their writers oozed mock courtesy towards opponents, whom they addressed more in sorrow than in anger, and they never descended to scurrility or scatology, but equally they never forgot a quarrel or forgave an enemy, and they carried their 'paranoid politics' into every corner—literature, history, science, architecture, and foreign travel.[14] To some extent this reflected the fact that party was beginning to permeate all walks of life, so that there was no such thing as a politically neutral poem, but that hardly accounts in full for what Walter Scott called their 'universal efforts at blackguard'.[15]

Clearly, there was a vigorous two-party atmosphere, but as to the reality the evidence is ambiguous. An analysis of printed division lists, distinguishing between MPs who always or usually voted with one side and those whose allegiance wavered, suggests a fairly high degree of independence in the Commons (17 per cent during 1820–6), but its definition of wavering is arguably too wide, since it includes MPs who voted against the Government on just three occasions out of the 214 for which Opposition lists were recorded.[16] Economic interest must have been of prime importance for many MPs, the party game being little more than 'a period of light relief after the dinner hour or even after the opera, when a well-dressed mob would arrive to hear a peroration by Mackintosh, Canning or Plunket and then clamour for the question to be put'.[17] Taking Whigs and Radicals together, the average Opposition strength was only about fifty during 1821–3, a difficult period for the Government. Since the identity of most of these voters is unrecorded, it is not known whether a few MPs voted against ministers regularly or if many did so occasionally, but either way it did not amount to much in a House of 658.[18] Moreover, there were

[13] William Hazlitt, 'A Letter to William Gifford, Esq.', in *The Collected Works of William Hazlitt*, ed. A. R. Weller and Arnold Glover (1902–6), i. 365; Southey to ?, 12 Nov. 1816, in *The Manuscripts of Lord Kenyon*, ed. W. J. Hardy (1894), 564.

[14] The phrase is taken from Kim Wheatley, 'Paranoid Politics: The *Quarterly* and *Edinburgh* Reviewers', *Prose Studies*, 15 (1992), 319–43.

[15] W. Scott to George Ellis, 18 Nov. 1808, in *The Letters of Sir Walter Scott*, ed. H. J. C. Grierson (1932–7), ii. 129; Derek Roper, *Reviewing before the 'Edinburgh' 1788–1802* (1978), 32. Any number of friendships were destroyed by misattributed reviews.

[16]

Parliament	Government	Government fringe	Waverers	Opposition fringe	Opposition
1812–18	253	78	102	83	149
1818–20	261	80	48	16	171
1820–6	250	99	114	66	154

(Austin Mitchell, *The Whigs in Opposition 1815–1830* (Oxford, 1967), 66).

[17] Peter Fraser, 'Party Voting in the House of Commons, 1812–1827', *EHR* 98 (1983), 777, 783.

[18] Peter Fraser, 'Comment', *EHR* 102 (1987), 85–8.

occasions when ministers were defeated on a run of minor issues, only for their supporters to rally whenever they threatened resignation. In 1819, for example, the Whig leader, Tierney, defeated the Government on the Windsor establishment and the criminal law, but when he called for a committee on the 'state of the nation', avowedly a motion of no confidence, he failed embarrassingly (357–178).[19] An Opposition threat that melted away whenever it came within sight of success was hardly credible.

More tangible evidence of a two-party system was the attrition of various personal or family sub-groups. Two disappeared in 1812, Sidmouth's when he joined Liverpool and Moira became Governor-General of Bengal, and the Prince's (known as Carlton House) due to Sheridan's election defeat and personal dissolution. More significant was Canning's claque, nearly forty MPs, over whom (according to an enemy) he had exerted 'an almost despotic sway, not only in their votes, but their opinions and conduct in the minutest concerns, such as who they must see and live with'.[20] Yet in 1813 Canning announced 'the dissolution and dismissal of my party'. Richard Wellesley's was absorbed into the ranks of ministerial supporters, and finally in 1817 the Grenvilles imploded, with roughly half formally joining their Whig allies and the remainder gravitating towards ministers. One effect of all this was to dilute the two main parties. Before 1806 each faction had stood for certain policies.[21] Pittites, Addingtonians, and Saints were for royal prerogative, Foxites, Grenvilles, and Carlton House against it. Foxites, Saints, and Carlton House favoured parliamentary reform whereas Pittites, Addingtonians, and Grenvilles did not. Grenvilles, Foxites, and many Pittites supported Catholic emancipation while Sidmouthites, Saints, and Carlton House were hostile. But as the two sides of the House crystallized into parties, all semblance of unity with regard to policy disappeared. Grey, Whitbread, and most Whigs opposed the war outright, Grenville supported maritime expeditions but no longer Continental ones, Holland and Horner were against the war in general but favoured military intervention in Spain, while Brougham condemned the 'Spanish madness' above all.[22] Between 1812 and 1815 only thirty nominal Whigs voted with their leaders in more than twenty out of sixty divisions. Finally, both parties remained deeply divided on economic and foreign policy, leading Palmerston to comment that 'the real opposition . . . sit behind the Treasury Bench', and Holland too observed that

---

[19] For similar events in 1821–2, see below, p. 274.

[20] *The Journal of Elizabeth Lady Holland (1791–1811)*, ed. Earl of Ilchester (1908), i. 216–18.

[21] A. D. Harvey, *Britain in the Early Nineteenth Century* (1978), 3; Peter Jupp, *Lord Grenville, 1759–1834* (Oxford, 1985), 421–3.

[22] Henry Brougham to Thomas Creevey, May? 1812, in *The Creevey Papers: A Selection from the Correspondence and Diaries of the Late Thomas Creevey, MP*, ed. Herbert Maxwell (1903), i. 154.

Political parties are no more. Whig and Tory, Foxite and Pittite, Minister and Opposition have ceased to be distinctions, but the divisions of classes and great interests are arrayed against each other,—grower and consumer, lands and funds, Irish and English, Catholick and Protestant.[23]

There were just two issues on which at least one of the parties was united. Virtually all Whigs supported Catholic emancipation, while ministerialists were seriously divided, Canning and Castlereagh being in favour, Liverpool, Eldon, Sidmouth, and Peel against; and most Whigs supported some degree of parliamentary reform, at least once the Grenvilles had sorted themselves out. Yet neither of these issues provided a basis for clear two-party politics. Ministers agreed to make emancipation an open question, which meant that it could not be brought forward as a Government measure, and for a long time defused the issue. Parliamentary reform was an issue during times of economic distress (1817–22), but outside those years the Whigs rarely raised the issue, and when they did they met with little public response. Grey even blew hot and cold on Catholic emancipation, sometimes refusing to present Catholic petitions in the Lords. His insistence on working through the ineffective Irish moderate Lord Fingall may have been responsible for the rise of militant agitation.[24] All in all, it seems that the two parties retained their cohesion despite internal policy disagreements and a lack of clear-cut differences between them.

Perhaps this paradox shows how *strong* party feeling was, but in that case it is necessary to ask what did bind the parties together. It was certainly not forceful leadership or organization. Although Disraeli was wrong to describe Liverpool as an 'arch-mediocrity', there was nevertheless a palpable lack of charisma about the man who was Prime Minister for fifteen years. Contemporaries noticed his 'ductility', his 'timid temper', his 'meek spirit—too meek for a premier', and in the final years his subservience to Canning.[25] Canning himself described him as 'not either a ninny—or a great and able man'. Pitt had thought him 'by no means a contemptible adviser'. As Liverpool was in the Lords, day-to-day responsibility for presenting the Government's case fell on Castlereagh, the Foreign Secretary and leader of the Commons until 1822. So too did most of the foul abuse hurled by Radicals and poets at what they thought was a highly repressive government.[26] Elegant and courteous, Castlereagh could also be charming and affectionate in private, but in public he seemed (even to a friend) 'so cold that nothing can warm him'.[27] He was

[23] Holland to Grey, 21 Dec. 1826, in Keith Grahame Feiling, *The Second Tory Party 1714–1832* (1951), 401–2; Palmerston to William Temple, 17 July 1826, in Bulwer, *Life of Palmerston*, i. 171.

[24] Michael Roberts, *The Whig Party 1807–1812* (1939), 101–2.

[25] *The Autobiography, Times, Opinions, and Contemporaries of Sir Egerton Brydges* (1834), i. 181–3.

[26] Including Shelley's well-known diatribe 'I met Murder on my way, He wore a face like Castlereagh.'

[27] Cornwallis to Alexander Ross, 6 Nov. 1803, in *Correspondence of Charles, 1st Marquis Cornwallis*, ed. Charles Ross (1859), iii. 506.

also a wretched speaker, so although he commanded the respect of the House he could rarely command its attention, and it was not until Canning succeeded to both his offices in 1822 that the Government acquired genuine leadership. However, although Canning was adored by his coterie, he was so distrusted by everyone else that the ministerial party quickly split into pro- and anti-Canning factions, sometimes labelled 'liberal Tory' and 'high Tory' by historians.[28]

His only serious rival, Robert Peel, was the grandson of a Lancastrian yeoman turned calico-printer who had died in 1795 worth about £140,000. His father became squire of Drayton Manor and was 'the first "cotton king" to sit in Parliament',[29] in which capacity he sought to ease the plight of children in cotton mills. It suggests a tenderly philanthropic streak which his hard-nosed son did not inherit. Despite considerable wealth and squirearchical pretensions, this provincial manufacturing background marked Peel for life, but he did his best to assimilate into metropolitan society by cultivating art and science and by adopting its superior moral tone.[30] No politician ever referred more profligately to the dictates of his conscience. As a boy at Harrow he seemed prematurely mature (Byron, a contemporary, wrote, 'I was always in scrapes, and he never'[31]). At Christ Church he took a brilliant double first viva voce, but went down with a carapace harder than ever. He also had the outsider's fervent attachment to established institutions, especially the Protestant constitution in Church and State, which is why Whigs and Radicals insulted him by calling him a Tory. Yet such was his promise that, just five months after making his maiden speech as an MP, he was given junior office, and in 1812 at the age of 24 he became Chief Secretary for Ireland. Here he displayed an appetite and talent for administration, and became the undisputed champion of the anti-Catholics. Clearly he was a coming man, but hardly so becoming as to account for the behaviour of his father, who in 1819 informed a packed and tense House that on the occasion of his son's christening he had dedicated the baby's life to the service of his country, that he might follow in the steps of 'the immortal Mr Pitt'. Now this was trumpery paternal moonshine, especially as Pitt had hardly become recognized as one of the immortals by 1788, but instead of raising guffaws his maunderings were received seriously on the Government benches. It suggests that many MPs, frightened by post-war radicalism, were desperate to find a successor to the 'pilot that weathered the storm'. Peel was to be a second Pitt,

[28] For a discussion of the principles dividing liberal from high Tories, see below, Ch. 5.

[29] Thorne, iv. 741.

[30] Though in some respects Peel's social anxieties focused more on those below than above him. As a young and privileged child in rapidly industrializing Lancashire, he would apparently 'walk a mile round rather than encounter the rude jests of the Bury lads' (Lawrence Peel, *A Sketch of the Life and Character of Sir Robert Peel* (1860), 49).

[31] *Byron's Letters and Journals*, ed. Leslie A. Marchand (1973–94), ix. 43.

which meant that he was invested with political longings he did not himself share, a false position that was to dog him for the rest of his career.

Until 1817 Grenville was nominally the leader of the Opposition, being the only person on that side whom the King might have tolerated as Prime Minister. The leader of the Foxite Whigs was Charles Grey, and it says much for the cachet of an earldom that so envious, peevish, and occasionally vindictive a man should have commanded any loyalty at all. Mildly dissipated in his youth—mildly, that is, for a Foxite—he now led a somewhat aimless existence. 'Deficient in reading and even in general conversation', Grey was an unusual Whig in having no interest in literature, art, religion, science, philosophy, or political economy. 'He had few inner resources . . . Only politics [could] fill Grey's life and satisfy his need for occupation.'[32] Unfortunately, politics in the vulgar sense was put beyond his reach in 1807 when the first Earl's death relegated him to the House of Lords. From then on his fires burned intermittently. Between 1809 and 1812 he repeatedly refused to enter coalitions which just might have edged his party back into ministerial contention,[33] and inconsiderately blamed Lady Grey's hypochondria for his frequent refusals to get back to Westminster in time for the start of a session, even when the Government seemed vulnerable. His dereliction of duty became so blatant in the 1820s that he felt obliged to hand the leadership over to Lansdowne, but with characteristic selfishness he made no public pronouncement, so that hardly any one knew of it and Lansdowne himself did not quite believe it. Vainglorious, self-righteous, manic-depressive, Grey suffered the longest of all Fox's martyrs, before coming unexpectedly into a reward he hardly deserved in 1830.

Meanwhile in the Commons, 'Snouch' Ponsonby was a good-natured and garrulous Irishman who was too easily deflected by insincere flattery and had no understanding of tactics. That this 'old drone' should have survived as leader for ten years after 1807, despite the open contempt of many on his own side, is evidence of the party's apathetic state.[34] For the ten years after that it was led by George Tierney, a charmer and a dashing orator with an effective line in sarcasm, but despite his confrontational public image he was inclined to trim and intrigue in private, and hankered after coalition, disqualifying himself perhaps from leadership in an emerging two-party system. The party's '*effective* leader' was its 'whip and fixer' Viscount Duncannon, who was genial and popular but a reluctant and negligible speaker. There were several aspirants for Tierney's position, the most tiresome being Henry Brougham, a clever but bombastic Scotsman. There were also two lost leaders: Francis Horner, who died in 1817 at the age of 38, and Samuel Romilly, who cut his own throat a year

---

[32] E. A. Smith, *Lord Grey 1764–1845* (Oxford, 1990), 150, 324.
[33] Like Rockingham before him.   [34] Thorne, iv. 861.

later in grief over his wife's death. Romilly had just managed to capture radical Westminster and would have established the party's credentials in the contested area of legal reform, while Horner was virtually the only Whig with a mastery of economic theory. Even more to the point, Romilly's puritanical austerity and Horner's lugubrious projection of rectitude suited the times and might have acted as antidotes to memories of Fox's levity.[35]

Yet arguably it was mainly the memory of the former leader which made the party tick, for he like Pitt was subjected to a powerful posthumous cult. Both men were routinely referred to as 'immortal', and their birthdays continued to be celebrated as though they had been monarchs. Tribal loyalties were further strengthened by at least fifty-three local Pitt clubs, and a similar number devoted to the memory of Fox, many of which were run by James Perry, the editor of the leading Whig newspaper, the *Morning Chronicle*. Their widely reported proceedings consisted of dinners followed by speeches and toasts to ancestral ghosts like William Russell and Algernon Sydney. Many of these clubs folded or faded during the late 1820s as politics moved into a new phase, but until then they provided a modicum of local party organization, especially at election time.

There was inevitably much disputation over *how* Pitt and Fox should be remembered. For example, Canning proclaimed the Pitt of 1800–1 who fought for Catholic emancipation, whereas Liverpool and Eldon recalled the minister who had subsequently returned to office on George III's Protestant terms. Both interpretations were at least plausible, but there were other more bizarre representations, notably those of the great war leader and devout Christian gentleman. So far from being the 'pilot that *weathered* the storm', Pitt 'went down at the helm when the waves ran highest', as a sceptic disobligingly pointed out,[36] but the fact that he died young, a martyr to the war effort, at the darkest hour, and shortly before dawn, was enough to capture the imagination of the coming generation. Even more preposterously, Pitt's image was distorted so as to impress the evangelical constituency. He had hardly been devout, and certainly not devout in the nineteenth-century sense, and it was clearly attested by Pretyman-Tomline, the Bishop of Lincoln, that at the point of death he refused the sacrament, saying that he had 'neglected prayer too much to have any ground to hope that it can be efficacious on a death-bed'.[37] The most he would do was repeat after the bishop that he threw himself on the mercy of God through the merits of Christ. Yet within hours of Pitt's death, stories of his

---

[35] Though he was hardly leadership material, Whitbread's suicide in 1815 deprived the party of yet another of its powerful parliamentarians. The reasons for his sudden mental derangement are obscure, but a possible cause was the defeat of his hero Napoleon, and the realization that he himself had become 'an object of universal abhorrence' (Roger Fulford, *Samuel Whitbread 1764–1815: A Study in Opposition* (1967), 304).   [36] N. W. Wraxall, *Posthumous Memoirs of His Own Time* (1836), ii. 71.

[37] Whereas evangelicals believed that it *would* be efficacious so long as it was sincere.

conversion were being put about. George Rose apparently told Parliament that Pitt had 'taken the Sacrament with the most fervent and edifying piety',[38] while the *Morning Chronicle* averred that his last conversation on earth had been conducted with 'that spirit of devotion which was always a leading sentiment of his mind'. Soon afterwards Tomline threw veracity to the winds by referring to 'a religious principle which never forsook him.... And HE who was his guide through life, and his hope and consolation in death, will proclaim his fame in heavenly glory.'[39] And so it continued. In 1818 *Blackwood's Magazine* proclaimed Pitt to have been a martyr and a prophet, while the *Weekly Political Review* depicted him as 'arrayed in glory, himself an host. While he sleeps in death...the grave has gained no victory over HIM...whose deeds will be transmitted to the latest posterity.' These absurd fabrications were necessary if Pitt was to serve as the patron saint of post-war Conservatism.[40]

Fox's apotheosis was equally risible. At least no one had the bad taste to turn him into a closet evangelical, but they gave him a haircut and shave instead. The classical busts and statuary which decorated great Whig mansions like Holkham, Woburn, Chatsworth, Castle Howard, Wentworth Woodhouse, and Holland House invariably depicted the dishevelled and dissolute-looking playboy as a togaed senator of Augustan calm, 'the last of the Romans'. Others more cannily anticipated the image of the mid-Victorian liberal statesman by making him out to be a champion of parliamentary democracy, individual liberty, and what today would be called human rights. The Duke of Bedford erected a temple of liberty at Woburn with a dramatically top-lit bust of Fox and a pediment by Flaxman depicting 'liberty enthroned with emblems of peace, prosperity, trade and liberality'.[41] This patrician fixing of Fox was challenged, slightly half-heartedly, by advanced Whigs such as Whitbread and Hobhouse, who tried to convince their contemporaries that Fox had been a Radical, struck off the Privy Council for toasting 'our sovereign, the people', but as time passed, the more conservative interpretation gained ground. Monuments erected in the 1820s, such as Westmacott's in Westminster Abbey, as well as poems to his memory, referred to responsible issues like anti-slavery, trial by jury, and pacifism, while overlooking more controversial issues like Catholic emancipation, parliamentary reform,

---

[38] Henry Richard, Lord Holland, *Memoirs of the Whig Party during my Time* (1852–4), i. 208. In *A History of the Political Life of the Right Hon. William Pitt* (1809), iii. 778–9, John Gifford strongly implied that Pitt *had* received the sacrament, but interestingly he received no endorsement from Pretyman-Tomline, who may well have felt embarrassed by the rumour he had helped to spread. 'You will scarcely believe that the Bishop of Lincoln refused to give me the smallest information respecting the last moments of Mr. Pitt, or even to assign the motives for his conduct' (John Gifford to Lord Kenyon, 18 Oct. 1807, in *Manuscripts of Lord Kenyon*, 561).   [39] *British Critic*, 29 (1807), 166–7.

[40] J. J. Sack, 'The Memory of Burke and the Memory of Pitt: English Conservatism Confronts its Past, 1806–1829', *HJ* 30 (1987), 623–40.

[41] N. B. Penny, 'The Whig Cult of Fox in Early Nineteenth-Century Sculpture', *P&P* 70 (1976), 97.

and republicanism.[42] Likewise, in a series of historical works, Lord John Russell constructed a virtuous Whig tradition in which moderate reformers like Shaftesbury, Walpole, and above all Fox had sought to uphold English liberties in the teeth of despotism, but in a manner free from all taint of radicalism.[43]

These mythical cults of Pitt and Fox show how different the parties were in ethos if not in policies. Where Pittites appealed to nationalism, authority, and religion, Whigs cultivated a civic, pacific, and libertarian image. In the short term it damaged them badly—some outspoken peace Whigs were defeated in the 1812 election, when bellicose patriotism was at its height, e.g. Brougham at Liverpool and Romilly at Bristol—but it also opened up links to the 'Friends of Peace' and rejuvenated the old alliance between Fox and Dissenters, so enabling the Whigs to stage a recovery at the grass roots. In return, Russell agreed to chair Protestant Society meetings on occasion and Holland acted as host to leaders of the United Deputies. Meanwhile, there was a corresponding tightening of the bond between the Government Party and the Church of England. Of course, ambitious clergymen had always curried favour with the ruling clique. What was new was the way in which younger politicians began to absorb the values of evangelical religion. Scandals like the Duke of York affair in 1809[44] made people feel that there was something rotten in the State, and affected many of the more earnest young men entering politics. On the Government side these included Peel, Goulburn, Robinson, and Croker. They met each Wednesday at the Alfred Club, many of whose members were touched by evangelical religion and were keen to discuss subjects 'political, literary, scientific, dramatic'. It was also 'a haven of liberal Toryism in economic matters', which is unsurprising given the link between evangelicalism and market economics.[45] On the other side were the Young Whigs, whose 'outrage over the York scandal' 'brought them together and created a striking separation between themselves and their parents' generation'.[46] Althorp, Milton, Tavistock, Ebrington, and Lyttelton were aristocratic, morally earnest, deeply puritanical, and fervently evangelical (though they did not so describe themselves). Naturally they stood out like extremely sore thumbs in the Whig Party, not only for their religiosity but for their attachment to political economy.[47]

---

[42] Ibid. 101–3.

[43] Richard Brent, *Liberal Anglican Politics: Whiggery, Religion, and Reform 1830–1841* (Oxford, 1987), 44–51. [44] See below, pp. 216–17.

[45] Brian Jenkins, *Henry Goulburn 1784–1856: A Political Biography* (Liverpool, 1996), 22. A member commented in 1820, 'A duller place than the Alfred there does not exist . . . The bores prevail there . . . It is the asylum of doting Tories and drivelling Quidnuncs. But they are civil and quiet' (J. W. Ward to Edward Copleston, 16 May 1820, in *Letters of the Earl of Dudley to the Bishop of Llandaff*, ed. E. J. Copleston (1840), 251).

[46] Ellis Archer Wasson, *Whig Renaissance: Lord Althorp and the Whig Party 1782–1845* (New York, 1987), 44–53.

[47] Peter Mandler, *Aristocratic Government in the Age of Reform: Whigs and Liberals, 1830–1852* (Oxford, 1990), 87–96.

Being out of office the Whigs missed out on patronage. That they retained their cohesiveness was due in part to their 'aristocratic subculture', itself a protest perhaps against the increasingly individualistic attitudes of the gentry and the upper-middle classes. Intermarriage meant that Grand Whiggery was a 'cousinhood' in which established families like the Cavendishes, Bedfords, and Howards rubbed genes with more parvenu shoots such as the Ponsonbys and Foxes. At the same time salonnières such as Harriet, Countess of Bessborough, presided over a social set in which sexual intrigue, extravagance, and exotic travel mixed with an interest in classical learning, the arts, and the public weal. Such behaviour had seemed perfectly natural in the days of Georgiana, Duchess of Devonshire, but now it seemed somewhat forced, as though it were in conscious defiance of the new Puritanism.[48] Brooks's Club catered for Whig MPs, as White's did for Government supporters and Boodle's for independent country gentlemen, but from 1797 onwards the Opposition's most eligible important social base was Holland House in Kensington. Elizabeth, Lady Holland, was not invited out because as a divorcée she was considered ill-fit company for respectable women. (That she was also lecherous did not matter in these circles.) She took revenge by turning herself into the most desired hostess in town. From Byron in 1812 to Dickens in 1838 her house was somewhere where Whigs could admire Napoleon, damn the Tories, scoff at God, and preach progressive liberalism including anti-slavery, which was especially high-minded given that Holland's Jamaican estates employed 500 slaves.[49] Greville called it 'the only great house of reception and constant society in England', and it must also have been one of the very few where politics dominated the conversation rather than religion, grouse, horses, port, or sex. It was where young men of parts were put through their intellectual paces in competition with Sydney Smith, Samuel Rogers, Henry Luttrell, 'Conversation' Sharp, John Allen, James Mackintosh, and T. B. Macaulay as well as assorted roués, artists, illuminati, politicos, grandees, foreign ambassadors, French and Italian refugees. If they passed muster they would be recruited to the cause. It was largely thanks to the Hollands that the Whigs were able to attract so much aspiring political and intellectual talent despite their prolonged inability to reward clever men with official places or secure preferment for them in their professions.[50]

As often happens when there are few policy differences between two parties, both made a bid for the centre ground, which in turn left many on the outside feeling frustrated, especially Radicals and Ultra Tories. Radicals stood to the left

[48] Ibid., 44–71.
[49] High-minded or hypocritical? Was it hypocritical of Holland to oppose slavery politically while enjoying its proceeds privately, or was it the height of altruism to seek to undermine politically a system from which he benefited privately? Such dilemmas continue to bedevil progressive politicians (e.g. on the choice of schooling for their children).   [50] Leslie Mitchell, *Holland House* (1980), 172–95.

of the Whigs, while Ultras stood to the right of the Government party, but there were certain issues like retrenchment on which the two united against the centre.[51] This complicating factor qualifies the extent to which a two-party politics could be said to have operated.

In 1806 only two or three MPs could have been described as Radicals,[52] the most prominent being Sir Francis Burdett. Since 1796 he had served as an independent member for Boroughbridge, a small town with about 600 inhabitants and sixty voters, the seat having been purchased for him from the Duke of Newcastle by his father-in-law, Thomas Coutts the banker. This good fortune did not prevent Burdett from denouncing aristocratic borough-mongers as the main cause of the poison running through the veins of the Constitution. In doing so he diverged considerably from Foxites, who blamed the Crown for everything that was wrong, but then Burdett was close to the Prince of Wales and had a romantic notion that monarchy might provide national leadership through communion with the people. Where he agreed with Foxites was in his hatred of Pitt and the war, which he regarded as nothing more than a ruse to establish military despotism and take political prisoners ('government by secret and concealed torture'). His work on behalf of political prisoners[53] incarcerated in Coldbath Fields led to his election for Middlesex in 1802 on the cry of 'Burdett and No Bastille', but he was subsequently unseated on petition. Then in 1806 he was defeated in the same constituency, having refused as a matter of principle to spend any money on securing his own return. That election has been described as marking his 'decisive public repudiation of the Whigs',[54] and in the following year he was returned as Radical MP for Westminster after a highly organized campaign in which, perhaps for the first time, artisan agitators succeeded in defying the wishes of a local elite.[55] Despite his lack of common touch, or sense of fellow feeling with the people, whom he apostrophized so readily, Burdett's evident sincerity and integrity won him the adulation of the London crowd, forcing fellow reformers like Cobbett and Cartwright to follow him in attacking placemen and pensioners rather than campaigning for an extension of the franchise. It was an understandable response to the threat of a bloated wartime state, but in retrospect it can be seen that Burdett led radicalism off on a detour, and it was not until the emergence of Chartism in the 1830s that it reverted to its eighteenth-century priorities. By that time Burdett, who remained in Parliament until 1844, had become the Conservative member for North Wiltshire, but even in his radical days he had proclaimed adherence to

---

[51] The implications of this are discussed below, pp. 517–24.   [52] Thorne, i. 195.

[53] Including Colonel Despard. Burdett had associated with United Irishmen before the 1798 Rising and half-expected to be indicted himself.   [54] Thorne, iii. 305.

[55] J. M. Main, 'Radical Westminster, 1807–1820', *Historical Studies: Australia and New Zealand*, 12 (1965–7), 186–204; J. R. Dinwiddy, *Radicalism and Reform in Britain, 1780–1850* (1992), 109–23.

'the principles of those who were called Tories in the reign of Queen Anne',[56] and his patriotism always had an agrarian tinge.

From 1807 on there was a growing cohort of parliamentary Radicals whose significance lay mainly in their claim to represent popular opinion, especially that of the growing number of independent freeholders' clubs and associations. There are problems of definition, especially as between Radical and 'advanced' Whig, but in the 1820s the party numbered about twenty-four MPs and included the aristocrats Hamilton, Folkestone, and Sefton as well as the sons of artisans such as Robert Waithman and Matthew Wood. The popular constituencies of London, Westminster, and Southwark remained the most important strongholds, but Radicals were also returned for Norwich and for industrial areas in the Midlands such as Stafford. Though new to Parliament, Radicals were older than most MPs, and kept alive an eighteenth-century tradition of debate centred on individual rights and liberties: the entitlement of Dissenters to civic office, of foreign aliens to privacy, of criminals to justice, of children to education, of women to legal status within marriage, of soldiers not to be flogged, of animals not to be tortured, of the dead not to be anatomized. Some like Joseph Hume were equally passionate about retrenchment. Their motive was not so much to reduce taxation as to undermine Old Corruption and the Pitt system—that network of patronage and preferment which alone (as it seemed to them) kept the regime in power.[57] As a perceptive historian has written, 'Radicalism was a protest against both political parties. One was born (or adopted) a whig, one was raised by preferment or office to be a tory, but one became a radical as soon as one began to question whether birth or preferment should by themselves confer political power.'[58]

About twenty Whig frondeurs such as Whitbread, Brougham, H. G. Bennet, and Thomas Creevey associated informally with Radicals and strove to keep pace with them on civil, parliamentary, and economical reform.[59] Rather absurdly they were nicknamed 'the Mountain' after Robespierre, Danton, Marat, and Saint-Just in the Revolutionary Convention. Their activities placed more *bien pensant* Whigs in a tactical dilemma, evident in 1809 when Cartwright and Burdett swayed an emotional meeting at the Crown and Anchor over the iniquities of the Duke of York. Even sympathetic Whigs like Whitbread stayed

[56] Such as Bolingbroke (Thorne, iii. 313).
[57] In the 1820s, however, as parliamentary Radicals like Burdett almost merged into the constitutional Opposition, a more important division opened up between them (and Place's Westminster Committee) on the one hand and more populist extra-parliamentary Radicals such as Wooler, Carlile, and Hunt.
[58] William Thomas, 'Whigs and Radicals in Westminster: The Election of 1819', *Guildhall Miscellany*, 3 (1970), 184.
[59] Dean Rapp, 'The Left-Wing Whigs: Whitbread, the Mountain and Reform, 1809–1815', *JBS* 21/2 (1981–2), 35–66.

away on that occasion, since the Duke was the Prince of Wales's favourite brother and the reversionary interest still seemed their best hope of obtaining office. 'Oh, the damned *Whigs*!', expostulated Cobbett, who led the chorus of radical abuse against them. A similar situation arose in 1819, after troops dispersed a peaceful crowd of protesters with fatal results at St Peter's Fields in Manchester.[60] Radicals were incandescent, but the Whigs hesitated. While they were naturally anxious to take advantage of any issue that might bring the Government unpopularity, and were keen not to let Radicals make all the popular running, they were all too well aware that middle opinion was likely to react in an authoritarian direction. When Earl Fitzwilliam, the Whig Lord Lieutenant for the West Riding, called for an inquiry into the conduct of the Manchester magistrates, he was dismissed from his post by the Government, but it was probably the chill behind his back that Fitzwilliam noticed most. Even the sincerity of the Whigs' hostility to Old Corruption could be questioned. While they wished to eliminate those jobs and sinecures which kept ministers in office, they remained 'official expectants' themselves and did not wish to go all the way with the Radicals. Yet if most Radicals outflanked the Whigs on the left, others outflanked them on the right, especially romantic Radicals like Burdett and Cobbett, with their almost 'Tory' reverence for the Crown and their contempt for an increasingly capitalist aristocracy.

Notwithstanding this muddying of the waters, the lack of discipline, and the internal party divisions over policy, the fact remains that politics was polarized, bipartisan, and often bitter. This would appear to be a two-party system without parties to put in it, and one consequence was that the Lower House achieved a considerable degree of independence. Eighteenth-century governments had managed Parliament through influence, but a squeeze on placemen and patronage led to a breakdown of discipline and made it hard for Liverpool to get legislation through. He therefore had to devote an inordinate amount of effort to tactical manoeuvre, for example by 'throwing tubs to whales', disguising his real intentions, relegating difficult business to 'the dog-days' when attendances were thin, even deliberately agitating the Catholic question in 1826 in order to divert attention from a politically more controversial initiative on corn. Eventually a system of party discipline would emerge to supply the deficiency caused by the loss of the payroll vote, but until that happened the outcome of debates remained unpredictable. This suggests not an emerging party system but genuine parliamentary government, in which the focal point of politics was no longer the closet nor yet the ballot box but the division lobby. For a few brief decades in English history, what was said in the Commons actually swayed the outcome of legislation. Appropriately, it was also a golden age of parliamentary oratory.

[60] See below, pp. 252–3.

THE NARRATIVE RESUMED: ALL-OUT WARFARE

In 1807 Portland became Prime Minister for the second time[61] and immediately strengthened his position by calling a general election, from which he benefited substantially owing to a wave of no-popery opinion. Although still highly respected, he was now 69 years old and frequently too unwell to attend cabinets. This meant that, instead of operations being directed by an inner circle, decisions now had to be taken by the whole Cabinet, the dominant members of which were all of roughly equal age and standing,[62] and discussions dragged on sometimes for months. By contrast Napoleon could take lightning decisions, while Austria, Prussia, and Russia all developed chiefs of staff, including both politicians and fighting men, to decide overall strategy and direct operations.[63] Yet for all its shortcomings and despite setbacks and scandals, the new Government did inject a sense of purpose. Much of the credit goes to Canning, who combined Windham's energy and imagination with greater common sense. It helped that the anti-war faction had been undermined by the comprehensive failure of Fox's peace mission in 1806. There were still pacifists, but much less fraternizing with the enemy. In the 1790s many whose fundamental loyalty was unimpeachable had opposed the war, either because they sympathized with the Revolution or because they suspected the motives of their own Government, but treason of this sort was now rare—so rare that one historian has described its persistence in psychopathological terms as a 'Napoleonist Syndrome' (rejection of legitimate authority grounded in ambivalence towards a parent or quasi-parent, and a consequent projection of loyalty onto a foreign tyrant).[64] It also helped that British policy was now transparent. Whereas Pitt's Gold had mainly gone to fight an underground war, the new objective was to subsidize foreign allies.

Militarily and diplomatically the situation was bleak. A Fourth Coalition with Russia and Prussia had been confirmed in October 1806 and had followed the usual miserable trajectory. Almost at once Napoleon crushed the Prussian army at Jena and Auerstädt. In February 1807 Russia and France fought to a draw at Eylau,[65] but this was followed by a decisive French victory at Friedland in June. It led to the settlement of Tilsit, when Napoleon and Alexander met on a raft in the middle of the river Niemen and carved out Eurasia between themselves. Prussia was almost completely dismembered, a Kingdom of Westphalia was set up for Napoleon's brother Jerome, and most of Poland

---

[61]   After a period of nearly twenty-three years, the longest such gap in English history.

[62]   Canning, Foreign Secretary; Castlereagh, War and Colonial Secretary; Hawkesbury (who became second Earl of Liverpool in 1808), Home Secretary; and Spencer Perceval, Chancellor of the Exchequer.

[63]   A. D. Harvey, *Collision of Empires: Britain in Three World Wars, 1793–1945* (1992), 114–19; Rory Muir, *Britain and the Defeat of Napoleon 1807–1815* (New Haven, 1996), 9.

[64]   E. Tangye Lean, *The Napoleonists: A Study in Political Disaffection, 1760–1960* (1970), 208–9.

[65]   French losses were more than 10,000, Russian losses about 25,000.

became a French-controlled enclave called the Grand Duchy of Warsaw. Russia handed over the Ionian Islands and other Mediterranean possessions in return for vague promises of future pickings in Turkey. Finally it was agreed that, if Britain should refuse to come to heel, Napoleon and Alexander would combine to force Denmark, Sweden, and Portugal to join the war against her.

Tilsit marked the zenith of Napoleon's power, even if it also left his empire overstretched, and the Portland Government felt bound to react forcefully. Its first initiative in September turned out to be Britain's most ruthlessly brilliant coup of the entire war. Having got wind of a secret clause in the Tilsit Treaty whereby France would take over the Danish navy, it pre-empted matters with a military–naval expedition to the Baltic. When the Danish Government refused an ultimatum to surrender its fleet, Copenhagen was blasted for several days without even a declaration of war. Eighteen ships of the line and many smaller vessels were captured, almost 2,000 civilians were killed, and many prominent buildings destroyed, in a barrage of shells and round-shot which has been described as 'one of the most intensive ever recorded prior to 1914'.[66] Even George III said it was 'a very immoral act', and for a while the name of Britain stank throughout Europe, yet Canning (the main instigator) would have been more than gratified by Napoleon's reaction. For while the Emperor's outrage at this suspension of the normal rules of war was entirely simulated, his admiration was wholly genuine. Among British statesmen the bombardment of Copenhagen signified a moment of self-realization. As Canning put it privately, echoing Caligula, 'We *are* hated throughout Europe and that hate must be cured by fear.'[67]

While Napoleon was still getting over the shock, Britain hugely raised the stakes in the economic war. The two countries had been sparring against each other's commerce since 1793, and in May 1806 Britain declared a blockade of the European coast from Brest to the Elbe. Napoleon countered in November with the Berlin Decrees, which inaugurated the Continental System, a total commercial and postal blockade between the British Isles and the Continent, the confiscation of all British goods, and the seizure of all vessels engaging in trade with Britain or its colonies. His aims were to starve Britain into submission, cripple its commerce, and boost French industry in that order. The British Prime Minister, Grenville, being a committed free-trader, had not wanted to retaliate, but was eventually forced by mercantile pressure to issue an Order in Council (January 1807) prohibiting seaborne trade between one French or French-controlled port and another. This method of bypassing Parliament had symbolic value in showing that a constitutional State could take emergency action when necessary, but the measure itself was little more than a gesture since

[66] Harvey, *Collision of Empires*, 98–102.
[67] Canning to Gower, 2 Oct. 1807, Canning MS 42.

it did not prevent ships from the colonies from trading with France. With Russia joining Napoleon's Continental System, and Denmark, Sweden, and Portugal threatening to do likewise, the new Chancellor, Perceval, brought forward a proposal to ban all exports of cotton and quinine to France, and to interdict every European port from which British ships were excluded. Neutral vessels wishing to enter or leave French or French-controlled ports would be ordered to dock somewhere in Britain, where they would have to pay customs dues and purchase licences. Portland reacted timorously to this suggestion, and Canning (another free-trader) wanted to 'confine the measures to...countries in the occupation of the enemy [rather] than extend it to the whole'.[68] On the other hand Hawkesbury and Castlereagh, who had always advocated economic regulation, backed the scheme strongly. According to the latter, the war was 'no longer a struggle for territory or for point of honor, but whether the existence of Great Britain as a naval power is compatible with that of France'. Perceval got his way, and two further Orders were issued in November 1807.[69] 'Either France should trade through Britain or she should have no trade at all,' as one historian puts it. Not to be outdone, Napoleon immediately retaliated with the Milan Decrees, declaring that any colonial goods found in neutral vessels not carrying a certificate of origin would be treated as British and confiscated accordingly, and that any vessels landing in England or submitting to inspection by English patrols (something they could hardly avoid) would be seized. The labels 'Berlin' and 'Milan' reminded everyone that Napoleon controlled most of the Continent. Order in Council seemed parochial by comparison. On the other hand the Royal Navy proved better at enforcing legislation than French customs officers. Besides which, the mere fact that Napoleon had been driven to retaliate against unbridled British aggression was an indication, however tiny, that he was at last beginning to lose the initiative.

Auckland complained that Britain and France seemed intent on 'mutual destruction'. 'Such conduct could only be compared to the insanity of two maniacs.... cutting each other with knives across the veins.'[70] This was exaggerated. Smuggling remained endemic, and when it suited, the rules were relaxed by both sides. After all, Napoleon could hardly starve Britain without hurting his own farmers, nor cut off her trade without damaging his own merchants. What was breathtaking about the measures of 1806–7 was not the mutually assured destruction but the extent to which both countries were

---

[68] Canning, memorandum, quoted in Denis Gray, *Spencer Perceval: The Evangelical Prime Minister 1762–1812* (Manchester, 1963), 169.   [69] Castlereagh, memorandum, quoted ibid. 170–1.

[70] *HPD*1 x. 150–1 (27 Jan. 1808). Having abandoned Fox in order to take office under Pitt in 1785, William Eden, first Baron Auckland, was omitted from Pitt's second ministry and promptly went back to Fox, becoming President of the Board of Trade in Grenville's Government.

prepared to trample on the sovereign rights of other nations. Napoleon's Decrees covered not just France but appropriated territories, dependent countries, neutrals, and even allies.[71] In the same way, England sought to force all of Europe to cooperate in its struggle. Neutrals might have been forgiven for wondering whether, for all the rhetoric of liberation, the war was not a device by which the two greatest powers ordered the rest of the world about to their joint advantage. But though diplomatically ambiguous, the Orders in Council constituted a defining issue between the parties at home, and much of 1808 was occupied with petitions and Opposition motions to have them rescinded. Free-traders opposed the measures on principle, and Grenville asserted that they would backfire by stifling economic growth, without which the war could not be successfully prosecuted. Mercantilists warned that they would drain the country of specie, making it impossible to pay troops and bankroll allies. Humanitarians charged ministers with seeking to spread malaria among French troops by withholding quinine. Foxite Whigs objected that the Orders would alienate the country's most important trading partner, the United States (they had always admired American republicanism).

Portland's Government was determined to follow up the shelling of Copenhagen and the Orders by landing an expeditionary force in Europe, but where? The answer was provided by Napoleon who, anxious to strengthen the Continental System, decided in concert with Spain's rulers to attack Britain's staunchest ally, Portugal. A French army under Junot occupied Lisbon at the end of November 1807, causing the ruling Braganzas to flee to their colonial outpost in Brazil. Then, without declaring war, Napoleon turned to subdue Spain, an ally of France since 1796. By the end of March his forces had occupied Madrid and the most important fortresses, Ferdinand VII had been forced to abdicate, and Napoleon's elder brother Joseph had been designated King. The British Government responded to these developments vigorously. It was thought vital to destroy the Spanish Empire before France could gobble it up, just as it had been vital to destroy the Danish fleet rather than let France have it, but since it was clearly impossible to bombard all Spain's overseas territories, the method chosen was to encourage colonial resistance movements against Spanish rule.[72] Meanwhile, an expeditionary force of over 13,000 men was quickly mustered for the Peninsula from garrisons in Sicily and Copenhagen. However, before it could sail, the French were jolted by a series of popular risings, which prompted a small British force at Cadiz to help the Spanish resistance, and this in turn may have prompted a delegation of patriots from Asturias to visit London and solicit assistance. Here the public conscience seemed stirred by the

[71] Paul W. Schroeder, *The Transformation of European Politics 1763–1848* (Oxford, 1994), 308.
[72] See above, p. 108.

idea of a fledgling nation fighting against the French tyrant. Spanish fever swept the country, and the Asturian deputies were fêted and fawned on to such an extent that once, when they visited a theatre, the performance was held up for an hour. A profound ignorance of that part of Europe 'enabled every group in Britain to believe that the Spanish patriots reflected their own particular ideological views'.[73] Even such an inveterate opponent of the war as Grey argued that 'to assist the Spaniards is morally and politically one of the highest duties a nation ever had to perform'.[74] Money, arms, and equipment were immediately forthcoming, but significantly the Asturians did not want troops (after all, they had just been bitten in that way by the French). This meant that the British forces, which ministers were itching to send somewhere, went instead to Portugal, where Junot's army was still in occupation.

The decision to attack the French imperium by invading the Iberian peninsula can be seen in retrospect as decisive. It is impossible to quantify the various causes that contributed to Napoleon's eventual defeat, but the Spanish Ulcer, by draining France of men and material, to say nothing of confidence, was important. Unfortunately, the Portland Government received no credit because of an act of apparent irresolution. In July 1808 Lieutenant-General Arthur Wellesley, having made a reputation for himself in India and distinguished himself in the Danish campaign, set out from Cork with about 9,000 men, landed in Portugal, and swiftly defeated the French three times. He and two senior officers, generals Burrard and Dalrymple, then neglected to chase the enemy from the field and allowed Junot to negotiate the Convention of Cintra, under which 26,000 French troops were repatriated to France by the Royal Navy along with their baggage and booty.

It looked like a failure of nerve, and it caused a tremendous outcry in Britain. One moment the first military victory over the old enemy for forty-seven years was being celebrated with bells and bunting. The next moment it was learned that the French had been let off the hook, the Portuguese and Spaniards let down. Besides the sense of anticlimax, the Convention touched a radical nerve, a suspicion that the British Establishment was corrupt, that the military top brass were in league with the enemy, and that the war was just a device to feather the nests of elites in both countries at the expense of their peoples. Such was the furore that ministers got into a rare funk. Canning was for disowning Cintra and sacking the generals. 'This Convention must be distinctly *ours*, or *our* Commanders. We must judge *them* . . . or the public will judge us . . . I shall not be prepared to consent to take an atom of the responsibility for this work.'[75]

[73] Muir, *Britain and the Defeat of Napoleon*, 37–8.
[74] Grey to Brougham, 29 Sept. 1808, in *The Life and Times of Henry Lord Brougham, Written by Himself* (Edinburgh, 1871), i. 413.   [75] Canning to Perceval, 17 Sept. 1808, Canning MS 32.

The Cabinet listened instead to Castlereagh, whose priority was to exculpate Wellesley as the 'best instrument for future exertions'.[76] The Convention was endorsed, and an attempt made to fob off popular anger with a public inquiry. This turned out to be a lengthy exercise in obfuscation, leading to a declaration that Dalrymple and Burrard had forced through the Convention against the strong opposition of Wellesley. It was an untenable proposition, especially as Wellesley's own testimony contradicted it, and it did not deceive the public, whose admiration for Wellesley was diminished, but it was sufficient to save his face in Establishment circles and allow him to continue in his command. Dalrymple and Burrard, on the other hand, having been made official scapegoats, sank without trace. Wellesley would dismiss them later as 'two old women'.[77]

Why the cover-up? It is now clear that ministers not only approved of the Convention but had even laid down in general terms the policy on which the Army commanders had acted. They were anxious that the defeated French troops should leave the Peninsula at once. It was one thing to stir up disaffection in the Spanish colonies, but they had no desire to encourage popular nationalism among the Portuguese and Spanish guerrillas, especially as they were aiming to install a puppet government in Lisbon under the control of British Army chiefs.[78] However, ministers did not feel able to tell the public what they were about, and when the truth cannot be told, myths flourish. The most successful myth-maker was William Wordsworth, whose pamphlet *The Convention of Cintra* (1809) was stuffed with hyperbole regarding the Spanish freedom fighters, 'the rights of human nature', and 'eternal happiness...for all mankind'. Above all, Wordsworth regarded the Spanish situation as being, for Britain, both providential and penitential.

Do not forget that the Spanish and Portuguese Nations stand upon the loftiest ground of principle and passion, and do not suffer on our part those sympathies to languish which a few months since were so strong, and do not negligently or timidly descend from those heights of magnanimity to which as a Nation we were raised, when they first represented to us their wrongs and entreated our assistance, and we devoted ourselves sincerely and earnestly to their service.

Wordsworth insisted that, by treating the French invaders leniently at Cintra, British generals and politicians had proved themselves 'abject, treacherous, and

[76] 'My first object is your reputation; my second is, that the country should not be deprived of your services at the present critical conjuncture' (Castlereagh to Wellesley, 26 Sept. 1808, in *Memoir and Correspondence of Viscount Castlereagh*, ed. Charles William Vane (1848–53), vi. 454.

[77] Arbuthnot, *Journal*, i. 233.

[78] Richard M. Schneer, 'Arthur Wellesley and the Cintra Convention: A New Look at an Old Puzzle', *JBS* 19/2 (1979–80), 93–119. It is unclear whether Canning, who at about this juncture complained of being 'a cypher', was privy to this policy.

pernicious', unfit for association in Spain's 'sacred cause'.[79] His ardent and anguished pamphlet caught the public imagination, and made many English people actually believe their own propaganda—that they were engaged on a war for the liberation of nations rightly struggling like the Iberians to be free.

Napoleon now decided that his own presence was needed in Spain, though he did not come up against Wellesley, who was still in London being quizzed about Cintra. Before long the French once more held most of the north, and the British forces led by Sir John Moore were chased to Corunna, where they were forced to disembark for home. This retreat (January 1809) was not a disaster, but it was a deep disappointment after the heady expectations of the previous year. Ministers tried to save their own faces by blaming Moore—an obvious scapegoat because he was a Whig and because he was killed in battle—but public opinion was more discerning, and with the French apparently once more dominant in Spain, the general sense of disgust with Portland's Government deepened.[80]

This in turn helps to explain why a salacious scandal involving the Duke of York should have made such an impact that it occupied domestic politics for two and a half months. The Commander-in-Chief of the Army since 1798, he had not been blessed with much success in the field, and though far from being a nincompoop he was an obvious target for Radicals keen to emphasize the unmeritocratic nature of English society. However, it was his love life that got him into trouble, in particular his affair some years previously with Mary Anne Clarke, whose expense-account lifestyle put not inconsiderable strain on the Civil List. Since separating from her in 1805 the Duke had bought her silence with an annual pension, but in 1808 he broke off the payments, and she in turn broke her silence.[81] Throughout that summer the press worked up a lather over corruption in high places, the main charge being that Mrs Clarke had used her influence with the Duke in order to sell commissions.[82] These rumours might well have fizzled had it not been for a specific accusation by Brevet-Major Denis Hogan, who claimed that he had been passed over for promotion because he refused to 'kiss the petticoat'. Hogan's *Appeal to the Public* (1808) went through eleven editions in seven weeks, selling well over 10,000 copies.[83] But there was more to the fuss than radical attacks on corruption. There was also

---

[79] *Political Tracts of Wordsworth, Coleridge and Shelley*, ed. R. J. White (Cambridge, 1955), 139–40. For once Byron agreed with Wordsworth: 'Britannia sickens, Cintra, at thy name' (*Childe Harold's Pilgrimage* (1812–18), I. 26).

[80] Peter Spence, *The Birth of Romantic Radicalism: War, Popular Politics and English Radical Reformism, 1800–1815* (Aldershot, 1996), 73–107.

[81] Paul Berry, *By Royal Appointment: A Biography of Mary Ann Clarke, Mistress of the Duke of York* (1970), 48–52.

[82] A much-enjoyed cartoon entitled 'Military leap-frog—or hints to young gentlemen', depicted young officers jumping over the bottoms of their seniors in order to get to Mrs Clarke.

[83] Spence, *Birth of Romantic Radicalism*, 109–35.

a newly prurient tone, a suggestion that sexual licence in someone who was second in line to the throne was itself a cause for national shame.

Early in 1809 Burdett and Colonel Wardle tabled a motion accusing York of corruption. Confident of rebutting these charges, Perceval persuaded his colleagues to set up a committee of the whole House to inquire into the allegation, and for twelve days the bar of the Commons became the best theatre in town as the 'saucy' Mrs Clarke with her pretty turned-up nose made twelve separate appearances, during which she admitted to all the sordid charges and insisted that the Duke had been complicit. Ministers pleaded his ignorance, but with high society unable to talk about anything else, Frederick was persuaded that he should resign. In acknowledgement of this sacrifice, the Commons threw out Wardle's motion by 363 to 125, a decision which 'outraged the nation'.[84] Either Perceval had misjudged the public mood, or else he had correctly anticipated the furore and deliberately set up the inquiry in order to divert attention from Cintra. Whichever it was, addresses rained in from fifteen counties and thirty-one boroughs, virtually all demanding reform as the only way to check corruption and save the nation from the fate of Holland, Italy, and Prussia. It was like 1783–4 all over again.

This affair, the sort of scandal younger royals often provide in monarchies, can be seen as a frivolous distraction from the much more critical struggle for national survival. 'One can understand Napoleon's rage and frustration,' writes one historian. 'With all his power, he not only could not bring the British down, he could not even gain their full attention.'[85] Yet this is to misinterpret the scandal. The York affair was not displacement therapy to get people's minds off Napoleon. Radicals claimed that Britain was not only a nation at war but a military State, and that therefore military corruption placed the Constitution in peril. And, since there could be no distinction between public and private virtue, immorality in the Commander-in-Chief was indicative of a wicked State.

Meanwhile, the redeployment of French troops from the Rhine and Danube to Spain prompted the Austrians to launch yet another grand alliance in April 1809. This Fifth Coalition proved even feebler than its predecessors. Again Napoleon humiliated the Allies in the field, notably at Wagram in July, and again the Austrians sought an armistice. In an attempt to take pressure off Austria and keep her in the war, the British Government had already decided to send an expedition to the Dutch island of Walcheren in the mouth of the Scheldt. Ministers may also have hoped to stimulate a northern version of events in Spain by stirring the Germanic peoples to rise against the oppressor. At any rate, more than 600 ships (including 226 warships) set sail from the

[84] Ibid. 119; Philip Harling, 'The Duke of York Affair (1809) and the Complexities of War-Time Patriotism', *HJ* 39 (1996), 963–84.   [85] Schroeder, *Transformation of European Politics*, 384.

Thames, taking more than 40,000 troops, who landed on the island. Flushing was captured, and Antwerp would almost certainly have fallen too had not the British commander, Lord Chatham (Pitt's elder brother), dilly-dallied, allowing the French and Dutch forces to rally, while the Cabinet in London also havered over whether to order a disembarkation. Malarial fever attacked the British troops marooned among the dykes and polders, and by the time Chatham withdrew at the end of September he had lost 106 men in action and 4,000 to disease. This was probably England's single biggest disaster in the entire war.[86]

Walcheren might have brought the Government down in any circumstances, especially as Portland was terminally ill. As it happened, the Cabinet was in turmoil anyway, and it collapsed in melodrama after Castlereagh challenged Canning to a duel on Putney Heath, wounded him slightly with a pistol shot to the thigh, and promptly resigned along with his victim. The immediate reason was Castlereagh's discovery that several colleagues had been intriguing for months with the King's connivance to have him removed from office. He blamed Canning for this uncollegial behaviour, and with some justification, though to be fair Canning had offered to resign too, and it was Portland's fault that the plotting had been conducted behind closed doors.[87] The men were personal rivals anyway, and especially so since their official roles overlapped, but Canning's disparagement of the other was genuine. He had, to the surprise of some, shown brilliant talents as well as imagination and energy at the Foreign Office. He had been responsible for the Copenhagen coup, he had helped to transfer the Braganzas to Brazil and rescue the Portuguese fleet in the process, he had masterminded the strategy for liberating Spain, and he had opposed Castlereagh's Walcheren initiative, partly because it would divert troops from the Peninsula.[88] He was also cursed with what one historian has called 'the irritable impatience of a clever man. He was too clever either to be satisfied with the destructive and critical role of the Whig opposition, or with the pedestrian pace of those who retained power by their repute among steady men.'[89] Able plodders like Castlereagh, in other words.

On 4 October Spencer Perceval became Prime Minister. With his skeletal frame and skull-like face, he looked like something out of Golgotha, appropriately so since he was exceptionally devout, lived in Clapham, and is remembered as 'the Evangelical Prime Minister'. Charged with forming a government, he first offered to serve under Grey or Grenville, but they refused peremptorily. It was therefore necessary to shuffle the existing pack. Wellesley's brother Richard

---

[86] Gordon C. Bond, *The Grand Expedition: The British Invasion of Holland in 1809* (Athens, Ga., 1979).

[87] According to R. G. Thorne, Canning 'had never wished for this prolonged secrecy, for which'—such was his reputation as a schemer—'he foresaw that he would be blamed' (Thorne, iii. 390–2, iv. 769–70, v. 284–6).   [88] Muir, *Britain and the Defeat of Napoleon*, 84–7.

[89] J. Steven Watson, *The Reign of George III 1760–1815* (Oxford, 1960), 477.

became Foreign Secretary, Hawkesbury (now Earl of Liverpool) became Secretary at War, and Richard Ryder (the future Earl of Harrowby) became Home Secretary in an administration which was probably unparalleled for mediocrity and inexperience.

Having refused to take office with Perceval, the Whigs needed to invigorate their performance as an Opposition and to recapture some of the popular ground lost to Radicals over the York affair. They had been reluctant to go for the Duke because he was the Prince of Wales's favourite brother and the Prince was still their best hope of office, but they let fly over the Walcheren fiasco. They secured a committee of the whole House to inquire into its causes, but the decisive votes went against them and the ministers survived, probably because of a feeling among most independents that for all their failings they were still more patriotic than the Opposition. To Radicals these votes showed that corruption had infected Parliament as well as the executive and fighting forces. They were also angry that, although the inquiry had been minuted *officially*, there was no independent record of proceedings since the press—like the rest of the public— had been excluded from the proceedings. When a London Radical, John Gale Jones, advertised a public debate on the legitimacy of this action, he was convicted by the Commons[90] for breach of privilege and committed to Newgate prison. A few days later Burdett printed Gale Jones's speech in Cobbett's *Register* and was committed to the Tower. In attempting to resist arrest he sparked off serious and apparently spontaneous riots in London.[91]

All this high-profile radicalism was perturbing, yet it was something of a charade. It was nothing like as serious as the often treasonable activity of the 1790s, when English reformers had conspired with French and Irish malcontents. This can be gauged from the fact that the authorities met the crisis, not with spies and bully boys and the suspension of habeas corpus, but with pageants and propaganda centred around the celebration of George III's jubilee. In October 1809 the King's reign entered its fiftieth year, prompting gestures of public reconciliation and good-will. Debtors were let out of prison and the King donated £6,000 to launch a public subscription for repaying their creditors, an amnesty was declared for all deserters willing to rejoin their ships or regiments, non-French prisoners of war were allowed and even helped to go home, and in Brighton 2,000 poor inhabitants were royally dined and waited on at table by local notables.[92] Such ostentatious acts

---

[90] The House of Commons was primarily a legislative body, but it had the right to sit as a court in causes respecting its own privileges.

[91] For good measure Cobbett was also imprisoned in 1810, his offence being to have published an article critical of military floggings.

[92] Malcolm Chase, 'From Millennium to Anniversary: The Concept of Jubilee in Late Eighteenth- and Nineteenth-Century England', *P&P* 129 (1990), 141–2; Linda Colley, 'The Apotheosis of George III: Loyalty, Royalty and the British Nation 1760–1820', *P&P* 102 (1984), 117.

of public benevolence by the royal family, central government, and local authorities were the 'State's' way of responding to the radical critique of terminal corruption.

Ministers were far more worried about the currency, the national debt, and the state of trade, for the blockade was now biting hard. British exports to the United States fell badly in 1808 and again in 1811, while speculative attempts to open up export markets in Latin America mostly proved over-optimistic. A record number of bankruptcies led to increased unemployment in the manufacturing districts and to outbreaks of machine-breaking known as Luddism.[93] A profound gloom set in about the country's economic prospects, and this was compounded by a diplomatic crisis with the United States, which more than any other country had been caught in the crossfire of economic warfare between Britain and France. After a number of desultory and ineffectual attempts to retaliate, in December 1807 Congress passed an Embargo Act, the aim of which was to deprive Europeans of New World goods by ordering all American vessels, except those engaged in the coasting trade, to remain in port.[94] Britain and the United States both made some concessions during 1808–9, and it looked as though matters would be settled amicably when Canning settled down to discussions with William Pinckney, Washington's representative in London. However, after Perceval became Prime Minister and Richard Wellesley became Foreign Secretary, relations soured considerably, mainly because of visceral anti-Americanism on the British side.

Meanwhile the future of the ministry had been thrown in doubt by a serious recurrence of the King's madness in October 1810. Brought on by the fatal illness of his youngest and favourite daughter, Princess Amelia, it was at first expected to pass away in time, but it turned out to be permanent, and a few months later the Prince of Wales was at last installed as Regent. It was widely assumed that he would turn to his old friends the Whigs, and all the old arguments of 1788 were trotted out regarding the extent to which he should assume monarchical powers. In February 1811 Parliament legislated to the effect that the Regent should take no irreversible actions (to which his father might object on recovery) until the expiry of at least one year. This gave the Prince time to reflect, and the more he reflected the less he liked the idea of turning out the present ministers, however much he might affect to despise them on personal grounds. Of his closest friends among the Whigs, Fox was dead and Sheridan was decrepit. He had felt gravely let down by Grenville's Government in the matter of his own debts and with respect to the 'delicate investigation' into the conduct of his spendthrift and dissolute wife. (An official

---

[93] See below, pp. 586–7.
[94] Judith Blow Williams, *British Commercial Policy and Trade Expansion 1750–1850* (Oxford, 1972), 230–7.

commission of inquiry (1806) censured Princess Caroline for her 'levity of conduct' and for behaving like 'a female political', but the Cabinet resolved not to exclude her from court.) He shared his father's opposition to Catholic emancipation, was anxious to prosecute the war with vigour, and naturally loathed the more reformist Whigs like Whitbread. Therefore it is not particularly surprising that, when the restrictions on his freedom of action expired in February 1812, he should have written to his brother, but really for the information of Grey and Grenville, 'In the critical situation of the war in the Peninsula...I cannot withhold my approbation from those who have honourably distinguished themselves in support of it.'[95] It was a decisive act of betrayal.

In May 1812 Perceval became the first and last prime minister to be assassinated[96] and was succeeded by Lord Liverpool. Considering that the new Government was to last for fifteen years, the process of its formation was remarkably inauspicious. The details are not important except in so far as they throw light on the confused state of politics. Immediately after the assassination Castlereagh (who had recently returned to office as Foreign Secretary[97]) was confirmed in post, Sidmouth was appointed Home Secretary, and his follower Nicholas Vansittart became Chancellor of the Exchequer. Nine of the thirteen Cabinet members were peers; two others were complete nonentities. This disposition of places provoked a revolt among the independent country gentlemen, who felt that the crisis called either for a government of national unity or for a great man to step in as saviour. Liverpool was prepared to stand down, but unity was not in evidence and no great men available, though Richard Wellesley regarded himself in that light. His pretensions to the premiership— which if they had been satisfied would have united the civil and military powers in one family—complicated more than eleven weeks of frenzied negotiations, in which all the main participants except Canning were peers or (in Castlereagh's case) the son of one. A number of permutations were tried and failed. The Regent would not have the Whigs on their own, but seemed willing for a few of them to serve alongside Wellesley and Canning (now known as the Third Party). Gossipy Foxite epigoni were disdainful of this suggestion.

This is capital, two fellows without an acre of land between them, the one an actual beggar, both bankrupts in character, one entirely without Parliamentary followers, the other with scarce a dozen. These two bucks I say in the abundance of their high honor and character condescend to offer to Earl Grey of spotless character, followed by the Russells and the Cavendishes, by all the ancient nobility, and all the great property of the

[95] The Prince Regent to the Duke of York, 13 Feb. 1812, in *The Correspondence of George, Prince of Wales 1770–1812*, ed. A. Aspinall (1963–71), viii. 371.

[96] In the lobby of the House of Commons and at the hands of a deranged bankrupt who had a private grievance against the Government.

[97] In February 1812 following Wellesley's resignation from Perceval's Government.

Realm and by an unshaken phalanx of 150 of the best men in Parliament, these honorable worthies offer Earl Grey so circumstanced four seats in the Cabinet to him and his friends.[98]

The independent Whig and Regent's friend Lord Moira, first canvassed as a national saviour in 1797, attempted a coalition, but was resisted by Liverpool and Eldon. Wellesley would not serve other than as Prime Minister without Canning, and Canning would not serve unless he could have an office superior to Castlereagh. By the end of July everyone was weary and Liverpool was reappointed by default, still to some extent derided, but fortified by a general feeling that he was at least honest and dependable.

The central figure in all these negotiations was Canning, and the most significant aspect of Liverpool's new ministry was his absence from it. He was in several different minds about what to do, and wretched about the outcome, which he later called his 'political suicide'. As to whether he or Castlereagh should have the priority, a compromise seemed likely at various stages, but ultimately the point of honour proved decisive. Canning claimed that his friends were more sensitive on the issue than he was himself, though the most intransigent of them, Granville Leveson Gower, may have played up the difficulty in the hope that Canning would join the Whigs. Canning also believed, wrongly as it turned out, that a Government hewn from the materials available to Perceval would not prosecute the Peninsular War vigorously, and he was rightly concerned that Liverpool, Sidmouth, and Eldon would block Catholic emancipation. Then again, he cannot have relished the indignity of serving *under* his old friend and Christ Church contemporary. 'Old Jenkinson' was a man for whom he had genuine affection but to whose talents he had always condescended. Finally Canning, for all his boldness in office, had a marked degree of political timidity, born no doubt of his awareness that politics was not a level playing field for those of doubtful social origins. Even Eton and Oxford had not effaced the common prejudice, memorably expressed by Lord Grey, that 'the son of an actress is, *ipso facto*, disqualified from becoming Prime Minister'.[99] Having nailed his colours to Pitt's mast for so long, Canning was now unwilling to commit himself to any new vessel unless he could be sure that it would float. Hence his refusal to join the administration that delivered victory in Europe. He was very soon to lament 'the station in Europe and in history, which I have thrown away... having refused the management of the mightiest scheme of politics which this country ever engaged in, or the world ever witnessed, from a miserable point of etiquette'.[100]

---

[98] Creevey to his wife, 3 June 1812, in *Creevey's Life and Times: A Further Selection from the Correspondence of Thomas Creevey*, ed. John Gore (1934), 55.   [99] Smith, *Lord Grey*, 242.

[100] Thorne, iii. 399. In 1814 Canning accepted the Lisbon embassy, partly for the sake of its climate as his beloved eldest son was seriously ill, and in 1816 he returned to the Cabinet as President of the Board of Control.

LIBERATION AND LIBERALISM

While British politicians played musical chairs, a global turning point occurred with Napoleon's decision to invade Russia in June 1812. He narrowly defeated Kutusov's army at Borodino, but after he entered Moscow the Russians burned that city to ashes. Winter frostbite forced the Grande Armée to retreat through 600 miles of scorched earth, and by the time the remnants staggered back over the Niemen 400,000 men had been lost at the very least. Britain had nothing to do with these events, but they encouraged her to take the initiative. With Liverpool as Prime Minister, Castlereagh as Foreign Secretary, and the amiable, light-hearted, and shyly competent Bathurst as Secretary for War and Colonies, Britain seemed for the first time to be making things happen rather than simply reacting to events.

For a start, when Napoleon proffered peace terms in April 1812 the Government rejected them out of hand, ostensibly because they did not concede Ferdinand VII's right to be restored as King of Spain. Instead, 20,000 men were sent to reinforce the army in the Peninsula, making more than 150,000 British troops in the field overall. In June 1812 Britain and Russia formed the nucleus of the Sixth Coalition, to which Spain and Portugal quickly adhered. In February 1813 Prussia suddenly abandoned Napoleon and joined the allies. In June Austria was with difficulty persuaded to clamber on board once more,[101] in July Castlereagh secured the accession of Sweden, and in October Bavaria and Saxony joined up. With a united front of Great Powers in place for the first time since 1795, Napoleon was driven west of the Rhine following the massive battle of the Nations at Leipzig in October. Early in 1814 the allies invaded France, but there was a great deal of mutual mistrust among them, and it was largely Castlereagh's diplomacy, conducted in person on the Continent, that kept them together and led to the signing of the decisive Treaty of Chaumont on 1 March 1814.

Liverpool, Vansittart, and Castlereagh had made all this possible by insisting on massive subsidy payments to the allies, though this would not have been possible without an economic upturn. Pitt had initiated this policy at the time of the Third Coalition in 1805 when he promised £1,250,000 per anaum for every 100,000 men raised by Austria, Prussia, and Russia, even though those countries had no intention of accepting his plans for a post-war settlement. The actual amount paid out averaged about £2,650,000 per anaum during 1807–11, though much of the money lavished on Spain and Portugal was used for purposes other than those intended, leading to furious disputes between Viscount Wellington (as Arthur Wellesley had now become) and the politicians. There was a staggering climax under Castlereagh in 1813–15, when more than £26 million was

---

[101] Austria had sided with France during 1809–12.

transmitted mainly to Russia, Prussia, Sweden, Spain, Portugal, and Austria, as well as a further £2 million worth at least of *matériel*—muskets, artillery, ammunition, and uniforms. Castlereagh also directed that money for the Peninsula be sent via Wellington in order to ensure that it was not squandered. Though the amounts expended were as nothing compared with the total cost of the war to Britain—8 per cent perhaps at the outside—and though the recipients only fought Napoleon because they had other reasons to do so, the subsidies undoubtedly helped to knit the often fractious Third, Fourth, Fifth, and Sixth Coalitions together.[102]

A decisive factor was the British Government's ability to mobilize gold, not just to subsidize the allies but to clear arrears of Army pay, with the result that British soldiers did not have to resort to plunder and pillage like Napoleon's troops. On 11 January 1814 Vansittart wrote to his former secretary J. C. Herries, now Commissary-in-Chief, that he needed more money for Wellington's army than the 'usual channels' (notably the Bank of England) could supply.[103] This was a coy way of suggesting that Herries should raise funds clandestinely through Nathan Mayer Rothschild. The latter obliged with an offer of £600,000, but it was not just his vast accumulations of gold and coin from markets all over Europe that made him indispensable. In the course of building up his firm he had become the most glamorous blockade-buster of the day, chartering ships, employing special couriers to outwit Napoleon's customs officers, and maintaining a sophisticated spy system based on carrier pigeons and encoded Yiddish.[104]

It is often said that Napoleon was defeated not on the playing fields of Eton but in the banks and counting houses of the City of London. Nevertheless financiers, like statesmen, are incapable of winning wars without an effective fighting machine. Here it is important not to overlook the Navy's contribution. Though periodic invasion scares persisted for another four years or so, the victory at Trafalgar had been so decisive that it acted as a deterrent for about a century, and although Napoleon rebuilt his navy he never risked it in battle. (There would be no more grand engagements between the fleets of the Great Powers until the battle of Jutland in 1916.[105]) Nevertheless, the Royal Navy played a crucial role in policing the Orders in Council, patrolling the seas,

[102] John M. Sherwig, *Guineas and Gunpowder: British Foreign Aid in the Wars with France 1793–1815* (Cambridge, Mass., 1969), 345–56, 365–8.

[103] Rothschild Archive, London, T37/8; Niall Ferguson, *The World's Banker: The History of the House of Rothschild* (1998), 91–118.

[104] Rothschild learned about the outcome of Waterloo on the night of 19 June, but the Prime Minister refused to believe his news until official confirmation came through forty-eight hours later.

[105] There were a few sea battles between Great and non-Great Powers, such as Navarino (1827), Lissa (1866), and Tsushima (1905), but these too were uncommon, testimony perhaps to Britain's effective policing of the oceans.

convoying the British mercantile marine, beating off privateers, impounding defaulters, inspecting neutral vessels and their cargoes. Between 1808 and 1812, for example, Vice-Admiral Sir James Saumarez acted as an 'armed diplomat', skilfully deploying his forces to keep vital Baltic trade links open in the face of Danish naval attacks, while at the same time working behind the scenes to prevent a deterioration of relations with Prussia and Sweden.[106] Mean while, in the Mediterranean, Admiral Collingwood effectively policed the seas between Cadiz, Cairo, and Constantinople, again melding political and diplomatic functions. The Navy also played a crucial role in various amphibian operations, transporting British troops, horses, equipment, and other supplies to Spain, Italy, Denmark, and the United States, and then supporting those armies from the shore. Without such back-up the British Army would have proved no more successful in operating so far from home than it had done in the 1790s. Indeed, it was only in 1813, after the Navy had finally gained complete control of the seas against French coastal ships and privateers, that Wellington was able to transfer his logistical base (or main lines of communication) from Lisbon and Oporto to Santander, and go truly on the offensive. The Navy also played an essential part in the expeditions to capture French, Dutch, and Spanish colonies.

The Army had changed beyond recognition since 1793. Highly trained, disciplined, and well equipped, and with new weapons at its disposal, it deserved the limelight it was about to enjoy. Manpower had been completely transformed following the failure of Windham's plan to switch resources from the militia and Volunteers to the regular Army. The idea had been to conscript all men aged between 18 and 40, with enlistment for twenty-one years instead of life, and with better pay and pension rights and possibly even a county vote for all who served.[107] Unfortunately the Volunteers wound down much faster than the regular Army increased, so that when Castlereagh succeeded Windham the situation was grave. At least the diminished fear of invasion made it possible to reduce the home guard, and so Castlereagh was able to transfer 27,500 militiamen to the regular Army as well as raising 12,000 normal recruits. By the end of the war approximately one in six of Britons had been mobilized, a higher figure probably than that achieved by France.[108] In his competent and unflustered way Castlereagh also built up 'disposable forces' ready for embarkation at a moment's notice. They consisted of about 35,000 infantry and 9,000 cavalry and were concentrated near Cork and Portsmouth and in east Kent, where there

---

[106] *The Saumarez Papers: Selections from the Baltic Correspondence of Vice-Admiral Sir James Saumarez, 1808–1812*, ed. A. N. Ryan (1968), pp. xiv–xxv; A. N. Ryan, 'The Defence of British Trade with the Baltic, 1808–13', *EHR* 74 (1959), 443–66.   [107] Thorne, v. 627.

[108] Charles J. Esdaile, *The Wars of Napoleon* (1995), 144.

were also fleets of transport ships, ready equipped and victualled and capable of carrying about 10,000 men at one lift.[109]

The quality of troops improved as well, despite some unpromising raw material. Whereas French soldiers were conscripted from every class, the British Army was, so Wellington famously observed, 'composed of the scum of the earth—the mere scum of the earth . . . It really is wonderful that we should have made them the fine fellows they are.'[110] Wellington may have exaggerated the transformation, but certainly a degree of *esprit de corps* developed as a result of the Duke of York's organizational improvements. Training became more uniform, discipline tougher but fairer, and a slightly more rational system of promotion was instituted in all the infantry and cavalry regiments, though the artillery and engineers went unreformed, not being under York's control. (The contrast might explain why Wellington preferred to fight in line whereas Napoleon, whose superior artillery provided covering fire, preferred to fight in column.) It was largely thanks to these changes that the Army moved from the margins of society to something approaching respectability. The professional soldier entered the Army for life, modelled himself on his NCOs and sought to be one, 'wore his regimental uniform with pride', lived with his family at the depot, hoped that his sons would follow him, and looked forward to a pension for long service.[111] But perhaps the most important advance followed from York's enforcement of the Dundas *Rules and Regulations* (1792). Traditionally each infantry battalion had developed its own methods of performing manoeuvres, but gradually all were made to conform to eighteen codified close-order drill systems laid down by General David Dundas. The disastrous Dutch campaign of 1799 prompted the creation of specialist light infantry corps, which received intensive lessons in skirmishing by Sir John Moore, an expert coach, and then served in the front of each line.[112] Meanwhile, the much abused Ordnance was overhauled, especially the Quartermaster-General's Department, and its performance in 1813, when it had to distribute arms, ammunition, and equipment to almost every corner of Europe, has been described as superb.[113]

It is important not to exaggerate these gains, or forget that much was owed to the brilliance of Wellington, whose cautious, painstaking, and methodical approach was in sharp contrast to Napoleon's inspired, erratic, and dangerous

---

[109] Richard Glover, *Peninsular Preparation: The Reform of the British Army, 1795–1809* (Cambridge, 1963), 245–54. The militia ballot was also reintroduced, by which means the depleted militia was gradually brought back to strength.

[110] Philip Henry, fifth Earl of Stanhope, *Notes of Conversations with the Duke of Wellington 1831–1854* (1888), 14, 18.   [111] J. E. Cookson, *The British Armed Nation 1793–1815* (Oxford, 1997), 124–5.

[112] P. Mackesy, *Statesmen at War: The Strategy of Overthrow 1798–1799* (1974), 312–13; Michael Glover, *Wellington as Military Commander* (1968), 30, 241.

[113] Muir, *Britain and the Defeat of Napoleon*, 277.

genius. Words like 'methodical' and 'cautious' might seem to contradict the judgement of a noted authority that Wellington was 'the greatest improviser in the history of war', but improvisation here does not necessarily imply spontaneity. As the same authority goes on to say, 'No eventuality found him unprepared ... Wellington's genius lay in making the best of any situation and of the materials available.'[114] He had a good eye for ground, and knew how to deploy his troops so as to maximize fire power. He kept to the drill books and did not make tactical innovations, while his obsessional determination to ensure adequate supply lines meant that logistically his armies did not always move as quickly as they might have done. On the other hand, it also meant that Wellington's soldiers, unlike many of the French, did not go hungry. His men revered him because they knew that he would do all he could consistently with winning to keep them alive, again unlike Napoleon, who was far more prodigal. Wellington also had an advantage over his predecessors in exercising a degree of political as well as military control. At Lisbon, where he held supreme military and political power as Commander-in-Chief of the Anglo-Portuguese army, unofficial member of the Regency Council, and chief representative of the British Government, he was able to 'transform the political, social, and economic structure of the country to achieve his military goals'.[115] In Spain his authority was more circumscribed but still extensive, especially after he became Generalissimo of the Spanish armies in 1812. He was also held in high esteem by the Cabinet in England, despite his quarrelsome temperament. To some extent he compensated in his own person for the fact that a chief of staff had never developed, able to take command of operations at the highest level.

After returning to the Peninsula in 1809, Wellington quickly defeated the French under Soult at Oporto and again under Jourdan at Talavera. Then, doubting the quality of the Spanish and Portuguese troops under his command, he retreated westward towards Lisbon, scorching the earth as he went. At Torres Vedras, 25 miles north of the city, he constructed 3 defensive lines: 108 redoubts protected by 447 mounted guns and backed up by a sophisticated system for supplying victuals, ammunition, and instructions to the front line. Having meticulously prepared his parlour he was ready to play the patient spider, the unfortunate fly being Masséna, whom Napoleon dispatched to Portugal in 1810 with three strong army corps. After months of teasing inactivity, Wellington at last moved north in order to tempt the great French general, then allowed himself to be chased back to his dugouts at Torres Vedras, where the French were taken utterly by surprise. After a long siege during which his own troops went

---

[114] Glover, *Wellington*, 204, 240.
[115] Donald D. Horward, 'Wellington as a Strategist, 1808–14', in Norman Gash (ed.), *Wellington: Studies in the Military and Political Career of the First Duke of Wellington* (Manchester, 1990), 112–13.

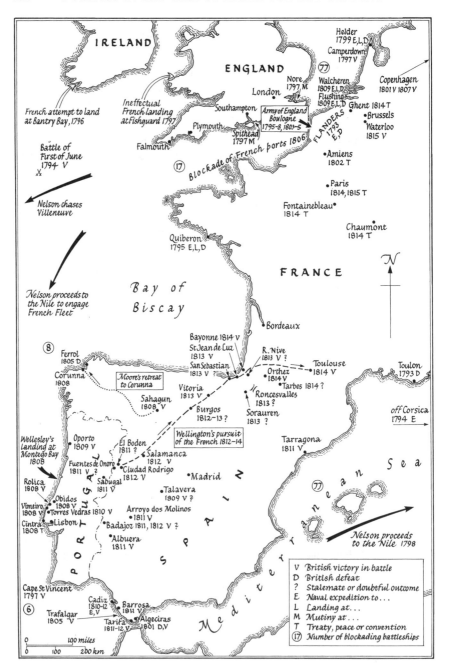

MAP 4.1. British participation in European warfare, 1793–1815

hungry, Masséna fell back, only to be followed by Wellington and defeated at
Fuentes de Onoro (May 1811). The rest of that year was a stalemate, with victories for both sides. Wellington, who was furious with the politicians in London
for not sending him enough specie, bided his time until, as a result of the
Russian campaign, French troops in the Peninsula had been reduced to fewer
than 200,000. At this point Wellington left his base, captured Ciudad Rodrigo in
January 1812, and then took Badajoz in April. The latter success came at the cost
of 5,000 men, a setback for which British troops took their revenge out on
Spanish civilians in a disgraceful three-day sack of the city. Throughout this
year's campaigns Wellington was assisted, much more than he was subsequently
prepared to admit, by first-rate intelligence on the enemy's plans and disposition. (This was thanks to an obscure lieutenant-colonel, George Scovell, who,
working from a little office in Abchurch Street, cracked the French military's
main cipher, the Grand Chiffre, in 1812.[116]) After a period of cat-and-mouse
marches, Wellington defeated Marmont at the great battle of Salamanca in July,
captured Madrid in August, and besieged Burgos in September. Salamanca has
been described as technically his finest victory—40,000 men defeated in forty
minutes—while the Burgos campaign has been described as 'the most unfortunate that he ever undertook'. Six precious weeks and 2,000 men were lost due to
rare bad planning, after which Wellington retreated towards Ciudad Rodrigo for
the winter to build up reinforcements.[117] By 1813 the French armies had haem-
orrhaged even further, but that hardly detracts from Wellington's excellent tactics, which culminated in the capture of Burgos and a dazzling victory at the
battle of Vitoria (June). However, his troops were unable to pursue the enemy
from the field, being 'totally knocked up' by a night of wine, women, song, and
plunder (a recurrent aspect of British behaviour in the Peninsula). In October
Wellington's army invaded France, and was still winning victories over Soult
when, in April 1814, Napoleon—unable to halt the allied armies' advance on
Paris, increasingly dependent on untrained boy soldiers, and facing a mutiny by
his own generals—abdicated.

    The Peninsular War was immensely complex. There were several theatres of
conflict besides Wellington's, and the single main reason for France's failure was
the fact that, as the British had discovered on a smaller scale in America thirty
years earlier, brutal and ruthless guerrillas, fighting on and for their own soil, can
defeat large, well-trained, and highly equipped armies.[118] Even so, the presence

---

[116] Mark Urban, *The Man Who Broke Napoleon's Codes: The Story of George Scovell* (2001), 181–237.
[117] Rory Muir, *Salamanca 1812* (New Haven, 2001); Richard Glover, *Wellington's Peninsular Victories*
(1963), 94.
[118] As usual in such cases, many of the guerrillas were itinerants, psychopaths, or bandits (Charles
J. Esdaile, *The Peninsular War: A New History* (2002), 250–80; id., *Fighting Napoleon: Guerrillas, Bandits,
and Adventurers, 1808–1814* (New Haven, 2004)).

of British troops was important because it prevented the French from dispersing their units and fighting the guerrillas on their own terms. In the final account, a maximum of about 50,000 British soldiers, together with about the same number of British-trained Portuguese regulars, pinned down not fewer than 150,000 (and sometimes as many as 320,000) French troops in the Peninsula for six years, besides finally defeating them. Wellesley was rewarded in the way the English knew best. Having been created Baron Douro of Wellesley and Viscount Wellington in 1809, he became Earl of Wellington in February 1812, Marquess of Wellington eight months later, and finally Marquess of Douro and Duke of Wellington in 1814.

Meanwhile, England had become engaged in a futile conflict with the United States. The Americans declared war in June 1812 for three reasons. They resented the Orders in Council, they were angered by the British habit of searching neutral vessels and of impressing foreign seamen captured on the high seas into service with the Royal Navy,[119] and they had designs on parts of Canada north of the Great Lakes and the St Lawrence River. The fortunes of war oscillated, with both sides winning and losing battles and capturing and surrendering fortresses in rapid succession, and at the end neither side could claim much more than a draw. American efforts to invade Canada were eventually repulsed, while a counter-attempt to invade the United States from the north was fended off as well. In August 1814, 5,000 British troops under Major-General Ross landed at Chesapeake Bay, swept aside 6,500 American militiamen, and occupied Washington for five weeks, burning the White House to the ground, firing cannon shot through into the Capitol, and desecrating other public buildings. As a shock tactic all this was awesome, but it could not be sustained. The war ended in January 1815 with a matching success for the Americans, when a British force of 14,250 under Sir Edward Pakenham sailed from Jamaica and marched towards New Orleans. They were checked by the war's one true hero, the future president Colonel Andrew Jackson, who, with just 700 regular troops and a handful of ring-ins, repulsed the invaders. The dead and wounded tally read: British 2,000; American 13. Naval campaigns in the Great Lakes and on the high seas were also inconclusive, though the Americans won on points, having the better of the set piece battles. Canning exaggerated when he told the Commons that 'the sacred spell of the invincibility of the British Navy was broken',[120] since the skirmishes had taken place between frigates, not ships of the line, but even so it was a war which partisans of the Royal Navy have preferred not to dwell on.

---

[119] The British claimed that this was justified by the prevalence of privateers, i.e. seamen licensed by the French Government to attack British merchant shipping. It has been estimated that one-fortieth of British trade was lost in this way during 1793–1841.   [120] *HPD*1 xxiv. 643 (18 Feb. 1813).

Francis Jeffrey commented that half the English people did not even know their country was at war with America.[121] The utter absurdity of the conflict is underlined by the fact that the main *causus belli* (the Orders in Council) was removed four days *before* it broke out, while the final decisive engagement took place two weeks *after* peace was signed,[122] the problem in both cases being that communications did not get through swiftly enough to those on the ground. But though the battle of New Orleans was strictly unnecessary, it was important. It ensured that Britain, while remaining resolute on the question of the Canadian border, made no further attempt to interfere with the position of the southern states, and even tacitly accepted the validity of the Louisiana Purchase.[123]

Given its military preoccupations, Liverpool's ministry could have been forgiven for neglecting domestic policy, yet here too there was a sudden flurry of activity. Significant inroads into the traditions of mercantile monopoly and religious persecution gave it a reputation for 'liberality',[124] and signalled a step forwards in the political mobilization of the commercial and Dissenting middle classes. To start with, there was a growing consensus in favour of repealing the Orders in Council. The cause was catching fire in the provinces and especially in Liverpool, the main port for American trade.[125] The repeal campaign, which was brilliantly coordinated by Brougham among others, brought a number of business leaders to prominence, Roscoe in Liverpool, Attwood and Spooner in Birmingham, Kirkman Finlay in Glasgow, Schonswar in Bristol. Perceval might have fought to retain the Orders but he was assassinated in May, and in the following month Castlereagh conceded repeal, admitting that American retaliation had not been anticipated and was doing great harm. In Yorkshire the issue divided clothiers from merchants, but at least the two groups could combine to campaign against the East India Company's commercial privileges. The outcome was a spectacular victory for private merchants and for the provinces over London.[126] Although the Company's China monopoly was retained,[127] from 1813 all Britons were allowed to trade with India and other parts of South-East Asia within the Company's territories, while other named British ports were granted equal rights with London for the first time. The importation of Indian

---

[121] *Diary of Joseph Farington*, xiii. 4492 (18 Apr. 1814).

[122] The Pacification of Ghent, December 1814.

[123] This refers to the huge area comprising the western basin of the Mississippi along its full length, seized by Napoleon from Spain in 1800, and sold to the United States for $15 million in 1803 in order to forestall a possible conquest by Britain.   [124] William Smith, *HPD*1 xxv. 1147–8 (5 May 1813).

[125] B. H. Tolley, 'The Liverpool Campaigns against the Order in Council and the War of 1812', in J. R. Harris (ed.), *Liverpool and Merseyside: Essays in the Economic and Social History of the Port and its Hinterland* (1969).

[126] David Moss, 'Birmingham and the Campaigns against the Orders-in-Council and East India Company Charter, 1812–13', *Canadian Journal of History*, 11 (1976), 173–88.   [127] Until 1834.

cotton manufactures (other than for the purpose of re-export) was prohibited from these other ports, thereby enabling Lancashire to conquer Eastern markets and eliminate the Indian cotton industry.[128] The legislation was clearly due to changes in official thinking as well as to provincial pressure. Dundas had protected the East India Company, but now Buckinghamshire and Rose, the former recently appointed as President of the Board of Trade, were determined to reverse his policy. Although Lancashire benefited, it seems that the two ministers were not so much concerned to boost British exports as to make India a source for the supply of vital raw materials such as raw cotton, sugar, and hemp, thereby lessening dependence on a hostile United States.[129] It was also a time of heightened concern about the social effects of inflation, and the East India monopoly was thought to keep prices artificially high, if only because, with its very great warehousing capacity in London's docklands, the Company could afford not to sell imported Indian goods at times when prices were low.

The most dramatic aspect of the legislation was the 'pious clause' whereby the Company, in return for a renewal of its charter, undertook to repeal its ban on Christian missionaries from entering the Subcontinent, and even to support their work. This decision came out of the blue. Charles Grant and Wilberforce argued that Hindu society was so utterly depraved as to require immediate Christianization, but most Company officials felt that the best way to prevent sepoy uprisings, such as the Vellore mutiny of 1806, was by respecting native religions and culture, not by trying to force conversions.[130] When the Company's charter had last come up for renewal in 1793, Wilberforce's missionary proposals had been rejected, but since then Grant and a number of like-minded persons had infiltrated the Company's Court of Directors, a good example of the way in which evangelicals combined private pressure and public propaganda. The practical importance of the 1813 decision should not be exaggerated, since the Court of Directors, governors-general, presidency governors, Army generals, and bishops continued to put spokes in the missionaries' wheels,[131] but it was important symbolically. The fact that the issue attracted an unprecedented avalanche of petitions entitles it to be classified alongside anti-slavery, the peace movement, and the campaign against the Orders in Council as signs that

---

[128] The Act of 1813 almost ruined the Indian economy, not only by destroying cotton manufactures but by forcing down raw material prices (Asiya Siddiqui, 'Money and Prices in the Earlier Stages of Empire: India and Britain 1760 to 1840', *Indian Economic and Social History Review*, 18 (1981), 243–52).

[129] Anthony Webster, 'The Political Economy of Trade Liberalization: The East India Company Charter Act of 1813', *EconHR* 43 (1990), 404–19. This privileging by politicians of primary imports over manufactured exports had a counterpart in the corn laws. See below, pp. 264–8, 305–7, 551–8.

[130] Charles Grant (1746–1823) was a director and many times chairman of the East India Company and the father of Charles Grant, Baron Glenelg (1778–1866), a Canningite.

[131] Penelope S. E. Carson, 'Soldiers of Christ: Evangelicals and India, 1780–1833', Ph.D. thesis (London University, 1988).

a popular liberal politics was emerging. It also led to a striking degree of interdenominational cooperation. To the disgust of many High Churchmen, Anglican evangelicals joined forces with sections of organized Dissent (notably Methodists, Scottish Presbyterians, and Particular Baptists[132]) so that 'a good part of England seemed obsessed by a frenzy for foreign missions'. It has been suggested that Methodist leaders channelled their flocks in this direction in order to divert them away from radicalism at home,[133] but there were other motives too, such as the desire of denominations not to be last among the godly, and even a sincere belief that such work was a divine imperative.

Nonconformity was anyway feeling politically buoyant just then. In 1811 Sidmouth had tried to persuade the Lords to amend the Toleration Act by restricting the award of preaching licences to those Dissenting ministers who were attached to a specific congregation and could produce testimonials from several 'reputable and substantial householders' in the community. Justices had granted as many as 2,386 new licences between 1795 and 1808, and Sidmouth was afraid that Britain was becoming divided between 'a nominal Established Church, and a sectarian people'.[134] His bill sparked off a tremendous outcry, especially among the Methodists, who relied on itinerant preaching, and Sidmouth was forced to back off. One historian has seen in this episode 'the politicizing of evangelical Dissent', with huge implications for the future. In 'seeking to defend the Anglican constitution, Sidmouth unwittingly unleashed the forces that helped to dismantle it'.[135] In 1813 Unitarians were at last admitted to the benefits of the 1689 Toleration Act. Their leader, William Smith, hailed this relaxation of the rules regarding oaths and meetings as 'the most complete [Act of Toleration] which had hitherto been passed in this country'.[136] The Prime Minister, who had secured the bishops' agreement to the changes in advance, argued that 'an enlarged and liberal toleration was the best security to the Established Church', a view which was beginning to take root among more open-minded Anglicans. Goodwill and mutual congratulation briefly abounded, though far from placating Nonconformists the concessions encouraged them to renew their political campaign.[137]

Attempts at retrenchment, and attacks on traditional notions of moral economy and just price, were further signs that liberalism was making headway. In 1812, and again in 1813, the Commons narrowly resolved to abolish all

---

[132] The prominence of Particular Baptists is problematic since, unlike General Baptists, they held a Calvinist belief in predestination, and in general Calvinists thought it was presumptuous and unnecessary to preach the Gospel to the unconverted.

[133] Bernard Semmel, *The Methodist Revolution* (1973), 152–66.

[134] *CPD* xix. 1131 (9 May 1811).

[135] Michael A. Rutz, 'The Politicizing of Evangelical Dissent, 1811–1813', *Parliamentary History*, 20 (2001), 187–207.   [136] *HPD* i xxiii. 1105 (20 July 1812).

[137] Bernard, Lord Manning, *The Protestant Dissenting Deputies* (Cambridge, 1952), 218–19.

sinecure offices, though on both occasions the decision was contemptuously overturned in the Lords. It was pressed by Bankes and Wilberforce, with support from Canning and Huskisson outside the Government, leaving Castlereagh and Eldon to argue that talented people would not enter public life unless they could secure provision for their families. Then in 1814 the last vestige of medieval guild regulations was removed by the repeal of the Elizabethan Statute of Artificers. This had required persons engaged in trade, whether as masters or as journeymen, to undergo seven years of training, and had empowered magistrates to regulate apprenticeship, settle industrial disputes, protect employment, and fix wages. Admittedly, the Statute had only ever applied to cities, incorporated towns, and market towns, and to trades which existed before 1563. Woollens had been excluded in 1809, and elsewhere the rules had been flouted, especially in the new mechanized mills and factories where children were often hired without any qualifications whatever. Even so, its repeal in 1814 was symbolically important as signifying the permeation of free-market ideas. The legislation was mainly the work of independent-minded and Opposition-leaning MPs, but ministers seem to have given it a fair wind, and the same is true with the repeal of the London Assize of Bread in 1815.[138] Traditionally magistrates had taken the cost of flour as supplied by the millers, added a baker's allowance, and calculated the price at which bread should be sold to the consumer. The trouble was that many bakers were in hock to millers, and millers had an interest in exaggerating their costs. It was believed that a competitive market in the manufacture and distribution of bread would benefit the more substantial bakers, and so allow the commodity to fall below its current artificially inflated price.[139] Finally, in 1816 the first serious debates took place on the Usury Laws. Such was the strength of biblical injunction against usury, however, that it seemed easier to allow them to fall into disuse, and formal repeal did not take place until 1854. The overall picture is complicated by the fact that the single most spectacular measure of these years, the Corn Law of 1815,[140] seemed to buck the trend against monopoly. However, this was a genuinely special case, and does not militate against the fact that MPs were gradually submitting to liberal notions on economic policy.

The last point must not be pressed too far. The avowed object of the Sinecure Bill was mainly political, being to curb the influence of the Crown, while in so far as it was motivated by economic considerations, pragmatic concerns over the bloated wartime state, commercial crisis, unemployment, industrial unrest, and Luddism[141] probably accounted for more than theory. The repeal of the Statute

---

[138] Provincial assizes were abolished in 1819.

[139] Boyd Hilton, *Corn, Cash, Commerce: The Economic Policies of the Tory Governments 1815–1830* (Oxford, 1977), 26–8.   [140] See below, pp. 264–8.

[141] See below, pp. 586–7.

of Artificers was also mainly political, being a victory for the master manufacturers, and carried in the teeth of strenuous objections by journeymen and apprentices, who argued that their seven-year period of training constituted a form of property which would now be rendered worthless. As for the role of ministers, this was somewhat ambiguous in that, although they responded to pressure for reforms and sometimes facilitated them, they never took the initiative. Even so, it hardly seems fair to describe Liverpool's Government in its earlier phase as 'arguably the most thoroughly anti-reformist since 1714'.[142] Far more significant were the stirrings of arguments that a decade later would come to define the differences between so-called high and liberal Tories.

VICTORY, THE SECOND EMPIRE, AND A MISTAKEN CASE OF NATIONAL IDENTITY

The objectives of British foreign policy were stated definitively by Pitt in a memorandum of January 1805. The first was 'to rescue from the dominion of France those countries which it has subjugated since the beginning of the Revolution, and to reduce France within its former limits, as they stood before that time'. The second was 'to make such an arrangement with respect to the territories recovered from France, as may provide for their security and happiness, and may at the same time constitute a more effectual barrier in future against encroachments on the part of France'. The third and final requirement was 'to form, at the restoration of peace, a general agreement and guarantee for the mutual protection and security of different powers, and for re-establishing a general system of public law in Europe'.[143] His plan for future collective security was problematic, if only because the partners had conflicting priorities. In particular Alexander wanted the French crushed and excluded from discussions, whereas Liverpool and Castlereagh were already looking to post-Napoleonic France as an ally against the three eastern autocracies.

Immediately after Napoleon's abdication, the Great Powers signed the Treaty of Fontainebleau (April 1814). The Bourbon dynasty was restored in the person of Louis XVIII, and the former emperor was exiled to the tiny Mediterranean island of Elba, which insultingly he was given to rule. In May the first Peace of Paris imposed on France a settlement which in the circumstances was remarkably generous: the borders of 1792 but with local rectifications which added more than half a million inhabitants. The unification of Belgians and Dutch within

---

[142] Eric J. Evans, *The Forging of the Modern State: Early Industrial Britain 1783–1870* (1983), 65.

[143] Harold Temperley and Lillian M. Penson (eds.), *Foundations of British Foreign Policy from Pitt (1792) to Salisbury (1902)* (Cambridge, 1938), 11. For Castlereagh's adherence to these principles, see John W. Derry, *Castlereagh* (1976), 147–8.

a new Kingdom of the Netherlands was the most important provision from Britain's point of view, since historic sensitivity to French designs on the Low Countries had led her into European war in the first place. In September the Powers met in Vienna to tidy up some details and consider future peacekeeping. The preliminaries dragged on for months, with interminable wrangles between the various delegations by day, and a frenetic round of feasting and festivity by night.[144] The Congress of Vienna had still not met formally when news came through towards the end of February that Napoleon had escaped from Elba. He marched on Paris, gathering armed supporters as he did so and forcing Louis to flee to Belgium. Hearing this, the several representatives heaved themselves into the fray again by forming the Seventh and final Coalition, to which the British Government pledged another £9 million. They also put aside their differences in drawing up a comprehensive settlement known as the Vienna Final Act, subsequently ratified at the only meeting of the Congress on 9 June. It confirmed the legitimate rights of the pre-war ruling dynasties of Europe. The Grand Duchy of Warsaw lost land to Prussia and Austria, while what remained became the Kingdom of Poland under the control of Russia. Prussia achieved hegemony in northern Germany with the accession of parts of Saxony, Pomerania, and Westphalia, while Austria gained Lombardy and Venetia and a preponderant influence in the rest of Italy.

Napoleon's Hundred Days ended with a series of bloody actions in and around Waterloo. On 14 June he disposed his army of 128,000 mainly excellent troops in three great columns to the south of Brussels. Wellington's army of just over 100,000 largely raw troops was spread out for 40 miles from north to south with a base in Antwerp and headquarters in Brussels. Further to the east, Blücher commanded an army of 117,000 Prussians from a base in Cologne. In the early hours of the 16th Wellington attended the Duchess of Richmond's ball in Brussels with its 'sound of revelry by night'. While he was thus off his guard, Napoleon managed to insinuate the French army between those of Britain and Prussia, with a view to finishing off each in turn. Later that same day, and having returned to duty, Wellington just managed to repel Ney's forces from Quatre Bras, while Napoleon inflicted heavy damage on the Prussians at Ligny. To this day it is disputed whether Wellington deliberately encouraged Blücher to engage at Ligny by falsely suggesting that his own troops were close by to lend a hand, or whether he honourably dispatched troops in Blücher's direction, only for them to lose their way in the fog of war.[145] At all events, the Prussians took the

---

[144] The social whirl was blamed on Metternich as host, and might well have been a deliberate attempt by him to delay a settlement long enough for relations between Russia and Prussia to sour, since he feared that otherwise the Tsar might gain a hegemony over central and eastern Europe.

[145] For the most recent and elaborate version of this charge, see Peter Hofschröer, *1815, The Waterloo Campaign: Wellington, his German Allies, and the Battles of Ligny and Quatre Bras* (1998), 192–247,

strain while Wellington's own army regrouped. At noon on the 18th, while Blücher was still licking his wounds, Napoleon engaged with Wellington at Waterloo. For several hours the French cavalry tried to break their opponents' infantry squares,[146] and it soon became clear that the outcome would depend on whether the latter could hold out until the Prussians arrived. With an uncharacteristic lack of lustre, but also hampered by wet weather, Napoleon held his Imperial Guard back longer than he should have done, Blücher's army arrived in early evening, and within an hour the French were being chased from the field.

Waterloo, which as Wellington famously said was 'a damned close run thing', became the most publicly celebrated battle in English history since Agincourt. It was presumed to have been decisive, although it is hard to see how, if it had gone the other way, Napoleon could have held out much longer against the Austrians and Russians, who were ready to field 450,000 men. France was exhausted, especially of manpower, and Napoleon was suffering from illness, perhaps the one that was to kill him in 1821.[147] No matter. Such was Napoleon's magnetism and will-power that no one could be sure of his defeat until Waterloo, followed by his second abdication and banishment, this time to St Helena in the remote South Atlantic. In November the second Peace of Paris broadly confirmed the terms of the first, though France was now made to surrender territory to her smaller neighbours, pay a 700 million franc indemnity, and submit to a five-year occupation of her northern departments.

Short of being made King, Wellington could not be given any more titles. Instead, Parliament granted him an additional £200,000 towards an estate fitting for a duke. The site eventually settled on in 1817 was Stratfield Saye in Hampshire, though grandiose plans for a classical palace to outdo Blenheim[148] were never realized. Wellington was also showered with foreign honours and displaced Napoleon as the most famous man in the world. Given that Castlereagh in his tenacious and methodical way had largely effaced Metternich, Talleyrand, and the Tsar in the Vienna negotiations, it can safely be said that Britain's military and diplomatic prestige touched a pitch it has never reached before or since.

331–51. Hofschröer also accuses Wellington of deliberately falsifying the subsequent record so as to conceal his treachery (id., *Wellington's Smallest Victory: The Duke, the Model Maker and the Secret of Waterloo* (2004)). For Wellington's defence, see David Hamilton-Williams, *Waterloo New Perspectives: The Great Battle Reappraised* (1993), 147–50, 171–7, 201.

[146] This was a tactic perfected and used extensively in the Peninsula. Wellington formed his infantry into squares in a chequered pattern, so enabling them to soak up the enemy's cavalry charges, while Wellington's own cavalry could then be used to counter-attack. Hamilton-Williams, *Waterloo*, 134–5.

[147] It has even been suggested that Napoleon was suffering from the effects of arsenic poisoning, deliberately administered by a disgruntled aide on Elba.

[148] Built by the nation between 1705 and 1722 for a previous conquering hero, the Duke of Marlborough.

With the Royal Navy able to control the English Channel and the North Sea, and with its tonnage (609,300) almost as large as the combined navies of France, Russia, the Netherlands, Spain, Portugal, Sweden, and the United States,[149] Britain enjoyed a maritime supremacy that made it, for the first time in history, entirely safe from invasion. With security went national self-confidence. For the next thirty years or so many British statesmen took it for granted that their views on international disputes would be respected, that they could lecture foreigners on how to govern, and that they could act the part of international policemen, especially on the high seas. They cherished the country's role as a haven for political refugees, and took steps in 1844 to facilitate the legal process of naturalization. It is an indication of just how genuine their self-confidence was that by and large they did not feel the need to boast about it. Macaulay exemplified this national self-satisfaction: 'Why is it that an Irishman's, or Frenchman's, hatred of England does not excite in me an answering hatred? I imagine that my national pride prevents it. England is so great than an Englishman cares little what others think of her, or how they talk of her.'[150] It was only in the 1850s, when French ironclads threatened British shores,[151] the Crimean War exposed military shortcomings, the Indian Mutiny revealed the fragility of empire, and the rise of Prussia highlighted the lack of clout in Europe, that an era of bombast ('Podsnappery') set in.

How the English perceived their role in the world in the late eighteenth century is not easy to clarify. Many historians have identified nationalism as a powerfully integrating force, and some have ascribed it to enthusiasm for Protestant mission and hatred of France as the foremost Catholic power.[152] Yet the temper of the times was generally tolerant, with little anti-Catholicism before the resurgence of the Irish problem in the 1820s. Aggressive Protestantism did not take off until the founding of the British Reformation Society (1827), the Protestant Association (1835), the National Club (1845), the Evangelical Alliance (1846), the Scottish Reformation Society (1850), and the Protestant Alliance (1851). As for Francophobia, although Britain and France were formally at war for a total of fifty-eight years between 1689 and 1815, antagonism between the two countries was mostly based on commercial rivalry rather than visceral hatred. Radical opponents of the mid-eighteenth-century aristocracy had attacked what they saw as its cultural cringe in the face of French sophistication, but this was a domestic quarrel, not an international one.[153] Fox tried to evoke similar sentiments—part

[149] Michael Duffy, 'World-Wide War and British Expansion, 1793–1815', in P. J. Marshall (ed.), *The Oxford History of the British Empire*, ii: *The Eighteenth Century* (Oxford, 1998), 204.
[150] Macaulay, diary, Aug. 1849, in *The Life and Letters of Lord Macaulay*, ed. G. O. Trevelyan (1876), ii. 263.
[151] And sparked off another militia initiative (in 1852) and another volunteer movement (in 1859).
[152] Linda Colley, *Britons: Forging the Nation 1707–1837* (New Haven, 1992), 11–54.
[153] Gerard Newman, *The Rise of English Nationalism: A Cultural History 1740–1830* (1987), 215–44.

Tory–Radical, part civic humanist—when he attacked the supporters of the Eden Treaty for being 'dazzled with the splendour of Louis XVI, so conscious of the eminence of power which France had lately attained, that they sunk before it... in their own despondency'.[154] His chum Philip Francis joined in: 'The nearer [England and France] are drawn into contact, and the more successfully they are invited to mingle and to blend with one another, in the same proportion the remaining morals, principles, and vigour of the national English mind, will be enervated and corrupted. We shall be civilized out of our virtues, and polished out of our character.'[155] However, these Foxite attempts to play the nationalist card did not resonate strongly at the time, and they made even less sense after the French Revolution, when the old French enemy (Bourbon and Catholic) gave way to a new one (Jacobin and atheist). Any semblance of an ideological war was confined to the years 1793–5. After that there was war to the death, but the enemy was always Bonaparte rather than the French, who continued to be regarded as civilized above all others. That is why so many hurried over to Paris after the Peace of Amiens. Even in the Peninsula 'the British and French, "enemies", liked and respected each other more than either liked or respected the Spanish'.[156] That is not so surprising given that guerrilla resistance fighters did not understand professional military conventions on the taking of prisoners, and their atrocities against French soldiers, famously etched by Goya, turned many Enlightenment stomachs. Again, once Napoleon had been defeated, most English people concluded that they had more in common politically, culturally, and ideologically with France than with their erstwhile allies. At a Pitt Club celebration in 1817, with Peel in the chair, verses were sung in honour of the Brunswicks (as the Hanoverian dynasty was generally called):

> No longer to France will defiance be hurl'd,
>> No more she'll contend for the throne of the world . . .
> Let Bourbon with Brunswick in amity join
>> And with England's fair Rose the French Lily entwine.[157]

The argument from nationalism also begs the question: which nation—England or Britain? The idea of Britishness is currently in vogue, and certainly from one perspective it can be argued that between 1780 and 1830 'a genuinely British landed elite came into being... on the ruins of a decaying local squirearchy'. 'The hitherto separate territorial elites of England, Ireland,

---

[154] *CPH* xxvi. 222 (23 Jan. 1787).   [155] Ibid. 420 (12 Feb. 1787).

[156] Geoffrey Best, *War and Society in Revolutionary Europe 1770–1870* (Leicester, 1982), 179–80. 'Enormous offence was given to the Spaniards by the way British and French officers would hob-nob with each other after battles; the British victors even, as in Vitoria, walking arm-in-arm through the streets with their surrendered French equivalents, and together snubbing their supposed Spanish equivalents.'

[157] *The Pitt Club: The Triennial Commemoration of the Anniversary of Mr. Pitt's Birth, at Merchant Taylor's Hall, London* (1817), 21.

Scotland and Wales gradually merged into a new, authentically British landed class.'[158] Yet it is probably no coincidence that 'Rule Britannia' had been written at a moment of heightened national paranoia (1740) and by a Scotsman. The Scots, and to a lesser extent the Welsh and Irish, embraced Britishness as a way of dealing with the English on equal terms within the Union,[159] and it was only after this concept lost its saliency, from the 1850s, that an alternative Scottish nationalism began to develop. Meanwhile, national identity mattered much less to the English. They might have subscribed to the notion of Great Britain in moments of bombast, but at moments of peril it was 'England' that expected 'every man to do his duty'. All that was admirable about Scotland was subsumed into Englishness, the rest was discarded.

A good deal of weight has also been placed on empire as an accompaniment of Britishness. According to a leading authority,

the French wars saw the greatest expansion of British imperial dominion since the creation of the colonies of settlement in Ireland and America in the seventeenth century. Most later extensions of the empire, whether in Africa in the 1880s and 1890s or in the Middle East after the First World War, were the slowly matured consequences of policies laid down by Pitt and Dundas.[160]

Against this, a leading diplomatic historian has seen the Napoleonic wars as marking the moment when Britain acknowledged her position as a Continental power. 'What happened in the end was not so much that Europeans joined Russia and Britain to overthrow Napoleon, but that Russia and Britain, in order to defeat France, joined Europe. The Continental System merely developed Napoleon's imperialism; it ultimately made Britain and Russia alter theirs, even partly abandon it.'[161] In their cruder forms these interpretations cannot both be true, yet considered separately each makes sense. They may perhaps be reconciled by recognizing that the English suffered from a fundamental schizophrenia, which looks like humbug in retrospect but which was probably genuine. It was partly a polarization between ideal types—little Englanders and pro-Europeans like Joseph Sturge and Richard Cobden against chauvinist imperialists like Palmerston—but the vast majority felt ambivalent, in consequence perhaps of the gap between what their country was doing in the world and what they perceived it to be doing.

---

[158] David Cannadine, 'The Making of the British Upper Classes', in Cannadine, *Aspects of Aristocracy: Grandeur and Decline in Modern Britain* (New Haven, 1994), 10–12.

[159] Although Walter Scott is usually thought of as inventing the tartan-and-bagpipe version of Scottish history, his more significant message was to elevate the virtues of fair-skinned British Saxons over those of swarthy Celts, and to trace British civilization back to Danish tribesmen and 'our common Teutonic stock'.

[160] C. A. Bayly, *Imperial Meridian: The British Empire and the World 1780–1830* (1989), 100.

[161] Schroeder, *Transformation of European Politics*, 310.

It is undeniable that having squandered the American colonies the English picked up a second empire during the course of the French wars. By 1815 theirs was once more a global power, with worldwide interests based on dominion and profit, on formal colonization here and informal influence there. Sugar islands were gobbled up, and trading stations and strategic naval bases established on major shipping routes. Gibraltar (British since 1713) was a vital base from which to monitor the French fleet as well as lying athwart the shipping lane to the West Indies and North America. A string of strategically placed islands, entrepôt ports, naval bases, and trading stations—white and non-white, Christian and infidel—were knitted together by the Navy, by the merchant marine, and by ordinary civilians doing business in distant countries with as much assurance of their right to do it as pedlars might formerly have shown in taking their wares from village to village. The Dutch Cape Colony[162] was appropriated together with Ceylon, Tobago, St Lucia, Mauritius, Heligoland, Malta, the Ionian Isles, Trinidad, and the Seychelles. By 1816 there were forty-three colonies as compared with just twenty-six in 1792, and the term 'empire' was increasingly used to refer to them rather than to the British Isles.

Historians have traditionally attributed these developments to profiteering rather than to a lust for dominion,[163] yet significantly the area of the most intense commercial interest, South America, was not one over which there was any sustained attempt to exert formal control. Considerations such as this have given rise to a powerful alternative case that imperial expansion was not mercantile but authoritarian, ideological, territorial, racist, aristocratic, and above all agrarian. 'Agrarian improvement was a moral crusade, the inner heart of English expansion; indeed, it was seen as the domestic precondition of overseas enterprise.... Agrarianism was to become the dominant discourse of the Second British Empire, with the fostering of foreign trade as a dependent second.'[164] In this light imperialism can be seen as part of a more general aristocratic resurgence, a counterpart to the interest which elite families now began to take in local government and charities. And yet, as suggested above, their participation in these latter activities could be seen as a capitulation to middle-class priorities,[165] and in the same way the fact that so many aristocrats put their backs into colonial administration—the Moiras and Cavendish-Bentincks in India, for example, Lord Charles Somerset and six other members of the Beaufort family in South Africa—could be interpreted in a negative light, as a displacement of aristocratic power from the centre to the periphery.

---

[162] Which had been taken in 1795, handed back at Amiens in 1802, and retaken in 1806.
[163] Notably Vincent T. Harlow, *The Founding of the Second British Empire 1763–1793* (1952–64).
[164] Bayly, *Imperial Meridian*, 80–1.   [165] See above, pp. 137–8.

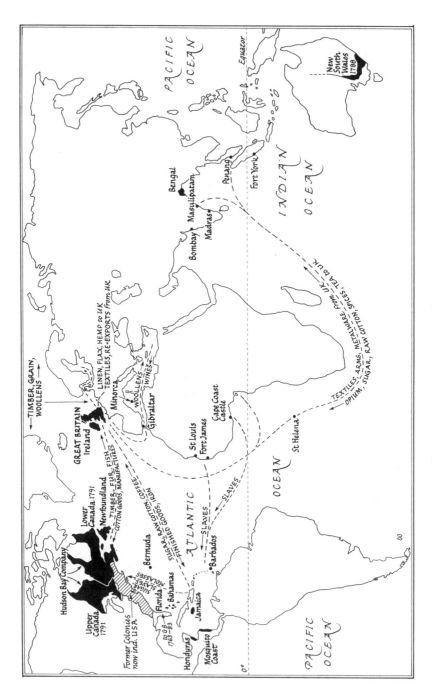

MAP 4.2. Overseas possessions and main trade routes, 1792

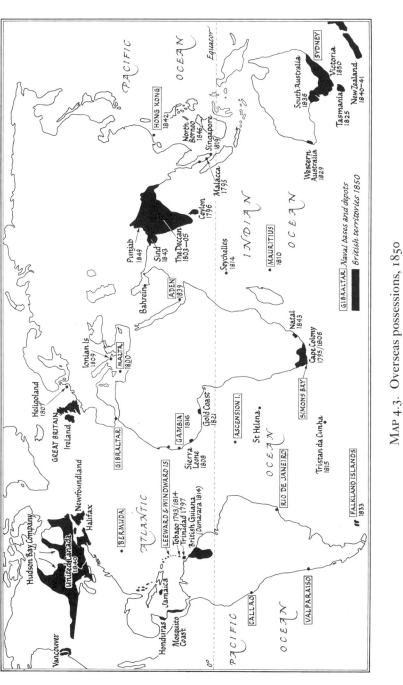

MAP 4.3. Overseas possessions, 1850

Vancouver

Hudson Bay Company

United Canada
1840

Newfoundland
Halifax

Honduras
Mosquito
Coast
Jamaica

BERMUDA

Leeward & Windward Is
Tobago 1793/1814
Trinidad 1797
British Guiana
(Demarara 1814)

ATLANTIC

OCEAN

PACIFIC

OCEAN

CALLAO

VALPARAISO

RIO DE JANEIRO

FALKLAND ISLANDS
1833

GREAT BRITAIN
Ireland

Heligoland
1807

Ionian Is
1809

GIBRALTAR

MALTA
1800

GAMBIA
1816

Sierra
Leone
1808

Gold Coast
1821

ASCENSION I.

St Helena

Tristan da Cunha
1815

ATLANTIC

OCEAN

Bahrein

ADEN
1839

Punjab
1849

Sind
1843

The Deccan
1803–05

Ceylon
1796

Seychelles
1814

MAURITIUS
1810

Natal
1843

Cape Colony
1795/1806

SIMONS BAY

INDIAN

OCEAN

HONG KONG
1842

North
Borneo
1846

Singapore
1819

Malacca
1795

Western
Australia
1829

PACIFIC

OCEAN

Equator

SYDNEY

South Australia
1836

Victoria
1850

Tasmania
1825

New Zealand
1840–41

GIBRALTAR Naval bases and depôts

■ British territories 1850

0°

Certainly, so far as the English were concerned, the acquisition of formal and informal empire was not accompanied by what might be called an imperial mentality,[166] whereas it probably was for many of the Irish and border Scottish gentry who went out as soldiers, administrators, businessmen, and engineers— the Elliots, Edmonstones, Elphinstones, Maitlands, Wellesleys, Macartneys, Castlereaghs, and Fitzmaurices.[167] The Scots especially had participated lustily in empire since the middle decades of the eighteenth century, when the juiciest jobs at home were mainly commandeered by Englishmen, and when up-and-coming Scotsmen—including many from Jacobite families—had been anxious to demonstrate their loyalty by assimilating into the British State. By 1800 Scottish engineers, architects, physicians, lawyers, and politicians no longer had difficulty in landing jobs in England,[168] but they continued to make a 'disproportional contribution to the Great Game' of empire,[169] perhaps because their parents had. It has even been claimed that their authoritarian approach to estate management fitted them for the militaristic indifference and brutality of proconsular rule. Whether or not that is true, Scots do seem to have been more comfortable in imperial jackboots than the English.

For, despite the long list of territorial acquisitions enumerated above, and despite the Navy's interference with the ships of rival empires such as the Spanish and Portuguese, the English genuinely believed that they were liberators and deliverers, fighting a defensive war to stop French imperialism and restore the autonomy of German and Italian states and of Sweden, Poland, and Spain. (Even after Waterloo, when Englishmen crossed the world—to make their mark, to prove their masculinity, to touch the hem of chivalry, or simply to find adventure—they were as likely as not to join the great *anti-*imperial game in Latin America, fighting to free Colombia, Brazil, and Argentina from Spanish and Portuguese rule.[170]) Canning's complacency on this point was typical:

Wherever this country has exerted herself, it has been to raise the fallen, and to support the falling; to raise, not to degrade, the national character; to rouse the sentiments of patriotism which tyranny had silenced; to enlighten, to re-animate, to liberate. Great Britain has resuscitated Spain, and re-created Portugal: Germany is now a nation as well as a name; and all these glorious effects have been produced by the efforts and by the example of our country.[171]

---

[166] Daniel Defoe's *Robinson Crusoe* (1719) was probably the best-selling novel of the early 19th century, and was usually interpreted as an anti-imperialist text.   [167] Bayly, *Imperial Meridian*, 133–6.

[168] Anand C. Chitnis, *The Scottish Enlightenment and Early Victorian English Society* (1986), 79–184.

[169] Colley, *Britons*, 132.

[170] Matthew Brown, 'Impious Adventurers? Mercenaries, Honour and Patriotism in the Wars of Independence of Gran Colombia', Ph.D. thesis (London University, 2004).

[171] *HPD*1, xxvii. 150 (17 Nov. 1813).

In maintaining this comfortable self-image, it helped that the most extensive, brutal, and unscrupulous extension of imperial power was effected at arm's length. Expansion on the Subcontinent was carried out by and in the name of the East India Company rather than the State, but this made little difference to the indigenous millions who were on the receiving end (the territories were not handed over to the Crown until 1858). The Company had effectively controlled Bengal since 1757, and had subsequently fought wars for the southern province of Mysore. A further struggle in 1789–92 ended with the Company dominating the richest parts, and in the fourth Mysore War (1799) it wrapped up practically all the remainder. This was where Arthur Wellesley first tasted action, and the killing of Tipu Sultan at Seringapatam in 1799—perhaps because it was commemorated in oils, first by the popular painter Henry Singleton and later by Sir David Wilkie—became one of the most vivid images of the Second British Empire: much agonized over, widely condemned, and as often extenuated. In combating Mysore the Company had had the support of the Marathas, but that did not stop it from turning on them, and the Second Maratha War (1803–5) extended its control over the Deccan. By 1815 the Company had an army of more than a quarter of a million (of whom 31,000 were Europeans), as compared with fewer than 90,000 at the start of the French wars. Notwithstanding all of which, the English were 'determined always to mark out the Raj as a moral, "civilized", and "civilizing", regime'.[172] This suggests that the English gained their Second Empire not in a fit of absence of mind but in a state of denial. Before the 1870s theirs was an imperialism that dared not speak its name, being dressed up first as religious mission, then as colonial trusteeship and white man's burden. In the same way bosscat and occasionally gunboat diplomacy, most commonly associated with Palmerston,[173] was larded with sententious appeals to high-sounding principles like nationality and constitutionality. Indeed, if language were all that mattered, one might conclude that English statesmen conducted an 'ethical foreign policy', but of course the concept is self-contradictory. For example, the determination—reaffirmed at Vienna—to rid the world of slave-traders and pirates seems laudatory, yet it was used by the Royal Navy on the high seas to justify a high-handed policy of stop and search and confiscate.[174] Equally hypocritical was the promotion of free trade on the grounds, much trumpeted by Cobden in the 1840s, that the mutual exchange of commodities would bring about international peace and goodwill. This ideal has been dubbed the *pax Britannica* yet, as will become clear, free trade was one of

---

[172] Thomas R. Metcalf, *The New Cambridge History of India*, iii/4: *Ideologies of the Raj* (Cambridge, 1994), 39.   [173] Foreign Secretary 1830–4, 1835–41, 1846–51, Prime Minister 1855–8, 1859–65.

[174] Bernard Semmel, *Liberalism and Naval Strategy: Ideology, Interest, and Sea Power during the Pax Britannica* (Boston, 1986), 18–23, 44–6.

a matrix of policies that had more to do with bellicose Britannia, meaning a determination to put the nation's finances on a sound footing so that, if war recurred, City financiers would be able to bankroll its fighting men as Rothschild had done.

They might have been hypocrites, but the English in this period were not in general racists, thanks in part to the sway of evangelical ideas. Sir James Stephen, who was born and bred among the Clapham Sect, served as Permanent Under-Secretary of the Colonial Office from 1836 to 1846 and was its presiding genius. He brought to his task a 'theology of empire' that was anything but imperialist in modern terms. Thanks to his confidence in the providential development of universal Christian mission, he not only opposed slavery with a passion but sought to protect the territorial rights of native peoples such as Aborigines, as well as those of ex-convicts. He envisaged a future in which the settler colonies at least would achieve self-government and even complete independence, though a prerequisite was that they should acquire British levels of evangelical awareness.[175] It was thanks to metropolitan officials like him that the Dutch farming community of the Cape was forced, not only to liberalize trade, but to abolish slavery, to frame vagrancy legislation in race-neutral terms, and to grant civil rights to everyone regardless of colour.[176]

The priorities of officialdom do not a Zeitgeist make, but the evangelicals' monogenism affected the culture more generally. English people's lack of interest in indigenous traditions now seems reprehensible, while their self-righteous belief in white trusteeship and an 'empire of mercy'[177] must have irritated the natives, but these traits were at least based on an idea of the fundamental sameness and not otherness of all peoples, whatever their current condition. Orientals might be benighted but they were not inherently inferior and were capable of being enlightened.[178] Similar monogenic beliefs governed other ruling ideologies in the period, notably Utilitarianism, which only made sense on the assumption that people are essentially the same. The same was true of political economy as reformulated by Ricardo, who abandoned the eighteenth

---

[175] Richard Ely, 'From Sect to Church: Sir James Stephen's Theology of Empire', *Journal of Religious History*, 19 (1995), 75–91.

[176] Elizabeth Elbourne, ' "To Colonize the Mind": Evangelical Missionaries in Britain and the Eastern Cape, 1790–1840', D.Phil. Thesis (Oxford University, 1992).

[177] *12th Anniversary Report of the C.M.S.* (1812), 438; Ian Bradley, *The Call to Seriousness: The Evangelical Impact on the Victorians* (1976), 90.

[178] In a distinguished study of the London Missionary Society, Susan Thorne has pointed out that evangelical Congregationalists often described 'darkest Africa' and 'darkest England' in similar terms. In her view, this shows that their view of the working class was 'raced'. More plausibly, however, it shows that (before 1850) their view of native peoples was *not* raced, as Elizabeth Elbourne has pointed out. Susan Thorne, *Congregational Missions and the Making of an Imperial Culture in 19th-Century England* (Stanford, Calif., 1999), 1–7, 53–88; Elizabeth Elbourne, reviewing Thorne in *Canadian Journal of History*, 36 (2001), 164–6.

century's preoccupation with national characteristics, and with relations between rich and poor countries, in favour of an analytical internal model of the economy based on the distribution of resources as between *classes*—landlords, capitalists, and wage-earners.[179] Of course, there were other factors besides ideology operating here, notably a simple recognition that the grotesqueries of the French Revolution had made the old polarity between European civilization and a barbarian other seem redundant. But at a time when ideas of nationality and national cultures were taking hold in many parts of Europe, it is worth emphasizing that feelings of Englishness, in so far as they existed, were far more bound up with institutions like the monarchy, Parliament, and the common law than with ethnicity. As in so many ways, the 1850s would bring great changes in this respect. It was then that the English began (gingerly at first) to buy into the idea of the British Empire, to talk about the Great Game in Asia, to build on theories of Anglo-Saxon greatness and inherent racial superiority, and to seek to civilize as distinct from simply convert the heathen.

   Inspired by globalization and the information revolution, recent studies of imperialism have shifted the emphasis from formal empire (territorial sovereignty) and informal empire (commercial exploitation) to more incidental techniques of coercion based on the possession and utilization of superior knowledge. However, before there can be knowledge, there has to be a means of discovering and recognizing it, an insight which has led to a renewed emphasis on institutions.[180] A Committee of the Privy Council for Trade and Plantations was established in 1784, immediately following the loss of America, and in 1801 a Secretaryship of State for War and Colonies was created. Both these departments spawned bureaucracies which naturally invented business to justify their keep. An even more striking example is provided by the Admiralty, which found itself reduced from constant red alert before 1815 to having not very much to do afterwards. The vacuum was filled by 'the father of exploration' John Barrow, who was Second Secretary to the Admiralty (1804–6, 1807–45) and as powerful an influence in his sphere as Stephen at the Colonial Office. In his enthusiasm to discover the river Niger by sailing down the Congo, and to find a North-West Passage through the Arctic, Barrow poured taxpayers' money and sailors' lives into a succession of reckless expeditions. His victims were mainly Royal Navy officers who had been 'mothballed on half-pay' and who 'yearned for something to do', even though it often led to hunger and sickness and death.[181] The less fortunate of 'Barrow's boys' were reduced to eating mice, raw meat, each other,

---

[179] For discussions of political economy and Utilitarianism, see below, Ch. 5.

[180] In the same way it will be argued below, pp. 284–5, that an institutional basis for providing social reform preceded the notion that social reform ought to be provided.

[181] The worst disaster was Sir John Franklin's ill-fated expedition to the North-West Passage in 1845–7.

even their own shoes, but they seem to have shared his almost manic resolve to fill in the missing bits of the atlas.[182] Others were fired by the prospect of scientific discovery, a tradition established by Captain James Cook, who died in 1779, and by the botanic passion for collecting native flora and fauna. The surveying voyage to Tierra del Fuego on which Darwin served as semi-official naturalist, instructed but not paid by the Admiralty, was merely the most portentous of many such expeditions.[183] The key official was Sir Joseph Banks, President of the Royal Society (1778–1820) and as close to the heart of the nation's patronage network as Dundas. He has been described as helping to disseminate a peculiarly 'English version of enlightenment', which drew on Newtonian natural philosophy and Paley's natural theology but lacked the anticlericalism that was central to its Continental counterpart.[184]

Banks was also the unofficial director of Kew Gardens, a site for the systematic display of native colonial flora, much as the British Museum was for bones and fossils, and the prototype of similar gardens throughout the empire. Significantly, however, Kew had begun to decline in importance well before Banks's death in 1820, and made much less impact than the Royal Geographical Society (RGS), which was founded in 1830 explicitly to promote a 'science of empire' and provide economic data and other information useful to the Government. The RGS's ethos in the early decades was strictly Utilitarian, and quite devoid of imperialist or racialist overtones. Kew's problem was that its philosophy contradicted this Anglican evangelical ethos, being not only agrarian but incarnational (or worldly as distinct from *other*-worldly). Its defence of the Englishman's right to 'intrude' on large areas of the globe's surface was based on his proven ability to 'improve' the land God had created, and to develop its natural resources.[185] In the same way Nonconformist missionaries often likened the work of saving native souls to that of planting Christian seeds.[186] Kew's day would come again, but only with the return of incarnational attitudes in the 1850s.

The stories of science and empire could intersect in complex ways. The Great Trigonometric Survey of India, conceived in 1799 and funded and undertaken by the British administration over the next seven decades, was unnecessarily elaborate and of considerably less practical use to revenue officers and military commanders than a simpler and cheaper method of mapping would have been.

---

[182] Fergus Fleming, *Barrow's Boys* (1998).   [183] See below, p. 442.

[184] John Gascoigne, *Joseph Banks and the English Enlightenment: Useful Knowledge and Polite Culture* (Cambridge, 1994); John Gascoigne, *Science in the Service of Empire: Joseph Banks, the British State and the Uses of Science in the Age of Revolution* (Cambridge, 1998).

[185] Richard Drayton, *Nature's Government: Science, Imperial Britain, and the 'Improvement' of the World* (New Haven, 2000), 50–128.

[186] Sujit Sivarundaram, 'Nature Speaks Theology: Colonialism, Cultivation, Conversion and the Pacific 1795–1850', Ph.D. thesis (Cambridge University, 2002), 89–115.

It was an enormous waste of taxpayers' money but, like NASA today, that was part of its attraction.

Trigonometric surveying, with its precision, cumbersome instruments, and complex calculations, invoked the apogee of metropolitan science. Its technical genealogy goes back to the great Enlightenment geodetic controversies, in which trigonometric surveys were used to measure the deformation of the earth's form, calculations that became the apotheosis of Newtonian mechanics. In essence...the British stuck to the ideal of trigonometric surveying not in spite of how hard it was, but because it was so hard. Anyone could sketch an ordinary topographic map using a compass and pedometer...but a trigonometric survey demanded the high-minded, rational, mathematical, co-ordinated efforts of an enlightened imperial administration. By performing the Great Trigonometric Survey, the British performed an elaborate masque of what it was to be British.[187]

In so far as empire *was* central to national identity, what counted were not its territorial and military aspects but the mercantile and scientific. Such imperialism was not confined to institutions, but was integral to the upper-middle-class social fabric. When the novelist Maria Edgeworth, for example, or her father, Richard Lovell, received letters from friends abroad, these would often be accompanied by ferns, birds' wings, bulbs, moss, seeds, and other such natural specimens to be collated and displayed back home, much as an earlier generation might have shown off Wedgwood vases. At a time when most other countries were absorbed in their own cultural entrails, many British citizens engaged in 'global pillage', and literally saw the whole world as their oyster.[188] But once again it bears saying that public and popular fascination with the 'mysterious [Far] East' and with the 'dark continent' was a later nineteenth-century development. In this period it was not the imperial possessions so much as Latin America, the South Seas, or, nearer to home, Greece, Italy, and Araby, that exercised the greatest hold over the imagination of the English.

Admittedly, any generalization about the mentality of the English is complicated by the succession of short-term mood swings, especially during the French wars. In 1812 plutocrats and aristocrats emerged from four years of subdued pessimism to behave with exaggerated swagger and self-confidence. This was the heyday of the dandy Beau Brummell, the blackmailing courtesan Harriette Wilson, and Lord Byron, who awoke one morning to find himself famous on account of the first two cantos of *Childe Harold's Pilgrimage*. Byron's brief but dizzy celebrity epitomized an age of exuberance, vice, and social whirl, qualities

---

[187] D. Graham Burnett, *Times Literary Supplement*, 20 Feb. 1998, 26, summarizing the central argument of Matthew H. Edney, *Mapping an Empire: The Geographical Construction of British India, 1765–1843* (Chicago, 1997).

[188] Larry Stewart, 'Global Pillage: Science, Commerce, and Empire' in Roy Porter (ed.), *The Cambridge History of Science*, iv: *Eighteenth-Century Science* (Cambridge, 2003).

which are indelibly associated with the label 'Regency' but which mainly belong to its first five years. It was a period when conventions were relaxed and traces kicked over, when aristocrats took advantage of high rentals to indulge in binge spending on everything from books to claret. It was the age of the waltz, of plays, balls, and masquerades, of silver forks, bucks and blades, dandies, beaux, bloods and swells, of West End clubbers and porter louts, their numbers boosted by returning officers on half-pay, as well as by foreign visitors coming to try their luck at dice and hazard on the London tables. By the same token, so many English people were going abroad, partly in order to dodge taxes, that the Treasury seriously considered a proposal to tax passports.

By 1815 the *Edinburgh Review* felt that it was time to call a halt. 'Artificial spirits, and mere frivolous glitter, we believe, were never so little in request among us. Aristocratic distinctions too, have been robbed of much of their importance, by the growing claims of opulence and respectability; and talents can no longer command general admiration, but by their union with some degree of integrity and moral worth.'[189] The prediction was slightly premature, but there were straws in the wind. Brummell and Byron exiled themselves to the Continent in 1816, the former to avoid creditors, the latter to avoid charges of buggery (a capital offence) and incest, while Wilson's 'days as a successful courtesan were over...The young men about town, who had taken their duties, regimental or otherwise, very lightly... were now marrying and settling down, and Harriette's part in their lives was over.'[190] A blanket of propriety came down after the brilliant 1817–18 season, which was notably cold and foggy, and brought five years of aristocratic and metropolitan bullishness to an end.[191] It had lasted long enough for the landed interest to secure one major piece of self-interested legislation, the notorious Corn Law of 1815, which restricted the importation of foreign wheat. Byron, who whatever his private behaviour was a genuinely radical Whig in the Whitbread tradition, condemned the way in which a landlord-dominated legislature had sought to 'make a malady of peace' by attempting to preserve indefinitely the naturally high food prices of wartime.

> Safe in their barns, these Sabine tillers sent
> Their brethren out to battle—why? for rent!
> Year after year they voted cent. per cent.,
> Blood, sweat, and tear-wrung millions—why? for rent!
> They roar'd, they dined, they drank, they swore they meant
> To die for England—why then live?—for rent!
> The peace has made one general malcontent

---

[189] [Francis Jeffrey], 'Paradise of Coquettes', *ER* 24 (1815), 398–9.
[190] Angela Thirkell, *The Fortunes of Harriette: The Surprising Career of Harriette Wilson* (1936), 196.
[191] Leonore Davidoff, *The Best Circles: Society, Etiquette and the Season* (1973), 23.

Of these high-market patriots; war was rent!
Their love of country, millions all misspent,
How reconcile? by reconciling rent!
And will they not repay the treasures lent?
No: down with everything, and up with rent!
Their good, ill, health, wealth, joy, or discontent,
Being, end, aim, religion—rent, rent, rent!

(Byron, *The Age of Bronze*)

'A MALADY OF PEACE': THE FOUDATIONS OF MONETARY POLICY

Ministers faced Parliament with 'unbounded' confidence in 1816, sure 'that the Battle would be fought and the triumph gained in discussions on our foreign policy'.[192] It therefore came as a shock when many of their warmest supporters rebelled on the Army estimates. Because they had to pay interest on a debt worth more than twice the national income,[193] they found themselves contending 'for what will be called a war expenditure in time of peace'.[194] The Property Tax was scheduled to end at the same time as hostilities, but since it is not as easy to cut expenditure as it is to sign an armistice, the Government proposed to continue the tax at half the rate. At this Brougham moved into philippic mode. Faced with almost 400 petitions and at least eighteen county meetings, Parliament threw the proposal out by 238 to 201. Ministers promptly gave up the war malt duties as well, presumably as a gesture to the lower orders, who might have resented the loss of a progressive tax alone. These developments, haughtily ascribed by Castlereagh to the public's 'ignorant impatience of taxation', led to the loss of about £16 millon or one-fifth of the Government's revenue, probably the sharpest reduction in English history. It also affected the subsequent direction of policy, especially by forcing retrenchment, and in that way may even be said to have made what came to be called 'liberal Toryism' inevitable.

The post-war years were scarred by distress and discontent. Prices and wages fell in all sectors, while discharged soldiers and sailors added to unemployment. To the upper classes it seemed that lack of 'all respect for established authority and antient institutions' was leading to revolution.[195] The Spa Fields riots of December 1816 followed a drunken meeting addressed by the Radical Henry Hunt, and ended in an armed attack on the Tower and the suspension of habeas

[192] Huskisson to Canning, 20 Apr. 1816, Canning MSS 67/83.
[193] Patrick K. O'Brien, 'The Political Economy of British Taxation, 1660–1815', *EconHR* 41 (1988), 1–32.
[194] Liverpool to Castlereagh, 16 Jan. 1815, in *Supplementary Despatches, Correspondence, and Memoranda of Arthur Duke of Wellington, 1797–1818*, ed. second Duke of Wellington (1858–72), ix. 538–9.
[195] Liverpool to Grenville, 14 Nov. 1819, Liverpool MS 38381, fo. 2.

corpus. Three months later hundreds of blanket-carrying weavers from Manchester ('Blanketeers') marched in the direction of London but were quickly dispersed. Three months after that a riot by textile workers at Pentrich in Derbyshire ended in the execution of Jeremiah Brandreth and two others and the transportation of thirty more. It had been encouraged by Oliver the Spy, the Home Office's notorious agent provocateur. The climax came on 16 August 1819 when a well-drilled but peaceful crowd of between 60,000 and 100,000 gathered at St Peter's Fields in Manchester to hear Hunt advocate universal suffrage and annual parliaments. In panic the local magistrates ordered a regiment of hussars to help the yeomanry disperse the crowd, which led to eleven being killed and more than 400 injured. Cobden referred to 'tory squires . . . coming into town and letting loose a troop of fox hunters disguised as yeomanry cavalry'. Finally, in February 1820 a group of Cato Street conspirators plotted to murder the entire Cabinet. They were foiled by Sidmouth's spies, who deliberately allowed them to approach a climax rather than nipping them in the bud, and Arthur Thistlewood and four others were executed for high treason.[196]

In a country whose history is relatively free of bloody reprisals, the Manchester Massacre or battle of Peterloo held great significance for Radicals, but for the political nation as a whole fear of the mob outweighed acknowledgement that on this occasion the local authorities had overreacted. Ministers were privately appalled by their 'precipitation', but endorsed their actions publicly. As Canning said, 'To let down the magistrates would be to invite their resignation, and to lose all gratuitous service, in the counties liable to disturbance, for ever.'[197] Later that year the Government introduced their controversial Six Acts, which drew on some of Pitt's repressive legislation but were in the circumstances quite mild. Public meetings of over fifty persons could not be held without the permission of a magistrate or sheriff, the laws against blasphemy and seditious libel were tightened, and the stamp duty on newspapers and cheap pamphlets was increased to 4d., significantly damaging the radical press. Ministers resisted calls by York and other old buffers for an increase in the standing Army. 'We must have an Army in peace to protect the Metropolis, including as it does the King, the Parliament, and the Bank. We must have a regular force likewise for the protection of our dock yards and other great public depots. But the property of the country must be taught to protect itself.'[198] Instead the Home Office made furious efforts to mobilize a loyal press as a counterweight to the rash of seditious publications. Public meetings were called to shower praise on the Government, loyal declarations were hurriedly 'got up',

---

[196] Despite this choice of venue, Thistlewood at his trial appealed to Brutus and Cassius as role models, not Cato.   [197] Canning to Huskisson, Aug. 1819, Huskisson MS 38741, fo. 315.   [198] Liverpool to John Beckett, 25 Oct. 1819, Liverpool MS 38280, fos. 205–6.

and local notables were encouraged to organize volunteer forces. It did the trick, but this was to be the last time ministers felt they could rely on symbols and propaganda to retain control. It was also the last time that the right to free speech and assembly was challenged with such contumely. By highlighting the creaky state of authority in industrial boom towns like Manchester, Peterloo stimulated a rethink on how best to maintain law and order.

Was it possible to prevent or mitigate economic distress? Here debate turned on whether the underlying cause was overproduction or under-consumption, a semantic distinction analytically but polemically significant. Ministers emphasized the former in order to avoid responsibility: 'Government or Parliament never meddle with these matters at all but they do harm.' There was no alternative but to wait 'till trade comes round and the population can find employment in a natural way'.[199] Whigs and Radicals, on the other hand, denied that time would 'correct the mischief'.[200] The root of the problem was 'an inability to consume', which could be corrected by lower taxes, public investments, or similar positive actions aimed at 'raising the consumption so as to make the produce and the demand meet each other'.[201] Lord Lauderdale, once known as Citizen Maitland for his radical views, had long argued against mistaking 'for the effects of abundance, that which in reality may be only the effect of failure of demand'.[202] He also criticized the ministerial doctrine that capital investment and not demand was 'the prime mover' in creating and extending industry.[203]

Some initiatives were taken. The Poor Employment Act of 1817 was a response to downturn in the Midlands armaments industry, which was particularly hard-hit by the coming of peace. Loan commissioners were authorized to advance up to £1¾ million in exchequer bills to individuals, corporations, vestries, and other statutory bodies for the purpose of completing canals, roads, bridges, docks, and other public work schemes authorized by Parliament.[204] Although not entirely unprecedented,[205] it marked a considerable extension of the scope of government, though its practical effect was marginal, especially as the money could not be used to initiate schemes, as was necessary in deprived

---

[199] Liverpool to Lord Kenyon, 18 Dec. 1819, Liverpool MS 38281, fos. 347–9; Liverpool, *HPD*2 vi. 710 (26 Feb. 1822).

[200] Sheffield to Sidmouth, 19 Jan. 1816, Devon RO, Addington MS 152M (1816–17).

[201] Lansdowne, *HPD*2 vi. 721 (26 Feb. 1822). One important Radical, however, supported the Government's position: Ricardo.

[202] Lord Lauderdale, *An Inquiry into the Nature and Origin of Public Wealth, and into the Means and Causes of its Increase* (Edinburgh, 1804), 264.

[203] Lauderdale to Holland [1821?], Holland MS 51692, fos. 58–65.

[204] These Commissioners were the forerunners of the Public Works Loan Commission set up in 1842 (M. W. Flinn, 'The Poor Employment Act of 1817', *EconHR* 14 (1961), 82–92).

[205] W. M. Stern, 'United Kingdom Public Expenditure by Votes of Supply, 1793–1817', *Economica*, 17 (1950), 196–210, analyses a 'modest trickle' of public spending on measures designed to improve 'the quality of life of the ordinary citizen'.

urban areas. More visible were the 1818 and 1824 Church Building Acts, which granted commissioners £1 million and £500,000 respectively for erecting new places of Anglican worship with free accommodation for the poor.[206] This was much more than just a make-work scheme. The brainchild of High Churchmen, it signalled an attempt to catch up with Nonconformity, especially in manufacturing areas, and to moralize the masses. Some 612 commissioner churches were built between 1818 and 1856, of which ninety-seven were initiated under the first grant. The vast majority were trabeated classical boxes, but whereas in London they mostly had Greek or Roman ornament, about two-thirds adopted newly fashionable Perpendicular details such as crockets, spires, finials, and upright tracery.[207] The effect of Gothic clothes on a classical body was somewhat artificial, appropriately so perhaps for an enterprise in which religion was wielded as an instrument of social control.

The single overarching problem facing ministers was the currency. Here it is necessary to refer back to the years 1810–11, when battle lines had first been drawn. At that time the economy had been suffering from the Continental blockade and from the collapse of a speculative boom in South American trade. As shares plummeted dangerously and bankruptcies hit record numbers (192 in July 1810 alone, 239 in the following January), a scapegoat had to be found, and was found in the 'speculator', henceforward branded as the enemy within. Speculators were the very opposite of rentiers, investing responsibly in government stock. Instead they were people who took advantage of paper money to get rich too quickly by overproducing, over-trading, and especially fictitious dealing. 'The STOCK EXCHANGE: it has so gangrened our hearts,' wrote an anonymous writer, who drew an analogy with the effects of American gold on Spain in the sixteenth century.

NO SOONER DID THEY OBTAIN WEALTH WITHOUT LABOUR, than unbridled passions began to predominate, and a love of immoderate enjoyments stamped the Nation with the horrible character of treachery and licentiousness! Woe to the people who obtain wealth without labour! Woe to the man, and to the million who can draw thousands from out of the mine, or from out of the TOWN and COUNTRY BANKS without inheritance, property, or labour. Woe to the man and to the millions who are enabled by such means to embark in flagitious speculations, and thereby to abandon an honorable and an industrious trade.[208]

---

[206] M. H. Port, *Six Hundred New Churches: A Study of the Church Building Commission, 1818–1856, and its Church Building Activities* (1961).

[207] e.g. James Savage's St Luke's, Chelsea (1820–4) and Charles Barry's St Matthew's, Campfield, Manchester (1822–5).

[208] *An Exposé of the Present Ruinous System of Town and Country Banks, etc, by a British Merchant* (1810), 7–8, 11, 19; Geoffrey Carnall, *Robert Southey and his Age: The Development of a Conservative Mind* (Oxford, 1960), 101–20.

The trouble with speculation was its contagion, its power to infect traders who had previously been manly and honest, so that Britain seemed poised like Nineveh and Tyre for a great fall. Burke had blamed the French Revolution on intellectual and currency speculation. Now a hundred moralists blamed financial speculation for the fact that public spirit and love of country had been displaced by private avarice. Such jeremiads are the common coin of commercial crises, and if this time the mood was more than usually febrile, that was partly owing to the fraught international situation and a feeling that the nation's destiny was in the balance.[209]

Interestingly Unitarians, as social outsiders, seemed able to view the likelihood of commercial calamity with equanimity. Harriet Martineau was only 8 but apparently experienced a certain amused *schadenfreude* at the prospect of national bankruptcy, especially as it would mean 'every body being brought to a state of barter; and all, except landowners, having to begin the world again, and start fair'.[210] Another Unitarian, Anna Letitia Barbauld, wrote *Eighteen Hundred and Eleven*, a controversial poem prophesying the decay of Britain's mercantile greatness and reversion to a primitive and pastoral condition. London was currently exultant, crazed by its 'midas dream',

> But fairest flowers expand but to decay;
> The worm is in thy core, thy glories pass away;
> Art, arms, and wealth destroy the fruits they bring;
> Commerce, like beauty, knows no second spring.

There was little of the Romantic apocalyptic in Barbauld's vision, rather a sober Augustan sense of an economic and cultural baton being passed from one commercial empire to another, with the Americas waiting in line. Jane Austen, who though not a Dissenter was equally detached, began her darkest story, *Mansfield Park*, in 1811. A morality tale and a 'condition of England' novel, it counterposes the heroine, Fanny Price, who clings rigidly to religion and propriety, against a worldly, witty, and sophisticated couple, Henry and Mary Crawford, whose only principle is hedonism. Unlike say Hannah More's *Coelebs in Search of a Wife* (1808), *Mansfield Park* avoids didacticism because the naughty characters are, superficially at least, much more attractive than the priggish Fanny. Nevertheless, the reader can be in no doubt that Austen endorses her values—i.e. stability, custom, and genuine feeling as against restlessness, novelty,

---

[209] In 1810 Abraham Goldsmid, the Government's leading loan contractor, added to the febrile atmosphere by committing suicide over allegations that he had bribed the Exchequer Bill Office to be allowed to subscribe to a loan early (S. R. Cope, 'The Goldsmids and the Development of the London Money Market during the Napoleonic Wars', *Economica*, 9 (1942), 180–206; John W. Houghton, 'Cultural Theory as Applied to the History of Economic Thought: A Case Study', *History of Political Economy*, 23 (1991), 512).

[210] Harriet Martineau, *Introduction to the History of the Peace: From 1800 to 1815* (1851), p. cclxiv.

pretence, and artificiality.[211] The latter qualities are encompassed by the term 'speculation', signifying not just economic risk-taking but the questioning of religious orthodoxies. In Chapter 25 Henry, Mary, Fanny, and Edmund Bertram (an ordinand) take part in a game of that name, the object being to bid for and gain certain of each other's cards. Mary of course plays recklessly: 'I will stake my last like a woman of spirit. No cold prudence for me. I am not born to sit still and do nothing. If I lose the game, it shall not be from not striving for it.' As the play proceeds in its desultory way, Henry brings the conversation round to the rectory which Edmund expects to acquire with his prospective living:

The farm-yard must be cleared away entirely, and planted up to shut out the blacksmith's shop. The house must be turned to front the east instead of the north—the entrance and principal rooms, I mean, must be on that side, where the view is really very pretty; I am sure it may be done. And *there* must be your approach—through what is at present the garden. You must make you a new garden at what is now the back of the house; which will be giving it the best aspect in the world—sloping to the south-east. The ground seems precisely formed for it. I rode fifty yards up the lane between the church and the house in order to look about me; and saw how it might all be. Nothing can be easier. The meadows beyond what *will be* the garden, as well as what now *is*, sweeping round from the lane I stood in to the north-east, that is, to the principal road through the village, must be all laid together of course; very pretty meadows they are, finely sprinkled with timber. They belong to the living, I suppose. If not, you must purchase them. Then the stream—something must be done with the stream; but I could not quite determine what. I had two or three ideas.

To these sweeping suggestions Edward replies primly that he cannot afford much 'ornament and beauty', and hopes merely that the 'premises may be made comfortable, and given the air of a gentleman's residence'. Henry retorts with another monologue, again betraying his metropolitan disdain for old landed pretensions.

The air of a gentleman's residence . . . you cannot but give it. But it is capable of much more. . . . By some such improvements as I have suggested . . . you may raise it into a *place*. From being the mere gentleman's residence, it becomes, by judicious improvement, the residence of a man of education, taste, modern manners, good connections. All this may be stamped on it; and that house receive such an air as to make its owner be set down as the great land-holder of the parish, by every creature travelling the road; especially as there is no real squire's house to dispute the point; a circumstance between ourselves to enhance the value of such a situation in point of privilege and independence beyond all calculation.

While this one-sided conversation is proceeding, Mary manages to buy the knave she has been coveting 'at an exorbitant rate'. Austen comments wryly: 'The game was her's, and only did not pay her for what she had given to secure it.'[212]

This was the cultural context in which an important debate was staged on the currency. Bullionists were anxious to get back to the gold standard. They claimed that the premium of gold over paper, the fall in the sterling exchanges, and the rise in prices relative to other countries—all of which were evident during 1801–3 and again much more dramatically during 1809–15—proved that paper money had been issued to excess and was therefore depreciated. See Table 4.1. Basing their views on the quantity theory of money and the specie flow mechanism, bullionists argued in effect that the level of money supply appropriate to any particular country was dependent on its economic performance relative to other countries (as measured by imports and exports). A successful nation might reward itself with higher prices, rents, and profits,[213] but a nation whose balance of trade was adverse should tighten its belt to match the drain of specie. This would engineer recovery as prices fell, making its goods internationally competitive, while the consequent rise in interest rates would attract inward investment. The vast majority of theorists were bullionists, including Ricardo, Malthus, and Henry Thornton, whereas anti-bullionism was rife among 'practical men', meaning politicians, businessmen, and most of the directors of the Bank of England. Anti-bullionists denied that the premium on gold, the fall in the exchanges, and the rise in prices were due to expansion of the money supply. They denied the possibility of currency being issued to excess so long as it was issued by bona fide bankers in order to discount 'genuine and sound short-term commercial paper' (this was called real bills doctrine). In their

TABLE 4.1. *Depreciation of sterling, 1797–1813 (percentage values)*

Year	Gold (£3 17s. 10½d. per oz)	Silver (60.84d. per oz)	Exchange on Paris (Fr 25.22 per £)	Exchange on Hamburg (36s. banco per £)	Commodity prices (1790)
1797	100.0	102.6		98	138
1801	109.0	117.3		113	142
1805	103.0	107.4	98.8	103	149
1811	123.9	120.7	139.1	144	158
1813	136.4	136.7	128.6	139	185

Source: Lords and Commons Committees on the Resumption of Cash Payment (1819), apps.

[212] Jane's brother Henry Austen was a banker and riding the crest of a speculative wave when *Mansfield Park* was published in 1814, but two years later he went bankrupt owing to the post-war loss of government orders for groceries and cloth. He was ordained shortly afterwards.

[213] The question of wages was considered more problematic. See below, pp. 344–6.

view a badly performing nation needed to increase and not diminish its accommodation to new businesses, so long as they were sound. Again, rather than reducing the money supply in response to falling exchanges, in the hope that this would lead back to equilibrium, anti-bullionists recommended counter-cyclical monetary policies.[214] Later, during the deflationary (post-1819) stage of the debate, a more theoretical anti-bullionism emerged. Its proponents conceded that the Bank restriction had led to excessive circulation and that individuals had suffered, but they defended it nevertheless because it had benefited *productive* classes—merchants, manufacturers, farmers, labourers—while those damaged had merely been 'drones'—rentiers, mortgagees, annuitants.[215]

The Bullion Report of 1810, the joint concoction of William Huskisson,[216] Francis Horner, and Henry Thornton, recommended the restoration of the gold standard (cash payments) within two years. Ideally Huskisson would have preferred a less precipitate resumption, but because the Bank directors were anti-bullionists on principle, he thought they should be coerced as quickly as possible.[217] The Report was debated in May 1811 and hotly disputed by many including Vansittart, Castlereagh, Perceval, Rose, and Herries,[218] who insisted that the Bank restriction made it much easier to obtain the specie needed for subsidies and for the armies in the Peninsula.[219] It was a good practical argument, and Castlereagh added a theoretical one. Attacking the bullionists' empiricist belief in a uniform measure of value, he postulated an 'ideal standard' or 'sense of value', a concept which was not without insight but puzzled the cognoscenti. Finally, Vansittart carried a series of resolutions, one of which (that promissory notes were equal to coin 'in public estimation') seemed to imply a permanent Bank restriction. However, it was also resolved that cash payments should be resumed six months after the end of the war.

In 1813 Vansittart, who was now Chancellor of the Exchequer, presented a New Plan of Finance, a complicated scheme which was carried only because virtually no one understood it. (Huskisson, who did, assailed it as a violation of Pitt's sinking fund and breach of faith with the public creditor.) Vansittart then launched into

---

[214] Jacob Viner, *Studies in the Theory of International Trade* (New York, 1937), 119–217; Frank Whitson Fetter, *Development of British Monetary Orthodoxy 1797–1875* (Cambridge, Mass., 1965), 26–63. See below, pp. 325, 548.

[215] Robert Torrens, *A Comparative Estimate of the Effects which a Continuance and a Removal of the Restriction upon Cash Payments are Respectively Calculated to Produce, &c* (1819), 52–69.

[216] Huskisson's expertise was unequalled. When he felt obliged to quit his official post along with Canning in 1809, Perceval remarked: 'This is the worst and most unexpected stroke of all' (Thorne, iv. 273).

[217] W. Huskisson, *The Question Concerning the Depreciation of Our Currency Stated and Examined* (1810), pp. xv–xviii.

[218] Liverpool also implied an adherence to the anti-bullionist position at around this time (*HPD* 1 xxvi. 1178–80 (9 July 1813)).

[219] e.g. Castlereagh, *HPD* 1 xix. 1007–11 (7 May 1811). This argument put bellicose bullionists like Canning on the defensive, but they rallied by insisting that the best guarantee of a nation's military energies were a sound currency and a sound credit rating.

what can only be called jiggery-pokery, 'mystic rites of which he was the attendant priest',[220] the purpose being to keep the Government's financial head above water in difficult circumstances. He had two main strategies. One was to borrow money in the City and give it to the sinking fund commissioners for purchasing stock some four times a week. By this means he kept the price of the funds perpetually high, which allowed him to meet any pressing deficit in the Government's finances by selling exchequer bills at short notice. Alternatively, he would apply to the Bank for an increase in the unfunded debt.[221] As a result of these machinations, which some-times involved buying stock in the dearest market and selling it in the cheapest, the Government made itself seem 'in all money matters little better than a Committee of the Bank',[222] as well as being in thrall to leading financiers such as Baring, Irving, Hart Davis, but especially Rothschild. The latter was only too willing to provide the Chancellor with accommodation at favourable rates in return for advance warning of Government moves on the money market. He made killings and the Exchequer stayed afloat.

Resumption of cash payments was postponed for a year after Napoleon's first abdication in 1814, for a further year in 1815, and then for two years in 1816, the ostensible reason being that the Bank restriction helped the Government to borrow money, which it would have to do to a greater than usual extent owing to the loss of the Property Tax. In 1818, following a poor harvest and loss of bullion, resumption was postponed again, but when the Prime Minister suggested yet another year's delay in January 1819, Huskisson was roused to angry recrimination.[223] In an important memorandum he denounced Vansittart's hand-to-mouth deficit financing and sham sinking fund, and called for a 'financial effort' in the form of retrenchment, new taxes, debt repayment, and resumption.

The mystery of our financial system no longer deceives anyone in the money-market; selling exchequer bills daily to redeem funded debt daily, then funding those exchequer bills once a year, or once in two years, in order to go over the same ground again; whilst the very air of mystery, and the anomaly of large annual or biennial loans in times of profound peace, create uneasiness out of the market, and in foreign countries an impression unfavorable with respect to the solidity of our resources . . . In finance, expedients and ingenious devices may answer to meet temporary difficulties; but for a permanent and peace system, the only wise course, either in policy or for impression, is a system of simplicity and truth.[224]

[220] W. R. Brock, *Lord Liverpool and Liberal Toryism, 1820 to 1827* (Cambridge, 1941), 172.

[221] Hilton, *Corn, Cash, Commerce*, 33–6.

[222] Arthur Young, diary, 17 Feb. 1816, in *The Autobiography of Arthur Young, with Selections from his Correspondence*, ed. M. Betham-Edwards (1898), 465–6.

[223] He had returned to office with Canning in 1814 as Commissioner for Trade, Forests, and Land Revenues (generally referred to as First Commissioner of Woods and Forests).

[224] Huskisson, 'Memorandum on the Resumption of Cash Payments', 4 Feb. 1819, Liverpool MS 38368, fo. 225; Charles Duke Yonge, *The Life and Administration of Robert Banks, 2nd Earl of Liverpool* (1868), ii. 382–4.

Liverpool seems to have been convinced, since Vansittart was apparently '*commanded* not to touch upon the principles of the question' in debate.[225] This was the Huskissonian moment, the point at which he began to dominate economic policy. Meanwhile, Whigs were also pressing for resumption, though they had ulterior political motives as is evident from Grey's private comment that it would be impossible 'to resume cash payments, without encountering a degree of distress, which no Administration can encounter'.[226] After secret committees of inquiry had been established in both Houses, Huskisson, Canning, and other bullionists seized the initiative, so that the question became *how* not *whether* to resume. The few witnesses who were of an opposite persuasion—Thomas Smith and the brothers Attwood—might as well not have turned up, since their interrogators did not seek any meeting of minds. In view of this stifling orthodoxy, most anti-bullionists, instead of attacking resumption per se, argued merely that the time was not yet ripe, a tactic which enabled their opponents to take the polemical high ground. As Peel reflected later, it was then or never. 'In 1819, the question came before the House for final decision. In my opinion, that question was, the choice between two alternatives—eternal Bank restriction, or the return to cash payments without further delay.'[227] After much wrangling in the corridors of power, first the Government and then Parliament accepted the committees' recommendations. The Bank was to return to the gold standard by redeeming its notes for gold bars on demand (the Ingot Plan) as from 1 February 1820. The amount of gold thus paid in exchange for paper was to increase periodically thereafter in stages according to a fixed timetable (the graduated scale). Payments in cash (gold coin) at the 1797 par value were to be restored by 1 May 1823 at the latest. Finally, all banknotes under the value of £5 were to be withdrawn from circulation within a period of two years from the date of resumption. Anti-bullionists argued that the policy would be so deflationary that many businesses would be strangulated. In Castlereagh's view, speculating ('over-trading') might have damaged individuals but it had benefited the community. Bullionists objected that the wealth created in wartime was not real or sustainable but 'shadowy', 'visionary', 'artificial', 'fictitious', 'speculative', 'ideal', 'drunken', to which Vansittart retorted dryly that Southwark Bridge (1814–19) must be 'real' because he had walked across it.

In retrospect the decision of 1819 can be characterized as a preference for deflation over reflation. However, ministers were motivated by financial rather than economic considerations, and it was only because of the consequences of resumption that concepts like deflation (not of course the term) came into play.

---

[225] Huskisson to his wife, 3 Feb. 1819, Huskisson MS 39949, fos. 58–61; C. R. Fay, *Huskisson and his Age* (1951), 198–9.   [226] Grey to Holland, 13 Dec. 1818, Holland MS 51545, fos. 215–16.
[227] *HPD*3 xvii. 512 (23 Apr. 1833).

It is therefore misleading of historians to interpret the policy in sectoral terms, as a victory for City merchants, bankers, and Lancashire cotton masters over landlords and Midlands ironmongers, that is to say, a victory for those with an interest in international trade (deflationists) over people who produced for the domestic market (reflationists).[228] Such an analysis is distorted by hindsight and misrepresents what the different economic interests thought at the time. Admittedly, it would not be very long before London and Lancashire came out in favour of the gold standard and sound money, but when the decision was taken in 1819 virtually all businessmen—whether manufacturers, merchants, financiers, brokers, or bankers—opposed resumption emphatically, just as they had done in 1811. In Birmingham's case this was only to be expected, since the town depended on buoyant home demand, but the great exporting centres were just as hostile. Businessmen always look first to short-term survival, and cash payments seemed to jeopardize that. Nearly all the memorials and petitions from merchants, bankers, and traders—400 to 500 such persons in London, 147 in Manchester, and many more in Bristol, Leeds, Halifax, and Bradford—urged the Government not to attempt such belt-tightening just when the economy was in cyclical depression anyway.

With regard to landowners, it is clear that in terms of material self-interest many of them *ought* to have opposed resumption. The Bank restriction had, after all, inflated the value of their prime asset. Furthermore, many landlords and farmers had taken advantage of high wartime food prices, low interest rates, and easy credit to borrow money on mortgage so as to extend their wheat crops, often on clay and other soils unsuitable for arable farming. Cash payments, by restoring the currency to its pre-war value, automatically increased the burden of their debts and reduced the price of their primary produce. Within months many agriculturists had come to regret the end of the Bank restriction, but at the time, and with very few exceptions, the landed interest supported the measure to resume cash payments.[229]

This degree of support was unexpected. For the crucial debates on 24–5 May the Commons was packed and the atmosphere slightly hysterical. A Canningite MP thought 'it was quite wonderful to observe how members' minds changed as the debate proceeded—at its commencement the numbers of those who were inclined to oppose the resolutions either from ignorance or apprehension were considerable, but every speech made seemed to gain the confidence of the House in the plan'.[230] The shift was partly due to a discourse by Ricardo, who

---

[228] Brock, *Liverpool*, 182; Asa Briggs, *The Age of Improvement, 1783–1867* (1959), 205; S. G. Checkland, *The Rise of Industrial Society in England, 1815–1885* (1964), 178.

[229] An exception was Sir John Sinclair, who paradoxically had opposed the Bank restriction in 1797.

[230] E. J. Littleton, journal, p. 248 (24–5 May 1819), Staffordshire CRO, Hatherton Papers.

was treated as an oracle, perhaps because he told MPs what they were anxious to hear—that cash payments could be restored without pain.[231] Seizing the moment, Canning daringly called for a unanimous declaration in order 'to show the public that the House was in earnest in its attempts to restore the ancient standard', and to everyone's amazement the resolutions were passed 'without a dissentient voice'. Yet, 'notwithstanding that extraordinary unanimity, everybody seems to differ'.[232] Firm opponents—mainly merchants, manufacturers, and bankers such as Hudson Gurney, Alderman Heygate, Joseph Cripps, William Manning, the elder Robert Peel—gurgled with rage but were 'at last...persuaded to be quiet'.[233] Matthias Attwood slunk away rather than appear to acquiesce. It was the same outdoors, where doubts were stifled in a simulated show of confidence. The funds fell dramatically, banks closed their doors, and panic gripped many sectors of trade and industry, yet deviants like Sinclair found themselves branded as public enemies, such was the 'delirium... in favour of a metallic currency'.[234] Even hardened bullionists were amazed. 'Canning says, "it is the greatest wonder that he has witnessed in the political world".'[235]

Whatever motivated MPs it was not economic rationality. Apart from a vague intuition that convertibility was 'manly and honest', the theme which rippled through all the speeches and pamphlets was the belief that cash payments would put an end to the social, economic, and moral instability that had so alarmed Jane Austen—'fictitious speculation', 'bubbles', 'adventures', 'mushrooms', 'frauds', and 'accommodations'—but without damaging honest and legitimate commerce. Astonishingly, they seemed to think that there was a clear line separating good and bad enterprises. Since most MPs owned land, they may have thought that agriculture, as the most 'natural' and 'legitimate' form of wealth creation, would survive the deflationary consequences of resumption, whereas overblown merchants, manufacturers, and financiers would be vulnerable. If so, they were wrong. Probably they failed to realize how greatly speculation had invaded the agricultural sector, i.e. how many Henry Crawfords there were. To landlords, speculation was something which merchants and manufacturers did, and anything which prevented it might also put a stop to the tidal wave of industrialization, with its attendant horrors of chimney stacks and child abuse. As a

[231] Ricardo's justification for this assurance was that in 1819 the premium on gold over paper was only 5%. As he was later to concede, this did not take into account the fact that the mere operation of returning to a gold standard (by other countries as well as Britain) would raise the value of gold, and so force an appreciation of paper by considerably more than 5%.

[232] Lord Sheffield to Lord Colchester, 19 May 1819, in *The Diary and Correspondence of Charles Abbot, Lord Colchester*, ed. second Baron Colchester (1861), iii. 76–7.

[233] *The Life of William Wilberforce*, ed. Robert Isaac and Samuel Wilberforce (1838), v. 27.

[234] *Memoirs of the Life and Works of Sir John Sinclair*, ed. J. Sinclair (Edinburgh, 1837), ii. 299.

[235] J. W. Ward to Edward Copleston, June 1819, in *Letters of Dudley*, 222.

witness to the 1819 committees put it, resumption would 'improve the quality, but *diminish the quantity* of commerce'.[236] So far as ministers were concerned, if the decision to return to gold was intended to help any particular sector, it was not productive industry, whether agriculture or manufacturing, but the fundholder interest, which was thought to deserve compensation for the recent decline in the value of money.[237] Back in the 1780s the Public Accounts Commissioners had cited 'justice to the public creditor' as an overriding duty. The idea moved from the realm of rhetoric to that of accepted public doctrine as a result of the debates of 1810–11 and 1819. Huskisson argued forcefully that, with an inviolable standard of value, London's status as 'the Emporium not only of Europe but of America north and south' would enable her to become in addition the 'chief bullion market' and the 'settling house of the money transactions of the world', thereby rendering its commerce more secure.[238]

The Act of 1819 (later referred to as Peel's Bill after the chairman of the Commons Committee and mover of the resolutions) did not settle the question. The moneyed interest led by Rothschild lobbied behind the scenes for a stay of execution, while the Bank directors, forced to implement a plan which most of them viewed 'with unabated solicitude', showed their pique with ministers by refusing to make the customary advances on forthcoming loans, and even threatened to withhold accommodation from the 'commercial world'.[239] The Bank was meant to reduce its circulation gradually and to achieve cash payments at the old parity by May 1822 at the earliest and May 1823 at the latest. In the interim it was to sell gold (in order to lower its value) but not contract its mercantile discounts. However, the directors chose to accelerate a process of which they did not approve so that, in the event, resumption of cash payments was arrived at a full year early in May 1821. This required them to *buy* gold (thus enhancing its value) and withhold accommodation from commerce more than was necessary. Cynics claimed that they acted precipitately in a deliberate attempt to discredit bullionism altogether. The effects were particularly noticeable in districts where paper circulation was restricted, such as south Lancashire, and also in the countryside.[240]

Rural opposition to the gold standard climaxed in June 1822 when 'Squire' Western, an agricultural leader from Essex, and the London banker Matthias

---

[236] *Reports from the [Commons] Secret Committee on the Expediency of the Bank resuming Cash Payments, PP* 1819 iii. 76.

[237] Huskisson condemned currency *depreciation*, but he was keen to diminish the *value* of money and was no crude deflationist. Before long he was seeking counter-cyclical reflation through lower interest rates, prolongation of the life of small notes, and bimetallism.

[238] Huskisson, 'Rough Draft on Coin and Currency', 12 July 1818, Huskisson MS 38741, fo. 252.

[239] Bank of England, Court of Directors Book, Pa 65–6, 105–7, 155–8, 208–11, Qa 63–9, 114–16, 236–8; Committee of Treasury Minute Book, 13, 15–17.

[240] Sir John Clapham, *The Bank of England in History: A History* (Cambridge, 1944), ii. 73.

Attwood moved for an inquiry into the possibility of devaluation. Huskisson then sealed the triumph of cash payments by carrying an amendment pledging Parliament never to alter the standard again. With hindsight it is clear that the vote of 1822 settled the matter until the First World War. It was a brave decision in so far as it challenged the views of the Government's landed supporters, but ministers had already vexed them sorely by their inclination, never explicitly announced, to reduce the level of protection on corn.

RETHINKING THE CORN LAWS

The 1815 Corn Law has been described as 'one of the most naked pieces of class legislation in English history'.[241] Peel was a junior minister at the time and actively supported the Law. Since he was also the Prime Minister who repealed the Corn Laws thirty-one years later, it seems as though a considerable somersault was turned, hence the charges of betrayal which were to be hurled at him. However, the shift in policy seems less dramatic when the intentions behind the 1815 Law are properly understood. Moreover, the decisive rethinking took place before 1827 and involved not just Peel but Liverpool, Canning, Huskisson, and Robinson. The fact that repeal was not achieved until 1846 was due partly to political difficulties and partly to the fact that the ministers involved in that rethinking were mainly out of office during the 1830s.

The Corn Laws were of medieval origin and were designed to ensure, through a mixture of import duties and export bounties, that English farmers grew sufficient grain. They became controversial only after the point, somewhere about 1793, when population increase meant that Britain became a chronic net importer. Export bounties being now irrelevant they were abolished in 1814, after which the Corn Laws simply signified controls on importation. As such, opponents regarded them as instruments of landed privilege and State mercantilism, and as standing between the consumer and cheap foreign food. They also fell foul of economic theory, for whereas Adam Smith had exempted matters of national security like food and shipping from his general strictures in favour of free trade, the cognoscenti now accepted Ricardo's view that market conditions should almost always prevail, whatever the short-term disadvantages.[242] Accordingly Corn Law repeal in 1846 was celebrated as the triumph of intellect over ignorance, of popular will over the aristocracy, and of manufacturing and trading interests over the land.

However, these social and ideological interpretations are not appropriate to the 1820s, when official thinking on corn was influenced by pragmatic

---

[241] Robert Blake, *The Conservative Party from Peel to Churchill* (1970), 15.
[242] Hilton, *Corn, Cash, Commerce*, 3–30, 98–126, 269–301.

considerations, especially the need to safeguard food supplies for a growing population. The French Revolution had begun during *la grande peur*, a panic partly sparked off by the prospect of starvation which had swept through France in 1789, and there had since been terrible domestic scarcities in 1795–6 and 1800–1. In 1810 a mini ice age hit western Europe, with damage to most crops and a recurrence of scarcity in the summer of 1812. These events seemed to confirm the dire message of Malthus' *Essay on the Principle of Population* (1798) that periodic famines were unavoidable. Food supply was the most anxious priority of governments throughout the first half of the nineteenth century, and it prompted Pitt to find out how many mouths needed feeding. The first national census was in 1801, but it was the second ten years later that alarmed contemporaries because it showed a 14 per cent increase. So, although the 1815 Corn Law had its origins in pressure from the landed interest (Byron's 'sabine tillers'), it was taken over by ministers as official policy and reflected their concerns about subsistence. Defying widespread popular protests, Parliament enacted that no foreign corn could be imported—or taken out of bonded warehouse and released on to the market—until the home price of wheat had reached an average of 80s. per quarter (equivalent prices being stipulated for barley, oats, and other types of grain). This involved a technical innovation, for whereas previous laws had merely *discouraged* imports by imposing a series of differential duties depending on price, the new Law actually *forbade* importation whenever corn was below the cut-off point, and allowed it to enter without any duty at all whenever prices were above the mark.[243] Opponents objected that wheat would never fall below 80s. again, but on closer inspection the Law turns out to have been much less of a capitulation to the landed interest than it appears at first sight.

Firstly, wheat from British overseas territories was to be admissible at 67s., a form of colonial preference. Secondly, foreign wheat could be stored freely in bonded warehouses at all times. This was deeply obnoxious to the gentry, but ministers insisted that such corn would constitute an emergency resource against famine. Thirdly, the cut-off point chosen for foreign wheat (80s.), while roughly representing the average price of the previous twenty years, was much below the average price of the previous quinquennium (107s. in 1809–13) and very much less than the 120s. that agriculturists were demanding. Finally, it is clear that the Government was anxious, not to maintain the price permanently,

[243] Because of this technicality, which continued until 1828, some contemporaries used the term 'free trade' to mean an absence of prohibition instead of the more usual sense of absence of protection. This usage has misled Norman Gash into thinking that Castlereagh ended up as a 'notable' free-trader (review, *EHR* 104 (1989), 137). For a similar misunderstanding, see Michael J. Turner, *The Age of Unease: Government and Reform in Britain, 1782–1832* (Stroud, 2000), 183.

but merely to avoid such a *sudden* fall from bloated wartime levels as would lead to capital being withdrawn from agriculture. Privately Huskisson referred to the Law as an example of 'management' designed 'to bring things gradually to their level and to prices approximating to those of other countries'.[244]

The most vulnerable agriculturists—whether landlords or tenants—were those who had taken advantage of dear food and cheap money to plough heavy wet clays that were unsuitable for arable in the long term. There is room for debate as to whether even these marginal farmers actually *needed* the protection provided by the 1815 Law—whether, that is to say, there was a vast mass of cheap foreign corn in northern Europe waiting to penetrate the British market and undercut the British producer. But even if in most years there was not, harvests varied hugely and in any particular year there might well be such a surplus. There was very imperfect intelligence as to the state of the crops in Lithuania, for example, and the amount of grain stored at Danzig and Riga, so that whenever even a trickle was imported English farmers could not know whether this was all there was or whether it heralded a flood. Fearing the worst, they would rush to sell their own corn instead of holding it back until the price was right in the manner prescribed by Adam Smith's theory of markets. In these circumstances the aim of the 1815 Law was to protect farmers from the *fear* of imports as much as from the *actuality*. Behind this was a still more fundamental rationale. Although ministers knew that it was no longer possible to rely on the domestic harvest every year, the strategy was still one of *autarky*, or self-sufficiency, in food supplies as far as possible. Another war might encourage another Napoleon to try to starve the country by blockading it. British agriculturists must be encouraged to invest capital in the land, and with luck it might even be possible to solve the Malthusian dilemma. High hopes were placed on Ireland, which, it was argued, could be integrated into the British economy by becoming the 'granary of England'.

In the event wheat prices fell to an average of 84*s.* in 1816–19 and 55*s.* in 1820–3, and in worst-hit areas such as the Fens there was extensive decultivation and an appalling catalogue of arrears, quittals, and bloody riots.[245] With its agricultural supporters demanding that the Corn Law be stiffened, the Government was reluctantly forced to investigate further by means of three select committees of which the most important sat in 1821. Its report was written mainly by Huskisson with encouragement from Ricardo, and it articulated what might be called a new agricultural policy, as well as stating the Government's overall monetary, fiscal, and financial strategy. Huskisson recognized that there could be no immediate reduction in protection, given the extent of rural distress, but

[244] Huskisson to Canning, 27 Mar. 1815, Canning MS 67.
[245] A. J. Peacock, *Bread or Blood: A Study of the Agrarian Riots in East Anglia in 1816* (1965).

he was adamant that future developments pointed the Corn Laws downwards, not upwards. Instead of seeking to extend the arable sector as in 1815, decultivation was now called for. Liverpool blamed agricultural distress on 'the quantity of land that was brought under the plough in the last years of the war', Castlereagh spoke contemptuously of soils being forced into 'an unnatural fertility, which was of course followed by a proportionate barrenness', and Robinson said that 'it was not by any act of the legislature that land had been called into cultivation, and it was not therefore to be expected that by any act of the legislature it should be continued in cultivation'.[246] Many reasons were given for this controversial switch of policy. The failure of so many farmers had undermined the heady ideas of self-sufficiency that had been entertained in 1815. Worse still a serious subsistence crisis in Ireland during 1816–17, when the grain and potato harvests failed, made it 'manifest, that the evil of a failing crop [in England] would be aggravated as our dependence on Ireland increased'.[247] Malthus and Ricardo among others had recently promulgated the law of diminishing returns to investment in agriculture, which further dashed hopes for an agrarian solution to the problem of overpopulation. It was therefore essential that supplies should be available overseas in times of scarcity, but recent travellers' reports indicated that foreigners were also cutting back on their production of grain. This contradicted the view, expressed very forcibly in 1815, that they would continue to grow corn even though there was no habitual market for them in Britain. Huskisson now argued that the maintenance of life-saving European supplies depended directly on whether or not the British ports were open constantly. Britain must take Saxon and Polish wheat on a 'constant and uniform' basis[248] in order to prevent farmers in those countries from turning to more profitable pursuits, such as cotton-spinning (the worry being not the threat to Lancashire but that to the consumer).[249] A further problem with the existing Law was that the sudden transition from a total prohibition to total free trade proved unsettling for everyone involved in food supply—farmers, merchants, factors, grocers—and therefore discouraged investment. In theory 80s. was meant to register scarcity following a poor harvest, but in practice such a price might not be reached until September, by when the Baltic might have iced over for the winter, making imports impossible. Another crucially important consideration was the effect of the Corn Laws on the currency. Under the system

---

[246] Liverpool MS 38281, fos. 347–9 (18 Dec. 1819); *HPD1* xxxiii. 1124 (9 Apr. 1816); *HPD2* i. 643 (30 May 1820).

[247] *Report from the Select Committee of the House of Commons on Petitions Complaining of the Depressed State of Agriculture* (1821), *PP* 1821 ix. 11.

[248] David Ricardo, *On Protection to Agriculture* (1822), in *The Works and Correspondence of David Ricardo*, ed. Piero Sraffa and Maurice Herbert Dobb (Cambridge, 1951–5), iv. 265.

[249] *Report on Petitions Complaining of the Depressed State of Agriculture*, 1821, 12.

established in 1815, the amount of corn imported was in inverse proportion to the size of the domestic harvest. It therefore fluctuated greatly from year to year, and since merchants often paid for foreign corn with gold coin it followed that bad harvests led to an exodus of bullion. This had not much mattered so long as there was no direct connection between the reserves and the amount of paper in circulation, but it mattered very much by 1821, the year in which Britain finally restored cash payments. The situation now was that sudden reductions in the country's gold reserves, due to bad harvests and high corn imports, would have to be accompanied by severe curtailments of domestic credit.

In as much as reciprocity of demand is the foundation of all means of payment, a large and sudden influx of corn might, under these circumstances, create a temporary derangement of the course of exchange, the effects of which (after the resumption of cash payments) might lead to a drain of specie from the Bank, the consequent contraction of its circulation, a panic amongst the country banks,—all aggravating the distress of a public dearth.[250]

The solution lay in the fact that corn could be kept for several years. Huskisson promised that a *freer* trade would lead to more regular imports and more regular remittances, with corn being paid for and stored in British warehouses until it was needed. In 1826 he made the same point even more starkly: 'To be consistent . . . with our system, if we keep our present prohibition of corn, we must reimpose the restriction on cash payments.'

For all these reasons it was believed that the corn trade should be permanently open and subject to more moderate duties than landlords were demanding. The need to safeguard food supply was still of overriding concern, but whereas in 1815 this consideration had pointed towards increased protection it now pointed towards freer trade. This new agricultural policy was in place by 1821, but it could hardly be implemented until the rural distress had lifted. Therefore, for the sake of his own political survival, Liverpool was forced to prevaricate as he faced the continuing wrath of the country gentlemen.

THE SQUIRES' REVOLT

The 'old, mad, blind, despised, and dying king' of Shelley's description finally expired on 29 January 1820. Southey, the Poet Laureate, wrote a fawning *Vision of Judgment* in which George III was escorted into Heaven by angels on the basis of a glittering curriculum vitae, universally favourable references, and popular approbation.[251] It invited a riposte by Byron, whose own *Vision of Judgment* featured a debate between Archangel Michael and the Devil as to whether the

---

[250] Ibid.

[251] Richard Garnett thought the poem was 'an experiment worth making' but that it 'should have been made by a more accomplished metrist, and upon some other subject' (*DNB*).

late King really deserved to go to Heaven. Southey is called as a witness on George's behalf, but his threat to read out some of his own poems causes such a pandemonium among the listening angels that George is able to slip into paradise while no one is looking:

> And when the tumult dwindled to a calm,
> I left him practising the hundredth psalm.

Back on earth the Regent's accession as George IV precipitated a crisis over his estranged wife. Having been offered £50,000 a year to repudiate her title and stay abroad, Caroline naturally responded by returning to London, where she received a popular ovation. As sympathetic addresses flooded in, and supporters demanded that her name be restored to the Liturgy, the Government brought forward a Bill of Pains and Penalties, the aims of which were to dissolve the marriage and deprive Caroline of all her titles and privileges. Despite heroic efforts by Brougham and Denman in her defence, witness after witness appeared at the bar of the House of Lords in order to blacken her character. In November the Bill passed its third reading, but only by nine votes, and Liverpool abandoned it. He considered that it had little prospect of success in the Commons. He was also afraid that the attempt to secure it might inflame the populace and even lead to the overthrow of the monarchy. Notwithstanding this solicitude, he was called 'all sorts of names' by the King for abandoning the Bill,[252] and even worse ones by the royal mistress, Lady Conyngham. Eight months later Caroline was forcibly repulsed while trying to gatecrash George IV's Coronation, and less than a month after that she was dead. There were serious riots as her cortège passed through London, and fatalities at Hyde Park Corner when the Life Guards opened fire on what ministers called the mob, Radicals called the People, and sensible folk were beginning to recognize as simply a crowd.

These riots have been described as 'arguably the largest movement of the common people during the early nineteenth century',[253] the storm before the calm. However, the political weather had begun to change *before* the Coronation. In 1820 many yeomen and gentry joined in pro-Caroline demonstrations, but during the first half of 1821, according to James Cottle's weekly journal *Brunswick; or, True Blue*, the 'temper of the public mind' underwent 'an astonishing change', as loyal addresses suddenly began to swamp radical ones.[254]

---

[252] Possibly because George IV wished to claim the credit for abandoning it himself (Norman Gash, *Lord Liverpool: The Life and Political Career of Robert Banks Jenkinson Second Earl of Liverpool 1770–1828* (1984), 164; Arbuthnot, *Journal*, i. 75).

[253] Craig Calhoun, *The Question of Class Struggle: Social Foundations of Popular Radicalism during the Industrial Revolution* (Chicago, 1982), 106.

[254] Jonathan Fulcher, 'The Loyalist Response to the Queen Caroline Agitations', *JBS* 34 (1995), 499.

Respectable reformers were alarmed by the popular element among the Queen's supporters, and also by the prevalence of women. The loyalist broadsides that appeared in T. E. Hook's newspaper *John Bull* were openly misogynist, but even without this factor the revelations of witnesses as to Caroline's immorality would have turned the tide. Having first presented her as an injured innocent, cartoonists gradually turned her into a coarse strumpet, while representations of the King became notably kinder.[255] His Coronation, at which no pomp was spared or circumstance omitted,[256] turned out to be an unexpected public relations triumph. Even his continual ogling of Lady Conyngham was forgiven.

Many of the manufacturing industries were recovering by this time, though not those that were mainly dependent on domestic demand. (It was claimed that in 1820 Birmingham's consumption of malt, beer, and other necessaries fell by one-third to one-half.) More worrying for ministers politically was the intensification of agricultural distress, which provoked the following characteristically thoughtful advice from Huskisson to the Government's business manager. He referred to a 'spirit' spreading through the country—

a soreness on every subject connected with expense, a clamour for economy, a feeling growing out of the present straitened circumstances of the yeomanry contrasted with the ease which they enjoyed during the war. Whilst this is the state of the yeomanry, the infection of radicalism, which is prevalent in the towns, is gradually making its way into the villages. In this state of things . . . the period may not be remote, in which we may find it necessary to do something to secure the affection and more cordial good will of some great class in the State. To bid for the lower classes or the manufacturing population is out of the question. Duty and feeling would equally forbid it; but the yeomanry are still within your reach, and to them in my opinion we must look.[257]

As wheat prices fell severely, and the landed interest clamoured for massively increased protection, a coordinated campaign was undertaken by the Central Agricultural Association led by George Webb Hall, once described as 'a species of "Hunt" in agriculture'. Representing about fifty local organizations from twenty counties, mainly in the South, it was driven by large tenant farmers, small landlords, solicitors, millers, gentlemen graziers, land agents, and squires suffering from rent arrears. They described themselves romantically (but mendaciously) in petitions and memorials as yeomen,

neither *Notables* nor *Radicals* but . . . UNQUESTIONABLY the most numerous class of inhabitants in the kingdom, possessing collectively the largest capital of any class seeking to gain a livelihood by skill, capital, and labour; employing UNQUESTIONABLY the greatest

---

[255] Tamara L. Hunt, 'Morality and Monarchy in the Queen Caroline Affair', *Albion*, 23 (1991), 719–21; M. Dorothy George, *English Political Caricature 1793–1832: A Study of Opinion and Propaganda* (Oxford, 1959), 199–201, 205; Fulcher, 'The Loyalist Response', 500–1.
[256] See Plate 10.   [257] Huskisson to Arbuthnot, 24 Mar. 1820, Huskisson MS 38742, fos. 6–9.

number of labourers ourselves; and maintaining, *almost exclusively*, all the labourers of every other class, when unemployed by their own masters.[258]

There was also concern for pastoral farming, and Sheffield's annual wool fair at Lewes, like Lord Somerville's London cattle show and the Holkham Sheep Shearing, was a regular scene of protectionist activity. Yet for some reason the agriculturists' campaign declined as suddenly as it erupted. Maybe they simply bowed to political reality following the 1821 Select Committee which, as Huskisson told Ricardo, they went into as plaintiffs and from which they emerged as defendants.[259] Whatever the reason, when Thomas Lethbridge moved for higher protection in May 1822, the motion was annihilated (243 to 24). It was not that the landed interest was any less dissatisfied, but its sights were now set on tax relief, public loans, and various expedients for increasing the supply of money. They were still protectionists in the sense of defending the existing Corn Law, but they no longer asked for more.

The agriculturists' abandonment of partisan solutions, which would have benefited themselves specifically, was accompanied by a shift in social analysis. Hitherto they had defined themselves in opposition to industrial manufacturers, but they now began to identify with them as fellow 'productive' members of society in contrast to the 'drones', meaning financiers, fundholders, annuitants, and what might be called the salariat, the latter with incomes fixed while prices were high. This newly perceived conflict locked into the division between creditor and debtor interests that had been developing in a subterranean way over thirty years, and complemented the arguments of those anti-bullionists who now defended the Bank restriction because it had benefited the enterprising.

According to one estimate the index of commodity prices fell from 138.7 in 1818 to 87.9 in 1822, while the price of banknotes appreciated commensurably. That the percentage fall was similar across a whole range of goods pointed to a common cause, namely the return to gold at the 1797 level. Thomas Attwood, the risk-taking Birmingham banker, had been a Government supporter hitherto, but he now decided that the only way to ward off ruin was by reforming Parliament so as to increase the strength of the country party. He claimed that resumption had been '*intended* to operate a total transfer of the landed rental of the kingdom into the hands of the fundholders',[260] likened Huskisson and Ricardo to 'Sin and Death guarding the gates of Hell', and prophesied that, unless Peel's Bill were repealed, 'the *Sword* will be the only arbiter that will

---

[258] *The Origins and Proceedings of the Agricultural Associations in Great Britain, in which their Claims to Protection against Foreign Produce, Duty Free, are Fully and Ably Set Forth* (1820), 20.

[259] Huskisson, as reported by Ricardo to Trower, 22 Aug 1821, in *Works and Correspondence of Ricardo*, ix. 37.

[260] T. Attwood to his wife, 11 and 13 Apr. 1821, in C. M. Wakefield, *Life of Thomas Attwood* (1885), 81–2.

remain. To that stern arbiter the landowners must appeal, or they must drop into the workhouse as the dried leaves of autumn to the ground.'[261] Attwood's hyperboles caught on 'like wildfire' in the countryside during 1821–2 and so, suddenly, did Cobbett's brutal slogan, 'the farmer versus the fundholder'. The latter had long denounced the Bank restriction, and he now lacerated the beneficiaries of resumption: annuitants, mortgagors, pensioners, placemen, stockjobbers. Hawking his message around the shires, he had the satisfaction of seeing his calls for economic and parliamentary reform adopted by shows of hands at a number of county and hundred meetings.

Broadly speaking, two different types of remedy were proposed. The first consisted of palliatives and was intended to help those who had suffered by shifting the tax burden from producers to drones, by reducing interest on the national debt, and by legislating for an equitable adjustment of existing dividends, debts, contracts, salaries, and taxes. The last idea was Cobbett's and was a genuine attempt to mitigate injustice, but it would have required an impossible degree of bureaucratic dirigisme. During 1821 the gentry had to settle for more practicable policies such as retrenchment and tax cuts, and they more or less forced ministers to abolish some minor offices and to give up the agricultural horse tax.[262] The Whigs were in their usual dilemma, keen to ingratiate themselves with the country gentlemen but wary about jettisoning too many places since, if they ever returned to office, they would need to compensate for four decades during which the most lucrative ones had gone to their opponents. Retrenchment therefore became the battle-cry of Radicals like Joseph Hume, with support from Whigs-cum-Radicals such as John Cam Hobhouse, Thomas Creevey, and H. G. Bennet. When P. G. Wodehouse commented that it was not difficult to tell the difference between a Scotsman and a ray of sunshine, he might have had Hume in mind. Angry, dour, and humourless, he regularly kept the House up until the early hours with seemingly interminable inquiries into the public accounts. 'We divided on every item of every estimate,' boasted Hobhouse, 'we were glued to these seats.'[263] However, these Radicals gave economical reform a bad name. Boring, obsessional, and vindictive, they threw away the aura of evangelical idealism that the cause had commanded when it was led by Saints such as Henry Bankes.

This may partly explain why, in 1822, the country gentry turned to a more dramatic type of remedy, which was to stimulate consumption by macroeconomic

---

[261] T. Attwood to E. Davenport, 9 June 1822, John Rylands University Library, Manchester, E. D. Davenport MSS, Attwood, fos. 21–34.

[262] When forced into tax cuts, ministers preferred to reduce a number of taxes rather than abolish any one, because for reasons of patronage they wished to retain the number of tax collectors (Edward Hughes, *Studies in Administration and Finance, 1558–1825: with Special Reference to the History of Salt Taxation in England* (Manchester, 1934), 505).   [263] *HPD*2 xv. 692 (27 Apr. 1826).

methods, such as suspension of cash payments, repudiation of the national debt, or devaluation of the standard. Western, who only two years previously had sought relief in higher corn laws, now described the resumption as 'almost the sole cause of the evil' and 'the greatest calamity the public had endured in modern times'.[264] At least eighteen county meetings were held in 1822, and many more in 1823, and most of them called for monetary adjustment.[265] Cobbett's ideas were clearly advancing, and it alarmed not only ministers but Whig grandees. In Kent and Sussex Darnley and Cowper lowered themselves by entering into public wrangles with him, while in Norfolk Cobbett humiliated Coke when, by twenty votes to one, he carried resolutions for an equitable adjustment and the appropriation of Church property and Crown lands.[266] Commentators noted a new class of agitator—millers, small farmers, and graziers who had done well out of the war, 'overgrown yeomen'—'these are the men who almost everywhere stand up for parliamentary reform and radical opinions, in opposition to the old gentry'.[267]

'It was not now a question between the owner and occupier of land, which should derive a particular share of the profit, but whether there should be a transfer of the whole land of England altogether into other hands.'[268] Whigs like Lord Dacre naturally welcomed an analysis which told farmers that their real enemies were not landlords and gentry but fundholders and placemen, yet they dared not stray too far away from what official circles considered sound political economy, and usually stopped short of advocating the suspension of cash payments or debt repudiation. According to Holland, the crisis required 'some very strong decisive measures and especially these two—Bankruptcy without the name of it—and the name of reform with as little real alteration as possible'.[269] Lauderdale demanded an end to a sinking fund which had invaded private property 'one hundred times more than all the thefts, acts of swindling, of house breaking, robberies, forgeries',[270] while a young Whig, Lord John Russell, denounced moneyed men and political economists, who 'care not for the difference between an agricultural and manufacturing population, in all that concerns morals, order, national strength, and national tranquillity. Wealth is the only object of their speculation. . . . Political economy is now the fashion; and the farmers of England are likely, if they do not keep a good look out, to be the

---

[264] *HPD2* vi. 1405 (1 Apr. 1822); vii. 430 (8 May 1822).

[265] Mitchell, *Whigs in Opposition*, 162.

[266] Travis L. Crosby, *English Farmers and the Politics of Protection 1815–1852* (Hassocks, 1977), 57–80.

[267] Mallet, diary, 4 Feb. 1822, iv. 20.   [268] Lord Dacre, in *The Times*, 2 Feb. 1822.

[269] Holland to Grey, 20 Apr. 1820, Holland MS 51546, fos. 112–15. Grey merely advised Holland not to say as much in public (Grey to Holland, 23 Apr. 1820, Durham University, Grey MSS).

[270] Lauderdale to Page, 14 Nov. 1821, Bodleian Library, MS Eng. lett. b. 3, fos. 50–3; Lauderdale to Holland, 2 Mar. 1822, Holland MS 51692, fos. 186–90; Hilton, *Corn, Cash, Commerce*, 141–2.

victims.'[271] All this made Whigs seem unsound in the eyes of most opinion-formers, writing in respectable newspapers and journals. As a well-informed public functionary put it,

a large and meritorious part of the community, the fundholders, who might as yet have considered the leading members of Opposition, as men of enlightened and liberal principles, found them at once ready to prey upon the public creditor, with a view of favouring that class of the community (namely the landed gentry) who have alone the power of bringing them into office.[272]

The squires' revolt of 1820–2 was a dress rehearsal for the rebellion that brought Wellington's Government down in 1830. It infuriated ministers, who could not understand why the country gentlemen acted 'in concert...and without consultation'.[273] Yet it soon became obvious that the latter as a body did not wish to topple the Government. After Western had carried the abolition of some malt duties by 149 to 125 (March 1821), ministers threatened to resign unless the decision were reversed, which it duly was a fortnight later by 242 to 144. Only five members changed their votes, but loyalists who had abstained previously now rallied. In 1822 the Commons abolished two lordships of the Admiralty and one of the postmasters-general, and came within four votes of repealing the salt duties, but again a resignation threat brought the gentry to heel, and soon afterwards the Radicals suffered huge defeats in their attempts to abolish the Swiss Mission and to reduce the Civil List. The Government's backbench supporters were evidently willing to wound and yet afraid to strike, or rather they were still afraid of letting in the Whigs.

'NEVER A CONTROVERSIAL CABINET': LORD LIVERPOOL'S SYSTEM OF POLITICS

Liverpool's Government did not attempt to deal with social problems such as poverty, housing, sanitation, and factory hours, while emigration was left to backbench initiatives, but it was the first to adopt a coherent economic policy. This was not a deliberate development. In part it was because of the markedly cyclical rhythm of business activity, which created a perception that national economies performed as a single system for which the government of the day should be held responsible. As a result, ministerial correspondence was full of allusions to the weather, the prospects for the next harvest, the state of the funds, the price of exchequer bills, the ease or difficulty of raising money on mortgage.

---

[271] 'Letters to the Yeomanry of Huntingdonshire', *The Times*, 18 and 22 Jan. 1822.
[272] Mallet, diary, 20 Feb. 1822, iv. 24.
[273] Wellington to Buckingham, 6 Mar. 1822, in *Memoirs of the Court of George IV, 1820–1830*, ed. Duke of Buckingham and Chandos (1859), i. 292.

Another reason may have been the current vogue for economic theory, though it seems likely that political economy became popular because governments adopted economic policies and not the other way round. In their own estimation, when ministers intervened in economic affairs they did so pragmatically, in response to difficulties as they arose, but having intervened they often felt bound to justify their actions in terms of principle, and so became theoreticians in spite of themselves.

They also succumbed to pressure from a proliferating number of vested interests. It was hardly surprising that, as the economy diversified, lobbies should have formed and that the Government should have been called on to arbitrate between them. Ministers were certainly aware of the antagonisms between different regions and interests. 'The question is... not a *national* but a local one between London and the country,' wrote Liverpool regarding the Spitalfields silk industry.[274] Again, while abolition of the preferential duties on West Indian sugar was often called for on ethical grounds, ministers were more concerned with whether or not it would be expedient to transfer 'the profit from one class of home manufacturers to another', that is from the Yorkshire woollen manufacturers, whose most important market was the West Indies, to the Lancashire cotton manufacturers, who mainly exported to the East Indies.[275] Liverpool also had to ensure that he did not offend the source of loans and the source of taxes simultaneously. As a Treasury official reminded him, 'ill humour among the landed interests' made it essential to 'put the monied interest in the City in good humour' by boosting the funds.[276] 'When so many interests are to be conciliated',[277] it was almost inevitable that sooner or later ministers would be sucked into commitments. However, the reason it happened so suddenly was that the transition from war to peace exposed a fissure that ran right through economic life.

Most wars leave hangovers, but in this case the difficulties were compounded by the fact that hostilities had lasted for twenty-three years, during which a whole new cohort of producers, middlemen, sellers, and purchasers had emerged. It had also been an economic war fought with subsidies and blockades, which meant that it affected almost everyone. There were many people who had been established in business *before* the war, whose livelihoods had been disrupted by it, and who now cried 'Back to normality!' But for a younger generation that had embarked on business during the war, the war *was* normality. There were manufacturers dependent on wartime industries, merchants reliant on colonial markets, and farmers whose soils were only viable in wartime price

---

[274] Liverpool to Huskisson, 11 Apr. 1824, Huskisson MS 38745, fo. 254.
[275] Huskisson, memorandum, 18 Feb. 1823, Huskisson MS 38761, fos. 95–100.
[276] George Harrison to Liverpool, 30 Nov. 1820, Liverpool MS 38288, fos. 221–4.
[277] Grenville to Huskisson, 27 Apr. 1825, Huskisson MS 38746, fos. 186–7.

conditions. The Government was pressed by some to restore the *status quo ante bellum*, and by others to leave things as they were. Its instinct was usually to do nothing, but that in itself was to take sides, because it meant ratifying the changed economic relationships which war had brought about.

For example, the timber trade was competed for between Baltic and Canadian merchants. It concerned a vital commodity since there was insufficient native wood for all the Navy's hearts of oak. Baltic houses had traditionally dominated but were badly hit by the Continental System, so from 1809 the Government deliberately encouraged an alternative source of supply by suspending all duties on timber from colonial North America, while imposing new and high charges on the Baltic product. Once the war was over, Baltic merchants clamoured for the preference to be removed, arguing that their product was superior in quality and that they should in fairness be enabled to recover their pre-war business. Canadian merchants protested that they would never be able to compete with the shorter haul under fair trade conditions, and that having sunk their capital in the North American trade in order to safeguard national security in wartime, Parliament's duty was to continue the preference. Both sides had a legitimate case, and ministers had no intrinsic predilections, as is evident from a remark by Canning, MP for Liverpool: 'I suppose I must vote as my constituents may wish me—that, I take it, will be for Canada, versus Norway.'[278] Eventually, after exhaustive lobbying and two conflicting Select Committee reports (1820–1), the preference was lowered from 65s. to 45s. per load, but not eliminated.[279]

This was a sensible though largely cosmetic concession to the Baltic lobby, but compromise was impossible in the dispute over the gold standard, an intergenerational conflict which affected almost everyone engaged in economic life above subsistence level. There were many who had owned money in 1793, had seen the value of their assets fall at certain periods during the war, and now looked to Government to restore the currency. But many others had borrowed money in order to launch themselves in business while money was already depreciated. There was no hiding place for ministers in this situation. If they left the currency as it was they would damage one part of the population, but if they restored it to its pre-war value they would damage the other. Compromise was not possible as it was in the case of the timber duties because virtually no one gave countenance to the possibility of devaluing the standard, i.e. of returning to gold at a lower rate than that which had existed before 1797. That would have been like Tudor governments clipping the coinage, a deliberate breach of faith with the holders of sterling, including foreigners. Exactly the same dilemma was

---

[278] Canning to Huskisson, 8 Mar. 1821, Huskisson MS 38742, fos. 187–97.
[279] Hilton, *Corn, Cash, Commerce*, 190–5.

to face policy-makers in 1925, when once again a post-war and post-inflation generation had to decide whether to return to gold at its former par.[280]

So, for each farmer, merchant, manufacturer, banker, or shipowner whom Liverpool's policies benefited, there was another that suffered. And since blame always speaks louder than praise, the Prime Minister felt exposed and vulnerable, a feeling no doubt exacerbated by his humiliation over the Property Tax in 1816. His response, possibly instinctive, was to devise a strategy for taking unpopular decisions while trying to dodge the political flak likely to arise from them. Accordingly, he strove to keep political and policy decisions in separate compartments. *Politics* was the art of parliamentary survival and was the function of Cabinet ministers. *Policy*-making, and so far as possible policy-*makers*, should therefore be kept *out* of the Cabinet. This strategy seems strange today, when Cabinet takes ultimate responsibility for policies, but it may seem less so when it is recalled that policy-making with this degree of intensity was a novel feature of the post-Napoleonic period.

George IV dismissed Mulgrave, Westmorland, and Bragge Bathurst contemptuously as 'ornaments', but then Liverpool merely *wanted* the members of his Cabinet to possess political (or ornamental) clout, either because they represented one of the various groupings which made up the governing coalition, or because they wielded electoral influence. As he once said, 'the great and material point to which the Government looked was strength in the House of Commons, and therefore whatever changes would take place in the cabinet were to be grounded on this consideration alone.'[281] Even allowing for the fact that the Cabinet was not an executive body, its discussions were haphazard, and hardly ever took place during the parliamentary recess. Any member could call a meeting , but was not obliged to invite all the others, and if he then forgot to turn up himself those present would not know why they had been summoned. There were no agendas or briefing papers, no minutes were kept, and usually no record was made of decisions taken. Cabinet dinners being bibulous were even more chaotic, but none of this mattered since the business to be done was largely ceremonial and tactical. Serious discussions occurred only when an issue had obvious political implications—Peterloo, for example, or Queen Caroline.

As far as possible Liverpool dealt with important matters of policy at informal meetings. Foreign affairs were decided by himself in concert with Castlereagh (Secretary of State), Canning, Bathurst, Harrowby, and Wellington if he was in

[280] A few businessmen, such as W. J. Denison and the Coventry MPs Edward Ellice and Peter Moore, advocated devaluation, as did a section of Liverpool's businessmen, but they were not taken seriously. However, even Huskisson had contemplated such a policy back in 1810, and Ricardo was not opposed in principle, though he thought that it was unnecessary since the premium on gold was only 5% in 1819. Keynes would have done the same in 1925.

[281] Fremantle's report of a conversation with Liverpool, Nov. 1821, in *Memoirs of the Court of George IV*, i. 232.

the country. He felt no need to consult the Cabinet before signing a secret treaty with France and Austria against Russia and Prussia (January 1815), even though it might have led to war.[282] Most of the influential advisers on economic policy were not even in the Cabinet, but formed a 'little committee' which met almost daily during sessions. They included Castlereagh and Canning, the financial experts Huskisson and Herries, Charles Arbuthnot (the Government's parliamentary manager), Peel when Irish matters came up, Treasury officials like George Harrison, and occasionally—for his experience—Lord Grenville, even though he was leader of the Opposition until 1817. When an issue was too prominent to be dealt with out of sight like this, Liverpool's other expedient was to appoint select committees. He first did this in 1813 over the East India Company's charter, but he was not really delegating power since by the time the committees met the Government was already committed to opening much of its trade.[283] Since Liverpool invariably hand-picked the members of such bodies to ensure that they arrived at the decision *he* wanted, their only real purpose was to enable him to present an unpopular policy as the joint decision of all parties. That was why the committees to decide on cash payments included a 'large sprinkling of Opposition';[284] why the Commons Committee was chaired by someone who was no longer officially connected with Government;[285] and why the Lords Committee was chaired by Harrowby, who, though a minister, was well known to regard resumption 'whenever it may happen as the consummation of certain ruin to the country'.[286] The crucial decision to resume cash payments was taken, not by these committees, but at Fife House, Liverpool's Whitehall home, on 3 April. On that occasion Canning, Huskisson, and Peel—one quite lowly Cabinet minister, one junior minister, and one backbencher—overruled four Cabinet ministers and senior office-holders in Castlereagh, Vansittart, Harrowby, and Bathurst.[287] As a well-informed diarist recorded, 'Lord Liverpool, Lords Grenville, Wellington and Lansdowne, Peel and Canning being agreed, no paper administration could be formed, and the reluctant multitude were obliged to yield.'[288] The two committees were then induced to come up with reports 'on right principles', so that the decision could be presented to

---

[282] C. K. Webster, *The Foreign Policy of Castlereagh 1812–1815: Britain and the Reconstruction of Europe* (1931), 374.

[283] Webster, 'Political Economy of Trade Liberalization', *EconHR* 43 (1990), 412.

[284] For example, seven out of twenty-one members of the Commons Committee (Huskisson to his wife, 3 Feb. 1819, Huskisson MS 39949, fos. 58–61.

[285] Peel had resigned as Chief Secretary in 1818, possibly from pique at Robinson's promotion to Cabinet ahead of him as President of the Board of Trade. Peel was intensely competitive.

[286] Thomas Grenville to Lord Grenville, 28 Jan. 1819, in *Historical Manuscripts Commission Report on the Manuscripts of J. B. Fortescue, Preserved at Dropmore*, ed. Walter Fitzpatrick and Francis Bickley (1892–1927), x. 445.   [287] Canning, diary, 2 and 3 Apr., 10 May 1819, Canning MS 29 D. 1.

[288] Mallet, diary, in *Works and Correspondence of Ricardo*, v. 365–6.

Parliament as the 'impartial' result of all-party discussions. The Cabinet was not informed until 8 May, more than a month after the meeting at Fife House, and two days after the committees' reports had been presented to Parliament. Even at this late stage the anti-bullionists tried to have the policy reversed, but as Canning noted laconically in his diary, 'Letter from Eldon protesting against the decision: too late'.[289]

When Liverpool wished to push ahead with tariff reform he again delegated responsibility to committees in each House (1820–4). The Lords' chairman was Lansdowne, a doctrinaire free-trader and conveniently a Whig; the Commons Committee was given to the Vice-President of the Board of Trade, Thomas Wallace, another zealot but sufficiently junior as not to compromise the Government *politically* if the policy went sour. The most blatant display of Liverpool's tactical cunning related to the Corn Laws. In 1813–14 he derogated the matter to select committees. Then in 1815 he held two 'very full' inter-party meetings at Fife House and secured the support of most Opposition gentry *before* introducing his Corn Bill. The tactic outraged Whig leaders, who denounced the meetings as 'a sort of legislative committee' and 'an unconstitu-tional kind of rehearsal' pre-empting Parliament.[290] When in 1820 landed MPs demanded a committee to inquire into distress, with the clear intention that it should recommend increased protection, Liverpool gave every appearance of submitting, but while they were off their guard he emasculated the Committee by restricting its remit to technical matters only. He was clearly playing for time in the hope that agricultural fortunes would revive before Parliament met again in 1821. When they did not, he was forced to appoint a second committee, and one that was allowed to consider the whole question, but he insisted that Huskisson and Ricardo should be on it, knowing that they would run rings round the protectionist witnesses. Several agricultural members gave up attending when it became clear what was happening. One of them was driven to 'wish this Committee had never existed',[291] and when Huskisson produced his anti-protectionist Report, even the nominal chairman (T. S. Gooch) denounced it as a 'piece of mystification' and 'worse than useless'.[292] In 1822 the agriculturists returned to the charge for a third time. Yet another committee was appointed, minus Huskisson, and a report was concocted by Henry Bankes and T. S. Gooch without any interference from ministers. It formed the basis of Castlereagh's 1822 Corn Law, which satisfied the landlords because it increased the level

[289] Liverpool to Eldon, 10 May 1819, in Horace Twiss, *The Public and Private Life of Lord Chancellor Eldon* (1844), ii. 329.   [290] Baring and Tierney, *HPD1* xxix. 784–7 (15 Feb. 1815).

[291] Denis Browne to John Foster, 9 June 1821, PRO NI, Foster/Massereene MS D562 16007; Ricardo to Trower, 21 Apr. 1821, in *Works and Correspondence of Ricardo*, viii. 369–70.

[292] *HPD2* vi. 463 (18 Feb. 1822). Apart from Althorp, none of the Committee members who sat for large agricultural constituencies signed their 'own' Report.

of protection above that enacted in 1815.[293] It looked like a defeat for the Government, but again Liverpool's cunning proved equal to the situation. He inserted a little-noticed clause stipulating that the new Law was not to operate until the price of wheat had reached 80s. in the market. It was patently a spoiling device, as became clear in 1825 and 1826. On the first occasion, when the price rose towards 80s., the Government passed a temporary measure to allow grain in cheaply; and on the second occasion it issued an Order in Council to allow wheat out of the bonded warehouses. It claimed to be acting for the sake of the consumer, but it was also making sure that the 1822 Corn Law never came into effect. In a candid moment Canning even boasted that the qualifying clause was 'an outwork, as it were, to prevent the body of the Law from being ever approached'.[294]

George IV was wrong to describe Liverpool's as a 'government of departments',[295] since the Prime Minister coordinated policy to a high degree. However, Wellington *was* correct to say in November 1821 that 'ours is not, nor never has been, a *controversial* Cabinet upon any subject',[296] though perhaps he did not properly understand why. The Whigs were frustrated by Liverpool's tactics, for they were rarely able to identify quite what Government policy was, let alone criticize it, and by 1820 even the ministry's own supporters were becoming restive over the way in which business was being delegated to 'committees of the House of Commons'.[297] It is therefore not clear how much longer Liverpool could have succeeded in neutralizing controversial policy decisions. What finally undermined his strategy, however, was a series of high political events—the Cabinet reshuffle of 1821–3.

THE RESHUFFLE OF 1821–1823 AND THE ORIGINS OF CABINET GOVERNMENT

The 1821–3 reshuffle has usually been regarded as marking the 'turn of the tide'[298] for Liverpool's administration, and it is easy to see why. The new men were more forceful, vigorous, and eloquent than their predecessors, and although they had the advantage of an economic upturn they were also more prepared to take initiatives instead of seeming to hide from events. Yet from another perspective the reshuffle could be regarded as the point at which things began to go wrong.

---

[293] Castlereagh succeeded as Marquess of Londonderry in April 1821 but will continue to be called Castlereagh here.   [294] *HPD2*, xvi. 767 (1 Mar. 1827).
[295] George IV to Liverpool, 6 Nov. 1823, in *The Letters of King George IV 1812–1830*, ed. A. Aspinall (Cambridge, 1938), iii. 39.
[296] Wellington to Fremantle, 3 Dec. 1821, in *Memoirs of the Court of George IV*, i. 237.
[297] Fremantle to Buckingham, 9 Feb. 1819, in *Memoirs of the Court of England during the Regency, 1811–1820*, ed. Duke of Buckingham and Chandos (1856), ii. 301.   [298] Gash, *Liverpool*, 171.

Liverpool was feeling pretty beleaguered in 1821. To start with, the King treated him as 'a sort of *maître d'hotel*'. He was also afraid of being winged by 'crossfire...from Mr Canning and Mr Peel and the Grenville connexion',[299] a comment which indicates how fluid the political situation was, for whereas historians see Canning and Peel as Government adherents who happened to be temporarily out of office,[300] Liverpool clearly regarded both them and Grenville as dangerous rivals. He therefore set out to neutralize all three, his first move being to recruit Peel, the rising star. He had little difficulty persuading Sidmouth to give up his post (in fact he had more difficulty persuading him to remain in the Cabinet), and in January 1822 Peel became Home Secretary. The next move, taken in February, was to bring the Grenvillite Charles Wynn into the Cabinet as President of the Board of Control. This, a dukedom for Buckingham, and some loaves and fishes for the kith and kin, tempted the remaining Grenvilles back to the Pittite fold. That just left Canning, whom Liverpool sought to deal with by offering the governor-generalship of Bengal.

Canning was terribly torn. He badly needed the money, and he knew that his future at Westminster was bleak with the King so hostile. On the other hand, he could not bear to think that he was so obviously being got out of the way, and it was even more galling that it should be his old friend, 'poor old Jenky', who was showing him the political exit. Eventually, in March, deciding that the financial security of his wife and children was more important than their immediate happiness, Canning accepted. 'The die is cast,' he told his mother. But for once events fell out in his favour. On 12 August 1822, before he could set out for India and oblivion, Castlereagh, who had been agitated for some time, slit his own throat. A blackmailer had threatened to expose him for 'doing a bishop of Clogher'. This referred to a recent scandal about the bishop and a guardsman, though there is no evidence of homosexuality in Castlereagh's case. Anyway his death opened the way for Canning's return to Government. Wellington (to his subsequent chagrin) persuaded the King not to object, and in September Canning became Foreign Secretary for the second time and Leader of the Commons. Castlereagh's death had a further implication in that it exposed Vansittart. No one questioned the Chancellor's assiduity, but his distaste for recent policies was obvious while his weakness at the dispatch box had turned him into a buffoon. Now that Castlereagh's protection was gone his position was untenable, and he was reluctantly persuaded to give way to a younger man, but only on condition that he be allowed to remain in Cabinet and change his name to Baron Bexley. His replacement was Frederick Robinson, lazy, irresolute,

---

[299] Liverpool to Charles Bathurst, 29 Dec. 1820, Liverpool MS 38288, fos. 386–8.
[300] Canning had resigned in 1820 because rumours about his affair with Queen Caroline made him unacceptable to the King.

and fairly incompetent, but good-natured, eloquent, and popular with the squirearchy.

The obvious person to fill Robinson's position at the Board of Trade was Huskisson, described by Pitt as 'one of the ablest men in the Kingdom'.[301] Even though Huskisson was a Canningite, Castlereagh had set his heart on getting him into the Cabinet, having consulted him 'daily . . . on all the interesting matters of internal policy'.[302] But that was the problem. Given Liverpool's aim of keeping *policy* and *politics* separate, Huskisson was too influential, and consequently too unpopular, to be promoted. Sensing his own dilemma, Huskisson had long since worked himself up into a lather of self-pity. 'I have been engaged in rowing the boat while the cabinet ministers . . . especially Lord Maryborough and Frederick Robinson . . . sit there like dead weights.'[303] 'The angry feelings which . . . [have] expanded themselves through the . . . agricultural part of the House and of the Country, have been concentrated upon me alone.'[304] He even had the temerity to compare himself with Wellington, who had 'only to hold up his little finger and the most unreasonable requests of brothers, cousins, and retainers are immediately justified', while he, on the other hand, had had to put up with 'vague and insincere promises' and 'empty compliments'.[305] In reply to all this, Liverpool pointed out that the King was already alarmed by Canning's promotion, and would not take kindly to one of his associates forcing his way forward. He therefore offered Huskisson the presidency of the Board of Trade but without the customary seat in Cabinet. Inevitably Huskisson saw this as 'a disparagement' and a 'cruel affliction'.[306] At this point Canning sent the now paranoid Huskisson into a further frenzy when he wrote to him: 'L[iverpool] asked me . . . whether you would insist upon Cabinet . . . [and said] there would be great objection to it. I asked if on the part of the K[ing]? He said, "Yes and elsewhere too".'[307] Here Liverpool was being disingenuous, since the King had sanctioned Huskisson's promotion long before this time,[308] and by 'elsewhere' he almost certainly referred to himself. During the following nine months it was the Prime Minister, not the King, who

---

[301] *The Diaries of Sylvester Douglas (Lord Glenbervie)*, ed. Francis Bickley (1928), ii. 29.

[302] Liverpool to Sidmouth, 21 Nov. 1822, Liverpool MS 38575, fos. 54–7.

[303] E. J. Littleton, diary, 20 Nov. 1821, Hatherton Papers, D260/M/F/5/26/5/148–50.

[304] Huskisson to Liverpool, 12 May 1822, Huskisson MS 38743, fos. 148–51.

[305] Huskisson to Liverpool, 14 Nov. 1821, 11 Jan. 1822, Huskisson MS 38743, fos. 13–14, 117–20. At one point Wellington essayed a man-to-man talk. 'Huskisson,' he said with a discrimination almost worthy of Jane Austen, 'this is more a matter of passion than of feeling with you' (Littleton, diary, 20 Nov. 1821).

[306] Huskisson to Canning, 3 Oct. 1822, Huskisson to Arbuthnot, 26 Dec. 1822, Huskisson MS 38743, fos. 223–6, 285–6.   [307] Canning to Huskisson, 3 Oct. 1822, Huskisson MS 38743, fos. 217–20.

[308] George IV to Liverpool, 2 Jan., 6 Nov. 1823, Liverpool MS 38575, fos. 82–3; *The Letters of George IV 1812–1830*, ed. A. Aspinall (Cambridge, 1938), iii. 38–9.

kept the door shut, not because he disparaged Huskisson, but because he wanted to keep the truly important policy-makers out of the political spotlight.[309]

Eventually, in January 1823, Huskisson agreed to accept Liverpool's offer in return for a promise of the first Cabinet vacancy, but he continued to moan throughout the following session.[310] The Board of Trade was 'constantly in contact with the feeling and interests which agitate the country at large', yet without a voice in Cabinet it could be no more than a 'Department of Hawkers and Peddlars'. Once he took delight in refusing the Prime Minister's request that he should attend a Cabinet meeting to explain a particularly complex minute which he had drafted on the Reciprocity of Duties Act. He clearly took the view that his superiors could stew in their own duties: 'I shall leave it to the Cabinet to deal with the whole matter as to them may seem best.'[311] Before too long Liverpool realized that Huskisson was going to be even more of a nuisance outside than in, so in November 1823 he opened the door, and Huskisson's 'nearly eight years of lingering expectation' were finally rewarded.[312]

This battle of wills between Liverpool and Huskisson was of much more than personal interest. In one of his many outbursts Huskisson wrote to Canning,

My own impression is . . . that L[iverpool] has some fanciful theory of his own about dividing public men into two classes—those who are, from the outset, destined to be drudges—and those who are marked for Cabinet—and that long ago he has thrown me into the former class.[313]

Historians have dismissed this as deluded self-pity,[314] but it was in fact correct. No doubt something which Canning had recently said brought Huskisson to this realization. Referring to the vacant chancellorship of the Exchequer, he informed his friend that ideally Liverpool 'would like you in Vansittart's room . . . [rather] *than a politician*'.[315] It was a thoughtless give-away remark and intended to soothe, but it brought home to Huskisson that Liverpool regarded him as merely a 'man of business' (albeit 'one of the best men of business in this country', as Liverpool himself had put it earlier), merely a member of the Court and Treasury Party, as the Prime Minister's father had once been. Huskisson by contrast saw himself as a career politician with his sights on the Cabinet. Their

[309] Thomas Wallace also had claims to Cabinet rank but, as the chairman of the Commons Committee on Foreign Trade, he, like Huskisson, was in much too exposed a position to be granted political status. He too moaned.   [310] Huskisson to Liverpool, 19 June 1823, Huskisson MS 38744, fos. 229–31.
[311] Huskisson to Canning, 25 Oct. 1822, 25 July 1823, Canning MSS 67/131, 68/20.
[312] Huskisson to Liverpool, 11 Jan. 1822, Huskisson MS 38743, fos. 122–7.
[313] Huskisson to Canning, 25 Oct. 1822, Huskisson MS 38743, fo. 259.
[314] J. E. Cookson, *Lord Liverpool's Administration: The Crucial Years 1815–1822* (Edinburgh, 1975), 387.
[315] Canning to Huskisson, 3 Oct. 1822, Huskisson MS 38743, fos. 217–20 (italics added). Bathurst too made a revealing private comment when he wrote that Robinson's appointment to the Exchequer was 'judicious, as it keeps *more in the background* one of the real objects of the change, viz. Huskisson's promotion' (Bathurst to Harrowby, 5 Jan. 1823, Sandon Hall, Harrowby MSS, 1st ser., XIV, fo. 123; italics added).

mutual miscomprehension is significant because it reveals something about the transitional nature of parliamentary government at this time.

A crucial factor was the very sharp reduction in the number of office-holding MPs or placemen from more than 120 in 1790–6, to about 100 in 1812–18, then eighty in 1818–20, and just fifty in 1830.[316] This diminution naturally led to a reconsideration of their status. At the same time there was a dramatic expansion of official business. For example, 20,000 papers were lodged in the Treasury in 1815 as against 1,000 in 1767, while the Foreign Office handled 30,000 dispatches in 1849 compared with only 6,000 in 1829.[317] This development forced a separation between administrative and political functions. In the 1770s there were two joint treasury secretaries with largely undefined roles, most of the business being undertaken by the energetic John Robinson, but after him a division of function took place, with a Financial Secretary whose job it was to prepare budgets and accounts, and a Parliamentary Secretary (George Rose) whose role was mainly political, e.g. dispensing patronage and managing elections. In time, even the Financial Secretary became partisan—inevitably so because he had constantly to defend the same ministers against the same opponents—and so in 1805 a further bifurcation occurred, whereby the Financial Secretary was recognized to be a political office, and a new post was created with the title Permanent Assistant Secretary, whose holder (George Harrison) was not permitted to sit in Parliament. A similar process of differentiation between political and bureaucratic functions, leading to the appointment of permanent under-secretaries, took place in the Home Office from at least 1806,[318] the Admiralty from 1807,[319] and the Colonial Office from 1825. When Huskisson and three other Canningites resigned from Wellington's administration in 1828, two Foreign Office under-secretaries resigned with them but a third, though also a Canningite, stayed put, thereby marking himself out as 'clearly a man of business, not a politician'.[320] By 1831, when the status of under-secretaries was recognized by Parliament, most departments had one temporary and one permanent official. The former were political appointees, while the latter formed the nucleus of a salaried and accountable public service, with regular office hours, annual holidays, fixed duties, and superannuation benefits (the Civil Service Compensation Bill of 1817 had provided for State pensions, as

[316] Thorne, i. 297–8. This reduction was despite the influx of twenty Irish office-holders on account of the Union.

[317] Zara S. Steiner, *The Foreign Office and Foreign Policy, 1898–1914* (Cambridge, 1969), 3.

[318] Though the terms 'permanent' and 'parliamentary' were not recognized until 1831 (J. C. Sainty, *Home Office Officials 1782–1870* (1975), 12–13).

[319] But called First and Second Secretary. Here the terms 'Parliamentary' and 'Permanent' were not used until after 1863. J. C. Sainty, *Admiralty Officials 1660–1870* (1975), 34.

[320] Charles R. Middleton, 'John Backhouse and the Origins of the Permanent Under-Secretaryship for Foreign Affairs: 1828–1842', *JBS* 13 (1973–4), 33–4. See below, p. 385–6.

being more acceptable to public opinion than sinecures for life).[321] Recruitment by competitive examination did not come in until 1870, but government service now offered careers in which promotion was open to talent and which were better paid and more secure than those in the armed services or the Church. A similar process affected the diplomatic corps. The Consular Act of 1825, brought in by Canning and Huskisson after much pressure from merchants, was 'a genuine attempt to convert a group of individual State servants overseas, whose only common denominator was the name of consul, into a single government service of full-time officials, paid and pensioned by the state'.[322] Once in place, it was almost inevitable that the new *corps administratif* in these several departments of government should extend their spheres of activity, leading to a process which has been called a 'revolution in government' in the 1830s,[323] but the intention behind it was the opposite. Centralization was meant to *limit* the freedom of action of the State, thereby increasing the freedom of citizens to live without interference.

Officers whose jobs were deemed to be incompatible with political participation naturally sought status by developing an alternative, non-political ethos. Many embraced the ideals of the Public Accounts Commissioners, and gradually came to envisage themselves as disinterested officers of State or civil servants, willing to serve whichever faction might be in power, rather than as personal servants of the King. However, it was not practicable to remove *all* the old placemen from the Commons, since aristocratic politicians could hardly be expected to master the details of naval victualling, Civil List auditing, Crown land surveying, and other such complicated matters. About fifty men of business (of whom Huskisson was one) remained in Parliament, and not surprisingly their relationship to the Government was rendered somewhat ambiguous. George III's madness meant that such MPs came to see themselves as Pitt's men or Perceval's men rather than as Crown servants, while the long monopoly of office by one set of politicians meant that some even came to see themselves as party men, constantly defending Government measures against criticism from the Foxite Whigs. Not only Huskisson but Viscount Palmerston, Henry Goulburn, Charles Grant junior, J. C. Herries,[324] and perhaps even Peel could be regarded

[321] Henry Parris, *Constitutional Bureaucracy: The Development of British Central Administration since the Eighteenth Century* (1969), 21–79; Norman Chester, *The English Administrative System 1780–1870* (Oxford, 1981), 286–95; G. E. Aylmer, 'From Office-Holding to Civil Service: The Genesis of Modern Bureaucracy', *Royal Historical Society Transactions*, 30 (1980), 91–108.
[322] D. C. M. Platt, *The Cinderella Service: British Consuls since 1825* (1971), 13–15.
[323] See below, pp. 377–8.
[324] Respectively Secretary at War 1809–28; Under-Secretary for War and Colonies 1812–21 and Chief Secretary 1821–7; Chief Secretary 1818–21 and Vice-President of the Board of Trade 1823–7; Commissary-in-Chief 1811–16, Auditor of the Civil List 1816–23, and Secretary to the Treasury 1823–7.

as this new type of career politician with aspirations to Cabinet rank. When the Pittite regime fell in November 1830, there was a complete change not only of Cabinet ministers but of junior ministers as well, thereby affirming that such officers were political appointees. Howick, for example, became Under-Secretary at the Colonial Office in 1830, and Secretary-at-War with a seat in the Cabinet in 1835; Spring Rice was Secretary to the Treasury in 1830–4, and Chancellor of the Exchequer in 1835–9.

Harriet Arbuthnot objected to the inclusion of ministers for Trade and War in the Cabinet. It gave those offices 'an importance which they ought not to have', and turned the Cabinet into 'a debating club', so that 'the public business was quite impeded by their eternal debates'.[325] Liverpool had thought the same, but had at last been forced to recognize that Huskisson's claims were irresistible, that *politics* and *policy-making* could no longer be kept separate. In other words, he discovered that politicians were no longer playing an aristocratic game, but were answerable for social ills. In other words, Huskisson's admission marked the beginnings, not only of Cabinet government, but of modern government itself.

DIVIDED CABINETS: FOREIGN AND ECONOMIC POLICIES

The prolonged Cabinet reshuffle invigorated Liverpool's ministry, which now seized the initiative on a number of fronts, but an immediate price was paid for this new strength in disunity. By 1826 several ministers were hardly on speaking terms, cabinets degenerated into shouting matches, and the Government broke apart in the following year.

Because the breach did not occur until immediately after Liverpool's sudden incapacitating stroke in February 1827, many historians have supposed that he personally kept the team together, and have therefore assumed that he must have been tactful, amiable, and conciliatory in his dealings.[326] Yet Liverpool was none of those things. Harriet Arbuthnot believed him to be 'upright, honest, excellent', yet referred to his 'disagreeable, cold manner' and 'querulous, irritable temper', both of which 'render it a difficult and unpleasant task to act in public life with him'. Her husband adored him yet acknowledged his 'gaucherie' with colleagues.[327] Nicknamed the 'Grand Figitatis', Liverpool was mercurial, nervous, irritable, and even violent (at least with inanimate objects and when he thought no one was looking). Having witnessed the fall of the Bastille, having become Prime Minister only because another one was assassinated, and having faced bomb plots as well as brickbats, he could never open his morning's post

---

[325] Arbuthnot, *Journal*, ii. 178 (27 Mar. 1828).

[326] e.g. Brock, *Liverpool*, 33, 75–6, 170; C. K. Webster, *Foreign Policy of Castlereagh 1812–1815*, 35; for a balanced account, see Gash, *Liverpool*, 193–5.   [327] Arbuthnot, *Journal*, i. 121.

without a spasm of 'anxiety and apprehension' lest it should bring dreadful news. The calm competence which he contrived to display in public was more a matter of tactics than of temperament.

In personality terms the most disruptive member of Cabinet was the new Foreign Secretary. Canning was a man of quicksilver spontaneity, who said what he thought and could not keep his own counsel as Castlereagh had done (colleagues might receive three or four of his bullet-pointed letters, always heavily underlined, in a single day). His enemies thought him deceitful, and even his friend Croker remarked that he 'could not take tea without a stratagem', but his real problem was the opposite one of ingenuousness and hypersensitivity to slights and intrigues, as Lord Dudley pointed out in his appraisal of this 'kind-hearted and affectionate man'.

He bore being opposed by his enemies... with a very good grace; but anything that he thought mean, or tricky, or an unfair advantage taken of him he could not endure. On such occasions he showed no mercy... He was quicker than lightning, and even to the very last gay and playful, so that it was very agreeable to do business with him, the more so because he was always inclined rather to disguise that immense superiority which must have made everybody else seem dull and slow to him than to make a painful use of it... He was very sensitive, and all his experience of the world had not blunted the natural acuteness of his feelings. More than once I have observed how much he was moved while mentioning some instance in which he thought that he had been kindly and generously used.[328]

Thomas Lawrence the portraitist described Canning as 'a modest man' who blushed whenever he looked at him intently.[329] He was of course socially insecure, and this was Huskisson's problem too. The latter's friends might insist postmortem that 'a purer and more honourable man in all the transactions of life never lived'[330] but his awkwardness caused problems. In order to compensate for social misgivings he strove to demonstrate his cleverness, which led him exaggerate the doctrinaire aspects of his policies, even though he was really a very practical statesman. This in turn alienated colleagues like Eldon and Sidmouth, who were baffled and frightened by political economy. He therefore came to be regarded— whether favourably or otherwise—as a 'philosophical statesman'.

Assertiveness on the part of Canning and Huskisson might not have mattered but for the vanity of Wellington, who complained bitterly about being presented with faits accomplis.

---

[328] Dudley to Helen d'Arcy Stewart, 21 Aug. 1827, *Letters to 'Ivy' from the First Earl of Dudley*, ed. S. H. Romilly (1905), 325–9.

[329] *The Diary of Joseph Farington*, ed. Kenneth Garlick, Angus Macintyre, Kathryn Cave, and Evelyn Newby (New Haven, 1978–98), 17 July 1809, x. 3513.

[330] A. Aspinall, 'Extracts from Lord Hatherton's Diary', *Parliamentary Affairs*, 17 (1963–4), 381 (22 Mar. 1845).

Deaf, Silent, thin as a lath, covered with all the honour the nation could give him, without much pride and without any pose, entirely devoted to the nation's weal, used not to discussion but to command, the Duke sat at the Cabinet Board, his hard eye on Canning, full of dislike, listening to his long harangues, not always hearing, but always suspecting. He was riddled with suspicion, the suspicions of a deaf man who is not always sure what they are saying, the suspicions of a soldier matched with talkative civilians, the suspicions of a hero who reasonably expects for his opinions a consideration that it is impossible to give them.[331]

Wellington alleged that Canning flew into ungovernable rages whenever a colleague disagreed with him, but he himself once stormed from the Lords and into a private party shouting, 'My Lord Liverpool is neither more nor less than a common prostitute.'[332] He mourned the days when business had been managed in a 'fair, honest, open way'.[333] What he meant, of course, was that Castlereagh had always consulted him. 'How foolish, how stupid, how blind I was to put that man [Canning] into the Cabinet!', he told Princess Lieven, clutching his head in his hands.[334]

Surprisingly perhaps, the issue which caused least strife was the Catholic question, over which ministers simply agreed to differ. The Whig Henry Grattan having died in 1820, the leadership of the Irish cause in Parliament passed to W. C. Plunket, a Grenvillite lawyer. His Emancipation Bill angered many Catholics because of certain built-in 'securities' (the most important being a royal veto on the Pope's choice of Irish bishops), but it passed on third reading by nineteen votes, before being thrown out in the Lords by thirty-nine. Soon afterwards, in August 1821, the King paid a state visit to Dublin. His gracious condescension to representatives of the majority population seemed to generate a deal of goodwill, but a detumescent aftermath brought a renewal of antagonisms—'the Catholics elated with extravagant hopes—the Protestant party, or rather Orange faction, reproved and humbled without being weakened or made wiser'.[335] In the same year the dispossession of tenants in arrears on Lord Courtenay's estates in Limerick sparked off a wave of resentful violence, and there were further rural disturbances following a potato failure. The Cabinet changes in December 1821 sent out a typically British mixed message in that an anti-Catholic Lord Lieutenant (Talbot) was replaced by a pro-Catholic (Wellesley), while a pro-Catholic Chief Secretary (Charles Grant) was replaced

---

[331] George Kitson Clark, *Peel and the Conservation Party: A Study in Party Politics 1832–1841* (1929) 21–2.

[332] Neville Thompson, *Wellington after Waterloo* (1986), 44.

[333] Arbuthnot, *Journal*, i. 339 (24 Sept. 1824).

[334] *The Private Letters of Princess Lieven to Prince Metternich 1820–1826*, ed. Peter Quennell (1937), 292 (4 Oct. 1823).

[335] Mallet, diary, 5 Dec. 1821, iv. 11–12. Mallet went on to observe, 'such a country as Ireland cannot be pacified by fair words'.

by an anti-Catholic (Henry Goulburn). Shortly afterwards a violently anti-Catholic Attorney-General (Saurin) was replaced by a strong pro-Catholic (Plunket). The adhesion of the Grenvilles to Government and the subsequent elevation of Canning tipped the administration in a pro-Catholic direction, though this was balanced to some extent by Peel's promotion. It was also becoming obvious that most active politicians among the younger generation supported Catholic emancipation, which led the *Morning Chronicle* to quip that it would be carried one day 'not by the march of improvement but by the march of death'.

In 1823 Daniel O'Connell formed the militant Catholic Association. Radicals and Whigs supported it wholeheartedly, whereas Government supporters were uniformly opposed, the anti-Catholics for obvious reasons and the pro-Catholics because they were afraid that it would make emancipation more difficult to achieve. All ministers agreed therefore on the need to suppress the Association by legal means, though for the sake of appearances the Bill which they enacted in 1825 (for two years) was directed against *all* unlawful societies in Ireland, Orange as well as Catholic. Ever the chameleon, O'Connell reacted to this provocation in the most conciliatory manner by agreeing that emancipation should be subject to additional 'securities', such as the disfranchisement of the Irish forty-shilling freeholders. On this basis Burdett's Catholic Relief Bill passed the Commons by twenty-one votes on third reading before being thrown out in the Lords by forty-eight. These events led to a ministerial crisis in May. Peel and Liverpool both contemplated resignation, while Wellington privately and preposterously suggested that he should become Prime Minister himself in order to carry emancipation, subject to still more securities.[336] However, the crisis died down as quickly as it had arisen, mainly because an older and wiser Canning decided to swallow his frustration over the Lords' intransigence.

In the case of foreign affairs, disagreements had as much to do with Canning's methods and pretensions as with policy. In 1824, for example, he and Wellington wrangled over whether he should make a personal visit to the new King of France. But what most offended more traditional colleagues was his tendency to publish diplomatic documents, to leak to the press and especially *The Star*, and to announce policy in Cabinet—or, worse still, in the Commons or in public—rather than to an inner circle of ministers and diplomats. Such unorthodox behaviour was partly a reflection of personality, but it was also a means to reassert control at a time when serious attempts were being made to undermine the Foreign Secretary's authority. As early as 1823 the ambassadors of Russia,

---

[336] His main suggestion was that Church of Ireland bishops should remain territorial but that Irish Catholic bishops should operate on a 'missionary system' (Wellington, memorandum, 1825, in WND ii. 592–607).

Austria, and France (respectively Lieven, Esterhazy, and Polignac), together with Neumann,[337] began to plot in secret with the King, his mistress, his physician-cum-factotum (Sir William Knighton), and at least two Cabinet ministers (Westmorland and Harrowby). The aim of this Cottage Coterie, so-called because it met in the Cottage at Windsor, was to stiffen George IV's legitimist instincts and undermine the new Foreign Secretary.

Conflict began almost at once with the crisis in Spain, a country that was widely perceived as an ideological battleground in the worldwide war between absolutism and constitutionalism. Its liberal revolution of 1820, which led to the establishment of an elected Cortes, was 'the first crack in the conservative structure' erected at Vienna.[338] Then in July 1822 the royalists attempted a military counter-coup which failed, after which radical constitutionalists expelled the more moderate liberals and tightened their grip on the government. Mob riots in the following February forced King Ferdinand to move from Madrid to Seville, where he was deposed by the Cortes in favour of a regency. By this time the country was embroiled in what is sometimes called the First Spanish Civil War, with royalists pitched against Jacobins (*exaltados*), and the liberals stuck nervously in the middle. It was almost inevitable that the Continental powers would feel called upon to intervene to root out the new revolutionary growth. The Tsar was keen to send in Russian troops, and while the rulers of Prussia and Austria would not sanction that, they did give guarded support to the French army, which invaded Spain in April 1823. It marched unhindered down the length of the country and forced the Cortes, now besieged in Cadiz, to capitulate, after which Ferdinand was restored to full authority.

Britain's response to these events had been foreshadowed in Castlereagh's State Paper of 5 May 1820. (Mainly focused on the Spanish danger, it had been discussed in Cabinet, and its tone had almost certainly been made more blunt at Canning's behest.) It was acknowledged that the Congress system had worked well at Aix-la-Chapelle in 1818, but there was concern about the way in which Tsar Alexander was seeking to turn it into a neo-Holy Alliance, a sort of ideological cosh for suppressing revolutions and upholding rulers. The British view was that the allies should act to uphold specific territorial guarantees and to prevent any military threat to the balance of power, but they were not entitled to interfere in the internal affairs of other European states, or wage war on 'democratic principles', or act on 'abstract and speculative principles of precaution'. There had then followed a year and a half of shadow boxing. Revolutions in Naples and Piedmont in July 1820 led in October to the Congress and Protocol of Troppau. The latter was a statement of ideological aims by the Tsar, and it met with a

---

[337] Baron Philip Neumann, the Austrian chargé d'affaires.
[338] Raymond Carr, *Spain 1808–1939* (Oxford, 1966), 139.

furious public rebuttal from Castlereagh. A further Congress at Laibach in 1821 endorsed Austria's right to suppress the Neapolitan revolt by force, and while Castlereagh supported this initiative as consonant with treaties, he objected to yet more circulars by the Tsar as being 'in defiance of the law of nations and the principles of common sense'.[339] In the same year the two Romanian principalities of Moldavia and Wallachia, followed by Greece, broke out in revolt against Turkish rule, raising a prospect that Russia might go to war against Turkey. In a desperate effort to prevent this, Castlereagh and Metternich agreed to summon yet another Congress, eventually held in Verona during October–December 1822.

By the time it met Castlereagh was dead, and in his place Wellington submitted a memorandum (30 October 1822) strongly opposing intervention in Spain.[340] From this point on Britain isolated itself from the other four Powers, and Wellington isolated himself from Canning. As French military preparations intensified, following Chateaubriand's appointment as Foreign Minister in December, Canning sought to prevent an invasion by threatening to intervene on the side of the Spanish constitutionalists. Yet, as he saw it, the deterrent effect of his warnings was fatally undermined by several unofficial statements—variously attributed to George IV, the Duke of York, Harrowby, Westmorland, and especially Wellington—which gave encouragement to the French. It was not just because he enjoyed histrionics, therefore, but because he wanted to establish in the minds of foreign diplomats that he and Liverpool made policy, not their recalcitrant colleagues, that Canning decided to embrace maximum publicity. On 14 April 1823, to the horror of several Cabinet ministers, he appeared at the bar of the House of Commons with a full set of official papers, including an important dispatch of 31 March to the French Government. As a student of his foreign policies has commented, 'His speech did little more than repeat the arguments of his State papers. But it made a great sensation that a minister should say the same thing in public as in private, and that the 31 March despatch should be published only five days after it had been communicated.'[341]

Another problem was that Wellington and Canning had different priorities. Whereas the Duke was mainly concerned about Russia's designs on the Ottoman Empire, Canning was more worried about French plans to help Spain recover its former colonies, and to place Bourbon princes on the thrones of Mexico, Colombia, Peru, Chile, and Buenos Aires. He had been keen to exploit

[339] *HPD*2 v. 1257 (21 June 1821).
[340] Apart from anything else, Canning was worried that a French army garrisoned in Cadiz might move from there to Ireland (Memorandum, Nov. 1824, Canning MS 131; Canning to Liverpool, 25 Nov. 1824, Canning MS 71).
[341] Harold Temperley, *The Foreign Policy of Canning 1822–1827: England, the Neo-Holy Alliance, and the New World* (1925), 86; Graham Warden Brook, 'British Policy toward the Concert of Europe, 1822–1832', Ph.D. thesis (Cambridge University, 1974), 57–9; Canning to Liverpool, 1 Feb. 1823, Canning MS 70; Wellington to Canning, 10 Feb. 1823, in WND ii. 29–31.

the commercial potential of Latin America since his first foreign ministry in 1807–9, and made it clear that he would wage war to preserve its newly gained independence. So when the French, backed by the Russians, proposed a Congress to discuss the region, he was at once suspicious. In October 1823 he told the French Ambassador, Polignac, in person that Britain had no aggressive intent on the former Spanish colonies, and sought nothing other than 'most favoured nation' status in commercial matters, 'equally with others' but 'after' Spain. Diplomatically Polignac said that France took exactly the same position, at which point Canning drew up a memorandum of the discussion, forced the dismayed Ambassador to sign it, and circulated it to the other governments of Europe. This was open diplomacy with a vengeance. Just as he had astounded the British public by saying 'the same thing in public as in private', now he had challenged a foreign diplomat, either to disown what he was alleged to have said, to else to stick by his words as published.

To forestall any lingering French designs on South America, Canning now proposed to recognize the republics. In his own ringing words, he 'called the New World into existence to redress the balance of the Old'. In truth this famous soundbite was something of a *pis aller*. He was instinctively aware of what would now be called his Euro-scepticism, and was anxious to offet it by establishing a 'special relationship' with the United States. His original aim had been that Britain and America should jointly warn off the Continental Powers from interfering in the New World. This hope had been thwarted by President Monroe's unilateral declaration to the same effect, the so-called Monroe Doctrine of December 1823. Nevertheless, Britain's unilateral recognition of the former Spanish colonies infuriated Wellington, who did not think that France was a threat to the colonies, and did not want to act independently of the Continental Powers. In May 1824 the Cabinet sided with Canning when it decided not to participate in a conference on the issue,[342] and in July–August it again followed Canning, and again defied the Concert of Europe, by recognizing Buenos Aires. Ominously Wellington, Sidmouth, Eldon, Westmorland, Melville, and Bathurst all opposed the decision. In November Canning proposed that Mexico and Colombia should also be recognized; otherwise the United States, which had already acknowledged them, would steal a commercial march. Wellington expostulated but, after Liverpool and Canning had threatened to resign, Peel came round to their point of view, which placed the Europhiles in a minority. (Peel's 'defection' devastated the Duke, and marked a significant moment in his own political development.) At this point Sidmouth resigned and Wellington talked about doing so, which emboldened the King to try to block the policy, but he backed off when Canning too threatened resignation,

[342] It sat at Paris for the whole of 1824, the British chair remaining empty.

and recognition was accorded on 3 January 1825. Three weeks later the King remonstrated again, only to be told in a statement by the whole Cabinet that a decision had been reached—despite differences of opinion and 'after as long and as continued a deliberation as ever has been given to any great question of national policy'—and that it was now 'irrevocable'.[343] This battle of wills between Crown and Cabinet was a significant episode in the story of the former's waning influence.

Meanwhile, a similar dispute had been affecting policy on the Eastern question. Canning and Wellington were both afraid that Russia might 'swallow up Turkey and Greece...in two mouthfuls'.[344] They also agreed that Britain should work with Austria to restrain the Tsar.[345] But, as over Spain and Latin America, Canning was unwilling to allow Britain to participate in another Congress to discuss the problem, whereas Wellington was as always anxious to maintain the integrity of the Alliance system. At first Liverpool sided with Wellington, being sure that 'the Turkish empire in Europe will fall to pieces sooner or later', and not wanting to leave Russia, Austria, and France free to pick up the pieces.[346] However, when towards the end of 1824 the Greek Government rejected the mediation of the Great Powers, Wellington, Canning, and Liverpool all agreed to have nothing to do with a conference, thereby seriously alienating Russia and Austria.

The stage was now set for an extraordinary few months during which the neo-Holy Alliance bent itself to suborn British foreign policy, possibly even to boost the cause of monarchy in England. The details are murky, but it seems clear that two of George IV's retrospective protests against his Government's 'erroneous' South American policies (in November 1824 and January 1825) were the result of pressure from Prince Esterhazy and Princess Lieven.[347] One historian goes so far as to refer to 'Metternich's intrigues...to bring down Liverpool's Administration...by influencing the King'.[348] It would have been a futile conspiracy but for the fact that Wellington, exasperated by Canning's anti-Europeanism, now threw in his lot with the Cottage Coterie. Relations between King and Foreign Secretary had been terrible ever since April 1824 when Canning attended the banquet of the Lord Mayor, Robert Waithman, a reforming MP and former champion of the Queen. According to Mrs Arbuthnot, who had it from Wellington, 'the King spoke of Mr Canning with the deepest

[343] Cabinet to George IV, 29 Jan. 1825, in Augustus Granville Stapleton, *George Canning and his Times* (1859), 419–21.   [344] Canning to Granville, 28 Dec. 1824, Canning MS 111.
[345] However, Canning went further than Metternich in March 1823 when he recognized the Greeks as belligerents.   [346] Liverpool to Canning, 18 Oct. 1824, in WND ii. 327.
[347] George IV to Cabinet, 27 Jan. 1825, in Stapleton, *Canning and his Times*, 416–19; H. W. V. Temperley, 'Canning, Wellington, and George the Fourth', *HER* 38 (1923), 206–25.
[348] Brook, 'British Policy', 118–19.

abhorrence, said he was the D—dest fellow in the world and that he could not bear him'.[349] Therefore, in January 1825 Canning decided on a showdown, hinting bluntly to the King that unless the conspiracies against him stopped he would feel obliged to reveal his suspicions to the Commons, and rely on what—thanks to the newspapers—he felt to be his own popularity in the country. The result of this démarche was quite astonishing. From that moment onwards the King took Canning's side almost obsequiously, while even Knighton (who had been very hostile hitherto) now made (according to Mrs Canning) 'an offer of himself body and soul to Mr C. in any way that he could be useful'.[350] George IV was known to be childishly fickle, but even so the suddenness and completeness of his capitulation took most people's breath away—and especially Wellington's—though it did not surprise the Prime Minister, who knew his capricious monarch by this time, and had counselled Canning throughout the crisis. The latter reported to his wife Liverpool's conviction 'that just now he [Liverpool] was sufficiently well with the King perhaps because I was his *bête noire* at the moment; but that all that might change any day, and that he enjoined me at least to do nothing myself that should make my going out my own act—that if I did not, he would answer for it, the King would never have courage to displace me'.[351] As Canning grew cockier in Cabinet, Wellington complained to Harriet Arbuthnot,

The alteration in Canning's position in my opinion is this. The King has communicated directly with him upon the only object which occupies his mind; and upon a matter relating to that object which is of all others the most delicate, and that upon which any man would be most desirous to avoid communicating with anybody. Then this has been done through Knighton; and has been kept a secret from us. It is very true that the K[ing] like other men nay more frequently than other men is in the habit of squeezing the orange and throwing the rind to the dogs! But I think that Mr C. feels as I do that these communications have altered his position; and he certainly gave the cabinet to understand that he had been apprized confidentially that there would be no difficulty on the part of the King as to the reception of the Plenipotentiaries from the new States in America.[352]

In 1826 yet another row erupted. When King John VI of Portugal died, his son Pedro, the Emperor of Brazil, abdicated in favour of his own 8-year-old daughter, and set his sister Isabella up as Regent under a liberal constitution. An Absolutist party quickly organized itself around Pedro's brother (Dom Miguel) and Isabella's mother (Carlotta), and looked to Madrid for assistance. Now Canning was as suspicious of Spain's designs on Portugal as he was of France's designs on Spain, so to deter the Spanish from invading in favour of Miguel, he first withdrew an ambassador and later dispatched 4,000 troops by water to the

[349] Arbuthnot, *Journal*, i. 309 (2 May 1824).   [350] Temperley, *Foreign Policy of Canning*, 249.
[351] Canning to his wife, 19 Dec. 1824, Canning MS 27, fos. 1–12.
[352] Wellington to Mrs Arbuthnot, 5 Aug. 1825, Stratfield Saye MSS.

Tagus, as a result of which the Spaniards climbed down. Once again Wellington castigated Canning, once again Liverpool backed his Foreign Secretary, and once again Wellington threatened to resign but did not do so. Three years later, however, as Prime Minister, Wellington was to withdraw the same troops, so allowing Miguel to establish a despotic hold.

That the Government was able to ride out these difficulties was owing to the economic boom of 1822–5 and the popularity of its fiscal policies, especially with the liberal press. Liverpool, Canning, Huskisson, and Peel would all have liked to restore the Property Tax, but that was politically impossible. In 1819, however, Huskisson won a crucial battle when he secured a £3 million increase in taxes to accompany the resumption of cash payments.[353] Vansittart and Herries opposed resumption but thought that if it had to happen it should at least be accompanied by counter-cyclical tax cuts. They would have preferred to borrow the money, but Liverpool sided with Huskisson on moralistic grounds, arguing that 'a strong and decisive effort can alone redeem our character and credit'.[354] The squires' revolt of 1822 subsequently cost the Government another £3.5 million in revenue, forcing it to cut official salaries by 10 per cent and to announce a reduction of departmental staffing levels to those of 1797. (This proved impossible: at the close of Liverpool's ministry there were still 43 per cent more government employees than in 1797, while the real cost of their salaries was twice as high.[355])

Once the commercial upturn began to deliver buoyant revenues, it became possible to reduce indirect taxes, starting with the duties on foreign timber in 1821. Excise taxes on windows, servants, horses, and carriages were abolished or reduced in 1823, as were import duties on wool, coal, rum, silk, cotton goods, woollens, linen, paper, glass, earthenware, and metals in 1824–5.[356] Many export duties (and bounties) were done away with, but significantly not those on machinery, while the Reciprocity of Duties Act (1823) seriously breached the navigation code by allowing the ships of any country which responded in kind to carry goods to the United Kingdom on the same terms as British ships. So long as prosperity lasted, these measures were welcomed by a mainly landed House of Commons. Only fifteen MPs opposed the third reading of the Reciprocity Act,[357] and Robinson's budget speech of that year was actually applauded.

---

[353] Mainly by increasing the excise duties on malt.

[354] Liverpool to Eldon, 10 May 1819, in Twiss, *Eldon*, ii. 329.

[355] Philip Harling, *The Waning of 'Old Corruption': The Politics of Economical Reform in Britain, 1779–1846* (Oxford, 1996), 176–7.

[356] The most controversial change was the substitution of a 30% duty on silk goods for a total prohibition on importation.

[357] Barry Gordon, *Political Economy in Parliament 1819–1823* (London, 1976), 164, describes the opposition as being composed of merchants and bankers, but in fact only seven of the fifteen could be designated as such.

Because free trade later assumed ideological importance, Huskisson and Robinson have often been seen as far-sighted, but in fact theirs was largely a tidying-up operation. The need to provide for interest payments on government loans in wartime had left a legacy of incidental import duties, the very complexity of which deterred merchants from engaging in business. In reducing over 1,000 customs acts to just eight categories, Huskisson acted in much the same way as Peel in codifying the criminal law.[358]

Judged as a proportion of customs to total central government revenue, protection jumped to more than 40 per cent following the loss of the Property Tax in 1816, and did not begin to fall again until after the introduction of income tax in 1842. But judged in relation to the retail prices of goods on which import

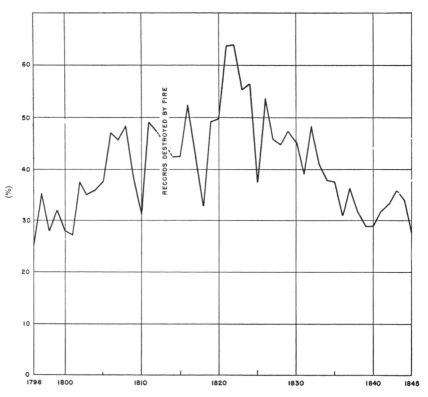

FIG. 4.1. Annual net customs revenue as a percentage of net import values, 1796–1845

[358] See below, pp. 318–19.

TABLE 4.2. *Total UK government expenditure as a percentage of gross national product, 1790–1850*

1790	12
1800	22
1810	23
1820	17
1830	15
1840	11
1850	11

TABLE 4.3. *Structure of central government tax revenue, 1771–1855 (%)*

Years	Direct	Customs	Excise	Total indirect
1771–5	22.4	26.8	50.7	77.6
1791–5	25.8	22.7	51.5	74.2
1811–15	39.8	20.4	39.8	60.2
1831–5	25.2	38.3	36.4	74.8
1851–5	31.4	40.1	28.5	68.6

duties were levied, it reached a peak in 1821 and fell thereafter. This suggests a sharp break in policy, coincident with changes in the Cabinet. Also, the fact that it came just after the 1820 London Merchants' Petition, which argued for unilateral free trade on the principle of 'buying in the cheapest market and selling in the dearest', suggests that the change might have been prompted by pressure from the commercial lobby or by economic theory. Moreover, given that low public spending, balanced budgets, sound money, and free trade became hallmarks of the mid-Victorian *pax Britannica*, Liverpool's ministers have sometimes been seen as anticipating Cobden and Gladstone and as acting from similar motives. This impression is strengthened by declarations such as Huskisson's that 'it was high time, in the improved state of the civilization of the world, to establish more liberal principles; and show, that commerce was not the end, but the means of diffusing comfort and enjoyment among the nations embarked in its pursuit'.[359]

---

[359] *HPD2* ix. 797 (6 June 1823).

However, the increase in protection relative to prices during 1819–21 was merely a fortuitous consequence of deflation, while notwithstanding the 1820 petition, protectionist sentiment remained strong in the City of London— among Harman's faction of Bank directors, in the East India Company, and in the shipping, timber, tea, and sugar interests, all of which benefited from imperial preference and the navigation code.[360] The petition was got up by Thomas Tooke with encouragement from ministers, who had already decided to embark on tariff reform, and wanted a declaration of public opinion so that they could pretend to respond to it. Many of the signatories including Tooke were Russian and north European traders, and had self-interested reasons for wanting to reduce duties on timber, the most pressing issue of the day. As this suggests, the commercial interest was fragmented, and its support for free trade partial. Most Manchester cotton merchants opposed the Corn Laws but supported the ban on the exportation of machinery. Many Yorkshire businessmen opposed the 6*d.* per pound duty on foreign raw wool (1819–24) but applauded the prohibition against exporting the raw British product.[361] East India merchants clung to their China monopoly but denounced the preference on West Indian sugar. It was only later, when the Corn Laws came to assume an overriding importance, that many merchants and manufacturers were prepared to trade in their own feather beds for the greater benefit of cheap food.

Furthermore, although the policies of the Liverpool Government anticipated those of the mid-Victorian *pax Britannica*, the motives differed. Firstly, it was keen to reduce smuggling, which was a highly organized big business and largely connived in by society at large. Strenuous efforts were made to stop illicit trade physically, with coastguards and pilots utilizing lookout stations in the Martello towers. Unfortunately, such labour-intensive methods were costly and, as the need for retrenchment intensified, attention switched instead to the possibility, earlier mooted by Pitt, of reducing the incentive for contraband by lowering duties on legitimate importation. A second principle, as enunciated by Wallace, was to make Britain 'the general dépôt, the great emporium of the commerce of the world'.[362] Reduced pilotage, light, and harbour dues, together with the Warehousing Act of 1823, boosted the entrepôt or transit trade by allowing commodities to enter the country and be stored in bonded warehouses duty-free for the purposes of re-exportation. The chief benefit to be gained from emporium status was that it would guarantee British consumers a ready access to necessary imports when they needed them, even in wartime. Whereas free trade was later to be based on the primacy of exports, and on the desire of making Britain the *workshop* of the world, Liverpool's ministers were more

---

[360] A. C. Howe, 'Free Trade and the City of London, *c.*1820–1870', *History*, 77 (1992), 391–410.

[361] E. Baines, jun., *The Life of Edward Baines* (1851), 134–5.   [362] *HPD*2 v. 1292 (25 June 1821).

concerned to complement her role as international 'mart and banker' by making her the *warehouse* of the world.

Again, the ethos of mid-Victorian or Cobdenite free trade was pacifist and cosmopolitan, whereas Huskisson's instincts were essentially nationalist. He was as determined as Canning to break free from European influence, and especially from the stranglehold that international financiers had enjoyed over Vansittart. The extended Rothschild family acted as bankers, not only to Britain, but to the French, Prussian, and Austrian governments, to crowned heads throughout Europe, and to many of the minor German states. Nathan Mayer's brother Salomon was close to Metternich in Vienna, while brother James was ensconced in Paris. It therefore comes as no surprise to find that the ministers most opposed to Huskisson's economic policies—Wellington, Harrowby, Westmorland, Bexley, and Herries—were also in favour of close contacts with Metternich and the neo-Holy Alliance.

A fourth objective, counter-balancing the rejection of Europe, was to attempt what Huskisson described as a 'great change in our colonial system'. This encompassed freer trade within the empire (but still in British ships); the completion of Pitt's plans for the abolition of tariff barriers with Ireland; greater latitude to the colonies to trade with non-British territories; warehouse facilities extended to the major colonial ports; and a preferential system whereby imperial produce could be imported into Britain at lower rates of duty than if it had come from a foreign country.[363] With regard to the sugar islands,

Every step in this change will contribute to introduce a greater proportion and a better description of white population, and gradually, I should hope, to diffuse a new spirit of enterprise, not only in commerce, but in agriculture—to stimulate endeavours, to raise other productions (indigo and silk, for instance) besides sugar, which will increase the cultivation and wealth of those colonies.[364]

And—he might have added—prepare them for the day when slavery was abolished. In 1825 Huskisson even allowed Canadian corn to be imported at a very low rate of duty for two years. The amounts were negligible but it was a significant gesture, identifying Canadian farmers with those in the homeland. It is therefore possible to depict Huskisson as an imperial statesman, schooled by Dundas, and prefiguring Joseph Chamberlain in his dreams of economic empire bound together in a single market, and of federated English-speaking, self-governing dominions.[365] To the extent that this was so, it points up another

---

[363] Barry Gordon, *Economic Doctrine and Tory Liberalism 1824–1830* (London, 1979), 67–9.

[364] *HPD2* xii. 1109 (21 Mar. 1825).

[365] Alexander Brady, *William Huskisson and Liberal Reform: An Essay on the Changes in Economic Policy in the Twenties of the Nineteenth Century* (1928), 132–67; C. R. Fay, *The Corn Laws and Social England* (Cambridge, 1932), 121–34.

difference from the policies of the 1840s, when the Peel and Russell governments swept away imperial preference in favour of general free trade. Yet this
may be to invest Huskisson's imperial policies and rhetoric with too much
significance. It seems more likely that he regarded both imperial preference and
reciprocity in instrumental terms, as weapons against mercantilism and half-
way houses towards free trade, rather than as ends in themselves. With regard to
sugar, for example, he wrote privately of 'the necessity of gradually weaning the
West Indians from their reliance on the perpetuity of the protecting system'.[366]

Until 1825 Huskisson and Robinson, cheered on by Canning and Peel,
carried all before them, but then there were repercussions. In the previous year
Joseph Hume had chaired a Select Committee to investigate the legal prohibitions
on workers' combinations, the emigration of skilled workers, and the export of
machinery. With Huskisson too busy for regular attendance, the Committee
listened somewhat uncritically to the political economists who appeared as
witnesses, notably McCulloch and Malthus, but even more influential was the
Benthamite tailor Francis Place, who, besides giving evidence himself, coached
scores of other working men on what to say. He claimed that the only reason
working men combined illegally, often under the guise of friendly societies, was
because they were forbidden to do so legally, and that if combinations were made
lawful they would cease to exist. This strange doctrine was based on an assumption
that individuals combined in order to assert political rights rather than to
achieve economic goals. Place also argued that no amount of industrial action
could push wages above their 'natural level' for more than a short period. He
won the argument, the Combination Laws were repealed in 1824, and the
immediate result was a barrage of strikes and industrial violence all over
the country, causing Peel his greatest headache since taking over the Home
Office, and forcing a somewhat shamefaced Huskisson to appoint a new Select
Committee followed by further legislation in 1825. The new Law was a fudge in
so far as it upheld the legal right of trade unions to exist, but undermined their
power to bargain collectively by enabling workers to make their own individual
contracts with an employer. Yet 'to the political economists and parliamentarians,
there was nothing absurd or inconsistent in their policy', since they were utterly
convinced that strike action was powerless to prevail against the authority of the
market.[367]

Meanwhile a comfortable bull market had turned into a raging bull market
(September–December 1825), primarily because the authorities lost control of
the money supply. Determined to revive 'dormant speculation', especially in

---

[366] Huskisson to Charles Ellis, 31 Mar. 1823, Huskisson MS 38744, fos. 194–6. Charles Ellis was a
Canningite MP and leader of the West India interest.

[367] P. S. Atiyah, *The Rise and Fall of Freedom of Contract* (Oxford, 1979), 528–31.

agriculture, ministers had reduced interest on government securities in 1822 and 1824, had extended the life of small notes for another ten years from May 1823, and had borrowed in order to spread out the cost of military half-pay and pensions. At the same time the Bank had got rid of excess liquidity by issuing £11½ million on mortgages, and had also increased its loans and discounts. Much of the extra cash was taken up by the private country banks, which competed with each other in an uncontrollable spurt of lending. As a result 624 companies were formed with a capital of £372 million in 1824 alone. However, with no new canals being projected and the yield on government securities low, much of the additional capital was deflected abroad.[368] Of about £30 million raised in Europe during 1824–5 for the purpose of lending to governments around the world, about £26 million was issued in London's foreign bond market. Of this amount, £17 million went in loans to the new Latin American republics[369] (and constituted an additional reason in favour of recognizing those countries), while most of the remainder was lent to the Continent. Yet more capital was invested in South American joint stock, as well as in a bewildering array of new company promotions at home, many of them highly speculative. As with the Anglo-Bengalee Disinterested Loan and Life Assurance Company in Dickens's *Martin Chuzzlewit* (1842–4), some prospectuses seemed to contain as many noughts as the printer could get into the same line.

Technically these new companies were subject to the Bubble Act of 1720. During the second half of the eighteenth century that legislation had fallen into disuse, but the courts had recently shown signs of enforcing it again, and so many would-be directors appealed to Parliament for incorporation. There they were cheered on by a vocal lobby of company promoters, led by Pascoe Grenfell and the two 'cheap money' MPs for Coventry, Peter Moore (who was soon to go spectacularly bankrupt) and Edward Ellice. There were 438 requests, of which 286 were successful in the 1825 session alone. High Tories like Eldon and Westmorland were horrified by all the share mongering, and wished to make the law on joint-stock formation even more restrictive. Huskisson was less horrified— especially as he was just then actively helping to promote a Liverpool and Manchester Railway Bill—and anyway he did not see it as the Board of Trade's job 'to probe to the bottom the merits of the various speculations, and to...decide which was likely to be a beneficial undertaking, and which a bubble'.[370] Liberals like Huskisson believed that individuals should be free to form companies without any restrictions, but they should also take the

---

[368] The loans to European governments were to facilitate the importation of foreign food during the shortages of 1828–31 and 1839–40.

[369] Frank Griffith Dawson, *The First Latin American Debt Crisis: The City of London and the 1822–25 Loan Bubble* (New Haven, 1990), 249.

[370] *HPD*2 xii. 717–19 (28 Feb. 1825). Huskisson had succeeded Canning as MP for Liverpool in 1823.

consequences, which he predicted would be disastrous in most cases. Liverpool agreed, and so the Act of 1720 was repealed. It had been born in a bubble and perished at the height of another.[371] The decision, which was a calculated snub to the Lord Chancellor in his own department, may well have excited still further speculation.

By early 1825 there were disturbing reports on the performance of South American silver mines, as well as indications of a glut in commodity markets. Three per cent consols fell drastically, a number of country banks failed in Bristol and elsewhere, and the Bank of England reduced its liabilities by selling exchequer bills and refusing to discount mercantile paper. Ministers approved of this overdue response to the external drain of specie, but the effect was to promote an internal drain as alarmed note-holders began to withdraw gold from the banks and hide it under their mattresses. By September exchequer bills were seriously below par, and to dissuade their holders from cashing them in, the Government deflated even further by raising interest rates. Liverpool called it the 'honest' policy, Robinson the 'legitimate' policy, but three past and present treasury secretaries—Arbuthnot, Herries, and Lushington—would have preferred reflationary measures to keep the funds up 'artificially', say by commissioning Rothschild to buy exchequer bills in quantity.[372] Bexley and Rothschild egged these cheap money rebels on, but they needed a ministerial champion and naturally looked to Wellington. Arbuthnot worked on him assiduously, describing Huskisson as a 'dangerous' man whose 'hasty and sudden innovations in trade are sending all the gold out of the country'.[373]

In October many of the newly promoted companies were traded below par for the first time, and there was a run on the country banks, with spectacular failures on both sides of the Pennines and in the West Country. On 12 December the London bank of Pole, Thornton, & Co. crashed, bringing down forty-three correspondent country banks, and with another suspension of cash payments looking only minutes away, the Bank of England at last bowed to long-standing ministerial pressure by raising its discount rate to the 5 per cent maximum. Yet coincidentally, on the same day the exchanges turned in favour and gold began to come back in. Following the mechanistic principles of political economy, ministers immediately demanded that the Bank adopt reflationary measures, such as the purchase of £500,000 of exchequer bills and the expansion of

[371] Ron Harris, 'Political Economy, Interest Groups, Legal Institutions, and the Repeal of the Bubble Act in 1825', *EconHR* 50 (1997), 675–96.

[372] Liverpool MS 38300, fo. 172; Robinson to Herries, 16 Sept. 1825, Herries MS 57402, fos. 5–7; Hilton, *Corn, Cash, Commerce*, 202–31. Liverpool's approach would eventually come to be identified as the Treasury view, but in the 1820s it was anathema to officials in that institution.

[373] Arbuthnot to Wellington, 25 Apr. 1825, in *The Correspondence of Charles Arbuthnot*, ed. A. Aspinall (1941), 74; Arbuthnot, *Journal*, i. 390–2.

discounts. The Bank directors agreed, but only in return for permission to leave the gold standard if their own liquidity was threatened. Wellington was compliant but Liverpool, Canning, and Huskisson would not hear of it, especially as they thought that Harman and 'the old school of Bank directors' had engineered the crisis deliberately in order to overturn Peel's Bill.[374] Huskisson also blamed Rothschild: 'I know of no one who would more rejoice at another Bank Restriction. It would be the Messiah of the Jews.'[375] In fact N. M. Rothschild was the *deus ex machina* who saved the situation by paying in £150,000 in gold sovereigns from France on the 16th.

Three things were at stake: the solvency of the Exchequer due to the unfunded debt, the solvency of the Bank of England which had implications for the gold standard, and business confidence. There seems little doubt that the ministers' overriding concern was the first, that is the roughly £30 million of exchequer bills in the market 'unprovided for' and '*virtually* payable on demand'.[376] Having persuaded a reluctant Bank to purchase exchequer bills, and seen them rise to par by 21 December, Liverpool felt able to relax at his country retreat, even though the Bank's reserve was still falling and did not touch its low point of just over £1 million on the 24th. Soon after that gold began to pour in and the crisis was over.

The financial crash of December 1825 was (still is perhaps) unprecedented in its ferocity. For a panicky week or so there were almost hourly meetings of ministers, Bank directors, and prominent private bankers, while Peel assembled troops to guard Threadneedle Street. Apart from Robinson, who in modern parlance 'wobbled' and whose reputation never recovered, most of those involved could look back on a good crisis. Even so, the mood had changed. As Huskisson gloomily anticipated, 'the Ultra Party...[were] now chuckling at the approaching distress...as affording a fair opportunity for raising a cry against all improvements'.[377] Meanwhile, behind the scenes acrimonious debates took place throughout 1826 over various remedial measures, starting with Huskisson's proposal for a return to pre-1797 bimetallism. Monetization of silver would help to foster trade with Latin America, and since most European business was conducted in that metal it might also enable London to compete with Paris as a 'clearing house' (it rankled that Paris had come to London's rescue with a £400,000 loan on 19 December). Bimetallism would also satisfy Huskisson's long-standing aim of making money 'as cheap as is consistent with the maintenance of [the antient] standard',[378] but Wellington strongly opposed

---

[374] Stapleton, memorandum of a conversation with Canning, 27 Dec. 1825, in Stapleton, *Canning and his Times*, 227.   [375] Huskisson to Canning, 16 Nov. 1825, Canning MS 68.
[376] Huskisson, 'Memorandum on the Present State of the Country in Respect to Currency and Finance', 8 Feb. 1826, Huskisson MS 38755, fos. 251–2.
[377] See e.g. Gordon, *Economic Doctrine*, 96–106; Huskisson to Canning, 5 Jan. 1826, Canning MS 69/80.
[378] Huskisson to Copleston, 1822, Huskisson MS 38761, fos. 77–89.

the idea and it was dropped. Ministers did agree on the immediate abolition of new, and the phased withdrawal of existing, £1 and £2 notes, to be completed by April 1829, not because small-note-holders had fuelled the speculation but because they had been less able to ride out the collapse. The measure was bitterly opposed by country bankers and by many merchants, and there were ructions inside Government when the Prime Minister yielded to pressure from Bexley, Wellington, and Herries, and announced that small notes might continue to be issued until September 1826. Canning was 'thunderstruck' when he heard about this concession, fearing that it would look like 'a relaxation in favour of the paper system'.[379] Finally it was agreed to invade the Bank of England's chartered privileges by allowing joint-stock banks to operate outside a radius of 65 miles from London, without any limit on the number of partners. In compensation the Bank was permitted to set up regional branches.

A fourth proposal almost broke up the Government. Eighty country banks failed during the early months of 1826, while of the 624 companies formed during 1824–5, about 500 had disappeared by 1827, and only fifteen were traded above their paid-up price. In earlier crises (1793, 1811) the governments of the day had issued distressed (but favoured) businessmen with exchequer bills, which they might then cash at the Bank of England, and there was very great pressure from the mercantile world for this procedure to be adopted again. Their demands were supported by most of the gentry, and by a number of ministers, but Liverpool, Peel, and Huskisson set their faces against it. Their view was that the Bank should *buy* exchequer bills and step up its discounting, so as to increase the circulation and relieve the business world *generally*. According to Croker, 'every man of the old Pitt party' hoped for an issue of exchequer bills, but had to keep quiet when Canning warned that ministers would resign rather than comply.[380] At one level the dispute was understandable enough. Politically an issue of exchequer bills would have gone down well in the City, which had traditionally supported the Government prior to the ascendancy of Huskisson and Robinson. The latter, on the other hand, were concerned about the unfunded debt, exchequer bills being once more at a discount, which is why they preferred the Bank to buy them rather than to issue new ones and have the Bank cash them.[381] They were also unwilling to bail out individual firms, partly because Liverpool had explicitly announced at an earlier stage, when the speculation was getting out of control, that he would never do this, partly because it would be difficult to decide which were the blameless firms, and partly because, as Huskisson said, if parties 'might always expect to obtain an asylum in government, it was as much calculated to encourage speculation as the poor-laws

[379] Canning to Liverpool, 20 and 21 Feb. 1826, Canning MS 72. Another concession was to exempt Scotland from the small-note ban, following a vigorous campaign of protest led by Walter Scott.
[380] Croker to Wellington, 20 Mar. 1826, in, WND iii. 209–12; *Croker Papers*, i. 314–17; *HPD2* xiv. 727–8 (23 Feb. 1826).   [381] Peel to Wellington, 3 Mar. 1826, in WND iii. 144.

were calculated to encourage vagrancy'.[382] These disagreements are perfectly understandable, the amount of heat engendered by them less so. At one point it looked as though the ministry would split up, which as Canning said 'would have been a mighty foolish kind of death'.[383] The explanation is that this technical point touched the raw nerve of ideological conflict.[384]

It was not the only thing to do so. 1826 was a general election year, and Wellington exploded when it was reported that Huskisson had advocated Corn Law repeal on the Liverpool hustings. The facts were disputed, but the Duke was right to fear the turn which this issue was taking. So long as the towns had boomed while agriculture languished, pressure for change had come from the landed interest. With the commercial crisis, however, the manufacturing sector started to clamour for amendment. In towns like Manchester, where there were serious riots,[385] the Corn Laws now displaced machinery as the main focus of radical and working-class demands. There was a cascade of petitions in favour of repeal, and while these predictably provoked counter-petitions from the landlords—only 59 in 1826, as many as 587 in 1827—most of the latter were much more defensive than hitherto, praying only that there should be no lessening of protection. This shift reflected, not only political realities, but an appreciation that former dreams of permanent self-sufficiency had been unrealistic. 'We cannot supply ourselves,' admitted Sir John Curwen in 1826. Formerly a passionate advocate of high protection, the MP for Cumberland was now despondent. 'I thought England might have gone on increasing her production almost to an unlimited extent. I spared neither myself nor my purse.' 'I once thought Great Britain could produce [enough] corn for itself, but I now think otherwise.' 'We had all or most of us at least ploughed too much' (a reference to wartime).[386]

Liverpool now took the initiative in consultation with Huskisson, Canning, and Peel (naturally the former was kept 'as much as possible in the background').[387] The first step was to send the Comptroller of Corn Returns, William Jacob, to find out how much corn was available in northern and eastern Europe waiting to come into Britain if the Laws were relaxed. This was not a genuine search for knowledge, since Jacob was well known to have an *idée fixe* about the inadequacies of Continental agriculture, and to believe that English agriculture had nothing to fear from foreign competition. In his view, the only way to convince farmers about this was to expose them to free markets, but once reassured they would, so Jacob argued, be willing to expand their undertakings until Britain became self-sufficient once more. The ministers had no such illusions. *They* wanted to lower the Corn Laws, not in

[382] *HPD2* xiv. 403 (14 Feb. 1826).
[383] Canning to Granville, 6 Mar. 1826, in Stapleton, *Canning and his Times*, 237–8.
[384] On which, see below, pp. 326–8.
[385] Donald Grove Barnes, *A History of the English Corn Laws from 1660–1846* (1930), 185–218.
[386] Edward Hughes, *North Country Life in the Eighteenth Century* (1952–65), ii. 232, 286–7.
[387] Liverpool to Canning, Oct. 1826, in *Liverpool*, ed. Yonge, iii. 450.

order to boost home production, but to sustain that of European farmers, now regarded as Britain's feeders of last resort. Jacob was merely their stooge.

Huskisson laid out the strategy in a memorandum as luminous as only a document by him could be. It repeated his earlier arguments for Corn Law reduction[388] but included an additional one, not emphasized before, that prohibitory Corn Laws deprived foreigners of the means of paying for British goods and forced them to manufacture for themselves, while dear food led to higher wages, which 'curtailed profits' and drove capital out of Britain. This doctrine, which was pure Ricardo, rested on the subsistence theory of wages and the inverse wage–profit ratio,[389] and was eventually to become the weapon most widely used to attack agricultural protection—that it damaged English manufacturing, or what was called 'native industry'—but it was a recent argument, not used when the Government had first turned its face against high corn laws.

Privately Huskisson would have liked to move swiftly to complete free trade, but this was politically impossible. His more limited aim was therefore to replace the current 'habitual prohibition' by a perpetual 'freedom of intercourse'. Though a differential would remain, it might then be possible to establish a 'sympathy' between British and Continental prices, so that they at least moved up and down together. The main point at issue was the appropriate level of duties to be charged on imported grain, which would in turn determine the amount of the differential. When the landed classes demanded protection, they meant such duties as would lift the price of foreign wheat to the level of British wheat or beyond. Huskisson rejected this in favour of Ricardo's prescription for countervailing protection, which meant just enough duty to lift the home price by an amount that would compensate landlords for the special burdens which they alone bore (poor rates, county rates, highway rates, tithes, and the land tax). By and large landlords were happy to bear these special domestic burdens since they were a mark of local power and influence. But, argued the theorists, if any of them were to abandon agriculture because they could not afford to pay, this would be just as contrary to market economics as if they were to remain in agriculture because it was over-protected. Countervailing duties, according to this reasoning, would reinforce rather than subvert the market. Having established this principle, Huskisson reasoned that it would be impracticable to allow British producers any duties at all in years of scarcity, since at such times the consumers' needs were paramount, so to compensate them for this sacrifice they were to be awarded a *more* than countervailing protection in years of plenty. The technical requirement was to devise a sliding scale of duties which would rise as the home price fell and would provide the farmers with a 'remunerating price', which, 'as matters now stand', Liverpool considered to be 60s.[390] By this he meant,

---

[388] See above, pp. 266–8.   [389] See below, p. 343–6.

[390] Huskisson, 'Memorandum on Corn Laws', 18 Oct. 1826, and Liverpool to Huskisson, 25 Oct. 1826, Huskisson MS 38371, fos. 182–217; MS 38748, fos. 184–6; Hilton, *Corn, Cash, Commerce*, 269–301.

presumably, that 60s. in 1826 was equivalent to 80s. in 1815, given the intervening price deflation and tax reductions. Before the Government could act on these plans, however, Liverpool had been removed from the scene. In 1827 Canning's Government introduced a bill that seemed likely to win general (albeit reluctant) acceptance, but it was wrecked by Wellington in the Lords, partly for political reasons. In the following year the Duke himself became Prime Minister and, after a great deal of quarrelling which helped to precipitate Huskisson and his fellow Canningites out of his Government, he forced the Cabinet to adopt a new bill with a shorter and steeper scale than that of 1827.[391] It stipulated a duty of 20s. 8d. per quarter when the home price was 66s., this duty to rise by 1s. with every 1s. fall in the price and to fall more steeply as the price increased.

Although it had become entangled in high politics as a result of a crisis within the governing party, the Corn Law of 1828 was essentially the outcome of hard, pragmatic thinking on technical issues by ministers mainly concerned to secure food supply and genuinely uncertain about how different systems would work. It was not an ideological bone of contention, and there were many practical points on which Huskisson and Wellington were agreed. The atmosphere was very different on the back benches, in clubland, and at county fairs and agricultural shows. Here the drift towards freer trade was identified with the faction increasingly demonized as liberal Tories. Wellington had described himself as the nation's 'protector against the political economists', and country Tories (that collective noun was now beginning to be widely adopted) looked to him to stop the rot. 'He feels he is looked up to by the great landed interest, and he is afraid of being reproached by his friends.'[392] His failure (as it was perceived) to stand up for agriculture in 1828 was one of the factors that turned his most natural supporters hostile.

It was once customary to divide Liverpool's administration into two distinct halves, separated by the prolonged Cabinet reshuffle of 1821–3, a period of civic disobedience and robust official repression followed by a 'liberal awakening' in which Peel amended the criminal law,[393] Huskisson and Robinson freed up the economy, and Canning asserted British interests abroad. By contrast it is now usual to emphasize continuity, to point out that many of the new policy directions preceded the reshuffle, that the ministers promoted then had held influential positions before they took up front-line Cabinet posts, and that two of the ministers most associated with the earlier period (Sidmouth, Vansittart) continued to serve in Cabinet following their demotion from office.

There is much to be said for this second view, but too many recent historians have supposed that, because there was no great discontinuity between the

---

[391] 'The Duke would not yield, though all were against him' (*A Political Diary 1828–1830 by Edward Law Lord Ellenborough*, ed. Lord Colchester (1881), i. 54). [392] Ibid. i. 57.
[393] For which, see below, pp. 318–20.

two phases of Liverpool's Government, there could have been no ideological division between ministers, and that the reason why the later ones achieved more than their predecessors was all to do with personality and the changed social, economic, and diplomatic conditions under which they operated. Yet the question of an ideological division is entirely separate from that of discontinuity, especially since membership of the Cabinet did not equate with influence over policy-making. There undoubtedly was an ideology of liberal Toryism, though it would be less misleading to call it liberal Conservatism.

Or Canningism. There is an obvious justification for calling this chapter after Liverpool. It might even have been called after Huskisson, in view of that statesman's immediate and long-term influence over policy. Canning's credentials are less obvious, given that he was in and out of Government and only reached the pinnacle at the very end of his life. He is also hard to place politically. Whigs regarded him as a natural ally who had turned his coat in order to truckle for office, while he insisted that Pitt was his guiding star, yet in his anti-Jacobin bellicosity and sense of national worth he was really more like Windham. He was the best and wittiest debater in a golden period of oratory, and the person on whose every action every other person hung, but even fond admirers recognized that these were superficial attributes.

His genius is a bright flame, but it is "Brillant comme le feu que les villageois font Pendant l'obscure nuit, sur le sommet d'un mont." It is liable to every gust of wind and every change of weather; it flares, and it flickers, and it blazes, now climbing the heavens, now stifled in its own smoke, and of no use but to raise the wonder of distant spectators, and to warm the very narrow circle that immediately surrounds it. If he does not take care the Canning bonfire will soon burn itself out.[394]

Croker wrote at a low point in Canning's career, but even so what he predicted seemed to happen. For all that Canning continues to warm historians, his long-term legacy has never seemed very significant. The so-called Canning*ite* party which survived him was never more than a clique, and it disappeared altogether when its most prominent surviving members joined Grey's Government in 1830. And yet, four of the five giants of mid-Victorian politics—Palmerston, Gladstone, Disraeli, and Derby (the other being Russell)—acknowledged the passionate nature of their youthful adherence to Canning. In order to understand why they did so, and why Metternich could call him 'a whole revolution in himself alone', it is necessary to place his career in the context of the early nineteenth-century wars of ideas.

---

[394] Croker to Vesey Fitzgerald, 20 Dec. 1821, in *Croker Papers*, i. 219. Coleridge deployed a similar metaphor when he said that Canning 'flashed such a light around the constitution, that it was difficult to see the ruins of the fabric through it' ('Specimens of the Table-Talk', ed. Carl Woodring, in *The Collected Works of Samuel Taylor Coleridge*, ed. Kathleen Coburn and Bart Winer (1960), xiv. 2, 86).

CHAPTER 5

Ruling ideologies

> The truth is this respecting Mr Canning. I stand exactly in the *Antipodes* in relation to him. I differ from his way of thinking, acting and conducting himself upon every subject...[But] excepting in the mode of acting ... I have not much to complain of in reality. Leaving out of the question the colonial affair... I don't know that I differ much with him upon any thing else. Indeed I have settled most of the other affairs myself; and in truth nobody has any reason to complain of anything excepting the mode in which they have been transacted and the manner of transacting them.
>
> (Wellington to Mrs Arbuthnot, 13 April 1825)

Many historians have argued that the antagonisms among Liverpool's ministers 'were more ones of emphasis and style than substance'.[1] However, Wellington's evident puzzlement suggests something more complex. Canning's 'mode of acting' might be a matter of style, but 'modes of thinking' are more fundamental. Similarly, when Huskisson referred to Vansittart as 'old Mouldy' the jibe seems personal, but when he called him 'the real *blot* and *sin* of the Government'[2] he implied profound disagreement. There does seem to have been, in embryo at least, a Canningite or liberal Tory mode of thinking. Whether it was an ideology or merely a temperament is debatable, but there surely was, as a wise historian has written, a 'deep antagonism between the spirit of Canning and the spirit of Eldon',[3] just as there was between the spirit of Canning and the spirit of Wellington.

'A LOVE OF SYSTEM'

It might be helpful to begin by saying what liberal Toryism was *not*. Some historians have characterized it—and in particular its key policy, the resumption of cash payments—as the 'virtual abandonment of the agriculturalists by the

---

[1] Neville Thompson, *Wellington after Waterloo* (1986), 44.

[2] Croker to Peel, 16 Aug. 1822, in *Croker Papers*, i. 229.

[3] W. R. Brock, *Lord Liverpool and Liberal Toryism, 1820 to 1827* (Cambridge, 1941), 34. The problematic nature of the word 'Toryism' was discussed in the previous chapter, and is used here simply in deference to a long–standing historiographical convention.

Government' and its 'conscious seeking' after commercial and manufacturing support.[4] This might seem plausible in so far as political disputes frequently boiled down to a battle between sectors. Until about 1850 it was by no means clear that urbanization and industrialization were irreversible developments, and so policy-makers were uncertain whether to promote or impede them. Their dilemma encouraged a polarization of values as between the landed interest and the rest, most notably in the so-called Spence–Mill debate of 1808. Like the French physiocrat Quesnay, Spence argued that wealth derived solely from land, and that dependence on exports would lead to crises of under-consumption, views echoed by Cobbett and Chalmers among others.[5] On the other side, James Mill, Torrens, Ricardo, and Brougham insisted that commerce was essential to the promotion of civilization.[6] There were echoes here of much older debates. Civic humanists had valued landownership as bestowing security, independence, and incorruptibility, and had disparaged commerce as leading to luxury and effeminacy, while Court Whigs had maintained that only commercial society could inculcate qualities of mutual trust, professionalism, specialization, and politeness. In this vein, one country MP talked unself-consciously about 'the *real* and the *false* people', and by the latter he meant the 'unfortunate proportion of the population which inhabited great manufacturing towns'.[7] Few expressed themselves quite so starkly as this, but everyone recognized the existence of a cultural distinction.

However, it was not the case that liberal Tories set out to promote trade and industry at the expense of agriculture. They cited Smith and were praised by Ricardo, and their policies probably helped Britain to become temporarily the workshop of the world, but they did not act with that end in mind, nor did liberal and high Tories appeal to different economic constituencies. For the former the point of freer markets and sound money was to restore the economy to a *natural* state, and there were many pundits like Chalmers who hoped that such policies would *reduce* the gross national product while giving agriculture a boost. This explains why most bankers, merchants, and manufacturers opposed cash payments in 1819, and for many years after that a majority of City businessmen, including Bank of England directors, supported the high Tories.

A second interpretation ventured by historians is that liberal Tories sought to stave off fundamental constitutional reform by demonstrating the regime's

---

[4] Ibid., 182; S. G. Checkland, *The Rise of Industrial Society in England, 1815–1885* (1964), 178; Asa Briggs, *The Age of Improvement, 1783–1867* (1959), 205.

[5] William Spence, *Britain Independent of Commerce* (1807); William Cobbett, *Perish Commerce* (1807–8); Thomas Chalmers, *An Enquiry into the Extent and Stability of National Resources* (Edinburgh, 1808).

[6] James Mill, *Commerce Defended* (1808); Robert Torrens, *The Economists Refuted: Or, An Inquiry into the Nature and Extent of the Advantages derived from Trade* (1808).

[7] Sir Thomas Lethbridge, *HPD*2 vi. 856 (28 Feb. 1822).

responsiveness to popular feeling.[8] Traditionalists might deplore the way in which Canning went 'round the country *speechifying* and discussing the acts and intentions of the Government',[9] but arguably he was thereby helping to make an exclusive political system more palatable. The dangers were apparent to Peel, who wrote a remarkable letter to Croker at the height of the radical disaffection.

Do not you think that the tone of England—of that great compound of folly, weakness, prejudice, wrong feeling, right feeling, obstinacy, and newspaper paragraphs, which is called public opinion—is more liberal—to use an odious but intelligible phrase—than the policy of the Government? Do not you think that there is a feeling . . . in favour of some undefined change in the mode of governing the country? It seems to me a curious crisis—when public opinion never had such influence on public measures, and yet never was so dissatisfied with the share which it possessed. It is growing too large for the channels that it has been accustomed to run through.[10]

This analysis reflects contemporary awareness of public opinion, but also indicates its nebulousness. Politicians invariably claimed to have public opinion on their side, but in reality there was no such thing. For most of the eighteenth century, and again after 1850, England could be said to have possessed a civic culture, meaning a normative set of values to which most privileged sections of society subscribed, but during the years between the Jacobin scare of 1792 and the last Chartist convention of 1848 there was no such consensus. That is why politicians who appealed to public opinion nearly always qualified the phrase with words such as 'respectable', 'rational', 'intelligent', 'sober-minded', 'right-thinking'—'the better sort of people'[11] or, as Huskisson put it, 'all that portion of public opinion which is worth having'.[12] In other words, not 'majority opinion' but those opinions judged by the politician in question to be 'public-spirited'. It is true that, in a reaction against post-Waterloo radicalism, the term 'middle class' increasingly came to stand for 'public', with the result that an 'imagined constituency' of the respectable began to emerge, but this development only really got under way with the debates leading up to the 1832 Reform Act.[13] Until then there were many deeply felt vertical divisions. James Mackintosh remarked in a debate on law reform that he felt as though he 'lived

[8] J. E. Cookson, *Lord Liverpool's Administration: The Crucial Years 1815–1822* (Edinburgh, 1975), 159–60.

[9] Arbuthnot, *Journal*, i. 275 (18 Nov. 1823). Wellington disparaged his attempts 'to seek popularity and to court the vulgar' (*Wellington and his Friends*, ed. 7th Duke of Wellington (1965), 53).

[10] Peel to Croker, 23 Mar. 1820, in *Croker Papers*, i. 170 (italics added). Contrast this with Huskisson's analysis, above, p. 270.

[11] Stuart Wortley to Liverpool, 18 Dec. 1820, in *The Life and Administration of Robert Banks, 2nd Earl of Liverpool*, ed. Charles Duke Yonge (1868), iii. 115.

[12] Huskisson to Granville, 9 Mar. 1826, Huskisson MS 38747, fos. 207–8.

[13] Dror Wahrman, *Imagining the Middle Class: The Political Representation of Class in Britain, c.1780–1840* (Cambridge, 1995), 184–272.

in two different countries, and conversed with people who spoke two different languages'.[14] In Thomas Peacock's satire *Crotchet Castle* (1831) a character seeks in conversation to evaluate 'the sentimental against the rational, the intuitive against the inductive, the ornamental against the useful, the intense against the tranquil, the romantic against the classical; these are the great and interesting controversies, which I should like, before I die, to see satisfactorily settled'. Of course, many people were ambivalent, and not all those of single mind were locked into some overarching war of ideas,[15] but Peacock's polarities did nevertheless reflect discursively an early nineteenth-century inclination to perceive the world in terms of opposites.

In 1818 the poet John Keats attended a lecture by Hazlitt on Shakespeare's genius. According to Hazlitt, Shakespeare

> was the least of an egotist that it was possible to be. He was nothing in himself; but he was all that others were, or that they could become. He not only had in himself the germs of every faculty and feeling, but he could follow them by anticipation, intuitively, into all their conceivable ramifications, through every change of fortune or conflict of passion, or turn of thought. . . . He had only to think of any thing in order to become that thing, with all the circumstances belonging to it.[16]

Ruminating on this, Keats was led to formulate a famous condemnation of contemporary English poets for their 'morbid feelings and devouring egotism'. What they conspicuously lacked was that which Shakespeare had had in abundance.

> I mean *Negative Capability*, that is, when a man is capable of being in uncertainties, mysteries, doubts, without any irritable reaching after fact and reason—Coleridge, for instance, would let go by a fine verisimilitude caught from the penetralium of mystery, from being incapable of remaining content with half-knowledge.[17]

In fact Coleridge was a less systematic thinker than this implies, being fascinated by 'contraries' and 'incompatible opposites', but Keats's general point stands, that at a time when knowledge seemed unsafe, being the victim both of Romantic subjectivity and of the French Revolution's assault on established verities, it was not enough to embrace isolated truths and insights. Only coherent syllogisms or homologies could impress the mind as infallible. Richard Whately made this point when he complained that 'love of *system*' prevailed over 'love of *truth*'.[18]

---

[14] *HPD2* xxiv. 1033 (24 May 1830).

[15] Marilyn Butler, *Jane Austen and the War of Ideas* (Oxford, 1975).

[16] William Hazlitt, *Lectures on the English Poets* (1818), in *The Collected Works of William Hazlitt*, ed. A. R. Weller and Arnold Glover (1902–6), v. 47–8.

[17] *The Letters of John Keats*, ed. Maurice Buxton Forman, 3rd edn. (1947), 72; Walter Jackson Bate, *John Keats* (1963), 233–63.

[18] Richard Whately, *Detached Thoughts and Apophthegms* (1854), 43.

The same striving for conviction led to a passion for cataloguing, mensuration, statistics, and for collecting and classifying phenomena.

In similar vein John Stuart Mill wrote in 1840 that 'every Englishman of the present day is by implication either a Benthamite or a Coleridgian; holds views of human affairs which can only be proved true on the principles either of Bentham or of Coleridge'. The two philosophers were 'the contrary of one another . . . inhabitants of different worlds'.[19] The most obvious interpretation of these remarks is political. Bentham was a Radical who sought far-reaching reform in the Church, the law, the legislature, and administration, whereas Coleridge—once he had got over an early pro-Jacobin, pro-Unitarian phase—became an arch-conservative and defender of establishments. However, Mill's more fundamental point was to contrast two conflicting views of nature. For those whose mode of thinking was like Bentham's, the world was a perfectly contrived machine. Individuals were also machines and should be left free to make their own choices (self-help). If they made the wrong ones, or behaved out of harmony with nature, the consequences would be painful, but the experience would be tutelary and induce correct behaviour in future. That the world did not operate as neatly as this in practice was owing to the fact that too many magistrates and parish officers told underlings what to do and think, which prevented the mechanism from operating naturally. Instead JPs should simply lay down rules, specify penalties for breaking them, and punish accordingly. In this way, Bentham virtually reduced governance to jurisprudence.

As one historian has written, 'by 1800 the machine philosophy had deeply permeated the thinking of all who were literate',[20] or as Thomas Carlyle more memorably put it, 'men are grown mechanical in head and in heart, as well as in hand'.[21] This is not to say that Benthamites were mainly responsible for its dissemination. It derived in part from evangelical religion, which was notably mechanical in the way it conceived of sin and grace as forces pulling souls respectively downwards and upwards, of the Atonement as the '*hinge* of Christian truth', and of Heaven and Hell as cosmic goalposts. It derived ultimately from the Newtonian natural philosophy (physics and mathematics) on which the English Enlightenment was founded. It was also integral to natural theology, which pervaded most religious thought whether evangelical, High Church, latitudinarian, rational, or pantheistic. It follows that Bentham was a less influential or representative thinker than, say, Archdeacon William Paley. Paley might have been politically authoritarian, but his belief that the mechanical harmonies

---

[19] J. S. Mill, 'Coleridge' (1840), in *Essays on Ethics, Religion and Society: Collected Works of John Stuart Mill*, ed. J. M. Robson (1963–91), x. 120–1.

[20] Larry Stewart, 'A Meaning for Machines: Modernity, Utility, and the Eighteenth–Century British Public', *Journal of Modern History*, 70 (1998), 265.   [21] See below, p. 439, 608–9.

apparent in the world were the benevolent contrivance of a divine clockmaker can plausibly be described as 'theological utilitarianism'.[22]

For those whose mode of thinking was like Coleridge's, the world was not expected to operate in a logical, rational, or predictable way, nor were consequences the inevitable outcomes of particular actions. Society was thought of as a web, an organism, a fabric, or a jungle, and was impossible for mortals to comprehend. It had developed over time and was the result of divine handiwork, but God was a stitcher or weaver rather than a clockmaker. He had, moreover, granted certain individuals temporal powers, and it was their duty to exercise tutelage over the lower orders, to protect, coerce, and think for them in a paternalistic sort of way. Coleridge laid great stress on the clerisy, an intellectual and cultural elite comprising 'the sages and professors of the law and jurisprudence; of medicine and physiology; of music; of military and civil architecture; of the physical sciences... in short, all the so called liberal arts and sciences, the possession and application of which constitute the civilization of a country, as well as the Theological'.[23] This clerisy constituted for Coleridge the true 'national church', and answered the question which Burke had left in the air when he observed that a State without the means of change was without the means of its own preservation. Secure in their endowed college fellowships and livings, these sages would distinguish between those aspects of existing society which should be retained for 'permanence', and those which should be surrendered to 'progression', and their wisdom would then be disseminated by subaltern members of the clerisy such as pastors and schoolmasters. Coleridge was anxious to prevent a situation like that in Ancien Régime France, when a disaffected intelligentsia had undermined social mores.[24] Instead the clerisy would provide paternal guidance, which Coleridge called 'the spirit of State', and which was the polar opposite of Bentham's belief in individual self-interest.

LIBERAL TORYISM VERSUS HIGH TORYISM

Politically liberal Tories were closer to Coleridge than to Bentham, but in terms of Mill's philosophical distinction they were the Benthamites while high Tories

[22] This is the Paley of *Natural Theology* (1802) and, to a lesser extent, of *The Principles of Moral and Political Philosophy* (1785), and it is the Paley that has dominated subsequent interpretations. However, it is important to remember that Paley *also* based Christian faith on revelation, as in *A View of the Evidences of Christianity* (1794), and on the possibility of direct communion with God, as in *Horae Paulinae* (1790). See Neil Hitchin, 'The Life and Thought of William Paley (1743–1805)', Ph.D. thesis (Cambridge University, 2000), 2, 245–300.

[23] S. T. Coleridge, *On the Constitution of Church and State According to the Idea of Each* (1830), ed. John Colmer, in *The Collected Works of Samuel Taylor Coleridge*, ed. Kathleen Coburn and Bart Winer (1960), x. 46.

[24] Christopher Kent, *Brains and Numbers: Elitism, Comtism, and Democracy in Mid-Victorian England* (Toronto, 1978), 4–5; Ben Knights, *The Idea of the Clerisy in the Nineteenth Century* (Cambridge, 1978), 37–71.

were Coleridgeans. This is not to disregard the large swathes of common ground. Most policy differences were ones of emphasis rather than substance—for example, Wellington conceded that, with respect to 'liberal principles of commerce', Huskisson might have 'gone a little too far, or not far enough, in some cases; but this is very certain, that in principle he is right'—and both groups were agreed in resisting parliamentary reform.[25] Moreover, the issue which most clearly divided ministers—the Catholic question—did not do so in terms of liberal and high Tory, since Peel opposed emancipation and Castlereagh supported it. Nor is it easy to say which camp the Prime Minister belonged to, for while he veered more towards Canning as time went by, this might simply have been due to 'the genuine warmth of old Christ Church feelings'[26] and a natural tendency to take the line of least resistance. Finally, both sides claimed Pitt's inheritance. For all these reasons, a 'still-life' portrayal of politics in 1825 (say) might suggest that a distinction between liberal and high Toryism is hardly worth making. However, since the former would later mutate via Peelism into Gladstonianism, its origins are worth attending to. Essentially what happened in the 1820s was that two important elements of Pittism—political authoritarianism and economic libertarianism—grew less and less compatible, leading to the ministerial divisions described in the last chapter.

A further caveat is that most Tories acknowledged Burke, whom Canning called 'the manual of my political philosophy', and Burke is impossible to tie down in these terms since he expressed himself mechanically on economic matters[27] and organically on political ones. In the same way Canning's diplomatic rhetoric was mechanistic, whereas his descriptions of the Constitution dwelled on images of oaks and ivy. ('Let the venerable fabric, which has sheltered us for so many ages, and stood unshaken through so many storms, still remain unimpaired and holy.'[28]) But though mechanists could occasionally slip into organic mode, the reverse was much less likely. It would have been unthinkable for a true high Tory such as Sidmouth or Eldon to have used Peel's metaphor of the 'social machine', or to have referred like him to 'the machine of government . . . beating with a healthful and regular motion—animating industry, encouraging production, rewarding toil, correcting what is irregular, purifying what is stagnant or corrupt'.[29] Ultimately there *were*, to quote Mackintosh, 'two different languages'.

While liberal and high Tories both favoured the devolution of authority to local magistrates, teachers, employers, and Poor Law guardians, they both accepted that there were certain inescapable functions of central government such as diplomacy and defence, preserving law and order, safeguarding food supplies, and managing the nation's accounts. High Tories believed that all

[25] Wellington, memorandum, 20 May 1828, in WND iv. 451–3.   [26] Thorne, iii. 400.
[27] Edmund Burke, *Thoughts and Details on Scarcity* (1800).   [28] *HPD*1 xvii. 161 (21 May 1810).
[29] *A Correct Report of the Speeches Delivered by Sir Robert Peel at Glasgow* (1837), 59–60.

government functions, whether local or central, required constant management, interference, and discretion, even if this meant pandering to monopolists
and preferentialists, whereas liberal Tories wanted the State to operate neutrally
according to rule. (During the scarcity of 1800, for example, Grenville denounced
attempts to lower prices 'either directly *or by contrivance*' as 'impious and heretical', since 'provisions, like every other article of commerce, if left to themselves,
will and must find their level'.[30]) Whereas high Tories tended to work ad hoc
through influential contacts and officials, liberals were strongly opposed to what
they saw as 'the encroachments of power, and the errors of empiricism',[31] and
sought to eliminate all such agency.

The distinction was particularly marked in respect of economic and social
policies, but it affected foreign policy too. Historians have agonized over how
far Castlereagh would have pursued similar policies to those of Canning. In all
likelihood he would have supported the royalist cause in South America, but
otherwise not have done things very differently. Even Wellington admitted that
most of Canning's policies were acceptable. Nevertheless, his and Castlereagh's
approach to diplomacy was genuinely different from Canning's, and not merely
in matters of style. It was Castlereagh who altered the Tsar's initial draft of
Article VI of the Treaty of Alliance with Austria, Prussia, and Russia (November
1815) to prescribe regular meetings of the allied sovereigns or their ministers
'for the purpose of consulting upon their common interests... for the repose
and prosperity of Nations, and for the maintenance of the peace of Europe'.
And it was Castlereagh who, during the Congress of Aix-la-Chapelle, boasted
that periodical meetings amounted to 'a new discovery in the European government, at once extinguishing the cobwebs with which diplomacy obscures the
horizon, bringing the whole bearing of the system into its true light, and giving
to the counsels of the Great Powers the efficiency and almost the simplicity
of a single state'.[32] Although he rejected utterly Continental attempts to turn
the Quintuple Alliance into a counter-revolutionary 'league for the defence of
thrones', arguing in his 1820 State Paper that it would be wrong to intervene in
Spain for ideological reasons or to 'act upon abstract and speculative principles
of precaution', this did not indicate any abandonment of his Aix-la-Chapelle
principles, and 'he never viewed British separation from the Alliance as anything
other than temporary'.[33] He remained committed to diplomacy by congress
and by personal negotiation, and never questioned the right of great nations to
manipulate small ones in their search for a balance of power.

[30] Grenville to Pitt, 24 Oct. 1800, in Stanhope, *Pitt*, iii. 247–50.

[31] Huskisson, *HPD*2 xxiii. 584 (18 Mar. 1830).

[32] Castlereagh to Liverpool, 20 Oct. 1818, in C. K. Webster, *The Foreign Policy of Castlereagh
1812–1822* (1925–31), i. 479–84, ii. 153.

[33] Graham Warden Brook, 'British Policy toward the Concert of Europe, 1822–1832', Ph.D. thesis,
(Cambridge University, 1974), 17.

Canning, on the other hand, argued that diplomatic 'cabal and intrigue' (or what he called 'the Age of Areopagus') had 'gone by'. 'Each nation for itself and God for us all.' He dismissed congresses in scornful tones as 'periodical sessions of legislation for the world' and a 'species of assessorship'.[34] His rhetoric was steeped in balance-of-power theory, but he saw this as a natural mechanism, not as something to be manoeuvred into place by Castlereagh's diplomats. Although high Tories criticized Canning for 'perpetually doing and undoing', he actually saw the world in terms of Newtonian equilibria. 'There is a balance between the forces of retrogradation and the forces of progress.' 'We are on the brink of a great struggle between property and population.' 'England should hold the balance, not only between contending nations, but between conflicting principles.' His famous declaration 'I called the New World into existence to redress the balance of the Old' sounds bombastic now, but expressed Canning's genuine sense of the harmonies of Creation. 'Foreign policy should be a scheme of policy regulated by fixed principles of action, and operating to produce definite and foreseen results.' In other words, rather than negotiating compromises, each country should clearly state its intentions, allowing God to act as ringmaster between them. Sometimes his mechanical metaphors took an astronomical turn: 'the true policy of England' was to move 'steadily on in her own orbit, without looking too nicely to the conduct of the Powers in alliance with her'.[35] However, the most coherent statement of Canningite principles was made by Lord Palmerston in 1829. In it he denounced the Wellington Government because it had not even attempted to prevent Dom Miguel's seizure of power in Portugal.[36] He also attacked its attempt to limit the boundaries of independent Greece, a policy which he associated with Austrian, Prussian, and Russian despotism. There were 'two great parties in Europe', the nobler of which listened to public opinion while the other wrongly sought to govern through physical force.

There is in nature no moving power but mind, all else is passive and inert; in human affairs this power is opinion; in political affairs it is public opinion; and he who can grasp this power, with it will subdue the fleshly arm of physical strength, and compel it to work out his purpose. Look at one of those floating fortresses, which bear to the farthest regions of the globe, the prowess and the glory of England; see a puny insect at the helm, commanding the winds of heaven, and the waves of the ocean, and enslaving even the laws of nature, as if instead of being ordained to hold the universe together, they had only been established for his particular occasion. And yet the merest breath of those winds which he has yoked to his service, the merest drop of that fathomless abyss which he has made into his footstool, would, if ignorantly encountered, be more than enough for his destruction; but the powers of his mind have triumphed over the forces of things, and the subjugated elements are become his obedient vassals. And so also is it, with the political

---

[34] Canning to Liverpool, 26 Aug. 1823, Canning MS 70.
[35] *The Speeches of George Canning*, ed. R. Therry (1828), v. 172–3.   [36] See above, p. 294–5.

affairs of empires; and those statesmen who know how to avail themselves of the passions, and the interests, and the opinions of mankind, are able to gain an ascendancy, and to exercise a sway over human affairs, far out of all proportion greater than belong to the power and resources of the state over which they preside; while those, on the other hand, who seek to check improvement, to cherish abuses, to crush opinions, and to prohibit the human race from thinking, whatever may be the apparent power which they wield, will find their weapon snap short in their hand, when most they need its protection.[37]

This quotation recalls Peel's earlier comment about public opinion. To say that he was a more 'liberal' Home Secretary than Sidmouth is not to suggest that he was more lenient. On the contrary, Peel was all for 'salutary terror'.[38] He disliked the bloody code, not because it was bloody but because it was not sufficiently codified and consistent. The worst anomaly was the frequent practice of 'pious perjury' when jurors, not wishing to see defendants hang for trivial offences, deliberately underestimated the value of items stolen, or even pretended to find criminals 'not guilty'. By reducing the number of capital offences, Peel was hopeful that a greater quantum of judicial punishment might result (much as economists predicted that lower tariffs would lead to increased revenues). One historian has called Peel 'a great hangman' because, whenever condemned felons or their loved ones petitioned the King in Council for clemency, they 'found little mercy in Peel . . . However high-mindedly, Peel still let more people hang in the 1820s than any predecessor in office, and he meant to go on killing them.'[39] Eldon, on the other hand, though often seen as reactionary in the matter of penal reform, was far less bloodthirsty and might even be described as squeamish.

Clearly Peel was not a humanitarian, but it hardly follows that his reduction in the number of capital offences was merely a 'holding operation', designed to outflank more wholehearted reformers such as Mackintosh.[40] On the contrary, he had a principled objection to Eldon's high Tory belief that it was 'salutary' to vest 'a very large share of discretion in the judges'. Eldon believed that it was 'not from the circumstances of the severity of the law being put into execution to the fullest extent, so much as the imaginary terrors of it on the mind, that produces the abhorrence of crime', and he therefore 'favoured the retention of severe laws that were rarely, if ever, enforced' in preference to a regime of lesser but more certain punishments.[41] Likewise, lower down the scale of criminality, JPs and victims were allowed to decide whether and at what level to indict an offender. Bentham campaigned against this *ancien régime* belief in judicial

---

[37] *HPD2* xxi. 1668 (1 June 1829). For an explanation of the philosophy behind this speech, see below, pp. 443–55.

[38] Peel to Sydney Smith, 24 Mar. 1826, in Parker, *Peel*, i. 401.

[39] Whereas soft–hearted George IV was invariably for leniency (V. A. C. Gatrell, *The Hanging Tree: Execution and the English People 1770–1868* (Oxford, 1994), 553, 566–7, 585).   [40] Ibid. 568–9.

[41] *HPD1* xix, app., p. cxii (30 May 1810); xx. 301 (24 May 1811).

discretion and latitude. In his view, sentencing should be scientific, taking into account the circumstances of an offence (consequences, intentionality, consciousness, disposition) and the qualities of a punishment (variability, equability, commensurability, characteristicalness). By these means judges would be able to arrive with some precision at a correct 'proportion between punishments and offences'.[42] As one historian has put it, 'gross and capricious terror should be replaced by a fixed and graduated scale of more lenient but more certain punishments'.[43]

Peel too wanted citizens to make rational prudential calculations on the disutility of criminal behaviour. They should know with a reasonable degree of certitude what punishments attached to different felonies, since inability to calculate consequences rendered all behaviour speculative. The less often discussed corollary of Peel's removing the death penalty from relatively minor offences was a more precise and systematic application of secondary punishments. For example, traditionally all persons stealing vegetable matter from an orchard or garden had been sentenced to transportation, but in 1826 Peel distinguished between the type and value of property; between stealing, destroying, and damaging; and between a first and subsequent offence. His belief was that, having refined and defined culpability in this way, it would be possible to specify an appropriate range of punishments such as transportation, solitary confinement, the treadmill, and 'whipping (public or private) once, twice, or thrice'.[44] A Whig lawyer, Thomas Denman, accused him of 'placing too precise and exact limits to the conduct of magistrates' and of 'too technical a laying down of their duties',[45] while his three consolidating statutes have been described by one modern authority as 'not unlike Napoleon's methodical procedure prior to the enactment of the *Code Civil*'.[46] Certainly, he was convinced that the law should be as 'precise and intelligible as it can be made, [so] that it is almost needless to fortify by reasoning or authority, the first impressions of the understanding'.[47] The religious basis of such beliefs was clarified by the

---

[42] *An Introduction to the Principles of Morals and Legislation*, ed. J. H. Burns and H. L. A Hart (1970), in *The Collected Works of Jeremy Bentham*, ed. J. H. Burns (London, 1968–), 165–86.

[43] Douglas Hay, 'Property, Authority and the Criminal Law', in Hay *et al.*, *Albion's Fatal Tree: Crime and Society in Eighteenth-Century England* (1975), 23. For a recent and authoritative survey of the 18th-century legal system, confirming that this was 'the golden age of discretionary justice', but without Hay's Marxist slant, see Peter King, *Crime, Justice, and Discretion in England 1740–1920* (Oxford, 2000), 355–6.

[44] 'If it were intended to rely on transportation and imprisonment as the principal means for repressing crime, it would be satisfactory to have some precise information as to the effects produced on the conduct and habits of criminals by the duration of those punishments' (Leon Radzinowicz and Roger Hood, *A History of English Criminal Law and its Administration from 1750* (1948–86), i. 585–7.

[45] *HPD2* xv. 286 (17 Apr. 1826).

[46] Desmond H. Brown, 'Abortive Attempts to Codify English Criminal Law', *Parliamentary History*, 11 (1992), 17; Boyd Hilton, 'The Gallows and Mr Peel', in T. C. W. Blanning and David Cannadine (eds.), *History and Biography* (Cambridge, 1996).   [47] *HPD2* xiv. 1214–15 (9 Mar. 1826).

highly influential publicist Hannah More:

Even while we are rebelling against [God's] dispensations, we are taking our hints in the economy of public and private life, from the economy of Providence in the administration of the world. We govern our country by laws emulative of those by which he governs his creatures:—we train our children by probationary discipline, as he trains his servants. Penal laws in states, like those of the Divine Legislator, indicate no hatred to those to whom they are proclaimed, for every man is at liberty not to break them; they are enacted in the first instance for admonition rather than chastisement, and serve as much for prevention as punishment. The discipline maintained in all well-ordered families is intended, not only to promote their virtue, but their happiness. The intelligent child perceives his father's motive for restraining him, till the act of obedience having induced the habit, and both having broken in his rebellious will, he loves the parent the more for the restraint: on the other hand, the mismanaged and ruined son learns to despise the father, who has given him a licence to which he has discernment enough to perceive he owes the miseries consequent upon his uncurbed appetites.[48]

Historians have tended to assume that there was a simple spectrum of opinion ranging from advocates of harsh discretionary justice to those who believed in more lenient and relatively fixed penalties. The reality was more complex. Ellenborough wanted harsh discretionary justice, Eldon and Mackintosh soft discretionary justice, Bentham wanted lenient fixed penalties, Peel harsh fixed penalties.

With regard to crime prevention, Sidmouth was obviously a high Tory managerialist. His Bill to limit preaching licences to those Dissenters who could produce testimonials from householders deemed by JPs to be 'reputable and substantial' was a blatant attempt to enforce the 'arbitrary discretion of magistrates'.[49] As Home Secretary he accentuated that aspect of Pitt's legacy which relied on the secret services, and he sought to maintain law and order by working through whatever instruments came to hand. Peel, on the other hand, thought it distasteful to deploy spies and informers, and utterly opposed the use of agents provocateurs. 'God forbid that he should mean to countenance a system of espionage; but a vigorous preventive police, consistent with the free principles of our free constitution, was an object which he did not despair of seeing accomplished.'[50] When setting up the Metropolitan Police in 1829, he insisted that the new 'Bobbies' or 'Peelers' should wear uniform, despite objections that it would give them a military and therefore un-English aspect.[51] It was

---

[48] Hannah More, *Christian Morals*, 4th edn. (1813), i. 69–70.
[49] William Smith, *HPD1* xxiii. 1106 (20 July 1812). See above, p. 233.
[50] *HPD2*, vii. 803–4 (4 June 1822).
[51] Radzinowicz and Hood, *History of Criminal Law*, iv. 162. The significance of the 1829 legislation should not be exaggerated. There were watchmen and constables in London before 1829, though they were less subject to central control. Elaine A. Reynolds, *Before the Bobbies: The Night Watch and Police Reform in Metropolitan London, 1720–1830* (Houndmills, 1998).

his conviction that the State should be *visible* as well as small, rather than any misattributed *humanity*, that made Peel a liberal.

In the same year a classic confrontation occurred with the publication of *Colloquies of Society*, Robert Southey's idealized portrait of England before the dissolution of the monasteries. In it he demanded higher taxes and 'a liberal expenditure on national works', meaning 'liberal' in its old sense of generosity rather than its new sense of meanness. Reviewing the book, the Whig Thomas Babington Macaulay seized on this as Southey's cardinal error.

He conceives that the business of the magistrate is, not merely to see that the persons and property of the people are secure from attack, but that he ought to be a perfect jack-of-all-trades—architect, engineer, schoolmaster, merchant, theologian—a Lady Bountiful in every parish—a Paul Pry in every house, spying, eaves-dropping, relieving, admonishing, spending our money for us, and choosing our opinions for us. His principle is ... that no man can do anything so well for himself as his rulers ... can do it for him, and that a government approaches nearer and nearer to perfection, in proportion as it interferes more and more with the habits and notions of individuals.

Macaulay's alternative vision stressed the operations of 'public opinion' within the context of a minimal or nightwatchman State.

It is not by the intermeddling of Mr. Southey's idol—the omniscient and omnipotent State—but by the prudence and energy of the people, that England has hitherto been carried forward in civilisation ... Our rulers will best promote the improvement of the people by strictly confining themselves to their own legitimate duties—by leaving capital to find its most lucrative course, commodities their fair price, industry and intelligence their natural reward, idleness and folly their natural punishment—by maintaining peace, by defending property, by diminishing the price of law, and by observing strict economy in every department of the state. Let the Government do this—the People will assuredly do the rest.[52]

Macaulay came at liberalism from a Whiggish rather than a Pittite direction, but there was an important point in common. Whereas Palmerston in the same year denounced intermeddling governments that repressed the people, Macaulay denounced intermeddling governments that treated them too kindly.

An archetypal high Tory in Southey's managerial and paternal mould was Pitt's acolyte George Rose. He denounced the Bullion Report, secured legislation to protect friendly societies (1793) and trustee savings banks (1817), sought to introduce schemes for public employment, supported outdoor relief of the poor, opposed workhouses other than for the old and insane, piloted through an Act enabling London's Lord Mayor to influence bread prices (1800), called for statutory regulation of disputes between cotton bosses and their

---

[52] [T. B. Macaulay], 'Southey's Colloquies *on Society*', *ER* 50 (1830), 546, 565.

employees (1803–4), advocated a minimum wage, fought against the abolition of apprenticeship and instead tried to extend it (1813–14), preferred to suppress smuggling by means of physical management rather than mechanically by tariff reduction, and opposed the Corn Law of 1815 out of concern for the poor.[53] (The last is especially noteworthy given that high Tories are often said to have kowtowed to the landed interest. In fact, that highly protectionist Corn Law was supported by most liberal Tory ministers.) However, these were all losing battles. A more influential high Tory than Rose was the Chancellor of the Exchequer, Vansittart, whose hand-to-mouth methods invariably involved some intricate manipulation of the money market. He thought it perfectly natural that financiers like Rothschild and Baring should work hand in glove with government, giving and receiving favours, in order to keep the economy continuously under control, but his methods were excoriated by Edward Copleston, an Oxford philosopher–divine, adviser to Peel and Huskisson, and one of the few self-conscious liberal Tory intellectuals. He described Vansittart as the 'pilot… who has all along chosen to regulate his course, not by the sun and the stars and the immutable laws of nature, but by objects fleeting and variable, which move as he moves, and by the advice of those whose interest it is to keep him involved in these perplexities'.[54] Similarly in 1828–30, when Wellington's Government faced a severe financial shortfall, the Prime Minister devised schemes (which were not proceeded with) to privatize the management of the Government's finances and the administration of a recently acquired overseas possession. He was willing to give the Bank 'every possible advantage resulting from the transmission of the revenue and keeping the publick money, making the Bank pay handsomely for the same',[55] and he thought he might get the East India Company 'to take Ceylon off our hands, and thus save £100,000 a year'. According to Ellenborough, the Duke was anxious 'to get the City of London with the Government as Pitt had', but what these hare-brained suggestions also signified was his instinctive high Tory confidence in the benefits of making financial bargains with the private sector.[56] Huskisson by contrast was willing to sacrifice revenue in order to secure the Government's 'independence of the money market'.[57]

[53] Thorne, v. 52. For a local example of how high Tories proved more generous towards the poor than liberal ('Pittite') Tories, and also more supportive of strike action by cotton workers, see Donald Read, *Peterloo: The 'Massacre' and its Manchester Background* (Manchester, 1958), 87–91.

[54] [Edward Copleston], *A Second Letter to Robert Peel, on the Causes of the Increase of Pauperism, and on the Poor Laws* (Oxford, 1819), 6–7.

[55] Wellington to Goulburn, 6 Sept. 1828, Surrey RO, Goulburn MS II/12.

[56] *A Political Diary 1828–1830 by Edward Law Lord Ellenborough*, ed. Lord Colchester (1881), i. 184, 212; ii. 138.

[57] Huskisson, 'Memorandum: Proposal for Meeting the Financial Demands of the Year', 22 Mar. 1818, Huskisson MS 38741, fo. 207.

Liberal Tories supported *moral* paternalism, such as church-building and indecency and vagrancy legislation (1822–4),[58] but with regard to *material* welfare they preferred deterrence and self-help. They therefore took a dim view of legislation brought forward by Vansittart and Rose in 1817–18 to guarantee a 4½ per cent rate of interest to poor investors in savings banks and friendly societies in return for submitting to regulation by JPs. All such tax subsidies came under attack once liberal Tories gained the ascendancy. In 1829 the super-vision of friendly societies was transferred from magistrates to the National Debt Office, and reduced in intensity on the grounds that the State should not interfere in private finance.[59] Above all liberal Tories abhorred the escalation in Poor Law expenditure. Governments lacked the political will to tackle the issue until 1834, but the enactment then of a mean and minimalist policy[60] elicited predictable responses, with liberal Tories like Peel enthusiastically in favour and high Tories like Sidmouth, Eldon, and Vansittart (now Lord Bexley) strongly opposed to such a 'hazardous measure'.[61] Similarly, in the 1830s high Tories were more likely than their liberal colleagues to support moves for the legislative control of factory hours.

The defining issue was the resumption of cash payments, which was resisted by all high Tories (Bexley, Castlereagh, Sidmouth, Eldon, Herries, Bathurst, Harrowby[62]) and supported by liberals in both parties (Canning, Huskisson, Peel, Robinson, Grenville, Lansdowne, Althorp). Bexley's opposition to convertibility was partly constitutional, and followed from his first resolution of 1811, which had asserted that 'the right of establishing and regulating the legal money of this kingdom hath all times been a royal prerogative, vested in the sovereigns thereof'.[63] Convertibility was likely to undermine the Crown's freedom of action in that respect and would also 'shackle the Bank', but of course that was its main appeal for liberals. By taking control of the money supply out of the hands of ministers and financiers,[64] and by substituting a '*natural* system of currency

---

[58] A metropolitan moral panic, sparked in part by the Caroline riots, led to a substantial tightening of vagrancy legislation in 1822, including use of the treadmill as a punishment (M. J. D. Roberts, 'Public and Private in Early Nineteenth-Century London: The Vagrant Act of 1822 and its Enforcement', *Social History*, 13 (1988), 273–94).

[59] In 1846 the function passed to a newly elected office of Registrar of Friendly Societies, known as the 'minister for self-help'. There was widespread indignation when clergymen and other well-to-do members of the middle class and petite bourgeoisie took advantages of privileges not intended for them, and in an attempt to prevent such abuses, Parliament periodically reduced the legal maxima on members' initial investments in friendly societies and saving banks.

[60] The New Poor Law of 1834 reduced the amount of money spent on relief and theoretically made residence in a workhouse a condition of entitlement.

[61] Eldon to Lady Bankes, 23 July 1834, in Horace Twiss, *The Public and Private Life of Lord Chancellor Eldon* (1844), iii. 233.   [62] Wellington was an exception.

[63] *CPD* xx. 69 (15 May 1811).

[64] Some pundits advocated central discretionary control of the money supply; e.g. Thomas Attwood, who called for a managed currency, and David Ricardo, who recommended a national bank.

and circulation' for a '*discretionary* issue of paper money',[65] it would force all banks (including the Bank of England) to monitor both their own liquidity and the foreign exchanges, and adjust their liabilities accordingly. Huskisson promised that, once back on the gold standard,

the Bank would be the great steam engine of the State to keep the channel of the circulation always pressing full, and the power of converting its notes at any time into gold bullion at 78s. the ounce the regulator and index of the engine, by which the extent of its operations and the sufficiency of the supply would be determined and ascertained.[66]

Steam engines are self-regulating, mechanical, and repetitive. It was Huskisson's maxim that 'no restraint upon human actions can permanently or effectually countervail the nature of things'. It was therefore futile to suppose that a country with no gold standard could maintain an appropriate level of money supply by natural means, just 'as it would be, in mechanicks, to expect that a body impelled by two powers, acting in different directions, would continue in the same line of motion, if one of those powers were withdrawn'.[67] Peel was less theoretically explicit, but instinctively his mindset was alike. In 1819 he read the Bullion Report for the first time, and its central syllogism—based on the quantity of money and the specie flow mechanism—at once struck him as being 'true' in the same way as the 'proof of a proposition in mathematics'. He impatiently brushed aside some awkward statistics which had been dredged up by opponents in order to discredit the bullionists' theory.

There are facts apparently at variance with [bullionist] theory. If the demonstration is complete, this can only be so apparently. They are like the triangles that I used to bring to Bridge,[68] and declare that the angles of those particular triangles amounted to more than two right angles. The answer in each case is the same: There is some error in the fact, and in the triangle, not in the proof, which was as applicable to that fact, and that triangle as to any other.[69]

This is the politician whom many historians have seen as the embodiment of pragmatism, yet while it is true that Peel could make a fetish of facts that suited him, recalcitrant facts yielded to theory every time. In this he was probably influenced by Copleston, who argued that cash payments were 'natural' and

---

[65] *Report from the Select Committee on the High Price of Gold Bullion, PP* 1810 iii. 24 (italics added).

[66] W. Huskisson, 'Rough Draft on Coin and Currency', 12 July 1818, Huskisson MS 38741, fo. 251.

[67] W. Huskisson, *The Question Concerning the Depreciation of Our Currency Stated and Examined* (1810), 31–3, 102. This treatise is saturated with references to the 'natural order', 'natural forces', 'harmony', and 'law'. See Nathan Sussman, 'William Huskisson and the Bullion Controversy, 1810', *European Journal of the History of Economic Thought*, 4 (1997), 237–57.   [68] His former mathematics coach at Oxford.

[69] Peel to Charles Lloyd, 1819, Peel MS 40342, fos. 26–7.

would restore to the economy 'that principle of self-correction which the analogy of nature teaches us is the universal law of her constitution'.[70]

On 25 March the Bank directors reiterated their view that the link between the size of the note issue and the state of the exchanges remained not proven. To bullionists this was recalcitrance, or even heresy, and on the very next day the Secret Committee of the House of Lords recalled Ricardo in order to grill him about his Ingot Plan, something they had shown no interest in previously.[71] They were attracted, not by the plan itself, and its economical use of gold, but by its corollary the graduated scale, which would ensure that the process of transition towards resumption at the old par could begin *at once*, and so provide an 'additional security' that the Bank would not wriggle out of a policy it abhorred.[72] On 20 May the directors made a last throw of the dice, declaring that the Bank restriction had devolved on them 'duties to the community at large, whose interest in a pecuniary and commercial relation, have in a great degree been confided to their discretion', whereas the Ingot Plan would 'take away from the Bank anything like a discretionary consideration of the necessities and distresses of the commercial world'.[73] This declaration outraged the liberal Tories. 'The moment has arrived', declared Peel sombrely, 'when the nature of the relations existing between the Government and the Bank should be changed.'[74] This question of whether central bankers should act managerially or mechanically applied locally as well. Anti-bullionists thought that private bankers should determine which customers were creditworthy ('real bills'), whereas bullionists sought to establish guidelines—the state of the exchanges, say, or an individual bank's liquidity position—as to when accommodation should be granted. One high Tory commentator even went so far as to urge that bankers should act as 'a species of social police': 'spies, impelled by the strong impulse of interest to watch with the most careful attention the conduct and proceedings of the classes engaged in productive industry'.[75]

In view of these disputes it is no coincidence that what almost split the Government in 1826 was the liberal Tories' refusal to issue exchequer bills to certain firms in distress.[76] For them, businessmen like working people must

---

[70] [Edward Copleston], *A Letter to Robert Peel, on the Pernicious Effects of a Variable Standard of Value, Especially as it Regards the Condition of the Lower Orders and the Poor Laws* (Oxford, 1819), 37.

[71] See above, p. 260.

[72] *Reports from the [Commons] Secret Committee on the Expediency of the Bank resuming Cash Payments, PP* 1819 iii. 16–17. For example, 'Is it not a great advantage of such a Plan, that nearly the whole progress of its operation . . . would also thus be brought successively under the view of Parliament, instead of its being left to the discretion of the Bank, until the arrival of the time ultimately fixed for payment in cash or bullion at the mint price, without any such gradation?' (*[Lords] Reports respecting the Bank of England resuming Cash Payments, PP* 1819 iii. 197–8). [73] *HPD*1 xl. 601–4.

[74] Ibid. 688 (24 May 1819).

[75] Revd Edward Edwards, 'The Bank of England', *QR* 43 (1830), 352. For an explanation of real-bills doctrine, see above, pp. 257–8. [76] See above pp. 304–5.

stand on their own feet, and should not expect to receive outdoor relief when they got into difficulties. This in turns explains the need for a neutral monetary policy. If paupers were to be made to suffer the 'wholesome terrors of a work-house',[77] and failed businessmen were to be imprisoned for debt without limit of liability, then it was essential that they should not be able to blame their situation on unpredictable events beyond their control. In other words, citizens could not be expected to behave rationally—postponing marriage, procreating respons-ibly, saving in good years to tide themselves through bad ones, looking before they leapt into speculations—if, as under the Bank restriction, they were trapped inside a monetary system which was itself capricious and defeated ratio-nal expectations. The market was an arena in which God spoke directly to many people, and so played a constitutive part in what Peel called 'the great scheme of human redemption'. The liberal Tory vision of life as a game of moral snakes-and-ladders was further articulated by Peel in 1837, when he referred to a nat-ural 'system of social retribution', with its 'just reward of merit, and just penalty of folly and vice'. Society fluctuated like a

great ocean, whereof one part seems depressed and another elevated, if it be regarded hastily and only for an instant of time; but presenting, if viewed attentively for a longer period, constant vicissitude—that which is at one time the lowest, assuming, in its turn, the station of the highest. The fluctuations of the waves are caused by physical and fortuitous influences; but they are moral influences which affect the fluctuations of society. Industry, sobriety, honesty, and intelligence will as assuredly elevate the low, as idleness, profligacy, and vice will depress, and justly depress, those who are in high stations.[78]

Policies similar to those espoused by Huskisson, Canning, and Peel became widely accepted as public doctrine after 1850, but the spirit was by that time very different. It was then supposed that free trade, sound money, and retrenchment were recipes for economic growth and international peace ('Cobdenism'), any detrimental side effects such as welfare expenditure cuts being more than com-pensated for in the longer term by greater prosperity all round. Liberal Tories, by contrast, were sceptical about the prospects for peace and prosperity, and looked for social justice rather than economic growth. The point is not that they *wanted* the economy to fail, indeed they were delighted whenever it flourished, but, because of their Malthusian conviction that the world's resources were finite, they simply did not believe that progress was sustainable. Therefore, when seasons of distress came round, the liberal Tories' instinctual response was to blame it on speculation, over-trading, and excess. 'I anticipate more inconvenience from the glut of every article of consumption than I do from the recent failures,'

---

[77] [Edward Copleston], *A Letter to Robert Peel on the Pernicious Effects of a Variable Standard of Value* (Oxford, 1819), 34.   [78] *Speeches Delivered by Peel at Glasgow*, 42–3.

wrote Peel in December 1825. 'I fear we have been working too fast—building too fast—importing too fast—and that when confidence in banking establishments (in those at least which *ought* to be confided in) shall have been restored, we shall still find that there will have been much less demand for labour than there has been.'[79] Given his further belief that irresponsible businessman were most vulnerable to collapse, it is easy to understand the relish with which he reassured colleagues that 'ultimate good after some severe suffering will result'.[80] Any ruling-class interference in the lives of ordinary citizens, whether caring or coercive, would disrupt the social machine and thwart God's 'system of social retribution'.[81] So whereas Bentham believed that individual choice would lead to social harmony and the 'greatest happiness of the greatest number', Peel was an ethical pessimist whose object was to inculcate 'moral discipline' and tame 'the unruly passions and corrupt natures of human beings'.[82]

Peel was not a demonstrative man and only showed his feelings at times of stress, as in the peroration of his great speech of 16 February 1846, when he sacrificed his political career in order to repeal the Corn Laws.[83] While he assured MPs that, by embracing free trade, they would do 'whatever human sagacity can do for the promotion of commercial prosperity' and 'the continued contentment, and happiness, and well-being of the great body of the people', his emphasis was on the probability, even certainty, that bad times would recur. 'It seems to be incident to great prosperity that there shall be a reverse—that the time of depression shall follow the season of excitement and success. . . . The years of plenteousness may have ended, and the years of dearth may have come.' But when that happened, by repealing the Corn Laws MPs would at least have the satisfaction of knowing that they 'had anticipated the evil day, and, long before its advent, had trampled on every impediment to the free circulation of the Creator's bounty'.

When you are again exhorting a suffering people to fortitude under their privations, when you are telling them, 'These are the chastenings of an all-wise and merciful Providence, sent for some inscrutable but just and beneficent purpose—it may be, to humble our pride, or to punish our unfaithfulness, or to impress us with the sense of our own nothingness and dependence on His mercy'; when you are thus addressing your suffering fellow subjects, and encouraging them to bear without repining the dispensations of Providence, may God grant that by your decision of this night you

---

[79] Peel to E. J. Littleton, 23 Dec. 1825, Staffordshire RO, Hatherton MS D260/M/F/5 /27/2/110. Liberal Tories hoped that, by investing in savings banks, labourers would be able to take a rest from work whenever a market became over-stocked with commodities, whereas at present they were forced to produce even more goods to offset low prices, so glutting the market still further.   [80] Ibid.

[81] *Speeches Delivered by Peel at Glasgow*, 43.

[82] For the way in which this duality operated in economic and social policy, notably the Poor Law, see, Boyd Hilton, *The Age of Atonement: The Influence of Euangelicalism on Social and Economic Thought 1795–1865* (Oxford, 1988), 64–70, 237–48.   [83] See below, pp. 551–8.

may have laid in store for yourself the consolation of reflecting that such calamities are, in truth, the dispensations of Providence—that they have not been caused, they have not been aggravated by laws of man restricting, in the hour of scarcity, the supply of food![84]

In these remarks Peel melded Utilitarianism, natural theology, and political economy, all of which contributed to the mechanism and providentialist fatalism of liberal Tory social philosophy.

UTILITARIANISM

Jeremy Bentham (1748–1832) was an amiable fellow with a fondness for classi-fication, codification, neologisms, and impossible schemes of improvement. He had a legal training but did not practise, once describing lawyers as 'the scum of the earth'. He abhorred judge-made precedents, and sought to produce a 'pannomion', or comprehensive body of fixed legislation, to replace the common law. Cold-shouldered by most of the great and the good apart from his patron Lord Shelburne, first Marquess of Lansdowne, he inspired a number of devotees who made it their goal to popularize his ideas. These included Étienne Dumont, his Genevan translator, who spread his fame overseas; Sir Samuel Romilly, his follower in jurisprudence; James Mill, who is often held responsible for injecting a Puritan strain into Utilitarian philosophy;[85] and Francis Place, who tried to turn his ideas into practical politics. Virtually unknown for much of his life, Bentham's fame and influence grew rapidly in the 1820s. This was due in part to the *Westminster Review*, founded in 1824 by Henry Southern and John Bowring and with himself as proprietor; to publications such as the *Morning Chronicle* and *The Examiner*; and to the self-conscious discipleship of the so-called Philosophic Radicals, a handful of MPs who were to enter Parliament after the 1832 Reform Act and who included George Grote, John Arthur Roebuck, and Sir William Molesworth. His spirit suffused London University, the 'Godless institution of Gower Street', which opened in 1828 following a vigorous cam-paign by Brougham, James Mill, and Grote. Its Church-and-King counterpart, King's College in the Strand, was founded in the same year and made a corresponding obeisance to Coleridge.

   Like Coleridge, Bentham was lovelorn for the last forty years of his life, the victim of an unrequited longing for Fox's niece Caroline, and it is easy to imagine that this might help to explain his obsessive personality. He was not louche like Coleridge, but had a similarly childlike character. Both men had to be cosseted through the complexities of daily life by an entourage of friends and pupils who undertook their routine household affairs. But whereas Coleridge's

---

[84] *HPD*3 lxxxiii. 1043 (16 Feb. 1846).

[85] William Thomas, *The Philosophic Radicals: Nine Studies in Theory and Practice 1817–1841* (Oxford, 1979), 97–104, argues that James Mill was in many ways more influential than Bentham.

ideas were as chaotic as his lifestyle, Bentham's were clinically clear. He was particularly interested in chemistry, and saw his own approach to jurisprudence as scientific, in contrast to the self-interested antiquarianism of common lawyers. Even Macaulay, who castigated Bentham's views on democracy, thought him someone whom 'posterity will ... place in the same rank with Galileo, and with Locke, the man who found jurisprudence a gibberish, and left it a science'.[86]

He is most famous (or notorious) for his model prison, or 'panopticon', described as a 'mill for grinding rogues honest, and idle men industrious'.[87] The idea of systematic rewards and punishments designed to inculcate habits of hard work was hardly new, but Bentham added an ingredient which he thought had an operative force akin in importance to that of gravity. 'Morals reformed, health preserved, industry invigorated, instruction diffused, public burthens lightened, economy seated as it were upon a rock, the Gordian knot of the Poor-laws not cut but untied—all by a simple idea in architecture.' That idea was invigilation. Prisons, factories, workhouses, madhouses, hospitals, and schools were to be designed on the principle that 'the more constantly the persons to be inspected are under the eyes of the persons who should inspect them, the more perfectly will the purpose of the establishment have been attained'. The panop-ticon was to be circular with the cells arranged around the outside, while the inspector—'the spider in the web', as Burke called him when he read the plans—would occupy a vantage point at the centre. When dusk fell, brilliant artificial light would be reflected into each cell so as to blot out the night, but the inspector's office would remain throughout an 'utterly dark spot', all the better for seeing out of 'without being seen'. Although not every inmate could be watched every minute of every hour, 'at least he should *conceive* himself to be so'.[88] This would necessitate continuous sobriety and good behaviour until the point was reached at which sobriety and good behaviour became an ingrained habit of mind. It was, in Bentham's eyes, a humane form of punishment that would lead to rehabilitation.

The panopticon 'absorbed all his energies' in the 1790s[89] and intermittently later, but it was rejected by the Government in 1813, after two decades of prevarication and circumlocution, in favour of the evangelical penitentiary.[90] Bentham was awarded £23,000 in compensation, but even so the frustration

[86] T. B. Macaulay, 'The French Revolution', *ER* 55 (1832), 553.

[87] Bentham to J. P. Brissot, Nov. 1791, in *The Correspondence of Jeremy Bentham*, ed. T. L. S. Sprigge, A. T. Milne, I. R. Christie, J. R. Dinwiddy, S. Conway, and C. Fuller (London, 1968–94), iv. 342.

[88] J. Bentham, *Panopticon; or, The Inspection–House* (Dublin, 1791), 3, 23, 139–40; Gertrude Himmelfarb, *Victorian Minds* (1968), 32–81.   [89] Ross Harrison, *Bentham* (1983), 20.

[90] In 1811 a parliamentary committee reported against Bentham and in favour of John Howard's 'great new penal experiment' embracing 'penitential confinement, seclusion, employment, and religious instruction' (Janet Semple, *Bentham's Prison: A Study of the Panopticon Penitentiary* (Oxford, 1993), 273–4).

he felt may well account for his 'transition to political radicalism' in 1809–10.[91]
His later publications advocated republicanism, the compulsory rotation of MPs,
annual elections, universal male and female suffrage subject only to a literacy
test, and the secret ballot.[92] Emotionally he always sided with the underdog,
and did not share the fear of proletarian revolution that gripped so many of
his contemporaries. In seeking to inculcate order, regularity, visibility, accountability, and self-control in his fellow citizens, he saw himself as attacking inherited and institutional privilege, especially legal. Yet, because of the panopticon,
he has often been seen as trying to reinforce the subordination of the poor.
According to this myth, surveillance would take the part of physical subjection,
and the lower orders would be brainwashed into disciplining themselves, a case
of repression through freedom.

It is certainly true that Bentham had no time for natural rights, which he
famously called 'nonsense on stilts'. His Utilitarianism was rooted in two notions:
that 'self-regarding affections' predominate over the 'social', and that individuals
weigh up the consequences of alternative courses of action and choose that
which promises the greatest amount of happiness (the felicific calculus). Bentham
defended his system from the charge of selfish egoism by invoking Hartley's
doctrine that habit forms through the association of ideas, implying that people
take reflected pleasure in the pleasurable experiences of others. However, this
defence only works on the assumption that everyone is psychologically the
same, has the same basic likes and dislikes, wants the same ends, and fears
the same dangers. It is evident from James Mill's *History of British India* (1817),
for example, that Benthamites had little sense of racial or gender differences,
but then they had little sense of any kind of difference. This insensitivity led
them to believe that society might be so organized that everyone's interests—
that is to say, their true as distinct from superficial desires—might be mutually
and simultaneously satisfied through rational choice. Government would be
reduced to a 'tutelary role', rewarding good (i.e. socially motivated) actions and
punishing bad ones. Gover*nance*, in the sense of princes, ministers, priests,
lawyers, parish overseers, or municipal officers exercising discretionary rule,
would cease to exist, since even when it was well intentioned it was likely to be
based on arbitrary and subjective notions of what constituted right behaviour.

Such a brief account risks making Utilitarianism seem even more mechanical
than it was. Bentham was aware that much knowledge about the world is handed
down from generation to generation and serves to guide conduct much of the
time. Nevertheless, conventional knowledge of this sort needs constantly to be

---

[91] J. R. Dinwiddy, *Radicalism and Reform in Britain, 1780–1850* (1992), 273–90, ascribes this to Mill's
influence, but see James E. Crimmins, 'Bentham's Political Radicalism Reexamined', *Journal of the
History of Ideas*, 55 (1994), 259–81.
[92] Jeremy Bentham, *Plan of Parliamentary Reform in the Form of a Catechism* (1817).

questioned, if only to prevent it from sinking into superstition, and the principle of utility—that which leads to the 'greatest happiness of the greatest number'—was the best criterion by which to judge it. It was also a help when people found themselves at the margin, without inherited prejudices to guide them.

Utilitarianism was a tool of analysis rather than the a priori theory of human behaviour it has often been taken for, but even so it suffered from two fundamental implausibilities. First, the notion that people are essentially the same precluded any consideration of personality or character. In Bentham's formulation, the only important distinction related to disposition: socially conditioned citizens were disposed to do good, the rest to do harm. It was an instrumental view of human nature that led Bentham to take jurisprudential views which now seem odd. For example, he believed that someone who committed a crime under strong temptation should be punished more harshly than one who committed the same crime without much temptation. Since 'all punishment in itself is evil' because it causes unhappiness, judges should impose the minimum penalty necessary in each case to offset the temptation to commit the crime. Therefore, the greater the degree of temptation under which a guilty person has acted, the greater should be his punishment.[93] This was logical, but it overlooked the consideration that a wrongdoer who gives in to a slight temptation is more depraved than one who acts under the pressure of a strong one. James Mill's son John, who was subjected as a boy to a particularly rigorous form of Utilitarian education, came to realize how important it was to allow for variations in human personality. The principle of utility was only of any use if it was 'grounded on the permanent interests of man as a progressive being', meaning that under a properly regulated system of liberty people's characters would mature and improve over time.[94] But classic Utilitarians (like evangelicals) had no room for intermediate development. Either citizens had achieved a state of socialization (faithful), or else they were antisocial (damned).

As well as failing to distinguish between types of personality, Benthamism did not differentiate between pleasures, thereby bringing to the surface a problem which had been latent in most English philosophy since Locke. If humans have no innate knowledge or reason, and if all knowledge or understanding is rooted in sensation or experience of the world, then the *only* way to marshal that knowledge, say for transmission to later generations, is by dividing it into those sensations which give pleasure and those which are painful. Pleasure and pain thus cease to be subjective experiences and become the objective criterion by

---

[93] Bentham, *An Introduction to the Principles of Morals and Legislation*, 158, 166–8.

[94] J. S. Mill, 'On Liberty' (1859), in *Collected Works of Mill*, xviii. 224. John Mill's severe nervous breakdown in 1826–7 is generally attributed to a loss of faith in Utilitarianism, but as José Harris has recently suggested in the *Oxford Dictionary of National Biography*, maybe 'it was not so much finding Benthamism false but fearing that parts of it might indeed be true that generated his deepest depression'.

which to judge the merit of things, which means that only the amount and not the quality of a pleasure can be assessed. To cite the famous example, Bentham had to concede that pushpin (a childish game of throwing) was as good as poetry in the sense that it could give as much pleasure. Again, it required the younger Mill to retort that it was better to be Socrates dissatisfied than a fool satisfied.

It has been suggested that Bentham's economics, being predicated on a *natural* harmony of interests, contravened his jurisprudence, which envisaged an *artificial* harmonization of interests.[95] In fact the contradiction was more apparent than real, since political and economic liberalism have rarely cohabited, believers in a free market usually requiring an authoritarian State to police it. Bentham's real mistake lay in failing to realize that it is impossible in practice to limit central government agencies to mechanical functions like reward and punishment. Perhaps he thought that the democratic reforms he was also calling for would successfully confine them to such a role. But since, in practice, bureaucrats are blamed when social market outcomes seem unfavourable, they naturally intervene preventively and end up not so much policing the market as seeking to make it work according to subjective notions of fairness, precisely what Bentham himself had condemned in *ancien régime* officials and interfering local authorities. This process of 'bureaucratic creep' made it almost inevitable that Bentham's 'night watchman' State would slide imperceptibly towards a paternalist State during the later decades of the nineteenth century.

NATURAL THEOLOGY IN A FALLEN WORLD

Anglican evangelicals were prominent among those who campaigned for penal reform, but the lead was taken by Dissenters like the Congregationalist John Howard and the Quaker Elizabeth Fry. Disliking excessive capital punishment and barbarous prison conditions, Howard's ideal was the penitentiary, where criminals would be 'encouraged' through solitary confinement and the treadmill to see the error of their ways and repent.[96] In practice such a regimen was not all that different from what Bentham was advocating, and in fact Utilitarians and evangelicals cooperated, not only in penal and prison reform, but in other areas such as anti-slavery and temperance. On the face of it this seems surprising, since James Mill denied and Bentham ignored God.[97] On the other hand, their idea of how secular rulers and magistrates should operate mirrored the pervasive evangelical idea of the 'moral government of God by reward and punishment',

[95] Élie Halévy, *The Growth of Philosophic Radicalism* (1928; new edn. 1972), 489–91.

[96] Michael Ignatieff, *A Just Measure of Pain: The Penitentiary in the Industrial Revolution, 1750–1850* (1978), 44–79.

[97] Bentham's pseudonymous *Nor Paul, but Jesus* (1823), by 'Gamaliel Smith', emphatically rejected the Pauline doctrines that were at the heart of evangelicalism, and helps to explain his closeness to many Unitarians.

the world being seen as a cosmic panopticon in which every thought was monitored by the divine eye. Again like Utilitarians, evangelicals saw the world in terms of causes and consequences, and depicted human beings as inherently flawed but capable of being made good. Neither had much time for qualitative personality differences. What mattered to evangelicals was whether people were saved; what mattered to Benthamites was whether they had inwardly digested the principle of utility. Carlyle hit the comparison on the head when he referred to Bentham's concern for 'man's salvation as a social being'.[98]

Evangelicalism appealed to contemporaries as a religion of the heart and of the word, but just as importantly it was a religion of nature. Belief in God through divine inspiration was still largely discredited in upper-class eyes by the seventeenth-century Puritans with their antinomianism and disregard for the law. Belief in revelation, meaning the witness of God in the Bible and the formularies of an apostolic Church, was strong among High Churchmen, but it struck many eighteenth-century minds as superstitious, while by the 1820s there were alarming rumours that German critics were undermining the authority of the Bible. The only unassailable bedrock of belief was therefore natural religion or natural theology, reasoning upwards from nature and *inducing* 'the power, wisdom, and goodness of God' from the mechanics of his Creation. This idea of the divine watchmaker, famously associated with Paley, fits the so-called long eighteenth century chronologically since it originated in the Newtonian mechanics of the 1680s and 1690s, while its swansong was a high-profile series of eight Treatises, commissioned under the will of the eccentric Francis Egerton, eighth Earl of Bridgewater, and published between 1833 and 1836. The donor was a notable eccentric who dined at table with cats and dogs dressed up as men and women, each with a napkin and flunkey in attendance.[99] However, the authors—five distinguished scientists and three clergymen with an active interest in natural philosophy—were by no means intellectual flunkeys.[100] Only Bell and Buckland, and to a lesser extent Kidd and Prout, adopted the previous century's functional and teleological approach.[101] As an ensemble, the Treatises were much more than simply 'Paley updated', and yet they were widely interpreted as endorsing the belief 'that design and benevolence

[98] [Thomas Carlyle], 'Signs of the Times', *ER* 49 (1829), 448.

[99] Egerton's approach to design was hardly Paleyan. He thought that the best proof of the power, wisdom, and goodness of God was the existence in Britain of a landed aristocracy.

[100] John Kidd (the physical world), William Buckland (geology and mineralogy), Peter Mark Roget (physical and animal physiology), William Prout (chemistry, meteorology, and the function of digestion), Charles Bell (anatomy of the hand), William Whewell (astronomy and general physics), William Kirby (animal creation), and Thomas Chalmers (moral and social science, including political economy).

[101] And even they owed less to Paley than to Cuvier, on whom, see below, pp. 339–40; John Topham, ' "An Infinite Variety of Arguments": The *Bridgewater Treatises* and British Natural Theology in the 1830s', Ph.D. thesis (Lancaster University, 1993), 213–32.

were everywhere visible in the natural world'.[102] It seems as though the authors' many qualifications and idiosyncrasies were completely overlooked, as readers of the Bridgewater treatises 'roamed enchanted from barnacles to migrating swallows, from the habits of worms to mouths of whales, from the duodenal tube to electrical galvanism, and marvelled at the beautiful machinery of God'.[103]

Although the purpose of the Bridgewaters was affirmative, the tone was often defensive. This was partly owing to recent scientific trends, but more fundamentally it was because the horrors of the French Revolution had cast doubt on the very idea of design. Newton had demonstrated the perfection of the gravitation system, and Adam Smith the operations of self-interest and sympathy in harmonizing society, but to a generation brought up in the shadow of Jacobinism, food shortages, wars, and pestilence (Asiatic cholera returned in 1831) it must have seemed that God was either malign or powerless. In the words of a political economist, 'Paley, in his Natural Theology . . . assumes . . . that the order of the universe shows intelligence and design; and this proves an intelligent cause-designing mind. But the Atheist denies that the order of the universe shows intelligence and design.'[104] One response to this dilemma was to argue that God so loved humankind that he was about to wind the world up and usher in the millennium. From this perspective, which was adopted by certain apocalyptic evangelicals,[105] it could be argued that present horrors were really cause for hope. But this was not a line which the majority of believers (whether evangelical or otherwise) could take, given their commitment to the ideas of mechanism and uniform natural law. Their solution was rather to stand Paley's theory of providence on its head so that it became a theodicy, i.e. a means of defending God against the charge of cruelty. The machinery of Creation remained perfect, but the demonstration of its efficacy was now its propensity to produce not happiness but justice. Having granted fallen human beings free will, God dealt them perfect justice, usually and admonitorily in this world but occasionally reserving it for the next. As a contributor to the evangelical *Christian Observer* (almost certainly Wilberforce) pointed out,

The goodness of God is the only moral attribute which is apprehended by Dr. Paley to be manifest, from the appearance of the natural world. No observation occurs . . . concerning the holiness or justice of the deity; nothing of those tendencies of virtue to produce happiness, and of vice to produce misery, which are so judiciously collected and so unanswerably enforced by Bishop Butler, and analogically applied as proofs that the

---

[102] Charles Bell, *The Hand: Its Mechanism and Vital Endowments as Evincing Design* (1833), p. xi.

[103] Owen Chadwick, *The Victorian Church* (1976–70), i. 561. This type of science was synthesized in Mary Somerville's *On the Connexion of the Physical Sciences* (1834), which was hugely successful and went through several editions.

[104] Robert Torrens to Macvey Napier, 28 Oct. 1830, BL, Add. MS 34614, fos. 426–7.

[105] Including one of the Bridgewater authors, Kirby. See below, pp. 457–8.

world is not now in the state in which it originally proceeded from the hands of the Creator, but that it is evidently in a state of degradation and ruin—that the Creator is a *moral* governor.[106]

The philosopher Bishop Joseph Butler (1692–1752) was frequently appealed to, especially in the second quarter of the nineteenth century, and not only by evangelicals. He held as great a sway at Oxford as Paley did in the scientific culture of Cambridge, and shared with Aristotle the distinction of being a compulsory set author on the Greats syllabus until 1854. Butler shared the Utilitarians' mechanism and consequentialism, but in place of self-love and self-interest he highlighted the conscience, a moral governor within the breast that enabled people to know instinctively which actions were right and which wrong, irrespective of the quantum of pleasure they evoked. Butler helped his nineteenth-century readers to cope with disease and pain, phenomena which had always caused Paley difficulty, as the following comment makes clear.

Evil no doubt exists; but is never, that we can perceive, the object of contrivance. Teeth are contrived to eat, not to ache; their aching now and then is incidental to the contrivance, perhaps inseparable from it; or even, if you will, let it be called a defect in the contrivance; but it is not the object of it.[107]

Prompted by Butler, a later generation could argue, like the physician Thomas Watson, that 'bodily suffering and sickness' were, in the vast majority of cases, 'the natural fruits of evil courses; of the sins of our fathers, of our own unbridled passions, of the malevolent spirit of others'. It followed that illnesses should be welcomed as dispensations of providence, 'judgments, which are mercifully designed to recal men from the strong allurements of vice, and the slumber of temporal prosperity; teaching that it is good for us to be sometimes afflicted'.[108]

One of the most frightening of natural evils was famine. Paley had expressed an eighteenth-century commonplace when he wrote that the main aim of all rational politics was

to produce the greatest quantity of happiness in a given tract of country . . . The quantity of happiness produced in any given district . . . *so far* depends upon the number of inhabitants, that . . . the collective happiness will be nearly in the exact proportion of the numbers, that is, twice the number of inhabitants will produce double the quantity of happiness . . . Consequently, the decay of population is the greatest evil that a state can

---

[106] *Christian Observer*, 2 (1803), 373 (italics added). The evangelical geologist Adam Sedgwick likewise compared Paley unfavourably to Butler (and St Paul): 'By what right . . . do we assert the simple and unconditional benevolence of God; and, on this assumption, go on to found a moral system and rule of life? If he be a God of mercy, is he not also a God of justice? Sin and misery are often among us the means of bringing about the ends of his providence' (Adam Sedgwick, *A Discourse on the Studies of the University*, ed. Eric Ashby and Mary Anderson (Leicester, 1969), 55).

[107] Paley, *Natural Theology*, 501, 527.

[108] Thomas Watson, *Lectures on the Principles and Practice of Physic* (1843), i. 15.

suffer; and the improvement of it the object which ought, in all countries, to be aimed at, in preference to every other political purpose whatsoever.[109]

However, Malthus' generation took the opposite view, being inclined to agree with him that God had invited too many mortals to nature's feast. There is a good deal of uncertainty regarding Robert Malthus' intentions. The first (1798) edition of *An Essay on the Principle of Population as it affects the Future Improvement of Society* proposed that population growth (increasing geometrically) would always outpace food supply (increasing only arithmetically) leading to wars, famines, and pestilence, but this alarming prediction was mitigated by a cheerful chapter in which it was envisaged that the threat to subsistence would act as a stimulus to farmers and prompt an agricultural revolution.[110] Such optimism may have reflected Unitarian influences on Malthus at the Warrington Dissenting Academy and Jesus College, Cambridge, as well as his Foxite political views and amiable personality. However, the second (1803) edition was entitled *An Essay on the Principle of Population, or a View of its Past and Present Effects on Human Happiness, with an Enquiry into our Prospects respecting the Future Removal or Mitigation of the Evils which it Occasions*, a more rueful theme and more befitting an Anglican curate.[111] It turned him into an ogre in many circles. 'This vile, infamous theory, this hideous blasphemy against nature and mankind',[112] implied that the only way to avoid famine was by 'the preventive check to population', meaning sexual abstinence since Malthus had no truck with birth control. In both editions his main target was the republican atheist William Godwin's *An Enquiry concerning Political Justice, and its Influence on General Virtue and Happiness* (1793). Godwin had argued that social equality would increase the sum of human happiness, since vastly more people would gain than lose from the transaction. He also claimed that the creation of such a utopia would so increase civility and so diminish sexuality that the population dilemma would be solved. Now Malthus, like most Whigs, was in favour of inequality, but he realized that it was no longer efficacious to rely on the age-old argument that God had willed it so. Instead he sought to demonstrate that getting rid of social distinctions would have disastrous consequences for rich and poor alike. His key point was to argue that it was *only* 'the hope of bettering our condition, and the fear of want' that could force men—who were by nature 'inert, sluggish, and averse from labour', as well as highly sexed—to work hard and forgo animal pleasures.

[109] Paley, *Principles of Moral and Political Philosophy*, bk. VI, ch. 9, pp. 587–9.
[110] A. M. C. Waterman, *Revolution, Economics and Religion: Christian Political Economy, 1798–1833* (Cambridge, 1991), 58–112.
[111] From 1805 until his death in 1834 he was Professor of Political Economy at the East India College, Haileybury.
[112] Friedrich Engels, *Outlines of a Critique of Political Economy* (1844), in *Karl Marx Frederick Engels Collected Works* (1975–2001), iii. 437.

But if that argument were to carry any weight, Malthus had to show that laziness and sexual activity would have disastrous results. Hence his scaremongering about arithmetic and geometric ratios and the danger of population growth.[113]

It was the repressive second edition that caught the public's imagination, and in particular his argument for the gradual elimination of poor relief. Once that had been accomplished,

If any man chose to marry, without a prospect of being able to support a family, he should have the most perfect liberty so to do ... [But] he should be taught to know, that the laws of nature, which are the laws of God, had doomed him and his family to starve for disobeying their repeated admonitions; that he had no claim of *right* on society for the smallest portion of food, beyond that which his labour would fairly purchase.[114]

Malthus was widely denounced, not least for contradicting the biblical injunction to 'go forth and multiply', but in governing circles, and on what might be called the official mind, his impact was enormous. His views were endlessly reprised, and notably by John Bird Sumner, an evangelical who later became Archbishop of Canterbury.[115] The Scottish Presbyterian Thomas Chalmers made the message much more evangelical by arguing in his Bridgewater Treatise that population pressure was a sign of God's love, in so far as ecologically enforced sexual abstinence would awaken mortals unto salvation.

Political economy is but one grand exemplification of the alliance, which a God of righteousness hath established, between prudence and moral principle on the one hand, and physical comfort on the other. However obnoxious the modern doctrine of population, as expounded by Mr. Malthus, may have been, and still is, to weak and limited sentimentalists, it is the truth which of all others sheds the greatest brightness over the earthly prospects of humanity—and this in spite of the hideous, the yet sustained outcry which has risen against it. This is a pure case of adaptation, between the external nature of the world in which we live, and the moral nature of man, its chief occupier. There is a demonstrable inadequacy in all the material resources which the globe can furnish, for the increasing wants of a recklessly increasing species. But over and against this, man is gifted with a moral and a mental power by which the inadequacy might be fully countervailed; and the species in virtue of their restrained and regulated numbers, be upholden on the face of our world, in circumstance of large and stable sufficiency, even to the most distant ages. The first origin of this blissful consummation is the virtue of the people.[116]

---

[113] In the 1817 edition of his essay Malthus adapted his arguments to meet those of Robert Owen, who had succeeded Godwin as the main exponent of equalitarian doctrines (Donald Winch, *Riches and Poverty: An Intellectual History of Political Economy in Great Britain, 1750–1834* (Cambridge, 1996), 280–7).

[114] T. R. Malthus, *An Essay on the Principle of Population*, 2nd edn. (1803), 539–40.

[115] J. B. Sumner, *A Treatise on the Records of the Creation, and on the Moral Attributes of the Creator; with Particular Reference to the Jewish History, and to the Consistency of the Principle of Population with the Wisdom and Goodness of the Deity* (1816; 2nd edn. 1818), ii. 119–434.

[116] Thomas Chalmers, *On the Power, Wisdom, and Goodness of God as manifested in the Adaptation of External Nature to the Moral and Intellectual Constitution of Man* (1833), ii. 49–51.

Chalmers's most daring insight was in perceiving an analogy between Malthus' theories of population and capital. In his *Principles of Political Economy* (1820), Malthus had predicted that financial crises would recur as the country proved unable to consume all the goods and services it produced. Chalmers seized on this in order to argue that the quintessential sin of the middle classes— the 'desire to be rich'—led inexorably to an 'oversurplus' of capital, just as sexual incontinence among the lower orders led to overpopulation. And, just as wars, famines, and pestilence got rid of 'excrescent population', so cycles of national bankruptcy, occurring roughly every six or seven years, could get rid of speculation. At this stage in the argument, Chalmers pointed to a moralistic solution. Just as the *threat* of wars, famines, and pestilence could frighten the poor into 'elevating their minds above their passionate flesh', thereby restoring ecological equilibrium, so the apprehension of financial loss might promote proper Christian conduct in commercial behaviour, the need for which was a prominent feature of contemporary homiletic. That is why liberal Tories were so determined not to provide an asylum for businesses in distress, and why Liverpool's administration almost broke apart over whether to issue exchequer bills in 1826.[117]

Why do certain ideas catch on? Chalmers's analogy between overpopulation and over-speculation, and likewise between famines and bankruptcies, resonated because of a widespread tendency to explain current problems in terms of surfeit, and to seek solutions through evacuation and release. It was commonplace to talk about the 'fever of speculation', implying that the desire to be rich was an illness. Fever dominated the imagination of the second quarter of the nineteenth century, especially when it took the form of cholera morbus. Because that disease occurred spasmodically, with visitations in 1831–2, 1847–8, and 1853–4, it reinforced contemporary notions of providential government, and stole the limelight from more deadly but less dramatic killers such as enteric typhus. In the previous century most English doctors had seen fevers as contagious and debilitating, but now it was commonly assumed that physical disease was inflammatory, intrinsic to the individual organism, and therefore incapable of being transmitted (anti-contagionism). It was attributed to excitement, overload of the system, or excess, implying more often than not personal immorality. This explains why bloodletting was thought of as the best way to treat fevers, and why heroic bleeders such as John Armstrong and Henry Clutterbuck were such respected physicians.[118] Release was a familiar trope in the imaginative writing of the day, and medical and political debates crisscrossed at several points. For example, fashionable anti-contagionists were usually economic liberals who supported free trade. Those who wished to protect

---

[117] See above, pp. 304–5.   [118] Hilton, *Age of Atonement*, 154–62.

native industry and keep out foreign products offered an alternative, contagionist view on the causes of fever, seeing it as an invasion from abroad, and calling for strict quarantine arrangements to protect the nation's health. Again, the fashionable response to cholera was to designate a Fast Day, in the hope that prayer and abstinence would propitiate the Almighty, whereas Radicals insisted that cholera was a disease not of excess but of undernourishment, and that what was really needed was a Feast Day, or free food for the hungry. These bitter debates seem quaint today, if only because neither side had any understanding of how bacterial germs could spread disease.

Volcanoes were looked on as prime examples of the release mechanism, being thought to result from bubblings up of molten lavas in the bowels of the earth.[119] This was important because in the 1810s geology began to take over from chemistry as the fashionable science. It had to confront the Bible, which had its own view on the origins of planet earth. The chronological and genealogical information contained in the Old Testament had long since led to a belief that Creation had begun at dusk on 22 October 4004 BC, making the world less than 6,000 years old. And yet there was constantly unfolding evidence of the long sequence of 'events' in earth's history. It came from amateur geologists, ordinance surveyors, mappers, and miners as they uncovered yet more rock strata and layers of fossil remains. Owing to a series of prehistoric accidents, the British Isles contains specimens from nearly all ages—3,000 million years separate the Archaean rocks of northern Scotland from the more recent tertiary clays of the London basin, and most of the intervening periods are also represented— so when William Smith produced his remarkable coloured map of the nation's geology in 1815 it reinforced the impression of intensive past activity.[120] The only way to reconcile so many happenings with the earth's supposed youthfulness was by supposing that God had crowded a great deal of activity into a very short period—hence the emphasis on catastrophes such as volcanoes, earthquakes, and floods. The key contribution came from a French naturalist, Georges Cuvier, whose *Recherches sur les ossemens fossiles des quadrupèdes* (with its startling introduction *Discours sur les révolutions de la surface du globe*) was published in 1812 and translated into English the following year. Cuvier explained the discovery of fossil remains considerably older than the Garden of Eden by arguing that they were survivals from a previous world, which must have been wrecked by a general convulsion, and this was broadly the line taken by evangelical writers on geology such as Sumner and Chalmers. Now it should have been evident (and was to scholars) from James Hutton's *Theory of the Earth* (1785–8) that the world was at least billions of years old, but his ideas regarding

---

[119] e.g. Charles Daubeny, *A Description of Active and Extinct Volcanoes* (1826), 357–60, 390–3. Daubeny was an Oxford professor.   [120] See above, p. 171.

'deep geological time' only began to gain general acceptance in the 1830s.[121]
One reason may have been the instinctive willingness of contemporaries to believe
in catastrophist geology, since it chimed so well with evangelical ideas of providential dispensation.

According to Cuvier, the only world-destroying catastrophe that had taken
place during biblical history was Noah's flood, a crucially important occurrence
for all those who feared that science might be about to dethrone religion. Hence
the official and popular acclaim accorded to the Paleyan Oxford geologist
William Buckland, who claimed to have unearthed evidence in favour of the
scriptural account in his *Vindiciae Geologicae* (1820) and *Reliquiae Diluvianae*
(1823). Government ministers took Buckland's claim to have harnessed geology
to the cause of revealed religion very seriously. Liverpool made him a canon
of Christ Church in 1825, while Peel, a close friend, appointed him Dean of
Westminster twenty years later.[122] If liberal Tories had a spiritual guide, however,
it was not Buckland but Chalmers. Peel and Huskisson were both devotees,
and Canning was reported to have alternated between tears and 'raptures' as he
listened to one of his sermons. Chalmers was variously described as a second
Luther, whose influence rolled 'like a mighty wave of good over the whole surface
of the land',[123] 'a man greatly lifted out of the region of mere flesh and blood',[124]
who 'may be said rather to have created than to have belonged to an era'.[125] 'His
was a voice that filled the world . . . from end to end.'[126] 'Not one man [but]
a thousand men.'[127] A charismatic and captivating preacher, he was a parish minister
for many years before becoming Professor of Moral Philosophy at St Andrews
in 1823 and Professor of Theology at Edinburgh five years later. He mainly
operated in a Scottish context, but was widely revered and alternatively reviled
in the United Kingdom as a whole, and he was particularly close to members
of the English evangelical establishment such as Wilberforce, Bickersteth,
Teignmouth, Buxton, Elgin, Grenville, Zachary Macaulay, and the Grants.

Whether Chalmers merely dispensed conventional wisdom, the man on the
Clapham omnibus as it were, or whether (to use his own word) he 'impregnated'
the nation with his views is debatable. In the 1820s his fame partly rested on his

[121] And it was not until the 1860s that his cyclical theory regarding the symbiotic operation of erosion
and sedimentation became generally accepted (V. A. Eyles, 'James Hutton', in *Dictionary of Scientific
Biography*, ed. C. C. Gillispie (New York, 1970–90), vi. 584. See below, pp. 449–50).

[122] Hilton, *Age of Atonement*, 150–2, 235–6; Nicolaas A. Rupke, *The Great Chain of History: William
Buckland and the English School of Geology (1814–1849)* (Oxford, 1983), 31–88.

[123] Patrick E. Dove, *Account of Andrew Yarranton, the Founder of English Political Economy* (Edinburgh,
1854), 100–1.

[124] [W. E. Gladstone], 'Memoir of Norman Macleod', *Church Quarterly Review*, 2 (1876), 494.

[125] Hugh Miller, cited in John Anderson, *Reminiscences of Dr Chalmers* (1851), 401.

[126] *Reminiscences and Opinions of Sir Francis Hastings Doyle 1813–1885* (1886), 102.

[127] Sydney Smith, cited by Ian Henderson in Robert Selby Wright (ed.), *Fathers of the Kirk: Some
Leaders of the Church in Scotland from the Reformation to the Reunion* (1960), 130.

practical experiments in a poor district of Glasgow to demonstrate that private charity—properly organized on a parochial basis of home visiting, personal contact, and religious exhortation—could sustain the population happily without the need for compulsory poor relief and its encouragement to procreation. For the thousands who thought like Chalmers, private charity was always superior to public provision. First, it enabled the philanthropist to please his Maker and appease his conscience, which was no light matter given that God held the rich accountable for their wealth. They might not face the workhouse like the poor, but they were held to be spiritually inferior, and there was an eternity of less eligibility awaiting them in the bowels of the earth. It followed that charitable acts should be private, personal affirmations, conquering the selfish desire to keep one's money to oneself. It was after all one's state of mind and heart and not one's actions that would open the gates of Heaven. Secondly, private charity created a desirable 'gift relationship' between giver and receiver based on personal feelings such as condescension and what Chalmers called 'loving gratulation', whereas compulsory poor laws led the poor to think that they had a right to relief, which reduced charity to a matter of 'angry litigation'. Finally, it was only by visiting the poor in their own homes and getting to know them— things which bureaucratic boards of guardians did not do—that philanthropists could distinguish properly between deserving and undeserving poor. For if charitable giving was necessary to save the souls of the rich, indiscriminate giving might easily ruin those of the poor. God tested the rich according to what they did with their wealth, but he judged the poor by how they coped with their poverty.

There was no compulsory poor relief in Scotland before 1845, and Chalmers wanted the English to give up theirs. Few were prepared to go that far. Even Malthus, who acknowledged Chalmers as 'my ablest and best ally', was reluctant to press his own theories to such a logical conclusion. Nevertheless, a belief in deterrent poor laws and minimal social welfare was at the heart of liberal Toryism. It was advocated by evangelicals such as Chalmers, Wilberforce, and Sumner, but was not confined to them. Copleston, for example, ridiculed the idea of 'compulsory love', and argued that misplaced philanthropy did more harm than good.

In this lies the great merit and the everlasting value of [Malthus'] work. It was natural indeed to think that all truth would be harmonious and consistent—that the universe was not constructed upon a plan so preposterous, as to tempt to the execution of that which is abhorrent to the very nature and end of our being. It is the high distinction of the *Essay on Population* to have demonstrated that such is the fact—that all endeavours to embody benevolence in the law, and thus impiously as it were to effect by human laws what the Author of the system of nature has not effected by his laws, must be abortive— that this ignorant struggle against evil really enlarges instead of contracting the kingdom of evil—that it not only must fail, but that it involves great mischief both during the attempt and in its consequences.[128]

The case for deterrent poor laws and for preferring private to public poor relief was often put, by Chalmers and others, in utilitarian terms as a way of teaching citizens to help themselves, 'a hand up rather than a hand out', but Chalmers's real motive was the religious one, which he put with chilling clarity in private: '*I should count the salvation of a single individual more important than the rescue of a whole empire from pauperism.*'[129] It summed up the conventional social thought of the period, and overturned the previous conventional wisdom, as expressed by Paley, that the poor had a claim of right founded in the law of nature, and that the care of the poor should be the principal object of all laws.

At this point a caveat is necessary. Although liberal Toryism was fired by an evangelical ethos, there were many self-styled evangelicals whose views were diametrically opposed. Welfare paternalists such as Lord Shaftesbury and Henry Drummond, for example, fell into the category of Chalmers's 'weak and limited sentimentalists'. However, these *so-called* evangelicals differed from Chalmers and the Clapham Sect in every possible way. In their expectation of an imminent Apocalypse (Adventism) and in their rejection of natural law, they had more in common philosophically with Coleridge than with Bentham, and more in common politically with high and Ultra Tories than with liberals.[130]

THE PARADOXES OF POLITICAL ECONOMY

Adam Smith's *An Inquiry into the Nature and Causes of the Wealth of Nations* (1776) made economics central to discussions of moral and political philosophy. The Continental blockade, Corn Laws, Property Tax, and cash payments brought fiscal and monetary issues to the forefront of debate. And David Ricardo's *On the Principles of Political Economy and Taxation* (1817) introduced enough analytical rigour to convince many that it was a genuine science with predictive qualities. In 1821 the Political Economy Club was founded with Ricardo as its chief luminary. One of its rules, drafted by James Mill, enjoined members to 'ascertain if any doctrines hostile to sound views . . . have been propagated', to 'refute such erroneous doctrines, and controvert their influence'. *Un*sound doctrines were of course mercantilist ones, especially government intervention to increase the balance of trade and the level of gold reserves. 'We hear nothing on all sides, at dinners, parties, in church and at the theatre, but discussions on political economy,' wrote a bored diplomat in 1826, and in the same year the diarist Charles Greville observed that 'all men are become political economists'.

[128] [Copleston], *Second Letter to Peel*, 22.
[129] Chalmers to James Brown, 30 Jan. 1819, Edinburgh University Library, MS DC. 2. 57, fo. 62.
[130] For these apocalyptic evangelicals, see below, pp. 401–6.

Whereas Bernard Mandeville, in *The Fable of the Bees* (1714), had argued for a surplus of exports over imports in order to bring precious metals into the country, Smith argued for a surplus of production over consumption in order to increase the capital stock. Whereas Mandeville had attributed growth mainly to demand-side factors, such as spending on luxuries, Smith emphasized the supply side, e.g. the division of labour and habits of saving and parsimony by the rich. Since in his view the main stimuli to production were population growth and men's natural desire to rise in society, it was best for wages to be high, but profits should be kept low in the interests of frugality and capital accumulation. Finally, Mandeville had called on 'skilful politicians' to promote that demand which he thought was all-important, whereas Smith insisted that growth would occur automatically so long as legislators forswore 'management' in favour of a 'system of natural liberty'. He opposed corporations, primogeniture, and entail because they interfered with market forces; even chivalry was suspect because it encouraged non-profit-maximizing behaviour.

Radicals such as Godwin opposed Smith's analysis on the grounds that 'any increase in the productiveness of labour achieved through capital accumulation, the extension of markets, and the division of labour merely impoverished those who were already poor'.[131] More relevant here were divisions among political economists, first between Smith and Malthus and then between Malthus and Ricardo. Smith welcomed population growth; Malthus saw in it the harbinger of catastrophe. Smith thought that hope of advancement was the surest incentive to labour; Malthus considered that the fear of downward mobility was more effective. Smith believed in market forces; Malthus wanted intervention (e.g. corn laws) to prevent too much capital from accumulating in the manufacturing sector. The shift from Smithian to Malthusian ways of thinking—from the natural harmony of interests to ecological competition—marked a transition from optimism to pessimism regarding the prospects for economic growth. Ricardo was also pessimistic if less fatalistic. He accepted Malthus' population theory and shared his sympathy with the opposition Whigs.[132] Both men were amiable and discussed their differences without rancour, but those differences were significant nonetheless. Ricardo wanted wages kept at subsistence level and the maximum possible investment in manufacturing industry in order to boost economic growth, Malthus was torn between wanting manufacturing to expand in the hope that it might *inhibit* growth, and not wanting it to on the grounds that industry was socially deleterious. To Ricardo there was always a need for more capital accumulation in order to avoid the horrors of a 'stationary state', whereas the latter appealed to Malthus as a natural way to cure economies that

---

[131] Godwin's views as glossed in Winch, *Riches and Poverty*, 258.

[132] In fact he had quite strong reformist tendencies, though he avoided party-political entanglements (Murray Milgate and Shannon C. Stimson, *Ricardian Politics* (Princeton, 1991)).

were running into glut. Ricardo disparaged landlords because their consumption of luxuries was largely unproductive, while Malthus defended them on the same grounds. Whereas Ricardo opposed public works, Malthus supported them, but not because he thought they would trigger the multiplier, as maintained by Keynesians a century later. Instead, like Lord Liverpool, he hoped that they would have the opposite effect by diverting resources from more productive private enterprise. That is also why Malthus defended expenditure by the idle rich—say on carriages, servants, and estate improvement. After 1815 such luxuries could even be seen as substituting for the much more unpleasant type of unproductive labour that had gone into fighting Napoleon.

Many of Ricardo's theories were superseded within a few years of his death in 1823, but in one crucial respect he won the argument over Malthus. His endorsement of Say's Law of Markets—that supply creates its own demand, meaning that overproduction could never be the cause of long-term or structural unemployment—was widely accepted by the 1830s and held sway for a century until Keynes reasserted the dangers of under-consumptionism.[133] The victory perhaps owed less to intellectual than to political factors. Britain's ability to export its surplus to Third World countries meant that Malthus' theory of general gluts was never put to the test. Secondly, Malthus' calls for pump priming and other means of regulating demand fell foul of the overriding desire of all Opposition politicians to cut taxes and jobs. The Whigs constantly blamed the Government when things went wrong with the economy, but they were inhibited from calling for government action to put them right, since that would have meant the appointment of yet more officials, all inclined to support their ministerial patrons.

Perhaps Ricardo's most important contribution was to make contemporaries think of society not as an aggregate of free-thinking individuals, but as landlords, capitalists, and workers locked together in a zero-sum economy. His adoption of Smith's labour theory of value, which held that the price or value of any product was mainly defined by the amount of labour that went into its production, led to the subsistence theory of wages, meaning that in a competitive market entrepreneurs would inevitably push down wages as far as they could, i.e. just enough to keep the labourer and his or her family alive. By postulating a single fund out of which wages, profits, and rents had to be paid, Ricardo proposed that any rise in wages above subsistence would be at the expense of employers (the inverse profits–wages theory) and would therefore impair growth. This was the obverse of a natural harmony of interests, and explains why political economy was called the 'dismal science', the butt of Victorian moralists such as Carlyle, Dickens, and Ruskin. The implication was that, however successful a firm and however

---

[133] Jean-Baptiste Say was a French economist.

successful the economy, wages could never rise above subsistence without jeopardizing the future. It was an unappetizing brew, and Chalmers's bromide— that the poor could raise their wages by limiting their own numbers through sexual abstinence—did not make it any more palatable.

By the 1830s it was obvious that, as a ruling-class apologia, Ricardianism would not do. A theory which defined value in terms of labour yet did not allow labourers to rise above subsistence was obviously flawed. There emerged a group of writers known ironically as Ricardian socialists because, like Marx, they used his theory of value to attack the capitalist system which he had celebrated. The most important of these was Thomas Hodgskin, a prolific journalist and one of many middle-ranking naval officers rendered footloose by the end of the wars. Like many self-made men he lived on the edge of frustration, was in constant expectation of social rebuffs, and solaced himself by becoming a radical reformer and scourge of the establishment.[134] In *Labour Defended against the Claims of Capital* (1825) Hodgskin argued that workers were the only source of wealth and that the employers' profits amounted to expropriation. Moreover, since society was a 'progressive organism', the workers would before long secure their just deserts.

All this prompted the capitalist classes to seek a new theory of value, one that did not attribute the credit for economic success entirely to labourers. It was provided by J. S. Mill, Nassau Senior, and Richard Cobden, who adopted the utility theory of value as expounded by Say and popularized by Marcet. This held that the price or value of any product (including labour) depended primarily on supply and demand.[135] In the 1840s this became the accepted view and, while it might not have converted many politicians to free trade, without it many fewer politicians would have been converted. The standard objection to free trade in corn, for example, in the days when the labour theory of value still held sway, was that it would lead to cheaper food, which would enable the bosses to drive down wages, thereby enabling them to sell their wares more cheaply, but leaving their workers no better and possibly worse off. Richard Cobden's polemical achievement was to persuade contemporaries that wages could rise while prices came down, that free trade would boost the economy, which would raise the demand for labour and also its remuneration. In 1847 Peel explained his apparent conversion to free trade by the 'many concurring proofs that the wages of labour do not vary with the price of corn'. 'Wages do not vary with the price

---

[134] David Stack, *Nature and Artifice: The Life and Thought of Thomas Hodgskin (1787–1869)* (Woodbridge, 1998), 34–61.

[135] The utility, or market, theory of wages was followed in the second half of the century by the development of marginal utility theory, which enabled the entrepreneur and the investor to displace the labourer from centre stage by making the successful anticipation of movements in supply and demand a key element in the success of manufacturing firms.

of provisions. They do vary with the increase of capital, with the prosperity of the country, with the increased power to employ labour; but there is no immediate relation between wages and provisions—or if there be a relation, it is an inverse ratio.'[136] In its insistence that all classes of the community could benefit, Cobdenism marked a return to optimism regarding the natural harmony of interests. The key ingredient was the promise of economic growth, which overturned Malthus' belief in a finite economy and a finite ecology.

Although belief in growth and development did not become conventional wisdom until somewhat later, it began to form in the public consciousness during the 1830s and 1840s. This was thanks in part to Whig pundits like Senior, who continued to believe that Malthusian pressures would reduce living standards to a minimum, but also thought that it was possible to raise tastes, and so raise the standard in absolute terms. If evangelical Malthusianism was the philosophy in office during the years from Pitt to Peel, the possibility of a modicum of progress was kept alive by the Opposition. It is time to return to the Whigs.

PHILOSOPHIC WHIGGISM

The leader of the Whigs in the Commons admitted in 1826 that they were virtually 'extinct'. 'The poor Opposition will never make any more whips about anything.'[137] His despair was understandable given that the party had tasted office for less than fourteen months in the previous forty-three years, and had now lost some of its smartest clothes to the Canningites. Prosperity seemed to have 'driven reform almost out of the heads of the reformers', and once-thriving Whig clubs, like the one at York, had sunk into torpor.[138] To many former Foxites, the situation appeared terminal.

One factor helping to sustain cohesion through the dark decades was intellectual, in which respect Holland House was less important than the Lansdowne salons in London and at Bowood in Wiltshire. In the 1790s the first Marquess (formerly Lord Shelburne) had assembled a coterie of savants including Bentham, Dumont, Price, Horne Tooke, Priestley and Romilly, and new members such as Ricardo, Hallam, and Maria Edgeworth were introduced by Henry Petty, who succeeded as Third Marquess of Lansdowne in 1809. He represented the mechanistic, Utilitarian, and political economy sides of Whiggism, which explains his growing rapprochement with the liberal Tories,[139] though he did not share

---

[136] *HPD*3 xxxiii. 72 (22 Jan. 1846); Peel, *Memoirs*, ii. 102.

[137] Tierney to Holland, 16 and 24 Mar. 1826, Holland MS 51584, fos. 111, 115.

[138] Lansdowne to Holland, 17 Jan. 1825, in Austin Mitchell, *The Whigs in Opposition 1815–1830* (Oxford, (1967), 182; Peter Brett, *The Rise and Fall of the York Whig Club 1818–1830* (York, 1989), 22–7.

[139] Especially from 1827 onwards, and especially with Huskisson on economic policy and with Peel on criminal law reform.

their evangelical moral sense. Gradually, however, a number of other Whig intellectuals began to mark out a more distinctive position. Their immediate aim was to redefine their position in relation to Radicals, so as to avoid being overtaken on the left, but the effect was also to put clearer water between themselves and liberal Tories.

For example, Whig historians such as Francis Palgrave, Henry Hallam, James Mackintosh, and John Allen had traditionally agreed with venerable radicals like John Cartwright in tracing the origins of Parliament to before the Norman Conquest.

Divine immortal Alfred! ... in whose manly bosom glowed the love of liberty, steady, ardent, inextinguishable! ... who in an ignorant age didst [see] ... that *free parliaments, juries, organization*, and *an armed people*, are the true foundations of national freedom and security; and who, with thine own hands, didst lay the deep foundations, and rear, to an adoring world, the glorious edifice![140]

Tragically this Anglo-Saxon 'democracy', in which knights of the shire had been elected by all freemen, including mere yeomen and archers, had since been compromised by fourteenth- and fifteenth-century statutes, which led to the growth of borough-mongers and of Old Corruption generally. Meanwhile, Tory historians such as Walter Scott, R. H. Inglis, and J. W. Croker claimed that these same statutes had *created* Parliament, which was therefore feudal in origin. During the 1820s, however, Whig intellectuals developed a new theory, partly to counter the democratic implications of the Anglo-Saxon thesis, and partly to steer a distinctive line between Tories and Radicals. First Thomas Creevey, and then Hallam, Palgrave, and Mackintosh, conceded that Parliament had originated in Edward I's writs of summons, but whereas Tories like Inglis and Croker argued that parliamentary representation by charter had rested in *particular* boroughs, Creevey claimed that Edward had ordered *every* city and *every* borough to send two representatives. He equally distanced himself from Radicals by affirming that it had originally been the electors' duty to pay their representatives' wages, thereby ensuring that only wealthy townsmen in thriving boroughs would respond to Edward's call.[141] The implication was that the rotten boroughs of the nineteenth century had been the Manchesters of the Middle Ages, and it foreshadowed the claims of Whig reformers in 1831 that parliamentary constituencies should be based on large centres of population rather than on historic boroughs.[142] As history it was bogus, and Creevey must have known it.

[140] John Cartwright, *An Appeal, Civil and Military, on the Subject of the English Constitution*, 2nd edn. (1799), 10. See also [John Allen], 'Constitution of Parliament', and 'History of English Legislature', *ER* 26 (1816), 347; 35 (1821), 3–12.
[141] Thomas Creevey, *Letters to Lord John Russell* (1826), 17–25; R. J. Smith, *The Gothic Bequest: Medieval Institutions in British Thought, 1688–1863* (Cambridge, 1987), 165–6.
[142] See below, pp. 431–2.

A more dramatic clash between Whigs and Radicals occurred when Mackintosh called Bentham a democrat, and Mill accused Mackintosh of favouring despotism. Since making his name with *Vindiciae Gallicae* (1791), a powerful riposte to both Burke and Paine, Mackintosh had acquired the reputation of a clever though indolent barrister, but he sprang back to life in 1818 by attacking Bentham's plans for universal suffrage and the secret ballot, which he thought would lead to a tyranny of the majority. Later he denounced Bentham's 'selfish system of morals', his conflation of ethics and jurisprudence, and his neglect of 'feeling' and 'intuition'.[143] James Mill responded by condemning Mackintosh's 'sentimental system', which encouraged judges to take a criminal's motives into account when sentencing, and thereby licensed them to act arbitrarily. Meanwhile, in 1829 Macaulay launched a vicious and 'devastating' attack on Utilitarians in the *Edinburgh Review*, firstly for advocating democracy, which would lead to revolution, and more fundamentally for their rational, a priori, deductive philosophy, which, he believed, had blinded them to beauty, ornament, fine art, poetry, literature, chivalry, sentiment, eloquence, and irrationality. The *Westminster Review* offered a feeble riposte, but Macaulay's assault undoubtedly 'caused havoc in the utilitarian ranks'. 'The rout of the utilitarians was complete.'[144]

Mackintosh's approach has been described as 'the very antithesis of Bentham's and Mill's. Where they saw society as a mechanism, he saw it as an organism. They appealed to reason; he appealed to history.'[145] So far this would align his Whiggism with high Toryism, but of course they were very different, as Macaulay's lambasting of Southey made clear.[146] In fact, a new Whig ideology was emerging, one which appealed to history but also and more importantly to the future. This philosophic Whiggism, as it is sometimes called, emanated from the 1790s when young grandees, cut off by war from Leipzig, Göttingen, and Leiden universities, went instead to Scotland where they imbibed the final draughts of the Scottish Enlightenment, a headier brew than was on offer at other Whig redoubts such as Trinity College, Cambridge, and Christ Church, Oxford. The spirit of David Hume, William Robertson, Adam Ferguson, and Adam Smith was now distilled in the teachings and writings of John Millar of Glasgow and Dugald Stewart of Edinburgh (the 'Athens of the North'). Many young Whigs sat at the latter's feet, including Mackintosh, Erskine, Lauderdale, Lansdowne, Brougham, Jeffrey, Horner, Cockburn, and Russell.[147] Stewart's

---

[143] James Mackintosh, *Dissertation on the Progress of Ethical Philosophy* (1830; 2nd edn. Edinburgh, 1836), 284–313.

[144] William Thomas, *The Philosophic Radicals: Nine Studies in Theory and Practice 1817–1841* (Oxford, 1979), 135–40; John Clive, *Thomas Babington Macaulay: The Shaping of the Historian* (1973), 128–33; Donald Winch, in Stefan Collini, Donald Winch, and John Burrow, *That Noble Science of Politics: A Study in Nineteenth-Century Intellectual History* (Cambridge, 1983), 91–126.

[145] Thomas, *Philosophic Radicals*, 125.   [146] See above, p. 321.

[147] Also Palmerston, a liberal Tory or Canningite who joined the Whigs in 1830 and later led them.

lectures 'were like the opening of the Heavens', rhapsodized Cockburn; 'I felt that I had a soul.'[148] The hyperbole reflects the fact that Pitt's Terror was especially brutal in Scotland. In such a feverish atmosphere, rather like the Prague Spring of the 1960s, political opposition was forced to take an academic guise. Mackintosh, Horner, and numerous other young Whigs were members of the Edinburgh Speculative Society, where they earnestly debated the possibilities of utopia.

What would they have learned from Stewart? To challenge Utilitarianism, to adopt Smith's economics but to place it in a physiocratic or agrarian framework, and to be relaxed about population growth and ecological catastrophe. Stewart had no time for Chalmers's 'miraculous' and market-led 'reformation in the moral character of a people', since changes in national 'habits and ideas' could only be effected through positive laws. He adhered to Thomas Reid's common-sense philosophy, with its assumption that moral feelings were innate and its emphasis on motives rather than consequences, and he developed a theory of collective psychology in opposition to the liberal individualism that was becoming fashionable in England. Alongside Stewart, John Allen gave extramural lectures on animal economy (1794–1802), which advanced 'the notion of life as process rather than principle; the idea of the body as an interdependent whole in which there was no predominant centre; the recognition that vital operations might be . . . subject to the same laws as inorganic matter . . . that function was, at least in principle, prior to structure'.[149] But above all young Whigs would have learned about the 'natural history of society' or 'conjectural history'. The central tenet of the Scottish Enlightenment was that societies progress through stages. So, in *Vindiciae Gallicae* for example, Mackintosh defended the French revolutionaries' legal innovations as legitimate adaptations to commercial society as it emerged naturally out of aristocracy. Five years later, in 1796, Richard Payne Knight, a Foxite MP, wrote a poem entitled *The Progress of Civil Society*, the first four books of which were devoted to hunting, pasturage, agriculture, and arts, manufactures, and commerce. In 1815 the sculptor Westmacott decorated the Woburn Temple of Liberty with an allegorical frieze showing the familiar progression from hunter–gathering to grazing or pastoral, then to arable farming, and finally trade.[150] And this was also the basis of the *Edinburgh Review*'s 'philosophic Whiggism', defined as an 'identification of modern European civilisation with the progress of commercial society' and a 'belief in the necessity for economic expansion'.[151]

---

[148] Henry Cockburn, *Memorials of His Time* (Edinburgh, 1856), 24–7, 45–6.

[149] L. S. Jacyna, *Philosophic Whigs: Medicine, Science and Citizenship in Edinburgh, 1789–1848* (1994), 72–3. See below, pp. 443–5.   [150] Penny, 'Whig Cult of Fox', *P&P* 70 (1976), 98–9.

[151] Biancamaria Fontana, *Rethinking the Politics of Commercial Society: The 'Edinburgh Review' 1802–1832* (Cambridge, 1985), 183–4.

So, whereas high Tories and most Radicals located truth in the past, and liberal Tories, Utilitarians, and natural theologians lived in a timeless mechanical present, philosophic Whigs looked to the future. Mackintosh challenged Peel's and Bentham's conception of jurisprudence as a set of timeless and universal rules to curb 'unruly passions', arguing instead that 'the criminal law could never be effectually administered, but when it was in perfect unison with the moral feelings and sympathies of the people'.[152] In this he anticipated the view of mid-nineteenth-century liberals like Gladstone, Bagehot, and Dicey that laws should evolve with changing social mores. But perhaps the most illuminating clash between the thinking of the liberal Tories and that of the philosophic Whigs was Scrope's attack on Chalmers's Bridgewater Treatise.

George Poulett Scrope was an advanced Whig MP (1833–67) and a prolific pamphleteer, who unconventionally placed articles in *The Quarterly* in the hope of converting the enemy.[153] He was also one of the first geologists to realize that Hutton's discovery of deep time made it possible to discard functional, cyclical, and catastrophist explanations such as deluges and volcanoes, and to depict the past in terms of gradual, smooth, non-violent progression instead. 'The leading idea,' he wrote in 1827, 'the sound of which to the ear of the student of Nature seems continually echoed from every part of her works, is—Time!—Time!—Time!'[154] In both his uniformitarian geology and his contagionist understanding of disease, Scrope challenged the prevailing dualism which attributed all natural changes to external forces. Domestically he defended 'the rights of industry' as against those of 'the banking system', thereby helping to shift the debate away from a town–country axis, and focusing instead on the antagonism between agriculture and manufacturing on the one hand, finance on the other. As a Whig he rejected Owenite socialism, believing that 'human society . . . has hitherto . . . proceeded on the principle of *competition*, that is to say, of individual exertion for individual gratification . . . The co-operative principle . . . has never yet been found to lead man one step forward in the improvement of his condition and the enlargement of his faculties.' Nor did he accept Hodgskin's doctrine that the labourer had a claim 'for the whole produce of industry', leaving nothing for the capitalist and landowner. 'The maintenance of the right of property is the *sine qua non* of production, wealth, and civilization.' Unfortunately, property had already been attacked, not by violent mobs, but 'silently and stealthily' as a result of the deflation caused by the resumption of cash payments. 'Few of the

---

[152] *HPD2* ix. 413 (21 May 1823); Randall McGowen, 'A Powerful Sympathy: Terror, the Prison, and Humanitarian Reform in Early Nineteenth-Century Britain', *JBS* 25 (1986), 312–34.

[153] This must be why so many historians have mistaken him for a Tory.

[154] G. Poulett Scrope, *Memoir on the Geology of Central France* (1827), 165; Martin J. S. Rudwick, 'Poulett Scrope on the Volcanoes of Auvergne: Lyellian Time and Political Economy', *British Journal for the History of Science*, 7 (1974), 205–42.

sufferers can explain or understand how it happened, but the fact is very plain to them, that they have somehow lost a great deal of money, and other persons have got hold of it.' Worse still, the 'currency juggle' had confiscated £1.5 million from the wealth-creating, productive, and industrious classes—'the country gentleman of not over-grown estate . . . the farmer, the tradesman, the merchant, the manufacturer, and the labourer'—whereas tax receivers, moneyed men, and placemen had found that their incomes, while remaining nominally the same, could purchase more. Reflation, by contrast, would give a 'great and constant impulse to industry', but Scrope did not (like Attwood) want to devalue the standard, since that would merely destroy credit and create new injustices. The only solution was to remove the Bank of England's monopoly of note issue within 65 miles of London. Free banking would make credit more elastic, and enable it to 'adapt itself to the necessities of commerce'.[155]

Holding these views, it is no wonder that Scrope should have loathed Chalmers's Bridgewater Treatise, with its 'monomania' on the subjects of over-population and overproduction. Regarding 'excrescent' or 'redundant' population as a 'blotch' and a 'distemper', Chalmers subordinated all other considerations to 'the great object of retarding the increase of our numbers'. Worse still, he regarded any social welfare policies such as poor relief, home colonization, or assisted emigration as 'evil', on the grounds that anything that improved the material condition of the labouring classes would merely increase their numbers and their poverty. 'Evil, be thou our good!' was Scrope's comment on that doctrine. Worst of all, Chalmers blamed poverty on personal improvidence, and wanted to make its relief voluntary, 'a thing of love, not law'. Scrope expostulated,

The poor have a decided claim, in justice, to a support from off the land on which Providence has placed them . . . Such a provision, therefore, instead of being a matter of charity and benevolence . . . is but the legal concession of a right antecedent even to that of the owners of the soil—a divine right—a right based on the eternal and immutable principles of intuitive justice.

Underlying the bitterness was a chasm of mutual incomprehension. Scrope applied his discovery of 'Time' forwards as well as back. He conceded that the Malthusian nightmare might strike in the distant future, but since there were lands still to be cultivated in England and elsewhere, the enemy was not yet 'at the gates'. He complained that Chalmers, in wishing to 'starve the present race of man . . . for the comfort of his posterity in the hundredth generation', was mistaking 'ultimate for immediate effects', and 'assuming ultimate effects to be constantly present'. Scrope was equally perplexed by Chalmers's confidence that, were the relationship between food supply and demand for food to alter,

---

[155] [G. P. Scrope], 'The Rights of Industry and the Banking System', *QR* 47 (1832), 409–19.

adjustment to a new market equilibrium would occur 'with almost the speed of an explosion'.[156] Scrope could not see that, for Chalmers, with his finite sense of time, his awareness of mechanical and cyclical motion but *not* progression, and his search for a Final Cause rather than historical causes, it simply made no sense to say that food supply was a long-term rather than a short-term problem. In the evangelicals' cosmogony one could not distinguish between a present and an ultimate threat, for the Judgement of souls was here and now, ubiquitous and continual.

Both were passionate free-marketeers, but they envisaged very different outcomes. Chalmers's view that society would be cured, 'not by means of economic enlargements, but of moral principles and restraints', baffled Scrope, who ridiculed the 'Utopia of a "self-contained" nation'.

If there be any one desire or design more manifest than another throughout the works of nature, or more worthy of the benevolence of nature's great Author, it is that there should be the utmost possible multiplication of beings endowed with life and capacity for enjoyment. We do not see that nature has contented herself with establishing little groups of organized beings in snug corners, to thrive there in security and content, through a nice adjustment of their numbers to the food within their reach . . . No! abundance, extension, multiplication, competition for room, is the order of creation.

What emerges is Scrope's enthusiasm for manufacturing civilization, in contrast to Chalmers's agrarian bias and 'Godly commonwealth ideal'.[157]

It is a constant principle of human nature, that our wants increase with the means of gratifying them. And well is it that we are so constituted. Were man the sober, chastened, and easily contented animal, which moralists have sometimes, with false views of human welfare, attempted to make him . . . his species would probably have forever remained in a condition little superior to that of the cattle he has domesticated. Art, science, literature,—all the pleasures of refinement, taste, and intellectual occupation, would have been unknown . . . and the prospect . . . of a progressive and indefinite amelioration in the circumstances of mankind, would have been closed at once. But it is not so . . . [158]

At the end of the seventeenth century so-called 'country', 'civic humanist', or 'republican' Whigs had presented a static vision of society, based on landownership as the source of all wealth and the only title to political power. For much of the following century they were challenged by 'court' Whigs, whose social vision was based on economic growth and on commerce as the highest stage of civilization. The governing ideology of the first half of the nineteenth century—broadly liberal Tory and fed by evangelicalism—was also based on commerce, but the vision was non-progressive in so far as it sought to maintain and justify the

[156] Thomas Chalmers, *The Christian and Civic Economy of Large Towns* (Glasgow, 1821–6), iii. 315.

[157] Stewart J. Brown, *Thomas Chalmers and the Godly Commonwealth in Scotland* (Oxford, 1982).

[158] [G. P. Scrope], 'Dr. Chalmers *on Political Economy*', *QR* 48 (1832), 40, 44, 49, 61–6.

status quo. A new challenge came from Whigs like Scrope, who hailed manufacturing industry as representing an even higher stage, and as bringing with it
'wealth, comfort, splendour, taste, civilization—all that distinguishes us from
a horde of barbarians'. Philosophic Whiggism thus envisioned a new type of
society, one that was to be launched into political orbit by Macaulay in the
reform debates of 1831 when he eulogized the 'progress of society', the 'development of the human mind', and 'the law which regulates the growth of
communities'.[159]

Country, Court, and philosophic Whiggism all reflected masculine perspectives, yet without constraining the freedom of women to express themselves.
The only barrier to making oneself heard during the Whig ascendancy before
1780 was one of rank, not gender. Under Pitt and his successors, by contrast,
women seem to have been silenced, yet they found ways of asserting themselves,
and invisibility may even have enhanced their influence. Despite appearances,
it is appropriate to include them in a chapter on ruling-class ideologies.

THE STATUS OF WOMEN AND IDEAS ABOUT GENDER

English society in the first half of the nineteenth century was ostensibly patriarchal. The vast majority of upper- and middle-class men assumed that their
womenfolk were included in themselves as wives, daughters, aunts, and sisters,
and it never occurred to them that dependants of either sex should vote on their
own behalf. A wife had no legal identity as distinct from her husband's. If she
had property it passed to him at marriage,[160] and whereas he could divorce or
dump her, she would find it very hard to escape. When, in 1848, a Mrs Dawson
brought a bill of divorce on account of her husband's adultery, backed up by
the fact that he had beaten her with riding whip and hairbrush, her petition was
laughed out of court in the House of Lords.[161] Among the labouring classes,
failed marriages usually ended in his desertion or her eviction, though the
practice of selling wives at market, strongly condemned by moralists, rose to a
peak in the 1820s and 1830s and served the purposes of divorce, since the
publicity prevented either party from subsequently claiming marital rights.[162]
The reform of the representative system in 1832 skewed matters even further.
In the first session of the reformed Parliament a widow's legal right to dower
was abolished, and in the second the bastardy laws were tightened. (The authors
of the 1834 Poor Law Report were outraged by the fact that unmarried mothers
had hitherto been able to claim child maintenance from any man whom they

[159] *HPD3* ix. 388 (16 Dec. 1831).
[160] By 1790 it had become possible for a woman carrying on a separate business to hold and manage
property separately so long as she had her husband's consent.
[161] Lawrence Stone, *Road to Divorce: England 1530–1987* (Oxford, 1990), 361–2.
[162] Ibid. 143–8; E. P. Thompson, *Customs in Common* (1991), 409–11.

cared to cite, with or without evidence. In their view, the female was almost always at fault, since 'a single illegitimate child is seldom any expense, and two or three are a source of positive profit'.[163] The only significant step in the opposite direction was the Infant Custody Act of 1839, passed after a long campaign of publishing and lobbying by Caroline Norton, whose children had been snatched by her estranged but not divorced husband. From now on the custody of children under seven was vested in the mother, provided that she had not been found by a court of law to have committed adultery, while the other parent was accorded right of access.

Meanwhile, the scope for women to participate in public life became even more circumscribed. Admittedly, it made no difference in practice when the 1832 Reform Act explicitly confined the franchise to 'male persons' for the first time, since women who were also substantial householders had not voted in parliamentary elections for at least 150 years. But it did make a difference three years later when the Municipal Corporations Act imposed the same limitation, since property-owning widows and spinsters had been allowed to vote in most parish and Poor Law elections thanks to a court ruling of 1739.[164] Even the People's Charter, which represented the high point of working-class protest, only called for universal *manhood* suffrage.[165] The general opinion remained that of the late eighteenth-century radical Major Cartwright, who argued that parliamentary election was 'an essential part of dominion, and that the female is by a law of nature put under the dominion of the male'.[166]

The scope for exercising informal political influence was also narrowing. So long as elections had been primarily social affairs, revolving around family influence more than national issues, women could direct campaigns and exploit local contacts. They participated in treating and canvassing, and though Georgiana, Duchess of Devonshire, was abused for allegedly kissing butchers in the Westminster campaign of 1784, her offence was to break a class taboo, not a gender one.[167] The adjudication of controverted elections—a significant political process—was frequently affected by testamentary depositions, a circumstance that privileged women since they were most likely to know which of their neighbours owned a hearth (the qualification for voting in potwalloper boroughs), and

[163] *Report from His Majesty's Commissioners for Inquiring into the Administration and Practical Expenditure of the Poor Laws, PP* 1834 xxvii. 93.

[164] Hobhouse's Vestries Act had formally recognized this female right to franchise as recently as 1831, but it has been suggested that MPs did not realize what they were doing, being preoccupied with the Reform Bill (James Vernon, *Politics and the People: A Study in English Political Culture, c.1815–1867* (Cambridge, 1993), 16–29).   [165] See below, pp. 620.

[166] Dinwiddy, *Radicalism and Reform,* 288.

[167] Elaine Chalus, ' "That Epidemical Madness": Women and Electoral Politics in the Late Eighteenth Century', in Hannah Barker and Elaine Chalus (eds.), *Gender in Eighteenth–Century England: Roles, Representations and Responsibilities* (1997).

to remember which ones had exercised the franchise in the past. Such oral testimony was vital in determining who got to vote at a time when records were few and contradictory, but its importance ceased in 1832 when jurisdiction was transferred to the registration courts.[168] Again, in the old freeman and burgage boroughs some male voters had exercised their rights by virtue of their spouses' estates, prompting local party organizers to canvass both man and wife. This too came to an end in the 1830s.

Before 1783 aristocratic women had often played an important role in high political infighting, a notable example being Rockingham's use of his wife in trying to woo the elder Pitt in 1765.[169] Grand Whiggery still existed, and society hostesses like Lady Jersey, Lady Melbourne, and the Duchess of Sutherland continued to oil its wheels, but since their party was perpetually out of office they no longer wielded 'power' exactly. The Duchess of Devonshire might possibly have helped in the gestation of the Talents Ministry in 1806, but that was all.[170] The Lennox girls lived glitteringly stellar lives, yet exercised not the slightest political clout. Harriet Granville, the wife of a British ambassador to Paris, was a worldly-wise and witty correspondent, yet her letters steered clear of public and political events.[171] Ideology and economic interest had driven out the older politics of family and faction, much to women's detriment. When after 1850 the threat of revolution disappeared, the social side of politics reasserted itself to some extent, allowing mid- and later Victorian women to serve as politicians' 'incorporated wives', working in 'active partnership' at dinners, balls, and assemblies to advance the family interests and their husbands' careers.[172] But this hardly ever occurred in the first half of the nineteenth century.

On the ministerial benches Pitt was celibate while Liverpool, Canning, Huskisson, and Peel—all highly uxorious—kept their family lives private. Wife and home represented release: 'My own dearest love, I long to get to town to you and to escape the insistent torments of business. I am quite bewildered.' Thus wrote Peel, who sustained this level of anguish in almost daily letters for three decades.[173] But the saddest document of the period is the diary of Harriet Arbuthnot, a feisty, opinionated, intelligent high Tory who was Castlereagh's confidante and Wellington's lover. She constantly fretted and chafed over

---

[168] Elaine Chalus, 'Women, Electoral Privilege and Practice in the Eighteenth Century', in Kathryn Gleadle and Sarah Richardson (eds.), *Women in British Politics, 1760–1860: The Power of the Petticoat*, (2000), 19–38. On the 1832 changes, see below, pp. 516–17.

[169] Elaine Chalus, 'Elite Women, Social Politics, and the Political World of Late Eighteenth-Century England', *HJ* 43 (2000), 669–97.

[170] Amanda Foreman, *Georgiana: Duchess of Devonshire* (1998), 377–90.

[171] *A Second Self: The Letters of Harriet Granville 1810–1845*, ed. Virginia Surtees (Salisbury, 1990).

[172] K. D. Reynolds, *Aristocratic Women and Political Society in Victorian Britain* (Oxford, 1988), 129–87; Pat Jalland, *Women, Marriage, and Politics 1860–1914* (Oxford, 1986), 189–249.

[173] Robert to Julia Peel, Nov. 1830, in *The Private Letters of Sir Robert Peel*, ed. George Peel (1920), 126.

the feeble and ineffective way in which those two fought their political corners, as well as over the failure of her wimpish and cuckolded husband (the Government's unofficial Chief Whip) to promote his own career. Her journal conveys very powerfully the frustrations felt by a politically minded woman in a system that had no room for her. Frances, Lady Shelley, observed that Mrs Arbuthnot 'had a man-like sense' and was 'devoid of womanly passion', thereby helping to perpetuate the conventional assumption that any woman who took an interest in men's affairs must by definition be in want of feminine sensibility.

Needless to say, women were not permitted to reinterpret Scripture. God's was so obviously a masculine way of thinking that such direct inspiration as to his purposes for mankind was beyond their capability. The Oxford philosopher Richard Whately was only half-joking when he apologized to his head of House for Mrs Whately's forwardness in such matters. 'I am afraid that my wife was rather saucy in finding many faults with some parts of your sermon. She has been what I would call spoiled in that respect, having always been allowed to maintain her opinions against mine whenever she sees fit.'[174] Even within the republic of letters it came to be accepted that women should steer clear of public affairs. The schoolteacher Anna Letitia Barbauld gave great offence with her poem *1811*, which predicted that the torch of Western civilization was about to pass from Britain to America.[175] She was unlucky in her timing, since the out-break of war with the United States a year later made her look unpatriotic, but what annoyed the crabby high Tory John Wilson Croker, writing in the *Quarterly Review*, was not what Barbauld thought but the fact that she should presume to think at all on such matters.

She must excuse us if we think that she has wandered from the course in which she was respectable and useful, and miserably mistaken both her powers and her duty, in exchanging the birchen for the satiric rod...We had hoped, indeed, that the empire might have been saved without the intervention of a lady-author...Not such, however, is her opinion; an irresistible impulse of public duty—a confident sense of commanding talents—have induced her to dash down her shagreen spectacles and her knitting needles, and to sally forth...in the magnanimous resolution of saving a sinking State, by the instrumentality of...a pamphlet in verse.[176]

More significant perhaps than Croker's condescension was the absence of voices on the other side. There was hardly any pressure for women's rights, except among groups that opposed the establishment in *all* its guises, such as Unitarians, Owenites, and the followers of Richard Carlile.

[174] Richard Whately to Edward Hawkins, 2 Mar. 1831, Oriel College, Oxford, MS Ca.
[175] See above, p. 255.
[176] [J. W. Croker], 'Mrs Barbauld's *Eighteen Hundred and Eleven*', *QR* 7 (1812), 309.

This may seem odd given that Mary Wollstonecraft's iconic text *A Vindication of the Rights of Woman* (1792) has often been seen as the first feminist call to arms. It was, however, a theoretical rather than a practical work. Although herself an Anglican, she wrote for a section of the chattering and discontented classes in the metropolis, mainly Unitarians and other rational Dissenters, who were excluded by religion from formal power.[177] She had already achieved notoriety as the author of *A Vindication of the Rights of Men* (1790), a riposte to Burke's *Reflections*. In it Wollstonecraft, who was a friend of Brissot and other leading Girondins, denounced the Bourbon tyrants and monkish priests of the Ancien Régime, and celebrated the National Assembly's 'glorious change' of direction. She also insisted that it was 'possible to render the poor happier in this world, without depriving them of the consolation which you gratuitously grant them in the next' (a sarcastic hit, not just at Burke, but at all those who used eschatology as a reason for withholding alms), and denied that it was 'always blasphemy to suggest that the law might not be omnipotent'. Clearly, this first *Vindication* was a radical rather than a feminist tract—the men referred to in the title were humans, not males—but it contained a powerful message about gender, sparked off by the author's revulsion against the purplest and most hackneyed passage in the whole of Burke's œuvre, his drooling over the doomed Marie-Antoinette:

It is now sixteen or seventeen years since I saw the queen of France, then the dauphiness, at Versailles; and surely never lighted on this orb, which she hardly seemed to touch, a more delightful vision. I saw her just above the horizon, decorating and cheering the elevated sphere she just began to move in,—glittering like the morning-star, full of life, and splendor, and joy. Oh! what a revolution!... I thought ten thousand swords must have leapt from their scabbards to avenge even a look that threatened her with insult.— But the age of chivalry is gone.—That of sophisters, œconomists, and calculators, has succeeded; and the glory of Europe is extinguished for ever. Never, never more, shall we behold that generous loyalty to rank and sex, that proud submission, that dignified obedience, that subordination of the heart, which kept alive, even in servitude itself, the spirit of an exalted freedom.[178]

This image of revolution as an act of proletarian rape infuriated Wollstonecraft and she responded with great passion, though her point had once again to do with class rather than gender—namely, that Burke defended the Queen only because of her rank and not because of her sex. Wollstonecraft's brilliant conceptual leap was to link the passage to something Burke had written more than thirty years earlier, that 'the beauty of women is considerably owing to their

[177] Marilyn Butler (ed.), *Burke, Paine, Godwin, and the Revolution Controversy* (Cambridge, 1984), 1–17, 74–5; Janet Todd, *Mary Wollstonecraft: A Revolutionary Life* (2000), 152–68; Barbara Taylor, *Mary Wollstonecraft and the Feminist Imagination* (Cambridge, 2003), 95–142.

[178] Burke, *Reflections*, 126–7.

weakness or delicacy, and is even enhanced by their timidity, a quality of mind analogous to it'.[179] Wollstonecraft let fly at this:

You may have convinced [ladies] that *littleness* and *weakness* are the very essence of beauty; and that the Supreme Being, in giving women beauty in the most supereminent degree, seemed to command them, by the powerful voice of Nature, not to cultivate the moral virtues that might chance to excite respect, and interfere with the pleasing sensations they were created to inspire. Thus confining truth, fortitude, and humanity, within the rigid pale of manly morals, they might justly argue, that to be loved, women's high end and great distinction! they should 'learn to lisp, to totter in their walk, and nick-name God's creatures'.[180]

Although the *Vindication of the Rights of Woman* powerfully extended these thoughts, its specific target was not Burke but Rousseau, its generic target not royal tyranny but 'the oppressor, sovereign man'. Wollstonecraft's demand for equality between the sexes was partly to achieve a fair distribution of happiness— why should woman be no more than man's 'rattle and toy', why should females shoulder unpaid the drudgery of housework?—but it was mainly motivated by distaste for the way in which their dependent status could turn women into vain spoiled brats. As with 'the rich of both sexes ... their senses are inflamed, and their understandings neglected, consequently they become the prey of their senses, delicately termed sensibility, and are blown about by every momentary gust of feeling', until rendered virtually incapable of moral judgement.[181] Wollstonecraft blamed the fashionable philosophy of education which derived from Rousseau's fable of Émile and Sophie. While boys were taught to ratiocinate and generalize, girls performed routine and repetitive tasks. They developed strong sensations, passions, emotions, sensibilities, imagination, but could not reason. They learned how to attain given ends, but not how to discover ends for themselves. They were able to enslave men by their coquetry, but were themselves enchained within a patriarchal scheme of values. Although the *Vindication* was not ostensibly religious, its arguments were steeped in assumptions about divine providence.[182] So long as women submitted blindly to male authority like soldiers, their prospects of eternal happiness were diminished. This was a bit like evangelicals fretting about the impossibility of black slaves making it to Heaven, though for Wollstonecraft the process of salvation came through moral behaviour and the exercise of reason rather than through an investment in faith.[183]

    [179] Burke, *Philosophical Enquiry*, 275–6.
    [180] Mary Wollstonecraft, *A Vindication of the Rights of Men* (1790), in *The Works of Mary Wollstonecraft*, ed. Janet Todd and Marilyn Butler (1989), v. 45.
    [181] Mary Wollstonecraft, *A Vindication of the Rights of Woman: With Strictures on Political and Moral Subjects* (1792), in *Works of Wollstonecraft*, v. 129, 133–6.
    [182] Jane Rendall, *The Origins of Modern Feminism: Women in Britain, France and the United States, 1780–1860* (Houndmills, 1984), 60.   [183] Wollstonecraft, *Rights of Woman*, 88–106, 147–84.

1. 'Pitt entered the Commons . . .
his head erect and thrown back,
looking neither to the right nor to
the left, nor favouring with a nod or
a glance any of the individuals seated on either side, among whom
many who possessed five thousand
pounds a year would have been
gratified even by so slight a mark of
attention' (Sir William Nathaniel
Wraxall). Portrait by George
Romney, c.1783

2. Nicknamed 'Holy Hannah'
by Horace Walpole and 'the old
bishop in petticoats' by William
Cobbett, Hannah More appears
here in a portrait by James Heath,
1787

3 (*right*). Disloyal Opposition? Erskine (with finger raised), Whitbread, C. J. Fox, Sheridan, Grey, and other Opposition MPs listening to Pitt informing the Commons that France has declared war in February 1793. Detail from a painting by Karl Anton Hickel

4 (*below*). An intellectual opposition 1791: Gillray's depiction of the Revolution Society's toast to 14 July, as drunk by Sheridan, Priestley, Wray, Fox, Horne Tooke, and Lindsey. According to Priestley, 'the social millennium will be brought about by the influence of the commercial spirit aided by Christianity and true philosophy. Public money no longer wasted [on war] will be spent on . . . public buildings, public libraries, and public laboratories. The empire of reason will ever be the reign of peace.'

5. Expiration and expiation: Nelson mortally wounded on the quarter-deck of HMS *Victory* in the battle of Trafalgar, October 1805. Fearless and single-minded, he saw himself as an instrument of providence, and may possibly have willed his own death at Trafalgar by wearing gaudy apparel

6. 1812. The battle of Salamanca was 'Wellington's finest victory' and marked the turning of the tide in the Peninsular War

7. 'Morals reformed, health preserved, industry invigorated, instruction diffused, public burthens lightened, economy seated as it were upon a rock, the Gordian knot of the Poor-laws not cut but untied—all by a simple idea in architecture.' Certain of his own ability to solve social problems and for all time, Bentham directed that his clothed skeleton should be pickled and preserved in University College London. The head is of wax, while the real head is kept in the College safe.

8. Canning's greatness was most clearly recognized by his reactionary opponents. Metternich said that he was 'a whole revolution in himself alone'. Coleridge said that he 'flashed such a light around the constitution, that it was difficult to see the ruins of the fabric through it'. This is an early portrait of 1797 by John Hoppner

Who, peaceably Meeting
    to ask for Reform,
Were sabred by Yeomanry Cavalry,
    who,
Were thank'd by THE MAN,
    all shaven and shorn,
All cover'd with Orders——
    and all forlorn;
THE DANDY OF SIXTY,
    who bows with a grace,
And has *taste* in wigs, collars,
    cuirasses, and lace;
Who, to tricksters, and fools,
    leaves the State and its treasure,
And when Britain's in tears,
    sails about at his pleasure;
Who spurn'd from his presence
    the Friends of his youth,
And now has not one
    who will tell him the truth;
Who took to his counsels, in evil hour,
The Friends to the Reasons of lawless Power,
That back the Public Informer, who
Would put down the *Thing,* that, in spite of new Acts,
And attempts to restrain it, by Soldiers or Tax,
Will *poison* the Vermin, that plunder the Wealth,
That lay in the House, that Jack built.

c

" Portentous, unexampled, unexplain'd !
    What man seeing this,
And having human feelings, does not blush,
And hang his head, to think himself a man?——
    I cannot rest
A silent witness of the headlong rage,
Or heedless folly, by which thousands die——
Bleed gold for Ministers to sport away."

THESE ARE

THE PEOPLE

    all tatter'd and torn,
Who curse the day
    wherein they were born,
On account of Taxation
    too great to be borne,
And pray for relief,
    from night to morn;
Who, in vain, Petition
    in every form,

9. A typical stanza from William Hone's comic but vicious anti-Government squib *The Political House that Jack Built* (1819)

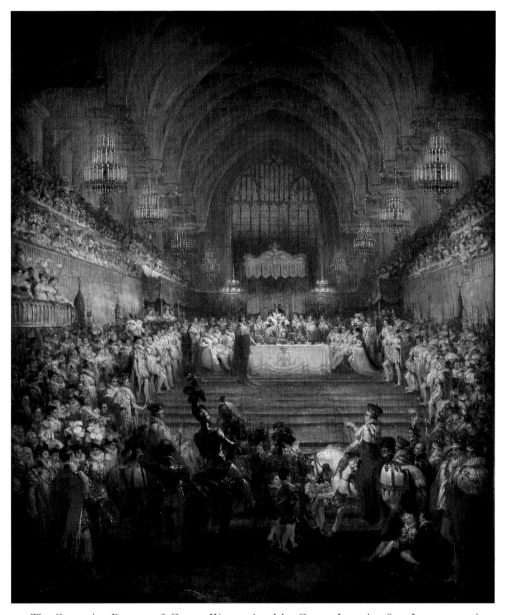

10. The Coronation Banquet of George IV, as painted by George Jones in 1821. Later generations remembered him as 'a dissolute and drunken fop, a spendthrift and a gamester, a bad son, a bad husband, a bad father, a bad subject, a bad monarch, and a bad friend, whose word was worthless and whose courage doubtful' (*Dictionary of National Biography*, 1885–90). Yet undoubtedly he had style, and could be fun

11. Lord Byron, painted here by Thomas Phillips, 1814, was the object both of unbounded adoration and sniffy disapproval.

'O God! that so many souls of mud and clay should fill up their base existence to its utmost bound; and this the noblest spirit in Europe should sink before half his course was run' (Jane Welsh Carlyle, 1824).

'Among that large class of young persons whose reading is almost entirely confined to works of the imagination, the popularity of Lord Byron was unbounded. They bought pictures of him; they treasured up the smallest relics of him; they learned his poems by heart, and did their best to write like him, and to look like him. Many of them practised in the glass in the hope of catching the curl of the upper lip, and the scowl of the brow ... A few discarded their neck-cloths in imitation ... The number of hopeful under-graduates and medical students who became things of dark imaginings, on whom the freshness of the heart ceased to fall like dew, whose passions had consumed themselves to dust, and to whom the relief of tears was denied, passes all calculation. This was not the worst. There was created in the minds of many of these enthusiasts a pernicious and absurd association between intellectual power and moral depravity. From the poetry of Lord Byron they drew a system of ethics, compounded of misanthropy and volup-tuousness, a system in which the two great commandments were, to hate your neighbour, and to love your neighbour's wife' (Lord Macaulay, 1831)

12. One of John Martin's celebrated apocalyptic visions, *The Deluge*; mezzotint of 1828 based on a painting exhibited at the British Institution in 1826. The previous year's financial crash had prompted many capitalists to suppose that cosmic events were 'visibly marching forward to a great visible era of doom and triumph'

13. The London & North Western Railway's Stockport Viaduct, seven miles to the south of Manchester, was built in 1841–2 and remains the longest brick structure in Europe. The booming industrial towns caught many people's imaginations, but visual representations were comparatively rare. Yet according to Benjamin Disraeli in 1844, Manchester, if 'rightly understood', was 'as great a human exploit as Athens'

14. Early Victorians often imagined the Tudorbethan, or 'olden', time as a riot of bay windows, battlements, great halls, banqueting suites, long galleries, inlaid chambers, marquetry, heraldry, rafters, hammer beams, plaster ceilings, carved oak wainscoting, elaborate mouldings, armorial cartouches, halberds, and suits of armour. It was also seen as an age of revelry. This picture, from Joseph Nash's *The Mansions of England in the Olden Time* (1839), shows liege lords, courtiers, wassailers, feasters, jesters, jousters, duellists, minstrels, mummers, morris dancers, hobby-horses, dragons, giants, cats, and dogs all enjoying the Christmas Festivities at Haddon Hall

15. Chivalric longings. Around the time that Victoria came to the throne, many members of the gentry liked to imagine themselves in armour-plated medieval mode. The proud paterfamilias in Daniel Maclise's family portrait of 1837 is Sir Francis Sykes. Given the size of Sir Francis's weapon, it is just as well he did not yet know that the artist was having an affair with his wife, Henrietta

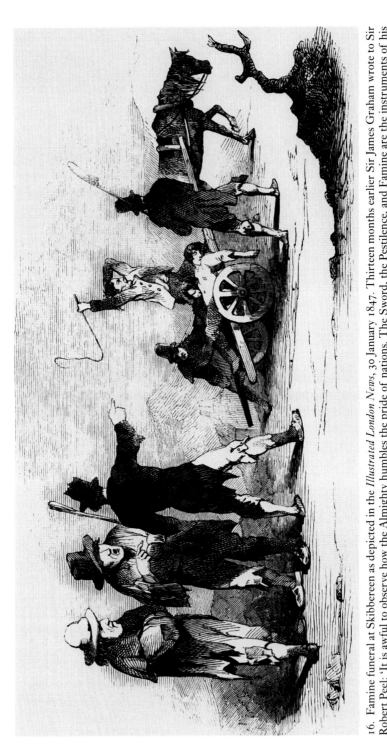

16. Famine funeral at Skibbereen as depicted in the *Illustrated London News*, 30 January 1847. Thirteen months earlier Sir James Graham wrote to Sir Robert Peel: 'It is awful to observe how the Almighty humbles the pride of nations. The Sword, the Pestilence, and Famine are the instruments of his displeasure; the Canker-worm and the Locust are his Armies; he gives the word; a single Crop is blighted, and we see a nation prostrate, and stretching out its Hands for Bread. These are solemn warnings, and they fill me with reverence; they proclaim with a voice not to be mistaken, that "doubtless there is a God, who judgeth the earth"

It is hard to see the *Vindication* as a feminist tract, if only because the author obviously despised her own sex as much as she resented the other. It was not widely purchased, it was probably not widely read except by fringe groups like the Owenites (nineteenth-century 'new-agers' who read it as a paean to free love), and it only began to be taken seriously by middle-class and intellectual women in the 1850s.[184] Admittedly, there was a special reason for its neglect, since following Wollstonecraft's death in childbirth in 1797, her grieving husband, William Godwin,[185] published a loving memoir in which he revealed that she had had a number of sexual affairs. This made her *persona non grata* in society, but it is unlikely that the *Vindication* would have made much headway even without the moral issue, so out of tune was it with the times. In fact, it is best understood, not as a starting point, but as the culmination of a long tradition of free and vigorous public comment by women in the mid-eighteenth century. Members of the Bluestocking Circle—such as Hester Chapone, Hester Thrale, Elizabeth Carter, Elizabeth Montague, and Catharine Macaulay—had all engaged in salon conversations without constraint, but theirs was only the most prominent of many such coteries. A craze for debating societies was just one manifestation of a 'cultural world that traversed boundaries of gender and class, that connected the high-born with the poltroon, that allowed everyone who could afford the price of admission an equal chance to speak and be heard'.[186]

This tolerant state of affairs had come to an end in the trauma caused by the loss of the American colonies. Whereas other eighteenth-century wars were fought against an external enemy, typically France, this was a war within the family, a daughter's denial of patriarchy, parricide even. According to one historian, it precipitated male 'gender panic', a sublimated fear of women (and also perhaps of children), reinforcing rigorous sexual norms.[187] 'Amazon', formerly a term of admiration, now became an insult (it was often applied to Wollstonecraft), females began to dress in more explicitly feminine ways, and de-sexing garments like ladies' breeches and jodhpurs went out of fashion. The events of 1789 made this fear of women still more explicit. The French Revolution first turned nasty

---

[184] Pam Hirsch, 'Mary Wollstonecraft: A Problematic Legacy', in Clarissa Campbell Orr (ed.), *Wollstonecraft's Daughters: Womanhood in England and France 1780–1920* (Manchester, 1996).

[185] Whom she had dearly loved but whom she had *married* only because of her pregnancy.

[186] Donna T. Andrew, 'Popular Culture and Public Debate: London 1780', *HJ* 39 (1996), 405–23.

[187] Dror Wahrman, '*Percy*'s Prologue: From Gender Play to Gender Panic in Eighteenth-Century England', *P&P* 159 (1998), 113–60. Wahrman has divided 18th-century plays into those that took a rigid, prim, and retributive view of homosexuality and cross-dressing, and those that found such subjects commonplace or funny. He finds that out of nearly 600 plays written during 1711–80 only six showed any anxiety about gender boundaries, whereas only four out of about 200 written during 1780–1800 took a flippant or questioning attitude. Even Hannah More, the foremost moralist of domesticity, propriety, and sexual difference, had taken a jovial attitude to cross-dressing in *Percy* (1777). Following her prolonged evangelical conversion in the 1780s, she refused to attend revivals of the play.

in October when 7,000 hungry, armed, and bloodthirsty housewives marched on Versailles to revile the members of the National Assembly as they gorged on ostrich and goose eggs. As the King was taken back to Paris, a virtual prisoner, he had to endure what Burke described as 'horrid yells, and shrilling screams, and frantic dances, and infamous contumelies, and all the unutterable abominations of the furies of hell, in the abused shape of the vilest of women'.[188] Working-class females especially were prominent in revolutionary *journées*, the assassin Charlotte Corday became a figure of dread, the guillotine was 'Madame'. This was the context in which Horace Walpole called Wollstonecraft 'a hyena in petticoats', and it helps to explain why her ideas made so little headway.[189]

Many women do seem to have accepted the view, attributed to Burke, that littleness or weakness was the essence of beauty, and to have imbibed the notion of separate spheres, a concept frequently deployed by historians of this period. Excluded from public life, spinsters are said to have become dependent and expendable, while married women became 'angels in the house', founts of authority, discipline, and affection and repositories of sensibility, but leaving strategic decisions to the paterfamilias as sole breadwinner. Hannah More's heroine Lucilla Stanley in *Coelebs in Search of a Wife* (1809) if often said to have personified the new ideal—active in charity, houseproud, taciturn, submissive to her menfolk, and devout. The book went through eight editions in two months. Romantic love also began to be represented as a feminine quality, while husbands were half-expected to seek sexual gratification with mistresses or prostitutes.

> Man's love is of man's life a thing apart,
>   'Tis woman's whole existence; man may range
> The court, camp, church, the vessel, and the mart;
>   Sword, gown, gain, glory, offer in exchange
> Pride, fame, ambition, to fill up his heart,
>   And few there are whom these cannot estrange;
> Men have all these resources, we but one,
> To love again, and be again undone.
>
>   (Byron, *Don Juan*, canto i, stanza cxciv)

By the 1840s, it has been suggested, even men were starting to chafe against a double standard that increasingly excluded them from the intimacies of domestic life.[190]

---

[188] Burke, *Reflections*, 122.

[189] Karen Green, *The Woman of Reason: Feminism, Humanism and Political Thought* (Cambridge, 1995), 104, argues that there was 'no marked progress in philosophical content between Wollstonecraft's text and John Stuart Mill's *Subjection of Women*' in 1869.

[190] John Tosh, *A Man's Place: Masculinity and the Middle-Class Home in Victorian England* (New Haven, 1999), 53–101.

Separate-spheres ideology certainly did operate to some extent, but it can hardly be the case that the doctrine was socially determined, a function of the growing physical distance under capitalism between home and workplace,[191] since no such changes occurred for the vast majority of those middle-class families that are supposed to have been affected by the doctrine. Since very few lawyers, bankers, or businessmen had worked from home before the 1780s, the so-called Industrial Revolution changed little in this respect. In so far as separation of home and workplace did occur, it mainly affected labourers' families, notably those that had once combined farming and weaving. Yet plebeian women showed no sign of retreating into gender passivity.

True, their involvement in public affairs was sporadic, but then it always had been. It was well known for housewives to seize potatoes from market stalls, and to take a prominent and sometimes violent part in food riots,[192] but they were largely absent from political demonstrations, such as those against the Duke of York and the Covent Garden price rises in 1809. After the war there was a brief flurry of exclusively female radical societies in places like Blackburn and Manchester, but they were mostly short-lived. A female brigade was very visible at Peterloo, where the mere presence of so many women in white, waving their own flags, was thought to have provoked the yeomanry's ferocious response. (It was even thought by some to have justified that response.)[193] All over the country women met exclusively to pledge support for Queen Caroline (as many as 7,800 signed petitions in Nottingham, 11,047 in Bristol), while in London their sex was heavily involved in rioting on her behalf, and accused of instigating mutiny among the Regiment of Foot Guards.[194] Far from promoting the cause of women, however, their involvement probably contributed to the sudden demise of radicalism.[195] They played a modest part in the struggle for parliamentary reform—a Female Political Union was formed in Manchester in 1832—and many demonstrated against the New Poor Law with its tough bastardy regulations and provision for the separation of families.[196] Chartism too mobilized armies of women in the early stages, though their participation rapidly declined, partly owing to its neglect of female suffrage.

However, far from adhering to notions of feminine submission, many lower-class women were asserting themselves more aggressively than ever in daily life.

[191] As argued forcefully by Leonore Davidoff and Catherine Hall, *Family Fortunes: Men and Women of the English Middle Class 1780–1850* (1987). For a balanced assessment, see Robert B. Shoemaker, *Gender in English Society, 1650–1850: The Emergence of Separate Spheres?* (1998).
[192] Malcolm I. Thomis and Jennifer Grimmett, *Women in Protest 1800–1850* (1982), 28–46.
[193] M. L. Bush, 'The Women at Peterloo: The Impact of Female Reform on the Manchester Meeting of 16 August 1819', *History*, 89 (2004), 209–32.
[194] See the articles by Hunt, Fulcher, Laqueur, Clark, and Wahrman in the Bibliography. See below, p. 680.   [195] See above, p. 270.
[196] Ruth and Edmund Frow (eds.), *Political Women 1800–1850* (1989), 76–81.

Admittedly, it is hard to generalize because the impact of economic change on family structure varied from place to place. Women had few employment opportunities in mining areas, where their role was to bear children, especially boys. In textiles, on the other hand, females often found work more easily than men, both in traditional sectors like Nottingham lace and in mechanically sophisticated Lancashire, where 38 per cent of women were employed in the cotton industry. As machinery increasingly displaced brawn, master manufacturers relied more and more on women and children, since it was customary to pay them less.[197] (One reason for the growth of combinations or trade unions was to protect men against such cheap labour.) In the Yorkshire woollen industry separate spheres worked in reverse as the men wove at home while women and children carded, spun, and finished in the mills. The shift from country to town did not at once disrupt older family patterns, since it was a rapid process in which newcomers latched onto relatives and friends who had preceded them. Moreover, kith and kin frequently operated as teams within the cotton factories, at least until the 1830s when more impersonal working patterns began to be introduced.[198] Families remained affective units, but their precise dynamics were affected by various strategic decisions aimed at maximizing income in times of uncertainty. Where adult male wages were adequate and reliable, women might give up work at parturition. If on the other hand their wages were needed for survival, mothers would probably rely on childminders. In times of high unemployment, wives might even become breadwinners by taking advantage of the opportunities which towns provided for domestic service, schoolteaching, laundering, and nursing, in which case their husbands would tend the children, clean the house, and prepare meals. Far more grown-up children struck out on independent paths than in pre-industrial times, but, if they were required to contribute to the family income, they might be discouraged from marrying or made to carry on living in the parental home. Other strategies for survival involved theft, credit, the pawnshop, charity, poor relief, and the whole gamut of 'calculative short-run instrumentalism' in negotiations with neighbours and especially relatives.[199] At its fiercest 'calculative instrumentalism' could turn into a full-scale 'struggle for the breeches', as the sexes battled—often violently—for control of the weekly wage packet. At the same time, leisure activities began to diverge along gender lines. Most men liked to cap exhausting shifts by congregating in pubs, and, since these were increasingly 'no go' premises for

[197] In 1851 there was a slight preponderance of women (generally earning from 9s. to 17s. a week) in the Lancashire cotton industry (David Chadwick, 'On the Rate Wages in Manchester and Salford and the Manufacturing Districts of Lancashire, 1839–59', *Journal of the Statistical Society*, 23 (1860), 1–36).

[198] Neil J. Smelser, *Social Change in the Industrial Revolution: An Application of Theory to the Lancashire Cotton Industry 1770–1840* (1959), 180–224.

[199] Michael Anderson, *Family Structure in Nineteenth-Century Lancashire* (1971), 136–7, 162–9.

respectable women, there developed an atmosphere of male libertinism and aggressive misogyny that was largely lacking in older rural environments.[200]

Perhaps in reaction to these developments, by 1850 bourgeois values of domesticity and respectability were beginning to trickle down to many plebeian women, a tacit retreat on their part that 'solved the sexual crisis but narrowly defined the working-class movement as masculine'.[201] Paradoxically, their acceptance of separate-spheres ideology occurred just at the point when a significant minority of middle-class females at last began to reject the doctrine; that is, if they had ever *truly* subscribed to it. There is no doubt that the vast majority of upper- and middle-class women appeared to observe the conventions, but that should not necessarily be taken as a sign of submission. To be an angel in the house was no bad bargain given that so much more emphasis was placed on family, home, and private life than in previous centuries. Thus at first sight the strictures addressed to women by moralists such as the Quaker-turned-Congregationalist Sarah Stickney Ellis seem limiting. She ordered them to be 'content to be inferior to men—inferior in mental power, in the same proportion that you are inferior in bodily strength'. However, her real point was to assert the superior moral authority of women in the domestic sphere.[202] Furthermore, any sense of deprivation with regard to their position outdoors must have been assuaged by the feeling that, however circumscribed still, the roles allotted to women were wider than ever before. In this context, it has been argued very plausibly that 'separate spheres' was an ideological construct, and what is more, a masculine one and a defensive one. In other words, it was an index of male anxieties and a covert sign that 'more women were seen to be active *outside* the home rather than proof that they were so confined'.[203] Similarly, there is a case for saying that, as gender boundaries became more rigid, and it became less acceptable for one sex to behave like the other, women lost a public voice but gained a distinctive platform from which to address their contemporaries. To natural theologians this was illustrative of God's providential dispositions.

The fin was not more clearly bestowed on the fish that he should swim, nor the wing given to the bird that he should fly, than superior strength of body and a firmer texture of mind given to man, that he might preside in the deep and daring scenes of action and

---

[200] Anna Clark, *The Struggle for the Breeches: Gender and the Making of the British Working Class* (1995), 119–40, 177–219.

[201] Ibid. 218–19, 264–71. See also Sonya O. Rose, *Limited Livelihoods: Gender and Class in Nineteenth-Century England* (1992), 126–53.

[202] Mrs [Sarah Stickney] Ellis, *The Daughters of England: Their Position in Society, Character, and Responsibilities* (1842), 3, 10–11.

[203] Amanda Vickery, 'Golden Age to Separate Spheres? A Review of the Categories and Chronology of English Women's History', *HJ* 36 (1993), 400. Vickery's criticism of the idea that there was a necessary link between 'separate spheres' ideology and 'middle-class formation' is effective. However, she underestimates the changes that took place in the late 18th century.

of council; in government, in arms, in science, in commerce, and in those professions which demand a higher reach, and a wider range of powers. The true value of woman is not diminished by the imputation of inferiority in *these* respects; she has other requisites better adapted to answer the purposes of her being, by 'HIM who does all things well'.[204]

At any rate, the conventional view of feminine submission needs to be qualified. Women might have been inaudible but they were encouraged to be visible, almost as though their presence lent a benediction. They wangled access to the gallery of the Commons, lapped up fashionable sermons, and attended scientific meetings such as those of the British Association. They prepared speeches for their husbands to declaim, handed round religious leaflets, and, although they were not permitted to reinterpret Scripture, they wrote any number of expository tracts. It is possible to be apocalyptic about their situation.

The marginalisation of women in the political world has to be understood as part of a larger process whereby women were being marginalised from, or indeed excluded from, the public world generally. The debate over what part women should play in philanthropy illustrates this very clearly. As long as they were concerned with private philanthropic work, visiting people in their homes in particular, there was no problem. The difficulties arose when they attempted to step outside that domestic arena and take on a more public role.[205]

Yet women who handed out leaflets and visited the poor arguably exercised more real power than men who wrote improving tracts in the remoteness of their studies.

Two crucially important aspects of politics in the first half of the nineteenth century worked in women's favour: the central role played by pressure groups and the importance attached to humanitarian causes. Between 1790 and 1810 about 10 per cent of subscribers to philanthropic societies were women,[206] and they continued to be highly prominent in the campaigns against slavery, suttee, Jewish disabilities, the Corn Laws, and the demon drink.[207] Missionary activity, canvasses, networking, committee work, even stuffing envelopes all provided an entrée to the back corridors of power. There was scope for effective lobbying in private, so that Sarah Austin was able to bend Gladstone's ear on the need for

---

[204] Hannah More, *Strictures on the Modern System of Female Education* (1799), ii. 23–4.

[205] Catherine Hall, 'Private Persons versus Public Someones: Class, Gender and Politics in England, 1780–1850', in Carolyn Steedman, Cathy Urwin, and Valerie Walkerdine (eds.), *Language, Gender and Childhood* (1985) 25.

[206] Clare Midgley, *Women Against Slavery: The British Campaigns, 1780–1870* (1992), 17.

[207] F. K. Prochaska, *Women and Philanthropy in Nineteenth-Century England* (1980); Clare Midgley, 'From Supporting Missions to Petitioning Parliament: British Women and the Evangelical Campaign against *Sati* in India, 1813–30'; Nadia Valman, 'Women Writers and the Campaign for Jewish Civil Rights in Early Victorian England'; and Simon Morgan, 'Domestic Economy and Political Agitation: Women and the Anti-Corn Law League, 1839–46'; all in Gleadle and Richardson (eds.), *Women in British Politics*; Shoemaker, *Gender in English Society*, 248–66.

compulsory education on the Prussian model in 1839. Also, women had more leisure for letter-writing in a period when letters carried special conviction, being technologically cutting-edge while allowing scope for reason and reflection. 'Correspondence gave women effective contacts with male politicians and other male public figures whilst shielding them from the social opprobrium that would have accompanied more open campaigning' (or publication).[208] It was only later, with the growing importance of political parties and the development of a civil service, that women found themselves shut out from the policy-making process.

If these were the only points to be made on this side of the ledger, they would not add up to a convincing case for female empowerment, but they can be supplemented by a still more powerful cultural argument. Policy-makers always suppose that they are making rational deductions on the basis of concrete evidence, even when they are really slaves of conventional beliefs about society and human nature. However, this was especially so during the half-century following the French Revolution, when structures of ideas or paradigms displaced the older emphasis on loyalties and style as determinants of political allegiance. And not only was ideology more than usually significant, but women played a bigger than usual role in its formulation and dissemination.

One reason for this was the Great War against France, which as newspapers and private diaries make clear was at the forefront of everyone's consciousness. It created danger, disruption, and romantic possibilities, as Jane Austen emphasized. Women have been depicted as participating enthusiastically in the war effort, organizing patriotic subscriptions and knitting winter woollies for the troops, thereby contributing to the growth of British national identity,[209] and no doubt this was the case to some extent. Yet this war was not the usual, comfortable, eighteenth-century away match. Fear of invasion led to the press-gangs, which meant the forcible enlistment of women's sons and husbands, and prompted Wollstonecraft to condemn the Government as a bad parent. By and large women writers on the war took a much more pacifist line than men, were more concerned about its cruelties, worried more about the proper care and management of the wounded and bereaved, and were more likely to empathize with the plight of enemy soldiers.[210] Women were also prominent in the various pacifist movements of the first half of the nineteenth century. If, as was argued in Chapter 4, the tone of society was fundamentally and predominantly non-militaristic and anti-imperialist, then women contributed significantly to that mentality.

---

[208] Sarah Richardson, 'Well-Neighboured Houses: The Political Networks of Elite Women, 1780–1860', in Gleadle and Richardson (eds.), *Women in British Politics*.

[209] Linda Colley, *Britons: Forging the Nation 1707–1837* (New Haven, 1992), 261–2.

[210] Emma Vincent Macleod, *A War of Ideas: British Attitudes to the Wars against Revolutionary France 1792–1802* (Aldershot, 1998), 158–78.

Another factor helping to empower women was the extent to which contemporary politics focused on domestic issues that were particularly important to them (though it might be more accurate to say that issues that had once been gender-neutral were now redefined as women's issues, thanks to separate-spheres ideology). It can be argued, for example, that monetary policy was conducted in the interest of fundholders. Fifty years earlier the typical fundholder was a City speculator or Dutchman; now it was a widow, an orphan, or a dependent female relative. Second only in importance to the politics of money was the politics of food. Corn laws mattered not only to farmers but to the managers of households. Malthus' *Essay on the Principle of Population* led to serious consideration of birth control for the first time, and there were other prominent issues with an obvious gender slant, such as education, restrictions on female and child labour, poor relief, and bastardy. Unsurprisingly, female novelists such as Charlotte Elizabeth Tonna, Frances Trollope, and Elizabeth Gaskell pioneered the notion that there was something fundamentally rotten in the condition of England.

The explosion of print culture has often been seen as a form of self-assertion by the bourgeoisie, a way of demonstrating their intelligence to the aristocracy while excluding all but a chosen few from the working classes, yet the gender aspect is just as striking. Barbauld argued, for example, that women novelists could represent subjectivity better than men precisely because their domestic lives were restricted. Male novelists had wider casts of characters, more humour and zest, and were better at battle scenes, but women understood sentiment and morality. 'Where have order, neatness, industry, sobriety, been recommended with more strength than in the agreeable tales of Miss Edgeworth?'[211] Now this was a period when political reform was considered secondary to moral reform, and when even men acknowledged that women had superior insight in the question of morals, so it could be argued that, while women lost ground in terms of being allowed to behave like men, they gained ground in terms of establishing their claims to superior powers of discrimination on moral questions.

'Everywhere one looks in the literature of the period, one sees women reading,'[212] and rightly so since female literacy rose dramatically during this period. For the first time, moreover, women made up a large part, perhaps even the bulk, of the readership. And since 'reading permits critical engagement with issues of authority', it provided women with combustible material of conversation which they could exchange while mutually engaged in apparently submissive activity

---

[211] Anna Barbauld, 'On the Origin and Progress of Novel-Writing', in Barbauld, *The British Novelists*, 2nd edn. (1820), i. 47–8.

[212] Jacqueline Pearson, *Women's Reading in Britain 1750–1835: A Dangerous Recreation* (Cambridge, 1999), p. ix.

like needlework.[213] It was a way of remaining 'domestic yet public', and fell 'somewhere between the private and the social'. Authors of both sexes began to write with this audience in mind, especially novels whether romantic, silver-fork, supernatural, or Gothic horror—Wollstonecraft's daughter Mary Shelley wrote *Frankenstein* (1818)—while apart from Scott, nearly all the best-selling novelists of the early nineteenth century were women: Maria Edgeworth, Elizabeth Hamilton, Amelia Opie, Mary Brunton, Jane and Anna Maria Porter, and Lady Sidney Owenson.[214] Their work was rarely didactic, but it carried a punch. The greatest of all, Jane Austen, was once thought to have been interested only in romances and balls, gossip and snobbery, yet now she is invariably interpreted in political or ideological terms. Joanna Baillie was the top dramatist of her day, while sentimental poets such as Felicia Hemans and the louche Letitia Landon were best-sellers, the former staggeringly so. There were more than 900 female poetizers between 1780 and 1835, of whom at least 339 published under their own names and another eight-two appeared in print anonymously,[215] and there were probably as many as a thousand novelists as well. There were also vogues for conduct books, educational tracts, travel writing, history, political economy, science, letters, journals, and memoirs, all genres that enabled women writers to influence public culture. It seems likely that Croker's viciousness towards lady authors such as Barbauld was provoked more by masculine anxiety—that dreaded 'pencil under the petticoat'—than by genuine condescension.

Science—so central to the public culture of the period—was another area in which women held an advantage. Schoolboys invariably concentrated on classics, but girls were frequently exposed to science because it was thought that their powers of 'application, curiosity, attention to detail, practicality' were peculiarly suited to it.[216] Some became popularizers after the manner of Jane Marcet, whose *Conversations on Chemistry* (1806) went through sixteen editions in forty-seven years, and whose *Conversations on Natural Philosophy* (1819) was also a best-seller, but others made significant original contributions, notably Caroline Herschel, Mary Somerville, Charles Babbage's collaborator Ada Lovelace, and the palaeontologist Mary Anning, condescendingly described as the 'handmaiden' of real male geologists. So long as collecting specimens remained central to

---

[213] Rozsika Parker, *The Subversive Stitch: Embroidery and the Making of the Feminine* (1984), 125–77; Gary Kelly, *Women, Writing, and Revolution 1790–1827* (Oxford, 1993).

[214] Roy Porter, *Enlightenment: Britain and the Creation of the Modern World* (2000), 327.

[215] Anne K. Mellor, *Mothers of the Nation: Women's Political Writing in England, 1780–1830* (Bloomington, Ind., 2000), 3. That so few have survived is partly because women excelled in republican writing—i.e. in discussions of morality, reason, and the 'domesticated sublime'—whereas the canon that was formed in the later 19th century, mainly by male anthologists, privileged imagination, egoism, romantic sensibility, and the ideal of the 'man of genius' (Anne Mellor, *Romanticism and Gender* (New York, 1993)).

[216] Patricia Phillips, *The Scientific Lady: A Social History of Women's Scientific Interests 1520–1918* (1990).

scientific endeavour, women were in the thick of it. It was only towards the middle of the nineteenth century, with the development of laboratory science and sophisticated instrumentation and the increasing emphasis on mathematics, that they were edged out.

Much the same can be said about economic science. The conventional reading of separate spheres is that the market was thought to be masculine and amoral, and the family a locus of love and religion, presided over by wives whose sensibility might yet redeem their endangered menfolk,[217] despite which women were at the forefront in disseminating market ideology. Maria Edgeworth's conduct books, notably the Harry and Lucy stories, held up entrepreneurs and professionals for admiration while depicting effete aristocrats as spoilt and useless. Jane Marcet's *Conversations on Political Economy* (1816) went through seven editions in twenty-three years and, like her earlier book on chemistry, was 'intended more especially for the female sex'. She is usually dismissed as a mere popularizer, yet she anticipated Ricardo in some respects while dissenting from his and Smith's theory of value. Harriet Martineau's *Illustrations of Political Economy* (1832–4), *Poor Laws and Paupers Illustrated* (1833–4), and *Illustrations of Taxation* (1834) purported to describe everyday life under market capitalism. It is often said to have presented the subject in a rigid and didactic way, yet the abstractions of macroeconomic theory were bound to seem glib and formulaic when applied to everyday reality. Nevertheless, the main impact of political economy for good or ill was not on policy but on household management. Martineau's homilies were written, partly at Brougham's request, for use by the Society for the Diffusion of Useful Knowledge and mechanics institutes, and her corner-shop economics based on thrift and prudence would affect the lives of thousands of respectable artisans. She and Marcet were convinced of the trickle-down effect of private affluence, never doubting that 'the comforts of the poor [were] derived from the riches of the rich'.[218] So, if the main thrust of early nineteenth-century governance was to convince the lower orders of the virtues of the market, it was not Ricardo or Mill who achieved this but these two women writers who mediated political economy for the masses by placing it in the context of domestic household management. Their confidence in the natural harmony of individual interests was consistent with the views of Smith, but at odds with those of many contemporary male economists.

More vital still was the role of women in propagating evangelical religion. If Thomas Chalmers was the man on the Clapham omnibus, Hannah More was undoubtedly behind the wheel. A remarkable propagandist and fine writer, she aimed to inoculate the lower orders against Paine and Wollstonecraft in a vast

---

[217] Davidoff and Hall, *Family Fortunes*, 108–18.
[218] [Jane Marcet], *John Hopkins's Notions on Political Economy* (1833), 10.

proliferation of Christian homilies and didactic morality tales. 'Following a strict Evangelical logic of causes and consequences, the typical More plot sets improvident vice against tested virtue, rewarding spiritual self-examination and devotion to local obligations with a modest rise in the world.'[219] It could be argued that More just happened to be a woman, and yet her stories all celebrate the power of 'Christian heroism' (conventionally 'the property of the power-less—women, the poor') to 'save England from external threat and internal dis-integration'.

Hers is peculiarly a woman's answer, a domestic endurance derived from women's moral traditions, now deemed appropriate for poor and rich, female and male alike... For the female teachers who embraced them, such remedies signaled anything but quietism and social apathy. They located the only real ground of power. And they sanctioned female exercise of that power... Defining social problems as essentially moral and religious made woman's role focal. She was, in More's frequent phrase, God's instrument. Socializing the young and rehabilitating the laboring poor—two groups key to moral renovation—were woman's rightful obligation.[220]

Certainly there are various respects in which her brand of evangelicalism was a predominantly female ideology. First, it was centred less on congregations (which were sites of patriarchy) than on family life (where matrodoxy was the norm). At a time when more emphasis was being placed on love in choosing marriage partners, and less on money or social standing,[221] more emotional capital was also being invested in children. Evangelical piety was partly a response to the very great incidence of infant mortality, and served a consolatory as well as admonitory function. Secondly, middle-class men were often simply too busy to bother about religion except on the sabbath, whereas feminine domesticity made it possible to undertake the relentless introspection which More's 'hard school of moral discipline' demanded. For if the world was a place of trial, designed not for happiness but to test faith, and if every tiny eventuality was loaded with providential meaning, then true believers were not to be allowed any spiritual time off. Thirdly, a faith centred on emotional commitment suited women, who were more able to love Christ with the intensity required, if only because God the Father and the Son were masculine symbols—Chalmers frequently referred to Christ in martial terms as the 'captain general of salvation'.[222] Finally, women were conceived of as embodying in themselves the duality that was central to

---

[219] Mitzi Myers, 'Hannah More's Tracts for the Times: Social Fiction and Female Ideology', in Mary Anne Schofield and Cecilia Macheski (eds.), *Fetter'd or Free? British Women Novelists, 1670–1815* (Athens, Ohio, 1987), 271. [220] Ibid. 274.

[221] This development has sometimes been caricatured, as though love counted for nothing before the late 18th century, but the trend is clear.

[222] In contrast to the third quarter of the 19th century when Christ the manly redeemer turned into a passive and almost feminine Jesus, or 'lamb of God'.

evangelical religion, being both the source of sexual temptation, Eve and serpent combined, as well as the fountainhead of sexual continence and redemptive virtue.[223]

Wollstonecraft's hope that women would 'every day grow more and more masculine' went unrealized,[224] but on the other hand public life did become more feminine. The discourse of eighteenth-century Whiggism had been masculine in ethos. It portrayed corruption as feminine,[225] and financial speculation as irresponsible, skittish, even hysterical. Elaborating this conceit, it might be suggested that Pitt inaugurated a feminine polity. This is partly because his rule was based on the virtues of commercial society, polite, amiable, sentimental, and restrained. Speculation was deemed a greater social evil than ever, but it was now conceived of as aggressive, masculine, and predatory. More specifically, Pitt began the adaptation of household virtues to government with his liking for order and 'œconomy', his understanding of the need for moral reform, and his underlying belief in the market as instrument for achieving it. There is therefore a case for describing the ruling regime of the first half of the nineteenth century as a type of gentlewomanly capitalism.

It may seem somewhat backhanded to rescue women from the condescension of posterity, only to saddle them with responsibility for the psychological terrorism and repression that characterized public doctrine in the first half of the nineteenth century. In mitigation, it bears repeating that this was a polarized society, and if some women were the main proponents of evangelicalism, others were among its main antagonists. They included rational Dissenters with their contrasting idea of God,[226] and aristocratic matrons with their contempt for religious fashion, especially the morbid cult of deathbeds. When Catherine Stanley fell ill during 1841, her sister Mary wrote to her aunt Lady Stanley of Alderley,

All hope is gone and the last 10 hours we have all been in her room and we have been raised above this earth. The Soul seems already winged for flight—she is lying in the most heavenly state, speaking a word of comfort to each, quite alive to everything that passes.

To which mawkishness her aunt replied impatiently,

I want to hear more of the dear child's bodily state and less of her mental or spiritual, because I consider the instances given of that as bordering on fever, and certainly proving great excitement, and it is incomprehensible to us all that she should have been allowed

---

[223] It has been claimed, not wholly implausibly, that 'the turn to Evangelicalism' was 'a female strategy for allaying anxiety about the body', and an example of 'female complicity in patriarchal class operations' (Elizabeth Kowaleski-Wallace, *Their Fathers' Daughters: Hannah More, Maria Edgeworth, and Patriarchal Complicity* (New York, 1991), 56–93).   [224] Wollstonecraft, *Rights of Woman*, 74.

[225] J. Barrell, *The Birth of Pandora and the Division of Knowledge* (Houndmills, 1992), 64.

[226] See below, pp. 462–4.

to be so surrounded, and to talk so much, and above all, the extreme excitement of constant Cathedral musick—keeping her hearing and *feeling* on the constant strain. I really think you have all lost your wits—have got into the seventh heaven of enthusiasm and forgot every thing sublunary. You gave her over and then seemed to think she must be indulged in all her fancies without considering whether they might be hurtful—and have fancied her under inspiration almost, forgetting that the greatest criminals and villains frequently go out of the world exulting at the gallows in their assurances of eternal happiness and really, I have no doubt, feel what they say.[227]

Lady Stanley's put-down is a reminder that not everyone had given up on eighteenth-century good sense.

---

[227] *The Ladies of Alderley*, ed. Nancy Mitford (1938), 17–18.

CHAPTER 6

The crisis of the old order, 1827–1832

> Trade and South America and...corn bills [and the] Catholic question... such are in truth the only questions now at issue—and the great parties in Parliament must ultimately be distinguished by their respective and opposite opinions on one or most of these topics. In that case a jumble of *men* must ensure a liberal ministry with an intolerant court opposition, or an intolerant court ministry with a liberal opposition.
>
> (Holland to Grey, 2 September 1825)

Holland was by no means alone in supposing that economic and religious disputes would shatter the existing party system. However, it took Liverpool's sudden seizure in February 1827 to precipitate events. The next five years were characterized by ideological confrontation and political confusion, and so call for a quickening of the narrative pace.

COALITION AND THE CANNINGITE FLAME

The King turned to Canning, who managed to form an administration, but only after more than seven weeks of wrangling. Six Cabinet colleagues (half of them, in other words: Peel, Wellington, Bathurst, Eldon, Westmorland, Melville) and thirty-six junior ministers[1] refused to serve under him, while Wellington also resigned as Commander-in-Chief. All the seceders except Peel opposed liberal Toryism *in toto*. All except Melville were strongly opposed to Catholic emancipation, and in their mandatory explanations to Parliament they cited Canning's well-known Catholic sympathies in justification. In particular, this was the line that Peel took in a speech which was embarrassing, boastful, and self-conscious. From this point on, the Commons was a stage on which Peel would parade, not quite the pageant of his bleeding heart, but the injured innocence of his beaten breast. It became his habit to speak 'with many protests of candour and humble

---

[1] Collectively described by Huskisson as 'worn out rubbish' (Huskisson to Sturges Bourne, 16 Jan. 1828, Huskisson MS 39948, fos. 104–6). Wellington wanted the premiership but held back, probably for fear of being beaten by the despised Canning.

consideration, in a sort of beseeching tone'.[2] His mature self-exculpatory style led an acute commentator to imagine a Home Office file labelled 'My Conscience', and containing papers 'designed to show that "my conscience" was sincere'.[3]

To be fair, Peel was in a difficult position. Eighteen years junior to Canning, he was nevertheless close enough to be a rival. Back in 1821 the then unemployed Canning had certainly seen him as such, anticipating that if Peel were to get back into office ahead of him, 'the door is closed to me for ever'.[4] Now the positions were reversed, in that if Canning succeeded in forming a stable administration, the premiership might skip over Peel's generation altogether. And though Peel might not have been motivated by personal considerations, he must have known that others thought he was. Unlike the other seceders he claimed 'an entire union of opinion' between himself and Canning 'on all public questions except one',[5] and he made it clear to Parliament that he had no wish to be associated with fellow *refuseniks* such as Eldon and Bathurst. Even on the Catholic question his position was ambiguous, since two years earlier he had secretly offered to resign in order to facilitate emancipation. In stepping down now, Peel almost certainly hoped, not that Canning would *fail* to carry a Catholic Relief Bill (as everyone supposed), but that he would carry it swiftly and decisively, while Peel himself enjoyed the obscurity of the back benches, temporarily out of the fray. If this was indeed Peel's calculation, Canning's unanticipated death on 8 August 1827 must have been a severe blow. If only he had stayed in office he would have been in line for the succession. Moreover, in that case, when the time came (as come it must) to concede the Catholic claims, he might have been able to persuade his followers that he was acting in good faith and for sound *raison d'état*. What was to weigh against him so strongly, when he finally proposed emancipation in 1829, was that only two years earlier he had helped to split the party in order (apparently) to prevent the policy.

Deprived of so many former ministers, Canning turned to the Whigs, and split them as well. Lansdowne, Tierney, and the sixth Earl of Carlisle entered the Cabinet, the first as Home Secretary. They did so on the basis of an April memorandum stating that the Catholic question should remain open, that the Test and Corporation Acts should be maintained, and that parliamentary reform should be resisted (Lansdowne owned a borough and Tierney sat by courtesy of the Duke of Devonshire). More puristic Whigs like Grey and Russell were furious. The former's detestation of Canning apparently 'went deeper than rational explanation',[6] and centred on the unaccountable fact that, despite being

---

[2] *The Autobiography of Sir Egerton Brydges* (1834), i. 200. George IV, a brilliant mimic, could endear himself even to his detractors by impersonating Peel in this mode.

[3] Walter Bagehot, 'The Character of Sir Robert Peel', in *The Collected Works of Walter Bagehot* ed. Norman St John-Stevas (1965–86), iii. 242.   [4] Canning to his wife, Canning MSS.

[5] Parker, *Peel*, i. 479.   [6] E. A. Smith, *Lord Grey 1764–1845* (Oxford, 1990), 243.

brilliant, Canning had adored Pitt rather than Fox. When Holland—the apostolic successor to Foxite Whiggery—and Brougham also offered Canning goodwill and support, the former even crossing the floor of the Lords, Grey was driven to despair. 'I now feel myself almost a solitary individual... I shall not... again embark upon the troubled sea of politics, upon which, all my life, till now, I have navigated—God knows with how little success.'[7] Shortly afterwards he attacked Canning so bitterly in the Lords that the Prime Minister considered recommending himself for a peerage in order to answer him in person. Clearly, both parties were 'split to pieces'.[8] Moreover, there was common ground between the liberal Tories and the more economically liberal Whigs, as reflected in the very close alliance between Huskisson and Lansdowne. Liberal individualism was a shoot pushing up through and dividing both main parties, and while Canning's was not quite a coalition government, since Pittites predominated, it was not far short of one.[9]

It is interesting to speculate on what would have happened if Canning had lived and his administration had succeeded. In that case the 'revolution of parties', which Holland had predicted two years previously, could well have occurred. A liberal centre party might have developed incorporating Canning, Huskisson, Robinson, Grant, Palmerston, Melbourne, Lansdowne, Tierney, Brougham, and Carlisle. This might have prompted high Tories and true Whigs—Wellington, Eldon, Grey, Ellenborough, Russell, Lauderdale, and Sir James Graham—to coalesce against them. In those circumstances, Peel and Althorp would have been forced to choose between their liberal instincts and their party allegiances.

How realistic was this possibility? Certain inferences can be drawn from what happened after Canning died. His immediate successor, Robinson (raised to the peerage as Viscount Goderich), was unable to sustain his liberal coalition, and was succeeded by Wellington (January 1828), who at once sent Lansdowne and Tierney packing.[10] His half-hearted attempts to work with Huskisson and Palmerston foundered within a few acrimonious months, after which he wanted nothing more to do with them. On the other hand, he was 'extremely anxious to have Ld Grey in the Cabinet', perhaps as Foreign Secretary,[11] though that would have required the Whig leader to keep constant intercourse with the King, who

---

[7] *HPD2* xvii. 732–3 (10 May 1827). Althorp was almost certainly offered and refused a place in Canning's Cabinet, but he offered the new Prime Minister 'qualified support' (Ellis Wasson, *Whig Renaissance: Lord Althorp and the Whig Party 1782–1845* (New York, 1987), 137–51.

[8] Greville, *Memoirs*, i. 127 (25 Feb. 1828).

[9] Joe Bord, 'Patronage, the Lansdowne Whigs and the Problem of the Liberal Centre, 1827–8', *EHR* 117 (2002), 78–93.

[10] He did half-heartedly offer a post to Carlisle, but probably in the hope and justified expectation that it would be refused (Peter Jupp, *British Politics on the Eve of Reform: The Duke of Wellington's Administration, 1828–30* (Houndmills, 1998), 77). [11] Arbuthnot, *Journal*, ii. 178 (27 Mar. 1828).

still hated him. For his part, Grey might well have agreed to serve under Wellington had it not been for the death of the Ultra Tory Duke of York in 1827. It meant that the heir to the throne was now the Duke of Clarence, who was on record as saying that Grey was the finest politician in the land. The Whigs had at last acquired a reversionary interest, which was a powerful temptation to hold out and wait for George IV to die.[12] Grey let it be known, therefore, that he would only take office if he could bring in some of his friends as part of a 'general arrangement', an obvious non-starter. Nevertheless, speculation that Grey might join Wellington continued, though when at last in November 1830 a coalition between high Tories and Whigs did take place, it was directed *against* the Duke and brought him down. (A defining moment had come when two of the most ardent Ultra Tory peers, Eldon and Cumberland, crossed the floor to sit among the Whigs.) During 1831 parliamentary reform so polarized politics on Whig–Tory lines that all talk of realignment disappeared, but it surfaced again in 1833 on the currency and Poor Law issues. In other words, when social and economic issues were to the fore a realignment seemed likely, whereas political and religious issues shook the pieces up differently and reinforced the old Whig–Tory polarity. The prospect of a centre coalition was finally killed off during 1834–5 by a furore over the Irish Church and the reaction to Peel's hundred-day administration (1834–5). The dashing of a centre coalition meant that both parties would remain split on economic and social policy.

If Liverpool's stroke brought the differences between liberal and high Tories into the open, Canning's death led at once to an ideological polarization between them. His personality had been so vivid that, while he was alive, their differences had seemed personal, but once he was dead, as though to cover the void his supporters mounted a rhetorical call to arms in favour of 'Mr Canning's system', 'Mr Canning's principles', and 'liberal politicks'. The last adjective had retained its mainly negative connotations ('Liberality is the word of the day ... and it is seriously threatening the British Empire with the overthrow of all its ancient institutions, by which it has hitherto flourished'[13]), but in 1827 it also began to be used in a strongly positive sense, prompting opponents like Mrs Arbuthnot to designate themselves proudly as 'illiberals'.[14] At the same time the word 'Tory' came to be used unself-consciously as a term of identity rather than an insult.[15] Palmerston's ideological assault on Wellington in 1829, when he divided Europe

[12] The Whigs overestimated monarchical influence, perhaps because it provided them with an alibi for their continued exclusion from power.

[13] Redesdale to Colchester, 27 July 1823, in *The Diary and Correspondence of Charles Abbot, Lord Colchester*, ed. second Baron Colchester (1861), iii. 300–1.

[14] See also Bastard to Vyvyan, 2 Sept. 1829, Cornwall RO, Vyvyan MS BO/48/32–3.

[15] For example, Mrs Arbuthnot did not use the term before 1827, and in that year she used it mainly to denote the Ultras, referring to them as 'they' rather than 'we', but by 1828 she had identified completely with the Tory Party.

into 'two great parties', only makes sense in the context of the intellectual battles which Carlyle, the Mills, Coleridge, Southey, Macaulay, and Mackintosh suddenly began to engage in from 1828 onwards. It was an obvious bid for the Canningite mantle after twenty-two years as a junior minister.[16] Wellington himself did his best to stand aloof. 'We hear a great deal of Whig principles, and Tory principles, and Liberal principles, and Mr Canning's principles; but I confess that I have never seen a definition of any of them, and cannot make to myself a clear idea of what any of them mean.'[17]

THE GODERICH FILE

Without Canning's charismatic pertinacity, it seemed very unlikely that the husk of his administration could survive. His successor was known to contemporaries as 'Prosperity Robinson'[18] and 'Goody Goderich', but is remembered by posterity as Disraeli's 'transient and embarrassed phantom' and the 'Duke of Fuss and Bustle', whose Government collapsed after three months without having faced Parliament. Nevertheless, the reasons for its failure shed light on some shadowy but powerful forces that gripped the political world.

As soon as Goderich became Prime Minister, Wellington resumed command of the Army. This led to a blazing row with Mrs Arbuthnot, who complained that it made the Duke's earlier resignation look like a personal slight on Canning rather than a protest against Canningite liberalism. Wellington replied that as a soldier he had a duty to his country, and that he could not be expected to behave like a politician since he was not one. '*Then be one*,' was the gist of Mrs Arbuthnot's reply. 'I told him . . . that it was ridiculous nonsense for him to stand up and tell me he was *no politician* . . . that a large body in the State looked to him as their protector against the political economists, and that he must be quite aware that they did not do so on account of his military talents.' At which point the Duke '*swore* (which he never does) and said he would do as he liked'.[19]

The King insisted that the new Chancellor of the Exchequer (in place of Goderich) should be John Charles Herries, a Treasury Secretary and formerly Vansittart's private secretary. Palmerston surmised that he was a 'live shell', planted with the deliberate intention of blowing the enterprise sky high. Certainly Tierney, Lansdowne, and Carlisle were furious, since Herries was thought to be strongly anti-Catholic and he had opposed many of Huskisson's policies including cash payments. Instead of resigning like other high Tories on the formation of Canning's Government, he had remained in office as a junior minister, and then as a Cabinet minister under Goderich. This enabled him to

[16] See above, pp. 317–18.   [17] Wellington, memorandum, 20 May 1828, in WND iv. 451–3.
[18] The sobriquet was meant ironically as in 'Miracle Lawson' 160 years later.
[19] Arbuthnot, *Journal*, ii. 137–40.

pass on copies of confidential documents (invariably marked 'Burn this!') to Arbuthnot and Holmes for onward transmission to Wellington and Knighton. At one point Arbuthnot became alarmed at the mole's blatant disloyalty: 'I think it better not to send me the papers.... It is certainly advisable that I should not see them ... I believe however that I am pretty well acquainted with their contents.'[20] Whether or not it was the King's intention, Herries did finally sink Goderich's Government by quarrelling with Huskisson[21] over the appointment of a Chairman of the Finance Committee, an ad hoc body which Lansdowne and Tierney had insisted on as a condition of joining Canning, and whose remit was to supervise hefty cuts in public expenditure. Briefly, Huskisson and Tierney agreed that Althorp would make a suitable Chairman, and then discussed the possibility with Herries, who as Chancellor was technically responsible, but without telling him that they had already sounded Althorp out. When Herries afterwards discovered this from a casual conversation, he exploded. Huskisson wrote in a conciliatory tone apologizing for lack of consideration, and Herries seemed to be mollified, but then on 21 December he suddenly re-took umbrage, informing Goderich that he had been insulted and threatening to resign if Althorp became Chairman. This démarche was probably in response to a letter which Goderich—in conjunction with Lansdowne and Huskisson—had just written to the King, pleading with him to admit Wellington and Holland into his Cabinet. They did not really want Wellington but they knew the King did, and they probably used him as a decoy to conceal their real purpose, which was to seal the realignment of parties by co-opting Holland. Unfortunately, the demoralized Goderich had added a personal paragraph admitting to a 'protracted state of anxiety' about his own and his wife's health, which meant that he could not give the premiership his full mental attention.[22] Now, George IV was no workaholic, but even he could hardly ignore such a declaration of incapacity. When, shortly afterwards, Goderich burst into tears over his inability to control the two warring ministers, the King is said to have lent him a pocket handkerchief and sent for the Duke of Wellington.

So what was going on? Huskisson complained paranoically of a 'deep malignity', a 'fiendish', 'baneful and secret influence' working to undermine him. Herries meanwhile clearly regarded Huskisson's high-handed behaviour as part of an insidious attempt to dictate economic policy. He also pointed out that those who were apprehensive about the Finance Committee would be even more so if 'the most prominent member of the most reforming party in the House' were made Chairman, whereas Huskisson retorted that responsibility would have

---

[20] Arbuthnot to Herries, 12 Sept. 1827, Herries MS 57370, fo. 54.

[21] Who was now War and Colonial Secretary like his old mentor Dundas.

[22] Goderich to George IV, 11 Dec. 1827, in *The Letters of King George IV 1812–1830*, ed. A. Aspinall (Cambridge, 1938), iii. 344–6.

the beneficial effect of shackling Althorp.[23] Beyond this, the quarrel seems to have been purely personal and devoid of substance. On the other hand, Herries and Huskisson hardly needed to articulate points of disagreement by this time. Ever since 1810, when they clashed over the Bullion Report, they more than anyone had epitomized the clash between manipulative high Toryism and mechanistic liberal Toryism. As wartime Commissary-in-Chief responsible for subsidy payments and transmitting gold to the front, Herries had become extremely close to Huskisson's *bête noire* Rothschild. In 1819 he brooded about the 'under game' that Huskisson was playing for Liverpool's ear.[24] Since then Herries's influence had been limited, but he continued to be regarded by the business community as its champion. 'The great stockholders . . . *all* put their trust in you,' wrote a backbencher from Bristol,[25] and the same could be said of all but one of the Bank of England directors, while throughout 1827 Herries received advice and encouragement from Rothschild.[26] Back in 1810 no one could have foreseen that a dispute between two junior lackeys would one day bring down a government, but in 1827 Huskisson and Herries, Colonial Secretary and Chancellor of the Exchequer, were the most prominent commoners in Cabinet. The men of business had moved centre stage, signifying that politics was no longer the sport of aristocrats, but was crucial to the way in which the country was governed.

The Huskisson–Herries affair may have had another 'meaning', though not one that was made explicit. Throughout the dispute Herries received alarmist letters from Arbuthnot as the Duke's amanuensis, pleading that the Finance Committee should not be allowed to effect reductions in an Army which was 'even now not equal to the exigencies of our extended empire'. Wellington was said to be 'in despair' over the prospect of reducing British forces in Gibraltar and the Mediterranean, 'just at the very moment that we have had the folly to make Russia a naval power in the Greek Archipelago'.[27] This referred to the one substantial act of Canning's Government, the Treaty of London (July 1827), by which Britain, France, and Russia recognized the autonomy of Greece under Turkish suzerainty, while allowing the Russian fleet to enter the Mediterranean. This initiative displeased Tory Russophobes and with some justification, for the accord quickly broke down,[28] and in the ensuing naval war against Turkey

[23] Herries to Huskisson, 29 Nov. 1827, Huskisson to Herries, 30 Nov. 1827, Huskisson MS 38752, fos. 101–2, 112–13.   [24] Herries' diary, 1819, Herries MSS.

[25] R. Hart Davis to Herries, Nov. 1827, Herries MSS.

[26] Spearman to Herries, 31 Dec. 1827, Herries MS 57374, fos. 56–8; Boyd Hilton, *Corn, Cash, Commerce: The Economic Policies of the Tory Governments 1815–1830* (Oxford, 1977), 242–5.

[27] Herries to Arbuthnot, 29 and 31 July, 2 and 5 Aug. 1827, Herries MS 57370, fos. 47–53.

[28] Contradictions in policy were exposed at the battle of Navarino (October 1827) when Vice-Admiral Edward Codrington, leading a combined force of British, French, and Russian vessels, destroyed a Turkish–Egyptian fleet. This satisfactorily advanced the cause of Greek independence, but the damage to Turkey worked to Russia's advantage.

(1828–9) the Russians extended their position alarmingly. Possibly the real but unspoken reason Wellington resumed command of the Army was to fight proposed cuts in military expenditure. For, despite more than a decade of peace, contemporaries were afraid that war might break out at any moment—against Russia over Greece, France over Spain, Spain and Austria over South America, and the United States over trade. It is not far-fetched to suggest that Herries and Wellington might have staged a military–financial coup in order to bring down what looked to them like a dangerously insouciant Government. Yet in fact the ministers also had their eyes on the diplomatic dangers. A decade later Cobdenites would claim that reduced military spending led to international peace and obviated the need for large armies. Canningite liberals were much less complacent, and in supporting defence cuts they were paradoxically preparing the country for war. Huskisson was gravely alarmed by 'our want of adequate preparation, in respect to the arrangement of our currency and finance, to meet those demands which war may at any time render necessary',[29] while his ally Charles Grant, the President of the Board of Trade, spoke of 'trimming the vessel . . . to prepare her for the storm which might in time gather around her'.[30] In cutting back on all expenditure, including that on the forces, it seems that Huskisson was reflecting a view that creditworthiness was a more effective arm of defence than large military arsenals.

THE FIRST BLOW: TEST AND CORPORATION ACT REPEAL

For a few months Wellington's administration approximated to Liverpool's, since the coalition Whigs were discarded and several Tories who had refused to serve under Canning returned. It was only stitched together with difficulty, however. Wellington needed Peel as Home Secretary to lead in the Commons, but Peel refused to serve unless the Canningites (now Huskissonites) were included and rampant illiberals like Eldon and Westmorland left out. Eldon was outraged, and everyone sensed that his exclusion marked a symbolic ditching of the past. There was trouble in the rival camp as well. Joan Canning was furious with Huskisson for taking office under her late husband's enemy. In an effort to placate her, he announced publicly that the Duke had pledged himself to govern according to Canning's principles, which had high Tories fluttering in alarm and Wellington spluttering with rage. Speculation that Grey might enter the Government came to nothing, but his 'acolyte' Lord Ellenborough did so, and so too in 1829 did Lord Rosslyn and Sir James Scarlett. The last two thereby abandoned lifetimes of Whiggery just one year before the party's long period of exclusion came to an end, and missed out on the rewards that would have been

---

[29] Huskisson, memorandum, 8 Feb. 1826, Huskisson MS 38755, fo. 229; Hilton, *Corn, Cash, Commerce*, 232–5.   [30] *HPD*2 xix. 603 (12 May 1828).

theirs. Brougham was luckier. He had angled for office under Goderich and was ashen with disappointment when Wellington took over, but it meant he got the Woolsack in 1830.

At least Wellington had managed to put a Cabinet together, even if its members differed 'on almost every question of importance', as Palmerston observed, and behaved towards each other with exaggerated politeness like people who had just fought a duel.[31] However, they had hardly had time to breathe, as Peel ruefully remarked, when they faced an unexpected problem, and one whose portentousness they may have underestimated. Among other things, the Corporation Act of 1661 required holders of municipal office to take the sacrament of Holy Communion in an Anglican church, and the Test Act of 1673 imposed the same burden on all holders of civil and military office under the Crown. Roman Catholics were the main intended target, but Protestant Nonconformists were caught in the scatter fire. Even so, agitation against the Acts had been subdued since the 1780s. A venerable body known as the Protestant Dissenting Deputies, led by the Unitarian William Smith MP, brought pressure to bear, but its watchword was the uninspiring one of 'vigilance, not action'. The problem was tactical, and stemmed from the fact that repeal of the Acts would be impossible without the full cooperation of the Whigs, most of whom cared more for the Catholic cause than for that of Protestant Dissent. This posed no problem for Unitarians and most Old Dissenters, who were happy to deliver political and civil rights for all, but the last thing many so-called New Dissenters and especially Methodists wished to do was liberate Catholics. For example, the Protestant Society for the Protection of Religious Liberty (1811), the most active and outspoken Nonconformist body, was passionately anti-papist, and became even more so with the resurgence of what it saw as 'extraordinary' Irish Catholic 'bigotry and violence' in 1823.[32] In these circumstances, Smith simply sought to stifle public expressions of rabid anti-Catholicism in his ranks,[33] while watching for an opportune moment. It seemed to come when Canning became Prime Minister, but he insisted that the Catholics' disabilities were more important and must be repaired first. Unexpected frustrations often serve to galvanize human rights movements more than prolonged ineffectuality, and Canning's rebuff stirred Smith to mount a propaganda campaign of unprecedented vigour. Hundreds of petitions were presented, and about 22,000 broadsides stitched into the *Quarterly* and *Edinburgh* reviews. Lord John Russell, always on the lookout for a cause, and sensing a chance to reinstate the old alliance

---

[31] *A Political Diary 1828–1830 by Edward Law Lord Ellenborough*, ed. Lord Colchester (1881), i. 3.

[32] J. Pye Smith to William Smith, 29 Nov. 1824, CUL, William Smith Papers, Add. MS 7621/142.

[33] Richard W. Davis, *Dissent in Politics 1780–1830: The Political Life of William Smith, MP* (1971), 212–45.

between Dissent and Whiggism, brought forward a Bill to repeal the two Acts in February 1828, catching ministers entirely off their balance.

Peel consulted his old tutor Charles Lloyd, now the Bishop of Oxford. In England as a whole Anglican privileges were mainly symbolic, but they meant something at Cambridge University, where only subscribers to the Church of England could graduate, and they meant even more at Oxford. where non-Anglicans could not even matriculate. A scholarly High Churchman, Lloyd proffered several pedantic seventeenth-century arguments such as that of Bishop Sherlock (1678–1761), who denied that Nonconformists were disqualified from office for religious reasons, since their failure to pass the sacramental test was merely the *evidence* of their lack of qualification and not the *cause* of it.[34] Peel rejected this as being not 'a House of Commons argument'.[35] Just as significantly, he refused Lloyd's advice to react in an alarmist manner, observing that one should only take the 'high ground' in Parliament if one was sure of winning the vote. 'If you are to be beaten, the higher the tone you take, the more creditable it may be to the individual or the party who takes it; but . . . the more complete is the triumph *over* the party on whose behalf it is taken.' In other words, it would be dangerous to argue that the survival of the Church of England depended on the Test and Corporation Acts, for then their repeal might make the destruction of the Church a self-fulfilling prophecy. 'I should be sorry for the sake of the Church to argue that she would infallibly cease to be the Established Church, if you were once to admit equality of civil privilege. We might be taken at our word.'[36]

Peel was just as candid in the Commons: 'I do not think . . . that the Church of England must fall if the Test and Corporation Acts are repealed.'[37] He stolidly took the low ground, arguing that the existing system worked, that there was very little pressure for change, that only six petitions had been received between 1817 and 1826, that many of those recently presented had been manipulated, and that the grievances complained of were merely symbolic, and easily surmounted by Nonconformists attending Anglican Communion once a year or else signing a certificate of indemnity. All this fell far short of what Lord Holland had grandiloquently called the Dissenters' condition of 'civil death'. On the other side reformers argued that, if the grievances were merely symbolic, then the privileges were hardly worth preserving; that, if Nonconformists 'were dangerous, they ought to have been excluded altogether; and, if not, they should have been

---

[34] Significantly Lloyd had to dredge these arguments up from the literature. They did not trip off his tongue, which they would have done had belief in a confessional state been habitual. See above, pp. 24–5.

[35] 'House of Commons arguments' were for the 'blockheads' in his party, for 'people who know very little of the matter—care not much about it—half of whom have dined or are going to dine—and are only forcibly struck by that which they instantly comprehend without trouble' (Peel, *Memoirs*, i. 66–7; Parker, *Peel*, ii. 30).   [36] Peel to Lloyd, 20 Mar. 1828, Peel MS 40343, fos. 217–26.

[37] *HPD2* xviii. 751 (26 Feb. 1828).

fully admitted'; that the law tempted hypocritical Dissenters to cheat their way into office, while depriving the public service of more scrupulous brethren who declined to profane the Anglican sacrament; that religious tests were 'a bungling and fallacious proof of loyalty';[38] and that attempts to 'clothe the State with the sacred mantle of religion' reduced religion to the status of a 'mere handmaid of the Government'.[39]

Only one MP seriously sought to defend the Test and Corporation Acts with reference to the Protestant Constitution. Because Robert Harry Inglis had personal links with the Clapham Sect, he is often referred to as an evangelical, but he should probably be designated a High Churchman.[40] Taking his stand by 'the principles of the Constitution, as established at the Revolution', and claiming that he did not 'desire to be a better Whig than Lord Somers', Inglis argued that the Test and Corporation Acts had been outworks, directed not against Charles II but against Oliver Cromwell, and that if they fell 'we should have to fight for the citadel'. He then referred to the cheers with which some MPs had greeted Russell's statement that the Test and Corporation Acts were a restriction on 'the natural rights of man'.

The question of power is one of pure unmixed expediency: no man has an abstract right to it: power, as Burke has stated it, is the creature of society: when once established, indeed, its sanctions are from a higher source: but, in the beginning it is not like the right of life, or of liberty, original and absolute, but it is the arbitrary and artificial arrangement of men, modified and distributed in different ages and countries in every possible variety of combination . . . The question, therefore, whether any man or any body of men, ought to be eligible to power is a question of pure expediency, not of justice; and such power may be regulated by sex, by age, by property, or by opinions, without any wrong to any one's natural claims.[41]

As Burkean rhetoric this was splendid, but it met with ridicule in the Commons. Nor is there evidence to suggest that it struck any chords outside Parliament.

The debates on the Test and Corporation Acts were important, not so much in their own right but because they impacted on the Catholic question. Supporters of repeal argued that the latter issue would be unaffected, since the Declaration against Transubstantiation and the Oath of Supremacy would remain in place, but few were deceived. Many who voted for Test and Corporation Act repeal explicitly did so because it would prise open the door for Catholics.[42] Others opposed it for the same reason. But some (including

[38] Russell, *HPD2* xviii. 683, 686.   [39] George Wilbraham, *HPD2* xviii. 703.
[40] He is described in the *DNB* as being 'of no great ability' but as accurately reflecting 'the feelings and opinions of the country gentlemen'. Both statements are plain wrong.
[41] *HPD2* xviii. 710–15 (26 Feb. 1828).
[42] 'Every step we make this night will be in favour of Ireland—every advance we make for the relief of the Dissenters will be so much gained in the great cause of Catholic emancipation. Break but once

Huskisson and Palmerston) voted against a measure they approved in principle because it might make emancipation *more* difficult to achieve, their fear being that if Protestant Dissenters were relieved first, many of them would then turn against their Catholic 'allies'.[43] Finally, there were twenty to thirty Ultra Tory MPs who disliked Dissenters but disliked papists even more, and who voted to repeal the Test and Corporation Acts in the hope that it would actually stymie Catholic emancipation.[44] The result of all these conflicting prejudices was that Russell's repeal motion was carried by forty-four votes.

At this point Peel requested a four-day postponement while he decided what to do, and when the House refused he stormed out. (He subsequently glossed over this piece of ill temper by saying that he had gone for something to eat.) Then he tried to persuade a backbench loyalist to bring forward a compromise measure. Only when that ruse failed did he resolve to beat the retreat himself. He summoned several of the higher clergy to a meeting, which paved the way for a settlement. The sacramental test was to be abandoned in favour of a declaration by each office-holder and corporation member that he would not, 'on the true faith of a Christian', do anything to subvert the Established Church. It was presented as a compromise but was really a capitulation to the Dissenters. It may be a slight exaggeration to say that Peel 'orchestrated' the Church into submission,[45] but his refusal to fight on 'high ground' was certainly significant, as Russell pointed out privately: 'Peel is a pretty hand at hauling down his colours. It is really a gratifying thing to force the enemy to give up his first line, that none but Churchmen are worthy to serve the State, and I trust we shall soon make him give up the second, that none but Protestants are.'[46] Although Wellington said later that he could have thrown the Bill out in the Lords,[47] the peers did not even bother to divide on the issue. Eldon cursed and raged, yet even he saw that it was by now 'somewhat impracticable' to form an administration 'conformable with [his own] opinions and principles'.[48] And so, in a fit of absence of mind, or rather with their minds on a different problem, the legislators casually cut down the sacred ivy that for nearly two centuries had graced the Constitutional oak.

through the line of bigotry and prejudice, and the victory is our own' (G. Wilbraham, *HPD*2 xviii. 708–10 (26 Feb. 1828)).

[43] 'He was convinced that the present step, so far from being a step in favour of the Catholic claims, would be the means of arraying an additional power against them' (W. Huskisson, *HPD*2 xviii. 734).

[44] G. I. T. Machin, *The Catholic Question in English Politics 1820 to 1830* (Oxford, 1964), 113–15.

[45] J. C. D. Clark, *English Society 1688–1832: Ideology, Social Structure and Political Practice during the Ancien Regime* (Cambridge, 1985), 395.

[46] *Early Correspondence of Lord John Russell 1805–40*, ed. Rollo Russell (1913), i. 272.

[47] WND iv. 411.

[48] Eldon to Mrs Ridley, 3 Mar. 1828, in Horace Twiss, *The Public and Private Life of Lord Chancellor Eldon* (1844), iii. 34.

THE SECOND BLOW: CATHOLIC EMANCIPATION

The Catholic Association had been founded by Daniel O'Connell and Richard Lalor Shiel in May 1823. It was partly a response to the increasingly active and semi-secret Orange societies whose remit was to advance the cause of Protestantism in Ireland, but it broke new ground by levying a tax ('Catholic rent') on its members, thereby binding them fiscally to the cause. To the Anglican Bishop of Limerick, 'the system of collection [was] a complete system of organization. In each parish . . . a "Master" is appointed; he appoints deputy Masters for each townland; they collect from the people, and take down their names, reporting to the Master; the Master to the Priest, &c. &c.' 'In Dublin', he added, 'a system of terror has lately commenced', with the names of all who refused to pay, including Protestants, being entered on a 'proscription list'.[49] In March 1825 the Government legislated to suppress all Irish associations on the grounds that they were usurping the authority of Parliament, even imitating its forms and procedures. Though their target was the Catholic Association, the pretence of even-handedness marked a symbolic break from a policy of automatically favouring the Protestant cause.[50] O'Connell sidestepped the ban by forming a New Catholic Association (July 1825), ostensibly for worship, charity, education, agriculture, and other permitted activities, but really to continue the political work of the old Association. A patient and determined mobilizer with a capacious knowledge of local politics, he organized his supporters— mainly priests, gentry, professional men, and shopkeepers—into Liberal clubs in eighteen counties, with the intention of persuading Catholic forty-shilling freeholders to defy their (mainly) Protestant landlords. This was despite the fact that he had little faith in their actually doing so, and was ready to go along with Plunket's proposal to disfranchise them in return for Catholic emancipation. This pragmatic willingness to pursue alternative strategies was typical, and may have owed something to O'Connell's experience as a successful barrister.

In one special sense, his politics were passive. He was inured to adverse or otherwise unpleasing decisions being handed down by an exterior authority; only momentarily would these depress or irritate him. There were always other cases, other means. This strange amalgam of acquiescence and resilience, of cutting losses and planning their recoupment—the professional's carapace hardened by the years of practice—was the very stamp of his political behaviour.[51]

As it happened, O'Connell underestimated the forty-shillingers. At the general election of 1826, which has been called 'the great turning point in Irish popular

[49] Bishop Jebb to R. H. Inglis, 18 Jan. 1825, Canterbury Cathedral Archive, Inglis Papers, U210/3/1.
[50] Oliver MacDonagh, *The Hereditary Bondsman: Daniel O'Connell 1775–1829* (1988), 215.
[51] Ibid. 188.

politics',[52] gains for anti-Catholic candidates in three nomination boroughs counted for nothing as against six for pro-Catholic candidates, half of them in the popular and hard-fought county constituencies of Monaghan, Waterford, and Louth. Even at the time Shiel commented that 'Ireland has been to a large extent revolutionised'. In England a modest Protestant backlash led to net gains of sixteen MPs, but this was many fewer than had been expected, nor could they all be taken at face value. At Leicester, for example, Anglican aldermen and councillors went in for pope-bashing, but only because they were afraid that civil rights for Catholics would spill over in favour of Protestant Dissenters, who would then compete with them for control of the local Corporation,[53] another example of how Catholics and Nonconformists got in each other's way. With regard to the election in general, 'the grand point', according to Palmerston, was 'that the No Popery cry has been tried in many places and has everywhere failed; and we may now appeal to the experience of facts to show that there does *not* exist among the people of England that bigoted prejudice on this point which the anti-Catholics accused them of entertaining'.[54]

It had been clear for some time, even to ardent anti-Catholics like Lord Liverpool, that 'whenever the *crisis does come*, the *Protestants* must go to the *wall*'.[55] Canning's elevation finally provoked that crisis by bringing the question to the top of the agenda. Accordingly, when Wellington became Prime Minister in January 1828, he immediately sounded out Bishop Phillpotts as to whether and on what the terms Churchmen might agree to a settlement. In May Burdett's motion for emancipation passed the Commons by six votes, only to be flung out in the Lords by 44. Peel flew his Protestant colours for the last time, but his speech contained a 'get-out' clause, when he said in a low-key way that he 'would do all in his power' to bring emancipation about *if* he could be persuaded— which he was not at present—that it would tranquillize Ireland. In similar vein, Wellington informed peers that, while he would never concede to agitation, a settlement might be possible if only there were peace in Ireland. But what really brought emancipation forward was the departure of its main supporters from the Cabinet in May–June 1828. Acutely conscious of their late leader's legacy, Huskisson, Palmerston, Dudley, and Grant had worked closely together, particularly over the Corn Law, on which Wellington found himself isolated.[56] He therefore seized the first opportunity to flush them out. It had already been decided to suppress the constituencies of Penryn and East Retford on account of gross electoral corruption, but there was disagreement over whether the vacant

[52] Fergus O'Ferrall, *Catholic Emancipation: Daniel O'Connell and the Birth of Irish Democracy 1820–30* (Dublin, 1985), 143.
[53] A. Temple Patterson, *Radical Leicester: A History of Leicester 1780–1850* (Leicester, 1954), 148.
[54] Palmerston to William Temple, 17 July 1826, in Henry Lytton Bulwer, *Life of Palmerston* (1870), i. 171.
[55] Liverpool to Bathurst, 4 May 1825, in *Historical Manuscripts Commission Report on the Manuscripts of Earl Bathurst*, ed. Francis Bickley (1923), 581.   [56] See above, p. 307.

representation should be given to Manchester and Birmingham, or whether the seats should be 'thrown into the hundreds', i.e. made larger by incorporating adjacent parishes. The former course would concede the case for parliamentary reform, while the latter would resist it, especially as the parishes around East Retford were owned by the Ultra Tory Duke of Newcastle, who was soon to outrage reformers by evicting some tenants for political disobedience and demanding contemptuously, 'Is it not lawful for me to do what I please with mine own?'[57] The Cabinet decided in favour of expanding the constituencies, after which Huskisson broke ranks by voting with the Commons minority in favour of Manchester. Since this was a breach of Cabinet responsibility, he wrote to place his office at Wellington's disposal. Craftily, Wellington interpreted it as a letter of resignation and forwarded it to the King. Huskisson protested but was too proud to rescind in writing, so out he went, as contumaciously as he had come in, together with his three allies. The balance in Cabinet now tilted from eight-to-five in favour of emancipation to six-to-five against, and anti-Catholics were delighted. Eldon gave 'one cheer more' for the Protestant ascendancy to a raucous company assembled for the annual dinner of the Pitt Club. But they gloated too soon since, as Palmerston noted in his diary, Wellington might feel more able to attempt emancipation if he could seem to be doing it spontaneously and not at the behest of Canningites.[58]

Peel was left stranded by these events. On the East Retford question he apparently supported Huskisson in Cabinet with 'such a furious passion he became as pale as death',[59] and even Palmerston acknowledged that he was now 'perfectly liberal and enlightened on all subjects except the Catholic Question'.[60] From the opposite perspective Mrs Arbuthnot described him as 'over liberal' and 'for giving up everything'.[61] He was reconciled to emancipation, if only to heal a prolonged and damaging breach between the two Houses, but his own past record seemed to preclude him from doing the business himself. So he asked to be allowed to follow Huskisson onto the back benches, from where he would support a Government-sponsored emancipation bill, only returning to office when the hoo-ha had died down. Like Liverpool in 1825, Wellington fought to keep Peel in the Government, and in this respect at least he was helped by the turn of events in Ireland. Newly appointed ministers were constitutionally required to seek endorsement from their constituents, so the departure of the Canningites led to a number of by-elections, including one in County Clare, the seat of the new President of the Board of Trade, Vesey Fitzgerald. It was due to

[57] The reformers had their revenge on 10 October 1831 when the Nottingham mob razed his mansion, Nottingham Castle.   [58] Bulwer, *Life of Palmerston*, i. 282.

[59] Arbuthnot, *Journal*, ii. 173.

[60] Kenneth Bourne, *Palmerston: The Early Years 1784–1841* (1982), 291.

[61] Arbuthnot, *Journal*, ii. 171.

be held on 5 July, just four days after the three-year ban on bodies like the 'old' Catholic Association was due to lapse. The Association had not previously opposed the election of pro-Catholic candidates like Fitzgerald but, being anxious to make up for lost time, it now decided to oppose *all* Tories, irrespective of their individual views. However, it could find no one to challenge Fitzgerald, who was a popular landlord, and with just a few weeks to go O'Connell was reluctantly persuaded to stand himself, even though as a Catholic he would not be able to take up a seat. Far from laying a trap, he seems to have been as astonished by the outcome as everybody else. He expected the forty-shilling freeholders to follow their landlords. Instead they followed their priests. In Peel's words, 'tens of thousands of disciplined fanatics, abstaining from every excess and every indulgence, and concentrating every passion and feeling on one single object',[62] gave O'Connell a majority of more than 1,000. 'No man can retire in the face of immediate peril.'[63] The election of an ineligible candidate briefly prompted fears of rebellion, forcing Peel to remain in post until he was sure the danger had passed. By September he was confident enough about this to propose resignation once more, but again Wellington resisted, and Peel eventually decided to remain in office and drink from the poisoned chalice. It was a harrowing decision, yet he seems to have felt a touch of relish for the martyrdom (or 'self-devotion', meaning devotion *of* self) that would soon be his. He claimed later that the Anglican hierarchy's refusal to cooperate in emancipation as they had over the Test and Corporation Acts forced him to stay in post, since it meant that Wellington would need his help in persuading the King and the Lords to swallow the potion.

Although it was now clear to Wellington and Peel that emancipation was inevitable, the decision was not announced until 5 February 1829, nor did rumour of their intentions leak out until a few days before that date, when they caused storms of 'indignation and contempt' among those who felt themselves betrayed.[64] The cause of this prolonged governmental paralysis was that Wellington stupidly accepted the King's interpretation of Canning's April Memorandum, which was that the Prime Minister should not even discuss the *possibility* of emancipation with anyone unless he had obtained royal permission.[65] This was to resurrect George III's 1801 veto with a vengeance, and was a doctrine which Liverpool, Canning, and even Goderich would have treated with contempt. It meant that Wellington wasted his energy for months on end, merely trying to get permission to broach the issue, first with Peel and Lyndhurst, then with certain bishops, and finally with his own Cabinet.

[62] Peel to Sir Walter Scott, 3 Apr. 1829, in Parker, *Peel*, ii. 99–100.
[63] Peel to Lord Hotham, 7 Feb. 1829, in Parker, *Peel*, ii. 91.   [64] *Annual Register*, 71 (1829), 4.
[65] Arbuthnot, *Journal*, ii. 198 (29 July 1828); Wellington to George IV, 1 Aug. 1828, in WND iv. 564–70; R. W. Davis, 'The Tories, the Whigs, and Catholic Emancipation, 1827–1829', *HER* 97 (1982), 89–98.

If Wellington had responded to the Clare election with an immediate announcement of his intention to bring emancipation forward, he might have defused the Irish problem, but as time went by and nothing happened, tension rose on both sides. Shiel denounced the Government's 'almost imbecile indecision' and 'fantastical irresolution', while O'Connell, notwithstanding his own socially conservative instincts, felt impelled to hold mass meetings and to step up agitation. This meant that emancipation, when it finally came, looked like a concession to physical force—always a bad precedent—rather than a generous recognition of the will of the electors, which in a roundabout way it was. Meanwhile the Protestant extremists, sensing that all might not be lost, and that ministers might have the bottle to stand up to O'Connell after all, bent every nerve. Throughout Ulster Orangemen formed themselves into more than one hundred Brunswick clubs,[66] and matched O'Connell's tactics by collecting a 'Protestant rent'. 'Almost all the [Protestant] peasantry, the farmers, and mechanics belong, or are on the eve of belonging, to the Brunswickers,' wrote one MP in November. 'The majority of the upper and middle ranks do not belong to them, but wish them all success.'[67] In England, meanwhile, the Brunswick Constitutional Club and its noble spokesmen—Cumberland, Newcastle, Kenyon, Eldon, Colchester, and Winchilsea—made a great deal of noise, though its impact was scattered, being strongest in remote rural parts such as Dartmoor, the Weald of Kent, and the Welsh marches, as well as in certain industrial towns like Birmingham and Sheffield. When rival mobs faced each other on Penenden Heath in Kent (24 October), the Brunswickers out-shouted their rivals. Then there was the battle of petitions, which the Protestants won at the rate of about three to one—over 2,000 protests had been received by the end of March. Yet for all this frenzied activity, most historians have stressed the Brunswickers' ineffectiveness, especially in the political heartlands.[68] Their unconstitutional extremism may well have divided the anti-Catholic forces, which in turn may have persuaded Wellington that he could get away with emancipation politically.

All this while ministers sent out conflicting signals which elated and dejected each party in turn, especially in Ireland where there was a total breakdown of executive government. The new Lord Lieutenant was the one-legged and likeable Marquess of Anglesey. He had gone to Dublin with Protestant views, but had since developed a romantic attachment to the idea of a Gaelic Ireland,

[66] The name Brunswick referred to the senior branch of the House of Hanover.

[67] Hereward Senior, *Orangeism in Ireland and Britain, 1795–1836* (1966), 226.

[68] Machin, *Catholic Question*, 131–56. For a more upbeat assessment, see Clark, *English Society*, 397–8. It is essential to Clark's thesis (see above, pp. 669–70) that Brunswickism should be regarded as the authentic voice of the English people, much as he claims Jacobitism to have been a century earlier. In his view, Brunwickism continues to be underestimated because historians are still in thrall to secular and patrician Whigs like Holland, who were disdainful of the 'Kentish clodpolls and bigots', as they were of 'most manifestations of English democratic opinion'.

and from the moment of O'Connell's election he bombarded Peel and Wellington with letters on the need for an immediate concession of the Catholic claims.

You will, I am sure, appreciate the motive that engages me to revert again to the great question. Few, very few, even of the reputed Orangemen, now dispute the fact that it must at no distant period be adjusted. Every hour increases the difficulty of adjustment. What would have been considered as a perfect boon but a few years—I may say but a few months ago—would not, I apprehend, be now very gratefully received.[69]

In all his replies to Anglesey Peel prevaricated, prevented by the royal veto from letting him know what was in his mind. The Lord Lieutenant naturally concluded that his political masters intended to do nothing, in which case it seemed to him that *he* must do something, so that autumn he began to court the Catholic Association very publicly, inviting its members to parties and giving them audiences, all in a desperate attempt 'to keep this country in a quiet state for a little time longer' by charm. The situation was becoming ridiculous and ended in farce. On 16 November, having warned the King that 'nobody can answer for the consequences of delay', Wellington at last secured permission to raise the matter with certain clerics, though still not with the Cabinet or Lord Lieutenant.[70] Accordingly he wrote on 11 December to the Roman Catholic Primate of Ireland, Dr Patrick Curtis, explaining that he expected to settle the Irish question satisfactorily, and merely wished to 'bury it in oblivion for a short time', presumably to let the Protestant flames die down. Curtis showed this letter to Anglesey, who reacted as though scales of incomprehension had fallen from his eyes. He informed Curtis in writing that he should have trusted Wellington's judgement and made more 'ample allowance . . . for the difficulties of his situation'. Unfortunately, the Cabinet had already decided that Anglesey had gone too native and should be recalled, yet the sacking of so popular a Viceroy—'this gallant and high-minded man', O'Connell called him—reinforced the impression that Wellington meant to defy the Catholics. And so, to calm tempers, Anglesey gave the game away by publishing his own private letter to Curtis. Even allowing for the difficulties of his situation, Wellington had made a very botched job of it.

Encouraged by Ultra peers including his brother the Duke of Cumberland, the King held out for several months, pleading his Coronation Oath. On 4 March he went so far as to dismiss his ministers, no doubt in the hope that Cumberland and Eldon would be able to form a Protestant administration. They could not. Wellington was then called back to Windsor where the King, still 'saying he would ne'er consent, consented', and on the very next day Peel proposed a motion 'to incorporate the Catholics into the Constitution'. The resignation

[69] Anglesey to Peel, 26 July 1828, in Peel, *Memoirs*, i. 164–5.
[70] Wellington to George IV, 16 Nov. 1828, in WND v. 252–4.

may well have been a charade, calculated to make it look as though George IV had done his best by his friends. From this point on the result was hardly in doubt, despite frenzied last-ditch efforts by Inglis, Sadler, Wetherell, Lowther, Cumberland, Jebb, Winchilsea, Newcastle, and others, and the Bill passed by huge majorities in both Houses.

The last-ditchers were sincere but did not argue on what Peel would have called the 'high ground'. Reliance on the Coronation Oath, and Inglis's claim that the King was a deliberative part of the Constitution like Parliament, were transparent ruses and not taken seriously. Inglis also dwelled on the history of the question and the geography of religious toleration, but his only substantive points were pragmatic ones, such as his claim that Irish priests would take advantage of emancipation to demand a Catholic King, a Catholic establishment, and repeal of the Union. 'One step more, and we are prostrate.'[71] Other Ultra Protestants like Michael Thomas Sadler, a Leeds merchant and the Duke of Newcastle's protégé, used apocalyptic language to describe the fissure that had opened up between public and parliamentary opinion.

I know how dear this sacred, this deserted cause, is to the hearts and to the understandings of Englishmen. The principle may be indeed weak in this House, but abroad it marches in more than all its wonted might ... To their representatives the people of England committed their dearest birthright, the Protestant Constitution. They have not deserted it, whoever have. If it must perish, then, I call God to witness, that the people are guilt-less! Their voices are heard, in their numerous and earnest petitions, calling aloud, as it were, for water, to wash their hands from the stain of all participation in this foul transaction.

Finally there was the argument, also emphasized by Sadler, that Ireland needed poor laws, philanthropy, resource development, and employment, not emancipation.

Ireland—degraded, deserted, oppressed, pillaged—is turbulent; and you listen to the selfish recommendations of her agitators. You seek not to know, or, knowing, you wilfully neglect, her real distresses. If you can calm the agitated surface of society there, you heed not that fathomless depth of misery, sorrow, and distress, whose troubled waves may still heave and swell unseen and disregarded. And this forsooth is patriotism! Ireland asks of you a fish, and you give her a serpent; she sues for employment, for bread—you proffer her Catholic Emancipation.[72]

According to Greville, half a million copies of Sadler's speech were sold and it was also printed in the *Morning Journal*.

The Ultras were bitter, but their opponents were far from elated. Catholics were still excluded from the throne, the lord lieutenancy, and some other positions. Worse, the Relief Bill was accompanied by legislation to suppress societies such

[71] *HPD*2 xix. 525–7 (9 May 1828).   [72] *HPD*2 xx. 1150–4, 1168–9 (17 Mar. 1829).

as the Catholic Association and to disfranchise the Irish forty-shilling freeholders, those 'disciplined fanatics' who had precipitated the crisis. The proscription of political clubs was probably aimed at the Orange Association and designed to prevent a violent Protestant backlash, especially in Ulster, but it looked like petty vindictiveness against O'Connell, and far from deterring Protestant radicals it may have galvanized them into activity, in England as well as Ireland, for example in the Birmingham Political Union. As for disfranchisement, O'Connell had acquiesced in this idea in 1825, but he was furious about it now that the forty-shilling freeholders had unexpectedly done their stuff. Peel defended the move by stating that the right to vote 'differs in its character from the rights of property, and other strictly private rights. It is a public trust given for public purposes—to be touched, no doubt, with great caution and reluctance; but still, which we are competent to touch, if the public interest manifestly demands the sacrifice.'[73] It might have been a debating point, but the distinction he made between public and private rights had ominous implications for any Tories who still looked to Peel as their champion.

THE EMANCIPATION OF PEEL

Wellington and Peel took no pleasure in emancipation, but they knew that without it many more Irish counties would do a Clare at the next election. That would inevitably lead to an alternative Parliament in Dublin and the end of the Union. The latter was less than thirty years old, yet it was held to be sacrosanct by most Englishmen, partly because of their anti-Catholicism, which had recently become far more virulent, partly because of their fears for absentee landlords' property rights, partly because Ireland was still a likely back door for French invasion, and partly because the consciousness of being an imperial power made loss of John Bull's other island unthinkable.

It is often said that Wellington and Peel acted as they did in order to prevent a civil war in Ireland, and certainly Wellington sometimes referred to the 'Spanish danger'. To an extent this reflected his more pragmatic temperament. Supposing, he mused, Irish Catholics refused to pay tithes. 'The clergy and the landlords might have recourse to the Law. But how is the Law to be enforced? How can they distrain for rent or tithes millions of tenants?'[74] But it must also be borne in mind that Wellington anticipated huge resistance from his fellow peers (wrongly as it turned out), and used every argument to hand. Peel had no such imperative, since the Commons was sure to pass emancipation now that it was proposed by ministers, and it must be significant that he did not employ the civil war argument, either in public or in private, even though he could have made

---

[73] Ibid. 771–2 (5 Mar. 1829).   [74] Wellington to George IV, 14 Oct. 1828, in WND v. 133–6.

things easier for himself by doing so. His confidant Charles Lloyd realized this when he urged Peel to announce 'that your original opinions remained altogether unchanged, although the circumstances of the Empire had rendered it necessary that you should consent to a satisfactory adjustment of the question'. Without such a disclaimer, people might think that there had been a 'total abandonment of your former opinions'.[75] But Peel would not make things easier for himself. 'I have not the slightest apprehension of the result of civil commotion.' 'I believe it could be put down at once.'[76] The point about the recent by-election was not that it had been disorderly but that it had been so peaceful. 'In this case of the Clare election, and of its natural consequences', he wrote later, 'what was the evil to be apprehended? Not force—not violence—not any act of which law could take cognizance. The real danger was in the peaceable and legitimate exercise of a franchise according to the will and conscience of the holder.'[77] Or, as he put in debate, 'I yield . . . to a moral necessity which I cannot control.'[78] While mere physical necessities like civil war were manageable, the evil here was 'not casual and temporary, but permanent and inveterate'.

Whereas the Duke wanted to accompany Catholic relief legislation with 'wings' or safeguards—such as a royal veto on the ordination of priests, or the imposition of oaths, or some form of concurrent endowment[79]—Peel objected that such compromises would merely 'give power to the Roman Catholics without giving satisfaction'. One of the reasons he gave so much offence to his supporters in 1829 was the apparently self-righteous (albeit defensive) way in which he presented the case for emancipation, as though it were self-evident to all but fools. Gladstone wrote later about 'the agony' of 1829 as a process during which Peel grew to 'ripeness', and certainly it brought his policy on this most important issue of the day into line with his liberal instincts on most other matters. In this sense it was a moment of truth, and entailed a change of political personality. Understandably contemporaries were slow to perceive this. Mrs Arbuthnot, for example, was unwilling to believe in Peel's conversion, and so put his behaviour down to cowardice. 'The fact is, Mr Peel's fear of the liberals in the House of Commons gets the better of his judgment and temper.'[80]

Clearly Peel's change of policy on Ireland was not pragmatic in the most straightforward sense. That is to say, he did not adopt a new policy in order to prevent a practical evil, while continuing deep down to believe in the merits of the old one. On the contrary, he changed his whole approach to Irish governance, as well as his language and tone. Whether it was an intellectual or

[75] Lloyd to Peel, 1 Feb. 1829, Peel MS 40343, fos. 334–9.

[76] Peel, memorandum, 12 Jan. 1829, in Peel, *Memoirs*, i. 293.   [77] Peel, *Memoirs*, i. 117.

[78] *HPD*2 xx. 730 (5 Mar. 1829).

[79] Meaning the payment of State salaries to Catholic priests, with the intention naturally of subordinating them to political control.   [80] Arbuthnot, *Journal*, ii. 173 (21 Mar. 1828).

ideological conversion is more questionable. It can plausibly be argued that Peel never really *believed* in any policy because he was not the type of politician to feel commitments. An intellectually and socially diffident outsider, despite his privileged education, his attachment to the established Church was more functional than intellectual or emotional, a way of conforming and of confirming his own membership of the establishment. He was too young for Canning's eighteenth-century sceptical cosmopolitanism, having grown up while Britain was intellectually and physically isolated from the Continent. Surely there was something sacred about the Constitution of the country that had overwhelmed Napoleon, and Protestantism seemed an integral part of its Constitution.[81] Unfortunately, most of those whom Peel called 'the intelligence', and whose esteem he most craved, were in favour of Catholic emancipation, and this situation could only get worse, since 'the opinions of the young men who are now entering into public life, and who are likely to distinguish themselves, are, with scarcely an exception, if with one, in favour of an adjustment of the question'.[82] Looked at in this light, it could be said that he did not so much change his mind on the Catholic question, merely that his former attitudes lost their relevance as circumstances changed.

This is all part of the picture. On the other hand, there are good grounds for thinking that Peel really did undergo a conversion, a claim that seems more plausible in light of the ideological polarization taking place at that time. In 1829 he offered four main arguments in favour of emancipation, each in its way a declaration of liberal principle. First, he succumbed to the Whig–Liberal belief in progress:

They must advance, or they must recede. They must grant further political privileges to the Roman Catholics, or they must retract those already given. They must remove the barriers that obstruct the continued flow of relaxation and indulgence, or they must roll back to its source the mighty current which has been let in upon us, year after year, by the gradual withdrawal of restraint.[83]

'The time is come.' 'The time has at length arrived.' Some Tories were still trying to resist the spirit of the age, yet from 1829 onwards Peel claimed to accept the direction in which society was moving, and merely sought to ensure that it did not move too rapidly. This collusion with Whigs in a rhetoric of progress helped to make change a self-fulfilling prophecy, enabling Peel's later disciple Gladstone to make a virtue of his many similar conversions.

Secondly, Peel's conversion was liberal in so far as he now sought to get the mechanism of Irish society right, rather than govern the country through management and influence. He had been a high Tory in Irish matters only

<hr />

[81] For interesting reflections on these lines, see Norman Gash, *Mr Secretary Peel: The Life of Sir Robert Peel to 1830* (1961), 586–98.   [82] Peel to Jebb, 8 Feb. 1829, in Peel, *Memoirs*, i. 361.
[83] *HPD2* xx. 729–30 (5 Mar. 1829).

because he thought that to keep the peace in Ireland it was necessary to work through the 'exclusive agency' of landlords, stipendiary magistrates, vestry men, and police authorities, almost all of whom were Protestants. It was like Vansittart operating through financiers, Sidmouth through informers, Castlereagh through diplomatists. It had seemed essential not to offend the only section of the community which could deliver sound administration and impartial justice, to provide education and (one day perhaps) a measure of poor relief. If he had come to the Irish question fresh from the outside, as with economic policy in 1819, he would probably have adopted a more theoretical approach from the start, but he had got to know Ireland from the *inside*, as Chief Secretary, and had learned too well how to manage the 'Protestant system' to want to dismantle it. By 1828, however, he had come to realize that this attempt to rule through the Protestant ascendancy was *ipso facto* to colonize Ireland and render her ungovernable. He may have been influenced by the Canningite Charles Grant, who had argued that the exclusion of Catholics 'deranged the whole system'. By giving to numbers what they would not give to property—i.e. by allowing Catholic freeholders to vote while not allowing Catholic landlords to stand— Parliament had 'destroyed the influence of rank and property' and delivered 'the body of the people at the feet of the priest or incendiary'. An alternative structure of authority had therefore evolved, 'a vast and compact body, exercising a power not recognized by the Government'. However, if only Catholics could be incorporated, 'the moderate party will then come forward, while the violent party will be constrained and kept within bounds'.[84] Grant's response was typical of imperial statesmen facing national movements, and compared with similar appeals to 'loyal' Americans, Indians, and Arabs. Peel appropriated many of Grant's arguments in 1829, apparently oblivious of the fact that they contradicted most of his previous statements. 'The system of governing Ireland by patronage'[85] would have to be abandoned because 'there are not adequate materials or sufficient instruments for its effectual and permanent continuance'. In other words, there were simply too few Protestants, especially in the South and West.[86] But if high Tory management did not work, then it was necessary to make the system less deranged, to create a natural self-regulating society based on conciliation and consent:

Surely, government, civil government, means something more than the rigid enforcement of penal law . . . There is a willing moral obedience, founded on the sense of equal justice, without which the terrors of the law would be vain . . . God grant that . . . by the admission of the Roman Catholics to a full and equal participation in civil rights, and by the establishment of a free and cordial intercourse between all classes of his majesty's subjects,

---

[84] *HPD*2 xix. 598–600 (12 May 1828).

[85] For this phrase, see Wallace to Herries, 8 Aug. 1821, Herries MS xxxvi, fos. 105–7.

[86] Castlereagh's high Tory response to this situation was the same as Wellington's: concurrent endowment of Irish Catholic priests and Presbyterian ministers (Wendy Hinde, *Castlereagh* (1981), 98).

mutual jealousies may be removed ... God grant that the moral storm may be appeased—
that the turbid waters of strife may be settled and composed—and that, having found
their just level, they may be mingled, with equal flow, in one clear and common stream.[87]

'Intercourse.' 'Just level.' This was the language of political economy. A third
reason for describing Peel's conversion as liberal derives from his essentially
economic vision of how Ireland should henceforward be governed. In the hope
that mutual goodwill would provide opportunities for individual elevation, as well
as attracting 'the enterprise and capital of England', he insisted on repealing
remnants of the old penal laws against Catholics owning property.[88] A decade later
he developed a policy for land reform, with the intention of building up a Catholic
middle class. Meanwhile, 'public money in aid of local improvements' should be
scaled down as part of the system of 'moral evil' now being dismantled. Even where
such funds were not misappropriated, their mere existence discouraged local
landlords and businessmen from exerting themselves to improve their localities.[89]

Economic liberals believe in markets and markets have to be policed: one
reason why economic liberals tend to be authoritarian. It is therefore not
surprising that Peel's capitalist vision of Ireland's future incorporated proposals
for firm government. Emancipation may even have been a secondary concern.
Once the law officers had advised Peel against trying to suppress the Catholic
Association under existing legislation, he may have seen emancipation as the
political price which would have to be paid in order to persuade Parliament
to pass tougher measures of coercion.[90] Conversely, he predicted that emancipation would do no good unless the Irish could be habituated 'to a vigorous unsparing
enforcement and administration of the law, criminal and civil'. Policing and
punishment must come first, while 'extensive schemes for the employment,
and education, and improvement of the condition of the people' would have
to wait. 'The time is come when it is unnecessary any longer to pet Ireland.'[91]
Or to 'spoil' her with subsidies from the public funds.

We may no doubt repress any actual violence by military force; but I think some severe
discipline must be permanently administered, and discipline for which Ireland ought to
pay ... Why should England pay the charge of civilising Ireland, either by direct pecuniary advances or indirectly by maintaining a great military force? ... Let Ireland, as is
but just, pay the charge of suppressing her own disorders, and have therefore an inducement to keep the peace.[92]

---

[87] *HPD*2 xx. 730, 748, 778–9 (5 Mar. 1829).

[88] Ibid. 757, 772 (5 Mar. 1829). Hopes that Ireland might become better integrated into the British
economy had been boosted by the assimilation of the two countries' exchequers in 1817 and currencies
in 1826.   [89] Peel to Anglesey, 26 July 1828, in Peel, *Memoirs*, i. 175–6.

[90] Peel, memorandum, 12 Jan. 1829, in Peel, *Memoirs*, i. 286.

[91] Peel to Leveson Gower, 30 July 1829, in Parker, *Peel*, ii. 122–3.

[92] Peel to Wellington, 27 July 1829, in Parker, *Peel*, ii. 120–1; WND vi. 52–3. In 1825 five-sixths of Britain's
30,000 armed troops were stationed either in Ireland or else on the west coast, ready for embarkation.

It would take another fifty years for most English politicians to accept that Ireland was never going to respond to the stimulus of competitive markets, and that collectivist policies such as public works and State-sponsored peasant proprietorship were necessary to prevent social breakdown. One purpose of Gladstone's Home Rule Bill (1886) was to separate the two fiscal systems and devise a mechanism whereby, ultimately, better-off Irish citizens could be made to reimburse the British Exchequer for any sums spent on social and economic development. For, as Peel might have put it in Gladstone's situation, why should England pay the charge of modernizing Ireland?[93]

Peel's biggest polemical somersault was to argue that emancipation was necessary in order to avert 'an imminent and increasing danger' to the Protestant Church. 'This is my defence—this is my consolation—this shall be my revenge.'[94] Yet for many years he had warned that to 'open wide the door of political power to the Roman Catholics' would be to endanger the 'pure faith' by creating a 'priestly ascendancy'.[95] This was the standard view, held by High or Orthodox Churchmen, but most members of the Clapham Sect and other evangelicals of their type—people whose world-view was close to Peel's—supported emancipation, not because they sympathized with Catholics but because they thought that discriminatory laws helped the enemy. They advocated 'free trade in religion', being confident that Protestantism was a superior product and would prosper under competition. This doctrine was memorably enunciated by Chalmers in a celebrated sermon of 1827, when Peel was among the congregation. According to Chalmers, Protestantism had triumphed over popery at the Reformation, but had lost ground from the moment it swapped spiritual weapons for 'carnal' ones.

The moment that the forces of the statute-book were enlisted on the side of Protestantism, from that moment Popery, armed with a generous indignancy against its oppressors, put on that moral strength, which persecution always gives to every cause that is at once honoured and sustained by it. O, if the friends of religious liberty had but kept by their own spiritual weapons, when the cause was moving onward in such prosperity, and with such triumph! But when they threw aside argument, and brandished the ensigns of authority, then it was that truth felt the virtue go out of her; and falsehood, inspired with an energy before unknown, planted the unyielding footstep, and put on the resolute defiance.[96]

---

[93] Whereas the Conservative Party was willing to spend British taxpayers' money on Irish improvement, hoping that such kindness would kill demands for Home Rule.

[94] *HPD2* xx. 754, 779 (5 Mar. 1829).   [95] *HPD2* xix. 581–2 (9 May 1828).

[96] *Works of Thomas Chalmers* (Glasgow, 1836–42), xi. 152–3; *Memoirs of the Life and Writings of Thomas Chalmers*, ed. William Hanna (Edinburgh, 1852), iii. 161–2. Chalmers's confidence that Protestantism would benefit from the removal of laws designed to protect it was analogous to his belief that agriculture would benefit from the removal of the Corn Laws. See above p. 310.

Grant and Huskisson deployed the same argument in 1828,[97] and then a year later—most unexpectedly—so did Peel. Why was it, he asked rhetorically, that the 'Reformation in Ireland has hitherto made no advance?'

Where are our conversions? In what part of the world is the adherence to the errors against which we protest more inveterate than it is in Ireland? Let us maturely consider, whether penalties and disabilities may not have enlisted pride on the side of conscience . . . may not have raised defences round prejudice and superstition, which have been and will continue to be impenetrable by terror or force.[98]

With luck emancipation would conciliate the Catholics, but if it did not and they sought to use their new powers to turn themselves into an intolerant 'ascendancy', at least Protestants would be able to fight back on the basis of their own 'intrinsic purity'.

We shall have dissolved the great moral alliance that has hitherto given strength to the cause of the Roman Catholics. We shall range on our side the illustrious authorities which have heretofore been enlisted upon theirs;—the rallying cry of 'Civil Liberty' will then be all our own. We shall enter the field with the full assurance of victory.[99]

So sanguine was Peel about 'the expansive force of the Protestant faith', that four years later he still felt able to congratulate himself on 'the spreading of the Reformation in Ireland'.[100]

Clearly, Peel was not the sort of liberal who prioritized individual rights. He still hated Catholics, especially rootless and itinerant Jesuits engaged in Catholic mission,[101] and he abhorred the hold which that Church exercised over poorer Irish freeholders. 'The landlord has been disarmed by the priest,' thereby 'severing every remaining tie between the landed proprietor and the Roman Catholic tenantry of Ireland.'[102] Wellington thought that emancipation was essential if the nobility and gentry were ever to 'recover their lost influence',[103] but for Peel it was already too late, hence his insistence on disfranchising the Irish forty-shilling freeholders. As with the suppression of the Catholic Association, perhaps he felt that the only way to force such a drastic measure through Parliament was to offer emancipation as a quid pro quo.

MONEY AND THE MILLENNIUM

'The world seems altered in every way. It seems that seasons, people, and principles, are so altered that I can hardly believe that I am still in poor Old

---

[97] *HPD*2 xix. 665–6 (12 May 1828).   [98] *HPD*2 xx. 753 (5 Mar. 1829).
[99] Ibid. 779 (5 Mar. 1829).   [100] *HPD*3 xvii. 999 (6 May 1833).
[101] Memorandum on Catholic emancipation, Jan. 1829, Peel MS 40398, fos. 52–61.
[102] *HPD*2 xx. 746, 764 (5 Mar. 1829).   [103] Wellington to Peel, 12 Sept. 1828, in WND v. 43.

England.'[104] Many Tories shared the bitterness of Lord Kenyon's aunt over Catholic emancipation. One cartoonist depicted Wellington and Peel as 'murdering the Constitution' and handing the body over to be dissected by grinning Jesuits. (This was a reference to the notorious killers Burke and Hare, who sold their victims' corpses to the Edinburgh anatomy schools.[105]) Wellington was widely condemned for accepting a challenge to a duel, while Peel was widely condemned for declining one. He was, however, obliged to stand for re-election at Oxford University, was heavily beaten, and forced to seek refuge in a close borough. His conqueror was Inglis, who had taken the Chiltern Hundreds in order to humiliate him. Virtually everything that the Prime Minister did in 1829 was criticized. In particular, the establishment of the Metropolitan Police, together with his penchant for appointing old soldiers to political positions (namely, Anglesey, Murray, Hardinge, and Rosslyn), led to complaints that he wanted 'to make all Europe a military camp and to govern upon arbitrary principles'. Wellington was even blamed for events in France, where Martignac was replaced by the ultra-royalist Polignac as head of the Government.[106]

The political panic was exacerbated by economic crisis. The December 1825 banking and Stock Market crash, the first and worst of the century, came out of a clear blue sky and appeared to strike 'the innocent and the guilty' alike.[107] Several major banks failed, and 1,650 bankruptcies were recorded during the first half of 1826 alone. Shortage of specie led to non-payment of wages, which provoked riots in industrial districts, for example among the weavers of Blackburn from where they spread to Manchester, Bury, Rochdale, and Oldham. In all these places county magistrates were few and far between, and lacked personal links with working people. Significantly there were no disturbances in Preston, which had corporate status and a householder franchise, and where resident JPs provided for adequate poor relief and a uniform rate for piecework, something that had been refused in nearby Blackburn. In Lancashire as a whole ten people died, scores were injured, and thousands of pounds, worth of damage was done, mainly to power-looms. The rising was eventually smothered by military terror, but it had demonstrated 'a powerful unity' on the part of the working classes, and appears to have 'lasted long in the collective consciousness'.[108] It also scared the middle classes and confirmed Peel's view that methods of policing needed to be completely restructured.

[104] Machin, *Catholic Question*, 180.
[105] Hare turned King's evidence and Burke was hanged in 1829.
[106] Richard Vyvyan's opinions, as reported in Palmerston to Laurence Sulivan, 7 Oct. 1829, in *The Letters of Viscount Palmerston to Lawrence and Elizabeth Sulivan 1804–1863*, ed. K. Bourne (1979), 233; Robert Heron, *Notes* (Grantham, 1851), 181. As the French Ambassador to London (1823–9), Polignac had been a member of the Cottage Coterie. See above, p. 290.
[107] G. C. Babington to T. Babington, 23 Dec. 1825, Trinity College, Cambridge, Babington Papers, 2⁷⁴.
[108] David Walsh, 'The Lancashire "Rising" of 1826', *Albion*, 26 (1994), 601–21.

While food got dearer, the movement of industrial prices, profits, wages, and investment was downwards from 1827 to 1832, creating a state of stable stagnation.[109] Commerce and manufacturing languished, and London lay blighted by unfinished building projects as a phase of hectic development came to a sudden halt. (Although no one knew it at the time, the age of grand projects and metropolitan improvements was over for good.) So-called professionals, artists, writers, and entertainers all suffered badly. Yet the psychological shock of December 1825 was even worse than the actuality. For decades moralists had warned against the moment when the bubble burst, and for everyone who lost a fortune there were scores who wondered how close they had come to doing so. Their personal assets might be sound, but in a system of unlimited liability innocent investors could find themselves plunged from riches to penury overnight and through no fault of their own. Frenzied whisperings as to who might be next to fall inaugurated a preoccupation with business crashes, those cyclical visitations that were to cut further great swathes through Society in 1837, 1847, 1857, and 1866. No other subject so forcefully gripped the imagination of novelists and homilists.

The fear, not the fact—the fear of overtrading may so excite the mind of the man of vast enterprize, that he may, by finesse and contrivance, seek to veil the vastness of his transactions from other eyes, lest they should suspect, what by-and-bye may be the fact, that he has gone beyond his balance, and that a crash may follow the indiscretion, by which millions may suffer.[110]

When danger threatened, businessmen dared not even warn their families for fear of making the situation worse, 'and this suppression of misery is worse than the misery itself'.[111] When the crash came it brought immediate oblivion. 'The erasure of the name from the doors and the memory of the firm from their friends were almost simultaneous.'[112] No wonder so many cracked, went mad, turned hermit, converted, or killed themselves.

The most celebrated victim of 1825 was Walter Scott, whose gestures of friendship had left him responsible for the debts of three of his publishers, Ballantyne & Co., Constable & Co., and Hurst, Robinson, and Co. 'My extremity has come,' Scott noted in his diary on 18 December; 'I suppose it will involve my all.' 'London chooses to be in an uproar . . . in the tumult of bulls and bears,' and 'a poor inoffensive lion like myself is pushed to the wall'. Despite liabilities of £104,081, Scott managed to avoid bankruptcy, having transferred his Abbotsford estate to his eldest son in the nick of time. He spent the last seven

[109] A. D. Gayer, W. W. Rostow, and A. J. Schwartz, *The Growth and Fluctuation of the British Economy 1790–1850* (Oxford, 1953), i. 211–41.
[110] Revd George Fisk, *Lectures to Young Men in Exeter Hall* (1848), 278–9.
[111] Edward Irving, 'Remarks on Commercial Distress', *The Pulpit*, 6 (1826), 27–8.
[112] Edmund Yates, *Kissing the Rod: A Novel* (1866), iii. 88.

years of his life there writing potboilers, which enabled him to pay a dividend of 9s. in the pound. He thereby managed to salvage his honour and his creditors, not to mention more than 4,000 bottles of wine and 400 bottles of spirits.[113] His unfortunate partner Archibald Constable lived only nineteenth more months, squeezed into squalid digs with a wife and eight children, the eldest of whom apparently went mad with shame. Yet according to Benjamin Disraeli, he had initially faced up to his 'fatal and shattering bankruptcy' in an 'ecstasy of pompous passion'.[114] The 21-year-old Disraeli also crashed but remained shameless. Pale and handsome, with black curly locks, Jewish and bejewelled, extravagantly dressed in ruby and canary waistcoats and lavender trousers—this was a time when sober greys were fashionable—Disraeli reacted to the crisis with all the insouciance of a man who had nothing to lose (and a very rich father).

Evangelical businessmen, whether or not they crashed, invariably invoked divine providence. The Gurneys—bankers of Norwich and evangelical Quakers— were able to stay calm as the crisis developed, 'feeling the Lord to be near to us'.[115] The crisis struck Clapham when Henry Thornton junior was brought down by a dissembling and speculating partner. According to his sister, 'There was something in the sight of so youthful a pilot weathering such a storm... A special Providence seems to watch over those walls. Those same qualities of high honour, strict principle, and fearless integrity which once built it up, have now saved it from falling.' 'This is just the scene to make a man of you,' wrote the Governor of the Bank of England to Henry.[116] Allowing for family piety, this account exemplified the widespread belief that bankruptcy was a moral trial sent by God for the improvement of mankind, which is what Peel meant when he referred to 'ultimate good after some severe suffering'.[117] God sent thunderbolts on individuals in the deaths of children and accidents at work, but to smite whole communities he targeted economies and ecologies, thereby spreading the wings of his wrath over as many individuals as possible. Naturally there was much debate over whether commercial failure justly punished individual guilt in the form of fraud or over-trading, or whether it visited merchants and financiers indiscriminately, in which case bankrupts were sacrificial victims atoning for the sins of society. In both cases commercial failure was a 'dispensation of providence', but the first approach conceived of providence as for the most part acting mechanically, whereas the second more messianically identified

---

[113] For the heroic Scott myth, see Paul Johnson, *The Birth of the Modern: World Society 1815–1830* (1991), 895–8; for a more jaundiced view, see John Sutherland, *The Life of Walter Scott: A Critical Biography* (Oxford, 1995), 272–321.

[114] *Disraeli's Reminiscences*, ed. Helen M. Swartz and Marvin Swartz (1975), 10.

[115] J. G. Gurney, Journal, 25 Nov. 1825, *Memoirs of Joseph John Gurney*, ed. J. B. Braithwaite (Norwich, 1854), i. 300.

[116] E. M. Forster, *Marianne Thornton 1797–1887: A Domestic Biography* (1956), 106–24.

[117] See above, p. 327.

the crash as a 'special providence', a departure from the ordinary course of natural law, a punishment for national sins, even a signpost to the end of the world.

Most Christians looked forward to the millennium, when Christ would come to reign in glory with his saints prior to the General Resurrection and Judgement. For post-millenarians or millennialists (the terms are used interchangeably here), this would only happen when the world was morally and spiritually fit to receive the Messiah. But although they envisaged the millennium as a distant event, they believed that the world was gradually preparing itself under divine guidance. Improvement might be imperceptible, but it was still the job of humankind to accelerate the process by engaging in missionary movements at home and overseas. Some stricter millennialists believed that the Second Coming could not occur until the whole of the world was Christianized, the signal for which would be the restoration and conversion of the Jews. In 1841 the British and Prussian governments set up an Anglican bishopric in Jerusalem with a view to hastening just such an event. Pre-millenarians or pre-millennialists (again the terms are used interchangeably) had no understanding of incremental progress, and believed that the Second Coming must *precede* the millennium. The world, in other words, must sink into wickedness and chaos, like Babylon or Sodom and Gomorrah, before there could be a sudden transformation and 'the light of a morning which is to know no night breaks gloriously forth'. The prophetic books of Daniel were scoured for clues to the exact date of Christ's return, and as favourite years went by and nothing happened, undaunted messianists plucked out new ones. Many, like G. S. Faber and J. H. Frere, believed that the vial of the Apocalypse had begun to pour with the French Revolution, that Napoleon was the beast from the abyss, and that his victories were successive breakings of the seals, all as adumbrated in Revelation. The taste for apocalypse explains the extraordinary popularity of John Martin's paintings, especially *The Fall of Babylon* (exhibited in 1819 and issued in mezzotint in 1831)[118] and *The Deluge* (which first went on show in 1826). It also explains why the 1825 bank crash should have prompted so many to suppose that 'events were visibly marching forward' to a 'great visible era of doom and triumph'.

Historically, pre-millenarianism had appealed mainly to the poor and dispossessed. Powerless on earth, they could at least claim the consolation of knowing the future. In the 1790s the best-selling and pro-revolutionary doomsayer Richard Brothers 'saw Satan walking leisurely into London: his face had a smile, but under it his looks were sly, crafty, and deceitful'.[119] He called on Britain's 'hidden Jews', among whom he numbered William Pitt, to meet in Jerusalem in preparation for the Second Coming. This was all a bit too juicy for the authorities at a time of radical ferment, and after it was claimed that crowds of people 'resorted to him

118 See Plate 12.
119 Richard Brothers, *A Revealed Knowledge of the Prophecies and Times* (1794), 40.

daily', he was incarcerated in a madhouse at the instigation of the Home Secretary. Many of his followers switched allegiance to Joanna Southcott, an 'inspired' writer whose presence attracted hordes of admirers in many provincial towns. According to supporters, her sixty-five *Books of Prophecies* (1792–1814), each dramatically sealed for a number of years, accurately predicted the outcome of battles and harvests. The chief 'inheritor of the Southcottian mantle' was a mad shoemaker, John Ward, known as Zion Ward or Shiloh, whose spellbinding harangues on radical reform and revolution won him huge followings in London, Nottingham, Birmingham, Derby, and Leeds. He propagated a new calendar in which 1826 was designated Year One. Meanwhile, a more cautious and socially conservative strand of pre-millenarian thought was carried by the Dissenting *Evangelical Magazine* from 1793 onwards. Many of its readers were far from being socially oppressed, but they nevertheless saw themselves as outsiders and so were less prone to guilt feelings than Anglicans. Charles Wesley's words

> Ah, lovely Appearance of Death!
> No Sight upon Earth is so fair,
> Not all the gay Pageants that *breathe*
> Can with a dead Body compare

might appear masochistic but were in fact affirmative, and expressed his longing for holy fulfilment, like a 'bride or bridegroom impatient for the wedding-night'.[120] In the same spirit, most Nonconformists envisaged the Second Coming more as Jubilee than Armageddon, more as liberation than Judgement.

The second quarter of the nineteenth century was unusual in that pre-millenarian ideas were taken up widely by elite members of the Establishment. A few, like the Whig Lord Morpeth, seem to have envisaged the Apocalypse as a jolly tea party affair, but the prevailing tone was now overwhelmingly Tory and apprehensive. However glorious the outcome, the process would assuredly be painful. This was the line taken by Henry Drummond, a country MP and partner in the family banking firm at Charing Cross until 1817, when he became 'satiated with the empty frivolities of the fashionable world' and embraced a life of austere religiosity instead. He urged Tsar Alexander, another radical evangelical, to accelerate the conversion of the Jews by establishing a colony for them in the Crimea. During 1825 the insane speculation in Latin American mining shares began to direct his attention to 'the events connected with the close of the Christian dispensation'. According to rumour, he sold his life insurance policies during the reform crisis of 1831, believing that the Second Coming really could not be far off.[121] Another key figure was the Scottish Presbyterian and protégé of

[120] E. P. Thompson, *The Making of the English Working Class* (1965), 373–4.
[121] *Autobiography of Dean Merivale with Selections from his Correspondence*, ed. J. A. Merivale (1899), 127; Timothy C. F. Stunt, *From Awakening to Secession: Radical Evangelicals in Switzerland and Britain 1815–35* (Edinburgh, 2000), 95–7.

Chalmers, Edward Irving, who had been Minister of the Caledonian Chapel in Hatton Gardens since 1822, and was something of an ecclesiastical lion. It was said that Lord Liverpool once had to climb into the building by one of the windows, such was the throng of politicians and other notables struggling to hear the celebrated preacher, while the queue of carriages waiting for the congregation to debouch was sometimes 4 miles long. Before long, however, Irving began to develop unconventional ideas, as in a sermon of 1824 to the London Missionary Society in which he assailed the entire missionary philosophy. He absorbed Frere's prophetic writings and fell under the influence of Coleridge's personality.[122] (On seeing them together, Chalmers was disturbed to note 'a secret and to me as yet unintelligible communion of spirit betwixt them, on the ground of a certain German mysticism and transcendental lake-poetry which I am not yet up to'.[123]) In 1826, when his father-in-law was ruined by rash investments in a joint-stock bank, Irving was sure that God had determined to 'wound us in the part we deem most invulnerable'. He eagerly compared the 'boundless ruin and desolation, spreading on all sides, to the Day of Judgment'.[124]

In the same year Drummond gathered a group of about forty like-minded zealots, two-thirds of them Anglicans, to a series of conferences at his Albury estate in Surrey.[125] Among those present were Irving, Frere, Lord Mandeville, Hugh McNeile, and Alexander Haldane, a prominent religious publisher.

That time was clearly a time of expectation. An age of great events was just over ... At home the internal economy of the country was swelling with great throes—agonies in which many people saw prognostics most final and fatal. Out of all the visible chaos, what a joyful, magnificent deliverance, to believe—through whatsoever anguish the troubled but short interval might pass—that the Lord was coming visibly to confound his enemies and vindicate his people.[126]

Accordingly the Conference resolved 'that the present Christian dispensation is not to pass insensibly into the millennial state by gradual increase of the preaching of the Gospel', but that it was to be 'terminated by judgments, ending in the destruction of this visible Church and polity, in the same manner as the Jewish dispensation had been terminated'.[127] One indication that the event was imminent was that Satan had come down to the earth in great rage, knowing that his time was short, and the hour of temptation almost come.

[122] Coleridge disabused Irving of the belief that 'the present world is to be converted unto the Lord, and so slide by a natural inclination into the Church'. Instead it would be 'burned up and destroyed' in a 'glorious and overwhelming revolution'. Margaret Oliphant, *The Life of Edward Irving* (1862), i. 190–1.

[123] *Memoirs of Chalmers*, iii. 160; D. W. Bebbington, *Evangelicalism in Modern Britain: A History from the 1730s to the 1980s* (1989), 80–1. [124] Irving, 'Remarks on Commercial Distress', 27.

[125] Columba Graham Flegg, *'Gathered under Apostles': A Study of the Catholic Apostolic Church* (Oxford, 1992), 37–8. [126] Oliphant, *Life of Irving*, i. 397.

[127] Henry Drummond, *Dialogues on Prophecy* (1828), vol. i, pp. ii–iii, quoted in Flegg, *'Gathered under Apostles'*, 39.

These . . . are the grounds of our alarm for our beloved country. We quail not before the machinations of the discontented, or the forces of the incendiary, or the assemblies of the seditious, or the assaults of the profane. These are nothing in themselves, and in themselves we fear them not. But we tremble at the recollection of our guilt, our unGodliness, and our rebellion.[128]

These views were disseminated by two new journals, Alexander Haldane's *Record* (1828) and Irving's *Morning Watch* (1829–33). *The Record* was highly political, its parliamentary champion being J. E. Gordon MP, who attacked all liberals— but especially post-millenarian evangelicals—with 'vulgarity and vitriol'.[129] In 1827 he had founded the British Society for Promoting the Religious Principles of the Reformation, a body with close links to the Albury group through McNeile, Drummond, and Mandeville. By 1834 the Reformation Society had acquired fifty-three affiliated branches.[130] *The Record* was just as successful, rapidly eclipsing the *Christian Observer* in terms of circulation, a sign that respectable and moderate evangelicalism was being swamped by Pentecostal, Adventist, and charismatic versions. This explains why so many sons of Clapham gravitated to the High Church, including Gladstone, Stanley, Acland, Newman, Manning, and Robert Wilberforce. Irving, himself, however, went from strength to disaster. It was at the consecration in 1827 of his new Scottish National Church in London's Regent Square that Chalmers delivered his famous sermon in favour of Catholic emancipation. It was almost certainly a rebuke to Irving, who, since meeting Coleridge and taking his pre-millenarian turn, had become violently antipathetic to Rome, which he now identified with Babylon. By 1830 Irving's congregations were known to be 'speaking in tongues' as a sign of divine inspiration, as well as attesting to miraculous cures. More dangerous still was Irving's suggestion that at his incarnation Christ had assumed fallen human nature. This was all part of his desire to assert the worldliness of Christ, in contrast to the excessively spiritual approach of the despised Clapham Sect, but it was obviously heretical and it led to his deposition from the Church of Scotland by the Presbytery of Annan in March 1833. He then helped to found the Catholic Apostolic Church, but died a broken and abandoned man in the following year, aged only 42. Drummond, by contrast, soared up the new Church's hierarchy, becoming in turn an Apostle, Evangelist, Prophet, and eventually Angel.

It was in this context of heightened millennial awareness that repeal of the Test and Corporation Acts suddenly took place. It has to be said that, despite

[128] *The Record*, 29 July and 2 Dec. 1830.
[129] W. J. C. Ervine, 'Doctrine and Diplomacy: Some Aspects of the Life and Thought of the Anglican Evangelical Clergy, 1797 to 1837', Ph.D. thesis (Cambridge University, 1979), 299; Grayson Carter, *Anglican Evangelicals: Protestant Secessions form the Via Media, c.1800–1850* (Oxford, 2001), 152–94.
[130] John Wolffe, *The Protestant Crusade in Great Britain 1829–1860* (Oxford, 1991), 36, 50.

its retrospective significance, 'hardly a dog barked' at the time.[131] Eldon 'fought like a lion' and cursed his former colleagues for a 'parcel of cowards', but he was much less hysterical in private, acknowledging that most people cared more about the latest opera star than about the Protestant Constitution.[132] Another staunch high Tory, Mrs Arbuthnot, barely mentioned the subject in her very detailed political diary. Most Churchmen stayed silent, and Lloyd admitted that even in Oxford there was 'very little feeling about the matter'. There were only twenty-eight petitions against the measure and very few pamphlets.[133] But the few who did oppose got very worked up about what they saw as 'the poison of liberality' and 'the march of intellect'. Most of these were pre-millenarians like Drummond, who stressed the eschatological consequences. By privileging Anglicans, the Test and Corporation Acts recognized the distinction which God had made between religions, but Satan's object was to level distinctions, and 'liberalism is this very principle of Satan in action at the present day'. 'The day of awful retribution' must be at hand, 'when he will come again in power and glory', having 'prepared other instruments of punishment'. Irving was if anything even more excited about the prospect of a divine scourging.[134] Needless to say, the second instalment of 'national apostasy' (Catholic emancipation) multiplied such apocalyptic fantasies a thousandfold. England had 'thrown off her Protestant shield', had 'supped with Anti-Christ', and was now 'grovelling at the cloven feet of Satan, disguised as an Irish Popish demagogue'.[135] 'If we desert our God, will he not desert us? will he not be avenged upon such a nation as this?'[136] 'The curse of God hangs upon the measure.' 'God's people are solemnly warned, that, unless they come out from idolatry, and avoid all union with it, of whatever description; they must expect to receive of those temporal plagues, which are prophetically announced as impending over idolatry.'[137] 'As great and flagrant a rebellion against Christ the King as any ever committed.'[138] Et cetera, et cetera!

Not everyone who opposed Catholic emancipation was pre-millenarian, but all pre-millenarians opposed emancipation, for example the revds William 'Millennial' Marsh and Edward Bickersteth, earls Roden and Winchilsea, and

---

[131] G. F. A. Best, 'Church and State in English Politics 1800–33', Ph.D. thesis (Cambridge University, 1955), 297–8.   [132] Twiss, *Eldon*, iii. 37, 44, 46.

[133] One historian found only four (G. I. T. Machin, 'Resistance to Repeal of the Test and Corporation Acts, 1828', *HJ* 22 (1979), 128–9.

[134] 'A Letter to the King against the Repeal of the Test Act by a Tory of the Old School' (1828), in *Speeches in Parliament and Some Miscellaneous Pamphlets of Henry Drummond*, ed. Lord Lovaine (1860), 51, 54–9; Edward Irving, *A Letter to the King on the Repeal of the Test and Corporation Laws* (1828), 14–15.

[135] Fourth Duke of Newcastle, *Thoughts in Times Past Tested by Subsequent Events* (1837), pp. xx–xxi.

[136] Fourth Duke of Newcastle, *A Letter to Lord Kenyon* (1828), 8, 10. Newcastle blamed Lord Liverpool, under whom the 'vile and accursed system of liberalism, neutrality, and conciliation' had begun.   [137] G. S. Faber, *Four Letters on Catholic Emancipation* (1829), 12–13.

[138] Henry Drummond, *A Letter to Dr Chalmers* (1829), 10–11.

Viscount Mandeville. Conversely, the great majority of post-millenarian evangelicals—including Wilberforce, Chalmers, John and Charles Sumner, Thomas Acland, Daniel Wilson, W. A. Shirley, and Thomas Gisborne—supported the policy. The difference between the two groups was basically theological, as Drummond lucidly explained in a published *Letter to Dr Chalmers* (1829). Introduced as 'the most redoubted champion of Evangelical liberalism', Chalmers was accused of peddling the 'spurious theology' that had 'pervaded the land', of placing expediency ahead of 'pagan virtues' such as patriotism and chivalry, and of blinding Englishmen to the great fact that all power was held of Christ. But the fundamental error of evangelical liberals was to deny the relevance of the Old Testament to present-day circumstances. Because they were fixated with the 'economy of the Gospel' (or 'Pauline analogy') they thought it was God's will that the Church and the State should be separate, and that Churchmen should confine themselves to preparing individuals for the joys and exercises of Heaven. In other words, that Christ's Kingdom could never be of this world. Against this, Drummond sought to re-establish the ancient Jewish economy in which Church and State had blended, authorizing clerics to interfere in temporal politics. Christ was not merely the redeemer but *King* of the Jews, and though he exercised power at present through earthly vice-regents, he would soon return to exercise it directly. 'Surely it must be admitted, that wherever Christ is King, there can be no free trade in creeds.'[139]

ULTRA TORY BACKLASH

Drawing an analogy between false Christianity and false economics, Drummond proceeded to define liberalism as 'a system of letting loose all ties and bonds whatever, but that of selfish interest'.[140] Since, in his view 'the comfort of the labouring class' was 'the exclusively infallible test of all equitable government', he assigned Chalmers contemptuously to the 'Satanic School of Scotch political economy', the aim of which was to protect capital rather than the poor.

Whereas post-millenarian evangelicals like Chalmers believed in general providence, meaning that God ruled according to fixed laws 99 per cent of the time, pre-millenarians regarded all events as special providences.

The common phrase, 'second causes', may be allowable; but we like it not, nor that which it is generally taken to express. Means are appointed to educe certain effects; but the one sole cause of all things is the will of God—we, of course, except from this wicked works, of which we can but say 'an enemy hath done it', the Lord not interposing to prevent, but for some wise purpose permitting the evil.[141]

---

[139] Ibid. 1–4, 14, 18–21.   [140] Ibid. 22–5.
[141] Charlotte Elizabeth [Tonna], *Second Causes: or, Up and Be Doing* (Dublin, 1843), 2.

In rejecting ideas of mechanism in favour of a perpetually intervening God, pre-millenarians also rejected natural-law-based social theories such as political economy. Not only Drummond but Shaftesbury, Sadler, Bickersteth, Charlotte Elizabeth Tonna, Patrick Brewster, Richard Oastler, William Marsh, George Bull, R. B. Seeley, and S. R. Bosanquet combined belief in an imminent Second Coming with advocacy of generous welfare payments to the poor and with social interventionism (or paternalism) generally. In their view it was the duty of magistrates, who held power under the Lord, to exercise their authority with similar discretion. There is a paradox here. To modern eyes, it looks as though these pre-millenarians were active in seeking to improve the world, whereas post-millenarians were fatalistic and indifferent. But that is only because modern eyes are accustomed to see improvement in predominantly material terms. At the time, both parties were *other*-worldly in their aspirations, and both conceived of improvement in spiritual rather than material terms. Once this is grasped it becomes clear that the post-millenarians were really the improvers and the pre-millenarians were the fatalists. (Some of the latter even opposed 'improvement' because it might delay the Apocalypse.) Hence Drummond denounced the soul-saving Clapham Sect as 'boasters of their charitable, and missionary exploits',[142] and as presuming to do God's work for him, instead of reacting to misfortunes properly, that is to say with resignation and redoubled devotions. Likewise, according to Irving, 'bereavements, losses, crosses, persecution, perils, and sword' were 'so many fostering and nutritious measures to hasten ourselves into premature perfection, and raise us to a preternatural purity; and those who endure such afflictions patiently are to account themselves highly favoured of the Lord, and to reckon that His grace and His providence are working together for their good'.[143] As this suggests, pre-millenarians had more assurance of faith than post-millenarians, and consoled themselves that God used earthly tribulation as a launching pad for the thousand-year reign of felicity. Their paternalism did not stem from a desire to raise the poor in station, but reflected their view that it was the duty of those whom God had placed in the upper ranks of society to protect those below them, as the millennial waters rose and the flames grew hotter. Another difference was that post-millennialists prioritized the soul or spirit, whereas their opponents concentrated on the body and its ultimate resurrection.

Paternalism and pre-millenarianism were factors in the thought of many Ultras. As many as 200 MPs might be regarded as dissident Tories in so far as they were furious about emancipation and the direction of economic policy, but

---

[142] Henry Drummond, *A Defence of the Students of Prophecy* (1828), 116. Clapham types hit back, accusing the pre-millenarians of 'vanity, pride, and carnality' (C. Simeon to J. J. Gurney, 26 Jan. 1832, in *Memoirs of the Life of Charles Simeon*, ed. William Carus (1847), 688–90).

[143] *Miscellanies from the Collected Writings of Edward Irving* (1865), 306.

408 THE CRISIS OF THE OLD ORDER

in order to be classed as an Ultra it was necessary to share Newcastle's metaphysical despair

The whole nation is convulsed—trade, commerce, agriculture are in the utmost distress and confusion... alteration of the currency being the evil, and new doctrines of free trade and free action in everything, have overturned the balance of men's understandings as well as their money accounts.[144]

Possibly as many as ninety MPs fell into this category, including the Marquess of Blandford, Edward Knatchbull, Richard Vyvyan, Robert Inglis, Colonel Sibthorpe, M. T. Sadler, and Sir Charles Wetherell, and they were egged on by peers such as Newcastle, Rutland, Richmond, Winchilsea, Mansfield, Chandos, Roden, Lyndhurst, Cumberland. Although Orangeism was very important to them, emancipation was a done deal and could not possibly be undone. Instead what mainly sustained the Ultra campaign was a Cobbettian critique similar to that of the early 1820s. Newcastle acknowledged the importance of economic factors when he suggested that they should ditch the names Whig and Tory and call themselves 'the Country Party'.[145] Similarly, when Vyvyan somewhat improbably sought to recruit Palmerston to the cause, he asked him whether he would 'detach' himself from Huskisson (who 'frightened the country gentlemen') and whether he was 'free' on the currency and trade questions (he was not).[146] Several Ultras also flirted with the idea of parliamentary reform on the grounds that members for nomination boroughs were often dangerous intellectuals,[147] and that a Parliament more truly representative of the people—with more county MPs and more open constituencies—would not have agreed to Catholic emancipation or the restoration of the currency. Late in 1829 Blandford moved for the suppression of rotten boroughs in order to prevent wealthy Roman Catholics from purchasing seats. Then in the following February he demanded the transfer of all nomination and close boroughs to counties and large towns, a ratepayer and residential franchise, payment of MPs, and the dismissal of all placemen.

This opened up a link between some Ultras and the Whigs. Hitherto the latter had distanced themselves from Cobbett's analysis, but now Grey declared that

[144] Newcastle, diary, 3 Apr. 1827, Nottingham University Library, Newcastle MS Ne2 F3/1, p. 204. For an inclusive analysis of Ultra-ism, see D. G. Simes, 'The Ultra-Tories in British Politics, 1824–1834', D.Phil. (Oxford University, 1974); for a more exclusive version, see Simon P. Karginoff, 'The Protestant Constitutionalists and Ultra-Toryism in Britain, 1792–1846', Ph.D. (Murdoch University, 1994). Many of the more sincere anti-Catholics despised the Ultras for their willingness to use religious issues for political ends (Wolffe, *Protestant Crusade*, 65).
[145] Newcastle, diary, 13 Feb. 1830. Most Ultras would by this time have identified themselves as Tories, but Stanhope still called himself a Whig, and most contemporaries also referred to Blandford as a Whig.
[146] *Letters of Palmerston to Sulivan*, 231–6.
[147] Ricardo had sat for Portarlington, and Huskisson's first constituencies had been the tiny boroughs of Morpeth and Liskeard.

he had an open mind on the currency. Another prominent Whig, Sir James Graham, an evangelical with apocalyptic leanings, had published a best-selling tract, *Corn and Currency* (1826), in which he attacked the resumption of cash payments for having brought about a revolutionary confiscation of property.

The capitalist and the economist ruled the day; and an administration, more connected with annuities than with land, possessed of few acres, and haunted by general principles, introduced, in 1819, a measure which will render that year memorable in the history of our misfortunes, if it be not the real date of our decline.[148]

Despite which, Graham did not think that it would be expedient to go off the gold standard again, nor did he think Cobbett's solution of an equitable adjustment practicable. His prescriptions for agricultural recovery were an open trade in corn subject to a moderate fixed duty, an end to all commercial monopolies including those of the Bank of England and East India Company, drastic retrenchment and tax relief, and a levy on funded wealth.

In 1826 it had been decided that £1 and £2 notes should be withdrawn by April 1829.[149] Most banks left it until the last moment, so their sudden disappearance then must have struck baffled contemporaries like the loss of eleven days from the calendar in 1752. It added a further deflationary twist to the economy, and, according to Graham, brought an already 'unhappy country to the verge of ruin'.[150] In 1830 he highlighted individual cases of abuse, such as the £650,164 paid to just 113 privy councillors, and raised cheers in the House by demanding that all salaries (except military stipends) should be reduced to their level at the time of the Bank restriction in 1797. He also struck a populist note by observing that 'Kings, Ministers, East India-men, Jew Loan Contractors, India Nabobs all had splendid palaces', and asking,

Where was the furniture which adorned the poor man's cottage? all was gone—pinching hunger and despair now held their place in the labourer's habitation . . . If the fund-holder, the political economist, the lawyer, Whig and Tory, are to rally under the banners of the Wellington Government, the time is come when, on the part of the tax-payer, it is necessary to form another party to reduce the burthens of the country.[151]

Several Ultras took up Graham's arguments on currency and taxation. Sadler, for example, denounced the whole drift of economic policy—free trade and competition, dear money, deflation—and traced all these errors to one fundamental misconception: the Malthusian law of population. Fashionable political economy had instilled a 'passion for cheapness' and for 'buying in the cheapest

[148] Sir James Graham, *Corn and Currency; in an Address to the Land Owners* (1826), 37–8. For the record, Huskisson—the main proponent of the 1819 measure—was not a fundholder.
[149] See above, p. 304.
[150] Edward Hughes, *North Country Life in the Eighteenth Century* (1952–65), 273–92.
[151] *HPD2* xxii. 443–4, 450 (12 Feb. 1830).

market', but this merely benefited those on fixed incomes, like place-holders and annuitants. As a result, 'every class of society ... except the *mere* monied capitalist, the fund-holder, and the pensioner, was in a state of extreme suffering'. 'Ministers meant, though they starved the *industrious* people, to pay the debt of honour they had contracted to the public creditor.'[152] Blandford was even shriller. England had become 'a nation of paupers and of placemen', having been laid low by 'loan-mongers and borough-mongers, wallowing in the stagnant and *unproductive* accumulations of their joint and several monopolies'. Parliament was held in 'utter hatred' by the people for ruining 'the great *productive* interests,...the farmers, traders, and other honest and *industrious* subjects'. An 'accursed and unnatural funding system [was] in its last agonies', and MPs who had supported that system must make 'a sincere and contrite confession of their sins, and a total and immediate alteration of their conduct'.[153] A printed version of Blandford's speech was circulated eagerly throughout the country-side. Ultra fury was further roused when ministers referred to distress as partial. They did so, presumably, because any admission that it was general would trigger a search for a common cause, such as the gold standard. And, as Sadler com-plained, 'the currency was one of those few questions which were never to be considered; it was a sort of political blasphemy to allude to it'.[154]

Politically and tonally, the currency critique was indebted to Cobbett, who had been pounding away for decades against fundholders, stockjobbers, and placemen, key ingredients of what he called 'THE THING' or 'OLD CORRUPTION'. It was Cobbett who laboured the distinction between unproductive drones and the industrious classes, and it was he who coined the simplistic but widely publicized slogan 'The farmer versus the fundholder'. Economically, however, the analysis owed less to Cobbett, who like Graham defended the gold standard despite its faults, but to Thomas Attwood and other members of the Birmingham School. That town was opposed to fashionable political economy for much of the nineteenth century. Because its industries were small in scale and geared to the British market, its businessmen were more concerned with buoyant home demand than with international competitiveness. Many therefore opposed the gold standard, while few showed much interest in free trade. Much later, when mid-Victorian boom gave way to *fin de siècle* depression, Birmingham would lead the way, first for fair trade and bimetallism, and then for full-scale protective duties. Meanwhile, interest in the domestic economy gave the town an affinity with agricultural spokesmen such as David Robinson, who from 1826 onwards urged cheap money policies in *Blackwood's Magazine*. The *Morning Herald* was equally strident, and has been credited with causing several

[152] *HPD*2 xxiii. 412 (16 Mar. 1830) (italics added).
[153] *HPD*3 i. 68 (2 Nov. 1830) (italics added).   [154] *HPD*2 xxiii. 416 (16 Mar. 1830).

ministerial losses in the 1830 election.[155] Just how widespread such views were at the grass roots remains questionable, however. Twenty-two counties 'met' to discuss distress in the first quarter of 1830, the first such meetings for seven years, but not much is known about what was said at them. It *is* known that almost every speaker gave prominence to the currency at an agricultural meeting in Aylesbury (February 1830), despite which the formal resolutions did not mention the subject,[156] a silence that seems to bear out Sadler's complaint that it was 'a sort of political blasphemy' to allude to monetary matters.

Before long the struggle for parliamentary reform would generate a debate in which an idealized urban middle class was pitted against a demonized rural aristocracy. The rhetoric of 1829–30 was more realistic in recognizing that many aristocrats had industrial and commercial interests, while merchants, manufacturers, and so-called professionals were often dependent on the rural economy. Like Graham and Chandos, many ultras were heavily in debt, being either failed improvers or ideological backwoodsmen who despised agrarian capitalism. They found themselves on the wrong side of a regime that benefited those on fixed incomes—whether rentiers, fee-earners, or office-holders in receipt of pensions and salaries—but worked against the interests of labourers (whose wages could be expected to decline with prices), of landlords encumbered with debts and mortgages, and of producer interests generally, whether manufacturing or agricultural. It was a dear-money and deflationary regime, which benefited those who *owned* money and damaged those who *owed* it, and its contradictions were about to be exposed.

THE FALL OF THE PITTITE REGIME

According to Whig myth, the Pittite regime (by now increasingly identified as Tory) collapsed in 1830 amid country-wide demands for parliamentary reform. In reality no petitions calling exclusively for reform were presented between 1825 and 1829,[157] despite many thousands on the subjects of Catholics, slaves, and corn. Even Grey abjured reform in 1827, and the issue seemed dead. Moreover, its eventual revival was more a consequence than a cause of Wellington's fall, which was due to discontent within his party rather than in the country at large.

---

[155] David Cresap Moore, *The Politics of Deference: A Study of the Mid-Nineteenth Century English Political System* (Hassocks, 1976), 190–242; Harold Perkin, *The Origins of Modern English Society* (1969), 244–52.

[156] See the debate between D. C. Moore ('Is "the other Face of Reform" in Bucks an "Hallucination"?') and R. W. Davis ('Some Thoughts on Thoroughness and Carefulness'), in *JBS* 15 (1976), 150–61; 17 (1977), 141–2.

[157] Though fourteen petitions mentioned reform collaterally, i.e. as a means to achieve some other object or objects.

The Government's majority was much attenuated during the 1830 Session. Ultras and Canningites were increasingly hostile, though some Opposition MPs, including Grey's son Howick, voted with the administration. The Whigs were in their usual dilemma, being tempted to join the crusade against Old Corruption, yet unwilling to throw up the opportunity to reward their friends should they ever gain power themselves. As it happened, partly for political reasons and partly from genuine conviction, especially in Peel's case, ministers pre-empted the Whigs in this respect. Goulburn's budget cut public spending by about £1 million, nowhere near the reduction to 1797 levels demanded by Graham, but even so an enormous amount which would have been met with enthusiasm at any other time. But because it seemed to have been conceded by a government on the run, it merely provoked Radicals such as Joseph Hume and Poulett Thomson to demand more. Besides which, a regime partly based on patronage cannot reduce public spending without to some extent pulling the rug from under its own feet.

Meanwhile the reform issue began to stir a little. It was generally agreed that a reformed Parliament would not have passed Catholic emancipation, so some Ultras took up the cause in order to prevent a similar calamity in future, while Whigs and Canningites felt that it was safe to press for reform, now that the Catholic question had been satisfactorily settled. The Whigs needed a new rallying cry anyway to replace emancipation, and Althorp's somewhat reluctant assumption of leadership in the Commons (March) ensured that it would be reform. The issue also surfaced at county meetings, and was boosted by a new phenomenon, the political unions. The first of these was founded at Birmingham in January 1830 by an Ultra Tory group including Thomas Attwood. Though sneered at by most local Whigs and ministerialists, it was to be 'the most powerful political force in the Midlands' for nearly a decade.[158] By May 1832 there were organizations in Leeds, Manchester, Bristol, Blackburn, and about 120 other towns. Many of them 'grew in size and standing with every hour'.[159] Whereas the Birmingham Political Union was a single-issue pressure group in favour of a paper currency, later unions homed in on the system of parliamentary elections and may well have forced the Whigs' hands. At all events, in late February Russell moved to give seats to Manchester, Leeds, and Birmingham, and thanks to support from Canningites and some Ultras his motion failed by only forty-eight votes.

Nevertheless, the Whigs hardly looked like a government-in-waiting. Russell, who had been so hostile to coalition in 1827, now contemplated a junction with

[158] Carlos Flick, *The Birmingham Political Union and the Movements for Reform in Britain 1830–1839* (Connecticut, 1978), 17–18.

[159] Michael Brock, *The Great Reform Act* (1973), 295; Nancy D. LoPatin, *Political Unions, Popular Politics and the Great Reform Act of 1832* (Houndmills, 1999), 174–7.

the Canningites—'They have what we want, men of official experience, and we have what they want, numbers'—and negotiations opened in the summer.[160] Lansdowne and Graham were particularly keen to recruit Huskisson, but taking him in would alienate the Ultras, whom the Whigs were also courting. The mercurial Grey continued to dither. Constantly declaring disinterestedness in public, yet always so calculating in private, Grey kept trying to weigh up how strong the Government was, and how much support he would obtain if he made a strike. Unable perhaps to bear the prospect of another failure after a lifetime's futility, he stayed away from London during the early months of the Session, despite the ministers' evident weakness, and after that he offered them 'friendly neutrality'. But then on 30 June he suddenly decided 'to emerge from harbour, his sails bellied out by the rising winds of public and personal discontents',[161] and in a furious tirade he denounced the ministry as utterly unfit to govern. Why this sudden 'declaration of war'? With his northern connections he was highly aware of the reality of industrial distress. He may genuinely have believed that pig-headed ministers were behaving like the old French aristocracy in 1789, and that the country was on the brink of a revolution from which only he could save it. But the most obvious reason was political. Just four days previously Grey's old enemy George IV had died, which meant that at long last he had a prospect of achieving office independently. The King's death also meant that there was now no reason why Wellington should not take Grey into his own Cabinet. Very possibly Grey spoke out as he did in order to forestall any such offer.

Meanwhile, the Government was in terminal disarray. Wellington's strategy was much the same as at the climax of the battle of Waterloo when his staff officers had begged him for orders and he allegedly replied, 'There are no orders, except to stand firm to the last man.' Even Mrs Arbuthnot, his most fervent admirer, conceded that 'the whole of this session the Treasury Bench in the H. of Commons has been a disgrace to the country'. Most of the junior ministers stayed 'mute' through resentment of their indifferent treatment by Peel, who therefore dominated debates, which meant that his stock rose in Cabinet, which in turn annoyed Wellington, whose need to dominate all around him extended beyond his immediate family. Cross that his colleagues should disregard his own words and hang on Peel's, he threatened at one point to 'resign the Government into his hands'. 'Don't do any such thing,' barked Mrs Arbuthnot. Peel would immediately make 'a junction with the Huskisson party', and revolutionary principles would gain a powerful boost throughout Europe.[162]

The accession of William IV required a general election to be held within six months. Wellington decided not to wait, hoping perhaps to catch his opponents

by surprise. Only about one-third of English seats went to the polls, fewer than
in 1826, though there were many more contests in Ireland. Party feeling was not
particularly high, hence the large numbers who were prepared to split their votes
and the small number of plumpers.[163] Of course there were local exceptions.
In Great Yarmouth, with a long tradition of party organization and interest in
national politics, not one of the 1,702 voters split, but very high proportions
did so in Bristol (77 per cent), Lewes (53 per cent), Shrewsbury (45 per cent),
Beverley (44 per cent), and Northampton (43 per cent).[164] No doubt many voters
were confused by recent events at Westminster, with some front-bench Whigs
defending the Government from its own Ultras, and it was hard for pundits to
compute the results for the same reason. Even a month after the election the
Government's election manager listed thirty-seven MPs as 'doubtful favourable'
and twenty-three as 'doubtful unfavourable'. He counted on more than twenty
Government gains overall, whereas Opposition whips boasted (less plausibly)
that they had gained forty. But whatever the technical score, ministers had several
reasons to feel uneasy. One was the unprecedented degree of disrespect shown at
the hustings by non-voters, which meant that in order to succeed many candidates had had to pledge themselves to retrenchment and parliamentary reform.
Another was the Government's failure in open constituencies. It won only three
out of the twenty-eight most popular urban seats, and only twenty-eight out of
eighty-two in English and Welsh counties. It did especially badly in counties
where landlord influence was limited, like Norfolk, Essex, and Cambridgeshire,
while the defeat of an archetypal backbencher (Edmund Pollexfen Bastard) in
Devon marked a spectacular victory for the Whigs. Suffolk had regularly
returned one Whig and one Tory since 1790, but this year two Whigs were elected
with ease. Substantial gains in Ireland (thanks to the disfranchisement of the
forty-shilling freeholders), Scotland, and the close boroughs were little compensation. Politically motivated corporations and borough-mongers may have
exerted less pressure than usual because of what had happened to East Retford
and Penryn, while in popular constituencies voting must have been affected by
the uprising in Paris, news of which reached England on 31 July and created
enormous 'interest and excitement'.[165] At any rate, the return of Joseph Hume for
Middlesex (unopposed), of Brougham for Yorkshire, and of Huskisson for
Liverpool were ominous signs for Wellington.

The 1830 elections marked a return to denominational politics, with the vast
majority of Anglicans voting for the Government and Dissenters for the Opposition.

    [163] See App. 6.2.
    [164] These statistics are taken from John A. Phillips, *The Great Reform Bill in the Boroughs: English
Electoral Behaviour 1818–1841* (Oxford, 1992).
    [165] Greville, *Memoirs*, ii. 19 (31 July 1830); Roland Quinault, 'The French Revolution of 1830 and
Parliamentary Reform', *History*, 79 (1994), 377–93.

This is significant because it suggests that, far from destroying a Tory–Anglican identity, as sometimes supposed, the events of 1828–9 did much to create one. Protestant Nonconformists had often supported Liverpool's Government because they were socially conservative and hated Catholics (some Welsh Calvinist Methodists in London were excommunicated by their minister for signing a petition in favour of emancipation).[166] They were naturally shocked by Wellington's sudden betrayal of the Protestant Constitution, and many embraced parliamentary reform for the same illiberal and populist reasons as some Ultras.[167] Another feature of the elections, and one that alarmed Whigs as much as Tories, was the collapse of traditional influence. Large pockets of deference persisted, as on the Bedford estates in Cambridgeshire,[168] but in many places small gentlemen and independent farmers seemed willing for the first time to follow the lead of recalcitrant millers and grocers against the wishes of their magnates. The Duke of Rutland suffered rebuffs, Lord John Russell was ejected from the family fief at Bedford, the Grosvenors only avoided a contest by surrendering one of their Chester seats, while others survived only after a scare. As one historian has written, 'everywhere the men of the establishment found themselves naked to the wind'.[169]

The most sensational result was Brougham's success in Yorkshire. Although this was a Whig victory, it was a blow to local Whig grandees. The county does not like to employ 'foreigners', whether parliamentarians or cricketers, and Brougham was the first outsider to be elected to represent it since the seventeenth century. Like Wilberforce, one of his predecessors in the seat, he galvanized the West Riding by focusing on slavery. This was why the Leeds Bainesocracy[170] invited him to stand and why the Dissenters largely voted for him. But once adopted as a candidate, Brougham held a series of town rallies at which he pledged himself to the cause of household suffrage, redistribution of seats, and triennial parliaments. He seemed 'intoxicated' with demagogic fervour,[171] which may have been genuine, or may have been a way of working off his frustration at having been pipped to the leadership by Althorp. Whatever the spur, local Whig magnates like the Howards abhorred his tub-thumping, barnstorming methods. Partly thanks to Brougham, the leading Opposition newspaper, the *Morning Chronicle*, became fully committed to reform for the first time, and even *The Times* began to toy with the cause as it slowly but surely turned against the Government.

[166] Machin, *Catholic Question*, 145–6.
[167] Front O'Gorman, *Voters, Patrons, and Parties: The Unreformed Electorate of Hanoverian England 1734–1832* (Oxford, 1989), 367–8.   [168] Moore, *Politics of Deference*, 88–9.
[169] Brock, *Great Reform Act*, 93.   [170] See above, p. 163.
[171] Chester W. New, *The Life of Henry Brougham to 1830* (Oxford, 1961), 408–10. Gash explains but may exaggerate the way in which the mercantile Bainesocracy hijacked the Whig–Dissenting anti-slavery crusade and turned it in favour of parliamentary reform (Norman Gash, 'Brougham and the Yorkshire Election of 1830', *Proceedings of the Leeds Philosophical and Literary Society*, 8 (1956), 19–35).

The 1830 election was the first since 1708 to be followed by the fall of a Government. However, it is unclear whether this was a case of cause and effect, since Parliament did not meet for another three months or so, during which time political tension heightened considerably. The July Revolution, the third and final overthrow of the Bourbons, was regarded as a portent; even some Ultras, true to 1688 Whiggism, hailed the 'late glorious events in France' as a blow against Catholic military despotism and in favour of liberty.[172] Pre-millennialists described them as a 'symbolical earthquake', and the pouring out of the seventh vial.[173] Unsurprisingly, Wellington blamed the July Revolution for his loss of support: 'Men fancied that they had only to follow the examples of Paris and Bruxelles, and that they would acquire all that their imaginations had suggested as the summit of public happiness and prosperity.'[174] In June 1830 a huge meeting of trade unionists in Manchester brought together delegates of the National Association for the Protection of Labour, a pioneering body that had been mobilized by John Doherty in the previous year, and which represented spinners in Manchester's various out-towns. This meeting led in turn to the formation of a number of committees to prevent a reduction of wages, which was indicative perhaps of a shift in popular concern from political to economic rights. In August Burdett and other London Radicals addressed a number of monster meetings, where tricolour ribbons and cock-ades were sported. There were riots against the new Metropolitan Police, and at the end of October the Tower of London and Bank of England had to be guarded against invasion by over 6,000 working men from Brixton and Deptford. There were similar incidents throughout the provinces, and in Ireland a number of demonstrations against the Act of Union, but none of these problems caused half so many jitters as the series of events known as the Swing riots or Last Labourers' Revolt.

This was a manifestation of disaffection in the rural heartlands, beginning in Kent and spreading westward and northward in an arc from Hampshire via Buckinghamshire to Norfolk. According to Buckingham it 'spread consterna-tion throughout the countryside', and was far more unsettling to most MPs than anything that might happen in Manchester. It involved the burning of ricks and farm buildings, especially in Kent and Sussex, while in Wiltshire, Berkshire, and Hampshire the main object was the destruction of threshing machines. The vandals operated mainly at night, and often left threatening messages:

> Revenge for thee is on the Wing
> From thy determined Capt Swing.

---

[172] Vyvyan, *HPD2* xxv. 934–42 (2 July 1830).

[173] James Hatley Frere, *Eight Letters on the Prophecies, relating to the Last Times* (1831), 1.

[174] WND vii. 383; *Memoirs of the Courts and Cabinets of William IV and Victoria*, ed. Duke of Buckingham and Chandos (1861), i. 25.

This is to inform you what you have to undergo Gentlemen if providing you Dont pull down your messhenes and rise the poor mens wages the maried men give tow and six pence a day a day the singel tow shillings or we will burn down your barns and you in them this is the last notis.

Wherever Swing struck there would be reported sightings of mysterious strangers, and allegations against Methodist preachers and atheistic Radicals. There were also rumours of foreign intervention, prompting the Cabinet to look into cases of incendiarism ('which seem very much to resemble ours')[175] in Normandy and Picardy. These suspicions were reasonable, given that the troubles originated in east Kent just one month after the French Revolution, and coincided with a Belgian revolt against Dutch rule.[176]

However, most historians prefer to place the Swing riots in a socio-economic context. Threshing machines represented the introduction of capitalism into the agriculture of southern England by bourgeois farmers. They reduced the amount of winter employment, and—along with the loss of commons and other customary rights, and a squeeze on poor relief in many parishes—they added to the farm labourer's sense of proletarianization. This interpretation is based on the idea of class conflict, but the riots can also be regarded as manifestations of rural deference. Why else did so many farmers and gentry support the rioters and protect them from detection?[177] Given the perceived struggle between town and country, the Swing riots may have been an appendage to the Ultra revolt against a decade of liberal Tory economics, in which case it may be significant that 60 per cent of all disturbances took place in the single month of November 1830, when Ultra indignation was at its peak. Another possibility is that farmers secretly colluded in the destruction of machines, since the growing rapidity with which they enabled corn to be brought to market after a harvest was leading to severe autumnal price falls. A legislative ban on machinery was out of the question, while voluntary agreements merely allowed unscrupulous farmers to steal a march, so direct action by farmhands against everyone's machines might have seemed expedient.[178] But allowing for all these possibilities, the burnings and smashings certainly terrified landed society as a whole, and added to the sense that ministers had lost control of events.

Even so, the general view was that Wellington would survive so long as he could strengthen his front bench. Hertford and Grenville tried hard to bring about an accommodation between Huskisson and the Duke, and saw a chance at

---

[175] 'The object [of the fires] seems to be to spread general terror. It is clear that they are effected by the discharge of some chemical preparation, which ignites after a time. No watching has any effect. Fires take place where no one has approached' (Ellenborough, *Political Diary*, 5 Nov. 1830, ii. 415–16).

[176] Quinault, 'The French Revolution of 1830', 390.

[177] E. J. Hobsbawm and George Rudé, *Captain Swing* (1969), 15–17; K. D. M. Snell, *Annals of the Labouring Poor: Social Change and Agrarian England, 1660–1900* (Cambridge, 1985), 220–6.

[178] Hobsbawm and Rudé, *Captain Swing*, 359–65.

the opening ceremonies of the Liverpool to Manchester railway on 15 September. There was to be a cavalcade of eight trains, the first of which would be driven by the engineer George Stephenson and would consist of several coachloads of celebrities, including one for the Duke's personal entourage. The Prime Minister was in charge of invitations and had to decide where to place Huskisson, a local MP and a moving spirit behind the project. Much significance was attached to his decision, and when Huskisson learned that he was not to be in the ducal carriage but relegated to the 'Opposition long Coach', he commented: 'The great Captain, you know, is to be there with all his tail. Of course one object is to throw me into the background at the ceremony.'[179] There was the usual touch of paranoia in Huskisson's analysis, but it was swamped by tragic irony. When the day came the eight trains set off from Liverpool, running a few miles before pausing at various vantage points. At roughly mid-way in the journey Stephenson's VIP train moved ahead of the other seven and came to a halt on an embankment over a quarry where there was a stretch of double track. Here some of the company descended from their coaches and milled around, waiting for the other seven trains to sweep by in cavalcade. Either of his own accord, or because someone suggested it, Huskisson went over to the Duke and they shook hands. Immediately afterwards the oncoming trains were spotted, Huskisson tried to clamber into the Duke's coach, fell back, panicked, was hit by the third train (*The Rocket*), and was taken to Eccles where he died in agony a few hours later. He had been a thoroughly inept politician—too awkward, too prickly, too conscious of his lack of breeding, perhaps too clever for a country which was beginning to despise intelligence—but as a statesman he was unparalleled, combining theoretical expertise with a practical awareness of how economic agents function better than anyone before Keynes.

His death undoubtedly improved the prospect of the remaining Canningites' return to the fold. Palmerston, their new leader, was soon receiving approaches from both parties, and told the Duke in person that he would join the Government if he could bring several leading Whigs in with him. When that offer was rejected, Palmerston lowered his terms, intimating (via intermediaries) on 1 November that he and Grant, as well as Graham, and Stanley, could be won over by a promise of moderate reform.[180] Then on the very next day Wellington made a speech which has gone down as one of the great parliamentary blunders of all time. In it he not only declared his implacable opposition to reform, but went so far as to say that 'Britain possessed a Legislature which answered all the good purposes of legislation, and this to a greater degree than any Legislature ever had answered in any country whatever.'[181] Maybe this

---

[179] Huskisson to Graham, 26 Aug. 1830, Graham MSS, General Series, 3/26.
[180] Arbuthnot, *Journal*, ii. 395; Parker, *Peel*, ii. 163–7.   [181] *HPD3* i. 52–3 (2 Nov. 1830).

hyperbole was intended as a coded rebuff to Palmerston. Maybe he thought that his supporters, still sore at the surrender of 1829, would appreciate a gesture of defiance now. Whatever the motive, the speech made him seem dangerously complacent and out of touch.

When Wellington sat down, a colleague told him that he had just announced the fall of his Government, but this was premature. It is true that the speech caused the nation to polarize very swiftly over reform, and the sight of London crowds shouting slogans like 'No police! No Polignac!' made Princess Lieven feel that the country was 'just on the brink of a revolution'.[182] But Wellington might well have benefited from this development if he had possessed more political acumen, and when his Government fell shortly afterwards it was somewhat inadvertently. The final crisis stemmed from a proposal by Goulburn to cut £161,000 from a budget of about £1,250,000 for the new King's Civil List. This was a lot, but the Opposition said it was not enough, and on 15 November Henry Parnell, backed by Althorp and Hume, moved for the appointment of a select committee. In the vote that followed, a substantial number of members normally thought of as pro-Government voted with Parnell, and to the ministers' amazement the motion was carried by 233 to 204.[183] Wellington resigned at once, the first Prime Minister to fall as a result of a Commons vote since Shelburne in 1783. Bruised by his recent experiences, Peel seemed delighted by this outcome, and most observers believed that the delight was genuine, not mere bravado.

The Tory rebels included Knatchbull, Vyvyan, and about forty of their faction, so it could be said that the Ultras brought Wellington down. However, since they had voted against him throughout the previous session, the real significance of 15 November was that the Whigs were no longer willing to sustain the Government. It fell to a combination of Whigs, Radicals, Irishmen, Canningites, and Ultras, with collateral damage from some MPs whose discontents were more personal than principled. Only fifteen English county MPs voted with the Government. Yet ministers did not *have* to resign over the Civil List vote, which was hardly an issue of confidence. They did so because Brougham was scheduled to propose a motion for parliamentary reform on the following day, and they felt that it would be 'more advantageous to go out upon a question in support of the King's prerogative . . . than upon a more serious question'.[184] As Wellington explained, 'the country was in a state of insanity about Reform'.

---

[182] Lieven to her brother, 9 Nov. 1830, in *Letters of Dorothea, Princess Lieven, during her Residence in London, 1812–1834*, ed. L. G. Robinson (1902), 268.

[183] When Wellington was first told the voting figures, he assumed that his Government must have been in a majority of twenty-nine rather than a minority, and expostulated: 'What, no *more*! I don't understand it. There must be some mistake' (Denis Le Marchant, diary, Nov. 1830, in *Three Early Nineteenth Century Diaries*, ed. A. Aspinall (1952), 1).

[184] Hardinge to Arbuthnot, 16 Nov. 1830, in *The Correspondence of Charles Arbuthnot*, ed. A. Aspinall (1941), 132.

This had created 'the necessity of resigning at an hour's notice, in order to prevent Reform being carried by storm'.[185] He clearly hoped it would shake sense into the rebels, making it difficult for Grey to form a government.

Yet this was to suppose that the rebels would have supported Brougham's reform motion, whereas it seems likely that many would not have done. Ellenborough believed that the Ultras were 'sorry for the work they have performed, and regret their vote. They had intended to stay away on the question of Reform—now they mean to vote against it.' It is, of course, impossible to be sure. The fact that all but twenty-eight of the rebels would vote against the crucial division on the second reading of the first Reform Bill is inconclusive,[186] since they might have supported more moderate proposals, but even so it seems likely that the rebel votes and abstentions of 15 November were meant to warn the Government, not destroy it, much as country gentlemen in the early 1820s had defected on little issues but proved loyal on motions of confidence. Liverpool had understood this, but Wellington as a soldier was not prepared to hold office on such terms. It is sobering to think that the fall of the Pittite regime, which had momentous consequences, was partly accidental.

THE STRUGGLE FOR REFORM

Grey was on tenterhooks at the opening of the new Parliament in case Wellington should steal his thunder just as he had on emancipation. He need not have worried. The Duke's declaration against reform roused so much feeling in the country that the Whigs, who had taken up the issue tentatively, even reluctantly, suddenly found themselves in the unaccustomed position of being popular. By 1 March 1831 more than 1,000 petitions had been presented in favour of reform and only two against; those from Birmingham and Edinburgh had over 21,000 signatories, Manchester's 12,500. Naturally there was no agreement over what reform should mean in practice, but it was clear that something would have to be done to satisfy this sudden surge of feeling. But first Grey had to form a government. The point most often made is that his Cabinet was the most aristocratic of the century, with nine peers, one Irish peer, one heir to the peerage, and only two commoners, of whom one was a baronet. More importantly it was a coalition. The three secretaryships of State and the Board of Control went to Canningites,[187] while the Ultra

---

[185] Wellington to Buckingham, 26 Jan. 1831, in WND vii. 399.

[186] On 23 March 1831. Of the MPs listed by Aspinall as Ultra Tories elected in 1830, 111 opposed the first Reform Bill and 28 supported it (Aspinall, *Three Early Nineteenth Century Diaries*, p. xxix). A Treasury secretary estimated the number of Ultras more conservatively at sixty, who subsequently divided 47–10 against the Bill. Twenty-five were still MPs after the 1832 election, by which time twenty were firmly back in the Tory Party.

[187] Palmerston (Foreign Secretary), Melbourne (Home Secretary), Goderich (War and Colonies), Grant (Board of Control).

Tory Richmond became Postmaster-General. Althorp (Chancellor of the Exchequer) was a Whig, but nevertheless came from Pittite stock. All this meant that there was no room for genuine Whigs apart from Lansdowne, Graham, Durham, and Holland, though Duncannon, Russell, and about twenty of Grey's personal relations became junior ministers.[188] The most remarkable appointment was Brougham's to the Woolsack. Very likely Grey was anxious to get him out of the Commons, where he might have undermined Althorp's gentle style of leadership. But although this was not a predominantly Whig Government, the Reform Bill was a Whig measure. Russell, Graham, Duncannon, and Durham were appointed a Committee of Four to draft proposals in conjunction with Grey and Althorp.[189] Such was the momentum that they sailed through Cabinet, and even the King only objected to the secret ballot. In fact, none of the proponents wanted the ballot except Durham. It was only included as a ruse to draw the King's fire and deflect him from the main issue.

The fifteen-month struggle for reform was more significant than the changes that resulted, which is what Bright meant when he described it as 'not a good Bill, though . . . a great Bill when it passed'.[190] Very briefly, Russell introduced the first Bill on 1 March 1831, and this passed its second reading by a single vote on the early morning of the 23rd.[191] On 19–20 April a spoiling motion was carried by eight votes and the King agreed to grant Grey a dissolution. The subsequent elections gave him an overwhelming majority, with about thirty-five gains in counties and twice that number in the boroughs. Only six of the thirty-four county MPs who had voted against the measure got back in. On 6–7 July Russell's second Bill passed the Commons by 136 votes, though it was amended (in some respects significantly) during forty days in committee (July–September). It then faced an uphill struggle in the Lords, where it was eventually defeated by a majority of forty-one on 7–8 October, the bishops dividing twenty-one to two against. This provoked serious rioting in London, Derby, Nottingham (where the Duke of Newcastle's castle was destroyed by fire), and Bristol (where the Bishop's Palace, prisons, and forty-five houses were likewise razed to the ground). In the hope of finding a compromise, Tory waverers led by Wharncliffe and Harrowby entered into negotiations with more moderate ministers such as Palmerston and Grey, while die-hard Tories held out for death in the last ditch.

[188] Russell entered the Cabinet in 1831. Perhaps he was left out initially so that the Cabinet would not seem too soiled were the Reform Bill to flop.
[189] According to Russell, 'Grey formed [the Bill] in his own mind.'
[190] *Public Addresses by John Bright*, ed. J. E. Thorold Rogers (1879), 29.
[191] The decisive vote was that of John Calcraft, who had been an Opposition MP during Liverpool's administration, held minor office under Wellington during 1828–30, turned Whig again in 1830, then— finding his own seat (Wareham) threatened with disfranchisement—spoke violently against the Reform Bill, but changed his mind at the last moment and voted for the second reading. He killed himself six months later, correctly imagining himself to be hated by both sides equally.

On 22 March 1832 a third Bill passed the Commons after twenty-two days in committee. Meanwhile, Grey extracted a promise from the King to create additional peers in order to force the Bill through should the Lords prove intransigent. On 13–14 April the Bill passed its second reading in the Upper House by 184 to 175, but three weeks later the Government was defeated on an Opposition motion to postpone certain key clauses.[192] Despite his earlier promise, the King refused to create additional peers, and Grey resigned. The King now called on Wellington and the Speaker (Manners-Sutton) to form an administration on the basis of the Reform Bill as amended by the Lords. Peel refused to join, arguing in effect that a second U-turn by him would destroy all 'confidence in the declarations of public men'.[193] Without Peel, Wellington had no hope of sustaining a ministry, but the matter was put beyond doubt by the threat of popular violence during the so-called Days of May. On the 15th of that month Wellington caved in, realizing both that reform was inevitable and that only Grey could carry it. The Whigs resumed office, the King tearfully agreed to create peers, and in order to prevent that necessity the Lords surrendered. The Bill passed on 4 June by 106 to 22, and in December the Whigs were rewarded by a thumping election victory (483–175). The Pittite regime seemed not only dead but buried.

Parliamentary reform affected both the distribution of seats and the way in which citizens might qualify for the franchise. Under the first Bill—which is the best guide to ministerial intentions—most of the existing county seats were divided into two smaller double-member constituencies, increasing the number of English county MPs from eighty-two to 137; the respective figures for the United Kingdom as a whole were 188 and 253. Sixty small boroughs—ranging from tiny hamlets like Old Sarum and Gatton to towns with fewer than about 2,000 residents—lost their representation entirely, and forty-seven medium small boroughs (roughly 2,000–4,000) lost one of their two members. Eleven large towns including Manchester, Birmingham, and Leeds were awarded two members each, twenty-one other towns gained one, and London's representation rose from ten to eighteen. Ownership of a forty-shilling (£2) freehold remained the basic qualification for a county vote, but two wealthier categories were added: £10-a-year copyholders (a variation of freehold), and £50-a-year leaseholders provided that the lease was for at least twenty-one years. Arguably this was to make the county franchise *less* 'democratic', not more. In the boroughs

---

[192] Those relating to the disfranchisement of small boroughs.

[193] Peel to Croker, 12 May 1832, in *Croker Papers*, ii. 181. Littleton took a jaundiced view of Peel's motives. 'He means ... to lie on his oars, and let others do the work—he will then return to office—a vacancy will be made for him. He will meantime do all he can to support the Bill that the new Administration may bring in, no matter how extensive, and the country will not discover the juggle till it is over.' 'His talent is eminently fitted for turning things to his own account.' E. J. Littleton, diary, 11 and 14 May 1832, in Aspinall, *Three Early Nineteenth Century Diaries*, 249, 253.

a uniform qualification was introduced for the first time,[194] enfranchising all adult males who *occupied* houses with a rental value of £10 per annum or more (usually the lowest rent at which a householder was assessed for poor rate). Owner–occupiers of borough property worth £10 or more were assured of a vote in the borough, but were no longer allowed to vote in the surrounding county; however, those whose property was worth more than 40s. but less than £10 might continue to do so. Those who owned but did not occupy a borough property worth £10 would be prevented from voting in the borough by the new residency principle; and, if their property was occupied by an adult male, they would not be able to vote in the county either, on the principle that a single dwelling should not confer two votes. Finally, all existing franchise-holders were to keep their votes for life so long as they were resident in the constituency. Other detailed provisions related to the constituency boundaries and the conduct of elections, and included the introduction of a registration system, an increase in polling places, and a two-day limit on the polling process. The system of plural voting, whereby a person with several properties in different constituencies could vote several times over, was not affected.

The Act as finally passed was slightly modified. A third member for seven counties raised the total of English county seats to 144.[195] The criteria for disfranchising boroughs was changed from simple population to the number of houses and amount of tax paid. As a result the number to lose their representation entirely was reduced from sixty to fifty-six, while the number that lost just one member fell from forty-seven to thirty. At the same time the number of towns gaining two members was raised from eleven to twenty-two, the number gaining one member stayed at twenty. Sons and apprentices of existing freemen were allowed to inherit the right to vote on certain conditions. After much wrangling it was decided to allow those who owned but did not occupy borough property worth more than £10 to vote in the surrounding county. Finally, an amendment moved by the Marquess of Chandos, and carried by an alliance of Tories and Radicals, enfranchised the £50 tenants-at-will, sometimes known as 'opulent serfs'. Tories supported it because the beneficiaries were opulent and yet, having no security of tenure, were subservient to their landlords. More deviously, some Radicals supported it in the hope that possession of the vote by people who were so obviously not independent would strengthen the case for a secret ballot. This clause, the one serious setback for the Government, increased the county electorate by about one-third, rendering it less 'democratic' still.

---

[194] Existing boroughs had developed in different ways over the centuries, so that by 1831 there was a bewildering variety of franchise qualifications—householder, freeman, corporation, scot and lot, burgage, and freeholder.

[195] Despite this substantial increase, in comparison with boroughs, counties continued to be underrepresented in relation to their population.

It is difficult to estimate the size of the Hanoverian electorate owing to the lack of a register and the infrequency of contests, but the Reform Act probably increased it by about 45 per cent, that is from 3.2 to 4.7 per cent of the population. The restriction on non-resident freemen voters (known as outvoters) meant that in some towns the size of the electorate was reduced, for example in Leicester where it was almost halved. The balance of representation followed the distribution of population northwards. Thus Cornwall lost thirty borough seats, Wiltshire eighteen, Sussex fourteen, Hampshire and the Isle of Wight ten, while the industrial areas of south-east Lancashire and south-west Yorkshire—both previously lacking in borough representation—gained thirteen and ten respectively. Five seats were added in Wales, and in July and August 1832 separate Reform Acts were carried for Scotland (where the electorate increased from an estimated 4,500 to 64,500) and Ireland.

Historians, anxious to know how far the legislation altered the balance of power and privilege, do not regard it as particularly daring. Contemporaries, anxious to know where it might lead, thought it momentous. MPs whose seats were to be abolished naturally thought it was cataclysmic. In this respect the Government's proposals went very much further than expected. When Russell recited the list of boroughs to be abolished, he was greeted with hoots from the Opposition benches, that is hoots of dismay from Tories and of elation from Radicals,[196] though some of the former laughed with relief, calculating that proposals so extreme could never pass. As to why the Government went so much further than expected on this one point, the clue may lie with Peel, who was now emerging as the dominant player in the game. 'Every one, Court, City, Ministers, Tories, all agree that the Government holds its seat at the mercy of Sir Robert.'[197] Many Tories were confident of a swift return to office, or would have been but for Peel, who 'keeps rather aloof from the Duke and is determined to make Ultras come on their knees to him'. Mrs Arbuthnot now despaired of the man she once described as a 'determined hater'.

We are at *sixes and sevens* . . . Peel, saying he does not wish to return to office . . . treats all the Tory party with arrogance and insolence, affects to consider himself as an *individual* and not the leader of the party, and has hitherto positively rejected all the advances of the ultra-Tories who now desire nothing better than to make up past differences and unite cordially with us.

But Peel had no intention of making it up with 'the fellows who turned us out three months ago'.[198] Aside from personal animus, it was obvious to all that he was preparing to acquiesce in a moderate degree of Constitutional change.

---

[196] Most Radicals sat in opposition with the Tories during these early debates.
[197] *Croker Papers*, ii. 108.   [198] Arbuthnot, *Journal*, ii. 415–16 (21 Mar. 1831).

Several times already Croker had tried to get him 'to pledge himself, like the Duke, against all parliamentary reform, but . . . he will pledge to nothing'.[199]

Now this prospect frightened Whigs as well as Tories. After almost fifty years in opposition they craved a decisive victory, not a parliamentary compromise in which Peel played the statesmanlike role of broker. It seems likely that they went to extremes in the matter of abolishing borough seats in order, deliberately, to drive Peel into outright opposition. If so, the tactic worked triumphantly. The single most crucial moment in the whole saga came after Russell and his seconder had finished speaking on 1 March, when everyone waited for Peel to get up and bury reform as Canning had done in 1822. But instead Peel sat shaking with anger, aware no doubt that because of the Government's unexpectedly aggressive attack on rotten boroughs he had been left with no alternative but to make up with the despised Ultras. The shrewd Croker believed that if only Peel had divided the House as soon as Russell had sat down, reform would have been scotched there and then.[200] Yet despite the taunts and goadings of Whigs and the imploring of his own party managers,[201] Peel did not speak until the third night, by which time the argument had begun to slip away from the anti-reformers. Then, admitting to 'feelings of pain and humiliation', he acknowledged that he had been prepared to accept moderate reforms, 'founded on safe principles, abjuring all confiscation, and limited in their degree', but as for Russell's plan he 'so wholly despair[ed] of modifying its provisions' that he could give it nothing but 'positive dissent'.[202] Before long the anti-reformers fell out among themselves. Some, such as Vyvyan and Knatchbull, called for a compromise by which seats would be given to large towns and the small boroughs spared. Others, like Wetherell, inveighed hysterically against any concession, and Peel and Wellington took the same line.

The dilemma for the Whigs was that, popular expectations having been raised, they dared not let the Bill fail, yet it could hardly succeed 'except under a degree of apprehension excited from without which one can hardly wish to see'.[203] Twenty-three counties had met to petition for reform by 8 April, and there were monster meetings in many large towns including Westminster, where Place and Hobhouse took the lead. A sustained press campaign spearheaded by *The Spectator* demanded 'the Bill, the whole Bill, and nothing but the Bill', and for once Radicals such as Cobbett, O'Connell, Carlile, Attwood, Hunt, Place,

[199] Croker to Hertford, 19 Jan. 1831, in *Croker Papers*, ii. 101.

[200] [J.W. Croker], 'Stages of the Revolution', *QR* 47 (1832), 564–5.

[201] 'It is right you should know that the Government have determined to say nothing more of their plan until they have heard from you . . . I trust that someone will make a speech which a Cabinet Minister will be forced to answer, for the intention certainly is to hear you before another word is said by any member of the Government' (C. Arbuthnot to Peel, 3 Mar. 1831, in Parker, *Peel*, ii. 176).

[202] *HPD*3 ii. 1344–5 (3 Mar. 1831).

[203] Lansdowne to Grey, 4 Mar. 1831, quoted in Brock, *Great Reform Act*, 164.

and Parkes sang in unison. A Metropolitan Trades' Union was founded in March and became the National Union of the Working Classes and Others (NUWC) in May. As already noted, the Lords' rejection of the second Bill led to violent riots in Bristol, Derby, and Nottingham, and though there was local provocation in all three places, and elsewhere the reaction was 'quite tame',[204] they led to calls for the formation of civil guards, armed if necessary, for public safety and the protection of property. Much of the initiative was taken by the Birmingham Political Union (BPU) and by Place's National Political Union, formed in October 1831. (When it became known that Russell was corresponding with the BPU, there were predictable complaints that such 'mock parliaments' were governing the country.) A meeting of more than 100,000 protesters in October led the BPU to re-form on semi-military lines,[205] and the Government responded with a royal proclamation warning political associations not to take it upon themselves to act as public authorities. For, although ostensibly their role was one of civil defence, their scarcely hidden purpose was to put pressure on Parliament. In the Days of May, for example, while Wellington was trying to form a government, 200,000 delegates from various parts of the country met in Birmingham to hear Attwood hint that armed insurrection might be needed to reinstate the Whigs. A follow-up meeting brought together some 1,500 men carrying pikes and muskets, many of them former soldiers. Count Czapski, who had fought in Poland's struggle against the Tsar, was apparently on standby to take command.[206]

How close was all this to revolution? A Canningite MP (E. J. Littleton) thought the country was 'in a state little short of insurrection', while the Revd Sydney Smith later recollected a 'hand-shaking, bowel-disturbing passion of fear'.[207] Historians are more cautious, knowing that both reformers and anti-reformers had an interest in talking up the danger.[208] One interpretation insists that it was all a bit of a leg-pull. James Mill is credited with having master-minded a propaganda campaign in which middle-class newspapers like the *Morning Chronicle*, *The Examiner*, *The Times*, the *Manchester Guardian*, and the *Leeds Mercury* deliberately purveyed a 'language of menace' in order to convince parliamentarians that opinion in the country was violently in favour of the Bill. Place is supposed to have said, 'We must frighten them.' Ergo: 'We must pretend to be frightened ourselves.'[209] According to this interpretation, respectable

---

[204] Joseph Hamburger, *James Mill and the Art of Revolution* (New Haven, 1963), 181.

[205] Brock, *Great Reform Act*, 253–4.   [206] Ibid. 294–309.

[207] Littleton, diary, 14 May 1832, 253; Sydney Smith to Bishop Blomfield, 5 Sept. 1840, in *The Letters of Sydney Smith*, ed. Nowell C. Smith (Oxford, 1953), ii. 709.

[208] Moreover, Francis Place, on whose extensive archive historians are forced to rely, had a natural interest in exaggerating his own importance (Dudley Miles, *Francis Place 1771–1854: The Life of a Remarkable Radical* (Brighton, 1988), 199–207).

[209] Hamburger, *Mill and the Art of Revolution*, 117.

middle-class reformers were never in danger of losing control of events. The fact that many members of the political unions were men of property, even quite substantial property, has led one historian to describe the Days of May as marking 'the high point in co-operation between middle- and working-class reformers'.[210]

However, this version of events draws heavily on Birmingham, where there was a considerable degree of sans-culotte unity thanks to its small-scale units of production, its many skilled journeymen who aspired to become master manufacturers, and its master manufacturers who had once been workers. Currency reform was one on which bosses, workforce, and nearby Warwickshire farmers could all agree. Attwood had until recently described himself as an Ultra Tory, and his objection to rotten boroughs was that they provided seats for London rentiers. In this context it is pertinent to note that one of the BPU's most potent weapons was a politically organized run on the banks: 'To stop the Duke, Go for gold!' The effectiveness of placards calling on bank depositors to scuttle has been questioned, as has the campaign to withhold taxes and other forms of civil disobedience. Nevertheless, what made the political establishment so vulnerable was the financial pressure that followed the withdrawal of deposits. Not for the first or last time, Rothschild found himself working frantically to preserve the British Government's solvency.[211]

Given that Birmingham was unusual, there is a case for seeing the crisis in genuinely revolutionary terms. For a brief period control passed out of the hands of the parliamentary classes and into those of radicals. True, Place and Attwood colluded a little with ministers, and their motives were not dissimilar—to conjure impressive demonstrations of support which would appear to be more violent than they actually were, and to *prevent* a conflagration by persuading Tory diehards that there would be one if they did not yield. The difference was that, having less to lose, Attwood and Place were willing to sail closer to the wind. Presumably they calculated that Wellington—had he succeeded in forming a government—would not have ordered the regular Army to fire on Attwood's citizen guard, but in view of the Duke's 'publish-and-be-damned' mentality, this was a high-risk strategy. Then again, in many other towns the situation became confrontational as the unity demonstrated by radicals during the early summer of 1831 dissipated, and respectable reformers began to be outflanked on the left. In London, for example, reaction to the Lord's rejection of the second Bill has been described as 'staggering'. Within two days there were 'more meetings than ever before.'[212] The NUWC disseminated the ideas of

[210] Brock, *Great Reform Act*, 295.

[211] And in the process making mockery of the Chancellor of the Exchequer's recent boast that he had ordered 'his door to be shut against Rothschild' (Arbuthnot to his wife, 13 Feb. 1831, in *Correspondence of Charles Arbuthnot*, 136).

[212] Iorwerth Prothero, *Artisans and Politics in Early Nineteenth-Century London: John Gast and his Times* (Folkestone, 1979), 286.

Thomas Paine, Robert Owen, and Thomas Hodgskin through the pages of Henry Hetherington's *Poor Man's Guardian* and Richard Carlile's *Prompter*.[213] In their view the Reform Bill was 'the most illiberal, the most tyrannical, the most hellish measure that ever could or can be proposed'[214] because it failed to grant manhood suffrage and annual parliaments.

In the volatile North-West a merchant-turned-journalist, Archibald Prentice, sought to use the Manchester Political Union (MPU) to create class cooperation on Birmingham lines. He had some success until the Lords' rejection of the second Bill, but thereafter the situation deteriorated dangerously. Large-scale units of production made for a sharper cleavage between masters and workforce than in the Midlands,[215] and besides there was much bitterness left over from the spinners' strike of 1829. Although social *division* did not inevitably lead to social *conflict*,[216] it inhibited cooperation between three different groups of reformers. On the moderate wing was a band of local notables, mostly respectable business-men and liberal (often Unitarian) Dissenters led by Thomas and Richard Potter and J. E. Taylor, who had founded the *Manchester Guardian* (1821). They wanted reform, but merely as a step towards free trade, and thought the Whig Bill too democratic. To the left of this group was Prentice's MPU, whose main constituency was the shopocracy. Its members did not think the Bill went far enough but were prepared to accept it as a first step. Further left still was the Political Union of the Working Classes (PUWC), which condemned the Bill as worse than useless. Founded in 1831, the PUWC was led by radicals like Nathan Broadhurst and dominated by weavers, shoemakers, and other skilled workers. Their idol was Henry Hunt, MP for Preston and a frequent presence. Violent, stentorian, egotistical, boastful, vain and vainglorious, domineering, capricious, jealous, half-deranged, and handsome—he made the wearing of a white hat a badge of radical chic in the 1820s—Hunt never dissembled, and was quite incapable of the sort of revolutionary counterfeit which has been attributed to Place and Mill. In October 1831 a respectable indoor meeting called by the moderates was hijacked by the PUWC and dragged out into the open air. About 100,000 gathered at Camp Field, where Thomas Potter was forced to accept a motion for universal suffrage, annual parliaments, and the ballot. This putsch has been described as 'a decisive working class rejection of middle class political leadership' in Manchester. Amid rumours of nocturnal drilling by the MPU, the respectables kept their heads down until the Days of May when tensions broke out again. At another huge meeting the moderates called on their fellow

---

[213] Brock, *Great Reform Act*, 165–7.   [214] *Poor Man's Guardian*, 1 Apr. 1832.

[215] Asa Briggs, 'The Background of the Parliamentary Reform Movement in Three English Cities (1830–2)', *Cambridge Historical Journal*, 10 (1952), 293–317.

[216] V. A. C. Gatrell, 'The Commercial Middle Class in Manchester, c.1820–1857', Ph.D. thesis (Cambridge University, 1971), 11.

townsmen to withhold taxes until the Bill was passed. Meanwhile, the plebeian radicals, led this time by the cotton manufacturer John Fielden, denounced proposals for a creation of peers, since they wished to see the miserable Bill destroyed, not passed.[217]

Which was more typical, Birmingham or Manchester? The Leicester Political Union resembled Attwood's, a 'shadow town council' in which reformers from different backgrounds 'learned to work together, broadened their outlook, and developed their knowledge of social problems'.[218] Yet in Nottingham, another parliamentary borough almost twice as large and less than 30 miles away, the Political Union was almost exclusively a working-class organization, and much more threatening.[219] In Sheffield a skilled work force and influential shopocracy constituted a subaltern class of respectable reformers as in Birmingham, but Leeds was more like Manchester. When a local chemical, glass, and bottle manufacturer (Joshua Bower) tried to turn the local Political Union into 'a sort of connecting link between the middle and the operative classes', he was strongly challenged by the Leeds Radical Political Union (LRPU), which defended the 'artisan' against the 'capitalist', and called for working-class representation in order to obliterate 'degradation, misery and want'.[220] To the LRPU the Reform Bill was nothing more than a bribe to the middle classes that would leave the operatives weaker than ever.

A MIDDLE-CLASS BILL, OR A CASE OF LANDED REACTION?

The Tories deployed a plethora of arguments against reform. Abolition of parliamentary boroughs would render the Commons uncontrollable, making executive government impossible. It would jeopardize property in general, given that

the established Church of this country was a chartered body; that the Peerage held its privileges by instruments and patents, granted under the Great Seal; that the Bank of England and the East India Company, and every other great establishment of the country, possessed all their rights and property, and utility and value, public and private, individual and aggregate, under a charter, which, like that of the about-to-be-confiscated boroughs, might be hereafter violated, if the dangerous precedent were once supinely admitted.[221]

---

[217] Michael J. Turner, *Reform and Respectability: The making of a Middle-Class Liberalism in Early Nineteenth-century Manchester* (Manchester, 1995), 279–315; Gatrell, 'Commercial Middle Class', 215–24. See also Nicholas C. Edsall, *Richard Cobden: Independent Radical* (Cambridge, Mass., 1986), 30.

[218] A. Temple Patterson, *Radical Leicester: A History of Leicester 1780–1850* (Leicester, 1954), 188.

[219] Malcolm I. Thomis, *Politics and Society in Nottingham 1785–1835* (Oxford, 1969), 230–1.

[220] R. J. Morris, *Class, Sect and Party: The Making of the British Middle Class, Leeds 1820–1850* (Manchester, 1990), 125; Donald Read, *The English Provinces c.1760–1960: A Study in Influence* (1964), 35–7.

[221] Wetherell, *HPD*3 ii. 1236 (2 Mar. 1831). Peel could not use this argument, having justified his own disfranchisement of Irish forty-shilling freeholders in 1829 on the grounds that the right to vote was a public trust, and therefore different from 'the rights of property, and other strictly private rights' (*HPD*2 xx. 771–2 (5 Mar. 1829)).

Nomination boroughs were valuable as nurseries of talent,[222] for how else would men of parts but few means (Chatham, Fox, Pitt, Burke, Canning, Huskisson, Windham, Brougham, Romilly) become MPs without having to descend to demagoguery or 'mob oratory'?[223] Reform would undermine members' independence, or worse still make them 'free agents only in one direction', able to 'outrun the public cry and bid against each other as in a political auction', but preventing them from opposing '*any* proposition which the Press may call the wish of the People'.[224] In this way mercantile and manufacturing MPs would find themselves 'fettered by local interests and prejudices'.[225] Also, the criteria selected for borough abolition unfairly favoured the Whigs by sparing their own strongholds at Tavistock, Malton, Knaresborough, Portsmouth, and Calne.[226] Finally, Tories invoked the slippery slope. The change proposed could not possibly be final: 'We shall be bound to proceed further.'[227] As for the Whigs, neither in speeches nor in their private correspondence did ministers make out a theoretical case for reform, preferring to stick to details. Indeed, apart from a few comments by Burdett and Hunt, nothing was heard about natural rights, citizenship, the superiority of democracy to oligarchy, or any other of the abstract arguments put forward by Trenchard, Burgh, Wyvill, Cartwright, Tooke, and Jebb before the French Revolution. Instead Bankes, Hume, Place, Attwood, and Mill focused on the practical defects of the unreformed system such as corruption, high taxation, and loss of community. It was another sign that personal fulfilment had come to be associated exclusively with private life, while political systems were to be judged according to their utility.

The simplest argument in favour of reform was the need to root out Old Corruption. The 1832 edition of John Wade's *Extraordinary Black Book* (first published in 1820) contained a 700-page exposé of places, pensions, reversions, sinecures, nepotism, and pluralism in the court, the Church, the Privy Council, government departments, colonial establishments, municipal corporations, guilds, fraternities, the judiciary, the City, the military, and so on.[228] For some

[222] As well as providing bolt-holes for established politicians when their electors proved unworthy of them. In 1830, for example, Russell was defeated at Bedford and took refuge at Tavistock (maximum number of electors, twenty-seven); another Whig minister, E. J. Stanley, was beaten by Hunt at Preston and decamped to the royal borough of Windsor.

[223] Even though the Ultras had previously criticized rotten boroughs on precisely this ground—that they allowed men of avant-garde opinions into Parliament.

[224] Croker to Peel, 17 Oct. 1832, Peel MS 40320, fo. 222.

[225] This was the Tories' most interesting argument, that the current system of 'virtual representation' enabled the master cotton-spinner Thomas Houldsworth to represent Manchester, even though he sat for a rotten borough.

[226] Though Calne, controlled by Lansdowne and described by Hunt as 'that rottenest, stinkingest, skulkingest of boroughs', lost one of its members in a subsequent amendment (*HPD*3 ii).

[227] Peel, *HPD*3 ii. 1345 (3 Mar. 1831).

[228] The widespread sense that there was 'something rotten in the state of Denmark' may help to explain why *Hamlet* overtook *Macbeth* in critics' estimation as Shakespeare's greatest play at about this time.

reason the cause of all this mass of putridity was held to be the suborning of Parliament by a borough-monger faction. Following a line of argument begun by Thomas Oldfield in the 1790s, Wade calculated that 487 out of 658 MPs were returned by nomination. (In fact only about 200 MPs were dependent on wealthy or aristocratic patrons, though between 50 and 60 others benefited in some degree from ministerial influence.[229]) According to the Whig historian Creevey, the borough franchise had originally been uniform and was based on an ability to contribute to MPs' wages. However, successive kings had deliberately abandoned the financial qualification in order to create a subordinate class of needy boroughs.[230] It is possible that ministers swallowed this rigmarole. Introducing the Bill, Russell claimed that his scheme was restorative rather than revolutionary in seeking to re-create a uniform borough franchise of taxpaying citizens. He followed Hallam in arguing that all large towns without representation must have emerged from obscurity *since* the days of Henry VIII, and conversely that the present rotten boroughs must have been metropolises by thirteenth-century standards. 'Our ancestors gave Old Sarum representatives, because it *was* a large town; therefore we give representatives to Manchester, which *is* a large town. I think we are acting more as our ancestors would have acted, by letting in representatives for our great commercial and manufacturing towns, than by excluding such representatives.'[231]

Russell sat down and Peel declined to speak, so the task of answering him fell to Inglis. An antiquarian who just eleven days later was appointed a Commissioner of Public Records, Inglis had no difficulty in showing that, despite what Hallam and Russell claimed, representation had *never* been linked to population. When a medieval king had needed money he had summoned his free barons (Lords) and the representatives of communities (Commoners), but he had chosen the latter 'arbitrarily, and without reference to numbers'. Old Sarum had been favoured, not because it was populous (it never had been) but because Edward I had wished to bestow a personal favour on the Earl of Salisbury by giving him a right of nomination to the Commons. In other words, nomination had always been the basis of the franchise; because it was linked to taxation it was originally a burden, but now it was seen as a privilege. 'Nothing is more certain than that boroughs were created by the mere will of the King, sometimes at the requisition of a favourite.'[232] Academically Inglis was carrying all before him, but polemically he was condemning the *ancien régime* out of his own mouth,[233] so much so that Russell might even be suspected of having laid a

---

[229] O'Gorman, *Voters, Patrons, and Parties*, 18–23.   [230] See above, pp. 347.
[231] *HPD*3 ii. 1085–6 (1 Mar. 1831).   [232] *HPD*3 ii. 1098, 1103 (1 Mar. 1831).
[233] As Inglis himself seems suddenly to have realized mid-speech: 'I am not defending this, though I am perfectly willing to defend it. I say only, that those who talk of *restoring* the Constitution, are bound to shew at what period in our history our Constitution has been purer, or other than at present.'

trap. More generally Inglis's diehard Tory legalism and his reverence for procedure, precedent, and propriety struck the wrong note.

The standard interpretation of the Reform Act is that it was designed to incorporate the middle classes into the Constitution and detach them from the workers. In one sense this is self-evident. The Whigs clearly intended to increase the number of voters on the basis of property, whether owned or occupied, and inevitably the vast majority of those who benefited might be described as middle-class, but that does not make it the main intention of the Bill. Russell made no such claim in his introductory speech. Althorp, the second minister to speak, mentioned the 'respectable middle classes' once, but only off the cuff following an ironic interjection by Peel. A turning point was Macaulay's speech on the second night with its ringing peroration: 'Renew the youth of the State . . . The danger is terrible. The time is short.' It raised cheers on the Government benches, put anti-reformers on the defensive, and provided a rationale for reform which set the terms of all subsequent debate. Its central point, that appeals to prescription were no guide to policy ('We are legislators, not antiquaries') was a rebuke to Inglis, but also to Russell for his talk of restoring the Constitution to its condition under Edward I. Macaulay was willing to congratulate the Whig barons of the twelfth and thirteenth centuries for having 'framed a representative system . . . which was well adapted to the state of England in their time.' Since then, however, a 'great revolution' had taken place.

New forms of property came into existence. New portions of society rose into importance. There were in our rural districts rich cultivators, who were not freeholders. There were in our capital rich traders, who were not liverymen. Towns shrank into villages. Villages swelled into cities larger than the London of the Plantagenets. Unhappily, while the natural growth of society went on, the artificial polity continued unchanged. The ancient form of the representation remained; and precisely because the form remained, the spirit departed. Then came that pressure almost to bursting—the new wine in the old bottles—the new people under the old institutions . . . All history is full of revolutions . . . A portion of the community which had been of no account, expands and becomes strong. It demands a place in the system, suited, not to its former weakness, but to its present power. If this is granted, all is well. If this is refused, then comes the struggle between the young energy of one class, and the ancient privileges of another.[234]

Such had been the struggle of the plebeians against the patricians in ancient Rome, of the American colonists against the British Crown, of the third estate against the clergy and nobility in France, of the Jamaican blacks against an 'aristocracy of skin', and 'such . . . is the struggle which the middle classes in England are maintaining against [an] Aristocracy of mere locality'. Russell had not mentioned them, Althorp had only done so incidentally, yet following Macaulay most

[234] *HPD*3 ii. 1196, 1204–5 (2 Mar. 1832).

MIDDLE-CLASS COUP OR LANDED BACKLASH

speakers assumed that the main point of the Bill, for good or ill, was to enfranchise the middle classes. Palmerston, who spoke next day, affirmed that the latter were 'distinguished by morality and good conduct—by obedience to the laws— by the love of order—by attachment to the Throne and the Constitution... [and] devotion to their country', and that the purpose of the Bill was to 'include' more of them in the Constitution.[235] Grey too argued for 'a greater influence to be given to the middle classes, who have made wonderful advances in property and intelligence', 'who form the real and efficient mass of public opinion, and without whom the power of the gentry is nothing'.[236]

Macaulay undoubtedly provided a rationale for ministers, who 'had a policy but needed a philosophy',[237] but he was not a minister, this was only his third speech as an MP, and he was not privy to the thoughts of those who had drafted the Bill. His interpretation caught on partly because it registered with opponents of the Bill, both Radical and Tory. Hunt had been pleasantly surprised by Russell's speech, but Macaulay's gave him pause. If the aim of the Bill was to empower the middle classes, then mere mechanics—the sinews of the nation— would be consigned to 'political slavery'.[238] His reaction was not lost on Peel, whose 'fatal objection' to the Reform Bill was that it 'severs all connexion between the lower classes of the community and the direct representation in this House'. 'It is an immense advantage that there is at present no class of people, however humble, which is not entitled to a voice in the election of representatives.' Admittedly, not many MPs were elected by potwallopers or by scot and lot, but the fact that there were *some* meant that 'the [working] class is represented' and 'has its champion within your walls'. That was why the MPs for Preston and Coventry were accorded special attention whenever issues pertinent to the lower orders were being discussed. But to exclude everyone below an arbitrary £10 line would mean either that the line would have to be lowered bit by bit, or else that those below it would turn against parliamentary institutions altogether.[239]

The Reform Act debates undoubtedly created a strong conception of the middle class or classes.[240] Brougham defined them as 'generally speaking... a class above want, having comfortable houses over their heads, and families and homes to which they are attached'. To Peel, by contrast, they constituted a 'vulgar privileged pedlary... the class just above physical force, which has no quality attracting respect, whose arrogance is at all times intolerable to those

[235] Ibid. 1327–8 (3 Mar. 1831).
[236] Grey to Palmerston, 10 Oct. 1831, quoted in G. M. Trevelyan, *Lord Grey of the Reform Bill* (1920), 313.
[237] Joseph Hamburger, *Macaulay and the Whig Tradition* (Chicago, 1976), 160–1.
[238] *HPD*3 ii. 1209, iii. 18–19 (2 and 4 Mar. 1831).   [239] Peel, *HPD*3 ii. 1346 (3 Mar. 1831).
[240] Dror Wahrman, *Imagining the Middle Class: The Political Representation of Class in Britain, c.1780–1840* (Cambridge, 1995), 298–327.

immediately below it'.[241] Rhetoric apart, however, the middle class was too diverse, materially and mentally, to explain much about the Government's motives. The Committee of Four had originally proposed a £20 franchise. This was later lowered to £10, partly in response to the ballot being dropped, but of course £10 was an arbitrary line which included many more occupiers in wealthy communities where rents were high than it did in poorer ones.[242] Many working-class occupiers would creep under the net in London, whereas some middle-class citizens would fail the hurdle in remoter places. To that extent the borough qualification was a self-adjusting mechanism, allowing a higher proportion of residents to vote in the more respectable localities.

If an intention to incorporate the middle classes was very likely a red herring, just what did ministers intend when they spoke of enfranchising 'the property, the wealth, the intelligence, and the industry of the country'?[243] Clearly, they were keen to uphold 'legitimate' influence, based on genuine deference, while eliminating that which was based on coercion or a 'cash nexus'. They were also more concerned about the distribution of seats than the level of enfranchisement. Population was to be a factor in deciding which towns should return members, since small boroughs could be subjected to 'undue influence', but it was not the only one. Frome was awarded a seat, despite having only 12,000 inhabitants, because it represented the woollen manufacturers of the South-West; Walsall because of its iron and leather industries; Whitby and Sunderland because they were shipping towns.[244] This concern for interests (which, incidentally, contradicted a fundamental tenet of the Constitution, that MPs should be representatives and not delegates) explains why *residence* was made a requirement of the borough franchise. In the counties, by contrast, *property ownership* or 'a stake in the soil' remained paramount. However, these are all generalities. In considering whether the Government had any more specific sense of what it was doing, it is pertinent to recall what Russell had said in 1822 when he proposed to remove one member from each of the 100 smallest boroughs, and to give 60 additional MPs to the counties and 40 to large towns. His main objection to small boroughs was that businessmen could buy their way in, not to represent the commercial interest as a whole, but in order to obtain personal favours, such as wartime licences for the West Indian trade. This was not only inherently wrong, but rendered those members wholly subservient to Government. Analysing recent division lists on popular issues such as retrenchment and the Queen's case, Russell calculated that MPs for boroughs with fewer than 500 voters had supported the Government by a ratio of 19 to 1, whereas it was

---

[241] Peel to Croker, 15 Apr. 1831, in *Croker Papers*, ii. 114–15.

[242] Norman Gash, *Politics in the Age of Peel: A Study in the Technique of Parliamentary Representation 1830–1850* (1953), 98–100.   [243] Althorp, *HPD3* vii. 424 (21 Sept. 1831).

[244] Gash, *Politics in the Age of Peel*, 24.

only 3 to 1 in boroughs with between 500 and 1,000 voters. MPs for counties, on the other hand, had voted with the Opposition by a ratio of 3 to 2, and those sitting for boroughs with more than 5,000 voters by 5 to 3. He naturally concluded that county members were 'the real representatives of the people', but even they had displayed less virtue than the House of Lords, which had often been closer to the feelings of the people than the Commons, on the Queen Caroline affair for instance.[245] Russell suggested that, rather than ennobling commoners, it would be better to put peers into the Commons, since they had a real stake in the country and would never damage its true interests. This was hardly a manifesto against the aristocracy, being reminiscent of Fox's rhetoric about the 'virtuous band', independent of self-interest and of the Crown. However, it needs to be placed in the context of Russell's attempts in the early 1820s to counter the influence of 'monied men', 'capitalists', and 'political economists', and to identify the Whigs as the party of tax relief, currency depreciation, and agricultural protection.[246]

It is hard to say whether Russell was still an agrarian populist in 1831, or whether he was on the way to becoming the committed free-trader of the 1840s. What can be said is that, for all the razzmatazz about large industrial towns, the main effect of the Act was to increase the power of the landed interest, at least in the short term.[247] The number of English county seats rose from eighty-two to 144, while the creation of separate seats for places like Manchester, Birmingham, and Leeds benefited agriculture was well as industry and commerce, because it reduced the number of urban voters in South Lancashire, North Warwickshire, and the West Riding respectively. Right at the start of the saga Russell counselled Graham, 'it is essential that . . . we do not give members to all the manufacturing parishes of the North'. Respectable towns and counties were the best bodies to receive new seats.[248] In debate, no sooner had Palmerston echoed Macaulay's paean to the middle classes than he backtracked by declaring that, 'without meaning to disparage the manufacturing or commercial interests, he . . . considered the soil to be the country itself'. The purpose of the Act, with its additional votes for copy-holders, additional seats for counties, and (as initially proposed) exclusion of certain borough freeholders from the county franchise, was to 'restore to the landed interest that influence which he thought indispensable to the safety and prosperity of the country'.[249]

---

[245] *HPD2* vii. 51–88 (25 Apr. 1822). As early as 1807 Jeffrey attacked Radicals such as Cobbett for their opposition to aristocratic influence over elections. Now that all power resided in the Commons, it was essential that peers should have influence there if the 'balance of the constitution' was to be maintained. Besides which, the danger to parliamentary government came not from the aristocracy but from 'stock jobbers and nabobs'. [Francis Jeffrey], 'Cobbett's *Political Register*', *ER* 10 (1807), 414–17.

[246] See above, p. 273.   [247] But not in the longer term. See below, pp. 505–6.

[248] Russell to Graham, Mar. 1831, Graham MSS, General Series, 4/26.

[249] *HPD3* ii. 1329–30 (3 Mar. 1831). On the exclusion of certain borough freeholders, see below, p. 437.

If the landed interest was meant to benefit from the Reform Act, the intended victims were not the provincial retailers and manufacturers, who had been friendly to the Foxites since the 1780s, but those upper-middle-class types that had given such sustenance to the Pittite regime. The point was not lost on anti-reformers. Inglis warned that London lawyers, bankers, and merchants could 'bid farewell to Parliament's walls forever', since in future MPs would need either to be local or else have the leisure in which to cultivate voters. Twiss insisted that small boroughs were vital for 'the professional classes . . . the colonial interest . . . the interest of the fundholders and money capitalists'.[250] Even Russell conceded privately that the 'monied interest' had reason to be discontented, since reform would leave a 'want of means for the great funded and commercial interests to enter Parliament, "the usual avenues", as these gentlemen call them, being closed. Certainly in reason and common sense they have a better claim than others to complain.'[251]

Finally, it remains to be considered *why* the Whigs were keen to strengthen the landed interest by increasing the number of county seats. It was a spectacular own goal, since the Tory–Conservative Party's rapid revival between 1835 and 1841 was centred on these agricultural constituencies.[252] The only explanation is that the Whigs had deluded themselves into supposing that the landed interest—the 'stamina of the country'—was once more behind them. Despite their long exclusion from office, they had signally failed to develop an inferiority complex, and had never doubted their title to be considered the country's natural leaders. Pickled in self-esteem, they attributed their decades of failure to three external factors: royal malignancy, Old Corruption, and the fact that the country gentlemen, in their post-French revolutionary funk, had preferred to cling to the coat-tails of Pittites than risk the impetuosity of Fox and Grey. But in the 1830 election the Whigs had prospered in the counties, only fifteen of whose representatives supported Wellington in the crucial vote of 15 November. Observing the Government Party consumed with venom over Catholic emancipation, the economic crisis in town and countryside, the threat from Captain Swing, and the emergence of militarized political unions, the Whigs could be forgiven for thinking that the long-standing (and always slightly incongruous) alliance between Pittite ministers and the bulk of the country gentlemen was finally over. When reformers swept the counties and the open boroughs in the 1831 election,[253] it merely confirmed Whigs in the belief that their time had come.

[250] *HPD*3 ii. 1132–3 (1 Mar. 1831).
[251] Russell, memorandum, 4 Apr. 1831, TNA, Russell MSS 30/32/22/1B/27–37.
[252] See below, pp. 499, 501–2.
[253] Reformers captured seventy-three out of eighty-two English county seats; only six of the twenty-five English county members who had voted against the second reading of the first Reform Bill survived; only Shropshire returned two anti-reformers.

However, with hindsight it is clear that there was yet life in the alliance between Pittites and gentry, if only because the Corn Laws remained on the statute book and the Conservative Party seemed more likely to defend them.[254] It would not take the Whigs long to realize their mistake. Before the 1830s were out, they would be forced to turn for support to those retailing and manufacturing middle classes to whom they had offered rhetorical tributes and cosmetic sops in 1832, but whom they had not at that stage sought to empower.

APPENDIX 6.1. THE STATUS OF THE BOROUGH FREEHOLDERS

The electoral status of borough freeholders played a prominent role in the reform debates. Whereas before 1832 a forty-shilling freeholder, in order to exercise a county vote, had had to be assessed to the land tax, the Reform Act removed this requirement. In many rural towns the change made little difference to the numbers qualified to vote, and even if it had it would not have signified much since country townsmen were bound up with the agrarian economy. But in places like Manchester, where few forty-shilling freeholders were assessed, the number entitled to vote increased considerably, and since those whose properties were worth less than £10 would not be able to vote in the newly created borough, this naturally heralded an invasion of the South Lancashire constituency by Manchester voters whose interests were perceived to be antagonistic to agriculture. Peel anticipated the problem, warning Hobhouse that 'town property gives a facility for the creation of little freeholds, which has not yet been called into action, but which infallibly will be if the Reform Bill is to pass, and town freeholders, backed and stimulated by the press, will overpower the influence of land.'[255] Banishing the borough freeholders (i.e. those whose property was worth between £40 and £10) from the county was the main plank in the abortive attempt by Wharncliffe's waverers to modify the Reform Bill, and it was to remain Conservative Party policy for many decades. (For example, Disraeli sought to restrict the borough freeholders to voting in the boroughs in his failed Reform Bill of 1859, while in the second Reform Act of 1867 he achieved the same end by surreptitious means, when he widened the borough franchise sufficiently to include all those who had previously voted in the county.) There was also much debate in 1831 about the other type of borough freeholder, he who owned *but did not live in* borough property worth £10 or over, and whose property conveyed a vote on the occupier. The first Reform Bill would have prevented such a borough freeholder from voting in the surrounding county, but a concession made by the Government in August 1831 allowed him to do so.

APPENDIX 6.2. SPLIT VOTING, STRAIGHT VOTING, AND PLUMPING

Nearly all constituencies returned two members and all voters were entitled to cast two votes. If two Tories and two Whigs stood for election, voters could choose either to split

---

[254] Especially as the most prominent Canningites had joined Grey's Government.
[255] Peel to Henry Hobhouse, July 1831, Peel MS 40402, fos. 98–101.

between a Whig and a Tory or to vote 'straight' for two Whigs or two Tories. If two Whigs and one Tory stood, then a Whig voter could either split or vote straight, but a Tory voter would 'necessarily' have to split or else 'plump', i.e. vote for the Tory candidate and not use his other vote. There is a presumption among historians that voters did not like to waste either of their votes. Hence it is assumed that 'necessary plumping' was a sign of political partisanship, and that splitting (and especially unnecessary splitting) was a sign of low partisanship. Calculations of the incidence of split voting and plumping are based on contemporary poll books, which recorded the way in which each voter exercised the franchise, and are inevitably affected by the chance fact that some poll books have survived and others have not. The introduction of the secret ballot in 1872 brought poll books to an end, and the introduction of single-member (one man, one vote) constituencies in 1885 brought split voting to an end.

CHAPTER 7

Contesting mechanical philosophy

Chapter 5 described a ruling-class ideology steeped in evangelicalism, natural theology, utilitarianism, political economy, and a muscular–corpuscular understanding of the body. This chapter considers those who, whether from left- or right-wing perspectives, railed against all such mechanical philosophies. The most savage critique was Thomas Carlyle's in 1829:

> It is the Age of Machinery ... Nothing is now done directly, or by hand; all is by rule and calculated contrivance ... The living artisan is driven from his workshop, to make room for a speedier, inanimate one ... Not the external and physical alone is now managed by machinery, but the internal and spiritual also. Here, too, nothing follows its spontaneous course, nothing is left to be accomplished by old, natural methods ... Thus we have machines for education: Lancastrian machines; Hamiltonian machines—monitors, maps, and emblems ... Then, we have Religious machines, of all imaginable varieties— the Bible-Society ... a very excellent machine for converting the heathen ... Philosophy, Science, Art, Literature, all depend on machinery. No Newton, by silent meditation, now discovers the system of the world from the falling of an apple ... The same habit regulates, not our modes of action alone, but our modes of thought and feeling. Men are grown mechanical in head and in heart, as well as in hand.[1]

The diagnosis was penetrating but Carlyle's windily Germanic appeal to the 'Invisible'—to beauty, virtue, and spiritual truth—meant nothing to most of his readers. His was a 'trumpet inciting to the battle and induing men with the resolution "to do with all their might"', to assert in other words the 'everlasting yea', but alas, he offered no 'prescriptive rule of life'.[2]

George Eliot's novel *Middlemarch* (1871–2) offered a subtler analysis. Set in a fictional Warwickshire town between 1829 and 1832, the mechanical mentality is represented by the 'provincially, solidly important' Nicholas Bulstrode, 'a banker, a Churchman, a public benefactor'. In the course of the novel it transpires that twenty years or so earlier he was engaged in some dodgy pawnbroker dealings. His business partner has no qualms about this, having 'never conceived

---

[1] [Carlyle], 'Signs of the Times', *ER* 49 (1829), 442–4.

[2] Geraldine Jewsbury, *Religious Faith and Modern Scepticism* (1849), quoted in *Womens' Writing in the Victorian Period 1837–1901: An Anthology*, ed Harriet Devine Jump (Edinburgh, 1999), 66.

that trade had anything to do with the scheme of salvation', but Bulstrode's evangelical conscience stirs, and brings about 'a moment of transition', 'his first moments of shrinking'. As in one of Hannah More's homilies, bad behaviour leads inexorably to worse. Bulstrode swindles his late partner's daughter out of her inheritance, and then brings about the death through wilful neglect of a blackmailer who threatens to expose him. Eventually, however, these secrets leak out, and the banker is subjected to public exposure and humiliation. What most exercised Eliot was not the wickedness itself but Bulstrode's attempts to justify it on Utilitarian grounds—although his wealth has been gained unworthily he has spent it in the service of the Lord. 'God's cause was something distinct from his own rectitude of conduct.' Just as seriously, Bulstrode denies the reality of causal sequence by mentally breaking his own evil behaviour up into a number of separate actions, each of which taken separately might be regarded as venial. In other words, it is Bulstrode's dual and divided self, the separation between reality and consciousness, between past and present, that is truly reprehensible. By contrast, the novel's noble characters—Dorothea Brooke, Will Ladislaw, Fred Vincy eventually—strive to lead organic and integrated lives within the community. 'For there is no creature whose inward being is so strong that it is not greatly determined by what lies outside it.'[3]

Yet Eliot's final judgement on Bulstrode was surprisingly gentle. She disparaged his evangelical–mechanical world-view, yet was almost equally critical of attempts by contemporary intellectuals to counter its influence. Another denizen of Middlemarch, Edward Casaubon, is a desiccated antiquarian and etymologist, whose mission is to carry on the work of the eighteenth-century mythologist Jacob Bryant, and to 'reduce truth to its original purity' by tracing the scattered tribes of Israel back to a single unitary source. His introverted pedantry is contrasted unfavourably with the altruism of the novel's other intellectual, young Dr Tertius Lydgate, whose ambition is to extend the experimental findings of M-F-X. Bichat. The latter was the first biologist in Eliot's words to insist 'that living bodies, fundamentally considered, are not associations of organs which can be understood by studying them first apart, and then as it were federally, but must be regarded as consisting of certain primary webs or tissues of which the various organs—brain, heart, lungs, and so on—are compacted'. Following Bichat, Lydgate's ambition is to discover a 'primitive tissue' or 'unitary source' from which the entire animal and vegetable kingdom originated. The analogy with Casaubon's research is obvious, and they are equally futile. If Casaubon had read German he would have known that K. O. Müller had undermined the whole basis of his etymological inquiries in 1825. Lydgate was

<hr />

[3] Tess Cosslett, *The 'Scientific Movement' and Victorian Literature* (Brighton, 1982), 74–100; Sally Shuttleworth, *George Eliot and Nineteenth-Century Science: The Make-Believe of a Beginning* (Cambridge, 1984), 143–8, 154–5.

unlucky, since he could not have known that, just a few years later, advances in cell theory by Matthias Schleiden and Theodor Schwann would undermine the notion of a unitary source of life. Yet although Lydgate is less culpable than Casaubon, his basic error is the same—a doomed attempt to combat Enlightenment dualism by supposing that there must be a single overarching principle, in Casaubon's case 'The Key to all Mythologies', in Lydgate's the concept of primitive tissue. To Eliot, a generation later, all such attempts to explain development in unitary terms seemed hopelessly Whiggish. She believed in 'organic heterogeneity', or webs of multiplicity, 'the many in the one, the one in the many'.[4]

This chapter considers a number of intellectual currents that opposed the ruling mechanical philosophy. Although some looked forward like Lydgate and others backward with Casaubon, all were in revolt against Enlightenment dualism, and all were in search of connectedness and organic wholeness in a world seemingly rendered atomistic by social change. But first it is necessary to consider the impact of Casaubon and Lydgate on each other, since it was during their fictional working lifetimes—the second quarter of the century—that the challenge of science led to a national crisis of faith.

THE EVOLUTIONARY MOMENT: THE SCIENTIFIC THREAT TO BELIEF

The last claim might seem perverse given that outwardly England remained intensely religious, with its thousands of devotional publications, its religious missions, its sabbatarian pall, its spiritual revivals, and its militant Dissent. Conventionally it has been assumed that the 'age of doubt' did not occur until the *third* quarter of the century, characterized as that was by a series of individual 'crises of faith', beginning in 1848–9 when Arthur Hugh Clough and J. A. Froude resigned their Oxford fellowships. It was not until the 1850s that the ontological doubts raised by Kant and Schopenhauer or the Bible criticism of Strauss and Vatke began to register with the public at large, and it was not until 1859 that Charles Darwin published *On the Origin of Species*, his theory of biological evolution by natural selection, as a result of which (it used to be thought) 'a great chasm seemed to have been opened between God and Nature', and 'it seemed to many . . . that God had been banished from the world'.[5]

---

[4] W. J. Harvey, 'The Intellectual Background of the Novel: Casaubon and Lydgate', in Barbara Hardy (ed.), *Middlemarch: Critical Approaches to the Novel* (1967); Michael York Mason, '*Middlemarch* and Science: Problems of Life and Mind', *Review of English Studies*, 22 (1971), 151–69.

[5] Noel Annan, 'Science, Religion, and the Critical Mind', in Philip Appleman, William A. Madden, and Michael Wolff (eds.), *1859: Entering an Age of Crisis* (Bloomington, Ind., 1959), 35–7.

Recent research has considerably revised this picture. Intellectuals who jettisoned faith in the 1850s did so as a result of moral revulsion against orthodox religion and not because of philosophical and scientific developments with which they had long been familiar. In many cases deconversion represented a thankful release following long periods of agonized indecision, a resolution rather than a realization of doubts, and it only occurred because society was now more tolerant of agnosticism. It is also clear that, except in a few biblically literalist circles, the *Origin of Species* was absorbed painlessly, being interpreted in an inappropriately optimistic and even progressive way that was deemed compatible with Christian belief.[6] By contrast the decades before 1850 really *were* crisis-ridden, if only because renunciation of faith was still such a difficult option. Very few savants shared the open scepticism of James Mill and George Grote, yet many suppressed the doubts they undoubtedly felt, being in denial of denial. This was probably true of Edward Pusey, who visited Göttingen and Berlin as a young man in 1825. Three years later he published *An Historical Enquiry into the Probable Causes of the Rationalist Character lately Predominant in the Theology of Germany*. Yet almost immediately afterwards, alarmed by the prospect of social disorder during the reform crisis, Pusey decided that rationalism could not be countered by argument, only by blind faith and reliance on authority.[7]

Developments in science seemed every bit as frightening. In 1831 Charles Darwin, just down from Cambridge, secured a post as naturalist on a scientific expedition to South American waters. The voyage of the *Beagle* (1831–6) enabled him to collect and study the fossil mammals and hermaphrodite molluscs of the Galapagos Islands. By 1837 he had become an evolutionist (or 'transformist'), and by 1838 he had formulated a theory of natural selection. Yet he kept silent, partly because publication would have damaged his claims to respectability, and partly because he was concerned about the effect that his theories might have on an insubordinate populace.[8] In other words, he wished to avoid the type of hostile and hysterical reception that just a few years later was accorded to Robert Chambers's anonymous *Vestiges of the Natural History of Creation* (1844). That electrical and embryological stab at a theory of evolution really *did* seem to banish God from the world. It scandalized polite society, and

[6] See below, pp. 635–6.

[7] Apparently he bought up and destroyed copies of his own book, and never allowed it to be reprinted (H. C. G. Matthew, 'Edward Bouverie Pusey: From Scholar to Tractarian', *Journal of Theological Studies*, 32 (1981), 101–24).

[8] David Kohn, 'Theories to Work By: Rejected Theories, Reproduction, and Charles Darwin's Path to Natural Selection', *Studies in History of Biology*, 4 (1980), 67–170; Adrian Desmond and James Moore, *Darwin* (1991), 240–338; Janet Browne, *Charles Darwin: Voyaging* (1995), 343–72. See also the essays by David Kohn, Phillip R. Sloan, and M. J. S. Hodge in David Kohn (ed.), *The Darwinian Heritage* (Princeton, 1985).

prompted a witch-hunt by Christian vigilantes, anxious to discover and punish its author.[9] One effect of *Vestiges* and of publications like it was to ensure that by 1859 the concept of evolution had been silently absorbed by the vast majority of educated people. Besides which, at the later date it was no longer thought necessary to uphold belief in a transcendent Deity in order to preserve social order. These considerations, plus the fact that Alfred Russel Wallace was breathing down his neck and threatening to trump him, finally persuaded Darwin to publish.

In 1844 Darwin confessed to a friend, 'at last gleams of light have come, & I am almost convinced (quite contrary to opinion I started with) that species are not (it is like confessing a murder) immutable'.[10] Murder, because belief in Special Creation had long been ingrained in the culture.

The contemplation of the works of the creation, necessarily leads the mind to that of the Creator himself... [The naturalist] sees the beautiful connection that subsists through-out the whole scheme of animated nature. He traces, from the bulk and strength of the massive elephant to the almost invisible structure of the minutest insect, a mutual depend-ency, that convinces him nothing is made in vain. He feels too, that at the head of all this system of order and beauty, pre-eminent in the dominion of his reason, stands Man. He sees himself the favoured creature of his Creator, and the finest energies of his soul are roused to gratitude and devotion.[11]

Darwin and Wallace claimed to have been inspired by Malthusianism.[12] The animal kingdom was a struggle for existence in which those species best fitted to a particular environment (i.e. taller, faster, cleverer) survived and procreated, while weaker specimens became extinct. In this sense the *Origin* was a tract for the times, even though it was too hot to publish until those rough times had passed and calmer water had ensued. In some ways the Malthusian analogy is misleading, however, since population theory was conceived within the static–mechanical–equilibrium framework of natural theology, by which it was assumed that time moved cyclically: seasons came round, empires rose and fell, famines and trade depressions recurred. The evolutionists' notion of continuous gradual change was based on an alternative linear view of time, and was related to other radical developments in early nineteenth-century science.

As explained in Chapter 5, establishment scientists—mainly Anglican in reli-gion, liberal Tory or Whig–Liberal in politics—melded Lockean epistemology,

[9] Adam Sedgwick was one of many who thought at first that only a woman could have leapt to such an elegant but unsubstantiated conclusion (Sedgwick to Lyell, 9 Apr. 1845, in *The Life and Letters of Adam Sedgwick*, ed. J. W. Clark and T. McK. Hughes (Cambridge, 1890), ii. 85).
[10] Darwin to J. D. Hooker, 11 Jan. 1844, in *The Correspondence of Charles Darwin*, ed. Frederick Burkhardt *et al.* (Cambridge, 1985–), iii. 2.   [11] *Zoological Journal*, 1 (1824), p. vii.
[12] Robert M. Young, 'Malthus and the Evolutionists: The Common Context of Biological and Social Theory', *P&P* 43 (1969), 109–45.

Newtonian natural philosophy, and Paleyan natural theology into a mechanical philosophy based on the concept of design.[13] The mind was a sheet of blank paper, devoid of innate ideas, but capable of reasoning about sense impressions received from the outside world. Matter was solid, inert, passive, and subject to outside forces such as gravitation, in the same way that a billiard ball is subject to the cue. All aspects of Creation had their appropriate function and were indicative of divine design. God governed by unvarying or general laws; 'and when a particular purpose is to be effected, it is not by making a new law, nor by the suspension of the old ones, nor by making them wind and bend and yield to the occasion'.[14] On the other hand there were political Radicals, often from freethinking or rational Dissenting backgrounds, who attacked this Newtonian science and emphasized materialist or necessitarian explanations of phenomena.[15] The most influential was Joseph Priestley, who asserted that 'matter is not the inert substance that it has been supposed to be'. 'Powers of attraction and repulsion are necessary to its very being.' He also rejected the idea that matter and spirit (mind) were 'two entirely different and independent principles in man, connected in some unknown and incomprehensible manner... I rather think that the whole man is of some uniform composition.'[16] Priestley was certainly no atheist and yet, if matter possessed gravity as well as extension, divisibility, mobility, and *vis inertiae*, there was reason to conclude that it was somehow responsible for creating 'thought and life themselves'.[17] This was clearly seen as a challenge to the doctrine of free will. Furthermore, by insisting on the 'homogeneity of man' and a single underlying principle to explain all phenomena (monism), Priestley questioned the conventional sharp distinction between organic and inorganic matter.

Priestley's writings stimulated many later attacks on Enlightenment dualism. During 1817–19, for example, William Lawrence, Thomas Charles Morgan, and John Elliotson all questioned the traditional view, as upheld by conservatives like John Abernethy of St Bartholomew's Hospital, that life was caused by an independent, God-given principle of vitality, electrical, chemical, or ethereal. Life, for these radicals, was rather a function of the nervous system, and there could be no basic discontinuity between living and non-living

---

[13] To avoid confusion: as used here the term 'mechanical' refers to the finished *design* of the universe, as in Newton's mechanics and Paley's natural theology. By definition it does *not* apply to arguments for evolutionary development, though some historians do use the term in that context.

[14] Paley, *Natural Theology* (1802), 43. The most significant 19th-century modification of Paley's schema was to make it more retributive, judicial, evangelical, 'Butlerian'. See above, pp. 332–42.

[15] For an authoritative as well as thrilling account of this approach, see Adrian Desmond, *The Politics of Evolution: Morphology, Medicine, and Reform in Radical London* (Chicago, 1989).

[16] Joseph Priestley, *Disquisitions relating to Matter and Spirit* (1777), pp xii–xiii, xxxviii.

[17] Arnold Thackray, *Atoms and Powers: An Essay on Newtonian Matter-Theory and the Development of Chemistry* (Cambridge, Mass., 1970), 146, 189–92, 244–52.

matter.[18] By analogy, the etymologist Horne Tooke broke away from the classical view that words represented acts of the mind and universal ideas. He argued instead that they were simply 'the signs of other words' with their own power to evolve syntactically over time.[19] And John Allen, an Edinburgh medic who in 1805 became the resident intellectual of Holland House, proclaimed that 'voluntary motion is never to be regarded as the effect of volition'. Bodily movements were caused by physiological changes to the fibres of sensation in the brain, which could not be controlled by mind, will, or 'consciousness'.[20] Another savant to attack the old mind–body dualism was Erasmus Darwin, a respectable provincial doctor and Charles's grandfather, but whereas Allen did this by reducing mind to a physical phenomenon, Darwin argued that mental powers were not confined to the human brain, and that even plants possessed intelligence. Whereas Allen attributed bodily movements to unconscious reflex actions of the nervous system, Darwin believed that reflex foetal movements were voluntary and accompanied by consciousness.[21] Their views were diametrically opposed, but both embraced a form of monism as defined here. Darwin's target was the Swede Linnaeus' influential classification of plants and animals according to their natural or God-given affinities. Darwin argued *per contra* that species had undergone a constant process of change over millions of years. In order to survive, organisms had had to adjust to environmental conditions, and so were modified as individual organs fell out of or came into use. Characteristics thus acquired had then been inherited.[22]

The most sophisticated debates were taking place among officials of the Musée National d'Histoire Naturelle in Paris. Here the establishment position was upheld by Georges Cuvier, who was allowed to pick out bits of skeletons while Napoleon rebuilt his capital in imperial splendour. From these he sought to reconstruct what extinct species had been like, and to compare the bones of fossils with those of living animals. His working hypothesis was the principle of correlation, meaning that all the constituent parts of any animal must cohere. Each species was unique and invariable, and God had given to each the organs peculiarly suited to its habitat. The mummified cats discovered in Egyptian

[18] L. S. Jacyna, 'Immanence or Transcendence: Theories of Life and Organization in Britain, 1790–1835', *Isis*, 74 (1983), 311–29.

[19] J. Horne Tooke, *The Diversions of Purley* (1786–1805); Hans Aarsleff, *The Study of Language in England, 1780–1860* (Princeton, 1967), 44–114; Olivia Smith, *The Politics of Language 1791–1819* (Oxford, 1984), 110–53.

[20] John Allen, 'Mania' (late 1790s), quoted in L. S. Jacyna, *Philosophic Whigs: Medicine, Science and Citizenship in Edinburgh, 1789–1848* (1994), 61–5.

[21] Edwin Clarke and L. S. Jacyna, *Nineteenth-Century Origins of Neuroscientific Concepts* (Berkeley and Los Angeles, 1987), 108.

[22] Erasmus Darwin, *Zoonomia; or, The Laws of Organic Life* (1794–6). Charles Darwin admitted having read this book as a young man, and originally thought of calling *On the Origins of Species* by the same title, but he denied that it had influenced him.

tombs were then proclaimed identical to nineteenth-century tabbies. This functional anatomy, based on the hypothesis that God had contrived each body part for a particular purpose, was directly opposed to that of Cuvier's great rival Jean-Baptiste Lamarck. The latter believed that species had mutated in response to environmental change, and that they were capable of passing on their acquired 'higher' characteristics to their offspring.

The political implications of these disputes are obvious. Darwin and Allen were uncompromising freethinkers whose neurological speculations (according to Dugald Stewart) denied mankind any 'freedom of choice between good and evil'. Tooke was an active political Radical whose philology aimed to undermine the linguistic basis of authority, especially in the law courts, while Lawrence, Morgan, and Elliotson were also anti-Establishment thinkers. In so far as materialism left any room for God, it was as an immanent First or Final Cause whose laws pushed constantly upwards from below, a 'democratic' concept as opposed to vitalism and dualism, which were transcendental theories symbolizing political power and submission. Priestley commented that his doctrines were 'grains of gunpowder' to which his enemies were 'providing the match',[23] a prophetic comment in that one year later, in 1791, his house in Birmingham was destroyed by fire in a Church-and-King riot. Yet once the immediate tensions of the revolutionary period had cooled, it became possible once more to discuss such issues with relative equanimity. As late as the 1820s Christians could feel confident that the debate was going their way, and there was much rejoicing in the rectories when Buckland revealed what looked like evidence for the historical truth of Noah's Flood.[24]

So what happened to give these issues a life-and-death character, prompting Charles Darwin to feel it was 'like confessing a murder'? Partly it was a question of audience. It was one thing to publish challenging theories between expensive leather covers, quite another to insert them in the Revd Dionysius Lardner's *Cabinet Cyclopaedia*, directed at the working classes from 1829 onwards. Partly it had to do with the political and intellectual polarization of the late 1820s, the immediate cause of which was a conservative backlash against the 'march of mind'.[25] At any rate, there was something of a Paleyan fight-back among establishment scientists. In 1828 a German chemist Friedrich Wöhler succeeded in partially synthesizing an organic substance (urea) from a mixture of inorganic ones. Historians used to think that this laboratory experiment must have discredited vitalism by indicating a link between organic and inorganic substances, but this was not the contemporary perception. Indeed it has been suggested that, by only being partial, Wöhler's synthesis might have given

[23] *The Theological and Miscellaneous Works of Joseph Priestley*, ed. John Towill Rutt (1831), xix. 311.
[24] See above, p. 340.   [25] See above, pp. 401–11.

vitalism 'a new lease of life'.[26] Then, two years later in Paris, amid the tensions of
another revolution, a famous set-piece debate took place between Cuvier and
Étienne Geoffroy Saint-Hilaire. It led Goethe to reflect, 'the volcano has
erupted; everything is in flames, and it is no longer a negotiation behind closed
doors'. Following Lamarck's death the previous year, Geoffroy was the foremost
proponent of the view that all animals were formed of the same elements in the
same number ('unity of animal composition'), that self-organizing material
transmuted, that the same patterns of organic structure ran through the animal
scale, and that human anatomy could only be understood comparatively.[27]
Cuvier's response, a robust restatement of functional anatomy, was widely but
simplistically reported in Britain as a restatement of the argument from design,
and paved the way for the celebrated Bridgewater Treatises of Bell (1833) and
Buckland (1836).[28] It was probably this rearguard action by conservatives, rather
than the inexorable rise of radical science, that led to the bitter clashes of the
1830s. At any rate their position was stated in increasingly uncompromising
fashion. In the words of Adam Sedgwick, a Cambridge evangelical Whig, 'As a
matter of fact, species do not change, and the fixed organic laws of nature are the
first principles of physiology; in the same way that the fixed laws of atomic
combination are the first principles of philosophical chemistry. Were nature
changeable, there could be no philosophy.'[29]

Another factor was the way in which conflict between comparative and
functional anatomists became enmeshed in a political struggle within the
medical world, which was not immune to the nationwide clamour for institutional reform. By and large, the Oxford- and Cambridge-trained Anglican elite
of society doctors who dominated the royal colleges, the medical schools, and the
teaching hospitals regarded the human body as a perfectly created machine.
Conversely the jobbing, lower middle-class, artisan, and frequently Dissenting
doctors who staffed the public and Poor Law infirmaries, private anatomy
schools, and medical unions embraced the newer evolutionary biology as a complement to their radical and reformist politics. As one historian has memorably
expressed it, they 'saluted the new anatomists for having brought nature, man,
and mind under the control of the laws of progress and development'.[30] More
dangerously, their belief that nature was self-regulating and not God-regulated,
that ideas were a product of matter and organization, and that acquired

---

[26] John H. Brooke, 'Wöhler's Urea, and its Vital Force?—a Verdict from the Chemists', *Ambix*, 15
(1968), 102.

[27] Toby A. Appel, *The Cuvier–Geoffroy Debate: French Biology in the Decades before Darwin* (New York,
1987); Dov Ospovat, *The Development of Darwin's Theory* (Cambridge, 1981).

[28] See above, p. 333–4.   [29] [Adam Sedgwick], 'Natural History of Creation', *ER* 82 (1845), 73.

[30] Desmond, *Politics of Evolution*, 199.

characteristics might possibly be inherited seemed cumulatively to suggest that humankind might have evolved from animals. Such suppositions were too dangerous to appear in English textbooks, but they circulated in the medical underworld, in lecture halls and mechanics institutes, in provincial venues like the Manchester Royal Infirmary; in the *London Medical and Surgical Journal* and *The Lancet*, the latter directed by the reforming doctor Thomas Wakley MP. Many radical doctors had absorbed the theories of Geoffroy and Lamarck during their student days in Edinburgh, the main conduit for Continental ideas.[31] One such was the Unitarian Thomas Southwood Smith, who moved to London in the early 1820s to work in East End hospitals, and became Bentham's personal physician. A prominent contagionist and sanitary environmentalist, Southwood Smith argued that the mind had no existence independent of the body.[32] Another was Robert Grant, who became a professor at London University in 1827, and Robert Knox who, after oscillating between Paris and Edinburgh, finally settled in London in 1842. They in turn influenced native London surgeons such as William Lawrence and John Elliotson. Lawrence broke with his mentor Abernethy, while Elliotson rejected orthodox medicine symbolically in 1826 when he forsook knee-breeches and silk stockings for trousers, and became one of the first men in the country to sport a beard.[33] He became a London University professor in 1831, but was forced out seven years later, partly owing to his enthusiasm for mesmerism.

Such brief life histories do not convey the extent to which scientific disagreements disrupted old loyalties and friendships, causing much personal heartache. They also aroused political passions, as can be glimpsed from the proceedings of a Select Committee (1835–6) on the British Museum. The point at issue concerned its displays of fossils and other zoological specimens. Robert Inglis and John Children regarded these as 'attractive' ornaments, and were adamant that 'the specific names of Linnæus ought never to be abandoned' in classifying them. Robert Grant, on the other hand, complained that the traditional nomenclature rendered the Museum 'almost useless to the public' as a teaching instrument. Exhibits should appear in 'strict zoological order' so as to demonstrate evolutionary progress— 'the whole continuous chain of beings, from the lowest corals up to the highest animal forms that exist'.[34] He was supported by

---

[31] Eliot's fictional doctor, Lydgate, declined to take up a place at Oxford University, preferring to study in Edinburgh, Paris, and London.

[32] T. Southwood Smith, *The Philosophy of Health: or, An Exposition of the Physiological and Sanitary Conditions Conducive to Human Longevity and Happiness* (1835; 11th edn. 1865), p. xi. For contagionism, see above, pp. 338–9.

[33] The Pitt and Peel generations were clean-shaven. Whiskers did not come back until the 1850s, and then they came back with a vengeance.

[34] *Report from the Select Committee on the Condition, Management, and Affairs of the British Museum*, PP 1836 x. 27–39, 132–45, 229–40.

two Dissenting and Radical MPs, Henry Warburton and Benjamin Hawes, who also demanded that the Museum should become a place of education, open to non-ticket-holders. It was all too much for conservative evangelicals such as Children, who expostulated privately in 1831 against 'the abominable trash vomited forth by Lamarck and his disciples, who have rashly, and almost blasphemously, imputed a period of comparative imbecility to Omnipotence, when they babbled out their puerile conditions about a progression in nature'.[35] The Warburton–Hawes proposals were duly squashed, but it is noteworthy that the dispute occurred before Darwin had returned from his voyage on the *Beagle*.

Related debates took place in other areas of natural philosophy. Despite the speculations of Werner, Hutton, and latterly Scrope, the orthodox view that the earth was created at the start of biblical history held the field until the appearance of Charles Lyell's *Principles of Geology* (1830–3), a powerful statement of uniformitarianism. Lyell 'practically gave the death-blow to the catastrophic school of geologists',[36] by implying that there had been sufficient geological time for such 'natural' processes as sedimentation and erosion to have brought the earth imperceptibly to its current condition. It made it possible, in Scrope's words, to 'dispense with . . . revulsions and convulsions, deluges or cataclysms', and suchlike indications of divine intervention.[37] Traditionalists were of course perturbed. Sedgwick praised Lyell's 'geological dynamics' but protested against his doctrine of 'equal intensity' over time. 'Volcanic action is essentially paroxysmal,' he objected. The earth had been subjected to 'periods of feverish spasmodic energy, during which the very framework of nature has been convulsed and torn asunder'.[38] Meanwhile, scientists responded excitedly to Laplace's nebular hypothesis, suggesting that the earth and other planets had been formed out of condensed gas or dust. In a volume of Lardner's *Cabinet Cyclopaedia*, John Herschel went so far as to surmise that new solar systems might be forming before astronomers' very eyes, as debris broke loose from existing planets and began to swirl around in space.[39] There was further unease in establishment circles when the Regius Professor of Astronomy in Glasgow, John Pringle Nichol, included the theory in his popular volume *Views of the Architecture of the Heavens* (1837),

[35] Desmond, *Politics of Evolution*, 145–51.   [36] G. A. J. Cole, *DNB*.
[37] [G. Poulett Scrope], 'Lyell's *Principles of Geology*', *QR* 53 (1835), 407, 410. Lyell did not, however, share Scrope's belief in progress. See above, pp. 350–3; John Burrow, 'Images of Time: From Carlylean Vulcanism to Sedimentary Gradualism', in Stefan Collini, Richard Whatmore, and Brian Young (eds.), *History, Religion, and Culture: British Intellectual History 1750–1950* (Cambridge, 2000).
[38] Adam Sedgwick, *Addresses delivered at the Anniversary Meetings of the Geological Society of London* (1831), 21–7; Crosbie Smith, 'William Hopkins and the Shaping of Dynamical Geology: 1830–1860', *British Journal for the History of Science*, 22 (1989), 37–8.
[39] John Herschel, *Preliminary Discourse on the Study of Natural Philosophy* (1830), 274–81.

and when Chambers incorporated it in *Vestiges*, which also sold in cheap editions.[40]

It is disputed whether James Joule was religiously motivated in seeking to demonstrate the unity of forces in nature, or whether he simply wanted to replace steam power by electricity in his father's Salford brewery. Either way his paddle-wheel experiments of the 1840s led him to discover the mechanical equivalent of heat, and to conclude that 'an enormous quantity of *vis viva* exists in matter'. This was analogous to Priestley denying mental volition, and to Lawrence rejecting the principle of vitality. Hitherto it had been assumed that heat was caused by the presence in bodies of a weightless calorific fluid. By showing that heat was the effect of energy transferred from work, Joule helped to formulate the First Law of Thermodynamics (known as Conservation of Energy, or Persistence of Force), which holds that the world of phenomena manifests a single principle of continuous causation called energy.[41] As the physicist William Grove put it in a significant lecture series at the London Institution in 1843, 'humanly speaking, neither matter nor force can be created'. 'An essential cause is unattainable—Causation, is the will, Creation, the act, of God.'[42] This interest in thermal agency was neatly counterbalanced by studies in the dynamic role of glacial cooling. Meanwhile, a mistaken belief that electricity must form part of the unified forces of nature, along with heat, light, magnetism, and chemical affinity, prompted Michael Faraday's experiments in electromagnetism and field theory from the 1830s, further helping to undercut mechanism and to promote a linear view of development. Another more down-to-earth example was the new zymotic pathology. Whereas sewage had once been regarded as waste, fit only for expulsion like Malthus' excrescent population, some now considered it fit for recycling as agricultural fertilizer, metamorphosing 'from one beautiful and useful occupation to the next'.[43] Underlying these developments was a shift within mathematics from an earlier Newtonian emphasis on fluxions towards more Continental models, notably algebraic calculus and probability. (Advances in the latter field paradoxically undermined the basic Enlightenment assumption that, in Butler's words, 'probability is the very guide of life' by

[40] For the way in which J. S. Mill and J. P. Nichol fused nebular theory, political economy, phrenology, and Comtism in order to support arguments for political reform, see the seminal article by Simon Schaffer, 'The Nebular Hypothesis and the Science of Progress', in James R. Moore (ed.), *History, Humanity and Evolution* (Cambridge, 1989).

[41] For the religious promptings behind William Thomson's complementary work in Glasgow, see Crosbie Smith and M. Norton Wise, *Energy and Empire: A Biographical Study of Lord Kelvin* (Cambridge, 1989), 643–5.

[42] W. R. Grove, *On the Correlation of Physical Forces* (1846), 50.

[43] Christopher Hamlin, 'Providence and Putrefaction: Victorian Sanitarians and the Natural Theology of Health and Disease', *Victorian Studies*, 28 (1984–5), 381–411. For the sanitary movement, see below, pp. 578–81.

demonstrating that so much happens counter-intuitively.) The key figures here were William Frend and later Augustus De Morgan, who left Cambridge on grounds of conscience to become London's first Professor of Mathematics in 1828.[44] It has been argued that these developments led to a cultural shift— nascent in the 1820s, dominant in the 1830s, and consolidated in the 1840s— whereby the idea of evolution replaced that of balance, and a sense of dynamics replaced that of static equilibrium. At the same time, design gave way to development, and dualism to uniformitarianism.

Phrenology was another Continental 'science' that infiltrated the country via Scotland. Its progenitors were Franz Joseph Gall and Johann Gasper Spurzheim, the second of whom lectured in Edinburgh in 1816 and inspired a number of disciples. The most zealous was George Combe, for whom phrenology appeared to be 'a true system of human nature'[45] and a way of escape from the scarifying Calvinism of his own town. Its fundamental premiss was that the lineaments of a person's character are determined by the shape of the bumps on the head, and in particular by the size of various organs or faculties—e.g. amativeness, combativeness, conscientiousness, and philoprogenitiveness (Malthus' bugbear). This was a reassuring message in such a shifting and fluid society, where commercial trust was essential yet so many people rose without trace. Being based on faculty psychology, phrenology obviously contravened notions of free will, at least on a day-to-day basis, though Combe's hope was that people would fight against their bad propensities once they had been shown scientifically what those were.[46] His chief work, *The Constitution of Man, Considered in Relation to External Objects* (1828), was the standard manual for self-improvement before the publication of Samuel Smiles's *Self Help* in 1859, by which time it had sold more than 300,000 copies in Britain and America. That means it was possibly the fourth best-selling book of the second quarter of the century after the Bible, *The Pilgrim's Progress*, and *Robinson Crusoe*. At first it attracted evangelicals like Chalmers, who saw in it an anatomical basis for the doctrine of original sin, but a rupture occurred in the early 1830s as it became clear that Combe did not subscribe to depravity, Atonement, or hellfire.[47] On the contrary, his New Testament-inspired vision of tender Christian charity pointed towards the

[44] Joan L. Richards, 'The Probable and the Possible in Early Victorian England,' in Bernard Lightman (ed.), *Victorian Science in Context* (Chicago, 1997); Kevin Craig Knox, 'Disputes about Nothing: Natural Philosophy in Late-Georgian Cambridge', Ph.D. thesis (Cambridge University, 1995), 92–161.

[45] George Combe to Thomas Chalmers, 19 Feb. 1823, New College, Edinburgh, Chalmers Papers, CHA 4. 24. 82.

[46] There is a parallel here with J. S. Mill, who turned against free-will individualism on a day-to-day basis under the impact of Robert Owen's environmental determinism, but nevertheless argued that people had the freedom to develop their personalities.

[47] Roger Cooter, *The Cultural Meaning of Popular Science: Phrenology and the Organization of Consent in Nineteenth-Century Britain* (Cambridge, 1984), 127–31.

religion of the third quarter of the century, and was strongly influenced by that of his friend the American Unitarian William Ellery Channing.

As an attack on ruling-class assumptions about free-will individualism, phrenology was a liberating force. Political Radicals such as J. S. Mill and J. P. Nichol exploited it, along with political economy and Comtean positivism, in order to develop a 'science of progress' based on fundamental laws of human nature. It was also democratic, in so far as anyone could learn how to interpret bumps without having to attend university or be initiated into a clerical coterie. Phrenologists certainly saw themselves as promoters of social mobility, blowing away the cobwebs of mercantilist privilege in favour of free trade. Maybe that is why Manchester provided Combe with some of his most enthusiastic audiences, making one of his stays there a 'constant Jubilee', a fact which Cobden, himself a keen phrenologist, attributed to 'the enlightening chemical and mechanical studies with which our industry is allied, and to the mind-invigorating effects of our energetic devotion to commerce'.[48] On the other hand, phrenology's impact downwards—on the labouring classes—was anything but liberating, since its doctrines were used to rationalize emerging industrial society, and to discipline the workforce. It became more or less institutionalized in mechanics institutes during the 1830s, but especially in those where the middle classes wrested control from their original working-class founders. This has prompted one historian to describe phrenology as a form of 'secular Calvinism' or 'secular Methodism',[49] which is apt given that it was spread by itinerant lecturers, perhaps as many as 200 at its peak. It is also undeniable that in *The Constitution of Man* Combe sought to inculcate thrift, timekeeping, order, industry, regularity, and cleanliness, while discouraging degeneracies such as early marriage and the consumption of spicy foods.

Phrenology went into 'precipitous decline' after 1850, but as a craze it had already been displaced by animal magnetism, or mesmerism. This was displaced in its turn by spiritualism, but for about a decade it seemed as though everyone was doing it.[50] Originated by the Austrian physician Franz Anton Mesmer in the 1790s, it was revived by French doctors in the 1820s, and then took England by storm from 1837 onwards, thanks especially to a series of experiments conducted by Elliotson at University College Hospital (UCH) on Elizabeth and Jane O'Key, domestic servants who had been diagnosed as suffering from hysteria and epilepsy. Elliotson, who was also an ardent phrenologist, claimed to influence his subjects' nervous systems by making certain hand movements, and causing the warmth of his body to penetrate theirs in the form of some ubiquitous but invisible magnetic fluid. The experiments were discredited when it

[48] Cobden to Combe, 1836?, quoted in Charles Gibbon, *The Life of George Combe* (1878), i. 314–15; ii. 10.
[49] Cooter, *Cultural Meaning of Popular Science*, 132, 194–8; Hilton, *Age of Atonement*, 189–202.
[50] Cooter, *Cultural Meaning of Popular Science*, 256.

became evident that the O'Key sisters were manipulating the proceedings, an alarming subversion of accepted doctor–patient (not to mention male–female) relationships.[51] As a result, most 'professional' doctors turned against mesmerism, with one very important practical result. As mesmeric anaesthesia for surgical patients gained ground during 1842–6, hospital doctors were stung into developing an alternative chemical version. In December 1846 Robert Liston of UCH performed the first operation under ether, and chloroform was used for the first time by Edinburgh's James Young Simpson in the following year.[52] The prospect of painless surgery probably affected the way in which contemporaries viewed their whole lives, but its discovery owed less to a desire to prevent pain—then still regarded as part of the scheme of things—than to the need for hospital doctors to maintain their authority. Chloroform had the added advantage that it knocked patients out, whereas mesmeric anaesthesia enabled them to play a part—often even the leading part—in their own operations.

The surgical *locus* is appropriate since mesmerism was above all a theatrical movement. It went with belief in miracles and the supernatural, was rife among ecstatic sects like the Irvingites, and was taken up by some of the clergy as a useful pastoral tool to match Roman Catholic ritual and Nonconformist hymn-singing. Moreover, by demonstrating how one person could exercise physical power over another—with the implication that there was a material interconnectedness between minds—mesmerism undermined Utilitarian and evangelical notions of individualism, and encouraged more corporate conceptions of society. Phrenology, mesmerism, and phreno-mesmerism also appealed to provincial elites as a means of cultural assertion against metropolitan hegemony, but whereas phrenology was predominantly artisanal, mesmerism attracted social extremes, from bishops (Samuel Wilberforce) and aristocrats (Lord Morpeth) down to peripatetic fairground artists appearing alongside dwarfs and bearded ladies. Also, whereas phrenology promised to explain character, mesmerism questioned whether any such thing existed, being just one example of the Victorians' fascination with the idea of 'altered states' or different forms of consciousness, whether induced through drink, drugs, hysteria, dreams, trances, or insanity.[53] Eventually the Unitarian William Carpenter, yet another important naturalist whose career hovered between Edinburgh and University College London, would undermine the claims made for mesmerism by providing physiological reasons, not only for the phenomena themselves, but also for the credulity of the people who believed them. His materialist theory of mind

[51] Worse still from the doctors' point of view was Harriet Martineau's much-trumpeted view that mesmerism had cured her uterine tumour.

[52] Alison Winter, *Mesmerized: Powers of Mind in Victorian Britain* (Chicago, 1998), 60–78, 163–86.

[53] Davy's experiments with nitrous oxide set Coleridge cackling and Edgeworth capering and gave Anne Edgeworth Beddoes an orgasm, further blurring the line between vitalism and materialism.

was based on the notion of consensual mental reflexes in the brain and on the correlation of mental forces with external stimuli. As such it directed attention away from the supernatural, and helped to inculcate the view that over time social reform (specifically education) and will-power were capable of civilizing society.[54]

FROM ROMANTIC SCIENCE TO PEELITE COMPROMISE

Scientific debates were politically important because of the ways in which the world of ideas and the world of public affairs overlapped. Lord Althorp, for example, was absorbed in such matters, writing to Brougham on one occasion,

> Instinct in all cases operates by the impressions originally made by the Deity on the natural organization of his creatures and not by his special interposition in individual cases . . . My view raises I think rather higher than yours the wisdom and design which directed the divine mind in the Creation, but yours is much more impressive as to the continued government of the universe and the constant dependence in which we exist on the divine will.[55]

So, was the universe mechanical in operation and unchanging in composition, or had it developed organically over time? Could it be explained materially in terms of itself, or was God an active agent, instilling the created world with vital powers? These binary permutations gave rise to four main intellectual positions.

Most Establishment scientists were political conservatives and philosophical dualists. Their universe was a mechanism created and set in motion (i.e. given vitality) by an external or transcendent God. They distinguished between body and soul, organic and inorganic substances, the here and hereafter, the sacred and the secular, living minds and inert matter.[56] They adhered to atomic, corpuscular, and muscular theories of motion, and were comforted by the argument from design. They differed only in whether they took a benign view of Creation—God having ordered everything for the happiness of humankind (Paley)—or whether they took the evangelical and retributive view (Chalmers),[57] an important distinction in terms of tone, less so in terms of analysis. But if dualists were relatively homogeneous in their opinions, their opponents differed greatly. Some scientists adopted the Radical position described in the last section, arguing that the world had undergone a continuous process of organic development according to principles inherent in its structure at the Creation. Others took the view, which was common among Ultra Tories, that God

---

[54] W. B. Carpenter, *Principles of Human Physiology* (1842; 4th edn. 1853); Winter, *Mesmerized*, 287–305.

[55] Althorp to Brougham, 8 June 1836, BL, Althorp MS. H14.

[56] Hence the saliency of Palmerston's observation, as applied to politics, that 'there is in nature no moving power but mind, all else is passive and inert'. See above, p. 317.

[57] See above, p. 334–5.

exercised a continuous and active control over the operations of the world. Now the Radicals' belief in divine immanence and the Ultra Tories' belief in an interventionist God were vastly different, but in context the two modes of thought were linked by their rejection of New Testament dualism. Radicals and Ultra Tories were in this context monists, being convinced that God was in active control of the universe, although one explained his power in terms of special providence and the other in terms of 'continuous creation'. Priestley was unusual in that he believed both in materialism and in an interventionist God. But then Priestley was a pre-millenarian who believed in an imminent Apocalypse and special providence, which was also unusual for a Unitarian. His friend Richard Price summed up the puzzle: 'The parts of the machine which he calls man were put together by Divine wisdom.' 'The motions of this machine are produced not by the matter itself that composes the machine, but by the constant operation of the Deity whom he makes the only agent in nature.'[58]

Though largely neglected by historians, the science of special providence was very significant, especially in the fashionable field of chemistry. Here dualistic orthodoxy was represented by John Dalton, whose *A New System of Chemical Philosophy* (1808–27) explained combination in mechanical terms: solid atoms combined according to weight and proportional equivalence in a purely mathematical way. His views met with scepticism from Humphry Davy, who could not help condescending to someone he saw as a naive provincial. The biggest scientific celebrity of his day, who turned chemistry into public theatre, Davy asserted that there were forces of chemical affinity or romantic attraction between different elements, and he demonstrated electrolysis to show, first, how 'the same ponderable matter in different electric states, or in different arrangements, may constitute substances chemically different', and, conversely, how two compounds could be chemically identical and yet have very different physical properties. This proved that 'powers' could modify 'matter', that 'powers' rather than 'matter' were the main agents of order and change, and that the student of chemistry could himself intervene in nature.[59]

Science has given to him an acquaintance with the different relations of the parts of the external world; and . . . has bestowed upon him powers which may be almost called creative; which have enabled him to modify and change the beings surrounding him, and by his experiments to interrogate nature with power, not simply as a scholar, passive and seeking only to understand her operations, but rather as a master, active with his own instruments.[60]

---

[58] Richard Price to Lord Monboddo, 2–12 Aug. 1780, in *The Correspondence of Richard Price*, ed. W. Bernard Peach and D. O. Thomas (Durham, NC, 1983–94), ii. 67.

[59] Humphry Davy, *Elements of Chemical Philosophy* (1812), 488; David Knight, *Humphry Davy: Science and Power* (Oxford, 1992), 75–80.

[60] *The Collected Works of Humphry Davy*, ed. John Davy (1839–40), ii. 318–19.

It was a commonplace to depict scientists as explorers charting vast new seas of knowledge (George Eliot described 'the dark territories of Pathology' as 'a fine America for a spirited young adventurer'), but Davy saw himself in true Romantic fashion as a scientific general, campaigning to master nature by modifying matter.[61]

A poet as well as chemist, and a self-conscious hero in the Romantic mould, Davy identified with Coleridge, Wordsworth, and Southey, all of whom took the same journey from youthful radicalism to authoritarian Ultra Toryism. In claiming that there were hierarchical properties in nature, he drew an analogy with human societies, where an unequal division of property provided 'the sources of power in civilised life'. Davy's belief in hierarchy and 'progressiveness', and his claim that force and not mechanism was primary in nature, delighted Romantic philosophers.[62] Coleridge, for example, was very concerned in a post-Kantian way about the relationship of the laws of nature to those of mind, and he appealed directly to Davy's electrochemistry ('philosophic alchemy'), as well as to 'dynamic geology', in arguing that the mechanico-corpuscular theories of matter peddled by Establishment liberals was mistaken, and that nature underwent a constant process of organic development. However, he had no time for those democratic 'ruffians' who attributed this process of change to self-empowered atoms, and who argued by analogy that individuals should govern themselves in human society. For Coleridge, the 'unfolding' of nature was caused by 'inward powers of matter'—'active', 'causal', and 'constructive powers, excited in Matter by the influence of God's Spirit and Logos'.[63] So, although Davy and Coleridge were as strongly opposed to Enlightenment dualism as Elliotson, Lawrence, and Erasmus Darwin, they attacked it from a different angle. Whereas most radical scientists dissolved mind–body dualism by describing mental problems as a function of matter, these Tories argued in effect that matter could think. Not living creatures only, but matter too, was subject to providence,

that Divine Power which behind the cloud & veil of Worldly Events and seeming Human Agency controls, disposes, and directs both events and actions to the Gradual unfolding and final Consummation of the vast Scheme of Redemption, in and by which the evil and

---

Davy may have influenced the heterodox currency theorist Thomas Attwood, who claimed that banknotes were 'alive'. As such they were 'capable of breaking open prison doors, and of feeding the hungry, and clothing the naked'. [Thomas Attwood], *Prosperity Restored: or, Reflections on the Causes of the Public Distresses and on the Only Means of Relieving Them* (1817), 61, 207.

[62] David Knight, *Ideas in Chemistry: A History of the Science* (1992), 70, 74–6; Christopher Lawrence, 'The Power and the Glory: Humphry Davy and Romanticism', in Andrew Cunningham and Nicholas Jardine (ed.), *Romanticism and the Sciences* (Cambridge, 1990), 222; Trevor H. Levere, *Affinity and Matter: Elements of Chemical Philosophy 1800–1865* (Oxford, 1971), 30–1.

[63] Trevor H. Levere, *Poetry Realized in Nature: Samuel Taylor Coleridge and Early Nineteenth-Century Science* (Cambridge, 1981), 60, 79, 98–100, 106; Desmond, *Politics of Evolution*, 44, 206.

alien Nature shall be cast forth, & the Union effectuated of the Creature with the Creator, of Man with God, in and thro' the *Son* of Man.[64]

These older Romantics all believed in an interventionist God. To Southey the cholera of 1831–2 was a 'chastisement', albeit one that was 'sent rather to give us an awful warning than to punish us. This good it will do, that it will make known the extreme misery of the lower classes.' On another occasion he anticipated some modern residents by averring that 'nothing but a special Providence [can] save Keswick'.[65]

Richard Vyvyan will be remembered for leading the Ultra Tory charge against Wellington's Government, but he also engaged in secret night-time experiments designed to show that nature was 'one great system of progressive development'.[66] His aim was to forge a theory that would combine creationism, trans-cendentalism, Lamarckian transmutation, animal magnetism, phrenology, abstract geology, psychology, and chemistry in an attempt to meet the radical anatomists on their own ground and yet, *by leaving room for an active God*, refute their materialism. By emphasizing the interstices between particles, rather than the particles themselves, he developed his 'electrochemical hypothesis', a theory of 'supreme creative energy, which is constantly engaged in promoting the auto-matic development of successive series of individual beings'. Not surprisingly Vyvyan was a prime suspect when the hunt began for the author of *Vestiges of Creation*.[67] Another Ultra (though nominally a Whig) was the fourth Earl of Stanhope, who searched obsessively for medico-botanic solutions to ill health, being convinced that a benign providence would not inflict on the fauna of a country any disease that was incapable of being treated by the extracts of its indigenous fauna. Notorious for his adoption of the wild boy of Bavaria in 1832, he argued that the mind was 'necessarily immaterial', and he speculated that inferior animals might possess reasoning and moral faculties.[68] There was Andrew Crosse, who was known as Dr Frankenstein for his country house experiments in electrocrystallization, in which he claimed to have created insects from inert matter.[69] Finally, there was the Hutchinsonian William Kirby,

[64] S. T. Coleridge to Mrs Basil Montagu, 1 May 1827, in *Collected Letters of Samuel Taylor Coleridge*, ed. Earl Leslie Griggs (Oxford, 1956–71), vi. 677.

[65] *Selections from the Letters of Robert Southey*, ed. J. W. Warter (1856), iv. 242–9, 262, 269, 285.

[66] Richard Vyvyan to H. T. De la Beche, 10 June 1842, National Museum of Wales, Geology Department MSS.

[67] Others suspected of writing *Vestiges* were George Combe, Ada Lovelace, William Carpenter, Andrew Crosse, J. P. Nichol, and Francis Newman, all of whose thought was in the monistic tradition.

[68] Edward Binns, *The Anatomy of Sleep: or, The Art of Procuring Sound and Refreshing Slumber at Will*, 2nd edn., with additions by Earl Stanhope (1845), 490–1.

[69] James A. Secord, 'Extraordinary Experiment: Electricity and the Creation of Life in Victorian England', in David Gooding, Trevor Pinch, and Simon Schaffer (edn.), *The Uses of Experiment: Studies in the Natural Sciences* (Cambridge, 1989).

'the naturalist of the right-wing Hackney Phalanx'.[70] His Bridgewater Treatise on animal creation differed markedly from all others in the series, since it postulated a system of 'inter-agents' existing between God and the visible material world, a 'cherubic chain of spiritual vice-regents [whose] powers initiated every event in nature, and in society realized God's Will through His Church'.[71] In this way Kirby put his own spin on Lamarckian transformism in order to deny materialism, assert the stability of species, and portray God as a 'kind', 'watchful', 'fatherly', 'interventionist Providence'.

> The Deity superintends his whole Creation, not only supporting the system that he has established . . . but himself, where he sees fit, in particular instances dispensing with these laws: restraining the clouds, in one instance, from shedding their treasures; and in another, permitting them to descend in blessings. Acting every where upon the atmosphere, and those secondary powers that produce atmospheric phenomena, as circumstances connected with his moral government require.[72]

Preoccupied with prophecy and the Second Coming, Kirby 'watched' intently for signs of a time 'when there should be *one* great Antichrist,—a single being reigning supreme, until the fiat of God should go forth to overwhelm him with a sudden confusion and destruction'.[73]

In political affairs Radicals and Ultra Tories were diametrically opposed, yet they sometimes came together on a programme of social welfare against the free-marketeers of the centre. In the same way transcendental Ultra Tory scientists like Vyvyan, Crosse, and Kirby were diametrically opposed to immanentist and materialist radicals, yet the two could make common cause against the natural law scientists of the Establishment, who were invariably liberal Tory or Whig in their political sympathies. Thus assailed from right and left, Establishment scientists had to update the argument from design, and rescue it from charges of materialism. They had somehow to acknowledge God's active agency, and to accommodate the irrefutable evidence of changes that had taken place since the Creation, while retaining the idea of natural law—a predictable mechanism of cause and effect, susceptible to human understanding and the basis of God's moral government. They did this by building on Cuvier's theory of 'punctuated progression', according to which prehistoric fossils were the

---

[70] Pietro Corsi, 'A Devil's Chaplain's Calling', *Journal of Victorian Culture*, 3 (1998), 129–37. Corsi points out that in the late 1830s evolutionary ideas were embraced by many who were neither artisans nor 'dangerous radicals' (e.g. Baden Powell, W. B. Carpenter, Robert Chambers, and Francis Newman).

[71] Desmond, *Politics of Evolution*, 114; Jacyna, 'Immanence and Transcendence', 325–6.

[72] William Kirby, *On the Power, Wisdom, and Goodness of God as Manifested in the Creation of Animals and in their History, Habits, and Instincts* (1835), vol. i, pp. xci, 46.

[73] John Freeman, *Life of the Rev. William Kirby* (1852), 46, 168–9; John Topham, ' "An Infinite Variety of Arguments": The Bridgewater Treatises and British Natural Theology in the 1830s', Ph.D. thesis (University of Lancaster, 1993), 213–32.

remains of previous worlds that had eventually succumbed to some 'general convulsion' or 'revolution'. God had been actively responsible for the earth's passage from one dispensation to the next by creating new organisms to suit each new environment.[74]

It is when new systems emerge from the wreck of old ones, and from the ruins of a former catastrophe there is built up another modern habitation, and peopled with new races both of animals and vegetables—it is then that we demand the interposal of a God. Whence did those new genera and species come into being? Nature gives no reply to this question . . . There is no spontaneous generation, and no transmutation of species.[75]

This came from Chalmers, whose geology was avowedly scriptural, but exactly the same point was made by Buckland and Sedgwick, who conceded that 'great changes' had taken place in organic structure, and that these had not evolved naturally one into the other but had been *created* by a 'prospective and active intelligence . . . at successive times and periods contriving a change of mechanism adapted to a change in external conditions'.[76] All three men were adamant, however, that *at any particular point in time* the Creation was held in equilibrium by the 'functioning' of general laws. Even volcanoes and floods were not *necessarily* indications of arbitrary providence, since occasional 'paroxysms of internal energy', leading to the formation of mountains and seas, were 'a part of the mechanism of nature', part of its 'glorious workmanship'. The organization of living matter was 'as mechanical as the works of our own hands', and differed from them 'only in complexity and perfection'.[77] Of course they had to believe this, otherwise all their other assumptions would have come tumbling down.

A similar compromise based on 'punctuated progression' was reached in zoology by Richard Owen, who rose from a fairly ordinary social background to a place at the heart of the Anglican scientific establishment, becoming friendly with Whewell, Buckland, Sedgwick, Cuvier, Peel, and Prince Albert. Intellectually he moved in the opposite direction from Lawrence. Unhappily exposed to comparative anatomy as a student at Edinburgh University, he left to study under John Barclay, a professed anti-materialist who ran a private school, and from there he went to London to work with Abernethy. His ultimate achievement was to devise a modified form of comparative anatomy, which dispensed with vital fluids and other crudely Paleyan devices, and which accepted

---

[74] A variant was to suggest that God included the 'new' organisms in the original Creation but had allowed them to remain dormant until needed.

[75] [Thomas Chalmers], 'Morell's *Modern Philosophy*', *North British Review*, 6 (1847), 315.

[76] Sedgwick, *Addresses at the Geological Society*, 35–6. For William Whewell's variation on the theory, see Michael Ruse, 'William Whewell: Omniscientist', and M. J. S. Hodge, 'The History of the Earth, Life, and Man: Whewell and Palaetiological Science', in Menachem Fisch and Simon Schaffer (eds.), *William Whewell: A Composite Portrait* (Oxford, 1991), 112–13, 275–6.

[77] Sedgwick, *Addresses at the Geological Society*, 35–6.

much of the evidence provided by Lamarckian scientists like Grant, but which nevertheless left room for God to play a part at crucial moments in fossil history by giving forms to—and laws for—newly minted archetypes. The key moment came in 1839 when, helped by Buckland, he ingeniously interpreted certain disputed specimens (the Stonesfield fossil jaws) as being mammalian *Amphitherium* and not, as Robert Grant believed, reptiles. This 'marsupial diagnosis' was to hold the field for a generation, after which British and American geologists returned to the Stonesfield jaws and reconceptualized them as generalized sub-marsupial mammals.[78]

Owen's transcendentalism held the Lamarckian chain and the theory of natural selection at bay—for a while. It has been called a 'Peelite strategy', partly because of the personal connection,[79] but also because he was willing to make judicious concessions to the Radicals in order to preserve the substance of Establishment thought. It was this pious compromise that *Vestiges* challenged in 1844. Like Lamarck and Geoffroy before him and Darwin later, Chambers refused to accept that there had been *any* gaps in evolution or *any* miraculous leaps forward. Not only did God not intervene from day to day; he had not even done so at specific moments in the past. Law was all in all, and there were no archetypes, only ancestors.

FROM UNITARIANISM TO LIBERAL ANGLICANISM

Price, Priestley, Southwood Smith, Grant, De Morgan—a very high proportion of radical scientists and social reformers came out of rational Dissent, a genuinely counter-cultural religion, so contra in fact that one of its most prolific scholars described Charles Fox as Britain's 'angel of redemption'.[80] It attracted seceders from many different traditions including the Church of England, but the most important line of descent was the dwindling band of English Presbyterians. Its numbers included many with strong theological views, like Arians and Socinians,[81] and also persons of great learning such as Thomas Belsham, its leader from 1805 to 1829, but for the most part rational Dissenters had put doctrinal niceties behind them in favour of a simple scriptural approach to worship, and were now simply known as Unitarians to signify their disbelief in a triune God. A small sect numerically, amounting at most to about 2 per cent of all Dissenters, it was declining in many parts of rural England, but it

---

[78] For thrilling accounts of this episode, see Desmond, *Politics of Evolution*, 22–3, 318–19, and Adrian Desmond, *Archetypes and Ancestors: Palaeontology in Victorian London, 1850–1875* (Chicago, 1982), 43–4, 200–1.   [79] Desmond, *Politics of Evolution*, 318, 355–8.

[80] *Memoirs of the Life of Gilbert Wakefield, Written by Himself*, 2nd edn. (1804), ii. 300.

[81] In brief, Arians accepted that Jesus was divine but denied that he was the redeemer, whereas Socinians believed in his perfect humanity but not his divinity.

flourished in major commercial centres, attracting not only shopkeepers and petty capitalists but also members of the haute bourgeoisie. The esteem enjoyed by members of the Cross Street Chapel within the Manchester business community has already been noted.[82] In Hull merchants and shipowners, led by the Pease family and joined by doctors and solicitors, patronized the Bowl Alley Lane Chapel, which has been described as the town's 'genteelest' congregation. A merchant-ship owner, Ralph Carr, led a similar group at the Hanover Chapel in Newcastle upon Tyne, and there were comparable chapels in Leeds, Liverpool, Wakefield, Birmingham, and Nottingham. In Bristol, where Dr Lant Carpenter presided (1817–39), 'some of the Unitarian families were more powerful and established than their Anglican merchant peers... In no sense was the Unitarianism founded on the Lewin's Mead Meeting an outsider culture... [It] was an intrinsic part of upper-class activity within the city.'[83] In London the worshippers at Theophilus Lindsey's fashionable conventicle on Essex Street (1774) included a large number of peers and MPs as well as physicians. Furthermore, Unitarian chapels became increasingly ornate, with fine three-decker pulpits and brass candelabra, while dancing, cards, theatre, even 'lust of the flesh', were condoned in moderation.[84] Their famous academies (Warrington, Manchester, Hackney) grounded pupils in Latin and Greek, but differed from the 'public schools' by teaching science and modern languages as well, and they kept up contact with the leading universities elsewhere, notably Paris, Edinburgh, Leiden, and Glasgow.

Yet, as an alienated intelligentsia, Unitarians also featured prominently on the Home Office list of 'Disaffected & Seditious persons'. In the late eighteenth century they were dominant members of the remarkable group centred around Joseph Johnson's house in St Paul's churchyard. Johnson was Paine's publisher and the founder of the *Analytical Review* (1788–99).[85] His milieu included Price, Priestley, Godwin, Barbauld, and Mary Hays as well as pro-revolutionary non-Dissenters such as Mary Wollstonecraft, the mystic poet William Blake, and the novelists Elizabeth Inchbald, Helen Maria Williams, and Thomas Holcroft. Other more exclusive coteries formed around William Turner in Newcastle, William Gaskell in Manchester, Josiah Wedgwood in Stoke, William Roscoe in Liverpool, Henry Crabb Robinson in Colchester, and in London William Johnson Fox, the editor of the *Monthly Repository*.[86] Their irrepressible

[82] See above, p. 164–5.

[83] Michael Neve, 'Science in a Commercial City: Bristol 1820–60,' in Ian Inkster and Jack Morrell (eds.), *Metropolis and Province: Science in British Culture, 1780–1850* (1983), 181, 185.

[84] John Seed, 'Gentlemen Dissenters: The Social and Political Meanings of Rational Dissent in the 1770s and 1780s', *HJ* 28 (1985), 310–11.

[85] A radical journal which eventually fell victim to anti-Jacobin hysteria.

[86] *Youth and Revolution in the 1790s: Letters of William Pattisson, Thomas Amyot and Henry Crabb Robinson*, ed. Penelope J. Corfield and Chris Evans (Stroud, 1996).

questioning of the status quo naturally exposed Unitarians to the full force of anti-Jacobin reaction. Priestley's house was razed, William Frend was formally expelled from Cambridge University in 1793, Joseph Johnson was fined and imprisoned in 1797, the journalist Benjamin Flower likewise in 1799. Admitted to the benefits of the Toleration Act in 1813, Unitarians enjoyed their period of greatest influence in the 1820s when their leader William Smith MP spear-headed the successful campaign for Test and Corporation Act repeal. Since Smith was an intimate friend of Grey and Holland, Unitarians might have been expected to come into their own after the Whigs took power in 1830, but power was something with which they could never be comfortable. Before long they had seceded from the Dissenting Deputies, and then became further isolated as the latter became more strident and militant. The 1844 Dissenters' Chapels Act brought Unitarians further recognition, but at the price of alienating them still further from mainstream Nonconformity.

Unitarians were genuinely counter-cultural because their denial of the divinity of Christ was a stab at the symbolic heart of the Establishment. This was partly because rejection of God the Son entailed rejection of God the Father as well, yet God's fatherhood was emblematic of all earthly authority as exercised by kings, lords, magistrates, and heads of households from Adam onwards. Equally important was the point made in Chapter 3 that the division of labour between the first two persons of the Trinity—the belief that Christ had redeemed humankind's debt to God—was a very common trope used to sanc-tion capitalist market relationships based on debts and contracts. Unitarians, however, condemned the doctrine as a corruption of Pauline teaching, not to be found in the Old Testament or the Gospels.[87] Indeed, they condemned all the ingredients of the evangelical scheme of salvation, including the Fall, original sin, moral trial, the need for redemption, the Atonement, and eternal punish-ment. Priestley, for example, was unable to 'feel a proper repentance for the sin of Adam'. Believing in a God of love rather than justice, and in the essential goodness of human nature, they took a benign view of the Creation and an optimistic view of the prospects for society.

Philosophically, rational Dissenters rejected both the dualistic idealism of Descartes and the dualistic empiricism of John Locke.[88] That so many of them attended Scottish universities may account for their debt to Thomas Reid's theory of common sense. They profited from the aesthetics of Francis Hutcheson,

[87] Joseph Priestley, *Defences of the History of the Corruptions of Christianity* (1783–86). See above, pp. 183–4.
[88] Descartes posited a distinction between mind and body, Locke a distinction between mind and the external world. Some recent attempts to play down Locke's influence on the thought of the 'long eigh-teenth century' have missed the mark by concentrating on his political writings to the neglect of his epis-temology and psychology.

with its emphasis on concepts such as motion, action, abruptness, speed, spontaneity, momentum, and force. But the temporal book which more than any other formed the basis of their thought was David Hartley's *Observations on Man* (1749), which Priestley said threw 'more useful light' on the theory of the mind than Newton did on nature, so that reading it was 'like entering upon *a new world*'.[89] Its central doctrine was the association of ideas, a theory based on a complicated series of neurophysiological and psychological responses ('vibrations') which allowed the nerves and particles of the brain to interact with the physical universe, according to Newton-like laws of attraction and repulsion. External objects created sense impressions in several parts of the body, impressions created sensations, sensations sparked off simple ideas, simple ideas combined with emotions to form more sophisticated concepts, and—so long as the stimuli were repeated often enough—all this happened without the individual being conscious of the process. The theory implied that original sin did not exist and that, appropriately stimulated, everyone could become 'partakers of the divine nature', leading to universal salvation.[90]

In simple terms, Unitarians believed that sense perceptions determined character and character determined actions, a doctrine sometimes called environmental necessarianism. The analysis allowed no scope for individual freedom but made room instead for social progress and moral reform. The key to all such improvement was knowledge, and the key to knowledge was education— many of the Dissenting academies and later the mechanics institutes were promoted and run by Unitarian reformers. In the words of Gilbert Wakefield, 'an intimate connexion subsists between letters and morality'.[91] It was important to ensure that young children were subjected to favourable sense impressions so that a properly moral character could be nurtured. Their emphasis was on what, even today, would be recognized as progressive education, such as the need to develop powers of reflection rather than cramming the mind with facts, while corporal punishment was eschewed. The inspiration came from two Swiss pioneers, Pestalozzi and Fellenberg, who insisted that children were like plant seeds. They should be nourished through kindness, and given the freedom to develop their individual personalities according to their own inner lights and desires. Spontaneity and activity were encouraged, the concrete was privileged over the abstract, and the work of the hands and the heart was prized as highly as mental ability. Compulsory spontaneity is of course elusive, and these pedagogical methods may have been as oppressive in their own way as those at Dr Keate's Eton (just as phrenology was much less liberating for the poor than

[89] Joseph Priestley, *An Examination of Dr. Reid's 'Inquiry', &c.* (1774), pp. xix, 2.
[90] David Hartley, *Observations on Man, his Duty, and his Expectations* (1749), i. 1–114, 500–12.
[91] *Memoirs of Gilbert Wakefield*, ii. 311.

it was for the middle classes), but they were nevertheless distinctive. Many Unitarians gave strong support to the energetic campaign of the Quaker Joseph Lancaster, who between 1798 and 1810 claimed to have founded fifty new schools for 14,200 poor scholars, overcoming the obvious financial problem through the monitorial system, whereby senior children tutored the less advanced.[92] Unitarians were also keen on adult and female education. Indeed, in so far as there was anything approaching a women's rights movement during the second quarter of the nineteenth century, it was to be found among radical Unitarians such as the Harriets (Martineau and Taylor) and the Flowers (Eliza and Sarah).[93]

By this time it was becoming clear that Unitarians, as the main intellectual opposition to the Pittite regime, were beginning to win the argument. One sign of this was the increasing prominence within the Establishment of so-called Liberal Anglicans, as the evangelical and High Church parties became increasingly extreme. In part this was a political development. The ecclesiastical legislation of 1828–9 had undermined the logical basis of Anglican privilege by opening the civil realm to non-Anglicans. In response, Liberals called for the Church to open itself up as well, by 'absorbing' or 'comprehending' moderate Dissenters such as Methodists and Congregationalists within its walls, and by granting further rights to more extreme Dissenters such as Jews, Catholics, Unitarians, and some Quakers. This, they hoped, would detach Nonconformists from political Radicals, many of whom were itching to abolish the Establishment altogether.[94] Such a programme would require the Church of England to encompass an even wider variety of opinion and ceremony than it did already, but this was not a problem for Liberal Anglicans since, as Thomas Arnold wrote in *Principles of Church Reform* (1833), a key text, the Establishment was to be justified by 'the good rather than by truth'. Like Unitarians, Liberal Anglicans were pious but undogmatic, concerned for personal salvation but even more anxious to bring about communal regeneration. Although they did not, like Unitarians, explicitly deny the Trinity, they moved in that direction by switching attention from Scripture as the basis for right conduct, and from Christ's spiritual role as a sacrificial redeemer, to Jesus' earthly ministry and ethical teachings. To quote Arnold again,

Will it be said, that all worldly objects are too insignificant to engage the attention of an heir of immortality? Yet it is only by the pursuit of some worldly object that we can

[92] Lancaster became embroiled in a fierce dispute with an Anglican educationist, Dr Andrew Bell. Ostensibly the argument was about which of them had originated the monitorial system, but it was really a salvo in the long war between the Established and Free churches for control of educational provision. See below, pp. 532–8.

[93] Ruth Watts, *Gender, Power and the Unitarians in England 1760–1860* (1998), 33–52, 99–118, 203–5; Kathryn Gleadle, *The Early Feminists: Radical Unitarians and the Emergence of the Women's Rights Movements, 1831–51* (Houndmills, 1995).

[94] For the politics of Liberal Anglicanism, see below, pp. 520–2.

perform our worldly duty, and so train ourselves up for immortality; it is by improving the various faculties that are given to us that we can fit ourselves for our everlasting habitations.[95]

Liberal Anglicans were convinced that religion would not be able to foster national unity and heal social divisions unless it faced up to the challenges of German philosophy and French science. Thanks in part to Coleridge's influence, they took Lessing, Kant, Hegel, Fichte, and Schelling on board, and learned to accept that not everything in Scripture was an immutable and universal truth, or the product of divine inspiration. On the contrary, the Bible had been composed by human beings writing in given historical contexts, and expressed only so much of the truth as God had chosen to reveal to his witnesses in any particular generation. It followed that, if religious doctrine was to continue developing, biblical scholars everywhere must adopt German methods of inquiry, disposing of superstitious and outdated elements.[96] Liberal Anglicans were probably the first group of savants to emerge from particular university backgrounds. Many had attended Trinity College, Cambridge, where they might have been members of a secret undergraduate society known as the Apostles,[97] and influenced by liberal practitioners such as the classicists Julius Hare and J. W. Blakesley, the historian Connop Thirlwall, the mathematicians De Morgan and George Peacock, or the scientists William Whewell, Charles Babbage, and George Airy.[98] Hare and Thirlwall, especially, mobilized the methods of German scholars, such as Schleiermacher and Niebuhr, in a self-conscious attempt to combat the excessive rationalism of British thought. Intellectually Trinity's counterpart at Oxford was Oriel College, and a group of luminaries known as Noetics, notably Renn Dickson Hampden, Henry Milman, and—by far the most important—Thomas Arnold.[99]

The year 1826 was a significant stage in the latter's intellectual development, as it was for many others. It was then that he woke up to the 'deep disease' affecting society and to the omnipresent struggle between good and evil.[100] An obscure country deacon who coached private pupils for the universities, he was unexpectedly chosen to become headmaster of Rugby School in 1828, chiefly on

[95] Thomas Arnold, *The Christian Duty of Granting the Claims of Roman Catholics* (Oxford, 1829), 13.

[96] Charles Richard Sanders, *Coleridge and the Broad Church Movement* (Durham, NC, 1942).

[97] Peter Allen, *The Cambridge Apostles: The Early Years* (Cambridge, 1978).

[98] Susan Faye Cannon, *Science in Culture: The Early Victorian Period* (New York, 1978), 29–71; Robert O. Preyer, 'The Romantic Tide Reaches Trinity', in James Paradis and Thomas Postlewait (eds.), *Victorian Science and Victorian Values: Literary Perspectives* (New York, 1981).

[99] Duncan Forbes, *The Liberal Anglican Idea of History* (Cambridge, 1952); Richard Brent, *Liberal Anglican Politics: Whiggery, Religion, and Reform 1830–1841* (Oxford, 1987), 144–83; Pietro Corsi, 'The Heritage of Dugald Stewart: Oxford Philosophy and the Method of Political Economy', *Nuncius, Annali di Storia della Scienza*, 2/2 (1987), 89–144.

[100] Arthur Penrhyn Stanley, *The Life and Correspondence of Thomas Arnold*, 5th edn. (1845), i. 50.

the strength of the Provost of Oriel's prediction that he would 'change the face of education'. Thanks in part to the hagiography of adoring pupils, Arnold came to be seen as a prototype of the mid-Victorian headmaster, and under him Rugby became a factory for producing manliness. The last concept must be understood in its mid- rather than late Victorian sense. Towards the end of the nineteenth century public school manliness would come to denote a coarse, hearty, games-playing, Tory imperialism, but under Arnold it was an essentially Christian brew, composed of earnestness, gentleness, truth-telling, dutifulness, compassion, and turning the other cheek. Late Victorian manliness would imply masculinity, whereas under Arnold it implied humanity. Indeed, many of the values he inculcated were feminine ones. His pedagogic mission was to root out violence and debauchery and to produce Christian gentlemen who would not be afraid to pray on their knees in front of a mocking dormitory. Thomas Hughes's account in *Tom Brown's Schooldays* (1857) of how Arnold single-handedly transformed Rugby is mythical, since his predecessor Wooll had done much to rescue the school from its grisly condition in 1797, when a pupil rebellion involved a bomb, a bonfire, the reading of the Riot Act, and the summoning of the military. Nevertheless, there is no doubting the impact of Arnold's personality on those who were under him at Rugby, nor its still greater impact on the many thousand more who had not been under him but fantasized that they had.

Despite an acknowledgement that he 'craved' the support of 'liberal Tories', Arnold is difficult to categorize both politically and ecclesiastically. 'Most earnestly would I be Conservative', he wrote in 1831, 'but defend me from the Conservative Party.'[101] He is usually designated a Liberal Anglican because of his tolerant attitude to Roman Catholics and his desire to comprehend moderate Dissenters within the Church of England, yet his religion had more intensity and commitment than was typical of that school. His theocratic notion of the Church as 'a sovereign state' dominating the entire life of society was apostolic and Catholic in tone, yet he vowed never to 'join with the High Church party'. As for the evangelicals, he was 'repelled' by their narrow, cliquish 'party' views and their spiritual other-worldliness, which directly contradicted his own ambition to make 'the kingdoms of the world indeed the kingdoms of Christ', yet he recognized that only evangelicals shared his 'lively sense of social evils', and he bitterly regretted his separation from them. He was as obsessed as they were by original sin, never sparing the rod in his attempt to extirpate the elemental 'wickedness of boys' (especially their propensity to violence),[102] and like evangelicals he saw life as a series of trials, sent by God to punish, test, and refine

---

[101] Arnold to Whately, 7 Mar. 1831, ibid. i. 296.

[102] Arnold believed that the movement by certain reformers to abolish flogging in schools was un-Christian and 'essentially barbarian'. He meant that it harked back to a feudal age when personal honour counted for more than law and justice. *The Miscellaneous Works of Thomas Arnold* (1845), 365.

humankind. As he lay dying from a heart attack in 1842, he apparently thanked God 'for giving me this pain: I have suffered so little pain in my life, that I feel it is very good for me: now God has given it to me, and I do so thank Him for it'.[103] Like apocalyptic evangelicals he believed that 'the day of the Lord is coming', and that 'calamities, wars, tumults, pestilences, earthquakes' marked all of 'God's peculiar seasons of visitation', but he also said (in the same letter) that he had 'not the slightest expectation of what is commonly meant by the Millennium'.[104] The fact that he is so hard to categorize may help to account for his influence over the mid-Victorian generation of the 1850s and 1860s, forced as it was to come to terms with life after the black-and-white certainties of the first half of the century.

For all his ambiguities, Arnold's success was one sign that the views of Liberal Anglicans were beginning to spread. Another sign was their ability to win over many who started out as conservative High Churchmen, including Whewell at Cambridge and Baden Powell, Savilian Professor of Geometry at Oxford, both of whom felt the need to synthesize the new scientific ideas with revelation.[105] Despite his association with the Hackney Phalanx, Powell was keen to meet dreaded Unitarians and materialist medics on their own ground.

Scientific knowledge is rapidly spreading *among all classes* EXCEPT THE HIGHER, and the consequence must be, that that Class *will no longer remain* THE HIGHER. If its members would continue to retain their superiority, they must preserve a real *preeminence in know-ledge*, and must make advance at least in proportion to the Classes which have *hitherto* been below them.[106]

Blindly confident that the laws of nature, once *properly* expounded, would supplement and not undermine the scriptural proofs of Christianity, Powell ended up by virtually accepting the idea of progression. It aligned him with types of thinker whom he had formerly despised, such as the Unitarians Francis Newman and William Carpenter, and the radical Robert Chambers.[107] His defection to liberalism naturally alarmed High Churchmen, like Hugh James Rose[108] and Francis Newman's brother John Henry. They fought back, often aggressively, thereby contributing to an increasingly febrile and confrontational atmosphere. As J. H. Newman put it in the first of a series of ninety *Tracts for the*

---

[103] Stanley, *Life of Arnold*, i. 50, 90, 286; ii. 337.   [104] Ibid. i. 311.

[105] Richard Yeo, *Defining Science: William Whewell, Natural Knowledge, and Public Debate in Early Victorian Britain* (Cambridge, 1993), 235–50. The former Spanish Catholic priest and Oxford Whig intellectual Blanco White moved from Anglicanism to Unitarianism in 1835.

[106] Baden Powell, *The Present State and Future Prospects of Mathematical and Physical Studies in the University of Oxford* (Oxford, 1832), 27.

[107] Pietro Corsi, *Science and Religion: Baden Powell and the Anglican Debate, 1800–1860* (Cambridge, 1988), 194–208, 261–90.

[108] David A. Valone, 'Hugh James Rose's Anglican Critique of Cambridge: Science, Antirationalism, and Coleridgean Idealism in Late Georgian England', *Albion*, 33 (2001), 218–42.

Times against Popery and Dissent (1833–41), it was time for Christians to *choose their side*.

THE OXFORD MOVEMENT

The Oxford Movement, otherwise called Tractarianism after its series of publications, was germinated during the 1820s at Oriel College, where besides those already mentioned the senior common room included Keble, Pusey, Froude, and J. H. Newman, but it erupted as a result of political events. The bishops' failure to make a spirited fight against Test and Corporation Act repeal showed these ardent young High Churchmen how enervated the Establishment had become. The campaign to exclude Peel from his university seat gave them the taste of blood. Then in November 1830 the Whigs came to power. As Newman recollected much later,

> The vital question was, how were we to keep the Church from being liberalized? There was such apathy on the subject in some quarters, such imbecile alarm in others; the true principles of Churchmanship seemed so radically decayed...I felt dismay at [the Church's] prospects, anger and scorn at her do-nothing perplexity. I thought that if Liberalism once got a footing within her, it was sure of the victory in the event.[109]

In 1833 John Keble delivered an assize sermon entitled *National Apostasy*, in which he complained that 'the Apostolical Church in this realm is henceforth only to stand, in the eye of the State, as *one sect among many*'.[110] His sermon was directed against 'the fashionable liberality of this generation',[111] and more specifically against the Whig Government's suppression of ten Irish bishoprics, and it rallied support from young High Churchmen of all types. Significantly, many of these—including John Newman, Henry Manning, Robert and Henry Wilberforce, and George Dudley Ryder—had been brought up as evangelicals. Politically and culturally their change of allegiance was surprising, but theologically the distance between post-millennial evangelicalism and High Churchmanship was not great. Evangelicals placed more stress on justification and conversion, High Churchmen on sanctification and reserve,[112] but both had a horror of religious liberalism, both had a high sense of 'the Satanic significance of contemporary events',[113] and both stressed the need for holiness, though

[109] J. H. Newman, *Apologia Pro Vita Sua: Being a History of His Religious Opinions*, ed. Martin J. Svaglic (Oxford, 1967), 39–40, 254–62.   [110] John Keble, *National Apostasy* (Oxford, 1833), 2.
[111] Ibid. 16.
[112] The Tractarian doctrine of reserve, which their enemies called equivocation, held that God vouchsafed his truth gradually to worshippers as they grew in faith. It was memorably enunciated by Isaac Williams in Tracts 80 and 87.
[113] Sheridan Gilley, 'Newman and Prophecy, Evangelical and Catholic', *Journal of the United Reformed Church History Society*, 3 (1983–7), 160–88.

evangelicals conceived of this in personal and Tractarians in corporate terms. Very probably these young men had been alienated from parental tradition by the growing prominence within evangelicalism of the pre-millenarians, the Recordites and Watchmen. That was certainly the case with W. E. Gladstone, who was brought up on Clapham Sect lines, then as an undergraduate (1828–31) was briefly fascinated but finally alienated by the Calvinist Pentecostalism of the Oxford St Ebbe's set. He also considered the evangelicals' reliance on private judgement too 'individualizing' for a period of liberal advance and social unrest, and he turned to the High (or, as he called it, the 'historic') Church mainly because it offered order, discipline, community, and tradition.[114]

Edward Pusey, now Regius Professor of Hebrew, was the dominant figure in the early political phase of the Movement, which culminated in 1836 when the Tractarians led a united front of High Churchmen and evangelicals in protest against the appointment of Hampden, a Liberal Anglican, to the Regius Chair of Divinity. Some college tutors forbade undergraduates from attending the new Professor's lectures, with the predictable result that his audiences multiplied. For the liberals, Arnold retaliated by denouncing the 'moral wickedness' of the 'Oxford Malignants' and their 'habitual indulgence of evil passions'.[115] From this point on the controversy became more theological and very much more rancorous. Hampden's main offence was to have supported abolition of subscription to the Thirty-Nine Articles by arguing that 'the University is not the Church. It is only accidentally a society of church-members; and considered as a literary society, it has surely no right to rest on authority, as the *foundation* of its lessons in any department of knowledge.'[116] He could hardly have angered the Tractarians more if he had said 'secular' instead of 'literary', since both implied that Oxford existed to impart knowledge independently of revelation, like London University. Yet, as one historian has observed, 'if Hampden was heretical, so were Bishop Watson, Archdeacon Paley, Professor Hey, Bishop Hoadly and a row of eighteenth-century divines'.[117] Unfortunately, Newman and Keble were coming to think precisely that.

John Henry Newman was fast becoming the cynosure of all attention. Peevish and poignant by turns, since 1828 he had been the charismatic vicar of the University Church of St Mary, where his winning and insinuating ways had won a growing number of acolytes. It was his idea, as well as Keble's, to bring out an edition of Froude's *Remains* (1838–9), thereby precipitating the next crisis.

[114] *The Prime Ministers' Papers Series: W. E. Gladstone*, ed. John Brooke and Mary Sorensen (1971–81), i. 140–61; Perry Butler, *Gladstone. Church, State, and Tractarianism: A Study of his Religious Ideas and Attitudes, 1809–1859* (Oxford, 1982), 24–7.

[115] [Thomas Arnold], 'The Oxford Malignants and Dr Hampden', *ER* 63 (1836), 225–39.

[116] Renn Dickson Hampden, *Observations on Religious Dissent with Particular Reference to the Use of Religious Tests in the University*, 2nd edn. (Oxford, 1834), 38–9.

[117] Owen Chadwick, *The Victorian Church* (1966–70), i. 116.

Hurrell Froude had died in 1836 at the age of 32, and the decision to publish was prompted more by loyalty to his memory than by an intention to be polemical. Nevertheless, the revelation that he had been obsessed with hagiography, martyrology, and medieval saints caused an uproar. Froude, according to Newman,

had a severe idea of the intrinsic excellence of Virginity; and he considered the Blessed Virgin its great Pattern. He delighted in thinking of the Saints; he had a vivid appreciation of the idea of sanctity, its possibility and its heights; and he was more than inclined to believe a large amount of miraculous interference as occurring in the early and middle ages. He embraced the principle of penance and mortification.[118]

The fact that Newman and W. G. Ward idealized celibacy, and the taste of some Tractarians for flagellation and wearing hair shirts, led some twentieth-century historians to see the Movement in a homoerotic light. But what most worried evangelicals were the Romish tendencies evident in Froude's *Remains*. The final break with their former allies came with another political decision. In October 1841 Peel's new Conservative Government secured the passage of a bill to establish a joint Anglo-Prussian bishopric in Jerusalem with jurisdiction over the tiny handful of British and German Protestants in the Holy Land. The plan had the backing of Prince Albert, Archbishop Howley, Bishop Blomfield, and the powerful evangelical party of Lord Shaftesbury, but Newman and his followers hated this alliance with Lutheran heretics, as well as the attempt to proselytize among Orthodox adherents of the Eastern Church.

Events at base now became increasingly fractious, while the rest of the country looked on in appalled fascination. 'The Oxford Tract men have got the bit in their mouths,' wrote Gladstone's brother-in-law. [119] By this time at least as many as 1,000 clergymen out of a total of some 18,000 had Tractarian leanings. Many of them were impressionable former undergraduates who had taken Puseyism into the parishes. But some of Newman's followers still in Oxford, including some at his retreat in Littlemore, now began to place him in an impossible position by converting to Rome, while *he* clung desperately to the Church of England as a *via media*. Another crisis occurred with Tract 90 (1841), in which Newman claimed that the Thirty-Nine Articles could be read in a Catholic sense as endorsing (*inter alia*) the doctrine of transubstantiation, or real presence in the Eucharist. It caused a sensation and prompted his enemies to commence the fight-back. In March 1841 the Hebdomadal Board censured Tract 90 by nineteen to two. Then in 1843 the Vice-Chancellor's court suspended Pusey from preaching within the University for two years on account of a sermon in which he too leant towards transubstantiation.[120] This was a green light for

[118] Newman, *Apologia*, 34.
[119] G. W. Lyttleton to J. W. Blakesley, 6 Sept. 1841, Trinity College, Cambridge, Blakesley Papers, Add. MS a. 244[48].   [120] E. B. Pusey, *The Holy Eucharist: A Comfort to the Penitent* (1843).

anti-Tractarian priests and prelates to weigh in with anathemas of their own. By this time

the counter-revolution was having things all its own way. The Provost of Oriel was refusing testimonials to young men of his college, candidates for Holy Orders, who were known sympathizers with the Romanizing party. High Churchmen stood no chance of obtaining Fellowships. Colleges changed their dinner-hour on Sundays to prevent undergraduates from attending the sermon at St Mary's. Espionage, *agents provocateurs*, ruthless interrogations ... were appearing on the small ecclesiastical stage of Oxford in the early 'forties. The Party was on the run. The whole academical pack snapped and snarled at their heels.[121]

In February 1845 Convocation stripped Ward of his Master's degree for having written *The Ideal of a Christian Church* (1844), in which he claimed the right to propagate Roman Catholic (or 'ideal') doctrines while remaining an Anglican communicant. A similar move was then made against Newman in respect of Tract 90. The attempt was vetoed but the strain became too much for him, and on 9 October 1845 he was finally received into the Roman Catholic faith.[122] This may have been a testament to his suggestibility, since it was what his enemies had been predicting for at least five years, but they saw it as proof of his treachery. To them, Newman's 'Lead, kindly Light' (1833), with its famous lines

> Keep thou my feet; I do not ask to see
> The distant scene; one step enough for me,

was stuff and nonsense, since in their view the Oxford Movement was a long-meditated plot to subvert the Church of England from within. And it is true that many Tractarians *were* destructive, demanding tolerance and understanding for themselves, but rarely willing to extend those qualities to others, yet there was pathos in their situation, and in most cases their losses were greater than their gains. Newman's last sermon as an Anglican was entitled 'The Parting of Friends', a fitting subject since many families and communities were sundered by the crisis he had brought about.[123] Between 1845 and 1900 about 450 Anglican clergymen, as well as more than seventy peers and peeresses, followed Newman to Rome.[124]

---

[121] Geoffrey Faber, *Oxford Apostles: A Character Study of the Oxford Movement*, 2nd edn. (1936), 429–30.

[122] For a severe and sceptical but compelling and (in a strange way) sympathetic account, see Frank M. Turner, *John Henry Newman: The Challenge to Evangelical Religion* (New Haven, 2002). However, Turner's claim that Newman was originally driven by opposition to the evangelicalism of his upbringing rather than by opposition to liberalism is mistaken. Certainly, he loathed evangelical Dissent and Bulteel's style of apocalyptic evangelicalism, and he disapproved of orthodox evangelicals' reluctance to oppose them head on, but liberalism was always the enemy.

[123] As sensitively described in David Newsome, *The Parting of Friends: A Study of the Wilberforces and Henry Manning* (1966).

[124] W. Gordon Gorman (ed.), *Converts to Rome: A Biographical List*, 11th edn., (1910).

It is in the nature of militant reformers to disparage their predecessors, and the Tractarians certainly helped to establish the view that the Hanoverian Church in general, and the High Church in particular, had been moribund. This was probably unfair on the eighteenth century, and it certainly ignored the High Church revival of the early nineteenth, which was sustained through the 1830s and 1840s by divines such as Henry Phillpotts, William Palmer, H. J. Rose, W. F. Hook, and Edward Churton. Liturgically this High Church tradition appeared drier than it really was because of an aversion to anything emotional or fervent that had set in after the French Revolution. There was no hymn-singing or music or poetry, hardly any ritual, and nothing that appealed to the visual or olfactory senses, or went beyond the words and rubrics of the Book of Common Prayer. However, in this respect it differed little from Tractarianism. As one historian has puts it,

High Church fastidiousness was as much a matter of culture as of religion; as a mark of refinement, it was a badge of social class, and passed into the Oxford Movement as the doctrine of the *disciplina arcani*, the practice declared to exist in the early church of with-holding the Christian mysteries from catechumens too recently converted to understand them in the fullness of faith.[125]

During the 1830s bishops such as Blomfield and Phillpotts took steps to enforce the rubrics, and to make services somewhat less austere. The real difference therefore was not between old High Churchmanship and Tractarianism, but between Tractarianism and the next generation's brand of Anglo-Catholicism known as Ritualism. The latter was sometimes referred to as 'the second Oxford Movement' because it was also led by Pusey, but this was misleading. As an attempt to proselytize among the urban proletariat by adopting some of the beauties of Roman Catholic worship, it owed less to the Oxford Tractarians than to the Cambridge Ecclesiologists.[126]

If there was little to choose between Tractarianism and Old High Churchmanship in terms of liturgy, there were significant doctrinal differences. Broadly speaking the old High Churchmen cleaved to the Anglican tradition of the Elizabethan and Caroline divines, notably Richard Hooker and William Laud. Far from being Erastian, as Tractarians alleged, they were highly apostolic. They preached the unity—meaning the 'organically implied single entity'—of Church and State, and they considered that the first duty of the latter was to defend and promote the former. Old High Churchmen believed in the supremacy of

---

[125] Sheridan Gilley, 'Introduction', in John Keble, *The Christian Year*, ed. S. Gilley (1977), pp. xiv–xv. See also Peter Benedict Nockles, *The Oxford Movement in Context: Anglican High Churchmanship, 1760–1857* (Cambridge, 1994), 212–17.

[126] John Shelton Reed, *Glorious Battle: The Cultural Politics of Victorian Anglo-Catholicism* (Nashville, Tenn., 1996), 175–7. See below, p. 480.

Scripture but not in *sola scriptura*, or the realm of private judgement, and they placed great weight also on the testimony of creeds, Prayer Book, and catechism. They emphasized the doctrine of sacramental grace in both Eucharist and baptism, while steering well clear of the Roman Catholic principle of *ex opere operato*. Any traces of religious mysticism, such as had characterized Hutchinsonianism in the mid-eighteenth century, were suppressed in the wake of the French Revolution, with the result that High Church apologetic in the late Georgian period consisted mainly of a rationalistic natural theology based on 'evidences'.

The Tractarians by contrast argued that the Church of England needed to go back beyond Hooker to pre-Reformation ideals of Catholicity. 'I saw that Reformation principles were powerless to rescue her,' wrote Newman. 'There was need of a second reformation.'[127] Whereas old High Churchmen merely paid lip-service to patristics, the Tractarians revered the writings of the early Fathers as guides to how the nineteenth-century Church might be respiritualized.[128] Whereas old High Churchmen emphasized practical spirituality, based on good works and self-denial, Tractarians advocated saintly holiness, asceticism, and an unworldly piety that varied in tone from Keble's sober temperate devotionalism to Froude's 'emotional and ecstatic spirituality'.[129] Though not at first in favour of disestablishment, Tractarians never emphasized the need for the Church to consecrate the State or for the State to promote the Church, and they set no particular store by the practical trappings of Establishment such as clerical provision, endowment, or tithes. By the 1840s Newman, Froude, and fleetingly even Keble had come round to the view that the Church should be independent of the State. In matters of ecclesiology the Tractarians mainly followed old High Churchmen, but they sought a more positive or 'high sacramental understanding' of doctrines such as Apostolicity.[130] They took a higher view of episcopacy in theory, but a much lower view of real live bishops, some of whom they lacerated unmercifully. Finally, whereas most old High Churchmen held strongly to the doctrine of ministerial absolution, some Tractarians went further in demanding auricular confession and other manifestations of sacerdotal authority. They were far more critical of the Prayer Book, and reacted against what they saw as old High Church rationalism by developing more mystical approaches to truth such as rites, ceremonies, prophecies, and typology. Theirs has been described as 'a new romantic feeling for the past, a new tenderness for Anglican parochial life, a sturdy Protestantism not unsympathetic to monasticism and the Middle Ages, a new depth of devotion to the Blessed Virgin, even to her immaculate Conception'.[131]

---

[127] Newman, *Apologia*, 40.

[128] 'In proportion as I moved out of the shadow of that liberalism which had hung over my course, my early devotion towards the Fathers returned' (ibid. 35).   [129] Nockles, *Oxford Movement*, 198.

[130] Ibid. 151.   [131] Gilley, 'Introduction', p. xv.

Looking back in later life on the years immediately prior to Keble's 1833 assize sermon, Newman wrote, 'I was beginning to prefer intellectual excellence to moral; I was drifting in the direction of the Liberalism of the day.' He meant that he had succumbed to a widespread 'anti-dogmatic principle',[132] a tendency to suppose that truth could be arrived at through introspection and ratiocination. The purpose of the *Tracts* was to delve behind the doctrinal bric-a-brac of centuries to the origins of the Church of England, with the hope of uncovering a specifically *Anglican* truth which might then be proclaimed as a means towards national regeneration. Unfortunately, the Anglican Church had never had a doctrinal basis, having been founded for political reasons and to secure Henry VIII a divorce. Those Tractarians who turned to Rome did so because they realized this, and realized too that only the universal Roman Church was in a position to order its adherents (in Newman's words) 'not to reason, but to obey'.[133] A related point is that Newman's understanding of what constituted truth changed dramatically. The young evangelical, approaching the concept mechanically, had sought 'to erect a coherent dogmatic edifice' by melding elements of Patristic and Caroline theology. He had hoped that a systematized Anglicanism, shorn of anomalies, 'when one thing fits into another, when each part mutually supports and is supported', would be able to stand up to Roman Catholicism and Calvinism by being likewise 'self-balanced and self-sustained and entire.'[134] As late as 1836 he counselled Pusey, 'Let us preach and teach, and develop our views into system.'[135] Having failed, however, to uncover any such schema in the writings of sixteenth-century Anglicans, Newman tried to work out what they must have thought by reconstructing the oral traditions from which they had sprung, starting with the Arians of the fourth century. This historicist investigation led him to adopt an evolutionary conception of truth, culminating in *An Essay on the Development of Christian Doctrine* (1845), in which he felt able to reconcile discrepancies between the Fathers and the Council of Trent. In this way the convert of 1845 could confidently proclaim that modern Rome was the repository of Christian truth.[136]

The philosopher Mark Pattison, an 'intimate disciple of Newman from 1842 to 1846', wrote to him three decades later, 'Is it not a remarkable thing that you

[132] Newman, *Apologia*, 26, 54, 254.

[133] A spate of High Church secessions to Rome followed the 1850 Gorham Judgment, in which the jurisdiction of the Church courts was shown to be inferior to that of the Judicial Committee of the Privy Council, a lay body. The Judgment effectively denied the right of a bishop to deny preferment to a clergyman on doctrinal grounds alone.

[134] [J. H. Newman], 'Palmer's Treatise on the Church of Christ', *British Critic*, 24 (1838), 349; Nockles, *Oxford Movement*, 129–31, 174.

[135] Newman to Pusey, 24 Jan. 1836, in *The Letters and Diaries of John Henry Newman*, ed. Charles Stephen Dessain, Thomas Gornall, Ian Ker, and Gerard Tracey (London, Oxford 1961–), v. 215.

[136] Nockles, *Oxford Movement*, 144–5.

should have first started the idea—and the word—Development, as the key to the history of church doctrine, and since then it has gradually become the dominant idea of all history, biology, physics, and in short has metamorphosed our view of every science, and of all knowledge?'[137] Just as remarkably, Newman was led to the idea of temporal evolution through studying developments in the past, which shows that the dividing line was not merely between forward-looking radicals and backward-looking Ultra Tories. Equally if not more significant was the conflict between those who conceived of time as moving in a linear direction, whether they were radicals or Tories, and the majority of Establishment savants, for whom time in that sense did not exist.

THE MIDDLE AGES, THE 'OLDEN TIME', AND IDEAS OF NATION

Tractarianism reflected changes that were transforming Oxford visually in the two decades before the railways arrived in 1844. The city's 'first great refacing' began in 1824 as Lincoln College followed by All Souls, Pembroke, Exeter, Merton, and others turned themselves into scrubbed Gothic halls, building 'new ranges so that they should appear old ranges, with a gate tower, with windows with arched lights, and with oriels in appropriate places'.[138] Oxford, in other words, was beginning to whisper the last enchantments of the Middle Ages, as to a lesser extent were towns and cities throughout the country. Given that this was the world's most dynamic and developing society, it is not surprising that some people should have been fixated with the past, or that steam locomotives should have been named after Knights of the Round Table, but such nostalgia contradicted what might be called the ruling ideology of the period, which was essentially ahistorical. Liberal Tories subscribed to Enlightenment mechanism, while even Whigs, despite their attachment to stadial theory, had little sense of history as *process*. When Macaulay spoke of revolutions between classes successively leading to higher stages of civilization, he was talking the language of Adam Sedgwick on the creation of new worlds out of old ones. To that extent the growing and in some quarters almost obsessional interest in England's Gothic past was counter-cultural.

The Gothic backlash is an immensely complex topic, but in tracing its development it is possible to distinguish three partially overlapping phases, the first of which lasted from the early 1790s to the mid-1820s. Gothic or 'Gothick' had never completely disappeared, having survived as a low-level vernacular

---

[137] Mark Pattison to J. H. Newman, 5 Apr. 1878, in *Letters and Diaries of Newman*, xxviii. 339 n. 3; Owen Chadwick, *From Bossuet to Newman: The Idea of Doctrinal Development* (Cambridge, 1957), 96–163.

[138] Jennifer Sherwood and Nikolaus Pevsner, *Oxfordshire: The Buildings of England* (Harmondsworth, 1974), 52–4.

tradition with the odd significant outcrops, like Horace Walpole's architectural extravaganza Strawberry Hill (1753–77). Having begun to turn that house into an eighteenth-century version of Gormenghast, Walpole suffered a nightmare one night while sleeping there, and this apparently prompted him to write one of the first Gothic horror novels, *The Castle of Otranto* (1764). It had few imitators before the French Revolution, but then inspired a number of popular novels, notably Ann Radcliffe's *The Mysteries of Udolpho* (1794), Matthew Lewis's *The Monk* (1796), and Jane Austen's satire on the genre, *Northanger Abbey*, written in 1798 and published posthumously. Readers surfeited on ghosts and spectres, mad monks and sinister nuns, smugglers and banditti, sex and sensation. A favourite device was the discovery of a cryptic note telling of some fair-skinned daughter incarcerated in some locked chamber or dungeon, while the overriding theme was conspiracy, whether by Catholic priests or by Freemasons.[139] It seems obvious that such obsessions had something to do with events in France, a point recognized by one reviewer when he wrote of 'the strange luxury of *artificial* terror',[140] but their success owed much to new marketing practices. William Lane's Minerva Press, for example, created a retailing revolution by publishing books in unprecedented quantities, approximately one-third of them with Gothic titles.[141]

After 1800 the subject matter of this first phase of literary Gothic diversified. Many popular writers like Selina Davenport purveyed a domestic and sentimental mode, possibly in reaction to the wartime interruption of family life. At the other extreme, a succession of epics, tales, and romances set in the mysterious East testified to the enduring fascination of William Beckford's oriental fantasy *Vathek* (1786–7), but it was mainly stimulated by Napoleon's adventures in Asia and Araby. The strangest and most original was Coleridge's opium-induced *Kubla Khan*, subtitled *A Vision In a Dream* and probably written in 1797, though not published until much later. The most famous was the runaway success *Childe Harold* (1812–18), in which Byron turned the Grand Tour into a crusading epic.[142] There was much fascination with the clash of cultures, especially as between Christians and Muslims and between Greeks and Turks. Byron exploited it in *The Giaour*, *Lara*, and *The Corsair*, three sensational verse-tales of 1813–14, and so too did Percy Bysshe Shelley in *The Revolt of Islam* (1817–18). Similarly, Walter Scott explored relations between East and West and

---

[139] The most notable of many non-fictional conspiracy theorists was the Edinburgh natural philosopher John Robison, author of *Proofs of a Conspiracy against all the Religions and Governments of Europe* (1797).   [140] *Monthly Review*, 15 (1794), 280.

[141] Coral Ann Howells, *Love, Mystery, and Misery: Feeling in Gothic Fiction* (1978), 81; James Watt, *Contesting the Gothic: Fiction, Genre and Cultural Conflict, 1764–1832* (Cambridge, 1999), 70–101; E. J. Clery, *The Rise of Supernatural Fiction, 1762–1800* (Cambridge, 1995), 133–67.

[142] As pointed out in Christopher Hart, ' "Fiction is the Mask of History": Contextual Readings of Byron's Poetry', Ph.D. thesis (Cambridge University, 1996), 32–72.

between Norman and Saxon in *Ivanhoe* (1819), *The Betrothed* (1825), and *The Talisman* (1825), three novels set in the time of the Third Crusade. Another Gothic fashion was for scientific fantasy, as in John Polidori's *The Vampyre* (1819) and Mary Shelley's best-selling *Frankenstein: Or, The Modern Prometheus* (1818), in which it was envisaged that monsters might be created by sparking corpses into life. Shelley was almost certainly inspired by Davy's electrochemical experiments and Galvani's demonstrations of animal magnetism, and her fantasy may well have reflected an impatience to improve human nature instantaneously, bypassing the slow evolutionary processes envisaged in Erasmus Darwin's treatise on sexual selection.[143]

A similar chronology was evident in matters of design. Like *Otranto*, Strawberry Hill had few serious imitators before the mid-1790s, when the mad degenerate William Beckford created Fonthill, but thereafter wealthy housebuilders showed a growing taste for picturesque Gothic, Tudorbethan, or Scottish baronial as at Belvoir (1801–30), Eaton Hall (1803–25), Panshanger (1806–21), and Lowther Castle (1806–11). Even staid John Nash caught the mood, rebuilding Brighton Pavilion in oriental style (1815–22). Designer cottages also came into vogue, with at least one book on the subject appearing each year between 1790 and 1810. As for picturesque landscaping, this too had mid-eighteenth-century origins, with the villa revival and 'controlled wildernesses' of Capability Brown, but again it was only in the 1790s that the style became normative.[144] This was partly the result of a series of publications during 1794–5 by Richard Payne Knight, Uvedale Price, and Humphry Repton, who despite differences broadly agreed that the picturesque represented raw nature and supplemented Burke's categories of the sublime and beautiful. They also believed that each estate had its own peculiar genius, which it was the improver's duty to develop.[145] Yet it is important not to get carried away by this catalogue of books and buildings, impressive though it is. Castellated turrets were eye-catching, but the established architectural style remained that of the classicists Soane and Smirke. Though several of Scott's novels were about the Middle Ages, many more of his tales had seventeenth- and eighteenth-century settings. Poems might be full of 'thees' and 'thous', and palely loitering knights-at-arms, but the loitering was not with any serious intent, being essentially escapist.

---

[143] Anne K. Mellor, *Mary Shelley: Her Life, her Fiction, Her Monsters* (New York, 1988), 91–105. Mary Shelley was the daughter of Mary Wollstonecraft and William Godwin and the husband of P. B. Shelley.

[144] John Summerson, *Architecture in Britain 1530 to 1830* (1953), 291.

[145] Stephen Daniels, *Humphry Repton: Landscape Gardening and the Geography of Georgian England* (New Haven, 1999), 1–25, 103–47; Andrew Ballantyne, *Architecture, Landscape and Liberty: Richard Payne Knight and the Picturesque* (Cambridge, 1997), 138–89. One historian has defined as anti-phenomenalist 'monists' those landscape artists who believed in an 'ontological continuum between human beings and their environment' (Charlotte Klonk, *Science and the Perception of Nature: British Landscape Art in the Late Eighteenth and Early Nineteenth Centuries* (New Haven, 1996), 39).

Byron recognized as much in his sardonically Augustan masterpiece *Don Juan* (1819–24), in which he repeatedly undercut the Romantic excesses of his own tales.

> And the sad truth which hovers o'er my desk
> Turns what was once romantic to burlesque.

A more serious form of Gothicism originated with Robert Southey, whose political opinions veered with age from republicanism to ultra-royalism, but whose fascination with the Middle Ages was constant from the time of *Wat Tyler* (1794)[146] and *Joan of Arc* (1796) through to *Madoc* (1805), *Roderick, the Last of the Goths* (1814), and *Sir Thomas More* (1829), already noted as a red rag to Macaulay's bull. His work differed from that of his fellow Romantics in that it formed the basis of a concerned paternalism.[147] He even sanctioned the agency of the central State ('civil government'), which was most unusual for a high Tory. Like Cobbett and Coleridge, Southey was fiercely anti-Catholic, yet like them he came to regret the loss of community care which the pre-Reformation monasteries had provided, and their replacement by workhouses. The most polemical manifesto was *The Broadstone of Honour* (1822–7) by a convert to Catholicism, Kenelm Digby. It was a compendium of facts and fiction in praise of the Middle Ages, 'when all men were parts of one family, when great and low dined together at a single board, when all classes joined together in sports on the village green, and when the Church gave charity with kindness and tact'.[148] Digby's volumes inspired many others to write in favour of organic societies and paternalist governors, and mostly in a serious rather than wistful way.[149] In 1835 William Dansey published *Horae Decanicae Rurales*, 900 pages of medieval ecclesiastical lore in heavy, archaic, Gothic typeface, but this was by no means nostalgic antiquarianism, nor even an attempt to defend Old Corruption by medieval precedent. Dansey realized the need for the Church to undertake urgent structural reforms, and his work served to advertise a pre-existing diocesan revival.[150] Perhaps the most influential author in this organicist tradition was Carlyle,

---

[146] *Wat Tyler* was written but not published in 1794. A pirated edition was brought out by radicals in 1817, explicitly to embarrass the new Poet Laureate by reminding the world of his youthful republicanism. It sold two or three times more than all Southey's other works put together. William St Clair, *The Reading Nation and the Romantic Period* (Cambridge, 2004), 316–18.

[147] For assessments of Southey's paternalism, see David Eastwood, 'Robert Southey and the Intellectual Origins of Romantic Conservatism', *EHR* 104 (1989), 308–31; David M. Craig, 'Republicanism Becoming Conservative: Robert Southey and Political Argument in Britain, 1789–1817', Ph.D. thesis (Cambridge University, 2000), 96–121.

[148] Alice Chandler, *A Dream of Order: The Medieval Ideal in Nineteenth-Century English Literature* (1971), 156; Mark Girouard, *The Return to Camelot: Chivalry and the English Gentleman* (New Haven, 1981), 55–66.

[149] For its extent and variety, see David Roberts, *Paternalism in Early Victorian England* (1979).

[150] Arthur Burns, *The Diocesan Revival in the Church of England c.1800–1870* (Oxford, 1999), 79–96.

whose Teutonic inspiration was evident in *Chartism* (1839) and *Past and Present* (1843), two withering attacks on political economy, cash payments, mammonism, and the 'condition-of-England'.

To whom, then, is this wealth of England wealth? Who is it that it blesses; makes happier, wiser, beautifuler, in any way better? ... As yet no one. We have more riches than any Nation ever had before; we have less good of them than any Nation ever had before ... In the midst of plethoric plenty, the people perish; with gold walls, and full barns, no man feels himself safe or satisfied. Workers, Master Workers, Unworkers, all men, come to a pause; stand fixed, and cannot farther. Fatal paralysis spreading inwards, form the extremities ... [151]

According to Carlyle there was no salvation in orthodox religion but only in aristocracy, the descendants of Hengst and Horsa, 'the corporation of the Best, of the Bravest'.

To this joyfully, with heart-loyalty, do men pay the half of their substance, to equip and decorate their Best, to lodge them in palaces, set them high over all. For it is of the nature of men, in every time, to honour and love their Best; to know no limits in honouring them. Whatsoever Aristocracy *is* still a corporation of the Best, is safe from all peril, and the land it rules is a safe and blessed land. Whatsoever Aristocracy does not even attempt to be that, but only to wear the clothes of that, is not safe; neither is the land it rules in safe! For this now is our sad lot, that we must find a *real* Aristocracy![152]

The architectural equivalent of this serious medievalism was the Gothic revival proper. Its origins may be traced to a highly influential work of academic archaeology, Thomas Rickman's *An Attempt to Discriminate the Styles of Architecture in England from the Conquest to the Reformation* (1817), which ran through many editions and has had an enduring influence on popular typology. Its high priest was Augustus Welby Northmore Pugin, whose *Contrasts* (1836) and *True Principles* (1841) proclaimed the doctrine that 'there should be no features about a building which are not necessary for convenience, construction, or propriety', and that 'all ornament should consist of enrichment of the essential construction'.[153] (This is why, despite their retro style, Pugin's buildings have been seen as originating the twentieth-century 'modern movement'.) He insisted that Gothic was *true*, that it represented the revealed word of God, and that crockets (for example) signified the Resurrection. By contrast the

---

[151] Carlyle, *Past and Present: Shilling Edition of the Works of Thomas Carlyle* (1888), bk. 1, ch. 1, pp. 5–6.

[152] Carlyle, 'Chartism,' in *Works of Carlyle: Critical and Miscellaneous Essays* (1888), vi. 146–7.

[153] A. W. N. Pugin, *The True Principles of Pointed or Christian Architecture* (1841), 1. Pugin's *Contrasts: Or, A Parallel between the Noble Edifices of the Middle Ages, and Corresponding Buildings of the Present Day; Shewing the Present Decay of Taste*, first appeared in 1836 and again in much-expanded form in 1841 (Rosemary Hill, ' "To Stones a Moral Life": How Pugin Transformed the Gothic Revival', *Times Literary Supplement*, 18 Sept. 1998, 21–2).

symmetrical fenestration and stuccoed classical pilasters of modern architects were 'deceitful', 'artificial', and 'sham' (his chief *bête noire* was Soane). Pugin's influence on Church architects was immense, but what most seduced his readers was a plate contrasting a pagan modern town, dominated by smoky chimneys and warehouses, and an idealized medieval city, shown as a jumble of cloisters, almshouses, and churches with steep roofs, rough masonry, and delicate pointed spires. The drawing celebrated the Middle English (or Second) Pointed style of the thirteenth and fourteenth centuries. According to Pugin, that age of faith and social justice had given way to one of bastard feudalism and faithless fidelity, expressed in the flamboyant and Perpendicular styles of the fifteenth and sixteenth centuries. Then, by way of reaction, had come the still-greater evil of the Protestant Reformation. Pugin, who converted to Rome in 1834, could be called the Tractarian of the Gothic revival, in so far as he was dogmatic and confrontational and regarded architectural propriety as a route to moral and spiritual regeneration. The same was true of members of the Cambridge Camden Society and of the contributors to its journal *The Ecclesiologist*. Founded in 1839 by a group of undergraduates under the leadership of an obsessive antiquarian, John Mason Neale (yet another young High Churchman who had fled from parental evangelicalism), the society mustered more than 750 members within four years, including both archbishops and sixteen bishops.[154] The Camdenians cleaved to pointed Gothic, though they declined to acknowledge Pugin's example, deplored his Romish apostasy, and went much further in their attempts to introduce mystery and symbolism into Anglican worship. They 'loved screens, priests' doors, sedilia, piscinas, gargoyles, concealed frescoes, fragments of brasses, poppy-heads, hammer-beams'.[155] Some of this was more high jinks than High Church, but it caught a mood.

At the same time a conviction gained ground that community buildings should be Gothic, especially if they were ecclesiastical, or educational, while great Whig mansions like Chatsworth and Castle Howard were increasingly dismissed as vulgar, ostentatious, and 'un-English'. These views were of course hotly contested, like every other strongly held belief in this period, which is why the architectural history of the second quarter of the century is often depicted as a 'battle of the styles'. Gothic was very far from dominant, and classicism fought back, as in Joseph Hansom's Birmingham Town Hall (1831–4) for example, but it was definitely in the ascendant. Any doubts on this score were stifled by what happened after large parts of the Palace of Westminster went up in flames on the evening of 16 October 1834, a conflagration caused by carelessness but which anti-reformers naturally ascribed to Satanic influence. Somewhat unexpectedly,

[154] James F. White, *The Cambridge Movement: The Ecclesiologists and the Gothic Revival* (Cambridge, 1962), 41–2.   [155] Chadwick, *Victorian Church*, i. 213.

the commissioners appointed to superintend an architectural competition for its replacement insisted on either the Gothic or Elizabethan style. The stipulation enraged Utilitarians and especially Joseph Hume, who fought a long rearguard action against it, but Elizabethan was redolent of Shakespeare and Francis Bacon, while Gothic was thought to be eminently English and natural, its vaults like the overhanging trees in a forest glade, its silhouettes responding romantically to stormy northern skies.[156] What the commissioners eventually got was a composite—an essentially classical plan and structure by a mainly classical architect Charles Barry, with façades and interior surfaces in a sumptuous Perpendicular Gothic that owed much to Pugin, acting as Barry's draughtsman.

In so far as the new Palace contradicted Pugin's own tastes—notably his dislike of superficial ornament and preference for Middle Pointed—it marked the onset of a third phase of Gothicism. Certainly, if Royal Academy paintings and book illustrations are anything to go by, high medievalism lost ground in popular taste during the 1830s to a fashion for the grand-vernacular picturesque, an archaic but not archaeological style combining late Gothic Perpendicular motifs with sixteenth- and early seventeenth-century elements. A dominant image was that of the romantic ivy-covered ruin, like the Great Hall of Kenilworth Castle. It conjured up what was called the Olden Time, an imagined period stretching roughly from the Wars of the Roses to the Civil War (c.1450–c.1650).[157] An architectural mishmash of Tudor, Elizabethan, and Jacobean—in which hips, gables, dormers, brick, half-timber, and thatch mingled with late Gothic features—was strikingly illustrated in a highly popular series of lithographs of *The Mansions of England in the Olden Time* (1839–49) by Joseph Nash. One shows Lyme Hall to the south-east of Manchester, which is famous for its porticoed quasi-Palladian front by Giacomo Leoni (1720) and its Grinling Gibbons panelling, but tellingly Nash preferred to illustrate the Elizabethan drawing room. His favourite houses were Compton Wynyates, Haddon Hall, Audley End, Hardwicke, Hatfield, Hampton Court, Knole, and Bramhall Hall, all with bay windows and battlements, great halls and banqueting suites, long galleries, inlaid chambers, marquetry, heraldry, rafters, hammer beams, plaster ceilings, carved oak wainscoting, elaborate mouldings, armorial cartouches, halberds, and suits of armour. In his illustrations liege lords and their extended families mingle with courtiers in ruffs and doublets, feasters,

---

[156] Only six entries out of ninety-seven took the Elizabethan option (M. H. Port and Phoebe B. Stanton, in M. H. port (ed.), *The Houses of Parliament* (New Haven, 1976), 30–1, 73–80).

[157] The classic account is Peter Mandler, *The Fall and Rise of the Stately Home* (New Haven, 1997), 38–69; id., ' "In the Olden Time": Romantic History and English National Identity, 1820–50', in Laurence Brockliss and David Eastwood (eds.), *A Union of Multiple Identities: The British Isles, c.1750–c.1850* (Manchester, 1997).

jesters, jousters, duellists, minstrels, mummers, morris dancers, not to mention cats and dogs in scenes of wassail, sport, and revelry.[158] Not surprisingly painters caught this Olden Time mood. The most notable was Daniel Maclise, whose extravagant oil *The Chivalric Vow of the Ladies and the Peacock* (1835) re-created a banquet from Scott's *Lay of the Last Minstrel*. His watercolour *Portrait of Sir Francis Sykes and his Family*, exhibited at the Royal Academy in 1837, was even more remarkable in so far as it depicted a nineteenth-century domestic group in armour-plated medieval mode.[159] But first prize for risibility must go to a staging of performance art, the Eglinton Tournament in 1839. Piqued by a cheese-paring decision to omit some of the usual medieval pageantry from Queen Victoria's 'Penny Coronation' the previous year, the thirteenth Earl of Eglinton resolved to hold his own Round Table at his estate in Ayrshire. Twelve mainly aristocratic jousters attired as Black Knight, Black Lion, Knight of the Griffin, Knight of the Red Rose, etc. were cheered on by 100,000 tourists who had sailed from Liverpool, or else travelled by excursion trains on the just-built railway line. Unfortunately torrential rain stopped play early, the thirteenth Earl was declared the winner, and the sightseers went home in sopping period dress.[160] A similar taste for late Gothic and Tudor–Jacobethan infected authors, as in the highly successful *Bentley's Miscellany*, launched in 1837. Its publisher, Richard Bentley, was at the centre of a London literary clique which for a time included Dickens. The editor was Harrison Ainsworth, a middlebrow popularizer of Olden Time and Gothic romances, and a prominent contributor was the Revd Richard Barham, author of *The Ingoldsby Legends* (1840–7). Admittedly, much of its output was comic whimsy—Barham was associated with his friend Thomas Hood of the *New Monthly Magazine*, and with the humorous journal *Punch* (1841)—but it also had a serious social edge, as Hood's angry ditty on worker exploitation *The Song of the Shirt* (1843) makes clear.

As already noted, those people in the early nineteenth century who were obsessed with history can be considered counter-cultural, since the dominant metropolitan values of liberal Tories and Whig–Liberals were a-historical. They were counter-cultural in another way, which is that those metropolitan values were also universalist and monogenetic, whereas the historicist imagination frequently appealed to ideas of nation and race.[161] Walter Scott, for example, frequently emphasized England's Danish origins and the existence of a common

---

[158] See plate 14.

[159] Though possibly Maclise was sending the armour-plated baronet up. Not only is Sykes made to look like a prat, but the painter was sleeping with the baronet's wife, Henrietta, at the time. Shortly afterwards Sir Francis caught the couple in bed and threatened to sue, prompting Charles Dickens, a friend of Maclise, to use a variant spelling of his name for the villain of his current novel, *Oliver Twist*. See Plate 15.

[160] Girouard, *Return to Camelot*, 87–110.

[161] However, this did not apply to the Catholic convert Pugin or to the Anglo-Catholic Neale.

Teutonic stock, while many of his 'medieval chivalric' romances celebrated Saxon bravery under the Norman (for which many must have read Napoleonic) yoke. The Society of Antiquaries pronounced Gothic to be the English style in 1800, reflecting a fascination with primitive archaeology and the origins of the Saxon race.[162] (The brothers Hengist and Horsa, ideal types for Carlyle's new aristocracy, had led the first Saxon revolt against native Britons in AD 441.) King Arthur and Robin Hood each enjoyed a 'literary apotheosis' in the three decades following the outbreak of the French Revolution, and in 1818 alone the Sherwood Forest legend was reworked by Scott, Keats, and Peacock.[163] A non-mythical national hero also emerged in Sharon Turner's *History of the Anglo-Saxons* (1799–1805), which set the scene for what has been called the 'apotheosis of King Alfred the Great'. Alfred had played a prominent enough role in the eighteenth-century imagination, but only became a focus for national sentiment during the 1790s and 1800s, with numerous plays, poems, paintings, and engravings. (His role in building up the Royal Navy and his heroic defence against the Danes added symbolic significance to the bombardment of Copenhagen in 1807.) The bandwagon continued with Richard Payne Knight's *Alfred: A Romance in Rhyme* (1823) and G. L. N. Collingwood's *Alfred the Great: A Poem* (1836), and when a competition was held for a royal statue to decorate the new Palace of Westminster, he and Queen Elizabeth led the field.[164]

   Yet, despite its incipient appeal, Englishness never gelled into a usable set of racial or nationalist ideas. There were two main reasons. The first is that the passion for antiquarian learning fed a loyalty to particular localities. The market for urban histories, for example, expanded rapidly in the later eighteenth century as 'a direct beneficiary of the Gothic Revival'.[165] A further surge of interest followed the debates on the borough franchise and municipal corporations: at least twelve new antiquarian societies were formed between 1834 and 1846, including the Camden. Investigation of the legal rights and responsibilities of historic boroughs, guilds, and parishes informed the work of (among others) the philologist J. M. Kemble, the leading Anglo-Saxonist of the 1840s, to be exploited in the following decade by fierce opponents of the centralized State like Toulmin Smith. A second reason for the failure of a national myth to flourish at this time is that there was so much history and it was so hotly disputed. For simplicity's sake it is possible to distinguish three contemporary

[162] Rosemary Sweet, *Antiquaries: The Discovery of the Past in Eighteenth-Century Britain* (2004), 261–8.
[163] Stephanie Barczewski, *Myth and National Identity in Nineteenth-Century Britain: The Legends of King Arthur and Robin Hood* (Oxford, 2000), 7–8, 39–9, 44. The Camelot myth probably lent added resonance to the Duke of Wellington's forename.
[164] Simon Keynes, 'The Cult of King Alfred the Great', *Anglo-Saxon England*, 28 (1999), 289–341. The millennial anniversary of Alfred's birth in 1849 was celebrated enthusiastically.
[165] Rosemary Sweet, *The Writing of Urban Histories in Eighteenth-Century England* (Oxford, 1997), 62.

versions of the national past—Gothic, Whig, and Catholic—the first two of which offered competing national stories, while the last denied the concept of a national story altogether. The Whig view, which formed the basis of histories by Sharon Turner (1814–23) and T. B. Macaulay (1848–55), dwelt on the shortcomings of medieval Christendom, the strength of the common law, the country's destiny as the leading Protestant nation, the religious settlement and national achievements of Elizabeth, and the Glorious Revolution. Much of this was accounted conventional wisdom, but academically the interpretation was on the defensive, having been powerfully challenged by the Catholic historian John Lingard, whose *History of England to the Accession of William and Mary* (1819–30) comprised ten volumes of meticulous scholarship, dispassionate language, and quietly polemical intent. In defending the medieval Church and in reasserting the importance of canon law, Lingard effectively implied that the Reformation had been imposed from above by force, and that England was merely an imagined nation, the fabrication of a succession of Protestant historians in the Tudor and Stuart periods.[166]

Gothic (or Saxon) history was based on the Teutonic thesis, which held that England's institutions, language, and customary beliefs—including the much-vaunted love of liberty—derived from the North German tribes and village communities of the Dark Ages. Like related trends in architecture and literature, the theory had survived since the late Stuart period, but it gained fresh inspiration in the early nineteenth century, thanks partly to the German War of Liberation against Napoleon, and partly to new ideas of biological development. The historian Francis Palgrave, for example, believed that nations formed habits like children, and that characteristics thus acquired were then handed down to later generations in the blood, a sort of 'Lamarckian history'.[167] Here was the basis for a credible theory of English nationality and race, but it stalled in the 1830s when, without entirely abandoning the Teutonic thesis, Palgrave muddied his own waters by adopting elements of Whig history.[168] Influenced in part by the pre-millenarian Edward Irving, he now claimed that imperial Rome was the fourth and final monarchy providentially foretold in the book of Daniel, and that Roman law, not Teutonic customary law, was still the basis of authority in Europe, having passed to Germans and then (in England's case) to Normans at the Conquest. Palgrave's ideal polity was the federation or commonwealth of

---

[166] Edwin Jones, *John Lingard and the Pursuit of Historical Truth* (Brighton, 2001); id., *The English Nation: The Great Myth* (Stroud, 1998), 168–217.

[167] For this phrase, and for the subject in general, see Roger Smith, 'European Nationality, Race, and Commonwealth in the Writings of Sir Francis Palgrave, 1788–1861' in Alfred P. Smyth (ed.), *Medieval Europeans: Studies in Ethnic Identity and National Perspectives in Medieval Europe* (Houndmills, 1998): J. W. Burrow, *A Liberal Descent: Victorian Historians and the English Past* (Cambridge, 1981), 187–8; R. J. Smith, *The Gothic Bequest: Medieval institutions in British Thought, 1688–1863* (Cambridge, 1987), 140–64.   [168] Francis Palgrave's *The Rise and Progress of the English Commonwealth* (1832).

historic peoples, a notion of pressing relevance to the multinational and multiracial British Isles and Empire. He thus had no time for Mazzinian notions of the unitary state enjoying undivided sovereignty, uniform laws, and defined borders. In other words, Palgrave 'used nationality to oppose nationalism, at least in its dominant early nineteenth-century form'.[169]

These and other intellectual disagreements may help to explain why medievalism, for all its popularity, made so little political impact. Among the few MPs to take it seriously were the young high Tory William Gladstone and the young radical Tory Benjamin Disraeli. Like many others, Gladstone was exercised about the status of the religious Establishment following the legislation of 1828–9. Liberal Anglicans, it will be remembered, responded to the opening-up of civil society by demanding that the Church follow suit, while Tractarians responded to what they saw as the secularization of the State by demanding greater independence for the Church. Gladstone, by contrast, argued that the State had been contaminated, and therefore that the Church must be placed in a position of authority over it. In a remarkable manifesto of 1838, inspired by Coleridge and containing much second-hand Hegel, he challenged the supremacy of 'individual conscience', and argued that 'the system of ... individual morality' was a 'degraded' and 'injurious legacy' of Locke. Citizens should be regarded 'not as individuals, but only as constituents of the active power of ... the [national] life'. 'The state is the self-governing energy of the nation made objective.'[170] His arguments were not entirely coherent, but taken literally Gladstone seemed to be calling for the clerical elite to advise Parliament and to proclaim truths for the nation—a commonplace enough notion on some parts of the Continent, but in the British context a breathtaking return to the ideas of Filmer and Leslie in the late Stuart period. Peel was dismayed by the book (which he called 'trash'), Macaulay mocked its author as 'the rising hope of ... stern and unbending Tories', and Keble, while sympathetic, argued that the State could never be remoralized from within. A much better answer was 'the violent separation of Church and State', for even though that would lead to persecution of the former by the latter, such conflict would be redemptive. 'There is no blood of martyrs in [Gladstone's] prospect,' and therefore 'no seed of future diffusion and victory'.[171] Within ten years Gladstone had abandoned his theocratic ideas, telling a friend that he was engaged on a

---

[169] Smith, 'European Nationality', 249. Appointed Deputy Keeper of Her Majesty's Records in 1838, Palgrave began the essential task of preserving, cataloguing, and even publishing some of the thousands of official documents that had lain virtually neglected until then.

[170] W. E. Gladstone, *The State in its Relations with the Church* (1838; 4th rev. edn. 1841), i. 73–8, 88, 124, 149–50, 296–7.

[171] [John Keble], 'Gladstone—the State in its Relations with the Church', *The British Critic and Quarterly Theological Review*, 26 (1839), 396.

'process of lowering the religious tone of the State, letting it down, demoralizing it—i.e. stripping it of its ethical character, and assisting its transition into one which is *mechanical*.[172] For 'the State cannot be said now to have a conscience ...inasmuch as I think it acts...as no conscience—that is, no personal conscience (*which is the only real form of one*) can endure'.[173] There were various reasons for Gladstone's change of heart, but an important one was the collapse of the Oxford Movement, since he had looked to Tractarians to train the required clerisy of ecclesiastical leaders.

Gladstone was a leading member of a group called the Young Gentlemen, whose aim was to establish an Anglican near-monopoly of education. The same epithet was adopted by members of Young England, but their movement was very different in content and style, being social and economic rather than religious and moral. Its main texts both appeared in 1845: a newspaper of the same name, published by Bentley, and *Sybil: Or, The Two Nations*, Disraeli's brilliant exposé of the moral and economic gulf between rich and poor. At one level Disraeli, Lord John Manners, George Smythe, and Alexander Baillie-Cochrane were frondeurs, out to make their mark within the Conservative Party by attacking a Peelite leadership that showed little sign of promoting them. Even so, their criticisms cannot be dismissed, if only because so many contemporary writers agreed in decrying the 'whirlwind of money-making', as Disraeli called it, and the resulting decay of paternalism and deference.[174] Young England's solution was to go backwards to the Middle Ages, to a decentralized agrarian society based on great estates and smallholdings, and to modes of manufacture based on guilds and apprenticeship. This was not whimsy or fantasy, but intended as practical politics. It would, however, cease to be practical politics in 1846 when the Corn Laws—the only realistic instrument for carrying such policies into effect—were repealed, after which Disraeli like Gladstone was forced to start again.[175]

Gladstone had been concerned to promote religious nationality, while nationality and Englishness would remain the most significant planks of Disraeli's political philosophy,[176] weapons against Cobdenite cosmopolitanism and middle-class internationalism generally. But although the Gothic, the

[172] Gladstone to Henry Manning, 19 Apr. 1846, in *Correspondence on Church and Religion of William Ewart Gladstone*, ed. D. C. Lathbury (1910), ii. 272 (italics added); Hilton, *Age of Atonement*, 340–72.

[173] Gladstone to Newman, 19 Apr. 1845, in *Correspondence on Church and Religion of Gladstone*, i. 72 (italics added).

[174] 'The principle of the feudal system, the principle which was practically operated upon, was the noblest principle, the grandest, the most magnificent and benevolent that ever was conceived by sage, or ever practised by patriot' (*Selected Speeches of the Earl of Beaconsfield*, ed. T. E. Kebbel (1882), i. 47–52, 57).

[175] His antiquarian father had helped to create the public's fascination both with the past and with national identity (Isaac D'Israeli, *Commentaries on the Life and Reign of Charles I* (1828–31))

[176] J. P. Parry, 'Disraeli and England', *HJ* 43 (2000), 699–728.

Middle Ages, the Olden Time, the State, and the nation all had powerful literary advocates, the mix fell very far short of a Risorgimento. Most Englishmen continued to regard themselves as citizens of the world, and took genuine delight in landscapes and cityscapes not their own.

FROM ROMANTICISM TO SOCIALISM

Among those who did like to extol the beauties of home—the Lake District, say, or the Wye Valley—were the first-generation Romantics. Most of what was discussed in the last section could be described as Romantic, but the concept of a Romantic movement is problematic, partly because it is so capacious. Even if confined to poetry it has to take in the first wave (Wordsworth, Coleridge, Southey), who abandoned their youthful republicanism for high Toryism, as well as the second wave (Byron, Shelley, Keats), all of whom died before they could make the same transition. Then there was William Blake, who was thirteen years older than any of the first group, lived three years longer than any of the second, yet never abandoned his radicalism. Despite these variations, many generalizations have been put forward. Whereas eighteenth-century moralists tempered sensibility with sense, Romantics are said to have spiced it with sublimity. Or it is claimed that they valued fancy more than facts, imagination more than reason, enthusiasm rather than earnestness. They privileged egotism, self-consciousness, and subjectivity, especially in relation to artistic creation. Being uncertain about their audience they had to 'create the taste' by which they were to be comprehended,[177] as a result of which originality became the main criterion of merit. They cultivated feelings of guilt, loss, and wretchedness, and fantasized about altered states of consciousness. They felt themselves to be living in epochal times, and their poetry was political in the sense of engaging with the great moral and intellectual questions of the day. Yet while all these statements apply to some Romantics, none applies to all of them, and the composite impression that emerges is a caricature.[178]

The problem is highlighted by the changing literary reputation of Lord Byron. In terms of biography and personality, of course, he has always seemed the epitome of Romantic existentialism ('The great object in life is sensation.' 'To feel that we exist, even though in pain'), the embodiment of its restlessness ('Anything rather than conjugate that terrible verb *ennuyer*'), the archetype of its tortured and tormented genius, the exemplar of its world-weary heroism. The young Tennyson would not have run along the beach wailing 'Keats is dead', nor

[177] Jon P. Klancher, *The Making of English Reading Audiences, 1790–1832* (Madison, Wis., 1987), 1, 18–46.

[178] For a shrewd analysis, see Kelvin Everest, *English Romantic Poetry: An Introduction to the Historical Context and the Literary Scene* (Milton Keynes, 1990).

was there any other writer about whom Jane Welsh would have written, 'If they had said the sun or the moon was gone out of the heavens, it could not have struck me with the idea of a more awful and dreary blank in the creation than the words, "Byron is dead".'[179] It was thanks to the products of Byron's morbid imagination, not Coleridge's, that crying, swooning, and fainting became part of the armoury of the young of both sexes. Having been held in low esteem for much of the last century and a half, his poetry is once more critically admired, correctly so, but also thanks in part to the present-day's concern with style, marketing, and self-invention, rather than with content. Likewise, his cynical empiricism pleases the postmodern desire for inconsequentiality much more than the other Romantics' Platonic concern for transcendental truths. And whereas Wordsworth and Coleridge believed that poetic acts of creation obeyed organic laws of development, Byron's pretence in his masterpiece *Don Juan* that he had no control over where his text was going suits the present-day tendency to see Romanticism in historicist terms.

Yet if Romanticism is judged in terms of its content—i.e. as one of the ways of thinking that contested mechanical philosophy—then Byron can hardly count as a Romantic at all. Take religion, for example. As young men, Blake and Coleridge were strongly influenced by Unitarian friends. Wordsworth was staunchly Anglican, but Unitarians such as Crabb Robinson were his earliest admirers and promoters. All three were creationists and universalists.

> To see a World in a grain of sand,
> And a Heaven in a wild flower,
> Hold Infinity in the palm of your hand
> And Eternity in an hour.[180]

Like Unitarians they believed that God was exclusively a God of love and that human beings were born innocent. In Wordsworth's famous lines, the child came into the world 'trailing clouds of glory'.[181] By contrast Byron, for all his scoffing bravado, accepted the other-worldly beliefs of the evangelical Establishment. Indeed, his conviction of original sin and damnation was laden with extra doom in his case because of an inherited Calvinism. Secondly, most Romantic poets purveyed the evolutionary scientists' sense of optimism. For example, John Keats, licensed apothecary and general practitioner, was fascinated by the interaction of mind and matter and considered poetry to be a healing art like medicine.[182] Wordsworth regarded the natural growth of human

---

[179] Jane Welsh to Carlyle, in J. A. Froude, *Thomas Carlyle: A History of the First Forty Years of His Life 1795–1835* (1882), i. 214. See plate 11.   [180] William Blake, *Auguries of Innocence* (written 1800–3). [181] Stephen Prickett, *Coleridge and Wordsworth: The Poetry of Growth* (Cambridge, 1970); id., *Romanticism and Religion: The Tradition of Coleridge and Wordsworth in the Victorian Church* (Cambridge, 1976), 70–90.   [182] Hermione De Almeida, *Romantic Medicine and John Keats* (New York, 1991).

communities as analogous to geological processes, and in *The Excursion* (1814) he imagined a complex series of interactions taking place between national, natural, and individual histories. The poem is said to have influenced the uniformitarian scientists of the 1830s in their search for physical laws of Creation that were 'directionalist', but not based on scientific materialism.[183] Davy's experiments inspired Coleridge to believe in 'causal powers of matter', while in *Prometheus Unbound* (1820), Percy Bysshe Shelley proffered a utopian view of 'progressive, willed evolutionary change' as informed by the ideas of Laplace, Lagrange, Davy, and Erasmus Darwin. Byron was equally interested in such matters, yet took an entirely different view. In the first place, he emphasized the contingent, chaotic, contradictory nature of creation, and had little sense of organic development; while in so far as he did have any sense of change over time, he was a degenerationist. These opinions led him to side with the 'enlightened' and mechanical scientists of the Establishment. His *Prometheus* (1816) and *Cain* (1821) have been seen as ripostes to Shelley, explicitly appealing to Cuvier's ideas of 'Christian deteriorationism', catastrophism, and 'eventual extinction'.[184] Shipwrecks rather than fruitfulness dominated his imagination. So, for all his anti-Establishment attitudes and naughty-boy rebelliousness, and the enormous popularity of his poetry among the working classes, including Chartists and radicals,[185] ideologically Byron was the opposite of counter-cultural.

Two real counter-culturalists were Southey and Coleridge, who as very young men became enthused with the idea of Pantisocracy, or utopian socialism, meaning communities of equals where all labour was shared and no property was held in private. That brief flirtation apart, Romantics endorsed the individualism at the heart of the mechanical philosophy while rejecting its rationalism, whereas with socialists it was the other way round. Needless to say, no one had any conception of what would now be called state socialism, and the ideas of Frenchmen such as Saint-Simon, Fourier, Blanqui, and Blanc made little impact. The only effective brand of socialism was Owenism, which one historian has described as 'probably the most radical counter-culture that had existed in England since the time of the Civil War'.[186] Robert Owen, a self-made Welshman, was first employed by a firm of Manchester cotton-spinners as one of the new breed of industrial managers. In 1800 he was given a share of his father-in-law's mills at

[183] John Wyatt, *Wordsworth and the Geologists* (Cambridge, 1995), 128–92.

[184] Ralph O'Connor, 'Mammoths and Maggots: Byron and the Geology of Cuvier', *Romanticism*, 5 (1999), 26–42.

[185] Engels commented that Byron's poetry was 'cherished' by working men, and certainly, if the number of cheap and pirated editions means anything, *Don Juan* had as great an impact on the popular imagination as any work since Paine's *Rights of Man* (St Clair, *Reading Nation*, 322–36).

[186] Jose Harris, in *London Review of Books*, 5/17 (1983), 8–9. See Barbara Taylor, *Eve and the New Jerusalem: Socialism and Feminism in the Nineteenth Century* (1983).

New Lanark on the Clyde, made himself the dominant partner, and established a model factory, model village, and model schools. At this stage his key idea—paternalist rather than socialist—was that benevolent management would improve both behaviour and productivity. Operatives were not to be exploited, children were not to be overworked, while instead of alcohol he prescribed singing, dancing, and physical exercises to provide the required uplift. Owen wrote up his achievements in *A New View of Society: Essays on the Principle of the Formation of the Human Character* (1813–16) and *Report to the County of Lanark* (1821), as a result of which thousands of visitors came to see the mills for themselves. By this time he was a national celebrity, and had come to see himself as a seer, capable of reforming the world. His next step was to establish a number of farming villages based on the communal ownership of land, the largest being Harmony Hall at Queenwood in Hampshire (1839). It is tempting to dismiss such projects as pastoral and nostalgic, but the enthusiasm shown for these and similar schemes by Spence, Cobbett, and O'Connor indicates how deeply felt was the desire for self-sufficiency and for independence of the business cycle.[187]

Owen*ism* dated from the 1820s, during which its founder devoted much time and even more money to setting up a number of communities in America, starting with New Harmony in Indiana (1824). Some succeeded, some did not, depending on locality and personality, a truth which Owen did not want to acknowledge, being anxious to establish the viability of a system, but the movement as a whole was an astonishing success, and soon spread to the British Isles. However, two of its greatest sources of strength—religion and gender—were also causes of internal tension. Owen professed himself a militant atheist, yet in America especially and also in England many of his communities developed millenarian and ecstatic tendencies. Most previous utopian sects had been inspired by godly zeal, and the revivalist mode was probably essential to the successful transmission of Owenism, but the idea of a 'secularized version of millennial sectarianism' jarred with various elements of the founder's philosophy.[188] Meanwhile, women joined the movement in droves, attracted partly by Owen's advocacy of equal education, collectivized family life, legalized divorce, and birth control (he regarded marriage as a priestly rite and a form of sexual slavery). No other cause gave anything like as much scope for women to participate actively in political and social protest, and it was under its banner that militant feminists such as Anna Wheeler, Emma Martin, Fanny Wright, and Eliza Macauley became iconic figures. In some instances a shared concern for female equality, especially in matters of sexual relations, brought Owenites

---

[187] Malcolm Chase, *'The People's Farm': English Radical Agrarianism 1775–1840* (Oxford, 1988), 121–89.

[188] J. F .C. Harrison, *Robert Owen and the Owenites in Britain and America: The Quest for the New Moral World* (1969), 91–139.

together across wide disparities of status and wealth. However, developments at the grass roots often proved more troublesome than platform rhetoric. Attempts by some community leaders to institutionalize free love proved destructive, while more prosaically it often turned out that men were happy to let women share in masculine tasks but drew the line at helping with the housework.[189]

The third stage of Owen's career was political. He was one of the first to mobilize unskilled labourers, and founded the short-lived Grand National Consolidated Trades Union (1834). He also helped to establish the workers' co-operative movement, the first manifestation of which was the Rochdale Society of Equitable Pioneers in 1844. By that date there were sixty-five branches of the Rational Society, the aim of which was to spread the Owenite message by means of schools, libraries, and meeting houses, while its journal, *The New Moral World* (1834–45), had an estimated readership in the hundreds of thousands. It was also largely thanks to Owen that child-centred approaches to education moved from the old narrow Unitarian circles into something approaching the mainstream. Among those influenced were Samuel Wilderspin (a Swedenborgian and a phrenologist), James Buchanan (who helped to found the infant schools movement), and the Chartists William Lovett and John Collins.

Leslie Stephen described Owen as 'one of those intolerable bores who are the salt of the earth',[190] while Engels dismissed his followers as peaceable utopians and 'utterly hopeless'. The movement certainly collapsed very suddenly. Within three years of Owen being thrown off the governing body of Queenwood (1845), the Rational Society shut up shop. His insistent claim that cooperation was compatible with technological advance and economic growth was decisively rejected, and capitalism triumphed with the adoption of ever more measures tending towards free trade.[191] Furthermore, middle-class ideals of domesticated womanhood had percolated down to working-class communities, and militated against the prospect of a sexual revolution. And yet, certain of Owen's ideas, like certain of Wordsworth's,[192] proved more congenial to the following generation than to his own. In particular his psychological theories, which were heterodox in his own day, influenced public doctrine in the mid-Victorian period. He held that actions were determined by character, and that free will and moral responsibility were therefore non-existent. Character in turn was formed by circumstances, but in the case of children especially it might be possible to develop characters for the better by environmental controls. Few in the later generation agreed with

---

[189] Taylor, *Eve and the New Jerusalem*. Coleridge, who was not a house-proud person, had nevertheless anticipated this problem by seeking, back in his Pantisocracy days, to develop a houseworking machine.

[190] *DNB.*

[191] Gregory Claeys, *Citizens and Saints: Politics and Anti-Politics in Early British Socialism* (Cambridge, 1989), 208–60; id., *Machinery, Money, and the Millennium: From Moral Economy to Socialism, 1815–1860* (Princeton, 1987), 130–65.   [192] See below, p. 634.

his inference that the legal punishment of crime should be abolished, but many accepted the premiss about character and free will and allowed it to soften their approach to malefactors.

As this chapter has demonstrated, by 1840 post-millennial evangelicalism and Utilitarian rationalism were in the process of losing their importance as solid centres for the governing classes, and were giving way on the one hand to Liberal Anglican and evolutionary perspectives, and on the other to Tractarian and pre-millenarian longings. Sir James Stephen of the Colonial Office, a late representative of the Clapham Sect, expressed contempt for all the many do-gooding misfits who were clamouring for attention:

It is a prophetical age. We have Nominalists who, from the monosyllabic 'Church' educe a long line of shadowy forms, hereafter to arise and reign on Episcopal or patriarchal thrones—and Realists, who foresee the moral regeneration of the land by means of union workhouses, of emigrant ships, or of mechanics' institutes—and Medievals, who promise the return of Astræa in the persons of Bede and Bernard redivivi—and Mr Carlyle, who offers most eloquent vows for the reappearance of the heroes who are to set all things right—and profound interpreters of the Apocalypse, who discover the woes impending over England in chastisement of the impiety which moved Lord Melbourne to introduce Mr. Owen to the Queen of England.[193]

Stephen's mocking tone betrayed his complacency. So many voices were raised against mechanism, and from so many directions, that such protesters might seem to have been in the majority, stymied only by their own diversity and lack of political unity. On the other hand, it is often those who sense that they have lost the battle for opinion who shout the loudest and write the most.

---

[193] Sir James Stephen, 'The Clapham Sect', *ER* 80 (1844), 304–7.

CHAPTER 8

Politics in the time of Melbourne and Peel, 1833–1846

Grey was cockahoop following the election of December 1832, and confident that he could rely on 'the sterling good sense of the people of England' to resist the violent designs of Radicals and republicans, and to see through the 'infatuated violence' of the Tories.[1] Even the lugubrious James Graham, the able First Lord of the Admiralty, looked forward to the 'great experiment' and feared 'no danger' from 'the rapid progress of knowledge, the spirit of liberty and independence'.[2] One manifestation of that spirit was the large number of petitions against slavery, which was duly abolished throughout British dominions in 1833. Some Radicals complained about the generous compensation offered to slave-owners, but could not puncture the smug mood of national self-satisfaction. Yet for Whigs this was the high point, to be followed by a decade of decline.

FROM REFORM TO REPEAL: THE NARRATIVE RESUMED

Part of the problem was political. The Cabinet was full of prima donnas who unmanned the Prime Minister, and none more so than his bullying son-in-law Lord Durham. 'Resolute in his own escapism and feeble in everything else',[3] Grey was soon looking for an excuse to get out. Althorp, who had been so reliable during the reform debates, also sought 'happiness' in retirement. Russell, on the other hand, was feeling like a tennis player who has won the Grand Slam in his first season and then has nothing left to play for. The impetuosity for which he became notorious was really an attempt to recapture the glamour that had been his during the reform crisis. Then there was Brougham, a potentially great statesman in so far as he possessed energy, vision, and steadfastness, but he was also irritable, vain, domineering, and quarrelsome. It was one of the leakiest cabinets there has ever been.

[1] Grey to Graham, 29 Dec. 1832, Graham MSS, Old Files, 54.
[2] Graham to Joseph Saul, 3 Jan. 1833, and Graham to Thomas Acland, 14 Jan. 1833, Graham MSS, General Series, 20/28.
[3] William Thomas, *The Philosophic Radicals: Nine Studies in Theory and Practice 1817–1841* (Oxford, 1979), 356.

Outdoors, and especially in the rural South, there was a serious crisis of authority, to which the Home Secretary, Melbourne, responded with brutal vigour. He offered huge rewards for information on the Swing rioters, exhorted magistrates to punish them vigorously, and used the regular Army to deal with trouble spots. Admittedly, only nineteen of the 252 rioters sentenced to death were actually hanged, but four or five hundred were exposed to the hazards of the voyage to Australia in convict ships. In 1834 Melbourne sought to counter the 'democratic tyranny' of trade unions by securing the prosecution of six agricultural labourers from a village near Dorchester. These so-called Tolpuddle Martyrs were transported for having undertaken a perfectly respectable and lawful demonstration,[4] and took their place in line with Levellers and Luddites as milestones on the long march of Labour. These actions, which were surprisingly robust for someone with Melbourne's reputation for amiable nonchalance, damaged the image of a Government ostentatiously dedicated to liberty and popular rights.

Worse still was the state of Ireland, which as Althorp foresaw was 'incompatible with the existence of an administration wishing to act and being supported upon liberal principles. It will turn us out.'[5] The ministers most responsible were Melbourne, Graham, Chief Secretary Stanley, and Anglesey, who had resumed the post of Lord Lieutenant. Well-meaning, well-informed, and determined to take advantage of the goodwill which they hoped had been created by emancipation, they advanced nineteen bills for solving the country's social and economic problems. In a major concession to the Roman Catholic hierarchy, a Board of Education was established in 1831 to oversee a new system of state-aided national schools, open to children of all denominations, and offering non-denominational religious instruction. A Board of Works was established, and a Commission to examine the question of tithes. Yet instead of calling his agitation off, O'Connell merely turned his attention to the repeal of the Union and restoration of the old Dublin Parliament. Likewise many priests, having been drawn into politics on the emancipation issue, now seemed reluctant to resume a purely spiritual and pastoral role. Before long Anglesey's letters, like those of so many viceroys before him, were painting 'a fearful picture of impending civil war', denouncing 'dastardly and mischievous' agitators, and begging for armed forces to quell the 'unruly spirit of triumphant insubordination'.[6] 'Things are now come to that pass that the question is whether [O'Connell] or I shall govern Ireland.'[7] In January 1831 the Irish leader was briefly arrested, the first of many

---

[4] Joyce Marlow, *The Tolpuddle Martyrs* (1971).

[5] Althorp to Ebrington, 30 Dec. 1832, BL, Wellesley Papers, Add. MS 37306, fo. 308, quoted in Ellis Archer Wasson, *Whig Renaissance: Lord Althorp and the Whig Party 1782–1845* (New York, 1987), 307.

[6] Graham to Anglesey, 9 July and 21 Aug. 1832, Graham MSS, Old Files, Letters, A/49.

[7] Marquess of Anglesey, *One-Leg: The Life and Letters of Henry William Paget, First Marquess of Anglesey 1768–1854* (1961), 247.

colonial malcontents to be demonized by the Government in London as though they were personally responsible for anti-British sentiment. It was an unwise move since, besides commanding thirty-nine Irish MPs committed to repeal, O'Connell was actually a force for legality and moderation, but the British Establishment could not see this because of its visceral objection to the idea of a separate government for Ireland, even one that remained subject to the Crown. Such an outcome would signal the 'total eclipse of the power and glory of the British empire', and was 'utterly and entirely out of the question'.[8] When O'Connell moved for repeal of the Union in 1834, he was defeated by 523 votes to thirty-eight, only one English member voting in the minority.

Long before then Graham had come to the conclusion that there was 'no alternative left but to govern by force, or to yield to combined violence... Ireland is rent asunder by violent extremes, and if the middle course be not safe or expedient, then we must either revert to Protestant Ascendancy, or rule by the mandate of Catholic agitators.'[9] In January 1833 he was even more blunt: 'Until that unhappy and insane people be re-conquered there will be no peace.'[10] Determined to be tough on Irish crime as well as on the causes of Irish crime, Grey allowed Stanley to introduce a draconian measure of coercion, including a ban on all public meetings. Althorp was dismayed, and Brougham attempted to defuse the situation by entering into secret negotiations with O'Connell,[11] in which he apparently promised that coercion would be watered down. There was a fuss when rumours of these talks leaked out, and the Government was criticized for having truck with terrorists, but the main damage was to Cabinet solidarity.

Since public works and education would take years to have any beneficial effects, a dramatic gesture was needed. Anglesey's most insistent refrain was that British government concessions always came too late. 'The only way of rendering O'Connell harmless is by anticipating him, and preventing him from having the advantage of the initiative in all healing measures.' What was needed was for Government to 'legislate for Ireland with the rapidity of lightning'. 'Rapidity of lightning is not our characteristic,' noted Graham drily, but he agreed that 'every measure of an ameliorating and soothing character should emanate from the Government and not appear to be forced on them by O'Connell'.[12] There was scope for such a gesture in the area of ecclesiastical

[8] Ibid. 243.
[9] Graham to Anglesey, 21 Aug. 1832, in *The Life and Letters of Sir James Graham 1792–1861*, ed. Charles Stuart Parker (1907), i. 173.
[10] Graham to Anglesey, 21 Aug. 1832 and 17 Jan. 1833, Graham MSS, Old Files, Letters, A/49.
[11] The negotiations were conducted through E. J. Littleton, who had succeeded as Chief Secretary after Stanley became Colonial Secretary in April 1833.
[12] Anglesey to Graham, 12 Feb. 1832 and 30 July 1833, Graham to Anglesey, 2 Aug. 1831, Graham MSS, Old Files, Letters, A/49.

policy. Emancipation had been offered too grudgingly to have done any real good, but maybe the orange was not yet sucked dry. Accordingly it was decided to tackle a problem which the Irish had not yet focused on. The Church of Ireland—effectively the Church of England *in* Ireland—was enormously wealthy, with a notional revenue from tithes, property, and endowments of over £800,000 per annum, yet it served only a tiny fraction of the population[13] and allegedly more than one-third of its incumbents were non-resident. So, however one looked at it, the institution failed the Benthamite test of utility. Accordingly, the Government's Irish Church Temporalities Bill of 1833 proposed *inter alia* to suppress ten out of twenty-two bishoprics, tax large stipends, augment low ones, abolish Church rate or cess, and use the money saved for social and charitable purposes. The last proposal (Clause 147) was Russell's initiative and backed by Althorp and Durham, but it was strenuously opposed by Stanley and other ministers, by the King, the peers, most Churchmen, and most Opposition MPs on the grounds that to confiscate Church funds and use them for non-religious purposes (lay appropriation) would be a breach of faith with donors. No doubt some of the opposition was synthetic, but it was understandable. During fifteen months of fierce debate the Whigs had promised that their Reform Act would not lead to de-Christianization or the confiscation of property, yet here they were, in the first Session of the reformed Parliament, advocating the spoliation of an Apostolic Church. So bitter was the opposition that in June 1833 Russell agreed to surrender Clause 147 on the grounds that 'this country could not stand a revolution once a year'. Wellington, Peel, and Blomfield then urged acceptance of the amended Bill, given that the Conservatives were hardly in a position to form a Government, and this was hardly the issue to fight an election on. The Bill passed, but instead of appeasing it merely angered the Irish Party, whose members felt let down by the last-minute compromise.

Political events then moved rapidly. In May 1834 Russell 'upset the coach' by again proposing to use the confiscated revenues of the Church of Ireland for the purposes of poor relief and education. Within the month Stanley, Graham, Richmond, and Ripon (the so-called 'Derby Dilly' group) resigned from the Cabinet, and about forty other MPs signalled their disaffiliation from the Government. In July Althorp quit in protest against renewed coercion, and this in turn prompted Grey's immediate resignation. Melbourne became Prime Minister, after which Althorp reluctantly agreed to remain on condition that the prohibition on public meetings was lifted. Grey was furious because, although he had wanted to go, it looked as though he had been the victim of a coup, and he continued to bully his successor for some time to come. Althorp was just as

---

[13] It was reliably calculated in 1834 that 80.9% of the population was Catholic, 10.7% belonged to the Anglican Church of Ireland, and 8.1% was Presbyterian.

unhappy to have stayed, and when in November his father died and he became Earl Spencer, he resigned for good. Then, while the Whigs were arguing over who should succeed him at the Exchequer, William IV 'kicked out' the lot of them,[14] and called instead on Wellington, who sensibly deferred to Peel,[15] who immediately dissolved Parliament.

Peel was the last Prime Minister to be installed by the King against the wishes of a large Commons majority, and the first to issue an explicit address, ostensibly to his constituents but really to the country. He called his Tamworth Manifesto a 'frank and explicit declaration of principle', unlike the usual 'vague and unmeaning professions' espoused by politicians. In reality his promises to correct 'proven abuses', redress 'real grievances', and support 'judicious reforms' were platitudinous. The document's significance was not substantive but political. Firstly, it signalled Peel's willingness to lead the party after two years when this had seemed in doubt, not least because of his 'war with Wellington'.[16] (Still smarting from his rejection by Oxford in 1829, Peel was especially embittered when the Duke became Chancellor of the University in June 1834.) Secondly, Tamworth indicated that the Conservative leadership would pursue liberal Tory rather than Ultra Tory policies, notably by accepting the Reform Act as 'a final and irrevocable settlement'. The Manifesto must have had some effect, since in the ensuing election (January 1835) the number of Conservative MPs increased from 175 to 273, but that still left them in a minority of 112. Nor could it prevent Whig, Liberal, Irish, Dissenting, and Radical leaders from making the Lichfield House Compact in March. In it they pledged their joint opposition to Peel's Government, and a few weeks later, following a series of reverses in the Commons, the last on Russell's motion for appropriation, Peel was obliged to resign. It is often said that the election was a defeat for the King, because he failed to emulate his father's success in 1784, when the voters endorsed the decision to install Pitt. It was indeed a defeat for the King, but for a different reason. George III's triumph had been pyrrhic, in so far as it polarized politics on party lines, and thereby reduced the monarch's power to mediate. It seems likely that William IV was aiming not so much to dish the Whigs as to recover some freedom of action by bringing about a coalition. During the 1833–4 Session Peel had voted with ministers in fourteen of the twenty-four divisions,[17] hoping thereby to stiffen their resolve against the Radicals, and the King felt encouraged by this to hope that Melbourne might

[14] Greville, *Memoirs*, iii. 144 (16 Nov. 1834).
[15] But he acted as locum tenens from 17 November to 10 December, running the Government virtually single-handed while Peel hurried back from Italy.
[16] Élie Halévy, *A History of the English People in the Nineteenth Century*, iii: *The Triumph of Reform 1830–1841*, trans. E. I. Watkin, 2nd edn. (1950), 171.
[17] That is, more frequently than 87% of the Government's own nominal supporters (Ian Newbould, *Whiggery and Reform, 1830–41: The Politics of Government* (Stanford, Calif., 1990), 326 n. 36).

offer places to Wellington and Peel. Unfortunately for him, his subsequent sacking of Melbourne and the Lichfield House Compact polarized parties along the old lines, leaving the monarch more squeezed out than ever.

These events did not bring all cooperation between the front benches to an end—it was said in 1836, for example, that 'Peel and J. Russell completely frater-nise'[18]—but the terms were different now that there was no prospect of a realignment. Everyone sensed that the Conservative leader was biding his time, controlling the midfield, keeping ministers on the defensive, and waiting for the right moment to strike. He also displayed a degree of tactical acumen not evident before, most notably over local government reform. Passed in September 1835, the Municipal Corporations Act replaced 178 closed boroughs by bodies of councillors elected by ratepayers and with power to levy rates. It reflected min-isters' genuine concern for community and responsible citizenship, but it also had a partisan purpose since the closed boroughs, with their powers of local patronage and control over charitable bequests, were havens of Toryism. Joseph Parkes, an indefatigable Birmingham solicitor who helped to coordinate the Government's electoral and registration campaigns, gleefully prophesied that the Act would 'break to pieces the Tory cliques of the old corporators'.[19]

The Corporation Bill will be poison to Tory-ism . . . I am organising for country meetings and local deputations from the towns . . . When the Bill is public the meetings will go off like minute guns in Martello towers. Nothing but *agitation—agitation—agitation* will on this question keep the Cabinet up to the mark or beat off the Tories. The Household Suffrage will be the grand field of battle . . . [that and] a thorough purge of the existing Corporators. Peel must denounce it: that will place him in his proper anti-reforming position.[20]

As it turned out, Parkes was mistaken on two counts. Although Peel insisted on certain amendments, he defended the Government against much more robust ones from Opposition peers, and so helped the measure to pass.[21] Secondly, the Act in practice did 'hardly any, if any mischief' to the Conservative Party.[22] One reason was that, contrary to what many historians have assumed, the new municipal franchise was actually narrower than that enacted for parliamentary boroughs in 1832. For although household or ratepayer suffrage might seem a good deal *more* generous than the £10 occupier qualification decreed for Westminster elections, it was limited by a stipulation that voters must have

---

[18] Morpeth to Mulgrave, Sept. 1835, quoted ibid. 187.

[19] Parkes to Durham, 23 Oct. 1835, Lambton MSS, quoted in Philip Salmon, *Electoral Reform at Work: Local Politics and National Parties, 1832–1841* (Woodbridge, 2002), 215.

[20] Joseph Parkes to Lord Durham, 1 June 1835, Lambton MSS, quoted in Thomas, *Philosophic Radicals*, 280.

[21] G. B. A. M. Finlayson, 'The Politics of Municipal Reform, 1835', *HER* 81 (1966), 673–92.

[22] Francis Bonham to Peel, 27 Oct. 1840, Peel MS 40428, fo. 342.

resided and paid rates for at least three years, whereas only one year was requisite in the case of the parliamentary franchise. So although Liberals and Radicals swept the board in the first municipal elections (1835), and consequently dominated most of the new councils, this may have had less to do with the social composition of the electorate than with a natural desire for change on the part of first-time voters. That would also explain why the Conservatives did best in the few places (such as Nottingham and Bristol) where Liberals had been in control of the old corporations.[23] In many towns the Conservatives' fight-back began in 1836, since one-third of councillors had to be re-elected annually, and their efforts registered in 1839 when they captured twenty-four corporations from the Liberals.[24] Municipal reform was the supreme achievement of Melbourne's second Government, but from a narrow party perspective it was a grave disappointment.

In 1837 another general election had to be held as a result of the death of William IV and succession of the 18-year-old Queen Victoria. The Conservative representation jumped from 273 to 313, leaving them only thirty-two adrift of the Government, and they also had a majority in English seats, forcing Melbourne to depend on his Irish allies.[25] The political scene now appeared extremely confused. Peers scented a Conservative backlash in the country, and were anxious to compensate for their loss of influence over the Commons by establishing their independence. Accordingly many followed Lord Lyndhurst, who directed a number of wrecking amendments against Government legislation, notably on Irish municipal reform. Ministers probably welcomed some of these, and only pretended to be cross, whereas Peel was fearful that Lyndhurst's tactics would undermine his attempt to present the Conservatives as middle-of-the-road. Several times he divided with the Government, partly to save it from the Radicals but also to marginalize his own Ultras. Meanwhile, Wellington could almost be regarded as an 'honorary member' of the administration, so often did Melbourne consult him over how to steer legislation through the Lords. 'The Duke of Wellington and Sir Robert Peel have behaved very well,' Melbourne told the Queen 'with tears in his eyes'. 'They have helped us a good deal; some of the *other* Tories have not behaved so well, and have been factious; when Sir Robert Peel is not there they give trouble; but they don't dare to do so when he is there.'[26]

In these circumstances the Government naturally proceeded with caution. The Corn Laws and ballot were declared to be open questions, and Russell

[23] B. Keith-Lucas, *The English Local Government Franchise: A Short History* (Oxford, 1952), 57–8.
[24] Philip Salmon, 'Local Politics and Partisanship: The Electoral Impact of Municipal Reform, 1835', *Parliamentary History*, 19 (2000), 370–1; id., *Electoral Reform*, 210–48.
[25] And also on the few remaining Radicals, whose group had fared even worse at the polls.
[26] Queen Victoria's journal, 23 Dec. 1837, quoted in L. G. Mitchell, *Lord Melbourne, 1779–1848* (Oxford, 1997), 186.

acquired the contemptuous sobriquet 'Finality Jack' for declaring that further electoral reform was off the agenda (though that did not prevent ministers from being charged with 'radicalism by association' when Grote and Molesworth demanded secret voting and triennial parliaments). This abdication of responsibility mirrored the apparent passivity of the Prime Minister, of whose many aphorisms the most memorable (but possibly apocryphal) was 'What are we to say? I don't care, but we had better all be in the same story'. For all his laconic cynicism, Melbourne was an enigma, so much so that his three twentieth-century biographers might have been writing about different people. The first portrayed him à la Watteau, a languid amateur, salonard wit, erudite, charming, stylish, aristocratic, and quintessentially Whig.[27] The second presented him as a hard-nosed careerist, more Huskissonian than Whig, but above all 'ambitious, cynical, and almost wholly without principle'.[28] The last biographer depicted him as a political nonentity, who rose without trace for the simple reason that being insignificant he had hardly any enemies. Yet others have credited Melbourne with being a progenitor like Russell of philosophic Whig–Liberalism, based on a pragmatic application of political economy, historical awareness, and a belief in social progress and citizenship.[29]

Whichever view one takes, it is irrefutable that Melbourne's personal life was problematic. Spanking sessions with aristocratic ladies were harmless, not so the whippings administered to orphan girls taken into his household as objects of charity, besides which he seemed strangely dependent on a sinister and low-born private secretary. He had always been irresolute, having been smothered from birth by a protective cocoon of sisters, cousins, and aunts who took all important decisions for him. His marriage as William Lamb to Lady Caroline was a very public disaster. He became a serial cuckold, most famously of Byron (who also consorted with his mother), and had to endure Caroline's nasty kiss-and-tell novel *Glenarvon*. He seems to have shrivelled emotionally under the exposure, and it was not until after his wife's death in 1828 that his personality began to bloom. But bloom it did, for outwardly Melbourne came to seem the most composed, detached, kindly, and sagacious of counsellors. If his air of debonair imperturbability was an act, it fooled young Queen Victoria, with whom he developed a close and protective relationship, he avuncular and she coquettish. It reached a peak of intensity, and at the same time provoked a constitutional furore, in the so-called Bedchamber Crisis of 1839. Faced with the West India

[27] Lord David Cecil, *The Young Melbourne* (1939); id., *Lord M* (1954).

[28] Philip Ziegler, *Melbourne: A Biography of William Lamb* (1976), 66–7, 84–6. Huskisson was Melbourne's cousin, and regarded very much as his country cousin, i.e. gawky and gauche, but Melbourne nevertheless described him as 'the greatest practical statesman he had known' (Greville, Memoirs, ii. 46 (14 Sept. 1830)).

[29] Jonathan Parry, 'The Real Founder of the Liberal Party', *London Review of Books*, 19/19 (2 Oct. 1997), 22–3.

planters' continuing refusal to abide by the terms of the Slave Emancipation Act, the Government proposed to suspend the Jamaican Assembly and to institute direct rule for a period of five years. It was not an issue of tremendous importance to most politicians, and it seems likely that the decision of Peel and some Radicals to oppose it was taken on political grounds. At all events, in May Melbourne came within five votes of defeat and promptly resigned, as a result of which Victoria was forced, inwardly kicking and screaming, to offer his position, first to Wellington, who refused it, and then to that 'nasty wretch' Peel.[30] The latter stated that he would only accept if she gave him a public token of confidence by dismissing some of the ladies in her household, who were virtually all Whigs, and replacing them with Conservatives. This she gleefully refused to do, and so Melbourne was obliged, less gleefully, to soldier on. This episode is sometimes seen as evidence that monarchs still mattered. In reality Peel would almost certainly have taken office, with or without the ladies, if it had suited him. But he had already undertaken one minority government, and all it had done was to allow his squabbling opponents to sink their differences. Far better from his point of view to force the Liberals to stagger on in office, divided and discredited, until the electorate could have its say.[31]

These years were probably the most enjoyable of Peel's career. Editorial opinion was moving in his favour (significantly *The Times* had turned Conservative in 1834[32]), and by mid-1837 Stanley, Graham, and about thirty followers had nailed their colours firmly to his mast.[33] He held the balance in the Commons, sustaining ministers against attacks from the Radicals, while waiting for an opportunity to pull the rug from under their feet, just as Grey had pulled the rug from under Wellington's in November 1830. Indeed, Peel's withdrawal of support from Melbourne was almost sadistically gradual and calculating. Even when he attacked them over Jamaica in 1839, it was not with an intention to bring the Government down (since he was not yet ready for office), but was designed to force ministers into supporting Irish and Radical motions, which in turn would make them look extreme, and damage their prospects at the next election.

The leadership of the Liberal coalition had changed considerably since 1830. Gone were Grey, Althorp, Brougham, Graham, and Stanley. In had become

[30] Mitchell, *Melbourne*, 81, 183, 211–31, 241–3, 259–60.

[31] This lesson was lost on Peel's successor as leader of the Conservative Party, Edward Stanley, later the fourteenth Earl of Derby, who undertook minority governments in 1852, 1858–9, and 1866–8. It was *not* lost on Disraeli, who refused to form a minority government in 1873, but waited for the warring Liberals to go down to electoral defeat in 1874.

[32] Not least because of its proprietor John Walter's passionate hostility to the 'cruel' New Poor Law— not that he would receive any joy from Peel on that subject.

[33] This had been coming for some time. Stanley and Graham moved from neutral benches below the gangway to the Conservative side on 1 July 1835.

TABLE 8.1. *Election results in English counties, 1826–1841*

Year	Whigs, Liberals, Radicals	Tories, Conservatives
1826	34	48
1830	44	37
1831	73	9
1832	104	40
1835	74	70
1837	47	97
1841	20	124

Grey's son Howick, Spring Rice, Francis Baring, Duncannon, Normanby, Poulett Thompson, and Morpeth. These changes help to account for some significant policy shifts, but in the case of the most important—the adoption of free trade—political tactics also played a part. The Whigs had strengthened the landed interest by their Reform Act on the doubtful assumption that it was preponderantly on their side, so they were naturally anxious not to offend it. This explains why they punished rural malcontents so heavily, and put a brake on the slide towards free trade in corn. Here they were helped by the commercial and manufacturing boom of 1833–6, during which the Corn Laws and other urban grievances retreated into the background. However, it became clear from the results of the 1835 and 1837 elections that their agricultural support was dissipating (see Table 8.1).

Even if it was not obvious to Whig–Liberal strategists after the 1837 election that the counties were a lost cause, the immediate sequel must have convinced them. For in that year the situation changed fundamentally with the onset of the century's most acute manufacturing depression. This brought the Corn Laws back to centre stage, not because of the politicians—neither party dared to alienate the landed interest—but thanks to pressure from without. In 1839, following the Commons' contemptuous dismissal of a free-trade motion, a national Anti-Corn Law League was formed from a Manchester base. Within six years there were 225 local affiliated associations in England alone, the vast majority in Lancashire, London, and the West Riding.[34] Its parliamentary stars were Richard Cobden, a Manchester merchant and calico-printer who was elected in 1841, and a Quaker mill owner from nearby Rochdale, John Bright, who became an MP two years later. Its managing directors were George Wilson and J. B. Smith, who were responsible for the organization of meetings and mailshots—more than 9 million tracts were sent out in just one week during February 1843—and for a saturation press bombardment by *The League*, the *Anti-Bread-Tax*

---

[34] There were also thirty-five in Scotland, mainly along the Clyde–Forth–Dundee axis.

Circular, and the *Anti-Corn-Law Circular*.[35] What was new about the League was its 'culture of theatre',[36] its forays into literature (notably Ebenezer Elliott's *Corn Law Rhymes*), its money-raising bazaars, fancy dress balls, opulent banquets, ritual festivals, tea parties, lectures, and dramatic performances. Meetings were punctuated with cheering and applause, even in religious meeting houses like Exeter Hall in the Strand, and women were encouraged to participate. The emphasis on excitement, exuberance, and fun was far removed from the Clapham Sect's moralistic and retributive approach to free trade. The campaign was also defiantly provincial and Nonconformist in tone, notwithstanding London's sixty-one affiliated associations.

Unlike O'Connell's Catholic Association, from which they took some of their tactics, Leaguers could not feed on atavistic prejudices. They had to make their own music, and did so brilliantly. Rather than promote free trade on purely materialistic grounds, they made a pitch for the high moral ground. On the negative side this meant associating protectionism with trade wars, military establishments, and armaments manufactures: 'War is the aristocratical trade; war is the aristocratical passion; war is the aristocratical convenience for bringing forward the junior members of titled families, instead of providing for them out of the family property.'[37] On the positive side it meant associating free trade with universal and everlasting peace, a point first emphasized in August 1841 when a celebrated meeting took place of nearly 700 ministers to proclaim the 'politics of the Gospel', and to indulge post-millennial fantasies of 'Christian brotherhood and commerce'.[38] 'I see in the Free Trade principle', said Cobden, 'that which shall act on the moral world as the principle of gravitation in the universe—drawing men together, thrusting aside the antagonism of race, and creed, and language, and uniting us in the bonds of eternal peace.'[39] God had created a 'harmonized and mutually dependent system' of differing climates, natural resources, and national aptitudes:

All these belong to each other! Let their influence be reciprocal: let one minister to another; be the interest of each the interest of all, and let all minister to each; they are one in wisdom and beneficence, and show forth as resplendently as the starry heavens the glory of benevolent Providence.[40]

[35] Norman McCord, *The Anti-Corn Law League 1838–1846* (1958), 137–87.
[36] Paul A. Pickering and Alex Tyrrell, *The People's Bread: A History of the Anti-Corn Law League* (2000), 191–216.
[37] W. J. Fox, 'English Wars: Their Causes, Cost, and Consequences', cited in Richard and Edward Garnett, *Life of W. J. Fox: Public Teacher and Social Reformer 1786–1864* (1910), 271–2.
[38] *Report of the Conference of Ministers of All Denominations on the Corn Laws, held in Manchester* (1841).
[39] *Speeches on Questions of Public Policy by Richard Cobden*, ed. John Bright and James E. Thorold Rogers (1870), i. 362–3 (15 Jan. 1846).
[40] W. J. Fox, 'Religious Aspect of Free Trade', *The League*, 19 May 1845, cited in Richard Francis Spall, Jr., 'Free Trade, Foreign Relations, and the Anti-Corn-Law League', *International History Review*, 10 (1988), 405–32.

Likewise, in the words of a Methodist minister:

First: Free Trade is implied in the primeval benediction God pronounced on Man;

Secondly: Free Trade is sanctioned in Sundry other Scriptures of the Old Testament;

Thirdly: Free Trade is favoured by God's providential arrangements in the Government of the World;

Fourthly: Free Trade accords with the genius of Christianity;

Fifthly: Free Trade is promoted by Christian Missions; and

Sixthly:—Free Trade will be exemplified when Christianity gains the final triumphs in the conversion of the world.[41]

So what might have seemed like a sordid piece of lobbying, or an exercise in class warfare, took on the role of a moral crusade, with a membership which overlapped with those of the anti-slavery, peace, and temperance campaigns.

The Corn Laws would have been repealed sooner or later without the Anti-Corn Law League. Even so, it had an exhilarating effect on English politics, greater probably than any single-issue group before or since. Admittedly, it takes two to tangle, and the free trade controversy derived much of its sharpness from the determination of the protectionists to fight back hard. The initiative came from local associations of tenant farmers, starting in Essex and Lincolnshire and then spreading to most of the Midlands, and culminating in the formation of an *Anti*-League (1843) under the leadership of the Ultra Tory Duke of Richmond, President of the Central Protection Society.[42] In this way the Corn Laws replaced religion as the central political issue, and once that had happened it was widely assumed that the Whig–Liberal Party was the party of repeal and that the Conservatives were the protectionists. It frequently happens in politics that perception counts for more than deeds, and in this case it did not seem to signify that Liverpool's and Wellington's governments had done more for free trade than Grey's and Melbourne's. As a result the movement of agriculturists towards Peel, already under way, became a stampede.[43]

These political developments would have forced ministers to change policy irrespective of whether they accepted the Cobdenite line on free trade (which some of them did). But because of past inaction, they needed an excuse for their sudden volte-face. They therefore appointed a Select Committee on Import Duties (1840) under the free trade Radical Joseph Hume. It was, even more than usual, an exercise in propaganda rather than a genuine investigation. Witnesses

---

[41] [Revd William J. Shrewsbury], *Christian Thoughts on Free Trade* (Bacup, 1843), 40–55, cited in Spall, 'Free Trade', 414–15.

[42] Travis L. Crosby, *English Farmers and the Politics of Protection 1815–1852* (Hassocks, 1977), 130–8.

[43] In Cornwall, for example, farmers had traditionally been Whiggish, partly under the influence of Methodism, but in 1841 protectionism made most of them Conservative (Edwin Jaggard, *Cornwall Politics in the Age of Reform 1790–1885* (Woodbridge, 1999), 95–102).

were drilled, and there was concerted pressure from Board of Trade officials such as the joint secretaries James Deacon Hume and John McGregor, the commercial diplomat John Bowring, and the statistician G. R. Porter, all failed businessmen and all true believers in the market. Having lapped up their evidence, Joseph Hume's committee reported in line with the growing Manchester School orthodoxy, i.e. that free trade would work to Britain's comparative advantage and lead to export-led growth.[44] It gave Baring an excuse to include in his 1841 budget a proposal to reduce the preference on colonial over foreign sugar drastically from 39s. per hundredweight to 12s. Most Conservatives were outraged by this, as were several Whig protectionists, and so too were many Liberal anti-slavers, since foreign sugar was largely still produced by indentured labour. These forces combined to defeat the proposal (317–281), whereupon Melbourne dissolved Parliament and appealed to the country on a variety of freer-trade proposals, including a fixed 8s. duty on foreign wheat.

Gladstone called the ministers' conversion to free trade 'a deathbed repentance', and certainly it came too late to impress the electorate. The Conservatives swept back to power with an overall majority of 367 to 291, and a lead in England of almost 100. Benefiting especially from the votes of the £50 tenants-at-will,[45] they won more than 85 per cent of English county seats, sensationally beating the Whig aristocrats Milton and Morpeth in the West Riding, and they also did handsomely in smaller rural boroughs, as Table 8.2 demonstrates.

On the other hand, Liberals retained their lead in the fifty-four largest English boroughs (those with populations of more than about 20,000)[46] and made gains at Bath, Bolton, Brighton, Ipswich, Norwich, Preston, Stockport, Stoke, and Wakefield. The only big towns where Conservatives did well were those with strong protectionist lobbies: the City of London and the ports of Hull,

TABLE 8.2. *Election results in the ninety-four smallest English boroughs, 1835–1841 (i.e. with populations under c.10,000 in 1831)*

Party	1835	1837	1841
Conservatives	73	80	95
Liberals	82	75	60

[44] A privately printed summary of the Report sold 30,000 copies.

[45] David Eastwood, 'Toryism, Reform, and Political Culture in Oxfordshire, 1826–1837', *Parliamentary History*, 7 (1988), 115, describes the tenants-at-will as 'the shock troops of the Tory counter-offensive' in that county.

[46] By an extraordinary coincidence, Liberals led the Conservatives in these boroughs by seventy-eight seats to thirty in each of the 1835, 1837, and 1841 elections.

Liverpool, Rochester, and Southampton, where the shipping interest mattered. Finally, the Liberals led by fifty-four seats to thirty-two in English boroughs north of the Trent. All this suggests that, having adopted free trade hesitantly, the Whig–Liberal Party was at last facing in the right direction. Despite its defeat in 1841, it was shortly to enter on forty-five years of political hegemony based on the support of provincial businessmen, manufacturers, and retailers, many of whom were Nonconformists. These were groups to whom rhetorical obeisance had been made in 1832, but with whom Grey's ministers had never really identified before, and to whom they had certainly never intended to hand over power. What happened in 1841 was that the Whig–Liberal Party abandoned its attempt to be the party of aristocracy, and turned to face its destiny.

But if Liberals now pointed in the same direction as their natural supporters, Peel in victory found himself facing the opposite way from most of his. This was not because he was trying to transform his party, or to make it more middle-class. A good deal of nonsense has been written about Peel's attempt to appeal to the bourgeoisie. True, he was anxious to counter the influence of Ultra Tories and rabid agrarians—but then so too were Liverpool, Canning, and Wellington before him. True, the party had solid support among what might be called the *upper*-middle classes—yet so it had always done. As for the £10 householder class, the industrialists and shopocracy, these were people whom Peel had sneered at as a 'vulgar privileged pedlary', and whose predominantly Nonconformist grievances he had gone out of his way *not* to assuage. No, the reason he was at odds with many in his party was that he wished to continue liberal Tory policies and they wished to put the clock back, only they were explicit about their hopes while he kept quiet until after the election was won. And the plain fact is that it was won in the counties and small boroughs on a platform of saving the Church and maintaining protective duties on corn.[47] Leader and led were on course for collision right from that moment.

Looking back on the years from 1841 to 1846, Gladstone told Peel that he had exercised more personal authority than any prime minister since Pitt. 'Your Government has not been carried on by a Cabinet but by the heads of departments each in communication with you.'[48] There was much truth in this. Although Goulburn was nominally Chancellor of the Exchequer, Peel introduced the eventful budgets of 1842 and 1845.[49] Irish affairs were handled in

[47] Ian Newbould, 'Sir Robert Peel and the Conservative Party, 1832–1841: A Study in Failure?', *EHR* 98 (1983), 529–57.

[48] *The Gladstone Diaries*, ed. M. R. D. Foot and H. C. G. Matthew (Oxford, 1968–94), iii. 559 (13 July 1846).

[49] Perhaps not much should be made of this, since Peel was the first Prime Minister in the Commons not to be his own Chancellor of the Exchequer. On the other hand, the job had grown enormously in recent times, and the only subsequent prime ministers to act in both capacities simultaneously were Gladstone (August 1873–February 1874, April 1880–December 1882) and Baldwin (May–October 1923).

collaboration with successive viceroys (De Grey, Heytesbury) and secretaries (Eliot, Fremantle), but again it was Peel who single-handedly determined strategy. Ripon was a cipher at the Board of Trade; Gladstone, who succeeded him in 1843, was a tyro; while Graham at the Home Office was an assiduous administrator but largely subordinate as a policy-maker. Only in external affairs was Peel willing to delegate, to Aberdeen in the case of foreign policy and to Stanley where colonial matters were concerned. Such sense of purpose and mastery of business could be intimidating, and even Dalhousie, one of the most devoted ministers, was heard to complain that they were treated like schoolboys. (A more jaundiced critic referred to 'a cabinet of Peel's dolls'.[50]) As for backbench critics, he admitted that he lacked the 'patience to listen to the sentiments of individuals whom it is equally imprudent to neglect, and an intolerable bore to consult'. Or, as he put it on another occasion, 'heads see, and tails are blind'.[51] Such expressions of contempt added a leaven of insult to those who felt injured by his policies.

Since Peel was electorally committed to upholding Protestantism and protection, his moves in the opposite direction had to be presented as unpremeditated changes of mind, justified by events. In debate after debate Peel wielded statistical and theoretical arguments to justify apparent shifts in policy, including finally a proposal to repeal the Corn Laws. This naturally gave him the *appearance* of a man who kept on changing his mind. The Liberal journalist Walter Bagehot proclaimed that Peel had a talent for latching onto policies just at the point when they became acceptable to the general public. 'He was converted at the conversion of the average man.'[52] Peel's Conservative antagonists were more brutal. Disraeli, as will be seen, accused him of constantly falling for the latest intellectual fashion. Yet Disraeli and Bagehot were equally mistaken. The key to Peel's dominance was his clarity of vision, and the key to that was an increasingly doctrinaire approach to policy-making. More specifically, as Cobden reported to the phrenologist George Combe, 'his mind has a natural leaning towards politico-economical truths'.[53] If he *appeared* to change his mind it was because he had kept his cards close to his chest for tactical reasons. Thus almost immediately on taking office he wrote to Graham, Goulburn, Ripon, Gladstone, Stanley, Herries, and Eliot on issues such as taxation, the Corn Laws, and Ireland. These letters advanced possibilities and invited responses, so that superficially Peel appeared to be seeking advice, but their tone was deceptive. He knew exactly what needed to be done, and was actually seeking to persuade.[54]

---

[50] Ashley, diary, 1 Feb. 1845, in Edwin Hodder, *The Life and Work of the Seventh Earl of Shaftesbury* (1886), ii. 84.   [51] Peel to Hardinge, 24 Sept. 1846, in Parker, *Peel*, iii. 474.
[52] Bagehot, 'The Character of Sir Robert Peel', in *The Collected Works of Walter Bagehot*, ed. Norman St John-Stevas (1965–86), iii. 245. For the concept of an average man, see below pp. 610.
[53] Cobden to Combe, 7 Mar. 1846, BL, Add. MS 43660, fos. 33–6.
[54] Peel's motives are discussed below, pp. 543–58.

The first step, in 1842, was to introduce income tax, lower the 1828 Corn Law, and cut tariffs generally. This went more smoothly than might have been expected, the only casualty being the egregious Duke of Buckingham, who resigned from the Cabinet. The Canadian Corn Bill of the following year even appeased protectionists to some extent because it reaffirmed the principle of colonial preference. The Bank Charter Act of 1844 offended many City firms but, helped by economic recovery, it bolstered Peel's reputation for competence. However, in the same year two blatant pieces of railroading soured the atmosphere. First ninety-five Conservative backbenchers rebelled in support of a motion by Ashley to limit the labour of women and youngsters in the textile industries to ten hours a day. Shortly afterwards sixty-two Conservatives voted against the Government's proposal to lower the import duties on free-grown foreign sugar, a move which was aimed to discriminate against slave-owners but which threatened collaterally to damage colonial interests as well. On each occasion Peel forced the rebels into line by threatening very gracelessly to resign and leave them to the mercy of the Liberals.[55] In the following year he ignored clamour from agriculturists for tax relief, and flouted his party's Protestant sensitivities by nearly tripling and making permanent the grant to the Roman Catholic seminary at Maynooth near Dublin. Conservatives divided 150–148 against on the third reading, though the Bill passed easily thanks to Opposition members. As Graham rightly observed, 'A large body of our supporters is mortally offended, and in their anger they are ready to do anything either to defeat the Bill or to revenge themselves upon us . . . We have lost the slight hold which we ever possessed over the hearts and kind feelings of our followers . . . In a party sense it has been fatal.'[56]

Clearly the Conservative Party was in a fractured and fractious state even before Peel proposed to suspend the Corn Laws at the beginning of November 1845. His motives are discussed below; what matters here is the political impact, which was dramatic. Stanley and Buccleuch rejected the proposal outright, other Cabinet members were deeply unhappy, and Peel was more or less forced to resign on 5 December. The Queen then called not on Melbourne but on Russell, the Opposition leader in the Commons, to form a Government. Russell was himself committed to repeal—his 'Edinburgh Letter' to that effect, published in the *Morning Chronicle* on 26 November, had helped to provoke Peel into resignation—but after lengthy negotiations he was unable to put a Cabinet together, the main reason being the refusal of Howick (who had recently become the third Earl Grey) to serve in a government of which Palmerston was Foreign

[55] Very few Conservative MPs changed their votes as a result of Peel's threats, but many former rebels abstained while many loyalists came up to London to support him (Robert Stewart, *The Foundation of the Conservative Party 1830–1867* (1978), 187–90).
[56] Graham to Heytesbury, 12 Apr. 1845, in *Life and Letters of Sir James Graham*, ii. 10.

Minister. Disraeli claimed that Russell deliberately handed the 'poisoned chalice' back to Peel because he believed that repeal would divide whichever party undertook it,[57] but that motive can be discounted since Russell never got over his despair at the fact that Peel had trumped him and was therefore awarded the popular tributes which Russell felt were due to himself. At any rate Peel returned to office, but without Stanley. His mood even more self-exalted than usual, he declared that he was 'determined to carry repeal'.[58] This was less of a challenge than he made it sound, given that most Liberals were willing to support him. As in 1829 the hard work was in the Lords, and again it was Wellington—disliking repeal, but disliking disloyalty even more—who steered the policy through. Whether Peel thought he could achieve repeal and retain office is unclear. There seemed a fighting chance, but he was more than ready to relish a second dose of martyrdom should it come to that.

It did come to that. The Commons debate lasted thirty-two nights and was incredibly bitter. Peel's torturers-in-chief were Benjamin Disraeli and Lord George Bentinck. Without the first the protectionists would have lacked forensic power; without the other they might have lacked integrity. Yet it was Bentinck who inflicted the nastiest single wound when he accused Peel of having joined with high Tories in hounding his mother's brother-in-law (Canning) to death in 1827. Unfair, but with just sufficient truth in it to unnerve the Prime Minister. Disraeli's sustained and devastating invective has often been written off (probably wrongly) as the pique of a man who had been denied office in 1841. Whatever the spur, his brilliant mingling of grandiloquence and sarcasm added to the impact of speeches which O'Connell said were the greatest he had ever heard in Parliament. His main theme was that Peel had adopted free trade, not because he understood it, but because it was intellectually fashionable.

Between thirty and forty years, from the days of Mr. Horner to the days of [Mr. Cobden], that right hon. gentleman has traded on the ideas and intelligence of others. His life has been one great appropriation clause. [Shouts of laughter and cheers.] He is a burglar of others' intellect... There is no statesman who has committed political petty larceny on so great a scale. [Peals of laughter from all parts of the House.] I believe, therefore, when the right hon. gentleman undertook our cause on either side of the House, that he was perfectly sincere in his advocacy; but as, in the course of discussion, the conventionalisms which he received from us crumbled away in his grasp, feeling no creative power to sustain him with new arguments, feeling no spontaneous sentiments to force upon him conviction... the right hon. gentleman, faithful to the law of his nature, imbibed the new doctrines, the more vigorous, bustling, popular, and progressive doctrines, as he had imbibed the doctrines of Mr. Horner—as he had imbibed the doctrines of every leading

[57] Benjamin Disraeli, *Lord George Bentinck: A Political Biography*, ed. Charles Whibley (1905), 21.
[58] In fact the Corn Laws were to be phased out, so that by 1849 there would be nothing left but a 1s. duty levied for registration purposes.

man in this country for thirty of forty years, with the exception of the doctrine of Parliamentary reform, which the Whigs very wisely led the country upon, and did not allow to grow sufficiently mature to fall into [his] mouth . . .

In a withering peroration, Disraeli denounced 'the huckstering tyranny of the Treasury bench [loud cheers]—these political pedlars that bought their party in the cheapest market, and sold us in the dearest'.

I know, sir, that there are many who believe that the time is gone by when one can appeal to those high and honest impulses that were once the mainstay and the main element of the English character. I know, sir, that we appeal to a people debauched by public gambling—stimulated and encouraged by an inefficient and a shortsighted Minister. I know that the public mind is polluted with economic fancies; a depraved desire that the rich may become richer without the interference of industry and toil. I know, sir, that all confidence in public men is lost. [Great cheering.] But, sir, I have faith in the primitive and enduring elements of the English character. It may be vain now, in the midnight of their intoxication, to tell them that there will be an awakening of bitterness; it may be idle now, in the springtide of their economic frenzy, to warn them that there may be an ebb of trouble. But the dark and inevitable hour will arrive. Then, when their spirits are softened by misfortune, they will recur to those principles that made England great, and which, in our belief, can alone keep England great. [Prolonged cheers.] Then too, sir, perchance they may remember, not with unkindness, those who, betrayed and deserted, were neither ashamed nor afraid to struggle for the 'good old cause'—the cause with which are associated principles the most popular, sentiments the most entirely national—the cause of labour—the cause of the people—the cause of England![59]

Peel's self-conscious rectitude was proof against Bentinck's accusation that he had deliberately 'sold' his party, but he was never very steady under ridicule, and Disraeli's imputation that he was intellectually challenged caught him at his most vulnerable. The minister flinched but said little in response, and when he did defend himself, mainly in perorations of his own, it was in a stilted, pompous, self-congratulatory tone that brought him little credit.

In relinquishing power I shall leave a name severely censured I fear by many who, on public grounds, deeply regret the severance of party ties—deeply regret that severance, not from interested or personal motives, but from the firm conviction that fidelity to party engagements—the existence and maintenance of a great party—constitutes a powerful instrument of government; I shall surrender power severely censured also by others who, from no interested motives adhere to the principle of protection, considering the maintenance of it to be essential to the welfare and interests of the country; I shall leave a name execrated by every monopolist who, from less honourable motives, clamours for protection because it conduces to his own individual benefit; but it may be that I shall leave a name sometimes remembered with expressions of good will in the

---

[59] *HPD*3 lxxxvi. 675–7 (15 May 1846).

abodes of those whose lot it is to labour, and to earn their daily bread by the sweat of their brow, when they shall recruit their exhausted strength with abundant and untaxed food, the sweeter because it is no longer leavened by a sense of injustice.'[60]

Disraeli crucified Peel in 1846, but Peel was more than a little willing to shed his own mediatorial blood. Hence the curious mood of exaltation that suffused the inner circle of Peelites, meaning a number of young acolytes such as Gladstone, Herbert, Dalhousie, and Lincoln, who had already begun to turn him into a cult figure (somewhat oddly, since he had nothing but contempt for their intense High Churchmanship). It began as soon as Peel had snatched the poisoned chalice back. 'Peel was most kind, nay fatherly,' wrote Gladstone; 'we *held* hands instinctively and I could not but reciprocate with emphasis his "God bless you".'[61] When the hour of his political destruction was come, the Prime Minister wrote to Hardinge: 'We have fallen in the face of day, and with our front to our enemies...Here...feasting on solitude and repose...I have every disposition to forgive them.'[62] For after all they knew not what they did— 'How can those, who spend their time in hunting and shooting and eating and drinking, know what were the motives of those who are responsible for the public security, who have access to the best information, and have no other object under Heaven but to provide against danger, and consult the general interests of all classes?'[63] As late as 1850 Peel's devotees looked forward to his political resurrection, for he was still a fit and vigorous man when, aged 62, he was thrown from his horse and died on the kitchen table after eighteen hours of agony. This not surprisingly called forth more messianic imagery from his disciples: 'He was a tower in Israel—and so, if ever the Philistines come, we shall keenly feel.'[64]

Repeal was carried in the Commons thanks to the Liberals and Radicals, who supported Peel by 235 to 10 on the third reading, while the Conservatives divided against him by 241 to 114. The question arises as to whether there was any correlation between the constituencies MPs represented and the way they voted. In fact MPs saw themselves as *representatives* rather than *delegates*, and were more beholden to party whips than to constituency organizations, but for what it is worth 86 per cent of Conservatives who sat for counties voted against repeal, as did 63 per cent of those who sat for rural boroughs with fewer than 500 voters, whereas only 50 per cent of those whose electorates exceeded 500 did so.[65]

---

[60] *HPD*3 lxxxvii. 1054–5 (29 June 1846). [61] *The Gladstone Diaries*, iii. 506–7 (22 Dec. 1845).
[62] Peel to Hardinge, 4 July 1846, in Peel, *Memoirs*, ii. 309–10.
[63] Peel to his wife, 16 Dec. 1845, in *The Private Letters of Sir Robert Peel*, ed. George Peel (1920), 273. Not that Peel was averse to hunting, shooting, eating, or drinking himself.
[64] Dalhousie to Sir George Couper, 24 Aug. 1850, in *Private Letters of the Marquess of Dalhousie*, ed. J. G. A. Baird (Edinburgh, 1910), 137–8.
[65] Stewart, *Foundation of the Conservative Party*, 215–16. However, there was no obvious correlation between votes on the Corn Laws and Conservative MPs' personal sources of income.

More interesting is the fact that over 97 per cent of Conservative frontbenchers supported the Maynooth Bill, and nearly 86 per cent supported repeal, whereas of those holding local county office (deputy lord lieutenants, sheriffs, magistrates) nearly 80 per cent opposed repeal and 60 per cent opposed Maynooth.[66] This reflected long-standing tensions between central and local government and between front- and backbenchers. Quite apart from the substantive issues, many of the latter simply detested the centralizing tendencies of an overbearing executive. Thus, of the 148 Conservative MPs who had opposed Peel over Maynooth, only seventeen subsequently supported him on the Corn Law;[67] the ninety-two who had opposed him on Ashley's ten hours amendment divided two to one against the Maynooth grant, and five to two against Corn Law repeal. It was therefore no surprise when, on the same night that repeal was carried in the Lords (25 June), the Prime Minister suffered another Commons rebellion over an Irish Coercion Bill. This time the rebels had no objection to the policy, but were simply out for revenge. This time the Liberals had no reason to rescue him, he was duly defeated, and Russell became Prime Minister after all.

It is important to emphasize the fundamentally divided nature of the Conservative Party because there is a tendency to think that Peel might have got away with it but for Disraeli's malevolence. Yet the truth is that his Government had been elected on a lie, while the final split was along normative lines and was inevitable. To be fair to Peel, the lie assumed a significance he could not have anticipated a few years earlier. The Corn Laws' sudden burst to prominence polarized opinion between agriculture and the rest—more crudely between the aristocracy and the people—obscuring the cleavage between the *upper-* and the *lesser-*middle class, and eroding many of those upper-middle-class values on which the Pittite regime had been founded. Peel acknowledged these new realities when he commented that the 'real old Tory, Church of England, Protectionist, Protestant party' was now completely alienated from himself and his supporters.[68] It follows that the idea put about by some historians, that Peel was the 'unchallengeable... founder of modern Conservatism', is terribly wide of the mark.[69] Corn Law repeal led to a formal split, the loss of five consecutive general elections, and virtual exclusion from power for almost thirty years. Moreover, when the Conservative Party eventually revived, first under Disraeli and then under Salisbury in the later nineteenth century, it owed almost nothing

[66] Heera Chung, 'The Church Defence Problem in Conservative Politics, 1841–1847', Ph.D. thesis (Cambridge, University 2001), 45.

[67] Ibid. 39–40. The 150 pro-Maynooth Conservatives were less predictable: seventy-nine voted for Corn Law repeal and fifty-five opposed it.

[68] Peel to Graham, 2 Jan. 1848, Graham MSS, General Series, 105; Robert Stewart, *The Politics of Protection: Lord Derby and the Protectionist Party 1841–1852* (Cambridge, 1971), 1–32.

[69] Norman Gash, *Sir Robert Peel: The Life of Sir Robert Peel after 1830* (1972), 709.

to Peel, whose name Salisbury and Balfour could hardly bear to hear mentioned, regarding him as little better than a traitor. In so far as Peel left any legacy, it was contained in his economic policy and his approach to the Irish problem, and the beneficiary was the later nineteenth-century Liberal Party under Gladstone. Yet Peel could have no place in the Liberals' pantheon either. To them he was merely a facilitator of reforms he had previously resisted, and by no means to be compared with Fox, Grey, and Russell, who had borne 'the burden and heat of the day'.[70] Only in the 1920s did historians begin to think that Peel had founded the Conservative Party, the reason being that it then took ownership of liberal economic policies as the Liberal Party declined. An inescapable conclusion is that the political events of 1846 did not point forwards, but brought to a close the hegemony of a governing order and a set of political ideas that had preponderated since 1783.

THE ANALYSIS RESUMED: PARTY POLITICS WITHOUT PARTIES

In many ways the Great Reform Act made little difference. Some voters would continue to be coerced by landlords, or intimidated by angry mobs, or subjected to ritual treating until the Ballot Act of 1872 and the Corrupt Practices Act of 1883. It is true that the number of aristocratic MPs fell from 217 in 1826 to 169 in 1835, but this was a side-effect of the Tory Party's collapse, not a new social dispensation.[71] Yet in other respects politics changed profoundly. There had long been a two-party feel to politics but this became so marked as to constitute a qualitative difference. Looking back ten years later on 'the good old days of party government, before the great break up of 1846', Gladstone wrote,

Ah! those were times indeed. What close-running! what cheering! what whipping in! No loose fish; no absentees: if a man broke his leg before a great division, it was a kind of petty treason.... It was a time, no doubt, of strong antipathies; but it was also a time of strong attachments, of unwavering confidence, of warm devotion. If a man detested one half of the House of Commons, at least he loved the other.[72]

In many ways this was misleading, as will appear, but it captures a feeling.

Influenced by comments such as Gladstone's, historians have often written about the 'decline of the independent members of Parliament'. In reality there was no statistical decline,[73] but their power to influence legislation diminished for two reasons. The first was an increase in the number of Government order

[70] Bagehot, 'Character of Peel', 245.
[71] The number of Tory aristocrats fell from about 300 to under 100 while Whigs stayed steady at about seventy-five.
[72] [W. E. Gladstone], 'The Declining Efficiency of Parliament', *QR* 99 (1856), 527–8.
[73] See below, pp. 517–18.

days and consequent reduction in private members' bills. Perhaps there is a tendency for political parties which spend a long time in opposition to abuse power when they finally get it. Certainly Peel had a point in complaining, as early as 1833, that only 'this government' would exploit a huge majority to allow such short amounts of time to consider important measures or treat the Commons so badly.[74] A second factor was the development of what has been called 'club government'. Its effects were especially marked on the Conservative side, if only because it is easier for oppositions to communicate and agree. Cohesion and morale undoubtedly benefited from the foundation of the Carlton Club in 1832, while the chief whip (Thomas Fremantle), the principal agent (Francis Bonham), and what today might be called the party chairman (Lord Granville Somerset) formed an important nucleus which helped for a while to bridge the gap between Peel and his backbenchers.[75] On the other side, a Reform Association was founded in 1835 to liaise with newly forming local bodies, and the Reform Club was established in the following year. The latter, especially, was seen by metropolitan Liberals and Radicals as a forum in which to browbeat the Whigs with superior arguments, but its actual effect may rather have been to smother Radicals in an aristocratic embrace, as one historian has astutely pointed out.

> Whig contact, whig habits, whig sociability were in the long run calculated to work a profounder change in the outlook of the radicals than doctrinaire arguments were on the whigs. In politics . . . proximity can be a more seductive instrument than principle. The single-mindedness, the integrity, the characteristic acidity of the radicals that flourished in frigid isolation, could not easily survive transplantation to the convivial atmosphere of the Pall Mall clubrooms . . . If Molesworth and Parkes had seriously envisaged the Reform Club as a kind of Trojan horse within the whig camp, the horse was soon docilely eating from the whig manger.[76]

Because it came after a period of confusion and cross-voting, no one knew whether the 1830 election had strengthened or weakened the Government until Parliament met three months later. There was no such uncertainty in 1841, since nearly all candidates had stood for one side or the other.[77] As this implies, the two-party battle was especially marked in the country. The size of the potential

---

[74] *HPD2* xvi. 483 (8 Mar. 1833); Gary W. Cox, *The Efficient Secret: The Cabinet and the Development of Political Parties in Victorian England* (Cambridge, 1987), 46–51.

[75] Norman Gash, 'The Organization of the Conservative Party, 1832–1846. Part I: The Parliamentary Organization', *Parliamentary History*, 1 (1982), 137–59.

[76] Norman Gash, *Politics in the Age of Peel: A Study in the Technique of Parliamentary Representation 1830–1850* (1953), 410–11.

[77] Bonham informed Peel in January 1840 that there were just eight Radicals and eight other MPs whom it was impossible to classify definitively as either ministerial or Opposition supporters (Gash, *Sir Robert Peel*, 240; id., *Reaction and Reconstruction in English Politics 1832–1852* (Oxford, 1965), 202).

electorate had increased by at most 45 per cent in 1832, but the numbers actually voting increased by about 500 per cent,[78] thanks to the greater frequency of contested elections (see Table 8.3). Equally significant was a marked polarization among the electorate. On the assumption that a voter who 'split' could not have felt a strong sense of party identity, it would seem that party affiliation rose strongly in English boroughs during the 1830s, reached a peak in 1841, went into rapid decline following the Conservative split of 1846, and reasserted itself in 1865 and 1868. Such a pattern is evident from Table 8.4 on English boroughs, but even those figures probably underestimate the situation in 1841, since in two-thirds of the most active constituencies the splitting ratio may have been as low as 6.2 per cent. Despite huge variations from place to place, there was increased polarization from 1818, and then much more during the 1830s, but the 1841 election was the most polarized on record, which could explain the sudden

TABLE 8.3. *Number and percentage of contested seats at general elections, 1826–1841*

Year	No.	%
1826	88	36
1830	83	34
1831	75	31
1832	188	74
1835	153	60
1837	176	69
1841	138	54

TABLE 8.4. *Percentage of voters who split their votes in English boroughs south and north of a line from the river Mersey to the river Humber, 1832–1868*

	1832	1835	1837	1841	1847	1852	1857	1859	1865	1868
South	25.3	18.0	15.1	8.6	26.3	18.3	16.0	18.5	12.5	12.6
North	20.8	26.8	13.8	10.7	26.7	19.5	22.4	26.7	16.1	8.1

Source: T. J. Nossiter, *Influence, Opinion and Political Idioms in Reformed England: Case Studies from the North-East 1832–74* (Hassocks, 1975), 178.

[78] Derek Beales, 'The Electorate before and after 1832: The Right to Vote, and the Opportunity', *Parliamentary History*, 11 (1992), 139–50, calculates that 2.49% of adult males in England and Wales actually voted in 1830, 2.11% in 1831, 11.03% in 1832, and 7.7% in 1835.

drop in the number of contested elections. (Contests being expensive, there was no point in pressing ahead with one if it was obvious who would win, and it was more obvious who would win when opinion was polarized.) Just as telling was the decline in the number of floating voters. According to longitudinal analysis, only 24 per cent of eighteenth-century voters had supported the same party over four elections, whereas nearly 40 per cent did so during 1820–32, and more than 70 per cent between 1832 and 1841.[79]

This rise in partisan loyalties has been attributed to a switch of emphasis from local to national issues, and from faction to 'a politics of principle'. A more likely reason was the growth of local party organization. This tended to be a feature of Opposition politics in the nineteenth century, and it was particularly true of the Conservatives in the 1830s. A central election committee, run by Granville Somerset and Francis Bonham, headed a formal network of constituency associations designed to raise money, coordinate activity, mobilize the press, encourage the formation of local operative and tradesmen's societies, and exercise some control over the excesses of the Orange lodges.[80] Despite the efforts of Parkes, the Liberals did not achieve the same level of coordination,[81] but the most important development was common to both parties and arose directly from the Reform Act. The creation of large anonymous electorates, with qualifications based on complex property and residence qualifications, meant that it was no longer feasible to expect a person's right to vote to be determined at the poll (and then open to dispute afterwards). Instead, the names of eligible voters were to be recorded in advance. Each party hired local solicitors to promote the registration of sympathetic voters, to challenge the credentials of persons proposed by the other side, and even to manufacture voters by creating leaseholds and splitting up freeholds. As the omni-prescient Peel somewhat gloomily observed,

The Reform Bill has made a change in the position of parties and in the practical working of public affairs, which the authors of it did not anticipate. There is a perfectly new element of political power—namely, the registration of voters, a more powerful one than either the Sovereign or the House of Commons. That party is the strongest in point of fact which has the existing registration in its favour . . . We shall soon have, I have no

---

[79] Admittedly, the frequency of elections in the 1830s will have been a factor (John A. Phillips and Charles Wetherell, 'The Great Reform Act of 1832 and the Political Modernization of England', *American Historical Review*, 100 (1955), 411–36; John A. Phillips, *The Great Reform Bill in the Boroughs: English Electoral Behaviour 1818–1841* (Oxford, 1992), 15–61).

[80] These developments are comprehensively described in Norman Gash, 'The Organization of the Conservative Party, 1832–1846. Part II: The Electoral Organization', *Parliamentary History*, 2 (1983), 131–52; Stewart, *Foundation of the Conservative Party*, 128–50.

[81] Ian Newbould, 'Whiggery and the Growth of Party 1830–1841: Organization and the Challenge of Reform', *Parliamentary History*, 4 (1985), 137–56.

doubt, a regular systematic organisation of it. Where this is to end I know not, but substantial power will be in the Registry Courts and there the contest will be determined.[82]

In 1843, accordingly, Conservatives sought to disfranchise certain Dissenters on technical grounds, while Anti-Corn Law League officials tried to create bogus freeholds in the counties.[83]

Voter registration was further boosted as a consequence of the Municipal Corporations Act of 1835. Whereas, not so very long before, most parliamentary elections had turned on local factors, right from the start most municipal elections were dominated by national issues and fought on a party basis, which kept the political pot stirred on an annual, not to say continuous, basis. At about the same time, by-elections began to be regarded as indices of a government's popularity, as they are today. The Attorney-General's defeat at Dudley in 1834 was seen by Grey as a warning shot from Dissenters, while Lincoln's defeat at South Nottinghamshire in February 1846 was seized on as indicative of rural dissatisfaction with Peel. Another consequence was that governments began to be judged on whether the economy was performing well or badly, thus tempting them to time elections with reference to the trade cycle. A final point worth noting is that the 1841 election was the first since 1708 to bring about the fall of a government enjoying majority support. On other occasions when elections were associated with a change of ministry, the latter preceded the former as in 1710, 1783–4, 1806, and 1807.[84] What happened in 1841 was therefore a foretaste of 'democracy' in so far as the electorate decided who should run the country.

In many ways, therefore, this looked like a two-party political system. There was just one problem: the nature of the two parties. The period began with the defection of the Stanleyites, which was followed by several years in which Melbourne held office by courtesy of Peel, and when the administration was run on departmental rather than Cabinet lines.[85] Indeed, as Table 8.5 conclusively demonstrates, loyalty to a particular party—as expressed in several hundred recorded division lists—was significantly less strong in the 1830s than in the previous decades. Since both parties were divided on a range of issues, and neither front bench could be sure of getting its policies enacted, it looked at times as though the different sections of each might recombine to form more stable units. It could not happen, however, because both parties were split upon

---

[82] Peel to Arbuthnot, 1839, in Parker, *Peel*, ii. 368.

[83] John Prest, *Politics in the Age of Cobden* (1977), 72–102; D. Hamer, *The Politics of Electoral Pressure: A Study in the History of Victorian Reform Agitations* (Hassocks, 1977), 58–90.

[84] A case might be made for 1830, except that between the election in July and the fall of Wellington in November there was a four-month time lag during which many significant political events took place. See above, pp. 416–20.   [85] Mitchell, *Melbourne*, 156, 186.

TABLE 8.5. *Voting records of Whig, Liberal, and Radical MPs, 1831–1841* (%)

Years	Always voted with the Liberal government	Voted against the Liberal government in up to 10% of divisions	Voted against the Liberal government in more than 10% of divisions
1831–2	23.0	54.0	23.0
1833–4	18.0	54.0	28.0
1835–7	9.0	72.0	19.0
1837–41	10.5	75.5	14.0

Note: It would be impossible to provide a meaningful table on these lines for the Conservative Party. During 1833–4 as many as 184 out of 211 Opposition MPs voted with the Whig Government in more then 10% of the twenty-four recorded divisions, but then they were simply obeying their leader, Peel, who, it will be rememebered, voted with ministers on fourteen occasions.

Source: Ian Newbould, *Whiggery and Reform, 1830–41: The Politics of Government* (Stanford, Calif., 1990), 17–23.

two quite different axes, which complicated the situation beyond the capacity of a two-party system to accommodate.

First, there was the division between reformers and reactionaries along a political axis. In the shadow of the French Revolution, this was the polarity which contemporaries were most aware of, and it broadly corresponded to the distinction between Liberals and Conservatives. In this sense a Liberal was someone who wanted a more inclusive society and less privilege. It was what Peel meant when he said that 'the tone of England ... is more liberal ... than the policy of the Government'.[86] If he was a liberal Conservative, his equivalent at the other end of the spectrum, though still some way short of Ultra, was the raffish, sarcastic, and slightly saturnine Lyndhurst.[87] Admittedly, the differences between the two men were partly tactical and personal—they disliked each other intensely and may even have considered themselves leadership rivals—but there were principled disagreements too, as highlighted by Lyndhurst's protégé Disraeli in his *Vindication of the English Constitution* (1835). This was a paean to the hereditary peerage as more truly representative of the people than the 'Venetian oligarchy' which controlled the Commons. It proclaimed the virtues of decentralization and 'the great unpaid', attacking the Whig penchant for stipendiary magistrates beholden to the Home Office. And it drew a new lineage for the party by privileging Bolingbroke, Chatham, and Canning at the expense

---

[86] Peel to Croker, 23 Mar. 1820, in *Croker Papers*, i. 170. See above, p. 311.
[87] Lord Chancellor 1827–30, 1834–5, and 1841–6.

TABLE 8.6. *Political spectrum across parties from right to left, late 1830s*

Ultra Tory	Newcastle, Londonderry, Plumtre
high Tory	Gladstone, Lyndhurst, Inglis
moderate Tory–Conservative	Wellington, Aberdeen
liberal Tory–Conservative	Peel, Goulburn, Stanley
Whig	Holland, Melbourne
Whig–Liberal	Russell, Morpeth, Clarendon
Liberal	Lansdowne, Howick
Radical	Hume, Roebuck

of North, Pitt, and Liverpool. 'The Tory party in this country is the national party; it is the really democratic party of England.'[88]

According to this political definition of the word 'liberal', and leaving Irish MPs out of account, a cross-section of the political community in the late 1830s would read as shown in Table 8.6. On this scale the crucial line was that which separated the liberal Tories from the Whigs, i.e. Peel from Melbourne, and there was another important gap between Liberals and Radicals. The distinction between Whigs and Liberals seems insignificant by comparison, the latter lying a little further to the left along the political spectrum. Seen from this perspective, the party simply switched labels unthinkingly as it moved in that direction.[89]

This political spectrum shows where individuals stood on civil rights issues such as parliamentary and ecclesiastical reform, but it cannot explain Tory–Radicals such as Cobbett, Burdett, Attwood, and Disraeli. Evidently the two ends of that spectrum had some things in common. In 1833, for example, Radicals and Ultra Tories voted to quit the gold standard while centrists defended it. This is because there was another unrelated division, which contemporaries probably regarded as secondary, but which had come to prominence in the late 1820s. The debate between writers such as Carlyle, Coleridge, Southey, the Mills, and Macaulay had turned, it will be remembered, on a less benevolent meaning of the word 'liberal'—a preference for low taxes and public spending, for non-intervention in the operations of the workplace and the market, and for minimal (meaning harsh) welfare systems. This second

[88] Benjamin Disraeli, *Vindication of the English Constitution in a Letter to a Noble and Learned Lord* [i.e. Lyndhurst] (1835), repr. in *Whigs and Whiggism: Political Writings by Benjamin Disraeli*, ed. William Hutcheon (1913), 216.

[89] See e.g. Gash, *Reaction and Reconstruction*, 165–6: 'The name Liberal was in common use by 1834–5, applied both to Government and party; the difficulty was to translate the idea into reality.'

polarity—occurring along what might be called the social policy spectrum—has already been seen to explain the differences between market-oriented liberal Tories like Peel and interventionist high Tories like Eldon, but, as Table 8.7 shows, it also created divisions within the Whig–Liberal Party, though the parallels are not exact. At the risk of oversimplification, it could be said that economically liberal *Tories* were more likely to adopt a moralistic or evangelical approach to non-intervention, by arguing that it made individuals more virtuous in the long run, whereas the economic liberals in Grey's and Melbourne's governments were more likely to take a secular or utilitarian view, arguing that it would eventually lead to greater prosperity and happiness for all. Meanwhile, high Tories were fierce localists as well as being paternalists, whereas Whigs were more willing to call on the central state to improve the lot of the poor. This was partly because so many of them were great magnates with the mentality of minor German princes, but they may also have fallen for the Foxite myth that Whigs were in business to protect the people, formerly against despotic kings and now against poverty and social exploitation.

Such interventionists mainly came from solid Whig soil and included Grey, Russell, Holland, Carlisle, Duncannon, Hobhouse, Morpeth, and Normanby. They honoured their 'commitment to intervention and centralization' by promoting education, public health, factory reform, and a more enlightened Irish policy, but on strictly economic issues they were usually outgunned by their free-market liberals colleagues.[90] These included successive chancellors of the Exchequer (Althorp, Spring Rice, and Baring), the Lord President (Lansdowne),[91] the Lord Chancellor (Brougham), presidents of the Board of Trade (Auckland and Poulett Thomson), and several former Canningites (besides Spring Rice, Ripon, Palmerston, Melbourne, Grant, and George and Thomas Villiers). It was these economic liberals who sponsored the harsh New Poor Law of 1834, and who fought to keep to a minimum any reduction of hours of work in factories.

To complicate the matter further, from 1833 onwards the most important political issues concerned the civic rights of Dissenters. Here the significant movers were the Liberal Anglicans, whose ideals of a Broad Church and pluralist state were discussed in the last chapter. Russell, Normanby, Morpeth, Howick, Spring Rice, Hobhouse, and Duncannon all looked forward to the abolition of compulsory Church rates, the disendowment of the Church of Ireland, the extension of primary education and non-denominational Christian

[90] See the powerful analysis in Peter Mandler, *Aristocratic Government in the Age of Reform: Whigs and Liberals, 1830–1852* (Oxford, 1990), 23–4, 170–99. Normanby and Duncannon even held out against Corn Law repeal, quite a brave stand to take against political economy in the Liberal Party of December 1845.
[91] Lansdowne was, however, very keen on national education.

TABLE 8.7. *Economic 'liberals' and interventionist 'Whigs',*
1830–1841

Economic 'liberals'	Interventionist 'Whigs'
Althorp	Cowper
Auckland	Duncannon
Baring	Ebrington
Graham	Hobhouse
George Grey	Holland
Labouchere	Howick
Lansdowne	Morpeth
Milton	Normanby
Poulett Thomson	Russell
Ripon	
Tavistock	
Villiers	
Wood	

teaching, and the admission of Dissenters as full members of Oxford and Cambridge colleges.[92] They were opposed by others in the party who were happy to have seen the Test and Corporation Acts repealed and the Catholics emancipated, but who did not wish to go much further. The latter included sceptical older Whigs like Grey and Holland, but the most passionate antagonists of Liberal Anglicanism were the (mainly) younger generation of devout evangelicals, as well as a few equally pious High Churchmen (see Table 8.8). One way or another, Fox's old party had finally caught up with the religious temper of the times, provoking Holland to confide that he found some of his colleagues so serious he was afraid to talk before them.[93]

What emerges clearly from a comparison between Tables 8.7 and 8.8 is a taxonomy in which economic liberals were either High Churchmen or evangelicals, whereas economic and social interventionists were liberals in religion (see Table 8.9). Conversely, economic liberals were *illiberal* in terms of religious and civil rights, while religious liberals were invariably social interventionists.

[92] These policies would eventually be achieved by the Liberal Party under Gladstone between 1868 and 1871, but back in the 1830s the young High Churchman and high Tory was hostile to all of them. He was still hostile to the last two in 1871.

[93] Richard Brent, *Liberal Anglican Politics: Whiggery, Religion, and Reform 1830–1841* (Oxford, 1987), 134. Stanley and Graham are often designated High Churchmen, but this can only be an extrapolation from their opposition to anticlerical legislation. In terms of Churchmanship they were clearly evangelicals. Moreover, Stanley was a convinced free-trader notwithstanding his opposition to Peel on political grounds in 1846. Angus Hawkins, *The Forgotten Prime Minister: The 14th Earl of Derby 1799–1869* (forthcoming).

TABLE 8.8. *Religious affiliations of Whig and Liberal politicians, 1830–1841*

Evangelicals	High Churchmen	Liberal Anglicans	Indifferent or indefinable
Althorp	Auckland	Duncannon	Lord Grey
Francis Baring	Cottenham	Hobhouse	Melbourne
Cowper	Richmond	Howick	Palmerston
Ebrington	Ripon	Morpeth	Holland
Graham		Normanby	Brougham
Grant		Russell	
George Grey		Spring Rice	
Labouchere			
Parnell			
Poulett Thomson			
Radnor			
Stanley			

TABLE 8.9. *Taxonomy of politics 1830–1846, showing (1) the association of economic liberalism with moderate evangelicalism and High Churchmanship, and (2) the association of economic interventionism with Liberal Anglicanism and pre-millenarian evangelicalism*

Economic Liberals		Economic interventionists	
Evangelicals	High Churchmen	Liberal Anglicans	Pre-millenarian evangelicals
Althorp	Auckland	Duncannon	Ebrington
Francis Baring	Ripon	Hobhouse	Cowper
Graham		Howick	
Grant		Morpeth	
George Grey		Normanby	
Labouchere		Russell	
Milton			
Parnell			
Poulett Thomson			
Radnor			
Stanley			
Tavistock			
Wood			

(Ebrington and Cowper are the two ministers who seem not to fit the pattern, being evangelicals who were also social interventionists, but that is because they were pre-millenarian evangelicals like Ashley, Sadler, and Drummond, whose belief in perpetual special providence led them to reject self-help in favour of a paternalistic interventionism.[94]) The fact that those who were liberal in a religious and political sense were illiberal in a social and economic sense (and vice versa) is logical, since when used in a religious or political context the term 'liberalism' implies a generous treatment of underdogs such as Dissenters, but when used in a social or economic context it implies an *un*generous treatment of underdogs such as the poor. Economic liberals were less tolerant of dissent in all its forms than Whigs, just as liberal Tories were less tolerant than high Tories. For example, Melbourne's liberal toughness as Home Secretary was in marked contrast to his Whig successors, Russell and Normanby. In 1836 Russell defied and implicitly rebuked his own Prime Minister by pardoning two Tolpuddle Martyrs, while his penal reforms went far beyond Peel's. Russell, Normanby, and Holland were also far more relaxed about trade union activity than Peel and Melbourne, with their addiction to political economy.[95] None of this is surprising, however, since in all periods economic liberals have usually been dogmatic and intolerant. After all, the main point of free markets for those who believe in them is to inculcate social discipline and correct behaviour, so no wonder their champions have wished to promote an authorized version of social morality, and to prohibit the transmission of alternative (non-market) messages. In 1840 a market liberal might be an evangelical or a High Churchman, since both styles of belief promoted orthodox codes of behaviour (such as restraint and deferment of gratification), but he was unlikely to be a religious liberal in his attitude to religion or politics.[96]

The point has been made already that whenever social and economic issues predominated, as they did in 1827, 1830, and 1833–4, a realignment, whereby the paternalist and interventionist wings of both parties came together against the free marketeers of the centre, seemed a realistic possibility. Each time, however, a constitutional or Church issue cropped up to reinforce the existing polarity between the Conservative and Liberal parties: first emancipation, then the reform crisis, finally lay appropriation. Consequently, both parties remained divided over the conflict between free-market liberalism and social paternalism. It always seemed likely that one of them would eventually split, and maybe it was always likely to be the Conservatives, since they were more divided on that

---

[94] For this distinction, see above, pp. ooo–o. Like several other pre-millenarians, Cowper was later to become a Liberal Anglican.   [95] Mandler, *Aristocratic Government*, 142–3.

[96] A recent parallel is provided by the free-marketeer Margaret Thatcher's determination to subordinate the churches, the unions, the universities, the BBC, local government, and any other institutions suspected of inculcating non-market values.

issue.[97] Another reason was Peel's determination to railroad his policies through at all costs. By forcing his followers to accept policies they did not support, he tested the system to destruction, proving that parties only worked so long as one did not try to put them to any practical use. As for whether such behaviour means that Peel should be seen as a doctrinaire politician rather than a pragmatic moderate, it depends on which perspective one views him from. Politically he was a centrist who thought that the best way to preserve the substance of the old Establishment was to reform abuses, but he was at the far end of the social policy axis, and dogmatic in his addiction to self-help and individualism.[98]

THE POLITICS OF MILITANT DISSENT

The Conservatives may be assured that the siege of the constitutional citadel will be indefatigably pushed by every means and in every shape—by stratagem—sap—blockade—assault... If we are to fight *toto de corpore regni*, the Church is the clearest and the highest ground, on which that great Conservative battle can be fought—it is in fact the key of the whole constitutional position.[99]

The reform crisis inflamed the ecclesiastical atmosphere. Bishops were hissed and pelted, their Church was described in a widely read pamphlet as 'a machine of Anti-Christ', and even Thomas Arnold thought it to be in such a state as 'no human power can save'.[100] Protestant Nonconformists now made up about one-tenth of the population and almost one-fifth of the electorate, and were determined to assert their civil rights and claims to leadership. Peel was convinced that they had a 'preponderating influence', and was disinclined to resist it. 'The great question, then, is this,' he wrote submissively with regard to the tactics which his party should adopt on one anticlerical proposal, 'Is it best for the Church to submit to this Bill, or to speculate upon the chance of a better?'[101] It was 1828 all over again—the line of least resistance—and it dismayed many of his supporters.

The Church also faced internal problems, epitomized by the widely touted fact that the Bishop of Durham earned £19,000 a year while the stipend of the average curate was only £86. Yet these were dealt with effectively—even

---

[97] Another difference was that the Conservatives' fault lines tended to separate the front- and backbenchers, whereas in the Whig and Liberal Party the frontbenchers were divided among themselves.

[98] Significantly, between 1841 and 1847 the pattern of voting among Conservative MPs on social and economic issues was different from that on Constitutional and ecclesiastical issues (W. O. Aydelotte, 'The Disintegration of the Conservative Party in the 1840s: A Study of Political Attitudes', in William O. Aydelotte, Allan G. Bogue, and Robert William Fogel (eds.), *The Dimensions of Quantitative Research in History* (Princeton, 1972)).   [99] [J. W. Croker], 'Political Affairs', *QR* 63 (1839), 274.

[100] R.M. Beverley, *A Letter to His Grace the Archbishop of York, on the Present Corrupt State of the Church of England*, 5th edn. (1831), 16; Arnold to J. E. Tyler, 10 June 1832, in Arthur Penrhyn Stanley, *The Life and Correspondence of Thomas Arnold*, 5th edn. (1845), i. 326. Beverley's pamphlet went through twelve editions within a year.   [101] Peel to Goulburn, 24 June 1833, in Parker, *Peel*, ii. 223.

triumphantly—by Ecclesiastical Commissioners in cooperation with both political parties. Peel upset Conservatives by refusing public funds for Church extension, but his insistence that the money could be found through better management of clerical revenues proved correct. Over 2,000 new places of Anglican worship were built between 1831 and 1851, and at last the Church of England could punch its weight in the industrial North.[102] The grossest abuses relating to simony, pluralism, and non-residence were attended to; many of the worst sinecures were abolished;[103] the glaring gap between stipends in different sees was modified; deans were robbed a little in order to pay archdeacons more. Another part of the solution lay in persuading the Church to be more hard-nosed. There was a significant revaluation of cathedral property to bring it into line with market rates, and a commensurate increase in the twenty-one-year fines which lessees paid on renewal. The knottiest problem was tithe. Being levied on produce, it burdened agriculture to the tune of £4 million a year, and it was also a disincentive to improvement, since the harder a farmer worked, the more he paid. Hence the well-known parody of the harvest hymn, 'We plough the fields and scatter the evidence from the parson!'[104] In 1836 Russell commuted all tithes into a fixed money payment related to the price of corn, under the supervision of central and assistant commissioners. Peel would have preferred a voluntary system, based on the views of two-thirds of tithe-owners and -payers in each parish, while Inglis likened Russell's plan to the Civil Constitution of the Clergy, the great attack on the Catholic Church at the time of the French Revolution, but in the event the new system worked smoothly. Less successful was Peel's New Parishes Act of 1843, which enabled the Ecclesiastical Commissioners to create parishes in districts with more than 2,000 residents. It was a well-meaning attempt to encourage the establishment of schools, provident associations, visit-ing societies, and clothing clubs in the manufacturing areas, but it did not take into account the probability that parishes only worked well in the countryside because the population was already predisposed to religious belief. This was not the case in large towns, as the first religious census in 1851 would reveal.[105]

---

[102] Brian Lewis, *The Middlemost and the Milltowns: Bourgeois Culture and Politics in Early Industrial England* (Stanford, Calif., 2001), 151–220.

[103] For example, the Pluralities Act (1838) tightened rules for future incumbents; the Ecclesiastical Duties and Revenues Act (1840) reduced cathedral establishments and reallocated money for parochial purposes; the Deans and Chapters Act (1840) suppressed all the 360 or so non-resident prebends which were attached to cathedrals. It fluttered many belfries but especially at Lincoln, where the ensuing controversy could have come straight out of Trollope.

[104] In fact, more than one-third of tithes were owned by laymen, but radical rhetoric invariably portrayed them as a specifically clerical abuse (Eric J. Evans, *The Contentious Tithe: The Tithe Problem and English Agriculture, 1750–1850* (1976), 8).

[105] Olive J. Brose, *Church and Parliament: The Reshaping of the Church of England 1828–1860* (Stanford, Calif., 1959), 198–206. The census suggested that only 38.8% of the population attended religious services. Worse, only 18.4% attended Anglican churches as against 19% for the Protestant Nonconformist sects.

The hallmarks of ecclesiastical reform are generally taken to be 'utility, thrift, efficiency',[106] its heroes the Bishop of London (Charles Blomfield), the Archbishop of Dublin (Richard Whately), Peel, and Russell. Yet it was not an exclusively utilitarian or top-down process, and much of the renewed impetus for social work and parish reform came at diocesan level or below in the form of episcopal visitations and in the enhanced roles accorded to rural deans and archdeacons. Dr W. F. Hook, the High Church Vicar of Leeds, is remembered for his parochial efforts and philanthropy, but he was not such an anomaly as is often supposed. At the grass roots the impetus for reform long preceded the 1830s, and what that decade brought, in response to public concern, was bureaucratization (diocesan societies, boards, committees, and red tape).[107] From this perspective the growing ascendancy of rural deans and archdeacons can be seen as a victory for middle management and a defeat for community laymen such as churchwardens, parish clerks, sextons, and schoolteachers.[108] While Anglicans marshalled their defences, recognizing that theirs was now just one denomination among many in a competitive religious market, Dissenters felt sure that their hour had come. In 1833 a United Committee of Dissenters was established, and two years later a Dissenters' Parliamentary Committee was set up to help Liberal candidates in elections. Most of its leaders were moderates who were anxious to cooperate with Russell and Morpeth, but they were in danger of being left behind by the 'remarkable upsurge of Dissenting feeling that adopted the disestablishment cry' during the winter of 1833–4.[109] When the Congregationalist Thomas Binney asserted that the Church of England was 'a great national evil', which destroyed more souls than it saved, it was widely taken to be an outright declaration of war.[110] In May 1836 a large rally in London, chaired by the moderate John Angell James of the Birmingham Congregation, led to the formation of the Church Rate Abolition Society. At the same time, municipal reform gave Nonconformists a huge boost, most spectacularly in Leeds where the old Anglican corporation gave way overnight to a council more than half of whose forty-eight elected members were Dissenters,

    [106] Ibid. 35–6, 93–5; Kenneth A. Thompson, *Bureaucracy and Church Reform: The Organizational Response of the Church of England to Social Change 1800–1965* (Oxford, 1970); G. F. A. Best, *Temporal Pillars: Queen Anne's Bounty, the Ecclesiastical Commissioners, and the Church of England* (Cambridge, 1964), 239–347.

    [107] Arthur Burns, *The Diocesan Revival in the Church of England c.1800–1870* (Oxford, 1999), 260–75.

    [108] Frances Knight, *The Nineteenth-Century Church and English Society* (Cambridge, 1995), 167–200; Stewart J. Brown, *The National Churches of England, Ireland, and Scotland 1801–46* (Oxford, 2001), 168–246.

    [109] D. W. Bebbington, *Evangelicalism in Modern Britain: A History from the 1730s to the 1980s* (1989), 98–9; Owen Chadwick, *The Victorian Church* (1976–70), i. 60–4; G. I. T. Machin, *Politics and the Churches in Great Britain 1832 to 1868* (Oxford, 1977), 42–3.

    [110] Herbert S. Skeats and Charles S. Miall, *History of the Free Churches of England 1688–1891* (1894), 479–80.

as were the first ten mayors. These developments prompted Whig ministers to abandon their policy of moderate concessions,[111] while the antics of the Tractarians and the Conservative victory in 1841 soured relations even further. Gradually the Dissenters' campaign for civic equality was overtaken by Voluntarism, meaning the total disestablishment of the Church of England. To this end Edward Miall's British Anti-State Church Association, later called the Liberation Society, was established in 1844. One historian has characterized the change as a transition 'from Dissent to Nonconformity'.[112] In general the terms have been used interchangeably in this book, but it can be argued that Dissent implied resentful opposition to a political establishment from which its members felt excluded, whereas Nonconformists more positively basked in the sure and certain hope that God was on their side. This would make Nonconformity a cultural movement in its own right, with a unique institutional setting—chapel—and traditions of full-throttle hymn-singing and communal participation. And there were compelling reasons for optimism in that member-ship rose much faster even than that of the population as a whole. Baptist congregations increased from under 400 in 1773 to more than 2,300 in 1851, by which date there were over 6,000 Wesleyan Methodist congregations and more than 4,300 belonging to other Arminian Methodist groups.[113] As a result of expansion, brains came to matter less than numbers. Therefore, Unitarians lost much of their old authority,[114] and the lead was taken more and more by Congregationalists (formerly Independents), Baptists, and Methodists, the latter being the most numerous and the most centrally organized,[115] despite being more widely dispersed, in mining villages for example. This denomina-tional shift in power might have signalled the triumph of evangelicalism, except that the sects were losing much of their old spiritual fervour. This was owing to four trends that were barely noticeable before 1830, seemed unstoppable by 1846, and would develop even more forcefully over the next half-century.

The first was a perhaps inevitable consequence of the turn to politics. Dissenters had once despised such matters, but now it was widely felt that 'Not to be a politician in these days is to be a traitor to those principles which are identified with the advancement of Christ's kingdom.' Perhaps it would be more accurate to say that the nature of their political activities changed. Dissenters

[111] Richard Brent, 'The Whigs and Protestant Dissent in the Decade of Reform: The Case of Church Rates, 1833–1841', *EHR* 102 (1987), 887–910.

[112] Clyde Binfield, *So Down to Prayers: Studies in English Nonconformity 1780–1920* (1977), 31–142.

[113] Michael R. Watts, *The Dissenters*, ii: *The Expansion of Evangelical Nonconformity* (Oxford, 1995), 23.

[114] In 1836 the Unitarians even seceded from the Dissenting Deputies and from the General Body of London Ministers following a dispute with evangelical Nonconformists over rights to an endowment fund (Lady Hewley's Trust).

[115] Causing their most prominent minister, Jabez Bunting, to be dubbed by detractors 'the Methodist Pope'.

had traditionally acted on the public stage as Friends of Peace or opponents of the slave trade. Such campaigns were assertions of middle-class identity, with overlapping leagues and societies, each giving rise to its own newspaper and journal, and with regular congresses and conferences which processed from town to town like medieval courts, but they were also highly idealistic ventures. Early pacifism, for example, was a predominantly metropolitan movement, despite the fact that its leader was the Exeter draper Jonathan Dymond, and its moving spirits were Quakers, with their belief in the inner light. Thanks to their conviction that the Creation was benign, and that there was a particular providence guarding the country, pacifists thought it safe to disarm unilaterally. Their confidence in the possibility of universal brotherhood challenged head-on the orthodox evangelical and Malthusian belief that wars, like famines and pestilence, were part of the natural order. Such Quaker pacifism survived into the second quarter of the century, but it then lost out to the view that disarmament should only proceed on a reciprocal basis. This more pragmatic and provincial strand of the peace movement was associated in the 1830s with Joseph Sturge, the Birmingham Quaker, and then in the 1840s with Cobden, Bright, Henry Richard, and a largely Manchester contingent for whom peace was less an end in itself than a concomitant of free trade and commercial benefit.[116]

A second trend was the desire for a more professional ministry. In place of spontaneity, homespun simplicity, and a talent for converting sinners, it now seemed important that ministers should be able to stand their ground in theological controversy with Anglican clergymen. This required them to serve full-time, attend theological colleges, and obtain qualifications (the first training institution for Methodists was established in 1834).[117] It meant a widening gap between themselves and the laity, though a few sects such as the Primitive Methodists and Bible Christians maintained their enthusiasm for itinerancy, recruitment, and mission. A third and related trend was for Dissent to become socially respectable,[118] which at least removed one incentive for its members to turn Anglican. Congregationalists especially were by this time overwhelmingly

---

[116] Martin Ceadel, *The Origins of War Prevention: The British Peace Movement and International Relations, 1730–1854* (Oxford, 1996), 222–469; Alex Tyrrell, *Joseph Sturge and the Moral Radical Party in Early Victorian Britain* (1987), 139–52.

[117] Dale A. Johnson, *The Changing Shape of English Nonconformity, 1825–1925* (New York, 1999), 15–32; Deryck W. Lovegrove, *Established Church, Sectarian People: Itinerancy and the Transformation of English Dissent, 1780–1830* (Cambridge, 1988), 66–87.

[118] K. S. Inglis, *Churches and the Working Classes in Victorian England* (1963), 9, 13–14; R. Tudur Jones, *Congregationalism in England 1662–1962* (1962), 235–44; W. R. Ward, *Religion and Society in England 1790–1850* (1972), 129; David Hempton, *Methodism and Politics in British Society 1750–1850* (1984), 227, 236; A. D. Gilbert, *Religion and Society in Industrial England: Church, Chapel, and Social Change, 1740–1914* (1976), 66–8, 144–57.

middle-class. The most visible manifestation of this development was architectural. Up to the mid-1830s almost all Dissenting preaching houses were plain, vernacular, and brick-built; on the few occasions when grandiloquence was essayed, the preferred style was Greek. Yet in 1837 the Unitarians chose thirteenth-century Gothic and stone for Charles Barry's Upper Brook Street Chapel in Manchester. The Congregationalists had done the same at March in Cambridgeshire the previous year, and from then on chapels were made to look a bit like parish churches. Admittedly, this often caused acrimony, as did the installation of organs. Many of the new places of worship seated several thousands, and organs were needed to enable congregations to sing in time together, but some suspected that the real reason for their introduction was liturgical. It was just such a controversy at Leeds in 1827 which led to the secession of 900 Wesleyans, and to the formation of the Protestant Methodists, who became the umpteenth splinter group to claim that it represented John Wesley's true beliefs.[119]

Thanks to some relatively accurate statistics, the class composition of Wesleyans can be discussed with some confidence. It appears that the great surges in recruitment of the mid-1790s and mid-1800s coincided with falling real wages, whereas during 1820–3, 1831–4, and 1848–50 they occurred at times of rising wages, at least in the towns.[120] The most likely explanation is that Wesleyanism was transformed by the many secessions from its ranks. In the earlier period most conversions were driven by apocalyptic anxiety, what the historian E. P. Thompson famously called 'the chiliasm of despair'.[121] The prospect of a Paradise in which the last would be first offered solace in adversity, and spawned among the poorest sections of the community waves of revivalism characterized by heavy pietism, love feasts, belief in miracles, and a good deal of ranting. From the 1810s, however, working-class Methodists were more and more likely to secede (as Primitive Methodists, Bible Methodists, Reformed Methodists, Independent Methodists, etc.) leaving the parent Wesleyan stem ever more middle-class in composition.

Between the 1830s and the 1840s the proportion of businessmen, retailers, and white-collar workers among the Leeds Wesleyans doubled while the proportion of unskilled workers halved and the weavers disappeared. While the proportion of higher-skilled workers among Leeds Wesleyans remained fairly steady from the 1830s to the 1860s, the proportion of middle-class men rose from 25 per cent in the 1830s to 46.5 per cent in the 1860s, the proportion of labour aristocrats also nearly doubled, and the proportion of [lower and unskilled labourers and depressed weavers] fell from 46.5 per cent in the 1830s to 18.1 per cent in the 1860s.[122]

---

[119] Watts, *Dissenters*, ii. 34, 185–7, 414–16, 605–7.   [120] Ibid. 72–3.
[121] E. P. Thompson, *The Making of the English Working Class* (1965), 350–400.
[122] Watts, *Dissenters*, ii. 303–27, 600–1.

In these circumstances it seems likely that later Wesleyan revivals reflected the successful, associational side of urban life—along with the cooperative movement, trade unions, mechanics institutes, and public libraries—rather than with immiseration and despair.

A final development was even more destructive of evangelical enthusiasm. Bunting's strict Methodist parents, seeking the best, had sent him to Unitarian ministers for his education in Manchester,[123] but by 1846 such ecumenism was unthinkable. So long as Dissenters had been on the defensive against Anglicanism, they had enjoyed a strength which comes from unity, but now that they felt that they were winning, differences emerged and jealousies arose. This was most evident among Methodists with their various secessions, but it was also characteristic of Nonconformity as a whole. A staggering growth in devotional magazines reinforced these sectarian barriers. Table 8.10, based on the 1851 Religious Census, gives a sense of how fissiparous Nonconformity had become by this time, but even it ignores the distinction between evangelical and mainstream Quakers, between Particular and General Baptists, and scores of smaller sects.[124]

Such subdivision was bound to cause internal friction, as in 1844 when Peel's Government introduced the Dissenters' Chapels Bill, giving statutory recognition of the Unitarians' legal right to retain some 200 buildings and certain charitable funds originally owned by Presbyterians and other orthodox sects. In the case of the buildings they had to prove twenty-five years' continuous usage and show that Trinitarian worship was not explicitly stipulated in the original trust deed. Most High Churchmen and 102 Conservative MPs opposed the Bill, and so too did many orthodox Dissenters, notably Methodists, Congregationalists, and Baptists, on the grounds that Unitarians were not entitled to any property granted to them before 1813, the year in which they had been recognized as a lawful denomination. The same unlikely combination of High Churchmen and Dissenters recurred in 1845 with the formation of the Evangelical Alliance in protest against Peel's decision to increase the Maynooth grant. Some Anglicans such as Edward Bickersteth teamed up with anti-papists in Europe and America as well as with Nonconformists at home. Wesleyans were especially keen members of the alliance, having nowhere else to go. Many retained a residual loyalty to the Establishment and were further distinguished among Nonconformists by their support for the Conservative Party,[125] so they felt especially betrayed by Peel's actions. A mammoth demonstration against the Maynooth Bill was orchestrated from Exeter Hall with

---

[123] Ward, *Religion and Society*, 4.

[124] Roughly speaking, evangelical Quakers such as J. J. Gurney believed in original sin rather than the inner light and in the operations of general (rather than particular) providence most of the time. The distinction between Particular and General Baptists referred not to the operations of providence but to the Calvinist doctrine of pre-election.

[125] However, most rank-and-file Wesleyans voted Liberal (Hempton, *Methodism*, 179–223).

TABLE 8.10. *Number of Protestant Nonconformist worshippers in England, 1851*

Denomination	No. (to nearest 000)	% population	Main regions of strength
Congregationalists	656,000	3.88	Wales, south and east England
Baptists	500,000	2.95	Hunts, Beds., Camb., Wales
Quakers	17,000	0.10	
Unitarians	34,000	0.20	Hackney, Hampstead, Manchester, Bristol, Birmingham, Exeter
Presbyterians	28,000	0.17	Northumb.
United Presbyterians	22,000	0.13	
Calvinistic Methodists	19,000	0.11	North and west Wales
Lady Huntingdon's Connexion	22,000	0.13	
Wesleyan Methodists	924,000	5.46	Corn., Lincs., Yorks., Derby., Notts., Wales
Wesleyan Methodist Association (1835)	62,000	0.36	Corn., Lancs.,
Methodist New Connexion (1797)	62,000	0.37	West Riding, Staffs. Notts.
Independent Methodists (1805)	2,000	0.01	Lancs., Ches.
Primitive Methodists (1812)	330,000	1.95	North-east, East Midlands
Bible Christians (1815)	48,000	0.28	Corn., Devon
Protestant Methodists (1827)	?		Leeds
Wesleyan Reformers (1849)	62,000	0.37	
Moravians	7,000	0.04	
New Church (Swedenborgians)	8,000	0.04	Lancs., Yorks.
Brethren	7,000	0.04	
Others	70,000	0.41	

Source: Adapted from Michael R. Watts, *The Dissenters*, ii: *The Expansion of Evangelical Nonconformity* (Oxford, 1995), 28.

over 10,000 petitions mustered in four months, one of which had more than a million and a quarter signatures. Perhaps as many as one in twenty of the entire population of Britain and Ireland registered opposition.

Of course, many issues still brought Dissenters together. They all resented Church rates, which cumulatively contributed about 12 per cent to the Establishment's revenues. Since at least the fourteenth century all local ratepayers had been charged for the upkeep and repair of parish churches and the running costs of services. The burden had increased as a result of the Church Building Acts, but there were no formal protests until 1832, when parish vestries up and down the country refused to levy the rate.[126] This civil disobedience was followed up by a large meeting of Dissenters, held in Manchester in 1834 and fronted by the Congregationalist George Hadfield. The simplest solution would have been to exempt non-Anglicans. This would have been just about manageable for the Church financially, but would have boosted the number of Dissenters, so instead Althorp brought in a Bill to replace the rates with an addition to the land tax, the proceeds of which were to be handed over to the Church. It was carried in the Commons by 256 to 140, but aroused so much resentment among the Government's own supporters that it was quietly withdrawn. The fact that all but three out of 140 opponents were Whigs, Radicals, and Dissenters, while 111 of the 265 MPs who supported it were Conservatives, including Peel and even Inglis, proves that the Bill was bad for Dissenters, who would still have had to pay ('out of one pocket instead of out of the other'[127]) but would have had less power to influence the rate at which the tax was levied than they currently possessed in local vestries. Furthermore, Scottish and Irish taxpayers would have been called on to help maintain edifices in England for the first time. In 1837 Spring Rice won Dissenters' support for a scheme to maintain the Church's buildings from a fund created by the better management of its leaseholds, but this time the bishops cried foul and the Government backed off. Church rates were to remain legally compulsory and a bone of bitter contention until 1868. Meanwhile, in 1834 Russell had introduced a Bill which would have allowed Dissenters to marry outside the parish church, while still requiring them to publish banns there. It too was withdrawn after an outcry by Nonconformists, who regarded the qualification as insulting, but the introduction of civic registration three years later meant that at last Dissenters could enter and leave the world, as well as marry, without making obeisance to the hated vicar.

Education was coming to be regarded as another rite of passage. London University finally got its charter in 1836, after strong opposition from Oxford and Cambridge, and so became University College London. Its professorial structure,

---

[126] J. P. Ellens, *Religious Routes to Gladstonian Liberalism: The Church Rate Conflict in England and Wales, 1832–1868* (University Park, Pa., 1994), 1–69.

[127] J. D. Hume, *HPD*3 xxii. 1020 (21 Apr. 1834).

modelled on Scottish and German precedents, and its rejection of clerical trappings, were meant to appeal to Nonconformists, but many were repelled by its secular ethos, some referring to it as 'the synagogue of Satan'. Unfortunately, their own institutions of general education were—with a few notable exceptions like the Unitarian Manchester College—much weaker than in the eighteenth century. Many therefore set their sights on storming Oxford and Cambridge, recognition perhaps that the institutions once described by Priestley as 'pools of stagnant water' had begun to flow a little intellectually, although it may also have owed something to the socially aspirational nature of Nonconformity at this time.

Repeal of the Test and Corporation Acts posed the problem of the 'confessional university in an increasingly non-confessional state'.[128] Since the Oxford Examination Statute of 1800, which decreed that undergraduates receive religious instruction and take holy communion at least once a term, the rule requiring them to matriculate by subscription to the Thirty-Nine Articles had been enforced with increasing rigour. The situation was somewhat more relaxed at Cambridge, where subscription had never been required for matriculation, while since 1772 it had also been possible to graduate by simply declaring oneself a bona fide member of the Church of England. In 1834 attempts by reformers to open up both systems caused mayhem. The heads of houses in Oxford decided by one vote to replace subscription with a bland declaration, but were forced by Convocation (voting 459–57) to rescind the decision a year later. Similarly, in Cambridge a petition by sixty-two resident dons (and one other) for Dissenters to be allowed to drop even the declaration, and also to become fellows of colleges, was swamped by a counter-petition from 258 others, more than half of whom were non-resident. One reason why such high-table controversies were followed so avidly in the country at large was the involvement of the 'external university'. In each institution the supreme legislative body was composed of all MAs who were willing to make the journey to attend in person, and about three-quarters of them were in holy orders.[129] It could even be argued that the Convocation of Oxford and the Cambridge Senate were the only forums in which Anglicans could engage in ecclesiastical and theological debate since the convocations of Canterbury and York were prorogued in 1717.[130]

---

[128] H. C. G. Matthew, 'Noetics, Tractarians, and the Reform of the University of Oxford in the Nineteenth Century', *History of Universities*, 9 (1990), 195–225.

[129] M. C. Curthoys, 'The Careers of Oxford Men', in M. G. Brock and M. C. Curthoys (eds.), *The History of the University of Oxford*, vi: *Nineteenth-Century Oxford, Part 1* (Oxford, 1997), 482.

[130] The Convocation of the Church of England was finally re-established as a debating forum in 1855, one year after the power of the Convocation of Oxford had been weakened by the establishment of Congregation to represent the tutors and professors, and one year before a similar reform was effected at Cambridge.

Eventually a Unitarian, G. W. F. Wood, brought in a Bill to allow anyone of good character to be admitted to any university. It succeeded in the Commons but was thrown out in the Lords by 102 votes. Nonconformists argued that the right to attend the ancient universities was a ticket of citizenship; Anglicans countered that those institutions were primarily religious seminaries. There were even calls in debate to revive Church courts and to enforce religious attendance at parish level. It would be simplistic, however, to portray the dispute as one between pluralism and privilege, since Wood thought that Nonconformists should submit to university discipline once they had been admitted, whereas Conservatives realized that this would be improper as well as impossible. As Gladstone hinted, if Dissenters attended they would have to be excused compulsory chapel, and that would make it harder for the dons to hold the line against the drinking societies. A more profound concern, expressed by Goulburn among others, was that the presence of non-Anglicans would inhibit teachers from bringing religious considerations to bear on secular subjects, thereby 'separating religious from literary education', the sacred from the secular.[131] 'If you unchurch your universities you must unchristianize them.'[132]

The English school system in 1800 was exceptionally diverse. There was a handful of public schools for aristocrats and aspirants, a number of endowed grammar schools in older and more prosperous towns, and at least 1,500 privately run charity and trade schools. Some of these were endowed, some relied on subscriptions, and some offered free education for the very poor. Some were organized under the auspices of the Society for the Promotion of Christian Knowledge, and some belonged to the various Dissenting sects. In addition, most towns and villages had dame schools, and parents at all levels of society would scrape together a farthing a week to secure their children's attendance. Monitorial, industrial, and workhouse schools proliferated from the 1800s onwards, and networks of cellar schools in towns like Manchester. By the 1830s several mainly charitable 'ragged schools' had been established to provide education for a lucky few from the most destitute classes, but the most spectacular development was the Sunday school movement. Thousands of new Sunday schools were established (see Table 8.11), while the number of pupils enrolled in them (actual attendance is of course a different matter) increased to a quite staggering degree: from under 60,000 in 1788 to almost 750,000 by 1821, and more than 2 million in 1851. By that time enrolments took in 12.5 per cent of the population, including many adults, 56.5 per cent of children aged 5–15, and 75.4 per cent of working-class children.[133]

[131] *HPD*3 xxv. 646 (28 July 1834).
[132] 'The Cambridge Controversy: Admission of Dissenters to Degrees', *QR* 52 (1834), 472.
[133] Thomas Walter Laqueur, *Religion and Respectability: Sunday Schools and Working Class Culture 1780–1850* (New Haven, 1976), 44.

TABLE 8.11. *Number of Sunday schools built or founded,*
1780–1851

Years	No. of Sunday schools	% affiliated to Church of England
1780–1801	2,290	56.4
1802–11	4,687	48.8
1812–21	8,236	45.7
1822–31	11,910	45.0
1832–41	17,168	45.0
1842–51	23,135	45.0

Source: T. W. Laqueur, *Religion and Respectability: Sunday Schools and*
Working Class Culture, 1780–1850 (New Haven, 1976), 44.

Although affiliated to church or chapel, most Sunday schools were run on independent (and sometimes even antagonistic) lines, and the education they provided was mainly secular, with just a small amount of denominational religion thrown in.[134] Their popularity probably owed a lot to the fact that they were grass-roots organizations, and if they inculcated an ethos of respectability, it came from working-class men and women themselves, not from bourgeois pressure.[135] By contrast most of the subscription-based charity schools, responsible for a very large part of elementary instruction, were absorbed by one of two controlling bodies, the British and Foreign School Society (BFSS, 1808) and the National Society for the Education of the Poor in the Principles of the Established Church (1811). The National Society, founded by Joshua Watson, was highly catechetical and was passionately supported by High Churchmen and Anglican evangelicals, whereas its rival the BFSS promoted a generalized, unsectarian form of religious education and was championed by Nonconformists and Liberal Anglicans.

Most popular schooling in the eighteenth century had mixed book-learning with practical skills such as sewing and spinning, whereas in the schools of the two societies and the surviving charity schools the curriculum was more purely academic. Their pupils were tempted to think of themselves as forming an upper stratum of the working classes—'children of the deserving poor'—and fit for a more exalted education than was available in the Sunday, industrial, and cellar schools. Learning to read and write would fit them for what later came to be

---

[134] It was only with the expansion of elementary state schooling after 1870 that the Sunday schools abandoned secular instruction. Their new role was to inculcate that religious dogma which state (Board) schools were not permitted to teach.   [135] Ibid. 241–5.

called white-collar occupations, for example as bookkeepers in the expanding retail trades.[136] Here lay the origin of a snobbish distinction between theoretical and technical knowledge, pure and applied, which may account for a long-term decline in England's success in producing inventive entrepreneurs. But whatever the strengths and weaknesses of such schools, at least 2 million children missed out altogether. Illiteracy among females (as measured by those who could not sign their names in marriage registers) probably fell slightly during 1800–40, whereas among men it may even have increased during 1783–1810 and only fallen slightly thereafter.[137] The 1840s brought mild improvement, but still at mid-century about 30 per cent of men and 45 per cent of women could not sign. There was to be no dramatic improvement until after the passing of the 1870 Education Act, when illiteracy went into a nosedive, being down to 1 per cent by 1911. However, these national figures mask considerable variations between different occupations, and also within and between regions, with the worst-performing counties forming a broad horizontal band between the Ribble and the Thames. All that can be said with certainty is that education varied from the excellent to the dire. As in the mid-twentieth century, the main ones to suffer were probably not the children of the poor, but rather the sons of those who sought to purchase a would-be genteel education at somewhere like Dotheboys Hall, Dickens's fictional boarding establishment in *Nicholas Nickleby* (1838–9).

Apart from a few Tory diehards, most commentators accepted that 'the education of the children of the poor . . . should not be left to their ignorant and corrupted parents; it is a public concern, and should be regarded as a public business'.[138] In making such claims, the underlying objective was usually conceived to be social and moral regeneration rather than economic efficiency. In France, Austria, and several German states including Prussia there was a move towards state control, but because of an ingrained antipathy to centralization, the only way to have established public provision and control in England would have been through the rates. In 1820 Brougham brought in an abortive bill to force parishes to provide for elementary education, as in Scotland, and he continued to press for such a solution in the 1840s. However, by the time that local government had been reformed, Parliament had already ventured on a different model. One of the first acts of the reformed Parliament was to devote

---

[136] M. G. Jones, *The Charity School Movement: A Study of Eighteenth-Century Puritanism in Action* (Cambridge, 1938), 160–1.

[137] On the relation of writing to reading, Schofield suggests that the number able to sign was roughly equal to the number able to read fluently, while half as many again could probably read to some extent (R. S. Schofield, 'Dimensions of Illiteracy in England 1750–1850', in Harvey J. Graff (ed.), *Literacy and Social Development in the West: A Reader* (Cambridge, 1981)).

[138] Mrs [Sarah] Trimmer, *The Oeconomy of Charity* (1801), i. 12.

£20,000 per annum for elementary education, to be shared between the two national societies in proportion to the amounts which they each raised privately. Scoffers observed that six times as much was spent on rebuilding the royal stables that year, but even so it was something of a breakthrough that money should be spent on the people as well as the monarch. The size of the grant increased with the creation of new schools, and had reached £100,000 in 1846, but instead of inspiring gratitude all round, Nonconformists succumbed to feelings of relative deprivation owing to the fact that 70 per cent of the money went to the National Society, simply because the bulk of voluntary schools were Anglican.

Another point of controversy was the place of religion in grant-aided schools. Hardly anyone was yet prepared to suggest that weekday education should be entirely secular. Most Whigs and Liberal Anglicans believed that multi-denominational schools were necessary to instil a sense of English identity and to restore organic unity to a palpably disintegrating society, but this required that religious instruction should be non-denominational, non-doctrinal, and inoffensive. Utilitarians broadly concurred, and in 1836 the Radical MP J. A. Roebuck founded a Central Society of Education to press for just such a solution. In 1839 Russell brought forward proposals for non-sectarian elementary schools, along the lines of Ireland's national schools, which appeared to be working well. There was to be a national inspectorate, answerable to an Education Committee of the Privy Council, which would be composed entirely of laymen, would administer the annual grant to National Society and BFSS schools, and would be responsible for ensuring common standards. He also devised a scheme for a teacher training college, or 'normal school', and a model school to pioneer a form of Bible-based teaching. The idea was that this should incorporate the highest common factors of faith, on top of which the various denominations including Catholics would be free to teach their own particular dogmas at particular points in the timetable.[139] No one was pleased. Anglicans protested that Bible-based instruction would favour Protestant Nonconformity, which was relatively undogmatic anyway. Inglis denounced the idea of mixed-religion, or 'comprehensive', schools. Disraeli attacked centralization on the grounds that 'wherever everything was left to the government the subject became a machine'. But the greatest anguish came from a high-pressure group of youthful High Churchmen nicknamed the Young Gentlemen, whose leading lights were Gladstone, Ashley, Acland, and Sandon. Faced with such intensity of opposition, Russell backed down on a central point by conceding that inspectors of National Society schools should be appointed and directed by the Church of England.

[139] Jonathan Parry, *The Rise and Fall of Liberal Government in Victorian Britain* (New Haven, 1993), 138.

When Graham became Home Secretary he sought to exploit the education clauses of recent legislation covering textile workers.[140] His Bill of 1843 proposed that children between the ages of 8 and 13 should work for a maximum of six and half hours with at least three additional hours a day for education, including compulsory Scripture readings in the authorized version. These factory schools would be inspected by the Committee of the Privy Council and run on a day-to-day basis by local trusts. Their masters would be appointed by elected local boards of managers, but bishops were to have an ultimate right of veto (thus ensuring that almost all of them would be Anglicans, and that none of them would be Roman Catholics or Unitarians). The Dissenters exploded with anger, not only Congregationalists and Baptists but even Wesleyans, who had taken the Church of England's side against Russell in 1839, and Graham was forced to withdraw his Bill.[141] Peel called it 'a sorry and lamentable triumph that Dissent had achieved',[142] thereby echoing the feelings which Russell had had about the Establishment four years earlier. Education was to remain stuck in this denominational quagmire for decades to come.

CLOUDS IN THE WEST

'That sweet sleep in which Irish agitation had slumbered' was how Russell described the years of Lord Melbourne's administration. One reason for this was a temporary lull in sectarian and ethnic bitterness, despite continuing agrarian crisis. Since 1815 prices had fallen much faster than rents, which led to many smaller tenant farmers (cottiers) and conacre tenants being evicted. However, their oppressors were just as likely to be large Catholic freehold farmers as Protestant landlords, and much of the resulting violence was by papist on papist. Meanwhile, in urban areas there was increasing cooperation between the traditional Protestant Dissenting middle class and a Catholic bourgeoisie which was rapidly expanding in size and wealth. In particular the two groups worked together in chambers of commerce to attack the closed corporations, which had traditionally monopolized control over Irish business. There was also a rare degree of goodwill at Westminster. Liberal and Radical losses in the 1837 election left the Government dependent on the Irish Parliamentary Party (IPP), which put an onus on O'Connell to act responsibly.[143] He was inclined to move cautiously anyway because of the IPP's own losses following its initial triumph in 1832 (see Table 8.12). Although about half of

---

[140] See below, pp. 589–90.

[141] J. T. Ward, *Sir James Graham* (1967), 193–7; G. I. T. Machin, *Politics and the Churches in Great Britain 1832 to 1868* (Oxford, 1977), 151–60; D. G. Paz, *The Politics of Working-Class Education in Britain, 1830–1850* (Manchester, 1980), 122–4.

[142] Peel to Ashley, 16 June 1843, Peel MS 40483, fos. 110–11.

[143] Angus Macintyre, *The Liberator: Daniel O'Connell and the Irish Party 1830–1847* (1965), 126–66.

TABLE 8.12. *Irish general election results, 1832–1841*

Year	Conservatives	Whig/Liberals	Repealers
1832	30	38	39
1835	39	34	32
1837	34	40	31
1841	40	47	18

the forty Whig and Liberal MPs cooperated with O'Connell, others such as William Smith O'Brien were keen to engage constructively with ministers, and to grab the reform initiative for the United Kingdom as a whole, offering Ireland as a laboratory for social experiments.[144]

The Government also deserves credit for the improved atmosphere. Thomas Spring Rice, MP for Cambridge University, was a genial Irishman, former Canningite, the main force behind the promotion of national schools in Ireland, and one of Melbourne's more resourceful and imaginative ministers. Unfortunately he is mainly remembered as a failed Chancellor of the Exchequer, having held that office through the onset of a serious economic depression (1835–9).[145] The Government officials responsible for Ireland—Normanby (Viceroy 1835–9), Morpeth (Chief Secretary 1835–41), and Thomas Drummond (Under-Secretary 1835–40)—were all genuinely likeable and devoid of racial condescension. In particular Drummond, an indefatigable and fair-minded Scotsman, brought highly effective executive talents to bear until his early death in 1840. Morpeth was less astute, and in the West Riding was regarded as 'sleek and oily', but in Dublin he went down like a charm. He treated the natives cordially, gave sartorial advice, cracked jokes, held galas and balls, and held his own in blarney. Above all he tried to ensure that Catholics got their fair share of patronage, as in the bonanza of jobbery which followed the Constabulary Act of 1836. Almost all the judges, stipendiary magistrates, and police inspectors appointed during 1835–41 were Liberals, and about half were Catholics; so too were a fair number of ordinary magistrates.[146] Catholics were allowed to work in Dublin Castle for the first time, and even invited to sit on juries, a particularly sensitive issue since it meant they were trusted to adjudicate on acts of civil disobedience perpetrated by their co-religionists. Orange marches were

[144] In this they anticipated the IPP of the 1880s. See Alan O'Day, *The English Face of Irish Nationalism: Parnellite Involvement in British Politics 1880–86* (Dublin, 1977).

[145] Jennifer Ridden, *'Making Good Citizens': Irish Elite Approaches to Empire, National Identity, and Citizenship* (forthcoming).

[146] Oliver MacDonagh, 'Politics, 1830–45', in W. E. Vaughan (ed.), *A New History of Ireland*, v (Oxford, 1989), 179, 213–14.

prohibited, Catholic meetings to protest against tithe were allowed to proceed, and green bunting was ostentatiously deployed on official occasions. In another symbolic but significant gesture, the Government sought to have state prayers commemorating the Fifth of November omitted from the Lord Lieutenant's chapel in Dublin; the date marked both the discovery of the Gunpowder Plot and the 'day of deliverance' wrought by William of Orange in 1688.[147] Most important of all was the extension of the New Poor Law to Ireland in 1838, for though that legislation was roundly hated by the populace in England, where it reduced the amount of spending on poor relief,[148] it looked very much more generous in a country where there had never been any compulsory assessment for the poor. Most Irishmen also recognized that Russell was making genuine attempts to resolve the problems of voter registration, tithes, and municipal corporations, and was not to blame for the way in which the Conservative majority in the Lords kept thwarting his intentions. The worst example was the Irish Corporations Bill, which was effectively destroyed by Lyndhurst's Ultras in the Upper House each year from 1836 until finally a watered-down version was passed in 1840. There are many 'if onlys' in the history of the Anglo-Irish Union, such as 'if only Home Rule had succeeded in 1886', but arguably this was more important. 'If we can get the Corporation monopoly put an end to', O'Connell had promised a supporter in 1833, 'we will break a gap in the enemy's fortifications',[149] and that of course explains why Conservative peers were so hostile. Yet in reality municipal reform offered the best opportunity for the development of a non-sectarian urban middle class.

A significant downside in all this was that the Conservative Opposition was inevitably demonized, so when Peel returned to power in 1841 it was almost inevitable that violence would recur. The Loyal National Repeal Association, founded in the previous year, immediately stepped up agitation. Then in 1842 the National Repeal Convention of America was founded, and quickly divided into physical- and moral-force wings, the former of which marked the origin of Fenianism. A series of monster meetings were held in 1843, culminating in one at Clontarf which prompted the Government to have O'Connell arrested and thrown into prison, a move which further soured the atmosphere. Country areas were still disturbed by Ribbonism, which was the latest in a series of underground subversive nationalist movements, successors to the Defenders, and inheriting much of their underground communication and disciplinary networks.[150] A new development of the 1840s was the foundation of Young

---

[147] Peter Nockles, 'Church or Protestant Sect? The Church of Ireland, High Churchmanship, and the Oxford Movement, 1822–1869', *HJ* 41 (1998), 473.   [148] See below, pp. 590–8.

[149] O'Connell to P. V. FitzPatrick, 11 Mar. 1833, in *The Correspondence of Daniel O'Connell*, ed. Maurice R. O'Connell (Dublin, 1972–80), v. 16–17.

[150] Tom Gavin, 'Defenders, Ribbonmen and Others: Underground Political Networks in Pre-Famine Ireland', in C. H. E. Philpin (ed.), *Nationalism and Popular Protest in Ireland* (Cambridge, 1987).

Ireland, a movement led by John Mitchel, William Smith O'Brien, Thomas Davis, and Charles Gavan Duffy. It placed great emphasis on emotion and ethnicity—such as Gaelic language, the harp, and other symbols of cultural nationalism—and it owed much to Continental revolutionary movements in Italy, Hungary, and Czechoslovakia, but it was wholly non-sectarian, and most of its leaders, including the first three mentioned above, were Protestants. It was nevertheless symptomatic of the progressively deteriorating situation that O'Brien moved from being a loyal pro-Unionist in the 1830s, to a member of O'Connell's Repeal Association in 1843, a Young Irelander in 1846, and finally a supporter of the revolutionary Irish Confederation in 1847.

Peel's response to this situation was characteristically gloomy. 'We cannot hope to pass coercion bills. If we did pass them, could we execute them through any other instrumentality than that of the known and recognised Law—that is Trial by Jury? What I fear is that that instrument will break short in our hands.'[151] It was therefore necessary to respond constructively and to kill repeal by kindness. His economic initiatives did not have long enough to work, while possibly the Devon Commission on Irish land (1843–5) did more harm than good by raising false hopes that peasant proprietorship might shortly be on the agenda.[152] His religious concessions were much more significant. As recently as 1833 Peel had expressed his confidence in 'the expansive force of the Protestant faith' to effect 'the Reformation in Ireland'. Even as late as 1839 Graham believed that 'Protestantism is the only weapon with which we can encounter republicanism.'[153] Yet by 1844 it was obvious that the 'Protestant crusade' was dead in the water. It seemed equally obvious, to Peel at least, that much of the agitation was orchestrated by 'a confederacy of twenty or thirty priests', many of whom were alumni of Maynooth. He tried lobbying Metternich in an attempt to have the Pope proscribe clerical involvement in Irish politics. When this failed he decided that he must somehow placate the Catholic clergy instead, hoping that the latter would in turn exercise a moderating influence over the peasantry. 'I know not what remedy there can be . . . but the detaching from the ranks of Repeal, agitation, and disaffection a considerable portion of the respectable and influential Roman Catholic population.'[154] This strategy led him to inaugurate a three-pronged programme of religious concessions. The Charitable Bequests Act of 1844 made it easier to donate gifts of money or land to the Roman Catholic Church in the hope that this would 'make its inferior position less galling'. Unfortunately, as Peel told the Queen, many Irishmen seemed to

[151] Peel, Cabinet memorandum, 17 Feb. 1844, Peel MS 40540, fos. 230–7; Donal A. Kerr, *Peel, Priests and Politics: Sir Robert Peel's Administration and the Roman Catholic Church in Ireland, 1841–1846* (Oxford, 1982), 117 and *passim*.

[152] Peter Gray, *Famine, Land and Politics: British Government and Irish Society 1843–1850* (Dublin, 1999), 55–94. [153] *HPD2* xvii. 999 (6 May 1833); J. T. Ward, *Sir James Graham* (1967), 171.

[154] Peel, Cabinet memorandum, 17 Feb. 1844.

'prefer the grievance to the remedy', and so in the following year he went further down the road of conciliation with his Maynooth Bill, arguing that it was preferable for Irish priests to be trained locally in a college dependent on a parliamentary grant, than to go off to Rome and pick up wild Ultramontanist ideas. Immediately afterwards came the Academic Colleges Bill to establish three new universities at Cork, Galway, and Belfast. The real aim was to cater for Catholics and Presbyterians, but since any attempt at state endowment of specifically anti-Establishment institutions would have caused an outcry in Parliament, it was decided to make them non-denominational along the lines of London's University College and the Irish national schools. As a result they were denounced from all sides as 'godless'.

Peel's Irish policy tore the Conservative Party apart, but he would have regarded that as a price worth paying for reconciliation in Ireland. Was there any prospect that he would achieve this? Much turned on the response of the Catholic hierarchy, a lively and self-confident group of men with a sure hold on the loyalty of the faithful, and a growing consciousness of their role in public life. The situation was complicated by a struggle for power between Daniel Murray, the elderly Archbishop of Dublin, and the charismatic John MacHale, Archbishop of Tuam. A *politique* noted for his angelic mildness of disposition, Murray had almost been killed in the 1798 rebellion, and he nursed a deep suspicion of popular movements, including O'Connell's. Like many of the older bishops, he had been educated on the Continent, and had no wish to offend the Protestant Establishment by overt displays of Catholic devotion. The Maynooth-trained MacHale by contrast was an aggressive nationalist, thanks partly to the fact that his was the poorest province and also the one in which the attempt at a Protestant crusade had been fiercest. Murray thought that MacHale was one of those 'fools who become quite suspicious of every kind of mischief, if we come at all into contact with people in power'. MacHale thought Murray a Protestant lackey, and too much 'under the influence of the vice-regal court in Dublin'. Time and again MacHale successfully frustrated Murray's attempts to cooperate with Peel's Government, despite the fact that most of the other bishops were closer to Murray. His success owed partly to the machinations of Paul Cullen, Rector of the Irish College in Rome, who influenced the Curia in his favour, but there was also the more general reason that ginger groups are only as conciliatory as the least conciliatory member. Where extremists are willing to rock the boat, ultimately moderates must go along with them for the sake of maintaining that unity which only moderates crave.

Historians have often praised Peel's Irish policies, and regretted that they had so little time in which to work. But although the attempt to defuse nationalism by conciliating the clergy was just the sort of elegant solution to be expected of him, it was based on three false premisses. He mistakenly thought that the violence and mass demonstrations of 1842–4 signalled a surge in repeal sentiment, when more likely they were signs that it was on the wane. He condescendingly assumed that Irish peasants were putty in the hands of priests. And he could not see that even conciliatory Catholics like Murray would take the gifts he offered without compromising their underlying nationalism a jot. For these reasons it would be wrong to see his ministry as one of those 'if only' moments. Equally characteristic was Peel's inability to calculate practical effects. Confident that a policy so well conceived must succeed if pushed hard enough, in 1848 he even proposed endowing Catholic clergy, a wholly unaccept-able offer given that it would have rendered them subservient to the British state. As a shrewd historian has observed, Peel 'ignored the force and validity of other men's enthusiasms', not only in Ireland but behind the Treasury Bench.[155]

TOWARDS FREE TRADE: 'MIGHTY ATHLETE' OR 'WOUNDED GIANT'?

Between 1830 and 1850 the East India Company monopoly, the West India sugar preference, the Corn Laws, and Navigation Acts were all abolished, the powers of the Bank of England were curbed, while public expenditure remained level, despite a population increase of almost 4 million. The fiscal–military state was fast becoming a minimal state,[156] while mercantilism was retreating before free-market attitudes. Historians sometimes attribute this development to parliamentary reform, but in fact there are grounds for thinking that the coming to power of the Whigs in 1830 delayed rather than accelerated the process.

The Whig Budget of 1831, their first for twenty-four years, was bungled. Althorp, Poulett Thomson, and Parnell were devotees of political economy, and their proposals went much further than Huskisson in the direction of unilateral free trade by reducing the preference on colonial timber, and by repealing import duties on manufactured articles such as printed calicoes and finished cotton goods. In opposition they had boasted about how they would pay for tax cuts by retrenchment, but it was difficult to trim expenditure much beyond the nearly £3 million worth of savings that Wellington's Government had already effected. (Althorp announced the suppression of more than two hundred places, as 'confirmation . . . that the Government of this country would no longer be carried on by patronage', but he was forced to admit that in the short term there would be no 'great economy in point of money'.[157]) They could hardly make up the lost revenue with a property tax, having attacked the last one so vociferously,

[155] G. Kitson Clark, *Peel* (1936), 126.
[156] Martin Daunton, *Trusting Leviathan: The Politics of Taxation in Britain, 1799–1914* (Cambridge, 2001), 32–57.   [157] *HPD*3 ii. 405 (11 Feb. 1831).

so instead they proposed a duty on imported raw cotton (which flatly contradicted free-trade policy) and a half per cent tax on the transfer of landed and funded property. Placing duties on raw cotton, while removing duties from the manufactured product, doubly damaged those Lancashire manufacturers who are often thought to have been the intended beneficiaries of the Reform Bill, and is further evidence that the Whigs at this stage still regarded themselves as the party of the landed interest. So too is the transfer tax, which conformed to a Cobbett-type agrarian populism. It was targeted by Peel and Goulburn as a breach of faith with the fundholder, and caused such a mighty outcry in the City that Althorp withdrew the proposal. Nor was this the only fiasco. On 18 March, just four days before the crucial first vote on the Reform Bill, the Canadian merchants and shipowners mustered a successful bid to preserve the preference on colonial timber. The Whigs' first and only really enterprising budget had unravelled completely.[158]

Clearly caution was required, which explains why the most significant aspects of economic policy under Lord Grey were both roads *not* taken. Many people had supported (or opposed) parliamentary reform in the belief that it would lead to repeal of the Corn Laws or to abandonment of the gold standard, respectively the Manchester and Birmingham nostrums, though it must not be supposed that opinion in those towns was monolithic. Expectations proved false in both cases. In March 1833 a proposal by Thomas Attwood implicitly to go off the gold standard was only narrowly defeated (192–158), with both front benches united against Radicals and Ultra Tories. About half of the agriculturists and more than half of the Conservatives lined up behind a man whom only a year before they had regarded as a dangerous political unionist. It seemed to many that Birmingham must triumph, and when Croker called on Peel shortly afterwards he found him

apparently resolved to accept office and make battle. He spoke with great firmness and spirit, said he would do his duty, and, if necessary, venture to attempt a ministry . . . He seemed to think there would be an entirely new combination, of which the currency questions would be the basis. On that he was firm, but foresaw that Radicals and Ultra-Tories would unite against him.[159]

When Attwood raised the matter again a month later, Peel made the speech of his life, invoking concepts such as 'conscience', 'duty', 'the manly course', 'the integrity of the empire', and 'sacred trust'. Meanwhile, Althorp lobbied furiously behind the scenes, and although Conservative county MPs lined up nineteen to nine for Attwood, the motion was heavily defeated (271–134).

---

[158] Lucy Brown, *The Board of Trade and the Free-Trade Movement 1830–42* (Oxford, 1958), 14, 45–50.
[159] *Croker Papers*, ii. 205.

Shortly afterwards Parliament received a very important select committee report on agriculture, written by its chairman, Graham. It conceded that large classes of the community had been affected by changes to the currency. Creditors and persons on fixed incomes had suffered from the restriction in 1797, while 'the active capitals of the country' had benefited. In 1819 resumption had affected the same interests in the opposite direction. Both events had been equally traumatic and equally unjust so far as individuals were concerned, but resumption had been worse for the economy as a whole since it had put a blight on the productive classes. Despite this concession, the report insisted that a line must be drawn in the sand, for fear of creating further injustices.[160] As Althorp put it privately, although 'a gross robbery on the public was committed by Mr Peel's bill in 1819', the repeal of Peel's Bill would constitute 'a similar robbery'.[161] This tactic of admitting the diagnosis[162] while rejecting the cure pulled the rug from under the anti-bullionists, and it was probably wise. Had some sort of 'equitable adjustment' been attempted, the country might have become embroiled in a bank war like that of Jacksonian America. As it was, complaints against the currency diminished with the recovery in wheat prices from 1837 onwards. The subsequent commercial and manufacturing depression turned attention to the Corn Laws, and by the time that issue was finally settled, the effects of Peel's Bill really had been dissipated, with those unjustly affected having died or else adjusted to their losses.

In June 1833 a motion calling for the almost total repeal of the Corn Laws was lost by just twenty-six votes (in a thin House, admittedly), yet in the event no alteration was made until after the Conservatives had returned to office. This was a surprising omission since, although Grey supported agricultural protection and Melbourne was indifferent, most of the truly dogmatic free-traders were on the Liberal side of the House, starting with Althorp, Poulett Thomson, Lansdowne, Howick, Parnell, Palmerston, Brougham, and Villiers, and these Zealots were in turn egged on by their Radical allies and the *Edinburgh* and *Westminster* reviews. From the back benches the lead was taken by Joseph Hume and a Shropshire Whig, William Wolryche Whitmore, two men who epitomized the different but complementary approaches to free trade that were current at the time.[163] Whereas Hume was a secular Radical and utilitarian, who thought like Cobden that Corn Law repeal would lead to economic expansion, Whitmore was a moralistic and retributive type of free-trader like Chalmers, whom he knew and admired. (An evangelical and 'Saint', he treated

---

[160] *Report from the Select Committee on Agriculture, PP* 1833, vol. v, pp. x–xi.

[161] *A Portion of the Journal kept by Thomas Raikes* (1856–8), i. 171.

[162] By admitting the diagnosis Graham must have offended Peel, who still could find no fault in his eponymous Bill, but by rejecting the cure Graham took his first big step towards becoming a Peelite.

[163] C. P. Villiers took the lead in Parliament from 1838 onwards.

the poor with characteristic harshness in his role as chairman of the Bridgnorth Poor Law guardians.)

No one could say that the 1828 law was working well. The sudden large jumps in the scale of duties (1s. at 73s., 2s. 8d. at 72s., but as much as 13s. 8d. at 69s.) meant that importers held onto their corn as the price crept upwards, and then when the duty reached the nominal shilling they flooded the market together. Also, the prospect that a slight fall in price would greatly increase the duty discouraged merchants from bringing food from distant ports where transport costs were high. The result, according to Whitmore, was a market '*deluged* far beyond the demand', as well as 'endless scheming, and speculation, and gambling, and uncertainty, and revulsions, which placed the foreign corn-trade on quite another footing than that wholesome system of supply and demand which under an honest and free system of trade alone did and alone ought, to regulate the price'.[164] Accordingly, in May 1833 Whitmore moved to have the 1828 law replaced by a moderate (or roughly 'countervailing') fixed duty, but he was heavily defeated (305–106). A few months later the Select Committee on Agricultural Distress produced a soporific report, causing Poulett Thomson to complain that it had been 'composed wholly of landowners'.[165]

During 1834–6 the Corn Law issue retreated into the background, owing to the coincidence of acute agricultural distress and commercial boom. It was a time of cheap food and plenty—wheat imports for the six-year period 1832–7 were no more than those for 1831 alone—but also of disinvestment and decultivation (especially on the inferior wet clays of the Midlands), which pointed to a future in which Britain would be *ordinarily* dependent on overseas supplies, as the Agricultural Report acknowledged. Yet in an important polemical shift, Whitmore and Hume based the case for reduced protection less on the need for food supplies than on the need to boost manufactures. 'Every import must be paid for by an export.' 'Every quarter of wheat imported put into employment some manufacturers to pay for that import... There was a limit to the cultivation of land; but there was no limit to the increased employment of hands in manufactures, save a want of demand.'[166] Joseph Hume's view seems to have reflected that of the official mind, at least as represented by James Deacon Hume, the respected Joint Secretary of the Board of Trade and devotee of Huskisson.

We have long since passed that point up to which the prosperity of a country is based upon its land. Our trade has outgrown our agriculture, because it has led to an increase of population which the land can neither profitably employ nor plentifully feed... I know

[164] *HPD*3 xvii. 1351 (17 May 1833).
[165] Thomson to Melbourne, 30 Jan. 1836, Hertfordshire RO, Melbourne Papers.
[166] Joseph Hume, *HPD*3 xvii. 1359 (17 May 1833).

[the landed interest] think that there is a cycle of employment to be found in the home trade, in which the same internal elements of prosperity may be perpetually revolved and improved . . . [But] if the increase of population should not comprise a new body of manufacturers, capable of supplying commodities for the foreign market . . . the home trade and the agriculture would languish together, and the country would become little else than one great poor-house. On the other hand, if the additional population consist chiefly of manufacturers, who produce commodities suitable to foreign markets, and the export of those commodities materially exceed in quantity the corn which had formerly been exported, in return for the imports—the case of the country is thenceforth entirely changed, and its future prosperity will be based upon trade, and not upon land; and no imaginable measure can be so injurious to land as that which may impede the progress of trade.[167]

The debate over which of the two sectors constituted the ultimate source of wealth was an old one, but the fact that great national prosperity could coincide with so much agricultural distress brought it sharply into focus. Still, it was in neither party's interest to stir the Corn Law issue, given the strength of the landed interest. It was only after Peel had won back power on an implicit promise to defend the Corn Laws that he moved decisively against them, and he did so then in the context of an economic slump and a financial deficit.

The shortfall for 1841–2 was estimated to be nearly £2½ million, and the accumulated deficit about £7½ million. Peel, who could not be expected to take the Keynesian view that running a deficit was an appropriate way to deal with economic depression, called it 'a mighty evil'. In 1842 he inaugurated the first ever peacetime income tax, levied at 7d. in the pound on incomes of £150 and over. It was presented as a temporary measure to deal with the legacy of public debt, but the claim is doubtful given that Peel had 'hankered' for it as far back as 1830, long before the deficit had emerged. He had said then he wanted to tap the wealth of 'great capitalists' like Rothschild, Baring, and his own father, to reconcile class antagonisms, and to commute 'taxes bearing on the industry and the comforts of the labouring poor'.[168] These aims were repeated in 1842, but not emphasized. Now the talk was of revenue and rationalization (there were extant 1,142 dutiable items, of which just ten yielded 91 per cent of customs revenue, while the remainder merely added to the administrative burdens on business-men). Peel estimated a yield from income tax of £4 million, which would make up the existing shortfall and create a £1½ million surplus, enabling him to reduce import and excise duties as an experiment to see 'whether increased consumption under a lower rate of duty will give you equal or nearly equal

[167] J. D. Hume, *Letters on the Corn Laws, and on the Rights of the Working Classes* (1834), 45.
[168] Peel to Arbuthnot, 16 Feb. 1830, in *The Correspondence of Charles Arbuthnot*, ed. A. Aspinall (1941), 124; *A Political Diary 1828–1830 by Edward Law Lord Ellenborough*, ed. Lord Colchester (1881), ii. 203–16.

revenue'.[169] (This 'demand elasticity' theory was the new orthodoxy as laid down by the 1840 Select Committee on Import Duties, and earlier in Herries's report to the 1828 Finance Committee.) Accordingly, he reduced the import duties on some 750 articles, observing a maximum of 5 per cent on raw materials, 12 per cent on partly manufactured goods, and 20 per cent on wholly manufactured goods. Despite the lower rates, revenue from indirect taxation remained steady, establishing Peel's reputation as a sound finance minister, but he was of course lucky in that shortly after his first budget the economy entered a cyclical upturn. In 1845 he went still further, abolishing all export duties and 430 import duties, including that on raw cotton.

He has also received credit for the Bank Charter Act of 1844, described by him as 'the complement and defence of the Act of 1819'.[170] The hope then had been that, by going back to the gold standard, and by imposing on banks the obligation of convertibility, Parliament had reduced the likelihood of over-speculation and instability. That hope had been dashed by successive periods of boom and bust, culminating in 1839 when four factors—a worsening balance of trade, the need to pay for essential corn imports, the requirement to compensate the former slave-owners, and a rise in short-term debts to America—all led to massive outflows of gold. The situation was in turn exacerbated by a panic run on the banks at home. Allegedly the Bank of England came close to a stoppage, though the day was saved (humiliatingly) by the Bank of France, which agreed to discount British bills. As before, bankers were blamed for having failed to discourage over-speculation, and a committee was appointed to assess the situation. It sat through 1840–1 and Peel was a prominent member.

The proceedings of the Select Committee on Banks of Issue gave rise to a debate between adherents of the so-called Currency School (S. J. Loyd, Robert Torrens) and Banking School (J. W. Gilbart, J. S. Mill). The currency theorists, like today's monetarists, blamed the reckless speculation on over-issue, and called on bankers to reduce the money supply whenever the balance of trade deteriorated. Their opponents argued that bankers should use their discretion in order to accommodate sound business ventures ('real bills') irrespective of the state of the economy.[171] Neither side suggested that Britain should abandon the gold standard, but because the Banking School theorists used a 'real bills' argument similar to the one that anti-bullionists had used in 1819, Peel considered them to be wolves in sheep's clothing. He kept asking Banking School witnesses *why* they wished to retain the gold standard 'if the legitimate demands of commerce may always be relied upon as a safe criterion by which the

[169] Peel to Goulburn, 22 Dec. 1844 and Feb. 1845, Surrey RO, Goulburn MSS, Acc. 304/41–2; Brian Jenkins, *Henry Goulburn 1784–1856: A Political Biography* (Liverpool, 1996), 315.
[170] Peel to Brougham, 9 May 1844, Peel MS 40482, fo. 42.   [171] See above, p. 257.

country issuers can determine the proper amount of currency'. One of them, bewildered, could only reply: 'I do not see the connexion between the two.' Clearly Peel was stuck in a time warp, still fighting the battles of 1819.[172] In his defence it can be said that he sincerely believed the 'vast majority' of the population to be in favour of abandoning convertibility. He was almost certainly mistaken, but it explains why he feared that an official endorsement of 'real bills' doctrine would open the floodgates.[173]

In so far as the problem was a political one, Peel came up with a characteristically elegant solution. His main aim was to acquire some control over note issues. To achieve this it was first necessary to centralize issues in the Bank of England, and then to restrict its discretionary powers. By stipulating that private banks of issue should not increase the amount of their notes in circulation beyond the average of the previous twelve weeks, Peel ensured that they would wither away gradually as the economy expanded. This avoided the brouhaha which would have ensued had he simply legislated their rights away. The problem posed by the Bank of England was that of a private corporation performing a public function. It had a legal duty to maximize the profits of those who held its own stock, yet one way of doing that—expanding its note issues—might well be inflationary and detrimental to the community. Peel reluctantly rejected Ricardo's idea of a national bank, since Conservatives could not confiscate powers which the corporation had enjoyed since 1694. His alternative solution was to divide the Bank into watertight compartments (for note issues and banking), each of which had no cognizance of what the other was up to. Henceforward, the Issue Department could only circulate notes that were backed by bullion in its vaults, except for a fiduciary leeway over and above that amount of just £14 million, which would constitute the credit element in the system. However, in order to forestall any complaint by the Bank directors that this entailed a loss of discretion, Peel offered them a quid pro quo. Now that the Banking Department was entirely separate, it was to be allowed to pursue its interests in the loan market like any other bank. Profits lost by the restriction on note issues could be made up instead with interest-bearing loans.

Now the Bank had not lent much money in the ordinary way for several decades. Under a succession of governors, of whom J. Horsley Palmer was the best known, it had deliberately kept its discount rate above that obtaining in the

---

[172] *PP* 1841 v. 109–10 (QQ 959–69). In fact some of the leading 'banking' theorists, such as John Fullarton and Thomas Tooke, had been bullionists in 1819, whereas Torrens—a 'currency' theorist—had been an anti-bullionist.

[173] Anna Gambles, *Protection and Politics: Conservative Economic Discourse, 1815–1852* (Woodbridge, 1999), 117–43, has emphasized the surviving importance of anti-bullionism in the Conservative Party. Even so, by the 1840s Birminghamismus in the form pursued by Thomas Attwood and Richard Spooner seems to have been fairly marginal.

market. Businessmen did not borrow from it, but other banks applied to it for rediscount facilities when necessary. This made the Bank a lender of last resort, and as such it was able to impose a degree of regulation over struggling private banks. Following the Bank Charter Act, however, it began to discount competitively, with disastrous results.

The history of the next few years is to some extent that of the Bank's attempt to reconcile its split personality. The day after the Act became law, on 5 September 1844, the directors, taking Sir Robert's advice to heart, announced a new rate and policy for discounting, a minimum rate of 2½ per cent being accepted for first-class three-month bills. This was competition indeed; market rate, though it had stood below 2 per cent, was tending to rise, and for the next three years minimum bank rate was consistently lower than market rate.[174]

The consequence was an orgy of cheap money (that which Peel abhorred above all else), which in turn fuelled a speculative railway boom and led to the financial collapse of October 1847, at which point the Act was temporarily suspended. Thereafter, the Bank directors reverted to their previous practice, but it had been a disastrous episode, and one for which Peel must take much blame, his political ingenuity having led to the economic ruin of thousands.

In order to understand his motives, the most important point to focus on is his decision to limit the fiduciary to £14 million. This was a minuscule amount of credit for a country whose gross national income was about £500 million, and it gives the lie to those historians who suppose that Peel shared Adam Smith's belief in free markets as a means to economic growth.[175] Peel did not dissemble about his intentions, and made it clear that his overriding aim was to kill speculation. If the Bank Charter Act had had the effects which he intended, then there could have been no mid-Victorian boom, and nothing like as many public buildings, roads, railways, schools, asylums, prisons, hospitals, houses, parks, squares, or sewers as in fact were built during the 1850s and 1860s, nor would there have been such a proliferation of consumer goods. That explains why the Act was opposed so strenuously by Thomas Attwood and the Birmingham School, as well as by a free banking lobby which argued that anyone should be allowed to issue notes, so long as they and their clients were prepared to take the consequences of mismanagement.[176]

---

[174] C. N. Ward-Perkins, 'The Commercial Crisis of 1847', in E. M. Carus-Wilson (ed.), *Essays in Economic History* (1954–62), iii. 264.

[175] For example, Robert Blake in *The Times*, 30 Nov. 1990, aligning Peel with Thatcher: 'Peel believed in an enterprise culture. He thought that if the barriers on trade were removed the increased wealth of the commercial and business classes would have a "trickle-down effect" and benefit all classes.' See also Gash, *Sir Robert Peel*, 439.

[176] The Bank Act was complemented by the Companies Act, also in 1844, which similarly introduced registration and central regulation, with the explicit intention of reducing 'reckless speculation' and ensuring 'the legitimate reward of industry'.

In the event, and no thanks to Peel, the new Bank Charter did not have the dampening effects intended. Like many of his contemporaries, Peel assumed that paper currency 'stands in a certain relation to the gold coin and the foreign exchange in which other forms of paper credit do not stand'.[177] In practice, however, the restriction on banknotes did not reduce the money supply, since it simply led to a greater use of cheques, bills, and deposit banking. Also, significant gold finds in California and Australia from the late 1840s brought to an end three decades of international deflation. Since Britain's balance of payments was highly favourable thanks to invisible earnings, much of the additional bullion ended up on deposit in the Bank of England. The Bank Charter regime might well not have survived without this sudden increase in the world's supply of gold. Conversely, the gold finds meant that tying the circulation to the amount of bullion in the Bank of England proved much less restrictive than Peel had intended. Indeed, the 1844 Act may have helped to ensure sustained but gentle price rises throughout the next two decades, instead of runaway inflation. At all events, and despite further suspensions in 1857 and 1866, it remained a cornerstone of the British (and international) economy until the First World War.

The climax of Peel's economic strategy was of course Corn Law repeal. He had undoubtedly been complicit in Huskisson's project for eventual free trade in grain, at least so long as population continued to rocket upwards, and though it cannot be proved that his own determination went back as far as the 1820s, it certainly went back a long way. He could hardly come clean about his intentions before the 1841 election, but his speeches were sufficiently equivocal to leave the door open. 'Unless the existence of the Corn Law can be shown to be consistent . . . [with] the improvement of the condition of the labouring classes, the Corn Law is practically at an end.'[178] His Cabinet memorandum written soon after taking office echoed all Huskisson's concerns, the most important being food supply and monetary stability. Peel was adamant that, 'notwithstanding the immense improvements in agriculture, the tendency of population is to increase more rapidly than the internal production of corn'. 'A diminution in the supply of wheat from Ireland' had also occurred, which meant that 'we must calculate on the necessity (excepting in seasons of extraordinary productiveness) of a considerable annual import of grain from foreign countries'.[179] Peel was also made aware of a collective deficiency in the customary sources of supply in north-west and central Europe, shortages that were to climax in 1846–7, and in the same memorandum he wrote of the need to 'widen the range' from which supplies were drawn. However, merchants would not import from as far afield as

[177] *HPD*3 lxxiv. 733 (6 May 1844).

[178] *HPD*3 xlvi. 757 (15 Mar. 1839). For a similar 'get-out' strategy prior to Catholic emancipation, see above, p. 385.   [179] Peel MS 40507, fos. 193–231: 203, 207; Peel, *Memoirs*, ii. 327–41.

the United States or Black Sea steppes unless they were insulated against the possibility of costly tariffs.[180] Peel's second point was the need to make corn imports more regular so as to minimize their impact on the currency. Huskisson's warnings on this head had been borne out in the later 1830s, when a series of poor harvests made it necessary to import food. Whereas regular imports could be accommodated in the normal course of trade, any sudden influx of foreign wheat, such as that demonstrated in Table 8.13, had to be paid for in bullion and was bound to 'derange' the circulation.[181] This suggests a direct link between the Bank Charter Act and Corn Law repeal. Having tied the money supply so tightly to the amount of gold in the Bank of England, it was essential to prevent sudden drains of gold, and therefore to render the corn trade 'as little fluctuating as the circumstances of the case will admit of'.[182]

Peel's 1842 Corn Law kept the sliding scale but reduced duties to slightly less than half of existing levels. Even this did not go far enough for Gladstone, Vice-President of the Board of Trade, who privately suggested a much greater lurch towards free trade. Never much given to initiative in others, Peel slapped him down angrily, but added revealingly that he would have had 'no hesitation' in going further had he not had 'to look to *other than abstract considerations*', meaning opinion in the Cabinet and the difficulty of getting legislation through the Lords. Clearly his thoughts were running well ahead of his deeds, and this is confirmed by a comment of Graham, his closest confidant, who described the legislation as 'the euthanasia of the Corn Laws; if we maintain it ten years, I shall be satisfied: and then I trust that our agriculture will not want [i.e. need] it'.[183]

TABLE 8.13. *Official values of corn imports, 1836–1840 (£)*

Year	Value
1835	334,000
1836	746,000
1837	1,501,000
1838	2,388,000
1839	6,060,000
1840	5,156,000

[180] S. Fairlie, 'The Nineteenth-Century Corn Law Reconsidered', *EconHR* 18 (1965), 562–75.

[181] Peel to Ripon, 28 Nov. 1841, Peel MS 40464, fo. 105.

[182] Peel, Cabinet memorandum (Winter 1841), in Peel, *Memoirs*, ii. 335.

[183] Quoted in Gladstone, memorandum, 9 Mar. 1842, in *The Prime Ministers' Papers: W. E. Gladstone*, ed. John Brooke and Mary Sorensen (1971–81), ii. 172, 175. Soon afterwards Graham wrote to Peel: 'It is a question of *time*. The next change in the Corn Laws must be to an open trade; and if our population increase for two or three years at the rate of 300,000 per annum, you may throw open the ports, and British

It is impossible to be sure, but it seems likely that Peel was preparing the ground. Maybe he planned a further reduction of duties in, say, 1845. Then at the next election (due not later than 1848) he could have argued that two downward revisions had done no harm to farmers, and that if re-elected he would repeal the Corn Laws together. But if this was indeed the prospectus, something must have happened to disrupt it. At the end of 1843 Peel commented almost casually to Gladstone 'that the next change in the Corn Laws would be to total repeal',[184] and he evidently meant *before* the next election. Maybe he was moved by the sufferings of the poor in places like Paisley and Stockport during the winter of 1842–3. Maybe industrial strife prompted him to reflect that 'the *worst* ground on which we can fight the battle of true Conservatism'—at the next election presumably— 'is on a question *of food*'.[185] According to Prince Albert, Peel's aim was to 'remove the contest entirely from the dangerous ground upon which it has got—that of a war between the manufacturers, the hungry and the poor against the landed proprietors'.[186] It has also been suggested that his motives were party political. Since 1841 the Anti-Corn Law League had not only mobilized powerful support in urban areas, it had also begun to exploit the borough freeholder provisions of the Reform Act by registering town residents for votes in counties. Peel may therefore have feared that he would lose the next election to the Liberals unless he could get rid of the League, and the only way to get rid of the League was to give it what it wanted. Whatever his motives, Peel suddenly began to manufacture pretexts to justify a volte-face. During the row about Ashley's ten-hour proposal in 1844, he kept on intimating that, if the amendment were to pass, adjustment of the Corn Law would follow as a 'certain consequence'.[187] The episode is usually cited as an example of his high-handedness, but it is possible that Peel hoped his back benchers would *not* back down, that he *wanted* them to call his bluff, so that he would then have an excuse to punish them by repealing the Corn Laws. In the following year he and Graham put it about that the reduction in agricultural taxation which landlords were demanding would 'destroy the principal defence of the Corn Law, and leave no ground of resistance to the League'.[188]

agriculture will not suffer. But the next change must be the last; it is not prudent to hurry it; next session is too soon' (Graham to Peel, 30 Dec. 1842, in Parker, *Peel*, ii. 551).

[184] Gladstone, note, 20 Dec. 1843, in *Prime Ministers' Papers: Gladstone*, ii. 226.

[185] Peel to Arbuthnot, 7 Jan. 1846, in *Correspondence of Charles Arbuthnot*, 240; Betty Kemp, 'Reflections on the Repeal of the Corn Laws', *Victorian Studies*, 5 (1961–2), 201–4. On the industrial strife, see below, pp. 612, 616.

[186] 'Memorandum by Prince Albert', 25 Dec. 1845, in *The Letters of Queen Victoria 1837–1861*, ed. A. C. Benson and Viscount Esher (1907), ii. 78.

[187] His argument was that a ten-hour day would lead to lower wages, thereby requiring cheaper food (Peel to Brougham, 21 Mar. 1844, Peel MS 40482, fo. 29).

[188] Graham to Peel, 23 Feb. 1845, Peel MS 40451, fo. 43; Peel to Graham, 23 Feb. 1845, Graham MS, General Series, 86. This was to imply that the special burdens on agriculture constituted 'the principal defence of the Corn Law'.

If Peel was indeed searching for a pretext to undertake repeal, a much more compelling one occurred in October 1845 when reports came through of the catastrophic failure of the Irish potato crop. That it elicited such a 'spontaneous reaction'[189] from Peel and Graham in favour of repeal suggests they had been waiting for the opportunity. As the former reflected subsequently in his *Memoirs*. 'The Minister who foresaw ... that there would be "cruel distress" in Ireland from the scarcity of food, might surely advise the removal of restrictions on its import without justly incurring the reproach of treason and perfidy to his party connections.'[190] Yet Peel cannot really have thought that repeal would alleviate the famine. And if he *had* thought so he should have suspended the Corn Laws immediately, not phased them out over three years. Goulburn advised him that repeal would not 'materially affect this year's supply, or give us any corn which will not equally reach us under the law as it stands',[191] and in January 1846 Peel himself admitted that 'if there be any part of the United Kingdom which is to suffer by the withdrawal of protection, I have always felt that that part of the United Kingdom is Ireland' (presumably because Irish tenants needed to sell their corn at inflated English prices in order to pay their rents).[192] He defended his timing on the grounds that it was 'better to make the *inevitable* change in a time of comparative calm and quiet than to be compelled to make it in a season of commercial and manufacturing distress, and amid the clamours of a starving population'.[193] And in Parliament he pleaded for the question to be settled 'in this the present hour of comparative prosperity, yielding to no clamour, impelled by no fear', and before 'the years of dearth' should *return*.[194] There can be no doubt at all that repeal was a policy designed to meet British rather than Irish interests, but by linking it in his *Memoirs* to the famine he was able to castigate protectionists as selfish and uncaring.[195]

Ireland was not the only red herring. After it was all over, Peel praised Cobden publicly as the man whose name ought to be associated with repeal.[196] The accolade astonished contemporaries and still puzzles historians, since previously Peel had censured Cobden severely, he loathed the tactics of the League, he had made his decision independently and from different motives, and he was a proud man who had never before admitted to being bounced. Besides which, the tribute was both unnecessary and politically inexpedient. Indeed, it seems inconceivable that Peel had been converted by Cobden, notwithstanding the well-known story about him turning to his colleague Sidney Herbert during one

---

[189] Gash, *Sir Robert Peel*, 552.   [190] Peel, *Memoirs*, ii. 155.

[191] Goulburn to Peel, 30 Nov. 1845, ibid. 202.   [192] *HPD*3 lxxxiii. 273 (27 Jan. 1846).

[193] Peel to Charles Harding, 5 Feb. 1846, Peel MS 40584, fos. 159–60.

[194] *HPD*3 lxxxiii. 1042–3 (16 Feb. 1846).

[195] By then about 1 million Irish had died, but this was wholly unanticipated at the time of Corn Law repeal, at which point no one had died.   [196] *HPD*3 lxxxvii. 1054 (29 June 1846).

of Cobden's parliamentary orations and whispering, 'You must answer this for
I cannot.' Nevertheless, Cobden's explanation of how free trade could benefit all
classes and all interests alike might well have had an effect. Bagehot called Peel 'a
nearly unequalled master of the art of political advocacy'. 'He hardly ever said
anything which struck you in a moment to be true; he never uttered a sentence
which for a moment any body could deny to be plausible.'[197] Bagehot's own word
for this sort of oratory was 'specious'. However, it would be more charitable to say
that Peel could sincerely believe in the case he was making so long as it continued
to stack up, but that when an argument lost its syllogistic force it also lost its truth.
Sooner or later he would have repealed the Corn Laws anyway, owing to practical
necessities like food supply and economic stability, but by presenting the case for
free trade so forensically, Cobden made it a theoretical necessity as well.

It could be argued that, in moving from reciprocity to unilateral free trade,
eliminating colonial preference in regard to corn, and denying agriculturists even
so much as a countervailing protection, Peel had stepped over a decisive threshold
separating the Huskissonian tradition from Cobdenism.[198] Many landlords who
had loathed Huskisson's policies now said that they could live with those but not
with Peel's. Even so, the tribute to Cobden was profoundly misleading for at least
three reasons. In the first place, Huskisson's policies would probably have evolved
in the same way had he lived, while colonial preference was a victim of changing
food supply conditions. The case for countervailing duties had been undermined
by a fall in the poor rates, the introduction of rate-support grants, and a broader
fiscal base resulting from the income tax. With regard to reciprocity, the situation
had been turned on its head since 1828 as successive German states joined the
Prussian *Zollverein*, or customs union. It meant that Britain could no longer
engage with its fiercest industrial competitors on a reciprocal basis, leaving
unilateral free trade as the only route out of mercantilism. In these ways Peel's
policy can be represented as a gear shift but not a change of direction.

Secondly, Peel considered Cobden's idea of class conflict between the aristocracy
and bourgeoisie, the 'field of corn' and the 'field of barley', abhorrent. It was,
anyway, a wild over-simplification. Many improving agrarians had little fear of
free trade, while there were staunch protectionists among the merchants and
manufacturers, especially in shipping and sugar. Opinion in the City of London,
moreover, remained tilted in that direction. Its reorientation towards free
trade came later, and was a consequence rather than a cause of the ending of
protection.[199] Nor, despite occasional expressions of exasperation, did Peel fall

---

[197] Bagehot, 'Character of Peel', 261.

[198] Anthony Howe, *Free Trade and Liberal England 1846–1946* (Oxford, 1997), 1–69.

[199] Russell's Liberal Government commenced abolition of the preference on colonial sugar in 1846,
and repealed the Navigation Laws in 1849 (Howe, *Free Trade*, 17; M. J. Daunton, ' "Gentlemanly
Capitalism" and British Industry, 1820–1914', *P&P* 122 (1989), 119–58).

for the League's view that landlords wanted to tax the poor man's breakfast simply to keep themselves in clover. He appreciated that a serious case was being made for agricultural protection by conservative economic 'nationalists'. Such theorists, who included the journalist Archibald Alison, saw the Corn Law as just one part of a comprehensive mercantilist package along with discretionary note-issue, allotments, home colonization, generous systems of social welfare, imperial preference, colonial (as distinct from foreign) emigration, and the Navigation Laws. These policies, it was argued, would ensure agricultural self-sufficiency, the pre-eminence of home demand, and balanced sectoral growth.[200] Peel's legislation decisively contradicted such a strategy, but at least he recognized it for what it was.

Thirdly, Cobden presented free trade as a 'secular religion'. Once it had spread sufficiently, the international economy would expand. As the mightiest

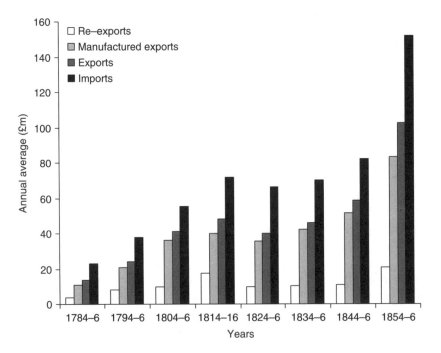

FIG. 8.1. Computed values of British trade, 1784–1856

Source: Ralph Davis, *The Industrial Revolution and British Overseas Trade* (Leicester, 1979), 86.

[200] Gambles, *Protection and Politics*, 1–22, 50–85.

athlete and the workshop of the world, Britain would enjoy the fastest growth, but wealth would eventually trickle down to other countries. His optimism proved justified, at least as far as the stimulus to British trade was concerned, as Figure 8.1 reveals. Nevertheless, Peel never shared Cobden's vision. The most *he* would promise MPs was that, if they embraced free trade, then

You will have done whatever human sagacity can do for the promotion of commercial prosperity. You may fail. Your precautions may be unavailing. They may give no certain assurance that mercantile and manufacturing prosperity will continue without interruption. It seems to be incident to great prosperity that there shall be a reverse— that the time of depression shall follow the season of excitement and success. That time of depression must perhaps return; and its return may be coincident with scarcity caused by unfavourable seasons. Gloomy winters, like those of 1841 and 1842, may again set in. Are those winters effaced from your memory? From mine they never can be ... These sad times may recur. 'The years of plenteousness may have ended,' and 'the years of dearth may have come'.[201]

But at least in future, when calamities recurred, they would clearly be seen as 'dispensations of Providence', and not caused by 'laws of man restricting, in the hour of scarcity the supply of food'.[202] Peel's rhetoric was all about the need to 'revive' (not expand) commerce at a time of terrible distress, and to prevent a 'retrogression' in manufacturers. He wrote a series of well-known (but less well-understood) letters to Croker during 1842 in which he observed that one 'might on moral and social grounds prefer cornfields to cotton factories, an agricultural to a manufacturing population. But our lot is cast, and we cannot recede.' There were now so many people dependent on the export trade that they must do everything they could in an increasingly competitive world to retain market share. Peel was desperate to increase export markets because, like Huskisson and Malthus, he saw the world economy in zero-sum terms, and rejected Cobden's view that countries could all get rich together. Nor did he agree with Deacon Hume, who cheerfully admitted that 'a change to a totally free system' might lead in the short term to the 'relinquishing of some branches of the silk, and even of cotton manufactures',[203] but who considered that such misfortunes were a price worth paying for the sake of the national economy as a whole. Even more tellingly, Peel insisted that 'we must make this country a cheap country for living'.[204] This alone confirms that for him the end of free trade was not Cobden's technical specialization and a high-wage economy. It was based rather on the conviction that, by adjusting the standard of living *downwards* so as to

[201] *HPD*3 lxxxiii. 1042 (16 Feb. 1846).   [202] See above, pp. 327–8.
[203] *Report from the Select Committee on Import Duties*, *PP* 1840 v. 113 (Q. 1363).
[204] Peel to Croker, 27 July, 3 Aug., and 30 Oct. 1842, in Parker, *Peel*, ii. 528–31.

conform to wage costs operative in other countries, it might be possible to avoid the horrors of a stationary or even retrogressive state.

Peel's philosophy of free trade, based as it was on rectitude and conscience, is linked to the question of when he first became committed to it. For if he really had been converted *after* taking office in 1841, as he pretended, then he would have done so at a time when Cobden's ideas were in the ascendancy among journalists and publicists. But if, as seems certain, Peel's instinctive attachment to free trade went back to the 1820s, then the more moralistic, Malthusian, liberal Tory world-view provides a better context. Here Britain was seen less as a mighty athlete than as a wounded giant, suffering worsening terms of trade and increased economic rivalry as European and American competitors girded their loins.

TOWARDS THE *PAX BRITANNICA*

The question of free trade cannot be separated from wider considerations of Britain's role in the world. Most obviously, the movement towards minimal government meant the dismantling of the fiscal–military state, which had reached its zenith between 1800 and 1815. Gross income from all forms of taxation fell from just under £80 million in 1816 to well under £60 million in 1846, despite a nearly 50 per cent rise in population, and the main cause of this reduction was the sudden slashing of military spending once the Napoleonic wars were over (see Table 8.14). Not only were there drastic cuts in manpower, but what was left of the Army suffered from atrophy between 1820 and 1850, so that its capability to defend the country from external enemies was much impaired. In these circumstances the belief that free trade would lead to universal peace was not just a pious theory but an important source of national reassurance.

Unfortunately, there were all too many issues of a geopolitical nature which Britain, as the leading naval and economic power, could not afford to ignore.

TABLE 8.14. *Military expenditure, 1815–1845*
(£m.)

Year	Army and ordnance	Navy	Total
1815	49.6	22.8	72.4
1825	9.0	6.2	15.2
1835	7.6	4.5	12.1
1845	8.1	5.4	13.5

The year 1830, like 1820 and 1848, was one of those years in which different parts of Europe seemed to catch fire. In Paris the July Revolution threw out the Bourbon Charles X and installed the Orléanist Louis-Philippe as a constitutional monarch. On balance this was regarded as highly satisfactory by the new Whig–Liberal hierarchy in Britain. In Warsaw there was a rising against the Polish government established in 1815. It was a relatively liberal regime but also a puppet of the Tsar, who swiftly crushed the revolt and reduced the country to the status of a Russian province. This caused much hand-wringing in polite metropolitan circles, but lacking a powerful expeditionary force there was nothing to be done about it. Finally, the Belgians revolted against the decision taken in 1814 to squash them into a United Netherlands under the House of Orange. Access to the mouth waters of the river Scheldt was a historic concern, anxiety over which had led to war in 1793. In February 1831 there were uprisings against Austrian rule in Bologna, Parma, Modena, and the Papal States, and there was continuous strife in the Iberian peninsula, ostensibly between royal absolutists and liberal constitutionalists. In Portugal the absolutists held power in the person of the pretender Dom Miguel, while liberals fought to have Queen Maria restored. In Spain the liberals held power under Queen Isabella, but were under attack from forces supporting her uncle Carlos. These struggles polarized the Great Powers. Britain and France supported the liberals in both cases, while Austria, Prussia, and Russia declared their support for the absolutists at the Convention of Münchengrätz (1833). The Spanish civil war especially was portrayed in highly ideological terms— liberal democratic atheism versus Catholic absolutist royalism—and it stirred a number of Englishmen to go off and fight Carlism in person. Some of these volunteers must have been psychopaths and freebooters, still hankering for the good old days of Napoleonic adventure, but others were soldiers of conscience. They resembled the international brigades in Spain a century later, and the freedom fighters in Greece a decade earlier, but their cause never quite took fire in England—never found its Byron—and was soon forgotten. Greece itself was now quiet, having been declared independent in 1830 under the protection of France, Russia, and Britain, but the Ottoman Empire soon faced another national revolt. The Egyptian pasha Mehemet Ali captured Syria from the Turks, and by 1840 seemed poised to secure complete independence, threatening yet further instability in the Near East.

Further problems arose in what was left of British North America. Since 1783 ministers had been anxious not to repeat the mistakes of their predecessors, whose policy of taxation without representation had ostensibly led to the loss of the thirteen colonies. In 1791 they had attempted to resolve the problem, not by relieving colonials of taxation or according them direct representation at

Westminster,[205] but by establishing autonomous legislatures in Upper and Lower Canada (now Ontario and Quebec). The arrangement had worked reasonably well in wartime, when there was a flourishing demand for North American timber, but post-war economic depression exacerbated tensions between the two locally elected houses of representatives and their respective executives, which were still appointed and mainly staffed by British personnel. As in Ireland before the Union, a system of devolved legislature and centralized executive proved unworkable. In 1837–8, after a period of stand-off during which the parliaments refused supply and the ministers exacted revenues illegally, there were rebellions in both Ontario and Quebec. The former, led by a Scottish Radical, William Lyon Mackenzie, was mainly constitutional in its aims, whereas the latter, led by Louis Joseph Papineau, was fuelled by separatist ideology. French nationalism in Lower Canada was a disturbing ingredient, since it revived fears of the successful Franco-American alliance of the 1770s.

And this mattered because, in the argot of the day, 'those damned Yankees' were getting ever more pesky. Americans feared the hostility—and questioned the legitimacy—of Britain's Canadian colony, especially as there were long-standing border disputes remaining to be settled. They were angered by British attempts to prevent Texas from being incorporated in the United States, and there was yet further resentment over the slave trade. In its determination to eliminate this traffic, Britain had signed treaties with a number of states permitting the Royal Navy's West Africa Squadron to stop and search suspected ships. Americans rejected Britannia's assumption of the role of global policewoman, and persistently refused to sign any such treaty. They were therefore furious when British commanders insisted on checking American ships in order to make sure that they really *were* American, and not just flying the Stars and Stripes as a flag of convenience. Problems also arose when slaves escaped from American ships to a British West Indian port and then claimed freedom on the grounds that they had 'once breathed English air'. Governments in London upheld such claims, but contended that their own citizens could never alienate their birthrights and duties, and could therefore legally be pressed into naval service if caught in foreign ships. Just as inconsistently, Americans denied the right of slaves to escape, but insisted that immigrants from tyrannical European regimes (including Britain's) should have the right to transfer allegiance at will.

The ministers mainly responsible for dealing with these issues were Palmerston and Aberdeen, who between them held the office of Foreign Secretary for twenty-three and a half years, apart from 142 days in 1834–5 when Wellington

---

[205] Direct representation of the colonies was contemplated by the Whig framers of the 1832 Reform Act, but abandoned as problematic.

occupied it.[206] In terms of temperament and method they were vastly different. Palmerston was flippant and aggressive with a penchant for bluff, though these characteristics were held in check by a sharp sense of realpolitik. Like many compulsive womanizers, he was in most social contexts a man's man. He was also one of those men who take pleasure in browbeating and insulting their colleagues and associates. When their victims collapse in a heap, that is to their liking. When one of them complains or fights back, they innocently protest that it is all just good fun, all part of the rough and tumble of collegiality. On the whole this technique served him pretty well in domestic policies but less so in diplomacy, where how things are said matters as much as what is said. Aberdeen by contrast was conciliatory and timid. Whereas Palmerston went out of his way to insult foreign statesmen, including allies like the French, Aberdeen was unfailingly courteous, and genuinely close to Guizot, Metternich, and the Lievens. He loathed war, having surveyed the carnage at the battle of Leipzig, and did not mind if those with whom he was negotiating knew it. Possibly because he came from Jacobite nonjuring stock, he took no pride in the idea of Greater Britain. Gladstone commented admiringly that Aberdeen never showed any 'regard to the mere flesh and blood . . . of Englishmen', even unconsciously, or allowed such prejudice to prevent him from 'putting the most liberal construction upon both the conduct and the claims of the other negotiating state'.[207] Palmerston described this as 'antiquated imbecility'. Whereas Palmerston was incapable of nuance, Aberdeen seemed unable to lay anything on the line. Yet most aristocratic Whigs were Francophiles like Lord Holland, and closely linked to the reigning Orléans dynasty, and they much preferred Aberdeen's way of doing things. Concern over Palmerston's diplomatic brinkmanship was the ostensible reason for Russell's failure to form a ministry in December 1845.

It is tempting to see in Aberdeen a follower of Castlereagh and Wellington, given that all three shared a European outlook and liked to negotiate compromises, whereas the aggressive, insular, nationalist Palmerston more resembled Canning. The comparison seems even more apt in the light of Palmerston's claims to support liberal constitutional regimes. On the other hand, it is now generally agreed that his proclamation of lofty principles was for domestic political consumption, and that the key to his policies was pragmatism, as he once candidly and famously admitted.

> I hold with respect to alliances, that England is a power sufficiently strong, sufficiently powerful, to steer her own course . . . I hold that the real policy of England—apart from questions which involve her own particular interests, political or commercial—is to be

[206] Palmerston was Foreign Secretary during 1830–4, 1835–41, and 1846–51; Aberdeen during 1828–30 and 1841–6.

[207] John Morley, *The Life of William Ewart Gladstone*, 3 vols. (1903), ii. 641.

the champion of justice and right; pursuing that course with moderation and prudence, not becoming the Quixote of the world, but giving the weight of her moral sanction and support wherever she thinks that justice is . . . We have no eternal allies, and we have no perpetual enemies. Our interests are eternal and perpetual, and those interests it is our duty to follow . . . The interests of England ought to be the shibboleth of . . . policy.[208]

In other words, Britain was to champion justice and right, but only moderately and only when its own interests were not at stake. Palmerston instinctively saw problems in material rather than ideological terms, regarding Carlism, for example, as nothing more lofty than an instrument for enabling Basques to defend their privileges against the Liberals' centralizing policies. As for diplomatic styles, Aberdeen differed sharply from Castlereagh and Wellington in that he disliked congresses.[209] Conversely, it was the supposedly go-it-alone Palmerston who locked Britain into the Quadruple Alliance (1834), a western bloc which included France, Spain, and Portugal and was designed to counter the three eastern autocracies, Russia, Austria, and Prussia.

In terms of cold war ideology Britain's closest ally was France, yet in terms of interest France (along with Russia) was also its greatest antagonist.[210] Thus it was mainly to scupper French designs that Palmerston took the initiative in the Belgian crisis, his efforts bearing fruit when the great powers signed the Treaty of London (1839), by which an independent kingdom was established under a minor German prince, and its neutrality guaranteed.[211] With regard to Italy the Government limited itself to vague expressions of sympathy for the patriots, but again was mainly anxious to prevent the French from interfering. The most worrying situation was in the Peninsula. In May 1834 forces loyal to Maria, and backed by a British naval squadron under Napier, succeeded in defeating and deposing Miguel, thereby effectively ending the Portuguese civil war, but the Spanish struggle lingered on, and it was reluctantly conceded that military intervention by French troops would be necessary. How to encourage that, while preventing France from obtaining a preponderant influence, became the central problem.[212] At one point Palmerston was moved to side with Spanish radicals (whose politics he loathed) when it seemed that the Liberals (whom he much

---

[208] *HPD*3 xcvii. 122–3 (1 Mar. 1848).

[209] M. E. Chamberlain, *British Foreign Policy in the Age of Palmerston* (1980), 48; ead., *Lord Aberdeen: A Political Biography* (1983), 297–385.

[210] A parallel might be found in the United States' attitude towards the United Kingdom in and immediately after the Second World War.

[211] The 1839 Treaty was the infamous 'bit of paper' which the Germans tore up in 1914, thereby provoking Britain's entry into the First World War. The prince in question was Leopold of Saxe-Coburg, who came to seem much less minor when his nephew Albert married Queen Victoria in 1840.

[212] There was no question of British military intervention, but Palmerston encouraged volunteers by suspending the Foreign Enlistment Act, which forbade Britons from serving in alien armies. Carlos was eventually defeated in 1839.

preferred) were cosying up to France. Similar ambiguities prompted the British Government to defend the Ottoman Empire against Egypt. Rudely bypassing France, Palmerston joined the three eastern autocracies in forcing on Egypt a Convention to guarantee Turkey's integrity (July 1840). Then when Mehemet Ali made a show of recalcitrance, he was quickly brought to heel by the bombardment of Acre (48,000 rounds causing thousands of casualties), after which he was forced to give up Syria. The French were furious, since they regarded Egypt as a client state, but nevertheless they felt obliged to cooperate with the other powers in securing the Straits Convention (July 1841), which further guaranteed Turkish independence. Since the real need was to prevent France and Russia from fishing in nationalist waters, the main achievement of the Convention from Palmerston's point of view was to have all warships barred from the Bosporus and Dardanelles during peacetime, thereby reversing an agreement which Russia and Turkey had arrived at eight years earlier.[213]

When Peel and Aberdeen took over the reins there was a serious prospect of war with both France and America, as well as actual wars in China and Afghanistan.[214] Accordingly they at once proceeded to rein back, and in particular to establish better relations with Guizot and Louis-Philippe. Palmerston was furious, and did his best to stymie the new policy with a series of anti-French outbursts, of which the following gratuitously offensive blast, delivered to a public meeting in 1841, was typical. His theme on this occasion was the contrast between French colonial behaviour in Algeria and that of the British in India.

The French army . . . sally forth unawares on the villagers of the country; they put to death every man who cannot escape by flight, and they carry off into captivity the women and children (*shame, shame!*). They carry away every head of cattle, every sheep, and every horse, and they burn what they cannot carry off. The crop on the ground and the corn in the granaries are consumed by the fire (*shame!*). What is the consequence? While in India our officers ride about unarmed and alone amidst the wildest tribes of the wilderness, there is not a French man in Africa who shows his face above a given spot, from the sentry at his post, who does not fall a victim to the wild and justifiable retaliation of the Arabs (*hear, hear!*).[215]

A natural consequence of such public Francophobia was that Guizot retaliated immediately after Palmerston resumed office in 1846. His goad was to secure the marriage of Queen Isabella's sister to a son of Louis-Philippe, in defiance of an earlier agreement that the crowns of France and Spain should never be united. The protracted and complex affair of the Spanish marriages was the bizarre final act of a centuries-old soap opera based on European dynasties. Within two years

---

[213] By the Treaty of Unkiar Skelessi (1833). The most authoritative account of Palmerstonian diplomacy in this period is in Kenneth Bourne, *Palmerston: The Early Years 1784–1841* (1982), 332–638.
[214] See below, pp. 565, 570–1.   [215] Herbert C. F. Bell, *Lord Palmerston* (1936), i. 316–17.

the French monarchy had ceased to exist, and before very long the issue of royal loins ceased to be a diplomatic issue. An immediate consequence of the quarrel was that French and British statesmen were looking the other way when in November 1846, and in defiance of their wishes, the three eastern powers took advantage of an internal uprising to eliminate the independent Polish state of Cracow and assign it to Austria.[216]

Meanwhile it had fallen to Aberdeen to settle disputes with the Americans, and characteristically he did so mainly on their terms. The Webster–Ashburton Treaty of August 1842, which *inter alia* fixed the border between Maine and New Brunswick, was described as a 'capitulation' by Palmerston, who complained that foreign policy generally had 'got upon a sliding scale'.[217] Texas was swallowed up by the United States in 1845, and in June of the following year the north-west frontier between Oregon and Vancouver was determined at the 49th parallel.[218] Peel's Government thereby effectively conceded Yankee predominance in the New World. There would be no Great Game in Latin America. By way of reward the value of British exports to the United States almost trebled between 1846 and 1856, though that signified less than it would have done earlier, owing to the remarkable reorientation of trade that had occurred in the first half of the century. Whereas in 1815 the value of trade with India and Asia had been little over one-twelfth of the total, by the early 1840s it amounted to about one-sixth. In absolute terms its value increased by 132 per cent, thereby overtaking American and West Indian trade, which fell slightly (see Table 8.15). At the same time African trade increased by 325 per cent, but from a very much lower base.[219]

TABLE 8.15. *Percentage of British manufactured exports by destination, 1699–1856*

Years	Europe	North America, West Indies	Australia, Latin America, Africa, Near East, Asia
1699–1701	83.6	13.3	3.1
1772–4	45.0	46.9	8.1
1804–6	37.3	49.4	13.3
1834–6	36.3	34.7	29.0
1854–6	28.9	28.1	43.0

Source: N. F. R. Crafts, *British Economic Growth during the Industrial Revolution* (Oxford, 1985), 145.

---

[216] Foreshadowing the events of 1956, when an Anglo-French Middle Eastern adventure that went wrong provided cover for a Soviet takeover of Hungary.

[217] Palmerston to Lansdowne, 4 Nov. 1842, in Bell, *Palmerston*, i. 330, 443.

[218] Chamberlain, *Foreign Policy*, 32–59.

[219] Albert H. Imlah, *Economic Elements in the Pax Britannica: Studies in British Foreign Trade in the Nineteenth Century* (New York, 1958), 128–31.

There is little evidence to suggest that policy-makers were influenced by these trends. Palmerston sometimes spoke about looking to Asia and Africa to replace European markets lost through increased competition, and he once commented privately that it was 'the business of the Government to open and secure the roads for the merchant',[220] but the only unequivocal case in which such motives operated was the infamous Opium War of 1839–42. The problem here was that the Chinese exported quantities of tea, silk, and porcelain to Britain but had little desire to buy its goods in return. In order to avoid loss of bullion, the Government acquiesced in the development of a triangular trade, whereby opium grown in India was used as remittance. This was resented by some Chinese officials, and a crisis arose when a commissioner in Canton subjected the British consul and a number of British merchants to house arrest. Imperial honour was satisfied when the authorities in India (without properly consulting London) sent a squadron of frigates to scatter a number of junks, but there was also a good deal of anguish over this too easy victory—in debate the first Gladstonian bleat was heard of what was later to become the liberal pacifist *Manchester Guardian*-reading conscience of Victorian England. The war ended in 1842 with the Treaty of Nanking, whereby Britain acquired Hong Kong as well as a right of access for British goods through Shanghai and three other treaty ports. It was the only time when commercial considerations definitely drove foreign policy.

To sum up, Britain in the second quarter of the century had no territorial ambitions in Europe and was invulnerable to invasion.[221] Result: happiness! If only geopolitics could have stayed like that for ever. But the world was already about to change. A new anxiety began to trouble metropolitan dinner parties in 1846, rumours of the latest developments in steam-driven ironclad warships capable of crossing the Channel within thirty minutes. In the 1850s France was once again thought to threaten invasion, and topics such as the militia, volunteering, and national defence returned to the agenda. As Prime Minister in 1855–8 and 1859–65, Palmerston blithely continued with the old methods of foreign policy, but was to find that bluster worked much less well from a position of weakness.

IMPERIAL ONSET

Imperial acquisition continued after the battle of Waterloo. The Gambia (1816), Singapore (1819), the Gold Coast (1821), Malacca and part of western Burma (1824), Western Australia (1829), the Falklands (1833), South Australia (1836),

---

[220] Palmerston to Auckland, 20 Jan. 1841, University of Southampton Library, Broadlands Papers.

[221] Partly thanks to improved naval administration, especially during Sir James Graham's tenure of the Admiralty (1830–4).

Aden (1839), New Zealand (1840), Hong Kong (1842), Natal and Sind (1843), and North Borneo (1846) all fell under British rule. Even so, there was still little sense of imperial destiny. Overseas missions continued apace, but had lost some of their religious fervour. Many Anglican expeditions in particular now seemed to have less to do with conversion than with exploration, museum collecting, and scientific discovery. To Liberals overseas possessions were merely vested interests demanding protection, and intimately bound up with a discredited mercantilist regime, while even Disraeli, who might have been expected to defend them on those grounds, dismissed the 'wretched colonies' as 'a millstone round our necks'.[222] Such imperial enthusiasm as there was tended to be cerebral rather than visceral. Malthusian economists hoped that overseas settlements would provide homes for Britain's excrescent population, markets for its redundant manufactures, and outlets for its surplus capital, as well as supplies of raw materials.[223] The most influential proponent of 'systematic colonization' on these lines was a scapegrace diplomat, Edward Gibbon Wakefield, who was keen to put colonial landholding onto a commercial basis, ending the system whereby settlers were given free grants of land. In 1836 he inspired the creation of a new colony by the joint-stock South Australian Association. The territory was to be governed by Crown Commissioners, from whom the company bought plots of land and sold them at a profit. The sequel was not untypical of such experiments. The Governor overspent on lavish buildings, and the consequential budgetary crisis forced British ministers to suspend the company's charter and to make South Australia a Crown colony (1841). It was this sort of haphazard and unforeseen outcome that caused some to regard the Second British Empire as having been won in a fit of absence of mind.

Nevertheless, it was important that imperial possessions, once acquired, should not be surrendered, otherwise the entire edifice might collapse, and with it the nation's power and prestige. There was a widespread consciousness that the garrisons deployed around the globe were spread very thinly, hence the jitters when French sailors landed in Tahiti, expelled its English missionaries, and proclaimed a protectorate (1842). Tahiti was tiny, and well over 2,000 miles from New Zealand, which the British had annexed two years earlier, but the French initiative was nevertheless perceived as a threat to hegemony in the Pacific. Russell referred privately to 'vultures' that were circling over the country's head, waiting to pounce at the first sign of weakness.[224] This was why the 1837

[222] Disraeli to Malmesbury, 13 Aug. 1852, in Earl of Malmesbury, *Memoirs of an Ex-Minister: An Autobiography*, 3rd edn. (1884), i. 343–4. However, this might have been an offhand, ill-considered remark.

[223] Bernard Semmel, *The Rise of Free Trade Imperialism: Classical Political Economy, the Empire of Free Trade, and Imperialism 1750–1850* (Cambridge, 1970), 48–129.

[224] Russell to Grey, 19 Aug. 1849, TNA, Russell MS 30/22/8A, fos. 90–1.

Canadian rebellions were so frightening. In terms of their intrinsic value, Britain's possessions in North America might easily have been jettisoned. The problem was that any abandonment would look like a defeat at the hands of the United States. It was also feared that, if the Canadian rebels were allowed to secede, it would have a domino effect in Ireland, and perhaps in Asia as well. Melbourne's Government therefore responded with unusual alacrity, though they may also have been motivated by a desire to get rid of a troublesome colleague, Lord Durham, who was shipped out to investigate. In 1839 his famous report paved the way for the amalgamation of the two Canadas in the following year, with full autonomy from both Whitehall and Westminster. It provided a template for the development of overseas possessions generally,[225] and presaged the twentieth-century Commonwealth of independent nations. Not that any such vision informed policy-makers at the time. The autonomy which was conceded, though considerable, was calculated to be the minimum that the Canadians would accept while consenting to remain in the British Empire. Anything less, and it was obvious that they would submit to be annexed by the United States. Pragmatic calculations such as these were far more important than visions of imperial trusteeship.[226]

Canada's experience supports the argument that Britain's fiscal–military state was not so much dismantled as exported to the colonies.[227] Firstly, the empire offered impecunious younger sons status, adventure, and well-paid careers.[228] Secondly, many former Napoleonic war generals went on to become colonial governors, responsible for both military and civil administration.[229] They included George Napier at the Cape (1837–43) and Sir Henry Hardinge in India (1844–8), both of whom were younger sons. The satisfactions of empire might explain, incidentally, why so few Army officers became involved in domestic politics as compared with the United States and many Continental countries. Thirdly, there was a long-standing belief that colonists should pay for their own defence, even though they would have needed less defending had they not been part of the empire. They were to be taxed, in other words, in order to uphold Britain's world role. So whereas governments were able to placate the English by

[225] The Australian Colonies Government Act (1850) was followed by the grant of autonomy to Victoria, New South Wales, Tasmania, South Australia, and later Queensland. In 1867 Ontario and Quebec were federated with Nova Scotia and New Brunswick in the Dominion of Canada.

[226] Phillip A. Buckner, *The Transition to Responsible Government: British Policy in British North America, 1815–1850* (Westport, Conn., 1985), 6–8.

[227] C. A. Bayly, 'Returning the British to South Asian History: The Limits of Colonial Hegemony', *South Asia*, 17 (1994), 1–25; id., 'The British Military–Fiscal State and Indigenous Resistance: India 1750–1820', in Lawrence Stone (ed.), *An Imperial State at War: Britain from 1689 to 1815* (1994); Daunton, *Trusting Leviathan*, 124–35.

[228] C. A. Bayly, *Imperial Meridian: The British Empire and the World 1780–1830* (1989), 134–5.

[229] Hew Strachan, *The Politics of the British Army* (Oxford, 1997), 74–91.

paring public expenditure to a minimum, many overseas possessions approached the mid-century in a state of fiscal contention, with civil disobedience at the Cape and in New South Wales, Jamaica, and Ceylon. To make matters worse, the colonists' commercial advantages were whittled away during the 1840s with the reduction of fiscal preferences on timber, corn, and sugar.

The main appeal of the East India Company, so far as the British Government was concerned, was its effectiveness as a tax-collecting machine in the three presidencies (Bengal, Madras, and Bombay). When its charter came up for revision in 1833, Parliament therefore decided to perpetuate its nominal rule, though the withdrawal of the China monopoly meant that its functions were little more than cosmetic.[230] Real power was now shared between the Board of Control at home and a new Supreme Council in Calcutta, though the façade of Company rule was maintained until 1858 when the colony was transferred to the Crown. This arrangement made for considerable tension in the governing counsels of what was now recognized as the epicentre of empire. Most sensitive Britons in the Subcontinent were aware that they were there on sufferance as tax-gatherers and policemen, having failed to establish any sense of identity with the natives or any 'reciprocity of feeling'. A typical lament was to wonder 'why the Russians in their empire seemed to have "a magic wand whose touch makes everything Russian" whereas the British in India were still strangers after a hundred years'.[231] Likewise Lord Ellenborough, the Conservatives' Governor-General (1842–4), argued that the empire had been acquired only by arms, and therefore 'by arms alone could it be preserved, for in the heart of the people it has no foundation. Ours has been a repulsive government. It has established no sympathy with the governed . . . It rests only upon the continuance of military success by which the fidelity of the troops is mainly preserved.'[232]

On the surface these might seem to be expressions of regret, even apology. More likely they were statements of a determination that in future military priorities should rule. The 'magic wand' referred to was presumably the Russian bayonet, and Ellenborough was a soldier *manqué*, notorious for the robustness of his policies. As he saw it, India needed to be rescued from the woolly idealism of his predecessor but one, Lord William Bentinck, who had been Governor-General of Bengal (1828–33), then of all India (1833–5), and afterwards a Liberal MP. Unlike Ellenborough, Bentinck was a real soldier, but he had made a heroic attempt to win the affections of native Indians through a programme of civil reform. The second son of the third Duke of Portland and an uncle of Lord George, Bentinck has been described as a precursor of later liberal imperialists,

---

[230] Its India monopoly had been withdrawn in 1813. See above, pp. 231–2.

[231] John Rosselli, *Lord William Bentinck: The Making of a Liberal Imperialist 1774–1839* (1874), 182–3.

[232] M. E. Yapp, *Strategies of British India: Britain, Iran and Afghanistan, 1798–1850* (Oxford, 1980), 442–3. Contrast this with Palmerston's Panglossian view, above p. 563.

viewing empire as a means of guiding backward countries into independent nationhood. A prominent example of his fervour was the suppression of *sati* (the burning of Hindu widows on the pyres of their late husbands) and thuggee (religiously inspired murder by roving gangs, or Thugs). He undertook strict retrenchment in both the civil and military departments, bore down on fraud, and reformed the tax and judicial systems.[233] Much of this antagonized the princes and other local potentates, but the most controversial of Bentinck's reforms was his rigidly monocultural plan of national education. In the heated debate between orientalists and Anglicists, he came down decisively in favour of the view that 'our great object ought to be the promotion of European literature and science among the natives of India'.[234] Along with a zealous official, Charles Trevelyan, he was mainly responsible for the famous Education Minute of 1835. Vigorously drafted by Macaulay, who had joined the Supreme Council of India in the previous year, it prescribed English as the proper language of instruction in the most uncompromising terms.[235] These policies have led Bentinck to be accused of blind addiction to the Utilitarian theories of Bentham and James Mill, and he was certainly conscious that most up-to-date science was to be found in Western languages rather than in Sanskrit or Arabic. But more importantly he considered that 'education and the knowledge to be imparted by it, can alone effect the *moral* regeneration of India'.[236] He was preoccupied by feelings of guilt and inadequacy, saw life as a 'constant state of preparation for another world', engaged continually in prayer and self-scrutiny, and was anxious that persons of other cultures should also seek salvation.[237] Almost all the evangelicals involved in Indian education policy—Bentinck, Trevelyan, Charles Grant,[238] and, by upbringing at least, Macaulay himself—plumped strongly for Anglicization mainly on religious and moral grounds. It is yet another illustration of the way in which evangelicalism and Utilitarianism could work from entirely different premises towards the same ends.

[233] Previously, as commander of British troops in Sicily (1811–14), he had bullied King Ferdinand of Naples into setting up a liberal government and parliament on the British model, and into reforming the fiscal, judicial, and landholding systems.

[234] Lord William Bentinck, 'Draft on Educational Policy', Feb. 1835, in *The Correspondence of Lord William Cavendish Bentinck*, ed. C. H. Philips (Oxford, 1977), ii. 1413–14. For the dispute between 'orientalists' and 'Anglicists', see John Clive, *Thomas Babington Macaulay: The Shaping of the Historian* (1973), 343–76, 424–5; Rosselli, *Bentinck*, 208–25. Some leading orientalists (e.g. H. H. Wilson) were servants of the Company, which meant by and large that they were more sympathetic to indigenous traditions.

[235] *Correspondence of Bentinck*, ii. 1403–13. Macaulay also drafted a consolidated Penal Code for India in 1835–7 (Eric Stokes, *The English Utilitarians and India* (1959), 219–33).

[236] *Correspondence of Bentinck*, ii. 1395 (italics added).

[237] For an exceptionally sensitive discussion of these themes, see Rosselli, *Bentinck*, 61–6, 82–6.

[238] Grant was President of the Board of Control 1830–4, was created Baron Glenelg in 1835, and was Secretary of State for War and the Colonies 1835–9.

That Bentinck's policies bore little immediate fruit was partly his own fault in fuelling panic over the Russian threat to India's northern borders. This led to the First Afghan War (1839–42) and a huge rise in military spending, which meant that, although his plans for university education went ahead, his proposals for improved schools were simply not affordable. The war also brought about a general coarsening of British rule that was alien to his intentions. However, Bentinck was far from alone in magnifying the Russian threat. It had long been obvious that India's security against invasion depended on unreliable native troops, or sepoys. The aim had been to establish Persia as a buffer state, but by 1838 it was widely believed that the policy had failed, and that Russia had established an unassailable hegemony in that country. In so far as this fear was justified, the blame must lie with Palmerston, who had been dilatory both in winning over Persians and in warning Russians off. In so far as the fear was unfounded, blame lies partly with British representatives in Tehran, who probably exaggerated Russian influence there in order to excuse their own lack of clout.[239] Military commanders in India also exaggerated the Russian threat in calling for additional troops, but they were actually more apprehensive of internal revolt.

At any rate, Bentinck's successor, Lord Auckland, Governor-General in 1836–42, decided that if Persia was unsound then an alternative buffer state must be erected in Afghanistan. This meant becoming involved in tribal warfare, which the British did not understand, and in alliances which shifted with bewildering rapidity. Dost Muhammad, the Emir of Afghanistan, was thought to be pro-Persian and therefore by proxy pro-Russian, so—with the vague encouragement of Palmerston—Auckland hatched a plan to replace him by Shah Shuja, who had been exiled for the past thirty years in India.[240] Like recent Western powers contemplating warfare in that country, it was hoped that the brunt of the fighting would be borne by locals, in this case Sikh warriors from Punjab, but their ruler, Rajit Singh, refused the starring role, meaning that the British had to use their own mainly Hindu troops. The outcome was horrible. Kabul was taken and Shah Shuja installed as a British puppet, but the situation of the occupiers was precarious, for they were marooned with no hope of reinforcements. Eventually, overzealous attempts to reform fiscal practices on British lines, and interference with the rights of local chieftains, led to a riot (November 1841) in which the British consul was shot and hacked to pieces. It was quickly decided that the entire garrison should retreat to Jalalabad. Like Napoleon in 1812, though more understandably given his proximity to the

---

[239] Yapp, *Strategies of British India*, 134–7, 148–50, 302–3, 415–17.

[240] It is unnecessary to elucidate who or what Dost Muhammad and Shah Shuja were, since it is certain that hardly anyone in England had a clue.

Equator, Major-General William Elphinstone, commanding, reckoned without the freezing cold of the mountain passes and the danger of frostbite; he was also surprised by the fanaticism of the exiled Dost's supporters. In January 1842, assailed by Afghans with knives, between 12,000 and 16,000 perished on the Jagdalak pass. Just one lone medical officer made it safely to Jalalabad.

It was a humiliating disaster. The Duke of Wellington, as Commander-in-Chief, wrote to the new Governor-General Ellenborough: 'It is impossible to impress upon you too strongly the notion of the importance of the restoration of our reputation in the East.'[241] 'Honour' was accordingly restored by the British Army marching on Kabul, blowing up the bazaar, administering some random and collective punishment on nearby villages, and then retreating, leaving Shah Shuja in the lurch. He was (unsurprisingly) murdered and Dost Muhammad reinstalled. The longer-term consequences were profound. Now that the buffer was gone it was necessary to strengthen India's north-west frontier itself. This was done by the annexation of Sind in 1843 and Punjab in 1849. Secondly, the Afghan War strengthened the hands of the military in relation to the political officers of the Company, who were, inevitably, blamed for the disaster. Thirdly, the imperial Army had for the first time met the equivalent of today's suicide terrorists, frightening because they seemed oblivious to the conventions of chivalrous warfare. The shocked wife of a British officer wrote, 'It was very like the scenes depicted in the battles of the Crusades. The enemy rushed on and drove our men before them like a flock of sheep with a wolf at their heels.'[242] More perhaps than any other single episode, the Jagdalak pass massacre destroyed the optimistic monogenetic assumptions that had underlain evangelical-ism, Utilitarianism, and other Enlightenment projects—i.e. that human beings were the same under the skin, and simply differed in their stages of develop-ment. Commentators dwelled on the 'irredeemable savagery' of the Afghans, their 'bloodthirsty butchery' and 'consummate treachery'—it was claimed that they had offered the British safe passage before slaughtering them. Consciousness of racial difference and of racial superiority began to characterize English culture to a far greater extent than hitherto.[243] In return the Afghan War transformed the way in which Asians regarded the 'mother country', for it broke the bubble of imperial prestige, encouraged native Indian opposition, and so contributed to the rebellion, or Mutiny, of 1857.

And yet, for all that the war was a disaster, there was surprisingly little sense of shock back home. One reason was the time it took for intelligence to get

---

[241] Wellington to Ellenborough, 30 Mar. 1842, in Yapp, *Strategies of British India*, 452.

[242] *Lady Sale: The First Afghan War*, ed. Patrick MacRory (1969), 100–2, quoted in Richard Holmes, *Redcoat: The British Soldier in the Age of Horse and Musket* (2001), 304.

[243] Catherine Hall, *Civilising Subjects: Colony and Metropole in the English Imagination, 1830–1867* (Chicago, 2002), 338–441.

through (Reuters, the future news agency of the British Empire, was not founded until 1851). The Afghan disaster happened on 12–13 January, but did not surface in the British press until the late editions of 4 April. A more significant reason was the absence still of any emotional investment in empire. *The Times* devoted just three leading articles to the subject and was far more interested in the provisions of Peel's budget. When the first intimations of trouble surfaced, it blamed the governments in London and Calcutta for their 'blind lust' of empire and of treasure. Instead of repaying the 'large moral, religious, and political debt' that was owed to India, they had preferred to set out on a policy of endless acquisition. 'We have been intoxicated with military success,' and it was to be hoped that current events would teach a 'terrible, perhaps useful, lesson to those rulers who think that a territory may be gained by a few military successes—blowing open a few gates, storming a few forts, and shooting down a few hundred wild Afghans!'[244] Even when the full horror was revealed, there was nothing like the amount of hysteria that was manifested in September 1879 when a British legation was massacred at Kabul in the Second Afghan War. Elphinstone's destruction did not scar the national psyche because there was not yet any sense of imperial destiny.

This chapter has stressed the extent to which developments dating from the late eighteenth century were brought to a close. However, the second quarter of the nineteenth century also registered some important beginnings, most notably the determination at last to tackle the appalling social consequences of industrialization and urbanization.

[244] *The Times*, 1 Mar., 5 and 6 Apr. 1842

CHAPTER 9

The condition and reconditioning of England

In developing capitalist systems there is often a point at which inequality and absolute poverty peak before both are reined back. In Britain the second quarter of the nineteenth century marked that point, intensifying anxieties over what Carlyle called the 'Condition-of-England question'.[1] London, for example, had recently enjoyed a speculative building boom, and its best social circles were agog with excitement about the wave of 'metropolitan improvements', but at the same time more disobliging writers began to draw attention to the seamier and more squalid side of urban life, and to the lack of a developed infrastructure. It was becoming clear that investment in public amenities, unlike investment in private enterprise, had been 'crowded out' during the wartime years, and with distinctly negative consequences for health, life expectancy, and morals. On the positive side, the growing recognition that England was out of condition led to demands that something be done about it. Many barriers remained, and it would take another hundred years and two more world wars before any government seriously attempted to slay the 'five giants' of want, disease, ignorance, squalor, and idleness. But at least it can be said that in the 1830s social reform moved irreversibly onto the public agenda.

SOCIAL CRISIS

In calculating trends in living standards, it is obviously not enough to divide gross national income by the size of the population. An individual's circumstances depended on his or her wages, patterns of consumption, the cost of essential consumables, family size and the number of dependants, the frequency of unemployment and short-time working, the availability of community support or charitable funds, and access to payments in kind and to customary rights such as raw materials, timber, and grazing facilities. Between 1783 and 1846 as a whole there was probably a modest increase in most people's material standards, although the quality of life often deteriorated with the move from countryside to town. Between 1825 and 1850, however, there was no overall improvement in

---

[1] Thomas Carlyle, *Chartism* (1839).

real wages, while those of agricultural workers declined.[2] The most successful workers were in leading-edge factory industries like textiles, but they were also the ones who suffered the worst assault in terms of gruelling conditions, disease, deformity, and early death. If one indication of economic well-being is early marriage, it is noteworthy that, whereas the average age had been coming down steadily since 1750, after 1825 it shot up again, and by mid-century was back where it had been a hundred years earlier.[3]

All this has been seen as evidence of a demographic catastrophe. 'The 1830s and 1840s may well have been the worst ever decades for life expectancy since the Black Death in the history of those parishes which were now experiencing industrial-isation.'[4] Mortality rates had declined in the decades to 1830, but then rose sharply for twenty years before falling off again. The year 1831 was notorious for the return of Asiatic cholera, which was especially frightening because it pounced so suddenly, but endemic infectious diseases such as typhus, whooping cough, measles, dysentery, and diarrhoea had even higher mortality rates and were responsible for 40 per cent of deaths in rapidly growing industrial towns. In London about one-third were due to tuberculosis, or 'consumption', a malady with romantic associations but horrific symptoms.[5] There were of course large regional and class differentials. A death rate of eight per thousand in Hereford contrasted with twenty per thousand in Middlesex, while in 1840s Liverpool the gentry and professional classes had an average life expectancy of 35, tradesmen 22, mechanics, servants, and labourers—the vast majority of whom lived in cellars—only 15.[6]

Trends in national physique tell the same story. The average height of 20-year-olds in the Army rose steadily from 1770 to 1845, but in the next generation—i.e. those born between 1826 and 1850—it fell by about two inches before bottoming out and starting to rise again after 1870. The experience of working-class 15-year-olds was more complicated, since a marked loss of stature among those born in the final quarter of the eighteenth century was followed by a recovery in the first quarter of the nineteenth, and then by a loss of two inches for those born between 1825 and 1850.[7] One explanation must be

---

[2] Charles H. Feinstein, 'Pessimism Perpetuated: Real Wages and the Standard of Living in Britain during and after the Industrial Revolution', *Journal of Economic History*, 58 (1998), 625–58.

[3] A factor here may have been the New Poor Law of 1834. However, the 'if' is important. See above, p. 5.

[4] Simon Szreter and Anne Hardy, 'Urban Fertility and Mortality Patterns', in Martin Daunton (ed.), *The Cambridge Urban History of Britain, 1840–1950* (Cambridge, 2000), esp. 671; Simon Szreter, 'Economic Growth, Disruption, Deprivation, Disease, and Death: On the Importance of the Politics of Public Health for Development', *Population and Development Review*, 23 (1997), 693–728.

[5] An abiding image was of John Keats spitting blood on the Spanish Steps in Rome.

[6] The national average life expectancy at birth was 40–1 years in 1841, whereas in Manchester it was only 27 and in Liverpool 28.

[7] Roderick Floud, Kenneth Wachter, and Annabel Gregory, *Height, Health and History: Nutritional Status in the United Kingdom, 1750–1980* (Cambridge, 1990), 134–95, 287–306.

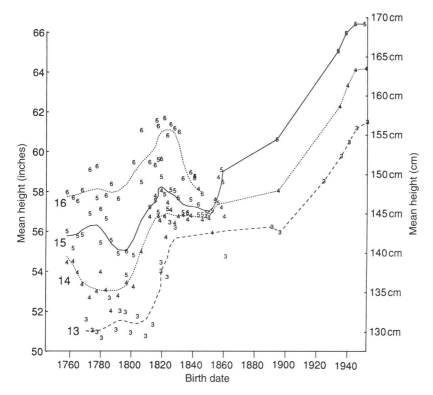

FIG. 9.1. Mean height of working-class 13-, 14-, 15-, and 16-year-olds, 1758–1940

Source: Roderick Floud, Kenneth Wachter, and Annabel Gregory, *Height, Health and History: Nutritional Status in the United Kingdom, 1750–1980* (Cambridge, 1990), 166.

nutritional, since in 1840 the per capita consumption of sugar was only half of what it had been in 1801, while that of tea and bread probably fell as well.[8] Another factor must have been squalid living conditions as people in search of work crowded into places like Birmingham, Leeds, Liverpool, and Manchester from Ireland, the Scottish highlands, and their surrounding countrysides. The population of London ('the modern Babylon') more than doubled to nearly 2½ million during the first half of the century, while in the 1820s alone Manchester and Salford grew by 47 per cent, West Bromwich by 60 per cent, and Bradford by 78 per cent. In the absence of local authority housing and philanthropic intervention, market forces ruled. In London about 2s. a week secured a rented room in a tenement house, many of them former single

[8] John Burnett, *Plenty and Want: A Social History of Diet in England from 1815 to the Present Day*, 2nd edn. (1979), 24–9.

dwellings which had been divided up, giving rise to a hated new intermediary, the tallyman. Workers in the new industrial centres crowded into common lodging houses, many of which had mixed dormitories, making them hotbeds of prostitution. Families were often forced to live in fetid, overcrowded basement cellars; in Liverpool several were infiltrated by 'fluid matter of the court privies', in one reported case forming a ravine 4 feet deep below the family bed. Less insalubrious but just as cramped were the one-up, one-down brick back-to-backs erected to house textile and metal workers (two-thirds of Birmingham's population lived in such dwellings in 1850).[9] All large industrial towns had brothels, gin shops, alehouses, thieves' dens, filthy courts, rookeries, communal privies, cesspools, middens, dung heaps, and dangerous ill-paved streets crawling with wild dogs, wolves, and rats. Most were noisy, smelly, filthy, smoky, dark at night time,[10] blisteringly cold in winter, fly-ridden and dusty in summertime, flea- and lice-ridden at all times. Townspeople were no less crowded in death, as urban graveyards groaned at the seams with bodies. Reformers demanded new out-of-town cemeteries but met resistance from the Church of England, which had a financial stake in the status quo.

In such conditions the concept of lawfulness was elusive. About 5,000 people were committed for trial in England and Wales in 1810, and more than 18,000 in 1830, yet policemen were virtually non-existent, especially outside the metropolis. Soldiers stood by in urban barracks to curb radical discontent, but played no part in routine law enforcement. Affluent people who walked the streets were at perpetual risk from pickpockets or worse, much as in frontier societies. Beggars were a particular hazard—there were scores of thousands of highly organized professional fraudsters in London alone.[11] Indoors was safer, yet the crime of 'larceny by the servant' was a constant source of anxiety. Much abuse fell on Irish immigrants, who had legal rights to residence as citizens of the United Kingdom but were rarely able to establish entitlement to poor relief, and often lived in destitution. As in parts of today's Third World, the greatest urban nuisances were the almost feral street urchins who roamed their neighbourhoods in violent gangs.[12] Many other children were family breadwinners, whether as wage-earners—e.g. piecers in spinning mills—or else as thieves and beggars. Either way, traditional parental authority was subverted, childhood was coarsened, and juvenile delinquency began to be conceptualized as a specific and oppressive social problem.[13] While young girls were considered innocent,

[9] John Burnett, *A Social History of Housing 1815–1985*, 2nd edn. (1986), 54–96.
[10] Though gas lighting spread rapidly in the principal thoroughfares of principal towns from 1816 onwards.   [11] A Society for the Suppression of Mendicity was founded in 1818.
[12] 'Artful Dodger' is too cute a term to describe the way in which such hooligans were regarded, but then Dickens represented a new wave of sensibility regarding childhood.
[13] Heather Shore, *Artful Dodgers: Youth and Crime in Early Nineteenth-Century London* (Woodbridge, 1999), 1–16.

working-class women were widely blamed for the illegitimacy rate, which also seems to have increased in the 1830s and 1840s before declining thereafter.[14] Not only were they thought to be hyper-sexed, but they were widely suspected of deliberately acquiring bastards in order to increase the size of their handouts from the parish.

Alcohol was blamed as well as sexual incontinence. Concerns about the safety of drinking water had led to a surge in the consumption of whisky, gin, and wine. This in turn prompted Parliament in 1830 to deregulate the beer and cider trades in the hope of promoting them as manly alternative beverages. Now for a small fee anyone could set up an alehouse without reference to a magistrate. As a result, more than 24,000 beer shops opened in the course of six months, and the amount of malt on which excise was paid rose by 40 per cent between 1829 and 1831. This 'beer binge'[15] in turn provoked a rash of organizations against the demon drink, the most prominent being the British and Foreign Temperance Society (1831), which was especially popular in Lancashire (where almost 2 per cent of the population enrolled) and Cornwall. The temperance movement has sometimes been attributed to industrial capitalism and the factory owners' need for a regular and reliable workforce. On the other hand there are stories of operatives who were rabid teetotallers being dismissed because they threatened factory morale, sustained as that often was by yards of ale. More likely temperance was part of the moral panic that gripped society in the late 1820s. As with the associated peace and anti-slavery movements, Quakers and evangelicals were prominent in the campaign, their women especially so, while religious and moral exhortation far outweighed any secular arguments in favour of sobriety.[16] This was also true of the discussions of the Select Committee on the Sale of Beer in 1833, and the Select Committee on Drunkenness in 1834, both of which focused on the causes of working-class degeneration.[17] Eventually, recognition that alcohol was addictive helped to undermine belief in free will and to promote environmentalist solutions to social problems, but this shift did not register until after 1850.

Friedrich Engels's famous account of Manchester describes how radial roads leading to leafy suburbs were lined with a better class of housing in order to mask the slums behind. While acknowledging that such 'hypocritical town-planning' was universal, he insisted that the town was 'unique in the systematic way in

---

[14] Though the statistics are particularly unreliable for this period (Peter Laslett and Karla Oosterveen, 'Long-Term Trends in Bastardy in England: A Study of the Illegitimacy Figures in the Parish Registers and in the Reports of the Registrar General, 1561–1960', *Population Studies*, 27 (1973), 255–86).

[15] Nicholas Mason, ' "The Sovereign People are in a Beastly State": The Beer Act of 1830 and Victorian Discourse on Working-Class Drunkenness', *Victorian Literature and Culture*, 29 (2001), 109–27.

[16] Brian Harrison, *Drink and the Victorians: The Temperance Question in England 1815–1872* (1971), 93–113.

[17] It was sometimes suggested that alehouses should have clear plate glass frontages in order to shame their occupants.

which the working classes have been barred from the main streets. Nowhere else has such care been taken to avoid offending the tender susceptibilities of the eyes and nerves of the middle classes.'[18] But although the slums were kept out of sight, they were certainly not out of mind. Three of the most graphic accounts of the early 1830s also featured Manchester, reflecting its reputation as the world's shock city. Dr James Kay (later Kay-Shuttleworth) published *The Moral and Physical Condition of the Working Classes employed in the Cotton Manufacture in Manchester* (1832), which was followed by Peter Gaskell's *The Manufacturing Population of England* (1833), and then came *The Philosophy of Manufactures* (1835) by a former Professor of Chemistry at Glasgow, Andrew Ure. These commentators went beyond mere reportage to advocate bourgeois norms from which, as they saw it, the working classes were sadly deviating. They expressed pity for the wretchedness on view, but what really alarmed them was the 'extinction of decent pride', as evidenced by the absence of furniture from many working-class homes. Similarly, William Cooke Taylor acknowledged the squalor in his *Notes of a Tour of the Manufacturing Districts of Lancashire* (1842), but as a prominent member of the Anti-Corn Law League he was also anxious to stress the potential benefits of industrial capitalism. It took a Frenchman, Alexis de Tocqueville, who had visited Manchester in 1835, to suggest that anarchic capitalism was itself the problem. 'Everything in the exterior appearance of the city attests the individual powers of man; nothing the directing powers of society. At every turn human liberty shows its capricious creative force. There is no trace of the slow continuous action of government'.[19]

Investigators were drawn to places like Manchester by a series of parliamentary reports, or blue books, on conditions in the industrial districts. They culminated in the remarkable *Report on the Sanitary Condition of the Labouring Population of Great Britain* (1842), written and compiled by the most prominent public servant of the period, Edwin Chadwick. Manchester-born, trained in law, and an intimate of Bentham, Chadwick played a decisive role in policing, Poor Law, and factory legislation before taking up the sanitary idea. When the civil (and compulsory) registration of births, marriages, and deaths was introduced in 1837, he insisted that causes of mortality be recorded in each case.[20] Thanks to this, the *Sanitary Report* was able to show how closely a map of disease reflected the spread of towns and the distribution of higher-, middle-, and lower-class residential areas.[21]

[18] F. Engels, *The Condition of the Working Class in England*, ed. W. O. Henderson and W. H. Chaloner (Oxford, 1958), 56. Friedrich Engels was a resident of Manchester and the book was largely based on that town and its environs, but though it was published in German in 1845 it was not translated until 1887, and therefore cannot have affected contemporary perceptions.

[19] Quoted in Steven Marcus, *Engels, Manchester, and the Working Class* (1974), 61.

[20] Another motive was to help in the detection of murder.

[21] Edwin Chadwick, *Report on the Sanitary Condition of the Labouring Population of Great Britain* (1842), ed. M. W. Flinn (Edinburgh, 1965), 219–54.

The same exercise led to the growth of a new type of social science based on epidemiology and to a new interest in public health, as pioneered by doctors such as Neil Arnott and the first Registrar-General, William Farr.

As already noted,[22] most members of the medical Establishment were anti-contagionists, and so contributed to the fatalistic and Malthusian assumption that population pressure must inevitably lead to poverty, disease, and a falling birth rate until an equilibrium between numbers and food production had been restored. Chadwick disposed of this argument robustly.

> If, in the most crowded districts, the inference is found to be erroneous, that the extent of sickness and mortality is indicative of the pressure of population on the means of subsistence, so is the inference that the ravages act to the extent supposed, as a positive check to the increase of the numbers of the population. In such districts the fact is observable, that where the mortality is the highest, the number of births are more than sufficient to replace the deaths.[23]

Many other Radicals argued, against the anti-contagionists, that fever was—if not *caused*—then *spread* by destitution, which invariably weakened the resistance of human bodies to disease. This was the line taken by Dr W. P. Alison, an influential social reformer who inverted Malthus' premiss when he wrote, 'It *is not the fear of lowering, but the hope of maintaining or bettering* their condition, which really constitutes [the] preventive check.'[24] Alison's solution was a more generous system of social welfare, which Chadwick, as a proponent of the harsh New Poor Law, could not go along with. He therefore needed to devise an alternative form of environmental activism, and fastened on contagionism. Not being able to anticipate developments in bacteriology, Chadwick wrongly believed that disease was due to 'pollution of the air by the retention of ordures and refuse', or 'miasma',[25] but he was instinctively right in wishing to discard the existing unhygienic system by which sewage was taken away in handcarts, and to install hydraulically operated, arterial–venous systems of drainage which would bring healing streams of fresh water into houses with water closets, while disposing of sewage in suspension to the nearest farms, where it could be used as fertilizer. With Benthamite rigour, Chadwick detailed exact specifications regarding size and shape of sewer; he had a horror of amateur bumbling, and suspected that private companies would cut standards as they competed for the right to install drainage. In a supplementary report he attributed some of the miasmatic disease to the working-class habit of laying dead bodies out for viewing at home. Realizing that the poor could not afford the cost of commercial undertakers,

---

[22] See above, pp. 338–9.   [23] Chadwick, *Report on the Sanitary Condition*, 243.

[24] William Pulteney Alison, *Observations on the Management of the Poor in Scotland, and its Effects on the Health of the Great Towns* (Edinburgh, 1840), 98.

[25] Chadwick, *Report on the Sanitary Condition*, 134.

he came up with visionary proposals for 'suburban Valhallas', meaning state-directed mortuaries and cemeteries.[26]

It has been suggested that Chadwick deliberately highlighted filth as a metaphor for the most brutalized, dangerous, and revolutionary members of society. 'Because they were determined and not independent beings, it was easy enough to wash those ideas right out of their heads. Thus, sanitation was simultaneously a mechanism for fostering fear and for neutralizing it. The *Sanitary Report* is then an ideological manifesto, not an empirical survey of conditions affecting health'.[27] Chadwick stood somewhere between evangelical moralists like Chalmers and socially committed Whigs such as Robert Slaney, leading light of the Health of Towns Association. All three wished to pare material social welfare down to a minimum and for the Government to sponsor environmental improvements. They shared a vision of the model town in which walks, parks, loan societies, schools, mechanics institutes, public libraries, and public laundries would combine to teach the workers thrift, 'useful instruction, and rational recreation', but whereas Slaney believed in 'a quality of the human mind named Benevolence, Kindness of Heart',[28] Chadwick and Chalmers thought that the mass of humankind was ill-motivated. And whereas Chalmers blamed this on sin, which was intrinsic to the human condition, Chadwick (like Slaney) was an environmental determinist who regarded human characters as socially constructed.

There are clear signs that the softer attitudes of Slaney and Alison were gaining force by the 1830s. Demonization of the poor as potential revolutionaries had been commonplace since the last two decades of the eighteenth century. Even sympathetic caricaturists like Gillray invariably depicted them as demoralized, skeletal, bestial creatures, their pinched faces staring malevolently from the margins of his prints at the ladies and gentlemen corpulently occupying centre stage. 'Unable to challenge the propertied directly, [the poor] appear in windows and at doors, importuning from a distance.... A vision of a society separated into distinct and hostile groups has replaced the more fluid, ambiguous worlds of Defoe and Hogarth.'[29] Such images were symptomatic of polite society's inability to distinguish between poverty and various types of deviance, such as

[26] Edwin Chadwick, *A Supplementary Report on the Results of a Special Inquiry into the Practice of Interment in Towns*, PP 1843 xii; Mary Elizabeth Hotz, 'Down among the Dead: Edwin Chadwick's Burial Reform Discourse in Mid-Nineteenth-Century England', *Victorian Literature and Culture*, 29 (2001), 21–38.

[27] Christopher Hamlin, *Public Health and Social Justice in the Age of Chadwick: Britain, 1800–1854* (Cambridge, 1998), 186–7.

[28] Slaney, notebook, 1854, quoted in Paul Richards, 'R. A. Slaney, the Industrial Town, and Early Victorian Social Policy', *Social History*, 4 (1979), 87.

[29] Lynn Hollen Lees, *The Solidarities of Strangers: The English Poor Laws and the People, 1700–1948* (Cambridge, 1998), 94. See also M. Dorothy George, *Hogarth to Cruikshank: Social Change in Graphic Satire* (1967), 13–17.

crime, delinquency, lunacy,[30] sexual depravity, and Jacobinism. In their imaginations all these horrors merged into one great phantasmagoria of the mad, bad, and dangerous people, an infectious disease threatening to destroy civilization. 'Pauperism we consider nearly as infectious as smallpox,' wrote one official. 'Without constant vigilance it would soon overspread the whole parish.'[31] Like speculation and disease, poverty seemed capable of being spread through personal contact until it engulfed the whole of society.

These phobias affected mainstream thought for as long as revolution seemed a possibility, i.e. until the mid-century, but among opinion-*formers* a new tone began to be heard long before then. The publishing sensation of the 1820s was Pierce Egan's journal *Life in London* (1820–1), also called *Tom and Jerry*, which was plagiarized and imitated in at least sixty-five other publications. Illustrated by George and Robert Cruikshank, its racily picaresque accounts of bohemian low life in the teeming alleyways of the East End and Seven Dials were not exactly glamorized, but in their unremitting gusto they were at least morally neutral. Egan's gin-sodden pimps, prostitutes, and pickpockets were lively, witty, and interesting, while their comic Cockney slang brought them into intimate contact with the reader. Operatic performances of *Tom and Jerry* virtually dominated the London stage throughout the 1820s, prompting Carlyle to observe that '*no* play had ever enjoyed such currency'. (Apparently the Lord Chamberlain was urged to suppress W. T. Moncrieff's adaptation at the Adelphi, but he enjoyed it so much that he not only went to see it again the following night but took his wife.) Its success has been called a 'formative moment in the cultural history of the metropolis',[32] and it paved the way for *Sketches by Boz* from 1834 onwards. In these Charles Dickens did not disguise the seamy side of working-class life, but his mood was jovial and even cosy, his working-class characters eccentric, but full of vitality and rarely grotesque. As in his novels, the plots emphasized the interconnectedness of different social worlds; meaning that his poor were neither out of sight nor out of mind. Such tonal changes probably reflected a rueful awareness that the working class was as much sinned against as sinful.

Certainly, it was hard to deny the problems caused by industrial machinery. Many economists clung to the view (which Ricardo posited in 1817 but retracted four years later) that labour-saving innovations created wealth and so increased

---

[30] In 1800, following an attempt on George III's life, provision was made for the indefinite detention of criminal lunatics.

[31] *Extracts from the Information received from His Majesty's Commissioners as to the Administration and Operation of the Poor Laws* (1832), 177.

[32] John Marriott (ed.), *Unknown London: Early Modernist Visions of the Metropolis, 1815–45* (2000), vol., pp. xv, xxxix; Robert L. Patten, *George Cruikshank's Life, Times, and Art* (1992–6), i. 226–31; Deborah Epstein Nord, *Walking the Victorian Streets: Women, Representation, and the City* (Ithaca, NY, 1995), 31–6.

wages in the long run. But even if machines were beneficial in macroeconomic terms, their effect on workers' lives caused a good deal of anguish. Because they were expensive to install, the best way to pay for them was to keep them going for as long as possible, and in many trades factories operated from 6 o'clock in the morning until 8 o'clock at night, six days a week, with hardly any time off for meals.[33] Industrial tasks were not intrinsically harder or more prone to drudgery than those in agriculture and domestic industry, nor did exchanging seasonal rhythms for those of the clock necessarily entail loss. But the transition must have been painful for those who experienced it—learning to associate bells with work rather than worship, being locked out for turning up late, counting time in terms of hours and minutes instead of tasks accomplished. Moralists were aghast at the opportunities for promiscuity in large impersonal workshops, and complained that the relatively high wages merely led to drunkenness. Many entrepreneurs overcame this problem by paying their employees in vouchers exchangeable for goods,[34] but this practice allowed the less benevolent of them to exploit their workers even further by offering shoddy goods at inflated prices. 'Tommy shops' were widely criticized as contrary to the principles of a cash economy, and the Truck Act of 1831 made payment in kind illegal. Yet despite these concerns, proposals to limit factory hours by legislation met with fierce opposition. According to Nassau Senior, it was only the final half-hour or so of each current working day that allowed mill owners to make any profit and so compete with foreigners.[35] Long hours were also justified as a motor of social mobility, since the high wages that resulted enabled more enterprising workers to amass savings quickly and set themselves up as small masters, retailers, or teachers. This claim was backed up by anecdotal evidence suggesting that, whenever an enlightened employer unilaterally reduced working hours, some of his operatives would move to rival factories in search of better pay. There was also the ideological argument that wage-earners were free agents who had entered voluntarily into contracts with their employers. Reformers might retort that it was 'perfect nonsense' to talk of them as free agents since they were merely 'free to starve or to obey the will of their masters',[36] but such sentiments were slow to make headway.

Reformers had therefore to concentrate on the plight of those workers who were obviously not free agents. It is often claimed that mechanization made it more attractive to employ children because it reduced the level of skill and

[33] A prominent casualty was the tradition of 'St Monday' (i.e. taking Mondays off in return for working extra hard at other times).

[34] Sidney Pollard, *The Genesis of Modern Management: A Study of the Industrial Revolution in Great Britain* (1965), 203–4.

[35] Senior was especially doctrinaire, even opposing the regulation of child labour.

[36] *Report from the Committee on the Bill to Regulate the Labour of Children in the Mills and Factories of the United Kingdom, PP* 1831–2 xv. 459 (Oastler's evidence).

dexterity required in the workforce, though any adults who have had to have mobile phones and video timers explained to them by a 7-year-old may find that argument unconvincing. More importantly children could be paid less and were easier to discipline. Yet when adult male operatives campaigned for a statutory limit to children's hours of labour, they were accused of bad faith. It was said that they really wished to limit their own hours, since if juniors were not on hand to tend the steam-powered looms and mules as piecers, cleaners, and scavengers, then the machines could not work at all. Alternatively, it was said that they looked on children as competitors, and saw legislative restrictions as a means of protecting their own jobs. It was also alleged that the worst cases of cruelty to children occurred in factories where families worked in teams; this suggests that the problem was not the boss's thirst for profit, but the wish of the child's parents and uncles to maximize the family's earnings in the form of piece-rates. Opponents of factory legislation therefore argued that it was impossible 'by legislative enactments, to supply the place of parental affections in behalf of the child. If these natural ties were unavailing, legislative enactments would prove equally useless.'[37] Some employers sought to rescue children from the pressure of family greed by placing them under the control of foremen.[38] It was a humane move, but led to complaints that the patriarchal family unit was being undermined.

Way back in 1802 Robert Peel the elder had sponsored an Act to protect pauper apprentices assigned to cotton, woollen, and some other mills by the Poor Law authorities. Theoretically this protection was extended to all cotton mill children in 1819, but the legislation was largely ineffective. In 1825 Hobhouse sought to restrict the employment of children under 16 to eleven hours a day. His Bill was 'mutilated' by Robert Peel the younger, acting in concert with the Manchester Chamber of Commerce, but at least a twelve-hour limit was secured.[39] It was followed by a severe and prolonged depression which galvanized the Manchester-based Grand General Union of Cotton Spinners under John Doherty to mount a campaign of unionization and strike action.[40] All this was in anticipation of the Ten Hours Movement, which began in 1830 on the other side of the Pennines. Numerous short-time committees were established to liaise with political unions, to prepare mass petitions, and to hold monster meetings and 'pilgrimages'. Whereas the Lancashire spinners had sought

[37] John Hope, *HPD*3 xi. 386–7 (16 Mar. 1832).

[38] Neil J. Smelser, *Social Change in the Industrial Revolution: An Application of Theory to the Lancashire Cotton Industry 1770–1840* (1959) 196–202, 220–4.

[39] Peter Mandler, *Aristocratic Government in the Age of Reform: Whigs and Liberals, 1830–1852* (Oxford, 1990), 143–4; J. T. Ward, *The Factory Movement 1830–1855* (1962), 28–9.

[40] R. G. Kirby and A. E. Musson, *The Voice of the People: John Doherty, 1798–1854, Trade Unionist, Radical and Factory Reformer* (Manchester, 1975), 85–152; John Rule, *The Labouring Classes in Early Industrial England, 1750–1850* (1986), 290–304.

to redress the balance of power between masters and workers, the Yorkshire campaign was a howl of rage against the process of industrialization itself,[41] and took its tone from three local notables. One was George Stringer Bull, a former African missionary and strong temperance reformer, now a parish priest near Bradford and known as the Reverend Bruiser.[42] Then there was Richard Oastler, a large and powerful man with a very loud voice, sometimes called 'the Danton of the factory movement'. A former Leeds cloth merchant and New Connexion Methodist, he had since become steward to a large landowner and was a staunch Anglican. A fierce protectionist and a spirited opponent of the New Poor Law, he called himself a Tory, investing that term with a conscious sense of traditional obligation, social duty, and paternal care.[43] His rhetorical coup was to compare wage-slaves with negro slaves and 'the children of Israel', and to liken the factory system to the 'Egyptian bondage'.

Thousands of our fellow-creatures . . . are this very moment existing in a state of slavery *more horrid* than are the victims of that hellish system, '*colonial slavery*'. . . . The very streets which receive the droppings of an 'Anti-Slavery Society' are every morning wet by the tears of innocent victims at the accursed shrine of avarice, who are *compelled* (not by the cart-whip of the negro slave-driver) but by the dread of the equally appalling thong or strap of the over-looker, to hasten, half-dressed, *but not half-fed*, to those magazines of British infantile slavery—*the worsted mills in the town and neighbourhood of Bradford!!!*[44]

Finally there was Michael Thomas Sadler, another Leeds merchant who in 1829 became MP for Newark, a seat controlled by the Ultra Tory Duke of Newcastle. Even Oastler failed to excel him in moral outrage.

Even, at this moment, while I am thus speaking in behalf of these oppressed children, what numbers of them are still at their toil, confined in heated rooms, bathed in perspiration, stunned with the roar of revolving wheels, poisoned with the noxious effluvia of grease and gas, till at last, weary and exhausted, they turn out almost naked, plunge into the inclement air, and creep shivering to beds from which a relay of their young work-fellows have just arisen;—and such is the fate of many of them at the best while in numbers of instances, they are diseased, stunted, crippled, depraved, destroyed.[45]

Like many Tory MPs sympathetic to factory reform, Sadler lost his seat in December 1832, being defeated in the new constituency of Leeds by two Government candidates, Macaulay and John Marshall, the latter a local mill owner and flax-spinner. It was a notably bitter contest, with Baines's *Mercury*

---

[41] One scholar goes so far as to call the campaign a 'jihad' (Diana Davids Olien, *Morpeth: A Victorian Public Career* (Washington, 1983), 99).   [42] J. C. Gill, *Parson Bull of Byerley* (1963), 62–77.
[43] Cecil Driver, *Tory Radical: The Life of Richard Oastler* (Oxford, 1946), 29–33, 42–3.
[44] Eileen Groth Lyon, *Politicians in the Pulpit: Christian Radicalism in Britain from the Fall of the Bastille to the Disintegration of Chartism* (Aldershot, 1999), 136–8.   [45] HPD3 xi. 384 (16 Mar. 1832).

denouncing Oastler, and Macaulay going one better than Burke by comparing the swinish multitude to 'hyenas'. The leadership of the Ten Hours Movement now passed to Lord Ashley, the future seventh Earl of Shaftesbury, whose lachrymose concern for the victims of industry went with an apparent indifference to the fate of his own Dorset labourers. His judgemental religiosity, his propensity to see himself as St Sebastian, and his aristocratic contempt for mill owners put many people off, yet his genuine humanitarianism made him the social conscience of the age, the champion and protector of lunatics, climbing boys, and ragged schoolchildren as well as factory operatives. Ashley, Sadler, and Bull—like their Manchester ally the powerful preacher Joseph Rayner Stephens—were Ultra Tories and evangelicals of that apocalyptic, liberationist, pre-millenarian type that opposed economic liberalism. They were joined in the cause by Radical MPs such as William Cobbett and Thomas Duncombe, by the Unitarian John Fielden and the Bible–Christian temperance reformer Joseph Brotherton, both manufacturers from the Manchester area, and by the arch-conservative Inglis. The same kaleidoscopic quality characterized the local short-time committees, described as a 'strange combination of Socialists, Chartists and ultra Tories'.[46]

Unfortunately for them all, the key economic ministers believed in market forces. A Bill of Hobhouse's in 1831 was seriously watered down by business interests acting through Althorp, and when Sadler attempted another in the following year he was forced, again by Althorp, to submit the question to a select committee. This was a blow, since the hope had been to secure legislation before a new Parliament could be elected on a middle-class franchise, but at least it gave Sadler an opportunity to bring the plight of the factory children to public notice. In 1833 Ashley moved in favour of a ten-hour working day, and again ministers colluded with the manufacturers' lobby in getting the issue referred, this time to a Royal Commission of Inquiry comprising the ubiquitous Chadwick, the political economist Thomas Tooke, and Southwood Smith, a physician. So began the battle of the blue books. Sadler's report, based on the evidence of twenty-one doctors and sixty working people, was a catalogue of beatings and sexual abuse, accidents and deformities, but its impact was lessened by its compiler's obvious animus against industry and by his over-emotive language. He exaggerated and distorted medical evidence, took hard cases for the norm, and idealized such alternatives to factory work as agriculture and the domestic industries. The Commissioners were equally biased in so far as they set out 'to supersede the ruinous measure then before the House', and to prevent 'children being used as the instruments of agitation'.[47] Nevertheless, their report, based on interviews

[46] *Leeds Mercury*, 23 Mar. 1844.
[47] Chadwick to Senior, 1834 ?, quoted in Mandler, *Aristocratic Government*, 148.

with hundreds of witnesses, probably came 'somewhat closer to the truth' than Sadler's committee, as even Engels acknowledged.[48]

Machines created lives of drudgery for factory operatives, but they brought ruin to the more than 800,000 domestic producers scattered about the country-side who were forced to compete with them in the cotton, linen, silk, and woollen textile industries. Though they lacked the romance attaching to yeomen allegedly driven off the land by enclosures, the hand weavers' plight elicited much hand-wringing in political circles. As well as loss of status, the prices such handicraftsmen were able to command for their cloth fell steadily, especially if they worked for one of the many smaller middlemen, or 'grinders', who paid minimal piece-rates. In the West Riding, for example, earnings sank to as little as 4s. 6d. a week during the 1830s, a pittance which ruled out meat as an article of diet. So rapid was the progress of the textile industries, cottons especially, that displaced outworkers might have been absorbed into the factories fairly swiftly, with loss of dignity but not of livelihood, but instead they lingered on distress-ingly. This was partly due to obstinacy, but it owed more to the way in which bosses ran the factory and domestic systems side by side. Benjamin Gott, for example, continued to put work out in the 1830s despite employing 1,300 workers in his three mills, and Fielden Brothers continued to employ more than 1,000 domestic workers despite running a huge up-to-date spinning and weaving mill at Waterside.[49] Generally speaking, entrepreneurs installed only so much machinery as was necessary to supply goods at the lower reaches of each trade cycle. Then as business improved they would put out work to hand weavers, who picked up just enough crumbs to keep them going, despite being chronically underemployed most of the time. This strategy might have been due to compas-sion on the part of the masters, or it might be that they did not want their plant and machinery to stand idle in times of depression. Either way, the result was to drag out the transition from home to factory production unconscionably.

When domestic workers responded by smashing power-looms—the most sustained violence occurred during 1811–16—they were named after Ned Ludd, a Leicestershire halfwit who had destroyed a number of stocking-frames in a fit of temper in 1779. In the Nottinghamshire lace and hosiery industries Luddism mainly took the peaceful form of 'collective bargaining by riot', thereby sub-stituting for trade unions, which were illegal, but in Lancashire and Yorkshire there was genuine insurrectionary intent, at least if the testimony of government spies is to be believed.[50] The Luddites were eventually crushed with the help of

[48] Engels, *Condition of the Working Class*, 192.

[49] Stewart Angus Weaver, *John Fielden and the Politics of Popular Radicalism 1832–1847* (Oxford, 1987), 20–8.

[50] Roy A. Church, *Economic and Social Change in a Midland Town: Victorian Nottingham 1815–1900* (1966), 44–6; J. R. Dinwiddy, 'Luddism and Politics in the Northern Counties', in Dinwiddy, *Radicalism and Reform in Britain, 1750–1850* (1992).

12,000 troops, and a number of leaders executed or transported. Thereafter, despite notable weavers' riots in Blackburn and Burnley in 1826, Manchester in 1829, and throughout the North in 1833–4, it was obvious that any redress would have to come from Parliament. The snag was that parliamentary reform had made the House of Commons even less responsive than before to the cause of working people.

The only hand-loom workers with a tradition of legislative protection against unscrupulous employers were the Spitalfields silk-weavers in London's East End, where wages had traditionally been determined through collective bargaining and then enforceable through the courts.[51] However, as recently as 1824 Huskisson and Hume had joined forces to secure the repeal of the Spitalfields Acts, on the grounds that London had lost out to low-wage areas such as Macclesfield and Paisley, and would inevitably lose out to Lyon now that it had been decided to replace the prohibition on imported French silk by a 30 per cent duty. Given this blow against old mercantilism, it was unlikely that Parliament would renege so soon by reimposing wage controls on the textile industries as a whole. Nevertheless, that is what the weavers demanded in their submissions to John Maxwell's Select Committee of 1834–5. Delegates of local trade associations and members of mechanics institutes, they were earnestly committed to radical politics and confidently able to argue against the laws of political economy, for example by appropriating Thomas Hodgskin's labour theory of value. Their cause was taken up by the usual assortment of Tories and Radicals (Oastler, Sadler, Bull, Fielden, Cobbett) and by two heterodox political economists, Robert Torrens and E. S. Cayley, but the arguments employed on their behalf were contradictory. The hand weavers were praised for self-reliance, probity, and idyllic family lives, yet in the same breath it was said that poverty was driving them to drink, embezzle, and engage in premature marriages. What seemed to shock commentators most was that on Sundays many weavers would go for 'skulking walks in the country', being too ashamed of their threadbare suits to attend church.[52] That such an argument was thought to carry weight suggests that religion was coming to be regarded as a badge of respectability. It is hard to imagine Wilberforce's generation, with its intense concern for personal salvation, fretting about sartorial shabbiness.

Another straw in the wind was the fate of Sir Andrew Agnew's 1834 Bill on behalf of the Lord's Day Society to outlaw Sunday sport and recreation. Like many evangelicals Agnew was a passionate Sabbatarian, and his proposal was wildly popular, with over 650 petitions presented in the previous year, more

[51] I. J. Prothero, *Artisans and Politics in Early Nineteenth-Century London: John Gast and his Times* (Folkestone, 1979), 224.

[52] *Report from the Select Committee on Hand-Loom Weavers' Petitions, PP* 1835, vol. xiii, p. iv; Maxine Berg, *The Machinery Question and the Making of Political Economy 1815–1848* (Cambridge, 1980), 232–52.

than on any other subject except slavery. He also had considerable support in Parliament, where he was only narrowly defeated (161–125).[53] However, nearly all those who *spoke* treated the subject with either levity or vitriol. The Bill was a disastrous case of 'hyper-legislation'. It was conceived in a 'spirit of dictation'. It 'trench[ed] too much on the proper domain of conscience'. It went against 'the genius of the times' in seeking to make the law more severe. It reflected the 'tyrannical' jurisdiction of Agnew's 'gloomy, mortifying God'. 'Religion to be effective, must be spontaneous and sincere. It was useless to attempt driving the people into it.' Sunday was the day of Creation and Resurrection, and should be 'festive' and 'joyful'. 'Innocent' recreations (re-creations) like cricket fitted men for the performance of their moral and religious duties. Factory workers toiled throughout the hours of daylight each weekday, and should be permitted to saunter in the countryside on their only day of rest. Nor should policemen be made to labour on the Sabbath, merely in order to arrest people caught enjoying themselves.[54] Such sentiments had been expressed before, but only in holes and corners. What is interesting is the confidence with which they were now being uttered, throwing Sabbatarians on the defensive. In the country at large moralists were probably still in the majority, but it was an increasingly silent one.

THE ORIGINS OF SOCIAL POLICY

Social welfare policy began with the education grant and first systematic regulation of working hours in 1833, the New Poor Law of 1834, enhanced regulation of emigrant passenger traffic in 1835, and so on until 1848 when Morpeth established a permanent Board of Health with Chadwick its first Secretary. These developments have been described as 'a revolution in government', yet the process was not sustained. Victorian England's magnificent sewers, for example, were not dug until long after the *Sanitary Report*. One problem was a residual evangelical moralism, which half-welcomed epidemics as the natural desert of workers who had crowded into towns in the hope of higher wages. From such a perspective sanitary intervention—like the Corn Laws—might seem to thwart the dispensations of providence. The idea of public health—*sanitas sanitatum*—would not take off until the 1860s, by which time it was generally accepted that towns were here to stay. Another problem was that proposals for social expenditure ran up against the determination of successive governments to achieve a fiscally minimal state. A final difficulty in the way of national solutions was the widespread prejudice in favour of local government. In 1841, when Normanby sponsored a Bill to introduce rudimentary building regulations, its centralizing

---

[53] It was eventually carried in 1837, but never became law owing to the dissolution of Parliament in that year.   [54] *HPD*3 xxiii. 314–57 (30 Apr. 1834).

tendencies alarmed MPs and caused it to be withdrawn. The dilemma was summed up in an extremely frank letter from Russell to Chadwick.

We are endeavouring to improve our institutions. I think they have been lax, careless, wasteful, injudicious to an extreme; but the country governed itself, and was blind to its own faults. We are busy introducing system, method, science, economy, regularity, and discipline. But we must beware not to lose the co-operation of the country—they will not bear a Prussian Minister, to regulate their domestic affairs—so that some faults must be indulged for the sake of carrying improvement in the mass.[55]

This situation left little scope for manoeuvre, as became obvious in discussions on the three big social issues of the mid-1830s—the protection of factory children, the Poor Law, and the plight of the hand-loom weavers.

On factory reform the Government reaffirmed its refusal to interfere with adult labour, but went one better than the ten-hour day, which Ashley and other reformers were demanding for 9- to 12-year-olds, by legislating a maximum of eight hours. It looked like a remarkably generous gesture, but the beauty of the plan from the point of view of free-marketeers, like Althorp at the Treasury and Thomson at the Board of Trade,[56] was that it enabled children to be used in relays, and so allowed adults to go on being worked up to sixteen or seventeen hours a day. Obviously it would be necessary to employ many more children overall, but Chadwick was confident that these could be supplied from the workhouses which were likely to be built as a result of his Poor Law reform, already in the pipeline. The Act which eventually passed in 1833 stipulated that no children under 9 should work in textile factories (other than silk), that 9- to 12-year-olds should be limited to eight hours a day,[57] that 13- to 17-year-olds should be limited to twelve hours a day, and that no one under 18 should be made to work at night-time. Finally, it was proposed that factories should be turned into educational institutions providing twelve hours' a week of instruction for 9- to 12-year-olds.

For all the Act's limitations, younger children were now well protected, and a Statutory Commission had been placed over the employers in certain industries. Even so, the legislation may have been counter-productive. Because large factories were more amenable to inspection, there was probably a shift of business to smaller workshops where exploitation was greater, at least according to anecdotal evidence. Certainly the reformers were far from satisfied. Short-time committees kept up the momentum with frequent monster meetings in the manufacturing districts, and were patronized by religious leaders of all denominations as well as

[55] Russell to Chadwick, University College London, Chadwick Papers, 1733/I.

[56] Thomson 'did not apprehend that 69 hours work in the course of the week would be found injurious to [12- to 13-year-olds] in any way' (*HPD*3 xxxiii. 739 (9 May 1836)).

[57] Actually to forty-eight hours a week with not more than nine in any one day. The lace industry was exempted from the operation of the Act.

by Young England MPs. Ashley, meanwhile, turned his attention to the suffering of chimney sweeps or climbing boys and to the state of children in coal mines, luridly depicted as circles of Hell with naked bodies writhing underground. His hopes were pinned on a Conservative return to power, which took place in 1841, but he was furious when Peel tried to buy his silence with a lowly post in the royal household ('a department in which I could have exhibited nothing good but my legs in white shorts'[58]), and was soon complaining that the new Government was 'ten times more hostile to my views than the last'.[59] Even so, in 1842 he secured a ban on underground employment for all females and boys under 10, and two years later he triumphantly carried a motion limiting the hours of 13- to 17-year-olds in textile industries from twelve to ten.[60] At this point, however, Peel forced his party to reverse the decision by threatening to resign,[61] which caused an incandescent Ashley to describe him privately as an ethical 'heathen', who 'sneered at moral legislation, at attempts to make people moral by Act of Parliament; maintained that Government had nothing to do with the morality of the people; it should provide them with walks and spaces and means of amusement! What a Minister! What a Conservative! What a Christian!'[62] Ashley could at least console himself that leading Whigs and Liberals such as Russell, Grey, Macaulay, and Palmerston had come out strongly in his favour for the first time. Two years later those politicians found themselves unexpectedly in office, and in 1847 a ten-hour day was enacted for females and for males aged between 13 and 17. However, the glory went to the Radical MP John Fielden and not to Ashley, who had lost his county seat the previous year, having scrupulously put himself up for re-election on changing his mind in favour of Corn Law repeal.

If legislation on factory hours was a victory for paternalist Tories and interventionist Whigs, the New Poor Law with its 'workhouse test' was an even clearer victory for laissez-faire, or social market, liberals in both parties. Admittedly it might seem paradoxical to describe as laissez-faire an Act which 'gave a dogmatically uniform direction to English Poor Law policy', and established 'the principle of centralised executive control of local administration',[63] but this simply reflects an ambiguity in the term itself. One reason why historians have disagreed so much about the influence of laissez-faire ideas has been their failure to distinguish between the administrative sense of the term on the one

[58] Ashley, diary, Aug.–Sept. 1841, in Edwin Hodder, *The Life and Works of the Seventh Earl of Shaftesbury* (1886), i. 349–61.   [59] Ashley, diary, 3 Mar. 1842, in Hodder, *Shaftesbury*, i. 409.
[60] This was an amendment to Graham's Bill, which as passed imposed a limit of six and a half hours on 8- to 12-year-olds, and of twelve hours on all females over 12 and on 13- to 17-year-old males.
[61] See above, p. 508.
[62] Ashley, diary, 16 Mar. and 4 May 1844, quoted in Geoffrey B. A. M. Finlayson, *The Seventh Earl of Shaftesbury 1801–1885* (1981), 175, 212, 220.
[63] Sidney and Beatrice Webb, *English Local Government: English Poor Law History Part II: The Last Hundred Years* (1929), i. 1.

hand and its socio-economic implications on the other. By and large, those like Chadwick who wanted to *increase* the powers of central government also wanted to *reduce* the power of government in so far as it affected the lives of individuals. That is to say, they were opposed to laissez-faire in an administrative sense but supported it in a social sense. Conversely, those like Ashley who believed in giving local authorities freedom to exercise discretion also believed in high levels of protection and welfare to individuals.

The traditional system of poor relief, referred to as the 43rd Elizabeth, was a form of dole administered by parochial officers or overseers and monitored by county magistrates. From 1780 onwards it was increasingly subjected to statutory interference, until in 1834 magistrates were stripped of all remaining powers. At that point the more than 15,000 parishes of England and Wales were grouped into about 600 unions, to be run by boards of guardians elected by local ratepayers, with a system of plural voting to ensure that the largest landowners had most influence. The country as a whole was divided into districts, each comprising about forty unions and under the control of an assistant Poor Law commissioner, and these in turn were to answer to a permanent Commission in London, directly responsible to Parliament. Chadwick was its first Secretary (1834–42), and its overriding function was to prevent a return to JP-style paternalism. Viewed in this administrative light, the New Poor Law obviously ran directly counter to the principle of laissez-faire. But of course the reason for giving control to ratepayers rather than to JPs was that the former were more likely to count the cost of poor relief, and less likely to act in a benevolent or paternalist manner. Similarly, the reason for giving additional influence to large landowners was that they paid the highest rates. Judged therefore in terms of social philosophy, the legislation of 1834 was in the spirit of laissez-faire, being designed to prevent high welfare intervention and to promote social independence.

The central principle of the Old Poor Law was that the poor had a *right* to relief in their parishes of settlement, meaning paid labour for those who were capable of it, and alms for those who were not. Sturdy beggars who refused work, and vagrants outside their own parishes, were confined to prisons or houses of correction and frequently whipped. From the mid-eighteenth century outdoor relief was offered to some of those in paid employment who were unable to make ends meet, perhaps because of seasonal fluctuations, or the decline of cottage industry, or else the confiscation of allotments as farmers sought to engross more and more arable land.[64] Then, when prices shot up suddenly in the mid-1790s, these money payments were frequently allowed to increase with the cost of living and the size of the recipient's family. The combination of the last two practices was usually referred to as the Speenhamland system after the

[64] George R. Boyer, *An Economic History of the English Poor Law 1750–1850* (Cambridge, 1990), 23–43.

Berkshire village where magistrates adopted it in 1795, though there had been similar experiments elsewhere before then. By 1820 it had spread to most parts of southern England, a region blighted by agricultural distress and lacking in industrial towns to absorb 'excrescent population'.

'Speenhamland' became a shorthand term to depict a profligate system of relief, the main effect of which was 'to spread pauperism and improvidence over the greater part of the South'.[65] The ostensible reason for this was that, 'in abolishing punishment, we equally abolish reward... All the other classes of society are exposed to the vicissitudes of hope and fear; [the labourer] alone has nothing to lose or to gain.'[66] Yet most of the available evidence suggests that, rather than causing poverty, it was adopted in those parishes where poverty was already greatest.[67] The cost of poor relief generally peaked following the second of consecutive bad harvests (1796, 1801, 1813, 1818), but average real per capita expenditure remained steady from 1790 to 1813, then rose very sharply with the demobilization of soldiers and sailors, before levelling off in the 1820s. Yet there is no evidence that spending rose more in Sussex than in Kent, even though the former was the most notorious Speenhamland county of all and the latter was largely unaffected. Nor does it appear that within counties Speenhamland parishes were more spendthrift than the rest.[68] Nonetheless, the myth was a powerful one. In 1817 a Select Committee under the Canningite William Sturges Bourne laid down a number of doctrines which came to be accepted as orthodox. Firstly, that the allowance system encouraged the poor to marry early and have children. Secondly, that entitlement to relief demoralized the poor and led to a dependency culture. Thirdly, that the system of rates-in-aid-of-wages was open to exploitation by tenant farmers, many of whom served as magistrates and so were able to set the scales of relief. They were charged with paying their labourers less than a subsistence wage in the knowledge that ratepayers—predominantly landlords—would have to make up the difference. Sturges Bourne's committee considered this subsidy to farmers as subversive of the 'natural order of things', because it prevented landlords, tenants, and labourers from working together for mutual benefit 'by following the dictates of their own interests'.[69] One outcome of the committee's work was the Parish Vestries Act (1818), which gave up to six additional vestry votes to higher ratepayers on the assumption that they were least likely to be lenient towards the poor. The Sturges Bourne doctrine also sparked off a welter of anti-poor-relief

---

[65] [J. R. McCulloch], 'Causes and Cure of Disturbances and Pauperism', *ER* 53 (1831), 46.

[66] *Report from His Majesty's Commissioners for inquiring into the Administration and Practical Operation of the Poor Laws, PP* 1834 xxvii. 33, 44.

[67] Mark Blaug, 'The Myth of the Old Poor Law and the Making of the New', *Journal of Economic History*, 23 (1963), 151–84.

[68] D. A. Baugh, 'The Cost of Poor Relief in South-East England, 1790–1834', *EconHR* 28 (1975), 50–68.

[69] *Report from the Select Committee on the Poor Laws, PP* 1817 vi. 10.

propaganda, which culminated in the 1832–4 Poor Law Commission Report. Meanwhile, a number of local parishes were encouraged to make 'experiments in deterrence', notably in Nottinghamshire, Berkshire, and Sussex, even as others moved in the opposite direction by adopting Speenhamland practices for the first time. The situation cried out for uniformity.

The Poor Law Amendment Act of 1834 imposed such a system, in theory at least, by forbidding outdoor relief to the able-bodied. The destitute could keep themselves alive by seeking relief within the workhouse, where they would receive food and shelter but no more than that, since their lives were to be made 'less eligible' than those of the lowest independent labourers. 'No relief shall be given to the able-bodied, or to their families, except in return for work, and that work as hard as it can be made, or in the workhouse, and that workhouse as disagreeable as it can be made.'[70] Hopefully, such a regimen would deter all but the most unfortunate and the most feckless from entering in the first place. As one of the new assistant commissioners put it, the 'prison-like appearance' of the workhouses was deliberately 'intended to torment the poor', and to inspire a 'salutary dread of them'.[71] As a result they ceased to be places of *work*, and consequently sites of moral reformation, as they had been in the late eighteenth century. Then, a sharp rise in Poor Law expenditure (1775–85) had provoked a moral panic over drop-outs, and many market towns and industrialized parishes had responded by operating their workhouses as centres of industry. The expectation was that forced labour would have a beneficial effect on inmates, while at the same time contributing usefully to the national product.[72] However, by 1834 the advance of mechanized industry meant that workhouses were much less effective economically, and the legislation of that year tacitly acknowledged this by reconceptualizing the workhouse as a site of incarceration rather than of work. Reformation also went off the agenda, since it was now thought necessary to deprive inmates of *all* hope (including that one) in order to achieve the main objective, which was to deter people from entering in the first place.

Ministerial responsibility for the Act of 1834 lay with Althorp and Brougham, both liberals in the economic sense of the term, while paternalist Whigs such as Russell and Morpeth kept discreetly quiet on the issue. Behind the ministers were two officials, Senior and Chadwick, joint authors of the 1832–4 Poor Law Commission Report. Senior commented in private that there was no need for inquiry, since 'Chadwick has the Bill in his head', but he recognized that it would be prudent to take some evidence first, and to 'make our report in the way

[70] Nassau Senior to Brougham, 9 Mar. 1833, University College London, Brougham MS 44843; *Report on the Administration and Practical Operation of the Poor Laws* (1834), 127.

[71] E. C. Tufnell, *Second Annual Report of the Poor Law Commissioners*, PP 1836 xxix. 1, 452.

[72] Joanna Innes, 'The State and the Poor: Eighteenth-Century England in European Perspective', in John Brewer and Eckhart Hellmuth (eds.), *Rethinking Leviathan: The Eighteenth-Century State in Britain and Germany* (Oxford, 1999), 247–62.

in which I should wish, that is constantly referring to the evidence and defending ourselves not on general principles, but by facts, and opinions of magistrates and clergymen and practical people, and figures'. He had little doubt that witnesses would say what he wanted them to, since Chadwick 'has an admirable faculty of endowing the purposes of his examinees with words', just like 'a French cook who can make an excellent ragout out of a pair of shoes'.[73] This makes Chadwick and Senior look like ideologues who exploited the gullibility of witnesses, but perhaps they were exploited in their turn. It has been argued that 1834 was not so much a Whig–Liberal measure as the 'last great liberal Tory reform', plotted by former Canningites in Grey's Government while most minds were on parliamentary reform.[74] One of these, T. H. Villiers, Vice-President of the Board of Control, was acutely conscious of the need for an unpopular poor law to restore rustic discipline following the Swing riots,[75] and as early as January 1832 he urged the appointment of a Commission so that 'Government might at once relieve themselves from difficulty and responsibility'.[76] Moreover, although the 1834 Report spelled out the doctrine of less eligibility with more relish than before, many of its essential points had been enunciated in Graham's 1833 Agricultural Report (written with Peel's help) as well as by Sturges Bourne in 1817, and by Christian political economists such as Copleston.

Perhaps it does not matter who precisely was responsible for what, since there was a convergence on policy, but motivations varied. The civil servants (Chadwick, Senior) believed that harsh welfare policies would lead to greater individual effort and overall economic growth, while the politicians (Althorp, Peel, Brougham) and Commissioners (bishops Blomfield and Sumner, Sturges Bourne) emphasized the moral evil of pauperism and the desirability of retribution. But they all agreed on the need for an impersonal 'self-acting test of the claim of the applicant'[77] in place of the old discretionary paternalism. Instead of overseers or magistrates deciding who was worthy of relief, henceforward citizens would determine their entitlement for themselves, but they would not entitle themselves lightly owing to the doctrine of less eligibility. Impetuous as ever, Brougham blurted out the Government's intention when he denounced Speenhamland as a soppy system that said to the poor, in effect, 'The sweat shall trickle down that brow no more.' Conversely, the new law was based on the principle that 'A right in one man to be supported out of the industry or property of another is destructive of providence, frugality, and diligence.'

[73] Senior to Le Marchant, 28 June 1833, Senior to Brougham, 4 Jan. and 9 Mar. 1833, University College London, Brougham MSS 10857, 44437, 44843.

[74] Mandler, *Aristocratic Government*, 136.

[75] The Swing rioters attacked thirteen workhouses and destroyed two (M. A. Crowther, *The Workhouse System 1834–1929: The History of an English Social Institution* (1981), 21).

[76] T. H. Villiers to Howick, 19 Jan. 1832, copy in National Library of Wales, Senior MS C855.

[77] *Report from the Poor Law Commissioners* (1834), 148.

His colleagues, anticipating Radical and Tory attacks, had begged Brougham 'for God's sake to say nothing of the kind',[78] and instead to emphasize the fact that 'no man, whatever his misconduct, shall want the means of subsistence'. They need not have worried, for the vast majority in both Houses apparently shared Brougham's prejudices. There was muted opposition from Ultra Tory paternalists such as Kenyon, Newcastle, Redesdale, Eldon, and Vyvyan, who deplored both the deterrent and the centralizing aspects of the Bill, and from some Radicals, who argued that relief was a matter of 'natural right', not charity. However, the Conservative front benches supported the Bill to the hilt,[79] and it passed its Commons second reading by 319 to 20, while nine of the dissenting MPs sat for Irish constituencies which were not even affected by it.

The ease with which the legislation passed has prompted a lively debate as to its ideological origins. Could it really have reflected bourgeois capitalist attitudes, given that so many landlords and farmers supported it so fervently? Revisionist historians have suggested that the New Poor Law might actually have strengthened rather than weakened local paternalism, with peers and gentry able to exploit the system of dual votes for elections to Poor Law unions. No doubt many did do this, especially in aristocratic counties like Northamptonshire, but a more convincing reason why so many landlords supported the Bill is that they had themselves assimilated capitalist attitudes, which were not the exclusive property of some notional bourgeoisie.[80]

In the country at large the New Poor Law met with considerable resistance, which made for a good deal of continuity in practice. The Act of 1834 did not even abolish outdoor relief to the able-bodied, thanks largely to Wellington's amendment in the House of Lords replacing a specified date of abolition (1 July 1835) by a mere statement of intent. The Outdoor Relief Prohibitory Order of 1844 sought to apply the workhouse test rigidly, but could not eliminate the large number of exceptions. In January 1849 only 28,058 adults designated as 'able-bodied' were assigned to workhouses as against 171,472 receiving outdoor relief.[81] During 1834–9 as many as 350 workhouses were constructed,[82] nearly all in the rural South, but many unions still lacked the necessary accommodation, while elsewhere a defiant strain of paternalism persisted, especially in

---

[78] Mandler, *Aristocratic Government*, 137; *HPD*3 xxv. 230–1 (21 July 1831).

[79] Peel frequently claimed, both in public and in private, that he had had 'more responsibility for the passing of the Poor law' than any Government minister (Peel to Croker, 13 Dec. 1838, in *Croker Papers*, ii. 335–7).

[80] For the paternalist interpretation, the bourgeois capitalist interpretation, and a plausible reconciliation between them, see respectively the works by Brundage, Dunkley, and Mandler cited in the Bibliography, p. 721. For the subsequent decline in outdoor relief, see Karel Williams, *From Pauperism to Poverty* (1981), 59–107.   [81] *Eleventh Annual Report of the Poor Law Board*, PP 1859 ix. 741.

[82] Anne Digby, *The Poor Law in Nineteenth-Century England and Wales* (1982), 16.

Lancashire and Yorkshire.[83] However, where the new law was implemented properly it often proved to be as cruel and ruthless as its authors had hoped. Worse even than the gruel, the uniform, the regulation haircut, the delousing, the degrading and mind-numbing drudgery, were the separation of sexes and the tearing apart of families. There were several scandals, the most gruesome being at Andover workhouse in 1845, where paupers were apparently forced to stay alive by eating the bones they had first been given to crush. Some of the allegations may have been exaggerated, but what is undeniable is that spending on poor relief fell by 35 per cent from an annual average of £6,736,000 in 1831–4 to £4,603,000 in 1835–8, and it was still only £4,664,000 in 1839–42, despite the most intense depression of the century.

Because the New Poor Law was more tight-fisted than Speenhamland, it might be inferred that attitudes towards the indigent became harsher between 1795 and 1834. In fact the opposite was true. In the first place, the older system was nowhere near as lax as the reformers made out. The 1792 Vagrancy Act had led to much harsher treatment of those identified as rogues and vagabonds, while even in Speenhamland parishes outdoor relief had rarely been afforded to the able-bodied except in return for some form of labour.[84] Throughout southern England, moreover, almost all non-Speenhamland parishes had adopted the labour rate system, by which tenant farmers were forced to employ those who could not find work.[85] Finally, an important enactment of 1795 had stipulated that persons could only be removed back to their parishes of settlement if they actually applied for relief. At first sight this abolition of pre-emptive removal seems like a concession to the poor, but it must have deterred persons from applying for relief, just as later the New Poor Law's workhouse test was intended to do.[86] A second consideration is the time lag that often occurs between the high tides of public opinion and the passage of legislation. The judiciary's generosity in the 1790s, such as it was, reflected attitudes that had been current some decades before and were already beginning to come under attack from moralists and economists.[87] Likewise, feelings of hostility towards the poor peaked two or

---

[83] There also remained fifteen 'Gilbert unions' (named after the promoter of an Act in 1782) in which outdoor relief was officially permitted under certain conditions. Graham sought in vain to have these abolished in 1842.

[84] This might take the form of community duty at ratepayers' expense, or might involve being assigned to local employers on a rotational basis in what was called the roundsman system (Blaug, 'The Myth of the Old Poor Law', 156; Lees, *Solidarities of Strangers*, esp. 103–4, the best of recent synoptic accounts of the subject).

[85] Under this scheme, the cost of employing all the available labourers in any parish was assessed, and employers were charged a share of that sum according to rateable value, minus whatever actual sums they had expended in payment of wages.

[86] Michael E. Rose, 'Settlement, Removal, and the New Poor Law', in Derek Fraser (ed.), *The New Poor Law in the Nineteenth Century* (1976).

[87] It has been argued that the Berkshire magistrates acted as they did in Speenhamland in order to pre-empt utilitarian Poor Law reformers.

three decades before the Poor Law Amendment Act of 1834. Although the latter passed through Parliament easily enough, it quickly acquired notoriety, thanks in part to Charles Dickens's *Oliver Twist* (1837–9), and the widespread opposition to it probably says more about the mentality of the period than the Act itself.

The New Poor Law as enacted contradicted some of the principles on which it was supposed to be based. To start with, a solution designed for the over-populated South was also inflicted on the North, where Speenhamland-type policies had not operated on anything like the same scale. 'Less eligibility' might have had merit as an inducement to civil responsibility in the countryside, where there was time to ponder about one's long-term prospects, but it was meaningless in the whirlwind economies of towns, where hundreds might be thrown out of work overnight.[88] Secondly, the new system failed to include the repeal of the 1662 Law of Settlement, which stipulated that paupers had a right to relief only in their own parishes.[89] Many political economists had demanded this, as had Sturges Bourne's Committee and the 1833 Agricultural Committee, and its omission must have impaired that labour mobility on which Chadwick and his fellow Commissioners relied when they wrote: 'The poor man's only commodity is his labour, and there should be no legal interference... to his carrying it to the best market.' As Secretary to the permanent Poor Law Commission, Chadwick was to establish a Migration Agency to relocate children from stagnant rural pools to the industrial areas. Apparently over 10,000 families took advantage of the scheme (1835–8), which was attacked by many operatives as a cynical instrument for strike-breaking.[90] Despite all of which the Law of Settlement was not repealed, presumably because feelings in favour of local control ran so deep. Settlement and removal continued to be a frequent practice until 1865, when the Union Chargeability Act switched responsibility for rating from individual parishes to the union. Only then could a national labour market begin to develop.

Finally, the new system blurred the differences between the *deserving* poor and the feckless *undeserving* pauper, despite a lot of rhetoric affirming the importance of that very distinction. Chadwick and his colleagues proposed separate buildings for different 'classifications' of inmate, with less eligibility applying only to able-bodied paupers. They took for granted the community's continuing obligation to look after the young, the elderly, and the sick with

[88] Russell was apprehensive about inflicting the New Poor Law on the North, but Chadwick was keen to use it as a means to discipline the insubordinate operatives of the Ten Hours Movement (Anthony Brundage, *England's 'Prussian Minister': Edwin Chadwick and the Politics of Government Growth, 1832–1854* (University Park, Pa., 1988), 47–8).

[89] Persons could make parishes their own by fulfilling certain requirements regarding residence, employment, or apprenticeship. Otherwise, the parish of settlement was deemed to be that of the father, or in the case of married women the husband, or—if that was unknown—the place of birth. All this naturally made for very complex legal searches.

[90] S. E. Finer, *The Life and Times of Sir Edwin Chadwick* (1952), 123–4.

kindness and dignity. But because it cost money to build separate workhouses, the latter were all too often sent to mixed, or 'general', institutions, and subjected to the same punitive regimen as the able-bodied. Between 1848 and 1870 only 13–17 per cent of those in workhouses were able-bodied adults; about 40 per cent were children, while 30–40 per cent were aged or infirm,[91] and for them 1834 really did mark a loss of traditional rights, albeit unintentionally. Their plight was made even worse by the 1832 Anatomy Act, which assigned the bodies of those who died in public care, and which were not 'claimed' by bona fide relatives, to the various medical schools in proportion to their enrolments.[92] It was a well-meaning attempt by Benthamites like Henry Warburton to address the rocketing cost of cadavers, as hospitals competed with each other to obtain teaching and research materials on the black market. (In 1829 the notorious case of Burke and Hare in Edinburgh had highlighted the prevalence of grave-snatching and commercial murder, while in London seven gangs of 'resurrection men' were arrested during a fifteen-month period in 1830–1.) Victorians' dread of the workhouse probably had as much to do with what would happen to them after death as before it. For, apart from anything else, how could a dissected corpse rise at the Last Trump and participate in the General Resurrection? In other respects the system became progressively softer, with greater emphasis on medical provision and education. By the 1860s workhouse inmates were in many districts treated better than those on outdoor relief,[93] and then in the twentieth century the latter benefited as working men gained more control over scales of relief in inner city unions. A system introduced to curb the excessive generosity of Speenhamland finally succumbed to its own excessive generosity (commonly called Poplarism), and was dismantled in 1929.[94]

The abolition of outdoor relief (in theory) and the failure to curb factory hours effectively, brought the problems of the hand-loom weavers to a head.[95] In 1835 Maxwell's committee recommended a plan for masters and weavers to come together in local boards of trade, and to fix legal minimum wages based on the average paid by the largest manufacturers in each region. 'The effect of the measure would be to withdraw from the worst-paying masters the power which they now possess of regulating wages, and to confer it upon those whose object it

[91] Peter Bartlett, *The Poor Law of Lunacy: The Administration of Pauper Lunatics in Mid-Nineteenth-Century England* (1999), 15, 40, 44. Likewise in 1845 local authorities were required to provide specialized asylums for the insane, despite which a quarter of pauper lunatics were still being treated in workhouses in 1890 and another 8% were receiving outdoor relief.

[92] Ruth Richardson, *Death, Dissection and the Destitute* (1987).

[93] For Norfolk, see Anne Digby, *Pauper Palaces* (1978), 143–96, 215–28.

[94] Given the widespread phobia about dissection, it was notably tactless of the authorities to turn so many former workhouses into local authority hospitals.

[95] They were also disadvantaged by the failure of the 1833 legislation seriously to restrict the hours of labour in factories. A stronger bill might have driven up costs, and so eased the position of the domestic workers.

is to raise the condition and character of the workpeople.'[96] The riposte was that, while such a scheme might indeed protect domestic labourers from exploitation, it would also protect the larger manufacturers from competition.[97] Following a stern exhortation by Poulett Thomson, the Commons threw the proposal out by 129 votes to 41 in 1835. In 1837 Senior and S. J. Loyd were put in charge of a Royal Commission, which reported in 1841 to the effect that wage regulation was out of the question, and that hand-loom weavers, as the unfortunate victims of supply and demand, should simply switch to alternative employments: 'All that remains ... is to enlighten [them] as to their real situation, warn them to flee from the trade, and to beware of leading their children into it.'[98] Not surprisingly, many of them fled from the trade to trade unionism, and were prominent in Chartism.

This repudiation of the weavers' case has been described as a triumph for cap- italist ideology.[99] The message was that intervention in living and working con- ditions was allowable, but not in the labour market. That contemporaries were aware of the significance of the decision is clear from Maxwell's speeches, in which, besides attacking the 'prejudice for free trade and sound currency', he offered a fully fledged if futile under-consumptionist analysis.[100] He also claimed that his scheme would reinforce regional autonomy, whereas under free-market capitalism economies were mistakenly envisaged as national entit- ies. The point was significant, since tension between centre and locality was another complicating factor facing policy-makers in the 1830s and 1840s.

'SYSTEM, METHOD, SCIENCE, ECONOMY': DEFINING THE LIBERAL STATE

'Administrative ecstasy', a delicious term, was used by a disgruntled politician to describe the bewildering proliferation of diktats, ukases, and red tape that flowed downward from central government in late tsarist Russia.[101] This condi- tion, not unknown to public sector workers in the twenty-first century, also characterized English government in the 1830s and 1840s. The Factory Act of 1844, for example, contained seventy-four clauses, the following extract from just one of which is typical in its specificity:

XXXI. And be it enacted, That in any Factory in which the Labour of young persons is restricted to Ten Hours in any One Day it shall be lawful to employ any Child Ten Hours

[96] *Report on Hand-Loom Weavers' Petitions* (1835), p. xiv.   [97] Berg, *Machinery Question*, 245–6.

[98] *Hand-Loom Weavers: Report of the Commissioners*, *P&P* 1841; Duncan Bythell, *The Handloom Weavers: A Study in the English Cotton Industry during the Industrial Revolution* (Cambridge, 1969), 148–75; Geoffrey Timmins, *The Last Shift: The Decline of Handloom Weaving in Nineteenth-Century Lancashire* (Manchester, 1993).

[99] Paul Richards, 'The State and Early Industrial Capitalism: The Case of the Handloom Weavers', *P&P* 83 (1979), 91–115.   [100] *HPD*3 xxiii. 1090–6 (15 May 1834).

[101] Gregor Alexinsky, *Modern Russia*, trans. Bernard Miall (1913), 183.

in any One Day on Three alternate Days of every Week, provided that such Child shall not be employed in any Manner in the same or in any other factory on Two successive Days, nor after Half past Four of the Clock in the Afternoon of any *Saturday*: Provided always, that the Parent or Person having direct Benefit from the Wages of any Child so employed shall cause such Child to attend some School for at least Five Hours between the Hours of Eight of the Clock in the Morning and Six of the Clock in the Afternoon of the same Day on each Week Day preceding each Day of Employment in the Factory, unless such preceding Day shall be a *Saturday*, when no School Attendance of such Child shall be required: Provided also, that on *Monday* in every Week after that in which such Child began to work in the Factory, or any other Day appointed for that Purpose by the Inspector of the District, the Occupier of the Factory shall obtain a certificate from a Schoolmaster, according to the Form and Directions given in the Schedule (A.) to this Act annexed, that such Child has attended School as required by this Act . . .

This looks like the Benthamite mind in full pedantic rigour, anticipating, investigating, counting, recording, regulating, inspecting, enforcing, and adjusting. Such precision legislation must have made running a textile factory extremely difficult. Ashley's counter-proposal for a 'normal day' of ten hours to apply to all workers would have been much simpler and could have been monitored locally. If gas- or candlelight or noise had emanated from a factory after a certain hour, neighbours and rivals could have shamed the perpetrator into compliance.[102] But the complexity of the 1833 and 1844 Acts—for example, the different rules for different age groups, the trade-off between weekly and hourly maxima, and calculations as to the exact amount of time which might be made up for breakdowns of machinery—virtually necessitated an elaborate system of bookkeeping and a national system of inspection to support it.

It was suggested in Chapter 5 that, whereas high Tories believed in the need for society to be 'managed' from above, liberal Tories and economic liberals generally thought that individual citizens should take responsibility for themselves. The New Poor Law was a liberal measure in that sense because it allowed poor people to decide whether or not they should become paupers. In practice, however, life proved too varied and messy to fit any formulaic mechanisms, so laws had to become more precise in order to take account of special cases. The outcome was an administrative as distinct from a managerial culture. Hence Peel's comment on the subject of criminal law consolidation that, whenever he saw 'exceptions to the general principle, he considered it owing to negligence in drawing up the statute'.[103] Likewise, as the discretionary jurisdiction of magistrates was curtailed, so it was necessary for Parliament to lay down their modes of operation with bureaucratic rigidity.[104] The high Tory Ashley, on the

---

[102] Robert Gray, *The Factory Question and Industrial England, 1830–1860* (Cambridge, 1996), 62.
[103] *HPD2* xv. 290 (17 Apr. 1826).
[104] For Peel's wish to codify secondary punishments, see above, p. 319.

other hand, could prescribe a simple ten-hour rule, since in his universe JPs would have retained the power to interpret it in common-sense ways.

A similar problem bedevilled education policy, on which everyone except diehard Tories agreed that Britain was falling behind.[105] Given the reluctance of local ratepayers to meet the cost, in 1833 it was decided to make direct grants from national taxation. Given also the current attacks on Old Corruption and demands for accountability, it was inevitable that schools benefiting from the scheme would be monitored regularly. Local inspection could have been performed humanely, but the only practical way to conduct a nationwide audit was by applying a rigid curriculum based on the 3 Rs, even though this was anathema to fashionable educational theorists, who were mainly child-centred, progressive, and anti-utilitarian.[106] In *Hard Times* (1854) Dickens mocked rote learning in the persons of Mr Gradgrind and an anonymous government inspector, who instructs a class of young children that they 'are to be in all things regulated and governed by fact. We hope to have, before long, a board of fact, composed of Commissioners of fact, who will force the people to be a people of fact, and of nothing but fact. You must discard the word Fancy altogether.' Most of his readers would have sympathized with the satire, for Gradgrindism was the product of an administrative system, not a creature of educational ideology.

The same inspector was never without 'a system to force down the general throat like a bolus'. What was novel about the 1830s was not the search for legislative solutions to social problems, but the search for *national* solutions. The regulation of working conditions, administration of courts, and various policies of social amelioration had been in force for centuries, but all had been administered on a local basis, by unpaid justices at quarter sessions, by parish vestries (originally ecclesiastical bodies), or by ad hoc bodies which were either self-financing or maintained from the county rate. The effects of this administrative revolution have been characterized by one historian as follows:

The JP was the maid of all work . . . even developing what the Webbs called 'inchoate provincial legislation' in the form of orders in Quarter Session which derived what strictly legal force they possessed from old statutes, common law, or the mere habit of unchallenged authority . . . It was not an efficient mode of administration. Indeed, as the [eighteenth] century wore on, there accumulated that impenetrable thicket of competing and overlapping powers and jurisdictions which horrified reformers after Waterloo. But it worked; whatever was urgently wanted was accomplished: after a fashion, locally, and at surprisingly little cost to the public at large.[107]

[105] *Pace* E. G. West, *Education and the Industrial Revolution* (1975).
[106] This was partly owing to the influence of Fellenberg and Pestalozzi.
[107] Norman Gash, *Pillars of Government and Other Essays on State and Society c.1770–c.1880* (1986), 13.

Despite the decline of guilds and apprenticeship, local authorities retained into the nineteenth century considerable scope for intervention, having responsibility for hospitals, workhouses, dispensaries, public utilities, summary justice, and the enforcement of paternity obligations. The vagrancy laws were extended from the 1790s in order to punish loitering, pilfering, and embezzlement of raw materials. Vagrants were pressed into the Navy, prostitutes were impeded, and potential troublemakers (especially females) expelled from large towns.[108] Whenever new legislation was required—it might be for turnpike roads, enclosure of land, provision of water and gaslight, or improvement of pavements—it took the form of 'local and personal' (or 'private') Acts, promoted and scrutinized by committees representing the region's MPs. Local improvement commissions and trusts were sometimes appointed with powers to levy rates or to impose charges on the users of their services. (There were over 1,000 turnpike trusts in operation by 1835.) In such cases tensions frequently arose between the locals, who clamoured for improvements, and the property owners—not always resident—who paid the rates and would have to foot the bill.

In the 1830s Parliament began to turn its back on these traditions and to legislate for the whole country on a one-size-fits-all basis, hence the extremely complex draughtsmanship designed to anticipate all possible circumstances. However, complicated statutes are difficult to enforce, so there was also recourse to so-called delegated legislation, where Parliament laid down its broad intentions and left it to salaried officials to achieve those intentions in practice. This would eventually lead to the emergence of government departments staffed by civil servants possessing considerable discretionary powers of a quasi-statutory nature,[109] but at first the task of applying legislation was devolved on less permanent officials called commissioners. The latter have been described as 'statesmen in disguise', in recognition of the fact that they personified the State for the vast majority of citizens, whereas in 1783 that role had been performed by the county magistrate or parish overseer.

The second quarter of the nineteenth century could be called an age of commissions. Some were deputed to investigate pressing problems such as municipal government, Canadian disaffection, hand-loom weavers, Irish land tenure, or gas explosions in collieries. Such inquiries were traditional, but there were now many more of them (seventy-two during 1832–46 as against thirty-nine in 1815–31).[110] Much more significant were the commissions (some

[108] Nicholas Rogers, 'Vagrancy, Impressment and the Regulation of Labour in Eighteenth-Century Britain', *Slavery and Abolition*, 15/2 (1994), 102–13.

[109] Such as the General Board of Health 1848, the Local Government Board 1871, the Board of Education 1899.

[110] H. M. Clokie and J. W. Robinson, *Royal Commissions of Inquiry: The Significance of Investigations in British Politics* (Stanford, Calif., 1937), 54–79.

TABLE 9.1. *Major legislative commissions, 1831–1845*

Years	Commission	Prominent commissioners	Prominent inspectors or assistant commissioners
1831	Constituency boundaries		
1833	Factory Commission	E. Chadwick Thomas Tooke T. Southwood Smith James Wilson	Leonard Horner H. S. Tremenheere
1834–45	Criminal law digest	Henry Bellenden Ker John Austin Thomas Starkie Andrew Amos William Wightman	

1834–47	Poor Law Commission	E. Chadwick
		W. Sturges Bourne
		Thomas Frankland
		   Lewis
		John Shaw Lefevre
		George Nicholls
		George Cornewall
		   Lewis
			E. C. Tufnell

1835	Prisons	William Crawford	William Crawford Whitworth Russell
1836–45	Ecclesiastical Commission	Bishop Blomfield	
	Emigration		T. F. Elliot Robert Low
	Tithe Commission	Richard Jones	
1839	Schools		H. S. Tremenheere J. Kay-Shuttleworth
1843	Mining districts	H. S. Tremenheere	
1845	Lunacy	Lord Shaftesbury	
1845	Enclosure		

of them semi-permanent) to apply and monitor legislation already passed. As Table 9.1 indicates, commissioners were requested to redraw the boundaries of parliamentary constituencies, remodel the internal finances of the Church of England, adjudicate tithe commutations and land enclosures, inspect grant-aided schools, mines, and factories, and achieve uniformity of treatment across Poor Law unions. Official assignees were appointed in 1831 to take control of bankrupts' estates and distribute the assets among creditors. An Act of 1835 transferred authority for prisons from local magistrates to an inspectorate, again with the intention to standardize conditions. In 1828 commissioners in lunacy took over the inspection and control of London's madhouses from the College of Physicians, and in 1845 they relieved JPs of the same responsibilities throughout the rest of England and Wales. Meanwhile, in 1843 revising barristers were established to update the rolls for parliamentary and local elections. Moreover, if the relevant legislation had succeeded, commissioners would also have been given responsibility for a fund to replace Church rates and to supervise the leasing of ecclesiastical property. The intention behind all this was emphatically *not* to establish a centralized bureaucratic state, but four factors caused a movement in that direction. First there was the fascination, already mentioned, with nationwide solutions. Thus Bentham's panoptical theory, reinforced by observation of American practice, led to the model prisons of Pentonville (1842) and Millbank (extended 1844) with their 'separate' cells, solitary confinement, and intensive evangelical preaching.[111] Secondly, there was the centralizing zeal of individuals such as Chadwick, whose determination to extend the powers of the Poor Law Commission led to rifts with his first Chairman, Lewis. Thirdly, even commissioners less zealous than Chadwick often arrogated power to themselves, if only because they were likely to be held responsible when things went wrong. That probably explains why Horner and Tremenheere proved more tenacious factory inspectors than most MPs had intended. Finally, some of the cost of local government began to be met from central taxation. In 1835, for example, the Treasury provided a grant to pay for the removal of prisoners from local gaols to convict depots, as well as half the cost of assize and quarter session prosecutions. Then in 1846 Peel agreed to relieve ratepayers of the other half in compensation to property owners for the loss of the Corn Laws.[112] Such fiscal adjustments were defensible on the grounds that central government had taken over effective control of gaols from town halls,[113] but it was also a licence for additional interference in future. Also in 1846, a modest portion of Poor Law expenses (covering medical care and industrial training) was switched to central taxation.

Nevertheless, these were rogue developments in so far as they ran counter to a prevailing ethos in favour of local autonomy, voluntary action, and minimal rates and taxes. It was not only Ultra Tories like Wetherell who thought that

---

[111] These new prisons reduced the percentage of convicts held in the hulks from 72% in 1842 to 44% in 1844.

[112] Seán McConville, *A History of English Prison Administration*, i: *1750–1877* (1981), 256–9.

[113] A gradual process which can be traced back to Peel's Gaols Act of 1823.

allowing boundary commissioners to adjudicate on the size of constituencies was 'a direct jacobinical division of the country'.[114] Likewise, during the cholera panic of 1831–2 many commercial and industrial spokesmen denounced compulsory quarantine and hospitalization as unacceptable 'dictation'.[115] Some who accepted the need for legislation against antisocial behaviour, such as child exploitation or over-indulgence to the poor, drew the line at positive intervention in health and education. Others like Joshua Toulmin Smith genuinely supported the latter, yet were fanatically hostile to Chadwick and centralization.[116] What transpired from all these cross-currents was a 'legislative and administrative give-and-take' between activist Whig ministers and local elites anxious to retain their traditional responsibilities.[117] Sometimes permissive legislation was enacted in order to encourage local authorities to help themselves, as in the case of policing. Model clauses made it easier for those instituting private legislation to cut through legal minefields.[118] Alternatively, it was possible to establish what would now be called quasi or non-government organizations. One example was the granting of authority in all matters regarding lighthouses to Trinity House (1836), thereby terminating centuries of private profit-making.[119] Another example was the Bank Charter Act of 1844. Sometimes provision was made for intervention in the future. Faced with a railway boom which was spinning out of control, Gladstone was anxious to set safety standards and to prevent rival companies from laying redundant track. His *étatisme* was thwarted by Peel, but he did obtain a clause (1844) allowing for the future nationalization of railways, subject to compensation. He also stipulated that companies should cater for the working classes by running at least one cheap 'parliamentary train' at a penny a mile in each direction each day.[120] Such compromises were typical, making it impossible for someone in the mid-1840s to guess how the conflicts between intervention and non-intervention, centre and locality, would eventually be resolved.

Whig initiatives in the sphere of jurisprudence had been foreshadowed in Brougham's great speech of 1828, prepared in collusion with Bentham. Many of its more than fifty suggestions for making litigation cheaper and more accessible were recommended by commissions of inquiry into the common law courts and

---

[114] Wetherell, *HPD*3 v. 1243 (11 Aug. 1831); also Peel, *HPD*3 v. 1233 (11 Aug. 1831).

[115] e.g. Poulett Thomson, *HPD*3 ix. 309–15 (15 Dec. 1831); R. J. Morris, *Cholera 1832: The Social Response to an Epidemic* (1976), 30, 47–53.

[116] David Eastwood, *Government and Community in the English Provinces, 1700–1870* (Houndmills, 1997), 155–6.

[117] Philip Harling, *The Modern British State: An Historical Introduction* (Cambridge, 2001), 73–111.

[118] John Prest, *Liberty and Locality: Parliament, Permissive Legislation, and Ratepayers' Democracies in the Nineteenth Century* (Oxford, 1990), 6–13.

[119] James Taylor, 'Private Property, Public Interest, and the Role of the State in Nineteenth-Century Britain: The Case of the Lighthouses', *HJ* 44 (2001), 749–71.

[120] H. C. G. Matthew, *Gladstone 1809–1874* (Oxford, 1986), 67; H. Parris, 'Railway Policy in Peel's Administration, 1841–1846', *Bulletin of the Institute of Historical Research*, 33 (1960), 180–94.

the Law of Real Property (1829–34), and while on the Woolsack Brougham did his best to get them implemented.[121] With regard to the criminal law, Peel had chewed away at the edges of the old penal code, but Russell virtually dismantled it, so that by 1841 the only mainstream capital offences left were actual and attempted murder and high treason. As a result the number of felons sentenced to death fell in one decade from almost 4,000 in 1828–30 to 249 in 1838–40, while the number hanged dropped from 178 to twenty-six. Equally significant was a reform of the way in which criminal trials were conducted. Traditionally barristers for the accused had only been allowed to speak on matters of law and to cross-examine witnesses. Defendants had been required to answer for themselves, with a presumption that the judge would protect their rights. However, the Prisoners' Counsel Act of 1836 introduced the adversarial system whereby evidence on both sides was filtered through advocates, as in civil cases. This meant that 'there was no longer any place for the activism and paternalism of the judge', whose role henceforward was to referee the contest impartially and sum up for the jury.[122] The new procedure reflected a mechanistic or Benthamite understanding of justice, where what counted was not the prisoner's story with its muddle of motives and intentions, but legally admissible facts concerning actions and consequences. A similar adjustment was made to the role of constables, those 'Paul Prys in every parish' who made presentations of what was happening on their patches. Hitherto they had often seen fit to give evidence *for* rather than *against* persons whom they had themselves arrested, but now such discretionary procedures were outlawed in favour of a more competitive, advocacy-based system.

Reformers such as Chadwick were anxious to establish a centralized system of 'preventive police' such as in Ireland and Prussia.[123] London had pointed the way in 1829, but elsewhere there was strong attachment to the traditional system whereby policing was the responsibility of parishes. In 1832 Melbourne responded to social unrest by preparing a bill to establish a nationwide network of police forces, each controlled by a stipendiary magistrate responsible to the Home Office. However, he realized that the country was 'not yet prepared' for such a step,[124] which may explain why he never introduced the bill and why, three

---

[121] Chester New, *The Life of Lord Brougham to 1830* (Oxford, 1961), 390–401. For a more guarded assessment which stresses the piecemeal and even haphazard nature of Brougham's reforms, see Michael Lobban, 'Henry Brougham and Law Reform', *EHR* 115 (2000), 1184–1215.

[122] David J. A. Cairns, *Advocacy and the Making of the Adversarial Criminal Trial 1800–1865* (Oxford, 1998), 86–7.

[123] Edwin Chadwick, 'Preventive Police', *London Review*, 1 (1829), 252–308. The Irish Constabulary Act of 1836 established a semi-military armed police force under the direct control of Dublin Castle.

[124] Melbourne to Grey, 17 Mar. 1832, University of Durham Archives, Grey Papers. Stipendiaries ruled in Scotland, Wales, and Ireland but in England they had hitherto been confined to London and a few of the large industrial towns. Conservatives objected that, being financially dependent on their employment, they would be subservient to central government.

years later, his own Government adopted a judicious balance between compulsion and permission. The 1835 Municipal Corporations Act *required* new borough councils to establish police forces, whereas the County Police Acts of 1839–40 merely *empowered* JPs to establish the same, and to place the cost on the rates. There was a certain cunning here, since once most boroughs had established police forces, criminals would very likely turn their attention to the countryside; likewise, whenever a particular county adopted the new procedures, there was an incentive for its neighbours to do likewise.[125] Over two-thirds of counties took advantage of the possibility before it was made compulsory in 1856.

These developments help to explain how the British State was able to deal so effectively with the supreme crisis of authority that was Chartism.[126] At Peterloo in 1819 everything had depended on local magistrates and yeomanry, with Parliament's role reduced to the hugely blunt instrument of suspending civil liberties. At the time of the Reform Bill public security had depended on the dubious loyalties of the political unions. But in 1841–6 Graham coordinated action from the Home Office, often bypassing Parliament and local magistrates alike. He hated using spies even more than Peel had done, and spent much less on the secret service than all his recent predecessors.[127] He prohibited particular meetings rather than imposing blanket bans on public assembly, and used railways to facilitate troop movements, with Crewe emerging as an important junction for surveillance of the North and Midlands. In three towns deemed particularly dangerous—Birmingham, Bolton, and Manchester—the Home Office took over direct control of policing for three years (1839–42), and even adopted quasi-military procedures such as ostentatious drills and parades.[128] This centralization of authority marked the end of Sidmouth-style high Tory management, a development that was highlighted by an extraordinary scandal. In 1844 Graham acceded to the Foreign Secretary's request to open letters from Giuseppe Mazzini, an Italian nationalist exiled in Britain, and hand them over to the Austrian authorities. Governments had been opening mail for 140 years in an attempt to identify subversives, but in the new 'liberal' climate it was no longer deemed acceptable, and as a result of the outcry the Secret Department of the Post Office was abolished. During the next three decades—and for the only time in history—the State refrained from surveillance either of its own

---

[125] David Philips and Robert D. Storch, *Policing Provincial England, 1829–1856: The Politics of Reform* (1999), 136–66.

[126] John Saville, *1848: The British State and the Chartist Movement* (Cambridge, 1987); F. C. Mather, *Public Order in the Age of the Chartists* (Manchester, 1959).

[127] J. T. Ward, *Sir James Graham* (1967), 209–10.

[128] Michael Weaver, 'The New Science of Policing: Crime and the Birmingham Police Force, 1839–1842', *Albion*, 26 (1994), 289–308.

citizens or of visitors,[129] making Britain a haven for asylum-seekers like Karl Marx, especially following the failed European revolutions of 1848. It became a land where revolution was plotted but not attempted.

'We are busy introducing system, method, science, economy, regularity, and discipline.' Russell's list of desiderata calls to mind the evangelical, utilitarian, and political economy model of governance which went back rhetorically to Pitt and in practice to the liberal Tories. There were, however, two important differences. The first, which has already been alluded to, is that the liberal Tories were more moralistic and retributive in their attitudes to human behaviour, and less optimistic about the prospects for earthly prosperity and happiness. But even more fundamentally, liberal Toryism was rooted in the classical Newtonian scientific revolution, whereas Russell and his colleagues owed more to the Scottish Enlightenment and to Mackintosh's philosophic Whiggism, with its organic conception of the natural history of society and its understanding of time as developmental rather than cyclical.[130] Both traditions embraced mechanical ways of thinking, but in very contrasting ways, the difference being due in part perhaps to the subliminal cultural impact of more recent machine technology. The late eighteenth-century proliferation of steam engines, pulleys, gantries, cranes, precision tools, and clocks inevitably affected thinking about society. One of the most furious thinkers was Sir Samuel Bentham, Jeremy's brother, a marine architect and engineer, who first dreamed up the idea of the panopticon. As Inspector-General of Navy Works during the years of maximum national peril (1795–1805), he masterminded the reform of the royal dockyards in Deptford and elsewhere. Having inherited a chaotic regime with a hopelessly undisciplined labour force, despite the brutal punishments regularly meted out *in terrorem*, he at once introduced detailed rosters, specifications, and shift systems to ensure smooth running for twenty-four hours. Procedures were timed, parts standardized, artisans ranked according to ability, diligence, and conduct, and obstreperous workers 'crushed' by a 'new analytical form of labour discipline' based on piece-rate wages. Devices measured exactly the 'objective' amounts of work accomplished, and employees were made accountable for any wastage of raw materials.[131] Dockyard reform was a stark example of a general development whereby the irregular labour rhythms of pre-industrial times gave way to the dominion of the clock, and to a pervasive rhetoric enjoining workers to practise 'time-thrift'.[132]

---

[129] David Vincent, *The Culture of Secrecy: Britain, 1832–1998* (Oxford, 1998), 1–2.

[130] See above, pp. 348–53.

[131] Peter Linebaugh, *The London Hanged: Crime and Civil Society in the Eighteenth Century* (1991), 371–401, 440; William J. Ashworth, ' "System of Terror": Samuel Bentham, Accountability and Dockyard Reform during the Napoleonic Wars', *Social History*, 23 (1998), 63–79.

[132] E. P. Thompson, 'Time, Work-Discipline, and Industrial Capitalism', *P&P* 38 (1967), 56–97.

There was, however, a big difference between the natural mechanisms imagined by philosophers—such as the celestial physics of Newton and Laplace or Paley's biological adaptations—and real machines, which suffered from friction and resistance, imprecision and mismeasurement, not to mention the different reaction times of the people who operated them. And when it came to organizing human machines, the degree of unpredictability was magnified. Such difficulties encouraged a subtle shift in what might be called the mechanical imagination away from liberal Toryism's systematic, repetitive, and essentially static conception. In its place came an idea of the machine as process, as the creator of work, force, and energy. Moreover, now that actual machines were producing measurable results, more satisfying types of proof seemed possible than the deductive, a priori, and hypothetical reasoning of a Dugald Stewart or a Ricardo. It was noted in Chapter 7 that 'time was rediscovered' during the second quarter of the century, and that 'temporal change became an essential feature of the economy of nature'.

Temporality now entered in an essential way into the explanation of natural systems... Over a wide range of subjects 'economy' came to mean evolution rather than balance, temporal dynamics rather than equilibrium... Rather suddenly, temporal change became an essential feature of the economy of nature, as represented in political economy, astronomy, geology, natural philosophy, mathematics, and engineering.[133]

At Cambridge Babbage and Herschel sought with some success to switch the emphasis of teaching from Newton's simple (geometrical) analysis to French-style algebra, from fluxions to calculus, and this had its counterpart in scientific culture generally as experiment and observation displaced mathematical hypothesis and deduction. Functional analysis, it was claimed, could explain the workings of the mind. Here the crucial machine was Babbage's Analytical Engine, sometimes dubbed the first computer, which produced logarithms and similar calculations mechanically and did away with laborious calculations. It has been claimed that, in so condemning the traditional geometry which had hitherto dominated English mathematics, Herschel and Babbage threatened the prevailing model of the world.[134] 'The analyticals were on a quest to find a mental technology that was universal, efficient, visible, and, consequently, immune to ambiguity and corruption—a trait they believed characterized the old paternal world of interests propped up by Scripture'.[135]

[133] M. Norton Wise (with Crosbie Smith), 'Work and Waste: Political Economy and Natural Philosophy in Nineteenth-Century Britain', *History of Science*, 27 (1989), 263, 392; 28 (1990), 221. See above, p. 443.
[134] William J. Ashworth, 'Memory, Efficiency, and Symbolic Analysis: Charles Babbage, John Herschel, and the Industrial Mind', *Isis*, 87 (1996), 637; Harvey W. Becher, 'William Whewell and Cambridge Mathematics', *Studies in History and Philosophy of Science*, 11 (1980), 1–48.
[135] Ashworth, 'Memory', 636.

In similar vein, William Whewell and Richard Jones promoted social science with a view to replacing deduction by inductivism or 'Baconianism'.[136] The aim was to discover empirically how people had behaved in different places and under different circumstances, rather than to reason from universal postulates such as desire for profit maximization, aversion from labour, 'the hope of bettering our condition, and the fear of want'. Induction implied inference— generalizing on the basis of the familiar and the particular—and took for granted a 'statistical regularity in moral affairs'. 'Man is now seen to be an enigma only as an individual; in the mass he is a mathematical problem.'[137] (The last insight derived from the ideas of the Belgian statistician Adolphe Quetelet, who had recently adumbrated the idea of an 'abstract being, defined in terms of the average of all human attributes in a given country'—an *homme moyen*, in other words, who 'could be treated as the "type" of the nation, the representative of a society in social science comparable to the center of gravity in physics'.[138]) The Board of Trade and the British Association set up statistical sections in 1832 and 1833 respectively, while more than twenty local statistical societies were formed, the largest and most successful being those in Manchester and London. A General Register Office was established in 1837 to monitor births, marriages, and deaths, leading to an expanded and more rigorous census in 1841. This is not to deny that normative values often got in the way. When the Statistical Society of London investigated a notorious district in St Giles, it marshalled figures to prove the need for 'religion, virtue, truth, order, industry, and cleanliness', yet its underlying purpose was almost certainly to deflect the blame for wretchedness *from* industrial capitalism, and *onto* collateral factors such as alcohol, immorality, and the Church of England (castigated for its obstructive attitude towards popular education).[139] Even so, mathematical advances clearly made an important contribution to government, especially perhaps the insight that statistical irregularities could exist in events themselves and were not necessarily due to failures of perception, in other words that nature could be deviant.[140] Althorp, it will be recalled, argued that 'vital functions' all arose from the original perfection of God's machinery at the creation, whereas Brougham, impatient of deductive hypotheses, believed in God's 'continued government of the universe and the constant dependence in which we exist on the divine will'.[141]

[136] After the philosopher Francis Bacon (1561–1626), whose works were becoming increasingly fashionable at this time (Lawrence Goldman, 'The Origins of British "Social Science": Political Economy, Natural Science and Statistics, 1830–1835', *HJ* 26 (1983), 587–616).

[137] [Robert Chambers], *Vestiges of the Natural History of Creation* (1844), ed. James A. Secord (Chicago, 1994), 331.

[138] Theodore M. Porter, *The Rise of Statistical Thinking 1820–1900* (Princeton, 1986), 52–4.

[139] M. J. Cullen, *The Statistical Movement in Early Victorian Britain: The Foundations of Empirical Social Research* (Hassocks, 1975), 147.   [140] Porter, *The Rise of Statistical Thinking*, 78–83.

[141] Althorp to Brougham, 8 June 1836, BL, Althorp MS H14.

Both had a providential understanding of nature, but Althorp's was static, Brougham's dynamic and progressive. Macaulay's reform speeches repeatedly emphasized the progress of society, the development of the human mind, and 'the law which regulates the growth of communities',[142] and before long such concepts came to seem normative, not to say commonplace. It brought discretionary judgements back into governance (what Huskisson had called 'the errors of empiricism'), but now they were to be exercised—not by financiers, judges, and local elites—but by experts (including statistical experts) in London.

Of course, such conflicts did not seem so clear-cut at the time. When John Austin resigned from Brougham's Criminal Law Digest Commission in 1836 out of frustration at the slow pace of codification, the quarrel was presented (and probably understood) in tactical terms. 'We could not ... persuade him, that it was better to obtain codification by saying nothing about it directly,' wrote a fellow commissioner. 'He was for taking all by storm.'[143] Yet the difference was really one of principle. As the most radical of the commissioners and the only one clearly under Bentham's spell, Austin sought to continue the process of rationalization begun under Peel,[144] whereas Brougham never had any intention of undermining the concept of English common law—or of removing the interpretative discretion of judges—in order to establish a Continental-style civil code.[145] To take another example, the Prisoners' Counsel Act was presented above as an exercise in Benthamism, because the prisoner's story was suppressed in favour of legally admissible facts, but it could be interpreted in an opposite light. In moving away from the idea that facts were 'self-evident', and in acknowledging narrative complexity and ambiguity, it harmonized with Brougham's inductivist and developmental approach to jurisprudence.

It is impossible to generalize about attitudes to governance during these two decades of acute social crisis. Localists clashed with centralizers, interventionists with free-marketeers, and there were many different permutations of opinion. Everyone agreed that something had to be done about the condition of the working classes, but until 1838 there was little conception of the workers *as* a class. However, all that changed when for almost the only time in history England experienced what could legitimately be called class conflict.[146]

---

[142] *HPD*3 ix. 388 (16 Dec. 1831).

[143] Ker to Brougham, n.d., University College London, Brougham MS, 18176.

[144] See above, Ch. 5.

[145] Michael Lobban, 'How Benthamic was the Criminal Law Commission?', *Law and History Review*, 18 (2000), 427–32. On the other hand, the Municipal Corporations Act of 1835 reduced the discretion allowed to borough magistrates by codifying lesser penalties.

[146] The General Strike of 1926 might be regarded as another such moment.

CHARTISM

The People's Charter was drawn up by William Lovett (cabinetmaker) and Francis Place (tailor) in May 1838 for the London Working Men's Association, founded two years earlier. Its Six Points were all demands related to parliamentary representation: universal manhood suffrage, secret ballot, annual elections, constituencies of equal size, payment of MPs, and abolition of the property qualification for becoming an MP in the first place. Soon afterwards elections were held for a General or National Convention of the Industrious Classes, which met in London in February 1839. Three months later this 'anti-parliament' or 'people's parliament' moved to Birmingham,[147] where the Bull Ring riots occurred in July. In the same month the Chartists' first National Petition, signed by about 1,280,000 people, was dismissed in the House of Commons by 235 votes to 46. This act of patrician disdain set off a wave of strikes, or so-called National Holidays, which in turn provoked a sustained government clampdown involving the imprisonment of several Chartist leaders. Then, following a pause in activity, the National Charter Association was launched from Manchester in July 1840 to campaign for the election of MPs and town councillors. It has been called 'the first working-class political party',[148] having acquired 50,000 members and more than 400 branches, and it introduced many townspeople to associational activity for the first time. The violent platform rhetoric of 1839 gave way to an emphasis on organization and on cooperation with other protest groups,[149] yet when a second National Petition with about 3,320,000 signatures was presented in 1842, it was defeated even more heavily than before (287–49). This second rebuff was followed by an outbreak of industrial disruption, which came to a head during the third quarter of 1842 with a general strike affecting twenty-three counties. Centred mainly on the Potteries and the textile districts between Manchester and Halifax, the so-called Plug Plot[150] was a protest against wage reductions, redundancies, and threats of lockouts, but it was adopted by Chartists, who sought to exploit the proceedings at a delegates' conference in Manchester in August 1842. Once again, however, the protesters were ground down by police and military, leading to a further 15,000 arrests by October 1843.

[147] The Convention reconvened during 1842–5 in London, Birmingham, and Manchester, and sat again in London in 1848.

[148] John Belchem, 'Beyond *Chartist Studies*: Class, Community and Party in Early Victorian Populist Politics', in Derek Fraser (ed.), *Cities, Class and Communication: Essays in Honour of Asa Briggs* (Hemel Hempstead, 1990), 111.

[149] Robert Sykes, 'Physical-Force Chartism: The Cotton District and the Chartist Crisis of 1839', *International Review of Social History*, 30 (1985), 235.

[150] So called because in textile areas strikers drew out boiler plugs, temporarily depriving mills of power (Robert Fyson, 'The Crisis of 1842: Chartism, the Colliers' Strike and the Outbreak in the Potteries', in James Epstein and Dorothy Thompson (eds.), *The Chartist Experience: Studies in Working-Class Radicalism and Culture, 1830–60* (London, 1982)).

There followed a four-year lull during which Feargus O'Connor sought to divert Chartism into new channels. His Land Plan for the resettlement of urban workers on two-, three-, or four-acre plots built on the ideas of Spence, Cobbett, and Owen, as well as on suggestions for peasant proprietorship in Ireland. If his Land Company had succeeded it would have provided some hundreds of families with subsistence, security, cheap rents, and independence, and by soaking up surplus labour might also have increased the wage-bargaining power of industrial workers generally.[151] In the event it collapsed and was wound up in 1851, in part due to mismanagement for which O'Connor himself must take some blame.[152] Meanwhile in 1847–8 the final phase of Chartism had come and gone, and is usually seen, not as a climacteric, but as an anti-climax. This is because of what happened at Kennington Common on 10 April 1848, when about 150,000 demonstrators (estimates vary) dispersed after being faced down by 4,000 police and 85,000 volunteer special constables, many of whom were working men themselves.[153] The event stiffened elite resolve, and prompted the Commons to throw out a third petition with derision just a few days later, but the idea that it was a fiasco and that Chartism died with a whimper is a myth. Certainly the meeting passed off peacefully, just as its conveners intended, but the situation in London grew more dangerous afterwards, with serious disturbances at Bishop Bonner's Fields on 4 June, while Manchester, Liverpool, and Bradford stood in even greater peril.[154] Although the protests were less spontaneous than in 1839 and less widespread than in 1842, they were arguably more deadly, because more conspiratorial. Chartists formed links with the revolutionary hotheads of Young Ireland and through them with French and Italian activists. The European context was of course vital. A Parisian rising in February led to the establishment of the Second Republic, sparked off revolutions in Vienna, Berlin, several minor German states, and parts of Poland, Spain, Italy, and Hungary. Shrewdly the British Government bided its time, but when it sensed that the bloody 'June days' in Paris had turned middle-class opinion against the Chartists, it pounced with a number of strategically timed arrests and prosecutions. By September the movement was dead, but it had been killed by the strong arm of the State, not died from its own inanition.

But what was Chartism in the first place? A loose definition would sweep in all forms of popular protest—the anti-Poor Law movement, the war of the unstamped,[155] demonstrations against the new police, the revolutionary

---

[151] Edward Royle, *Chartism*, 3rd edn. (Harlow, 1996), 39–41.

[152] Joy MacAskill, 'The Chartist Land Plan', in Asa Briggs (ed.), *Chartist Studies* (1959).

[153] There were also 12,000 troops kept in reserve, just in case.

[154] David Goodway, *London Chartism 1838–1848* (Cambridge, 1982), 129–49; Saville, *1848*, 130–65; Royle, *Chartism*, 44–7.

[155] A 4*d.* stamp duty prevented working people from being able to afford newspapers, and prompted the rise of an illicit 'unstamped' press, which successive governments sought to eliminate through fines

religious nationalism of the Newport rising in South Wales (1839), and action by small tenant farmers against improving landlords (e.g. the Rebecca riots). The nature of the Chartism varied from place to place, and there were well over 1,000 places showing at least some taint of it, as well as more than 120 local newspapers aligned to the cause. It would be unfair to blame leaders for failing to unite a movement defined as broadly as this (even supposing a popular movement could be led like a political party anyway), yet alleged leadership failures have dominated discussion. Despite inventing stump oratory in 1838–9 (four tours and 147 meetings squeezed into sixteen weeks),[156] O'Connor's reputation has only recently begun to recover from Graham Wallas's damning early verdict.

There can be little doubt that O'Connor's mind was more or less affected from the beginning, and that he inherited tendencies to insanity. He was insanely jealous and egotistical, and no one succeeded in working with him for long. In all his multitudinous speeches and writings it is impossible to detect a single consistent political idea. The absolute failure of Chartism may indeed be traced very largely to his position in the movement.[157]

This echoes Lovett's resentful view that O'Connor was 'the great "I AM" of [radical] politics'.[158] Yet the fact remains that the tall, handsome, patrician-looking, yet slightly foppish Irishman was one of only two supremely gifted extra-parliamentary politicians in the first half of the nineteenth century. The other was Francis Place, popular radicalism's 'Duke of Newcastle', a behind-the-scenes manipulator and linkman with parliamentarians and ministers.[159] An intimate of Bentham and former moderate member of the London Corresponding Society, he was committed to advancing Lancasterian theories of educational improvement. Although he helped to draw up the Charter, Place never saw himself as a Chartist, but his moderate views were represented within the movement by his fellow draughtsman William Lovett. He too was an adept organizer, and an ardent believer in the power of education to transform society, but he was appalled by the violence of the Newport rising and was inclined to melancholia, especially after a spell in prison. In 1841 he launched the National Association for Promoting the Political and Social Improvement of the People by means of

and prosecutions. In 1836 the Chancellor of the Exchequer (Spring Rice) effectively acknowledged defeat when he reduced the duty to 1d., though even this remained a major grievance of Radicals until all paper duties were abolished by Gladstone in 1861. Patricia Hollis, *The Pauper Press: A Study in Working-Class Radicalism of the 1830s* (1970), 62–92.

[156] James Epstein, *The Lion of Freedom: Feargus O'Connor and the Chartist Movement, 1832–1842* (1982), 90–193. Sceptics claimed that his provincial itinerary matched that of his mistress Louisa Nisbett, a touring actor.   [157] *DNB.*

[158] *The Life and Struggles of William Lovett, in his Pursuit of Bread, Knowledge, and Freedom* (1876), 161.

[159] Dudley Miles, *Francis Place 1771–1854: The Life of a Remarkable Radical* (Brighton, 1988), 178–255.

self-help, school education, libraries, and public meeting houses. Like temperance Chartism and O'Neill's Chartist Church, Lovett's initiative was part of the New Move, and was denounced by O'Connor, who claimed that 'knowledge Chartism, temperance Chartism, and Christian Chartism' were all covert means of collaborating with the enemy. That charge seemed justified when Sturge and Lowery sought to make common cause with the Anti-Corn Law League, and Lovett founded the People's League (1848) to unite the middle and working classes. Likewise in Birmingham, when Arthur O'Neill and John Collins called for cooperation between working- and middle-class reformers, they were assailed by a colleague for proposing the nonsense of 'a union between the profit-hunters and the productive classes'.

Robert Lowery of Newcastle and later Edinburgh, a leading temperance Chartist, eventually drifted out of the movement and into militant Nonconformity, ending his life as a confirmed Liberal.[160] Joseph Sturge was a Quaker who founded the Complete Suffrage Union in 1842. Like Henry Vincent, nicknamed Demosthenes on account of his impassioned oratory, Sturge saw the parliamentary franchise as a panacea. Other prominent moderates included the London printer and publisher Henry Hetherington, who had moved into Chartism as a result of his efforts on behalf of the unstamped press. All four men were desperately sincere, but of each it could be said—as it was of Lovett—that he had 'no smouldering fire of personal resentment to make him feel the will to smite', or— as was said of Hetherington—that he had 'indignation without anger'.[161] They therefore had little in common with the combustible O'Connor, the tub-thumping Lancashire Methodist and Tory–Radical Joseph Raynor Stephens, the intellectual poet and proto-socialist Ernest Jones, the biblicist and millennialist Thomas Cooper, the fiery orator Bronterre 'Inebriate' O'Brien (alternatively dubbed the Danton and Robespierre of Chartism), the hard-headed socialist Alexander Hutchinson, or Julian Harney. The latter was a Crown and Anchor agitator, friend of Engels, and heir to an underground tradition stretching back to the corresponding societies and Jacobinism of the 1790s. These conflicts were characterized at the time in terms of 'physical force' versus 'moral force'. The distinction resonated with twentieth-century historians, perhaps because it corresponded to the struggle between Bolsheviks and Mensheviks, but its significance can be exaggerated. Terrorist movements have usually deployed military and political wings to produce the right degree of menace (Harney called this 'physico-moral-force'[162]). O'Connor was as keen as Lovett on workers asserting their cultural autonomy through reading groups and suchlike societies,

[160] Brian Harrison and Patricia Hollis, 'Chartism, Liberalism and the Life of Robert Lowery', *EHR* 82 (1967), 503–35. [161] G. D. H. Cole, *Chartist Portraits* (1941), 62; G. J. Holyoake, *DNB*. [162] *Northern Liberator*, 25 May 1839, quoted in F. C. Mather (ed.), *Chartism and Society: An Anthology of Documents* (1980), 74.

while most moderates recognized that 'moral force is moral humbug, unless there is physical force behind it'.[163] While addressing large crowds baying for violence, even Vincent could get carried away by the occasion, and even the teetotal Lowery could get drunk on applause.

Many historians have regarded Chartism as an economic ('knife and fork') question. A commercial upturn collapsed in 1837, food prices rose dramatically during 1838–9, and industrial unemployment probably peaked in 1842, the year of the Plug Plot. The lull of 1843–7 coincided with recovery, while the 1848 outbreak followed a financial crash. Then from 1849 the long mid-Victorian boom set in, and it was possible to think that Chartism had been anaesthetized by economic success. To the question 'Why then did Chartists seek a *political* solution in the form of the vote?', the answer was provided by O'Brien: 'Knaves will tell you that it is because you have no property you are unrepresented. I tell you, on the contrary, it is because you are unrepresented that you have no property. Your poverty is the result not the cause of your being unrepresented.'[164] Their votelessness also explained why taxes fell so heavily on bread, malt, hops, tobacco, sugar, glass, spirits, newspapers, and other working-class staples. This socio-economic interpretation is valuable because it explains the 'who' and the 'where' as well as the 'when' of Chartism. It was strongest in the industrial districts of Lancashire, the West Riding, the East and West Midlands, Durham, Northumberland, and Scotland. It was weakest in agricultural areas and in country towns, except for places like Trowbridge where the old weaving industry had decayed. Large centres of population like Manchester experienced less militancy than the less economically diversified out-townships such as Stalybridge, Stockport, and Ashton under Lyne. Craft-based domestic workers threatened by mechanized production (hand-loom weavers, framework knitters, fustian-cutters, wool-combers, stockingers, nail-makers) formed a persistent hard core,[165] while downtrodden factory operatives provided shock troops at the moments of maximum industrial depression (1841–3). There was little Chartism in the engineering trades, thanks to the railway boom, but hard-pressed navvies were often attracted along with former soldiers, criminals, tramps, and the unemployed. So too were marginal and downwardly mobile types such as briefless barristers, failed businessmen, and others with solid pasts but precarious futures, as well as shoemakers and tailors, skilled artisans who were respectable, self-educated, often ambitious, and bored with their work. Binding these disaffected types together, it is sometimes suggested, was an ideology of class, based on a new proto-Marxian political economy which

---

[163] *Northern Star*, 19 Feb. 1848.   [164] *Bronterre's National Reformer*, 15 Jan. 1837.
[165] It has been calculated that 130 out of 853 prominent Chartists were hand-loom weavers in 1841 (David Jones, *Chartism and the Chartists* (1975), 30–2).

TABLE 9.2. *Acts of legislature and other events perceived as hostile by the working classes, 1832–1839*

Year	Event
1832	Working class systematically excluded from the franchise
1833	Irish coercion
	Rejection of factory operatives' demands for a ten-hour day
1834	New Poor Law
	Transportation of the Dorset labourers
	Formation and collapse of Owen's Grand National Consolidated Trades Union
1835	Abandonment of the hand-loom weavers to their fate
	Inauguration of borough police
1836	Sinister new system of registering the civilian population
	Climax of official campaign of terror against the unstamped press
1837	Collapse of the Radical Party in the general election
	Erection of Poor Law 'bastilles' in the North of England
1838	Institution of county police

stressed the labour theory of value, economic exploitation, and the iron law of wages.[166] This may explain why most Chartist leaders, despite being gentlemen of independent means themselves, appealed in their speeches to the 'workers' rather than to 'citizens' as of old.

However, the socio-economic interpretation of Chartism overlooks the fact that—to invert Cobbett—it is often most difficult to agitate a man with an empty stomach (since simply staying alive absorbs all his energies). It has recently lost ground to a political interpretation which focuses on the series of body blows suffered by the working classes immediately following the Reform Act (see Table 9.2). Whereas socio-economic interpretations of Chartism were structuralist, the political approach is post-structuralist in so far as it identifies the movement by the millions of words poured out in newspapers, cheap journals, pamphlets, tracts, and broadsides, as well as in reported speeches up and down the country—'a complex rhetoric binding together, in a systematic way, shared premises, analytical routines, strategic options and programmatic demands'.[167] Sales of stamped newspapers rose from under 33 million in 1835 (just before the reduction of duty) to over 53 million in 1838.[168] Those of the Leeds-based *Northern Star* alone touched a phenomenal 50,000 a week nationwide during

---

[166] See above, Ch. 5.

[167] Gareth Stedman Jones, *Languages of Class: Studies in English Working Class History 1832–1982* (Cambridge, 1983), 107.

[168] Joel H. Wiener, *The War of the Unstamped: The Movement to Repeal the British Newspaper Tax, 1830–1836* (Ithaca, NY, 1969), 260–1; A. Aspinall, *Politics and the Press, c.1780–1850* (1949), 23.

1839, making perhaps as many as 1 million readers-cum-listeners in pubs and halls. According to one historian, 'its columns were the arteries through which the blood of Chartism flowed, bringing the whole body to life.'[169] Not surprisingly, perhaps, this emphasis on language reveals strong continuities with the radicalism of Hardy, Cartwright, and Paine fifty years earlier. Like them, contributors to O'Connor's *Northern Star* and Hetherington's *Poor Man's Guardian* defended natural rights (both individual and customary), defined citizens so as to include the propertyless, denounced privilege and idle wealth, and exalted virtuous labour.[170] They evinced a stronger sense of vertical social divisions—as between workers and drones, the pure and the corrupt—than of the horizontal gulf separating capital and labour. The franchise was therefore coveted for its own sake, as a badge of citizenship and dignity, and not merely as a means to economic advancement. Furthermore, to the extent that workers did become more class-conscious, this may well have been a positional move following their abandonment by the middle classes after 1832. Before that date radicals such as Cobbett had targeted Old Corruption. Parliament had been suborned by vested interests—by landlords, rentiers, placemen, pensioners, annuitants, pluralists, the military and clerical establishments—but once *re*-formed Parliament would resume its former position as the guardian of the liberties of the people.[171] This expectation was, however, undermined by a Reform Act which for the first time defined a borough citizen in strictly economic terms. As Peel predicted, one effect of the £10 occupational franchise was to 'sever all connexion between the lower classes of the community and the direct representation in this House'.[172] The consequence was that, when Parliament acted in the disobliging ways listed above, and then when distress came round again, the blame was laid on Parliament itself, not on the vested interests.

The state . . . increasingly came to be viewed as the tyrannical harbinger of a dictatorship over the producers. As the 1830s progressed, the predominant image was no longer merely of placemen, sinecurists and fundholders principally interested in revenues derived from taxes on consumption to secure their unearned comforts, but was something more sinister and dynamic—a powerful and malevolent machine of repression, at the behest of capitalists and factory lords, essentially and actively dedicated to the lowering of the wages of the working classes.[173]

---

[169] Royle, *Chartism*, 75.

[170] However, this raises the question of how far these two were representative of other Chartist newspapers (e.g. *The Operative*, *The Charter*, the *London Mercury*, the *London Dispatch*) in which some historians have detected more anti-employer than anti-corruption rhetoric.

[171] Unlike the Whigs, Radicals such as Cobbett and Burdett did not include the monarchy among those agencies that had corrupted Parliament.   [172] See above, p. 433.

[173] Stedman Jones, *Languages of Class*, 173–4. An aggravating factor was the way in which employers increasingly took over the magistracy in industrial districts (David Philips, 'The Black Country Magistracy 1835–60: A Changing Elite and the Exercise of its Power', *Midland History*, 3 (1975–6), 161–90).

O'Connor's great weapon was his 'rhetoric of exclusion', his ability to suggest that all grievances could be traced to the systemic workings of a middle-class-dominated Parliament. For all their differences, Chartists were held together by a shared perception that the State was their common enemy.

The political interpretation is beguiling because it offers a subtler reason for the movement's decline than crude economic reductionism. For if Chartism was rooted in a sense that the State was systemically corrupt, all that politicians had to do was prove that it was not so. Hence—so the argument goes—it was the *political* aspects of Peel's economic reforms, rather than Whig and Liberal attempts at *social* reform, that did the trick; not so much that he helped the poor as that he 'vexed the mighty'.[174] By taxing upper-middle-class incomes in 1842, by clamping down on financial speculation with the Bank Charter Act of 1844, and above all by removing the landlords' corn monopoly in 1846, Peel effected the moral rehabilitation of the State, and thereby undermined Chartism more effectively than any mere repression could have done.[175]

More recent approaches to Chartism have concentrated less on political ideology than on cultural experience, including non-verbal and symbolic communication—displays, processions, banners, and songs. Perhaps what O'Connor said was less important than the fact that he wore fustian and the red cap of liberty, or that he rolled his sleeves up, or that youngsters were initiated into Chartism through various rituals of remembrance, such as 16 August dinners to mark the anniversary of Peterloo.[176] Such activities were often extremely localized, being limited to particular neighbourhoods, kinship groups, or factories. A whole street might turn Chartist because a single denizen had been imprisoned or because a national leader like O'Connor had happened to pass that way.[177] When that happened, working men might rally as a way of asserting a claim to regard in their own communities, just as some landed gentlemen went into Parliament in order to win prestige in their counties. More significant than their omission from the parliamentary franchise were the positive opportunities opened up to working men (franchised and unfranchised) by the Municipal Corporations Act of 1835. Encouraged by the local press, even relatively tiny towns like Ashton under Lyne could forge a vivid sense of political activity by placing local events in national and even international perspectives.[178] Indeed,

---

[174] This phrase was originally applied to Gladstone (J. R. Vincent, *Pollbooks: How Victorians Voted* (Cambridge, 1967), 45).   [175] Stedman Jones, *Languages of Class*, 90–178.

[176] James A. Epstein, *Radical Expression: Political Language, Ritual, and Symbol in England, 1790–1850* (Oxford, 1994), 150, 156–7.

[177] Paul A. Pickering, *Chartism and the Chartists in Manchester and Salford* (Basingstoke, 1995), 44–55, 139–58.

[178] Patrick Joyce, *Democratic Subjects: The Self and the Social in Nineteenth-Century England* (Cambridge, 1994), 153–92.

much that went on in Chartist halls and clubs and at alehouse meetings was merely the stuff of ordinary town meetings.

This was a predominantly masculine culture, which may explain why Chartists seemed blind to the need for female suffrage, even in the case of spinsters and widows.[179] At first the movement mobilized tens of thousands of women from all over Britain, and briefly united female and working-class aspirations. The Birmingham Women's Political Movement led the way, and soon there were about 150 such associations, but as it became clear that their role was limited to cheerleading they gradually 'dropped out'. By 1848 only fourteen societies are definitely known to have been extant, and women's presence in crowd scenes was also diminished.[180] One historian has referred to the 'militant domesticity' of 'household Chartism', which held that the whole duty of woman was not to steal men's jobs but to nurture children and to organize the home on middle-class lines.[181] Even working-class newspapers took little interest in industrial disputes if they only involved female labourers, such as the subcontracted and sweated lace-makers of Nottingham.[182] Unlike Owenism, a genuinely counter-cultural movement, Chartism did not even try to break away from the dominant gender norms of early Victorian England.

Part of the explanation lies in what might be called its modus operandi. The outward face of Chartism was its journalism ('the platform'), monster meetings (Kersal Moor, Blackheath, Blackstone Edge, Peep's Green), and torchlight processions, but its inner life was bureaucratic, consisting of local and national committees, unions, conventions, and associations, each with its own carefully defined rules and constitutions. Participation in such bodies conferred status on the unfranchised, but a fascination with agendas, motions, resolutions, and minutes may explain why most Chartists retained a subaltern mentality, unable to develop any genuinely alternative vision of society.[183] But then it was generally the case that Chartists exploited popular culture rather than trying to change it. They successfully hijacked traditional fairs, festivals, circuses, and wakes weeks, and insinuated their own propaganda into various types of ceremonial, such as rites of passage and church worship.[184] Folk joined Chartist associations for the

---

[179] The first draft of the first petition contained such a clause but it was dropped, partly for fear of delaying the achievement of manhood suffrage. The 1843 rules of the National Charter Association used the word 'males' instead of 'persons'.   [180] Dorothy Thompson, *The Chartists* (1984), 120–51.

[181] Anna Clark, *The Struggle for the Breeches: Gender and the Making of the British Working Class* (1995), 220–47.

[182] Helen Rogers, *Women and the People: Authority, Authorship and the Radical Tradition in Nineteenth-Century England* (Aldershot, 2000), 23–32, 80–123.

[183] For the subsequent narrowing of political activism, and reliance on mailshots and ticketed meetings, see James Vernon, *Politics and the People: A Study in English Popular Culture c.1815–1867* (Cambridge, 1993), 207–30.

[184] J. M. Golby and A. W. Purdue, *The Civilisation of the Crowd: Popular Culture in England 1750–1900* (1984), 63–114.

same reasons that they joined friendly societies and benefit clubs or became teetotallers, i.e. to find companionship, mutuality, and a sense of purpose. Here at the grass roots the dispute that so bedevilled the leadership—whether to employ moral or physical force—was irrelevant. Many who cheered the violent language of O'Connor and O'Brien also engaged in moral force activities: temperance, Sunday schools, pacifism, vegetarianism, anti-slavery, anti-vivisection, even in some cases free trade. In other words, Chartism was a totalizing experience, having less to do with the world of work than with that of leisure, and may even have been for some a substitute for older Christian certainties. There were Chartist hymns, sermons, libraries, reading classes, discussion groups, lectures, clubs, camp and class meetings, orchestras, oratorio societies, choirs, and sports teams, all organized (it should be said) by working men themselves. Indeed, it was probably at this point that associational culture, for so long the hallmark of the upper-middle and middle classes, began to engage sections of the so-called proletariat as well. From this perspective, Chartism was not so much a violent *prelude to* as *part of* the gradual process of working-class acculturation and accommodation.[185]

What this suggests is that, however violently some of them sought to subvert an unjust political order, Chartists did not seriously challenge the norms (which some would call bourgeois) of the ruling class. Deep down they seem to have accepted the Peelite vision of a society in which individual effort, thrift, and moral desert should bring its reward. They differed from self-satisfied middle-class moralists only in their insistence that the desired state of society had not yet been attained. And, because they accepted basic social norms, it might take only a slight shift in political and economic conditions for subversive instincts to elide into apparent submission and accommodation.[186] More important in this context than Peel's and Russell's reforms or movements in real wages was the psychological effect of the Anti-Corn Law League's economic optimism. By presenting free trade as a way to explode the zero-sum economy, and by promising *both* economic growth *and* high wages, Cobden released the national psyche from its Malthusian and Ricardian straitjackets.[187] The only coherent economic strategy adopted by Chartists was O'Connor's Land Plan, which was powerless in the face of the League's 'great truth'. It is significant, however, that the leader who vainly sought to keep Chartism going in the 1850s was that inveterate back-to-the-land protectionist Ernest Jones.[188]

[185] Eileen Yeo, 'Robert Owen and Radical Culture', in Sidney Pollard and John Salt (eds.), *Robert Owen: Prophet of the Poor* (1971), 104–8.

[186] Trygve R. Tholfsen, *Working Class Radicalism in Mid-Victorian England* (1976).

[187] See above, pp. 556–7.

[188] Miles Taylor, *Ernest Jones, Chartism, and the Romance of Politics 1819–1869* (Oxford, 2003), 141–50, 232–44.

CLASS AND COMMUNITY

If, as the foregoing analysis suggests, there were certain dominant values affecting all levels of society—rational, evangelical, individualist—where does that leave considerations of class, for so long indelibly associated with this period in English history? Throughout much of the industrial North and Midlands, Chartism seems to have fed on a sense of working-class consciousness, but not in a crude materialist way. Class was just one of a number of 'imagined communities' with which individuals sought to identify, and competed alongside race, nation, region, religion, gender, and occupation. Worker solidarity was often frayed by racial and denominational loyalties, two categories which came together in anti-Catholic and anti-Irish feeling, and which were very strong in towns like Stockport.[189] Also, class was experienced one way in a town like Birmingham, with its small, family-run workshops, and quite differently in Manchester, with its huge factories and stark opposition between masters and men. For a long time it was thought that Birmingham offered a typology of inter-class cooperation,[190] yet it seems more likely that large-scale modes of production released tensions by offering scope for social mobility, for shop floor camaraderie, and for more acceptable (because more impersonal) forms of employer paternalism.[191] Besides, the larger the workforce, the harder it often was for masters to manage, especially where subcontracting was the norm. Nevertheless, and leaving local variations aside, there is a strong case for saying that what had formerly been characterized as the 'labouring poor' now became identified as a 'working class'. But it still leaves the question, if tensions were so marked in the 1840s, why did they dissipate so quickly thereafter?

One trenchant explanation has focused on Oldham, a steam-driven spinning town north-east of Manchester. Whereas in the 1830s and 1840s workers there joined forces in violent attacks on the New Poor Law and the new police, and then again in support of the Charter, this unity fragmented in the 1850s as skilled artisans adopted petty capitalist and petit bourgeois values, so leaving the manual labourers leaderless. This development has been ascribed to conspiratorial cunning on the part of the local bourgeoisie, who are said to have first divided and then satisfied the proletariat through a programme of 'liberalization'. Back in the 1830s and 1840s mill owners had tried to break the dominance of the skilled male spinners (or minders) over their dependent piecers by installing self-acting mules which were light enough for anyone (including women) to operate.[192] Then in the 1850s, when it was clear that this tactic had failed in its purpose, they sought

---

[189] Robert Glen, *Urban Workers in the Early Industrial Revolution* (1984), 20–4.

[190] Asa Briggs, *Victorian Cities* (1963), 184–92; id., 'The Background of the Parliamentary Reform Movement in Three English Cities (1830–2)', *Cambridge Historical Journal*, 10 (1952), 297–302.

[191] Clive Behagg, *Politics and Production in the Early Nineteenth Century* (1990), 13–19, 104–57.

[192] William Lazonick, *Competitive Advantage on the Shop Floor* (Cambridge, Mass., 1990), 78–114.

instead to turn the spinners into a labour aristocracy by giving them marks of status—separate canteens, superannuation benefits, and licensed as distinct from unofficial authority. At the same time they laid on annual dinners to appease the unskilled, and civic authorities chipped in with sponsored processions and similar baubles to brighten the labourers' lives.[193] It is possible, however, to think of less melodramatic reasons why the recently achieved working-class solidarity might have fractured at the mid-century. They relate to changes in the spatial organization of industrial communities, the increased role of saving in the family economy, and the cultural legacy of Chartism.

Manual labourers and skilled craftsmen had always been inclined to differ temperamentally. They can be caricatured as the rough and the respectable, wife-beating beer-swilling hedonists on the one hand and earnest (sometimes devout) autodidacts on the other. Before 1850, however, such differences did not prevent them from cooperating politically, at least in Oldham. They dwelled in the same streets, their children frequently intermarried, and they shared a thriving tradition of popular culture. Paradoxically, communal sports and pastimes dating back centuries—such as football, snowballing, bonfires, bear-baiting, and cockfighting—all survived longer in the new industrial regions than they did in rural villages and smaller market towns.[194] One reason is that manufacturing centres had developed very rapidly as young farmworkers flocked from the countryside. Some were propelled by agricultural depression and the consequent casualization of labour, others were tempted by higher wages, and many were virtually commandeered by vestries and employers. However, except in the case of Irish immigrants, the average distance travelled by these displaced workers was only about 20 miles.[195] While the rural South remained overcrowded, in Lancashire and Yorkshire whole villages decamped as new mills opened in the vicinity. Traditional practices including blood sports were often transplanted into new industrial centres, even as in smaller market towns they were being suppressed by local elites, anxious to clear the rabble from the main squares and streets in order to reserve such public spaces exclusively for commercial and ceremonial use. But if the anarchic condition of industrial towns enabled popular practices to survive, the fact that they survived may have enabled their inhabitants to remain culturally united despite disparities in

[193] John Foster, *Class Struggle and the Industrial Revolution: Early Industrial Capitalism in Three English Towns* (1974), 129–250; Patrick Joyce, *Work, Society and Politics: The Culture of the Factory in Later Victorian England* (Brighton, 1980), 134–200. See Bibliography, pp. 676–7.

[194] Emma Griffin, 'Popular Sports and Celebrations in England, 1660–1850', Ph.D. thesis (Cambridge University, 2001), 104–72.

[195] Arthur Redford, *Labour Migration in England, 1800–50*, 2nd edn. (Manchester, 1964), 63–7, 182–7. Internal migration has recently been subjected to analysis too sophisticated to summarize, but Redford's findings are broadly confirmed (Colin Pooley and Jean Turnbull, *Migration and Mobility in Britain since the Eighteenth Century* (1998)).

material interest and personal temperament. In which case the fracturing of the working class into unskilled and skilled or rough and respectable elements after 1850 may have been an unintended consequence of civic improvements, leading to residential segregation, following the local government reforms of the 1830s.[196]

The growth of friendly societies may also have helped to prevent skilled and unskilled workers from pulling apart until after mid-century. Membership rose from an estimated 600,000 in 1801 to over 2.8 million or about one-half of adult males in 1850. At that point many of the 25,000 or so societies were locally based, with a concentration in the manufacturing parts of the North and Midlands, though there were a few national affiliates (Oddfellows, Manchester Unity). They offered conviviality and mutual protection in a rapidly changing economy, and also tangible benefits such as insurance against sickness, old age, and death. Membership rose rapidly in the wake of the Anatomy Act and New Poor Law, as did that of burial societies, which safeguarded workers from the stigma of a pauper funeral. But friendly societies could not protect skilled workers against unemployment, or from being *de*skilled by new inventions, which meant that their situation, though superior, *felt* as precarious as that of manual labourers, and even worse in so far as they had more to lose. Here the slowness of trustee savings banks to take off, despite much official encouragement, was crucial. The number of such private philanthropic and non-profit-making organizations rose from six in 1812 to 465 by 1819, thanks in part to Rose's legislation,[197] but thereafter growth was slow: 476 by 1829, and still only 573 twenty-one years later. In fact, it was not until the 1850s that 'a watershed in the history of working-class thrift' occurred.[198] The single most important landmark came in 1844 with the foundation of the Rochdale Society of Equitable Pioneers, which was followed by many more consumer cooperatives, especially in the North. They gave better-off workers a measure of future security, on the basis of which many must have begun to form ambitions for their children. In the words of a contemporary moralist,

The man who has invested a portion of his earnings in securities, to the permanence and safety of which the peace and good order of society are essential—will be a tranquil and conservative citizen. . . . To have saved money and invested it securely, is to have become a capitalist . . . To have become a capitalist is, for the poor man, to have overleaped a great gulf; to have opened a path for himself into a new world.[199]

---

[196] Another factor may have been the breakdown of the old 'pan-evangelical consensus', as a hardening of denominational boundaries put an end to an older tradition of promiscuous and cooperative worship (Mark Smith, *Religion in Industrial Society: Oldham and Saddleworth, 1740–1865* (Oxford, 1994), 227–42).   [197] See above, pp. 321, 323.

[198] Barry Supple, 'Legislation and Virtue: An Essay on Working Class Self-Help and the State in the Early Nineteenth Century', in Neil McKendrick (ed.), *Historical Perspectives: Studies in English Thought and Society* (1974), 210–54.

[199] [W. R. Greg], 'Investments for the Working Classes', *ER* 95 (1852), 407–8.

Paradoxically, this development owed nothing to ministerial policy. Indeed, one reason for the Rochdale Society's success may have been that it was not just another attempt at middle-class philanthropy, but was founded and run by artisans themselves.

MAD METROPOLIS

In most of its peaceable activities Chartism belonged to a provincial and especially Northern industrial culture which was rooted in Nonconformist chapels and Sunday schools. For the next four decades that culture was accepted as normative in English life, and provided a context for Gladstone's populist brand of Liberalism. London by contrast was entering on a period of introverted marginality from which it would not recover until its reinvention as the great imperial city towards the end of Victoria's reign. The world of high fashion moved decisively back to Paris, and even its bohemianism went downmarket: Count D'Orsay and Captain Gronow were much more rackety dandies than the stylish Brummell. London's radicalism had always differed from that of the North, being secular, republican, and artisanal in outlook, a tradition that encompassed Tom Paine, Robert Owen, Richard Carlile, George Jacob Holyoake, and the sober-minded members of the London Working Men's Association,[200] but during the second quarter of the century the dominant tone was escapist and frivolous. The transition is exemplified by George Cruikshank and William Hone. In 1819 they brought out a vicious political satire, *The Political House that Jack Built*,[201] and followed it up with equally hateful squibs on the Queen Caroline affair, yet before long both men had retreated, Hone to bring out harmless calendars,[202] Cruikshank his amiable *Tom and Jerry* illustrations, which, it has been said, created a vogue for realistic urban drama. 'The city itself became seen as a great theatre.'[203] While the public's passion for melodrama continued, preoccupation now shifted from Gothic battles between vice and virtue, played out in medieval convents or in castles inhabited by wicked aristocrats,[204] to the social degradation of the contemporary city, with its heartless bailiffs, its alcohol, homelessness, poverty, illegitimacy, and crime. A typical example was

[200] E. J. Hobsbawm, *Labouring Men: Studies in the History of Labour* (1964), 371–85.
[201] See Plate 9. Extract from *The Political House that Jack Built* (1819).
[202] e.g. *The Every-Day Book: Or, Everlasting Calendar of Popular Amusements: forming a Complete History of the Year, Months, & Seasons, and a Perpetual Key to the Almanack for Daily Use and Diversion* (1826); *The Table Book* (1827–8); *The Year Book of Daily Recreation and Information, concerning Remarkable Men, Manners, Times, Seasons, Solemnities, &c.* (1832).
[203] Marriott (ed.), *Unknown London*, vol. i, pp. xliii–xlvi; Louis James (ed.), *Print and the People 1829–1851* (1976), 71–80.
[204] Paul Ranger, *'Terror and Pity Reign in Every Breast': Gothic Drama in the London Patent Theatres, 1750–1820* (1991), 42–68.

W. H. Ainsworth's *Rookwood* (1834), which with the help of Cruikshank's illustrations mythologized and even celebrated the violent real-life highwayman of yesteryear Dick Turpin. The two men repeated the trick five years later with *Jack Sheppard*, which enjoyed a brief but giddy period of acclaim and any number of stage adaptations.[205] The popular taste for depravity was further intensified by the introduction in the 1830s of penny bloods and dreadfuls, horror comics, and serialized novels, the latter format reflecting and reinforcing the desire for suspense. Successive instalments of *Sweeney Todd: The Demon Barber of Fleet Street* appeared in *The People's Periodical* from 1846. Londoners seemed obsessed with their own anonymity and with the dangers lurking in every alleyway and rookery.

Melodrama was not the only avenue of escape for the capital's ex-radicals. In the early 1820s the once ardent Spencean George Cannon suddenly abandoned radical publishing for joke books, comedy, trivia, and gardening tips. Like many other writers he also drifted into scatology, flagellation, and erotica, a cocktail that was turning large parts of the capital into the pornographic underbelly of evangelical England.[206] (According to one account, pornography was not more plentiful than in the previous century, but it became more psychopathic. Flagellatory literature, for example, had been comparatively rare and elitist until the 1780s, but from then on it proliferated, as an older enjoyment in honest bawdy gave way to 'a realm of fantasy in which sexual activities of a frequency, complexity and elaboration of accompaniments which could not be realized in practice are described'.[207] There was Robert Wedderburn, an ex-Methodist mulatto who steered close to the Cato Street conspirators. There was Thomas Evans, who exploited his preacher's licence to promulgate radicalism from brothels, taverns, and Dissenting chapels. Clowns, dwarves, ragamuffins, prize-fighters, and criminals added to the burlesque atmosphere. Most remarkable of all was a theatrical counter-culture centred on the Blackfriars Rotunda, where Robert Taylor, a mystical atheistic preacher, sent audiences of more than 1,000 into ecstasy with witty and would-be erudite tirades against the elite. His 1830 party piece was 'Raising the Devil' when, dressed in canonicals, he incanted the words 'Satan, Beelzebub! Baal, Peor! Belial, Lucifer, Abaddon, Apollyon, thou King of the Bottomless Pit, thou King of Scorpions: Appear!—Appear!', and then by a trick of electricity the Devil did appear, but only to be immediately

[205] Matthew Buckley, 'Sensations of Celebrity: *Jack Sheppard* and the Mass Audience', *Victorian Studies*, 44 (2001–2), 423–63.

[206] For a classic account of this 'ribald saturnalian anti-establishment culture', see Iain McCalman, *Radical Underworld: Prophets, Revolutionaries and Pornographers in London, 1795–1840* (Cambridge, 1988).

[207] Gordon Rattray Taylor, *The Angel-Makers: A Study in the Psychological Origins of Historical Change 1750–1850* (1958), 76 n.

'transformed into an angel of light'.[208] Taylor's mixture of 'esoteric eastern mythology and astrology' was intended to be subversive, especially of orthodox Christianity, but its appeal had more to do with the fashion for shows and spectacles, Punch and Judys, panoramas, scientific experimentations, exhibitions, and displays. Evangelical preaching had always carried an emotional punch, but now it became overtly theatrical. Exeter Hall in the Strand, with seating for about 4,000, opened in 1831 and made an immediate sensation.

This irreverent and raucous side of London's popular culture has sometimes been seen as a survival from the eighteenth century, now under threat from the Puritanism of the nineteenth. ('Perhaps the most significant legacy of this tiny metropolitan underworld was to keep alive a tradition of plebeian unrespectability and irreverence in the face of powerful countervailing forces.'[209]) More realistically, it can be seen as part of a detumescent post-war generation of footloose adventurers and chancers, actors, and mountebanks, attracted by and sympathetic to the second wave of Romanticism associated with Byron and Shelley. And although not all of London's radicalism was carnivalesque in tone, it undoubtedly had a strong performative aspect. Many Chartist leaders were charismatic charmers who pitched their stalls alongside messianists, mesmerists, fortune-tellers, table-tappers, and phrenologists. As has been observed, many of the movement's leaders 'came from the persuading professions and vocations— the law, evangelical ministry, quack medicine, the theatre, the bookstall, the newsdesk and the print-shop. In their hands and mouths words became weapons, with the power to capture and convert.'[210]

The public life of the 1830s and 1840s, as described in the last two chapters, was a mass of contradictions: a two-party system without coherent parties; attempts to find national solutions to social problems while reducing the size of the State and allowing scope for greater local independence; a determination to export British freedom by extending Britain's control over more and more of the world. Yet no feature was quite so paradoxical as that of a working-class protest movement, the most dangerous in English history, which ultimately fostered an ethos of self-improvement and respectability. Somehow the mad, bad, and dangerous classes of the later Hanoverian period became the loyal, docile, and dutiful subjects of Queen Victoria.

---

[208] I. D. McCalman, 'Popular Irreligion in Early Victorian England: Infidel Peachers and Radical Theatricality in 1830s London', in R. W. Davis and R. J. Helmstadter (eds.), *Religion and Irreligion in Victorian Society: Essays in Honor of R. K. Webb* (1992), 55–6. McCalman suggests that Taylor's 'astronomo-theological critique . . . contained . . . the same mix of ingredients that had contributed to the immense success [with working-class readers] of Byron's *Don Juan* a decade earlier'.

[209] McCalman, *Radical Underworld*, 237.

[210] Miles Taylor, 'Knife and Fork Question', *London Review of Books* (29 Nov. 2001), 28–9.

CHAPTER 10

Afterwards: 'There are no Barbarians
any longer'

It was suggested in Chapter 1 that, despite the pace of economic and technological change, the English did not feel so very different in the 1840s from how they
had in the 1780s. Yet the climate was just about to change utterly. The historian
G. M. Young, a Victorian by birth, illustrated the transformation with a memorable metaphor inspired by his having lived through two world wars:

> The difference... between the England of the last Chartist demonstration in 1848 and
> the Great Exhibition of 1851, is like the difference in one's own feelings at the beginning
> and end of a voyage in wartime through waters beset by enemy ships, or like the opening
> of the city gates after a long wintry siege ... It was in that Maytime of youth recaptured
> that Gladstonian Liberalism was conceived. It was the only atmosphere in which it could
> have been conceived, an atmosphere composed in equal measure of progress, confidence,
> and social union: from which the image of the Beleaguered City had faded—out of sight,
> and almost out of memory[1]

Young was careful to write about perceptions. The realities of existence for
the squalid, ragged, and undernourished masses will not have changed very suddenly, but upper-class assumptions about them certainly did. When Lord
Morpeth had spoken in 1846 about the 'glory of drying the tears, of brightening
the hopes, of elevating the character, of recasting the history of man, of making
freedom the guarantee of order, toleration the ally of religion, government the
object of love, and law the helpmate of virtue',[2] he must have sounded hopelessly
utopian to most members of the elite, reeling as they were from Chartism,
stunned by Irish disaffection and famine, appalled by the tactics of the Anti-Corn
Law League, horrified by the Scottish Disruption, and worried lest Newman
provoke a similar schism in the English Church. Yet miraculously much of
Morpeth's optimism quickly became commonplace. Lord Shaftesbury wrote
from Manchester in 1851, admittedly not without a touch of self-congratulation,

[1] G. M. Young, *Today and Yesterday: Collected Essays and Addresses* (1948), 32–3.
[2] Quoted in Peter Mandler, *Aristocratic Government in the Age of Reform: Whigs and Liberals,
1830–1852* (Oxford, 1990), 239.

Chartism is dead in these parts; the Ten Hours Act and cheap provisions have slain it outright. Often as I have seen these people, I never so them so ardent, so affectionate, so enthusiastic. But then, praised be God, they are *morally* and physically improved. The children look lively and *young*; a few years ago they looked weary and *old*.[3]

And looking back, Mark Pattison wrote about the 'enormous effect' on Oxford of Newman's conversion to Rome.

It was not consternation; it was a lull—a sense that the past agitation of twelve years was extinguished by this simple act . . . Theology was totally banished from Common Room, and even from private conversation. Very free opinions on all subjects were rife . . . If any Oxford man had gone to sleep in 1846 and had woke up again in 1850 he would have found himself in a totally new world . . . [a world] suddenly changed as if by the wand of a magician.[4]

There was an economic dimension to this development in that at last the country began to surmount the constraints on growth. Even income per capita began to increase, while to provide an immediate sense of well-being the value of imports and exports almost doubled between 1844–6 and 1854–6. A still more important consideration was that England in 1848 escaped the violent revolutions experienced throughout the Continent. The final act of Chartism, though not a fiasco, was sufficiently diminuendo for the upper classes to present it as such. At once the myth of the country's essential soundness began to be cultivated, a belief (which the working class seems to have swallowed) that revolution was a foreign disease. Macaulay said that it was about as likely to happen in this country as 'the moon dropping out of the sky'. It was as though the dreaded barbarians had suddenly decommissioned their tumbrils and dismantled their barricades. The relief was palpable.

Once fear of the mob had receded, it became possible to come to terms with towns and industry, to recognize that Britain's was an increasingly urban society and that there could be no going back. Until then it was widely assumed that the country was alone in taking the manufacturing route, which might therefore prove to be a profoundly unnatural process and liable to a terrible recoil. Economic growth was especially to be feared because it went hand in hand with population increase, the dangers of which were underlined by Ireland's terrifying experience. Yet perceptions were soon to change. A turning point came with the 1851 census, which revealed that for the first time more Britons were living in towns than in the countryside. Ten years later the Registrar-General announced that there was no longer any need to worry about starvation, since thanks to free trade it would always be possible to import food from the rest of

---

[3] Shaftesbury to Russell, 26 Nov. 1851, in *The Later Correspondence of Lord John Russell 1840–1878*, ed. G. P. Gooch (1925), i. 214.

[4] *Mark Pattison: Memoirs*, ed. Jo Manton (Fontwell, 1969), 212–13, 244–5.

the world in return for manufactures. Official doctrine thus returned to where it had been in the eighteenth century, before Malthus' fateful essay. Now that population growth was welcomed as benefiting both the economy and the armed services, the pundits began to worry about a falling birth rate instead.

Three other factors helped to reconcile the English to industrialization. All were psychologically significant, and one was of practical importance as well. The Great Exhibition of 1851 attracted 6 million visitors to London from all over the country, including many respectably dressed working-class families, and seemed to affirm the recently acquired sense of social cohesion. (It helped that many of the goods on display seemed likely to adorn the lives of all, and not just the elite.) The Exhibition also served to celebrate England's manufacturing supremacy as the workshop of the world, but perhaps a deeper message was that Britain was no longer on her own, and that other nations were hard on her heels. In these circumstances the old ambivalence about economic growth quickly gave way to the view that it was both natural and necessary. This feeling was strengthened by the visual impact of railways, the building of which reached a peak in the 1850s and greatly enhanced the consciousness that England was essentially urban. As the novelist Thackeray commented, 'They have raised those railroad embankments up, and shut off the old world that was behind them . . . We who lived before railways, and survive out of the ancient world, are like Father Noah and his family out of the Ark.'[5] The repeal of the Corn Laws, meanwhile, was not only important symbolically, but removed the only instruments by which it might have been possible to turn the economic clock backwards, as the Young England politicians and cultural medievalists discussed in Chapter 7 had fervently hoped to do. Immediately following repeal there was a credible push to revive the Corn Laws, but when the new mid-century mood kicked in, it at once became obvious, even to Disraeli, that protection was 'not only dead but damned'. A free-trade consensus made it inevitable that the economy would submit to market forces, preventing any regression to a rural past. A cult of medievalism persisted, but it differed from that of the Pugin era in its leftward-leaning political stance, and in its nostalgic rather than practical bent. John Ruskin, William Morris, and members of the Pre-Raphaelite Brotherhood (founded in 1848) idealized the Middle Ages as a rebuke to nineteenth-century materialism, but unlike their predecessors they never supposed that it might be literally possible to bring them back.

In 1846 it looked as though the business middle classes might be about to seize control. Instead the traditional ruling families rallied, with the consequence that a fully fledged entrepreneurial politics never developed. Having torn down the Corn Laws, the industrial bourgeoisie lost its radical menace, much to the

---

[5] 'Roundabout Papers' (1863), in *The Works of William Makepeace Thackeray* (1871–86), x. 57.

frustration of Cobden and Bright. Some of them sought gentrification for their children by sending them to the new rash of boys' public schools, about fifty of which were founded between 1840 and 1900, mainly for the middle classes. Still more opted for local notability. In Bolton, for example, the political parties rallied behind an Improvement Act of 1850, sinking decades of bitter hostility in an enthusiasm of civic pride. Throughout the industrial districts generally urban squalor gave way to improvement, rough sports to rational recreation. Preston's Moor Park (1844) was one of the first of a wave of municipal amenities offering fresh air, a bandstand, a lake, grass, and public conveniences. Factory employers laid on annual dinners for their workers, corporations organized civic processions, the churches came together in Whitsuntide walks. While more or less ungoverned London continued to stink, provincial towns and newly designated cities battled not to be last in the race for sanitation. Many also enjoyed an overdue architectural renaissance as the old upper-middle-class and metropolitan-minded elites[6] ceded leadership to local manufacturers and tradesmen. Vigorous and magnificent municipal buildings, banks, offices, and warehouses made of stone, brick, or terracotta in Greek, Gothic, or Italianate style largely effaced what was going up in the capital, which apart from the Palace of Westminster had little to match the work of Dyer and Gingell in Bristol, Lockwood & Mawson in Bradford, or Waterhouse, Worthington, Walters, and Gregan in Manchester. Many of the great private collections of nineteenth-century art that found their way into civic galleries were founded by industrialists, especially following the spectacular Manchester Art Treasures Exhibition of 1857. Such entrepreneurs might have lacked self-confidence in matters of taste, relying on the advice of middlemen concerning which were the best Pre-Raphaelites to buy, but magnates such as Joseph Whitworth collected art as a route to both personal and civic improvement. Taken together with the founding of symphony orchestras, oratorio societies, clubs, concert halls, and music festivals, mid-nineteenth-century towns have been convincingly depicted as 'sites of cultural display' in which urban patriciates were able to bury their former sectarian differences.[7] The Liverpool Philharmonic (1840) and Manchester's Hallé (1857–8) led the way in symphony orchestras and Huddersfield in choral societies (1836), while Leeds (from 1858) and Birmingham (from 1849) hosted the most prominent music festivals. It is probably no coincidence that these years of provincial chic were also ones in which the Parliamentary Liberal Party was in the ascendant. After about 1885 the Liberal Party—like the Nonconformity that sustained it—was to enter on a protracted albeit uneven decline, and when it did so the English provinces

---

[6] For whose indifference to civic improvement, see above, pp. 166–7.
[7] Simon Gunn, *The Public Culture of the Victorian Middle Class: Ritual and Authority in the English Industrial City 1840–1914* (Manchester, 2000).

retreated once more, allowing London ('the imperial city') to regain the cultural and architectural pre-eminence that it had enjoyed in the Georgian era, when aristocrats had provided most of the inspiration and money.

As suggested above, one reason why provincial ruling groups in the first half of the century had placed so little store by civic and social improvement was the other-worldly nature of their religion, especially evangelicalism. The earth was but a place of moral trial, and what mattered was the soul's salvation. However, religious ideology changed dramatically at the mid-century, especially among upper- and middle-class Anglicans. There are various explanations, but a simple one is that the strain of a faith requiring constant moral attention and threatening such dire penalties became too great. Evangelicalism with its 'win all, lose all' eschatology has been presented here as type of spiritual capitalism, and as a reflection of the economic insecurity felt by plutocrats whose wealth could so easily blow away overnight. The poor, in their view, were spiritually superior to themselves. Being worse off in *this* world, and so less subject to temptation, beggars were more likely to make it to paradise. Of course, this is how the rich have consoled the poor throughout history, but during the first half of the nineteenth century they seem really to have believed their own propaganda. That is, they saw themselves as carrying the spiritual can for capitalism, perhaps as a way of justifying their earthly privileges. Often it was women who, having been quick to buy into this 'flogging theology' fifty years earlier, now called for a truce. One such was a society lady whose agonies were described as follows by her friend Charlotte Williams-Wynn in 1858:

What religious teaching she had in her youth was of a so-called evangelical nature. No sooner did affliction come upon her, than these teachers came about her, wrote, and in short, kept her in a state of high nervous excitement. This will not do for everyday 'wear and tear', and for the last three years she has been in a constant alternation of feeling, obliged from position and circumstances to be always in society, and all the time fearing that she is falling from God because she can no longer find in herself the highly wrought emotions which existed when she was in stronger health. Loved by all who come near her ... devoted to her poor ... she is thoroughly unhappy from the constant fear of the wrath of this inexorable Judge.[8]

Women were repeatedly told that they were better at heightened emotions than men, but it is hard to keep heightened emotions up for ever. This distressed lady was allegedly cured by being given to read a volume of sermons by Frederick Denison Maurice with its confident reassurance 'that God is a God of love, and that He does not punish in anger.' In 1853 Maurice was dismissed from his professorial post at King's College London for arguing in effect that Hell did not

---

[8] Charlotte Williams-Wynn to F. D. Maurice, Apr. 1858, in *Memorials of Charlotte Williams-Wynn*, ed. by her sister (1877), 246–7.

exist in any literal sense, yet within ten years of that date his 'more indulgent Gospel' was on the way to becoming a commonplace.

Described by one of his friends as 'the most saint-like individual I ever met—*Christ-like*, if I dare to use the word',[9] Maurice was undoubtedly a pivotal figure. He took much from the Liberal Anglicanism of Thomas Arnold, but avoided its more anguished, quasi-evangelical, and disciplinary aspects. He was strongly influenced by Coleridge and Robert Owen, and was very sympathetic to Chartism. His *magnum opus*, *The Kingdom of Christ* (1838), attacked the prevailing philosophy of individualism, competition, and laissez-faire. His consolatory theology was taken up avidly by mid-century Christian Socialists such as Charles Kingsley (who always referred to him as 'my Master') and Thomas Hughes. He was undoubtedly sincere, but his theology also served a tactical purpose. From 1848 onwards a number of Anglican intellectuals, starting with James Anthony Froude and Arthur Hugh Clough, began to declare their loss of faith. Almost invariably their doubts arose, not from scientific discoveries or philosophical conundrums, but from moral revulsion against the cruelties involved in orthodox religion—Hell especially and the ideas of sin, moral trial, and vicarious sacrifice. Actual disasters being more immediate than theoretical ones, it was very possibly the Irish famine that discredited the idea of a deliberately vengeful God, rather as the Lisbon earthquake had awoken doubts among European intellectuals a century earlier. Whatever the reason, it now became fashionable in Anglican circles to believe that everyone would go to Heaven (universalism), or else that those who did not do so immediately would be offered a second chance in some purgatorial reform school. At the very worst, Hell was reinterpreted as a state of nothingness, devoid of literal torments. As Gladstone commented sadly, the doctrine of eternal punishment was banished 'to the far-off corners of the Christian mind...as a thing needless in our own generation'.[10] As a result people were deprived of the realization that there could be 'a kind of joy in salutary pain'.[11] As Liston had taken the physical terror out of surgical operations, so Maurice took much of the sting out of moral choices.

Anglicanism now became a one-sided religion in so far as Heaven remained firmly in place. However, it too was reconceived, being no longer imagined as a site of unimaginable but ecstatic bliss, and came instead to resemble a cosy domestic fireside where the deceased would be reunited with their former family, friends, and even pets.[12] At the same time the old fixation on Christ as sacrificial redeemer gave way to hero worship of Jesus as 'Lord and

[9] *The Life of Frederick Denison Maurice*, ed. Frederick Maurice (1884), i. 38.

[10] W. E. Gladstone, *Studies Subsidiary to the Works of Bishop Butler* (1896), 199–201, 206.

[11] W. E. Gladstone, 'True and False Conceptions of the Atonement', *Nineteenth Century*, 36 (1894), 327.

[12] Heaven also began to be conceived more in urban than in rural terms (Max F. Schulz, *Paradise Reserved: Recreations in Eden in Eighteenth- and Nineteenth-Century England* (Cambridge, 1985)).

Master'—exemplar, mentor, elder brother, in Arnoldian terms head prefect, for some even the first socialist, whose message to humankind was how to live, not how to die. Whereas the evangelical Chalmers had depicted him as the 'captain general of salvation', a military leader or freedom fighter, Broad-Churchmen like A. P. Stanley and Christian Socialists like Thomas Hughes, both impassioned devotees of Arnold, presented Jesus as possessing a tender rather than a heroic manliness, and an almost feminine capacity for suffering. At the same time the doctrine of the Atonement yielded primacy to that of the Incarnation, and Easter gave way to Christmas as the focus of the liturgical year. Charles Dickens's *A Christmas Carol*, published in December 1843, has been credited with helping to invent the commercial and semi-pagan festival that remains today. It is a simple tale of redemption. Early in the narrative Ebenezer Scrooge, a covetous and fun-hating businessman, sends a charity worker packing on the grounds that 'the poor might as well die, so as to decrease the surplus population'. Several ghostly visitations later he has come to understand the wickedness of his own heart, and devotes himself to spreading sweetness and light among those around him. The book was an immediate and quite extraordinary hit, itself a sign that Dickens's contemporaries wanted to be done with Malthus.

These developments can be seen as a victory for those Romantic writers who, throughout the first half of the nineteenth century, had battled against the spirit of the age to keep alive a strain of incarnational thought. Wordsworth, for example, had been regarded by orthodox Christians for most of his lifetime as little better than a pantheist, yet by the time of his death in 1850 he had become something of a guru. More than 2,000 people signed the Rydal Mount visitors' book in the 1840s, including Kingsley, who worshipped him as 'not only poet, put preacher and prophet of God's new and divine philosophy—a man raised up as a light in a dark time'.[13] Like Maurice's sermons, Wordsworth's poetry helped many who were burdened by evangelical guilt to survive a nervous breakdown. The same religious developments can also be seen as a victory for Unitarians,[14] who had opposed the ruling orthodoxy for seven decades, but in some respects it was a pyrrhic victory that threatened their own sense of identity. As their most dynamic leader James Martineau explained in 1858,

The difficulties which we have to encounter now are very greatly changed from what they were forty, fifty, or sixty years ago. Then Unitarians stood absolutely and hopelessly alone, objects of general abhorrence and antipathy. Now the difficulty appears to be to find any person who really differs with us ... We find within the limits of the Established

---

[13] Kingsley to his wife, 21 Apr. 1844, in *Charles Kingsley: His Letters and Memories of his Life*, ed. F. E. Kingsley, 4th edn. (1877), i. 120–1; Stephen Gill, *Wordsworth and the Victorians* (Oxford, 1998), 61.

[14] Maurice had been reared as a Unitarian in his early years.

Church itself every one of the favourite truths upon which we dwelt so many years ago, put forth with not less emphasis than they were in our own places of worship.[15]

During the following three decades most of the other (mainly Trinitarian) Dissenting sects followed the Church of England in abandoning strict evangelical doctrine, which caused Martineau to reflect even more gloomily that

The mission which had been consigned to us by our history is likely to pass to the Congregationalists in England and the Presbyterians in Scotland. Their escape from the old orthodox scheme is by a better path than ours. With us, insistence upon the simple Humanity of Christ has come to mean the *limitation of all Divineness* to the Father, leaving Man a mere item of creaturely existence under laws of Natural Necessity. With them the transfer of emphasis from the Atonement to the Incarnation means the retention of a Divine essence in Christ, as the Head and Type of Humanity in its realised Idea; so that Man and Life are lifted into kinship with God, instead of *what had been God* being reduced to the scale of mere Nature.[16]

Perhaps the Unitarians' real problem was their temperamental need to go against the grain, even to feel persecuted. At all events, while so many opinion-formers in the third quarter of the century moved *away* from belief in free-will individualism and towards a form of environmental or biological determinism, Unitarians such as Martineau abandoned that sect's long-held necessarian beliefs, played down scientific explanations of behaviour, and sought to formulate ideas of moral freedom instead.[17]

It might be supposed that, notwithstanding the spread of a more serene form of religion, the publication of the Darwin–Wallace theory of evolution by natural selection in 1859 would have shaken the Christian message to its foundations. That was indeed the case for some, especially for those mainly Nonconformist sects that held strictly to a literal truth of Bible Scripture. Yet the more obvious point is just how painlessly most of the well-educated classes swallowed *On the Origin of Species*. It was a savagely malevolent doctrine based on random development leading nowhere in particular—'the survival of the fittest' in Herbert Spencer's notorious phrase—which is why Darwin had kept it hidden for so long, and as such it was in marked contrast to the more benign versions of evolution developed previously by Erasmus Darwin and Lamarck. Yet paradoxically most mid-Victorians interpreted Charles Darwin's theory in a neo-Lamarckian light by filtering it through their own optimistic view of progress. It was widely assumed that human beings would become 'finer and fitter', 'better and more beautiful', and that society would move 'onwards and

---

[15] J. Estlin Carpenter, *James Martineau, Theologian and Teacher: A Study of his Life and Thought* (1905), 403.

[16] *Life and Letters of James Martineau*, ed. James Drummond and C. B. Upton (1902), ii. 231.

[17] Catherine Gallagher, *The Industrial Reformation of English Fiction 1832–1867* (Chicago, 1985), 62.

upward'. Gladstone's response was typical. He said that the doctrine of evolution actually enhanced his idea of the greatness of God because 'it makes every stage of creation a legible prophecy of all those which are to follow it'.[18] As a further irony, it was some of the more fundamentalist, more orthodox evangelicals, those who had always seen God in a cruel light, who understood and came to terms with the real Darwinian theory best.[19]

Richard Cobden, frequently lauded as the hero of Corn Law repeal, has been presented above as personifying the new optimism.

If we can keep the world from actual war—and I trust railroads, steam-boats, cheap-postage, and our own example in Free Trade will do that—a great impulse will, from this time, be given to social reforms. The public mind is in a practical mood, and it will now precipitate itself upon education, temperance, reform of criminals, care of physical health, &c. &c. with greater zeal than ever.[20]

Yet notwithstanding the Ten Hours Act of 1847, the Public Health Act of 1848, and the switch of emphasis from the other world to this, there was to be no sudden burst of social reform. Apart from anything else, respect for local autonomy and dislike of taxation continued to inhibit intervention. Nevertheless, there developed a considerably softer attitude to underdogs such as paupers, lunatics, and especially children, who were increasingly seen as 'trailing clouds of glory' rather than as embodiments of original sin.[21] A small but significant pointer was the Juvenile Offenders Act (1847), which gave JPs discretion not to throw first-time offenders into prison. An ardent proponent of the new ideas was the Unitarian social reformer and campaigner against corporal punishment Mary Carpenter. 'What rewards or punishments should then be employed in [reformatory] schools? As much as possible let them be of the same nature as those which the Heavenly Father has adopted in the treatment of His children... In a school where such views are adopted, *no punishments of a degrading or revengeful nature will ever be deployed*'.[22] Meanwhile, Poor Law regimes were also modified to the extent that experience of the workhouse often became more eligible than life outside. At the same time decades of highly personal charitable giving gave way to increasingly systematic philanthropy, epitomized by the Charity Organization Society, founded in 1869. The new practices were

---

[18] *Correspondence on Church and Religion of William Ewart Gladstone*, ed. D. C. Lathbury (1910), ii. 101.

[19] James R. Moore, *The Post-Darwinian Controversies: A Study of the Protestant Struggle to Come to Terms with Darwin in Great Britain and America 1870–1900* (Cambridge, 1979), 252–98.

[20] Cobden to Combe, 14 July 1846, BL, Cobden MSS, Add. MS 43660, fos. 46–51.

[21] Mary Carpenter, *Reformatory Schools for the Children of the Perishing and Dangerous Classes and for Juvenile Offenders* (1851), 85–7.

[22] It is true that prison regimes became crueller in the 1850s, which might seem to contradict the claim for a general softening of attitudes, but there was a special reason for this, which was that prisons were having to accommodate a much more hardened type of criminal, now that fewer felons were being hanged, and the system of transportation to Australia ceased in 1853.

undoubtedly more efficient, but surviving members of the Clapham Sect were not amused.

Ours is the age of societies. For the redress of every oppression that is done under the sun, there is a public meeting. For the cure of every sorrow by which our land or our race can be visited, there are patrons, vice-presidents, and secretaries. For the diffusion of every blessing of which mankind can partake in common, there is a committee.[23]

So long as the mid-Victorian boom continued, that is until the 1873 financial crisis followed by the Great Depression of the 1880s, it just about proved possible to encourage the adoption of national solutions to social problems without undermining the independence of local government. Permissive legislation (building on the work of non-government organizations like the Social Science Association, a sort of unofficial civil service), legal improvements, constructive planning, and the mobilization of private capital for philanthropic purposes brought improvements to society without major calls on tax- and ratepayers' pockets, or too much interference with individual freedom.[24] Discrimination in favour of the *deserving* poor continued, perhaps even intensified, but there was now less concern with morality and more with material need. The older Utilitarian and evangelical emphasis on free will was quietly dropped, as a later generation came to accept the view of Robert Owen—traduced throughout the first half of the century—that actions were the outcomes of character, and that character was shaped by circumstance, whether environmental, chemical, or hereditary. In consequence moral reformers began to emphasize prevention rather than the need for moral reformation. To cite just one striking example, for two decades the British and Foreign Temperance Society (BFTS) had sought to convert the poor from the demon drink by means of religious and moral exhortation within the context of a free trade in gin and beer. It was held that only a willing reform of heart on the part of individuals could possibly have a lasting effect on behaviour, and that for such a reform to take place, temptation must be placed in the sinner's way. Yet in 1848 the BFTS was wound up, to be replaced by the London Temperance League (1851) and the United Kingdom Alliance (1853), both of which organizations were devoted to tackling the same problem by means of licensing, prohibition, and other forms of prevention.[25]

Of course, the mid-century euphoria did not last. Fear of the barbarians within had at least presented society with clear and hard-edged choices, whereas the mid-Victorian generation would be forced to face up to the subtle complexities

---

[23] Sir James Stephen, *Essays in Ecclesiastical Biography*, 2 vols. (1849), i. 382.

[24] Lawrence Goldman, *Science, Reform, and Politics in Victorian Britain: The Social Science Association 1857–1886* (Cambridge, 2002).

[25] Brian Harrison, *Drink and the Victorians: The Temperence Question in England 1815–1872* (1971), 179–218.

involved in organizing a fully fledged industrial and urban society. But the euphoria was real while it lasted. In 1850 Tennyson succeeded Wordsworth as Poet Laureate. His haunted and in parts deranged poem of that year *In Memoriam* rehearsed many of the spiritual difficulties of the previous decades, resolving them (if that is the right word) in the vaguely optimistic spirit of Maurice's theology. For all the pious hopes expressed it is a frankly morbid poem, yet it contains twenty-two resonant lines that wonderfully caught the mid-century mood of national epiphany.[26]

> Ring out, wild bells, to the wild sky,
> The flying cloud, the frosty light:
> The year is dying in the night;
> Ring out, wild bells, and let him die.
>
> Ring out the old, ring in the new . . .
> Ring out the false, ring in the true.
>
> Ring out the grief that saps the mind,
> For those that here we see no more;
> Ring out the feud of rich and poor,
> Ring in redress to all mankind.
>
> Ring out a slowly dying cause,
> And ancient forms of party strife;
> Ring in the nobler modes of life,
> With sweeter manners, purer laws. . . .
>
> Ring out old shapes of foul disease;
> Ring out the narrowing lust of gold;
> Ring out the thousand wars of old,
> Ring in the thousand years of peace.
>
> Ring in the valiant man and free,
> The larger heart, the kindlier hand;
> Ring out the darkness of the land,
> Ring in the Christ that is to be.

---

[26] *In Memoriam* was started in 1833 and published in 1850. The quoted lines have been dated tentatively to 1846, but might have been written later (*The Poems of Tennyson*, ed. Christopher Ricks, 2nd edn. (Harlow, 1987), ii. 427 n.).

Chronology

Date	Political and Diplomatic	Legislative Affairs
1783	Fox–North Coalition: Portland Prime Minister (Apr.) Treaty of Paris concedes US independence (Sept.) Treaties of Versailles bring peace with France and Spain George III influences outcome of Lords debate on Fox's India Bill (Dec.) George dismisses Coalition and installs Pitt as a minority Prime Minister (Dec.)	Eleventh Report of the Commissioners for Examining the Public Accounts
1784	St Alban's Tavern group of MPs calls for government of national unity Fox makes tactical errors: his Commons majority dwindles progressively (Jan.–Mar.) Pitt mendaciously denies foreknowledge of King's moves against Coalition General election (Apr.) strongly endorses Pitt	Pitt's India Act Commutation Act drastically reduces tax on tea
1785	Pitt defeated on Westminster scrutiny, parliamentary reform, Irish trade proposals	Pitt initiates retrenchment in public offices Commission of Fees begins its work
1786	Prince of Wales's debts at crisis point, causing problems for the Opposition	Anglo-French trade agreement (Eden Treaty) Pitt's sinking fund Civil list reform
1787	Impeachment of Warren Hastings (May) Manchester anti-slave trade petition marks start of middle-class political awareness	First motion (proposed by Beaufoy) to repeal Test and Corporation Acts easily defeated (Mar.): Pitt deserts the cause and votes against Consolidation of customs duties Commencement of transportation to Australia
1788	Onset of George III's first madness (Nov.) Defensive alliances with United Provinces and Prussia (Triple Alliance)	Declaratory Act (India)
1789	George III recovers (Feb.)	Second Beaufoy motion to repeal Test and Corporation Acts almost succeeds

People, Projects, Military Events, Foundations	Publications
Arkwright installs Watt's rotary steam engine in a cotton mill for the first time	Blake, *Poetical Sketches*
Cort's puddling process in wrought-iron manufacture	
Wedgwood's General Chamber of Manufactures	Paley, *Principles of Moral and Political Philosophy*
Boulton–Watt rotary spinning operation applied in cotton	Cowper, *The Task*
Cartwright patents rudimentary power weaving mill	
	Beckford, *Vathek*
Wilberforce's Proclamation Society	More, *Thoughts on the Manners of the Great*
Association for the Abolition of the Slave Trade	
Commencement of transportation to Australia	
Soane commences rebuilding of Bank of England	
Price's address to Revolution Society	Bentham, *Principles of Morals and Legislation*
Perry buys *Morning Chronicle* (Foxite Whig)	Price, *A Discourse on the Love of our Country*
Fall of the Bastille (July) precipitates French Revolution	
French Declaration of the Rights of Man and of the Citizen	

Date	Political and Diplomatic	Legislative Affairs
1790	Rift between Fox and Burke over French Revolution General election confirms Pitt's position Nootka Sound crisis with Spain Third Mysore War (1790–2)	Third motion (proposed by Fox) to repeal Test and Corporation Acts overwhelmingly defeated
1791	Ochakov crisis with Russia Constitutional societies founded in Sheffield and elsewhere	Canada Act creates Upper and Lower Canada
1792	Foundation of London Corresponding Society (radical), Friends of the People (Whig), and Reeves's Association Movement (loyalist) Royal Proclamation against seditious meetings and publication (May) Insurrection scare leads to royal proclamation calling out militia (Dec.)	Fox's Libel Act Alien Act creates Alien Office Commons vote in favour of slave trade abolition Middlesex Justices Act (June)
1793	French declare war against Britain (Feb.) First Coalition formed Board of Agriculture established with Arthur Young as Secretary	Irish Catholic 40s. freeholders enfranchised
1794	Hardy, Thelwall, Tooke, and other radicals tried for treason and acquitted Jay Treaty between Britain and United States Portland, Windham, Fitzwilliam, Loughborough join Pitt (July); Opposition Whigs reduced to a rump Disastrous Fitzwilliam episode in Dublin	Habeas Corpus suspended (May) Failure of Catholic Relief Bill in Irish Parliament
1795	Hastings acquitted of treason 'Pitt's Terror' launched with the Two Acts (Dec.) Orange Order founded	Hunger and high prices: 'Speenhamland' system of local poor relief adopted in some southern counties Seditious Meetings and Treasonable Practices Act Seditious Meetings and Assemblies Act Irish Insurrection Act
1796	Failure of 'pacification' proposals with France Spain enters war against Britain General election confirms Pitt's political supremacy	

People, Projects, Military Events, Foundations	*Publications*
First steam-rolling mill	Burke, *Reflections on the Revolution in France*
Birmingham riots: Priestley's house destroyed United Irishmen formed (Wolfe Tone) Ordnance Survey commenced	Paine, *Rights of Man*, Part I Burke, *Appeal from the New to the Old Whigs* Mackintosh, *Vindiciae Gallicae* Bentham, *Panopticon* Boswell, *Life of Johnson*
Manchester loyalists attack radicals Midlands canal mania Prison massacres in Paris (Sept.)	Paine, *Rights of Man*, Part II Wollstonecraft, *A Vindication of the Rights of Woman* Paley, *Reasons for Contentment*
Execution of Louis XVI (Jan.) Start of the Reign of Terror in France Duke of York's futile campaign in Flanders Capture and loss of Toulon First of several expeditions to West Indies	Godwin, *Enquiry concerning Political Justice* *Evangelical Magazine* (Dissenting)
Battle of the Glorious First of June (Howe) Britain occupies Corsica Duke of York's army forced to retreat in Flanders Execution of Robespierre marks end of Reign of Terror (July)	Paine, *The Age of Reason* Darwin, *Zoonomia* Blake, *Songs of Innocence and of Experience* Godwin, *Caleb Williams*
Food riots in Manchester Invention of hydraulic press (Joseph Bramah) Acquisition of Cape Colony and Malacca Failure of counter-revolutionary invasion force to Brittany London Missionary Society (mainly Congregational)	More, *Cheap Repository Tracts*
Ceylon acquired from the Dutch Jenner begins vaccination against smallpox Hoche fails to land in Bantry Bay (Dec.)	Burney, *Camilla* Lewis, *The Monk*

Date	Political and Diplomatic	Legislative Affairs
1797	Commercial and financial crisis Suspension of cash payments (Feb.) Spithead and Nore naval mutinies (Apr.–May) Foxites secede from Commons	Act against Administering Unlawful Oaths Seduction from Duty and Allegiance Act
1798	Peace plan mooted	Newspaper Publications Acts Pitt's Triple Assessment: taxes on wealth
1799	War of Second Coalition starts (Jan.) Proscription of London Corresponding Society, United Irishmen, and other 'revolutionary' societies Fourth Mysore War	Suppression of Treasonable and Seditious Societies Act Combination Act makes trade unions illegal Pitt's income tax
1800	Royal proclamation against subversives (Sept.) Armed Neutrality of the North (Dec.)	Second Combination Act makes trade unions even more illegal Irish Act of Union Crown Estates Act
1801	Pitt resigns, ostensibly over Catholic emancipation (Feb.) Addington becomes Prime Minister (Mar.) Peace preliminaries Union of Great Britain and Ireland comes into force	Habeas Corpus suspended First national census
1802	Peace of Amiens (Mar.) Failure of Despard conspiracy General election: return of first Radical MPs	Peel senior's Factory Act Militia Act Partial disbandment of Volunteers Balloted Army of Reserve

People, Projects, Military Events, Foundations	*Publications*
Napoleon's Army of England near Boulogne: first invasion scare (1797–1801)	Wilberforce, *Practical View of the Prevailing Religious System of Professed Christians*
Jervis's naval victory at Cape St Vincent (Feb.)	Coleridge, *Kubla Khan* (published 1816)
Insignificant French landing at Fishguard (Feb.)	Canning's *The Anti-Jacobin* (1797–8)
Duncan's naval victory at Camperdown (Oct.)	
Arrests of prominent radicals	
Holland House, Kensington	
Rebellion followed by bouts of ethnic and sectarian killing in parts of Ireland (May–June)	Malthus, *Essay on the Principle of Population*
Nelson destroys French fleet at battle of the Nile (Aug.)	Wordsworth and Coleridge, *Lyrical Ballads*
Boulton–Watt rotary steam engine applied to spinning mule	Reeves and Bowles's *Anti-Jacobin Review and Magazine* (1798–1821)
Sale of Orléans collection	
Beckford's Gothic folly (Wyatt's Fonthill Abbey) projected	
Sir Sidney Smith checks Bonaparte at Acre	
Wellesley first tastes action: Tipu Sultan killed at Seringapatam	
Church Missionary Society	
York's futile Dutch campaign	
Royal Institution	
Onset of Blagdon controversy	
Acquisition of Malta (Sept)	Burke, *Thoughts and Details on Scarcity*
Poor harvest, food shortages, and high prices	Edgeworth, *Castle Rackrent*
Robert Owen's New Lanark 'model factory' opens	
Henry Maudslay's precision screw-cutting lathe	
Richard Trevithick introduces double-acting high-pressure steam engine	
Oxford Examination Statute	
Another poor harvest, more food shortages and high prices	Opie, *The Father and Daughter*
Abercromby's victories at Aboukir and Alexandria (Mar.)	
Nelson's victory in first battle of Copenhagen	
Baines buys *Leeds Mercury*	
John Dalton's table of atomic weights	Cobbett's *Political Register*
Society for the Suppression of Vice	Jeffrey's *Edinburgh Review* (Whiggish)
	Christian Observer (evangelical)
	Bentham, *Civil and Penal Legislation*
	Paley, *Natural Theology*

Date	Political and Diplomatic	Legislative Affairs
1803	Britain declares war on France (May) Emmet's Irish rebellion (July) Second Maratha War (1803–5) Junction between 'Old' and 'New' Oppositions	Addington's revised income tax deducts at source Levy en Masse Act
1804	Fall of Addington's Government (Apr.) Pitt resumes as Prime Minister (May) Spain declares war on Britain	Pitt's Additional Force Act (June)
1805	War of Third Coalition starts Trade dispute with United States	
1806	Impeachment of Melville (formerly Dundas) Deaths of Pitt (Jan.) and Fox (Sept.) Grenville's Ministry of All the Talents (Feb.) Failure of Fox–Lauderdale peace mission 'Delicate investigation' into Princess Caroline Fourth Coalition with Russia and Prussia (Oct.) General election strengthens Grenvillites (Dec.) Dutch Cape Colony finally acquired	
1807	Fall of Talents Ministry (Mar.) Portland Prime Minister: Canning Foreign Secretary General election strengthens Government: Burdett elected for radical Westminster Chesapeake affair leads to American trade embargo (Dec.)	British slave trade abolished
1808	Start of Peninsular War: 13,000 troops dispatched to the Peninsula Asturian delegation visits Britain Convention of Cintra (Aug.) Political agitation over Orders in Council	

People, Projects, Military Events, Foundations	Publications
The 'great terror' or invasion scare (1803–5)	Malthus, *Essay on the Principle of Population* (2nd edition) Lancaster, *Improvements in Education*
The 'great terror' or invasion scare continued British and Foreign Bible Society Trevithick's steam locomotive for Penydafren ironworks Decision to build Martello towers Coleridge's sojourn in Malta (1804–5)	
Battle of Trafalgar (Oct.); Nelson's death and 'apotheosis' British Institute for Development of Fine Arts	
British expelled from Buenos Aires and Montevideo Vellore Mutiny Britain blockades France and her allies (May) Napoleon blockades Britain: Berlin Decrees set up the 'Continental System' (Nov.) Battle of Austerlitz (Dec.): Britain left to fight alone Davy isolates the elements of sodium and potassium Gaslight installed in a Manchester cotton mill	Wilkie, *Village Politicians*
Joint-stock canal boom starts No-popery excitement at election Treaty of Tilsit marks zenith of Napoleon's power Canning's bombardment of Copenhagen (Sept.) Order in Council attacks French coastal trade (Jan.) Intensification of trade war with France (Nov.)	Wordsworth, 'Ode: Intimations of Immortality from Recollections of Early Childhood' Spence, *Britain Independent of Commerce* Cobbett, *Perish Commerce* (1807–8)
Manchester weavers' strike Royal Lancasterian Institution British and Foreign School Society Gains from Wellington's victories in Portugal thrown away by Convention of Cintra	Mill, *Commerce Defended* Hunt's *Examiner* Dalton, *A New System of Chemical Philosophy* (1808–10)

Date	Political and Diplomatic	Legislative Affairs
1809	Duke of York scandal Riots over Burdett's commitment to the Tower Fifth Coalition formed Canning and Castlereagh fight duel Portland resigns; Perceval becomes Prime Minister (Oct.)	Curwen's Bribery Act curtails sale of parliamentary seats
1810	George III goes permanently mad (Oct.)	Bullion Report (Huskisson, Horner, Thornton) recommends resumption of cash payments within two years
1811	British African squadron established to suppress foreign slave trade Sidmouth's attempt to license Dissenting preachers not only fails but leads to politicizing of evangelical Dissent	Act to establish the Prince of Wales as Regent Debate on Bank restriction postpones resumption until after the war Vansittart's resolutions on value carried in Commons
1812	War against United States (1812–15) Perceval assassinated (May) Sixth Coalition: Britain, Russia, Spain, Portugal (June) After long delay Liverpool succeeds as Prime Minister (July) General election: Government supporters outnumber Opposition by more than 2–1	Orders in Council repealed (June)
1813	Prussia joins allies against France (Feb.) Canningite 'party' disbands Austria joins allies against France (June)	East India Company's commercial monopoly in India ended; 'pious clause' inserted in its Charter Unitarians admitted to benefits of Toleration Act Vansittart's New Plan of Finance
1814	Treaties of Chaumont, Fontainebleau (Mar.–Apr.) Napoleon abdicates: end of French war (Apr.) Congress of Vienna (Sept. 1814–June 1815) Pacification of Ghent between Britain and United States (Dec.)	Repeal of Statute of Artificers (apprenticeship laws) Cash payments postponed for one year

People, Projects, Military Events, Foundations	*Publications*
Retreat of Sir John Moore's army to Corunna	Gifford's *Quarterly Review* (Tory)
Wellington's victories at Oporto (Portugal), Talavera (Spain)	Wordsworth, *Convention of Cintra*
Disastrous failure of Walcheren expedition	More, *Coelebs in Search of a Wife*
Royal Jubilee (Oct.)	Byron, *English Bards and Scotch Reviewers*
Covent Garden 'old price' riots; disturbances in Nottingham	
Nash starts work on Regent Street	
Wellington's defence of Torres Vedras (Portugal)	Crabbe, *The Borough*
Onset of 'Cambridge controversy' regarding overseas missions	
Wellington's victory at Fuentes de Onoro	Watson and Norris purchase *British Critic*
Severe commercial and financial crisis peaks	Austen, *Sense and Sensibility*
National Society for Promoting the Education of the Poor	
Second census shows frightening rise in population	
Climax of Luddite riots in East Midlands, Lancs., and Yorks.	
Mercantile campaign for repeal of Orders in Council	
Price of wheat rises to scarcity levels (120*s.* per quarter)	Barbauld, *Eighteen Hundred and Eleven*
Peak of Luddite riots	Davy, *Elements of Chemical Philosophy*
Nash begins to orientalize Brighton Pavilion	Byron, *Childe Harold* (1812–18)
Wellington's victories at Ciudad Rodrigo, Badajoz, Salamanca (Spain)	Crabbe, *Tales*
Napoleon's invasion and retreat from Moscow renders it likely that he will eventually lose the European war	
Wellington wins victories at Burgos and Vitoria (Spain); then invades France (Oct.)	Robert Owen, *A New View of Society* (1813–16)
Methodist Missionary Society	Austen, *Pride and Prejudice*
Battle of the Nations at Leipzig (Oct.)	Byron, *The Giaour*
	P. B. Shelley, *Queen Mab*
Allies invade France	Austen, *Mansfield Park*
Stephenson builds steam locomotive	Scott, *Waverley*
British troops overrun Washington, raze the White House (Aug.)	Wordsworth, *The Excursion*
Kean's passionate Shylock at Drury Lane: 'the defining moment in Romantic drama'	

Date	Political and Diplomatic	Legislative Affairs
1815	Napoleon's 'Hundred Days' (Feb.–June) After Napoleon's final defeat, Treaty of Paris imposes tougher terms on France (Nov.) Quadruple Alliance of Britain, Austria, Prussia, and Russia followed by Holy Alliance of Russia, Austria, and Prussia (Nov.)	Corn Law excludes foreign wheat unless home price is at or above 80s. per quarter Apothecaries Act points way to general practitioners Cash payments postponed for one more year
1816	Canning returns to Cabinet as President of Board of Control	Proposal for peacetime half-rate property tax defeated Cash payments postponed for two further years
1817	Grenvillite 'party' breaks up Death of Horner deprives Opposition of economic expertise Third Maratha War	Habeas Corpus suspended, seditious meetings banned Select Committee on high cost of relieving the poor Trustee Savings Banks Acts (1817–18) Poor Employment Act
1818	General election confirms Government's strength Congress of Aix-la-Chapelle introduces France to Concert of European powers Death of Romilly deprives Opposition of legal expertise Tierney becomes Opposition leader in Commons	Parish Vestries Act Habeas Corpus restored Church Building Act Cash payments postponed for yet one more year
1819	Singapore acquired by Stamford Raffles Political crisis following Peterloo massacre: Fitzwilliam sacked from lord lieutenancy	Act to resume cash payments by 1823 ('Peel's Act') £3m increase in taxes Act for Protection of Children in Cotton Mills Six Acts against radical press and agitation (Dec.)
1820	Death of George III; accession of George IV (Jan.) General election confirms Government's strength 'Trial' of Queen Caroline: Canning resigns Castlereagh's 'State Paper' criticizes Holy Alliance (May) Congress of Troppau (Oct.)	Bill of Pains and Penalties (to dissolve the King's marriage and deprive Queen Caroline of her titles and privileges) abandoned Select Committee on agricultural distress Select Committee on foreign trade (1820–4) London merchants' petition calls for free trade

People, Projects, Military Events, Foundations	*Publications*
British defeat in battle of New Orleans (Jan.) Wellington and Blücher defeat Napoleon at Waterloo (June) Whitbread commits suicide	

Economic depression and unemployment
Spa Fields riots
Hampden Clubs established in provinces:
    call for parliamentary reform
	Marcet, *Conversations on Political*
	    Economy
	Austen, *Emma*

Death of Princess Charlotte Augusta
March of the Blanketeers, Pentrich rising,
    St Bartholomew's Fair demonstration
	Wooler's *Black Dwarf* (radical)
	Wilson's and Lockhart's *Blackwood's*
	    Edinburgh Magazine (High Tory)
	Ricardo, *Principles of Political Economy*
	    and Taxation
	Bentham, *Plan of Parliamentary Reform*
	James Mill, *History of British India*

Institute of Civil Engineers Davy invents miners' safety lamp	Sherwood, *The History of the Fairchild* *Family* (1818–47) Mary Shelley, *Frankenstein* Keats, *Endymion* Hazlitt, *Lectures on the English Poets* Austen, *Northanger Abbey and Persuasion*

'Manchester massacre' or 'battle of
    Peterloo' (Aug.)
	Byron, *Don Juan* (1819–24)
	Martin, *The Fall of Babylon*
	Chalmers, *The Christian and Civic*
	    Economy of Large Towns (1819–26)

Cato Street conspiracy to murder Cabinet Launch of first iron steamship Manchester Chamber of Commerce	P. B. Shelley, *Prometheus Unbound* Hook's *John Bull* Malthus, *Principles of Political Economy* Buckland, *Vindiciae Geologicae* Egan, *Life in London* (1820–1)

Date	Political and Diplomatic	Legislative Affairs
1821	George IV's Coronation: exclusion of Caroline leads to pro-Caroline riots (July) Caroline dies (Aug.) Congress of Laibach	Reduction of preference on colonial timber Backbench revolt: abolition of malt duties (Mar.) Ministerial threat to resign brings backbenchers to heel Cash payments resumed two years ahead of schedule Select Committee on agriculture: Huskisson's report signals 'new agricultural policy' Catholic Relief Bill passes Commons, loses in Lords
1822	Peel replaces Sidmouth as Home Secretary (Jan.) Wynn's admission to Cabinet signals Grenvillite support for Government Castlereagh commits suicide (Aug.) and Canning becomes Foreign Secretary (Sept.) Congress of Verona reveals rifts with European allies (Oct.–Dec.)	Indecency and Vagrancy Acts (1822–4) Select Committee on agricultural distress Commons forces retrenchment on ministers Ministerial threat to resign again brings backbenchers to heel Proposal to increase agricultural protection decisively rejected by 219 votes (May)
1823	Robinson replaces Vansittart as Chancellor of the Exchequer (Jan.) Huskisson becomes President of the Board of Trade (Jan.); enters Cabinet (Nov.) O'Connell's Irish Catholic Association 'Cottage coterie' becomes active on foreign policy	Gaols Act: Peel's prison reform Reduction of protective and excise duties by Robinson and Huskisson Reciprocity of Duties Act breaches Navigation Code Warehousing Act aims to boost entrepôt trade
1824	Canning recognizes independence of Buenos Aires, Mexico, Colombia Canning provokes George IV's wrath by attending dinner of reforming Lord Mayor, Waithman (Apr.)	Repeal of Spitalfields Acts Repeal of Combination Acts against trade unions Church Building Act
1825	Canning ingratiates himself with George IV; Wellington is furious	Strikes lead to partial re-enactment of Combination Laws Suppression of Irish associations Catholic Relief Bill passes Commons, loses in Lords Bubble Act repealed Corn released from warehouses by Order in Council

People, Projects, Military Events, Foundations	Publications
Agricultural distress, county meetings and petitions King's state visit to Dublin	Southey, *A Vision of Judgment* Byron, *The Vision of Judgment* Constable, *The Hay Wain* James Mill, *Principles of Political Economy* *Manchester Guardian* Scott, *Kenilworth*
Agricultural distress, county meetings and petitions Last ever annual surplus on merchandise trade King's state visit to Edinburgh	De Quincey, *Confessions of an English Opium Eater* Wilkie, *Chelsea Pensioners Reading the Gazette of the Battle of Waterloo*
Law Society Royal Manchester Institution First mechanics institutes founded in London and Glasgow Wilberforce and Buxton found Anti-Slavery Society Monroe Doctrine enunciated (Dec.)	Wakley and Cobbett's *Lancet*
Lord Byron dies at Missolonghi in Greek War of Independence (Apr.) National Gallery Royal Society for the Prevention of Cruelty to Animals Lincoln College starts trend for Gothicizing Oxford's buildings Robert Owen's New Harmony settlement Economy overheats	Southern and Bowring's *Westminster Review* (radical) Hogg, *Private Memoirs and Confessions of a Justified Sinner*
Severe commercial and financial crisis (Dec.) Rothschild saves Bank of England from crashing Stockton–Darlington railway opens Fonthill Abbey's tower collapses for the last time	Hodgskin, *Labour Defended against the Claims of Capital* Hazlitt, *The Spirit of the Age*

Date	Political and Diplomatic	Legislative Affairs
1826	Ministerial crisis over issue of exchequer bills General election: pro-Catholic gains in Ireland Canning sends troops to Tagus to defend Portugal from Spain Straits Settlement incorporates Singapore, Malacca, Penang	Act to allow Bank of England branches Corn released from warehouses by Order in Council Liverpool, Peel, Wellington prepare new Corn Law Peel's revision of laws on theft and of administration of criminal justice
1827	Liverpool suffers stroke (Feb.), Canning Prime Minister (Apr.) Six Cabinet ministers refuse to serve under Canning, who forms coalition Government with three Whigs Treaty of London recognizes Greek autonomy within Turkish empire; allows Russian fleet into Mediterranean (July) Deaths of York, the Ultra Tory heir to the throne (Jan.), and of Canning (Aug.) Robinson (now Lord Goderich) becomes Prime Minister Bitter quarrel between Huskisson and Herries	Wellington destroys Canning's corn law in Lords Finance Committee to consider issues of expenditure, revenue, and debt Peel's consolidation, simplification, and mitigation, of the criminal law (Feb.)
1828	Goderich resigns, Wellington becomes Prime Minister, Peel Home Secretary (Jan.) Canningites (Huskisson, Palmerston, Grant, Dudley) quit Government (May–June) O'Connell elected at County Clare (July), but being a Catholic cannot take his seat George IV attempts to stifle discussion of Catholic emancipation Shouting match between Protestant and Catholic mobs at Penenden Heath (Oct.)	Repeal of Test and Corporation Acts extends civil liberties of Dissenters New Corn Law reduces levels of protection according to a sliding scale East Retford and Penryn disfranchised Finance Committee: Herries' report
1829	Peel and Wellington announce their conversion to Catholic emancipation (Feb.) King dismisses, then reappoints, ministers (Mar.) Ultra Tory revolt against ministers	Catholic Relief Act (emancipation) Suppression of Irish political societies Irish 40s. freeholders disfranchised Peel's Metropolitan Police Act Sinking fund abandoned
1830	Britain, France, Russia guarantee Greek independence (Feb.) George IV dies; William IV succeeds (June) General election (June–Aug.): indeterminate results but traditional influence under attack	Civil List Act Act to deregulate beer and cider Torrent of petitions in favour of parliamentary reform (from Nov.)

People, Projects, Military Events, Foundations	Publications
Bankruptcies proliferate Albury Group (Drummond, Irving, Haldane) anticipate the end of the world J. S. Mill suffers nervous breakdown Society for the Diffusion of Useful Knowledge (Brougham) Weavers' riots in East Lancashire London Zoological Society	Buckland, *Reliquiae Diluvianae*
Battle of Navarino (Oct.) Reformation Society	Clare, *The Shepherd's Calendar* Keble, *The Christian Year*
Arnold becomes headmaster of Rugby School Wöhler's partial synthesis of urea University College London	Pusey, *An Historical Enquiry into the Probable Causes of the Rationalist Character lately Predominant in the Theology of Germany* Combe, *Constitution of Man* Haldane's *Record* (radical evangelical)
King's College London Grand General Union of Cotton Spinners Manchester weavers' riots Shocking case of people murdered for the value of their bodies to medical schools: Burke and Hare in Edinburgh Oxford and Cambridge boat race	Southey, *Colloquies of Society* Carlyle, 'Signs of the Times' Irving's *Morning Watch* (radical evangelical)
Birmingham Political Union (Jan.) followed by others Huskisson killed at opening of Liverpool–Manchester railway (Sept.) Start of Swing riots in southern counties (from Aug.)	Macaulay, 'Southey's Colloquies on Society' Lyell, *Principles of Geology* (1830–3) Coleridge, *On the Constitution of Church and State* Cobbett, *Rural Rides* Tennyson, *Poems, Chiefly Lyrical*

Date	Political and Diplomatic	Legislative Affairs
	July Revolution in France Wellington's Government resigns after defeat on civil list (Nov.) Grey forms coalition Government (Whigs, Liberals, ex-Canningites)	
1831	Committee of Four drafts Reform Bill Fiasco over Budget (Mar.) Reform Bill checked: Grey dissolves Parliament (Apr.) General election: huge reform majority Riots in Bristol, Nottingham, etc. following rejection of Reform Bill in Lords	First Reform Bill carried in Commons by 1 vote (Mar.) Second Reform Bill passes Commons (July) Amended Second Reform Bill passes Commons (Sept.) Second Reform Bill thrown out by Lords (Oct.) Truck Act makes payments in kind illegal Hobhouse's Vestries Act
1832	Grey resigns after Tory spoiling motion in Lords Days of May (popular protest) Wellington's failure to form Government Grey resumes as Prime Minister, King consents to create peers if necessary, and Lords surrender General election: huge majority for Government	Third Reform Bill passes both Houses (Mar.–Apr.) Tory spoiling motion in Lords (May) Reform Act passes Lords after threat to create new peers (June) Sadler's Committee on Child Labour (1832–3) Poor Law Commission (1832–4) Anatomy Act
1833	United Committee of Dissenters Clause 147 of Temporalities Bill abandoned Crucial debates reaffirm gold standard (Mar.–Apr.)	Abolition of slavery in British territories Report of Commission on Children's Employment in Factories Factory Act inaugurates inspection regime (Aug.) Select Committee on Agriculture Marriages permitted in Nonconformist chapels Irish Coercion Act; Irish Church Temporalities Act First state grant to churches for building schools East India Company's China trade monopoly ended
1834	British squadron helps depose Miguel (Portugal) Quadruple Alliance with France, Spain, and Portugal Dorset, or Tolpuddle, martyrs transported Russell revives Clause 147 (May) Stanley, Graham, Ripon (Derby Dilly) resign	Poor Law Amendment Act, or 'New Poor Law' Bastardy Laws tightened Select Committee on drunkenness Maxwell's Select Committee on hand-loom weavers (1834–5) Althorp's Bill to end Church rates withdrawn

People, Projects, Military Events, Foundations	*Publications*
Disturbances in south London, strikes in North	
National Association for the Protection of Labour	
Geoffroy–Cuvier debate in Paris	
National Union of the Working Classes (May)	Sedgwick, *Addresses at the Geological Society*
National Political Union (Oct.)	Hetherington's *Poor Man's Guardian*
British Association for the Advancement of Science	Peacock, *Crotchet Castle*
	Grote, *Essentials of Parliamentary Reform*
Darwin begins voyage on the Beagle	
British and Foreign Temperance Society	
Exeter Hall opens in the Strand	
Carlton Club formed to focus Conservative parliamentary activity	Knight's *Penny Magazine*
	Martineau's *Illustrations of Political Economy* (1832–4)
Start of Brunel's Great Western Railway	Keble, *National Apostasy*
Manchester Statistical Society	*Tracts for the Times against Popery and Dissent* (1833–41)
Deposition of Edward Irving from the Church of Scotland by the Presbytery of Annan	Arnold, *Principles of Church Reform*
	Chalmers, *The Adaptation of External Nature to the Moral and Intellectual Constitution of Man* (one of eight Bridgewater Treatises, 1833–6)
	Carlyle, *Sartor Resartus*
Destruction by fire of the Palace of Westminster	
Robert Owen's Grand National Consolidated Trades Union	
Controversy at Oxford and Cambridge over admission of Dissenters	
Palace of Westminster largely destroyed by fire	

Date	Political and Diplomatic	Legislative Affairs
	Grey resigns, Melbourne Prime Minister (July) King sacks Melbourne, appoints Peel (Dec.) Peel's Tamworth manifesto (Dec.)	
1835	Lichfield House compact (Mar.): Whigs, Liberals, Irish, Radicals combine against Peel's minority Government General election: Conservatives gain c.100 seats but still outnumbered by 112 Melbourne replaces Peel as Prime Minister (Apr.)	Municipal Corporations Act paves way for urban local government reform (Sept.) Maxwell Committee on hand-loom weavers recommends legal minimum wage: proposal rejected in Commons
1836	Church Rate Abolition Society Reform Club (Whig–Liberal)	Tithe Commutation Act Ecclesiastical Commission Prisoners' Counsel Act Irish Constabulary Act Select Committee on Agricultural Distress report
1837	Death of William IV, accession of Victoria (June) General election: Conservatives gain 40 seats and have majority in England; Radical losses Rebellions in Ontario and Quebec	Civil registration of births, marriages, and deaths Royal Commission on hand-loom weavers headed by Loyd and Senior
1838	Russell's 'finality' speech against further reform Radicals continue to attack Government, demanding secret ballot, frequent elections, free trade in corn	Poor Law extended to Ireland Pluralities Act
1839	Treaty of London confirms Belgian independence First Opium War with China Suspension of Jamaica Assembly Melbourne resigns (May); Bedchamber crisis; Peel declines government; Melbourne resumes Chartists' first national petition rejected (July) Durham Report paves way for united Canada First Afghan War (1839–42) Aden acquired	County Police Act Education Committee of the Privy Council Infant Custody Act
1840	Loyal National Repeal Association (Ireland) Convention to guarantee Turkish integrity Upper and Lower Canada united (July)	Penny Post introduced (Jan.) Select Committee on import duties Select Committee on banks of issue (1840–1) Irish Corporations Act

People, Projects, Military Events, Foundations	*Publications*

Institute of British Architects
Protestant Association

Competition for new Palace of Westminster	Pugin, *Contrasts*
London Working Men's Association (June)	Dickens, *Sketches by Boz* and *Pickwick*
University College London receives charter	*Papers* (1836–7)
Central Society for Education	

Severe commercial and financial crisis	Dickens, *Oliver Twist* (1837–9)
(until 1843)	Carlyle, *The French Revolution*
Elliotson performs mesmeric experiments	Bentley's *Miscellany*
on O'Key sisters	O'Connor's *Northern Star*

Royal Agricultural Society of England	Dickens, *Nicholas Nickelby*
People's Charter: Six Points (May)	Gladstone, *The State in its Relations with*
Anti-Corn Law League, Manchester (Sept.)	*the Church*
Public Record Office	Froude, *Remains* (1838–9)
	Maurice, *The Kingdom of Christ*

Eglinton Tournament	Carlyle, *Chartism*
Richard Owen interprets Stonesfield	Neale's *Ecclesiologist*
fossil jaws	Turner, *The Fighting Temeraire*
Chartists' National Convention (Feb.)	
Bull Ring riots	
Newport rising (Nov.)	
Grand National at Aintree	

Marriage of Victoria and Albert	Dickens, *Master Humphrey's Clock*
National Charter Association	(including *The Old Curiosity Shop* and
Health of Towns Association	*Barnaby Rudge*) (1840–1)
Building starts on Barry's design for Houses	
of Parliament	

Date	Political and Diplomatic	Legislative Affairs
		Church reform: Ecclesiastical Duties and Revenue Act; Deans and Chapters Act
1841	Straits Convention guarantees Turkish independence; all warships banned from Dardanelles (July) Baring's proposal to reduce sugar duty defeated General election: Conservatives sweep counties and small boroughs; win by 76 seats (July) Melbourne resigns, Peel becomes Prime Minister (Aug.) South Australia becomes Crown colony	Act to establish Jerusalem bishopric Royal Commission on hand-loom weavers reports that the laws of supply and demand must prevail over the law of charity
1842	Massacre of British forces in Afghanistan (Jan.) Webster–Ashburton Boundary Treaty with United States Treaty of Nanking ends Opium War Chartists' second national petition rejected (May)	Peel's budget: first peacetime income tax and wide-ranging reduction of tariffs New Corn Law reduces levels of protection Introduction of long copyrights Chadwick's report on sanitary conditions Mines Act bans underground employment of women and children
1843	Monster meeting at Clontarf leads to O'Connell's arrest	Theatre Regulation Act ends monopoly of patent theatres in London New Parishes Act Graham forced by Nonconformists to withdraw bill for education of factory children Devon Commission on Irish Land (1843–5) Canadian Corn Act reaffirms colonial preference
1844	Young Ireland founded Ructions in Conservative Party over proposals on sugar duties and factory hours	Bank Charter Act (July) Joint Stock Companies Act Factory Act (Textiles) restricts working hours of women and children Dissenters' Chapels Act Charitable Bequests (Ireland) Act Royal Commission on the Health of Towns

People, Projects, Military Events, Foundations	*Publications*
National Association for Promoting the Political and Social Improvement of the People (Lovett's 'New Move') Serious economic distress Intense Chartist activity	Carlyle, *On Heroes, Hero-Worship, and the Heroic in History* Newman, Tract 90 Pugin, *True Principles of Pointed or Christian Architecture* Lemon and Mayhew's *Punch*
Pentonville Prison Further Chartist disturbances including Plug Plot Complete Suffrage Union	Duffy's *The Nation* Tennyson, *Morte d'Arthur*
Chalmers leads Disruption: Scottish Free Church (May)	Carlyle, *Past and Present* Dickens, *A Christmas Carol* and *Martin Chuzzlewit* Disraeli, *Coningsby* (1843–4) *The Economist* (free-trade newspaper)
Buckingham's last great splurge at Stowe Liston performs operation under ether anaesthesia Robert Owen's Rochdale Co-operative Society of Equitable Pioneers (Dec.) Miall's Anti-State Church Association Young Men's Christian Association	Chambers, *Vestiges of Creation* Thackeray, *Barry Lyndon*

Date	Political and Diplomatic	Legislative Affairs
1845	Russell's Edinburgh Letter calls for free trade in corn (Nov.) Peel resigns over Corn Law; Russell fails to form a ministry; Peel resumes office (Dec.)	Budget reduces import tariffs and eliminates all export duties Maynooth College grant increased Academic Colleges (Ireland) Bill Museums Act allows large towns to levy halfpenny rate for museums
1846	Corn Laws repealed after bitter debates Peel resigns after defeat on Irish coercion (June) Conservative Party divides into Peelites and Protectionists Imbroglio with France over Spanish marriages	Corn Law repeal carried in Commons (May) by cross-party alliance; only 112 Conservatives vote in favour Corn Law repeal carried in Lords, followed immediately by Peel's defeat on Irish coercion in the Commons Liverpool Sanitary Act paves way for appointment of local medical officer of health

People, Projects, Military Events, Foundations	*Publications*
Evangelical Alliance	Newman, *Essay on Development*
Andover workhouse scandal	Disraeli, *Sybil*
Chartist Cooperative Land Society	Browning, *Dramatic Romances and Lyrics*
Newman admitted into the Roman Catholic faith (Oct.)	
Serious failure of Irish potato crop becomes apparent (Oct.)	
National Club	
Famine in Ireland	Rymer, *Sweeney Todd, the Demon Barber of Fleet Street*
Standard railway gauge adopted	Dickens, *Dombey and Son* (1846–8)

Bibliography

The works cited below have been selected somewhat arbitrarily from the total number consulted. A few of them appeared after this book went to press. Primary sources and unpublished theses are referred to in footnotes to the text but are not mentioned in this Bibliography.

GENERAL SURVEYS

In the hands of historians, long stretches of chronology become shaped like landscapes, with peaks and troughs, fault lines and watersheds. The earliest attempts to map this terrain were made by so-called Whig historians beginning with T. B. Macaulay, who was also a prominent participant in events, and culminating with his great-nephew G. M. Trevelyan. Their key assumption, derived from the Scottish Enlightenment, was that countries progress naturally through stages, and that internal political struggles mainly reflect the tensions caused by underlying social processes. Specifically they argued that from 1783 to 1830 a conservative ruling elite sought to hold back the legislative clock in the face of rampant social change, and that it was only after Whig politicians finally achieved office that the necessary work of reconstruction was attempted, making the 1830s a great watershed. In *The Passing of the Great Reform Act* (1914), J. R. M. Butler wrote that 'the passing of the Great Reform Bill takes us suddenly into another air; we leave the remote world of the eighteenth century ... The old aristocratic system begins to crumble, and the feet of the nation are set on the path that leads to democracy' (p. vii). Likewise, according to A. V. Dicey's more schematic *Lectures on the Relation between Law and Public Opinion during the Nineteenth Century* (1905),

Passionate enthusiasm for parliamentary reform and all the innovations to which it gave birth, displaced, as it were, *in a moment* the obstinate toryism which for nearly half a century had been the accepted creed ... In 1830 legislative inertia came with apparent suddenness to an end ... The English people had at last come to perceive the intolerable incongruity between a rapidly changing social condition and the practical unchangeableness of the law.

What followed was a period of Benthamite reform in which power was transferred from the aristocracy to the middle class, individual liberty was extended, slavery abolished, and the law humanized (pp. 31, 110–11). The most explicit statement of this Whig interpretation came in the opening pages of George Macaulay Trevelyan's *British History in the Nineteenth Century* (1922).

In the ... fifty years, ending with the Great Reform Bill of 1832, the Industrial Revolution is, in its social consequences, mainly destructive. It destroys, in town and country, the forms and pieties of the old English life, that could not be harnessed to the new machinery. The government, while it prohibited all legal and political change as 'Jacobinism', urged on the economic revolution. The result was that by 1832 there was scant provision for the political, municipal, educational, or sanitary needs of the population, most of whom were not even tolerably clothed or fed. The laws and institutions had been kept back in one place, while the men and women had been moved on to another, where they were living as if it were outside society, under a guard of yeomanry and magistrates. The period [after 1832] is the story of the building up of the new world, of a wholly new type of society, infinitely more complicated and interdependent in its parts, more full of potential for progress or disaster, than anything the world has before seen. (pp. xv–xvi)[1]

The reference to possible disaster reflected post-First World War angst. Communism and fascism in Europe, as well as unemployment at home, had punctured Trevelyan's confidence in progress and civilization. By contrast historians of the Far Left, who broadly welcomed what was happening in Soviet Russia, retained their enthusiasm for the 1830s. Notably Sidney and Beatrice Webb, contrasting the enlightened administration of their own day with what they wrongly conceived to be the stagnant pool of local government in the eighteenth century, isolated the 1832 Reform Act and the Municipal Corporations Act of 1835 as crucial instruments of transition. Even more important was the New Poor Law of 1834, a 'revolutionary' piece of legislation which 'not only gave a dogmatically uniform direction to English Poor Law policy, but also incidentally transformed the system of Local Government which had endured for over three centuries, and established, for the first time . . . the principle of centralised executive control of local administration'.[2]

A more common inter-war response than the Webbs' was a modified version of Whig history, which retained its linear perspective and its emphasis on reform but was more circumspect about the consequences. This approach was pioneered by the hugely influential French historian Élie Halévy in his six-volume *Histoire du peuple anglais au XIXe siècle*. Volume I, *Angleterre en 1815* (1912), was a magnificent survey but gave an impression that the country had been set in aspic before the nineteenth century. The following volumes all emphasized progress and reform, but compared with Whig history the triumphalism was muted. Halévy's introduction to his second volume in 1923 faced up honestly to the change or mood following the First World War.

I very soon found myself in the presence of Canning . . . but I have been unable to see in him the great idealist, the hero of liberty, whose memory was revered by so many Englishmen fifty years ago. Am I mistaken in this? . . . I would not deny the possibility that my estimate has been influenced by the events of contemporary history . . . Had I been a contemporary of Canning, it is probable that . . . I should have rejoiced to watch him so successfully dividing, teasing, and flouting Governments so reactionary, so mean, and so mischievous that they were objects of scorn and hatred to every generous heart. And even if I had written ten years ago, I might possibly have pardoned Canning many of those dangerous decisions which were continually leading him to the brink of war . . . But in the interval I have learnt what war means; therefore I feel an instinctive distrust of a statesman who made a career for himself out of

---

[1] Trevelyan's understanding of the social effects of industrialization was largely based on the pessimistic writings of J. L. and Barbara Hammond, notably *The Village Labourer, 1760–1832: A Study in the Government of England before the Reform Bill* (1911) and *The Town Labourer, 1760–1832: The New Civilisation* (1917). He was to modify his view slightly after reading his Cambridge colleague J. H. Clapham's *An Economic History of Modern Britain*, i: *The Early Railway Age 1820–1850* (Cambridge, 1926).

[2] S. and B. Webb, *English Local Government from the Revolution to the Municipal Corporations Act. English Poor Law Policy Part II: The Last Hundred Years*, 2 vols. (1929), i. 1.

diplomatic crises, and shone most brilliantly when the condition of the world was darkest. I prefer to a Canning—possibly more liberal, at least in his speeches, but certainly more bellicose—a Robert Peel, who was proud to call himself a Conservative, but was a far more resolute friend of peace.[3]

Commentators had not hitherto held Peel in much esteem. To Conservative historians he was the man who had betrayed the party twice by his about-turns. Liberals had acknowledged his role in persuading the party of resistance to pass two crucial pieces of legislation, but to them he was merely a 'useful idiot' whose strategic concessions at specific junctures could not to be compared with the work of enthusiastic reformers such as Grey, Russell, and Gladstone, men who had borne 'the burden and heat of the day'. In the inter-war period, however, those reformers came to seem less self-evidently on the right side of history. Were they not woolly-minded Menshevik types whose headlong changes might well have led to a Russian-style revolution? Instead praise came to be heaped on Conservatives like Peel and Disraeli who, instead of behaving like the Tsar, had educated their party into the need for gradual concessions. Peel especially came to be regarded as someone who embodied the British genius for managed change, the statesman who 'saved the Church of England' by forcing it to reform itself, and by implication saved England from revolution.

Historians of the generation after the Second World War largely abandoned the evolutionary perspective in favour of structural (or modernist) approaches, one effect of which was to diminish the importance previously attached to the 1830s. Norman Gash, clearly influenced by Lewis Namier's work on the eighteenth century,[4] empha- sized how little the Great Reform Act changed the basic structure of politics in *Politics in the Age of Peel: A Study in the Technique of Parliamentary Representation, 1830–1850* (1953). Similarly, in *The Politics of Deference: A Study of the Mid-Nineteenth Century English Political System* (Hassocks, 1976), D. C. Moore showed how pockets of social and electoral deference survived well beyond 1832. Gash and Moore argued, though in different ways, that the intention behind the Reform Act was to rebuild the aristocratic system. Committed as they were to the view that society was made up of 'aristocracy and people', both historians regarded the so-called middle class as too fragmented and disparate, and too intent upon assimilation *into* the aristocracy, to have exercised any social or cultural authority of its own.[5] Peel remained a great statesman, especially for Gash, but his role appeared less heroic than in Halévy's work, if only because Gash's emphasis on deference, aristocratic paternalism, and social harmony suggested that the old order did not need much saving. At the same time, the vaunted reforms of the 1830s were made to seem less revolutionary by a clutch of historians who wrote about a 'revolution in government', but who meant by that phrase a conservative process of gradual and centrally directed social reform. The arch-bureaucrat Edwin Chadwick, hitherto neglected, was the subject of two biographies, by S. E. Finer and R. A. Lewis, in 1952. That coincidence prompted manifestos by Oliver MacDonagh and George

---

[3] É. Halévy, *The Liberal Awakening (1815–1830)*, trans. E. I. Watkin, rev. edn. (1961), pp. ix–x.

[4] Especially L. B. Namier, *The Structure of Politics at the Accession of George III.* (2 vols., 1929) and *England in the Age of the American Revolution* (1930).

[5] This is also the leitmotiv of Norman McCord, *British History, 1815–1906* (Oxford, 1991).

Kitson Clark in 1958–9,[6] and these in turn led to a number of detailed studies such as MacDonagh's *A Pattern of Government Growth, 1800–60: The Passenger Acts and their Enforcement* (1961), in which civil servants were depicted as participants in an 'official mind', reacting pragmatically to social evils as and when they were identified, rather than to some Whiggish notion of public opinion.[7] This Cambridge version of policy-making, dubbed 'tory' by Jennifer Hart,[8] owed much to Dicey and nothing to Max Weber, and was partly designed to cut the influence of Bentham and the Utilitarians down to size.

In contrast to these conservative approaches, left-wing historians in the 1950s and 1960s developed a Marxist analysis based on class-consciousness, class struggle, and the contradictions of capitalism, but much of their energy was dissipated in explaining why the expected English revolution never happened. Meanwhile, historians from the 'centre Left' proposed a marxis*ant* framework which focused on competition between different sections of society. The most important contribution here was Asa Briggs's *The Age of Improvement 1783–1867* (1959), but S. G. Checkland's *The Rise of Industrial Society in England 1815–1885* (1964), though less influential, was almost as stimulating. Their explanation of politics in terms of underlying social and economic tensions was similar to that of the Whig historians, but unlike the latter they were not fixated with political parties and ideologies, which they regarded as largely epiphenomenal. They too cut the Whig decade of the 1830s down to size by placing it in a longer continuum that stretched back to the 1780s and forward to the third quarter of the nineteenth century. Whereas MacDonagh and Kitson Clark were influenced by welfare state perspectives, historians like Briggs and Checkland seemed to respond to the neo-Keynesian and corporate politics of their own day, in which power was exercised less by political parties than by the Confederation of British Industry and the trade unions. Whatever the impulse, their explanations of nineteenth-century politics focused on movements in the value of money,[9] on rent and price indexes, and on profit maximization by extra-parliamentary interest groups. Prominent among the latter interventions were Patricia Hollis, *Pressure from Without in Early Victorian England* (1974), D. A. Hamer, *The Politics of Electoral Pressure: A Study in the History of Victorian Reform Agitations* (1977), Brian Harrison, *Drink and the Victorians: The Temperance Question in England 1815–1872* (1971), and Lillian Lewis Shiman, *Crusade against Drink in Victorian England* (Basingstoke, 1988).

Inspired perhaps by anthropologists and sociologists such as Durkheim, Talcott Parsons, and Lévi-Strauss, these structuralist studies sometimes took a linguistic turn

---

[6] G. K. Clark, ' "Statesmen in Disguise": Reflexions on the History of the Neutrality of the Civil Service, *HJ* 2 (1959), 19–39; Oliver MacDonagh, 'The Nineteenth-Century Revolution in Government: A Reappraisal', *HJ* 1 (1958), 52–67.

[7] Kitson's Clark's reliance on the idea (not the phrase) of an official mind resembled the work of two fellow Cambridge historians on imperial history: Ronald Robinson and John Gallagher, *Africa and the Victorians: The Official Mind of Imperialism* (1961).

[8] Jenifer Hart, 'Nineteenth-Century Social Reform: A Tory Interpretation of History', *P&P* 31 (1965), 39–61.

[9] It must be a tribute to Keynes's influence that the once obscure currency reformer Thomas Attwood should have been 'discovered' simultaneously by Asa Briggs, 'Thomas Attwood and the Economic Background of the Birmingham Political Union', *Cambridge Historical Journal*, 9 (1948), 190–216, and S. G. Checkland, 'The Birmingham Economists, 1815–50', *EconHR* 1 (1948), 1–19.

whereby cultural values and the language in which they were expressed were seen as reflecting the organization of society and the ways in which different groups made sense of their social experiences. This was how Harold Perkin explained the struggles and accommodations between what he called the aristocratic and entrepreneurial ideals—the former Anglican, landed, metropolitan, and literary, the latter middle-class, Dissenting, industrial, provincial, and scientific.[10] Likewise Trygve Tholfsen explored the dominant value systems affecting all social groups, and the fine linguistic line which separated working-class radicals from working-class conservatives.[11] Such histories had points in common with discourse analysis as practised by the highly influential modernist social philosopher Michel Foucault. Here politics was understood, not as the outcome of material struggles, but as a forum for competing discourses each of which expressed some aspect of power relationships. They included gender and race but especially class, for at the heart of bourgeois society as Foucault conceived it was a terrifying fear of the people, who were now too numerous and also perhaps too stroppy to be simply whipped into shape. Since flagrant shows of power could no longer subdue them, the magic having departed from ancient institutions like the Church and monarchy, the bourgeoisie invented subtle systems of surveillance to enforce docility—notably the asylum, the clinic, the hospital ward, and the schoolroom. Outright rebels would continue to be executed, transported, or thrown in prison, but the potentially rebellious majority would be forced to interiorize the messages being transmitted by these systems, and to incorporate them in what Foucault called 'the microprocesses of the body'. Society thus remained repressive at the edges, but most workers were 'disciplined' rather than 'punished' by being made to internalize new norms of subordination, living neatly and politely, 'ordering their selves', making sure not to invade another's body space, in short being 'respectable'—a process of 'conditioning', in other words, that was far more subtle than that of the Jacobins with their revolutionary *journées*. This was a repressive interpretation of social reform to set against Kitson Clark's emphasis on humanitarianism and on 'the tone of England' becoming 'gentler'.[12] Foucault's ideas have resonated widely,[13] partly perhaps because they anticipated a fashion for conditioning by targets, performance indicators, inspections, audits, and conformity, and partly because they could be extended post-structurally to a point where language was almost entirely dissociated from social reality, becoming instead the main constituent of group behaviour and sense of identity.[14]

Until recently most historians have assumed that late eighteenth-century industrialization (subliminally) and the French Revolution (very obviously) created new tensions in English society. More recently, however, it has become fashionable to talk about the 'long eighteenth century'. For example, where nationalism was once seen as a post-1760 or post-1780 phenomenon,[15] Linda Colley has presented it as an outcome of the

[10] H. Perkin, *The Origins of Modern English Society 1780–1880* (1969).

[11] Trygve Tholfsen, *Working-Class Radicalism in Mid-Victorian England* (1976).

[12] G. Kitson Clark, *The Making of Victorian England* (1962), 52–62.

[13] Explicit allegiance to his work was rare, an exception being Michael Ignatieff, *A Just Measure of Pain: The Penitentiary in the Industrial Revolution, 1750–1850.*

[14] See e.g. Patrick Joyce, *Visions of the People: Industrial England and the Question of Class 1848–1914* (Cambridge, 1991); Mary Poovey, *Making a Social Body: British Cultural Formation 1830–1864* (Chicago, 1995).

[15] Gerald Newman, *The Rise of English Nationalism: A Cultural History, 1740–1830* (1987; 2nd edn. 1997).

Reformation, a Protestant mission dating back at least as far as the 1690s when the long series of wars against France began.[16] John Brewer too has focused on the turn of the eighteenth century in describing the formation of a fiscal–military state, which he regards as the secret of Britain's success.[17] More recently the notion of continuity has been stretched even further in Richard Price's *British Society, 1680–1880: Dynamism, Containment and Change* (Cambridge, 1999). Evidently inspired by Briggs and Perkin, Price deploys insights derived from the nineteenth century in order to throw unexpected light on the earlier period, a questionable procedure perhaps, but productive of some stimulating results. The standard textbook in this vein is Frank O'Gorman's *The Long Eighteenth Century 1688–1832* (1997), while the most strident statement of the claim for continuity is by J. C. D. Clark in *English Society 1688–1832: Ideology, Social Structure and Political Practice during the Ancien Régime* (Cambridge, 1985). Clark depicts England's *ancien régime* as a society in which the vast majority of the population continued to believe implicitly in the doctrine of the divine right of kings, in the legitimacy of a hereditary and territorial nobility, and in the rites and privileges of the Anglican Church as by law established. Compared with these long-established verities, innovations like the Industrial Revolution, political radicalism, secularism, and middle-class consciousness made—it is claimed—little impact. At certain points in his analysis Clark concedes that urbanization and the spread of religious Dissent increased the proportion of the population which did *not* come under the sway of monarchical, aristocratic, and Anglican ideologies, but even so he would consider Trevelyan's central contention—that 'the laws and institutions had been kept back in one place, while the men and women had been moved on to another'—to be wildly exaggerated. In Clark's view, the *ancien régime* remained virtually intact until the threshold of the Great Reform Act, and only collapsed after the repeal of the Test and Corporation Acts (1828) had undermined its central symbolic prop, the Anglican supremacy. The consequences of this piece of legislative carelessness were held to be enormous, being nothing less than 'the shattering of a whole social order ... What was lost at that point ... was not merely a constitutional arrangement, but the intellectual ascendancy of a world view, the cultural hegemony of the old elite' (pp. 90, 409).[18] *English Society* was a conscious assault on the teleological assumptions of left-leaning or 'progressive' history, whether Whig, liberal, or Marxist, but it hardly deserved the counter-charge of being 'Ultra Tory' history, since its point was not to deny the collapse of the regime but rather to interpret that collapse in terms of contingency. The paradox, if any, was that Clark attacked progressive historians for having been subconsciously influenced by assumptions about social and economic development, whereas he himself seems to have been affected by the fashion of the 1980s for cutting the Industrial Revolution down to size.[19] Whatever one's views, no one could deny the stimulus that Clark's deliberate 'breach of the historiographical peace' gave to Hanoverian studies. Seventeenth-century historians might have invented 'revisionism', but even Conrad Russell was never referred to universally by his initials,

[16] Linda Colley, *Britons: Forging the Nation 1707–1837* (New Haven, 1992); David Armitage, *The Ideological Origins of the British Empire* (Cambridge, 2000).

[17] John Brewer, *The Sinews of Power: War and the English State, 1688–1783* (1989).

[18] See above, p. 24. Clark has toned down his argument slightly in a substantially rewritten second edition (Cambridge, 2000). [19] See below, p. 671–3.

whereas at seminars and conferences on the Hanoverian period the letters B.C. were for a while widely understood to mean 'before Clark'.[20]

Clark's 'shattering of a whole social order' resembles Butler's belief that the old aristocratic system began to crumble. The difference is partly that Clark does not regard the event as one necessarily to be celebrated, but more importantly he does not regard it as a *necessary* event. 'The accumulating forces hostile to the old order were as yet insufficient to destroy it...Its destruction in 1828–32 was political, not inevitable' (p. 90). It fell, not because the opinions of ordinary 'men and women' had forged too far ahead of the Constitution, as Dicey and Trevelyan had supposed, nor because the regime was unpopular from below or subject to 'pressure from without', but because of a betrayal from within and from the top. The analysis rests ultimately on Clark's belief in the primacy of politics.[21] For Whig and Marxist historians, political events were a function of social realities, whether those realities were defined in terms of ideas and opinions or in terms of the material clash of interests. However, the doctrine of the primacy of politics asserts that political outcomes depend on personality and contingency, and furthermore that they are more likely to determine than to reflect social developments. For while all citizens enjoy or endure private lives, the only forum by which they relate to other citizens whom they do not know is through the medium of public life. It follows that, if one political grouping with its own particular ideas and rhetoric triumphs over another, this may have a profound effect on how all citizens subsequently think and behave. According to this theory, sheer political pusillanimity led Peel and Wellington in 1828 to capitulate to routine and fairly half-hearted demands for the repeal of the Test and Corporation Acts. This 'betrayal from within' led on to Catholic emancipation in 1829 and parliamentary reform in 1832, and so brought a stable regime—the so-called 'Protestant Constitution'—together with 'its appropriate values and modes of behaviour', suddenly tumbling to destruction (p. 409).

Different chronological perspectives throw up different interpretations, and there is clearly some validity in the Hanoverian, or 'long eighteenth century', approach. It does, however, obscure the dramatic changes wrought by the American and French revolutions. There is also the point that, if aggressive Protestantism or assertive Anglicanism are regarded as hallmarks of the *ancien régime*, then both of these reached their peak immediately *after* its apparent destruction in 1828–32. But, if a focus on the Hanoverian period has its disadvantages, it at least avoids the mistake of taking off or landing in 1815, a date which was of no more than military significance. The volumes in the Arnold series[22] and in

[20] For tasters, see the symposia in *Albion*, 21 (1989), 361–474; J. lnnes, 'On Hitting the Buffers: The Historiography of England's Ancien Régime', *P & P* 11s (1987) 165–200; J. Clark, 'Social History and England's "Ancien Regime" ', *P & P* 117 (1987), 194–207; 194–207; R. W. Davis, 'The Politics of the Confessional State, 1760–1832', *Parliamentary History*, 9 (1990), 38–49; Frank O'Gorman, 'Eighteenth-Century England as an *Ancien Régime*', in Stephen Taylor, Richard Connors, and Clyve Jones (eds.), *Hanoverian Britain and Empire: Essays in Memory of Philip Lawson* (Woodbridge, 1998).

[21] A one-time Fellow of Peterhouse, Cambridge, Clark was presumably influenced by the work of Maurice Cowling and John Vincent, who mainly worked on the period after 1846.

[22] Ian R. Christie, *Wars and Revolutions: Britain 1760–1815* (1982); W. D. Rubinstein, *Britain's Century: A Political and Social History, 1815–1905* (1998); Norman Gash, *Aristocracy and People: Britain 1815–1865* (1979).

the last Oxford History of England series,[23] despite many merits, all laboured under a chronology that corresponded to neither the 'long eighteenth century' nor the 'age of revolution'. It is surely no coincidence that many of the most successful general political histories of the last fifty years have begun at or around 1783, not 1815.[24] Briggs's *Age of Improvement* is the most imaginative; Eric J. Evans, *The Forging of the Modern State: Early Industrial Britain 1783–1870* (1983; 3rd edn. 2001) and Michael J. Turner, *The Age of Unease: Government and Reform in Britain, 1782–1832* (Stroud, 2000) are both admirably clear and comprehensive;[25] while Jennifer Mori's *Britain in the Age of the French Revolution, 1785–1820* (Harlow, 2000) is probably the most reflective.

THE ECONOMY

Again it is impossible to do more than skim the surface. The clearest and most incisive single-author survey is probably M. J. Daunton, *Progress and Poverty: An Economic and Social History of Britain 1700–1850* (Oxford, 1995). Roderick Floud and Donald McCloskey (eds.), *The Economic History of Britain since 1700*, i: *1700–1860* (Cambridge, 1981; 2nd edn. 1994) and Roderick Floud and Paul Johnson (eds.), *The Cambridge Economic History of Modern Britain*, i: *Industrialisation, 1700–1860* (Cambridge, 2004) provide snapshots taken at intervals of a quarter-century. Joel Mokyr has edited *The Economics of the Industrial Revolution* (1985) and *The British Industrial Revolution: An Economic Perspective* (Boulder, Colo., 1993); the former contains his own important article on supply and demand factors. There is much wise reflection in J. Hoppit's review article 'Understanding the Industrial Revolution', *HJ* 30 (1987), 211–24, which calls for a 'statistical and literary, macro and micro, short, medium and long term, personal and impersonal, economic, social, political and intellectual', and yet also withal 'theoretical' history of the Industrial Revolution. Why are we still waiting?

Different interpretations have succeeded each other rapidly, sometimes in ways that reflect current preoccupations.[26] Older versions mainly stressed factors based on human agency such as mechanical invention, capital accumulation, a Protestant and profit-oriented society, and a favourable legislative climate. During the 1960s, when the white heat of technology was in the air, David S. Landes put forward a powerful interpretation based on changing entrepreneurial tactics: *The Unbound Prometheus: Technological Change and Industrial Development in Western Europe from 1750 to the*

---

[23] J. Steven Watson, *The Reign of George III, 1760–1815* (Oxford, 1960); E. L. Woodward, *The Age of Reform 1815–1870* (Oxford, 1938); likewise in the Short Oxford History of the Modern World: Wilfrid Prest, *Albion Ascendant: English History, 1660–1815* (Oxford, 1998) and Norman McCord, *British History, 1815–1906* (Oxford, 1991).

[24] But see the wonderfully compact and stimulating *The Nineteenth Century: The Short Oxford History of the British Isles: 1815–1901*, ed. Colin Matthew (Oxford, 2000).

[25] A. J. P. Taylor, the author of the 1914–45 volume in the previous Oxford History of England series, was once asked how he set about finding out what basically had happened in his period. 'I looked it up in Mowat,' was his reply, a reference to C. L. Mowat's, *Britain between the Wars 1918–1940* (1955). For Mowat, read Evans.

[26] See David Cannadine, 'The Present and the Past in the English Industrial Revolution 1880–1980', *P&P* 103 (1984), 131–72.

Present (Cambridge, 1969). At the other extreme, E. J. Hobsbawm suggested in *Industry and Empire: An Economic History of Britain since 1750* (1968) that economic take-off could be explained in terms of Britain's command of the burgeoning Atlantic economy; the insight was followed up in Ralph Davis, *The Industrial Revolution and British Overseas Trade* (Leicester, 1979), and has since been developed more analytically in Joseph E. Inikori, *Africans and the Industrial Revolution in England: A Study in International Trade and Economic Development* (Cambridge, 2002). Meanwhile, during the Thatcher years, it became commonplace to downplay Britain's economic performance by questioning some of the earlier and giddier estimates of increased gross national product. The key texts here were J. G. Williamson, 'Why was British Growth so Slow during the Industrial Revolution?', *Journal of Economic History*, 44 (1984), 687–712, and *British Economic Growth during the Industrial Revolution* (Oxford, 1985) by N. F. R. Crafts. In a similar spirit of scepticism, G. N. von Tunzelman, *Steam Power and British Industrialization to 1860* (Oxford, 1978) and G. R. Hawke, *Railways and Economic Growth in England and Wales 1840–1870* (Oxford, 1970) used econometric methods to question lazy assumptions about the importance of apparently key technological developments. Since then the Industrial Revolution has been reinstated, but as a more complex, unplanned, and (by contemporaries) largely unrecognized affair. For example, the central contention of E. A. Wrigley's important interpretative essays is the transition from an inorganic raw material economy to one based on mineral energy. *Continuity, Chance and Change: The Character of the Industrial Revolution in England* (Cambridge, 1988) and *People, Cities and Wealth: The Transformation of Traditional Society* (Oxford, 1987) leave room for human agency but less for individual heroes. There has therefore been an emphasis on the way in which, without being driven to it by capitalists, ordinary people began to work harder and in more market-oriented ways: see Jan De Vries, 'The Industrial Revolution and the Industrious Revolution', *Journal of Economic History*, 54 (1994), 249–70, and Hans-Joachim Voth, *Time and Work in England, 1750–1830* (Oxford, 2000).

Machines and manufactures were the most visible facets of economic change. Maxine Berg, *The Age of Manufactures: Industry, Innovation and Work in Britain 1700–1820* (Oxford, 1985) is an excellent introduction, and can be supplemented by the more detailed studies such as *Regions and Industries: A Perspective on the Industrial Revolution in Britain* (Cambridge, 1989) edited by Pat Hudson, and Hudson's own *The Industrial Revolution* (1992) and *The Genesis of Industrial Capital: A Study of the West Riding Wool Textile Industry c.1750–1850* (Cambridge, 1986). Entrepreneurship is the focus of A. E. Musson and Eric Robinson, *Science and Technology in the Industrial Revolution* (Manchester, 1969), Sidney Pollard, *The Genesis of Modern Management: A Study of the Industrial Revolution in Great Britain* (1965), and H. J. Habakkuk, *American and British Technology in the Nineteenth Century: The Search for Labour-Saving Inventions* (Cambridge, 1962). For the entrepreneurs themselves, there are François Crouzet's *The First Industrialists: The Problem of Origins* (Cambridge, 1985), Anthony Howe's *The Cotton Masters 1830–1860* (Oxford, 1984), and Katrina Honeyman's *Origins of Enterprise: Business Leadership in the Industrial Revolution* (Manchester, 1982). Turning to demand-side factors, a great deal of emphasis has recently been placed on consumerism, shopping, and material culture generally. The piece by Jan De Vries in John

Brewer and Roy Porter (eds.), *Consumption and the World of Goods* (1993) contains an analysis that is both comprehensive and subtle.

For all the recent caveats, it would be perverse to deny that there was an industrial revolution of sorts. Whether—as used to be assumed—there was also an agricultural revolution is more doubtful, but at least the rapidly expanding population managed to get fed (just). The classic account is J. D. Chambers and G. E. Mingay, *The Agricultural Revolution 1750–1880* (1966). E. L. Jones, *Agriculture and the Industrial Revolution* (Oxford, 1974) placed more emphasis on developments before 1783. Interventions since then have included Ann Kussmaul, *A General View of the Rural Economy of England, 1538–1840* (Cambridge, 1990), J. M. Neeson, *Commoners: Common Right, Enclosure and Social Change in England, 1700–1820* (Cambridge, 1993), Mark Overton, *Agricultural Revolution in England: The Transformation of the Agrarian Economy, 1500–1850* (Cambridge, 1996),[27] G. E. Mingay, *Parliamentary Enclosure in England: An Introduction to its Causes, Incidence and Impact, 1750–1850* (1997), and Robert C. Allen, 'Tracking the Agricultural Revolution in England', *EconHR* 52 (1999), 209–35. For reference there is the mammoth survey edited by Mingay, *The Agrarian History of England and Wales*, vi: *1750–1850* (Cambridge, 1989).

Ultimately, economic performance can only be judged in relative terms. Peter Mathias, *The First Industrial Nation: An Economic History of Britain 1700–1914* (1969) was one of the first books to focus on international comparisons. François Crouzet has explored the bitterest of all national rivalries in *Britain Ascendant: Comparative Studies in Franco-British Economic History* (trans. Martin Thom, Cambridge, 1985). For further comment, see Patrick K. O'Brien, 'Path Dependency, or Why Britain Became an Industrialized and Urbanized Economy Long Before France', *EconHR* 49 (1996), 213–49. But maybe divergences within Europe were less significant than those between Europe and Asia. Leading the field here is Kenneth Pomeranz, *The Great Divergence: China, Europe, and the Making of the Modern World Economy* (Princeton, 2000). Meanwhile, some geographers have emphasized divergences *within* Britain, thereby challenging familiar macroeconomic interpretations. Here the flagship article is John Langton, 'The Industrial Revolution and the Regional Geography of England', *Transactions of the Institute of British Geographers*, 9 (1984), 145–67.

SOCIAL CONDITIONS

Economic history used to encompass the social as well. For example, the *Economic History Review* and the *Journal of Economic History* traditionally carried articles descriptive of how ordinary people behaved in their working lives, but as those journals have become more analytical and econometric in approach, such social history now has to be sought in outlets like *Urban History*, *Business History Review*, the *Journal of Historical Geography*, and the *Transactions of the Institute of British Geographers*. Meanwhile, a vivid place to begin might be with the *Atlas of Industrializing Britain 1780–1914*, edited by John Langton and R. J. Morris (1986) and the *Atlas of British Social and Economic History*

---

[27] See also Mark Overton, 'Re-establishing the English Agricultural Revolution', *Agricultural History Review*, 44 (1996), 1–20.

since c.1700, edited by Rex Pope (1989). John Rule's *Albion's People: English Society, 1714–1815* (1992) provides an effective overview, as does *Eighteenth-Century English Society: Shuttles and Swords* (Oxford, 1997) by Douglas Hay and Nicholas Rogers. There are important thematic essays in Patrick O'Brien and Roland Quinault (eds.), *The Industrial Revolution and British Society* (Cambridge, 1993), and in the three volumes of *The Cambridge Social History of Britain 1750–1950* (Cambridge, 1990), edited by F. M. L. Thompson.

The long-standing debate about trends in working-class living standards has become too technically recondite to do more than nod to here. For glimpses at recent developments, see N. F. R. Crafts, 'English Workers' Real Wages during the Industrial Revolution: Some Remaining Problems', *Journal of Economic History*, 45 (1985), 139–53 (with a reply by Peter Lindert and Jeffrey Williamson); Joel Mokyr, 'Is There Still Life in the Pessimist Case? Consumption during the Industrial Revolution, 1790–1850', *Journal of Economic History*, 48 (1988), 69–92; Sara Horrell and Jane Humphries, 'Old Questions, New Data, and Alternative Perspectives: Families' Living Standards in the Industrial Revolution', *Journal of Economic History*, 52 (1992), 849–80; Peter H. Lindert's essay in Roderick Floud and Donald McCloskey's *Economic History of Britain*, i: *1700–1860* (2nd edn. 1994); S. L. Engerman, 'Reflections on the Standard of Living Debate: New Arguments and New Evidence', in John A. James and Mark Thomas (eds.), *Capitalism in Context: Essays on Economic Development and Cultural Change in Honor of R. M. Hartwell* (Chicago, 1994); N. F. R. Crafts, 'Some Dimensions of the "Quality of Life" during the British Industrial Revolution', *EconHR* 50 (1997), 617–39; and Simon Szreter and Graham Mooney, 'Urbanization, Mortality, and the Standard of Living Debate: New Estimates of the Expectation of Life at Birth in Nineteenth-Century British Cities', *EconHR* 51 (1998), 84–112.

Discussion of demographic factors has become equally technical, most of it conducted in the light of a magisterial volume by E. A. Wrigley and R. S. Schofield, *The Population History of England 1541–1871: A Reconstruction* (2nd edn. Cambridge, 1981). Wrigley's own subsequent contributions include 'Explaining the Rise in Marital Fertility in England in the "Long" Eighteenth Century', *EconHR* 51 (1998), 435–64, and 'British Population during the "Long" Eighteenth Century, 1680–1840', in Roderick Floud and Paul Johnson (eds.), *The Cambridge Economic History of Modern Britain*, i: *Industrialization, 1700–1860* (Cambridge, 2004). In conjunction with R. S. Davies, Wrigley has also edited a mammoth tome entitled *English Population History from Family Reconstitution, 1580–1837* (Cambridge, 1997). Much of the debate on population increase has turned on whether it was due to changes in nuptiality, fertility, and/or mortality. This clearly has implications for the argument between optimists and pessimists on the standard of living, though the connections are complicated. There is a notably depressing contribution by Simon Szreter and Anne Hardy entitled 'Urban Fertility and Mortality Patterns', in Martin Daunton (ed.), *The Cambridge Urban History of Britain*, iii: *1840–1950* (Cambridge, 2000). Not all deaths were due to unfavourable physical conditions. This period emerges as one in which the rate of suicide seems to have been exceptionally high, an under-studied topic but one usefully opened by Olive Anderson in her *Suicide in Victorian and Edwardian England* (Oxford, 1987).

There are vivid descriptions of countryside life in K. D. M. Snell, *Annals of the Labouring Poor: Social Change and Agrarian England, 1660–1900* (Cambridge, 1985) and Pamela Horn, *The Rural World 1780–1850: Social Change in the English Countryside* (1980). For the towns there is James Walvin, *English Urban Life 1776–1851* (1984) and also John Burnett's trilogy *Plenty and Want: A Social History of Diet in England from 1815 to the Present Day* (2nd edn. 1979), *A Social History of Housing 1815–1985* (2nd edn. 1986), and *Destiny Obscure: Autobiographies of Childhood, Education and Family from the 1820s to the 1920s* (1982). The strains which urbanization and industrialization placed on working-class family life were analysed in Neil J. Smelser, *Social Change in the Industrial Revolution: An Application of Theory to the Lancashire Cotton Industry 1770–1840* (1959), for a critique of which, see Michael Anderson, 'Sociological History and the Working-Class Family: Smelser Revisited', *Social History*, 3 (1976), 317–34. Anderson's own classic *Family Structure in Mid Nineteenth-Century Lancashire* (Cambridge, 1971), which also focused on the cotton industry, still holds the field. Anna Clark's *The Struggle for the Breeches: Gender and the Making of the British Working Class* (1995) shows vividly how working men and women battled for supremacy, whether through confrontation or negotiation depending on local circumstances.

E. H. Hunt, *British Labour History 1815–1914* (1981) and John Rule, *The Labouring Classes in Early Industrial England, 1750–1850* (1986) are good introductions to the state of working conditions. Robert Glen, *Urban Workers in the Early Industrial Revolution* (1984) is a perceptive study of the Stockport area. E. J. Hobsbawm, *Labouring Men: Studies in the History of Labour* (1964) is lively; E. P. Thompson, 'Time, Work-Discipline, and Industrial Capitalism', *P&P* 38 (1967), 56–97, famously showed how working-class life changed as the discipline of the clock replaced the older rhythms of the seasons and of nature. It should be read in conjunction with Hans-Joachim Voth's *Time and Work in England 1750–1830* (Oxford 2000), referred to above. Clark Nardinelli, *Child Labour and the Industrial Revolution* (Bloomington, Ind., 1990) examines econometrically one of the major downsides of industrialization. That process also made for a population more geographically mobile than ever before. Arthur Redford's *Labour Migration in England, 1800–1850* (Manchester, 1926) revealed that most moves were local, regional, and of short distance, a point confirmed by Colin Pooley and Jean Turnbull in their highly sophisticated investigation *Migration and Mobility in Britain since the Eighteenth Century* (1998). In 'Migration and Urbanization in North-West England circa 1760–1830', *Social History*, 19 (1994), 339–57, Colin G. Pooley and Shani D'Cruze even question the basic assumption that there was a ripple-like nature of sequential movement from countryside to town and from smaller towns to larger ones.

Education was an area in which Britain notoriously fell behind at this time. It is also a subject on which most of the best work was done some time ago, not least M. G. Jones's *The Charity School Movement: A Study of Eighteenth-Century Puritanism in Action* (Cambridge, 1938), Brian Simon's *The Two Nations and the Educational Structure 1780–1870* (1974), and Thomas W. Laqueur's *Religion and Respectability: Sunday Schools and Working Class Culture 1780–1850* (New Haven, 1976). John Hurt, *Education in Evolution: Church, State, Society and Popular Education, 1800–1870* (1971), D. G. Paz, *The Politics of Working-Class Education in Britain, 1830–1850* (Manchester, 1980), and

Neil J. Smelser, *Social Paralysis and Social Change: British Working-Class Education in the Nineteenth Century* (Berkeley, Calif., 1991) are useful, while W. B. Stephens has revealed immense regional differences in his study *Education, Literacy and Society, 1830–70: The Geography of Diversity in Provincial England* (Manchester, 1987). Richard Johnson emphasized the connections between 'Educational Policy and Social Control in Early Victorian England', in *P&P* 49 (1970), 96–119, and shortly afterwards, in *Education and the Industrial Revolution* (1975), E. G. West suggested that the drive (however slow) towards greater state involvement was damaging to the overall levels of provision. Children not at school were roaming streets and creating a largely new panic about juvenile delinquency, which is the subject of Heather Shore's *Artful Dodgers: Youth and Crime in Early Nineteenth-Century London* (Woodbridge, 1999).

WORKING-CLASS CONSCIOUSNESS, CULTURE, AND PROTEST

Thanks in part to Karl Marx—an excellent historian whatever else one thinks of him—the idea of class is indelibly associated with this period. Contemporary perceptions are examined in Asa Briggs's celebrated article 'The Language of "Class" in Early Nineteenth-Century England', in M. W. Flinn and T. C. Smout (eds.), *Essays in Social History* (Oxford, 1974), which was seminal in its day and remains pertinent. Harold Perkin's *The Origins of Modern English Society* (1969) has already been referred to. Craig Calhoun, *The Question of Class Struggle: Social Foundations of Popular Radicalism during the Industrial Revolution* (Chicago, 1982) addresses the problem head-on. David Cannadine's *Class in Britain* (New Haven, 1998) raises interesting questions of definition. However, working-class consciousness is no longer the talismanic concept it once was among historians. In retrospect it is clear that E. P. Thompson's magical evocation in *The Making of the English Working Class* (1963; rev. edn. 1968) brought a prominent line of inquiry to its culmination. Perhaps this should have been obvious at the time, given the author's determination to define class, not in material terms, but as a product of the daily experience of individual men and women.[28] Patrick Joyce is one of relatively few historians still to grapple positively with the question of class, as in *Democratic Subjects: The Self and the Social in Nineteenth-Century England* (Cambridge, 1994). Unfortunately his sophisticated *Visions of the People: Industrial England and the Question of Class 1848–1914* (Cambridge, 1991) focuses mainly on the years after 1846.

Elite members of society might have regarded the populace as mad, bad, and dangerous, but recent historians have mainly stressed its growing respectability. In *The London Mob: Violence and Disorder in Eighteenth-Century England* (2004), Robert B. Shoemaker detects a wind of change from about the 1790s, and the same theme is developed for a later period in F. M. L. Thompson, *The Rise of Respectable Society: A Social History of Victorian Britain, 1830–1900* (1988). This process of socialization obviously bears on whether the turnabout in working-class attitudes and behaviour after 1848 was real or apparent. One view is that of John Foster, who has argued in *Class Struggle and the Industrial Revolution: Early Industrial Capitalism in Three English Towns* (1974) that there

[28] On this theme, see also E. P. Thompson, *Customs in Common* (1991).

was a major discontinuity in Oldham's popular politics between the 1830s and 1850s. Counter-arguments in favour of continuity have been put forward, both on the basis of radical opposition to economic liberalism and on the basis of a persistent strain of working-class respectability and moral reformism. See, respectively, David Gadian, 'Radicalism and Liberalism in Oldham: A Study of Conflict, Continuity and Change in Popular Politics, 1830–52', *Social History*, 21 (1996), 265–80, and Michael Winstanley, 'Oldham Radicalism and the Origins of Popular Liberalism, 1830–52', *HJ* 36 (1993), 619–43. Both versions have merit but tend to cancel each other out, and on balance the case for discontinuity survives. Trygve Tholfsen's *Working-Class Radicalism in Mid-Victorian England* (1976), already mentioned, proposes a *via media*, and there are helpful observations in Neville Kirk's 'In Defence of Class: A Critique of Recent Revisionist Writing upon the Nineteenth-Century English Working Class', *International Review of Social History*, 32 (1987), 2–47.

A number of scholars, working separately but in parallel, have traced a 'shift from the demotic politics of the eighteenth century to the democratizing politics of the platform' in the first half of the nineteenth century. The phrase comes from Nicholas Rogers, whose *Crowds, Culture, and Politics in Georgian Britain* (1998) deals mainly with the earlier mode, what E. P. Thompson has called a 'plebeian counter theatre' with its rough music, burnings in effigy, and general cacophony. A similar point emerges in Charles Tilly's *Popular Contention in Great Britain 1758–1834* (Cambridge, Mass., 1995). Through close textual analysis of the language used in what he calls 'contentious gatherings', Tilly argues that within seven decades Britain 'moved from the alien world of the eighteenth century into our own era' as 'mass national politics [took] hold on a national scale' (p. 13). It was a move 'from donkeying to demonstrating', where the former signified ribald rituals aimed at scapegoating and humiliation.[29] Similarly but differently, Mark Harrison in *Crowds and History: Mass Phenomena in English Towns, 1790–1835* (Cambridge, 1988) depicts a process of acculturation into civil society, as multitudes came together to 'celebrate, commemorate, vilify or validate'. Focusing on Bristol, Liverpool, Norwich, and Manchester, Harrison suggests that crowd activity, being tightly organized and controlled, could actually contribute to 'order', and that urbanization could spawn 'consensus'. For a more gruesome take on mass participation, there is Thomas W. Laqueur, 'Crowds, Carnival and the State in English Executions, 1604–1868', in A. L. Beier, D. Cannadine, and James M. Rosenheim (eds.), *The First Modern Society: Essays in English History in Honour of Lawrence Stone* (Cambridge, 1989). M. Golby and A. W. Purdue, *The Civilisation of the Crowd: Popular Culture in England 1750–1900* (1984) stress the continuities between an older rural and newer urban England by showing how far pre-industrial leisure was already commercialized. (Forthcoming work by Emma Griffin will also stress continuity, but will do so by examining the transference of older sports and pastimes to the new towns.) Other books worth reading in this context include Robert W. Malcolmson, *Popular Recreations in English Society, 1700–1850* (Cambridge, 1973) and Bob Bushaway, *By Rite: Custom, Ceremony and Community in England, 1770–1880* (1982). Simon Cordery's *British*

---

[29] Noting that his book took a long time to produce, Tilly notes: 'The trouble with dawdling is that in the conscientious heart it stirs up guilt' (p. vii).

Friendly Societies 1750–1914 (Basingstoke, 2003) seems likely to remain the authoritative work for some time to come.

Communal action was inevitably challenged to some extent by the rise of private reading. Michael Sanderson, 'Literacy and Social Mobility in the Industrial Revolution in England', *P&P* 56 (1972), 75–104, was seminal in its day; David Vincent's *Literacy and Popular Culture: England 1750–1914* (Cambridge, 1989) is authoritative, as is the same author's *Bread, Knowledge and Freedom: A Study of Nineteenth-Century Working-Class Autobiography* (1981). Of course, learning to read brought access not just to improving literature but to subversion, filth, and trash, a topic on which Iain McCalman's *Radical Underworld: Prophets, Revolutionaries and Pornographers in London, 1795–1840* (Cambridge, 1988) is supreme. Almost as illuminating is the same author's 'Popular Irreligion in Early Victorian England: Infidel Preachers and Radical Theatricality in 1830s London', in R. W. Davis and R. J. Helmstadter (eds.), *Religion and Irreligion in Victorian Society: Essays in Honor of R. K. Webb* (1992). The classic account of this subject is Edward Royle, *Victorian Infidels: The Origins of the British Secularist Movement, 1791–1866* (Manchester, 1974).

Notwithstanding the move towards self-improvement, the fact remains that this period saw degrees of working-class subversion on an unprecedented scale,[30] as E. P. Thompson's *Making of the English Working Class* (1963; rev. edn. 1968) unforgettably demonstrated. Among the best introductory surveys are Edward Royle, *Revolutionary Britannia? Reflections on the Threat of Revolution in Britain 1789–1848* (Manchester, 2000); Edward Royle and James Walvin, *English Radicals and Reformers 1760–1848* (Brighton, 1982); John Stevenson and Roland Quinault (eds.), *Popular Protest and Public Order: Six Studies in British History, 1790–1920* (1974); H. T. Dickinson, *The Politics of the People in Eighteenth-Century Britain* (Basingstoke, 1995); and John Stevenson, *Popular Disturbances in England, 1700–1870* (1979; 2nd edn. 1992). On the question of radical organization and mobilization, Albert Goodwin, *The Friends of Liberty: The English Democratic Movement in the Age of the French Revolution* (1979) has recently been supplemented by Jenny Graham's *The Nation, the Law and the King, Reform Politics in England, 1789–1799* (Lanham, Md., 2000). David Worrall, *Radical Culture: Discourse, Resistance and Surveillance, 1790–1820* (New York, 1992) is suggestive, and there are important essays in H. T. Dickinson's brief but useful *British Radicalism and the French Revolution 1789–1815* (Oxford, 1985), and in Mark Philp (ed.), *The French Revolution and British Popular Politics* (Cambridge, 1991). John Bohstedt's *Riots and Community Politics in England and Wales 1790–1810* (Cambridge, Mass., 1983) on the Devon and Manchester areas slots popular violence into the vagaries of daily life, such as food riots. Roger Wells confirms the validity of this approach in *Wretched Faces: Famine in Wartime England 1763–1801* (Gloucester, 1988), while stressing radical mobilization, revolutionary intent, and the Irish connection in *Insurrection: The British Experience 1795–1803* (Gloucester, 1983).

---

[30] Whereas the events described in William Weber, 'The 1784 Handel Commemoration as Political Ritual', *JBS* 28 (1989), 43–69, seem more like a late manifestation of an 18th-century mode of political assertion. See also E. P. Thompson, 'The Moral Economy of the English Crowd in the 18th Century', *P&P* 50 (1971), 76–136.

Historians disagree over how far radical protest was driven underground by state repression, and how far it was swamped by an even greater degree of genuine popular loyalism and patriotism. The former was noticed in D. E. Ginter, 'The Loyalist Association Movement of 1792–3 and British Public Opinion', *HJ* 9 (1966), 179–90, but rose to prominence thanks to Linda Colley's *Britons: Forging the Nation 1707–1837* (New Haven, 1992) and also her formative article 'The Apotheosis of George III: Loyalty, Royalty and the British Nation 1760–1820', *P&P* 102 (1984), 94–129.[31] Robert R. Dozier, *For King, Constitution, and Country: The English Loyalists and the French Revolution* (Lexington, Ky., 1983) is good on the practicalities, while the Establishment's propaganda campaign is discussed in Thomas Philip Schofield, 'Conservative Political Thought in Britain in Response to the French Revolution', *HJ* 29 (1986), 601–22, and Gerald Newman, 'Anti-French Propaganda and British Liberal Nationalism in the Early Nineteenth Century', *Victorian Studies*, 18 (1974–5), 385–418. Most striking was the way in which clergymen wielded eschatological weapons (fear of hellfire) against would-be malcontents, a development revealed by Robert Hole in *Pulpits, Politics and Public Order in England 1760–1832* (Cambridge, 1989). Several historians have pointed out that loyalism was a two-edged sword, in that any form of popular mobilization carried the risk of awakening the masses to their own power. Prominent here are Mark Philp, 'Vulgar Conservatism, 1792–3', *EHR* 110 (1995), 42–69, and Kevin Gilmartin, 'In the Theater of Counterrevolution: Loyalist Association and Conservative Opinion in the 1790s', *JBS* 41 (2002), 291–328. Olivia Smith explores a similar theme with regard to public discourse in *The Politics of Language 1791–1819* (Oxford, 1984).

For the 'high politics' of the turn-of-the-century radicalism and its uneasy transition into the later and more sober movement led by Place, see J. Ann Hone, *For the Cause of Truth: Radicalism in London 1796–1821* (Oxford, 1982). Radical theory is examined in William Stafford, *Socialism, Radicalism, and Nostalgia: Social Criticism in Britain, 1775–1830* (Cambridge, 1987). Kevin Gilmartin's *Print Politics: The Press and Radical Opposition in Early Nineteenth-Century England* (Cambridge, 1996) studies the same subject with particular reference to the *Political Register* and the *Black Dwarf*. John Keane's *Tom Paine: A Political Life* (1995) is authoritative, as is Gregory Claeys, *Thomas Paine: Social and Political Thought* (Boston, 1989), Jack Fruchtman, Jr., *Thomas Paine: Apostle of Freedom* (New York, 1994), and Linda Nattrass, *William Cobbett: The Politics of Style* (Cambridge, 1995). The influence of American ideas on both these radicals is examined in David A. Wilson, *Paine and Cobbett: The Transatlantic Connection* (Montreal, 1988).

The submerged tradition of violent protest resurfaced in the East Midlands in 1811, on which, see Malcolm I. Thomis, *The Luddites: Machine-Breaking in Regency England* (Newton Abbot, 1970) and Adrian Randall, *Before the Luddites: Custom, Community and Machinery in the English Woollen Industry, 1776–1809* (Cambridge, 1991). Post-war activity is covered in David Worrall's *Radical Culture* (New York, 1992) already referred to. John Belchem, *'Orator Hunt': Henry Hunt and English Working-Class Radicalism* (Oxford, 1985) does some belated justice to the most active, flamboyant, and

---

[31] See also Linda Colley, 'Whose Nation? Class and National Consciousness in Britain 1750–1830', *P&P* 113 (1986), 97–117.

exasperating of the movement's gentleman leaders. It should be read alongside the same author's 'Republicanism, Popular Constitutionalism and the Radical Platform in Early Nineteenth-Century England', *Social History*, 6 (1981), 1–32. Donald Read's *Peterloo: The 'Massacre' and its Manchester Background* (Manchester, 1958) has been supplemented by Robert Reid, *The Peterloo Massacre* (1989), and there are interesting perspectives in Michael Lobban's 'From Seditious Libel to Unlawful Assembly: Peterloo and the Changing Face of Political Crime, *c*.1770–1820', *Oxford Journal of Legal Studies*, 10 (1990), 307–52, and in John Belchem's 'Manchester, Peterloo and the Radical Challenge', *Manchester Region History Review*, 3 (1989), 9–14. M. L. Bush has empha-sized the role played by women at Peterloo in *History*, 89/294 (2004), 209–32. However, when women took leading roles in the Queen Caroline demonstrations soon afterwards, they were thought by radical men to have overstepped the mark, and may even have caused the radical movement as a whole to falter. For contrasting views, see Tamara L. Hunt, 'Morality and Monarchy in the Queen Caroline Affair', *Albion*, 23 (1991), 697–722; Jonathan Fulcher, 'Gender, Politics and Class in the Early Nineteenth-Century English Reform Movement', *Historical Research*, 67 (1994), 57–74, and 'The Loyalist Response to the Queen Caroline Agitations', *JBS* 34 (1995), 481–502; Thomas W. Laqueur, 'The Queen Caroline Affair: Politics as Art in the Reign of George IV', *Journal of Modern History*, 54 (1982), 417–66; Anna Clark, 'Queen Caroline and the Sexual Politics of Popular Culture in London, 1820', *Representations*, 31 (1990), 47–68; and Dror Wahrman, ' "Middle-Class" Domesticity Goes Public: Gender, Class, and Politics from Queen Caroline to Queen Victoria', *JBS* 32 (1993), 396–432.

Dudley Miles, *Francis Place 1771–1854: The Life of a Remarkable Radical* (Brighton, 1988) seeks to rehabilitate a vitally important leader who was repeatedly denounced by E. P. Thompson for seeking cooperation between the middle and working classes[32] and for turning his back on both socialism and the tactics of menace. It also does justice to his part in instigating the movement for birth control. Iowerth Prothero has written two classic accounts of working-class political activity, *Artisans and Politics in Early Nineteenth-Century London: John Gast and his Times* (Folkestone, 1979) and *Radical Artisans in England and France, 1830–1870* (Cambridge, 1997). There are several import-ant essays in John Rule (ed.), *British Trade Unionism 1750–1850: The Formative Years* (1988). E. J. Hobsbawm and George Rudé, *Captain Swing* (1969) remains the standard account but it can be spiced with 'Rural Rebels in Southern England in the 1830s', Roger Wells's contribution to Clive Emsley and James Walvin (eds.), *Artisans, Peasants and Proletarians, 1760–1860: Essays Presented to Gwyn A. Williams* (Beckenham, 1985). Asa Briggs, 'The Background of the Parliamentary Reform Movement in Three English Cities (1830–2)', *Cambridge Historical Journal*, 10 (1952), 293–317, was a classic intervention and remains pertinent. The story told in Carlos Flick's *The Birmingham Political Union and the Movements for Reform in Britain 1830–1839* (Hamden, Conn., 1978) has since been broadened out by Nancy D. LoPatin in *Political Unions, Popular Politics and the Great Reform Act of 1832* (Basingstoke, 1999). These unions are contextualized in T. M. Parssinen, 'Association, Convention and Anti-Parliament in

---

[32] On which, see David Nicholls, 'The English Middle Class and the Ideological Significance of Radicalism, 1760–1886', *JBS* 24 (1985), 415–33.

British Radical Politics, 1771–1848', *EHR* 88 (1973), 504–33. Nicholas C. Edsall, *The Anti-Poor Law Movement 1834–44* (Manchester, 1971) remains the last and most comprehensive account of one of the main links between the reform riots and Chartism. A parallel link is examined in Patricia Hollis, *The Pauper Press: A Study in Working-Class Radicalism of the 1830s* (1970) and Joel H. Wiener, *The War of the Unstamped: The Movement to Repeal the British Newspaper Tax, 1830–1836* (Ithaca, NY, 1969). D. G. Wright's *Popular Radicalism: The Working-Class Experience, 1780–1880* (1988) places these events in a longer context. One response to the horrors of industrialization was to turn one's back on it, a tactic discussed in Malcolm Chase, *'The People's Farm': English Radical Agrarianism 1775–1840* (Oxford, 1988). In the same vein, Owenite socialism has attracted a number of important and analytical studies including J. F. C. Harrison's *Robert Owen and the Owenites in Britain and America: The Quest for the New Moral World* (1969); Anne Taylor's *Visions of Harmony: A Study in Nineteenth-Century Millenarianism* (Oxford, 1987); Barbara Taylor's *Eve and the New Jerusalem: Socialism and Feminism in the Nineteenth Century* (Cambridge, Mass., 1983); and two books by Gregory Claeys, *Citizens and Saints: Politics and Anti-Politics in Early British Socialism* (Cambridge, 1989) and *Machinery, Money, and the Millennium: From Moral Economy to Socialism, 1815–1860* (Princeton, 1987).

Chartism, unsurprisingly, dominates the literature on popular protest. There are some excellent general surveys, such as J. T. Ward's *Chartism* (1973), David Jones's *Chartism and the Chartists* (1975), Dorothy Thompson's *The Chartists* (1984), and Edward Royle's *Chartism* (3rd edn. Harlow, 1996). Despite its vintage, G. D. H. Cole, *Chartist Portraits* (1941) retains its savour, while Asa Briggs (ed.), *Chartist Studies* (1959) is a classic product of an era in which the movement was invariably depicted in economic and regional terms. Gareth Stedman Jones broke away from all such materialist explanations in his *Languages of Class: Studies in English Working Class History 1832–1982* (Cambridge, 1983), which includes a seminally influential essay ('Rethinking Chartism') on discourse. The challenge was taken up by Paul Pickering in 'Class without Words: Symbolic Communication in the Chartist Movement', *P&P* 112 (1986), 144–62, which was followed by James A. Epstein's *Radical Expression: Political Language, Ritual, and Symbol in England, 1790–1850* (Oxford, 1994). Pickering's *Chartism and the Chartists in Manchester and Salford* (Basingstoke, 1995) signalled a further advance for the 'cultural turn', as did John Belchem's 'Beyond Chartist Studies: Class, Community and Party', in Derek Fraser (ed.), *Cities, Class and Communication: Essays in Honour of Asa Briggs*, (Hemel Hempstead, 1990). James Epstein and Dorothy Thompson (eds.), *The Chartist Experience: Studies in Working-Class Radicalism and Culture, 1830–60*, (London, 1982) is in a similar vein. For a sample of leadership biographies, there are Alfred Plummer, *Bronterre: A Political Biography of Bronterre O'Brien 1804–1864* (1971);[33] James Epstein, *The Lion of Freedom: Feargus O'Connor and the Chartist Movement, 1832–1842* (1982); A. R. Schoyen, *The Chartist Challenge: A Portrait of George Julian Harney* (1958); and Miles Taylor, *Ernest Jones, Chartism, and the Romance of Politics 1819–1869* (Oxford, 2003).[34]

---

[33] Iowerth Prothero's biography of Bronterre is eagerly awaited.

[34] See Andrew Messner, 'Land, Leadership, Culture, and Emigration: Some Problems in Chartist Historiography', *HJ* 42 (1999), 1093–110.

682 BIBLIOGRAPHY

As for the refusal of a tightly organized and authoritarian State to buckle, F. C. Mather's *Public Order in the Age of the Chartists* (Manchester, 1959) has been followed by David Goodway's *London Chartism 1838–1848* (Cambridge, 1982) and John Saville's *1848: The British State and the Chartist Movement* (Cambridge, 1987). Moral force has proved less attractive to historians than physical, but David Stack is penetrating on 'William Lovett and the National Association for the Political and Social Improvement of the People', *HJ* 42/4 (1999), 1027–50. So too, on a wider canvas, is Miles Taylor, 'Rethinking the Chartists: Searching for Synthesis in the Historiography of Chartism', *HJ* 39 (1996), 479–95. Finally, one can turn to historical geographers for insight into how the movement kept itself alive through intensive networking, i.e. how the discrete local Chartisms uncovered by Briggs and his colleagues held together. See Humphrey Southall, 'Mobility, the Artisan Community and Popular Politics in Early 19th Century England', in G. Kearns and C. W. J. Withers (eds.), *Urbanising England* (Cambridge, 1991).

POWER, WEALTH, STATUS: THE UPPER AND MIDDLE CLASSES

To begin at the top: it was once supposed that this period saw 'the waning of "the influence of the Crown"'[35] and that there was little more to be said. The royal Court lacked Continental-style glamour, and George IV—the only king to show any extrovert tastes for the arts—was a political outsider, largely estranged from the ruling Pittite regime. The later Hanoverians, it was said, were all either madmen or wastrels, and it was not until after Victoria's succession in 1837 that the Crown's reputation began to recover. More recently, however, as historians have come to recognize the significance of informal influence, the monarchy has been somewhat rehabilitated in esteem, a process that owed much to Colley's article (already mentioned) 'The Apotheosis of George III: Loyalty, Royalty and the British Nation 1760– 1820', *P&P* 102 (1984), 94–129, and has continued as far as Christopher Hibbert, *George III* (1998). Steven Parissien, *George IV: The Grand Entertainment* (2001) does justice to its subject's wayward extravagances but also take pleasure in his sheer zest, while more surprisingly E. A. Smith (a historian who had not previously identified with liberated humanity) argued in *George IV* (New Haven, 1999) that 'it was he, rather than Victoria and Albert, who created the constitutional monarchy of nineteenth-century Britain and began the revival of its popularity'. Not to be outdone, Frank Prochaska has gone so far as to credit the dissolute royal dukes with having played their part in *Royal Bounty: The Making of a Welfare Monarchy* (New Haven, 1995). For the next King, his mistress, and his wife, read Tom Pocock, *Sailor King: The Life of King William IV* (1991), Claire Tomalin, *Mrs. Jordan's Profession: The Story of a Great Actress and a Future King* (1994), and A. W. Purdue, 'Queen Adelaide: Malign Influence or Consort Maligned?', in Clarissa Campbell Orr (ed.), *Queenship in Britain, 1660–1837: Royal Patronage, Court, Culture, and Dynastic Politics* (Manchester, 2002).[36] There remains much ground for dispute: see, for example,

---

[35] The title of an influential article by A. S. Foord, *EHR* 62 (1947), 484–507.
[36] Queen Adelaide exemplified the sort of 'new woman' referred to below in the comment on Nancy Armstrong's book.

David Cannadine, 'The Context, Performance and Meaning of Ritual: The British Monarchy and the "Invention of Tradition", *c.*1820–1977', in Eric Hobsbawm and Terence Ranger (eds.), *The Invention of Tradition* (Cambridge, 1983), and Walter L. Arnstein, 'Queen Victoria Opens Parliament: The Disinvention of Tradition', *Historical Research*, 63 (1990), 178–94. It may necessarily be so, for there was clearly a deep ambivalence in attitudes to royalty, a point explored by Marilyn Morris in *The British Monarchy and the French Revolution* (New Haven 1998) and by G. M. Ditchfield in *George III: An Essay in Monarchy* (Basingstoke, 2002).

Michael W. McCahill's *Order and Equipoise: The Peerage and the House of Lords, 1783–1806* (1978) is a rare but distinguished study of an institution which, in terms of formal political power, was at a low ebb. Nevertheless, and despite challenges, England remained an aristocratic society in terms of influence and status. So much is evident from any number of studies, including G. E. Mingay, *English Landed Society in the Eighteenth Century* (1963); F. M. L. Thompson, *English Landed Society in the Nineteenth Century* (1963); John Cannon, *Aristocratic Century: The Peerage of Eighteenth-Century England* (Cambridge, 1984); J. V. Beckett, *The Aristocracy in England 1660–1914* (Oxford, 1986); and Lawrence and Jeanne C. Fawtier Stone, *An Open Elite? England 1540–1880* (Oxford, 1984). Ellis Wasson thinks that the Stones underestimate the extent to which the elite was open to newcomers, yet his own analysis, in *Born to Rule: British Political Elites* (Stroud, 2000), shows that just 368 families out of 2,800 studied supplied more than two-thirds of all MPs and four-fifths of all peers between 1660 and 1945. Relevant to this debate is Harold Perkin, 'The Recruitment of Elites in British Society since 1800', *Journal of Social History*, 12 (1978), 222–34. Ruscombe Foster, *The Politics of County Power: Wellington and the Hampshire Gentlemen 1820–1852* (Hemel Hempstead, 1990) shows how important local influence remained to this section of society, though by the 1830s pressure from centralizing reformers was beginning to be felt. John Habakkuk, *Marriage, Debt, and the Estates System: English Landownership 1650–1950* (Oxford, 1994) examines the legal aspects of estate and family life, while David Cannadine's 'The Making of the British Upper Classes', in Cannadine, *Aspects of Aristocracy: Grandeur and Decline in Modern Britain* (New Haven, 1994) demonstrates the zest with which some aristocrats seized new opportunities to make money. The domestic lives of the great have always been lived vicariously by readers avid for descriptions of day-to-day existence in hall and manor. Recently, however, and as a by-product of the emphasis on gender history, there has been a vogue for minute and scholarly accounts of individual families, based on estate records and personal correspondence. To select two at random, Stella Tillyard's *Aristocrats: Caroline, Emily, Louisa and Sarah Lennox, 1740–1832* (1994) may be read against Joanna Martin's account of a slightly less exalted pedigree, the West Country Fox Strangways, in *Wives and Daughters: Women and Children in the Georgian Country House* (2004).

Landlords had the power to change the face of the English countryside dramatically, for which, see Oliver Rackham, *The History of the Countryside* (1997). Different traditions of husbandry and estate improvement sometimes had political and ideological implications, a point discussed in Stephen Daniels, *Humphry Repton: Landscape Gardening and the Geography of Georgian England* (New Haven, 1999), Nigel Everett, *The Tory View of Landscape* (New Haven, 1994), Ann Bermingham, *Landscape and*

Ideology: The English Rustic Tradition, 1740–1860 (1987), Andrew Ballantyne, *Architecture, Landscape and Liberty: Richard Payne Knight and the Picturesque* (Cambridge, 1997), and Charlotte Klonk, *Science and the Perception of Nature: British Landscape Art in the Late Eighteenth and Early Nineteenth Centuries* (New Haven, 1996).[37] Although nothing has been said about this in the foregoing text, this was the age of Mr John Jorrocks, Master of Foxhounds at Handley Cross; see Raymond Carr, *English Fox Hunting: A History* (1976), David C. Itzkowitz, *Peculiar Privilege: A Social History of English Foxhunting* (Hassocks, 1977), and Norman Gash, *Robert Surtees and Early Victorian Society* (Oxford, 1993).

The question whether late eighteenth-century society should be depicted in two- or three-class terms is discussed in Chapter 3. E. P. Thompson states the case for just two in 'Patrician Society, Plebeian Culture', *Journal of Social History*, 7 (1974), 382–405, in 'Eighteenth-Century English Society: Class Struggle without Class?', *Social History*, 3 (1978), 133–65, and again in *Customs in Common* (1991).[38] Like Roy Porter in his racy depiction of *English Society in the Eighteenth Century* (Harmondsworth, 1982), Thompson portrays the two-way relationship in an antagonistic, exploitative light. There is also, however, a cosier version in which Thompson's 'patricians and plebs' transmogrified into 'aristocracy and people'. Norman Gash's *Aristocracy and People: Britain 1815–1865* (1979), John Cannon's *Aristocratic Century* (Cambridge, 1984), J. C. D. Clark's *English Society 1688–1832: Ideology, Social Structure and Political Practice during the Ancien Régime* (Cambridge, 1985), and Ian R. Christie's *Stress and Stability in Late Eighteenth-Century Britain: Reflections on the British Avoidance of Revolution* (Oxford, 1984) all stress cosy paternalism and willing deference, Cannon going so far as to describe the landlord system as 'a great system of authority and subordination which formed the context for men's lives' (p. 170). Historians who subscribe to the opposing idea of a viable three-class society include Paul Langford in *A Polite and Commercial People: England, 1727–1783* (Oxford, 1989) and Nicholas Rogers, 'Money, Land and Lineage: The Big Bourgeoisie of Hanoverian London', *Social History*, 4 (1979), 437–54. There is further discussion in Alan J. Kidd and David Nicholls (eds.), *The Making of the British Middle Class? Studies of Regional and Cultural Diversity since the Eighteenth Century* (Stroud, 1998). Harold Perkin's view in *The Origins of Modern English Society* (1969) is that the bourgeois entrepreneurs were in fierce opposition to aristocratic culture until the 1860s when, having achieved the potential for hegemony, they suddenly succumbed to the charms of their enemy's outlook on life. Against this there is a more gradualist interpretation of entrepreneurial accommodation to aristocratic values, as put forward by F. M. L. Thompson in *Gentrification and the Enterprise Culture: Britain 1780–1980* (Oxford, 2001).

Some texts (including this one) emphasize the fractured nature of the bourgeoisie, in which case 'four-class' becomes a more appropriate term. No one has done more to press

---

[37] For a technical analysis, see Denis Cosgrove and Stephen Daniels (eds.), *The Iconography of Landscape: Essays on the Symbolic Representation, Design and Use of Past Environments* (Cambridge, 1988), especially the essays by Daniels, John Lucas, and Hugh Prince.

[38] See Peter King, 'Edward Thompson's Contribution to Eighteenth-Century Studies: The Patrician–Plebeian Model Re-examined', *Social History*, 21 (1996), 215–28.

its case, or to probe the distribution of usable wealth, than W. D. Rubinstein. See in particular three of his more important contributions: *Men of Property: The Very Wealthy in Britain since the Industrial Revolution* (1981), *Elites and the Wealthy in Modern British History* (Brighton, 1987), and 'The Structure of Wealth-Holding in Britain, 1809–39: A Preliminary Anatomy', *Historical Research*, 65 (1992), 74–89. Most recently, in *Men, Women and Property in England, 1780–1870* (Cambridge, 2005), R. J. Morris has taken Leeds as his focus in considering how the middle classes developed strategies for surviving a period of heightened economic insecurity. His detailed and sophisticated study of wills, trusts, property deeds, and account books reveals a group of 'essentially "networked" families created and affirmed by "gift" networks of material goods, finance, services and support with property very much at the centre', and likewise the enforcement of those debts and contracts that lay at the heart of capitalism.

Much emphasis has been placed above on the worlds of high finance and high commerce, but there are not many comprehensive surveys. David Kynaston, *The City of London*, i: *A World of its Own 1815–1890* (1994) covers important ground, as does L. S. Pressnell, *Country Banking in the Industrial Revolution* (Oxford, 1956). Niall Ferguson's *The World's Banker: The History of the House of Rothschild* (1998) reveals far more than was known before about that important *éminence grise* N. M. Rothschild. J. R. Ward, *The Finance of Canal Building in Eighteenth-Century England* (1974) charts the emergence of a widespread investing class, and the theme is picked up in Seymour Broadbridge, *Studies in Railway Expansion and the Capital Market in England, 1825–1873* (1970) and M. C. Reed, *Investment in Railways in Britain, 1820–44: A Study in the Development of the Capital Market* (1975). Iain Black, 'Geography, Political Economy and the Circulation of Finance Capital in Early Industrial England', *Journal of Historical Geography*, 15 (1989), 366–84, is illuminating. So is *The First Latin American Debt Crisis: The City of London and the 1822–25 Loan Bubble* (New Haven, 1990), in which Frank Griffith Dawson dissects the worst Stock Market crash of the century. Stanley Chapman's general studies *The Rise of Merchant Banking* (1984) and *Merchant Enterprise in Britain: From the Industrial Revolution to World War I* (Cambridge, 1992)[39] can be read in conjunction with Ralph Willard Hidy, *The House of Baring in American Trade and Finance: English Merchant Bankers at Work, 1763–1861* (Cambridge, Mass., 1949). P. G. M. Dickson, *The Sun Insurance Office 1710–1960: The History of Two and a Half Centuries of British Insurance* (1960) and Barry Supple, *The Royal Exchange Assurance: A History of British Insurance 1720–1970* (Cambridge, 1970) were two pioneering business studies, developing themes later explored by Clive Trebilcock in *Phoenix Assurance and the Development of British Insurance*, i: *1782–1870* (Cambridge, 1985).

The 'upper-middle class', as defined above, included groups that are now called 'professional'. A useful starting point is W. J. Reader, *Professional Men: The Rise of the Professional Classes in Nineteenth-Century England* (1966), which has now been supplemented by Penelope J. Corfield's *Power and the Professions in Britain 1700–1850* (1995). The law has received a steady stream of important monographs: Daniel Duman's *The Judicial Bench in England 1727–1875* (1982) and *The English and Colonial Bars in the*

---

[39] See also S. D. Chapman, 'British Marketing Enterprise: The Changing Role of Merchants, Manufacturers and Financiers, 1700–1860', *Business History Review*, 53 (1979), 205–34.

Nineteenth Century (1983); Wilfrid R. Prest's *The Rise of the Barristers: A Social History of the English Bar 1590–1640* (Oxford, 1986); and Christopher W. Brooks's challenging *Lawyers, Litigation and English Society since 1450* (1998). Doctors were slower to 'professionalize', a point emphasized by Roy Porter in any number of books, including *Health for Sale: Quackery in England 1660–1850* (Manchester, 1989), but that it happened at last is clear from Irvine Loudon, *Medical Care and the General Practitioner 1750–1850* (Oxford, 1986).

CIVIC CULTURES AND URBAN LIVES

The upper-middle class can only be understood properly in a civic and urban context. London was the greatest city in the world, though it ended the period in disarray with regard to its governance, as illustrated in Lynda Nead, *Victorian Babylon: People, Streets and Images in Nineteenth-Century London* (New Haven, 2000). The process of declension can be traced in Francis Sheppard, *London: The Infernal Wen 1808–70* (1971). There is a slightly more upbeat account in Deborah Epstein Nord, *Walking the Victorian Streets: Women, Representation, and the City* (Ithaca, NY, 1995), and a celebration of its diverse vivacity in Celina Fox (ed.), *London: World City 1800–1840* (New Haven, 1992). Dana Arnold, *Re-presenting the Metropolis: Architecture, Urban Experience and Social Life in London 1800–1840* (Aldershot, 2000) is also good on the self-conscious construction of an urban environment. However, the eyes of contemporaries were less on the capital than on the hectic growth of industrial towns, arguably the most important development of the period. Readers should start with *The Cambridge Urban History of Britain, ii: 1540–1840*, ed. Peter Clark, and iii: *1840–1950*, ed. Martin Daunton (Cambridge, 2000). Jeffrey G. Williamson, *Coping with City Growth during the British Industrial Revolution* (Cambridge, 1990) and Richard Dennis, *English Industrial Cities of the Nineteenth Century: A Social Geography* (Cambridge, 1984) give some idea of the enormous human problems such towns faced. In the circumstances local politics became sites of strife at least as bitter as Westminster. As a starting point Derek Fraser, *Urban Politics in Victorian England: The Structure of Politics in Victorian Cities* (Leicester, 1976) remains authoritative, as does Donald Read's *The English Provinces c.1760–1960: A Study in Influence* (1964). Specifically there are interesting essays on Manchester (V. A. C. Gatrell), Leeds (Brian Barber), and Bradford (Adrian Elliott) in Derek Fraser (ed.), *Municipal Reform and the Industrial City* (Leicester, 1982) and on Rochdale, Bolton, and Salford in John Garrard's *Leadership and Power in Victorian Industrial Towns 1830–80* (Manchester, 1983). Political struggles in Lancashire are covered in Michael J. Turner, *Reform and Respectability: The Making of a Middle-Class Liberalism in Early Nineteenth-Century Manchester* (Manchester, 1995); Martin Hewitt, *The Emergence of Stability in the Industrial City: Manchester, 1832–67* (Aldershot, 1996); Peter Taylor, *Popular Politics in Early Industrial Britain: Bolton 1825–1850* (Keele, 1995); and Paul T. Phillips, *The Sectarian Spirit: Sectarianism, Society, and Politics in Victorian Cotton Towns* (Toronto, 1982). The East Midlands are dealt with in A. Temple Patterson, *Radical Leicester: A History of Leicester 1780–1850* (Leicester, 1954) and Malcolm I. Thomis, *Politics and Society in Nottingham 1785–1835* (Oxford, 1969). Liverpool awaits its major study so far as this period is concerned. Eric Hopkins, *Birmingham: The First Manufacturing Town in the World 1760–1840* (1989) has more on the economy than on politics (perhaps reflecting the fact that some recent interpreters of the Industrial Revolution have come to see Birmingham's industrial organization as more typical than Manchester's), but Clive Behagg brings the two modes together in *Politics and Production in the Early Nineteenth Century* (1990), one of his aims being to get behind the 'myths of cohesion' that have coloured so much writing about that town.

Moving beyond the narrow ground of politics, Manchester and Leeds in particular have been presented as sites of conflict between an 'upper' and a 'lesser' middle class. On this theme Yorkshire towns are particularly well served, thanks to R. G. Wilson, *Gentlemen Merchants: The Merchant Community in Leeds 1700–1830* (Manchester, 1971); R. J. Morris, *Class, Sect and Party: The Making of the British Middle Class, Leeds 1820–1850* (Manchester, 1990); Gordon Jackson, *Hull in the Eighteenth Century: A Study in Economic and Social History* (1972); and Theodore Koditschek, *Class Formation and Urban-Industrial Society: Bradford, 1750–1850* (Cambridge, 1990). Brian Lewis, *The Middlemost and the Milltowns: Bourgeois Culture and Politics in Early Industrial England* (Stanford, Calif., 2001) is a highly detailed coverage of similar themes with respect to three Lancashire towns, while Howard M. Wach essays an important albeit speculative interpretation in 'Civil Society, Moral Identity and the Liberal Public Sphere: Manchester and Boston, 1810–40', *Social History*, 21 (1996), 281–303. Similar issues are addressed in Alan Kidd and David Nicholls (eds.), *Gender, Civic Culture and Consumerism: Middle-Class Identity in Britain, 1800–1940* (Manchester, 1999). Richard H. Trainor deals with a slightly different (i.e. lesser-middle-class) type of urban environment in *Black Country Elites: The Exercise of Authority in an Industrialized Area 1830–1900* (Oxford, 1993).

The habit of forming societies was central to middle-class civic culture. Peter Clark, *British Clubs and Societies 1580–1800: The Origins of an Associational World* (Oxford, 2000) is essential on the background, though its undoubtedly authoritative findings should not be allowed to obscure the fact that there was a distinctive change in the nature of such clubs towards the close of the eighteenth century. R. J. Morris provides another good introduction in his essay 'Voluntary Societies and British Urban Elites, 1780–1850: An Analysis', *HJ* 26 (1983), 95–118. There are also useful essays in *Class, Power and Social Structure in British Nineteenth-Century Towns* (Leicester, 1986), which is edited by Morris. R. S. Porter, 'Science, Provincial Culture and Public Opinion in Enlightenment England', *British Journal for Eighteenth-Century Studies*, 3 (1980), 20–46, was an eye-opener; some of those whose eyes were opened duly contributed to *Metropolis and Province: Science in British Culture, 1780–1850* (1983), edited by Ian Inkster and Jack Morrell. Turning to specific towns, Birmingham led the way in the eighteenth century, before falling slightly behind in the next one. John Money, *Experience and Identity: Birmingham and the West Midlands 1760–1800* (Manchester, 1977) provides a fine overview, while Robert E. Schofield, *The Lunar Society of Birmingham: A Social History of Provincial Science and Industry in Eighteenth-Century England* (Oxford, 1963) and Jenny Uglow, *The Lunar Men: The Friends Who Made the Future, 1730–1810* (2002) between them do full justice to that remarkable group of intellectual pioneers.

Robert H. Kargon, *Science in Victorian Manchester: Enterprise and Expertise* (Manchester, 1977) is highly informative, while Eddie Cass and Morris Garratt (eds.), *Printing and the Book in Manchester 1700–1850* (2001) serves as a reminder that a provincial town most famous for its proletariat also possessed a flourishing print culture and a sophisticated market in books. Art and architecture were also important ingredients of the new civic culture. See, for example, the essays on Liverpool by K. Hill[40] and A. Wilson[41] in Alan J. Kidd and David Nicholls (eds.), *The Making of the British Middle Class? Studies of Regional and Cultural Diversity since the Eighteenth Century* (Stroud, 1998); Alan J. Kidd and K. W. Roberts (eds.), *City, Class and Culture: Studies of Social Policy and Cultural Production in Victorian Manchester* (1985); Francis D. Klingender, *Art and the Industrial Revolution* (1947); John H. G. Archer (ed.), *Art and Architecture in Victorian Manchester* (Manchester, 1985); Janet Wolff and John Seed (eds.), *The Culture of Capital: Art, Power and the Nineteenth-Century Middle Class* (Manchester, 1988); and, for an interesting but slightly more patronizing account, see Dianne Sachko Macleod, *Art and the Victorian Middle Class: Money and the Making of Cultural Identity* (Cambridge, 1996). As in so many areas a little hindsight is requisite, and the civic culture of the earlier nineteenth century can only be properly understood in relation to what happened after about 1840. Here two recent studies are indispensable: Simon Gunn, *The Public Culture of the Victorian Middle Class: Ritual and Authority in the English Industrial City 1840–1914* (Manchester, 2000) and Tristram Hunt, *Building Jerusalem: The Rise and Fall of the Victorian City* (2004).

WOMEN AND GENDER

As in other areas the literature is too enormous to do more than nod to, the difference being that most of that literature is very recent. The first wave of feminist history emphasized the exclusion of women from public life. For example, in Jane Rendall's classic account *The Origins of Modern Feminism: Women in Britain, France and the United States, 1780–1860* (Basingstoke, 1984), 'origins' equates to the 'pre-history' of the women's movement. Hard though Ruth and Edmund Frow and their fellow contributors tried to unearth *Political Women 1800–1850* (1989), and despite the ingenuity of Malcolm I. Thomis and Jennifer Grimmett in cataloguing examples of *Women in Protest 1800–1850* (1982), still it seemed clear that even elite women were shoved out of 'high public' life in this period, and that they were much less visibly prominent than they had been in the eighteenth century.[42] Biographies of Mary Wollstonecraft continue to come thick and fast—see *Mary Wollstonecraft: A Revolutionary Life* (2000) by Janet Todd, and *Mary Wollstonecraft: A New Genus* by Lyndall Gordon (2005)—but she is seen as marking the end of the line.[43]

[40] ' "Thoroughly Imbued with the Spirit of Ancient Greece": Symbolism and Space in Victorian Civic Culture'.
[41] ' "The Florence of the North"? The Civic Culture of Liverpool in the Early Nineteenth Century'.
[42] On which, see Hannah Barker and Elaine Chalus (eds.), *Gender in Eighteenth-Century England: Roles, Representations and Responsibilities* (1997).
[43] See Karen Green, *The Woman of Reason: Feminism, Humanism and Political Thought* (Cambridge, 1995).

In what might be called the 'new historiography', women have tentatively begun to move towards centre stage. Clare Midgley's *Women Against Slavery: The British Campaigns, 1780–1870* (1992) has demonstrated a high degree of female participation in pressure groups. In *Small Change: Women, Learning, Patriotism, 1750–1810* (Chicago, 2000) Harriet Guest argues ingeniously that small changes in the contemporary understanding of patriotism allowed women, hitherto domestically bound, to 'imagine themselves as political subjects'. Helen Rogers makes some convincing claims in *Women and the People: Authority, Authorship and the Radical Tradition in Nineteenth-Century England* (Aldershot, 2000). There are similar contributions in Hannah Barker and Elaine Chalus (eds.), *Gender in Eighteenth-Century England: Roles, Representations and Responsibilities*, (1997) and in Kathryn Gleadle and Sarah Richardson (eds.), *Women in British Politics, 1760–1860: The Power of the Petticoat* (Basingstoke, 2000). And there are also two fine studies by Ruth Watts and Kathryn Gleadle: respectively, *Gender, Power and the Unitarians in England 1760–1860* (1998) and *The Early Feminists: Radical Unitarians and the Emergence of the Women's Rights Movements, 1831–51* (Basingstoke, 1995).

All this is impressive, yet the attempt to argue that women were politically significant can go only so far. (After all, the fact that Unitarian women were so active hardly helps the argument, since Unitarianism was counter-cultural in every respect.) Instead the case for female importance has to rest on their position within the wider public sphere, as several of the contributors to Amanda Vickery (ed.), *Women, Privilege, and Power: British Politics, 1750 to the Present* (Stanford, Calif., 2001) have noted (especially the editor herself and Peter Mandler). Science was important in culture and women were prominent in science, albeit not as superstars, a point nailed home in Patricia Phillips, *The Scientific Lady: A Social History of Women's Scientific Interests 1520–1918* (1990), and Patricia Fara, *Pandora's Breeches: Women, Science and Power in the Enlightenment* (2005). Private charitable work was also important, and that was an area which females dominated, as F. K. Prochaska shows in *Women and Philanthropy in Nineteenth-Century England* (Oxford, 1980). Education, and more generally pedagogy, was widely seen as the key to rescuing society from its thrall, and here too women were allowed a dominant voice, a point emphasized by Mary Hilton and Pam Hirsch in the introduction to their edited collection *Practical Visionaries: Women, Education and Social Progress, 1790–1930* (2000). Then there was religion, and the prominent influence of moralists like Hannah More (a topic reserved for the following section). Some of these themes can be explored in Lillian Lewis Shiman, *Women and Leadership in Nineteenth-Century England* (Basingstoke, 1992). Finally there was the prominent place which females occupied in the public sphere as readers and writers. The following studies are picked somewhat at random: Elizabeth Eger, Charlotte Grant, Cliona O'Gallchoir, and Penny Warburton (eds.), *Women, Writing, and the Public Sphere: 1700–1830* (Cambridge, 2001); Angela Keane, *Women Writers and the English Nation in the 1790s: Romantic Belongings* (2000); Joanne Shattock (ed.), *Women and Literature in Britain 1800–1900* (Cambridge, 2001); Jacqueline Pearson, *Women's Reading in Britain 1750–1835: A Dangerous Recreation* (Cambridge, 1999). Anne Mellor's *Romanticism and Gender* (New York, 1993) takes a different tack by arguing that Romanticism was a masculine strategy for feminizing nature and so marginalizing women.

Two other literary studies, Gary Kelly's *Women, Writing, and Revolution 1790–1827* (Oxford, 1993) and Nancy Armstrong's *Desire and Domestic Fiction: A Political History of the Novel* (New York, 1987), relate an increased awareness of gender directly to middle-class mores. More specifically, Armstrong argues that the 'new woman'—demure and domestic rather than titled and wealthy—was created as a template for new bourgeois notions of happy families. This is to place a more positive spin on 'separate spheres', a notion which gets its most authoritative airing in Leonore Davidoff and Catherine Hall, *Family Fortunes: Men and Women of the English Middle Class 1780–1850* (1987). Though skewed towards particular localities (the West Midlands, Essex) and social groups (Nonconformity), their powerful tome has provided historians with both a stimulus and a challenge. Its central argument—that the development of capitalism entailed a growing separation between home and workplace—has been gently questioned by Robert B. Shoemaker in his synoptic account *Gender in English Society, 1650–1850: The Emergence of Separate Spheres?* (1998), and it has also been powerfully challenged by Amanda Vickery in 'Golden Age to Separate Spheres?: A Review of the Categories and Chronology of English Women's History', *HJ* 36 (1993), 383–414. Katrina Honeyman, *Women, Gender and Industrialization in England, 1700–1870* (Basingstoke, 2000) weighs in by pointing out that women played a far more positive role than is usually thought in the development of industrialization, while conversely the process of industrialization helped to define ideas about gender, generally to women's disadvantage. Vickery's own study *The Gentleman's Daughter: Women's Lives in Georgian England* (New Haven, 1998) likewise emphasizes continuity. On the other hand Lawrence Stone's trilogy *Road to Divorce: England 1530–1987* (Oxford, 1990), *The Family, Sex and Marriage in England 1500–1800* (1977), and *Broken Lives: Separation and Divorce in England 1660–1857* (Oxford, 1993) depicts a family economy of affection that he believes was new in this period, a view that may be pondered in the light of James Christen Steward's *The New Child: British Art and the Origins of Modern Childhood, 1730–1830* (Berkeley, Calif., 1995). Of course increased affection can lead to increased strain, and many books deal with marital strife in the period, notably Anna Clark, *Women's Silence, Men's Violence: Sexual Assault in England, 1770–1845* (1987). In so far as separate spheres *did* operate, it is easy to see women as the victims (angelization as marginalization), but men could suffer too, as is evident from John Tosh's *A Man's Place: Masculinity and the Middle-Class Home in Victorian England* (New Haven, 1999), and also from Michael Roper and John Tosh (eds.), *Manful Assertions: Masculinities in Britain since 1800* (1990).

RELIGION, MORALITY, AND THE CHURCHES

This was in many ways an intensely religious period, though to some extent that very intensity masked an awareness of doubt. John Hedley Brooke, *Science and Religion: Some Historical Perspectives* (Cambridge, 1991) provides interesting insights, and although the contributors to Richard J. Helmstadter and Bernard Lightman (eds.), *Victorian Faith in Crisis: Essays on Continuity and Change in Nineteenth-Century Religious Belief* (Basingstoke, 1990) mainly address the years after 1846, they nevertheless throw light on this period as well. General surveys of worship include W. R. Ward, *Religion and Society in England 1790–1850* (1972); Robert Currie, Alan Gilbert, and Lee Horsley, *Churches and Churchgoers: Patterns of Church Growth in the British Isles since 1700* (Oxford, 1977); Alan D. Gilbert, *Religion and Society in Industrial England: Church, Chapel, and Social Change, 1740–1914* (1976); and K. D. M. Snell and Paul S. Ell (eds.), *Rival Jerusalems: The Geography of Victorian Religion* (Cambridge, 2000). For the Church as an institution, Owen Chadwick, *The Victorian Church* (1966–70) remains the starting point, followed by the various essays in (but especially the editors' introduction to) John Walsh, Colin Haydon, and Stephen Taylor (eds.), *The Church of England c.1689–c.1833: From Toleration to Tractarianism* (Cambridge, 1993). For organizational aspects, see Olive J. Brose, *Church and Parliament: The Reshaping of the Church of England 1828–1860* (Stanford, Calif., 1959); Stewart J. Brown, *The National Churches of England, Ireland, and Scotland 1801–46* (Oxford, 2001); Kenneth A. Thompson, *Bureaucracy and Church Reform: The Organizational Response of the Church of England to Social Change 1800–1965* (Oxford, 1970); Peter Virgin, *The Church in an Age of Negligence: Ecclesiastical Structure and Problems of Church Reform 1700–1840* (Cambridge, 1989); Frances Knight, *The Nineteenth-Century Church and English Society* (Cambridge, 1995); Arthur Burns, *The Diocesan Revival in the Church of England c.1800–1870* (Oxford, 1999); and G. F. A. Best, *Temporal Pillars: Queen Anne's Bounty, the Ecclesiastical Commissioners, and the Church of England* (Cambridge, 1964). The ancient universities remained to a large extent seminaries, and in the absence of Convocation provided virtually the only forum in which Churchmen could engage in public debate. Their condition is described in three excellent volumes: *The History of the University of Oxford, v: The Eighteenth Century*, ed. L. S. Sutherland and L. G. Mitchell (Oxford, 1986); vi: *Nineteenth-Century Oxford, Part 1*, ed. M. G. Brock and M. C. Curthoys (Oxford, 1997); and Peter Searby, *A History of the University of Cambridge, iii: 1750–1870* (Cambridge, 1997).

In the text above much importance has been attached to that protean phenomenon evangelicalism. The best introduction is by D. W. Bebbington in *Evangelicalism in Modern Britain: A History from the 1730s to the 1980s* (1989); G. M. Ditchfield's *The Evangelical Revival* (1998) is brief but makes some acute observations. For Anglican evangelicalism, Ford K. Brown, *Fathers of the Victorians: The Age of Wilberforce* (Cambridge, 1961) remains important, though it now needs to be brought up to date. Ian Bradley, *The Call to Seriousness: The Evangelical Impact on the Victorians* (1976) is a useful introduction. Grayson Carter, *Anglican Evangelicals: Protestant Secessions from the Via Media, c.1800–1850* (Oxford, 2001) is excellent on the divisions within the movement. Timothy C. F. Stunt, *From Awakening to Secession: Radical Evangelicals in Switzerland and Britain 1815–35* (Edinburgh, 2000) is an equally well-researched study of some fringe groups. Doreen M. Rosman, *Evangelicals and Culture* (1984) strips away some of the caricatures and stereotypes; Boyd Hilton's *The Age of Atonement: The Influence of Evangelicalism on Social and Economic Thought 1795–1865* (Oxford, 1988) relates the evangelicals' social and economic thought to their theology. That book placed much weight on an evangelical Presbyterian Scot, Thomas Chalmers, as a pundit who best articulated and also helped to spread the evangelical ideology. By far the best general account of his life is Stewart J. Brown, *Thomas Chalmers and the Godly Commonwealth in Scotland* (Oxford, 1982). Like Hilton, Herbert Schlossberg considers 'the struggle between evangelicalism and utilitarianism for intellectual domination' in *The Silent Revolution and the Making of Victorian England* (Columbus, Ohio, 2000). W. H. Oliver dissects the most important of many divisions within the so-called movement: *Prophets and Millennialists: The Uses of Biblical Prophecy in England from the 1790s to the 1840s* (Auckland, 1978). J. F. C. Harrison, *The Second Coming: Popular Millenarianism 1780–1850* (1979) shows how such ideas were played out by ordinary preachers and sectaries. There are many useful essays in Mark A. Noll, David W. Bebbington, and George A. Rawlyk (eds.), *Evangelicalism: Comparative Studies of Popular Protestantism in North America, the British Isles, and Beyond, 1700–1990* (New York, 1994). Finally, it is worth repairing to Gordon Rattray Taylor, *The Angel-Makers: A Study in the Psychological Origins of Historical Change 1750–1850* (1958), which place an interesting psychological gloss on some of the attitudes presented here as evangelical.

Students of High Churchmanship must begin with two brilliant studies, one evocative and the other analytical. These are David Newsome, *The Parting of Friends: A Study of the Wilberforces and Henry Manning* (1966) and Peter Benedict Nockles, *The Oxford Movement in Context: Anglican High Churchmanship, 1760–1857* (Cambridge, 1994). There are some fine biographies, such as *High Church Prophet: Bishop Samuel Horsley (1733–1806) and the Caroline Tradition in the Later Georgian Church* (Oxford, 1992) by F. C. Mather; *The Last of the Prince Bishops: William Van Mildert and the High Church Movement of the Early Nineteenth Century* (1992) by E. A. Varley; and above all *Science and Religion: Baden Powell and the Anglican Debate, 1800–1860* (Cambridge, 1988) by Pietro Corsi. Ian Ker, *John Henry Newman* (Oxford, 1988) is the standard biography; Frank M. Turner, *John Henry Newman: The Challenge to Evangelical Religion* (New Haven, 2002) is excitingly idiosyncratic; Stephen Thomas, *Newman and Heresy: The Anglican Years* (Cambridge, 1991) is theologically sophisticated. S. A. Skinner's very important *Tractarians and the 'Condition of England': The Social and Political Thought of the Oxford Movement* (Oxford, 2004) corrects long-held assumptions to the effect that this type of Churchman had little to say about social and economic questions. For the last gasp of 'High and Dry' Churchmanship, William J. Baker, *Beyond Port and Prejudice: Charles Lloyd of Oxford, 1784–1829* (Orono, Me., 1981) deals with the centre, and Clive Dewey, *The Passing of Barchester* (Rio Grande, Ohio, 1991), with the locality.

Liberal Anglicans—earlier called Latitudinarians, later called Broad-Churchmen—were less intense if no less sincere about religion. Three indispensable starting points are Charles Richard Sanders, *Coleridge and the Broad Church Movement* (Durham, NC, 1942), John Colmer, *Coleridge: Critic of Society* (Oxford, 1959), and Duncan Forbes, *The Liberal Anglican Idea of History* (Cambridge, 1952). Coleridge was not a Liberal Anglican himself, but his social and moral stance was influential, and Liberal Anglicans saw themselves as constituting the clerisy he had called for, a point discussed by Ben Knights in *The Idea of the Clerisy in the Nineteenth Century* (Cambridge, 1978). Thomas Arnold of Rugby School was the man who actually sought to create a 'manly' clerisy. A full-scale modern biography is desperately needed. Thomas Carlyle was a one-man clerisy in himself. The literature is vast, but there is good introductory material in A. L. Le Quesne (ed.), *Victorian Thinkers: Carlyle, Ruskin, Arnold, Morris* (Oxford, 1992) and Jonathan Mendilow, *The Romantic Tradition in British Political Thought* (1985). Peter Allen, *The Cambridge Apostles: The Early Years* (Cambridge, 1978) examines an important network, and can be read alongside N. Merrill Distad's *Guessing at Truth: The Life of Julius Charles Hare* (Shepherdstown, W. Va., 1979), and David Newsome, *Two Classes of Men: Platonism and English Romantic Thought* (Cambridge, 1974). Norman Vance, *The Sinews of the Spirit: The Ideal of Christian Manliness in Victorian Literature and Religious Thought* (Cambridge, 1985) is mainly on a later period but has important things to say about the liberal religion of Coleridge, Maurice, Carlyle, and Arnold. Similarly the earlier parts of J. W. Burrow, *Evolution and Society: A Study in Victorian Social Theory* (Cambridge, 1966) is crucial, as is the same author's *A Liberal Descent: Victorian Historians and the English Past* (Cambridge, 1981).

The view from London can lead one to exaggerate the importance of denominational differences. At any rate there was a degree of cross worship on the ground, as Mark Smith shows in *Religion in Industrial Society: Oldham and Saddleworth, 1740–1865* (Oxford, 1994). Having said that, those differences mattered politically. The starting point for students of non-Anglican Protestantism must be Michael R. Watts, *The Dissenters*, ii: *The Expansion of Evangelical Nonconformity* (Oxford, 1995). It can be followed by more concentrated studies such as Ursula Henriques, *Religious Toleration in England 1787–1833* (1961), Dale A. Johnson, *The Changing Shape of English Nonconformity, 1825–1925* (New York, 1999), and Deryck W. Lovegrove, *Established Church, Sectarian People: Itinerancy and the Transformation of English Dissent, 1780–1830* (Cambridge, 1988). Michael A. Rutz, 'The Politicizing of Evangelical Dissent, 1811–1813', *Parliamentary History*, 20 (2001), 187–207, tackles one important juncture. R. Tudur Jones, *Congregationalism in England 1662–1962* (1962) should be read alongside Clyde Binfield, *So Down to Prayers: Studies in English Nonconformity 1780–1920* (1977) and Susan Thorne, *Congregational Missions and the Making of an Imperial Culture in 19th-Century England* (Stanford, Calif., 1999). Rupert E. Davies, A. Raymond George, and E. Gordon Rupp (eds.), *A History of the Methodist Church in Great Britain* (4 vols., 1965–88) is a standard work, but see also Bernard Semmel, *The Methodist Revolution* (1973), David Hempton, *Methodism and Politics in British Society 1750–1850* (1984), and John Munsey Turner, *Conflict and Reconciliation: Studies in Methodism and Ecumenism in England 1740–1982* (1985). Much more than other types of Nonconformity, 'rational religion', or Unitarianism, has been presented here as the main antithesis of Anglican evangelical orthodoxies. The usual suspects are Price[44] and Priestley, but—as Barbara Taylor has ably demonstrated in *Mary Wollstonecraft and the Feminist Imagination* (Cambridge, 2003)—even that great 'feminist' can be understood properly only in religious terms. Knud Haakonssen (ed.), *Enlightenment and Religion: Rational Dissent in Eighteenth-Century Britain* (Cambridge, 1996) is a major contribution, as are H. M. Wach's 'A "Still, Small Voice" from the Pulpit: Religion and the Creation of Social Morality in Manchester, 1820–1850', *Journal of Modern History*, 63 (1991), 425–56, and three articles by John Seed: 'Unitarianism, Political Economy and the Antinomies of Liberal Culture in Manchester, 1830–50', *Social History*, 7 (1982), 1–25; 'Gentlemen Dissenters: The Social and Political Meanings of Rational Dissent in the 1770s and 1780s', *HJ* 28 (1985), 299–325; and 'Theologies of Power: Unitarianism and the Social Relations of Religious Discourse 1800–50', in R. J. Morris (ed.), *Class, Power and Social*

[44] D. O. Thomas, *Richard Price, 1723–1791* (Cardiff, 1976).

Structure in British Nineteenth-Century Towns (Leicester, 1986). David Young, *F. D. Maurice and Unitarianism* (Oxford, 1992) is indispensable on the way in which some of the Unitarians' attitudes gradually penetrated the Established Church. J. D. Holmes, *More Roman than Rome: English Catholicism in the 19th century* (1978) is a thoughtful consideration of the other end of the spectrum of religious Dissent. Finally, for two important studies of religious radicalism, see Richard Carwardine, *Transatlantic Revivalism: Popular Evangelicalism in Britain and America, 1790–1865* (1978) and Eileen Groth Lyon, *Politicians in the Pulpit: Christian Radicalim in Britain from the Fall of the Bastille to the Disintegration of Chartism* (Aldershot, 1999).

Religion obviously played a part in the pre-Victorian rise of respectability, a subject that can be approached through Marjorie Morgan's *Manners, Morals and Class in England, 1774–1858* (Basingstoke, 1994). Christopher Tolley discusses particular instances in *Domestic Biography: The Legacy of Evangelicalism in Four Nineteenth-Century Families* (Oxford, 1997). If Chalmers did much to disseminate evangelical ideas and mores, his English equivalent has to be Hannah More, than whom no one did more to promote the cause, especially as regards the populace. To the fine biography by H. G. Jones, *Hannah More* (Cambridge, 1952), one must now add Anne Stott, *Hannah More: The First Victorian* (Oxford, 2003). Also very important is Mitzi Myers, 'Hannah More's Tracts for the Times: Social Fiction and Female Ideology', in Mary Anne Schofield and Cecilia Macheski (eds.), *Fetter'd or Free? British Women Novelists, 1670–1815* (Athens, Ohio, 1987). Wackier but also very interesting is Elizabeth Kowaleski-Wallace, *Their Fathers' Daughters: Hannah More, Maria Edgeworth, and Patriarchal Complicity* (New York, 1991). Sexual prurience was of course a major component of respectability. Roy Porter and Lesley Hall illustrate the difference a new century can make in *The Facts of Life: The Creation of Sexual Knowledge in Britain, 1650–1950* (New Haven, 1995), while in *The Making of Victorian Sexuality* and *Victorian Sexual Attitudes* (Oxford, 1994), Michael Mason once again attributes the changing attitudes to evangelicalism.

SCIENCE

The history of science was once a recondite specialism, but is now seen as being central to intellectual and cultural concerns. This is most obvious in respect of the 'not quite sciences', on which Roger Cooter's *The Cultural Meaning of Popular Science: Phrenology and the Organization of Consent in Nineteenth-Century Britain* (Cambridge, 1984) and Alison Winter, *Mesmerized: Powers of Mind in Victorian Britain* (Chicago, 1998) lead the field quite brilliantly. But it also applies to those branches of science that came to be accepted as 'true', even though to say so now risks appearing reductive. The following survey is much too schematic, but may help to guide the reader through some complex issues. The Establishment science (i.e. essentially Newtonian science) of the earlier part of the period can be approached through *The Cambridge History of Science*, iv: *Eighteenth-Century Science*, edited by Roy Porter (Cambridge, 2003). More specific studies include Jan Golinsky, *Science as Public Culture: Chemistry and Enlightenment in Britain, 1760–1820* (Cambridge, 1992); Arnold Thackray, *Atoms and Powers: An Essay on*

Newtonian Matter-Theory and the Development of Chemistry (Cambridge, Mass., 1970); and Robert E. Schofield, *Mechanism and Materialism: British Natural Philosophy in an Age of Reason* (Princeton, 1970). Eighteenth-century counter-currents are covered in R. G. W. Anderson and Christopher Lawrence (eds.), *Science, Medicine and Dissent: Joseph Priestley (1733–1804)* (1987), and in Patricia Fara, *Sympathetic Attractions: Magnetic Practices, Beliefs and Symbolism in Eighteenth-Century England* (Princeton, 1996). For the period of Pittite hegemony between 1783 and 1820 there is John Gascoigne, *Joseph Banks and the English Enlightenment: Useful Knowledge and Polite Culture* (Cambridge, 1994), as well as several studies of the imperial dimension. These include Gascoigne's own *Science in the Service of Empire: Joseph Banks, the British State and the Uses of Science in the Age of Revolution* (Cambridge, 1998), Richard Drayton's *Nature's Government: Science, Imperial Britain, and the 'Improvement' of the World* (New Haven, 2000), and Patricia Fara's *Sex, Botany and Empire: The Story of Carl Linnaeus and Joseph Banks* (Duxford, 2003).

By this time, what might be called 'Opposition science' was beginning to make headway. L. S. Jacyna's *Philosophic Whigs: Medicine, Science and Citizenship in Edinburgh, 1789–1848* (1994) is one way in; another is John V. Pickstone's 'Establishment and Dissent in Nineteenth-Century Medicine: An Exploration of Some Correspondence and Connections Between Religious and Medical Belief-Systems in Early Industrial England', in W. J. Shiels (ed.), *Studies in Church History*, xix (Oxford, 1992). Coleridge the philosopher and Davy the chemist were Tories rather than Whigs, but in the eyes of the Pittite centre they were just as oppositional. Important contributions here include David Knight's *Ideas in Chemistry: A History of the Science* (1992) and *Humphry Davy: Science and Power* (Oxford, 1992); Trevor H. Levere's *Affinity and Matter: Elements of Chemical Philosophy 1800–1865* (Oxford, 1971) and *Poetry Realized in Nature: Samuel Taylor Coleridge and Early Nineteenth-Century Science* (Cambridge, 1981); Christopher Lawrence, 'The Power and the Glory: Humphry Davy and Romanticism', in Andrew Cunningham and Nicholas Jardine (eds.), *Romanticism and the Sciences* (Cambridge, 1990); Edwin Clarke and L. S. Jacyna, *Nineteenth-Century Origins of Neuroscientific Concepts* (Berkeley and Los Angeles, 1987); and L. S. Jacyna, 'Immanence or Transcendence: Theories of Life and Organization in Britain, 1790–1835', *Isis*, 74 (1983), 311–29.

These stirrings led to full-scale conflict between 'conservative' and 'radical' (including 'tory–radical') scientists in the 1830s and 1840s, for although Darwin did not publish his evolutionary theories until 1859, the formative years for evolutionary thinking occurred before 1846. So much is clear from two superb books (among others): Adrian Desmond, *The Politics of Evolution: Morphology, Medicine, and Reform in Radical London* (Chicago, 1989)[45] and James A. Secord, *Victorian Sensation: The Extraordinary Publication, Reception, and Secret Authorship of 'Vestiges of the Natural History of Creation'* (Chicago, 2000). There are also two superb articles: Simon Schaffer's 'The Nebular Hypothesis and the Science of Progress', in James R. Moore (ed.), *History, Humanity and Evolution: Essays for John C. Greene* (Cambridge, 1989) and

---

[45] See also Adrian Desmond, *Archetypes and Ancestors: Palaeontology in Victorian London, 1850–1875* (Chicago, 1982).

Martin J. S. Rudwick, 'Poulett Scrope on the Volcanoes of Auvergne: Lyellian Time and Political Economy', *British Journal for the History of Science*, 7 (1974), 205–42.[46] For Darwin himself, there are Adrian Desmond and James Moore, *Darwin* (1991)[47] and Janet Browne, *Charles Darwin: Voyaging* (1995). Robert M. Young, 'Malthus and the Evolutionists: The Common Context of Biological and Social Theory', *P&P* 43 (1969), 109–45, was seminal in its day and is still worth a ponder. Faced with these challenges, it was necessary for Establishment scientists to furnish a 'Peelite' or 'Whig–Liberal' compromise, one that would hold the line for a while longer. This development is discussed in Desmond's *Politics of Evolution* and also, more sympathetically, in Susan Faye Cannon's *Science in Culture: The Early Victorian Period* (New York, 1978), in Richard Yeo's *Defining Science: William Whewell, Natural Knowledge, and Public Debate in Early Victorian Britain* (Cambridge, 1993), in Menachem Fisch and Simon Schaffer (eds.), *William Whewell: A Composite Portrait* (Oxford, 1991), and in two books by Nicolaas A. Rupke, *The Great Chain of History: William Buckland and the English School of Geology (1814–1849)* (Oxford, 1983) and *Richard Owen: Victorian Naturalist* (New Haven, 1994).[48] Political positions need to be propagated, in science as in anything else, and after 1832 this meant taking the Whewell–Buckland–Owen compromise into the provinces. The definitive study is that of Jack Morrell and Arnold Thackray, *Gentlemen of Science: Early Years of the British Association for the Advancement of Science* (Oxford, 1981).

Meanwhile, of course, scientists continued to practise in ways that could not be interpreted in terms of political strategy. Geoffrey Cantor's *Michael Faraday, Sandemanian and Scientist: A Study of Science and Religion in the Nineteenth Century* (Basingstoke, 1991) depicts someone whose approach was largely independent, despite apparent baggage. Mathematics is perhaps the most value-free of all the sciences. A fascinating paper by M. Norton Wise (with Crosbie Smith), 'Work and Waste: Political Economy and Natural Philosophy in Nineteenth-Century Britain', *History of Science*, 27 (1989), 263–301, 391–449; 28 (1990), 221–61, hardly suggests that the mathematicians of the 1830s had a conscious agenda, yet by 'discovering' linear temporality they were to play a major part in softening the collective psyche up for ideas of evolution when these were put forward.[49]

LITERATURE, POLITICS, AND SOCIETY

The choice of books to cite must be even more arbitrary and eclectic than elsewhere. Over the last decade university literature departments have produced a flood of books (e.g. the Cambridge Studies in Romanticism series) that seek to place the period's imaginative writing in its historical context. Literature and History now meet on

---

[46] See also two important books by Martin J. S. Rudwick: *The Meaning of Fossils: Episodes in the History of Palaeontology* (1972) and *The Great Devonian Controversy: The Shaping of Scientific Knowledge among Gentlemanly Specialists* (Chicago, 1985).

[47] See the round-table discussion in *Journal of Victorian Culture*, 3 (1998), 123–68.

[48] See also N. Jardine, J. A. Secord, and E. C. Spary (eds.), *Cultures of Natural History* (Cambridge, 1996).

[49] See also Crosbie Smith and M. Norton Wise, *Energy and Empire: A Biographical Study of Lord Kelvin* (Cambridge, 1989).

common ground, though unfortunately it seems that the marriage will not be consummated any time soon. The historian can swallow—gratefully, but also without too much difficulty—books like Colin Campbell's *The Romantic Ethic and the Spirit of Modern Consumerism* (Oxford, 1987), Igor Webb's *From Custom to Capital: The English Novel and the Industrial Revolution* (Ithaca, NY, 1981), and Catherine Gallagher's *The Industrial Reformation of English Fiction 1832–1867* (Chicago, 1985). Ditto Richard L. Stein's *Victoria's Year: English Literature and Culture 1837–1838* (New York 1987), though snapshots of that sort ideally need to be placed in a more aggressively historical (i.e. generational) context. Slightly harder to swallow is James Chandler's *England in 1819: The Politics of Literary Culture and the Case of Romantic Historicism* (Chicago, 1998), a 'new historicist' take on a style of literature that is itself (plausibly) described as 'new historicist'. Chandler's central trope is derived from Shelley's sonnet 'England in 1819', and in particular its reference to 'golden and sanguine laws'. A political historian contemplating that poem and that year would be bound to think of the resumption of cash payments, a concept alien to Chandler's book, in which Shelley's 'gold' is meant to stand for 'doing-as-you-would-be-done-by', which is also what the gold standard stands for in economic terms. A reminder that one may arrive by different routes at common ground.

Studies of book production, marketing, and audience-making have helped to bring the two disciplines together. William St Clair's excellent *The Reading Nation and the Romantic Period* (Cambridge, 2004) caps a distinguished tradition that includes Jon P. Klancher, *The Making of English Reading Audiences, 1790–1832* (Madison, 1987) and William G. Rowland, *Literature and the Marketplace: Romantic Writers and their Audiences in Great Britain and the United States* (Lincoln, Nebr., 1996). Among the many general surveys that foreground political and intellectual concerns, one might pick Kelvin Everest, *English Romantic Poetry: An Introduction to the Historical Context and the Literary Scene* (Milton Keynes, 1990); Terence Allan Hoagwood, *Politics, Philosophy, and the Production of Romantic Texts* (DeKalb, Ill., 1996); and Philip Davis, *The Oxford English Literary History*, viii: *1830–1880: The Victorians* (Oxford, 2002). Walter E. Houghton, *The Victorian Frame of Mind 1830–1870* (New Haven, 1957) is in a different genre, but ranks alongside G. M. Young's impressionistic *Portrait of an Age: Victorian England* (1936; annotated edn. by George Kitson Clark, 1977) as unputdownable. *An Oxford Companion to the Romantic Age: British Culture 1776–1832* (Oxford, 1999), edited by Iain McCalman, is magnificent. Peter Conrad, *The Everyman History of English Literature* (1985) is a personal favourite. For ways in which literature, the stage, and painting became increasingly commercialized, see David H. Solkin (ed.), *Art on the Line: The Royal Academy Exhibitions at Somerset House, 1780–1836* (New Haven, 2001).

Turning to individual writers, Nicholas Roe's many distinguished contributions began with *Wordsworth and Coleridge: The Radical Years* (Oxford, 1987). There has not been time to discuss Blake in this text, but historically minded readers should repair first to E. P. Thompson, *Witness against the Beast: William Blake and the Moral Law* (Cambridge, 1993), a paean to the radical gospel of 'liberty against all laws', and then (when they have sobered up) to Heather Glen, *Vision and Disenchantment: Blake's 'Songs' and Wordsworth's 'Lyrical Ballads'* (Cambridge, 1983). To discover what happened to the first-generation-of-Romantic-radicals-turned-reactionary, read Stephen Prickett, *Coleridge and Wordsworth: The Poetry of Growth* (Cambridge, 1970) and the same author's *Romanticism and Religion: The Tradition of Coleridge and Wordsworth in the Victorian Church* (Cambridge, 1976). Stephen Gill's *Wordsworth: A Life* (Oxford, 1989) and *Wordsworth and the Victorians* (Oxford, 1998) are illuminating, as is John Wyatt's *Wordsworth and the Geologists* (Cambridge, 1995), which confirms (*inter alia*) Macaulay's dictum that, 'as civilisation advances, poetry almost necessarily declines'. That Wordsworth often looked for truth in dead geological matter is yet further evidence of the distance between him and his balladic collaborator; so much is evident from the essays in Nicholas Roe (ed.), *Samuel Taylor Coleridge and the Sciences of Life* (Oxford, 2001). Jane Austen was hardly a Romantic, but chronologically she was abreast of its first generation. Once regarded as a purveyor of social tittle-tattle,[50] her writing is now invariably mined for historical insights. There was a (thankfully brief) vogue for seeing her novels as driven by a consciousness of British imperial exploitation. Much more important was her recruitment to the conservative and evangelical cause in Marilyn Butler's two influential studies *Jane Austen and the War of Ideas* (Oxford, 1975) and *Romantics, Rebels and Revolutionaries: English Literature and its Background 1760–1830* (Oxford, 1981).[51] More recently Claudia L. Johnson in *Jane Austen: Women, Politics and the Novel* (Chicago, 1988) has posited a Whiggish Austen, and Peter Knox-Shaw, *Jane Austen and the Enlightenment* (Cambridge, 2004) an almost radical one. Michael Giffin, *Jane Austen and Religion: Salvation and Society in Georgian England* (Basingstoke, 2002) shows how it was possible to be both evangelical *and* enlightened, in so far as she belonged to 'that sceptical tradition within [the Enlightenment] that flourished in England and Scotland during the second half of the eighteenth century'. The literary war of ideas between 'Right' and 'Left' was of course a product of the 1790s, and in it both sides exploited the 'Gothic' mode, a point that is emphasized quite brilliantly in E. J. Clery's *The Rise of Supernatural Fiction, 1762–1800* (Cambridge, 1995). Her monograph shows how revolutionaries and conservatives engaged in a process of mutual demonization by projecting monsters onto each other: wicked monks as against freemasons, for example. Clery's work should be read alongside Coral Ann Howells, *Love, Mystery, and Misery: Feeling in Gothic Fiction* (1978) and James Watt, *Contesting the Gothic: Fiction, Genre and Cultural Conflict, 1764–1832* (Cambridge, 1999).

A good introduction to the second Romantic generation is Jeffrey N. Cox, *Poetry and Politics in the Cockney School: Keats, Shelley, Hunt and their Circle* (Cambridge, 1998). For a very long time now, ever since lyrics went out of fashion, Shelley's politics have overshadowed his poetics. Michael Henry Scrivener, *Radical Shelley: The Philosophical Anarchism and Utopian Thought of Percy Bysshe Shelley* (Princeton, 1982) is very useful, as is Anne K. Mellor's *Mary Shelley: her Life, her Fiction, Her Monsters* (New York, 1988). Hermione De Almeida, *Romantic Medicine and John Keats* (New York, 1991) and Nicholas Roe, *John Keats and the Culture of Dissent* (Oxford, 1997) are just two of many studies attempting to 'explain' that most aesthetic of poets by reference to his historical context. Byron is a much more obviously historical figure, and for many decades, when his poetry was discounted, it was as a volcanic person that he attracted so much attention. Paradoxically, now that historical context has become fashionable once again, Byron's

---

[50] There are many lives of Austen; a personal favourite is Claire Tomalin, *Jane Austen: A Life* (1997).
[51] See also Warren Roberts, *Jane Austen and the French Revolution* (1979).

poetry has come to be appreciated as art for its own sake. Leslie Marchand's *Byron: A Biography* (New York, 1957) is by far the best. It is a little staid, but far superior to some recent and seamier accounts. Perhaps men understand Byron better than women. A fine discursive sketch is Michael Foot's *The Politics of Paradise: A Vindication of Byron* (1988); for some excellent critical approaches, see Andrew Rutherford (ed.), *Byron: Augustan and Romantic* (1990).[52] A word finally about Tennyson, whose spiritual agonies over evolutionary theory were so common in the 1830s and 1840s. A good place to begin would be the chapter on *In Memoriam* in Michael Wheeler, *Death and the Future Life in Victorian Literature and Theology* (Cambridge, 1990).

THE STRUCTURE AND CULTURE OF POLITICS

This is a somewhat uncertain category, the line between it and the next section being somewhat blurred, but it has been included as a way of linking public life to some of the themes discussed above. As already indicated, Norman Gash's *Politics in the Age of Peel* (1953) and D. C. Moore's *The Politics of Deference* (1976) brought the structural perspectives of Namier to bear on the study of the second quarter of the nineteenth century. Gash's *Reaction and Reconstruction in English Politics 1832–1852* (Oxford, 1965) developed a similar analysis more discursively. However, as Namier himself acknowledged, this type of structural analysis has to be tweaked in order to accommodate the apparent rise of party. The insight was developed by Archibald S. Foord in *His Majesty's Opposition, 1714–1830* (Oxford, 1964), and also by D. C. Large in 'The Decline of "the Party of the Crown" and the Rise of Parties in the House of Lords, 1783–1837', *EHR* 78 (1963), 669–95. J. A. W. Gunn returned to the theme a decade later with his 'Influence, Parties, and the Constitution: Changing Attitudes, 1783–1832', *HJ* 17 (1974), 301–28. Two years later, with *The Growth of Parliamentary Parties, 1689–1742* (1976), B. W. Hill became one of the first historians to demonstrate successfully the importance of party in the first half of the eighteenth century as well, but his subsequent volume, *British Parliamentary Parties 1742–1832: From the Fall of Walpole to the First Reform Act* (1985), is less successful; certainly Namier emerges from it pretty well unscathed.[53] Frank O'Gorman's *The Emergence of the British Two-Party System 1760–1832* (1982) takes a similar line but is more judicious; Robert Stewart, *Party and Politics, 1830–1852* (Basingstoke, 1989) continues the story beyond the Great Reform Act. O'Gorman's definitive study *Voters, Patrons, and Parties: The Unreformed Electorate of Hanoverian England 1734–1832* (Oxford, 1989) makes a persuasive case for regarding the electoral system as much more open and representative than Namierite studies assume. The fact that in so many constituencies elections were not contested did not necessarily imply the absence of political strife, since all parties were inclined to avoid the expense of an election if the result was a foregone conclusion.[54] And even where

---

[52] Notably the essay by William St Clair on sales of Byron's books and on his extraordinary popular impact.

[53] For a novel conceptual approach, see J. C. D. Clark, 'A General Theory of Party, Opposition and Government, 1688–1832', *HJ* 23 (1980), 295–325.

[54] See Derek Beales, 'The Electorate before and after 1832: The Right to Vote, and the Opportunity', *Parliamentary History*, 11 (1992), 139–50.

certain elite families *did* manipulate their local freeholders, they often had to 'purchase' support by service to the community, thereby rendering the situation one of 'reciprocal' rather than simple one-way deference. The survival of several poll books has led historians to test all such theories psephologically, often using statistical techniques. This approach was pioneered by John A. Phillips in *Electoral Behaviour in Unreformed England: Plumpers, Splitters, and Straights* (Princeton, 1982) and *The Great Reform Bill in the Boroughs: English Electoral Behaviour 1818–1841* (Oxford, 1992). These volumes inevitably focus on particular constituencies and so take their place alongside such local political studies as T. J. Nossiter, *Influence, Opinion and Political Idioms in Reformed England: Case Studies from the North-East 1832–74* (Hassocks, 1975); Edwin Jaggard, *Cornwall Politics in the Age of Reform 1790–1885* (Woodbridge, 1999); R. W. Davis, *Political Change and Continuity 1760–1885: A Buckinghamshire Study* (Newton Abbot, 1972); R. J. Olney, *Lincolnshire Politics 1832–1885* (1973); and David Eastwood, 'Contesting the Politics of Deference: The Rural Electorate, 1820–60', in Jon Lawrence and Miles Taylor (eds.), *Party, State and Society: Electoral Behaviour in Britain since 1820* (Aldershot, 1997). Finally, for an authoritative summation of how the electoral system worked towards the end of the period, there is now Philip Salmon, *Electoral Reform at Work: Local Politics and National Parties, 1832–1841* (Woodbridge, 2002).[55] For a different, more instrumental perspective, see Gary W. Cox, *The Efficient Secret: The Cabinet and the Development of Political Parties in Victorian England* (Cambridge, 1987).

It is of course questionable whether politics in this period should be considered in terms of party in the first place. Perhaps it is no coincidence that most of the historical works that are explicitly devoted to parties are also devoted to parties in opposition. In the wake of Harold Wilson's election victory in 1964, three significant contributions to Opposition Whig politics tumbled over each other: Donald E. Ginter's *Whig Organization in the General Election of 1790* (Berkeley, 1967), Frank O'Gorman's *The Whig Party and the French Revolution* (1967), and Austin Mitchell's *The Whigs in Opposition 1815–1830* (Oxford, 1967). These were followed by E. Tangye Lean, *The Napoleonists: A Study in Political Disaffection, 1760–1960* (1970) and Leslie Mitchell, *Holland House* (1980). More recently William Anthony Hay in *The Whig Revival 1808–1830* (Basingstoke, 2005) has sought to rehabilitate Grey's party by stressing its gradual recovery at the grass roots, a story of which the main hero is Brougham. As for the later period, Donald Southgate's highly readable *The Passing of the Whigs, 1832–86* (1962) has now been superseded by Jonathan Parry's fine synoptic study *The Rise and Fall of Liberal Government in Victorian Britain* (New Haven, 1993). Meanwhile, the Conservatives, as they became known, had monopolized power for five decades before 1830, and it was only after losing it that they set about beefing up their party-political act, a task that required some retrospective manipulation of the facts, as J. J. Sack shows in his fascinating article 'The Memory of Burke and Pitt: English Conservatism

[55] See also, for example, D. G. Wright, 'A Radical Borough: Parliamentary Politics in Bradford, 1832–1841', *Northern History*, 4 (1969), 132–66; David Eastwood, 'Toryism, Reform and Political Culture in Oxfordshire, 1826–1837', *Parliamentary History*, 7 (1988), 98–121; John A. Phillips and Charles Wetherell, 'The Great Reform Act of 1832 and the Political Modernization of England', *American Historical Review*, 100 (1995), 411–36.

Confronts its Past, 1806–1829', *HJ* 30 (1987), 623–40. For the same reason, it is only after 1830 that historians have found the Conservatives worth studying. The classic account is in Norman Gash, 'The Organization of the Conservative Party, 1832–1846', *Parliamentary History*, 1 (1982), 137–59; 2 (1983), 131–52. Among the general party histories, Bruce Coleman's *Conservatism and the Conservative Party in Nineteenth-Century Britain* (1988) and Robert Stewart's *The Foundation of the Conservative Party 1830–1867* (1978) are the most important, backed up by Ian Newbould, 'Sir Robert Peel and the Conservative Party, 1832–1841: A Study in Failure?', *EHR* 98 (1983), 529–57. It was not quite a two-party system of course, but a full-scale history of parliamentary radicalism from its origins in 1802 has yet to appear. It might have been written by the late John Dinwiddy, whose *Radicalism and Reform in Britain, 1780–1850* (1992) pointed in that direction. Peter Spence's perceptive study *The Birth of Romantic Radicalism: War, Popular Politics, and English Radical Reformism, 1800–1815* (Aldershot, 1996) establishes the more conservative aspects of the party's ideology, while for a later period William Thomas's magnificent *The Philosophic Radicals: Nine Studies in Theory and Practice 1817–1841* (Oxford, 1979) examines how Bentham's disciples (and others) sought to exploit the political opportunities created by parliamentary reform. The first two retrospective chapters of Miles Taylor, *The Decline of British Radicalism, 1847–1860* (Oxford, 1995) are likewise indispensable.

After 1832 there was also an Irish dimension at Westminster to be reckoned with. Key texts here are Angus Macintyre, *The Liberator: Daniel O'Connell and the Irish Party 1830–1847* (1965), Kevin B. Nowlan, *The Politics of Repeal: A Study of the Relations between Britain and Ireland 1841–50* (1965), and Oliver MacDonagh, *The Emancipist: Daniel O'Connell 1830–1847* (1989). Jennifer Ridden's study of moderate Irish MPs in the 1830s is eagerly awaited,[56] but in the meantime there is her essay in Arthur Burns and Joanna Innes (eds.), *Rethinking the Age of Reform: Britain 1780–1850* (Cambridge, 2003).

One of the factors inhibiting the operation of party politics was 'interest', a much more specific and self-conscious concept by this time owing to the diversification of the economy. Norman McCord led the way in 1958 with *The Anti-Corn Law League 1838–1846*, a book which held the fort until *The People's Bread: A History of the Anti-Corn Law League* by Paul A. Pickering and Alex Tyrrell (2000). Unsurprisingly, pressure group politics was a central preoccupation of the 1970s, which had its own concerns about trade unions and other such single-interest demands. Among the key contributions were those of Patricia Hollis (ed.), *Pressure from Without in Early Victorian England* (1974); Travis L. Crosby, *English Farmers and the Politics of Protection 1815–1852* (Hassocks, 1977); and D. A. Hamer, *The Politics of Electoral Pressure: A Study in the History of Victorian Reform Agitations* (Hassocks, 1977). The relative significance of party and economic interest during the 1820s was then memorably debated by O'Gorman, 'Party Politics in the Early Nineteeth Century (1812–32)', *EHR* 98 (1983), 63–84, and Peter Fraser, 'Party Voting in the House of Commons, 1812–32' 102 (1987), 85–8.

[56] Jennifer Ridden, *'Making Good Citizens': Irish Elite Approaches to Empire, National Identity, and Citizenship* (forthcoming).

Putting party to one side, what assumptions did those in the political world make about the nature of power and authority? There are many brief attempts to answer that question in Stefan Collini, Richard Whatmore, and Brian Young (eds.), *History, Religion, and Culture: British Intellectual History 1750–1950* (Cambridge, 2000) and its companion volume *Economy, Polity, and Society*. For traditional viewpoints the reader should turn to Paul Langford, *Public Life and the Propertied Englishman 1689–1798* (Oxford, 1991); H. T. Dickinson, *Liberty and Property: Political Ideology in Eighteenth-Century Britain* (1977); J. G. A. Pocock, *Virtue, Commerce, and History: Essays on Political Thought and History, Chiefly in the Eighteenth Century* (Cambridge, 1985); R. J. Smith, *The Gothic Bequest: Medieval Institutions in British Thought, 1688–1863* (Cambridge, 1987); Lawrence Stone (ed.), *An Imperial State at War: Britain from 1689 to 1815* (1994); and John Brewer's *The Sinews of Power: War and the English State, 1688–1783* (1989).[57] For changing assumptions after 1783 a place to start might be J. A. W. Gunn, *Beyond Liberty and Property: The Process of Self-Recognition in Eighteenth-Century Political Thought* (Kingston, Ont., 1983), a theme picked up recently by Dror Wahrman. The latter's previous study, *Imagining the Middle Class: The Political Representation of Class in Britain, c.1780–1840* (Cambridge, 1995), argued for the discursive creation of the idea of the social centrality of the middle class in the debates on Pitt's Triple Assessment and income tax. In *The Making of the Modern Self: Identity and Culture in Eighteenth-Century England* (New Haven, 2004) Wahrman explains the 'transformation' of the 1780s and 1790s in terms of a 'revolution in the understanding of selfhood and of identity categories including race, gender, and class' (though it might be argued that all three were dependent on evangelical religion). Isaac Kramnick, *Republicanism and Bourgeois Radicalism: Political Ideology in Late Eighteenth-Century England and America* (Ithaca, NY, 1990) tests the new assumptions against some earlier theoretical categories. Also adopting a novel perspective is Michael Durey, *Transatlantic Radicals and the Early American Republic* (Lawrence, Kan., 1997). The ideological impact of the French Revolution is everywhere in the literature, but explicitly addressed in Gregory Claeys, 'The French Revolution Debate and British Political Thought', *History of Political Thought*, 11 (1990), 59–80, and in Marilyn Butler (ed.), *Burke, Paine, Godwin, and the Revolution Controversy* (Cambridge, 1984). Some historians explain what was happening in terms of the coming of 'modernity' and the predominance of material culture. Having written extensively about romantic subversives, misfits, and grotesques, Roy Porter towards the end of his life switched his attention to those aspects of the culture that were progressive and rational. *Enlightenment: Britain and the Creation of the Modern World* (2000) is a spirited compilation of positive cases, but it remains unclear how those cases should be understood in relation to the charlatans and fantasists who people his earlier books. John Brewer, *The Pleasures of the Imagination: English Culture in the Eighteenth Century* (1997) and Ann Bermingham and John Brewer (eds.), *The Consumption of Culture 1600–1800: Image, Object, Text* (1995) emphasize the rapidly broadening public sphere. In *The Scottish Enlightenment and Victorian English Society* (Beckenham, 1986) Anand C. Chitnis emphasizes the importance of the Scots as they began their 'conquest' of the metropolis. Larry Stewart takes a socio-psychological approach in 'A Meaning for

[57] See too John Cannon (ed.), *The Whig Ascendancy: Colloquies on Hanoverian England* (1981).

Machines: Modernity, Utility, and the Eighteenth-Century British Public', *Journal of Modern History*, 70 (1998), 259–94. Andrew W. Robertson brings an American concern for political rights to bear in *The Language of Democracy: Political Rhetoric in the United States and Britain, 1790–1900* (Ithaca, NY, 1995). Paul Johnson writes vivaciously about *The Birth of the Modern: World Society 1815–1830* (1991), though what he thinks modernity consists of is not quite clear. Anna Clark illuminates the changing attitudes to Crown and Constitution with reference to the lubricious behaviour of politicians in *Scandal: The Sexual Politics of the British Constitution* (2004). Two significant books have been published under the auspices of the German Historical Institute in London: *The Transformation of Political Culture: England and Germany in the Late Eighteenth Century* (Oxford, 1990), edited by Eckhart Hellmuth, concentrates mainly on aspects of political socialization and communication, while *Reform in Great Britain and Germany, 1750–1850* (Oxford, 1999), edited by T. C. W. Blanning and P. Wende, has made a start in breaking down the often lamented insularity of British political historiography. 'Reform' was of course a talismanic word in the period under question. It was tradition-ally conceived in simple terms as a case of politicians responding to popular grievances, but contributors to Burns and Innes (eds.), *Rethinking the Age of Reform*, mentioned above, emphasize its many elusive and varied meanings. Kathryn Gleadle, for example, links the new notions of gender and domesticity to the propaganda of physiological reformers and to moral reform movements like vegetarianism. For Philip Harling, on the other hand, the emphasis was on *The Waning of 'Old Corruption': The Politics of Economical Reform in Britain, 1779–1846* (Oxford, 1996). Despite which, as J. M. Bourne points out in *Patronage and Society in Nineteenth-Century England* (1986), place and favour continued to permeate English public life, albeit in different ways, even after the end of Old Corruption.

The linguistic and cultural 'turns' taken by historians in and since the 1980s has broadened the understanding of political history in many different ways, one of which has been the rediscovery of religion. J. C. D. Clark's *English Society 1688–1832*, men-tioned above, was immensely important in this respect. Having depicted a ruling regime based on Trinitarianism, it was but a short step to locating radicalism (i.e. rooted objec-tion to the regime) in rational Dissent or Unitarianism. The same author's *The Language of Liberty 1660–1832: Political Discourse and Social Dynamics in the Anglo-American World* (Cambridge, 1994) continued this denominational approach. By arguing that the main opposition to the regime was religious in nature, Clark aimed both to confirm his view that the regime itself was founded in religion, and also to deny the importance of twentieth-century-style secular radicalism. This approach found some support in James J. Sack's *From Jacobite to Conservative: Reaction and Orthodoxy in Britain, c.1760–1832* (Cambridge, 1993), the central contention of which was that 'defence of the Church of England, rather than nationalistic impulses, monarchical sentiment, or even economic self-interest, was the abiding concern of pre-1832 British conservatism'. Also focused on religion, and on the contrast between Trinitarianism and Unitarianism, but in a quite different way, is my *Age of Atonement* (Oxford, 1988), referred to above. This was an attempt to explain economic and social policy in terms of conventional religious tropes, notably the doctrine of vicarious suffering which was presented as a type of spiritual capitalism. More recently M. J. D. Roberts has approached similar themes from a different perspective in *Making English Morals: Voluntary Association and Moral Reform in England, 1787–1886* (Cambridge, 2004). Relevant too is the capacious article by Joanna Innes, 'Politics and Morals: The Reformation of Manners Movement in Later Eighteenth-Century England', in Eckhart Hellmuth (ed.), *The Transformation of Political Culture* (Oxford, 1990).

The crusade against slavery and the slave trade was led by evangelicals, though not of course by them alone. For example, Seymour Drescher in *Capitalism and Antislavery: British Mobilization in Comparative Perspective* (Basingstoke, 1986) and David Turley in *The Culture of English Antislavery, 1780–1860* (1991) relate the phenomenon to growing middle-class reformism, patriotism, and popular radicalism. The literature is vast and includes David Brion Davis, *The Problem of Slavery in the Age of Revolution 1770–1823* (Ithaca, NY, 1975) and *Slavery and Human Progress* (New York, 1984); Seymour Drescher, *Econocide: British Slavery in the Era of Abolition* (Pittsburgh, 1977); Roger Anstey, *The Atlantic Slave Trade and British Abolition 1760–1810* (1975); David Eltis, *Economic Growth and the Ending of the Transatlantic Slave Trade* (Oxford, 1987); Barbara L. Solow and Stanley L. Engerman (eds.), *British Capitalism and Caribbean Slavery: The Legacy of Eric Williams* (Cambridge, 1987); J. R. Oldfield, *Popular Politics and British Anti-Slavery: The Mobilisation of Public Opinion against the Slave Trade 1787–1807* (Manchester, 1995); Christine Bolt and Seymour Drescher (eds.), *Anti-Slavery, Religion and Reform: Essays in Memory of Roger Anstey* (Folkestone, 1980); and James Walvin (ed.), *Slavery and British Society 1776–1846* (1982). The perspectives vary, but thanks to this avalanche the crude Marxism of Eric Williams's classic *Capitalism and Slavery* (1944) has been left far behind. The further crusade to stop the slave trade internationally—including T. F. Buxton's ill-fated Niger expedition of 1841, an attempt to stifle it at source—is covered in Howard Temperley, *British Antislavery 1833–1870* (1972) and William A. Green, *British Slave Emancipation: The Sugar Colonies and the Great Experiment 1830–1865* (Oxford, 1976). Thomas L. Haskell's interesting essay 'Capitalism and the Origins of the Humanitarian Sensibility', *American Historical Review*, 90 (1985), 339–61, 547–66, seeks to get beyond interpretations based narrowly on evangelicalism. His argument for the emergence of a new type of mentality also helps to explain the rise of pacifism, a subject which should be approached through Martin Ceadel, *The Origin of War Prevention: The British Peace Movement and International Relations, 1730–1854* (Oxford, 1996), J. E. Cookson, *The Friends of Peace: Anti-War Liberalism in England, 1793–1815* (Cambridge, 1982), Alex Tyrrell, *Joseph Sturge and the Moral Radical Party in Early Victorian Britain* (1987), and Stephen Conway's articles on John Bowring and 'The Politicization of the Nineteenth-Century Peace Society', *Historical Research*, 64 (1991), 344–58, and 66 (1993), 267–83.[58] Charitable activity was another related phenomenon. David Edward Owen, *English Philanthropy: 1660–1960* (Cambridge, Mass., 1965) remains salient, as is Frank Prochaska's *The Voluntary Impulse: Philanthropy in Modern Britain* (1988).

What all this amounted to in the post-war era has been summarized by David Eastwood in 'The Age of Uncertainty: Britain in the Early-Nineteenth Century',

[58] See also Alex Tyrrell, 'Making the Millennium: The Mid-Nineteenth Century Peace Movement', *HJ* 21 (1978), 75–95.

Transactions of the Royal Historical Society, 6th ser., 8 (1998), 91–115, and by Michael Bentley in *Politics without Democracy 1815–1914: Perception and Preoccupation in British Government* (2nd edn. Oxford, 1996), a wonderfully 'inside' account of life at the top. By that time, however, new developments were beginning to set in, and were far from fully developed by 1846. Using postmodern techniques of textual reading, James Vernon, *Politics and the People: A Study in English Political Culture, c.1815–1867* (Cambridge, 1993) argues that the process of reform was a covert means of narrowing political partic- ipation and a means of thwarting long-held radical and democratic rights.[59] In *Conceiving Companies: Joint-Stock Politics in Victorian England* (1998), Timothy L. Alborn argues that the development of joint-stock companies reflected (and can therefore illuminate) prevailing attitudes towards society and the State; while Margot C. Finn in *The Character of Credit: Personal Debt in English Culture, 1740–1914* (Cambridge, 2003) likewise links the laws of personal credit and obligation to wider conceptions about the world.

As argued in the text, political life from the time of the French Revolution onwards was highly theatrical (just as the theatre was highly political), and there has been no shortage of historical attention. Marc Baer's *Theatre and Disorder in Late Georgian London* (Oxford, 1992) was followed by Gillian Russell, *The Theatres of War: Performance, Politics, and Society, 1793–1815* (Oxford, 1995), Jane Moody, *Illegitimate Theatre in London, 1770–1840* (Cambridge, 2000), and Julia Swindells, *Glorious Causes: The Grand Theatre of Political Change, 1789 to 1833* (Oxford, 2001). Katherine Newey's chapter in Burns and Innes (eds.), *Rethinking the Age of Reform* examines the reform of the London stage in the 1830s. As is evident from Hannah Barker's *Newspapers, Politics, and Public Opinion in Late Eighteenth-Century England* (Oxford, 1998), an excitable and frequently scatological press was all part of the culture, but despite many good individ- ual studies a truly synoptic early nineteenth-century volume is still needed. Cartoons somewhat better, however, thanks (among others) to M. Dorothy George, *English Political Caricature 1793–1832: A Study of Opinion and Propaganda* (Oxford, 1959), Vincent Carretta, *George III and the Satirists: From Hogarth to Byron* (Athens, Ohio, 1990), and Diana Donald, *The Age of Caricature: Satirical Prints in the Reign of George III* (New Haven, 1996).

THE POLITICAL NARRATIVE

Pitt dominated the politics of his time and John Ehrman's three-volumes *The Younger Pitt* (1969–96) dominate the historiography. It is hardly a biography, and indeed it is not clear that Pitt had an inner life to biographize, but it *is* a consummate account of the political 'life and times'. The author's determination to deal with every episode in detail sometimes blurs the perspective, but readers can be assured that each topic has been thoroughly researched and that Ehrman's analysis is invariably judicious. Epitomists and readers in a hurry may wish to consult one of the shorter biographies, of which Robin Reilly, *Pitt the Younger, 1759–1806* (1978) is particularly accessible, while Jennifer Mori's

[59] James Vernon (ed.), *Re-reading the Constitution: New Narratives in the Political History of England's Long Nineteenth Century* (Cambridge, 1996).

William Pitt and the French Revolution 1785–1795 (Edinburgh, 1997) offers a number of challenging interpretations. Fox, unlike Pitt, was obviously a charmer, but the flavour of his allure has proved difficult to convey. His most distinguished recent interpreter is L. G. Mitchell, a historian whose own amalgam of the Whig and high Tory enables him to convey successfully the same rich blend in his study of *Charles James Fox* (1992). There are also fresh insights in Penelope Jane Corfield, Edmund M. Green, and Charles Harvey, 'Westminster Man: Charles James Fox and his Electorate, 1780–1806', *Parliamentary History*, 20 (2001), 157–85. *The Duke of Portland: Politics and Party in the Age of George III* (2003) by David Wilkinson is a long overdue biography of a central but too easily neglected Whig; Peter Jupp's *Lord Grenville 1759–1834* (Oxford, 1985) accurately brings out the tomblike nature of that frigid statesman; *The Dundas Despotism* (Edinburgh, 1992) by Michael Fry is a major contribution, the title a reference to that politician's management of Scotland. The biggest biographical gap is that of the energetic maverick Windham, but there is at least a characteristically astute notice by R. G. Thorne, one of over 2,000 such potted biographies in *The History of Parliament: The House of Commons 1790–1820* (5 vols., 1986), edited by himself.

The political crisis leading to the launching of the Pitt regime has been explored in a series of articles by Paul Kelly[60] and in John Cannon's *The Fox–North Coalition: Crisis of the Constitution, 1782–4* (Cambridge, 1969). John W. Derry, *The Regency Crisis and the Whigs 1788–9* (Cambridge, 1963) is a definitive account, as is Leslie Mitchell's *Charles James Fox and the Disintegration of the Whig Party, 1782–1794* (1971). For extra-parliamentary perspectives on these events, there is Ian R. Christie, *Wilkes, Wyvill and Reform: The Parliamentary Reform Movement in British Politics 1760–1785* (1962), and N. C. Phillips, *Yorkshire and English National Politics 1783–1784* (1961). William C. Lowe, 'George III, Peerage Creations and Politics, 1760–1784', *HJ* 35 (1992), 587–609, supplements G. C. Richards's classic article 'The Creations of Peers Recommended by the Younger Pitt', *American Historical Review*, 34 (1928), 47–54. For the 1790s an obvious prism through which to delineate political disagreements is military strategy. Piers Mackesy's acclaimed series *The War in the Mediterranean, 1803–10* (1957), *Statesmen at War: The Strategy of Overthrow 1798–1799* (1974), *War without Victory: The Downfall of Pitt 1799–1802* (Oxford, 1984), and *British Victory in Egypt, 1801: The End of Napoleon's Conquest* (1995) is therefore as much about domestic intrigues as about external policy. Ehrman's thoroughness may have deterred younger researchers—he offers no aunt sallys—but D. Wilkinson's 'The Pitt–Portland Coalition of 1794 and the Origins of the "Tory" Party', *History*, 83 (1998), 249–64, usefully moves away from seeing the events of that year as a simple capitulation by one section of the Opposition to the Government. In the same issue (a collective tribute to Ehrman) Michael Duffy throws new light on 'The Younger Pitt and the House of Commons' (pp. 217–24). There are significant essays in H. T. Dickinson (ed.), *Britain and the French Revolution, 1789–1815* (Basingstoke, 1989). Though written somewhat telegraphically, Arthur Aspinall's introductions to his five-volume edition of *The Later Correspondence of George III* (Cambridge, 1966–70) are highly

---

[60] Paul Kelly, 'British Politics 1783–4: The Emergence and Triumph of the Younger Pitt's Administration', *Historical Research*, 54 (1981), 62–78; 'British Parliamentary Politics 1784–1786', *HJ* 17 (1974), 733–53.

informative, and especially useful on the political crises of the later 1790s. Richard Willis, 'William Pitt's Resignation in 1801', *Bulletin of the Institute of Historical Research*, 44 (1971), 239–57, is brief but important, since it woke historians up to the weaknesses of Pitt's position in the later 1790s. The appearance of C. J. Fedorak's *Henry Addington, Prime Minister, 1801–1804: Peace, War, and Parliamentary Politics* (Akron, Ohio, 2002) is one of many signs that Lord Sidmouth is beginning to emerge from under Pitt's historical shadow. It supplements Philip Ziegler's venerable *Addington: A Life of Henry Addington, First Viscount Sidmouth* (1965). There are new insights to be gleaned from R. E. Willis, 'Fox, Grenville and the Recovery of Opposition, 1801–1804', *JBS* 11 (1971), 24–43, and Stephen M. Lee, ' "A New Language in Politicks": George Canning and the Idea of Opposition, 1801–1807', *History*, 83 (1998), 472–96.

Historians have naturally wanted to assess the extent and reality of Pitt's so-called 'Terror'. E. P. Thompson, of course, delivered a stern judgement. His work on the treason trials has been taken further with great subtlety in John Barrell, *Imagining the King's Death: Figurative Treason, Fantasies of Regicide 1793–1796* (Oxford, 2000). The evidence is considered even-handedly in Clive Emsley's *British Society and the French Wars, 1793–1815* (1979) as well as in a series of supporting articles.[61] Bernard Porter, *Plots and Paranoia: A History of Political Espionage in Britain 1790–1988* (1989) puts the secret State in a long chronological context; for the Continental ramifications there is Elizabeth Sparrow's thoroughly researched *Secret Service: British Agents in France 1792–1815* (Woodbridge, 1999). War and invasion fears led to widespread albeit spasmodic panics between 1795 and 1805—Tom Pocock captures the atmosphere well in *The Terror before Trafalgar: Nelson, Napoleon and the Secret War* (2002)—and reinforced the need for national defence. This led in turn to the refining of techniques for impressment and recruitment. J. R. Western, *The English Militia in the Eighteenth Century: The Story of a Political Issue 1660–1802* (1965) still has much to offer on this. More recently J. E. Cookson has argued in *The British Armed Nation 1793–1815* (Oxford, 1997) that volunteering gave cohesion and identity to urban elites and encouraged them to stand up to aristocratic authority in the counties. Austin Gee claims, in a detailed and exhaustive study entitled *The British Volunteer Movement 1794–1814* (Oxford, 2003), that the Government's arming of 400,000 civilians was a 'calculated risk' which worked. Though independent-minded, and far from being manipulated by the authorities for crudely loyalist or law-and-order purposes, the privilege of bearing arms increased their loyalty to the State and their fundamentally conservative social attitudes.

Back in the days when so many histories began or ended in 1815, there was widespread neglect of the previous fifteen years, as though they did not belong properly to either century. Indeed, for a long time the only political histories to be soundly based in archival material were A. D. Harvey's *Britain in the Early Nineteenth Century* (1978), James J. Sack, *The Grenvillites 1801–1829: Party Politics and Factionalism in the Age of Pitt and Liverpool* (Urbana, Ill., 1979), and the occasional biography such as Denis Gray's

---

[61] e.g. Clive Emsley, 'The London "Insurrection" of December 1792: Fact, Fiction, or Fantasy', *JBS* 17 (1978), 66–86; 'An Aspect of Pitt's Terror: prosecution for Sedition during the 1790s', *Social History*, 6 (1981), 155–84; 'Repression, "Terror" and the Rule of Law in England during the Decade of the French Revolution', *EHR* 100 (1985), 801–25.

Spencer Perceval: The Evangelical Prime Minister 1762–1812 6 (Manchester, 1963). The gap has recently begun to be repaired with some fine studies, pre-eminent among which are *Britain and the Defeat of Napoleon 1807–1815* (New Haven, 1996) by Rory Muir, and Christopher D. Hall's *British Strategy in the Napoleonic War 1803–15* (Manchester, 1992), which like Mackesy's studies is as much about matters political as military.

Turning to the post-war period, there are relatively few full-length synoptic studies and an over-reliance on biographies. To start with the latter, Norman Gash, *Mr Secretary Peel: The Life of Sir Robert Peel to 1830* (1961) set a benchmark few other historians have emulated. The same author's *Sir Robert Peel: The Life of Sir Robert Peel after 1830* (1972) is less impressive, objectivity being sacrificed to what is largely a reflection of the statesman's own take on events. T. A. Jenkins, *Sir Robert Peel* (Basingstoke, 1999) does not seek to compete, but is a lucid and insightful analysis of conflicting interpretations. Donald Read, *Peel and the Victorians* (Oxford, 1987) comes alive in its discussion of the statesman's afterlife, the unexpected outpouring of grief that followed his fatal accident in 1850.[62] Gash has also written a judicious biography, *Lord Liverpool: The Life and Political Career of Robert Banks Jenkinson Second Earl of Liverpool 1770–1828* (1984), and has edited an important collection of essays on Wellington.[63] Wendy Hinde's *George Canning* (1973) and *Castlereagh* (1981) are the best biographies, while John W. Derry, *Castlereagh* (1976) and Peter Dixon, *Canning: Politician and Statesman* (1976) are more analytical. Even so, for sustained rumination on their politics one could do worse than revert to the studies of foreign policy by Webster and Temperley, mentioned below. Something on Huskisson is badly needed, though A. C. Howe's essay in *ODNB* points the way. Brian Jenkins, *Henry Goulburn 1784–1856: A Political Biography* (Liverpool, 1996) and J. T. Ward, *Sir James Graham* (1967) are highly efficient biographies of two important second-order statesmen; Angus Hawkins's forthcoming study *The Forgotten Prime Minister: The 14th Earl of Derby 1799–1869* (2005) is eagerly awaited. There are many fine biographies of three significant but somewhat maverick Conservatives. H. C. G. Matthew, *Gladstone*, i: *1809–1874* (Oxford, 1986) and Richard Shannon, *Gladstone*, i: *Peel's Inheritor 1809–1865* (1982) lead their particular field; Robert Blake's *Disraeli* (1966) remains indispensable, but needs to be updated with Jane Ridley, *The Young Disraeli* (1995) and Paul Smith, *Disraeli: A Brief Life* (Cambridge, 1996); while Geoffrey B. A. M. Finlayson's *The Seventh Earl of Shaftesbury 1801–1885* (1981) is a highly accomplished account, though G. F. A. Best, *Shaftesbury* (1964) is still worth perusal. All three were paternalists of different stripes, and the fact is that far more has been written about paternalist Conservatives[64] than about hard-nosed ones. The

    [62] For more limited and specific comments, see my three articles: 'The Ripening of Robert Peel', in Michael Bentley (ed.), *Public and Private Doctrine: Essays in British History Presented to Maurice Cowling* (Cambridge, 1993); 'The Gallows and Mr Peel', in T. C. W. Blanning and David Cannadine (eds.), *History and Biography: Essays in Honour of Derek Beales* (Cambridge, 1996); and, more synoptically, 'Peel: A Reappraisal', *HJ* 22 (1979), 585–614.

    [63] Norman Gash (ed.), *Wellington: Studies in the Military and Political Career of the First Duke of Wellington* (Manchester, 1990).

    [64] See also Cecil Driver, *Tory Radical: The Life of Richard Oastler* (Oxford, 1946) and Kim Lawes, *Paternalism and Politics: The Revival of Paternalism in Early Nineteenth-Century Britain* (Basingstoke, 2000), a study of M. T. Sadler.

most serious lack is a life of Lord Lyndhurst. Finally, a different but no less important style of 'Toryism' can be tracked down in Myron F. Brightfield's *John Wilson
Croker* (1940).

William Thomas, *The Quarrel of Macaulay and Croker: Politics and History in the Age
of Reform* (Oxford, 2000) links the two sides of the political divide. Here John Clive,
Thomas Babington Macaulay: The Shaping of the Historian (1973) should be read along-
side Joseph Hamburger, *Macaulay and the Whig Tradition* (Chicago, 1976). E. A. Smith,
Lord Grey 1764–1845 (Oxford, 1990), Patrick O'Leary, *Sir James Mackintosh: The Whig
Cicero* (Aberdeen, 1989), Ellis Archer Wasson, *Whig Renaissance: Lord Althorp and the
Whig Party 1782–1845* (New York, 1987), Richard W. Davis, *Dissent in Politics
1780–1830: The Political Life of William Smith, MP* (1971), and John Prest, *Lord John
Russell* (1972) are all highly authoritative biographies. So are Philip Ziegler, *Melbourne:
A Biography of William Lamb, 2nd Viscount Melbourne* (1976) and L. G. Mitchell, *Lord
Melbourne 1779–1848* (Oxford, 1997), though they paint very different pictures of that
elusive statesman. Kenneth Bourne's *Palmerston: The Early Years 1784–1841* (1982) is
not just a biography but an important and closely researched piece of political history.
Brougham is in desperate need of intellectual analysis, but his political activities are well
covered thanks to Chester W. New, *The Life of Henry Brougham to 1830* (1961) and
Robert Stewart, *Henry Brougham: His Public Career 1778–1868* (1985). Diana Davids
Olien, *Morpeth: A Victorian Public Career* (Washington, 1983) and Dorothy Howell-
Thomas, *Duncannon: Reformer and Reconciler 1781–1847* (Norwich, 1992) are useful
examinations of two second-rank politicians. A most serious lack is a life of Lord
Lansdowne.

Moving outside the two main parties, Donald Read's *Cobden and Bright: A Victorian
Political Partnership* (1967) remains useful, as do Keith Robbins, *John Bright* (1979),
Nicholas C. Edsall, *Richard Cobden: Independent Radical* (Cambridge, Mass., 1986),
and Wendy Hinde, *Richard Cobden: A Victorian Outsider* (New Haven, 1987). Three very
different sorts of Radical are dissected in books by David J. Moss, *Thomas Attwood: The
Biography of a Radical* (Montreal, 1990); Stewart Angus Weaver, *John Fielden and the
Politics of Popular Radicalism 1832–1847* (Oxford, 1987); and Ronald K. Huch and Paul
R. Ziegler, *Joseph Hume: The People's M.P.* (Philadelphia, 1985).

One very old monograph on the immediate post-war period is still worth reading for
its insights, even if its central contention must be discarded: W. R. Brock, *Lord Liverpool
and Liberal Toryism, 1820 to 1827* (Cambridge, 1941). Its most distinguished successor is
J. E. Cookson, *Lord Liverpool's Administration: The Crucial Years 1815–1822*
(Edinburgh, 1975), while I add my mite in 'The Political Arts of Lord Liverpool',
Transactions of the Royal Historical Society, 38 (1988), 147–70. My *Corn, Cash,
Commerce: The Economic Policies of the Tory Governments 1815–1830* (Oxford, 1977)[65]
contains much high political discussion, especially for the years immediately following
Liverpool's stroke. Neville Thompson's *Wellington after Waterloo* (1986) has since
been joined by Peter Jupp's exceptionally thorough micro-history, *British Politics on the
Eve of Reform: The Duke of Wellington's Administration, 1828–30* (Basingstoke, 1998).
Jupp has also raised a point of fundamental importance in 'The Landed Elite and

[65] If I were writing the same book today I would use the term 'conservative' rather than 'tory'.

Political Authority in Britain, *ca*.1760–1850', *JBS* 29 (1990), 53–79, for a response to which, see Philip Harling and Peter Mandler, 'From "Fiscal–Military" State to Laissez-Faire State, 1760–1850', *JBS* 32 (1993), 44–70. Relevant to the debate are Philip Harling, 'Rethinking "Old Corruption" ', *P&P* 147 (1995), 127–58; the same author's 'Parliament, the State, and "Old Corruption": Conceptualising Reform, c.1790–1832', in Arthur Burns and Joanna Innes (eds.), *Rethinking the Age of Reform* (Cambridge, 2003); and W. D. Rubinstein, 'The End of "Old Corruption" in Britain, 1780–1860', *P&P* 101 (1983), 55–86. Joe Bord's important ' "Our friends in the North": Patronage, the Lansdowne Whigs, and the problem of the liberal Centre, 1827–28', *EHR* 117 (2002), 78–93, discusses the tantalizing possibilities of political realignment.

The Pittite regime finally fell in 1830 because of an Ultra Tory revolt. The immediate cause was Catholic emancipation, on which, see G. I. T. Machin, *The Catholic Question in English Politics 1820 to 1830* (Oxford, 1964), Wendy Hinde, *Catholic Emancipation: A Shake to Men's Minds* (Oxford, 1992), and Boyd Hilton, 'The Ripening of Robert Peel', in Michael Bentley (ed.), *Public and Private Doctrine: Essays in British History Presented to Maurice Cowling* (Cambridge, 1993).[66] Rumbling away beneath the Ultras' anti-Catholicism, however, was their profound dismay about the drift of economic policy, on which D. C. Moore's highly original article 'The Other Face of Reform', *Victorian Studies*, 5 (1961–2), 7–34, is essential reading. The Pittites' fall led straight on to political reform. Michael Brock's *The Great Reform Act* (1973) was long awaited in its day, but is unlikely to be replaced in a hurry.[67] At the same time, John Cannon's *Parliamentary Reform 1640–1832* (Cambridge, 1973) situated the crisis of the early 1830s in its chronological context, and Joseph Hamburger offered some subtle suggestions as to motives and tactics in *James Mill and the Art of Revolution* (New Haven, 1963). The first significant action of the reformed Parliament can be followed up in two articles by I. Gross—'The Abolition of Negro Slavery and British Parliamentary Politics, 1832–1833', *HJ* 23 (1980), 63–85, and 'Parliament and the Abolition of Negro Apprenticeship 1835–38', *EHR* 96 (1981), 560–76—and two by Abraham D. Kriegel—'A Convergence of Ethics: Saints and Whigs in British Antislavery', *JBS* 26 (1987), 423–50, and 'Liberty and Whiggery in Early Nineteenth Century England', *Journal of Modern History*, 52 (1980), 253–78.

Four monographs dominate the historiography of the 1830s. Ian Newbould's *Whiggery and Reform, 1830–41: The Politics of Government* (Stanford, Calif., 1990) is utterly authoritative on high politics, but unlike the other three historians referred to he declines to distinguish Liberalism theoretically from Whiggism. Richard Brent's *Liberal Anglican Politics: Whiggery, Religion, and Reform 1830–1841* (Oxford, 1987) deploys both ingenuity and originality in defining the differences between Liberalism and Whiggism in religious terms.[68] In *Aristocratic Government in the Age of Reform: Whigs and Liberals,*

---

[66] Also G. I. T. Machin, 'Resistance to Repeal of the Test and Corporation Acts, 1828', *HJ* 22 (1979), 115–39, and 'Canning, Wellington and the Catholic Question, 1827–1829', *EHR* 99 (1984), 94–100.

[67] Which explains why most of the other pertinent contributions preceded it. For example, Moore's 'The Other Face of Reform', *Victorian Studies*, 5 (1961), 7–34, Norman McCord's highly sceptical 'Some difficulties of parliamentary Reform', *HJ* 10 (1967), 376–90, and John Milton-Smith's judicious 'Earl Grey's Cabinet and the Objects of Parliamentary Reform', *HJ* 15 (1972), 55–74.

[68] See also Richard Brent, 'The Whigs and Protestant Dissent in the Decade of Reform: The Case of Church Rates, 1833–1841', *EHR* 102 (1987), 887–910, and R. W. Davis, 'The Whigs and Religious

1830–1852 (Oxford, 1990), Peter Mandler deploys equal ingenuity and originality in defining the same difference in terms of social and economic policy, while J. W. Burrow, in *Whigs and Liberals: Continuity and Change in English Political Thought* (Oxford, 1988), brings older distinctions between civic humanism and court Whiggism to bear. At first sight the Brent and Mandler visions seem not to mesh, a point which I have sought to resolve in 'Whiggery, Religion and Social Reform: The Case of Lord Morpeth', *HJ* 37 (1994), 829–59. The overwhelming salience of religious issues, at least until the very end of the 1830s, is evident from G. I. T. Machin, *Politics and the Churches in Great Britain 1832 to 1868* (Oxford, 1977); John Wolffe, *The Protestant Crusade in Great Britain 1829–1860* (Oxford, 1991); Eric J. Evans, *The Contentious Tithe: The Tithe Problem and English Agriculture, 1750–1850* (1976); Timothy Larsen, *Friends of Religious Equality: Nonconformist Politics in Mid-Victorian England* (Woodbridge, 1999); J. P. Ellens, *Religious Routes to Gladstonian Liberalism: The Church Rate Conflict in England and Wales, 1832–1868* (University Park, Pa., 1994); and J. L. Alexander, 'Lord John Russell and the Origins of the Committee of Council on Education', *HJ* 20 (1977), 395–415.

By the time of the Conservative triumph in 1841, economic issues had pushed their way forward. An interpretation of Peel's intentions can be found in David Eastwood's two articles 'Peel and the Tory Party Reconsidered', *History Today*, 42/3 (1992), 27–33, and ' "Recasting our Lot": Peel, the Nation, and the Politics of Interest', in Laurence Brockliss and David Eastwood (eds.), *A Union of Multiple Identities: The British Isles, c.1750–c.1850* (Manchester, 1997). A somewhat different line is taken in Boyd Hilton, 'Peel: A Reappraisal', *HJ* 22 (1979), 585–614. It is important not to lose sight of the protectionist side of the argument just because it lost. That may once have been a danger, but is no longer thanks to three studies: Robert Stewart's *The Politics of Protection: Lord Derby and the Protectionist Party 1841–1852* (Cambridge, 1971); Angus Macintyre's 'Lord George Bentinck and the Protectionists: A Lost Cause?', *Transactions of the Royal Historical Society*, 39 (1989), 141–65; and *Protection and Politics: Conservative Economic Discourse, 1815–1852* (Woodbridge, 1999) by Anna Gambles.[69] Meanwhile, D. R. Fisher, 'Peel and the Conservative Party: The Sugar Crisis of 1844 Reconsidered', *HJ* 18 (1975), 279–302, examines the origins of the Conservative Party's disastrous split in 1846, while John Prest puts forward an ingenious 'political' explanation as to why Peel might have moved for Corn Law repeal when he did in *Politics in the Age of Cobden* (1977). Finally, it must not be forgotten that this was the age of Chartism; for the ministerial response, see A. P. Donajgrodzki, 'Sir James Graham at the Home Office', *HJ* 20 (1977), 97–120

BRITAIN IN THE WORLD AND QUESTIONS OF
NATIONAL IDENTITY

Although it deals with an earlier period, H. M. Scott's *British Foreign Policy in the Age of the American Revolution* (Oxford, 1990) is an indispensable scene-setter. Vincent T. Harlow,

Issues, 1830–1835', in R. W. Davis and R. J. Helmstadter (eds.), *Religion and Irreligion in Victorian Society: Essays in Honour of R. K. Webb* (1992).

[69] See also Anna Gambles, 'Rethinking the Politics of Protection: Conservatism and the Corn Laws, 1830–52', *EHR* 113 (1998), 928–52.

The Founding of the Second British Empire 1763–1793 (1952–64), famously argues for 'a swing to the East' in policy-makers' preoccupations following the loss of America. Equally challenging on a smaller scale is Daniel A. Baugh, 'Great Britain's "Blue-Water" Policy, 1689–1815', *International History Review*, 10 (1988), 33–58. Jeremy Black has written several books on international relations, including *Natural and Necessary Enemies: Anglo-French Relations in the Eighteenth Century* (1986), *A System of Ambition: British Foreign Policy 1660–1793* (1991), and *British Foreign Policy in an Age of Revolutions, 1783–1793* (Cambridge, 1994). There are also important essays by T. C. W. Blanning and Carl Haase and by Michael Duffy in Jeremy Black (ed.), *Knights Errant and True Englishmen: British Foreign Policy, 1660–1800* (Edinburgh, 1989). Paul Langford, *Modern British Foreign Policy: The Eighteenth Century, 1688–1815* (1976) is a useful synopsis. Paul W. Schroeder, *The Transformation of European Politics 1763–1848* (Oxford, 1994) provides the necessary Continental canvas, and C. A. Bayly supplies an intercontinental perspective in his magnificent overview *The Birth of the Modern World, 1780–1914: Global Connections and Comparisons* (Oxford, 2004). The diplomatic history of the 1790s is examined with great cogency by T. C. W. Blanning, *The Origins of the French Revolutionary Wars* (Harlow, 1986). Strategic policy is covered in the several volumes by Piers Mackesy mentioned above; likewise in A. B. Rodger, *The War of the Second Coalition: 1798 to 1801: A Strategic Commentary* (Oxford, 1964) and John D. Grainger, *The Amiens Truce: Britain and Bonaparte 1801–1803* (Woodbridge, 2004). Michael Duffy, *Soldiers, Sugar, and Seapower: The British Expeditions to the West Indies and the War against Revolutionary France* (Oxford, 1987) is indispensable on the Caribbean sideshow.

The literature of the revolutionary and Napoleonic wars is much too vast to cite here, but Charles J. Esdaile, *The Wars of Napoleon* (1995) may serve as an introduction, while two fine reference works are David G. Chandler, *Dictionary of the Napoleonic Wars* (1979) and Stephen Pope, *The Cassell Dictionary of the Napoleonic Wars* (1999). A. D. Harvey, *Collision of Empires: Britain in Three World Wars, 1793–1945* (1992) provides food for thought. Richard Glover, *Peninsular Preparation: The Reform of the British Army, 1795–1809* (Cambridge, 1963) is excellent on the home front; for the Iberian front, two further books by Charles J. Esdaile are supreme: *The Peninsular War: A New History* (2002) and *Fighting Napoleon: Guerrillas, Bandits, and Adventurers, 1808–1814* (New Haven, 2004). Michael Glover, *Wellington as Military Commander* (1968) is just one of many hundred assessments of Britain's most famous general. For whatever reason, the Navy has attracted much more attention. Clive Wilkinson makes its administration central to the maturation of a fiscal–military system in *The British Navy and the State in the Eighteenth Century* (Woodbridge, 2004). N. A. M. Rodger, *The Command of the Ocean: A Naval History of Britain, 1649–1815* (2004) is one of the finest books on the period, and covers a far wider brief than the subtitle might imply. (Even so, those who wish to imagine what life was like at sea will benefit from the novels of Patrick O'Brian.) Peter Padfield's *Maritime Power and the Struggle for Freedom: Naval Campaigns that Shaped the Modern World 1788–1851* (2003) is illuminating. And Margarette Lincoln's *Representing the Royal Navy: British Sea Power, 1750–1815* (Aldershot, 2002) admirably dissects the social world, political connections, and cultural significance of the Navy, first in wartime and then in its post-war doldrums. Roger Morriss's *The Royal Dockyards during the Revolutionary and Napoleonic Wars* (Leicester, 1983) and Brian Lavery's *Nelson's Navy: The Ships, Men and Organisation 1793–1815* (1989) help to complete the picture. The looming bicentenary of Nelson's death has led to a spate of excellent biographies; two more conceptual works (neither of which appeared in time to be taken account of here) are David Cannadine (ed.), *Admiral Lord Nelson: Context and Legacy* (Houndmills, 2005) and Adam Nicolson, *Men of Honour: Trafalgar and the Making of the English Hero* (2005). Armies and navies cannot win wars by themselves, of course. For what might be called the 'fourth arm' of attack, see John M. Sherwig, *Guineas and Gunpowder: British Foreign Aid in the Wars with France 1793–1815* (Cambridge, Mass., 1969).

For the post-war period two obvious starting points are, Harold Temperley and Lillian M. Penson (eds.), *Foundations of British Foreign Policy from Pitt (1792) to Salisbury (1902)* (Cambridge, 1938), and John Clarke, *British Diplomacy and Foreign Policy 1782–1865: The National Interest* (1989). More detailed studies include C. K. Webster, *The Foreign Policy of Castlereagh 1812–1815: Britain and the Reconstruction of Europe* (1931) and *The Foreign Policy of Castlereagh 1815–1822: Britain and the European Alliance* (1925); Harold Temperley's *The Foreign Policy of Canning 1822–1827: England, the Neo-Holy Alliance, and the New World* (1925); C. K. Webster, *The Foreign Policy of Palmerston 1830–41: Britain, the Liberal Movement and the Eastern Question* (2 vols., 1951); Muriel E. Chamberlain's *British Foreign Policy in the Age of Palmerston* (1980); and the same author's *'Pax Britannica'? British Foreign Policy, 1789–1914* (1988) and *Lord Aberdeen: A Political Biography* (1983). C. J. Bartlett, *Great Britain and Sea Power 1815–1853* (Oxford, 1963) contains admirable analyses of political decisions, while Roger Bullen, 'Party Politics and Foreign Policy: Whigs, Tories and Iberian Affairs, 1830–6', *Bulletin of the Institute of Historical Research*, 51 (1978), 37–59, focuses on one particularly defining moment. For the effects of peace on the key institutions, there are Michael Lewis, *The Navy in Transition 1814–1864: A Social History* (1965); Edward M. Spiers, *The Army and Society 1815–1914* (1980); and two books by Hew Strachan, *Wellington's Legacy: The Reform of the British Army 1830–54* (Manchester, 1984) and *The Politics of the British Army* (Oxford, 1997).

By 1815 it was impossible for Englishmen to ignore any longer that they headed an empire. Again it is impossible to do more than skim the surface. P. J. Marshall (ed.), *The Eighteenth Century* (Oxford, 1998)[70] and Andrew Porter (ed.), *The Nineteenth Century* (Oxford, 1999) comprise volumes ii and iii of the magnificent recent *Oxford History of the British Empire*. Eliga H. Gould argues in 'American Independence and Britain's Counter-Revolution', *P&P* 154 (1997), 107–41, that the loss of America served as a wake-up call with regard to the rest of the 'British' Empire. For C. A. Bayly the wake-up call had more to do with events in France in the 1790s. *Imperial Meridian: The British Empire and the World 1780–1830* (1989) contains an important statement about the polity and society of the United Kingdom, with empire seen as central to the process of state formation. All these historians regard the empire and the metropolis as inextricably connected. Earlier studies tended to be more strategically based, two distinguished examples being Edward Ingram's *Commitment to Empire: Prophecies of the Great Game in*

[70] See also P. J. Marshall, 'The First and Second British Empires: A Question of Demarcation', *History*, 49 (1964), 13–23.

Asia 1797–1800 (Oxford, 1981) and M. E. Yapp's *Strategies of British India: Britain, Iran and Afghanistan, 1798–1850* (Oxford, 1980). Inspired by the celebrated article of J. A. Gallagher and R. E. Robinson, 'The Imperialism of Free Trade', *EconHR* 6 (1953), 1–15, studies of the period after 1815 have tended to meld the strategic with the economic. Responses to Robinson and Gallagher constitute a large and distinguished historiography, including Oliver MacDonagh's 'The Anti-Imperialism of Free Trade', *EconHR* 14 (1962), 489–501, and a string of reservations and objections by D. C. M. Platt in *EconHR* 21 (1968), 296–306; 26 (1973), 77–91. Since then P. J. Cain and A. G. Hopkins, *British Imperialism: Innovation and Expansion, 1688–1914* (1993) has had an equally remarkable impact, not least for its thesis regarding 'gentlemanly capitalism'. Some earlier contributions are still well worth reading, however. For example, Albert H. Imlah, *Economic Elements in the Pax Britannica: Studies in British Foreign Trade in the Nineteenth Century* (New York, 1958), D. C. M. Platt, *Finance, Trade and Politics in British Foreign Policy, 1815–1914* (Oxford, 1968), and Bernard Semmel, *Liberalism and Naval Strategy: Ideology, Interest, and Sea Power during the Pax Britannica* (Boston, 1986). By 1846 it was clear that for economic reasons, such as the importance of the cotton industry, India would be the jewel in the crown. Three books are indispensable on the British approach to governance on the Subcontinent: Thomas R. Metcalf, *The New Cambridge History of India*, iii/4: *Ideologies of the Raj* (Cambridge, 1994); Eric Stokes, *English Utilitarians and India* (Oxford, 1959); and John Rosselli, *Lord William Bentinck: The Making of a Liberal Imperialist 1774–1839* (1974). Taking the empire as a whole, a wide range of explanations for expansion are considered in Ronald Hyam's lively synthesis *Britain's Imperial Century, 1815–1914: A Study of Empire and Expansion* (2nd edn. Basingstoke, 1993). They include sex. Finally, *Captives: Britain, Empire and the World 1600–1850* (2002) by Linda Colley opens up an altogether new way of looking at empire, bottom up but with a difference, since it considers the condition of poor whites overseas who got themselves caught up in its trammels. Implicitly at least, *Captives* qualifies the argument of Colley's earlier book *Britons: Forging the Nation 1707–1837* (New Haven, 1992) by emphasizing the complexities of English–British nationalism and also the many different varieties of 'otherness'.

Gerald Newman, *The Rise of English Nationalism: A Cultural History 1740–1830* (1987) and Colley, *Britons:* both showed how patriotism and nationalism shifted from being part of a radical posture to being part of a conservative one towards the end of the eighteenth century. Colley's book in particular, with its emphasis on anti-Catholicism and antipathy to France, provoked a huge interest in questions of national identity and of the role of empire within it. For positive views of empire in this context, one should turn to Catherine *Hall, White, Male and Middle Class: Explorations in Feminism and History* (Oxford, 1992) and Kathleen Wilson, *The Island Race: Englishness, Empire, and Gender in the Eighteenth Century* (2002). The present book, however, has tended to play down the concept of 'Britishness', since to the English it meant the same as 'Englishness'. It has also stressed the ambiguities of national identity, since though that was sometimes debated—particularly in the darkest hours of wartime—on the whole self-confidence meant that the English did not introspect about such things. And finally it has argued that empire played a relatively small part in national self-consciousness. Utilitarianism and evangelicalism were both monogenetic philosophies;

the English mission was to civilize and convert, not conquer; English identity rested more in law and institutions than in some Volkish tradition which, if it existed at all, was bound up with local (Anglo-Saxon) communities. Such issues are dealt with trenchantly by Peter Mandler in ' "Race" and "Nation" in Mid-Victorian Thought', his contribution to Stefan Collini, Richard Whatmore, and Brian Young (eds.), *History, Religion, and Culture: British Intellectual History 1750–1950* (Cambridge, 2000). His term to describe the English attitude is 'ethnocentric liberalism'. It would appear from a number of contributions, many too recent to have been absorbed properly here, that this is the new trend (or pendulum swing). For example, Bernard Porter argues the case for imperial indifference in *The Absent-Minded Imperialists: Empire, Society, and Culture in Britain* (Oxford, 2004); Krishan Kumar sees the prevailing 'missionary nationalism' as fundamentally anti-nationalist in *The Making of English National Identity* (Cambridge, 2003); and Stuart Semmel emphasizes the fractured nature of national identity in *Napoleon and the British* (New Haven, 2004). The case for anti-imperialism rests partly on the absence of evidence for its existence. Historians who take an opposite line argue that this is not so much an absence as a silence: early nineteenth-century English people did not talk about empire, either because they felt guilt about how important it was to them, or because it was so much a part of their mental furniture that they did not need to talk abut it. This is a perennial problem of historical interpretation. But assuming that there was indeed no imperial culture, when did it start? Most historians (but not Porter) would acknowledge its existence by (say) 1880. Several (but not Mandler) would accept that it was creeping in by (say) 1860, not yet overtly but in terms of the spread of polygenetic (i.e. racist) ideas. This would just about fit in with Catherine Hall's chronology in *Civilising Subjects: Colony and Metropole in the English Imagination, 1830–1867* (Chicago, 2002). It fits in too with Susan Kingsley Kent's interesting discussion in *Gender and Power in Britain, 1640–1990* (1999). In tracing how ideas of imperial masculinity developed in contrast to colonial effeminacy, there seem to have been two overlapping phases: a liberal one from 1815 to 1848 and an imperial one from 1825 onwards.

Leaving such complex problems of interpretation to one side, there are many thoughtful contributions to consider, including a number of essays by Colley.[71] For the antecedents, see Colin Kidd, *British Identities before Nationalism; Ethnicity and Nationhood in the Atlantic World, 1600–1800* (Cambridge, 1999), Rosemary Sweet, *Antiquaries: The Discovery of the Past in Eighteenth-Century Britain* (2004), Tony Claydon and Ian McBride (eds.), *Protestantism and National Identity: Britain and Ireland, c.1650–c.1850* (Cambridge, 1998), Roberto Romani, *National Character and Public Spirit in Britain and France, 1750–1914* (Cambridge, 2002), and G. M. Ditchfield, 'Church, Parliament and National Identity, c.1770–c.1830', in Julian Hoppit (ed.), *Parliaments, Nations, Identities in Britain and Ireland, 1660–1850* (Manchester, 2003). Seamus Deane, *The French Revolution and Enlightenment in England 1789–1832* (Cambridge, Mass., 1988) detects a 'sharpening of national consciousness' from the 1790s due to intellectual polarization over the French Revolution; something similar emerges from David Eastwood, 'Patriotism and the English State in the 1790s', in

[71] e.g. 'Britishness and Otherness: An Argument', *JBS* 31 (1992), 309–29; 'Whose Nation? Class and National Consciousness in Britain 1750–1830', *P&P* 113 (1986), 97–117.

M. Philp (ed.), *The French Revolution and British Popular Politics* (Cambridge, 1991)[72] Philip Schofield strikes a revisionist note in 'British Politicians and French Arms: The Ideological War of 1793–1795', *History*, 77 (1992), 183–201; in his view Britain fought France for counter-revolutionary rather than for strategic or economic reasons and simple survival. In *The King's Artists: The Royal Academy of Arts and the Politics of British Culture, 1760–1840* (Oxford, 2003), Holger Hoock shows how certain artists sought to promote a 'national school' of painting and statuary. Their celebration of heroes and victories in stone was apparently a deliberate attempt to create a sense of 'cultural patriotism'. The book should be read with John Barrell's *The Political Theory of Painting from Reynolds to Hazlitt: 'The Body of the Public'* (New Haven, 1996) and the same author's *The Birth of Pandora and the Division of Knowledge* (Basingstoke, 1992). Philip Harling has a new angle in 'The Duke of York Affair (1809) and the Complexities of Wartime Patriotism', *HJ* 39 (1996), 963–84, and there are important essays in David N. Livingstone and Charles W. J. Withers (eds.), *Geography and Enlightenment* (Chicago, 1999).

For further developments in the 1830s and 1840s, one should start with Peter Mandler's masterly discussion of 'Olden Time' ideas in *The Fall and Rise of the Stately Home* (New Haven, 1997). As a culture it had to compete with the 'medievalist revival', on which, see Alice Chandler, *A Dream of Order: The Medieval Ideal in Nineteenth-Century English Literature* (1971), Mark Girouard, *The Return to Camelot: Chivalry and the English Gentleman* (New Haven, 1981), James F. White, *The Cambridge Movement: The Ecclesiologists and the Gothic Revival* (Cambridge, 1962), and Paul Atterbury and Clive Wainwright (eds.), *Pugin: A Gothic Passion* (New Haven, 1994). Some Liberal Anglicans like Hare and Milman were eager to incorporate German theology and philosophy into English thought. In a wide-ranging and fascinating article, which takes in Prince Albert, the new art unions, and the 1830s fashion for medieval and devotional German art, Emma Winter argues, in 'German Fresco Painting and the New Houses of Parliament at Westminster, 1834–1851', *HJ* 47 (2004), 291–329, for a parallel attempt to redeem the working classes by forging a national English artistic culture by incorporating Germanic elements. Stephanie L. Barczewski, *Myth and National Identity in Nineteenth-Century Britain: The Legends of King Arthur and Robin Hood* (Oxford, 2000) explores one of many new obsessions with days of yore. For another, see Timothy Lang, *The Victorians and the Stuart Heritage: Interpretations of a Discordant Past* (Cambridge, 1995), which shows how the growing assertiveness of religious Dissent enabled Cromwell to be incorporated as an acceptable facet of the national history. Finally, Nigel Leask's *Curiosity and the Aesthetics of Travel Writing, 1770–1840: 'From an Antique Land'* (Oxford, 2002) examines aspects of self-identity as revealed in one fashionable genre, while Paul Langford in *Englishness Identified: Manners and Character 1650–1850* (Oxford, 2000) examines how foreigners saw the English.

---

[72] See also David Eastwood, 'Robert Southey and the Meanings of Patriotism', *JBS* 31 (1992), 265–87.

ECONOMIC AND SOCIAL THOUGHT AND POLICY

Until quite recently economic thought was taken to mean simply what economists thought. For a succinct, technical, and lucid account, see D. P. O'Brien, *The Classical Economists* (Oxford, 1975). B. A. Corry looks at the 'proto-Keynesian' opponents of Ricardianism, while Ronald L. Meek, *Economics and Ideology and Other Essays: Studies in the Development of Economic Thought* (1967) casts a Marxist squint at classical economics. Vivid essays on Bentham and Malthus in Gertrude Himmelfarb's *Victorian Minds: Essays on Nineteenth-Century Intellectuals* (1968) quickly redressed the ideological balance. Before long a huge Malthus industry developed as it became clear just how much he had dominated the public mind. That in turn led to an interest in Malthus' main antagonist, on whom, see Don Locke, *A Fantasy of Reason: The Life and Thought of William Godwin* (1980). For Adam Smith political economy had less to do with sophisticated technical analysis than with the science of legislation, and it was in his more humane guise that the subject first entered the political bloodstream, a process examined by Biancamaria Fontana in *Rethinking the Politics of Commercial Society: The 'Edinburgh Review' 1802–1832* (Cambridge, 1985), and by Winch in Stefan Collini, Donald Winch, and John Burrow (eds.), *That Noble Science of Politics: A Study in Nineteenth-Century Intellectual History* (Cambridge, 1983). This did not stop humanists from attacking the 'dismal science' as impersonal, arid, and philistine.[73] A case for the defence is mounted by Donald Winch in *Riches and Poverty: An Intellectual History of Political Economy in Great Britain, 1750–1834* (Cambridge, 1996), the most convincing account yet of the long 'conversation' between Hume, Smith, Godwin, Burke, Coleridge, Southey, and Malthus (Winch's hero). Some of the same topics are addressed, but from the standpoint of literary writers, in Philip Connell's subtle investigation *Romanticism, Economics and the Question of 'Culture'* (Oxford, 2001). In the post-war period technological changes forced experts (including Ricardo) to rethink, a process discussed in Maxine Berg, *The Machinery Question and the Making of Political Economy 1815–1848* (Cambridge, 1980). By then of course there was a highly developed critique of classical economics. On this, see Noel W. Thompson, *The People's Science: The Popular Political Economy of Exploitation and Crisis 1816–34* (Cambridge, 1984) and David Stack, *Nature and Artifice: The Life and Thought of Thomas Hodgskin (1787–1869)* (Woodbridge, 1998).

Meanwhile a different path of scholarship had been opened up by J. R. Poynter and Richard Allen Soloway. Poynter's *Society and Pauperism: English Ideas on Poor Relief, 1795–1834* (1969) and Solway's *Prelates and People: Ecclesiastical Social Thought in England 1783–1852* (1969) were two immensely important books in so far as they plugged thought about policy into wider issues of early nineteenth-century social and intellectual debate.[74] E. R. Norman, *Church and Society in England 1770–1970: A Historical Study* (Oxford, 1976) maintained an entertainingly sceptical stance—in his view ecclesiastical social thought was merely a case of trendy clerics seeking preferment

---

[73] David Eastwood, 'Robert Southey and the Intellectual Origins of Romantic Conservatism', *EHR* 104 (1989), 308–31.

[74] Whereas Gertrude Himmelfarb was more concerned to address later 20th-century preoccupations in *The Idea of Poverty: England in the Early Industrial Age* (New York, 1984).

by aping the latest ideas of the secular intelligentsia—but others took a more credulous view. *Churchmen and the Condition of England 1832–1885: A Study in the Development of Social Ideas and Practice from the Old Regime to the Modern State* (1973) was, like many of G. Kitson Clark's books, unfairly ignored. A. M. C. Waterman, *Revolution, Economics and Religion: Christian Political Economy, 1798–1833* (Cambridge, 1991) brought unrivalled theological and economic expertise to bear on the writings of certain clerical economists. In *The Age of Atonement (Oxford, 1988)* I tackled similar topics in a more impressionistic way.[75] Alternative attempts to explore the intellectual context of social policy have been made in two fine monographs: Robert Gray, *The Factory Question and Industrial England, 1830–1860* (Cambridge, 1996) and Christopher Hamlin, *Public Health and Social Justice in the Age of Chadwick: Britain, 1800–1854* (Cambridge, 1998). Michael Durey, *The Return of the Plague: British Society and the Cholera, 1831–2* (Dublin, 1979) and R. J. Morris, *Cholera 1832: The Social Response to an Epidemic* (1976) examine one particular episode that showed how much reform was urgently needed, while Geoffrey Finlayson provides a wide-ranging synthesis in *Citizen, State, and Social Welfare in Britain 1830–1990* (Oxford, 1994).

Erwin H. Ackerknecht, 'Anticontagionism between 1821 and 1867', *Bulletin of the History of Medicine*, 22 (1948), 117–55, placed the question of social (specifically health) reform in a European context by arguing that authoritarian regimes were more likely to favour sanitary measures (such as cordons and quarantines) than liberal ones. The thesis has been subjected to much subsequent investigation and has led to much subtler explanations, such as that contained in Peter Baldwin, *Contagion and the State in Europe, 1830–1930* (Cambridge, 1999). What *can* be said for the Ackerknecht thesis is that before nineteenth-century pundits could formulate social policies they had to develop a theory of government. Urbanization was placing the older, decentralized system under increasing strain, as is clear from a number of works including Norman Gash, *Pillars of Government and Other Essays on State and Society c.1770–c.1880* (1986). Chapter 1 on the Hanoverian constitution ('a centralized legislature and a decentralized administration') is especially relevant. David Eastwood analyses rural administration in *Government and Community in the English Provinces, 1700–1870* (Basingstoke, 1997) and, more specifically, *Governing Rural England: Tradition and Transformation in Local Government 1780–1840* (Oxford, 1994), while F. H. W. Sheppard, *Local Government in St. Marylebone 1688–1835: A Study of the Vestry and the Turnpike Trust* (1958) shows what could happen in the towns. The main force for reform came from Bentham and his circle, on whom, see Élie Halévy, *The Growth of Philosophic Radicalism* (1928; new edn. 1972); Ross Harrison, *Bentham* (1983); L. J. Hume, *Bentham and Bureaucracy* (Cambridge, 1981); Frederick Rosen, *Jeremy Bentham and Representative Democracy: A Study of the Constitutional Code* (Oxford, 1983); David Lyons, *In the Interest of the Governed: A Study in Bentham's Philosophy of Utility and Law* (rev edn., Oxford, 1991); and James E. Crimmins, 'Bentham's Political Radicalism Reexamined', *Journal of the History of Ideas*, 55 (1994), 259–81.

[75] Much too modestly, Waterman commented (p. 6) that, if viewed from one particular standpoint, his volume was an 'extended footnote or technical appendix' to *The Age of Atonement*. In return he once privately brought his analytical expertise to bear in reducing the latter's argument to a Venn diagram.

A 'wind of change' began to blow from the 1780s but reformers made little real headway before the 1830s. Henry Parris, *Constitutional Bureaucracy: The Development of British Central Administration since the Eighteenth Century* (1969), Henry Roseveare, *The Treasury: The Evolution of a British Institution* (1969), Norman Chester, *The English Administrative System 1780–1870* (Oxford, 1981), and John Roach's *Social Reform in England 1780–1880* (1978) survey the main developments.[76] Then there is F. David Roberts's trilogy *Victorian Origins of the British Welfare State* (New Haven, 1960), *Paternalism in Early Victorian England* (1979), and *The Social Conscience of the Early Victorians* (Stanford, Calif., 2002). William C. Lubenow, *The Politics of Government Growth: Early Victorian Attitudes toward State Intervention, 1833–1848* (Newton Abbot, 1971) is more chronologically specific, as are P. W. J. Bartrip's articles 'British Government Inspection, 1832–1875: Some Observations', *HJ* 25 (1982), 605–26, and 'State Intervention in Mid-Nineteenth Century Britain: Fact or Fiction?', *JBS* 23 (1983), 63–83. The collection of information about society and a growing belief in 'social science' were essential prerequisites of reform. These points are discussed in Philip Abrams, *The Origins of British Sociology, 1834–1914: An Essay with Selected Papers* (Chicago, 1968); L. Goldman, 'The Origins of British "Social Science": Political Economy, Natural Science and Statistics', *HJ* 26 (1983), 587–616; Theodore M. Porter, *The Rise of Statistical Thinking 1820–1900* (Princeton, 1986); Michael J. Cullen, *The Statistical Movement in Early Victorian Britain: The Foundations of Empirical Social Research* (Hassocks, 1975); D. Eastwood, ' "Amplifying the Province of the Legislature": The Flow of Information and the English State in the Early Nineteenth Century', *Historical Research*, 62 (1989), 276–94; and Mary Poovey, *Making a Social Body: British Cultural Formation 1830–1914* (Chicago, 1995). As well as 'facts' there had to be zealots. The most important 'statesman in disguise' is discussed in Anthony Brundage, *England's 'Prussian Minister': Edwin Chadwick and the Politics of Government Growth, 1832–1854* (University Park, Pa., 1988).[77] There was of course fierce local resistance to his plans, and reformers had to perform a balancing act between centre and locality, state intervention and the free market. These tensions are discussed in Oliver MacDonagh's *Early Victorian Government 1830–1870* (1977); John Prest, *Liberty and Locality: Parliament, Permissive Legislation, and Ratepayers' Democracies in the Nineteenth Century* (Oxford, 1990); and Philip Harling, *The Modern British State: An Historical Introduction* (Cambridge, 2001). Finally, there were tendencies in the opposite direction, as David Vincent's *The Culture of Secrecy: Britain, 1832–1998* (Oxford, 1998) makes clear.

Turning now from theory to practice. Economic policy as such started with Pitt, and the main thrust at that period was fiscal. Patrick K. O'Brien, 'The Political Economy of British Taxation, 1660–1815', *EconHR* 41 (1988), 1–32, and Patrick K. O'Brien and Philip A. Hunt, 'The Rise of a Fiscal State in England, 1485–1815', *Historical Research*, 66 (1993), 129–76, take the long view, while O'Brien's 'Political Biography and Pitt the Younger as Chancellor of the Exchequer', *History*, 83 (1998), 225–33, focuses on the specific. J. Torrance, 'Social Class and Bureaucratic Innovation: The commissioners for

[76] See also Gillian Sutherland (ed.), *Studies in the Growth of Nineteenth-Century Government* (1972).
[77] Though two earlier studies still have their uses: S. E. Finer, *The Life and Times of Sir Edwin Chadwick* (1952) and R. A. Lewis, *Edwin Chadwick and the Public Health Movement 1832–1854* (1952).

Examining the Public Accounts, 1780–1787', *P&P* 78 (1978), 56–81, brilliantly describes the formation of a Pittite public doctrine and places it in an appropriate social and ideological context; while Philip Harling, *The Waning of 'Old Corruption'* (Oxford, 1966), P. J. Marshall, 'The First and Second British Empires: A Question of Demarcation', *History*, 49 (1964), 13–23, and John R. Breihan, 'William Pitt and the Commission on Fees, 1785–1801', *HJ* 27 (1984), 59–81, serve as reminders that doctrine did not necessarily equal outcome. For richly detailed accounts of Pitt's policies, there are John Ehrman, *The British Government and Commercial Negotiations with Europe 1783–1793* (Cambridge, 1962); J. E. D. Binney, *British Public Finance and Administration 1774–92* (Oxford, 1958); and various essays in John Brewer and Eckhart Hellmuth (eds.), *Rethinking Leviathan: The Eighteenth-Century State in Britain and Germany* (Oxford, 1999).

Synoptic accounts of nineteenth-century policy include Martin Daunton, *Trusting Leviathan: The Politics of Taxation in Britain, 1799–1914* (Cambridge, 2001); Frank Whitson Fetter, *Development of British Monetary Orthodoxy 1797–1875* (Cambridge, Mass., 1965); Bernard Semmel, *The Rise of Free Trade Imperialism: Classical Political Economy, the Empire of Free Trade, and Imperialism 1750–1850* (Cambridge, 1970); William J. Ashworth, *Customs and Excise: Trade, Production, and Consumption in England 1640–1845* (Oxford, 2003); and S. G. Checkland, *British Public Policy 1776–1939: An Economic, Social and Political Perspective* (Cambridge, 1983). Post-war government policy is tackled in Boyd Hilton, *Corn, Cash, Commerce* (Oxford, 1977); conservative opposition to that policy is the subject of Anna Gambles, *Protection and Politics* (Woodbridge, 1999); while for ways in which the policy reverberated in business circles, three points of entry are Anthony Webster, 'The Political Economy of Trade Liberalization: The East India Company Charter Act of 1813', *EconHR* 43 (1990), 404–19; A. C. Howe, 'Free Trade and the City of London, c.1820–1870', *History*, 77 (1992), 391–410; and M. J. Daunton, ' "Gentlemanly Capitalism" and British Industry, 1820–1914', *P&P* 122 (1989), 119–58. Lucy Brown, *The Board of Trade and the Free-Trade Movement 1830–42* (Oxford, 1958) remains the only detailed study of economic policy in the 1830s, though for interpretation and context, see Peter Mandler's *Aristocratic Government in the Age of Reform* (Oxford, 1990). The years 1844 and 1846 were crucial for economic policy. J. K. Horsefield's study 'The Origins the Bank Charter Act, 1844', in T. S. Ashton and R. S. Sayers (eds.), *Papers in English Monetary History* (1953) remains authoritative, while Avner Cohen supplies an extremely subtle analysis in 'Cobden's Stance on the Currency and the Political Forces behind the Approval of the Bank Charter Act of 1844', *The European Journal of the History of Economic Thought*, 5 (1998), 250–75. It has often been assumed that, as a representative of Lancashire's export industry, Cobden ought to have opposed Peelite deflation, but Cohen points to the specific needs of calico-printing (Cobden's particular avocation), and also to his belief that stable exchange rates were essential for the maintenance of good international relations (and therefore peace). Two venerable but enduringly wise assessments of Peel's motives in 1846 are Susan Fairlie, 'The Nineteenth-Century Corn Law Reconsidered', *EconHR* 18 (1965), 562–75, and Betty Kemp, 'Reflections on the Repeal of the Corn Laws', *Victorian Studies*, 5 (1962), 189–204. More recent studies include Christine Kinealy, 'Peel, Rotten Potatoes and

Providence: The Repeal of the Corn Laws and the Irish Famine', in Andrew Marrison (ed.), *Freedom and Trade,* i: *Free Trade and its Reception, 1815–1960* (1998).

Social policy did not really commence until the 1830s, by which time Poor Law policy dominated attention. Lynn Hollen Lees, *The Solidarities of Strangers: The English Poor Laws and the People, 1700–1948* (Cambridge, 1998) is a fine synoptic discussion, while Karel Williams, *From Pauperism to Poverty* (1981), takes an interesting discursive approach, in part influenced by Foucault. For the economics of the question, see George R. Boyer, *An Economic History of the English Poor Law 1750–1850* (Cambridge, 1990) and D. A. Baugh, 'The Cost of Poor Relief in South-East England, 1790–1834', *EconHR* 28 (1975), 50–68. For what the pauper's life was like, there is M. A. Crowther, *The Workhouse System 1834–1929: The History of an English Social Institution* (1981); Anne Digby, *The Poor Law in Nineteenth-Century England and Wales* (1982); and most gruesomely Ruth Richardson's *Death, Dissection and the Destitute* (1988). The motives of the 1834 reformers have been a matter of considerable dispute among historians. See, for example, Mark Blaug in 'The Myth of the Old Poor Law and the Making of the New', *Journal of Economic History,* 23 (1963), 151–84; Anthony Brundage in *The Making of the New Poor Law: The Politics of Inquiry, Enactment and Implementation, 1832–39* (1978); and Peter Dunkley in *The Crisis of the Old Poor Law in England, 1795–1834: An Interpretive Essay* (New York, 1982). However, many areas of disagreement have been successfully adjudicated by Peter Mandler in 'The Making of the New Poor Law Redivivus', *P&P* 117 (1987), 131–57; 127 (1990), 194–201. Michael E. Rose, 'Settlement, Removal, and the New Poor Law', in Derek Fraser (ed.), *The New Poor Law in the Nineteenth Century* (1976), elucidates one of the law's biggest complexities. Tangentially, Paul Richards, 'The State and Early Industrial Capitalism: The Case of the Handloom Weavers', *P&P* 83 (1979), 91–115, reinforces the sense of ruling-class indifference to the travails of the poor.

Contemporaries often conflated paupers with criminals and lunatics. As explained in Leonard D. Smith's *Cure, Comfort and Safe Custody: Public Lunatic Asylums in Early Nineteenth-Century England* (1999), a network of publicly funded and predominantly custodial asylums were built following legislation in 1808. Then from the later 1830s there was a surge in 'therapeutic optimism' as systems of mechanical constraint began to be abolished in favour of softer (but arguably more sterile) regimes based on work. Smith's study, like Peter Bartlett's *The Poor Law of Lunacy: The Administration of Pauper Lunatics in Mid-Nineteenth-Century England* (1999), builds on Andrew Scull's earlier *The Most Solitary of Afflictions: Madness and Society in Britain 1700–1900* (New Haven, 1993). The background is covered in Roy Porter, *Mind-Forg'd Manacles: A History of Madness in England from the Restoration to the Regency* (1987).

For older attitudes to matters of crime and punishment, an exciting place to begin is with Douglas Hay's 'Property, Authority and the Criminal Law', in D. Hay *et al., Albion's Fatal Tree: Crime and Society in Eighteenth-Century England* (1975). For more nuanced accounts, turn to Peter King, *Crime, Justice, and Discretion in England 1740–1920* (Oxford, 2000); Peter Linebaugh, *The London Hanged: Crime and Civil Society in the Eighteenth Century* (1991); and Clive Emsley, *Crime and Society in England, 1750–1900* (1987). There is little nuance in V. A. C. Gatrell's *The Hanging Tree: Execution and the*

English People 1770–1868 (Oxford, 1994), but its passion stirs, and its psychological reconstruction of crowd behaviour is unparalleled. Randall McGowen's 'A Powerful Sympathy: Terror, the Prison, and Humanitarian Reform in Early Nineteenth-Century Britain', *JBS* 25 (1986), 312–34, is similarly stimulating. As for crime prevention, Elaine A. Reynolds, *Before the Bobbies: The Night Watch and Police Reform in Metropolitan London, 1720–1830* (Basingstoke, 1998) sets the scene and may be followed by Douglas Hay and Francis Snyder (eds.), *Policing and Prosecution in Britain 1750–1850* (Oxford, 1989); Stanley H. Palmer, *Police and Protest in England and Ireland 1780–1850* (Cambridge, 1988); David Philips, *Crime and Authority in Victorian England: The Black Country 1835–1860* (1977); and David Philips and Robert D. Storch, *Policing Provincial England, 1829–1856: The Politics of Reform* (1999). Seán McConville's *A History of English Prison Administration*, i: *1750–1877* (1981) is a straightforward account of what happened. Three other important books consider *how* and *why* reformers turned to rehabilitative techniques: Michael Ignatieff, *A Just Measure of Pain: The Penitentiary in the Industrial Revolution, 1750–1850* (1978); Martin J. Wiener's *Reconstructing the Criminal: Culture, Law and Policy in England, 1830–1914* (Cambridge, 1990); and William James Forsythe, *The Reform of Prisoners 1830–1900* (1987).

IRELAND

For the long view, start with *A New History of Ireland*, iv: *Eighteenth-Century Ireland, 1691–1800*, ed. T. W. Moody and W. E. Vaughan (Oxford, 1986) and v: *Ireland under the Union, 1: 1801–70*, ed. W. E. Vaughan (Oxford, 1989). R. F. Foster's *Modern Ireland 1600–1972* (1988) is excellent but should be balanced against J. C. Beckett's *The Making of Modern Ireland, 1603–1923* (1966), K. Theodore Hoppen, *Ireland since 1800: Conflict and Conformity* (1989), and Alvin Jackson's *Ireland 1798–1998: Politics and War* (Oxford, 1999). Jacqueline R. Hill, 'Popery and Protestantism, Civil and Religious Liberty: The Disputed Lessons of Irish History, 1690–1812', *P&P* 118 (1988), 96–129, is interesting, and Thomas Bartlett's *The Fall and Rise of the Irish Nation: The Catholic Question 1690–1830* (Dublin, 1992) is masterly.[78] For the turbulent 1790s there are many useful essays in Hugh Gough and David Dickson (eds.), *Ireland and the French Revolution* (Dublin, 1990) and David Dickson, Dáire Keogh, and Kevin Whelan (eds.), *The United Irishmen: Republicanism, Radicalism and Rebellion* (Dublin, 1993). E. W. McFarland, *Ireland and Scotland in the Age of Revolution: Planting the Green Bough* (Edinburgh, 1994) supplies a rare comparative dimension. Nancy J. Curtin, *The United Irishmen: Popular Politics in Ulster and Dublin 1791–1798* (Oxford, 1994), A. T. Q. Stewart, *A Deeper Silence: The Hidden Origins of the United Irishmen* (Belfast, 1993), and Jim Smyth, *The Men of No Property: Irish Radicals and Popular Politics in the Late Eighteenth Century* (Basingstoke, 1992) trace the build up to rebellion, while Marianne Elliott's *Partners in Revolution: The United Irishmen and France* (New Haven, 1982) explores Continental links. Thomas Bartlett, 'Defenders and Defenderism in 1795', *Irish Historical Studies*, 24 (1984–5), 373–94, examines one particularly portentous development. Thomas

---

[78] See also T. Bartlett, 'An End to Moral Economy: The Irish Militia Disturbances of 1793', in C. H. E. Philpin (ed.), *Nationalism and Popular Protest in Ireland* (Cambridge, 1987).

Pakenham, *The Year of Liberty: The Story of the Great Irish Rebellion of 1798* (1969) remains a standard account, to which Marianne Elliott, *Wolfe Tone: Prophet of Irish Independence* (New Haven, 1989) adds much fresh understanding. Problems of central governance are addressed in R. B. McDowell, *Ireland in the Age of Imperialism and Revolution, 1760–1801* (Oxford, 1979). James Kelly, *Prelude to Union: Anglo-Irish Politics in the 1780s* (Cork, 1992) and Gerard O'Brien, *Anglo-Irish Politics in the Age of Grattan and Pitt* (Dublin, 1987) cover the London-Dublin axis. The way in which Union was achieved is dissected in G. C. Bolton, *The Passing of the Irish Act of Union: A Study in Parliamentary Politics* (1966), and in Patrick M. Geoghegan, *The Irish Act of Union: A Study in High Politics 1798–1801* (Dublin, 1999).

London's increasingly desperate attempts to govern Ireland after 1801 are addressed in R. B. McDowell, *The Irish Administration 1800–1914* (1964), Brian Jenkins, *Era of Emancipation: British Government of Ireland, 1812–1830* (Quebec, 1988), Virginia Crossman, *Politics, Law and Order in Nineteenth-Century Ireland* (New York, 1996) and *Local Government in Nineteenth-Century Ireland* (Belfast, 1994), and Donal A. Kerr, *Peel, Priests and Politics: Sir Robert Peel's Administration and the Roman Catholic Church in Ireland, 1841–1846* (Oxford, 1982), as well as in Stanley Palmer's book on the *Police and Protest* (Cambridge, 1988), mentioned above. Fergus O'Ferrall's *Catholic Emancipation: Daniel O'Connell and the Birth of Irish Democracy 1820–30* (Dublin, 1985) is excellent, as is Oliver MacDonagh's fine two-volume biography of *Daniel O'Connell* (1988–9). For O'Connell's loyalist enemies, see Hereward Senior, *Orangeism in Ireland and Britain, 1795–1836* (1966), Peter Gibbon, *The Origins of Ulster Unionism: The Formation of Popular Protestant Politics and Ideology in Nineteenth-Century Ireland* (Manchester, 1975), and Desmond Bowen, *The Protestant Crusade in Ireland 1800–70: A Study of Protestant-Catholic Relations between the Act of Union and Disestablishment* (Dublin, 1978). For O'Connell's nationalist enemies, Richard Davis, *The Young Ireland Movement* (Dublin, 1987) can be supplemented by Brendan O'Cathaoir's *John Blake Dillon, Young Irelander* (Dublin, 1990). K. Theodore Hoppen, *Elections, Politics and Society in Ireland 1832–1885* (Oxford, 1984) is a pioneering study of political structures. Michael Beames, *Peasants and Power: The Whiteboy Movements and their Control in Pre-Famine Ireland* (Brighton, 1983) helps to explain the nature of agrarian unrest, on which, see also S. J. Connelly, *Priests and People in Pre-Famine Ireland 1780–1845* (Dublin, 1982), and Gearóid O'Tuathaigh, *Ireland before the Famine 1798–1848* (Dublin, 1972). On the famine itself, C. Woodham-Smith, *The Great Hunger: Ireland 1845–9* (1962) retains its descriptive power, but needs to be read alongside Peter Gray's very fine *Famine, Land and Politics: British Government and Irish Society 1843–1850* (Dublin, 1999); Christine Kinealy, *This Great Calamity: The Irish Famine, 1845–1852* (Dublin, 1994); Cormac Ó Gráda, *Black' 47 and Beyond: The Great Irish Famine in History, Economy, and Memory* (Princeton, 1999); and James S. Donnelly's 'The Great Irish Potato Famine (Stroud, 2001) and 'The Great Famine: Its Interpreters, Old and New', *History Ireland*, 1 (1993), 27–33. As a contribution to historiographical debate, Robert Haines's *Charles Trevelyan and the Great Irish Famine* (Dublin, 2004) does not always convince, and is too hectoringly defensive of its subject, but it is a mine of good information.

Index

Note: References in **bold** indicate sustained discussion of a particular topic.